FEMINISM
AND CHRISTIAN
TRADITION

Recent Titles in
Bibliographies and Indexes in Religious Studies

FEMINISM AND CHRISTIAN TRADITION

An Annotated Bibliography and Critical Introduction to the Literature

MARY-PAULA WALSH

Bibliographies and Indexes in Religious Studies, Number 51
G. E. Gorman, Advisory Editor

GREENWOOD PRESS
Westport, Connecticut • London

Library of Congress Cataloging-in-Publication Data

Walsh, Mary-Paula.
    Feminism and Christian tradition : an annotated bibliography and
critical introduction to the literature / Mary-Paula Walsh.
        p.   cm.—(Bibliographies and indexes in religious studies,
ISSN 0742–6836   ;   no. 51)
    Includes bibliographical references and indexes.
    ISBN 0–313–26419–8 (alk. paper)
    1. Feminism—Religious aspects—Christianity—Bibliography.
2. Feminist theology—Bibliography.   I. Title.   II. Series.
Z7963.R45W34   1999
[BT83.55]
016.2618′344—dc21   98–33137

British Library Cataloguing in Publication Data is available.

Library of Congress Catalog Card Number: 98–33137
ISBN: 0–313–26419–8
ISSN: 0742–6836

First published in 1999

Greenwood Press, 88 Post Road West, Westport, CT 06881
An imprint of Greenwood Publishing Group, Inc.
www.greenwood.com

Printed in the United States of America

The paper used in this book complies with the
Permanent Paper Standard issued by the National
Information Standards Organization (Z39.48–1984).

10 9 8 7 6 5 4 3 2

For

Marie Patricia Walsh
1913–1996

and for

Mary C. Schwartz

Letter writer par excellence,
for whom I have a similar and abiding affection.

Contents

Series Foreword

Had Jesus intended for women to be priests in his church, he would have chosen his mother.

Daphne Hampson, *Theology and Feminism*

Feminism's central insight contends that not only do women not shape and control their own lives, but that our most basic understandings of human nature are drawn primarily from men's experience.

Susannah Heschel, *On Being a Jewish Feminist*

To some degree these statements by Daphne Hampson and Susannah Heschel exemplify the two principal poles of Mary-Paula Walsh's present bibliographical study—feminist theology and feminist sociology, each informing and complementing the other in a uniquely creative synergy. It is high time that this cross-disciplinary approach be taken, for in the past three decades the contemporary women's movement, essentially a social and "political" phenomenon, has made a significant mark in the world of religion. Today, we think nothing of feminist investigations into the history of Christianity, and in many sectors of the Christian tradition feminism has forever transformed religious ritual, theology, leadership and institutional structures.

What a profound change this is from the situation of a few years ago. The Judaeo-Christian tradition, we must remember, has been heavily influenced by a patriarchal system in which the feminist perspective has been read, at best, as a sub-text. This is not to say that the feminine role has been consistently under-represented in traditional theology. For example, the role of Mary within the Catholic tradition has stood as a constant reminder of caring, material love and nurturing qualities in life—all significant aspects of the Christian message. However, while these feminine qualities have been recognized within Christianity, this has not meant that the views, opinions, and sensitivities of women have been equally respected. Indeed, women's experiences within Christianity have been viewed as other than normative, as external factors that merely supplement the dominant male perspective, which is regarded as the norm. So women have been forced to accept a patriarchal view of religion—God as stern judge has not on the whole been balanced by God as the loving mother of creation. At the risk of introducing heresy into the debate, we have for centuries lost the dual nature of divinity, the male and the female acting in concert.

Today, however, patriarchy has lost its primacy, and we see now that women are gaining acceptance within theology, within the power structures of the church. The genuine position of women within religion is being recognized and is no longer obscured by a dominant male paradigm. The feminine is half of the whole, with Christianity being equally male and female in its constructs, its beliefs system, it structures, its way of speaking and worshipping.

We are seeing the full development of a conscious, articulated relationship between male and female in the Christian tradition and a genuine recognition of feminine aspects of religion and of the equal place of women in the church. This development has generated perhaps more interest, more conflict and more debate than any other issue in the modern church. Battle lines were drawn early on and there have been countless skirmishes and many bloody battles in the last thirty years on virtually every aspect of feminism in the Christian tradition. 'Voluminous' is an inadequate description of the resulting corpus of literature, and it is this literature that forms the topic of Mary-Paula Walsh's guide.

From polemicists to pastoral theologians, from historians to biblical scholars, from psychologists to educationalists—all and sundry have felt compelled to add their ha'penny worth to the debate. Occasionally the ha'penny has turned out to be a gold sovereign, and it was with this goal of finding the sovereigns that we asked Dr. Walsh, at that time a professor at the Lutheran Theological Seminary in Gettysburg, Pennsylvania, if she might like to undertake an analysis of the literature in this field and to prepare a detailed bibliographical guide for this series. She clearly possesses the knowledge and expertise needed to assess the literature on feminism in the Christian tradition—this much is evident from her choice of entries and the quality of annotations in the bibliography. Moreover, her discussion of the principal issues and themes in the literature offers a comprehensive analysis of the principal developments and themes in the field, which are carefully delineated and comprehensively referenced in the extensive endnotes. Students new to the study of feminism within Christianity, as well as scholars seeking to order their more extensive knowledge, will find this discussion immensely beneficial. Furthermore, the bibliography itself succeeds in covering, in its six broad subject categories and 24 specific sub-categories, all key aspects of the field. In these sections the compiler has thoroughly and objectively annotated a fully representative range of the most important works in a wide range of disciplines—feminism, feminist theology and feminist sociology. Indeed, so extensive is Dr. Walsh's treatment that the bibliography will serve as an indispensable resource not only for newcomers to the topic but also for those engaged in advanced study and scholarship.

Putting this volume together has been a genuine labor of love for the compiler, and its gestation has been long and arduous; my correspondence with Dr. Walsh extends back a full decade and includes the most meticulous comments and queries of any author in the series. She has performed her task conscientiously, competently and professionally, and the result is a carefully structured and judicious survey that is accessible to students and useful to scholars. *Feminism and Christian Tradition* sets a high standard for the bibliographic treatment of feminism in the Christian tradition, and I am happy to commend it as a valuable addition to Bibliographies and Indexes in Religious Studies.

Dr. G. E. Gorman FLA FRSA
Advisory Editor
Victoria University of Wellington
March 1999

Preface

When I was a graduate student in 1973 I switched my academic program from religious studies to sociology. Shortly thereafter, my faculty advisor asked me to do a book review for a sociology of religion journal. The book was Rosemary Radford Ruether's *Religion and Sexism: Images of Women in Jewish and Christian Traditions.*

I had never read a book quite like it before. It was engaging, informative and in various ways, it just "made sense." It was different from Mary Daly's then recently published, *Beyond God the Father*, but at the same time, I could not exactly say how. So as I finished the review, I said this: "[Ruether's text] is a work which signals the development of a theology and religion beyond not *God* the Father, but *Church and/or Heritage the Father.*"

I liked the review and was particularly pleased with its ending, so I shared it with a friend and asked enthusiastically: "What do you think?"

"I love it," she said, "I think it's great! And I LOVE the ending."

I told her I liked the ending too. Not that I knew what it meant—for, frankly, I did not. But it sounded good, and I was sure it was important. My friend, Helen Delaurentis, now at the University of San Diego, agreed.

Naiveté is a wonderful thing, and while today Helen and I may each be less—or perhaps just differently—naive, we are nonetheless quite clear about what those "Church and/or Heritage" words mean. For in the years since those days, a time of hope and public humor has come and gone, and we live now with their memory.

This is a book written for sociologists and theologians, and particularly those sociologists and theologians who want to know more about the feminist movement in American Christianity. It is also a book written for students and members of the general public who may wish to know more about the literature of this movement, and who ask in various ways: "What *really* is it all about? When did it begin? What do feminist theologians believe, think, want, etc.,?

It is, I confess, a big book. It is thorough, and perhaps even so much so as to be a little "off-putting." But I hope its size is an asset rather than a liability, for if used carefully, it is a book that can identify trends and perspectives and perhaps provide a place of common ground for conversations across diverse, and at times, disparaging perspectives. This, at least, has been my goal, and if the book does that—if it provides a space for discussion across worlds now relatively separate—I shall be pleased and consider my task done.

It is not, however, without its limitations, and for these I take full responsibility. Most of these limitations are spelled out in the introductory chapters, but a few need mention at this point. First, while it is a big text, it only scratches the surface of what is now a serious corpus within the worlds of American religion and theological education. Hence, while I have tried to include as many authors and issue-defining texts as possible, there are many authors *not* included in the formally numbered 976 abstracts. This is not to say other authors and texts are never mentioned, for there is a considerable amount of additional bibliography embedded throughout the text, in both the introduction endnotes and individual abstracts. But many writing in the areas of feminist, womanist, evangelical, *Mujerista*, lesbian, Jewish, Asian and Asian-American feminist theologies will search the index for their names and no doubt ask: "Why was my work not included?" Hence,

I must state at the outset that the absence of a writer's work does not mean it is not worth reading. It just means that to the best of my ability, I have arrayed the sources historically and found those here to be (by and large) the grounding, defining or elsewise distinctive sources. Suffice it to say, for every one source that was included, there are at least five that were not. It has, after all, been a project nearly a decade in preparation.

Second, a word about cultures and language is in order at this point. An undeniable feature of late twentieth-century American culture is the continued wrestling with nearly three decades of social, legal and linguistic change. As I write, therefore, I do so within the milieux of the many revised and changing norms that govern the tasks of self-naming and ethnic identification. These changing norms are reflected in various sources reviewed for this work. For example, *Mujerista* is a term almost always italicized by its Hispanic and Latina spokeswomen, and it is almost always upper case. Likewise, "antifeminism" is now a term of accepted usage (and no longer a phenomenon becoming identified through its hyphenated predecessor "anti-feminism"), and in the area of sexuality, the phrase "same sex" appears as both two words and a hyphenated adjective as society struggles with the openness of gender, affectional, and sexual orientations.

Where changing linguistic norms are *everywhere* evident, however, is in the self-naming by members of various ethnic communities, and thus it is imperative that I state the norms I have followed through this text. First, as I have summarized various works, I have generally stayed with the language of individual authors. Hence, *Mujerista* is almost always italicized and it almost always upper case. Second, when speaking of African Americans, I have followed the conventions in use by various Black and non-African American authors, i.e., the word Black is upper-cased when used as a noun or adjective indicating ethnic identification, but lower-cased when used as an adjective for skin color. Thus, for example, 'Black clergy have historically been active in civil rights leadership, and women across the board (black and white) have benefited.' Similarly, when speaking about religion and African Americans, theological perspectives such as "Black Theologies of Liberation," are upper-cased, as are other ethnically specific theological perspectives, e.g., Asian and Asian-American feminist theology. This noted, however, reference to theologies written by Caucasian authors remains lower cased, unless the language is directly quoted from a specific author, or a summary statement of ideology (e.g., White Supremacy) is intended.

Finally, it goes without saying that regardless of my own feminist convictions (spelled out in the general introduction—and elsewhere unambiguous) certain religious conventions are upheld throughout the text. Thus Bible and Trinity are upper-cased, but "biblical" and "trinitarian" are not, and the nomenclature of the "Old" and "New" Testaments is used, although often in tandem with the more recent language of "First" and "Second" Testaments.

So! How does one thank all those who have helped and supported *this* long and detailed piece of work? This way. First. . .

For Hart M. Nelsen: My thanks for the initial invitation to review Ruether's book. And for all the good things since. If ever there was a mentor who "got it right," it has been you.

Second, my thanks go to specifically to each of the following:

To Alice Kroliczak, Vice President and Senior Study Director at The Gallup Organization in Washington, DC, who in spite of many, *many* drafts has remained my good and loyal friend—as well as one of my most consistent and helpful critics.

To Herman Steumpfle, President Emeritus of the Lutheran Theological Seminary at Gettysburg, who at some of the worst moments of my life, continued to support me—and this work—and insist that it must get done.

To Frances Taylor Gench and her beloved husband, Roger, each a friend and colleague who has nurtured me and kept me strong when the end seemed never in sight.

And a very particular thanks to Adair Lummis of Hartford Seminary, a friend and colleague of extraordinary talent, grace, accomplishment and kindness, whose home has always been a place of rest and refreshment, and who has reminded me regularly that I was a sociologist whose time had come.

Thanks also go to each of the following for their friendship and support. To Dean Hoge of the Sociology Department at The Catholic University of America (for things that have probably not even occurred to him); to Sandra Baxter, President and CEO of Applied Research Analysts of Fairfax, VA—for a vision given now more than two decades ago; to Myrna Goldenberg, now the Director of the Humanities Institute at Montgomery College in Rockville, MD, for a "Welcome" like too few others; to Lucy Laufe, also of Montgomery College, for "What's not to like?"; to Sara Mummert of the Gettysburg Seminary library staff in Gettysburg, PA—for things *way too numerous* to list; to Norma Wood now Dean of the Seminary faculty; to Richard Thulin, the Dean at Gettysburg during my last years there; to the library staff at Catholic University in Washington, DC—and particularly John Solorzano for his *consistent* patience with all my overdue returns; to Helen Delaurentis of the University of San Diego; to the Reverend Elinor Allison of Lewisburg,

Pennsylvania; and to Carolyn Lee, Lorraine D'Antonio, Diane Daniel, and Reba Spielman, each friends who have given differently to my psychic energies.

Thanks also go to various Greenwood editors: to Pamela St. Clair, Irene Lebov, Catherine Lyons, Alicia Merritt and Gary Gorman, who have each waited patiently for these pages finally to come together. Thank you, Pamela, Irene and Catherine, for your quick response and text production. Thank you, Alicia Merritt, for your kind and gracious patience. And thank you, Gary Gorman, for *your* patience and for your ongoing commitment to the development of this volume.

Last, for reasons also too numerous to list, I want to thank the members of my family. In particular, I am especially grateful to my sister, Margaret Verville; my aunt, Frances Cook; my cousin Joe O'Hare; and my very special niece, Ms. Kathleen Verville.

And to one of the most remarkable persons I have *ever* known, and to whom, together with my mother, this book is dedicated, I would like to say: "Dear Mary Schwartz: This is in response to your letter…"

The Bibliography: A General Introduction

A. THE PURPOSE OF THIS VOLUME

This book is about the literature on feminism and Christian tradition. It presents a survey of important writings, trends and sources, and it seeks to organize this literature in ways which are helpful to a broadly based and interdisciplinary audience. The principal disciplines represented in this discussion are theology and sociology, and by far the literature reviewed is drawn from American journal and book publications of the twenty-five year period 1968-1993, although important sources from the early 1960s, together with recent publications through the mid-1990s, are also included.

Many of these publications are well known (or at least well publicized) and as a consequence, there are few scholars in the areas of theology and sociology who will not at least recognize the entry titles and/or the names of writers in their respective disciplines. What is more likely, however, is that *apart from their own areas of specialization*, these same scholars will have only a passing or diffuse knowledge of the entries presented here, and that in the literature of the "other discipline," these scholars will have either no knowledge of the literature or worse yet, no means of immediate access to it. *This book has as one of its goals the accessible understanding of much literature from that "other discipline," whether that other discipline is theology, and specifically the writings comprising feminist and womanist theological perspectives, or whether that discipline is sociology, and specifically the published empirical literature on women in ordained ministry.*

Nor is access to these literatures the only goal of this work. A second and related goal of this book is to introduce readers to the issues raised by these respective literatures.

Obviously, there are several issues which one could identify as one examines the literature on feminism and Christian tradition, for with even a perusal of the literature, one could almost generate a list effortlessly and say: "Here they are. These are the issues. They are the equality of women, the destruction of sexism, the eradication of gender bias in research and writing, the full acceptance of women in ordained ministry, the need for inclusive rather than exclusive language, mutuality rather than hierarchy, etc., etc., etc." It is a list which could go on indefinitely, and in spite of its diffuse and vague character, it would not be inaccurate for this fact.

What separates such a listing from the discussion to be presented here, however, are three things. First, the discussion in this book seeks consistently to root the presentation of issues in a framework which is comprehensive and, as far as is possible, fully representative of major feminist theologians. Put somewhat differently, the discussion in this book seeks to root the presentation of issues in a framework which is historically developed and then synthesized topically in terms of core and current publications informed by feminist theology's several subdisciplines. This has meant a fairly focused population of writers, but the list is, by and large, representative of major feminist, Womanist, *Mujerista*, Asian and Jewish feminist theologians speaking to or out of the dialogue between feminism and Christian tradition.

Second, the discussion presented here focuses the presentation of issues in terms drawn from both feminist theological *and* feminist *sociological* sources, and thus from within a framework which is *cross*-disciplinary in scope and bridge-building in orientation. This is an important point and it merits strong emphasis, for not only have feminist theologians recognized the need for cross-disciplinary frameworks, a point evident in much feminist historical and ethical analysis, but sociological researchers have also acknowledged this need, when at various gatherings they have sought literature which seeks to bridge rather than isolate feminist theological, feminist sociological, and/or clergywomen directed research.

A final factor which distinguishes this work and the issues it will summarize is this. By specific design, the literature discussed and/or described in this general introduction is itself presented in Part II, in annotated and abstracted form so that readers may examine or review it at their own leisure and in terms of either the issues described in Part I or their own questions, research and/or other academic needs. The rationale here is obvious: it is hoped that this manner of presentation will facilitate the bridge-building process and serve to enhance rather than restrict cross-disciplinary reading, writing, research and conversation.

B. A VOLUME OVERVIEW

1. Structure and Organization. This volume is divided into two parts. Following the completion of this general introduction, Part II presents the volume's annotated bibliography on *Feminism and Christian Tradition.* This bibliography is made up of nearly 1000 sources arranged topically within six thematically related sections. The organizational and formatting conventions of these sections are summarized below, but it should be noted here that each of the bibliography's main sections includes an introduction that identifies developmental trends, authors, and discipline defining sources. Moreover, several individual chapters also include introductory comments that further identify issues, authors and current "flashpoints" within the literature. The volume's author and subject indices then complete the volume.

2. Formatting and Bibliographic Conventions. Four formatting conventions should be mentioned at this point. First, in an effort to maximize the use of both the introductory and bibliographic sections of this volume, a bibliography "identification system" has been put in place. Methodologically, this simply means that the bibliography's 976 entries have been numbered sequentially throughout the entire bibliography, so that apart from any other point of reference, each entry has a specific and unique ID number, printed in bold type, which can serve as its cross referencing device in textual discussion, other abstracts, and index listings. Typically, these ID numbers are printed individually in brackets (e.g., **[484]**), but they may also appear as elements of a series (e.g., **[132-135]**), as elements of a cross referencing list (e.g., the list in **[268]**), or together with a page reference to the abstract itself, with the latter separated from the abstract number by a colon (e.g., **[145:35]**). The point to remember here is this: this numbering system holds throughout the volume (beginning with the first entry of the bibliography on page one and ending with the last on page 424), and it is *always* the "ID number" of the abstract entry that is the identifying variable for locating the entry.

The second formatting convention here is that the sources in the bibliography are typically fleshed out in extended rather than brief annotations. The decision to present extended rather than brief annotations is based upon my several years of reading the literatures in both theology and the sociology of religion, and in the light of fostering an interdisciplinary dialogue, extended rather than brief annotations seem the most fruitful strategy to take. Thus, while some might argue that annotated entries should be limited to one or two sentences so that readers can move quickly to the original source; or alternatively, that such brief statements aid the librarian in her or his purchasing decisions, this author has found that the strategy most helpful to those seeking access to literatures beyond their own disciplines is that of extended rather than abbreviated annotations. Hence annotations are developed in terms of several things: an author's main or principal point(s), his or her supporting arguments, references to important documentation, and in many cases suggested and related literature not abstracted in the present volume, but nonetheless worthy of note.[1]

Third, the selection of text editions needs brief comment. Overall, I have tried to keep the editions selected for review current and up to date with distinctive features of revised editions noted or included in abstracts. In some cases, however, "more recent" does not necessarily mean "better," and in these cases I have indicated the reasons for the selected edition within the abstract itself.

Finally, several abstracts, as well as portions of the bibliography include a "**NOTE**" to the reader. These notes indicate related entries and/or additional abstracts for a given author, as well as listings of helpful but unabstracted sources. As illustrations of such "notes," see the "**NOTE**" in entry **[123]** and see the "**NOTE**" following entry **[823]**.

3. Definitions of Key Terms. Of obvious importance in a volume of this scope is the matter of definitions, and here specifically, the definitions of such terms as "feminism," "feminist theology," "womanism," "womanist theology," and of course, "tradition." Feminism shall be defined first, with the others to follow.

Following such writers as bell hooks **[29]**, Allison M. Jaggar **[32]**, Gerda Lerner **[35]**, and Janet Saltzman Chafetz **[98]**, the term "feminism" shall be taken to mean the political and social efforts of women and men directed toward ending sexist *domination*--with all that the latter may imply in terms of racial, economic and other patterns of stratification. From an analytical perspective this definition is useful in that it recognizes "solidarity" without disregarding "difference," and it thus permits the variable quality of feminist movement its expression. Moreover, because this definition stresses feminism as an historical movement, it identifies feminism as an organizational and attitudinal phenomenon, a social rather than privatized reality. Last, while it does not intend to ignore the differences between "liberal," "socialist," "radial" or even "postmodern" perspectives (cf., e.g, Castro [15] and Nicholson [38]), its key concerns are the behavioral outcomes of such perspectives, with the structural ending of sexist domination as paramount.

The second term to be defined here is "feminist theology." For the purposes of this volume, and unless it is otherwise specified, the phrase "feminist theology" will be understood in its widest possible sense, namely, as an umbrella term indicative of both those writings attached to the women's movement in religion which "...oppose any ideology, belief, attitude [structure] or behavior...[that]...establishes or reinforces discrimination on the basis of gender..."; and additionally, those same writings which oppose any ideology, belief, attitude, structure or behavior that establishes or reinforces feminism's *widest understandings of patriarchy and discrimination*, i.e., the varying racial, sexual, ethnic, heterosexual, economic and age-based patterns of stratification implicit in sexist domination. The first portion of this definition is adapted from Margaret Farley's discussion of feminism and feminist ethics [472], and while other definitions of feminist theology have subsequently appeared (cf., e.g., Chopp [264]), Farley's ethical emphasis remains useful for bridging various literatures within this volume. The second part of the definition then returns conciously to the pluralism of feminist movement itself, and its efforts to end the multiple patterns of stratification endemic to "sexist domination." Thus, to repeat the meaning of the phrase "feminist theology" as it shall be understood here, it is: (1) an umbrella term indicating those writings attached to the women's movement in religion that critique society's widest and most grounding patterns of social stratification (i.e., those of race, gender, ethnicity, age, social class and sexual orientation); and it is (2) a critique that extends to ideologies, beliefs, attitudes structures, and/or behaviors that establish or reinforce such wide and grounding patterns of social stratification.

Third and fourth to be defined here are the terms "womanism" and "womanist theology." The term "womanist" may be new to some, but it encompasses feminist writing from within the context of African American women's experience. It was first used by Alice Walker in her volume, *In Search of Our Mother's Gardens: Womanist Prose* to indicate "a commit[ment] to the survival and wholeness of [an] entire people, male and female..."[2] but it has since been widely adopted as a symbol for depicting the survival and communal dimensions of African American women's experience generally (cf., e.g., Grant's overview in [254], see Eugene [626], and see Delores Williams' several discussions, e.g., [632] and [639]).

To the best of my knowledge the term "womanist" was first used within the mainstream religious press by Toinette Eugene in a series of articles published in the *National Catholic Reporter* in 1984 (cf. *NCR*, 4/13/84, p. 4). It was subsequently developed theologically by womanist ethicist Katie Cannon in her essay, "The Emergence of Black Feminist Consciousness" [612] and then, again, in her doctoral dissertation, *Black Womanist Ethics* [253]. Current usage by, for example, sociologist Patricia Hill Collins [99] presents "womanism" as a term interchangeable with that of "Black Feminism," and this pattern has been adopted here. This said, the reader must not thereby presume that this usage identifies womanism as simply a Black analog to the emphases of early or contemporary mainstream, i.e., "liberal" American feminism. Rather, as Collins indicates in her discussion of such writers as Walker and hooks, Black feminism entails a "process of self-conscious struggle that empowers women and men to actualize a humanist vision of community," and it includes the many economic, occupational, cultural and social psychological dimensions embedded within this task (see Collins [99:39]).

Does Collins' usage of "womanism" exhaust the meaning of this term? Hardly, for as the background literature to womanist theology suggests (cf., e.g., Giddings [614]) the term "womanism" is yet evolving and yet being adapted to the many experiences that comprise the substance of African American women's history and religious-communal orientation.

What then, is "Womanist Theology?" At the very least, "womanist" theology is a theology indigenous to the religious experiences of African American women. That is, it is a theology which arises out of the distinctiveness of *African American women's* religious experience and not the religious experience of America's more dominant and specifically denominational and historically white, women's cultures.

On the face of it, this point may seem obvious, and even tautological. Moreover, it may even seem to suggest that to define womanist theology, one need only "adjust for race" within a given definition of feminist theology—with the latter, of course, presumed to be the more normative phenomenon because it is, statistically, the more apparant phenomenon. While such a strategy would be tempting for those seeking a summary definition, it would be an inadequate approach to the task of defining womanist theology, for it would ignore the intentions of several discussions now present in the literature (cf., e.g., [257], [258], and [259]), and affirming at least the following: First, that the phrase "womanist theology" itself signals something specific, i.e., the legitimacy of African American (and not other) women defining the theological ground, vision and horizon within which African American women stand. Second, that this defining process requires an accountability from history, society, *and its churches* for the waste, violence and other effects of racism in American society, and more, a recognition that this racism must end. Third, the process of defining womanism recognizes that in spite of America's racism *and* the roles it has assigned Black women, "womanist theology" is, as well, a celebrative phenomenon. It is an embracing and positive posture of Black women's solidarity, for it is a theology which speaks to the strengths hidden, preserved, and tapped on behalf of Black women's (racially) assigned social roles, and it is a theology which speaks now to the empowerment of Black women surviving and changing such roles, within and across American society. Put somewhat differently, womanist theology is an appropriated theology. It is a theology fought for and hewn from the experiences of African American women, and it is a theology which refuses an assimilation experience apart from the discussion of power, and specifically power relative to the racisms existing *within* as well as across race-gender interactions.

As the discussion of the literature progresses through this introduction (and further within the bibliography) other emphases of womanist theology (e.g., its communal character, its historical and often church based roots) will be introduced. But important to note here is that because African American women's history has differed radically from the histories of most American women (cf., e.g., Hull, Scott and Smith [49], Evans [74], Fox-Genovese [75], Malson et al. [79], and Giddings [614]), theological reflection on that history has also differed (cf., e.g., Dodson and Gilkes [613], Gilkes [615], Hoover [618], and Riggs [628]), and it serves now as an empowering and alternative core literature within the context of "feminism and Christian tradition."

The last term to be defined here is "tradition." As it shall be used within this text, the concept tradition shall refer to "...the repository of the lore about group boundary and about world-view, usually transmitted to the young of a society in preparation for full participation in the culture as adults." More concretely, a tradition includes the "stories, activities, memories and the rules governing group-boundary and world-view formation..." that typify a particular culture, and thus it provides the raw materials for "shaping identity" within that particular culture.

This definition is taken from Robert Schreiter's discussion, *Constructing Local Theologies*,[3] and because it recognizes both the historical and social dimensions of traditions (that is, their intergenerational and identity shaping power) *and* their communal or socially constructed character, it permits the recognition of traditions as malleable phenomena, or phenomena that are open to *re*construction as well as "reformation," and *"trans*formation" as well as "revolution." Second, because Schreiter's discussion frames the concept "tradition" in descriptive and functional terms, and not those of any one particular tradition, it permits application to a wide range of traditions--or tradition-like realities, whether the latter are cultural, institutional, theological, or philosophical. In particular, because "tradition" is a repository of "lore", it permits the recognition of enmeshed histories and social constructions, or the possibility of *multiply* rooted "stories, activities, memories and...rules governing group-boundary and world-view formation." Thus it provides a bridge concept to the multiple critiques of Christianity evident in feminist, womanist, *Mujerista* and other writings, and specifically their critiques of Christianity's doctrinal, institutional and organization features.[4] Finally, because its descriptive character is so fluid, Schreiter's concept of tradition is easily compatible with the many sources lifting up "tradition" itself as an object of critique and reconstruction (e.g., LaCugna [273], Loades [274], Plaskow [262], Schüssler Fiorenza [238], Chopp [239], Williams [259].)

Some final points about definitions here. Quite plausibly, one might expect the terms "sex" and "gender" to be defined here, if only briefly in terms of their respective "biological" (i.e., anatomical/chromosomal) and "socially constructed" (i.e., historically variable, symbolic, and role related) decriptors, for these latter *are* the stuff of "gender" studies in sociology. Recent work in feminist deconstructionist theory, however, has challenged this widely accepted distinction that sociologists (and others) tend regularly to take for granted.[5] In the present volume while this challenge is recognized, the more customary definitions will apply, with deconstructionist emphases noted as necessary. The reason for this choice is practical, and it is simply that the bulk of the sources reviewed here presume the traditional understandings of sex as a biological phenomenon and gender (or gender role) as a constructed or negotiated phennomenon.

Last, one might also expect a host of other definitions to emerge here, *viz.*, those of Latin American feminist theology (cf., e.g., [926]), *Mujerista* theology (cf., e.g., [256]), Jewish feminist theology (cf., e.g., [955]), Asian feminist theology (cf., e.g., [281]), and Han and Minjung theologies specifically (cf., e.g., [935, 937]). Definitions of these theologies appear throughout the text as each is introduced within the bibliography. For immediate overview discussions, however, the reader is referred to the respective entries in Russell and Clarkson's *Dictionary of Feminist Theologies* **[272]**, as well as entries **[265]** and **[275]** in the bibliography.

   4. Biases and Grounding Assumptions. It almost goes without saying that there are few (if any) writers who today would claim pure objectivity in the selection and development of material for a given research topic, for each of us is conditioned by the horizons of our personal and professional concerns and beneath these the values which guide our vision of the world. For my part, these values and horizons are largely "feminist" in orientation. That is, they are horizons "women identified," and thus fully supportive of women's autonomy, women's "equality" and women's social well being. After that, they are horizons formally sociological, and with a long standing penchant for the study of religious elites. Some of the latter stems from an early training in biblical theology and a love for the prophetic literature of the Hebrew Bible. But it stems, more recently, from those sociological studies which illuminate both the nature of power and the gendered--or more accurately, the *multiply* gendered (e.g., the racially gendered, heterosexually gendered, etc.) quality of virtually all interaction,[6] including those interactions one usually labels religious. Thus, as the reader will see from the bibliography's outline, I have prefaced the theological material of this bibliography with relevant sources detailing the literature and history of feminism and the American women's movement, and with sources from Women's Studies and feminist sociology which stress the multiple social, economic and cultural factors affecting women's history in the United States. This placement or structuring of material intends no deterministic argument about the theological sources which follow. Rather, it intends only that as I approach my subject, I do so with a certain amount of acknowledged feminist theological sympathy, but with at the same time a sociologically critical, if albeit cautious, edge. I trust, therefore, that theological readers will have patience with what may seem to them to be sociologically prejudiced (dare I say reductionistic?) statements, for there are many such statements in the abstracts prepared for this volume. My intent, however, is not any sociological reductionism, but to the best of my ability, clear analysis and a healthy respect for the dynamics of social interaction, social construction and the staying power of institutionalized phenomena. Similarly, I trust that sociological readers will forgive a certain level of feminist, womanist, and 'other' theological simpatico, should it creep across the pages undetected by editorial eyes. For again, there are many such statements in the abstracts prepared for this volume, and as above, my intent is not reductionism (here theological), but to the best of my ability, clear analysis and a healthy respect for the dynamics of social interaction, social construction and the staying power of now religious and 'other' institutionalized phenomena.[7]

   A second and important structural bias is this: that I have cast the literature of this volume widely as that of "feminism and Christian tradition," rather than narrowly, as that of "feminist theology" generally, or to take a more dichotomized perspective, the literatures of feminist theology (including womanism) on the one hand, and "feminist sociology" (including Gender and Women's Studies) on the other. There are several reasons for casting the literature of this volume in wide rather than narrow terms.

   First, and by way of a strategy designed to foster both an interdisciplinary perspective and its elements of conversation, it makes sense to keep the horizons of the conversation wide, so that options and opportunities for conversation abound rather than abate, and so that re-imagining (both sociological and theological) might flourish.

   Second, and equally important, there is the simple fact that the literature of this volume is virtually "paradigmatic" in scope, or to put the same somewhat differently, it is a literature which has ramifications for practically every aspect of mainline Christian experience as it has been lived and known, and it is a literature which either presently addresses those ramifications, or seeks to do so in the very near future. (Indeed, according to sociologist Marie Augusta Neal **[145**: 33], the women's movement in religion is a "reformation" as "far-reaching" in scope as that of the 16th century!)

   A number of feminist theologians (e.g., Elisabeth Schüssler Fiorenza **[283]**, Sally McFague **[200]**, and Letty Russell **[249]**) have called attention to this paradigmatic character of the literature, and while one might wish to debate whether a formal "paradigm change" has, in fact, *occurred* within Christian theology, few would dispute the paradigmatic *reach* of this theological literature. That is, at the level of culture and religious meaning there are discussions about the "gender of God,"[8] the ways in which one should or should not speak of God,[9] the impact of race and social class as factors within theological reflection,[10] the legitimacy of women's experience(s) as "sources" of revelation,[11] the significance of various "hermeneutics" as frameworks of interpretation,[12] and, at nearly all points, an attention to "praxis" as the watchword for all ethical, theological or religious symbolization.[13]

Similarly, and with respect to various institutional phenomena, one finds discussions about the interstructuring of racial, class and gender privilege,[14] the need to critique power and the abuses of religious authority,[15] the need to *re*construct long standing patterns of church organizational life,[16] and at local institutional levels (i.e., congregations), the difficult task of integrating women into an established [white and black] male-dominated profession.[17] To repeat, then, this second reason for keeping a wide and open-ended characterization of this volume's literature: it is a literature which is paradigmatic in scope, in that it is a literature that has ramifications for practically every aspect of mainline Christian experience as it has been lived and known, and it is a literature that either presently addresses those ramifications, or seeks to do so in the very near future.

Third, and relatedly, the literature of this volume is socially variegated and increasingly pluralized in terms of its religious and denominational bases. Put differently, while the literature of "feminist theology" was once thought to be a predominantly Roman Catholic literature addressing the issue of women's ordination within Catholicism (or alternatively, the often misunderstood theology of Mary Daly),[18] the literature of feminism and Christian tradition is now a *thoroughly* inter-denominational literature, with representative thinkers from practically all mainline churches and faith expressions. Thus, in addition to both the early and later Catholic feminist theological literatures (with their respective "women's ordination" and "womenchurch" emphases as detailed in Chapter 19 of the bibliography), one now finds feminist theological publications from writers across not only the denominational spectrum,[19] but too, the growing numbers of cultural and ethnically defined communities of women's discourse. To wit: the previously mentioned and the rapidly expanding "Womanist" theological literature;[20] the developing feminista/*Mujerista* theologies of Hispanic feminist theologians;[21] the feminist theologies of Latin American women[22] and American Jewish women;[23] the "Minjung" and "Han" theologies of Asian and Asian-American feminist theologians;[24] the feminist hermeneutics of Muslim women;[25] the feminist theologies of evangelical women;[26] the empowering forces of "out" lesbian spirituality—Catholic, Episcopal, evangelical and womanist;[27] the rising awareness of gender and spirit among Native American women;[28] and to cite but one more illustration, the developing critique of "anti-Judaism" in Christian feminism by contemporary Jewish feminist theologians.[29] Again, as with its paradigmatic reach, the variegated bases of this literature also suggest a wide rather than narrow approach to its description, i.e., its characterization generally as a literature of "feminism and Christian tradition," as contrasted, for example, with any other combination of the terms "feminism," "theology" and "sociology."

Fourth, and here, substance and strategy meet, there are obvious and practical reasons for casting the literature of this volume as that of "feminism and Christian tradition." Most directly, because the "experience" of women is, in fact, empirically varied (i.e., is *always* an experience which is racially, economically, ethnically, sexually, generationally, familistically and in numerous other ways specific), it is premature to presume that the literature of feminism and its encounter with Christian tradition is in any way exhausted or close to being finished; for in spite of its many publications, this literature is yet developing and yet to be completed. Indeed, if the development of literature from the wider field of Women's Studies generally is any indicator at all for the encounter of feminism with Christian tradition, then one must expect that the literature of this field will continue to grow rather than abate, and that the studies of this volume are but the tip of the proverbial iceberg.[30] What's more, that this is so seems obvious from the array of subdisciplines already encompassed by the literature. For example: among theological disciplines, the study of feminism and Christian tradition involves not only the fields of Hebrew and Christian biblical studies, but also biblical "hermeneutics" (the analysis and interpretation of biblical texts) and with this, the study of "theological method." Likewise, it includes the study of: "Church History" (including what is generally known as "patristics" or the writings of the "Church Fathers"); "Dogmatic Theology" (a broadly based topic with numerous subsections: e.g., Christology, Mariology, ecclesiology, soteriology, and eschatology);[31] Christian ethics and spirituality; and in the case of Roman Catholic writers, the study of "Canon" (or church) Law. Similarly, within the context of sociology, the literature of this volume includes not only the sociologies of religion, race, demography, gender, culture and ethnicity; but too, those of religious leadership, new religious movements, the self-conscious appropriation of secularized consciousness, and at a more general but necessary and obviously important level, the study of organizational change within American denominational life.[32] This range of perspectives, together with its internal and cross cutting topics, all suggest that a simple and dichotomous casting of the literature—as a literature of feminist theology (including womanism) on the one hand, and feminist sociology (including gender and women's studies) on the other—will simply not work. Rather, a very wide berth is needed.[33]

To sum up this second, structural and "organizing bias": There are strategic and substantive factors supporting the decision to cast the literature of this volume as that of "feminism and Christian tradition" and chief among them are: (1) the desire for a suitably wide context of conversation; (2) the paradigmatic scope or reach of the literature; (3) its highly pluralized social and religious bases, and (4) its extensive and internal interdisciplinary character within the subfields of theology and sociology per se. Each of these, and all of them together, suggest the necessity for a wide rather than narrow casting of the literature of this volume, its depiction as a literature of "Feminism and Christian Tradition," rather than as the literatures of feminist theology (including womanism) on the one hand and feminist sociology (including gender and women's studies) on the other.[34]

5. *Topics within the bibliography*. As indicated earlier in this chapter, the bibliography presented here contains six thematically related sections. These sections deal with the widest emphases of feminism, feminist theology and feminist sociology, and while they may each be read independently of one another, they together exhibit a developing and cohering logic.

Section I of the bibliography presents introductory and background literature on feminism and the women's movement. It is subdivided into four topically based chapters which introduce, in turn, "Feminism," "Feminism and Women's Studies," "Feminist Sociology," and "Women in American Religion." The literature in Section I covers a wide terrain, and its sociological, theoretical, and statistical dimensions provide several frameworks for understanding feminism and the women's movement vis a vis American religion, and particularly the many changes now in process around issues concerning women in institutional and para-congregational religious settings. Overall, these sources in Section I are current through the mid-1990s and they present easily readable and clear introductions to the topics they address.

Following these introductory materials, Section II provides an initial overview of the feminist theological literature. Entitled "Feminism and the Development of Feminist Theology," it organizes entries into three chronologically ordered units: (1) the "early" feminist theological sources, i.e., important grounding and transitional works published between 1968 and 1977; (2) the subsequent "core" or "established" feminist theological sources, i.e., key sources published between 1978 and 1985; and (3) recent and current literature, or sources published (by and large) through the mid-1990s. (The methodology for identifying these dates is spelled out in the next chapter, but in brief, it involves identifying the conceptual breakpoints in the literature and listing the emphases particular to those divisions.)

Section II of the bibliography is in many ways "the big picture." It reviews some of the most well known of the feminist theological sources, and where ever possible, it identifies writers by their specific affiliations: e.g., traditional Roman Catholic or Protestant contexts, the field of Women's Studies in Religion, and/or, the contexts of African American, *Mujerista* and Jewish feminist theologies.

Indeed, readers already familiar with the main lines of the feminist theological corpus will no doubt recognize many of the authors listed in Section II, for they are the writers whose works are standard within the discipline. Thus, the authors in Section II include (among others): Womanist ethicist Katie Cannon and feminist ethicists Carter Heyward and Beverly Harrison; Women's Studies scholar and Jewish feminist theologian Judith Plaskow; Catholic and Protestant biblical scholars Elisabeth Schüssler Fiorenza and Phyllis Trible; the very well known Roman Catholic historian and feminist theologian, Rosemary Radford Ruether; Protestant feminist theologian Sally McFague; Presbyterian feminist Letty Russell; and, of course, Mary Daly, whose initial work, *The Church and the Second Sex*, virtually precipitated the public discussion of feminism and religion within mainstream American churches during the mid and late 1960s. These, and others yet to be identified (e.g., Carol Christ, Rita Gross, Kari Borresen, Shiela Grave Davaney, Virginia Ramey Mollenkott, Nelle Morton, Dorothee Soelle, Arlene Swidler, Judith Weidman, Jacquelyn Grant, Kwok Pui Lan, Mary Hunt, Elizabeth Johnson, Sandra Schneiders, Rebecca Chopp, Susan Thistlethwaite, Emilie Townes, Delores Williams, Toinette Eugene, Daphne Hampson, Rita Nakashama Brock, Shawn Copeland, Reta Finger, Catherine LaCugna, and Mary Ann Tolbert--to name but a few) are some of the main contributors to the standard feminist theological literature presented in Section II of the bibliography.[35]

There are three additional points to be made here about the literature in Section II. First, the time frame encompassed by Section II is for the most part 1968-1993, although selected entries published through 1998 are also included. Thus, late 19th and early 20th century sources are omitted, although indicated by such historical sources as Bass and Boyd [130], Ruether and Keller [135], and Pellauer [271]. Second, the listings in Section II by no means exhaust the 1968 to mid-90s literature, but indicate instead its historical sweep. That is, they provide a chronology of key sources which have either generated the discussion of important issues in feminist theology, or, alternatively, proved pivotal in such discussion, as others have further developed selected issues and concerns. Last, the selected 1994-1998 entries presented in Section II provide an initial window into the now maturing moments of the feminist theological corpus, including its consistent recognition of diversity and theological pluralism and its widening horizon of cultural and religious dialogues. To repeat: Section II is the "big," largely "chronological" picture.

In contrast to these wide overview emphases, however, Section III of the bibliography reflects a deliberate attempt at synthesis, and if not an exhaustive listing of sources (for such is probably not possible by a single author) at least a fully representative introductory listing. More concretely, Section III of the bibliography is directed to a series of eight important and grounding "topical literatures" which have, in effect, become the literature of feminist, womanist, *Mujerista* and other multicultural women's theological studies. Further, these topics remain the galvanizing concerns around which a more comprehensive listing of sources can be organized. These topical literatures include the following: *Feminist Theology and Theological Anthropology; Feminist Theological Method; Feminist Biblical Studies; Feminist Theology and Historic Christian Symbols; Feminist Theological Ethics; Feminist Theology and Christian Worship; Feminist Spirituality;* and last, *Feminist Theology and the Critique of Heterosexism.* In Section III, while individual entries are arranged alphabetically by author, the effort here is toward *topical* syntheses, and as a consequence, affiliational emphases are largely ignored (although frequently identified within individual abstracts). Also, because the topics of this section are so important, every effort is made to cross-reference related sources so that areas of current and potential interdisciplinary discussion may be exposed.

Section IV of the bibliography presents entries from the rapidly expanding "Womanist Literature" within the study of feminism and Christian tradition. This literature is reasonably new to mainstream academic circles (both theological and sociological), but it dates from both the oral traditions of African American women surviving chattel slavery and the familistic, communal, social and literary traditions borne of that survival. It is an extremely important literature, and while many of its sources are presented and cross-referenced within the historical and topical literatures identified in Sections II and III, its emphases are sufficiently unique to warrant its characterization as an alternative "core literature" within the study of feminism and Christian tradition. Thus, as with previous sections, its bibliographic, specialized and theological sources are arranged accordingly, with subdivisions indicating the types and emphases of individual entries.

One further note is needed here in reference to Womanist theological literature. Because the defining emphasis of "Womanism" is the commitment of African American women to both themselves and to the familial, social and communal needs of African American children, families, women and men, as molded within the worlds of slavery, segregation and discrimination *and not those of European immigration and inclusion within America's mainstream denominational pluralism,* the variable of affiliational background (e.g., Roman Catholic or American Protestant) does not figure prominently within the womanist theological literature. As presented here, then, the literature is organized topically (e.g., womanist theology, womanist ethics, etc.) and within topics, alphabetically by author.[36]

Section V of the bibliography presents literature on the "The Religious Leadership of Women," and it is in this section that the published empirical literature on women clergy is surveyed. The section is divided into three major portions, with literature examining the experience of leadership among Protestant women surveyed first and the leadership of Roman Catholic women surveyed second. Both subsections include related historical and sociological sources indicating changes in American religious organization, and it is in the chapter on Roman Catholic women's religious leadership that the periodically controversial literatures of women's ordination and the "womenchurch" movement are surveyed. A final and brief chapter in Section V lists sources addressing "Feminist Theology, the Academy and Theological Education."[37]

The final section of the bibliography addresses recent developments, and as such, it provides material published largely from the late eighties and early nineties on four important and widely developing topics. These are: (1) "Antifeminism and Antifeminist Theology"; (2) "Patriarchy, Violence and Sexual Harassment within the Churches"; (3) "Feminist Theology's Global Voices"; and (4) "The Jewish-Christian Feminist Theological Dialogue." Because of the developing nature of these last four literatures, entries in Section VI are illustrative not exhaustive, and they point the reader in the direction of highlights rather than comprehensive listings.[38]

C. TRADITION, AUTHORITY and the WOMEN'S MOVEMENT in RELIGION

1. Feminist theology as a 'Second Reformation.' In an article following the height of feminist theology's early (1968-1973) prophetic literature, Catholic sociologist Marie Augusta Neal [**145**:35] described the women's movement in religion as a "second reformation." It was a "reformation" said Neal, "...as far reaching in its effect as the first" and this "...despite the fact that it was [then] hardly recognized by most sociologists of religion." This was no small suggestion, and in her discussion Neal suggested that this second reformation focused "...not on the mere insertion of women into the status roles provided within the present social system, but [instead] on change in the structure of [its] authority..." Moreover, she noted that "The values surrounding the family...with its traditional division of labor between men and women and children and parents...[were]...the values that religion...[had]...sacralized" and that these were the values that were both changing and in need of change, if religion was to continue as a creative force in modern society. Finally, Neal linked this change to the wider phenomenon of Western social change generally, and its shift from an ethic of "father right[s]" to one of "human right[s]."

2. *Feminist theology as a shift from "father rights to human rights."* Neal's discussion remains as valid today as when it was first published in 1975. First, as one examines the various sources addressing "Christianity and religious change" now published within the sociology of religion,[39] it becomes clear that late twentieth century Christianity is indeed experiencing a change, and that this change is very much tied to the experience and understanding Christianity has of its own "authority" in modern society. Second, it is also clear that this change is itself a process which is social and historical in origin, and that it involves the breakup of "hierarchy" and a growing awareness of "equality." Or, to return to Marie Augusta's exact words, it involves a "shift from father right[s] to human right[s]." Put in terms drawn from Max Weber, it involves the wide socio-cultural shift from "traditional" to "rational-legal" authority, and here specifically, one hastens to add, within the institutions of Christianity itself.

This shift is pivotal. For in very elemental terms, it entails (at the very least) the movement from "A," an obediance/compliance pattern of interaction between authority and its subordinates, to "B," a more *role negiotiated* pattern of authority-subordinate interaction. Moreover, although "hierarchy" (or the presence of super- and subordinate relations) is never removed from either "traditional" or "rational-legal" types of authority, its scope is clearly bounded in the rational (or "rational-legal") model of authority, whether because of such situationally specific factors as role expertise, or alternatively, the criteria of "efficiency" as dictated by the norms governing the specific roles in question. More concretely, while "hierarchy" is present in both traditional and rational-legal authority, it has, in effect, less "power over" people in the rational legal model, because power itself is more distributed.

An early discussion by sociologist Robert Nisbet captures this point clearly. As he summarized the understanding of "obedience" within Weber's traditional mode of authority, Nisbet noted that in the traditional model, "The object of obedience is *the personal authority of the individual which he enjoys by virtue of his traditional status*...[italics mine]" and futher, that "[the]...social essence [here] is *the direct personal relation between those affected:* teacher to student, servant to master, disciple to religious leader, and so on."[40] [Italics mine]. By way of contrast, however, in rational or rational legal authority, "All are equal under the rules governing them specifically...[and]...*the emphasis is on the rules* rather than on persons or on mores."[41] [Again, italics mine.]

Put somewhat differently, in the traditional model of authority, there is no distinction between the holder of authority and the boundaries of its exercise. Rather, the one is infused within the other, and obedience is an act of compliance to persons who are (in the eyes of subordinates) *indistinguishable from the positions or authority structures they occupy.* In the rational-legal model, however, there *is* a distinction between the authority to be exercised and the person who holds it, and in this model the authority of persons and the structures they occupy are separate. Moreover, in this model, the criteria governing authority role enactment are (at least, in theory) public and thus to some extent negotiable.

This distinction between persons and the "structures" they occupy may seem trivial or perhaps to some, even too subtle. But to persons unaccustomed to experiencing empowerment by and within *structures* of authority (whether religious, social, familial, occupational, or professional), the distinction between "persons" and "structures" is critical. For in the absence of such distinctions, persons of authority *are* authority—and in the case of Western Christendom—they are an authority which, historically, has stressed the physical, psychological and/or spiritual ownership of others, whether through sacralized ritual or family relations or, as is the case of some churches, a visible combination of both (e.g., clergy families). Illustrations aside, this point cannot be stressed strongly enough: in the "traditional" model, it matters little whether one is speaking of religious, familial, professional or social authorities, for the point is the same. The authority holder is not separate from the authority to be exercised. Hence, to return to Neal's discussion, it is this authority of "father right(s)" or an authority of ownership which in the 1960s and 1970s came publically under fire by the women's movement in religion, and which has continued to be so for nearly three decades.

Numerous theological writers have either presumed or made reference to this point, and it is this issue, which, has over time continued to ground the literature. Thus whether the terms of discussion are those involving "egalitarianism rather than hierarchy" or "inclusivity rather than exclusivity" or even the large and academically rich categories of a "paradigm" shift, the shift itself is about a restructuring of the connections between the holders and exercisers of authority, (i.e., the holders and exercisers of power), and relatedly, the recipients of that power and/or authority. Moreover, it is the almost palpable quality of this shift which seems to course through the various literatures of feminist theology, but especially those of its early and grounding years (i.e., 1968-1977), for it was during these years that authority's religiously cast "ownership" of women and children, of sisters and brothers, and of some men by others, its "father rights" if you will, began first, to unravel. And with this unraveling came the burst of literature now visible as the core sources of "feminism and Christian tradition."[42]

But there is more. For as this unravelling has continued, it has encompassed statuses apart from that of "gender," to include specifically, those "ascribed social statuses" over which individuals have no direct control—*viz.*, ethnicity, skin color, age, sexual orientation, and class origins—but to which society imputes value laden expectations. *It is this widened unravelling process which continues yet and which, together with the early literatures, now constitutes the literature of the women's movement in religion, or what is termed in this volume, the literature of "Feminism and Christian Tradition."*

When, then, did this literature begin? How has it developed? What are its main themes and principal emphases? Who are its key authors? And how have these various writings fared, since their establishment as an alternative perspective to the literature of traditional Christian theology? The next portion of this general introduction addresses these questions. It presents a brief history of the literature as a whole, together with a summary of its principal authors, ideas, theological and sociological contributions.

ENDNOTES

[1] Given the complexity of numerous sociological and feminist theological sources, the strategy of extended rather than abbreviated annotations has proved absolutely necessary, and I wish to thank those colleagues who reviewed various entries against original sources to give me a feel for appropriately helpful abstract lengths, and who "pre-tested" the use of specific abstracts as sources for lecture material.

[2] Alice Walker, *In Search of Our Mother's Gardens: Womanist Prose*. San Diego: Harcourt Bruce Janovich, 1983.

[3] Robert Schreiter, *Constructing Local Theologies*. Maryknoll, NY: Orbis, 1985, p. 106. I am particularly indebted here to the discussion on pp. 104-109 and all quotations are taken from these pages.

[4] Schreiter's discussion is rich in its implications for understanding religious change, and the reader is referred to chapters 2-5 of his text for details. Of particular salience is Schreiter's discussion of the "workability" of traditions. For traditions to "work," says Schreiter (that is, for traditions to give and ground social and personal identity), they must meet four functional criteria. First and foremost they must be "credible," i.e., the tradition's concerns must match or speak to those of the society or culture in question. Second, traditions (or a tradition) must be "intelligible," i.e., meaningful across various sectors of experience. Third, in order to work, a tradition must have "authority" or the "ability to mediate both identity and environment" and in a manner that is "beyond the level of the merely arbitrary." Last, a working tradition must be able to incorporate change. This is especially important, for the tradition must be able to absorb what is key to its survival as credible and intelligible. These "essentials" of a working tradition, says Schreiter, are what give it its integrating or meaning based quality, or alternatively, its character of dissonance and anomaly when either it or *its varying components* begin to fail (cf. Schreiter's discussion on pp. 104-112 of *Constructing Local Theologies*).

[5] For helpful introductions to the sociological literature here, see John Hood-Williams, "Goodby to Sex and Gender," *The Sociological Review* 44 (1996): 1-17 and Judith Lorber, "Beyond the Binaries: Depolarizing the Categories of Sex, Sexuality and Gender." *Sociological Inquiry* 66 (1996): 143-159.

[6] See, for example, the sociological discussions by Zinn and Dill [83], Andersen [84], Andersen and Collins [85], Collins [99], Basow [117], Feagin and Feagin [122]. Additionally, see the historical discussion by Giddings [614] and for a strong theological discussion see Copeland [278].

[7] An unfortunate effect of this first bias is that the literature on global feminism is thus relegated largely to bibliographic rather than single book length sources, although the entries by Morgan [9], Neft and Levine [10], Heise [28] and Jaggar [32] leave no doubt as to the fact that physical violence to women and the political support of policies dependent on women's poverty are the central, global-ethical issues which must be addressed, and especially so if organizational Christianity is to maintain its credibility as a tradition of "universal" love. For the theological literature here, see Chittister [754], Schüssler Fiorenza and Carr [493], and Schüssler Fiorenza and Copeland [275], and the literature generally in Chapter 23.

[8] Cf. the following entries: Susan Cady et al. [540], Carol Christ and Judith Plaskow [206], Elizabeth Moltmann-Wendel and Jürgen Moltmann [424], Sandra M. Schneiders [546], Dorothy Sölle [426].

[9]See, for example, the following entries: Mary Collins [517], Jackie Grant [254], Nancy Hardesty [519], Carter Heyward [242], Elizabeth Johnson [232, 422], Nelle Morton [202], Sally McFague [244], Virginia Ramey Mollenkott [247], Gail Ramshaw [523], and Miriam T. Winter [531].

[10]Cf. the entries by Katie G. Cannon [625], Ada Maria Isasi-Diaz [929], Kwok Pui-Lan [219], Letty Russell et al. [910], Susan Thistlethwaite [252], Delores Williams [259], and Marcia Y. Riggs [257].

[11]For examples here, see the entries by Adela Yarbro Collins [349], Rita Nakashima Brock [432], Beverly Harrison and Carol Robb [207], Carter Heyward [242], Clarice Martin [374], Rosemary Radford Ruether [366], Elisabeth Schüssler Fiorenza [369], Mary Ann Tolbert [372], Renita Weems [376].

[12]In its classical usage the term "hermeneutics" suggests a collective noun, the idea that a body of set principles exists by which the Bible and its meaning(s) can be understood. From a sociological perspective (cf. Rosabeth Kanter's discussion of commitment mechanisms in *Community and Commitment*, Cambridge: Harvard University Press, 1972) these principles are typically the norms of a religious community as defined by community leaders and as developed historically over several generations. Some examples from Christianity here are the Lutheran notion of "law and gospel," or alternatively, the Reformation principle that Scripture "interprets itself." As used by feminist theologians, the term hermeneutics still suggests a collective noun or the idea that there are "principles of interpretation," but these principles do not exist as communal norms divorced from the particularities of women's experience. Rather, these norms either arise from or seek to address various aspects of women's experience. Hence the literature identifies several idiomatic emphases, e.g., a "hermeneutics of suspicion" or the notion of a "feminist critical liberationist hermeneutic" to name but two. In these and other cases the idiom intends two things: (a) one or more interpretive principles identifying the normative authority of women's experience; and (b) the feminist critique of reified images of women's experience as drawn from either an earlier time or the assumptions of an androcentric frame of reference. For summaries of the early literature on feminist hermeneutics see Johnson [353] and Osiek [354], while for later literature see Castelli [358] and Trible [359]. Additionally, for Schüssler Fiorenza's work in hermeneutics see her many articles, but particularly [411], her discussion of the elements comprising a "feminist critical liberationist hermeneutic" and the ways in which it is to be distinguished from the more generalized framework of "liberation theology." Further, see [236] which includes her recent overview of the various hermeneutical strategies employed by feminist biblical theologians in their task(s) of interpreting biblical texts. Finally, for literature on womanist hermeneutics see Grant [254, 636], Williams [639], and Weems [642], while for the varying use of feminist hermeneutics within Judaism, see Plaskow [954] and Umansky [957].

[13]Cf. the following entries: Barbara Andolsen [468], Esther Bruland [474], Lisa Cahill [469], Ann Carr [549], Katie Cannon [253], Shawn Copeland [265], Rebecca Chopp [811], Margaret Farley [471], Ann O'Hara Graff [331], Eleanor Haney [473], Mary Hunt [479], Ada Maria Isasi-Diaz [928], Catherine LaCugna [234], Mollenkott [247], Letty M. Russell [250], Elsa Tamez [931], Johanna Bos [651].

[14]Cf. the following entries: Sheila Briggs [306], Virginia Fabella and Sun Ai Li Park [933], Aruna Gnanadason [916, 934], Marcia Riggs [508], and Rosemary Radford Ruether [172].

[15]Cf. the entries by Mary Daly [161], Letty M. Russell [249], Elisabeth Schüssler Fiorenza [175, 194, 237, 238], and in a somewhat different context, the literatures on "divine child abuse," e.g., Joanne Carlson Brown and Carole R. Bohn [863], Joanne Carlson Brown et al. [864]; and clergy sexual misconduct with adult women parishioners, e.g., Pamela Cooper-White [883], Marie Fortune [877], and Karen Lebacqz and Ronald G. Barton [878].

[16]Cf. the entries by Marie Kolbenschlag [756], Daphne Hampson [286], Rosemary Radford Ruether [759], Letty M. Russell [656], Leonard Swidler and Arlene Swidler [781], Mary Jo Weaver [762].

[17]Cf. the entries by Lynn Rhodes [655], Ruth R. Wallace [787], Delores Carpenter [644], Barbara Brown Zikmund [681, 682], Barbara Brown Zikmund, Adair Lummis and Patricia Mei Yin Chang [663] and much of the sociological literature cited later in this introduction.

[18]In several of her works, Daly notes the capacity of religious and church leaders to use ridicule and trivialization as the means of disparaging feminist theological analysis, literature and issues. Her own work was subjected to enormous trivialization when first published, although most of this was verbal rather than published and located within male clerical and academic circles. Of particular note was the response to her suggestion in *The Church and the Second Sex* that Catholic women should be ordained. As the first American woman theologian to criticize the hierarchical authority of Roman Catholicism in a manner which caught the public's eye, Daly has paid dearly for her integrity. Initially, her public challenge to Catholicism's authority cost Daly her teaching position as an assistant professor at Boston College (cf. *The Christian Century* 86 [April 9, 1969]: 471), although she was reinstated as an associate professor in 1969, following a critical protest within the institution. Presently, she continues to teach at Boston College and has published widely in the area of feminist philosophy (cf. Weaver [762:128] and Schneiders [761]). While Daly's identified mechanisms of ridicule and trivialization do not quite approach the level of what sociologists describe as "degradation ceremonies" (cf. Harold Garfinkel, "Conditions of Successful

Degradation Ceremonies" *American Journal of Sociology* 61 no. 2 [1956]: 420-424), they clearly qualify as mechanisms of status leveling as described by Kanter [728]. For Catholic feminist literature highlighting the significance of Daly's work, see Patrick [183] and Weaver [762]; additionally, see Loades [274] and Plaskow [262] for illustrative Protestant and Jewish perspectives, respectively.

[19]Cf. the anthologies edited by Weidman [213] and May [919]. At present, one can find several elements of theological consensus within the writings of women from differing denominational backgrounds (e.g., the need for theologically inclusive liturgical language, an attention to issues of poverty and social justice, and a clear preference for egalitarian rather than hierarchical patterns of interaction), and all of these because of the breadth of feminism's critique of historic Christian symbols. Where variation occurs, however, and where one might expect it to continue to occur, is in specifically "heritage" or historically based Protestant-Catholic differences such as an attention to the Bible as an "external" rather than communally grounded source of authority, or alternatively, an understanding of 'ministry' as grounded in local and familistic rather cosmopolitan and communitarian norms. While these kinds of differences are not formally discussed within the theological literature, several pieces allude to them or describe their more concrete expressions. For an insightful discussion of Protestant-Catholic differences by a biblical scholar, see Tolbert [284]. For the sociological literature see Briggs [137], Neitz [148], and Roberts [150].

[20]Again, the reader is cautioned not to equate the assumptions of African American feminism with those of "mainstream feminism," and particularly, the class based assumptions of feminist perspectives operative during the early years of the American feminist movement. Rather, as has been emphasized previously, the term 'womanist' is used by its originator Alice Walker and others to indicate the full personal and communal commitments of African American women to African American women, children and men, on behalf of African American families and communities, and in turn, all humanity. Hence, as a theological perspective, womanism suggests a Black feminist Christian tradition which transcends denominational lines and challenges the race/gender privilege of many established white feminist theologians

[21]See Isasi-Diaz [927, 928, 929, 256] and Tamez [930, 931]. The scope of the name "*Mujerista*" to designate the communal and empowerment aspects of many Hispanic women's theology is, in the mid-1990s, yet evolving, as Isasi-Diaz's work indicates. Further, while it is distinguished here from the "Latin American" feminist theology emanating from the Ecumenical Association of Third World Theologians [EATWOT] as represented, for example, by Maria Pilar Aquino [926], it is not inconsistent with the critical work provided through EATWOT. Rather, *Mujerista* theology and the feminist theology arising from EATWOT differ largely in terms of their organizational groundings: where Aquino's work builds from both Latin American publications and EATWOT Conference documents, Isasi-Diaz's work stems from both grass-roots activism on behalf of Spanish speaking women living in the United States and the religious community *Las Hermanas* and its efforts on behalf of Hispanic Catholics in the United States.

[22]See Maria Pilar Aquino [926].

[23]See, for example, Plaskow [953, 955], Falk [260], Gottlieb [261] and Umansky [957].

[24]The field-defining text is Chung Hyun Kyung's *Struggle to be the Sun Again* [935]. Additionally see the related literature in Chapter 23.

[25]See Ruether and Keller [132:432-433].

[26]See Gray [241], Scanzoni and Hardesty [251] and see the previously cited Bruland [474].

[27]See Hunt [556], Nugent and Gramick [587] and Zanotti [752] for the Catholic sources; see Heyward [217] and [242] for Episcopal sources; see Scanzoni and Mollenkott [574] and Mollenkott [247] for the evangelical literature; and see Hill [627] for womanist literature.

[28]Cf. [924] and [925].

[29]Judith Plaskow's work [970, 971] is pre-eminent here, although two early Catholic works should also be cited: Rosemary Radford Ruether's 1974 volume, *Faith and Fratricide* [299], a detailed history of the anti-Semitism endemic to Christian teaching since the beginnings of Christianity, and Charlotte Klein's *Theologie und Anti-Judaismus*, first published in 1975 and translated in 1978 as *Anti-Judaism in Christian Theology* [312]. Written from the perspective of a Jewish convert to Roman Catholicism, Klein's text first identifies and then documents several anti-Jewish themes taken for granted in key German exegetical and theological texts published from 1945 through the post-war period and used routinely in seminary teaching. In contrast, the Ruether text details the history of Christian anti-Judaism from its beginnings in the New Testament to its twentieth century expression in Nazi Germany. The recognition of "anti-Judaism" in Christian feminist theological writing is something to which Christian feminists are now becoming more sensitized (Cf. D'Angelo [397] and [433]), and it is one of the most important ecumenical dialogues now in process. Indeed, given the fundamentalism of much late twentieth century traditional Christian theology and its potentially Holocaust-denying implications, the dialogue between Jewish and Christian feminists cannot be emphasized strongly enough. By way of illustration, contrast the recent discussion by Lutheran theologian Paul Hinlickey ("A Lutheran Contribution to the Theology of Judaism." *Journal of Ecumenical Studies* 3, nos. 1-2 [Winter-Spring, 1994]: 123-152) with John Pawlikowski's text ("Christology, Anti-Semitism, and Christian-Jewish Bonding") in *Reconstructing*

Christian Theology, edited by Rebecca S. Chopp and Mark Lewis Taylor (Minneapolis, MN: Fortress, 1994, pp. 245-268). Hinlickey's discussion seems to suggest that Christianity's pre-Holocaust anti-Semitism—and especially its religious grounding in pre-World War II German Christianity—is not only not true, but is, at a very basic level, a gross misreading of what Christians actually thought, felt and believed about Jewish people in pre-WW II Germany. Alternatively, Pawlikowski's discussion synthesizes the more mainline (albeit androcentric) literature and the efforts of (male) Christian leaders to achieve healing and dialogue between Christian and Jewish traditions, *precisely because of* Christianity's twenty-centuries long history of anti-Semitism and violence to Jewish people. For a review of several recent "mainline" theological responses to the Holocaust, see Beverly Allen Asbury and Matthew C. Hawk, "Recent Perspectives on the Holocaust," *Religious Studies Review* 22 no. 3, (1996): 197-208. Additionally, see Peter Ochs' "Judaism and Christian Theology," in *The Modern Theologians*, edited by David F. Ford, 607-625, (2d ed.), Cambridge: Blackwell, 1997. Last, for examples of (male) Christian ecclesiastical and organizational literature, see the Jewish-Christian web site, *http://www.jcrelations.com*. It provides bibliography and selected articles dealing with institutional and theological issues of dialogue, although from perspectives uninformed by the literature of this bibliography.

30See, e.g., Stineman and Loeb [55], Hull, Scott and Smith [49], Loeb, Searing and Stineman [51], and Kramarae and Spender [66] to name but four now standard women's studies reference texts.

31Readers unfamiliar with these technical theological terms can consult any of the standard theological dictionaries, such as, e.g., *A New Handbook of Christian Theology*, edited by Donald W. Musser and Joseph L. Price, Nashville: Abingdon, 1992. At the risk of enormous oversimplification, however, the term "Christology" refers to theological writings about Jesus—and typically in terms of the history of Christian teachings that developed about him over the course of Christianity's first five or so centuries. Likewise, Mariology and ecclesiology refer, respectively, to theological writings about Mary (Jesus' mother) and "the church," with the latter understood as an organized community grounded in and at once expressive of what Christians perceive as God's absolute care for humanity. Similarly, soteriology refers to theological writings about redemption and "ultimate salvation," while eschatology refers to an understanding of temporal ultimacy. With respect to the latter, this ultimacy is sometimes conceptualized by the contrasting assumptions attached to the ideas of "time" and "eternity," while for others it means the process of history itself, as touched by the transcendence toward which (in the eyes of faith) history seems, itself, to be moving. These descriptions of time and its significance vary, but when speaking of 'eschatology,' it is time and its perceived significance *over time* that are being considered.

32Cf., e.g., the secularization literature cited in Chapters 18 and 19.

33Nor is this the only argument which can be made. As Plaskow [340] notes in a 1993 double issue of *Women's Studies Quarterly* [543], there is also a need for dialogue between religious scholars working in the area of women's studies and religion, as well as women's studies scholars working in feminist theology.

34Nor do these reasons even begin to tap the growth potentials within the literature. To cite but a few examples: Although feminist, Womanist, *Mujerista*, Minjung and other women's theologies all reflect the feminist perception of "the personal" as riddled through with "the political" (a long standing feminist emphasis), the literature of feminist civil religion—as expressed, e.g., by the leadership traditions of African American women—is yet to be developed, although it is clearly intimated in a number of historical and womanist theological sources. Cf. Giddings [614] and Townes [633].

35A present lacuna within the literature is the absence of "A Feminist Theological 'Who's Who,'" a biographical directory of feminist theologians working in seminaries and departments of religious studies nationwide. The beginnings of such a directory exist for African American feminist theologians in the 1991 *Directory of African American Religious Bodies* [599] where editor Wardell Payne presents a "selective" list of African American scholars in religion, including womanist and Black feminist theologians. A "second career" pastor within the Washington DC area, Payne's first career was as a Ph.D. sociologist demographer in criminal justice statistics. More recently, Russell and Clarkson's 1994 *Dictionary of Feminist Theologies* [272] provides academic addresses for more than 450 feminist, womanist and *Mujerista* contributors.

36This is not to suggest that denominations are not relevant within the womanist theological context. As Lincoln and Mamiya [598] indicate at the beginning of their study, more than 80% of Black Americans belong to the seven historical and totally Black controlled denominations formed after the "Free African Society of 1787." Further, as Delores Carpenter's doctoral dissertation research indicates (as cited by Lincoln and Mamiya [598:298], more than half of Carpenter's Black clergywomen thesis sample (N=380) were ordained and employed by established, mainline and white denominations. (See Carpenter's 1986 essay [644] for a brief description of her thesis data within the context of clergywomen and the professionalization of the ministry.)

37By way of background for both the women-church and related entries cutting across all of Section V, Elisabeth Schüssler Fiorenza is generally credited with the naming of "women-church" as a distinct movement and experience [195], and as used by her, the term suggests both an historical process of women gathering (e.g., the "ecclesia of women") and a hermeneutical principle [369], the latter being the setting for interpreting the salvific power of Scripture for women. The precise genesis of the term, however, is more fluid than specific footnotes can suggest. For example, in her 1977 discussion, *Mary: the Feminine Face of the Church* [448], Ruether refers to women as the image of the church. Similarly, in one of her earliest essays [179] Carter Heyward suggested the necessity for a community of women making church. Most recently [792] the literature speaks of the phenomenon of "womenchurch" as virtually "trans-Atlantic" in scope and as a distinctive and identifiable reform movement within institutional Christianity. Additionally, M. T. Winter (in Russell and Clarkson, [272:318]) credits the Women's Ordination Conference and the 1983 Catholic "Call to Action" with the genesis of the term, while in the conversational settings of women's worship groups, Diann Neu has often been credited with the genesis of the term. The fluidity of the term suggests the power of the symbol, and more deeply, the well springs from which it is emerging. Further, its recent appropriation by Chopp [812] as both a *reflection* of feminist theological education and a *principle* of feminist theological education, attests again, the power of the symbol—its authority, its depth, and its range.

[38]By way of additional literature for these topics, readers should consult both the bibliographies cited in Section VI and the more generalized bibliographies presented in Section I, and for literature on the developing discussion of "Native American Women's Theologies," in particular, readers should see Inez Maria Talamantez's discussion in Ruether and Keller [135], as well as Evans [74], Loeb, Searing and Stineman [51], DuBois and Ruiz [73], Zinn and Dill [83], Freeman [88], and the article entries in Mankiller et al. [52]. Also, for supplemental literature on Jewish feminist theology, the reader should consult Judith Hauptman, "Women and Prayer: An Attempt to Dispel Some Fallacies," *Judaism* 42 (1993): 94-103, and also by Hauptman, "Women and the Conservative Synagogue," in *Daughters of the King: Women and the Synagogue--A Survey of History, Halakhah and Contemporary Realities*, edited by Susan Grossman and Rivka Haut (Philadelphia: Jewish Publication Society, 1992).

[39]Included here are the ideas that Christianity is experiencing either a "secularization" process or a transposition from the public to the private sphere [686], and in the United States, a "struggle for America's soul" (cf. [687] and [688]).

[40]Robert Nisbet, *The Sociological Tradition*, NY: Basic Books, 1968, p. 142. Additionally, see Weber's own discussion which links patriarchy and traditional authority in religion in *From Max Weber: Essays in Sociology*, translated, edited and with an introduction by Hans H. Gerth and C. Wright Mills (NY: Oxford University Press, 1946), pp. 296 ff.

[41]*Ibid.*, p. 143.

[42]Nor do Neal's remarks pertain to Christians only. As the September 1995 United Nations Conference on Women held in Beijing evidenced, the shift from father rights to human rights is evident through the world generally, albeit at what for many are almost overwhelming levels of struggle. For a passionate and deeply moving account of one woman's experience of the Beijing Conference, see Joan Chittister, *Beyond Beijing: The Next Step for Women, A Personal Journal*, Kansas City, MO: Sheed and Ward, 1996. Additionally, see the data cited by Neft and Levine [10].

Mapping the Literature: 1968–1995

A. Feminism and Christian Tradition: An Overview of the Literature

1. Pin-pointing the beginnings. Pin-pointing the beginnings of any academic literature is always risky, and to pin-point the beginnings of the American feminist theological literature is riskier still. This is because, in accordance with one's definition of feminism, those beginnings may be identified with at least three historically and conceptually varied publications. These include (1) Elizabeth Cady Stanton's *The Woman's Bible,* a suffragist grounded text first published in 1895 and then reprinted in 1974 and 1993 (the latter with an excellent forward by Maureen Fitzgerald [346]); (2) Valerie Saiving's now classic discussion, "On the Human Situation" [163] an essay length exposure of male bias in theology first published in 1960, but not widely read until reprinted in 1979 in the feminist reader, *Womanspirit Rising,* edited by Carol Christ and Judith Plaskow [206]; and (3), Mary Daly's *The Church and the Second Sex* [157], an analysis of Christian (specifically Roman Catholic) misogynous teaching first published in 1968 (and angrily received by Church authorities at that time) and then re-issued by Daly in 1975 with its now famous "Post-Christian Feminist Introduction" in which Daly indicates her formal disaffiliation with Catholicism as her institutionally based religious framework.

For the purposes of this volume it is the last entry which shall be taken as the beginning point of the American feminist theological literature. The rationale for this beginning point stems from the literature on social movements which argues consistently that the presence of a galvanizing text, leader, or event is an early and necessary component in the successful launching of a social movement, in that without such an event, text or leader, the population frustrated by a given problem remains unmobilized as a movement resource.[1] Thus, while it is possible to argue a variety of starting points for the literature (cf. Schüssler Fiorenza [195], Christ [177], Plaskow [170], and Russell and Clarkson [272]),[2] it is Daly's text which is taken here as the beginning point of the literature, for it is Daly's discussion which meets the criterion of a galvanizing event.[3]

2. Three periods of development. With the decision about its beginning points made, the task of mapping the literature is significantly simplified. This is because the process of mapping requires only two basic tasks: the identification of a specific time frame, here the years 1968-1993; and an identification of those issues or distinguishing emphases which mark the development of the literature within that time frame. Put differently, the process of mapping becomes one of disclosing (a) the points of conceptual differentiation within the literature and (b) the times frames within which these points become visible. What, then, are those points of differentiation? And at what times are they visible?[4]

An examination of annual publications suggests three broad periods of development. The first is an early and classical period dating from 1968 through 1977. This period exhibits both critical and transitional pieces and it is distinguished clearly by its strong critique of patriarchy and misogyny within the history of Christian tradition. The second period of the literature's development stretches from 1978 through 1985. It continues many of the early and classical themes, but it is marked distinctively by a variety of methodological and discipline defining questions. Feminist theology's third period runs from 1986 through the early 1990s, and while it also includes critical and methodological pieces, its principal emphasis is on the reconstruction of the tradition from within the values established through the methodological phase of the literature.

A fourth period, the literature published from 1994 on, might also be distinguished, and perhaps characterized as feminist theology's "multicultural" period, in that the mid- through late-90s literature addresses issues of commitment and social location vis a vis theological sources and institutional applications. This characterization is, however, premature, and yet in tension with the literature of "identity politics." Hence, the more conservative framework of a three period development will be presented here.[5]

3. *Key themes within the literature*. The first period of the feminist theological literature encompasses the years 1968-1977. It takes in the early and classical sources published between 1968-1973 (a source group bounded at both ends by publications by Mary Daly) and it includes transitional sources published from 1974-1976 and a handful of early literature reviews published through 1977 including Carol Christ's [177] enormously influential "The New Feminist Theology: A Review of the Literature." Among the key themes emphasized in this period are (a) the prophetic critique of patriarchy, misogyny and the religious marginalization of women; and (b) the struggle to find a theological framework--a methodology, as it were--which respects the experience of women while yet acknowledging the results of women's marginalization from positive Christian themes and formal religious leadership.

Several important studies stem historically from this period. First, and of obvious importance, is Daly's grounding text, *The Church and the Second Sex*. With its panoramic view of Christian tradition as a history gripped by misogynist and androcentric thinking, Daly's text opened the feminist-Christian dialogue widely, with ramifications for virtually all mainline churches, in spite of Daly's then organizationally Catholic and late-'60s conciliar horizon.

Similarly, Daly's 1973 volume, *Beyond God the Father* [161], was equally, if not more influential, for its challenge to the "Father-God" and "Father-Son" symbolisms of Christian doctrine precipitated deeply felt questions which would echo through the literature for at least another decade, and some would argue even into the present time.[6] Moreover, with its symbolic coupling to Daly's first volume (by Carol Christ in 1977 as a means of framing the 1968-1976 literature [177]) *Beyond God the Father* was weighted with an almost indelible character, in that Christ's discussion identified virtually all feminist theological writing as either "reformist" in nature (i.e., more similar to Daly's first work) and thereby still within "the tradition" or alternatively, as "revolutionary" in nature (i.e., more similar to *Beyond God the Father)*, and thereby outside of or beyond "the tradition." Indeed, if there are any sources at all which powerfully define the early lines of the feminist theological literature, it is this threefold composite: Daly's first two volumes and the classificatory scope assigned them by Carol Christ in her 1977 review of the then developing feminist theological literature.[7]

But Daly's two books and the symbolism assigned them by Christ were not the only early and grounding sources of the feminist theological movement. Rather, a handful of additional sources also served to ground the literature, and in the long run, move it beyond its reformist/revolutionary polarization and into its core works (*viz.*, the sources prominent from 1978-1985). Among others, these additional sources include the following: Phyllis Trible's early essays on the study of gender and selected "Old" or First Testament texts ([164, 165]); the 1974 anthology *Religion and Sexism: Images of Women in the Jewish and Christian Traditions*, edited by Rosemary Radford Ruether [171]; Ruether's own essay collection, *New Women/New Earth* [172] published in 1975; Mary Daly's "Post Christian Feminist Introduction" to the 1975 edition of *The Church and the Second Sex;* Letty Russell's short but important 1976 collection, *Liberating Word: A Guide to Nonsexist Interpretation of the Bible* [174]; selected discussions published from within the American Academy of Religion (notably the reader edited by Rita Gross [187] and within it, Plaskow's early essay [170] on feminist theological method) and last, Margaret Farley's two critically important mid-'70s essays: (a) her deeply reflective discussion of gender and ethics [166] in the 1975 "women's issue" of *Theological Studies* [185]; and (b) her 1976 essay, "Sources of Sexual Inequality in the History of Christian Thought" [167]. All of these sources were significant in the development of the literature during its early years, for each attempted either a topically specific analysis of patriarchy within a given framework (e.g., the works by Ruether and Trible), or alternatively, a refocusing of the rapidly developing polarization which Carol Christ initially identified in her 1977 literature review.[8]

The second period of the feminist-Christian tradition corpus stretches from 1978 through 1985. It includes feminist theology's core or discipline defining works, and especially a variety of works published by Ruether [190], Heyward [198], McFague [200], Schüssler Fiorenza ([194, 195, 196]), Russell [210], Harrison (with Carol Robb) [207] and Cannon [612]. These works are described in the bibliography, but their most consistent emphasis is the attempt to identify the parameters of feminist theological method, and especially so in the light of feminist theology's reconstruction of the symbol "female" as also the "Image of God." Indeed, if the critiques of patriarchy, misogyny and women's marginalization are the markers for the early and classical sources, it is the redemption of women's experience from such perspectives which marks the literature from 1978-1985.[9]

In particular, it was during the years 1978-1985 that three things happened. First, a variety of biblical, historical, theological and ethical analyses of women's experience served to push reified and androcentric religious constructs aside, and to disclose thereby, the suppressed history of women in Christian tradition. (For some of the early literature here see Bass and Boyd [130].) Second, this process of exposure served to legitimate the positive experience of women within the tradition and to identify, thereby, its distortion throughout history. Third, as each of these processes occurred—whether in print, prayer, spirituality groups, and/or papers and caucuses at professional meetings—they each functioned to free up the discussion of women and Christian tradition and to make the suppressed history of women within the tradition available to others as a now legitimate source of religious insight and revelation.

Similarly, it was during this same period that the pluralism of women's experience became theologically visible, and particularly so for women within African American, Hispanic, Asian and Jewish religious communities. For by 1985, as the literatures in Sections IV and VI of the bibliography suggest--women within each of these communities had begun either to articulate their own theological histories, or alternatively, to identify the points of conflict (or consensus) which their communities held vis a vis Christianity's more dominant and established perspectives.[10]

The final period of feminist theology's general development is from 1986 through the mid- to late-1990s, and as with the first two periods, this period also critiques patriarchy and its negative images of women. However, unlike the first two periods, which are by and large respectively critical and methodological in focus, the current period is explicitly reconstructive. It is mindful of the necessity for a recasting of Christian themes and symbolizations along the lines of explicitly feminist ethical and feminist theological emphases (as identified during the second period of the literature's development), and thus it exhibits images and expectations which express inclusivity rather than exclusivity, egalitarianism rather than hierarchy, and mutuality rather than isolation.

Likewise, it is a literature yet attentive to the pluralism of women's experience. That is to say, it attends explicitly to the academic, existential, racial-ethnic, sexual, social, religious and ecclesiological horizons from within which women live, and the differences such differences make in the reconstruction of Christian or any religious tradition. This attention to pluralism is an important and still evolving emphasis within the literature. And, while it is grounded and held within the values of justice and mutuality, as established during the second period of the literature's development, its current expression is distinctively focused to address both (a) the commitments *and* the conflicts of the women's movement in religion (cf. Cannon and Schüssler Fiorenza [348], Bounds [485], Buhrig [652], Grant [214, 254], Jones [267], Kwok PuL-lan [219], King [338], Peskowitz et al. [339], Plaskow [968], Tolbert [284], Williams [341], Brock et al. [277], Graff [331], Hampson [286], Mercerdante et al. [648], and Copeland [278]); and (b) the expansion of feminist theology to an identification with ecology (cf. McFague [245], Johnson [233] and Ruether [235]); with issues of interreligious dialogue (cf. Brock et al. [277] and May [920]); and the needs of feminism globally on behalf of justice for women (Benevides [914], Finger [915], Hunt [919], Oduyoye [920] and Talbot [938]).

Finally, this last phase of the literature is also explicitly "populist" in terms of at least two issues, i.e., those of domestic and "ecclesiastical" [869] violence. In particular, as feminist theologians have examined various soteriological motifs, they have critiqued the sacralization of physical and sexual violence implicit in Christianity's history of misogynous and androcentric teaching, and concomitantly, the realities of domestic abuse within families and the sexual malfeasance of clergy against parishioners and/or congregational members.[11]

4. Classical Sources. Before turning to other concerns (specifically the sociological sources on women in ordained ministries), it will be helpful to review briefly some of the more classical statements from the feminist theological literature. This is because, like other literatures, this one too is grounded by its "classical" or discipline defining sources, or those texts which have served to shape its long term development. Some of these texts have been mentioned above (works by Mary Daly, Letty M. Russell, Rosemary Radford Ruether, Carol Christ, Margaret Farley, Judith Plaskow and Phyllis Trible. But there are a number of other sources which also ground the literature, and which have come to be looked upon as classics in spite of their publication beyond the early years of the feminist theological movement. Among these additional texts are the 1979 feminist spirituality reader, *Womanspirit Rising* [206], coedited by Carol Christ and Judith Plaskow; Rosemary Ruether's 1983 *Sexism and God-Talk* [190], Elizabeth Schüssler Fiorenza's *In Memory of Her* [195]; and Katie Cannon's essay, "The Emergence of Black Feminist Consciousness" [612].

The Christ and Plaskow reader is almost without precedent in terms of the wide area of women's studies and religion, for its multitraditioned entries challenge historical Jewish and Christian spiritualities and posit goddess experience as one of feminist theology's most significant resources.[12] Similarly, Ruether's *Sexism and God-Talk* falls also within this pale. With its systematic address of several historically specific Christian theological issues, ranging from methodology to eschatology, and with its description of transcendence as the unpronounceable "God/ess," it presents a first pass at feminist systematics, a discussion at once reformist and revolutionary and—antifeminist complaints notwithstanding--clearly within the tradition.[13]

The two remaining classics are Elisabeth Schüssler Fiorenza's *In Memory of Her: A Feminist Reconstruction of Christian Origins* [195] and Katie Cannon's essay, "The Emergence of Black Feminist Consciousness" [612].

Elisabeth Schüssler Fiorenza is one of the most widely known and internationally famous biblical and feminist theologians. She received her training in Germany before settling in the United States and teaching at a variety of American theological institutions. Her initial scholarship was well within the general lines of liberal and mainline biblical theology: an attention to the methodological issues of form and redaction criticisms, higher and lower criticism, the perception of the Bible as literature, the fully ecumenical or nondenominational appreciation of the Bible as an historical document, and so forth. Moreover, her commentaries on the book of Revelation[14] had established her credentials as a scholar of note, and her work was, as the saying goes, "rigorously academic." In 1984, however, Schüssler Fiorenza published two volumes [195, 196] which synthesized several earlier and more condensed discussions [194, 394, 440, 402] and challenged the then regnant assumptions about biblical criticism as an exclusively value free enterprise done quietly within the confines of academe—as contrasted with the lived-life of Christian parish and congregational experience. The first of these volumes was Schüssler Fiorenza's now famous, *In Memory of Her: A Feminist Theological Reconstruction of Christian Origins.*

In Memory of Her amassed mountains of scholarship to make several specific and related arguments: that women were among the very first of the early Christian disciples, that their presence in early Christianity was central not marginal, that women shared significantly in the leadership of the early church and its formal apostolic roles, and that the long history of Christian theology has, over time, suppressed this tradition of experience and leadership and that it continues to do so for the sake of its own organizational maintenance. Moreover, in the historical portion of her discussion, Schüssler Fiorenza argued that this process of suppression was neither sociologically inevitable (as a functional prerequisite to the development of Christianity), nor a mere accident of history. Rather, it was a sustained process of women's exclusion and marginalization from the "discipleship of equals," and it was and remains a process to which feminist hermeneutics and feminist biblical theological studies must ever be critically alert. No doubt, because it touched the core sources of religious authority for Christianity across the board, the Bible for Protestants and both "scripture and tradition" for Roman Catholics, *In Memory of Her* received instant and sustained attention to the point of citation by both the secular and religious press, with responses ranging from clerics fearful of its meaning to those acknowledging its courageous significance.[15]

Schüssler Fiorenza's second 1984 volume was *Bread Not Stone*, a collection of feminist hermeneutical essays critiquing the androcentric assumptions of exegesis and interpretation in both the Bible and established biblical scholarship. Although less programmatic than *In Memory of Her*, and presented as an essay collection rather than a sustained response to one fragment of biblical text (namely, Mark 14:9), *Bread Not Stone* also served feminist notice to the world of biblical studies. By way of particulars, its compact essays detailed Schüssler Fiorenza's "critical feminist liberationist hermeneutic," while its numerous footnotes on the history of biblical scholarship detailed the male dominance of biblical studies, literature and thought. Space precludes a listing of Schüssler Fiorenza's accomplishments within the pages of *Bread Not Stone* and *In Memory of Her*, but the discussion by Throckmorton [355] on the achievements of feminist biblical scholars presumes them at almost every point, and particularly Schüssler Fiorenza's work in *In Memory of Her.*[16] Further, in her various professional roles—as the Krister Stendahl Professor of Scripture and Interpretation at Harvard Divinity School, as faculty within the Boston Theological Institute, as a cofounder and coeditor with Judith Plaskow of the *Journal of Feminist Studies in Religion* [226], as the author and/or editor of several significant doctrinal and methodologically related texts (e.g., [238, 236]) and more recently, as the executive editor of the two volume series *Searching the Scriptures: A Feminist Commentary* [344-345]—Schüssler Fiorenza has generated extensive feminist biblical scholarship, and like Ruether and a handful of others, she has shaped virtually every aspect of contemporary feminist theological thinking.[17]

Similarly, although in ways differently institutional than those of Schüssler Fiorenza, Katie G. Cannon has also redefined the theological landscape, for her work has challenged the *racial* hegemony of much historically established theological study. Cannon's work, and particularly her 1985 essay, "The Emergence of Black Feminist Consciousness," is significant in at least three ways. First, it is in this essay Cannon that identifies the sectors of women's experience that undergird the theological assessment of African American women's courage and faith, and that, in Cannon's judgment, constitute a specifically "womanist" African American history. Thus Cannon moves beyond the early comparative discussions of Black and feminist theological literature (cf. Murray [181]), and she generates a perspective differentiated from Jacquline Grant's early work in womanism and Christology [254]. Second, as she traces this history out, Cannon puts the question of theological anthropology into clear ethical and sociological terms in that she names the historically existential question African American women had so regularly to face: that is, "Are African Americans, and particularly African American women, persons? Or are they property?" From a methodological perspective this question critiques not only the androcentric assumptions of much late-60s Black liberation theology. In addition, it critiques the middle-class biases inherent in many early feminist theological sources, and it identifies caste and class, or more widely, the various mechanisms of social stratification, as elements of feminist hermeneutical analysis. Thus it bridges feminist, womanist, and other communally defined women's perspectives, including lesbian and *Mujerista* perspectives. This linkage factor is important. In identifying slavery, which is one type of stratification, as a factor of hermeneutical analysis, Cannon's essay suggests the necessity of examining *all* ascribed statuses, including that of sexual orientation, from a critical hermeneutical perspective.[18]

The third significant element of Cannon's early essay is that it lays the groundwork for her subsequent and widely influential work in womanist ethics (cf. [253]). More concretely, with her attention to the history of African American women's experience as the emergence of an identifiable feminist ethical consciousness, Cannon's early essay suggests the lines of a specifically "womanist theological anthropology," or the recognition of African American women as distinct moral agents. Thus, in her doctoral thesis (cf.*Womanist Ethics* [253]), the "emergence of Black feminist consciousness" gives way to a specific model of African American "womanist ethics," namely, the model of "invisible dignity," "quite grace" and "unshouted courage," as exhibited the life and work of Zora Neal Hurston. To return then, to the original point concerning Cannon's work, like that of Schüssler Fiorenza, Cannon's work has also shaped the landscape of academic theological conversation—albeit in ways differently institutional than those of Schüssler Fiorenza, for Cannon's work has brought to the table voices that can no longer be overlooked, ignored, or elsewise unacknowledged.

Other "classics" published after the early period of 1968-1977 include such methodological pieces as Sally McFague's *Metaphorical Theology* [200], Beverly Harrison's *Making the Connections* [207], as edited by Carol Robb, Carter Heyward's *The Redemption of God* [198], and Letty M. Russell's *Feminist Interpretation of the Bible* [210], and from the period of the transitional literature but published in 1980, Judith Plaskow's doctoral dissertation, *Sex Sin and Grace* [203].

The text by Plaskow builds on Valerie Saiving's work [163] to critique the concepts of sin and redemption held by Protestant theologians Reinhold Niebuhr and Anders-Nygren. The McFague text briefly introduces her now famous 'mother, friend, and lover' imagery for God (an imagery she further extends in her 1987 *Models of God* [244]), and the Heyward and Harrison texts anchor "right relation" as the axis of feminist ethical method. Last, Russell's anthology presses readers to the social implications of feminist biblical hermeneutics, for in contrast to much earlier feminist biblical work (e.g., Phyllis Trible's 1979 *God and the Rhetoric of Sexuality* [205], or even Russell's own early feminist biblical work [173]), this mid-1980s collection connects feminist biblical study with such wide-ranging topics as the development of Black feminism on the one hand (i.e., Cannon's womanist essay) and the critique of pornography and the sexual abuse of women [384, 870]) on the other.[19]

Finally there are several current sources which ground the literature in feminist concerns, with the latter understood widely as the bridge building tasks so necessary across all communities of women.[20] These contemporary classics are too numerous to list, but of especial significance are Judith Plaskow's 1990 *Standing Again at Sinai* [262], Patricia Jung and Ralph Smith's 1993 *Heterosexism: An Ethical Challenge* [572], Rita Nakashima Brock's 1988 *Journeys by Heart* [432], and Chung Hyun Kyung's 1990 text, *Struggle to be the Sun Again* [935]. Each of these texts yet assails the reach of androcentrism and patriarchal bias into the lives of women and their loved ones, and each speaks loudly for their dismantlement and demise. Last, in terms of doctrinally specific Christian neo-classics, several additional discussions from the early 1990s also serve to ground the literature, and among these are Catherine LaCugna's trinitarian theology, *God for Us* [234], Elizabeth Johnson's widely acclaimed *She Who Is* [232], Letty Russell's *Church in the Round* [250], Delores Williams' *Sisters in the Wilderness: The Challenge of Womanist God-Talk* [259], Elisabeth Schüssler Fiorenza's *Miriam's Child, Sophia's Prophet: Critical Issues in Feminist Christology* [238], Rosemary Ruether's *Gaia and God* [235] and Emilie Townes' *In a Blaze of Glory: Womanist Spirituality as Social Witness* [258].[21]

One further note is necessary here concerning "classics" from the current period of feminist theological reconstruction. While it is not yet among the classics of the feminist theological literature, the developing discussion on "anti-Judaism within Christian feminist theology" is clearly headed for the status of classical feminist theological work. This discussion began formally in feminist circles in the late 1970s with Judith Plaskow's preliminary critique of the "Jesus was a Feminist" and other Christian feminist writings,[22] and it continued through the mid-'80s with her critique of Christian anti-Semitism as "the unacknowledged racism" [968] in feminist theological writing. More recently, the discussion has continued into the 1990s with Plaskow's essays ([970] and [971]) directed explicitly to an analysis of the way—one wants to say cultural and literary mechanisms—by which anti-Judaism is maintained in Christian writing, thought and symbols generally, albeit as described here in Plaskow's specific essays, in the literature of feminist theological writing particularly.[23]

5. The sociology of women's religious leadership. A development counterpoint to both the classical and general feminist theological literature is that of the research on women's leadership in various Christian denominations (Chang [658], Nesbitt [661] and Zikmund, Lummis and Chang [663]). It is an important literature, although less voluminous than that from the theological sphere. This said, its emphases have been manifold. First, this literature attends strongly to the recruitment and socialization of women to ordained ministry within mainline Protestant denominations, and here the co-authored work of Jackson Carroll, the late Barbara Hargrove and Adair Lummis of Hartford Seminary is preeminent, and particularly in terms of their benchmark overview of clergywomen from America's mainline denominations. Although published in 1983, their *Women of the Cloth* [657] remains a standard for subsequent research relative to the clergywomen population as a whole and the patterned experiences women clergy have, regardless of denominational affiliation. Likewise, it is the benchmark for a second and wider study of women clergy in American denominations (Zikmund, Lummis and Chang [663]) with the research for this second volume expanded to include (a) an increased number of denominations being surveyed; (b) research addressing the experience of ordained ethnic minority women in mainline, predominantly white denominations; (c) clergy boundary issues; and (d) research on gender differences across important occupational variables, including income, theologies of ordination, perceptions of ordained leadership, the career paths of female and male clergy, and the experience of women clergy serving in non-parish, as well as parish, church organizational settings).[24] Both are landmark pieces and sina qua nons of clergywomen research.

A second avenue of clergywomen research has been an attention to the differing patterns of placement, acceptance, benefits, and career patterns of women (and men) in mainline Protestant churches. And here Edward Lehman's work [695, 707] is preeminent. The bulk of Lehman's work has examined clergy experience from seminary to church placement ([700, 706, 710, 712]), and it has documented numerous gender and organizationally based clergywomen/clergymen differences. Additionally, it has tested the contact hypothesis (read: familiarity breeds friendship not contempt) in various denominations (cf. [707, 713]), and it has detailed several elements of the more broadly based "local/cosmopolitan" orientation [708, 709]. Last, Lehman's work has provided a context for numerous other studies addressing clergywomen career issues, including the socialization and gender sensitized experiences of women in seminaries (cf. Charlton [697]), the implications of egalitarian norms for both clergy socialization and issues of sexism in the parish (cf. Kleinman [698]), the impact of women's placements on financial giving in parish ministry (Royle [711]), and with respect to the ministry profession itself, the stratification of ministerial tracks now becoming evident within specific denominations (cf. Nesbitt [701]).

A third set of studies has examined the factors affecting laity perceptions of women in ordained ministry with data here drawn from both the United States and Great Britain. And here again, Lehman's work is distinguished. Lehman's British data on clergywomen from four denominations [713], set theoretically within the context of secularization and sex roles, replicates and confirms several American findings and is cast in his ever-readable, clear style. Similarly, the contrasting effects of theology and sexism vis a vis the ordination of women in Great Britain have been investigated by both Lehman [713] and Nason-Clark [714], with Nason-Clark's work focusing specifically on theology, attitudes, and perceptions of Anglican male clergy prior to the ordination of women [716] within Anglicanism. Nason-Clark's work is especially important for it provides an initial baseline of comparison for studies tracking change in Anglican circles relative to women priests.

A fifth area of research has also to do with "tracking," but here with respect to the demographic and denominational distribution of women in ordained ministry. The earliest study here (using Census data through 1960) is Bock [692], but more familiar and more frequently cited are the benchmark statistics provided by the late Constance Jaquet in his role as editor of the *Handbook of American and Canadian Churches*. In particular, Jaquet provided early clergywomen statistics for both mainline and evangelical churches, as well as data on clergy salaries and income [659]. More recently, various studies have updated these general statistics with numerous descriptions of seminary student populations (cf., e.g., King [660], O'Neill and Murphy [702], and Larson and Shopshire [699]). Moreover, the *Handbook of American and Canadian Churches* continues to provide ATS data on seminary enrollment by degree categories, gender, race and ethnicity.[25]

Sixth, the study of women clergy in African American churches has begun to take shape, with studies by Delores Carpenter [645] and Lincoln and Mamiya [141] taking center stage. Carpenter's work is preeminent: first because it constitutes the benchmark empirical work on African American women clergy and second, because her measures permit direct comparisons with the 1983 Carroll, Hargrove and Lummis study. Similarly, the social and religious leadership roles of women in Sanctified Churches has been pioneered by Cheryl Townsend Gilkes [615, 616]), and the Lincoln and Mamiya study incorporates both the Gilkes and Carpenter research into the historical and contemporary frameworks of African American churches as a whole.

Seventh (with significance for all of the above) the role of marital status in clergywomen's leadership has also been investigated: initially in terms of clergy couple data (Carroll, Hargrove and Lummis [657]), in somewhat more particularized contexts by others discussing clergy-family role conflict (Scanzoni [731], Nesbitt [723]), and most recently by Zikmund, Lummis and Chang [663] in terms of boundary issues attatched to work and family systems. Apart from these discussions, however, the role of marital status in clergywomen's careers is presently *under researched,* particularly in terms of both how conflicts are ameliorated and how theological orientations function in clergy marriages overall.[26]

As with several emphases within the theological literature, the research questions about women in ordained ministry are also evolving, although at a less rapid pace. For example, the bridge literature addressing "women in theological education" is also underdeveloped, although it is not without specific precedent (see Carroll, Hargove and Lummis [657]), and at least some preliminary issue-defining feminist theological sources[27] as well as, more recently, the Zikmund, Lummis and Chang update of *Women of the Cloth, Clergy Women: An Uphill Calling* [663], and Nesbitt's especially important research on clergywomen as a secondary labor market within the church as an occupational system [661].[28] Additionally, the study of ministry and sexuality, particularly the study of gay and lesbian clergy, is also underdeveloped, and yet to be shaped by a dialogue with both the Jung and Smith text [572], feminist theology's long standing critique of heterosexism, and Nesbitt's provocative reflections on backlash and gender construction.[29]

In an obviously related vein, the sociological research on women's religious leadership within Roman Catholicism is also underdeveloped, but nonetheless taking shape in key ways. In particular, Ruth Wallace's singular research on women pastors within Roman Catholicism [787] is without parallel, as is the Lummis and Stokes [742] study of Catholic feminist spirituality and social justice involvement.[30] Second, the literature on women's convent communities has begun to develop sociologically, and here with an attention to various organizational issues, i.e., organizational change [798, 799] and organizational decline [797], membership recruitment [803], group vision and mission development [800]. Likewise, the literature on Catholicism's women-church movement is also organizationally significant, although at present limited empirically to the work of Winter, Lummis and Stokes [153] and the sidebars it shares with various theological pieces, notably those by Neal [147], Hunt [789], Neu [790], Ruether [449], and Schüssler Fiorenza [369].[31] These topics—the study of Catholic women pastors, women in convent communities, the women-church movement—all bear further investigation, as do alternative spirituality and/or women's religious groups within traditions apart from Christianity: e.g., Rosh Hodesh and B'not Esh group(s) in feminist Judaism [958], Jewish women's Orthodox groups as identified by Davidman [973], and women's healing and spirituality groups within new religious movements as identified by Jacobs [901] and Neitz [148].

Finally, the *comparative* literature on women's religious leadership is also developing, and here the initializing pieces are interdisciplinary. Hence, from sociology, Simon, Scanlon and Nadell [719] contrast the ministerial experiences of women rabbis with those of Protestant women clergy, while from religious studies, Catherine Wessinger [136] and Ellen Umansky [946] provide historical work. In particular, Wessenger provides a collection on women's leadership in "marginal" traditions illustrating the conditions of women's religious leadership as identified by Bednarowski [665], while Ellen Umansky identifies several empirical questions about women's rabbinical experience which, in turn, await study and subsequent comparison with Protestant women clergy. All of these studies represent leading edge discussions, and they suggest one index into future research questions, agendas and needs.[32]

B.   Principal Contributions of the Literature

Clearly a literature of the scope presented here denies the possibility of a simple "listing" of its major contributions, the many twenty-year celebrations of "how far we have come" (cf. [268] and [279]) and the many new "keywords" in theological language and literature (e.g., *feminist* theology, androcentrism, womanism, marginalized, patriarchy, God/ess, women-church, clergywomen, mutuality, *Mujerista* and the "discipleship of equals") notwithstanding. How then might the contributions of this literature be detailed? Although several portions of the literature are yet developing, one portion of the literature is quite well developed, and within it, the contributions have been clear for over a decade. That portion of the literature is feminist biblical studies.

   1. *An early assessment.* In a panel discussion published in 1988, Burton Throckmorton [355] identified six ways in which feminist biblical scholarship had by that time contributed to the world of New Testament studies. These contributions, he noted, included the following: First, feminist biblical scholars have exposed the androcentric (male-centered) world of the whole Bible, including the synoptic gospels. Second, feminist biblical scholars have demonstrated that patriarchal assumptions have dominated (and continue to dominate) the field of biblical studies. Third, feminist biblical scholars have uncovered the "systematic silencing of women's voices... names, words and activities" within the tradition of the church's New Testament study, and they have exposed, thereby, "that our New Testament histories are to that extent falsified" (p. 87). Fourth, these same feminist biblical scholars have generated an important and necessary "hermeneutics of suspicion" which has, in turn, challenged the "value free" assumptions of the historical literary traditions of biblical scholarship. Finally, the work of feminist biblical scholars has pressed male scholars "to listen and [to] help [develop] a new mutuality in... critical theological work" (p. 88).

   2. *The wider framework.* Throckmorton's six areas of contribution could be extended to virtually all areas of the Christian theological enterprise: the study of worship, spirituality, Church history, Christology, ecclesiology, eschatology, soteriology, ethics, leadership, homiletics, sacramentology, theological anthropology, church structure and administration (i.e., polity and canon law) and ecumenism, to name those that come immediately to mind. For as a consequence of its sustained and ongoing development, the feminist movement in religion has made several theological inroads, and there are now no theological topics which can reasonably be discussed *apart from* feminist, womanist, multicultural, and "out" women's ecumenical concerns—that is, apart from the significance of an inclusive ethic which makes space for all at the widest of banquet tables. This is an enormously important point, for if there is one singular value which the feminist theological movement has incorporated into the tasks of Christian theological discourse it *is* that of *inclusivity*—read: the need to detach from androcentric and patriarchal patterns of thinking, theologizing and interacting, and the need to recognize, thereby, that all of the earth's six billion and more inhabitants are equally the image of God, equally the voice of creation, and equally the voice of one's neighbor before "She Who Is."

   This "wider framework" as it is being called here, might also be named differently. In particular, as both the global ecumenical movement among women has developed, and as the dialogue between Jewish and Christian feminists has developed—both through the now two decades and more efforts of such brave, creative and strong theologians as Mary Daly, Rosemary Ruether, Phyllis Trible, Carol Christ, Jaqueline Grant, Judith Plaskow, Margaret Farley, Letty Russell, Katie Cannon, Beverly Harrison, Elisabeth Schüssler Fiorenza, and quite literally, the scores of others who are their students and their students' students—it, the women's movement in religion, has changed the religious and theological landscapes of Western society. In a word, it has created a new and now *feminist* space within Western religion, a space within which *women also* construct and interpret "the tradition," and from within which the world's needs for peace and justice can be differently and more inclusively addressed. For some, this space is simply the opportunity to speak freely from within a gendered heritage. For others, it is the grace to "defect in place." Or as a third possibility, it is the opportunity to dialogue *deeply* with the conflicts inherent in Christianity's millenial Eurocentric history. Or, to cite a fourth and growing possibility, this space is now the time of *re-imagining* and of making "all things new."

The details of this space are diverse and they vary with both the speakers and their locations. But this space is now visible in both Jewish and Christian traditions, and the women's movement in religion has helped to create it. And in doing this—no matter the difficulties remaining *and they are many*—feminist theology, the women's movement in religion, has proved the reformation it was once named. Proved yet, that "the journey is home;" that it is a movement from "father rights to human rights;" that it is a movement from heaven to the world of God's body, and that *to this*, all who would befriend the earth and its life are welcome.

ENDNOTES

[1]For general discussions indicating the life history or path of social movements see the chapters on collective behavior and social movements in any introductory sociology text. Three very readable and regularly updated introductory texts are *Sociology*, by Beth Hess, Elizabeth W. Markson and Peter J. Stein (NY: Macmillan, 1995); *Sociology: A Down to Earth Approach*, by James M Henslin (Needham, MA: Allyn and Bacon, 1997), and Claire M. Renzetti and Daniel J. Curran, *Living Sociology* (Needham, MA: Allyn and Bacon, 1998). Each provides readable discussions of social movements—with several illustrations (e.g., the American Civil Rights movement, Nazism, American Antifeminism), and all are sensitive to multicultural and feminist concerns, with Hess at al. and Renzetti and Curran providing specific discussions of feminist sociology. Also, each details the role of media and propaganda in movement success or failure.

[2]Schüssler Fiorenza [195] credits Elizabeth Cady Stanton with the beginnings of the American feminist theological literature. Alternatively, Plaskow [170] points out that Saiving's discussion is the first feminist theological piece of the twentieth century, and that chronologically it represents the beginnings of the literature. Third, Christ's early "reformist/revolutionary" literature overview [177] cites both Stanton and Saiving. Fourth, at least two sources from the mid-90s (Russell and Clarkson's *Dictionary of Feminist Theologies* [272] and the 1995 edition of the *HarperCollins Dictionary of Religion* (edited by Jonathan Z. Smith, HarperSanFrancisco, 1995) follow Plaskow's lead and trace the literature through its organizational growth in the American Academy of Religion. From a strictly chronological perspective Plaskow is correct; but the effective significance of Saiving's work (when first published) was not that of galvanizing the early moments of a social movement. Rather with its reprint in the 1979 Christ & Plaskow reader, Saiving's essay served as an exemplar for the discussion of sin, redemption and feminist spirituality—and by extension—the discussions of women's self affirmation, women's religious community and women's transcendent possibilities. Last, while the importance of Stanton's *The Woman's Bible* cannot be denied (cf. Bass [352], Pellauer [271] and Schüssler Fiorenza [344]) the text itself *regained* rather than generated salience within the theological literature of feminism and Christian tradition. Further, to the extent that Stanton's text symbolizes the racial assumptions embedded within nineteenth century American feminism, it continues to be a symbol of painful differences which have historically separated black and white feminists. For helpful historical literature here see Lerner [77] and Giddings [614], as well as the sources which close Chapter 2. A final note on the beginnings of feminist theology: A fourth beginning point for the literature may also be identified here, although from a sociological perspective, it is more accurate to speak of this fourth beginning point as a premovement condition. In her discussion, "Toward a Critical Christian Feminist Theology of Solidarity" [278] M. Shawn Copeland indicates that with the creation of the Sacred School of Theology at St. Mary's College at Notre Dame, Indiana by Sr. Mary Madeleva Wolff in 1944, Sr. Madeleva "...quite directly 'mothered' feminist theology to life in the United States" (p. 4), and especially so, given that (among others) one of the school's early students was Mary Daly.

[3]It is not surprising that Daly's book generated an angry response on the part of institutionalized Christianity. To its credit, Daly's book both identified and dismantled the numerous theological arguments that traditionally had been used to support the inferiority of women in both the church and secular society. These included, that: following Eve, women were essentially sources of evil (the supposed teaching of Genesis); as a consequence, women were to be subordinate to their husbands (the supposed teachings of Genesis and Paul); according to the church Fathers, women were "fickle," "shallow," "garrulous," "weak," "intellectually slow," and "unstable of mind"; and that, according to Thomas (who followed Aristotle), women were naturally inferior to men because they represented, in fact, the results of a defective male offspring, born as a necessity for creation, but little suited for much else. Daly details these teachings in the second chapter of *The Church and the Second Sex*, where she cites repeated illustrations of the Church's "record of contradictions" vis a vis the essential Christian message of the worth, dignity and equality of all people. Moreover, through the patterning of her text after the criticisms of Christianity made by Simone de Beauvoir in the latter's own feminist treatise (Simone de Beauvoir, *The Second Sex*, NY: Bantam Books,

1961) Daly linked Christianity with its social and then current theological need for feminist analysis and critique, and she suggested the relevance of such a critique in the light of both the women's movement generally and the hopes generated among American Roman Catholics specifically by Catholicism's then recently completed Vatican Council. Daly closed her text with arguments for the following: (1) Christianity's "exorcism" of "its demon, sexism"; (2) its subsequent reinterpretation of much historical Christian dogma; and (3) a reorganization of church structures reflecting that reinterpretation: notably, the ordination of women and the inclusion of laity into positions of church leadership and policy formation. For the sociological literature identifying Daly's text as a social movement catalyst see Neal [145] and Porterfield [149]. For theological sources see Schneiders [761], Weaver [762] and the related literature in Chapter 8. For literature on the Vatican Council and its impact within American Catholicism, see Ebaugh [737], the introductory chapters in Wallace [787], Hoge [740], and D'Antonio et al. [736]. Curiously, as significant as this council was for the hopes of women, no research has (through the early 1990s) fully documented the functions of "gender" as a grounding concept in council documents.

4Although developed prior to Plaskow's recent overview of the literature [340], this strategy in many ways parallels her discussion there.

5That several texts published since 1993 follow the wider feminist framework of "difference" as a theological assumption is clear. See, e.g., Jaggar's *Living with Contradictions: Controversies in Feminist Social Ethics* [32] and DuBois and Ruiz [73] for the wider, secular feminist discussion; and see Russell and Clarkson's *Dictionary of Feminist Theologies* [272] and Schüssler Fiorenza and Copeland's *Feminist Theology in Different Contexts* [275] for the theological read. That the latter (as well as particular articles) indicate an attention to "difference" as a theological premise is obvious, but several reasons caution its immediate adoption as the defining characteristic of a specific time frame. First, while the premise of "difference" is distinct from the recognition of pluralism as evident in the literature after the mid-1980s, the particulars of the distinctiveness vary widely. Methodologically, this is played out in the current tensions between antifeminist and postmodernism reactions to much feminist theology, as illustrated, for example, in the critiques of feminist theology presented by Achtemeier [838] and Anne-Louise Eriksson [240]. While the one is visibly antifeminist and the other postmodernist, both undercut the authority of women's experience as legitimate sources of religious and ethical insight: Achtemeier's work because it assesses feminist theology from within misogynous assumptions and Eriksson's because it stops short of the theology it implies. What may, in fact, mark the beginning of a fourth developmental period, is that this attention to "difference" may signal the full differentiation of feminist theology into "transformational" and "post-institutional" (although not necessarily postChristian) organizational frameworks. The former would include the groups of women "defecting in place," as identified by Winter, Lummis and Stokes [153]; the latter, women organizationally distinct from denominational Christianity, but claiming its reconstruction as a legitimate source and object of feminist religious value. This distinction is implicit in Katzenstein [285], and is advocated by Copeland in her discussion of Christian feminist solidarity [278]. Also, it is consistent with much in the wider framework of postmodernist theology per se. For example, see Graham Ward's recent introductions to postmodern theology, *viz.*, "Postmodern Theology," in *The Modern Theologians* (edited by David Ford, Cambridge, MA: Blackwell, 1997, 585-602), and "Theology and Postmodernism" *Theology* 100, no. 798 (1997): 435-440. Finally, as a last example of "postmodernist" feminist theological potential—and as thereby, an illustration of the difficulty of classifying current feminist theology too closely, see Mary McClintock Fulkerson's work, *Changing the Subject: Women's Discourses and Feminist Theology* [Minneapolis, MN: Fortress Press, 1994]. A critique of contemporary academic feminist theology, with the experience of Appalachian Pentecostal women's religious experience as its philosophical and social locational case in point, *Changing the Subject* argues that "...academic feminist theology has failed to offer theories of language, social location, power and gender capable of displaying difference" (p. vii), and it thus well illustrates the multiple questions currently facing one who would too closely classify contemporary feminist theologies.

6Daly's text had charged that Christianity's symbols were "inherently" patriarchal, and thereby for all intents and purposes not open to change or reformulation. Given the date of Daly's publication, her position is, in retrospect, hardly surprising. In 1973, there was virtually no room in Roman Catholicism (or much else of American mainline Christianity) for adult feminist Christian perspectives. By the early 1990s, however, both the theological climate and the range of its possibilities had changed, such that the terms "feminist" and "Christian" were no longer *necessarily* incompatible, as LaCugna's 1993 collection [273] and the 1994 research by Winter, Lummis and Stokes [153] both demonstrate. This said, the continuing struggle between feminists and androcentrists within mainline Christianity cannot be denied, as several other entries (and Winter, Lummis, and Stokes) also indicate. See Bounds [484] and Russell [250] as examples of the struggle in mainstream Protestantism; see Daphne Hampson's post-Christian feminist theology [286]; see Bianchi and Ruether [733], Schneiders [761], Chittister [754], and the women's ordination movement as examples in Catholicism; and as a last example of the struggle, see "US Bishops, Pope at Odds on Feminism: Gender Neutral Bible Rejected by Vatican." *The Washington Post*, p.

A1, 4, November 12, 1994. Nor are the terms "feminist" and "Christian" as provincial as they once were in the early years of the feminist theology movement. Of deep significance here is the fact that among Jewish feminist theologians, Judith Plaskow [262] regularly attends to the influence of Daly's critique in *Beyond God the Father*, and in doing so, she sets a *very* wide frame for cross-tradition critique and conversation.

[7]The alignment of these two sources as representing the options open to feminist religious writers was first presented by Carol Christ in her 1977 review of the literature [177] and then presented again by Christ and Plaskow in the introduction to their 1979 co-edited feminist spirituality reader, *Womanspirit Rising* [206]. Also relevant to this alignment was Ann Barstow Driver's 1976 review essay "Religion," which focused the question underlying much early literature: "Can one remain within the Christian or Jewish traditions once one becomes conscious of sexism?" (See [178: 434]).

[8]The listing in Chaper 5 presents key sources, and while these sources easily represent the early feminist theological literature, the reader may wish to augment them from entries listed in both the 1986 annotated bibliography developed by Bass and Boyd [130] and the feminist theology chapter of Musto's research guide to liberation theology [270]. Additionally, the reader may wish to consult the *ATLA Database on CD-ROM* [129] by use of the program's date sorting feature.

[9]Obviously, this statement holds for the American and academic literature only. In much of the internationally directed literature and in much popularized feminist literature, this redemptive effort is still needed and still in process. See, for example, the circumstances of women as described by Morgan [9] and Heise [28], and for the theological read, see Carr [488], Schüssler Fiorenza and Carr [493], Benavides [914], Oduyoye [920], Park [936], and others from within Chapter 23. Additionally, see Leila Ahmed's recently published *Women and Gender in Islam* (New Haven: Yale University Press, 1992). Although not reviewed here, this text traces the history of ideologies governing women's status in Islam, and it highlights the distinctive feminist need Ahmed sees for Arab women: i.e., the necessity for a feminism which liberates from sexist oppression, but without complicity in an ideology of Western development. The literature here is only just beginning, with sources in Haddad and Findley [907] providing historical backdrops for religious material. Additionally, see Yvonne Yazbeck Haddad and Adair T. Lummis. *Islamic Values in the United States: A Comparative Study,* (New York: Oxford Univ. Press, 1987), and see the literature cited by Ruether in Ruether and Keller in [135]. Last, see Fatima Mersini, *Women and Islam: An Historical and Theological Enquiry,* translated by Mary Jo Lakeland, (Oxford: Blackwell, 1991).

[10]Thus, during this period Murray [181], Dodson [646], Grant [635], and Hoover [618] reflect variously on the experiences of African American women and Christian tradition, the term "*Mujerista*" enters the feminist theological vocabulary, Judith Plaskow identifies anti-Semitism as "the other racism" within feminist theology [968], and Kwok Pui-Lan [219] challenges the hegemony of Western Christian symbols generally, to name but a few of the "pluralizing" developments of this period. For an initial source here, see the 1984 reader, *Women's Spirit Bonding*, edited by Kalven and Buckley [208]. For an earlier and anticipating source, see Hageman [168]. And, of course, see the literatures in Chapters 16, 17, 23 and 24.

[11]See, e.g., the literature in Chapter 22, "Patriarchy, Violence and Sexual Harassment in the Churches."

[12] In fact, while the literature connecting feminist theology and women's studies generally is yet to be developed (cf. Plaskow [340]), it is this particular reader which regularly is cited as the grounding source for feminist spirituality in the wider context of women's studies literature. See, e.g., Carol Christ's own work [558, 559], see Eller [542], MacNichol and Walsh [539], and see the second co-edited spirituality reader published in 1989 by Plaskow and Christ [544].

[13]Ruether's work to find words expressive of the 'feminist' imaging of God have been both consistent and insistent over the last two decades. While she has never favored an abandonment of Christian tradition in the direction of "goddess worship," she has nonetheless consistently favored an abandonment of patriarchal religion and she has worked endlessly for ecumenical conversation on this point. The lines of this discussion are evident as one traces her work from her 1974 anthology *Religion and Sexism* [171], through her two volumes, *New Women New Earth* [172] and *Sexism and Godtalk* [190] published in 1975 and 1983, respectively, and last, her 1993 text, *Gaia and God: An Ecofeminist Theology of Earth Healing* [235]. Moreover, these lines are especially evident as one places them against some of Ruether's more comprehensive methodological pieces: e.g., her discussion of feminism and religion studies [326], of feminist theology and feminist spirituality [545], of Christology [441]—including her critique of Christologically based anti-Semitism (cf. her essay discussion [440] and her recently reprinted text, *Faith and Fratricide* [299]), her work in feminist hermeneutics [365-366], her work in the area of women-church experience and theology [193, 449], and last, her recent re-examination of dualism and evil [465]. For Ruether's own assessment of her work, see [334].

[14]See Elisabeth Schüssler Fiorenza, *The Book of Revelation: Justice and Judgment*, Philadelphia, Fortress Press, 1985. The revised edition, which fully incorporates Schüssler Fiorenza's attention to social location and rhetorical critical methodology, is *Revelation: Vision of a Just World*, Minneapolis: Augsburg, 1991.

[15]For the secular literature, see Cullen Murphy, "Women and the Bible," *Atlantic Monthly* (August, 1993): 39-64 and especially pp. 44-46. Alternatively, see "Radical Feminism Criticized," *National Catholic Reporter*, March 24, 1989, p. 6. Additionally, see the entries on antifeminism in biblical work in Chapter 22.

[16]Nor does Throckmorton's essay begin to cover the lot. Of no small merit is Schüssler Fiorenza's introduction of such phrases as the "discipleship of equals" into the general vocabulary of American religion and theology.

[17]Schüssler Fiorenza's work appears throughout the bibliography. For its formative biblical lines, see the notes on Schüssler Fiorenza in Chapter 10.

[18]The principal issue here is, of course, social control. This is because ascribed statuses are by definition, those which society imputes to individuals and *always* with the expectations of a stratified and thus controllable population. Again, see any introductory sociological text, or those mentioned in Note 1. By focusing her discussion in the manner she has, Cannon moves the conversation of current and historical complicity in race relations *beyond privatization*, but not beyond either individual ethical or institutional redress. From a sociological perspective this is particularly important, for it challenges the assumption that personal responsibility is encompassed by privatized faith and that this equation legitimately releases social leadership from working for justice on behalf of members within a given society. Indeed, much of the current "culture wars" literature (cf. James Davison Hunter, *Culture Wars: The Struggle to Define America*, HarperCollins, 1991) is premised on the privatization perspective and the notion that "rights" (human and civil) are a zero-sum entitlement. At its deepest levels Cannon's work challenges this assumption, and it thus implies an African American civil religious perspective, which to date has received little (if any) attention within the literature. For additional contrasts of Black and feminist theological perspectives, see the literature cited in Chapter 17 of the bibliography. For current contrasts see Volentine [650] and see hooks [29, 30]. Finally, for literature which promises an expansive and deeply ethical dialogue between Womanist and Jewish feminist perspectives, see Ringelheim's methodological discussion, "Thoughts About Women and the Holocaust" [966]. Cannon and Ringelheim each press the questions of racism, genocide and misogyny in ways the wider theological world simply cannot and *ought not* to ignore.

[19]See Chapter 22 for the recent literature here, with the collections by Brown and Bohn [863] and Horton and Williamson [900] constituting the discipline-defining texts for theological and pastoral counseling issues respectively, and the entry by Shupe [880] providing the current sociological norm. By way of background, the discussions by Lebacqz and Barton [878] and Marie Fortune [877] might also be thought of as offering discipline-defining perspectives for pastoral counseling, and specifically for the area of parishioner directed sexual abuse. This would, however, be a misnomer; for the issue in these works is the debate about sexuality and personal relationships between clergy and parish members, and not the wider concerns of pastoral counseling per se.

[20]See the Introduction to Jaggar [32] for an expansion of this point.

[21]Townes is a womanist ethicist who, like Cannon before her, details an exemplar of African American women's moral agency, here, Ida B. Wells-Barnett. That discussion, together with several implications of such agency, appeared in her doctoral thesis, *Womanist Justice, Womanist Hope* [633]. By way of the womanist literature, Townes' *In a Blaze of Glory* [258] unfolds womanist spirituality to assess (among other things) the parallels between the lynching of African Americans and the location of toxic waste sites in primarily poor rural and African American communities. Like other womanist authors (e.g., Sanders [631] and Riggs [257]), Townes' work reflects the "survival" motifs of the early womanist literature, but now together with an agenda for the Black church to re-ignite a communal liberation ethic within the now changing demography of contemporary Black America.

[22]Cf. Leanard Swidler, "Jesus Was a Feminist," *Catholic World*, Jan. 1971, pp. 177-183. For Plaskow's early work here see her essay, "Christian feminism and Anti-Judaism," *Cross Currents* 33 (Fall, 1978): 306-309.

[23]A theologian whose initial work was in the area of Women's Studies in Religion, Plaskow has emerged as a prophetic voice within both Jewish feminist theology and the Jewish-Christian feminist theological dialogue. She is currently a professor of religion at Manhattan College, and although she resigned her co-editorship of *Journal for Feminist Studies in Religion* (in 1994), she was, with Elisabeth Schüssler Fiorenza, the cofounder and coeditor of the *Journal* through its first decade. Her principle works include her doctoral dissertation, *Sex, Sin and Grace*, a women's studies critique of "sin" and "redemption" in the theologies of Paul Tillich and Reinhold Niebuhr [203] written in 1975 and published in 1980; an initial [170] and ongoing [339, 340] discussion of the pluralism so necessary for feminist theological method; a variety of articles linking her methodological study with the feminist critique of women's "otherness" in

Judaism **[953]**; her 1990 theological work *Standing Again at Sinai* **[262]**; and, in the mid-1990s, her work on Jewish feminist theology and the critique of anti-Judaism in Christian feminist theology **[970, 971]**. These last essays incorporate Katherine von Kellenbach's discussion, *Anti-Judaism in Christian Feminist Theology* **[288]**, a dissertation published through the *American Academy of Religion Cultural Criticism Series*, and they fruitfully locate it within the wider framework of the contemporary Jewish-Christian feminist theological dialogue. In particular, Plaskow incorporates von Kellenbach's three rules of formation into the wider contexts of (1) Plaskow's long standing recognition of insider/outsider status inconsistency, i.e., that feminist theologians typically participate in a combination of privileged and non-privileged statuses that can empower empathic understanding beyond one's own perspective and experience; and (2) the institutional, organizational and theological needs still to be realized within the current Jewish-Christian feminist theological dialogue. Plaskow's is a helpful use of von Kellenbach's work, which at many points, needs extensive editorial clarification.

[24]See Chang **[658]** for the early references to this work and see the text itself **[663]** *Clergy Women: An Uphill Calling,* with findings from the study on-line at *<www.hartsem.edu>.*

[25]See, for example, *Handbook of American and Canadian Churches: 1998,* edited by Eileen W. Lindner, 326-329, Nashville, TN: Abingdon, 1998.

[26]Although see the supplemental sources in Chapter 18. Adair Lummis of Hartford Seminary has done several commissioned pieces on stress in clergy families for churchwide agencies (cf. *The Washington Post* "Religion" section, 12/25/94 and see the literature cited in **[663]**). Hence, readers should contact her directly at Hartford Seminary for information about her work. Because the bulk of her work has been published specifically through denominational channels and in the format of denominational monographs, it has not been included in the literature reviewed for this volume. Apropos both Lummis' work and the study of patriarchy in clergy marriage generally (and particularly so with respect to lay spouses) are the early studies by Taylor and Hartley on "religious beliefs of clergy wives" **[726]**, the two-person career literature generally **[729]**, and various implications presently undeveloped in feminist ethicist Beverly Harrison's early work on sexuality and mutuality in **[497]**.

[27]For the theological literature here see the bulk of entries in Chapter 20, and see Harrison **[207]** passim. For the sociological literature, see Wheeler **[821]** (also in Chapter 20); and see the entry by Coleman as cited in Gilpin **[819]**. Last, see the journal *Theological Education,* passim and institutional publications from ATS. Worthy of note as a potentially disturbing feature of the early 1990's is the resignation of tenured women from Protestant seminaries, for reasons of feminist commitment. See, for example, "Theologian Resigns," *The Washington Post* 9/3/94, p. B7, and see the extensive controversy from the "Re-Imagining" conference as discussed in both the secular and religious press (e.g., *The Christian Century* and *Daughters of Sarah* among others).

[28]For Nesbitt's longer discussion, see her text, *Feminization of the Clergy in America: Occupational and Organizational Perspectives.* New York: Oxford University Press, 1997.

[29]See Chapter 15 for the feminist critique of heterosexism, and see Nesbitt's *Feminization of the Clergy in America: Occupational and Organizational Perspectives,* p. 8.

[30] As a further analysis of their *Defecting in Place* data, this study is especially important, not only because of the paucity of empirical studies on feminist spirituality and justice activities, but as well, for the wide range of subgroups it compares: lay and ordained Protestant women and the very underresearched population of Hispanic feminist women.

[31]Additionally, see Katzenstein's work (**[107]** and **[285]**), and see Jung and Smith **[572]** for interesting parallels between "defecting in place" and "ecclesiastical civil disobedience."

[32]Nor are these the only "cutting edge" areas of research. Of obvious importance *and need* are the studies— sociological and otherwise—which document the relationship(s) between religion and domestic violence, both within and beyond clergy marriages, and at a wider frame, the many and subtle ways in which the women's movement in religion ties to issues of the larger society. Some examples here include: (a) How does reimagining work for women's empowerment generally? That is, are local women-church groups religious analogs to local NOW groups? Have there been the mutual learnings in terms of "discourse" (cf. Katzenstein **[285]**) as a form of "defecting in place?" (b) Has not African American women's religious leadership functioned as an alternative civil religious tradition as Copeland's discussion **[265]** of Grant's work implies? And relatedly, what area the dimensions of civil disobedience as a means of social and organizational when practiced on behalf of gay and lesbian ordinations as Jung and Smith **[572]** suggest? (c) What ministry/military parallels go beyond sexual integration (Royle **[718]**) to include research on sexual harassment (Shupe **[880]**) and the institutional experience of gay and lesbian religious leaders? Finally, (e) how do feminist and womanist theologies handle America's changing work ethic(s)? Clearly several motifs in Harrison's *Connections* **[207]** as well as her discussion in **[497]** imply that feminist spirituality challenges capitalism as a spirituality, while works by Fischer **[490]** and Ruether **[492]** suggest numerous implications of various feminist "work ethics." In turn, how, then, do the latter suggest

alterations in social structure in the direction of inclusivity and "quality of life" issues as identified by Williams [259] and other womanists (Riggs [257])?

I

Introductory and Background Materials

The literature abstracted in this section includes reference works and theoretical sources that introduce the reader to four topics: "Feminism and the Women's Movement" (the literature in Chapter 1), "Feminism and Women's Studies" (the literature in Chapter 2), "Feminist Sociology," and last, "The Changing Status of Women in American Religion," Chapters 3 and I, respectively.

Chapter 1, "Feminism and the Women's Movement," introduces the reader to the many frameworks feminists have employed to critique and end "sexist domination" (see hooks, [29]). These frameworks are drawn primarily from philosophy, politics and the social sciences, and while the literature here is by no means exhaustive, it is representative and current through the mid 1990s, with Alison Jaggar's edited anthology *Living with Contradictions: Controversies in Feminist Social Ethics* [32], constituting a synthesizing and capstone source. For the sake of space, early literature is limited to bibliographic sources (e.g., Krichmar [2] and Williamson [5]) while more recent sources are addressed through summaries and/or essay collections (e.g., Boles [20] and Humm [31]). For introductory sources, readers new to the literature will find useful overviews in Buechler [13] and Carabillo [14], with more extended overviews provided by Castro et al. [15], Ferree and Hess [17], and Simon and Danziger [18]. Some definitional notes on the term "feminism": In addition to the overview entries mentioned above, formal and more specific discussions can be found in Lerner [35], Jaggar and Rothenberg [33], and Kramarae and Treichler [34], with feminism's global issues addressed by Morgan [9], French [24] and Neft and Levine [10]. In turn, Tobias [19] presents recent activist reflections, Drake [22] and Nicholson [38] synthesize "postmodern" definitions, and in an excellent, recent bibliography [7], Ryan synthesizes contemporary theory and practice, as well as sources available for funding and research opportunities. Finally, journal sources are listed at the close of the chapter, together with notes on selected Internet and feminist web sites.

Chapter 2 is "Feminism andWomen's Studies." It follows a format similar to that of Chapter 1 and it introduces the reader to the literature of Women's Studies, with attention directed respectively to two areas: again, an overview of standard bibliographic and reference materials, and second, a sampling of the theories and issues which make up the grounding concerns of Women's Studies as an academic discipline, including both its relation to feminist theory and the discussion of racial, class and gender interactions within the historical experience of American women. Here again, the literature is representative rather than exhaustive, and beginning readers are directed to the bibliographic discussions by Hull, Scott and Smith [49] and Stineman [55] for introductions to the early literature of Women's Studies, and to Loeb and Stineman [51], Redfern [53], Zinn and Dill [83], and Kramarae and Spender [66] for literature through the 1980s and early 1990s. Likewise, readers are directed to Bowles and Klein [62], Boxer [63], Howe [65] and Jackson [50] for literature on the history and development of Women's Studies, and to Lerner's classic *The Creation of Patriarchy* [68] as the conceptual bridge linking Women's Studies and Feminist Theory. Last, for encyclopedic overviews, two works synthesize the field well (Tierney's three volume set [57] and the more recent, *The Reader's Companion to U.S. Women's History* [52]), and Chapter 6 closes with several discussions on class, race and gender in American women's history. It should be noted that for reasons of space, these last sources are current through the early 1990s, and that for additional sources readers should consult the now numerous on-line bibliographies and/or women's studies web sites, or *The Reader's Companion...* [52] noted above.

Chapter 3 summarizes works in "Feminist Sociology." These works highlight the manifold impact of feminism on sociological theorizing: that it has generated reconceptualizations of both society and social processes, including the social construction of gender (Freeman [88], Kramer [90] and Lorber and Farrell [92]); that it has drawn attention to the political and ideological dimensions of social theory both in terms of the formulation of research questions and the opportunities for social change which such research can provide (cf. Chafetz [98], Cook and Fonow [100]); and last, that it has generated a wealth of empirically directed studies attesting the differential effects of gender in virtually all segments of society (cf., e.g., the overviews by Hess and Ferree [118], Feinberg and Knox [124], Taeuber [128], and Basow's comprehensive synthesis [117]). In brief, because the concept gender can be viewed as both a variable that is socially constructed *and* an analytical construct which goes far beyond that of "sex of respondent" (cf. Reinharz [112]), the implications of feminism for sociology are enormous, with the varying paradigmatic reconstructions only recently begun (cf., e.g., Wallace [115], Andersen and Collins [85], and Chafetz [97]). To introduce the reader to these issues, therefore, the materials in Chapter 3 are organized under four headings. These are: (1) Introductory Sources and General Anthologies; (2) Theoretical and Specialized Studies; (3) Selected Reference Works, and (4) Supplemental and Statistical Sources.

Overall, the introductory materials presume only a minimum of prior sociological knowledge. The subsequent listings presume a somewhat wider theoretical background. The reference works are handbook level overviews, and the supplemental and statistical sources are information based and in most cases user friendly. For the reader with no prior knowledge of sociology, the 1985 Lengermann and Wallace text [91] is an excellent beginning source. Other texts, such as Andersen [84], Chafetz [98], Lengermann and Niebrugge-Brantley [108], and Smith [114], can then supplement the reader's needs. Last, an extremely important text in this literature is Patricia Hill Collins' *Black Feminist Thought: Knowledge, Consciousness and the Politics of Empowerment* [99]. No understanding of feminist sociology can be complete without it.

Chapter 4, "Women in American Religion," completes the first section, and here the literature is sorted into two groups. These are "Reference Works" (including bibliographies and anthologies) and following these, several specialized studies indicating "The Changing Status of Women in American Religion." Apart from the bibliographies indicated at the beginning of the chapter, the materials in Chapter 4 are descriptive. They are historical and sociological sources which identify much of the suppressed and ignored history of women in American religion (cf. Wessenger [136], Hargrove, Davaney, and Schmidt [140], and MacHaffie [143]), and they indicate both the types and breadth of change which have occurred relative to women in institutionalized, American religious frameworks (cf. Briggs [137], Neal [147], and Neitz [148]). Of particular use to both beginning and seasoned researchers is the four volume Ruether annd Keller series [132-135]. It provides documentary literatures for women in American religion from the Colonial period through the early 1990s. Finally, of unparalleled significance for both its findings and interdisciplinary significance is *Defecting in Place: Women Claiming Responsibility for Their Own Spiritual Lives* [153]. This text is an empirical study of women's spirituality and feminist religious support groups, by M.T. Winter, Adair Lummis and Allison Stokes. Winter is a liturgical theologian known widely for her work in women's worship communities; Lummis is a well known sociologist of religion, and Stokes is a feminist ethicist. Together, they have produced a *sine qua non* which, when read with other sources from Chapter 4, provides a helpful framework for understanding the formally theological literature surveyed in subsequent sections of the bibliography.

Reminder: Although it has been mentioned previously at various points in this volume, it is worth repeating here: *all entries in the bibliography are numbered sequentially throughout the entire bibliography*, and thus for purposes of cross referencing, it is the ID number of a particular abstract which is needed to move in and around the bibliography, its indices and literature discussions.

1
Feminism and the Women's Movement

A. Reference Works

1. Early Reference Works

[1]   Flexner, Eleanor. *Century of Struggle: The Woman's Rights Movement in the United States*. 2d ed. Cambridge, MA: Belknap Press, 1975.
This revised edition of Flexner's 1959 work examines the history of the American Women's Rights Movement through the early 1970s. It presents an engaging analysis of the decades and events most salient for women in the American suffrage movement, and among its topics it includes: (1) the Seneca Falls Convention, (2) the tensions between feminists committed to women's rights and the rights of newly freed male slaves, (3) the presence and struggles of women in trade unions and political campaigns working organizationally on behalf of suffrage, and (4) the early twentieth century work of women in the labor movement and national politics and in the passage and efforts to ratify the nineteenth amendment. A closing chapter highlights 'second wave' ERA efforts and integrates the 'century of struggle' with women's political gains through the early 1970s.

[2]   Krichmar, Albert (With Virginia Carlson Smith and Ann E. Wiederrecht). *The Woman's Movement in the Seventies: An International English-Language Bibliography*. Metuchen, NJ: Scarecrow Press, 1977.
This partially annotated bibliography presents approximately 8600 entries describing various aspects of women's status in 100 different countries. The citations are limited to doctoral dissertations, pamphlets, periodical articles and books published between 1970-1975 (with some additional material from 1976), and all entries are arranged by country, with sectional subdivisions identified by either topical or geographical emphasis. A separate reference section presents over 200 entries, with 63 comprised by subject bibliographies, including early bibliographies on women of color and early and "near print" bibliographies on such topics as "religion and women/ordination/women in ministry." This is a wide reaching bibliography of Women's Studies and the women's movement during the first half of the 1970s, and while *annotated* entries range from 25% to 60% in any given category, its extensive references make it an especially helpful first line of investigation for national and international literature. Well organized subject, author and name indices close the volume. **NOTE**: See also Marie Barovic Rosenberg and Len Bergstrom, *Women and Society: A Critical Review of the Literature with a Selected Annotated Bibliography* [Beverly Hills, CA: Sage, 1975]. While not abstracted here, it covers a wide range of sources published from the mid-60s through the mid-70s, with extended entries from sociology, political science, history and "women in economics." Additionally, see Williamson [5] below.

[3]   Rossi, Alice S., comp. *The Feminist Papers: From Adams to de Beauvoir*. New York: Columbia Univ. Press, 1973.
This critically edited collection of feminist writings "From Adams to de Beauvoir" is now a standard source on the literature and history of the American feminist movement. Its excerpts span the full range of "first wave" American feminism and include entries from twenty-six feminist thinkers and/or advocates active during the period 1774-1953. Further, Rossi's introductions to both the volume's subdivisions and its individual writers are clear and informative, and her

extended essay, "Social Roots of the Woman's Movement in America" is especially insightful. A weakness consistent with much early feminist literature, however, is its almost exclusive attention to the history of white American women, and the concomitant absence of African American and other women's voices as either partners or participants in the conversation. Hence, see Hull, Scott, and Smith [49], Redfern [53], relevant essays in Mankiller et al. [52], and sources indicated later in this bibliography: e.g., Davis [72], Lerner [77], Collins [99], Loewenberg and Bogin [606], Giddings [614], and Jones [76], Gilkes [603], Ihle [604], and Townes [633].

[4]   Spretnak, Charlene, ed. *The Politics of Women's Spirituality: Essays on the Rise of Spiritual Power in the Feminist Movement.* Garden City, NY: Anchor, 1982/1994.

This collection of over fifty essays and/or essay excerpts on women and spirituality accomplishes two things: (1) it consistently evidences the empowering capacities of both feminism and religious "spiritualities" for women facing patriarchal power and its structures; (2) it specifies the range of experiences women identify as "spirituality." Three themes organize the entries ("Discovering a History of Power," "Manifesting Personal Power," and "Transforming the Political)," and each is further divided into analytical and existential emphases. Thus, for example, readings on goddess ritual are paired with readings on anti-nuclear activism. Spretnak provides helpful introductions for all sections, and in her preface to the 1994 edition she indicates various developments in women's spirituality (together with key bibliography) since her initial 1982 publication. This remains a standard introduction to sources on women's spirituality, and especially so for work outside the frames of denominational religion, although it is fruitfully read in conjunction with the latter (cf., MacNichol and Walsh [539] and Schneiders [547]).

[5]   Williamson, Jane. *New Feminist Scholarship: A Guide to Bibliographies.* Old Westbury, NY: Feminist Press, 1979.

This guide lists 391 major bibliographies and literature reviews for materials published across 30 categories of Women's Studies specializations through 1978. The largest sections are "General," "History," "Literature," and the "Professions," but other and smaller sections such as "Minority and Ethnic Women," "Reference Sources," "Women and Development," and the "Women's Movement" are equally helpful, and especially so for early literature. Williamson's locates the development of the bibliography in a brief history of Women's Studies as an academic discipline, and while she annotates only bibliographies and not literature reviews (or survey essays), her annotations are detailed and informative. Entries on religion, however, are quite limited. Title and author indices close the volume, together with a list of publishers for readers' use in ordering books. This is a useful resource for material on the history of the women's movement, although its religion references need supplements (e.g., the ATLA Database [129], Bass and Boyd [130], Ruether and Skinner Keller ([132], [133], [134], [135]), Finson [269], Musto [270], Ruud [951]).

2.   General Bibliography

[6]   Miller, Connie, with Corinna Treitel. *Feminist Research Methods: An Annotated Bibliography.* Westport, CT: Greenwood Press, 1991.

This bibliography details literature addressing the strategic and grounding assumptions of feminist research methods in the humanities and social sciences, with each of its disciplinary chapters (e.g., politics, economics, anthropology) preceded by a brief review of issues and important developments. Of particular relevance is Chapter III ("Sociology") with nearly fifty extensive descriptions of books and articles identifying and/or discussing feminist method(s) in sociology and sociological research. The entries are current through 1989, and subject and author indices provide relevant cross references. A limitation is that neither "religion" nor "feminist theology" are listed in the index, nor are studies on women in the sociology of religion. **NOTE**: For literature into the 1990s, See Ryan [7] below and Reinharz [112] in Chapter 13.

[7]   Ryan, Barbara. *The Women's Movement: References and Resources.* New York: . G. K. Hall, 1996.

This bibliography is an *excellent* beginning point for those seeking a thorough overview of feminist references and resources. Its six chapters are grounded in a social movements perspective and address, respectively, first and second wave feminisms, women activists, feminist discourse, cross cutting "issues," and in an especially helpful closing chapter entitled "Guide to Sources," feminist bibliographies, funding sources, library collections, primary documents, reference materials and anthologies and texts. Both hard copy and electronic sources (including established chat rooms) are detailed, and instructive and well formatted overviews guide the reader through the subdivisions of each chapter. Overall, 1,301 entries are abstracted, with sociological and religious entries falling in the "discourse" and "issues" discussions, respectively. Together with Loeb and Stineman [51], Mankiller et al. [52] and Kramarae and Spender [66] it covers the literature, although with an almost exclusive attention to goddess spirituality as its defining focus for religion and spirituality. This said, it remains a most highly recommended text. Its literature is current through the mid-90s, and its subject, author and title indices are fully comprehensive. **NOTE**: Also by Ryan (but not abstracted here) is her history of the women's movement [*Feminism and the Women's Movement: Dynamics of Change in Social Movement, Ideology and Activism*. NY: Routledge, 1992], with its clear summaries of movement changes and mobilization, the impact of the Reagan Bush years, issues of difference and the search for contemporary galvanizing issues in a post-ERA period.

[8]   Watson, G. Llewellyn. [With Janet P. Sentner.] *Feminism and Women's Issues: An Annotated Bibliography and Research Guide, Volumes I-II.* New York: Garland, 1990.

This excellent reference work provides the user with three research tools: a general bibliography of approximately 6900 entries on feminist issues (grouped into 14 distinct categories); an additional "general bibliography on feminism" (with nearly 400 entries); and, third, a listing of journals "partly or wholly devoted to the discussion of women's issues." The literature is current through 1986, and Watson's focus is on works that give full expression to feminism's critique of patriarchy in all institutional and social sectors. A brief introduction distills differences between 19th and 20th century feminisms and identifies Watson's Marxist framework for the selection of literature presented. A brief statement of "how to use the bibliography" explains cross referencing classifications, and the annotations then follow. While large numbers of entries remain unannotated, and while Llewellyn's "guide" lacks both author and subject indices, the text remains relatively easy to use, with the "Table of Contents" focusing topics by a very detailed "women and..." (education, law, religion etc.), listing. Users seeking material on religion will find general entries on women and religion, including many Christian feminist classics, but not other texts on feminist theology.

NOTE: For additional bibliography, see the listings in Chapter 2.

3.   Global Statistics

[9]   Morgan, Robin, ed. *Sisterhood is Global: The International Women's Movement Anthology.* Garden City, NY: Doubleday/Anchor, 1984/1996.

This anthology presents the writings of women from virtually all nations of the earth in an effort to witness to both the reality and need of "planetary feminism" and to invite all readers to 'share the vision' and participate in its work. An extended introduction pulls together the themes evident from international contributors: (1) that feminism is in varying degrees indigenous to all nations; (2) the control of women's bodies and fertility is yet in the hands of male power and its structures; (3) double standards of divorce, sexuality, and violence (both physical and economic) exist comfortably in most nations; (4) work done by women is devalued, denigrated, and/or else wise exploited throughout the world; (5) women's rights exist either precariously or not at all; (6) patriarchal religions continue to legitimate this global status quo, and last, the cultural and social ignorance of women is yet institutionally sustained across more than a third of the earth by entrenched systems that work against women's literacy, women's access to information, and thus the subsequent (albeit gradual) benefits that such provide. The documentation of these identified themes then follows as the reports of women across the globe cite statistics, ideologies, history, political struggles and the strengths and hope women have against such oppression. By way of presentation, reports are arrayed alphabetically by country with each preceded by a feminist fact-sheet. The latter describes that country's location, demography, government, economy, "gynography" (i.e., its marital, sexual and reproductive policies and practices), and last, the country's "herstory" and/or "mythology" (i.e., cultural/national symbols). This is a mammoth work with data current through the early 1980s, and it is yet to be contradicted by later research (cf., [10] and [11]). Its re-release in 1996 includes a new preface by Morgan indicating the impact of various geo-political shifts since the 1984 edition, together with additional sources on the global needs of women and particularly data published through the UN (cf. [12] below). Last, Morgan indicates efforts for a statistical update by 2000 and a "global statistics" web site.

[10]   Neft, Naomi and Ann D. Levine. *Where Women Stand: An International Report on the Status of Women in 140 Countries: 1997-1998.* NY: Random House, 1997.
This is, without doubt, one of the most readable, accessible, usable and helpful references on global feminism currently available. It draws from scores of governmental and international sources (e.g., the UN, WHO, numerous embassies, consulates etc.), and it provides clear data based overviews of several topics important to women globally, including women's education, employment, marriage and divorce rates, health, and experience of violence. Additionally, it provides statistical and narrative profiles for 21 countries on each of these issues, and it prefaces each profile with a brief history of the women's movement within that country. Data tables for women's status on the topics covered are then provided for 140 countries, with countries identified and ranked when they fall within either the top or bottom ten percent listing for the variables in the table. Resource names, addresses and phone numbers are listed throughout the text, and an extended chronology of "Significant Signposts on the Road to Equality" *globally*, together with a glossary, bibliography, and detailed index close the text. With a "forward" by former congresswoman Pat Schroeder, the text is a gem: it brims over with clearly written narrative and data presentations designed for wide lay and professional readership and use.

[11]   Schmittroth, Linda, comp. and ed. *Statistical Record of Women Worldwide.* Detroit: Gale Research Inc., 1991. [Rev. ed. 1995]
Using data from several different sources (e.g., published reports, articles, books and surveys of women worldwide) Schmittroth presents 814 well formatted data tables depicting the status (and/or responses) of women on variety of topics (e.g., abortion, income, politics, religion, sports, work and occupations, etc.). A well organized "Table of Contents" lists each of the 814 tables by number and title, and for the most part, tables are current through 1990. A closing brief discussion describes the references and/or organizations providing data for the volume, and Schmittroth lists addresses and contact phone numbers for organizational citations. A thorough "subject and geographical index" based on Library of Congress headings closes the volume. Of particular value in this volume are: (1) the numerous data tables presenting "girl" as well as "women" data, and (2) Tables 724-738, surveying women and religious practices, professions, and attitudes.

[12]   United Nations Department of Public Information. *The United Nations and the Advancement of Women, 1945-1996.* [The United Nations Blue Books Series, Volume VI, rev. ed.]. NY: The United Nations Reproduction Section, 1995/1996.
This text summarizes the history and efforts of the United Nations on behalf of the international movement for women's rights. It documents that history from the formation of the UN's "Commission on Human Rights" and its "Commission on the Status of Women" in 1946 through the "Fourth World Conference on Women" held in Beijing in 1995, and in all, 139 formal documents provide the resources for viewing UN politics and advocacy on behalf of women's rights. Boutros Boutros-Ghali, the Secretary General of the UN through 1996, traces the background to the volume and introduces many of the documents covered in the text. Helpful chronologies of events and seminars are included as guides to the text's more than 800 pages, and a listing of UN members' current positions (i.e., declarations, reservations, and objections) on the 1979 "Convention on the Elimination of All Forms of Discrimination Against Women" (Document 139) completes the text. Subject and document indices close the volume.

B.   Historical and Theoretical Works

1. Histories of Feminism and the Women's Movement

[13]   Buechler, Steven M. *Women's Movements in the United States: Woman Suffrage, Equal Rights and Beyond.* New Brunswick, NJ: Rutgers Univ. Press, 1990.
This volume presents an informative overview of women's movements in American history by examining both the movements themselves and their analysis from within the context of social movement theory. The book is organized into five chapters that deal respectively with: "Roots and Origins," "Organizations and Communities," "Ideologies and Visions," "Classes and Races," and "Opposition and Countermovements." Buechler's axis of organization is variation in movement and countermovement responses to the public-private split characteristic of "patriarchal" social organization, and his concluding chapter evidences this variation clearly. **NOTE**: For additional work by Buechler, see "Beyond Resource Mobilization? Emerging Trends in Social Movement Theory," *The Sociological Quarterly* 34(1993): 217-236 (not abstracted here). Additionally, see Chafetz and Dworkin [827], Klatch [833], Ferree and Hess [17], and Ferree and Martin [119].

[14]   Carabillo, Toni, Judith Meuli, and June Bundy Csida. *Feminist Chronicles: 1953-1993.* Los Angeles: Women's Graphics, 1993.
Carabillo introduces this text with an excellent overview of the American feminist movement from the period of "awakenings" in the 1950s through the accomplishments (and setbacks) of the 1990s. The actual "feminist chronicles" then follow, with an exceptionally readable and well-formatted annual listing of the advances and backlashes making up the history of American feminism--and the women's movement generally, from 1953-1993. The "chronicles" here identify important events, individuals, legislation, organizations etc., and the book's closing section reprints copies of precedent-setting early and recent legislative, organizational and task force documents. This is an excellent, highly readable source, well formatted for personal study and reflection, classroom and/or adult educational discussions, intergenerational and/or other group educational experiences.

[15]   Castro, Ginette. *American Feminism: A Contemporary History.* New York: New York Univ. Press, 1990.
This text is an especially readable and generalized overview of American feminism from the mid 1940s to the late 1980s. It is a translation of Castro's original 1984 French discussion, and it has been updated to cover events through 1989. It is particularly clear for the beginning reader who seeks an overview of the ideological issues distinguishing "egalitarian" and "radical" feminisms, and its synthesis of feminism in literature, the arts, media, politics, business and "the law" is exceptional. Additionally, its incorporation of Mary Daly's early work introduces the reader to the early feminist theological literature. Last, its "Chronology" of events from 1946-1989 is a handy ready reference. The notes and bibliography run through the late 1980s, but there is no index.

[16]   DuBois, Ellen Carol, Gail Paradise Kelly, Elizabeth Lapovsky Kennedy, Carolyn W. Korsmeyer, and Lillian S. Robinson, eds. *Feminist Scholarship: Kindling in the Groves of Academe.* Urbana: Univ. of Illinois Press, 1987.
An early and ongoing tension within the literature of feminism and Women's Studies focuses on whether [feminist] research on women should be "mainlined" (i.e., integrated within standard disciplinary sources), or developed independently in terms of Women's Studies programs per se, since Women's Studies represents the intellectual and academic arm of the feminist movement. This text both examines this issue and in fact expresses it, as it maps the history, development, and impact(s) of feminism in five specific disciplines: anthropology, education, history, literature and philosophy. The opening chapter summarizes the rise of feminism in the authors' selected disciplines, and subsequent discussions examine the initial incorporation of feminist research within these disciplines, together with the range of issues attached to understanding women's oppression, liberation and equality. The text closes with statistics on articles on women, women's issues and feminism in the major journals for each of the selected five disciplines for the period 1966-1980.

[17]   Ferree, Myra Marx, and Beth B. Hess. *Controversy and Coalition: The New Feminist Movement.* 2d ed. Boston: G. K. Hall, 1994.
The eight chapters comprising this discussion are premised on the assumption that [second wave] feminism has itself undergone sufficient differentiation to be considered a pluralized variable within American society. Thus the authors speak about "multiple feminisms," a plurality of "...movements focused with a common conviction that the present social system does not recognize the value of women or act to promote women's good" (p. viii). To synthesize elements of the movements comprising this new feminism the authors examine: (1) the organizational history and current achievements associated with this "new feminism"; (2) its attempts to yet accomplish several first and second wave feminist goals; (3) current issues and possibilities still facing feminist consciousness and movement, and specifically (4) the role of (ethnic, sexual and religious) diversity in feminist history and activity. Individual chapter discussions provide succinct, information packed overviews of various 19th century feminist ideologies, the organizational structures of America's second wave of feminism from 1963-1972, the tensions and ideological conflicts inherent in (and frequently absorbed by) those organizations, the role of interest groups in movement activity from 1973-1982 (including responses to backlash and anti-feminist ideology and activity), and finally, the new (and old) social and domestic issues (e.g., work harassment and domestic violence) facing feminist movement and consciousness in the 1990s and beyond. A detailed "chronology" of events beginning with President John Kennedy's 1963 Commission on Women and ending with Ruth Bader Ginsburg's appointment to the Supreme Court in 1993, together with a thorough bibliography and general index close this informative volume. While accomplished readers will appreciate the social movement based overviews of policy, organizational, diversity and other data based concerns, new users will find this a helpful

introduction, and especially if read with Hess and Ferree's 1987 reference volume [118] and Ferree and Martin's 1995 feminist organizations text [119].

[18]   Simon, Rita J., and Gloria Danziger. *Women's Movements in America: Their Successes, Disappointments, and Aspirations.* New York: Praeger, 1991.
The text examines historical and public data (including census, polling, and general demographic data) current through 1990 to identify and assess: (1) the status of American women since the colonial period generally, and (2) the "successes and failures" of the American women's movement from the 1830s through the 1980s. The discussion begins with an introductory overview of women's movements in the U.S. Subsequent chapters detail suffrage and women's political history in the U.S., "women in the work place", and the public/private nexus for women relative to marriage, family and divorce. A concluding chapter discusses "successes and disappointments." Simon and Danziger cover a number of topics in this text, with particular sensitivity to the legal history evident through the women's movement. It is an informed, well documented discussion. For additional work by Simon see [719]. NOTE: See also the Ryan text noted in [7].

[19]   Tobias, Sheila. *Faces of Feminism: An Activist's Reflections on the Women's Movement.* Boulder, CO: Westview Press, 1997.
Written for the wide breadth of lay and academic readership, Tobias' text surveys the feminist movement from its inception in the 19th century through its mid-90s "post-modernist" and "third wave" emphases. Tobias summarizes both feminism's accomplishments and failures, and although seemingly uncomfortable with current "third wave" perspectives, she concludes that "second wave" feminism, as it has traditionally been known, is over. Rather, she suggests, what must now characterize feminist activity are (1) increased local and intergenerationally based political efforts to assist the "mainstreaming" now coming into view (p.253) and (2) the development of a definition of "equality...that no longer depends on every one being the same" (p. 259). Her analysis focuses on several factors, e.g., the shaping of a movement around the changing issues attached to "role equality" and "role interchangeability," the influence of Phyllis Shafly's 'stopERA' and other antifeminist efforts, and the changing constituencies of support undergirding feminist activity, to name but three. But of equal importance to these is the impact of mainstreaming itself and the present possibility of a "remarginalization" of women's needs, as partisan issues assume priority and divide feminist support along sharp ideological lines. This is an important book, and it lays the groundwork for cooperative efforts on a variety of feminist concerns. It details the impacts of feminism's political and inclusive successes, it identifies the risks facing feminists today in their efforts to *not* jeopardize recent gains as issues such as identity politics and work comparability square off, and last, its many summary discussions of such key topics as race and gender conflicts, abortion and sexuality issues, women and the military, and feminism's initial insensitivity to family needs all press for dialogue across differences anow cknowledged and the need for a framework wide enough to implement the grounding premise of feminist vision, i.e., that all women (and men) are entitled to full participation in society's political and possibility-generating processes.

2. Recent Theory and Interpretation

[20]   Boles, Janet K., ed. *American Feminism: New Issues for a Mature Movement.* Newbury Park: Sage, 1991.
Initially published as volume 515 of *The Annals of the American Academy of Political and Social Science*, the 13 papers in this collection address varying aspects of feminist achievement, including women's political distribution and influence, various gender gaps, media obstacles, feminist ethics, women in the work force, and the impact of the Reagan administration on attitudes toward gender, the women's movement as a whole, and specific political strategies. Moreover, three papers move beyond second wave achievements, to address, as well, African American women in feminist politics, the future of antifeminism, and "Women's Rights as Human Rights: An International Perspective." Of these papers, the first traces the non-traditional political activities of African American women from the period of slavery through the 1980s. The second analyzes antifeminist ideology ([836]), and the third, the constraints (including religion) that work against "universal calls for equity" on behalf of women.

[21]   Collins, Patricia Hill. "The Social Construction of Black Feminist Thought." *Signs* 14 (1989): 745-773.
An important premise of the Berger/Luckmann volume, *The Social Construction of Reality*, is that all "knowledge" (or all of "that which passes for knowledge") is socially constructed, socially

mediated and socially distributed; and further, that the latter is critically dependent upon the power resources of the knowledge creators and distributors. Collins adopts this premise as a framework to indicate: (1) the factors affecting the knowledge legitimation process of Black women's socially rooted "standpoint epistemology;" (2) the four characteristics of this standpoint epistemology; (3) the parallels between African-American and feminist epistemologies; and (4) the cross-cutting pressures that play upon Black feminist scholars as they make their way through traditionally Eurocentric institutions of higher learning and the creation of new scholarship. This is a ground-breaking essay incorporating the literature of womanist reflection, feminist sociology and epistemology, and the tensions of an "insider-outsider" status as the means of mediating what are quite literally different *worlds* of experience. It is challenging, insightful, and well detailed with notes and bibliography. **NOTE**: For Collins' book length discussion, see **[99]**.

[22]   Drake, Jennifer. "Third Wave Feminism (Review Essay)." *Feminist Studies* 23 (1997): 97-108.
Writing from a perspective sympathetic to what she describes as feminism's "third wave," i.e., the political but title rejecting appropriation of feminist goals by "generation X" women, Drake reviews two edited readers that spell out the "feminist" commitments of this new generation. These texts are *Listen Up: Voices from the Next Feminist Generation*, edited by Baraba Findlen, [Seattle: Seal Press, 1995] and *To Be Real: Telling the Truth and Changing the Face of Feminism*, edited by Rebecca Walker [NY: Anchor Books, 1995]. Common to both--and to the wider framework of feminism's "third wave," is the recognition that women born in the 1970s grew up cognizant of various feminists' accomplishments as "taken-for granteds," e.g., the ownership of one's body (including the right to abortion, freedom of sexual expression, and available and safe contraception), adequate and affordable child care, equal pay for equal work etc., and that these accomplishments are yet worthy goals for younger women to be politically concerned about. At the same time, these women do not want what they see as "second wave" feminism's "uptight," "man-hating" and "anti-sex" attitudes and morality. Hence they reject the name "feminist," but remain committed to the political goals of the second wave, sans its almost "Puritan morality." The title, "feminist," they argue, stigmatizes its holder and requires a "victim" mentality that is alien to their generational perspective. Drake's discussion of the sources included in the texts she reviews is pointed, and although the (third wave) equation of feminism with its extreme positions may, in fact, be an empirically open question, her discussion nonetheless vividly portrays this late '80s developing orientation. **NOTE**: For a representative single author presentation of this orientation, see Rene Denfield, *The New Victorians: A Young Woman's Challenge to the Old Feminist Order*. NY: Warner Books, 1995. Additionally, see Tobias **[19]** above.

[23]   Fox-Genovese, Elizabeth. "From Separate Spheres to Dangerous Streets: Post-Modernist Feminism and the Problem of Order." *Social Research* 60, no. 2 (1993): 235-254.
In addition to introducing readers to the developing literature of "post-modern feminism," this essay critically summarizes feminism's critique of the public/private dichotomy as the vehicle for women's disempowerment and marginalization in twentieth century capitalist society. Two points are salient. First, Fox-Genovese argues that the public/private (contractual/consensual) metaphor has outlived its explanatory usefulness as a vehicle for describing how women are made "other" in androcentric society, for current data belie the clear political-economic and nurturing contexts the metaphor presumes. Second, in attacking this particular metaphor, the class bias of many feminist theories becomes clear, with privileged and non-privileged women becoming pitted against one another. **NOTE**: Also by Fox-Genovese is **[75]** and for her study of individualism and feminism, see *Feminism Without Illusion* [Chapel Hill, NC: Univ. of North Carolina Press, 1991].

[24]   French, Marilyn. *The War Against Women*. New York: Summit Books, 1992.
Defining feminism as "any attempt to improve the lot of any group of women through female solidarity and a female perspective," (p. 12) French introduces her text with a brief summary of recent feminist gains and an overview of what still is needed. And what is still needed is a full and "public discussion" of the violence men exert against women, and a discussion that recognizes this violence "as a global crisis" (p. 22). In a time of backlash (**[822]**), many may read French's words as angry rhetoric, but as she unfolds her four part discussion, the truth of her words becomes undeniably clear. Male violence against women is world wide and it is permitted and sustained in four general ways: *legally* through systemic discrimination supported by economic, political and religious norms; *institutionally* through educational, legal, penal, medical, juridical and economic structures; *culturally* through misogynist art including quite specifically, American (and

other) militaristic images of women as legitimate recipients of male social and sexual brutality; and finally, through *men's own personal violence*, which is tied regularly to male assumptions about women as necessary sexual and reproductive auxiliaries. This is a powerfully written book, and it presses for the political acknowledgment of violence against women so that a moral conversation about it can begin and be sustained. Its most extensive section is Part I, "Systemic Discrimination Against Women," where the economic, political and religious norms for numerous countries and major religious traditions are described. No one should avoid this book. While it is significantly longer than Heise's study [28], and proportionately shorter than Morgan's [9], French's description of violence against women alerts readers to the political character of its continuing existence and the necessity for world wide *political* action against it. **NOTE:** For recent related literature see Neft and Levine [10] above and for theologically cast discussions, see Section VI-3 on women's ecumenism and particularly the entries by Benavides [914], Gnanadason [915] and Chung Hyun Kyung [935]. Also, see Chittister [489], Schüssler Fiorenza and Carr [493] and Schüssler Fiorenza and Copeland [275].

[25]   Gunew, Sneja, ed. *A Reader in Feminist Knowledge*. New York: Routledge and Kegan Paul, 1991.
The essays here present "minority" feminist perspectives that challenge the assumption that feminism and feminist solidarity require a "monolithic theoretical" model for legitimacy as women centered perspectives. Indeed, Gunew's expressed purpose is to display the pluralism existing under the umbrella of feminism, and particularly the racial, national, ethnic and sexual pluralisms of feminist knowledge and theory. Twenty-seven essays--all powerful and well documented discussions--make up this volume, and (among others), the topics include epistemology, women's studies, philosophy, biology, religion, subjectivity, and psychoanalysis. Substantive overviews introduce each topical subsection, and an exceptionally helpful index closes the volume. Religion entries include works by Rosemary Ruether, Elisabeth Schüssler Fiorenza, Carol Christ, and Mary Daly. Other contributors include Jackie Higgins, bell hooks, Diane Bell, Susan Sheridan, Nancy Jay, Genevieve Lloyd, Ruth Bleier, Charlotte Bunch and Barbara Taylor to name but a few.

[26]   Harding, Sandra, and Jean F. O'Barr, eds. *Sex and Scientific Inquiry*. Chicago, IL: Univ. of Chicago Press, 1987.
This edited volume pulls together several discussions previously published in *Signs* between 1975 and 1986. Among others, it includes Londa Shiebinger's 1986 review essay, "The History and Philosophy of Women in Science"; Inez Smith Reid's "Science, Politics and Race" (first published in 1975); the co-authored 1980 essay, "Social and Behavioral Constructions of Female Sexuality" (by Patricia Y. Miller and Martha R. Fowlkes); Evelyn Fox Keller's (1982) "Feminism and Science" and Sandra Harding's (1986) "The Instability of Analytic Categories of Feminist Theory" [104]. In all, fifteen essays are grouped into five categories to address: "The Social Structure of Science"; "Misuses and Abuses of Science and Technology"; "Biases in the Sciences"; "Sexual Meanings of Science"; and last, "Epistemology and Metatheory". A brief bibliography lists related articles also published in *Signs,* and a subject index closes the volume.

[27]   Hawkesworth, M. E. *Beyond Oppression: Feminist Theory and Political Strategy*. New York: Continuum, 1990.
This text is discusses philosophical issues grounding the need for feminist analysis and theory. It approaches those issues through categories drawn largely from the sociology of knowledge, and it focuses its discussion in contexts familiar to western philosophical and theological thought (e.g., the need for gender analysis in theological anthropology etc.). Its distinctiveness, however, is its ultimate strategy for combating sexism. In brief, Hawkesworth argues for a reorganization of political life as based on the statistical realities of women's presence. Thus all political positions should reflect a 50/50 sex distribution so that women's voices find avenues of expression, regardless of partisan values. Hawkesworth's discussion is ordered, well documented, and frank about the remaining problems this solution does not address, i.e., social problems arising from other bigotries and notably racism. This said, she stands on her suggested political strategy.

[28]   Heise, Lori. "The Global War Against Women." *World Watch* (March/April, 1989). Reprinted in *The Washington Post*, 9 April 1989, Outlook Section.
This study documents the various forms of marriage-related violence that women experience--mostly from their husbands--but also from cultural norms and accepted traditions throughout third world countries. Heise began her work initially as a researcher intending to study the health problems of children in third world countries, but she found that as she interviewed women

everywhere, the consistently voiced reality was that "My husband beats me." Her report here provides documentation from a variety of sources: the women themselves, public statistics on violent deaths among women, and descriptions of widely held cultural assumptions about the acceptability of violence to women (e.g., dowry deaths and female circumcision). It is a frightening and sobering report that evidences the "risk factor of being female," and the necessity for governments to recognize that violence against women is sanctioned in virtually all countries, including the U.S., and that efforts to eradicate it are not panderings to a "women's issue," but needed priorities on all international agendas. For related literature see French [24], and the entries cross referenced there.

[29] hooks, bell. *Feminist Theory: From Margin to Center.* Boston: South End Press, 1984.
This frequently cited text is a sustained discussion of feminism as an effort to end sexist oppression, with the latter understood unequivocally in terms of its class and racially grounded gender ties. Writing from both her academic and existential experiences as an African American woman aware of the psychological definitions of feminism that have pervaded much middle class feminist rhetoric, hooks argues that feminism must become a [feminist] political movement committed to dismantling the oppressive linkages existing between race, sex and class in American society. Thus, feminism must come to include the experiences of all women--economically poor women, women of color, lesbian women, single women and single parenting women--rather than white women of privilege only. Further, feminism must be redefined to include bonds across several political lines (including coalitions with feminist men) so that feminist movement can in fact begin. hooks' commitments are clear: these changes will require political action geared to economic changes on behalf of African American and other families, a differing perception of feminist education, coalitions across racial, class and gender lines, a redefinition of sexual norms and mores to end sexual violence, and the ongoing work of establishing a mass based feminist constituency that incorporates women from society's margins *and* center, and works, thereby, for long term and institutionalized social change.

[30] hooks, bell. *Talking Back: thinking feminist•thinking black.* Boston: South End Press, 1989.
This collection of 25 brief essays by hooks runs the gamut of her published work and personal/professional development as a writer generally. She begins by telling the story of what 'back talk' and 'talking back' meant (and mean) in the world of "the southern black community" in which she grew up. It is to speak as an equal to an authority figure, and it is from this metaphor that she describes the pain of her earliest and recent writings: the necessity to write because too few people wanted to hear her truths; the criticism of homophobia she received for *Ain't I a Woman;* the radical nature of her feminist commitments; her perceptions of race, violence, rape, and the silence of so many in the face of it all; her personal struggles with finding her voice strongly enough to write autobiographically; her sharpening sense of the seriousness of society's personal-professional, public-private split; her commitments and strategies for feminist pedagogy and feminist ethics; and as a last illustration, her adamant emphasis on the structural ties between race and gender and the implications these suggest for black and white women advocating feminism and the social and institutional changes feminism requires. This is an engaging text with each essay bearing significance in its own right, and with all posing the political-ethical challenges for which hooks has become most known: her commitment to feminism as a fully political movement requiring structural change and coalition building for the long haul, and an acknowledged partnership of equals as various groups speak at the table of goal setting conversation. **NOTE**: For a "white feminist" response (not abstracted here) that works to dialogue seriously with Afrocentric feminism within the context of postmodernism, see Nancy Caraway, *Segregated Sisterhoood: Racism and the Politics of American Feminism*, Knoxville: The Univ. of Tennessee Press, 1991.

[31] Humm, Maggie, ed. *Modern Feminisms: Political, Literary and Cultural.* New York: Columbia Univ. Press, 1992.
This reader presents brief excerpts from feminist theory and philosophy together with clear commentaries on both sources and authors. Virtually all of its seventeen chapters present at least three sources on the topic at hand (with all "name" authors well represented), and each source is prefaced with an overview of the author's primary works, principal questions and investigations. Further, the entire volume is prefaced with a well formatted "Chronology of Events and Texts" that aligns political events and key feminist publications for the years 1903-1991. By way of topics, the text is true to its title in that political, cultural and literary sources from first and second wave

feminist writers--including lesbian, Asian, and African American writers--are all presented. The selections are well chosen, and although each is only two to three pages in length, each is expertly edited. Two final values of this reader: its introductory chapter provides a solid comparison of British and American feminism histories, and its "Glossary" of feminist terms is unbeatable save for lengthier enumerations. A full index closes this elegant, exceptional text. **NOTE**: Also by Humm, (but not abstracted here) is her revised text, *The Dictionary of Feminist Theory* 2d ed, Columbus, OH: Ohio State Univ. Press, 1995.

[32] Jaggar, Alison M., ed. *Living with Contradictions: Controversies in Feminist Social Ethics.* Boulder, CO: Westview Press, 1994.
This extended anthology runs nearly 700 pages and presents a variety of feminist perspectives grouped into seven topics of feminist ethical interest. These are: "Equality," "Women Working," "Marketing Femininity," "Women's Fertility," "Family Values," "The Personal as Political," and "Feminists Changing the World." Although these topics are not new, Jaggar's manner of selecting excerpts for their discussion is. For each topic she presents a range of liberal and conservative feminist entries, with anywhere from six to ten essays from each perspective illustrating the issue(s) of controversy. The contributors include feminists from numerous political, ethnic and sexual perspectives, and the selections are reprinted from works published through the late '80s and early '90s. Jaggar's introduction to the volume is clear and on the mark as it addresses the questions: "What is feminism?" and "What makes an issue feminist?" and each of her divisional introductions helpfully guide the reader. This a text to be read, studied, and read several times again, and in the end, more than appreciated--the lack of an index notwithstanding.

[33] Jaggar, Alison M., and Paula Rothenberg, eds. *Feminist Frameworks.* 3d ed. New York: McGraw-Hill, 1993.
This is a well known and widely used reader in feminist studies, with its main divisions directed to excerpts illustrating varying aspects of feminism, including: (1) the ways gender socialization defines women in and through numerous cultures and social worlds; (2) the subsequent need for pluralism in feminist theory; (3) the continuing problems women experience because of economic, social and sexual subordinations (both nationally and globally); and (4) the perception of contemporary issues (whether economic, familial and sexual) as seen through various factors of "difference" worldwide. Virtually all of the classical feminist sources are represented in this reader, and each section provides additional bibliography for suggested reading. An author-title index closes the volume.

[34] Kramarae, Cheris, and Paula A. Treichler. *A Feminist Dictionary.* Boston: Pandora Press, 1985. [Rev. ed., 1992]
This volume is patterned after the format of a traditional dictionary, and its text surveys literally hundreds of feminist words, phrases, acronyms and concepts, but here from the literature of feminist and womanist writers. Thus, as the meanings for any given term are presented, they are drawn from published feminist and/or womanist sources with full references to author and page number citations. The entry for "religion" illustrates this point. A first definition is taken from Ruether's *Religion and Sexism* [171], and reads: "[religion is]... 'The ideological reflection of...sexual domination and subjugation...' (Rosemary Radford Ruether, 1974, 9) and long a focus of feminist reform and revolutionary struggle" (p. 388). A series of five additional definitions then follow, with each documented from its primary source. A 73 page bibliography arranged alphabetically by author and presented at the close of the volume lists all sources from which the dictionary's nearly 500 pages of entries are developed. **NOTE**: The revised edition (with additional bibliography) is *Amazons, Bluestockings and Crones: A Feminist Dictionary*, by Kramarae and Treichler with assistance from Ann Russo. Also co-edited by Kramarae is [66].

[35] Lerner, Gerda. *The Creation of Feminist Consciousness: From the Middle Ages to Eighteen-seventy.* New York: Oxford Univ. Press, 1993.
Readers seeking a solid exposure to the history of Western women's religious literature will find this text well worth reading *and rereading*. It is the companion and sequel to Lerner's *Creation of Patriarchy* [68], and it identifies the patterns of support and voice developed by women from AD 700 to 1870 to combat the marginalization and exclusion of women from history since the beginnings of patriarchy. Lerner begins by noting the impact of patriarchy on social and political organization, and specifically the definitions of "persons" therein. She helpfully distinguishes the social and philosophical issues attached to defining "slaves" and "women" in Aristotelian and subsequent thought, and she documents the efforts of (Western) women's self-validation through

an analysis of religious and secular writings that lift up the two avenues of development open to Western women from 700 to 1870: their religious activities in the face of and apart from church authorities and their survival knowledge as mothers. This is a strong and detailed text, conscious that education is (for her selected years) a class based phenomenon--and conscious too that the hegemony of patriarchy can no longer have full sway in the definition of gender constructs. Feminist theologians may differ on the significance of this text. This is because there is no direct critique of contemporary religious authority, and because those who understand "feminist consciousness" as spelled by "difference" will find Lerner's definition perhaps too rooted in women's solidarity. These are red herrings. Lerner's purpose is to document the *rise* of feminist consciousness: the rise of a group knowing its difficulties are socially not naturally determined, and knowing too, that it needs its own validation to change the world lest marginalization again find its all too powerful voice.

[36]   Mansbridge, Jane. *Why We Lost the ERA*. Chicago, IL: Univ. of Chicago Press, 1986.
Mansbridge's discussion poses a simple but richly documented answer to the question, 'Why did the ERA fail, and especially so, when in its early years--if the polls are to be believed--there seemed to be so much support for it?' Her answer is that in spite of the poll data evidencing ERA support, the Equal Rights Amendment of 1972 failed, because deep down, both supporters and detractors sincerely believed that it would change America's actual experience of women's and men's gender roles. Moreover, what poll data actually had measured was less a sense of support for the amendment itself and more a general affirmation of individual democratic rights, regardless of gender. Mansbridge's discussion is well grounded. She reviews both the structural dynamics of the amendment process, the specific history of the ERA, the major poll findings spanning that history, and in several illuminating supplemental discussions, the factors affecting membership and commitment in voluntaristic and normatively grounded change-directed social movements.

[37]   McElroy, Wendy, ed. *Freedom, Feminism, and the State: An Overview of Individualist Feminism*. NY: Holmes & Meier, 1991.
This reader highlights 22 essays indicative of 19th century "individualist feminism" that McElroy introduces as the main emphases of what, historically, has become "libertarian feminism." The essays are by historical and contemporary writers, and they are grouped into eight "Women and...." categories that address ["women and...] government, sex, family, birth control, work, church, suffrage and war. McElroy's introduction traces "The Roots of Individualist Feminism in 19th-Century America." It is engaging and informative, and it sheds clear light on the struggles of pre-Civil war women abolitionists and post civil war feminists who eventually move to white supremacy perspectives. Second, it highlights differences between contemporary individualist and Marxist perspectives as it lays out the central emphases of contemporary libertarian feminism.

[38]   Nicholson, Linda J., ed. *Feminism/Postmodernism*. NY: Routledge, 1990.
This reader in feminist and postmodernist theory presents 13 essays grouped thematically around three issues: (1) "Feminism As Against Epistemology," (2) "The Politics of Location," and (3) "Identity and Differentiation." Seven of these articles have been previously published and include (among others) Jane Flax's "Postmodernism and Gender Relations in Feminist Theory," Christine Di Stefano's "Dilemmas of Difference: Feminism, Modernity and Postmodernism," Nancy Hartsock's "Foucault on Power: A Theory for Women?" and Andreas Huyssen's "Mapping the Postmodern." Others are new and reflect questions now familiar in feminist sociology, e.g., Harding's "Feminism, Science and Anti-Enlightenment Critiques" and Anna Yeatman's "A Feminist Theory of Social Differentiation." Nicholson's "Introduction" sets the framework for the debates about essentialism, relativism and nihilism, and her co-authored essay with Nancy Fraser ("Social Criticism without Philosophy: An Encounter Between Feminism and Postmodernism") provides a good summary of the "ad hoc" challenges of postmodernist thinking to feminist critique. NOTE: For examples of postmodernism's impact on feminist theory see Drake [22] above. Also, for theological examples see [240] and [287].

[39]   Offin, Karen. "Defining Feminism--A Comparative Historical Approach." *Signs* 14 (1988): 119-157.
This article reviews the history and usage of European, British and American understandings of the concept, feminism, so that a viable definition of this term may be obtained. The review suggests two historically evident trends: an "individualistic" emphasis that serves the needs of single women seeking parity with males in most social spheres, and a "relational" emphasis that recognizes the

"moral equality" of women and men and the implications of familism for social policy. After reviewing the strengths and weaknesses of each emphasis, Offin provides three criteria for identifying specifically "feminist" perspectives. These are: (1) the recognized validity of women's interpretations of their experience and needs; (2) consciousness of gender based institutionalized injustice; and (3) advocacy efforts to eradicate that injustice. Offin closes with the recognition that further constructive theoretical work is needed on behalf of a vision that can: (1) incorporate the best of both the individual and relational perspectives; (2) transcend stark individualism; and (3) open up new vistas for "the future of feminist politics." **NOTE**: For additional definitions of "feminism," see the subject index.

C.   Journals and Informational Sources

Too numerous to list are the feminist and Women's Studies journals currently in print, but obviously relevant are *Feminist Studies* [40] and *Signs* [41] (abstracted below), and in Chapter 2, *Women's Studies Abstracts* [59], the *Women's Studies Index 1989* [60], and *Women's Studies Quarterly* [61]. Also, for a *full* listing of early feminist and Women's Studies journals see Stineman and Loeb [55] with subsequent updates in Loeb, Searing and Stineman [51]. Additionally, see Kramarae and Spender [66] for the discussion of feminism in the professions and their supportive disciplines (with literature current through 1992), and see DuBois et al. above [16] and Boxer [63] in Chapter I-2 for early overviews of Women's Studies in selected disciplines within the humanities and social sciences. Finally, for journals addressing women's issues in religion generally, and feminist theology specifically, see entries [255] through [258].

[40]   *Feminist Studies*. Feminist Studies, Inc. 1972.
Published three times a year, this journal presents article length discussions of feminist literature, theory, and research together with regularly featured feminist resources, including extensive review essays on current topics, e.g., Gilkes [603], Dill [622], and Umansky [947].

[41]   *Signs: Journal of Women in Culture and Society* Chicago, IL: University of
       Chicago Press, Journals Division, 1975.
This journal regularly presents extended scholarly articles, topically grounded "forum" discussions, and regular review essays on subjects cutting across all aspects of feminist theory and practice. Additionally, each issue presents numerous single volume reviews of texts in feminist literature, history, art, social science and religion. Examples of articles presented in *Signs* and abstracted in this bibliography include Dill [602] and Gilkes [615].

D.   Internet and On-line Resources

As access to the World Wide Web continues to grow, users should seek and bookmark various feminist web resources, including on-line library catalogues and university course offerings, home pages for various feminist organizations, feminist publishing houses, Women's Studies programs, programs in diversity and multiculturalism, and web sites dedicated to the numerous topics covered in subsequent sections of the bibliography. Virtually all of these types of sources can be accessed through the standard search engines (e.g., "Yahoo" or "Alta Vista"), and all provide links to other sources. Two systems noted for their comprehensive listings and extensive connecting links are the Women's Studies program at the University of Maryland (<www.inform.umd.edu/EdRes/topic/WomensStudies>) and the Electronic Library at the University of Wisconsin (<www.library.wisc.edu/libraries/WomensStudies>). Additionally, the web address for the Feminist Majority Foundation is <www.feminist.org>.

Similarly, the number of theological and religious web sites is also vast, with links equally extensive. Useful sources include denominational and seminary web pages, typically listed by the name of the denomination or school: e.g., <http://www.ELCA.org> or, as is the case with New York's Union Seminary (which provides considerable links), <http://www.union.edu>. Second, just as college and university libraries are often on-line, so too are seminary libraries, and readers should search them out for journal and text literature. Finally, a third type of literature search simply asks the name (or book title) of a feminist theologian. Name searches are helpful because the user is frequently led to individual faculty web pages and/or on-line bookstores (such as AMAZON.com) which provide extensive source lists, summaries and user reviews.

2

Feminism and Women's Studies

A. References and Resources

1. Bibliographies and Informational Guides

[42] Ballou, Patricia K. *A Bibliography of Bibliographies*. Boston: G. K. Hall, 1980. 2d ed., 1986.
In the first edition of this bibliography (which is especially helpful for literature from the early years of the women's movement), Ballou classifies 557 bibliographies into four main divisions. With some modification, these organizing divisions carry over into the second edition and include: "general and interdisciplinary" bibliographies; various types of other "publications" (such as guides to dissertations and/or manuscript collections); geographically defined subjects (i.e., bibliographies subdivided by region, state or country of origin); and "topical subjects," or bibliographies organized by the familiar academic disciplines with their internal subject areas. Ballou's "topical subjects" is by far the largest section of the first edition, with eleven bibliographies indicated for Christianity and ninety-one for sociology. Her second edition continues with literature through 1985, and as with the first edition, entries are numbered sequentially throughout the volume and arranged alphabetically within subgroups.

[43] Capek, Mary Ellen S., ed. *A Women's Thesaurus: An Index of Language Used to Describe and Locate Information By and About Women* [A Project of The National Council for Research on Women and The Business and Professional Women's Foundation]. New York: Harper & Row, 1987.
This comprehensive (1,052 pages) research reference presents a "standardized vocabulary, a common language that reflects the complexity and subtlety of women's lives and work" (p. viii) so that researchers, bibliographers, catalogers and users of indices and literature by and about women may be aided in the task of presenting or accessing sources in as easy a manner as is presently possible. An introductory discussion by the editor provides both an overview of the notations grounding the structure of the thesaurus and a description of the many ways entries may be grouped, including a "Delimiters Display," which indicates generic search terms for both card-based and on-line electronic searches. Specialists in indexing and cataloging will find this thesaurus extremely helpful as they compile materials related to women's studies, while more "run of the mill" users of the literature will find it a stimulating source for cross referenced topics they might otherwise miss.

[44] Carter, Sarah, and Maureen Ritchie. *Women's Studies: A Guide to Informational Sources*. Great Britain: Biddles Lit., Guilford and King's Lynn, 1990.
This well indexed and comprehensive guide to sources in women's studies groups over 1,000 annotated entries into three main divisions. The first is "General Materials." It includes reference and bibliographic sources, periodical indices, special journal issues, dictionary and encyclopedic articles, thesauri, library and book trade sources, organizational sources, funding organizations and sources on statistical information about women. Part II, "Women in the World," presents a similarly broad scope, with entries grouped geographically in terms of African, Asian and Pacific

similarly broad scope, with entries grouped geographically in terms of African, Asian-and Pacific sources, sources from Australia and New Zealand, Europe, Latin America and the Caribbean, the Middle East and North America. Part III is the longest section of the guide. It synthesizes bibliographic, periodical and organizational sources on such specific subjects as: "The Arts and the media," "Black women," "Education," "History," "Law and politics," "Society and the environment," "Spirituality, myth and religion," and "Women in the labour force." The section on religion includes "Goddess Religion," "Jewish Women and Judaism," "Christianity," and "Other Religions." Overall, while its material on religion is scant, this is a useful introductory reference for those seeking information on the breadth of issues addressed by women's studies.

[45] Fenton, Thomas R., and Mary J. Heffron, comps. and eds. *Women in the Third World: A Directory of Resources.* Maryknoll, NY: Orbis, 1987.
This informative directory is ordered around five chapters that cover "organizations," "books," "periodicals," "pamphlets and articles," and "audiovisuals" on "women in the third world," with chapter materials further divided into "annotated entries," "supplementary" lists and "additional informational sources." The geographic spread is wide--Africa, Asia and the Pacific, Latin America, the Caribbean, and the Middle East--and the information is detailed, with listings for contact names, telephone numbers, prices and mailing lists for teaching and educational resources. All materials are indexed by page number and the result is a compact (104 pages), invaluable reference source. **NOTE**: Also by Fenton and Heffron is their *Third World Resources Directory,* which provides statistics on various issues important to women (e.g., aid, armaments, conflict, debt, democratization, environment, human rights), as well as statistical updates for much material in their 1987 volume. See *Third World Resources Directory: A Guide to Print, Audiovisual, and Organizational Resources on Africa, Asia and Pacific, Latin America and Caribbean, and the Middle East 1994-1995, A Data Center Guide,* compiled and edited by Thomas P. Fenton and Mary J. Heffron. Maryknoll, NY: Orbis, 1994.

[46] Gilbert, V. R., and D. S. Tatla, comps. *Women's Studies: A Bibliography of Dissertations 1870-1982.* Oxford, England: Blackwell Reference, 1985.
This reference text classifies 12,172 doctoral dissertations completed in Great Britain, the US, Ireland, and Canada on women, feminism and topics of related interest. The text lists theses published through 1982 with each classified within alphabetically arranged subjects (e.g., "the arts," "demography," "family dynamics," "health," "law," "religion," "society"). The religion section lists 315 theses, 284 of which deal with topics on women in Christian tradition. Although a separate author index is not included, the volume's thirty-nine page subject/author/topical index is most helpful. Additionally in a "checklist of bibliographic and reference sources" the compilers cite thirty-three other bibliographies on women's studies, together with indexing and journal sources.

[47] Haber, Barbara. *Women in America: A Guide to Books, 1963-1975.* Boston: G. K. Hall, 1978.
The 439 entries of this annotated bibliography address eighteen distinct but familiar categories. Those with the most entries are "history" (seventy-eight entries), "feminism" (forty-one entries), "work" (forty-one entries), "literature/arts" (thirty-eight), "sex roles" (thirty-two), and "Black Women and Native American Women" (twenty-seven). Those with the least number are "prostitution" (five entries), "rape" (nine entries), "crime and imprisonment" (ten entries), "health" (ten entries) and "life styles" (eleven entries). Remaining categories (religion, marriage, psychology, law and politics, education and sexuality) average eighteen to twenty-one entries each, and in all categories attention is paid to the author's expressed purpose of guiding one to and through books that depict the lived rather than abstracted qualities of women's experience. This book is a guide in the finest sense of the word. Readers seeking early feminist literature (as well as the salience of its topics) will find it useful, and especially so if coupled with the *Women's Annual* series [48] also spearheaded by Haber.

[48] Haber, Barbara, ed. *The Woman's Annual, 1980. The Year in Review.* Boston: G. K. Hall, 1981.
This volume is the first of five summary reviews of women's progress in several cultural and institutional American sectors, including the field of religion. Haber edits separate volumes for the years 1980 and 1981 and a third volume for the years 1982-1983. All are published through G. K. Hall and Co., with publications dates following the specific year in review. The final two volumes of the series are edited, respectively, by Sara Pritchard (*The Women's Annual, 1983-1984* [G. K. Hall, 1984]) and Mary McFeeney (*The Women's Annual 1984-1985* [G. K. Hall, 1985]). In all

volumes noted women scholars present essays from their respective fields and, in most cases, each provides extensive supplemental bibliography. A general author/subject index closes each volume.

[49] Hull, Gloria T., Patricia Bell Scott, and Barbara Smith, eds. *All the Women Are White, All the Blacks Are Men, But Some of Us Are Brave: Black Women's Studies*. Old Westbury, NY: Feminist Press, 1982.

This is one of the first sources to consult when seeking sources in Black women's literature through 1980. It features twenty-one article length entries organized around seven themes: (1) "Searching for Sisterhood: Black Feminism" (three entries); (2) "Roadblocks and Bridges: Confronting Racism" (four entries); (3) "Dispelling the Myths: Black Women and the Social Sciences" (three entries); (4) "Creative Survival: Preserving Body, Mind and Spirit" (four entries); (5) "'Necessary Bread:' Black Women's Literature" (five entries); (6) "Bibliographies and Bibliographic Essays" (seven entries); and (7) "Doing the Work: Selected Course Syllabi" (two entries). The bibliographic section is by far the largest with over 100 pages of reference material including historical sources, films, musical work, literature, near print sources and standard texts. The section on course syllabi is the shortest, but it includes several outlines, together with recommended bibliographies and supplemental materials. Numerous introductory prefaces serve to orient the reader, and a detailed index closes the work. This source is highly recommended and can be easily supplemented with womanist materials detailed in Section IV.

[50] Jackson, Stevi et al., eds. *Women's Studies: Essential Readings*. Washington Square, NY: New York Univ. Press, 1993.

This reader presents excerpts from over 150 key sources in feminist and women's studies literature, with sources organized into fourteen chapters as introduced by the volume's numerous editors. These categories and editors include: "Feminist Social Theory" [Stevi Jackson], "Women's Minds: Psychological and Psychiatric Literature" [Jane Prince], "Cross-cultural Perspectives on Women's Lives" [Teri Brewer], "Historical Perspectives on Women's Lives" [Deidre Beddoe], "Women, Education and Work" [Jane Prince], "Marriage and Motherhood" [Sue Faulkner and Stevi Jackson], "Sexuality" [Stevi Jackson], "Women and the Law" [Helen Power], "Women, Crime and Deviance" [Anthea Hucklesby], "Public/private: Women, Politics and the State" [Rose Pearson], "Science, Medicine and Technology" [Stevi Jackson, Jane Prince and Pauline Young], "Language and Gender" [Karen Atkinson], "Feminist Literary Criticism" [Pauline Young], and "Representations of Women in the Media" [Michele Ryan]. The excerpts are well edited and chapters include "further reading" bibliography.

[51] Loeb, Catherine, Susan Searing, and Esther Stineman [With assistance by Meredith J. Ross]. *Women's Studies: A Recommended Core Bibliography: 1980-1985*. Littleton, CO: Libraries Unlimited, 1987.

This volume is a follow-up to the excellent 1979 Stineman-Loeb, *Women's Studies: A Recommended Core Bibliography* described below [55]. Its arrangement, criteria of inclusion, and topical organization all parallel those of the 1979 volume, but with literature now extended through the mid-1980s. Expanded sections include the areas of "literature" and "reference materials" and in the latter, the subsections of bibliographies and journals are particularly helpful, with more than fifty women's studies and feminist journals described. Sociologists will find the sociology section expanded to "sociology and social issues" and religionists will find the "religion and philosophy" section updated to include important world religion and contemporary spirituality texts, although little in the way of mainline and formally theological literature--a need the authors readily recognize. As with their first bibliography, this volume also sets a standard for excellence in women's studies reference materials.

[52] Mankiller, Wilma, Gwendolyn Mink, Marysa Navarro, Barbara Smith, and Gloria Steinem, eds. *The Reader's Companion to U.S. Women's History*. Boston, MA: Houghton Mifflin, 1998.

This single volume text summarizes the major events, topics, and issues of "women's history" in the United States and the efforts of feminists and women's studies scholars to bring a consciously inclusive framework to the writing of "women's history" in the United States. As such, the text includes more than 400 alphabetized entries that touch upon or are associated with the widening parameters of women's studies and the range of perspectives opened out by its five editors, i.e., that every aspect of "class, race and sexuality" comprising the "experience" of women will be covered in this overview of American women's "gendered history." More than 300 scholars, activists, advocates, and "pioneers" have contributed to the volume, and they well meet the expectations of its editors. For example, nineteen different types of feminism are identified, a genuinely pluralized (rather than additive) framework grounds the handling of "difference" as an analytical quality, and points of conflict are acknowledged and detailed (e.g., racism in the women's movement). Many of the contributors are well known (e.g., the editors themselves, Bettina Aptheker, Catharine MacKinnon, Patricia Ireland) and several are those with works abstracted in the present bibliography (e.g., Martha Ackelsberg [958], Jo Freeman [88], Susannah Heschel [943], Rosemary Radford Ruether [190]). Most, however, represent the 'coming of age' of women's studies and its character as a field sufficiently populated to have lost the "all are stars" quality. Hence the text reflects both "second" and "third" wave perspectives and the racial, class and sexual inclusivity the editors expect. This is an important and helpful work. It reflects the breadth and depth of women's studies' twenty-five year long academic history, and with this, its deepening respect for the pluriform character of "women's experience." By way of organization, each of the editors briefly introduces the volume, a full list of contributors is included, and a well formatted general index enhances the already user friendly quality of this "companion" to U.S. women's history. It is an exceptional text. **NOTE**: While some religious topics receive specific treatment (e.g., Ruether summarizes "feminist theology"), most are embedded within wider discussions. Hence, see Ruether and Keller [132] through [135] and Russell and Clarkson [272] for detailed religious discussions.

[53] Redfern, Bernice. *Women of Color in the United States: A Guide to the Literature*. New York: Garland, 1989.
This "guide" to the literature is actually an annotated bibliography that synthesizes bibliographic, educational, feminist and women's studies, historical, literary-artistic and social scientific literature published since 1975 for four groups of racial-ethnic women: Afro-American women, Asian- and Hispanic-American women, and last, Native-American women. In all, 636 references are briefly described, with the section on African-American women comprising the largest proportion of materials (59%) and that on Asian-American women the smallest (10%). Overall, only "scholarly books, journal articles and significant chapters of books are presented," although some popular works are also included. Of particular value is Redfern's attention to doctoral dissertations on women of color, and her separate author and subject indices provide helpful cross-references. A limitation is the absence of a separate section for religion and women of color. (Nor is the subject index helpful here, for readers must find religious references under such subsections as politics or literature.) Limitations aside, Redfern's "guide" is helpful for literature about women of color through the late 1980s, and especially so for writings by African American women.

[54] Sahli, Nancy. *Women and Sexuality in America: A Bibliography*. Boston: G. K. Hall, 1984.
The focus of this 1,684 entry-long bibliography is historical. Sahli wishes to generate a reference source that shows the development of the notion of women's sexuality, as this concept emerged in American writing and reflection during the late 19th and early 20th centuries. Hence the bulk of her entries are from first editions, with exceptions made for such writers as Freud and Havelock Ellis, whose works are cited in terms of standard editions. By way of organization, Sahli includes social, political, legal, ethical, psychological and medical materials and such specific topics as "Prescriptive Literature" (both before and after 1920), "Masturbation and Nymphomania," "Lesbians," "Other Special Populations," and "Sexual Dysfunctions." In all, fifteen (unnumbered) chapters comprise the text, and for each, Sahli presents: (a) a brief introductory description of important trends and sources; (b) abstracts of key sources; and (c) supplemental (but not annotated) bibliography alphabetized by author. The abstracts are thorough and clearly written, with cross references to other materials helpfully cited. An "author/title index" 34 pages in length and a 24 page long "subject index" close this readable, informative volume.

[55] Stineman, Esther [With Catherine Loeb]. *Women's Studies: A Recommended Core Bibliography*. Littleton, CO: Libraries Unlimited, 1979.
Esther Stineman is the Women's Studies Librarian-at-Large for The University of Wisconsin System, and the "recommended core bibliography" she presents here lists 1,763 entries dispersed across 18 areas. Two of these areas, "literature" and "reference works," list additional subsections, with the category of "literature" broken down into various types of literature such as anthologies, drama, and poetry. Similarly, "reference works" are subdivided into "audiovisual[s]," "biographical materials," "bibliographies" and "general reference works." Most other organizing categories are quite general, and include such topics as anthropology, education, history, law, language and linguistics, psychology, religion and philosophy, sociology, sports, and "periodicals." Alphabetized entries are clearly presented within categories, and the sequential

numbering of all entries moves the reader comfortably along. Further, entries are *extensively* summarized *and* evaluated, and the reader is invited to examine entries closely and reflectively, rather than quickly as if on a title search only. Last, Stineman provides author and title indices, and an extremely thorough subject index. This is a superlative source both in terms of its scope and the attention it accords to literature on women of dual and multiple statuses (i.e., sex, race/ethnicity, class and sexual orientation). Its literature extends through 1977 and thus it should be used with more recent sources including [51] and [52] above, and [57] below. Stineman's introduction acknowledges the inevitable limitations that exist when one reviewer seeks to survey the breadth of topics included in her list. The limitations notwithstanding, this is still one of the finest sources available for women's studies materials published through 1977, and users unfamiliar with the interdisciplinary nature of women's studies will find it most helpful.

[56]   Straub, Deborah Gillan, ed. *Voices of Multicultural America: Notable Speeches Delivered by African, Asian, Hispanic and Native Ameicans, 1790-1995.* Detroit, MI: Gale Resarch, 1996.

This reference text presents more than 230 speeches by noted African-, Asian-, Hispanic-, and Native-Americans. All speeches are presented in full, and they span the range of American history from 1790-1995, with women and men both represented and an historical "timeline" included for historical reference points. In addition, each speech is prefaced with a brief biography of the speaker, and all are identified by time and place for use with the "timeline." This is an exceptionally well arranged text. It includes "ethnicity" and "speech category" indices, numerous photos of specific events, a helpful historical introduction and a closing "keyword index."

[57]   Tierney, Helen, ed. *Women's Studies Encyclopedia. Volume I: Views from the Sciences. Volume II: Literature, Arts and Learning. Volume III: History, Philosophy and Religion.* Westport, CT: Greenwood Press, 1989, 1990, 1991.

This three volume set presents articles encompassing feminist research in a variety of areas for use by scholars and others as a "handy" desk reference work. It is "written in a style and vocabulary a non-specialist can understand" (Volume I, p. xv), with articles arranged alphabetically in each volume and signed by the particular author who also provides a brief series of selected sources on the entry topic. Volume I presents articles grouped as *Views from the Sciences*, and it is here that articles on "feminism," "women's studies," "sex," and "gender" together with related topics receive their attention, as do a plethora of other topics ranging from "abortion" and "addiction" to "retirement" and "unemployment." *Literature, Arts and Learning* comprise the focus for Volume II, and here entries range from "aesthetics" to "African American...and/or [literature, prose and poetry]" to "Caribbean Writers in English" to "Women's Colleges." Similarly, Volume III hosts *History, Philosophy and Religion*, with entries encompassing various current and historical aspects of women's experience (and/or images of women) in all major religious and philosophical traditions. Thus, entries range, e.g., from "Abolitionism," "Abortion," and "Africa" to "Contraception," "Dowry," and "Gnosticism;" or again, from [the] "National Association of Colored Women," to "Prison Reform Movements," "Pro-Choice and Pro-Life Movements (U.S.)," to "Taoism" and the "Womanspirit Movement." While attention in all volumes is focused largely on American women, numerous entries address global and specific concerns, and various feminist perspectives are presented by female and male contributors. This is an exceptional and well indexed set, and users will find it an admirable desk reference.

[58]   Zophy, Angela Howard, ed. and Frances M. Kavenick, assoc. ed. *Handbook of American Women's History.* New York: Garland, 1990.

The editors of this handbook wish to present overviews of "those events, organizations, concepts and individuals that constitute a core of pertinent information" on American women's history, and their text is--with some clear omissions, exactly that. Its entries range from the contributions of women writers (e.g., Hellman, Hurston, Lorde, and Shange--but not Margaret Atwood) to such subjects as "Boston Marriages," "Title VII," "The American Red Cross," "Eating Disorders," "African Benevolent Societies," and "Asian American Women" (but not Hispanic-American women). Additionally, while some important topics in feminist theology and religion are omitted (e.g., womanism, feminist ethics and feminist spirituality), the editors have nonetheless included key writers and descriptions of their work. Thus Alice Walker's work receives specific attention, as does that of Rosemary Ruether and Mary Daly, with other feminist theologians (e.g., McFague, Letty Russell and Schüssler Fiorenza) cited in more generally based topical articles. Entries are arranged alphabetically, the majority are less than a page in length, and each is followed by a brief listing of critical bibliography and relevant cross references. By way of format, the volume is easy to use, and its list of "contributors" identifies scores of women's studies scholars who might otherwise be unknown to readers new to this topic.

2. Journals and Abstracting Services

[59] *Women's Studies Abstracts.* Rush, NY: Rush Pub. Co., 1972-.
This quarterly publication provides abstracts of women's studies and feminist literature from both academic and popular sources, with entries listed and cross-referenced numerically across various topical categories. It is a good resource for early and current feminist literature, and it should not be confused with the *Women's Studies Index* [60]. Its selections on religion are frequently limited to generalized topics, and thus readers will want to consult both the general theological bibliographies (such as ATLA Database [129]), and the specifically feminist and womanist theological bibliographies cited throughout the present bibliography (*viz.*, Bass and Boyd [130], DeBerg and Sherman [678], Finson [269], Gilton [595], Redfern [53] and Ruud [951].

[60] *Women's Studies Index: 1989.* Boston: G. K. Hall, 1991-.
This index synthesizes books, articles, reviews, discussions, videos, art, drama and music sources published variously in 78 women's studies journals, with all authors, subjects and cross-references interfiled alphabetically into a single listing. The index uses the Library of Congress classification system (with amplifications drawn from Capek [43]), and thus it presents one of the widest possible routes to material in women's studies for the year 1989, with subsequent volumes published on an annual basis. It is an excellent reference aid for women's studies generally, but it is limited in terms of feminist theological, womanist, clergywomen and other women/religious sources--the latter due, one suspects--because it indexes only three journals dealing with women/religious materials: *Signs* [41], *Journal of Feminist Studies in Religion* [226], and *Journal of Women and Religion* [227]. For material not found in the latter, the reader is directed to the bibliographic sources listed in the Index and the more standard religious and theological periodical indices. **NOTE:** A CD ROM version of this index, *Women Studies on Disc*, has been available since 1995.

[61] *Women's Studies Quarterly.* New York: The Feminist Press at CUNY, 19--.
Published four times a year, and with double issues for important and exceptionally broad topics such as "Spirituality and Women's Religions" [539], WSQ presents thematically grounded issues featuring articles and resources on topics of current feminist interest. Additionally, each issue typically emphasizes teaching and pedagogical discussions on the particular issue topic, together with a variety of other "resources" such as essay length literature updates, extended bibliographies and pertinent reviews.

B. Historical and Theoretical Sources

1. Theories of Women's Studies

[62] Bowles, Gloria, and Renate Duelli Klein, eds. *Theories of Women's Studies.* Boston: Routledge and Kegan Paul, 1983.
Published more than a decade after the advent of Women's studies, this anthology presents fourteen essays on issues of concern to academic programs of women's studies. Types of questions addressed include: What is the place of commitment in academic women's studies research? Is women studies an academic discipline? What is feminist methodology? Where do quantitative and experiential methodologies come into play? What are theories of women's studies? [and] What are the issues in the autonomy/integration debate? The endnotes and references for all essays are extensive and generally include literature dating from 1970-1982. The closing chapter presents an annotated bibliography addressing the various issues raised across the essays, with supplemental literature covering the years 1972-1982. A limitation, however, is the absence of material on religion and religious feminism.

[63] Boxer, Marilyn J. "For and About Women: The Theory and Practice of Women's Studies in the United States." In *Feminist Theory: A Critique of Ideology*, edited by Nannerl O. Keohane, Michelle Z. Rosaldo, and Barbara C. Gelpi, 237-271. Chicago: Univ. of Chicago Press, 1982.
This essay comprehensively reviews the literature on "women's studies as a field in American higher education" from its inception in 1966 to 1980. By way of organization, Boxer summarizes

not only the history of women's studies, but also the political issues, theories and structures that have grounded and developed in tandem with women's studies. Boxer's sources include print and near-print documents, theoretical works on feminism and women's studies, and works on women's experience generally. Her discussion of "theories" and "structures" highlights the organizational development of women's studies at several American universities, and the supporting documentation in her 128 footnotes is especially helpful for those seeking a chronicle of bibliographic sources. Boxer closes by noting the tensions still present in women's studies (e.g., the ongoing problematic of having separate women's studies departments as contrasted with the integration of women's studies across curricula subdivisions), and she identifies a "networking" model that blends both approaches as the emerging norm. Last, she acknowledges the need for "interdisciplinary" women's studies scholars who bridge both women's studies per se and the feminist critique of their own discipline's literature. **NOTE**: Loeb, Searing, and Stineman also call attention to this need, and specifically so for women's studies literature addressing religion. See **[51]** and see Plaskow **[340]** for literature through 1993.

[64]   Boxer, Marilyn J., and Jean H. Quataert, eds. *Connecting Spheres: Women in the Western World, 1500 to the Present.* New York: Oxford Univ. Press, 1987.
This detailed collection presents 13 essays organized historically under the rubrics of (1) "Women in the Age of Religious Upheaval and Political Centralization" (four essays); (2) "Women in Industrializing and Liberalizing Europe" (five essays); and (3) "Women in the Era of the Interventionist State" (four essays). In addition, each of these three sets is prefaced with its own 25-30 page summary of the cultural norms and social policies of the countries most salient in the periods of historical division, i.e., Europe, Russia and/or the United States during the years 1500-1750, 1750-1890 and 1890 to the mid-80s. The text then closes with supplemental bibliography and an exceptional index. This is an excellent resource for studying the rise of feminism since 1500, and particularly Western feminist history outside the US. Additionally, it highlights fascist antifeminism in both Europe and the US, with the latter via the Moral Majority and the New Right. Last, its bibliographic resources are exceptional, both in terms of supplemental and embedded sources.

[65]   Howe, Florence. "The First Decade of Women's Studies." *Harvard Educational Review* 49 (1979): 413-421.
As the introductory essay to a thematic issue on women and education, Howe's discussion examines the growth of women's studies from 1969-1979, with particular attention to: (1) the wide range of concerns distinguishing women's studies from more traditional male-centered curricula and (2) the substantive and methodological problems awaiting analysis by future women's studies scholars. For the latter, Howe identifies the need to understand both "the intersections of gender with race, class and sexual preference" (p. 418) and the impact of "inclusive" education (over time) and especially, in the light of comparative female/male data. Likewise, to illustrate the distinguishing concerns of women's studies, Howe cites not only the new understandings of women's experience in virtually all academic fields, but also the ongoing need for gender specific and gender comparative data on sex roles and socialization over the life course, and these as tied to social-institutional sectors. To close, Howe notes the absence of much necessary material in the special *HER* women's studies issue in which she writes, and she identifies Weskott's sociological essay **[116]** as a positive example of theoretical writing done in the service of gender equity and the critique of patriarchal ideology. **NOTE**: This is an informative early piece, but for a "before/after" view of how women's studies has grown since Howe's discussion here, see her essay, "'Promises to Keep:' Trends in Women's Studies Worldwide," *Women Studies Quarterly* 25, nos 1-2 (1997): 404-421. Additionally, see the editors' compilation in the same issue [*Women Studies Quarterly* 25, nos. 1-2 (1997): 422-455] of "Women's Studies Programs--1997," a listing of college and university programs in women's studies, indicating the type of degree and level of women's studies concentration per program.

[66]   Kramarae, Cheris, and Dale Spender, eds. *The Knowledge Explosion.* New York: Teachers College Press, 1992.
This is the premiere reference text for literature on the impact of feminism in the academy and the professions through the early 1990s. The editors present 44 essays written specifically for their volume to identify the impact of feminism and feminist theory on twenty-eight academic and applied professions and sixteen areas of current academic debate. Among the latter are such salient topics as abuse, pornography, and violence to women, technology (both reproductive and social), motherhood, sexuality, the information explosion, patriarchy, men's studies, and family sociology. Among the professions addressed are such traditional spheres as medicine and law, numerous

semi-professions historically identified as "Women's" professions (e.g., library science and home economics), various types of cultural and ethnic studies (e.g., language and peace studies, Black Studies and Women's Studies), and last, such traditionally identified academic areas as sociology, psychology, engineering etc.. The editors' introductory essay identifies the rationale and grounding expectations assigned the volume's stellar list of feminist scholars, and none of the essays disappoints. Other benefits include extensive embedded bibliography, an informative list of contributors, and an exemplary index.

[67]   Lerner, Gerda. *The Majority Finds Its Past: Placing Women in History.* New York: Oxford Univ. Press, 1979.
This brief volume presents twelve essays prepared by Lerner during the period 1969-1979. Eight have been published previously in academic journals, and four are papers or presentations edited specifically for this collection. Lerner's preface, "Autobiographical Notes--by Way of An Introduction," serves to frame and summarize each of the subsequent entries. Additionally, it summarizes the formative questions and experiences that have shaped Lerner's major work. These include her intellectual development as an historian who became a "feminist" historian; her ongoing concern for a conceptual framework that incorporates race, ethnicity, class *and* gender in the development of historiography; her sensed need for a more accurate periodocization of women's history (and a concomitant awareness of the relation between women's history and the nineteenth and late twentieth century "women's rights" and "feminist" movements); and last, her grounding recognition that "oppression" is not the most useful of starting points for the doing and development of women's history, but rather, that the class and racially contexted perceptions, experiences and activities of women are. Subsequent entries then well illustrate these themes. Thus, class, race and conceptual issues unfold in "The Lady and the Mill Girl...," in "Community Work of Black Club Women," and in "Black and White Women in Interaction and Confrontation." Likewise, definitional and formally theoretical issues emerge in "The Political Activities of Antislavery Women," in "Black Women in the United States...," and in "The Challenge of Women's History." Endnotes and a general index close the text. **NOTE**: For Lerner's related work see [77] and [69], and see her work on patriarchy [68] and feminist consciouness [35].

[68]   Lerner, Gerda. *The Creation of Patriarchy.* New York: Oxford Univ. Press, 1986.
If there is any definitive discussion on the meaning of patriarchy within feminist and women's studies, it is this text. In it Lerner examines both the historical development of (a) "the disvaluing of women in relation to the divine;" (b) the Aristotelian description of women as "incomplete and damaged human beings" (p. 10); and (c) the use of these symbolizations in the founding--and grounding--of Western civilization. Lerner's sources encompass the records, documents, texts, artifacts, and extended research governing the study of Ancient Mesopotamia (up to and through the writing of Genesis), and by distinguishing "History" (i.e., male identified and recorded reality) from "history" (what is visible and documentable from various data as the lived experience of peoples), Lerner raises to readership the central role of women in Western civilization. Her discussion documents the many roles males historically assigned to females in an effort to control female sexuality and female fertility--and over the course of several centuries, female access to divinity. Additionally, she illuminates the interlaced and uneven rates of gender, class and racial subordination, and in contrast to various single variable analyses (reviewed at the beginning of her study) Lerner evidences the *very* long process (from 3100-600 BC) by which patriarchy came to be institutionalized and seen, thereby, as "natural." In a word, women were (over time) "disvalued," taught to internalize their disvalued definition, and ultimately to comply with it. Lerner's powerful closing chapters (including her definitional appendices) all attest the potential for a cultural reconstruction apart from patriarchy (*viz.*, a "women-centered" reading of history) and her extensive chapter-specific bibliographies leave no stones unturned as to the scope of her research. The first of two volumes, its companion text is [35].

[69]   Lerner, Gerda. *Why History Matters: Life and Thought.* New York: Oxford Univ. Press, 1997.
This text brings together twelve papers prepared and/or presented by Lerner during the years 1980 to 1997. The topics vary and include both personal and professional reflections. They are synthesized, however, by the passion and wisdom of Lerner's conviction that "history matters," that it is "an obligation," and that "at a time when there is a virtual 'culture war' being fought about the meanings of history," (p. xvi) she finds herself compelled to speak from her fifty year experience as an historian whose consciousness has evolved first to that of a "feminist historian," and now more recently, to that of a "Jewish woman refugee...[whose]...work as a scholar [is] concerned with race, class and gender" (p. xii). Hence the collection. By way of overview, three

essays address Lerner's Jewish roots as the struggle to deal with "Otherness," the force of Nazi terror, and then her late in life academic acceptance. A fourth essay depicts both the re-appropriation of her native German language (which she had set aside for fifty years) and her conscious efforts to accept present day Germany after the Holocaust. Five more formally theoretical pieces take up "Nonviolent Resistance. The History of an Idea," "American Values," "The 20th Century: A Watershed for Women," "Looking Forward to the Year 2000," and "The Necessity of History," respectively, as Lerner discusses multiculturalism, political and social marginalities. Finally, in her closing essays, Lerner rethinks the race/class/gender paradigm to highlight the main processes by which dominance is institutionalized and historically maintained, *viz.*, the gendering, on the one hand, of class relations within structures of patriarchy, while dominants generate, at the same time, definitions of "deviant out groups" whose members internalize and retain dominant and "other" [deviant-based] self definitions. This is a powerful collection addressing much that has been background rather than foreground, and the mettle of Lerner's life is clear. Further, while its race/gender/class reconstructions provide a framework similarly detailed by sociologists and historians (cf., e.g,. Andersen and Collins **[85]**, Smith **[114]**, and Boxer and Quataert **[64]**), what sets it apart here is not only Lerner's keen observation of the realities before her, but the passion and strength of a woman who knows and shares—*to the bone*—why history matters.

2. Race, Class and Gender in American Women's History

[70] Amott, Teresa, and Julie A. Matthaei. *Race, Gender and Work: A Multicultural Economic History of Women in the United States.* Boston, MA: South End, 1991.
This book examines women's work lives though the "dynamic and complicated process ... called capitalist development" (p. 3) in order to: (1) highlight the multiple and diverse contributions of women's work (paid and unpaid) to US economic history; (2) expose the exploitation based interconnections of women's work within American economic history; and (3) "highlight major transformations in the gender, racial-ethnic, and class hierarchies accompanying" the history of America's capitalist expansion. It is strong study, with chapter length histories directed specifically to work by American Indian Women, Chicana Women, European American Women, African American Women, Asian American Women and Puerto Rican Women. The text is tightly argued and builds on the framework of gender, racial-ethnic and class interactive hierarchies to give sustained attention to the differences that socially constructed differences can make. Extensive notes, bibliography and data appendices flesh out the discussion.

[71] Bynum,Victoria. *Unruly Women: The Politics of Social and Sexual Control in the Old South.* Chapel Hill, NC: The Univ. of North Carolina Press, 1992.
This exceptionally well written social history examines the nuances of race and gender within three counties of the Piedmont area in North Carolina (Granville, Orange and Montgomery counties) for the period 1830-1865. The analysis draws upon archival county records to survey the similar and distinctively dissimilar experiences of slave and free Black women and wealthy and poor white women. In particular, Bynum presents three groups of women who, by all conventions of the time, were "unruly." These were women who "technically did not misbehave by challenging the rules...in North Carolina society," but who complained publicly about their husband's misbehavior. Second, they were women who "by the rules of society engaged in forbidden social and sexual behavior." Last, they were women who "implicitly or explicitly defied the authority of the Confederate State during the Civil War" (p. 1). It is a rich study, examining black and white womanhood, the state as patriarch, and the struggles of women to survive the American Civil War.

[72] Davis, Angela. *Women, Race and Class.* New York: Random House, 1981.
This short but semi-classic collection pulls together several of Davis's most urgent essays on the experiences of African American women in the United States. It identifies the race/gender tensions existing for black and white women during the suffrage movement, the American civil rights movement, and the second wave of American feminism. Additionally, it includes Davis's critique of capitalism, birth control and the dominant culture's taken for granted assumptions about "race, racism and rap," and specifically, the race gendered images of Black men as rapists and Black women as 'fallen' or promiscuous. Although no longer a widely cited text, it remains an historical marker for the discussion of race, class and gender in the United States.

[73] DuBois, Ellen Carol, and Vicki L. Ruiz, eds. *Unequal Sisters: A Multicultural Reader in U.S. Women's History.* New York: Routledge, 1990 (Rev. ed. 1994).
Both editions of this reader present thirty discussions addressing various dimensions of women's history in the United States, with attention focused primarily on the interactive effects of race,

gender and social class from the period of settlement onward. The opening essay (also the introduction in both editions) provides the reader with an overview of "...American Women's History in the 1980s...". Subsequent essays then chronicle the experiences of various women's groups: African American and Native American women, Japanese- and Chinese American women, working class women of rural and urban heritage, Mexican and Chicana women, lesbian women, and as one entry is entitled, "Unconventional Women," i.e., "...Puerto Rican Women in Religious Vocations Before Mid-Century." Several issues cut across the discussions (e.g., family violence, birth control, patterns of super- and subordinate role structure, bigotry, bias, women's wage work and corporate profits, and the role of women in the political system) and the majority of the essays address the experience of women through the mid-40s and 1950s. Four solid bibliographies (on African American Women, Asian American Women, Latinas and Native American women), together with an index and "contributor notes" close the text. NOTE: In the 1994 edition, Ruiz is first editor and DuBois the second. Also, for related literature see Anne Boylan, "Textbooks in U.S. Women's History" and Sarah S. Hughes, "Beyond Eurocentrism: Developing World Women's Studies" *Feminist Studies* 18 no. 2, (1992): 351-361 and 389-404.

[74]   Evans, Sara. *Born for Liberty: A History of Women in America*. New York: The Free Press, 1989.
This work richly details the history of "women's experience" in America, beginning with Iroquois women ["The First American Women"] and European and African women ["The Women Who Came to America: 1607-1770"]. Its subsequent chapters survey the experience of American women as chronicled through such key emphases as the political exclusion of women in the revolutionary era, the "watershed" of America's nineteenth century, all of America's wars, the Twenties, the Great Depression, modernity, "The Cold War and the 'Feminine Mystique,'" and last, the "Decade of Discovery" [the 1970s] when women found that "The Personal Is Political." Evans' style is light, journalistic, and ever attentive to the detail of personal diaries, anecdotes and other social and archival sources. Further, Evans regularly attends to the ways in which women's personal and political spheres do (and do not) intersect and mutually empower one another. Her closing chapter ["The Politicization of Personal Life: Women Versus Women"] addresses the tensions of differences glossed over by feminists during the 1970s , and it identifies points of tension and needed work. This is a very readable introduction, but with some limitations--e.g., an absence of material on women and such institutions as religion or the family. (Thus, see Ruether and Keller [132] through [135] and Matthaei [80]).

[75]   Fox-Genovese, Elizabeth. *Within the Plantation Household: Black and White Women of the Old South*. Chapel Hill, NC: The Univ. of North Carolina Press, 1988.
Using the "plantation household" as her fundamental unit of analysis, Fox-Genovese describes the racial, gender and class based relations of white and black women in the ante-bellum South. Her sources are archival and historical data, and the central theme grounding her analysis is the nature of resistance offered by enslaved African American women, who in contrast to white women of the ante-bellum South, had to struggle to define themselves as *selves*, rather than as gendered selves caught within the racial and class-based norms of the household plantation as defined by Southern slavery and paternalism. By way of overview, Fox-Genovese first details the rationale for using the plantation household as the unit of analysis: it, she argues, and not contrasts between Northern and Southern economies (and/or Northern and Southern perceptions of gender "spheres") most clearly evidences the relations between black and white women. Further, it is from within the household that the varying and violent bonds of racism and misogyny take their power. Following this, Fox-Genovese's develops her main argument. Namely, that the real resistance to slavery was brought by black women and not feminist-abolitionists, and that the nature of this resistance was largely psychological, i.e., the acts of will [to survive] that enslaved women bore in the face of absolute structural containment. To illustrate this argument the book's closing "Epilogue" presents a critical summary of Harriet Jacobs' *Incidents in the Life of a Slave Girl* (published under the name of Linda Brent), and it is in this particular discussion that the core dimension of resistance as an affirmation of self and the self's will to triumph becomes clear. Extensive notes, bibliography and a general index close out the text.

[76]   Jones, Jacqueline. *Labor of Love, Labor of Sorrow: Black Women, Work, and Family from Slavery to the Present*. New York: Basic Books, 1985.
This book details the work and family experiences of American Black women from the time of slavery to the early 1980s to indicate the variety of ways African American women have survived an exploitative white culture--first in slavery and later in domestic and clerical work, while

maintaining a separate and positive commitment to Black family life. The discussion of slave, rural, and working class black women comprises the first half of the book, while the familial and occupational experiences of Black women during migration, the Depression, and the American civil rights movement comprise the second half. Economic, political and ideological issues are consistently examined throughout the book, and Jones' final chapter ("The Struggle Continued and Transformed: 1955-1980") thoroughly critiques the welfare-matriarch myth of the Moynihan report, to which black feminists have so rightly objected. An "Epilogue: 1984" synthesizes the rich detail of Jones' historical discussion, and several data-based appendices, chapter notes and Jones' extended bibliography and index close out the text.

[77]   Lerner, Gerda, ed. *Black Women in White America: A Documentary History*. New York: Random House Pantheon Books, 1972.
This documentary history presents sources on the lives and experiences of black women from the time of slavery to the period of the early 1970s. It focuses largely on the experiences of "ordinary" black women (in spite of the difficulty, Lerner says, of obtaining "accurate, unbiased" sources), and it endeavors to show both the double jeopardy and double strength of being black and female in the United States. Lerner divides her materials into ten focusing categories. The first is "Slavery," and the documents here describe both the buying and selling of black women (and men) into slavery and the contributions and struggles of black women seeking freedom from slavery, both for themselves and others. Lerner's second category presents documents dating from 1832 to the period of the late 1920s. It addresses "The Struggle for Education" and identifies the efforts of black women teaching during and after slavery. Third is "A Woman's Lot," the documentation of sexual and other forms of violence done by white men and women to black women. Categories four through six detail, respectively, the domestic and factory based employment of black women, the resistance movements of black women in the face of slavery and segregation, and the political activity of black women from Harriet Tubman to Shirley Chisolm. In her remaining four chapters Lerner presents sources on "The Monster Prejudice," "Lifting As We Climb," (the Club Movement and black women's involvement in the YWCA), "Race Pride," and "Black Women [who] Speak of Womanhood." This is an extremely thorough set of materials and although its sources do not extend beyond 1971, it is required reading for anyone who wishes to know the *experiences, aspirations, efforts*, and *contributions* of black women who have worked against both racism and sexism in American history. Its divisions and sources are each prefaced with helpful commentaries and identifications, and an extended, closing bibliographic essay fleshes out the discussion of sources presented in Lerner's introduction. It is an invaluable companion to much womanist theological writing and a clear precursor to themes found in Lerner's other works, e.g., [67] and [69].

[78]   Lorde, Audre. *Sister Outsider*. Trumansburg, NY: Crossing Press, 1984.
This classic collection by the late poet/activist Audre Lorde provides an insightful and privileged entree into the experiences, struggles, dignity and joys of being a woman who is an African American lesbian feminist and mother. It synthesizes some of Lorde's most well known and frequently cited essays (including her "Uses of the Erotic: the Erotic as Power" and "Age, Race, Class, and Sex: Women Redefining Difference"), and it attests the potential of Black feminist conviction to withstand pervasive racism, heterosexism and class bias.

[79]   Malson, Micheline R., Elisabeth Mudimbe-Boyi, Jean F. O'Barr, and Mary Wyer, eds. *Black Women in America: Social Science Perspectives*. Chicago: Univ. of Chicago Press, 1990.
This volume is a collection of fifteen articles previously published in *Signs* between the years 1977 and 1990. It is, therefore, an important barometer of African American feminist research, as well as a major source of current (and established) womanist bibliography. The articles selected for separate description in the present bibliography include those by sociologists Collins [21], Dill [602], Brown [611], and Gilkes [615]. The volume's remaining authors address *historical and economic questions* (e.g., Susan Mann's "Slavery, Sharecropping and Sexual Inequality;" James Geschwender and Rita Carroll-Seguin's "Exploding the Myth of African-American Progress;" and Maxine Baca Zinn's "Family, Race and Poverty in the Eighties"); *literary questions* (Diane Sadoff's "Black Matrilineage: The Case of Alice Walker and Zora Neal Hurston"); and issues associated with *the interstructuring of racism, sexism and other ideologies* (e.g., entries by Patricia Williams and Deborah King). The editors' introduction locates the specifics of each essay, and a general index incorporating all essays closes the volume.

[80]   Matthaei, Julie A. *An Economic History of Women in America.* New York:
Schocken Books, 1982.
In thirteen tightly woven and expertly written chapters this book presents an economic history of
women in America as discernible from within the history of capitalism in the United States.
Matthaei's organizing focus is the nexus between familial and economic structures, with her
discussion encompassing: (1) white and slave families within the colonial economy; (2) white,
slave, immigrant, and husbandless families during the early period of industrialization; and in the
decades following slavery, (3) the differential effects of the "cult of domesticity" on these same
families. Matthaei's closing section describes the 20th century breakdown of the sexual division of
labor and the creation of "symmetrical marriage" with its implications for self-fulfillment vis a vis
the subordinating and subordinated role patterns of American family and occupational life. This is a
compelling and richly detailed Marxian analysis that focuses the history of male and female self-
fulfillment(s) as, respectively, the struggle to subordinate others to one's self (males), and to
subordinate one's self to others (females). Further, its consistent attention to the interaction of race,
class and gender highlights the various historical expressions of such self-fulfillment efforts,
including the exclusion of black men from such fulfillment, and the alternative views of
womanhood open to black and white women caught in tensions of differing subordination
experiences. These, and other emphases too rich and numerous to detail here, make this book
required reading for all interested in the "interstructuring" of race, class and gender as factors within
women's oppression.

[81]   Welter, Barbara, ed. *Dimity Convictions: The American Woman in the Nineteenth
Century.* Athens, OH: Univ. of Ohio Press, 1976.
Readers seeking an informative overview of the gender assumptions attached to white Protestant
women of the nineteenth century will want to begin with this frequently cited text. In it Welter
draws from several sources (women's magazines, personal letters, diaries and published novels of
the time) to portray the socialization patterns and expected roles of nineteenth century white women
vis a vis society, home and church. Of particular note (and near classic in status) is Welter's second
chapter, "The Cult of True Womanhood: 1800-1860." It vividly summarizes both the "four
cardinal virtues" of such womanhood ("piety, purity, submission and domesticity") and the
powerful force these virtues had for defining the nineteenth century white women's completely
other-directed and "self-sacrificing" sense of personal self. Likewise, Welter's sixth chapter, "The
Feminization of Religion: 1800-1860," is also noteworthy, for it thematizes the overlap between the
"genteel" Christian values of humility, meekness and submission, and those of "True Womanhood"
(as described in Welter's second chapter). As a social history of women, Welter's discussion is
limited in that it addresses only the experience of white women, and not women of color. This
said, her exposition of the role of "submission" in nineteenth century white women's lives and its
ties to religion remains valid, and still relevant to the aging populations of women (white *and black*)
in small town and rurally located congregations of many mainline American churches. **NOTE:**
For literature portraying the experience of nineteenth century African American women, see Lerner
[77], Jones **[76]**, Loewenberg and Bogin **[606]**, and Giddings **[614]**; see topical articles in
Mankiller **[52]** and Tierney **[57]**; and see Evans **[74]** and Malson et al. **[79]** *passim.* Last, for
additional literature on the "feminization" of American religion, see entries cited by Bass and Boyd
[130].

[82]   Yu, Diana. *Winds of Change: Korean Women in America.* Silver Spring, MD: The
Women's Institute Press, 1991.
Using both historical reference works and informal data borne of interviews with Korean women
living the Washington D.C. area, Yu presents an overview of American Korean women's
experience, with particular attention to the elements of assimilation Korean women face as they
enter the United States. Yu begins with a synopsis of Korean history from the "ancient period" of
c. 2330 BC through the "Japanese Occupation" in 1910 to the Republic of Korea [1948-1990].
She then details: (1) the influence of religion in Korean women's lives; (2) the traditional familial
and gender expectations held for Korean women; and (3) the assumptions made about women by
the structures of Korean law, education, politics, and presently, the Korean work force. In Part II
of her study, Yu examines both the typical ways Korean women have entered the United States (as
political refugees, students, Hawaiian laborers, "picture" and war brides, college students, adopted
children and "post-1965 immigrants") and the social networks, family structures, and
organizational involvements these women have since created. Overall, although based on anecdotal
data and a geographically limited sample, Yu's text conveys a clear and consistent sense of the
barriers facing Korean women who come to the United States. **NOTE:** For supplemental sources
see Amott and Matthaei **[70]**, Fenton **[45]**, Zinn and Dill **[83]**, and Feagin and Feagin **[123]**.

Also, for theological literature see Chapter 23, and for a specific discussion of how one woman has ministered to the needs of American Korean "war brides," see Letty Russell's description of Henna Han's ministry in **[250]** *passim.*

[83]   Zinn, Maxine Baca, and Bonnie Thornton Dill, eds. *Women of Color in the U.S.* Philadelphia: Temple Univ. Press, 1994.
This strong collection of essays is organized thematically around the metaphor of "the wall" as depicted in the novel, *The Women of Brewster Place.* In the novel, "the wall" serves to both enclose and enfold those living behind it, while blunting, as well, the possibilities outside it. Hence, in this collection various essays describe the "constraining walls of social location" while others present the tasks and examples of women "confronting those walls." The editors provide an engaging introduction and an informative, demographic overview of the numerous groups comprising "women of color." Subsequent essays fit within the elements of the metaphor, and the volume closes with selections reinterpreting the concept "gender" to indicate its pluralized character. Crucial to the volume are the four premises it unfolds through its sixteen discussions of work and family experience as lived by African American, Latina, Asian and Native American women. These are: (1) that gender is part of a "larger pattern of inequities" that are labor-based and structurally contained; (2) that women of color subsequently experience cultural affronts that frequently disempower them, but against which (3) they present personal and social resistance; and (4) that the demonstration of these points signals the necessity for clarifying feminism as "multiracial feminism" because gender is never experienced apart from the social locations of color, ethnicity and social class. Many of the volume's contributors are already well published (e.g., Zinn, Dill, and Cheryl T. Gilkes), but others are rising stars: e.g., Jennie R. Joe and Dorothy Lonewolf Miller, who co-author "Cultural Survival and Contemporary American Indian Women in the City." A detailed index closes the volume. **NOTE:** Also by Zinn and Dill (but not abstracted here) is "Theorizing Difference from Multiracial Feminism," *Feminist Studies* 22 no. 2(1996): 321-332, a discussion on the importance of race in the construction of gender.

NOTE: For additional literature addressing issues of class, race and gender see Lerner above **[69]**, see the Womanist literature in Chapter 17, see Chapter 18 on "Feminist Theology's Global Voices," and see Davidman and Tenenbaum **[949]** in Chapter 19.

C.   Internet and On-line Resources

See the notes at the end of Chapter 1 for feminist and women's studies web sites.

3

Feminism and Feminist Sociology

A. Overviews and General Anthologies

[84] Andersen, Margaret L. *Thinking About Women: Sociological Perspectives on Sex and Gender.* 3d ed. New York: Macmillan, 1997.
Now in its fourth edition, Andersen's text is an informative and comprehensive review of feminist social scientific research on women, with particular attention to feminist theory in sociology. Its twelve chapters cover the social construction of gender, women's internalization of gender imagery, sexuality and intimacy, women and work, families, health issues, religion, crime, politics and power. Of particular strength is Andersen's attention to inclusivity so that the variable "race" becomes neither an important addendum nor a qualifying exception within mainstream categories. Finally, in her closing chapters, Andersen contrasts the strengths and weaknesses of liberal, socialist and radical feminist perspectives, while a short concluding chapter focuses new directions in feminist theory. An extended bibliography and thorough subject and author indices close the volume.

[85] Andersen, Margaret L., and Patricia Hill Collins, eds. *Race, Class, and Gender: An Anthology.* Belmont, CA: Wadsworth, 1992.
Andersen and Collins are each noted for their feminist work on inclusivity. Here they present 54 diverse and challenging essays to address the multiple and interactive aspects of race, class and gender within social experience, and all with a conscious effort at illuminating the diversity of social experience as perceived from within self-affirming rather than "victim" categories, and visionary rather than problem perspectives. Clear introductions ground all subdivisions of the work, and helpful endnotes follow most entries. Two limitations are the lack of an index and supplemental bibliographies, but the text is suitable to classroom and reference use, and as a companion to both the individual works by Andersen [84] and Collins [99] an the general literature in feminist ethics.

[86] Benokraitis, Nijole V., and Joe R. Feagin. *Modern Sexism: Blatant, Subtle, and Covert Discrimination.* 2d ed. Englewood Cliffs, NJ: Prentice-Hall, 1994.
This text is one of the most succinct sociological statements on the dynamics, processes and consequences of sexism in American society available today. Its nine chapters locate the social and organizational aspects of sexism in the U.S., and as the authors develop their material, they identify and illustrate sixteen different mechanisms (with many having particular subsets) that permit the maintenance of sexism as both an ideology and an organizational reality. Their discussion of "blatant" sexism takes up issues of salary, as well as various occupational and familial aspects of sex discrimination. Likewise, their descriptions of "subtle" and "covert" discrimination illuminate the ways women and men intentionally *and* unintentionally participate in sustaining America's differential gender expectations. Equally important, the authors survey the "backlash" so well described by Faludi [822], "gendered racism" (the interactive effects of sexism and racism for women of color), and the unbelievable scope of social and personal damage accomplished by America's patterns of sex discrimination. A final chapter examines elements of social policy together with various means (legal, political, organizational and corporate) for changing America's

sexist and racist-sexist discriminatory patterns. A thorough index closes the volume. Without doubt, this is first source for readers seeking a clear, no holds barred primer on sexism in the United States. It is at some points frightening as it variously documents the problem, its mechanisms and entrenchment. At the same time, it is brief, pointed, and empowering as it evidences its solutions--and in the end--its "you don't have to take it" possibilities. In its first (1986) edition, this text was prophetic and compelling. Here it is again so, but with literature into the early 1990s, and no bookshelf is complete without it.

[87] Bernard, Jessie. *The Female World.* New York: Random House, 1981.
This volume discloses women's experience from within the multiple realities comprising the female world, which for Bernard means a discussion of the subworlds of children and girls, the structures of marriage, socioeconomic status, kinships, network and friendship groups, and the "structural" and "issue related faultlines" that cut across the varying dimensions of women's experience--to name but a few of Bernard's many topics. When first published, this text received mixed reviews. On the positive side were affirmations of its clarity, scope and vision; on the negative side, charges of eclecticism and an emphasis on general description rather than a specific theory. These judgments reflect varying degrees of accuracy, but do not detract from the ongoing value of Bernard's book and particularly its value for beginning readers: while its data need updating from more recent sources, its breadth, clarity and enormous supporting literature are still a useful baseline for beginners, and its closing 38 page-long bibliography, name and subject indices provide beginning readers with ready access to a wealth of women's scholarship published through 1980. Obviously, for more recent works, see the additional entries of this chapter.

[88] Freeman, Jo, ed. *Women: A Feminist Perspective.* 5th ed. Mountain View, CA: Mayfield, 1995.
Since its first edition in 1975, this regularly updated anthology has continued to serve as a major introduction to the wide range of issues and implications within women's studies generally and the sociology of sex and gender specifically. Presently, it contains 35 essays organized into seven categories: "Body Politics" [five entries]; "Relationships, Family and the Life Cycle" [five entries]; "Work and Occupations" [five entries]; "Words and Images" [four entries]; "Institutions of Social Control" [six entries]; "Feminism in Perspective" [five entries]; and "Feminism and Diversity" [five entries]. Virtually all of its essays are up to date on research through the early '90s, and while approximately a third are updates from the fourth edition of 1989 (and/or classics updated from the earlier editions, such as Freeman' own entry on the history of feminism), the majority are written specifically for this volume. Among the classics are Elizabeth Almquist's, "The Experiences of Minority Women in the United States: The Intersection of Race, Gender and Class," a clear and statistically documented discussion about the differential feminist expectations held by Native American women, African-American women, Mexican-American women, Puerto Rican women on the mainland, Cuban women in the United States and Asian-American women. Also classic are Martha J. Reineke's "Out of Order: A Critical Perspective on Women in Religion," and Rose Weitz' "What Price Independence? Social Reactions to Lesbians, Spinsters, Widows and Nuns," as well as several entries addressing general labor force statistics, clerical, blue collar and professional women's experiences, and "...Gender Differences in the Status of Students and Scholars." Examples of new pieces include discussions of inequality and marital conflicts, women and aging, and in Parts VI and VII, the widening plurality of feminisms now developing in various types of women's ethnic and other communities (e.g., "Afra-American," Chicana, Jewish and Lesbian feminisms). Selections reviewed in the present bibliography include: (1) Freeman's "The Revolution for Women in Law and Public Policy" [510]; (2) Pauline Terrelonge's "Feminist Consciousness and Black Women" [624]; (3) Susan Marshall's "Keep Us on the Pedestal: Women Against Feminism in Twentieth-Century America" [835]; (4) Alice Abel Kemp's "Poverty and Welfare for Women" [512]; and (5) Susan E. Martin's "Sexual Harassment: The Link Joining Gender Stratification, Sexuality and Women's Economic Status" [859]. Endnotes, additional bibliography, and subject and author indices are all helpful resources.

[89] Kandal, Terry R. *The Woman Question in Classical Sociological Theory.* Miami: Florida International Univ. Press, 1988.
This text presents clear overviews of the treatment of women in virtually all of the major sociological theorists from Comte to Mills. A general introduction frames the author's purpose as that of exploring the connection between contemporary feminism and classical theory, and Kandal's primary strategy is to examine the historical contexts in which classical "...debates about...the inequality and subjection of women" were formed (p. 3). And not surprisingly, the French and Industrial Revolutions, together with the Enlightenment, are the historical context for Kandal's

analysis. The discussions of specific theories include English theorists Mill and Spencer; French theorists de Tocqueville, Comte, and Durkheim; German theorists Weber, Simmel, Tonnies and Mannheim; Italian theorists Pareto and Michels; and American theorists Parsons and Mills. Introductory overviews precede all chapters and to conclude Kendel points to the prevalence of a "functionalist" and distorted view of women in classical theory, as well as an inattention to working class women. Endnotes, bibliography and a detailed index close the volume.

[90] Kramer Laura, ed. *The Sociology of Gender: A Text-Reader*. New York: St. Martin's Press, 1991.
This classic reader presents twenty-eight articles (and/or excerpts of articles) drawn from significant gender literature published during the mid and late 1980s. The entries are organized through the six frameworks of "culture and ideology," "socialization," "family and intimate relations," "the economy and work," "the political and legal systems," and "the potential for [social] change." Helpful overviews precede each of these topical sections, and entries are well balanced in terms of macro, middle range, and micro level emphases. A solid introduction focuses the meaning of feminist research and provides the rationale for entry selections. This is an informative introductory reader on the sociology of gender, and feminist ethicists particularly will appreciate its descriptions of social processes vis a vis race, class and gender in various institutional sectors. Name and subject indices close the reader. Entries reviewed in the present volume include Blumstein and Schwartz **[578]**, Wallace **[786]**, and Chafetz and Dworkin **[827]**.

[91] Lengermann, Patricia Madoo, and Ruth A. Wallace. *Gender in America: Social Control and Social Change*. Englewood Cliffs, NJ: Prentice-Hall, 1985.
Although the literature cited in this text is current through only the mid-1980s, its thoroughness and use of the 1980 Census data lend strong support to the social control and social change theories developed by the authors. Overall, Lengermann and Wallace approach gender as a "belief system," and in various chapter length discussions they unfold: (a) the six components of this belief system; (b) those mechanisms of socialization that reinforce it and promote gender inequality; (c) "new beliefs about gender," and (d) the macro and micro structures that promote these new beliefs and enhance efforts at gender equality. As regards social *control*, the factors of categorization, functional differentiation, segregation, unequal access to material resources, differential values and unequal power are crucial, for these generate and contribute to continued patterns of inequity. In contrast, *change* is accounted for through the impacts of industrialization, post-industrialism, contraception and mass media on levels of literacy, education, and leisure. In turn, the authors argue, these variables have prompted the recognition of (and social movement responses to) tensions existing between conventional and new beliefs about gender and the power arrangements attached to those beliefs. A detailed bibliography current through 1983, readable discussions of theory and data, and closing discussions on "resistance to change" and the future of American feminism make this an excellent historical reference for beginning students of the literature.

[92] Lorber, Judith, and Susan A. Farrell, eds. *The Social Construction of Gender*. Newbury Park, CA: Sage, 1991.
All but one of the 18 essays in this volume are culled from literature published in the feminist sociological journal, *Gender and Society* [Sage Pubs., Newbury Park, CA] during the period 1987-1990. The one new essay is editor Farrell's, "'It's our Church Too!' Women's Position in the Catholic Church Today," which reviews the gendered status of women in Catholicism, feminist critiques of Catholicism's theological rationales, feminist ethics and the characterization of feminist theology, and ethics as a "discourse of resistance." The earlier published essays address various aspects of gender construction from sources largely non-theological in nature: e.g., gender construction in family life (six entries), in the work-place (four entries), as an aspect of research strategies (two entries), and as a dimension of ethnic/racial identity (three essays). Remaining essays include an introductory section on "principles of gender construction" (three entries) and "efforts at de-construction" (three entries). All essays are clearly written, and while most are theoretical rather than empirical, virtually all synthesize findings from other empirical work. This is an important collection for understanding the *processes* of gender construction, in both social and formal organizational settings. **NOTE**: For additional literature on Catholic feminism as a "discourse of resistance," see Katzenstein **[285]**.

[93] Millman, Marcia, and Rosabeth Moss Kanter, eds. *Another Voice: Feminist Perspectives on Social Life and Social Science*. Garden City, NY: Anchor, 1975.
This collection of 12 essays is generally considered a classic for the initial range of issues it identified as necessary for the development of feminist sociological theorizing and research. Hence

the editors examine such topics as "Women and Medical Sociology: Invisible Professionals and Ubiquitous Patients" (by Judith Lorber, editor of [92] above); "Women and the Structure of Organizations: Explorations in Theory and Behavior" (by Rosabeth Moss Kanter, whose more formalized discussion is [728]); and last, a number of additional issues related to class, deviance, women's emotions and participation in informal networks, and the implications of feminist theorizing for research methodologies. An additional entry that yet bears strong reading is "Black Women and Self-esteem" by Lena Wright Myers. Myers examines the "Moynihan Report" to demonstrate the sources of self-esteem among African American women, and her research suggests that these sources are not the frameworks of either white society or Black men, but rather, other Black women. This is consistent with both womanist theological literature and Collin's research on Black feminism [99], and it serves as an early grounding for both.

B. Theoretical and Specialized Studies (1969-1993)

[94] Allen, Jessie, and Alan Pifer, eds. *Women on the Front Lines: Meeting the Challenge of an Aging America.* Washington, DC: The Urban Institute, 1993.
Ten essays, buttressed extensively with the facts and figures of America's aging population, including U.S. population projections for the years 2010, 2030 and 2050 all support the premise of this reader: namely, that women are on the "front lines," not only because they "…are a majority of the elderly …[and]…provide most of the care for the disabled elderly," but also because women "face economic disadvantages at older ages." Several essays address the issues of health care facing elderly American women, all address the diversity and ethnic pluralism of aging American women, and tied to both age and health care issues are those of work, poverty and the "expanding social roles" of older women. A closing essay examines both policy implications of the research and questions attached to practices and implementation. Cynthia M. Tauber [128] and Jessie Allen prepare the excellent overview, "Women in Our Aging Society: The Demographic Outlook," Alan Pifer addresses policy implications, and Julianne Malveaux looks at "Race, Poverty and Aging."
NOTE: For additional bibliography and a listing of important issues and resource organizations, see David Bender, Bruno Leone and Charles P. Cozic, eds. *An Aging Population: Opposing Viewpoints.* San Diego, CA: Greenhaven, Press 1996.

[95] Allen, Katherine R. *Single Women/Family Ties: Life Histories of Older Women.* Newbury Park, CA: Sage, 1989.
This study examines the life path of single (i.e., "never married") working class women from a 1910 birth cohort to identify the structural roles open to them, as contrasted with the structured roles open to women once married and now widowed. The data are based on an initial N of 104 women, with a smaller matched sample of 15 "never marrieds" and 15 "married but now widowed" women interviewed in detail. The life courses, socialization experiences, family roles, sources of support, and family support roles of the never marrieds and widows are compared in detail and the findings are integrated with various perspectives in family sociology. The study is well conceived, well written, sensitively done, and important for the research needs it yet identifies.

[96] Bernard, Jessie. "The Dissemination of Feminist Thought: 1960 to 1988." In *Feminism and Sociological Theory,* edited by Ruth Wallace, 23-33. Newbury Park, CA: Sage, 1989.
This brief essay identifies feminist sociology as the third "phase" of sociological theory, following the post-War period of structural functionalism and the "constructionist logico-deductive trends" of "Post-Parsonianism in the 1960s." Overall, Bernard: (1) characterizes the decade of the sixties as the period in which women recognized sexism; (2) chronicles the development of seven feminist journals during the 1970s [*Feminist Studies* and *Women's Studies* in 1972; *Quest* in 1974; *Women's Agenda,* [the] *Psychology of Women Quarterly,* and *Signs* all in 1976; and *Chrysalis* in 1977]; and (3) describes the "hostile" (and in her judgment premature) "wake" held for feminism in the 1980s. Last, she affirms "equality" as the yet relevant core issue of feminist thinking and activity, and she notes the ongoing question for all feminist sociological theory: "How can Feminism resolve the contradiction that gender consciousness is necessary to demand an end to prescribed gender roles?" (p. 31.)

[97] Chafetz, Janet Saltzman. *Feminist Sociology: An Overview of Contemporary Theories.* Itasca, IL: F. E. Peacock Publishers, 1988.
This text is one of the few comprehensive and theoretically developed discussions of feminist sociology that is open to widely based interdisciplinary usage in both philosophical and social scientific contexts. Chafetz's description of feminist sociology roots in both classical social theory

and feminist philosophy, and it includes not only the questions of social processes per se, but the general emphases of feminist theory in particular: (1) an attention to "gender as the central focus or subject matter of the theory;" (2) an awareness that gender relations are a problem--that is, related to social inequities, strains and contradictions; (3) a recognition of the variable quality of gender over time; and last, a commitment to the premise that theoretical work is to be actively engaged in changing the inequities borne of present and past gender relations. By way of overview, Chafetz takes this theoretical definition as a norm, and she examines numerous theories and/or schools of thought that attempt to address: (a) the causes of gender inequality; (b) the maintenance and reproduction of gender systems; (c) the social consequences of gender stratification; and (d) efforts at changing systems of gender inequality. Her scope is vast and varies from the development of Marxist-feminist theory to the writers of "socialization theories," "everyday-life theories," "anthropological" and "exchange theories." Further, as she examines each of these schools, she summarizes and assesses the arguments of individual theorists in terms of "what needs to change to produce gender equality" and how such change can come about. The range, readability, and clarity of this work make it especially attractive for readers seeking an introduction to the authors and issues current in feminist sociology through the mid-1980s. NOTE: Also by Chafetz are [98] and [827].

[98]   Chafetz, Janet Saltzman. *Gender Equity*. Newbury Park, CA: Sage, 1990.
This text synthesizes several of Chafetz's earlier works. It reviews and builds on the critique of general theories presented in [97] and it examines the factors that work variously to stabilize and decrease female disadvantage. It integrates macro and mezo levels of analysis and combines Chafetz's' work with Dworkin on antifeminism to present a well integrated theory of systemic change relative to female disadvantage and the role of male elites within those systemic processes. Last, it anticipates much of Chafetz's later work now integrated within stratification theory generally. (Cf., e.g., Randall Collins, Janet Chafetz, Rae Blumberg, Scott Coltraine and Jonathan Turner, "Toward an Integrated Theory of Gender Stratification." *Sociological Perspectives* 36 (1993): 185-216.)

[99]   Collins, Patricia Hill. *Black Feminist Thought: Knowledge, Consciousness, and the Politics of Empowerment*. New York: Routledge, 1990.
This text is far and away one of the most important theoretical discussions in contemporary feminist sociology. Working from the oral, anecdotal and published histories of African American women, Collins develops an African American feminist perspective that highlights the distinctiveness of African American women's experience *as, because of, and to the extent* that it has evolved historically. She details the development of several core themes that define the history and experience of African American women--Black women's work, family, mothering and political experiences--and last, "the sexual politics of black womanhood," with each of these further discussed in terms of: (a) the symbols and images geared historically to the control and disempowerment of black women's consciousness; (b) the distinctive social realities opened out by the exposition of sociological issues from within the linkages of America's historical race/gender hierarchies; (c) the dynamics of consciousness as affected by "passing" and the absence of "voice"; and (d) the gaining of strength to move beyond passing and into political (and social) self-empowerment. In sum and quite specifically, Collins' text entails the development of an Afrocentric epistemology from and for the experience of African American women. This is powerful text and in every way, required reading. Readers unfamiliar with the history of African Americans--and particularly African American women--will learn much from this text, while readers already familiarized will be stretched and energized. NOTE: For a theological work paralleling much of this text, see Williams [259].

[100]   Cook, Judith, and Mary Margaret Fonow. "Knowledge and Women's Interests: Issues of Epistemology and Methodology in Feminist Sociological Research." *Sociological Inquiry* 56 (1986): 2-29.
Drawing from the feminist sociological literature available in *Sociological Abstracts* from 1977 and 1985, Cook and Fonow identify five principles evident in feminist sociological method(s). These are: (1) an attention to the "pervasive influence of gender in all social reality" (whether in the private sphere, the male academic world or the researcher's own experience); (2) a recognition of consciousness-raising as a focus of research (both in terms of unanticipated experiences that raise women's consciousness--e.g., divorce, unemployment, violence--and consciousness-raising itself as a deliberate process); (3) an epistemological rejection of the "subject/object split" within research, since this split permits the masking of women's "political domination;" (4) an attention to ethical concerns (e.g., the use of language for social control and "gate-keeping"); and (5) an emphasis on

empowerment and transformation, including the need to disclose information helpful to women and to foster the awareness of social research as geared to social change. Their discussion is clear and easily readable by non-sociologists, and it echoes several themes current in feminist hermeneutics and theological method. The bibliography is extensive and the authors' main conclusions support the assumptions that: (1) feminist method is itself unfolding; (2) it cannot be understood as a series of research techniques only; and (3) it must work to change the asymmetry experienced by women in the social world. NOTE: A subsequent reader co-edited by Fonow and Cook (but not abstracted here) synthesizes fifteen classic, mid to late '80s essays illustrating the range of these conclusions in terms of feminism's impact in sociological research. See *Beyond Methodology: Feminist Scholarship as Lived Research* [Bloomingdale: Indiana Univ. Press, 1991.] Additionally, see Reinharz [112].

[101] Coser, Rose Laub. "Reflections on Feminist Theory." In *Feminism and Sociological Theory*, edited by Ruth Wallace, 200-208. Newbury Park, CA: Sage, 1989.
This closing discussion to Wallace's reader [115] identifies and discusses two ambiguities often posed by the description of sociological theory as "feminist." First, that the descriptor "feminist" might suggest a deconstruction of theory's traditional task of explanatory schemes that account for differences in social groupings and/or organizational processes; second, that it might suggest a restriction of "theory" to "the experience of women as women." To each of these ambiguities, Coser responds that sociological theory *is* explanatory in nature, and that the term "feminist" focuses sex as the most salient variable in the analysis of social inequity and interaction. Further, as a response to the use of "women's experience as women" as a base for theorizing, Coser argues that to use "women's bodily experience as a basis of theorizing is to reduce the gender gap to biological differences." More preferred, she suggests, is an explanation of gender based social inequities, patterns of super- and subordinate relations, and an identification of the processes by which society maintains such patterns. Finally, to the extent that a theory can and does explain the latter, it can and should work toward equality among social actors. Coser illustrates her discussion through a response to selected essays presented earlier in the Wallace reader, and she highlights the necessity for additional feminist theoretical efforts in the study of work and family structure. NOTE: For related sources see the volume itself together with Andersen [84], Basow [117] and Chafetz [97-98].

[102] Epstein, Cynthia Fuchs. "Women in Sociological Analysis: New Scholarship versus Old Paradigms." *Soundings* 64 (1981): 485-498.
This early article benchmarks several elements of the "neglect or misrepresentation of women within the social sciences" (p. 485). It gives examples of how sociological theory may illuminate patterns of gender interaction, and it critiques those theoretical positions that maintain the subordination of women (e.g., Parsons' early work on sex roles and family systems). By way of illustration, Epstein identifies three areas with the potential to reshape sociological thinking and research about women. These areas are socialization theory, political sociology, and the study of social stratification. For socialization theory, Epstein favors abandoning the early socialization model (which suggests that personality and identity are forever set early in life) both because her own research indicates the empirical inadequacies of the model, and because its ideological assumptions mask the adult socialization of women engaged in wage work. For political sociology, she suggests a necessary regrounding, both because a focus on the two-party system only assumes a low level of political involvement by women, and because this focus and its assumptions blind one to much politically effective activity of women outside the voting booth. As a third concern, Epstein suggests a regrounding of stratification theory; and here, the ideological link to the sociological neglect of women has been the Parsonian based "expressive-instrumental" dichotomy, the assumption that women do the emotional work in a society (i.e., nurturing) while men do the productive work (i.e., economic wage work). Such assumptions are faulty, and they block: (1) the study of women in economic and wage-work activities; (2) the expressive experience of males; and (3) the study of emotions generally, as phenomena that are "socially structured...to conform to [specific] social norms" (p. 496). A reconsideration of gender and stratification, argues Epstein, can help correct such faulty assumptions and open new avenues of long neglected research.

[103] Farganis, Sondra. "Social Theory and Feminist Theory: The Need for Dialogue." *Sociological Inquiry* 56 (1986): 50-68.
This discussion reviews the Frankfurt School's critique of positivism in sociology and the feminist theoretical critiques of both positivistic and phenomenological methodology in sociology. Both

critiques seek ways of analyzing human experience with methods other than empiricism, and both seek methods that direct such analysis to the betterment of the subject, not the researcher. The chief weakness of positivism is its affirmation of false neutrality, because "the consequence of its own approach is to have its findings used by those in power for purposes of controlling persons and dominating nature" (p. 51). Likewise, the chief weakness of phenomenological method is its lack of an activist component, a requirement for much feminist theory. Farganis sees critical theory as especially suitable for use by feminist theorists, and she argues that feminist social theory can benefit from a dialogue with the Frankfurt School, since the latter's attention both to emancipatory praxis and historical analysis permits a careful feminist reading of such problems as alienation, modernization, rationalization, community and equality--all factors tied ideologically and empirically to the historical oppression of women.

[104] Harding, Sandra. "The Instability of the Analytical Categories of Feminist Theory." *Signs* 11 (1986): 645-664.
This essay discusses the "instability" of feminist theory's analytic categories from within the assumption that such instability is desirable, lest feminist theory become caught in the epistemological binds that have characterized (and continue to characterize) androcentric theory. Harding begins by noting that two decades of feminist theory have comfortably revised both the androcentric perspectives of social science generally and its own feminist use of social science when the latter has proved ineffective as a resource for feminist insight and change directed critique. Further, she acknowledges that some revision has indeed been necessary lest feminist theory replicate androcentrism's empirically false universalism of white cultural hegemony, only in terms of white female rather than white male experiences. Last, she questions what a fully revised theory might look like since the scope of feminism is worldwide and it encompasses the experiences of half the human race. Harding does not pretend to have an answer to this second question, but she unfolds the minimal assumptions necessary for various feminisms to grapple with the pluralism of women's work and experience. Among others, these assumptions include the need to recognize that: (1) many "negative" features of androcentric social science contain their own subverting possibilities (e.g., feminism's appropriation of empiricist epistemology and feminism's use of standpoint methodologies); (2) in spite of feminism's critique of androcentric and sexist dualisms, some dualisms do exist and particularly with respect to embodiment (e.g., sex and gender and society and culture); and (3) these dualisms cannot be allowed to be used ideologically against women through a new "biology is destiny" style of argument. Last, Harding argues that a particular value of feminist theory and research is that it works against the "craft" image of social scientific research, or the formulation and investigation of research problems by elites who are insulated from the critique of their work by the subjects they investigate. Rather, she suggests, when feminists research questions and issues, they do so in conjunction with the subjects being researched, and with the subjects' ongoing input. **NOTE:** This essay is complex and difficult, but it reviews an extensive body of literature current through the mid-1980s. For Harding's longer discussion (not reviewed here), see *The Science Question in Feminism*. Ithaca: Cornell Univ. Press, 1986.

[105] Hess, Beth B. "Beyond Dichotomy: Drawing Distinctions and Embracing Differences." *Sociological Forum* 5 (1990): 75-89.
This essay synthesizes key feminist sociological sources published during the mid and late 1980s to describe the genesis, assumptions, resistances to and possibilities of feminist theory for the discipline of sociology. Its primary emphases include an attention to: (1) the diversity of feminist sociological perspectives (pedagogical, methodological and epistemological) that infuse the sociological study of "engendered" reality; (2) the elements of sameness and difference that cross-cut superordinate and subordinate populations (e.g., the differing implications of class and race within gender); (3) the "backlash" that has exerted itself within sociology in the face of feminist theorizing; and (4) the potential of feminist theory for a discipline-wide, paradigmatic restructuring of sociology, given the challenge posed to "objectivist," Enlightenment thinking by feminist sociology. It is clearly written, and it communicates the main lines of feminist theory without encumbering technicalities. It is recommended to readers seeking an informed and well illustrated overview of feminist sociological literature, regardless of their sociological background.

[106] Huber, Joan. "Trends in Gender Stratification, 1970-1985." *Sociological Forum* 1 (1986): 476-495.
This paper examines the "causes and consequences of sociological interest in gender stratification after 1970" (p. 76). By way of overview, Huber begins with a brief summary of the women's movement in the mid to late '60s and its influence (in 1969) on the development of "sex role"

studies within the American Sociological Association. She then details five general points. These are (1) her summary of sex role research through the early 1980s to note its limited theoretical development and particularly its focus on class analysis and not the *domestic* division of labor; (2), an examination of gender stratification in agrarian and industrial societies and particularly the mortality, fertility, educational, and women's labor participation trends within these societies *and* the role of "domestic" labor in each; and (3) her main point, that it is the *domestic division of labor* that "works to keep women out of elite positions" since "at the societal level, the most power and prestige accrue to those who control the distribution of valued goods beyond the family" and because for women to participate in such control, their work has to mesh with tasks of child rearing (p. 491). Following these points, Huber then examines the effects of contemporary mortality and fertility rates for women (i.e., they lower the number of years women spend in child bearing and child rearing activities), and, last, she suggests that in spite of the many institutional changes that must yet occur if women are to experience parity with men in American society, past and current gains offer a hopeful note.

[107] Katzenstein, Mary Fainsod. "Feminism Within American Institutions: Unobtrusive Mobilization in the 1980s." *Signs* 16 (1990): 27-54.
This article addresses the cultural perception that feminism has waned during the 1980s after its heyday in the late '60s and dissemination in the 1970s. The response to this perception is carried out in three steps, with the argument and its illustrations as instructive as they are interesting. First, Katzenstein cites national surveys indicative of America's changed and increasingly egalitarian attitudes about gender. Second, she suggests the concept of "gendered consciousness" to indicate a wider focus than that of "feminism" per se, so that the variety of "feminisms" may be observed. Third, she illustrates this feminist variation by a comparison of gender changes in two institutions traditionally deemed patriarchal: the Roman Catholic church and the U.S. military. Her discussion illustrates that gendered consciousness is, in fact, an ongoing social reality, but that it has become differentiated in diverse ways and (in at least two cases) under the influence of governing organizational norms. Thus, in American Catholicism, the differentiation of gendered consciousness has been governed by the wider organizational norm(s) of social justice and racial/ethnic inclusivity, while in the military its has been governed by bureaucratic authority. Given these norms, great areas of change are visible within these institutions. Also visible, though, are the apparent paradoxes that (a) where Catholicism advocates justice and racial-ethnic inclusivity, it does not yet ordain women, and (b) where the military advocates bureaucratic rationality, it promotes women on the criteria of careerism without necessarily holding to an egalitarian or justice based ethic of racial-ethnic inclusivity. The arguments of this piece are well developed, but questions remain. Specifically, sociologists may question the comparison between Catholicism and the military as total institutions, for in Catholicism, the "total institutional" quality is largely normative, but not remunerative or physically coercive, as is the case with the military. (Although precedent for the comparison does exist. In *The Future of Catholic Leadership: Responses to the Priest Shortage* [741] sociologist Dean Hoge directly contrasts staffing problems of the priesthood and the military, but without addressing sexism as institutionalized in Catholic leadership.) Similarly, feminist (and perhaps other) theologians will question the validity of identifying feminism apart from any attention to questions of social justice and racial-ethnic inclusivity. In sum, a refinement of indicators for "gendered consciousness" is needed. This said, Katzenstein's is an intriguing thesis, with excellent overviews of gender change in both the military and Catholicism. Her discussion merits extended circulation and studied reading. Also by Katzenstein is [285].

[108] Lengermann, Patricia Madoo, and Jill Niebrugge-Brantley. "Contemporary Feminist Theory." In *Sociological Theory*, 2d ed., edited by George Ritzer, 400-443. New York: Knopf, 1988.
This article reviews both the history of feminist theory and its relationship to the development of sociology. Additionally, it identifies the key trends and feminist perspectives currently evolving as a new paradigm of sociological theory. Several features mark this new paradigm: an attention to historical materialism as a grounding theoretical framework; a widening of the Marxian construct, social production, to include several sets of distinctive social arrangements involving the experience and relationalities of women; a women centered attention to the social construction of knowledge, and in particular, the ways in which patriarchy is recreated in women's consciousness; an extension of the theory's possible application to other subordinate groups, together with a recognition of variation within women's experiences; and last, an attention to the ways in which this new paradigm can utilize concepts drawn from conventional sociological theory. This is an especially informative source for literature on feminist sociology, and its typology of current literature--as

organized into theories addressing gender difference, gender inequality and gender oppression--surpasses the traditional division of feminist theories into cultural, liberal, radical and socialist frameworks, such that more creative theoretical syntheses can be developed and/or identified. It is strongly recommended as a major overview, and its bibliography is current through 1986. **NOTE**: For subsequent bibliography and discussion of literature trends, see the authors' "Feminist Sociological Theory: The Near-Future Prospects" in *Frontiers of Social Theory: The New Syntheses*, edited by George Ritzer, 316-344, NY: Columbia U. Press, 1990, and see Ferree and Martin [119]. Also, for earlier work by Lengermann, see [91].

[109] Lopata, Helena Znaniecka, and David Maines, eds. *Research in the Interweave of Social Roles: Friendship.* Greenwich, CT: Jai Press, 1981.
This volume presents ten essays on the sociology of friendship, all organized around one of three general themes. The first is "Friendship in the Life Course," which addresses friendship over the life span, including the friendships of children, feminist women, and widows. Part II examines how friendship is socially "situated" or embedded in other social roles, and here the authors examine factors that facilitate or constrain women's and men's friendships. Part III explores selected communal aspects of situated friendships, with essays on friendship in the military, in marriage and in an Israeli kibbutz. A major emphasis throughout the volume is the editors' attention to the disparity existing between social reality and the idealized perceptions of friendship that most respondents have, and with this, the multiple work-, family- and culturally-based factors that can constrain the development and growth of friendship. This is a rich and suggestive collection for feminist theologians (or ethicists) who use the metaphor of friendship to disclose inclusivity (and/or divinity), whether through written, preached or narrative forms. Further, its several essays suggest numerous implications for researching the effects of feminist beliefs, spiritualities and associations within women's religious networks. **NOTE**: Also by Lopata is [110].

[110] Lopata, Helena Znaniecka. "The Interweave of Public and Private: Women's Challenge to American Society." *Journal of Marriage and the Family* 55 (1993): 176-190.
This discussion presents an exceptionally clear description of "the social and ideological changes in American society that resulted in the definition of the world as containing two spheres, the private sphere of women and the public sphere of men, and the consequences of this view" (p. 176.) Lopata organizes her remarks around five general emphases: (1) the history and ideological supports of this two-sphere perspective; (2) its two consequences of generating both spheres of influence for women *and* (through various other ideological supports) the invisibility of women's public work; (3) the contemporary debate about women's multiple role involvements; (4) society's abandonment of communal support for child care, and (5) Lopata's prediction of a genuine "revolt" on the part of women against the circumstances surrounding society's expectations about women as the sole providers of child care in American society. An important emphasis distinguishing this "two spheres" discussion from related pieces (e.g., Welter [81]) is its contemporary and social (rather than historical and single institutional) perspective. Its survey of the literature is exceptional, and its discussion of women's contemporary role complexity provides a helpful balance to the sometimes conventional assumption that relationality precludes autonomous individualization.

[111] Nielson, Joyce McCarl, ed. *Feminist Research Methods: Exemplary Readings in the Social Sciences.* Boulder, CO: Westview Press, 1990.
Four essays addressing critical and epistemological questions, together with seven discussions addressing a variety of research topics (women and work, women and suicide, cognitive gender differences, and women and the legislative process) make up this feminist reader in social scientific research methods. Two of the theoretical pieces are reviewed elsewhere in this bibliography (Weskott [116] and Cook and Fonow [100]); others include Evelyn Fox Keller ("Gender and Science"), and a multiple authored piece, "Beginning Where We Are: Feminist Methodology in Oral History." Of particular significance is Nielson's 40 page introduction that charts the development of feminist thinking in social science relative to both "scientific method" and sociology's major theoretical shifts.

[112] Reinharz, Shulamit [With assistance from Lynn Davidman]. *Feminist Methods in Social Research.* New York: Oxford Univ. Press, 1992.
This is by far the most comprehensive synthesis of feminist methods currently available in sociological research. As such, it serves as a discussion text, a text on research history, on feminism in sociology, and of course, a text on "feminist methods." Reinharz begins with a

commitment to use a "working" and then increasingly refined definition of feminism, and specifically, so as the latter emerges from research pieces self-identified as feminist. She notes the necessity for a descriptive and pluralized orientation, and after noting the inadequacies of singular and monolithic definitions of feminism, she synthesizes vast amounts of research depicted by its authors as "feminist." By way of strategy, Reinharz addresses virtually all of the traditionally cast techniques (interviewing, survey Qs, experimental design, oral history, case studies, etc.) and for each, she presents a grounding or "defining quotation," a preliminary introductory discussion, and an overview of how the method has been and is now used by those defining their work as feminist. Her closing comments in each chapter then address controversies attached to the method in question. Her approach works. The "defining quotes" at the beginning of each chapter, the innumerable illustrations Reinharz presents, and last, her own reflections all serve to illustrate the history and current use of "feminist research methods." Equally important, the 130 pages of notes and bibliography document practically every word of the text. A thorough index closes the volume. NOTE: Reinharz' article length discussion (not abstracted here) appears in Kramarae and Spender **[66]** and Davidman's own research (on women in Judaism) appears in Section VI-4, *viz.*, **[949]**, **[973-974]**.

[113] Skevington, Suzanne, and Deborah Baker, eds. *The Social Identity of Women*. Newbury Park, CA: Sage, 1989.
This collection of ten essays--largely by British sociologists--utilizes the "social identity theory" developed by social psychologist, H. Tajfel, to examine how women's identity may fruitfully be studied as a group-related phenomenon. Tajfel's social identity theory focuses on identity as a *group* (and thereby stereotyped) reality that members of the "owngroup" or "ingroup" internalize in an effort to achieve positive self identification relative to an "othergroup" or "outgroup." A seemingly simple hypothesis, the theory posits several questions for persons who are members of non-voluntaristic groups (e.g., gender groups), for it raises the methodological question of which "othergroup" is an appropriate comparison group: Males? Other women? And if the latter, which other women: Traditional? Non-traditional? Editors Skevington and Baker emphasize that because gender varies by class, age, and race/ethnicity (and these all over time) there is no single "women's identity," but rather the need to understand how women come into their social identities, move from one group to another, work for individual mobility (or, alternatively, for collectively based social change), and do (or do not) identify with selected outgroups, dominant or non-dominant groups, and/or social perspectives. Because these are the substantive questions, Skevington and Baker press for their ethnographic (and quantitative) implications: i.e., methodological strategies that can illuminate identification(s) with group constructs and the ways women take such constructs in. All essays are well documented and clearly presented.

[114] Smith, Dorothy E. "Sociological Theory: Methods of Writing Patriarchy." In *Feminism and Sociological Theory*, edited by Ruth Wallace, 34-64. Newbury Park, CA: Sage, 1989.
As one element of feminist critique against perspectives that view actors and their social worlds as purely discrete entities, Smith argues three main points in this exceptionally important essay. First, she argues that sociology is itself a discussion borne of and sustained by certain patterns of social organization, and that these patterns are problematic for feminist sociology because they presume "through and through...a world known from within the relations of ruling, [and] presupposing the relations of gender, race and class that are already there" (p. 36). Further, Smith argues that to survive in this framework, one must become a part of the wide, social *process* that sociological discourse is. This, however, is exactly what is problematic for feminist sociology. Second, Smith argues that there are specific mechanisms by which theorists become a part of the ruling/ruled process that sociology is, and thus she identifies four mechanisms that (a) facilitate the process of separating subjects from their social worlds, and (b) thereby help locate the subject within the pale of sociological ruling/ruled relations. Smith's final point is that feminist work can and must resist this process of "writing patriarchy," and particularly by the inclusion of many voices within the sociological conversation, so that the relations of gender, race and class already present can and might be reorganized. This is an especially important essay with implications for both feminist sociology and feminist theology, for its emphases invite critical dialogue and extensive hermeneutical and ethical cross disciplinary work. Indeed, one immediate application is its relevance for understanding the dynamics by which some women clergy "write patriarchy:" that is, become theologically "male identified" and thus, theologically unsupportive of other women clergy. NOTE: For Smith's earlier, book length discussion, see *The Everyday World as Problematic: A Feminist Sociology*. [Boston: Northeastern Univ. Press, 1989.] The latter introduces Smith's concept of "standpoint" methodology, i.e., the premise that all knowledges are socially constructed

at specific "knowledge sites." Additionally, see her 1990 text, *The Conceptual Practices of Power* [Boston: Northeastern Univ. Press] which expands upon the dynamics of ruling and ruled processes as applied to case studies of women and mental illness. Last, for related sociological sources, see the literature cited by Lengermann and Niebrugge-Brantley [108], and for theological sources, see Copeland [265], Jones [267], Russell and Clarkson [272], Schüssler Fiorenza and Copeland [275], and the Driggs and Cannon entries in Cannon and Schüssler Fiorenza [348].

[115] Wallace, Ruth, ed. *Feminism and Sociological Theory.* Newbury Park, CA: Sage, 1989.
This volume is a solid primer for those seeking a clear statement of feminism's implications for sociological theory and research. Its three sections ("Enlarging the Horizons of Sociological Theory," "Criticizing and Re-Evaluating of Existing Theories," and "Emerging Feminist Theories") subsume nine substantive, thought provoking discussions. Contributors include: Jessie Bernard who traces the "Dissemination of Feminist Thought from 1960 to 1988" [96]; Dorothy Smith who details the "Methods of Writing Patriarchy" [114]; Joan Acker who discusses the "invisibility" of women in theory and research; Edith Kurtz who synthesizes the literature from psychoanalytic theory (a literature with which the reader must have some familiarity); and Miriam Johnson and Thomas Meisenhald who address, respectively, feminism and Parsonian thinking. and feminist and Habermas' critical theory. To close, Janet Saltzman Chafetz presents a compact version of her earlier book length treatment of gender stratification (cf. [98]), and Rae Lesser Blumberg discusses the "Janus-headed" question of "Development" and women world wide. Rose Laub Coser [101] responds to the volume overall with reflections on the nature of theorizing and what it takes to make a theory "feminist." Wallace's introductory essay opens up the questions addressed by contributing authors and introduces the meaning of "feminist" as a descriptor for sociological theory.

[116] Weskott, Marcia. "Feminist Criticism of Social Science." *Harvard Educational Review* 49 (1979): 422-430.
As described by its published abstract, this essay "discusses feminist criticism of the content, method and purpose of knowledge about women as defined by the social sciences and it offers a dialectical alternative to conventional analyses" (p. 442). Weskott begins with the awareness of women's dual status as social science researchers. As the latter, women are "insiders" in their profession. As women, however, they are "outsiders." The tensions of this dual status are evident as women approach the study of women, for the conceptual edifice of most social science is androcentric. Maleness is the norm and those not fitting the norm must be seen as either deviant or naturally subordinate. A feminist analysis, however, challenges this subordinated invisibility and calls for a new understanding of the human person, inclusive of women and women's experience. Second, a feminist analysis also challenges the notion of a congruence between the self and society (presumed by the functional understanding of successful socialization), for it lays bare the differential social worlds and experiences of women and men, and demonstrates thereby, the social alienation of women from all but the private sphere. Hence feminist analysis advocates a critical rather than a functional approach to social analysis, for the latter simply maintains the structural and ideological dependence of women. Third, if women are *not* to be assigned (theoretically) to the position of subordinates within social organization, and, alternatively, if women *are* to be integral to (rather than alienated from) the social world and its studied understanding, then the social scientific study of women's experience cannot be limited to "information about women" only, for this maintains the outsider status of women scholars and provides social science with an additional "fad" that may eventually disappear. Rather, a feminist analysis says that the purpose of women's studies in social science is to overcome the "subordination and devaluation" of women. Thus, the social scientific study of women's experience must become a social science *for* women, rather than only a social science *about* women. For Weskott, these criticisms have at least three implications for research on women, *viz.*, that social science must develop: (1) non-androcentric theoretical frameworks; (2) methodologies that overcome the "subject-object" split presumed by traditional "objective" social science; and (3) a self-consciously liberating posture towards women.

NOTE: For related literature see Buechler [13], Boles [20], and Harding and O'Barr [26].

C.   **Selected Reference Works (1985-1995)**

[117] Basow, Susan A. *Gender: Stereotypes and Roles.* 3d ed. Pacific Grove, CA: Brooks/Cole, 1992.
This is an undergraduate textbook on the meaning(s) of gender and the many ways it is socially constructed and influential in life and society. Its five sections examine and assess current gender

research in terms of: (a) roles and stereotypes; (b) male-female similarities with respect to "physical, cognitive, personality, social and sexual functioning;" (c) the historical development and transmission of gender patterns; (d) the "effects of gender stereotypes and roles on individuals, relationships and society" (including the patterning of same and cross sex relationships); and (e) "alternatives to traditional gender stereotypes and roles," together with ways of achieving them. It is designed for use by beginning students of gender research, and its more than 2000 research based references qualify it as one of the most comprehensive syntheses of gender research currently available. The author is a feminist sociologist who never loses sight of how "gender encodes inequality" and virtually every aspect of gender and the social world is examined in this text. Readers familiar with current research will find it an invaluable reference volume, while new users will appreciate its clearly written chapters, overviews and assessments. Additionally, feminist ethicists will find its data informative for several important issues. Basow's indices and reference bibliography are exceptionally thorough (albeit with occasional typo's), and the volume is strongly recommended as both an upper division text and resource for feminist ethics.

[118] Hess, Beth B., and Myra Marx Ferree, eds. *Analyzing Gender: A Handbook of Social Science Research.* Newbury Park, CA: Sage, 1987.
This handbook constitutes the best current source of social science literature on gender through the mid-1980s. It is arranged in five sections ("Gender and Ideology," "Social Control and Female Sexuality," "Gender Stratification," "Gendered Worlds," and "Gender and the State"), and each of these has on average, three to four additional subdivisions. For example, the section on "Gendered Worlds" includes essays on gender and class, family, religion **[137]**, and the women's health movement. All entries are clearly written and accessible by non-technical readers, and all provide additional, supplemental bibliography. An extremely helpful and well organized general index (27 pages in length)closes the volume. **NOTE**: For psychological literature on gender and "sex roles" current through the mid-1980s, see Janet T. Spence, Kay Deaux, and Robert L. Helmreich. "Sex Roles in Contemporary American Society." *The Handbook of Social Psychology* , 3d. ed., edited by Gardner Lindzey and Elliot Aronson, Volume II, 149-178. New York: Random House, 1985. Spence et al. review empirical and theoretical works on the "expressive-instrumental orientation," "sex roles and interpersonal behaviors" and "marital interactions," and all with particular attention to the social location of "conceptions of male and female differences." Their survey is detailed, but it presumes a strong professional background.

[119] Ferree, Myra Marx, and Patricia Yancey Martin, eds. *Feminist Organizations: Harvest of the New Women's Movement.* Philadelphia: Temple Univ. Press, 1995.
This volume presents 24 papers that variously detail the organizational outcomes of the twentieth century American feminist movement. They are organized into six categories: (1) Ferree and Martin's introductory section--a summary of the shift from traditional gender analyses to an organizational and resource mobilization perspective; (2) a series of seven papers that address "the politics of engagement..." in several mainstream organizational settings; (3) five papers documenting specific organizational efforts of feminist activity; (4) an additional five papers that examine conflicts and differences in feminist organizational strategies; (5) three papers on "expanding the scope of the political" toward an "inclusive vision of success"; and last, an "afterword" that synthesizes the movement as a whole "from seed to harvest" to describe "the transformations of feminist organizations and scholarship." An important emphasis throughout text is the recognition that feminism is presently a *form of discourse* in American society. Thus, it is a perspective that has evolved historically and organizationally, while learning both from and of its multicultural character. Additionally, as a movement to end "...male dominance and institutionalized privilege based on gender," it is now an institutionalized reality that cuts across time, class, generations and memories, to provide further opportunities for individual and collective feminist activity. This is an exceptional text, and in the light its scholarship, bibliography, and wide range of insights and observations, it is a *highly* recommended reference work. For representative selections, see **[285]** and **[621]**.

[120] Paludi, Michele A. *The Psychology of Women: A Manual of Resources.* Albany, NY: SUNY Press, 1990.
This manual pulls together countless resources from both academic and applied contexts for persons seeking teaching and research materials on the "psychology of women." It is divided into six sections--with each further divided into readable and well arranged chapters--and with each chapter presenting topically related course outlines, reference works, introductory and advanced textbooks, references for key journal articles, media listings (e.g., films and speakers' bureaus), methodological instruments, class room exercises and suggestions for further research. Its major

divisions include "general" and "foundational" resources, "life span development" and "women's health" issues, resources on "achievement and work," and last, a three chapter series on "victimization of women: rape, incest, battered women, gender and sexual harassment." **NOTE**: Also by Paludi but not abstracted here are *Sexual Harassment on Campuses: Abusing the Ivory Power*, ed. by Michele Paludi, [Albany, NY:SUNY Press, 1996] and *Workplace Sexual Harassment*, ed. by Anne Levy and Michele Paludi [Upper Saddle River, NJ: Prentice Hall, 1997].

D. Statistical and Related Literature (1986-1996)

[121] Crawford, Mary, and Jeanne Marecek. "Psychology Reconstructs the Female: 1968-1988." *Psychology of Women Quarterly* 13(1989): 147-165.
Drawing upon the psychology literature published from 1968 to 1988, the authors identify four periods of research and theory development about "women," "gender" and "feminism within psychology." The baseline for their discussion is psychology's initially "womanless" state, its years prior to the women's movement and during which women were essentially invisible in research. The discussion unfolds four distinct emphases: an attention to "exceptional women," to "problematic" women, to the "psychology of gender," and most recently, to a framework of "transformation." For supporting discussion, the authors cite literature, assumptions, and related themes for each of their four periods.

[122] Feagin, Joe R., and Clairece Booher Feagin. *Discrimination American Style: Institutional Sexism and Racism*. 2d ed. Malabar, FL: Robert E. Krieger Pub. Co., 1986.
This study examines the research and established theoretical perspectives on prejudice and discrimination relative to both gender and race in terms of four major concerns: (1) the general history of prejudice-discrimination theory and research; (2) a discussion of institutional discrimination as played out by individuals, small groups, and small and large organizations; (3) an overview of the impact of institutional discrimination in the economy (and specifically as it relates to employment), and (4) a similar discussion of institutional discrimination as evidenced in the areas of housing, education, health and social services, politics and the courts. Two further chapters survey possible remedies for ending discrimination, together with the conceptual and empirical frameworks currently governing the study and analysis of race/gender discrimination. A closing chapter critiques various "myths" about affirmative action, beginning with a clear and critical appraisal of the notion of "reverse discrimination" as a smoke-screening (and one wants to say scapegoating) technique in the development of social policy. Feminist theologians (and theological faculties generally) will find much to dialogue with in this volume. By way of format, the authors write to social scientists and policy maker audiences, but their clear presentation of theoretical and statistical materials, aided by helpful charts and diagrams, permits wide readership, including audiences unfamiliar with statistical and empirical formats and related research techniques. **NOTE**: For subsequent work by Feagin, see **[123]** below.

[123] Feagin, Joe R., and Clairece Booher Feagin. *Racial and Ethnic Relations*. 5d ed. Englewood Cliffs, NJ: Prentiss Hall, 1996.
This regularly updated textbook is a *sine qua non* for interdisciplinary research in questions of race/ethnicity, multiculturalism and the intersection of race, gender, class and the American economy. Among other things, its fourteen chapters provide detailed theoretical overviews on all issues relevant to migration and group contact, and with these, solid overview discussions for various ethnic groups: English Americans, Irish Americans, Italian Americans, Jewish Americans, Native Americans, African Americans, Mexican Americans, Puerto Rican and Cuban Americans, Japanese Americans, and last, Chinese, Filipino, Vietnamese and Asian-Indian Americans. By way of theoretical issues, the authors address definitional questions (the meanings of race, ethnicity, racism, ideology, stereotype, prejudice and discrimination); the role of America's dominant "Core Culture" in the development of various groups' contacts and social histories; the relative merits of assimilation and power/conflict frameworks for assessing racial and ethnic relations; and in the current (i.e., 5th) edition, the role of colonialism in the expansion of racism worldwide. This is an exceptional text. It is clearly written, well documented and attentive to the available research on women's contributions to American ethnic groups. **NOTE**: For additional work by Feagin, see **[86]** and **[122]** above. Additionally, see the following texts--not abstracted in this volume, but well worth the read: Joe Feagin and Melvin P. Sikes, *Living with Racism: The Black Middle Class Experience* [Boston: Beacon, 1994]; Joe Faegin and Hernan Vera, *White Racism: the Basics* [NY: Routledge, 1995] and *The Bubbling Cauldron: Race, Ethnicity and the Urban Crisis,* edited by Michael Peter Smith and Joe R. Feagin [Minneapolis: Univ. of Minnesota

Press, 1995]. Additionally, see the statistically detailed discussion of U.S. black/white differences by Andrew Hacker, *Two Nations: Black and White, Separate, Hostile, Unequal*, NY: Charles Scribner's Sons, 1992. Last, for recent article literature addressing the human rights, demographic, social and identity issues attached to American multiracial/multiethnic experience, see *The Multiracial Experience: Racial Borders as the New Frontier*, edited by Maria P. P. Root [Thousand Oaks, CA: 1996].

[124] Feinberg, Renee, and Kathleen Knox. *The Feminization of Poverty in the United States: A Selected, Annotated Bibliography of the Issues, 1978-1989.* New York: Garland, 1990.
In 1982 Feinberg published *Women, Education and Employment: A Bibliography of Periodical Citations, Pamphlets, Newspapers and Government Documents, 1970-1980* [Hamden, CT: Library Professional Publications/Shoe String Press Inc.], a bibliography listing more than 2500 (unannotated) references on women's education, training for and experience in the work place. Here, Feinberg and Knox present an extended *annotated* bibliography covering literally hundreds of items related to the "feminization of poverty," and/or its increased salience among female single parents, women in low paying jobs, and elderly women who experience the discriminatory impact of America's social security system. The literature cited here spans the period 1978-1989, and Feinberg and Knox collate their sources under eighteen topically based chapter headings (e.g., "Child-Care," Health, Nutrition and Hunger," and "Family Policy"). Additionally, they present excellent previews to each of their 18 chapters, with brief, informative descriptions of relevant material and issues. This resource is highly recommended to readers seeking recent literature and clearly described issues. For related social science and theological sources see the listings suggested for **[114]**. Additionally see the journal, *Feminist Studies* **[40]**, see Arnott and Matthaei **[70]** and Matthaei **[80]**, and for the theological literature see Andersen, Gudorf and Pellauer **[468]**, Fischer **[490]**, Ruether **[492]**, and Schüssler Fiorenza and Carr **[493]**.

[125] Grambs, Jean Dresden. *Sex Differences and Learning: An Annotated Bibliography of Educational Research, 1979-1989.* New York: Garland, 1991.
The 795 annotated entries of this bibliography span 23 research directed categories organized alphabetically from "academic achievement" to "toys/play/games." Entries are numbered sequentially, with multiple entries cross-referenced accordingly and with separate author and subject indices providing additional cross-references. The list itself focuses on the K-12 age range, and as the editors note in their clearly written introduction, there are some topics that have obviously received extensive research attention, e.g., "language, reading, literature," science, mathematics, and "sex role, socialization, stereotyping." Alternatively, other topics have received much less attention: e.g., those of "help seeking, helping behavior," "school attendance, dropouts" and "mental health, mental well-being." Finally, as the authors also note, there are seriously neglected areas within the literature itself, and thus within their bibliography. Hence because few studies: (1) utilize qualitative research methods; (2) integrate qualitative and quantitative data; (3) seek data on Hispanic and Asian students, and (4) incorporate variables dealing with personal creativity, religious affiliation, religious orientation and/or religious education and socialization, the literature on such topics is scant. Moreover, because the literatures from hard-to-tap populations such as "students from itinerant, dysfunctional and abusive families," bilingual students, gay and lesbian students, differently-abled students and students at risk for drug and alcohol use are also scant, so too are entries on these topics. These limitations notwithstanding, this bibliography is well synthesized, and social scientists, librarians, religious and other scholars will appreciate its scope.

[126] Ries, Paula, and Anne J. Stone, eds. *The American Woman 1992-1993: A Status Report.* New York: Norton, 1992.
Earlier volumes of this annually published status report on American women are summarized below **[127]**. This report (published prior to the 1992 November general election) addresses "Women in Politics," and the editors present four informative overview articles. First is Celia Morris' "Changing the Rules and the Roles: Five Women in Public Office." It surveys the careers of five "bridge women," i.e., women politicians socialized to traditional roles, but succeeding in the political world. Article #2 is Irene Natividad's "Women of Color and the Campaign Trail." It tracks the careers of several women of color in politics to examine the structural blocks they have faced. Article #3, by Ruth B. Mandela and Debra L. Dodson, is "Do Women Office Holders Make a Difference?" It contrasts voting records of female and male politicians on several issues, with controls for feminist orientation and other ideologically salient variables. Last, Celinda C. Lake and Vincent J Breglio examine data on gender and voting behaviors. The report's annual "statistical

portrait" of American women follows these articles with tabular, graphed and narrative discussions of gender statistics on such topics as population, health, child care and support, education employment, income, etc.. A summary of the "congressional caucus for women's issues for the 102nd congress" and a thorough index close the text.

[**127**] Rix, Sara E., ed. *The American Woman, 1990-1991: A Status Report.* [For the Women's Research and Education Institute of the Congressional Congress for Women's Issues]. New York: Norton, 1990.
The first edition of this informational resource appeared in 1987 [*The American Woman, 1987-1988: A Report in Depth*, edited by Sara Rix. New York: Norton, 1987]. It provided tabular and narrative discussions of several topics important to the study of American women, including lengthy essays on "Women in Twentieth Century America;" "Women and the Family;" "Women and the Economy;" and "The Women's Movement in Recent American Politics." Additionally, it surveyed such specific topics as women in business, broadcasting, sports, entertainment, the military, science, unions, and higher education, with each topic receiving a two to three page essay. Finally, this first volume presented data on "Women among Immigrants in the United States," "Women and Reproduction," "Latinas in the United States," and "Images of Black Women" [in the United States]. The 1990 edition continues this pattern of essays, overviews, and statistical summaries and adds extended discussions on: (1) the racial-ethnic pluralism of women in the US; (2) the activities of women in international development and the peace movement; (3) "The Emergence and Growth of Women's Studies," and (4) "The Congressional Caucus for Women's Issues in the 101st Congress." It then closes with a general statistical portrait of American women, additional bibliographical material, and the volume index.

[**128**] Taeuber, Cynthia Murray, comp. and ed. *Statistical Handbook on Women in America.* 2d ed. Phoenix, AZ: Oryx Press, 1996.
First published in 1991, this statistical handbook culls tabular data from the Census Bureau and other national databases to describe American women in terms of "demographic characteristics," "employment and economic status," "health aspects," and "social characteristics." Each of these four categories is further sub-divided into several topical units, and a "Guide to Related Informational Services" and "Glossary of Terms" are also presented. This is a useful guide, comprised largely of frequency based data tables and it is easily integrated with other statistical sources on women. Additionally, its glossary of terms clearly explains the variable measures assumed in the tabular materials. **NOTE**: Taeuber has also published various statistical sources on women and aging in American society (cf. [**94**]), with full text references available from on-line university libraries.

4

Women in American Religion

A. Bibliographies and Anthologies (1980-1995)

[129] *ATLA Database on CD-ROM.* Evanston, IL: The American Theological Library Association, 1993.
This is the premier starting point for literature searches on mainline religious and theological topics, with almost any term of concern usable as a point of entry into the literature: key words, authors' names, biblical passages, titles, journals, years etc. The database reviews "five distinct indexes searchable as a combined database" including *Religion Index One: Periodicals* [RIO, 1949-1964; 1975-1993]; *Religion Index Two: Multi-Author Works* [RIT, 1960-current]; *Index to Book Reviews in Religion* [IBRR, 1975-current]; *Research in Ministry: An Index to D. Min. Project Reports and Theses* [RIM, 1981-current] and *Methodist Reviews Index (1818-1985)*. Downloading features are available and the system is extremely easy to use.

[130] Bass, Dorothy C., and Sandra Hughes Boyd. *Women in American Religious History: An Annotated Bibliography.* Boston: G. K. Hall, 1986.
Five-hundred and sixty-eight (568) entries comprise this annotated bibliography and guide to sources on "Women in American Religious History." The entries are spread across seven areas: "General Works," (a strong and informative section); "Protestantism" (the largest section); "Roman Catholicism"; "Judaism"; "Afro-American Women"; "Native American Religions"; and "Utopian, Millenarian"; and "Other Alternative Religious Movements." As a guide to the literature, this text helpfully directs readers to other sources, both through specific titles and additional commentaries. Entries are indexed by reference numbers and the literature is current through 1985.

[131] James, Janet Wilson, ed. *Women in American Religion.* Philadelphia: Univ. of Pennsylvania Press, 1980.
This early anthology on women in American religious history presents an introductory overview by the editor and twelve subsequent essays addressing: congregational and Quaker women in Colonial America **[667]**, the religious experience and church involvement of women in 17th century New England, women's evangelical involvement (three entries), the experience(s) of Roman Catholic laywomen and women religious (three entries), an overview of Jewish women through the 1930s **[944]** and a case study on birth control among Missouri synod Lutherans. The introduction presents clear summaries of each entry and locates James' criteria for inclusion within the larger frameworks of "history of religion" and the "feminization" of American religion as described by Ann Douglass in *The Feminization of American Culture* [NY: Alfred Knopf, 1977] and Welter **[81]**. This is a solid volume, but without sources on African American women.

[132] Ruether, Rosemary Radford, and Rosemary Skinner Keller, eds. *Women and Religion in America, Volume 1: The Nineteenth Century: A Documentary History.* San Francisco: Harper & Row, 1981.
This volume is both an anthology and a *documentary history,* for in each of its essays contributors have organized their discussions around critical source materials that are, in turn, excerpted and

appended to the essay in question. An introductory essay by the editors sets the context of 19th century women's experience by contrasting the "perfectionist" and "liberal" visions of femininity prevalent during that period. The perfectionist image viewed woman as a moral auxiliary to the social order whether through motherhood, education, social work or social reform. In this view women's natural role was that of uplifting "mankind" from its more mired, "carnal" roots. In contrast, the liberal perspective stressed an "egalitarian doctrine of human nature," and while not applied consistently to "blacks, women and propertyless people" (p. xiii), it yet provided women an opportunity for religious leadership. The volume's topics and authors include: "Women and Revivalism" by Martha Tomhave Blauvelt [666]; Ruether's "Women in Utopian Movements"; "The Leadership of Nuns in Immigrant Catholicism" by Mary Ewens [804]; Ann Braude's "The Jewish Woman's Encounter with American Culture" [940]; B.B. Zikmund's "The Struggle for the Right to Preach" [681]; editor Keller's "Lay Women in the Protestant Tradition," and "Women in Social Reform Movements" by Carolyn de Swarte Gifford [668]. Although no single essay specifies the religious leadership of women of color, the editors note that the "ethnic diversity of religious roles for women" has been handled "by inclusion" within topical discussions. Likewise, they acknowledge the "largely unrepresented status" of "the religious activities of...Hispanic, Oriental, Indian, Eastern, and Southern European women" (p. xiv) in this volume--although all groups are widely represented in later volumes. An index links topics and sources, while bibliography is found in endnotes.

[133] Ruether, Rosemary Radford, and Rosemary Skinner Keller, eds. *Women and Religion in America, Volume 2: The Colonial and Revolutionary Periods*. San Francisco: Harper & Row, 1983.
In Volume II of this three volume series (cf., [132] and [134]), the editors "...chart women's [religious] role in the drama of colonization" (p. xiii) and again, via the medium of a "documentary history," a set of topically organized essays that introduce readers to key sources that are, in turn, excerpted and appended to their essay discussions. After noting the methodological difficulties attached to their task, the editors' well written introduction surveys the cultural and ethnic pluralism of women's religious leadership during the colonial period and especially the mosaic of women's ethnic, denominational and regional affiliations. The specific essays then follow: "American Indian Women and Religion" by Jacqueline Peterson and Mary Druke [925]; "Women and Religion in Spanish America" by Asuncion Lavrin; "Women in Colonial French America" by Christine Allen; "New England Women: Ideology and Experience in First-Generation Puritanism (1630-1650)" by Rosemary Skinner Keller; "The Religious Experience of Southern Women" by Alice C. Mathews; "Black Women and Religion in the Colonial Period" by Lillian Ashcraft Webb [620]; "Women in Sectarian and Utopian Groups" by Ruether and Catherine M. Prelinger; "Women and Revivalism: The Puritan and Wesleyan Traditions" by Martha Tomhave Blauvelt and editor Keller; and last, Keller's "Women, Civil Religion and The American Revolution." Embedded bibliographies in essay footnotes and an extensive index provide references for all sources and discussions.

[134] Ruether, Rosemary Radford, and Rosemary Skinner Keller, eds. *Women and Religion in America, Volume 3: 1900-1968*. San Francisco: Harper & Row, 1986.
Using the methodology set in their first two volumes, Ruether and Keller here "document the many roles of women in religion in twentieth century America" (p. xiii) through the use of introductory essays and the identification of historical source documents. In particular, Ruether identifies several figures among the "radical Victorians" (matriarchalists seeking alternative cultures and futures through both feminism and theosophy), and she provides bibliographic discussion and documentation of their work. Similarly, Kay Parker introduces "American Indian Women and Religion on the Southern Plains" [924]; Jualyne Dodson and Cheryl Townsend Gilkes describe the endurance of Black Christian women [613]; Ann Braude chronicles the history of American Jewish women in the 20th century [941]; Lorine Getz surveys Catholic women [748]; and several other authors examine, in turn, the religious leadership of Protestant laywomen [670], the struggle of women for leadership in evangelical and Pentecostal traditions [673], and last, the struggle for ordained ministry in "mainstream" Protestant traditions [682].

[135] Ruether, Rosemary Radford, and Rosemary Skinner Keller, eds. *In Our Own Voices: Four Centuries of American Women's Religious Writing*. HarperSanFrancisco: 1995.
Together with their three earlier volumes [132-134], Ruether and Keller here bring the documentary literature on women and American religion to its full synthesis, with themes from earlier works updated to the early 1990s and emphases subsequent to earlier works conceptually incorporated. The chapter organizers will be well known to those familiar with the

feminism/Christian tradition literature but seeking a one volume historical reference. Thus, Ruether and Keller survey "Catholic Women" and "Protestant Laywomen in Institutional Churches," respectively, and Ann Braude and Emilie Townes do the same for "Jewish Women" and "Black Women." Similarly, Nancy Hardesty synthesizes literature on "Evangelical Women," Joanne Carlson Brown surveys sources on "Protestant Women and Social Reform," and B. B. Zikmund continues the literature on "Women and Ordination," but here with an attention to ordination across traditions and denominations, with illustrative documents from mainline Pentecostal and holiness churches, historically black denominations, and last, American Judaism. The women's literature on "Utopian and Communal Societies" is again updated by Ruether, and the final topical chapter is by Ines Maria Talamantez who surveys literature on "American Indian Women." Framing these topical chapters are detailed syntheses by the editors, including Keller's "Introduction: Gender and the Multicultural Worlds of Women" and Ruether's closing overview, "Growing Pluralism, New Dialogue." Extensive endnotes, notes on the contributors, and an index 24 pages in length close the volume. By itself, this text is alone an invaluable reference, and with its predecessors it is virtually unmatched. Its editorial essays synthesize the interdenominational and multiply-traditioned aspects of current feminist theological and religious ethnic dialogue, and they include, thereby, the current discussions of Jewish, Womanist, Islamic, Mujerista, Asian, Buddhist, American feminist and Wiccan sources. In sum, the book is a documentary delight. A final note: Although the format of the Ruether Keller series was in some ways unique with its early volumes, it is now a standard structure in women's studies. See, e.g., Rittner and Roth, *Different Voices: Women and the Holocaust* [945] and Umansky and Aston, *Four Centuries of Jewish Women's Spirituality: A Sourcebook* [263].

[136] Wessenger, Catherine, ed. *Women's Leadership in Marginal Religions: Explorations Outside the Mainstream.* Urbana, IL: University of Illinois, 1993.
This anthology of eleven essays discussing and/or describing the leadership patterns of women in 19th and 20th century sectarian and para-denominational religious movements builds directly on the variables identified by Bednarowski [665] in her discussion of women's religious leadership "outside the mainstream." In that essay Bednarowski had identified four variables that foster women's inclusion within marginalized religious movements; here Wessenger expands these to a theory of charismatic leadership applicable to discussions ranging from 19th century movements to contemporary spirituality to gender specific theological reconstructions. In fact, it is Bednarowski who closes the text with an overview of women's theological reconstructions in Mormonism, Roman Catholicism and contemporary Theosophy. In addition to Bednarowski, other contributors include Wessenger, Robert Ellwood, Marjorie Procter-Smith, Elaine Lawless, Ann Braude, Cynthia Eller, Rosemary Ruether, David Estes, J. Gordon Melton and Dell deChant. Their essays include 19th and 20th century topics with the entries by Estes, Ruether and Eller (on respectively: African American women and Spiritualist churches, the Catholic women-church movement and contemporary women's spirituality) having particular salience for current feminist theological literature. This is a solid text for sociologists researching new religious movements, and its discussions are clearly written and well documented with extensive endnotes and embedded bibliography. For related literature see Section V.

NOTE: For more tradition specific bibliography see the denominational listings in both Bass and Boyd [130] and the Ruether and Keller series [132-135] above. Additionally, see DeBerg [678] for literature on women in Lutheran traditions, see Gilton [595] for early literature on Womanism, see Finson [269] for various tradition-based literatures, see Rowe (as noted in [672]) for literature on women in Methodist tradition, see Ruud [951] for literature on women in Judaism, and see the *Dictionary of Feminist Theologies* [272] generally (including its on-line index and entries) for bibliography attached to specific terms and concepts within feminist theology.

B. The Changing Status of Women in American Religion (1975-1996)

[137] Briggs, Sheila. "Women in Religion." In *Analyzing Gender: A Handbook of Social Science Research*, edited by Beth B. Hess and Myra Marx Ferree, 408-441. Newbury Park, CA: Sage, 1987.
This is one of the best sociological surveys on women and religion presently available for literature current through 1986. It thoroughly describes the main trends of Jewish and Christian feminist religious thought while identifying both the sources and limitations of feminist theology within organized "sectarian" and "mainstream" religion. It opens with a brief history of feminist and womanist religious thought and then addresses in sequence: "the struggle for ordination;" "the debate about language," "feminist theology," "feminist biblical studies," "feminist historiography,"

"feminist ethics," and in an especially informative section, the "distribution of religious feminism" via the multiple channels of "educational settings...conferences, journals and retreats." For closure, Briggs describes "the social class factor," i.e., the (then) current limitation of feminist theological thinking to a predominantly white middle class population, and the concomitant, diverse representation of various female populations within seminary and/or theological settings (viz., women of color, lesbian feminists, Roman Catholic nuns, women "in the Third World"). Overall, Briggs surveys a wide range of feminist theological sources, and while her discussion of women clergy could be expanded to include early empirical works by Lehman [700, 706, 708] and others (e.g., [711]), it is strongly recommended as an introduction to the study of women in contemporary American religion. NOTE: For theological overviews of the literature surveyed by Briggs, see the notes in Section C of this chapter.

[138] Chambers, Patricia Price, and H. Paul Chalfont. "A Changing Role Or the Same Old Handmaiden: Women's Role in Today's Church." *Review of Religious Research* 19 (1978): 192-197.
This article presents a content analysis of five independent religious periodicals (three Protestant and two Catholic) published between 1965 and 1974 to ascertain the following: (1) the extent to which women's entry into the ministry or priesthood is discussed; (2) whether it is discussed by female or male authors; and (3) whether from traditional or alternative role perspectives. As main findings, the authors note that (a) less than one percent of the more than 7000 articles they surveyed addressed the topic; (b) the preponderance of articles were by women; (c) no clearly defined alternative to the traditional (male) role perspective was developed; and (d) it is the period from 1970-1974 within which the majority of articles were published. To close, the authors speculate on the implications for change that such findings imply, and they conclude (among other things) that male editorship seems resistant to change and that the absence of an alternative ministerial role model for women works to maintain the status quo, indicating only token rather than real inclusion of women into the male occupation of ministry. NOTE: See Neal's [145] alternative perspective.

[139] Goldenberg, Naomi R. *Changing of the Gods: Feminism and the End of Traditional Religions.* Boston: Beacon Press, 1979.
Now a classic in the feminist critique of religion, Goldenberg's text synthesizes the feminist theological literature of the 1970s through the reformist/revolutionary framework developed by Christ [177], and it introduces readers to several aspects of feminism's critique of religion: viz., early discussions of women's experience as the basis for religious symbolization, a critical reading of Jung which precludes his prejudices around the area of religious symbolization, goddess religion, and the potential of dream analysis for unfolding women's spiritual and imaginative creativity. Of crucial importance in Goldenberg's discussion is that in the newer goddess religion of women and theology, God and/or the Goddess are not external to women and creation, but internal and celebrated as such. Hence her attention to Jungian analysis and dream interpretation.

[140] Hargrove, Barbara, Jean M. Schmidt, and Sheila G. Davaney. "Religion and the Changing Role of Women." *The Annals* 480 (1985): 117-131.
Working from feminist and feminist theological literature published through 1985, sociologist Hargrove and theologians Schmidt and Davaney survey several aspects of American religion and the 'changing status of women' within it. These include: (1) a survey of historical and cultural factors conditioning the development of women's role(s) in American religion (i.e., such factors as the cult of domesticity, the struggle of women for status within specific denominations, and the effects of race, ethnicity, immigration and religious volunteerism on that struggle); (2) the mid-20th century struggle for women's ordination (and conservative reaction to it); and (3) the feminist theological movement, with its general themes of (i) protest against patriarchy, (ii) the affirmation of religious and social inclusivity, and (iii) the validity of women's experience as a source of religious insight and value. By way of analysis, the authors note the potential conflicts facing feminist theologians if inclusivity is not realized as a social and structural value, and they highlight the growing movement of both women and religion from the private to the public sphere. This is a broad introduction to the study of women in American religion, easily supplemented by Ruether and Keller [135], Briggs [137], and Neitz [485]

[141] Lincoln, C. Eric, and Lawrence H. Mamiya. "The Pulpit and the Pew: The Black Church and Women." Chapter 10 in *The Black Church in the African American Experience*, 274-308. Durham, NC: Duke Univ. Press, 1990.
While the chapter-length historical and denominational discussions presented in Lincoln and Mamiya [598] generally identify the statistics pertinent to women in the seven black denominations

Lincoln and Mamiya study, Chapter 10 is concerned specifically with the discussion of African American women in preaching and leadership roles, including ordained roles, in the Black church. In particular, this chapter surveys: (1) the historical and cultural factors facilitating the rise of women preachers within the historically established Black churches; (2) contemporary Black clergy attitudes towards African American women preachers and pastors; (3) recent trends in African American women's theological education; and (4) the rise of womanist theology and the relationship of womanist theology and ethics to the Black church in its cultural and denominational history. Of special importance are the authors' data tables on Black clergy attitudes towards African American women clergy, as drawn from their nationwide survey of more than 2100 African American clergy. This is a benchmark synthesis of the historical and empirical research on the changing leadership status of women in African American churches; it should be read in conjunction with womanist and feminist theological sources on African American women and theological education, e.g., the literature in Chapter 20.

[142] Lindley, Susan Hill. *"You Have Stepped Out of Your Place": A History of Women and Religion in America.* Louisville: Westminster John Knox, 1996.
This is an exceptional text. It pulls together virtually all of the available resource materials to provide a chapter by chapter summary of "women in American religion," from the time of Anne Hutchinson to Lindley's own projections for the 21st century. It is clearly written, reasonably indexed, and well supported by its more than sixty-five pages of chapter notes cum embedded bibliography. Lindley begins with a brief statement detailing the sweep of the women's movement in American religion. Namely, that just as the search for a usable past has engendered various and new postures toward churches and American religion, it has also generated the materials needing synthesis into one text, and hence, the scope of her work. She then details the story of Anne Hutchinson (from whom the title of the text is taken) and moves steadfastly through the Quaker and Puritan diversity of colonial America, the periods of religious awakening, and, last, the nineteenth and twentieth centuries. En route, she describes the developing (and now well known) religious and domestic roles available to women, but with a recognized attention to the diversity of women's experience, and especially so in terms of nineteenth century women's experience. Thus in her twenty-two chapters she variously synthesizes: (a) women's activities and/or roles in a diversity of times and movements (e.g., "The Foreign Missionary Movement," "The Social Gospel," "Women's Religious Leadership in the Nineteenth and Early Twentieth Centuries"); (b) the experience of communal and denominationally based women in the nineteenth century (e.g., "Native American Women and Religion in the Nineteenth Century," "African American Women and Religion in the Nineteenth Century," "Jewish Women in Nineteenth Century America"); (c) specific reform movements and institutional changes (e.g., "A Nineteenth Century Feminist Critique of Religion," "Women's Religious Leadership in the Twentieth Century: Movement into the Mainline"), and possible lines of development yet to come ("Women and Religion in America: Looking Forward to the Twenty-First Century"). And at all points, Lindley attends to both the extraordinary and "ordinary" women who 'stepped out of their place.' While neither a theological nor sociological history of women in American religion, it is an unparalleled single text review.

[143] MacHaffie, Barbara J. *Her Story: Women in Christian Tradition.* Philadelphia: Fortress Press, 1986.
This text provides an introductory overview to the history of women in Christian tradition. Its ten chapters trace the status of women from the biblical period to the rise of mid-twentieth century American feminist theology, and its journalistic style permits a synthesis of historical, organizational and social factors illuminating that history. Its supportive literature is current through the early 1980s, and while virtually all mainline feminist theologians are incorporated into the text, the experience and leadership of African American and Native American women in American religion are noticeably absent. Supplemental bibliographies, subject and scriptural indices close the volume. **NOTE**: A subsequent volume by MacHaffie [*Readings in Her Story: Women in Christian Tradition.* Minneapolis: Fortress Press, 1991] provides a companion reader to MacHaffie's textual overview, with 75 excerpts (biblical and historical texts, church documents etc.) contemporary to the chapter periods described in *Her Story.* Additionally, see Ruether and Keller **[132-135]**, Ruether **[171]**, Clark and Richardson **[186]**, and sources in Chapter 8.

[144] McGuire, Meredith. "Extended Application: Women's Religion and the Social Definition of Gender Roles." In Meredith McGuire, *Religion: The Social Context,* 3rd ed., 111-130. Belmont, CA: Wadsworth, 1992.
This selection from McGuire's upper-division level text on the sociology of religion helpfully surveys the issues and research available on the linkages between religion and gender. Hence

where other sources might focus on the incorporation of women into roles of religious organizational leadership, the strength of McGuire's discussion is its emphasis on the norms and mechanisms involved in women's internalization of religion's definition of women as "other." Two questions ground McGuire's discussion. First, "*do* women accept their place?" And if not, what do women's alternative religious experience(s) look like? Second, "Can religions change to legitimate women?" McGuire's responses here are pessimistic as regards mainline American churches, but she sees alternative possibilities for women in "New Religious Movements." (Cf., e.g., Neitz [148] and Wessenger [136]).

[145] Neal, Marie Augusta. "Women in Religion: A Sociological Perspective." *Sociological Inquiry* 45 (1975): 33-39.
Using data from several secondary sources and her analysis of important sociological and religious sources published through the early 1970s, Neal argues that the women's movement in religion constitutes a "second reformation... as far reaching in effect as the first reformation [in 1517] despite the fact that it has been barely recognized by sociologists of religion" (p. 33). Further, through a discussion of Western society's transition from "fathers' rights" to "human rights" she demonstrates the urgency of recognizing this second reformation, together with its implications for religious organization: Namely, that it is not about the "the mere insertion of women into the status roles provided within the present social system, but change in the structure of authority... [which thus]... generates resistance on the part of those whose status is threatened by the correction of a basic inequality" (p. 36). Neal concludes with a description of current scholarly needs: that scholars should be studying "trends in religious institutions that bear upon changes in law, family life and language structure" (p. 37), for these, and not the traditional questions of human propagation, now constitute the critical areas of demographic and moral significance.

[146] Neal, Marie Augusta. "Women in Religious Symbolism and Organization." *Sociological Inquiry* 49 (1979): 219-250.
This classic essay by Neal examines several theories of symbolization and the specific ways the symbolization of women functions in religious and social milieux. Among other things, Neal addresses the relationship between female symbolization and priestly symbolization in Roman Catholicism, and specifically the priestly symbolization of celebrating the eucharist. She argues that one avenue of opposition to women's ordination in Catholicism lies with the (largely unconscious) perception of eucharist as community food, and in tandem with this, the social assumption of males as guardians of the community's food for survival. For closure, Neal notes: (1) the necessity for congruence between religious and social symbols (if religious socialization is to succeed) and (2) the current erosion of patriarchy as a social form, with the net effect of these two facts being that (3) women will no longer be socialized into social and cultural roles that validate those of Catholic religious organization. Subsequent research [147, 153] has proved her correct and underscored her near prophetic capacity for interpreting the status of women in American religion and in Roman Catholicism particularly.

[147] Neal, Marie Augusta. "Feminism: A Critique from a Socio-Historical Perspective." In *Defecting in Place: Women Claiming Responsibility for Their Own Spiritual Lives,* by M. T. Winter, Adair Lummis and Allison Stokes, 235-240. New York: Crossroad, 1994.
Writing as a consultant-respondent to the study *Defecting in Place* (a nationwide study of women's spirituality groups conducted through Hartford Seminary [153]), Neal reviews the high points of the "American Women's Movement" and its shift from an essentially "women's rights movement" to a formally "feminist movement." Important to this shift has been the increasing collapse of patriarchy as a social systemic network of "father rights" and "father privilege," and on the basis of parallels existing between the Hartford data and data from her "sister's survey" research, Neal hypothesizes the increasing development of women's spirituality groups such as those found in the Hartford study. Additionally, she notes their significance: in a world where father rights and father privilege decline, and in which women are no longer dependent upon males, women demand their rights to participate in decisions that affect them, and which affect, as well, the well being of the global community. Further, these women argue that it is religion that grounds these demands, for it is religion that bespeaks the retention or reinstatement of practices and symbols reflecting "God's steadfast love and abiding care [together with] God's relationships with the world as Creator, Redeemer and Sanctifier." Hence the religious commitment of women to social justice agendas, and the liturgically based efforts of women against racism, classism, ageism, and other forms of prejudice. Neal's is an especially important commentary on the Hartford study, for it identifies the

challenge yet facing feminism: i.e., the question of how to name God in the face of this circumstance.

[148] Neitz, Mary Jo. "Inequality and Difference: Feminist Research in the Sociology of Religion." In *A Future for Religion? New Paradigms for Social Analysis*, ed. by William H. Swatos, Jr., 165-184. Newbury Park, CA: Sage, 1993.
This review of feminist research in the sociology of religion highlights the "...long and ambivalent relationship [of feminism] to religion in America" (p.165), and it locates the continued evidence of that ambivalence through a survey of studies synthesized by Neitz in terms of: (1) women, ministry and oppression; (2) gendered experience within Abrahamic traditions; and (3) women centered religious groups and practices. Neitz's first category identifies the main literature for women and leadership issues in Pentecostal and mainline Christianity, with principal sources moving from the 1983 Carroll, Hargrove and Lummis [657] study to Wallace's [787] 1992 survey of Catholic women pastors. Category #2 highlights research on *gender* and leadership, including research on women in churches initially rooted in the "spirit based" leadership of women (but now routinized and masculinized in leadership--cf., e.g., [691]), research on "newly Orthodox Jewish women" (e.g., Davidman [973]), women in historically Black Churches, (e.g., Gilkes [615]), and last, the need for gender studies in New Religious Movements. Neitz's last category concentrates on women's spirituality groups, and particularly Jacobs' [901] research on women and ritualized healing. To close, Neitz indicates areas yet to be researched: (1) the gendering of religious roles in conversion experiences, spirituality and midwifery; (2) religious socialization and sexual abuse (but see Capps [873]); (3) gender and the structuring of religious emotions; and (4) gender and the *re*structuring of religious traditions, as evidenced, e.g., by Roman Catholic nuns and women in Asian-American religious milieux (e.g., Fabella, Lee and Suh [932] and Park [936-937]).

[149] Porterfield, Amanda. "Religious Feminism as a Revitalization Movement." *Sociological Analysis* 48 (1987): 234-243.
Working with the theoretical model of social movements as "mazeways" (as developed by Anthony Wallace), Porterfield identifies the American feminist theological movement as a movement of cultural revitalization. Three things are needed, she says, for the success of a revitalization movement: *viz.*, people must view their culture as a "system," they must be dissatisfied with it, and, last, members voicing the dissatisfaction must offer cultural peers a new "mazeway" (i.e., a new conceptual grid) which transcends the problems engendering the dissatisfaction. Citing both the cultural and gender mazeways of the 1950s-1960s and the staged based requirements of Wallace's formal "mazeway" model, Porterfield argues that Mary Daly's initial 1968-1973 writings meet the criteria needed for the prophetic stages identified by Wallace's model, while publications from the early 1980s (by, for example, Schüssler Fiorenza and Ruether) begin the work for remaining stages. Porterfield closes by noting that the movement is (at the time of her writing) still in its adaptation stage, and that the "the transformation of American society to a feminist mazeway" is still in the future, with the period of routinization "still more remote."

[150] Roberts, Keith A. "Religion and Prejudice: Christianity and Racism" and "Religion and Prejudice: Christianity and Sexism." In *Religion in Sociological Perspective*, 259-300. Belmont, CA: Wadsworth, 1990.
The first of these two chapters reviews data on Christianity and racism; it distinguishes "dominative" from "aversive" racism, the former being the "desire by some people to dominate or control members of another group," whereas the latter is "the desire to avoid contact" with members of another group. While institutionalized Christianity explicitly disavows dominative racism, it contributes unwittingly to the development and maintenance of aversive racism through three principal means: *meaning* factors (these are doctrines and/or symbols that generate antipathy for identifiable "other" group members); *belonging* factors (i.e., reference group norms that enhance we/they boundaries); and last, *institutional* factors or those practices and/or norms that reward non-prophetic religious roles. A similar discussion is presented for Christianity and sexism. Thus data on Christianity and gender prejudice are reviewed and summarized, and the *meaning, belonging*, and *institutional* factors contributing to Christianity's gender prejudice are identified. Among others, the misogynist norms and "hierarchical dualism" described by Ruether [172] evidence meaning factors, and the power of informal social norms together with several variables identified by Lehman's clergywomen research [706, 712] make up belonging and institutional factors. These chapters are located in an introductory sociology of religion textbook designed for use by seminarians and first year graduate students. Overall, Roberts introduces background material as needed, and all chapters may be read independently from one another. The bibliography is current through 1990, and the text is clearly written, well formatted, and well indexed.

[151] Swatos, William H., ed. "Religion and Gender Relationships." *Journal of Religion* 54 (1993): 1-122.
This thematic issue of the *Journal* presents eight articles on gender and religion with attention directed primarily to the effects of gender on religious leadership. Articles addressing this include: Edward Lehman's 1992 RRA Presidential Address, "Gender and Ministry Style: Things Not What They Seem" **[715]**; Paula Nesbitt's "Dual Ordination Tracks: Differential Benefits and Costs for Men and Women Clergy" **[701]**; "The Social Construction of a New Leadership Role: Catholic Women Pastors," by Ruth Wallace **[788]**; "The Limited Empowerment of Women in Black Spiritual Churches: An Alternative Vehicle to Religious Leadership," by Hans Baer **[643]**; a "Women Rabbis and Ministers," by Rita Simon, Angela J. Scanlan and Pamela S. Nadell **[719]**, and "Men Helping Women: A Monastic Case Study" by Penny S. Gold. Two other pieces address gender and specific religious norms within Judaism: "Gender and the Experience of Conversion: The Case of "Returnees" to Modern Orthodox Judaism" by Lynn Davidman and Arthur L. Greil **[974]**; and "Religious Rituals and Secular Rituals: Interpenetrating Models of Childbirth in a Modern Israeli Context" by Susan Starr Sered.

[152] Taves, Ann. "Women and Gender in American Religions." *Religious Studies Review* 18 (1992): 263-270.
This essay reviews eight recent, important volumes on women and gender in American religion and is recommended both for the substance of its discussion and the range of possibilities it introduces for the study of religion and sex role analysis. The volumes reviewed include: Lori Ginzberg, *Women and the Work of Benevolence: Morality, Politics and Class in the Nineteenth-Century United States* and Mark C. Carnes, *Secret Ritual and Manhood in Victorian America* (Yale Univ. Press, 1990 and 1989 respectively); Ann Braude, *Radical Spirits: Spiritualism and Women's Rights in Nineteenth-Century America* and Cynthia G. Tucker, *Prophetic Sisterhood: Liberal women Ministers of the Frontier, 1880-1930* (Boston: Beacon Press, 1989 and 1990, respectively); James Kenneally, *The History of American Catholic Women* (New York: Crossroads, 1990); Betty DeBerg, *Ungodly Women: Gender and the First Wave of American Feminism* (Minneapolis: Fortress Press 1990) **[828]**; Karen McCarthy Brown, *Mama Lola: A Voudou Priestess in Brooklyn* (Berkeley: Univ. of Calif. Press, 1991); and Will Roscoe, *The Zuni Man-Woman* (Albuquerque: Univ. of New Mexico Press, 1991).

[153] Winter, Miriam Therese, Adair Lummis, and Allison Stokes. *Defecting in Place: Women Claiming Responsibility for Their Own Spiritual Lives.* New York: Crossroad, 1994.
Using a denominationally pluralistic and admittedly "elite" sample of women (N=3746) who are approximately one third each members of feminist spirituality support groups, church related women's groups, and traditional parish/congregational members, the researchers in this Lilly funded study identify the following: (1) the many types of spirituality support groups to which feminist Protestant, Catholic and goddess directed women belong and/or participate in; (2) the experiences of alienation and church pain that undergird the involvement of these women in such groups; (3) the types of theological reflection and "god imagery" these women use in their prayer, meditation and/or worship experiences; and (4) the visions these women have for institutional and/or alternative religious affiliations. It is a moving and empowering study. Its *many, many* voices witness keenly to the alienation (and thus needed feminist empowerment) of its sample members, and in spite of its "elite" sample (*viz.*, its primarily white, educated and middle to upper middle class Christian professional religious base), it nonetheless evidences the struggles of both white feminists and feminists of color, as *both* struggle with issues of racism, sexism, heterosexism, classism and in the end, feminist inclusivity. For closure, the authors provide reflections from a variety of feminist theologian-consultants who contemplate both the significance of the study findings and (in many cases) the study's connections to women in the wider feminist movement in American religion. This is a benchmark text. Its data are ground breaking and informative, and its methodology and findings will surely be replicated and expanded by future research. It can serve as a study and discussion text for adult forums, for upper division college and graduate courses in women's studies and feminist theology, and for church related and/or goddess groups interested in women's spirituality. **NOTE**: For the study data on feminist spirituality and Roman Catholic sample members, see Lummis and Stokes **[742]**.

C.   Some Notes on Subsequent Sources

Additional sources on women in American religion (largely religious and theological) are presented in the remaining portions of this bibliography. Some of the early classics and most well known of these sources (as listed alphabetically) include the following: Christ and Plaskow [206], Daly [157] and [161], Harrison [654], Heschel [943], Heyward [198], Morton [202], Plaskow [203], Ruether [171-172], Schüssler Fiorenza [195] and Trible [205]. Also, for clergywomen studies, noted classics include Carroll, Hargrove and Lummis [657], early works by Lehman [706, 712], and for the comparative study of American with British women clergy in particular, Lehman [713] and Nason-Clark [714, 716]. For more recent literature, readers should see Zikmund, Lummis and Chang [663], a 'one of a kind' in the study of women clergy.

To return to theological literature, readers should consult Cannon [253], Grant [254], Gilkes [616], Townes [258] and Williams [259] for noted womanist sources, and Bendroth [825] and DeBerg [828] for sources on gender and Christian fundamentalism. Other topical overviews include Johnson [353] and Oseik [354] for general sources on feminist hermeneutics, and among Christian sources, Graff [331] and Williams [341] for feminist and womanist theological method(s), respectively, and Chopp [264] and Eugene [266] for definitions of feminist and womanist theologies. In turn, see Copeland [265] and Ross and Hilkert [268] for mid-90s overviews of the general feminist/womanist theological literature. Additionally, and citing still from Christian sources, see Cahill [469] and Robb [482] for sources on feminist theological ethics; see Procter-Smith [522] for work on feminist liturgy and worship; see MacNichol and Walsh [539] for feminist spirituality; see Arledge-Clanton [432], Darling-Smith [434], and Ruether [441] for literature on feminist christology; and for literature on feminist theologies of the Trinity, see LaCugna's chapter in [273] and her brief essay [459].

An important development in the 1990s has been the burst in Jewish feminist theology. Among Jewish authors, Judith Plaskow's work [262] is preeminent and rooted deeply in the multiple frameworks of feminist theology and women's studies [338], the Jewish Christian dialogue [971] and her long standing commitment to questions of feminist theological method ([170] and [953] through [955]). Also prominent in Jewish feminism are works by Ellen Umansky who examines the religious history of Jewish women (including women's ordination to the rabbinate [946]), the use of midrash as a form of feminist theological method [957], and with Diane Aston, the history of women's spirituality within Judaism [263]. Additionally, Falk's work in Jewish liturgy and spirituality [260, 960] addresses Judaism as a whole, while Gottlieb's recently published text provides a congregationally directed synthesis of Jewish feminist renewal [261]. Finally, Davidman and Tenenbaum [949] provide recent reviews of several theological and sociological "feminist studies in Judaism."

Two further important topics in the 1990s have been the backlash against feminism and, for a variety of reasons, the rising consciousness of clergy sexual misconduct. Faludi's text [822] together with articles by Marshall [835, 836] address the former, while a variety of theological [867, 869], pastoral [865, 887], canonical [896], and sociological ([879, 880]) sources address the latter.

Finally, for sociological literature on the impact of feminism on Roman Catholicism, see Lummis and Stokes [742] and Wallace [787], and see D'Antonio et al. [736] for data on the changing attitudes of Roman Catholics toward gender roles and questions of church leadership, ministry and ordination. (Also, see their follow-up discussion, "Gallup Survey Supplement" to the *National Catholic Reporter*, October 8, 1992.) Last, for theological literature on organizational change in Roman Catholicism, see Bianchi and Ruether [733] and see *The Gallup Monthly* [739] for data on Catholics and attitudes about religious practice, changes in the Church, and priest pedophilia. Other source overviews are listed in the introductions to each section of the bibliography.

II

Feminism and the Development of Feminist Theology

The literature reviewed in this section includes key feminist theological works published between 1968 and 1995. Grounding and transitional sources (i.e., primary works published between 1968 and 1977 together with critical assessments published through 1979) make up the initial or "early" feminist theological literature. These sources are abstracted in Chapter 5. "Core" or established writings (i.e., works published between 1978 and 1985, together with critical assessments published through 1986) appear in Chapter 6, and literature through the 1995 is surveyed in Chapter 7.

There are a handful of exceptions to the boundaries of these three periods of development. At the early end of the literature there are two. These are Valerie Saiving/Goldsmith's essay "The Human Situation: A Feminine View" [163] first published in 1960, but not widely read until its reprint in the 1979 Christ and Plaskow reader [206], and Mary Daly's 1965, "The Forgotten Sex: A Built-in Bias" [156], her essay precursor to *The Church and the Second Sex* [157]. On the more recent end, these exceptions include the 1996 publication, the *Dictionary of Feminist Theologies* [272], edited by Letty Russell and J. Shannon Clarkson, the *Concilium* reader on diversity in feminist theology [275], edited by Schüssler Fiorenza and Shawn Copeland, and last, Marcia Falk's elegant and grand *Book of Blessings* [260].

Several themes cut across the literatures of these chapters. In the early literature attention is focused on the critique of patriarchy and misogyny in the history of Christian teaching nad theology, while later writers work to identify and bridge the varying dimensions of women's culture, experience, denominational and religious differences. These themes have been described in the general introduction to the bibliography and they are reviewed briefly in chapter overviews throughout Section II.

Because the intent of this section is towards a general chronology of the literature in terms of its early, core and current principal sources, no attempt is made here to organize the literature in terms of its varying subject emphases (e.g., Bible, worship etc.). Rather, a developmental synthesis is presented, with the topical organization of additional and supplemental sources reserved for Section III. By way of "guide posts" to the literature, the entries by Plaskow [170], Driver [178], Murray [181], and Patrick [183] will help orient readers to the early literature, while Grant [214], Halkes [215], and contributors to Swidler and Conn [212] provide essay responses to early and "core" sources. Likewise, for essay length discussions of much core and current literature see the overviews by Copeland [265], Tolbert [284] and Graff [280] and--as interests warrant--overviews from chapters in Section III.

Finally, for edited collections by which to sequence the developmental sweep of the literature (including its Womanist and Multicultural dimensions), see the following: (1) the 1979 reader on women's spirituality cited above and edited by Christ and Plaskow [206]; (2) the 1984 reader on feminist theology edited by Weidman [213]; (3) Russell's 1985 collection on feminist biblical hermeneutics [210]; (4) Plaskow and Christ's 1989 collection on feminist spirituality [544] (listed in Section III-7); (5) Loades's [274] 1990 reader in feminist theology; (6) the 1993 Procter-Smith and Walton reader [526] on women's worship (listed in Chapter 12); (7) Townes' [638] 1993 collection on womanist ethics (listed in Chapter 19); (8) LaCugna's [273] 1993 collection on feminist theological reconstruction; (9) Schüssler Fiorenza's 1993 multicultural reader on feminist biblical hermeneutics **[344]** (listed in Chapter 10); and last, from the general literature in Chapter 4, the 1994 volume, *In Our Own Voices*, edited by Ruether and Keller **[135]**. Taken together, these collections provide a wide angled overview of the topics, trends and emphases grounding the development of feminist theology from its beginnings in the mid 1960s to its mid-1990s circumstance as a pluralized movement of inclusivity and theological reconstruction.

5

Early Feminist Theological Literature (1968–1977)

A. Grounding Sources: 1960, 1968-1973

[154] Bentley-Doely, Sarah, ed. *Women's Liberation and the Church: The New Demand for Freedom in the Life of the Christian Church.* New York: Association Press, 1970.
This early collection of seven essays depicts the status and concerns of Christian women working professionally in American churches during the late 1960s. The entries include: (1) Davida Crabtree's "Women's Liberation in the Church," a contrast of women's status in Christianity with the then salient goals of American feminism; (2) an historical-theological description of feminism by Rosemary Radford Ruether; (3) "A Christian Perspective on Feminism" by Sidney Callahan, a lay Catholic educator and professional journalist; (4-5) two essays (by Susan Barrabee and Norma Ramsey Jones, respectively) on the conflicts and roadblocks experienced by women in seminary and ordained ministry; (6) literature supporting the Sisters of the Immaculate Heart of Mary (a Los Angeles community of nuns) in their 1967 move to non-canonical community status vis a vis the Vatican; and last, Peggy Ann Way's powerful and frequently quoted essay, "Towards an Authority of Possibility." An appendix of materials from the December, 1969 Detroit meeting of the Women's Caucus of the Assembly of the National Council of Churches in Christ and a "Selected Bibliography" developed by Nelle Morton close the volume.

[155] Collins, Sheila. "Toward a Feminist Theology." *The Christian Century* 94 (1972): 796-799.
This essay describes four early feminist theological themes that in subsequent literature become characteristic emphases of feminist theological thought. These are the feminist rejection of theologically defined misogyny in the Bible, Christian theology and history; a subsequent acceptance of an "egalitarian and pluralistic schema;" the related call for a "re-thinking of the traditional doctrines of sin, incarnation and salvation...in terms consonant with the existential experience of all persons, not just [those] of White Western males;" and last, an "ethic based on the responsible self actualization of every person...[to]...achieve deeper awareness of the ties that bind all of creation together" (p. 799).

[156] Daly, Mary. "The Forgotten Sex: A Built-in Bias." *Commonweal* 81 (1965): 508-511.
This is Daly's first published critique of Catholicism's antifeminist bias against women, and it hints of all that will eventually be detailed in *The Church and the Second Sex:* (1) a perspective grounded in de Beauvoir's analysis of the marginality of women; (2) the many ways Christianity--and particularly Catholicism--has supported that marginality--and with it--the misogyny of the "Fathers"; and (3) a statement of hope, drawn from the recognition that not all of Catholicism's priestly caste is as androcentric as that of the magisterium and its authority. The article appears as one of two addressing the question: "Should women be priests?" with the second, by Gertrud Heinzelmann, (not abstracted here) presenting an early argument for women's ordination.

[157] Daly, Mary. *The Church and the Second Sex*. New York: Harper & Row, 1968/1978.
This discussion presents an historical, biblical and theological documentation of the charges leveled against Christianity by Simone de Beauvoir in her feminist treatise, *The Second Sex*. In particular, de Beauvoir had argued that Christianity or "Christian ideology" had: (1) oppressed women through a deceptive teaching of their inferiority; (2) enforced women's passive role through misogynist theology and "harmful [or antisexual] moral teaching;" (3) denied women a liberation that science has already made possible in both theory and practice; and (4) perpetuated the destructive myth of the "eternal feminine" that further serves to keep women subordinate. To demonstrate each of de Beauvoir's charges, Daly traced biblical and theological motifs that historically had projected negative and inferior images of women, and she cited specific papal and/or conciliar teachings evidencing the themes identified by de Beauvoir. Where Daly differed from de Beauvoir, however, was in her hope for the future. Thus, as she closed her discussion, she argued that the Church held within itself the possibility of a self-directed "exorcism," and that it could (at least in theory) rid itself of the "demon of sexism" both theologically and in church practice. The vehicle for this exorcism would be a theological renewal that would re-cast and redefine the symbolic tradition(s) that had so long defined Christianity as patriarchal, and Daly called upon the church to undertake this task. NOTE: Daly's suggestion notwithstanding, her hopefulness was short-lived. As she became increasingly involved with feminist literature and thought from 1970 to 1975, and as her call to exorcism went canonically unheeded, Daly eventually abandoned what she had perceived as Christianity's potential for self-directed exorcism, and in 1975 she formally separated herself from institutionalized Christianity to pursue what she described as "Post-Christian Feminism." It is this latter that is described in the 1978 reissue of this text.

[158] Daly, Mary. "After the Death of God the Father." *Commonweal* 94 (March 12, 1971): 7-11.
This brief and still provocative essay details how the "women's revolution can and should change our whole vision of reality...[and]...influence Western religious thought" (p. 7). In it Daly makes two points. First, the women's movement has reached a point of no return and it "may become the greatest single potential" for Christianity's undoing--not because it will attack Christianity, but because women may simply abandon Christianity. Second, radical feminism's real challenge to Christianity is its exposure of theologies that oppress human beings, rather than enhance their self actualization. Daly illustrates her discussion through a critique of male language for God and its *dis*empowering effects for women (e.g., alienation or self-reduction to stereotyped roles), and she notes the decreasing plausibility of such language. Finally, in a moment that anticipates ecofeminist theology, she argues for the necessity of linking feminist thought with planetary survival. The essay is vintage Daly: prior to *Beyond God the Father* [158] but anticipating its themes.

[159] Daly, Mary. "The Courage to See." *The Christian Century* 88 (1971): 1108-1111.
Shedding the internalized elements of sex role socialization (i.e., shedding male defined, stereotypical definitions of women) is a major theme in Daly's transitional pre-1973 essays, and here she refines her point by emphasizing the dimensions of "seeing clearly." To see clearly is to see that: (1) "sisterhood" is a revolutionary concept, not an analog to brotherhood, for the latter is exclusionary and divisive; (2) that theologians must abandon an exclusively male symbolism for God because such language is utterly oppressive to women in that it reinforces sexual hierarchy while suppressing women's self transcendence; and (3) that "theology is damaging if it encourages detachment from the reality of the human struggle against oppression in its concrete manifestations" (p. 7). Alternatively, women who are self-actualizing encourage others also to become so, and in turn, this "sisterhood of women" becomes also "a sisterhood of man:" a "creative and communal refusal of victimization by sex stereo-types" because there is a recognition by both women and men that oppression is the real enemy. NOTE: For an expanded description of her image, "the sisterhood of woman" (as a countermovement to the patriarchal structures of Christianity and a place of "sacred space" where liberation can happen), see Daly's essay, "The Spiritual Revolution: Women's Liberation as Theological Re-education," *Andover Newton Quarterly* 12 (1972): 163-176.

[160] Daly, Mary. "The Women's Movement: An Exodus Community." *Religious Education* 67 (1972): 327-334.
This essay includes Daly's November 14, 1971 Harvard Memorial Chapel sermon, and it highlights her perception that the women's movement in religion is a positive force moving women *away* from [patriarchal] oppression and *toward* the realization of a fully human church. In both the essay *and* the sermon Daly argues that women's professional thinking has been conditioned by the

prevalence of male culture and categories, and that it is the imagery of women's sex role socialization ["alienation"] that must be overcome if women are to develop as independent persons. She introduces the notion of sisterhood as "anti-church" (in that it is a counterworld to that of patriarchy), and she describes it as a symbol "...proclaiming dimensions of truth that organized religion fails to proclaim" (p. 332). She closes with her invitation to those present to "demonstrate our exodus from sexist religion..." and she proclaims the women's movement as an "exodus community." Letters written in response to her sermon and culled from local media then follow.

[161] Daly, Mary. *Beyond God the Father*. Boston: Beacon Press, 1973.
In her discussion of Daly's work, Loades [274:188] has characterized Daly's 1971 Ameican Academy of Religion paper, "Theology after the Demise of God the Father: A Call for the Castration of Sexist Religion," as "an attack on patriarchy...without quarter." The characterization holds for Daly's longer, book length work as well. What is more, Daly's genius for cutting to the theological bone is virtually unparalleled, as the rhetoric of this text makes clear with its references to "castration theology," "the tyranny of methodolatry," and the "end of phallic morality" etc. But beyond such excoriating rhetoric are the arguments that Daly's text brought to the religious and secular reading public: (1) her perception that feminist consciousness constitued a new and liberating spirituality for women; (2) her awareness that its power for women is the power of a new self-naming; (3) her conviction that the latter liberates women because it dislodges the traditional sex role expectations internalized by women during the course of socialization--and with such, the traditional male symbols of Christianity that support such socialization (i.e., Christianity's male identified doctrines, ethical assumptions, and misogynous aetiological myths); and (4) Daly's vision that feminist community involves building a "cosmic covenant," a normative framework fully grounded with feminist ethical, feminist religious, and feminist ecological values as espoused by and for women's communities. Often described as Daly's "transitional" text (in that she later moved exclusively to feminist philosophy per se), this volume presents Daly's final effort at a feminist rendering of traditional Christian symbols, and particularly her theology of God as "the Verb" through which women can confront the non-being of patriarchal definitions working to negate them. **NOTE**: For helpful overviews of Daly's work through 1973, see Weaver [762] and Carr [229].

[162] Morton, Nelle. "The Rising Woman Consciousness in a Male Language Structure."
       Andover-Newton Quarterly 12 (1972): 177-190.
This is one of the most well known of Nelle Morton's essays. In it she describes her perception of the process by which women come to feminist consciousness, and she suggests that this process is less a function of women's "protests" and "political action," and more the "new language" women experience as they come to consciousness through self affirmation and a rejection of "male" language. Her discussion is based on her notes, diaries and long experience of working with women in small groups and seeing the processes of defensiveness, pain, explosion and mutual empowerment women go through when experiencing support with one another. It is a process of seeing, hearing and speaking differently, and it entails a rejection of the "jarring" male words and structures that function to control and contain women. It entails the self-affirming and self-disclosing language of women finding independent consciousness in the presence of one another and literally "hearing" one another into existence. Although in many ways only a hint of what was to come, this essay remains an early statement on the development of "voice" as a major metaphor for the experience of feminism in Christian tradition. It is reprinted in *The Journey is Home* [202], Morton's collected essays attesting the power of women's voice against the multiple oppressions of sexism, racism, heterosexism and other prejudices based upon ascribed and stereotyped social characteristics.

[163] Saiving [Goldsmith], Valerie. "The Human Situation: A Feminine View." *The Journal of Religion* 40 (1960): 100-112.
Judith Plaskow [340] identifies this essay (also printed in [206]) as the beginning statement of American twentieth century feminist theology, for in it, Saiving asks directly how both a knowledge of and an attention to "women's experience" might affect the content of mainline Protestant theology, and in doing so she crystallizes the critique of mainline theology as "androcentric" or based on male--as contrasted with "human"--experience. To make these points, Saiving examines the notions of "sin" and "love" as understood by such theologians as Anders Nygren and Reinhold Niebuhr, and she argues that if 'sin' is as these theologians say it is, then it is not something applicable to women because women, by definition, cannot experience it, nor can they commit it. The linchpin of Saiving's argument is the Nygren-Niebuhr synthesis on sin and love: that sin is "hubris," or a Promethean like absorption of one's self for one's self and against

God, and further, that love is "agape" or self-sacrifice, or more concretely, the abandonment of one's self (after the manner of Christ) on behalf of others. The difficulty with such definitions, argues Saiving, is that women are socialized directly to the service of others (as their life role) and socialized consistently to the absence of any strong self-concept. Hence, women are virtually incapable of sin as understood by Nygren and Niebuhr, for they are defined throughout by selfless sacrificial giving. Saiving argues that the Nygren-Niebuhrian sin-love synthesis evidences the normativeness of male experience for Christian theology, and she explores the theological implications of concepts based on a more "human" (i.e., masculine and feminine) perception of experience. For related discussions see Plaskow [203], Andolsen [467], and Grey [477].

[164] Trible, Phyllis. "Depatriarchalizing in Biblical Interpretation." *Journal of the American Academy of Religion* 41 (1973): 30-48.

In later writings [356] Trible identifies three types of response that feminists may make to the Bible and its related literatures. These include: (1) documenting the patriarchal traditions of scripture; (2) text recovery and the identification of biblical critique(s) of patriarchy, and (3) the telling of scripture's tales of abuse to women "in memoriam." In this, her first extended discussion of feminism and the Bible, Trible focuses primarily on the second type of response. She acknowledges the legitimacy of response type #1, but she essentially eschews it, for in her judgment here, it would require an abandonment of scripture, something she cannot do. More to the point, there are several "themes that disavow sexism" and Trible here identifies them. These include: (1) the use of gynomorphic speech for Israel's God, YHWH (cf. Num. 11:12; Is. 42:14b; 49:15; 66:9,13; Ps. 22:9-10a; 71:6 and Job 3:12.); (2) the recorded revolutionary acts of women in the Exodus tradition (cf. Ex. 1:15-2:10); (3) the inclusive nature of Israel's concept of corporate personality, and (4) the egalitarian elements of gender relations in Gen 2-3 and Song of Songs, when both are read from non-misogynist perspectives. (And Trible's footnotes clearly indicate the misogyny of much conventional OT scholarship.) Several of Trible's main points here receive expanded treatment in separate articles (cf. [165]), and all become consolidated in her book, *God and the Rhetoric of Sexuality* [205]. Although dated and in places difficult, this essay is still a good introduction to Trible's work and a relevant critique of conventional OT scholarship through 1972.

[165] Trible, Phyllis. "Eve and Adam: Genesis 2-3 Reread." In *Womanspirit Rising: A Feminist Reader in Religion*, edited by Carol Christ and Judith Plaskow, 74-83. New York: Harper & Row, 1979.[First printed in *Andover Newton Quarterly* 13 (1973): 251-258.]

Textual re-interpretation is the careful rereading of texts once bound by misogynist horizons, and it is a major response feminists make to the patriarchy in Scripture [cf. 356]. Here, Trible exhibits its potential. She re-reads Gen. 2-3 to disclose and then dispel six inappropriate elements of the conventional exegesis and understanding of this text. These areas of disclosure include: (1) the relative status of the man and the woman as created entities; (2) their social position vis a vis the animals and each other; (3) their characterization as *ish* (man) and *ishah* (woman); (4) their moral capacities relative to the serpent; (5) the judgments they experience, and (6) the possible implications of the story for gender relations in the present time. In contrast to the traditional, conventional exegesis, Trible finds that: (1) The woman and the man are created equal; that is, they are a *sexually differentiated pair* borne of an androgenous *'adamah*. (2) They are *counterparts* to each other; that is, the woman is not a subordinate helper. Nor, (3) is she "named" by the man. She is simply *ishah* as he is *ish*. (4) Although there is much speculation about it, there is no real knowledge as to *why* the serpent spoke to the woman. Rather, the only sure knowledge is that the text "does not sustain the judgment that woman is weaker or more cunning or more sexual than man" (p. 78). (5) The judgments the woman and man experience are "descriptive not prescriptive." That is, these judgments are not curses, but observations: "...commentaries on the disastrous effects of their shared disobedience" (p. 80). (6) As regards the story's implications for current gender relations, they are (at least) that the story's judgments are culturally conditioned, and that "whatever form stereotyping takes in our own culture, [the implications of the story] are judgments upon our common sin and disobedience" (p. 81), not elements of gender identity.

B. Transitional Sources: 1974-1977

Listed below are additional sources that have grounded the development of the feminist theological literature. In particular, the works by Farley [166-167], Plaskow [170] and Ruether [171-172] significantly influenced the development of feminist ethics, theological anthropology and theological method; while those by Hageman [168], Pagels [196], and Russell [174] introduced issues of inclusivity, with Pagels and Russell addressing inclusive language, and contributors to the Hageman reader challenging linguistic, racial, class, gender, and heterosexist biases. Last, Russell [174], Schüssler Fiorenza [175] and Trible [176] variously laid grounds for feminist biblical and theological studies.

[166] Farley, Margaret A. "New Patterns of Relationships: Beginnings of a Moral Revolution." *Theological Studies* 36 (1975): 627-646.
This essay lays the wide ground for Farley's work in feminist theological ethics. After noting the emergence of society's growing shift from hierarchical to egalitarian patterns of relationships, Farley suggests that theology and ethics should help fill in the "gaps" in this process of transformation, and she examines how ideas of Christian love and justice can aid in this change. The gaps are clear. The old patterns assume women's general inferiority, the association of women with evil, and the identification of women as "derivative from and wholly complimentary to men" (p. 629). In contrast, the "new patterns of relationship" assume women's full autonomy as human beings and a call to "...equality and full mutuality with women and men" (p. 630). Hence theology and ethics should articulate the meaning of mutuality in ways that respect women's *full dignity* as persons, *and* their status as also *imago dei*. Thus theology and ethics must: (1) identify and reject the gendered patterns of understanding governing Protestant and Catholic notions of Christian love so that the notion of agape as "equal regard" can move beyond ideologies that variously consign women to invisibility and/or roles of subordination and auxiliary service; (2) reject the gendered and polarized ideas of reciprocity that undergird hierarchical patterns of interaction (i.e., patterns in which males give and females receive); (3) redefine reciprocity in terms of its deepest meaning (i.e., as the capacity of individuals to be fully and actively both givers and receiver--whether male *or* female); and (4) examine the Trinity as an ungendered symbol of full mutuality and reciprocity, so that the understanding of *women as fully givers and receivers* may also aid God's [trinitarian] self-disclosure (as fully giving and fully receiving). The latter is an especially important point, for although the traditional masculine language of the Trinity presumes that generativity is tied singularly to male generativity, contemporary consciousness knows generativity is tied equally to female generativity. Thus the language of "Mother," "Daughter," and "Spirit" also constitute an imaging of trinitarian self disclosure, and for Farley, one perhaps well suited for the contemporary cultural experience. This said, Farley notes that neither female nor male language has exclusive priority as speech for the naming of God, but crucial here is that women also function as the *imago dei*, i.e., as persons who also communicate God (giving and receiving) in fully equal and reciprocal terms. To close, Farley identifies other issues relevant to the shift from hierarchy to mutuality (e.g., questions of individual justice and the common good), but the steps described above are critical, for they identify women in egalitarian not hierarchical terms. **NOTE**: See [167] below and the entries cited there.

[167] Farley, Margaret A. "Sources of Sexual Inequality in the History of Christian Thought." *Journal of Religion* 56 (1976): 162-176.
This article builds on [166] above and summarizes Farley's ethic of mutuality and relationality. Farley begins by noting the need for a reconstruction of Christian thinking on the issue of equality between women and men. This reconstruction is needed both because of the dissonance contemporary Christian women experience vis a vis Christian tradition and the outmoded theologies that maintain the tradition. Farley then echoes Mary Daly's critique of Christianity (i.e., that its symbolism is sexist to the core and must be redefined or rejected [161]), and she begins the re-symbolization process. Key here are what Farley identifies as the two sources of gender inequality within Christian thought: the symbolization of evil as female, and the "attribution of the fullness of *Imago Dei,* to men." The first cannot be resymbolized without critical attention to the second, Farley argues, for to resymbolize women as good means that women also must be seen as the fullness of the *Imago Dei.* Can the "feminine" thus be resymbolized Farley asks? The answer is "yes," and especially so if one considers both (a) the pure mutuality, relationality and infinite reciprocity characteristic of God's trinitarian self, and (b) the relational capacities of women, as seen from a non-stereotypical perspective (that is, one which does not assign women an exclusively passive role, but rather, both activity and passivity). The assimilation of these concepts permits the "feminine" to be re-symbolized from such trinitarian insights as the fullness of mutuality and reciprocity and the fullness of activity and passivity characteristic of God's own self, and this, in turn, permits an abandoning of traditional superordinate and subordinate, hierarchical gender relations. Additionally, it demonstrates the reality of seeing women as also the fullness of *Imago Dei,* and it thus opens new avenues of trinitarian thought such that both female (and male) language may be used as revelatory of God. Farley's discussion is carefully nuanced, solidly theological, and ever committed to the assumptions of equality, mutuality, autonomy, and respect as the ethical

ground swell for understanding the nature of human persons. It should be read with [166] above, Farley's work in feminist ethics ([471], [472], [475], [568]) and biblical interpretation [364], and the literature on feminist theological anthropology (Chapter 8).

[168] Hageman, Alice L., ed. *Sexist Religion and Women in the Church: No More Silence!* New York: Association Press, 1974.
This collection of eleven essays addressing the various sources, types and extent of women's marginality in mainstream Christian churches is one of the early prophetic sources for American Protestant feminist theology. The essays stem from the women's caucus of the Harvard Divinity School and were first delivered in 1972 through Harvard's Lentz Lectureship series. Among the entries are such classics as Nelle Morton's "Preaching the Word," Theresa Hoover's "Black Women and the Churches: Triple Jeopardy" [618], and Mary Daly's "Theology after the Death of God the Father: A Call for the Castration of Sexist Religion" (cf. [158]). What still distinguishes this collection, however, is its early and clear recognition of the issues yet facing women in mainline religion: a continued denominational resistance to issues of inclusivity (whether over race/ethnicity, gender, age or sexual orientation); the painful conflicts yet experienced over the power of language in specific worship settings; and a continued resistance to the legitimacy of women's experience as a source of religious revelation, imagery and/or insight.

[169] Pagels, Elaine. "What Became of God the Mother? Conflicting Images of God in Early Christianity." *Signs* 2 (1976): 293-303.
This article (which also appears in *Womanspirit Rising* [206]) accomplishes three things: First, it reviews the illustrations and examples of feminine religious language evident in early Christianity prior to the formalized dichotomy between Christian and Gnostic beliefs. Second, it illustrates the numerous leadership and charismatic roles of women in what came to be called "gnostic" communities (and as evidenced in what came to be called the Gnostic gospels). Last, it raises the profound question implied by such reviews: i.e., how did it happen that such female symbols and activities were lost to Christian memory--or perhaps deliberately suppressed by patriarchal forces-- until retrieved by the efforts of critical and historical studies such as Pagels' own? Pagels does not answer this question. Rather, she suggests that when with further investigation it is answered, the history of Christianity may never again be able to be told in the same way.

[170] Plaskow, Judith. "The Feminist Transformation of Theology." In *Beyond Androcentrism: New Essays on Women in Religion,* edited by Rita Gross, 23-24. Missoula, MT: Scholars Press, 1977.
This early essay by Plaskow attributes the beginnings of the American feminist theological movement to the publication of Valerie Saiving's essay, "The Human Situation: A Feminine View" [163], and Plaskow here highlights two implications of Saiving's discussion. First, that as Saiving argued, theology is rooted in the particularities of human experience and specifically *male* experience, such that women are marginalized and males sacralized. Second, that because feminist theology is both feminist *and* theological, it is caught within two inherent and ethically grounded tensions. These are that: (a) while "women's experience" may (and does) constitute a normative source for theological reflection, it also evidences racial, class and religious pluralisms to which feminist theology should but does not attend; and (b) because feminist theology must, by definition, speak about *God*, it must work to avoid an absolutizing of its own thought, since theology is always particularized in specific social/historical terms. Plaskow's own feminist theological work is extensive. Her dissertation [203] builds on Saiving's work as it addresses feminist theological method and women's studies in religion, while her subsequent work continues to ground the feminist theology/women's studies dialogue [340]. Last, her publications through the mid-1990s ground the development of Jewish feminist theology [953-955] and challenge Christian feminists to abandon anti-Jewish assumptions carried uncritically from traditional theological sources [968, 970-971].

[171] Ruether, Rosemary Radford, ed. *Religion and Sexism: Images of Woman in the Jewish and Christian Traditions.* New York: Simon and Schuster, 1974.
One of the earliest of the classic anthologies in the feminist theological movement, this volume is still a rich source of preliminary material on "images of women in Jewish and Christian traditions." Its eleven essays examine various perceptions of women held in biblical texts [377], the writings of "Church Fathers" [319], the Talmud [942], Roman Catholic Canon Law [775], the Protestant Reformers [311], and among mid-twentieth century Protestant theologians, Karl Barth and Paul Tillich. Last, Judith Plaskow's midrash, "The Coming of Lillith" (reprinted in [192]) closes the volume. The essays provide comprehensive and well supported overviews of their respective

subject areas, with each detailing sexist attitudes, misogynist teachings, theories and/or practices. Supplemental bibliography and a name/subject index close the text. An example of what Trible [356] and others describe as "documentation" literature, this text reflects the concerns evidenced by early writers seeking to maintain credibility in both feminist and religious communities.

[172] Ruether, Rosemary Radford. *New Woman-New Earth: Sexist Ideologies and Human Liberation.* New York: Seabury Press, 1975/Boston: Beacon Press, 1995. This early text by Ruether "...lay[s] the groundwork for recognizing the interrelationship between ideology and social structure in the history of sexism" (p. xiv). More pointedly, in eight chapters it summarizes and assesses: sexism and religious symbolization (including Old and New Testament perceptions of nature, social structure, dualism, and justice); the tensions of race, gender and class; the repressive functions of Mariological doctrine, Freudian and Jungian psychology; the failure of Marxist and socialist revolutions (in both Europe and China); and with all these, the gender significant changes borne of industrialization, the doctrine of the "two spheres" [81], 19th century feminism, and its capitulation to the racism of 19th century American politics. Last, in manners consistent with her entire career, it describes the dynamics of demonization (whether of Jews, women, Blacks or that which simply cannot be controlled) and the standard sexist assumptions underlying clericalism, ministry, and Christianity's historical bent toward dualism and the domination of nature. This is a clear and comprehensive introduction to Ruether's feminist thought. It synthesizes several classic and contemporary issues that have characterized feminist theology its development, and often well before such issues attained heightened academic expression. For key subsequent, related works by Ruether see [299], [326], [191], [192], [193], [808], [743], [235], and [760]. NOTE: In her "preface" to the twentieth anniversary edition of *New Woman-New Earth* (Beacon Press, 1995) Ruether sketches the lines of her academic development, and particularly in terms of this book's key emphases.

[173] Russell, Letty M. *Human Liberation in a Feminist Perspective--A Theology.* Philadelphia: Westminster Press, 1974. This early "feminist" theology by Russell evidences the many themes that will characterize her more developed feminist theological work. Among others, these include: (1) Russell's consistent effort at integrating feminist affirmations within the framework of traditional Protestant evangelical categories and (2) her search within biblical images and experience for a usable past and future. Hence in this early text Russell casts the equality of women and men within the context of God's revelation in Christ and the new humanity that, historically (given her premises) God's revelation in Christ promises. Second, this text consistently evidences Russell's commitment to openness, praxis and inclusivity as she applies the biblical concepts of freedom, liberation, and new humanity to not only the wide issues of gender and racial equality--in both the United States and "third" world countries--but to as well, such concrete concerns as the problems facing women seeking positions in ordained ministry, the balance of work and traditional gender expectations within the context of social and family life, and, third, the struggles of women to appropriate their autonomy and selfhood. Finally, this early text indicates key images that will ground Russell's subsequent work, *viz.*, those of an "open ecclesiology" (later the "household of freedom" [249] and the "church in the round" [250]); and second, the image of "partnership" as an integrating or coordinating feminist theological theme. Where this text differs from Russell's later work is in its *under*developed assumptions about the nature of authority as a vehicle of "power over" groups rather than a medium of empowerment within groups. This latter discussion happens in her essays on ministry [656] and hermeneutics [367]. To complete this brief notation on Russell's work: Two additional texts by Russell (but not abstracted in this volume) are *The Future of Partnership* and *Growth in Partnership*, both published through Westminster Press, in 1979 and 1981, respectively. These expand upon, but do not substantively alter Russell's initial discussion as presented here in *Human Liberation in a Feminist Perspective*.

[174] Russell, Letty M. *Liberating Word: A Guide to Nonsexist Interpretation of the Bible.* Philadelphia: Westminster Press, 1976. Four essays plus "Suggestions for Study and Action" comprise this early guide for "non-sexist interpretation of the Bible." The guide's targeted audiences are "women, men, youth, pastors and laity in churches, study groups, college students and seminarians" (p. 10), and its four contributors take the pedagogical needs of these groups to heart. First, Sharon Ringe's essay, "Biblical Authority and Interpretation," introduces the reader to such notions as biblical criticism, canonical texts, hermeneutics and the common humanity of both reader and author. Second, Elisabeth Schüssler Fiorenza's "Interpreting Patriarchal Traditions" [380] looks specifically at the patriarchal and androcentric assumptions of Old and New Testament texts and notes how several of those same

assumptions carry over into contemporary biblical scholarship. In clear terms it is statement of much that will be expanded in her later work. Third, Joanna Dewey's "Images of Women," again picks up on Old and New Testament texts, but here with an emphasis on pastoral applications rather than studied analyses. Last, in "Changing Language and the Church," Russell addresses specific vocabulary needs of congregations, and she presents clear rationales for changing verbal behaviors. A closing section, "Suggestions for Study and Action" provides review questions and suggestions for the learners' assimilation of essay insights.

[175] Schüssler Fiorenza, Elisabeth. "Feminist Theology as a Critical Theology of Liberation." *Theological Studies* 36 (1975): 605-626.
This article is Schüssler Fiorenza's earliest exposition of feminist theology as a "critical feminist liberation theology." Further, it serves as an abiding introduction to her subsequent work. After her brief opening comments, Schüssler Fiorenza begins with Paulo Friere's definition of oppression--it is that which "hinders the pursuit of [one's] self-affirmation as a responsible person...because it interferes with [one's] ontological and historical vocation to be more fully human..." (p. 606), and she moves to the feminist critique of culture and religion as holding up "denigrated," "infantilized," and "idealized" images of women that preclude women's development as "independent and free human persons." She then details various aspects of feminist theology as rootéd in the desire to reform the established traditions of androcentric theology and scholarship. Thus, feminist theology is "critical" because it challenges the androcentrism and false objectivities of both theological and revelatory language *and* the profession of theology itself, which--as white, middle class and male--has sustained androcentric patterns of church life and experience. Second, feminist theology is "liberationist," because as directed to the full realization of the Christian vision as practiced in the early Christian community and presented in Gal 3:27-28, feminist theology directs Christianity to an emancipatory praxis on behalf of women via the re-surfacing of women's historically suppressed leadership roles and the incorporation of women into positions of ordained leadership. Third, feminist theology is visionary, for like earlier theologies, it also incorporates myths and symbols--but here, myths and symbols empowering to women. Hence, as a fourth point, feminist theology must critique traditional Christian images of women--and specifically those of Mary as traditionally understood, while retrieving more realistic "Mary myths," such as those of Mary Magdeline who, as the first witness to the resurrection, was the "apostle to the apostles." The latter, notes Schüssler Fiorenza, is an historically documented example of the suppressed leadership of women in the early church, and thus it exemplifies the feminist biblical reconstruction that must occur if women are ever to be know their history and full equality within the Church. Still a powerful and engaging read, this essay previews virtually all of Schüssler Fiorenza's later work: her stress on critical hermeneutics and feminist exegesis, the feminist reconstruction of biblical texts, the meaning of women-church, and the role of theology vis a vis the church, society and the academy--and all with rigor, humor, and her own passion for the profession she so clearly has loved.

[176] Trible, Phyllis. "God, Nature of in the O.T." In *The Interpreter's Dictionary of the Bible, Supplementary Volume*, 368-369. Nashville: Abingdon Press, 1976.
In this essay Trible describes several passages that exhibit female imagery for God and preclude, thereby, the unrestricted portrayal of the OT god as male. These images are rooted in the Hebrew *rehem* (womb) as "a basic metaphor for divine compassion" (p. 368), and they extend through a variety of OT writings: e.g., "creedal affirmations (Ex. 34:6, 33:19)," "descriptions of God's saving acts (e.g., Ps. 111:4, Neh. 9:17)," "petitions for deliverance (Ps. 86:15)," "calls for repentance (Joel 2:13, Jonah 4:2)," proclamations of unmerited forgiveness (Pss. 78:38, 103:8)," and some prophetic statements (Jer. 12:15, 30:18 and 31:20). Similarly, related female images include *shadayim* (breasts, [Hos. 9:14]), birth pangs (Is. 51:2 and Job 38:29), YHWH's identification with "comfort" for Israel (Is. 66:9), and in Numbers 11:12, "conception," as attributed to God indirectly by Moses. Trible closes by recognizing that while both female and male images of the OT god are appropriate, the OT faith nevertheless knows the "inadequacy of all analogies to the freedom and transcendence of YHWH and...has no resting place in God the mother or in God the father" (p. 369).

C. Overviews and Critical Assessments: 1975-1979

[177] Christ, Carol P. "The New Feminist Theology: A Review of the Literature." *Religious Studies Review* 3 (1977): 203-212.
In *Beyond God the Father* [161] Mary Daly critiques Christianity on two fronts. First, its core symbolization is inherently and hopelessly patriarchal; second, the *character* of its God is also

hopelessly patriarchal. Author Christ accepts Daly's critique as normative and on its basis reviews and catalogues feminist theological writing through 1976 as either "reformist" or "revolutionary." Reformist writers are those who do not address Daly's critique. Rather, in varying degrees, they maintain the legitimacy of the biblical tradition and seek various modifications of it on behalf of the liberation of women. The early writings of Rosemary Radford Ruether [172] and Letty Russell [173] illustrate this approach. In contrast, "revolutionary" writers are those who utilize women's experience as a starting point for theology, rather than as a corrective to it is as the case with reformers; and included here (among others) are Christ's own early works (cf. [206]) and the writings of Judith Plaskow [203]. In turn, Schüssler Fiorenza's early hermeneutical work [380], while identified as reformist, is taken as a reformist-revolutionary bridge. To close, Christ describes early sources (including her own) in feminist spirituality.

[178] Driver, Anne Barstow. "Religion." *Signs* 2 (1976): 293-303
This article reviews material published primarily by Christian feminists during the period 1967-1975 to indicate "...materials that criticize...religious traditions and find them to be our most deep-seated causes of patriarchy" (p. 434). Additionally, Driver raises two questions through the literature under review: *viz.*, "Can one remain with the Christian or Jewish tradition once one becomes conscious of sexism?" and if not, "Can one create a new religion out of the materials of patriarchal tradition?" (p. 434). According to Barstow, the definitive answers to these questions are lacking, but because the literature on such related concerns as the anger and skepticism of women is not, it--together with the growing number of works on women in religious history may be, and are here, described. Overall, the review is exploratory, and it falls into what Trible and others have described as the documenting literature on misogyny and patriarchy [356]. The discussion provides easy entree into the literature and is recommended for those seeking an initial introduction.

[179] Heyward, Carter. "Speaking and Sparking, Building and Burning." *Christianity and Crisis* 39 (1979): 66-72.
In contrasting the works of Roman Catholic feminist theologians Rosemary Radford Ruether and Mary Daly, Heyward suggests that methodological and epistemological assumptions underlie their respective writings and that these lead to predictable outcomes--in the case of Ruether, a focus on 'dualism and polarities' as the problem to be overcome for both a theology and praxis of liberation, and in Daly's case, a retreat into the subjectivity of her own mythological world, a kind of Bultmannesque reversal. Heyward notes that both perspectives have implications for feminist theology in that they invite rage against misogynist structures (Daly) and the temporal commitment to attempt systemic changes in churches (Ruether). NOTE: This essay predates published accounts of the women-church movement and Ruether's theology of it (cf., e.g., [193]), but Heyward anticipates both: while applauding Ruether's liberation theology, Heyward notes that "Ruether's theological praxis is not yet as fundamentally critical of and offensive to Christians as it must become if she...[and others with her]...are effectively to challenge--and change...Christendom, even insofar as to create among ourselves within the church a community of powerful sisters" (p. 68). Ruether's published work to that time suggests that Heyward's judgment here is overstated, but few statements so clearly anticipate the women-church movement.

[180] Lee, Marie Irene. "Religion and the Socialization of Women: A Working Bibliography." *Listening* 13 (1978): 176-182.
This bibliography is a basic listing of the early theological and popularized interdisciplinary literature on gender and religious roles published through the late 1970s. Thus entries are limited to the early writings of Mary Daly, Rosemary Radford Ruether, Letty Russell, Leanard Swidler and Phyllis Trible, with works by Schüssler Fiorenza not included, since her work did not assume wide salience until the 1983 publication of *In Memory of Her* [195]. These limitations aside, researchers new to the study of feminism and Christian tradition will find this listing of 39 books and 37 articles useful. The entries are succinct, substantive, and accessible from such journals as *Christianity and Crisis, Commonweal, The Christian Century* and *The Ecumenist* to name but a few. Alternatively, for more advanced discussions, researchers should begin with Patrick [183], Weaver [762], Bass and Boyd [130], Finson [269], Musto [270], and ATLA [129].

[181] Murray, Pauli. "Black Theology and Feminist Theology: A Comparative Review." *Anglican Theological Review* 60 (1978): 3-24.
This article pre-dates the ethical, exegetical and theological work of womanist scholars across the board, but it is nonetheless a classic and will remain so for its analysis of liberation theology, Mary Daly and James Cone. Specifically, Murray summarizes the characteristic features of liberation theology, and she contrasts the liberation perspectives of Daly [161] and Cone (cf., e.g., [591])

as "ultraradical" thinkers. She argues that each addresses only one factor of oppression (either race or gender but not both) and neither addresses class exploitation. For her discussion of the interplay of these factors she follows Ruether's early work [172] on the "interstructuring of gender, race and class" and she points to the necessity for a multidimensional analysis. She closes with a call to the church to recognize and exorcise this interstructuring and a call to Black theology to realize the potential of a dialogue with feminist theology. Murray's background as a professor of law and politics at Brandeis prior to her work in theology is clear throughout this essay, and it lends a sociological realism to her analysis of the possibilities and limitations of a late 1970s Black theology/feminist theology dialogue.

[182] Patricca, Nicholas A. "Religion and the Socialization of Women." *Listening* 13 (1978): 93-99.
This article reflects upon a 1977 dialogue at Mundelein College between social scientist Helen Lopata and theologian Rosemary Radford Ruether. For the dialogue, Lopata had argued that female students of Catholic high schools have "less realistic life-line projections" than do their public school counterparts, in that Catholic females focus almost exclusively on becoming wives and mothers without recognizing either the possibility of other life-fulfilling roles or the temporary nature of wife/mother roles given the potentials of divorce, death, possible later career interests, and/or the eventual adulthood of children. Moreover, Lopata noted that since the Industrial Revolution, American society has, overall, romanticized the institution of the family and pressed the identity of women into this idealized, privatized sphere. By way of response, Ruether noted the differing effects of traditional and liberal religion on family structure. The former, she argued, aligns itself with established society, equates natural law and revelation, and sees the family in terms of patriarchal hierarchy and authority, while the latter views nature as a "dynamic process in which all persons are equal" (p. 97). The article closes with the author's reflections on the dialogue and its implications for understanding other aspects of Catholic organization and structure (*viz.*, the concept of "religious vocation," the loss of "the egalitarian spiritual life promised in the gospels... [and the rise of]... "patterns [that] assume the inferiority of women" [p. 97], and the inevitable conflicts feminist critique would have with religion, given the conservative social function of religion as described by Durkheim (i.e., that religion attempts to "make sacred and absolute the values of culture and to conform individual thinking and behavior to society"). NOTE: While not detailed here, Maryanne Sawicki's *Faith and Sexism: Guidelines for Religious Educators*. [New York: Seabury, 1979] presents 90 religious educational guidelines for incorporating egalitarian gender roles and linguistic inclusivity into various areas of Catholic doctrine and social teaching.

[183] Patrick, Anne E. "Women and Religion: A Survey of Significant Literature, 1965-1974." *Theological Studies* 36 (1975): 737-765.
Because it surveys literature published between 1964-1975, and because its principal sources are Roman Catholic, Patrick's essay serves as a solid introduction to the religious and theological concerns of Roman Catholic feminists during the important decade of "discernment" following the close of Vatican Council II in December, 1963. Additionally, because it is published in the December, 1975 "Women: New Directions" issue of *Theological Studies* [185], it permits contrast with other readily available discussions appearing in that same journal, and particularly those by Farley [166], Brown [389], O'Neill [293], Schüssler Fiorenza [175], Ruether [492], and Carroll [767]. For her discussion, Patrick surveys four types of literature: (1) general analyses of women in religion, an assessment of much ecumenical and secular literature; (2) historical analyses that take up biblical and ecclesial issues; (3) discussions of particular topics (including ministry, liturgy and ordination), and (4) "constructive efforts and radical challenges" in which Patrick discusses works by Rosemary Ruether, Letty Russell and Mary Daly. Although now an historical source, Patrick's discussion of ministry, ordination and "radical challenges" remains fresh, with Catholic feminist echoes well into the late 1990s.

[184] O'Connor, June. "Symposium: Toward a Theology of Feminism." *Horizons* 2 (1975): 103-124.
This symposium is in two parts: an opening essay by June O'Connor ["Liberation Theologies and the Women's Movement: Points of Comparison and Contrast"] and a series of brief and pointed responses to Mary Daly's *Beyond God the Father* [161]. Contributors include organizer O'Connor, and theologians Wilma G. von Jess, Elisabeth Schüssler Fiorenza, John E. Burkhart and last, Daly herself, as a respondent to her critics. O'Connor's lead essay contrasts Daly's "liberation" directed message with others from mid and late twentieth century theology. It highlights Daly's grounding emphasis that Christianity's doctrines of God, the Fall, and

Christology are patriarchal to the core (and have legitimated, thereby, an ethically horrible world for women), and it notes Daly's prophetic judgment of Christianity for such horror and her assessment of sexism as *the* root of social evil. Thus O'Connor asks: (1) whether Daly has not somehow compromised Christianity's central symbols and (2) whether the case *can* be made that sexism is the root cause of other social evils such as racism and genocide. Other essays vary in quality: von Jess attempts a widened understanding of "suffering servant" motifs vis a vis women; Schüssler Fiorenza suggests the category "friend" as a symbol for God; and Burkhart argues that Daly's text is really an "ad hominem" argument, since she uses her own experience as a norm for the theologizing process. These questions (and re Burkhart, one wants to say insults) aside, the participants all acknowledge the "brilliant" and "prophetic" qualities of Daly's work and the threatening implications it poses for Christianity if true. To respond, Day restates her "feminist" and "theological" perspective by reaffirming the legitimacy of women's experience as a source of truth and her suggestion that women's experience is viewable as a revelation of God as "Verb."

D. Journal Issues and Edited Collections

[185] Burghardt, Walter J., ed. "Women: New Dimensions." *Theological Studies* 36 (1975): 577-724.
This thematic issue of *Theological Studies* contains some of the most grounding of early Catholic feminist theological sources. Among these are Schüssler Fiorenza's first (and yet engaging) description of feminist theology as a critical theology of liberation [175]; Margaret Farley's deeply prophetic description of feminist ethics as grounded in relationality--and here with specific reference to trinitarian symbolism [166]; an equally prophetic discussion by Ruether on gender and work [492]; an early identification of sources important to feminist theological anthropology [293]; Raymond Brown's exegesis of "Roles of Women in the Fourth Gospel" [389]; and last, two excellent overviews of the early feminist theological literature on, respectively, "Women and Religion" (Patrick [183]), and "Women and Ministry" (Carroll [767]).

[186] Clark, Elizabeth, and Herbert Richardson, eds. *Women and Religion: A Feminist Sourcebook of Christian Thought.* New York: Harper & Row, 1977.
This 1977 anthology is an excellent source for feminist literature on women and religion through the early 1970s. Its twenty entries begin with excerpts from Aeschylus, the Old and New Testaments, and selected church fathers (Clement of Alexandria, Jerome and Augustine). They then continue with medievalists (Aquinas, Julien of Norwich and Margerie Kempe), the *Malleus Maleficarum*, and Luther's writings on marriage and creation. Selections from Milton's "The Doctrine and Discipline of Divorce," various Shaker sources, the writings of Schleiermacher and Baader, John Humphrey Noyes' "Bible Communism" [an Oneida community source], and the reformist and feminist writings of Sara Grimke and Elizabeth Cady Stanton bring one to the contemporary period. Closing excerpts range from such bedfellow discussions as Pius XII's "Casti Connubii" and Karl Barth's theology of creation, to Mary Daly's "The Woman's Movement: an Exodus Community." This text is similar to what Ruether [132] terms a "documentary history," an anthology of critical commentary on sources excerpted and appended to their commentary discussions. The editors' detailed introduction and chapter endnotes are useful and informative, but the text lacks indices and supplemental bibliography.

[187] Gross, Rita, ed. *Beyond Androcentrism: New Essays on Women and Religion.* Missoula, MT: Scholars Press, 1977.
This early anthology on feminist method in both theology and the history of religions contains several essays describing the assumptions of androcentrism in biblical exegesis, in various American and cross-cultural religious settings, and in the use of feminist language for "constructs of ultimacy." Gross's introductory essay is especially helpful as it details the three assumptions of androcentric scholarship: *viz.*, the identification of the human norm with that of male experience, the subsequent marginalization of women, and the ontological and epistemic exclusion of women from philosophical and theoretical discourse). Also notable is Judith Plaskow's discussion on feminism and method in theology [170]. NOTE: For more recent literature on gender and the "history of religion/religious studies" literature, see Carol Christ, "Mircea Eliade and the Feminist Paradigm Shift" [337] and see Christ's essay in Kramerae and Spender [66].

[188] Kerr, Hugh T., ed. "In Christ...Neither Male Nor Female." *Theology Today* 34 (1978): 353-465.
This "special issue" of *Theology Today* presents seven position papers first presented at an interdenominational "In Christ...Neither Male Nor Female" Symposium held Nov. 3-4, 1977 in

Chicago and sponsored jointly by the "Council of Theological Seminaries" and the "Council on Women and the Church," both organizations of the United Presbyterian Church (p. 357). While now well surpassed by much subsequent literature, the papers remain as evidence of forward looking efforts on the part of churches to respond to "changes which will occur as women assume larger roles as clergy and lay leaders." Overall, the papers identify the needs of churches to: (1) develop inclusive and liberating biblical and theological anthropologies; (2) identify (and abandon) class and sex-based groundings of clergy roles and clergy role expectations; and (3) respond positively to the potential of the women's movement for the churches, with that potential identified variously by differing symposium contributors. Additional features in this issue include selected book reviews on women and religion and a series of anecdotal discussions grouped as "Women and the Pastorate" in which four clergywomen speak variously of gender and ministry, and the conflicts and opportunities such statuses hold.

NOTE: For other early and influential sources cited elsewhere in the bibliogaphy, see Goldenberg [139], Chambers and Chalfant [138], and Scanzoni and Mollenkott [574].

6

Core and Discipline
Defining Works
(1978–1985)

This chapter presents the core and discipline defining feminist theological works published between 1978 and 1985, which, together with the literature from the previous chapter, ground the reader for current sources and the topical literatures presented later in the bibliography. The early critical responses to these core sources are also surveyed (e.g., Grant **[214]**, Heyward and Hunt **[217]** and Kwok **[219]**).

Several emphases characterize these core sources. First, there is a decreasing salience of affiliational and/or denominational heritage relative to particular topics, such that a topic would be perceived as a specifically denominational (i.e., "Protestant" or "Catholic") issue. At the same time, there is the increased salience of collaboration as a feminist theological value. These shifts do not mean that inherited traditions are without value or impact. Rather, they suggest that--at least initially--the bridge of "women's experience" cuts across various aspects of male histories and theologies, and that this widening of horizons is recognized as a necessary and legitimate theological development. Put differently, this literature responds to the questions of how and in what ways women's experience is a theological resource, both in terms of the developing autonomy of women's spirituality, and the legitimacy of one's gendered-religious experience *and* the traditions of one's early and/or professional socialization. These emphases are evident in various biblical and systematic works published through 1985 (cf. Trible **[205]**, Schüssler Fiorenza **[194]**, **[195]**, **[196]**, Borressen **[189]**, Ruether **[190]**, **[191]**, **[192]**, **[193]**, Heyward **[198]**, McFague **[200]**, Plaskow **[203]**). They are also evident in the many edited and multiply authored works published during these years (e.g., Christ and Plaskow **[206]**, Harrison and Robb **[207]**, Ruether and McLaughlin **[209]**, Russell **[210]**, and Weidman **[213]**).

A third and related characteristic of this literature is its growing recognition of the tensions inherent in its acknowledged but not fully appropriated "multicultural" or pluralized social base. These tensions present conceptual and methodological challenges to feminist theology, both because stated positions and individual theologians carry uncritically held assumptions about "otherness" within their works (e.g., Grant **[214]** and Kwok **[219]**, and see Kalven and Buckley **[208]**) and because these premises are socially embedded within the profession of theology itself (cf. **[807]**, and see the literature in Chapter 20 on "Feminist Theology, the Academy and Theological Education."). The sources below reflect these varying concerns, with single-authored works presented first, and edited and/or multiply authored works then following.

Some final notes about the literature of this period: First, almost all of the topical literatures in feminist theology take shape in this period (e.g., feminist theology's formal methodological pieces, the early literature on women's spirituality, feminist biblical studies and feminist theology's critique of heterosexism), but because each of these literatures really *is* a topic in its own right, they are presented in Section III of the bibliography. (See for example, Chapters 9, 10, 14, and 15 respectively.) Second, while the main sources by such key thinkers as Beverly Harrison, Carter Heyward, Judith Plaskow, Rosemary Radford Ruether, Letty Russell, Elisabeth Schüssler Fiorenza and Phyllis Trible are all presented in this chapter, the reader is urged to consult the *Author Index* for the full listings for each of these authors, since their works cover such varying ranges of concern. Third and last, although they are few in number, the four journals most associated with feminist theology, i.e., *Daughters of Sarah* **[225]**, the *Journal of Feminist Studies in Religion* **[226]**, the *Journal of Women and Religion* **[227]**, and the Jewish feminist publication

Lillith [228], are also abstracted in this chapter, with the discussion of other journals noted in the general introducation, and with a listing of thematic journal issues listed in the "Subject Index."

A. Core Sources (1978-1985)

1. Roman Catholic Authors

[189] Borresen, Elizabeth Kari. *Subordination and Equivalence.* Lanham, MD: Univ. Press of America, 1981.
Together with Plaskow's *Sex, Sin and Grace* [203] and selected items from Ruether's 1974 anthology [171] this volume sets the framework for the feminist analysis of classical Roman Catholic--and ultimately Western--theological anthropology. Borresen examines and assesses the "nature and role of women" in Augustine and Thomas Aquinas, with attention directed specifically to the identification of androcentrism as the grounding premise for each as they discuss: "the order of creation," "the penalty of sin," and last, the "order of salvation." Two concepts facilitate Borresen's discussion. These are "subordination" and "equivalence," with the first identified (in both Augustine and Thomas) as an assumption about female identity (women) in "the order of creation," and the second, an assumption for both women and men (humanity) in the "order of salvation." In a closing discussion, Borresen relates both concepts to 20th century Catholic moral teachings on marriage, celibacy and sexuality, and she highlights their relevance for theological and ecclesiastical understanding(s) as evidenced in *Humanae Vitae* and *Inter insigniores.* Borresen's text identifies an important pattern in Catholic and Protestant traditions in that each variously affirms the *spiritual* equality of women and men (that is, equivalency in the "order of redemption"), while equivocating theologically about the social and historical equality of women and men (i.e., equivalency in the "order of creation"). **NOTE**: See the following by Borresen (but not abstracted here): *Images of God and Gender Models in Judeo-Christian Tradition* [Philadelphia, PA: Fortress, 1995] and see Kari Vogt and E. K. Borresen, eds., *Women's Studies in Christian and Islamic Traditions: Ancient, Medieval and Renaissance Foremothers* [Kluwer Academic:1993].

[190] Ruether, Rosemary Radford. *Sexism and God-Talk: Toward a Feminist Theology.* Boston: Beacon Press, 1983/1993.
This text is among the most noted in the literature of feminism and Christian tradition. It covers a variety of topics from within a formal feminist theological perspective, and it evidences the consistent use of what Ruether terms "the critical principle of feminist theology" or "the promotion of the full humanity of women" from within a formally theological framework. At its widest level, this principle recognizes both feminism and women's experience as sources of power and insight suitable to the tasks of systematic theology, and thus: "Whatever denies, diminishes or distorts the full humanity of women is...appraised as not redemptive... [while]...what does promote the full humanity of women is of the Holy" (pp. 18-19). Moreover, as it is brought to bear on such standard theological topics as theological method, God language, creation, theological anthropology, Christology, Mariology, ecclesiology, soteriology, sin, ministry, and redemption and eschatology, it permits a reconstruction of much Christian dogma as redemptive for women: e.g., (1) God is renamed as "God/ess," an unpronounceable symbol that preserves several prophetic and liberationist emphases of the biblical literature; (2) marginalizing and/or dehumanizing Christologies are identified and critiqued; (3) "Christic personhood" is subsequently identified as a dynamic perception of "Christ, as [both] redemptive person and Word of God" (p. 138); and as a last illustration, (4) the biblical image, "a new earth" is identified as the transcendent endpoint of humanity's ultimate liberation from patriarchy. This is an important text. It links Ruether's earlier work with her subsequent publications (see, for example, her 1975 *New Woman/New Earth* [172] and her 1993 *Gaia & God* [235]), and it formalizes several themes central to her thought, including Ruether's consistent effort to view Christianity in universal rather than parochial and ethnocentric terms and her ongoing attention to eschatology in Christianity's struggles with issues of justice, redemption and social kenosis. Although criticized extensively by fundamentalist and antifeminist writers (cf. [842]) it remains an important starting point for ecumenical and feminist conversation across denominations and feminist traditions. **NOTE**: In her re-release of this text in 1993, Ruether's new introduction traces her own theological development, together with her reflections on feminist theology's methodological and multicultural issues of the '80s and early '90s. Last, it states her own vision of how theological reflection, in fact, proceeds. It does not

begin with methodologies or other abstractions. Rather, as she recalls from one of her early professors, there is "First the God, then the song, and then the story..." (p. xvii).

[191] Ruether, Rosemary Radford. *To Change the World*. New York: Crossroad, 1983. Five essays, each a compact statement of Ruether's thinking, theology, and faith relative to Christology and selected ethical issues, comprise this text. First, in "Jesus and the Revolutionaries: Political Theology and Biblical Hermeneutics," Ruether criticizes the dualistic eschatology implicit in Oscar Cullman's christology to argue that "reconciliation with God means the revolutionizing of human social, political relations...[and]...over-throwing unjust, oppressive relationships" (p. 11). Second, in "Christology and Latin American Liberation Theology," Ruether continues this historical, redemptive emphasis by examining the contexts and advocacy theologies of liberation theologians Leanardo Boff, Jon Sobrina, and Jose Miranda. What distinguishes liberation theology, says Ruether, is that it "restores the kingdom to the centre of the gospel" and opens wide the possibility for the church to critique social sin as a sin of "collective and institutionalized violence and greed" (p. 25). In her third essay, "Christology and Jewish-Christian Relations," Ruether reaffirms her long-standing opposition to anti-Semitism (cf. **[440]** and see **[299]**). She examines three theological patterns that promote anti-Judaism" (p. 33) and she exposes their roots in the 'final/fulfillment' assumptions of traditional christology. Fourth, in "Christology and Feminism: Can a Male Savior Save Women?" **[441]** Ruether tracks the anti-women bias of christology and considers such alternative Christological images as the "androgenous" Christ and the "prophetic/iconoclastic" Christ. Finally, in "Ecology and Human Liberation: A Conflict between the Theology of History and the Theology of Nature" **[567]**, Ruether's emphasis on mutuality is extended through all the earth, with specific emphasis on eco-justice and the ideological critique of industrial and scientific domination(s).

[192] Ruether, Rosemary Radford. *Womanguides: Readings Toward a Feminist Theology*. Boston: Beacon Press, 1985/1996.
A quotation from her introduction to this collection--that "feminist theology cannot be done from the existing base of the Christian Bible" is often what one reads of this volume as commentators and critics assess it. But the quotation itself should not be read too rigidly, as if presented within a gestalt that jettisons rather than amplifies "the existing base of the Christian Bible." For that, in fact, is what the texts within *Womanguides* are about: they are selections from several sources, but largely the margins (and at times the centers) "...of that cultural matrix that has shaped Western Christianity: the ancient Near East, the Hebrews, the Greeks, the New Testament...[and]...marginated communities at the edges of Judaism and Christianity" (p. xi). It is a stimulating collection designed to jar imaginations and forgotten memories along twelve topics of religious symbolization: "Gender Imagery for God/dess;" "The Divine Pleroma;" "Stories of Creation;" "Humanity...", "The Origins of Evil;" "Redeemer/Redemptrix..." and so forth, right up through "New Beginnings," a category comprised by selections from two of Ruether's graduate students at the time of publication. This text is a valuable resource in at least four ways. First, it gathers a variety of important selections together into one volume. Second, the brief introductions to its twelve topics well synthesize Ruether's own work as it crystallized in the mid-1980s (cf. her feminist systematics **[190]** and the regathered themes from *New Woman/New Earth*). Third, these topics unfold her women-church and eco-feminist perspectives. Last, as with all of Ruether's works, the notes, bibliography and general index are clear and helpfully done. **NOTE**: In her re-release of this volume in 1996, Ruether relocates the collection within the wider frames of feminist theological history through the mid-90s, which she describes as midrashim similar to the early, but patriarchally thwarted, canonization of Christian Scripture. Thus feminist theology creates new "touchstones," that " must be open to criticism...particularly by those who have not yet been heard, by new voices that reveal how the liberative claims for some are nevertheless oppressive for others." Second, feminist theology must recognize that "there is no definitive end to this process...[but that]...the process is itself the end" (p. xiv).

[193] Ruether, Rosemary Radford. *Women-Church: Theory and Practice*. San Francisco: Harper & Row, 1985.
The first half of this two-part volume is "theoretical," with five essays describing the history and emphases of "women-church" as an evolving theological symbol. Specifically, Ruether surveys: (1) the genesis of women-church in the tensions between women's experience and Christianity as an androcentric and institutionally sexist church; (2) the mutual concern of religious and secular feminisms for communities genuinely respectful of women and women's experience; (3) male patriarchy within the institutional and theological notions of the church as 'ecclesia;' and (4-5) the "marks of the church" as "women-church." These last essays discuss both the exodus of women

out of patriarchy and the concrete "ministerial" needs that characterize the community called "women-church." These needs include: (i) a feminist, critical study and re-construction of Christianity's core symbols; (ii) community organizers and administrators; (iii) a communalization of roles and religious norms; and (iv) the need for liturgies and worship borne of and for the experience(s) of women. The second part of this text then presents a wide range of liturgies and celebration (complete with music and reflective commentary) that mark Christianity's justice traditions and the experience of women. These liturgies include rites of community celebration, rituals to help heal from patriarchal violence, rites of passage celebrating the life cycle, and among others, "seasonal celebrations" for events of cultural and social transformation. A final important feature of this text is its clear understanding of clericalism as not merely religious elitism, but rather, *"the relationship of a dependent adult to a dominant adult being assimilated into that of a child to a male parent... "* (p. 76). Endnotes, additional bibliography, and a subject index close the volume.

[194] Schüssler Fiorenza, Elisabeth. "You Are Not To Be Called Father: Early Christian History in a Feminist Perspective." *Cross Currents* 29 (1979): 301-323.
Of her early articles that address androcentrism as a grounding perspective in Christianity's beginnings, this is the most clearly developed and cogently argued. It may be summarized in terms of fiye main points. First, Schüssler Fiorenza introduces her task. It is the presentation of an interpretive model that can account for the possibility of women's autonomous leadership in the New Testament community. That such a model is needed and is a legitimate subject of New Testament scholarship derives from the facts that (i) all biblical scholarship is an attempt at ecclesial-political relevance for the contemporary Christian community and (ii) the women's movement has raised this issue. That women's leadership roles in the New Testament have previously been marginalized, however, is Schüssler Fiorenza's second point, for both androcentric interpretation and redaction have governed the study of NT texts. To illustrate this point, Schüssler Fiorenza identifies three ways in which androcentric redacting has been enhanced by like-minded translation and interpretation: first, key women's names have been masculinized in translation (e.g., Junia has become Junianus); second, key nouns indicating leadership roles have been feminized in translation (e.g., *diakonos* remains deacon for Paul, but is deaconess--with modern stereotypical assumptions--when applied, say, to Pheobe); third, contemporary exegesis evidences differential translations of masculine nouns with inclusive translations applying to group designations and [male] gender selectivity applying to individuals in authority positions. Such androcentric bias is also evident in the canonization of New Testament writings--Schüssler Fiorenza's third point--for where the New Testament exhibits obvious testimonies to women's leadership (e.g., in John and Paul), such testimonies are--in the patristic literature--discredited. The vehicle for this discrediting process is an "orthodoxy-heresy" model that governs the development of the New Testament canon and within which women's leadership is identified as heretical by virtue of its association with gnostic/charismatic motifs. To return to the question of accommodation and address the status of women in the Pastorals--her fourth main point--and specifically the "household codes" (e.g., I Tim. 2:19-15), Schüssler Fiorenza assesses the adequacy of G. Thiessen's "love-patriarchalism" model for New Testament beginnings. Like the orthodoxy-heresy model, this too, marginalizes women's religious leadership, but differently. Specifically, because this model argues the historical *necessity* of Christianity's patriarchal accommodation to Roman society and authority (when other albeit suspect egalitarian models were available), it presumes the theological credibility of the orthodoxy-heresy model. But this credibility is lacking, and the "love patriarchalism" model should be rejected. Therefore, to incorporate adequately both the Synoptic testimonies of Jesus' acceptance of women as disciples and the evidences of women's religious leadership found in John and Paul, Schüssler Fiorenza introduces an "egalitarian-conflict" model that identifies Christianity as a counter-cultural movement open to all of biblical society's outcasts as persons equal before God, both socially and theologically. For Schüssler Fiorenza, this model more accurately accounts for the New Testament "data" and it can better serve the emancipatory praxis of a contemporary church identifying itself with the New Testament/biblical heritage.

[195] Schüssler Fiorenza, Elisabeth. *In Memory of Her: A Feminist Theological Reconstruction of Christian Origins.* New York: Crossroad, 1983/1995.
This text synthesizes Schüssler Fiorenza's early feminist biblical and theological works (including [194] above), and it provides the transition to her fully critical feminist hermeneutical method as it links to and/or addresses questions of feminist theology's audience(s) and ecclesial and professional reference groups. It develops in three parts. In Part I Schüssler Fiorenza indicates the methodological needs for a feminist critical hermeneutics of liberation. She thus reviews: (1) the methodological inadequacies of various earlier feminist biblical critiques (i.e., secular, neo-orthodox and "sociology of knowledge" approaches); (2) the prevalence of androcentrism and

patriarchal norms in both the canonization of historical translations and subsequent professional literatures; and (3) and social world of the early Christians, as evidenced through recent sociological and women's studies perspectives, respectively. Her overall review establishes the methodological need to read the "silences" in the literature which open out the possibility for recognizing that women were a fully contributing and leadership population in the early years of both the Jesus movement in Jerusalem and the [Pauline] Christian missionary movement through the Greco-Roman world. Parts II and III of her text then make the case. Thus, in Part II Schüssler Fiorenza surveys the exegetical literatures relevant to these methodological needs, as (across three chapters) she addresses: (1) the social implications of inclusivity inherent in both the praxis and basaleia vision of Jesus and the Sophia symbolism identifying the Jesus' movement's community's norms; (2) the social and organizational development of Christianity's "house churches," missionary roles, and theological self-understanding (in which women play obviously enormous but often overlooked parts); and (3) the Pauline mixed bag construction of Galatians 3:28 ("neither male nor female") which affirms the religious and social equality of women and men across the Christian community, while yet restricting the religious roles of *wives* within mission-directed organizational needs. Part III of the text then summarizes Christianity's historical sex-typing of formal leadership roles (a process Schüssler Fiorenza presents as the "patriarchalization of church and ministers," and the "genderization of ecclesial office"), and a "Closing Postscript" identifies "ecclesia of women" as the basis for a feminist biblical spirituality. This is a sophisticated text which has well earned its reputation as a "classic." It is not beyond the grasp of beginning readers, but because it presumes the ability to dialogue with the various portions of established biblical-exegetical literatures, beginners might want to consult Schüssler Fiorenza's many individual articles presented in Chapter 10 of the bibliography. (See the Index for her full listing). Additionally, readers should see Schüssler Fiorenza's own reconsideration of this text (together with her customary review of the relevant literatures and comprehensive footnote citations) in her "Introduction to the Tenth Anniversary Edition."

[196] Schüssler Fiorenza, Elisabeth. *Bread Not Stone: The Challenge of Feminist Biblical Interpretation*. Boston: Beacon Press, 1984.
This collection of six essays unfolds the grounding assumptions of Schüssler Fiorenza's *feminist, critical theology of liberation* by contrasting the emphases of the latter with such alternative positions as Latin American liberation theology and the historical critical method of biblical interpretation. Generally speaking, the volume argues as a whole that: (1) a *feminist* critical theology of liberation is rooted in the experience of women, as women appropriate the Bible and its non-sexist texts; (2) a feminist *critical* theology of liberation is critical of its own methodological assumptions, including those of biblical scholarship that yet provide a conduit for transmission or legitimation of the Bible's patriarchal teaching and/or continued use as a tool of patriarchy; (3) a feminist critical *theology* of liberation is a specifically theological enterprise in that it speaks words of salvation to the faith community and (4) is accountable (as should be all biblical theological writing) both to the academic community (because of its critical methodological assumptions) and to the community of faith since the Bible is yet acknowledged as the community's founding document and norm of faith. All of the six essays presented in *Bread Not Stone* have either been previously published or presented as papers under differing titles, and each is abstracted (or discussed) in the present volume. See **[369]**, **[411]**, **[412]**, **[413]**, **[483]**.

NOTE: For additional work published by Roman Catholic feminists during this time period, see Collins **[517]**, Johnson **[421]** and **[438]**), and Weaver **[762]**, as well as the general literature in Chapter 19 on "Feminism and Women's Leadership in American Catholicism." Additionally, for backlash responses to the literature, see the entries in Chapter 21 on "Antifeminism and Antifeminist Theology."

2.   Protestant, Evangelical and Jewish Authors

[197] Davaney, Sheila Greeve, ed. *Feminism and Process Thought*. New York: Edwin Mellen Press, 1981.
This volume presents five papers delivered at the Harvard Divinity School in 1978 under the sponsorship of the Harvard Divinity School/Claremont Center for Process Studies. Davaney introduces the papers with an overview of themes common to both feminism and process thought. These include their mutual challenge of dualities and hierarchical patterns in social organization and philosophical analysis, and their similar affirmations of historicity, sociality, and the conditioned nature of human freedom. Additionally, Davaney summarizes Whitehead's philosophy, and she offers two suggestions concerning feminism's contribution to process thought: (1) not only can the

articulation of women's experience from within process categories provide a test of the latter's openness, but (2) the inclusion of women's experience into process categories can help overcome the latter's androcentrism. Subsequent contributors then address individualism and relationality (Valerie Saiving); the possibilities of mutual dialogue between process and feminist perspectives (J. Cobb); "openness and mutuality" (M. Suchocki); female experience and sexuality (P. Washbourn); and choices about pregnancy and abortion (J. Lambert). Endnotes follow the essays, but the volume lacks indices and supplemental bibliography.

[198] Heyward, Carter. *The Redemption of God: A Theology of Mutual Relation.* Lanham, MD: Univ. Press of America, 1982.
Originally Heyward's doctoral dissertation, this discussion is the grounding source for much feminist theological literature on concept of relationality, and particularly in the area of feminist social ethics. In five chapters Heyward movingly synthesizes questions of eschatology, christology, theodicy, justice as "right-relation," Christianity's moral failure in the face of the Holocaust, and all of these as grounded in Martin Buber's adamant affirmation--which Heyward shares--that "In the beginning is relation." Heyward addresses particularly the christologies (and eschatologies) of Irenaeus and Augustine, and she fits her critique of these christologies against the ethical challenges of Elie Wiesel's *Night* and related writings. Her analysis moves ultimately to an affirmation of panentheism and a christology directed ultimately to the praxis of historically real and politically visible liberation from unjust social structures--to God as "the power in relation." Similarly, Heyward's eschatology brooks no abstraction from the justice that must come to characterize concrete human relations, and in a closing epilogue Heyward responds directly to Wiesel's witness that "everything is question." A series of appendices addressing several issues ranging from feminism and sexuality to the concept of relation as understood in Council of Chalcedon further unfold the elements of her discussion, and they expand in expositional form what has frequently been cast in the text in existential and poetic form. This is a provocative and powerfully written text. It intimates much of Heyward's later work in ethics and Christology, and it remains, for many, the grounding source for feminist writing on God as "the power of relation" and justice as "right-relation."

[199] Heyward, Carter. *Our Passion for Justice: Images of Power, Sexuality, and Liberation.* New York: Pilgrim, 1984.
This collection of thirty "essays, addresses, sermons, homilies and liturgical prayers" prepared by Heyward during the years 1977-1983 provides an important, extended introduction to her more widely directed journal literature that critiques the social organizational assumptions of Protestant and Catholic thought, whether feminist, patriarchal or simply generically androcentric. The essays are organized thematically around four emphases that reflect the broadening scope of her work: an early commitment to the critique of patriarchal religious authority, whether in doctrine, religious organization or conventional sexuality; an embrace of moral passion (sexual, intellectual and emotional) as the grounding of human connectedness; an articulation of that passion as present in liberationist experience, existential wholeness and embodied spirituality; and last, a critique of liberalism (political, social and religious) for its almost narcotic like lack of such passion. Readers interested Heyward's specific analyses of feminism will want to consult the essays on feminist theology and philosophy per se, together with her entries on lesbianism, sexuality and commitment. However, none of these thirty entries lacks a "specifically feminist" emphasis, for Heyward's thought here is deeply integrated from beginning to end, and its "development" (as evidenced in these essays) reflects more an amplification of specific themes than the addition of new topics. It is a powerful collection, worthy in its own right, and clearly indicative of her more formal and extended analyses. For her additional work see **[179]**, **[198]**, **[216]**, **[217]**, **[242]**, and Davis's editing of her sermons in **[435]**. Additionally, see **[437]**, **[555]** and **[867]**.

[200] McFague, Sallie. *Metaphorical Theology: Models of God in Religious Language.* Philadelphia: Fortress, 1982.
McFague's purpose here is two-fold. She seeks, first, to establish metaphorical theology as a viable approach to the needs of twentieth century [Christian] experience, and particularly the experience(s) of those historically excluded from religious and theological involvement, i.e., women. Second, she seeks to demonstrate the value of friendship as a primary, although not exclusive, model for describing divine human interaction. The discussion develops in five chapters. Chapter one introduces McFague's main purpose by detailing several features prominent in contemporary theology, including the need for relevance and meaningfulness in religious language (as evidenced by various Protestant and Catholic discussions of theological method), the developing emphases of "parabolic" rather than incarnational Christology, and last, the feminist critique of patriarchy as a

framework for both religious (God 'the father') and social relations. Chapter two then explores the metaphor of Christ as the Parable of God, while chapters three and four summarize the use of models, paradigms and metaphors in both scientific and religious languages. Last, chapter five presents a "thought experiment" for the reader: an exploration into the contrasting implications of fatherhood and friendship as models for divine-human interaction, with the former exposed as language that has come to function idolatrously rather than meaningfully, and the latter as language that is inclusive, open-ended, transformative and empowering. NOTE: This text is largely methodological, and while it grounds McFague's initial "thought experiment," her wider discussion of the "friend" model is [244]. Also, for her discussion of creation as the "Body of God" see [245].

[201] Mollenkott, Virginia Ramey. *The Divine Feminine: Biblical Imagery of God as Female*. New York: Crossroad, 1983.
This text synthesizes early evangelical work identifying "non-sexist" biblical images of God. In it, Mollenkott acknowledges that sexist God imagery within the Bible has generated "the view that the Bible is the natural enemy of all womankind" (p. 6), but she urges a more optimistic and relationally grounded view of transcendence and its symbolization vis a vis women. To make her case, Mollenkott cites numerous "non-sexist," "inclusive" biblical images of God, but particularly God images that include: women giving birth (Is. 42:16; Acts 17:26, 28); women nursing (Is. 49:15 and Hos. 11:3-4); God as bakerwoman (Mt. 13:33); God as a female homemaker (Ps. 123); and God as Dame Wisdom (Wis. 1:6-7 and Prov. 8:22). It is best read with Mollenkott's subsequent work, and particularly [246] and [247].

[202] Morton, Nelle. *The Journey is Home*. Boston: Beacon Press, 1985.
One of the most important voices within the development of feminist theology, the late Nelle Morton wrote consistently about the power of language--images, symbols, words, stories, metaphors and myths--both to shape and create personal and social experience and the movement of people through both, to both. Hence the special importance of this text, for it brings together ten essays by Morton, all published previously between 1970-1984 (cf. e.g., [162]), but now gathered here and edited by Morton to synthesize her work and her hopes for those either beginning or well along their journey to feminist perception. Morton is frank about the difficulty of wresting one's self from patriarchy and its encompassing imageries, and particularly the difficulty for those who take church life and experience seriously. Thus, she writes for three distinct and at times disparate audiences: feminists who have "washed their hands of religion" because of their many painful experiences from it; feminist laywomen who are entering seminary and who may, thereby, work for the reconstruction of Christianity away from patriarchy ("stone by stone"); and third, lesbian women: women who are in all respects similar to the first two groups, save for the fact that homophobia has found its home in patriarchal Christianity and particularly its institutions of ministry and theological education. Each of these groups, together with the men who sympathize with them, is the audience of this text and its discussions of: (1) patriarchy and language--how patriarchy subverts preaching, the theologizing process and the access of people to their history and experience; and (2) the words of connection, of spirituality and of goddess that women are now learning to speak. This is a moving and thoughtful text. It brims with insight and compassion, and particularly in its appendix of "journal jottings" excerpted from Morton's own long struggle for feminist voice and the singularity of insight to be held when one bypasses footnotes, citations and other such specifics.

[203] Plaskow, Judith. *Sex, Sin and Grace*. Lanham, MD: Univ. Press of America, 1980.
This text is Plaskow's doctoral dissertation, a study articulating the impact of gender on the theologizing process, as evidenced by the assumptions attached to the concepts of "sin" and "grace" in the writings of Reinhold Niebuhr and Paul Tillich. By way of overview, Plaskow first examines the concept of "women's experience," both to demonstrate its consistent casting in culturally concrete assumptions and further, the specific assumptions (such as, e.g., passivity) that are identified with femaleness in American culture. Her principle sources here are the writings of Doris Lessing, and for her prototype of women's experience Plaskow takes the literary character of Martha Quest. Plaskow's second methodological step entails the description of "sin" and "grace" as found specifically in the writings of Niebuhr and Tillich, and as doctrines that are also culturally cast, but here with respect to the assumptions congruent with male experience, with the latter as normative for all human experience. Her final methodological step is the identification of various latent functions that are served in the casting of sin as "hubris" or pride (Niebuhr) and "estrangement, hubris and concupiscence" (Tillich). In brief, selfhood--as identifiable through

women's experience--is essentially omitted from discussion by these theologians, or more accurately, is relegated to a secondary ("Other") position, such that dialectical aspects of sin and selfhood remain suppressed from perception. Similarly, in the articulation of "grace" by these theologians, the assumptions of maleness preclude women as valuable bearers of salvific insight, and as with the concept sin, women remain marginalized: effectively unable to sin and needing salvation almost as if by proxy. Likewise, to the extent that the development of selfhood in women is suppressed, women do not recognize their real sin of non-development. This is a complex but clearly written study, and Plaskow draws out several implications for doctrines related to both sin and grace. It is an important analysis: both methodologically for its contribution to Christian feminist theological anthropology, and second, for its interdisciplinary grounding as a framework for all of Plaskow's work--as a women's studies scholar [340], a feminist theologian speaking to and within Judaism [953, 954, 955], and to and within the dialogue between Jewish and Christian feminist theologians [970-971] and [262].

[204] Soelle, Dorothee. *The Strength of the Weak: Towards a Christian Feminist Identity.*
    Philadelphia: Westminster, 1984.
Readers interested in exploring the interplay between experience, spirituality (described here by Soelle as mysticism), feminism and the struggles of post-World War II Christian theology, will find Soelle's text rewarding, informative and inspiring. The bulk of the 15 essays and/or sermons reprinted here date largely from the 1970s, but are translated and collected here because of their yet relevant recurring and prophetic themes: a critique of bourgeois society and its concomitant alienation; a critique of patriarchy and the need for feminine language for God; a critique of the "culture of obedience" that ties bourgeois and patriarchal thought together; the meaning of "work" in the oppression of women and men; and, last, a strong challenge to traditional religion to rethink its "father" and familistic language in the light of language borne of women's religious and secular experience. **NOTE:** Also by Soelle are [426] and [557].

[205] Trible, Phyllis. *God and the Rhetoric of Sexuality.* Philadelphia, PA: Fortress,
    1978.
Without doubt, this text is and will remain one of feminist theology's grounding classics, both for the methodology it exhibits and the exegesis it unfolds. Trible begins by introducing the reader to the idea that "The Bible is a pilgrim wandering through history to merge past and present..." (p. 1), and she notes its capacity to leave readers the clues necessary for its interpretation. These clues are diverse, and they include: *hermeneutical clues* ("clues within the text...[and]...clues between the text and the world"); *methodological clues* (i.e., clues from the "conventions" of form, narrative, poetry, metaphor, rhetoric and style); and last, *topical clues*, or the clues of "context," "text[s] within context[s]," and the subtexts of texts as metaphors. Each and all of these "clues" help to bridge the Bible's ability to interpret its readers and be interpreted by them. Further, when used with other interpretive strategies (and good writing), they help jettison conventional assumptions about human sexuality not actually supportable by the biblical text. The listing of these assumptions occurs in several shorter pieces by Trible ([164, 165]), but their general discussion is set here as she details "The Journey of a Metaphor" (an exegesis of the Hebrew "rhm" [womb], the fulcrum of Trible's interpretation); "Passages Along the Way" (a brief description of birthing texts evidencing "God and the rhetoric of sexuality"); "A Love Story Gone Awry" (Trible's exegesis of Gen. 2-4); "Love's Lyrics Remembered" (Song of Songs); and "A Human Comedy" (the story of Ruth). This text synthesizes previous work, and chapters may be read independently of one another. A scriptural index closes the volume. Trible's "Pilgrim" metaphor has been adopted widely and is a column format in the journal, *Daughters of Sarah*, and her strategy of "clues" has been well used in other theological contexts. An early bridge piece in feminist and biblical studies, this text is a resource for readers at similar points of development. **NOTE:** For an alternative view, see [196].

3. Edited and Multiple Authored Works

[206] Christ, Carol P., and Judith Plaskow, eds. *Womanspirit Rising: A Feminist Reader in Religion.* New York: Harper & Row, 1979/1992.
This text is indisputably a classic in the early feminist, women's studies/religion literature, and its four-fold focus continues to function as a platform of dialogue across feminisms of various communities. Part I presents essays by Saiving [163], Ruether, and Mary Daly to answer the question: "The Ecclesial Challenge: Does Theology Speak to Women's Experience?" In turn, contributors to Part II address: "The Past: Does It Hold a Future for Women?" with respondents including Shiela Collins, Phyllis Trible [165], Elisabeth Schüssler Fiorenza, Eleanor McLaughlin, Elaine Pagels [169] and Merlin Stone. Parts III and IV address "Reconstructing Tradition" and

"Creating New Traditions," and in these two sections numerous writers discuss Jewish feminism (Rita Gross, Naomi Janowitz and Maggie Wenig, Judith Plaskow, and Aviva Cantor), Christian spirituality (Elisabeth Schüssler Fiorenza, Nelle Morton, Sheila Collins), Goddess Spirituality (Carol Christ [558]), Witchcraft (Starhawk, Zsuzsanna E. Budapest) and religious motifs drawn from secular feminism (Mary Daly, Naomi Goldenberg, Carol Christ and Penelope Washbourn). Endnotes follow each entry, and an excellent introduction locates issues and authors. Lacking, however, are indices and supplemental bibliography. NOTE: An index and updated preface are included in the 1992 re-release of this volume.

[207] Harrison, Beverly W., and Carol S. Robb. *Making the Connections: Essays in Feminist Social Ethics*. Boston: Beacon Press, 1985.
All but two of the thirteen essays in this volume are reprinted from earlier sources, but significantly revised for this 1985 publication. Additionally, the text is *expertly* edited by Carol S. Robb, whose introductory essay outlines the methodological and substantive concerns of Harrison's work: *viz.*, an attention to economically rooted social justice, and with this, to personal respect and embodied mutuality as the bases and principles of a feminist/Christian/social ethics. Moreover, Robb's prefaces to each subsection of the text provide clear precis-length summaries of subsequent essays. Last, extensive endnotes and a detailed index permit a thorough use and study of both the text and its entries. Key topics addressed by Harrison include (but are not limited to): "Sexism and the Language of Christian Ethics," "Sexuality and Social Policy," "Theology and the Morality of Procreative Choice" [502], "Misogyny and Homophobia: The Unexplored Connections" [569], "Keeping Faith in a Sexist Church" [654], and "The Power of Anger in the Work of Love.". Long the single feminist ethical voice at Union Theological Seminary, Harrison's influence has been enormous and her contribution to feminist ethics is indisputable. Cf. [484], the *JFSR* issue published in her honor, and see [497] and [867].

[208] Kalven, Janet, and Mary Buckley, eds. *Women's Spirit Bonding*. New York: Pilgrim, 1984.
This volume presents the papers, presentations and panel discussions of an ecumenical conference on feminism and women's "bonding" held at the Loveland, Ohio adult educational center, Grailville, July 11-17, 1982. In all, materials from 36 feminists addressing nine topics are included. The nine topics are: (1) women and poverty; (2) women and nature; (3) racism, pluralism and bonding; (4) women as makers of literature; (5) war and peace; (6) lesbianism and homophobia; (7) resources from various traditions; (8) envisioning an alternative future; and (9) rituals and celebrations. An important feature of this conference was its "praxis" orientation-- everywhere reflected in the editors' and conference planners' comments, discussions and panel overviews--and reflected too in the themes raised by participants and addressed in subsequent feminist theological literature. These themes include a strong critique of racism within the feminist and feminist theological movements; the feminist critique of heterosexism; the relational ethic of feminist spirituality; and most widely, an awareness of the power of women's experience to transcend the culturally constraining barriers of religion, race, ethnicity and sexual orientation. Conference contributors include virtually all of the major feminist theologians publishing for the period 1975-1990, together with others beginning their careers in the mid to late '80s. Well documented and well formatted, this volume remains an excellent introduction to issues in feminist ethics, spirituality and community empowerment.

[209] Ruether, Rosemary Radford, and Eleanor McLaughlin, eds. *Women of Spirit: Leadership in the Jewish and Christian Traditions*. New York: Simon and Schuster, 1979.
This is the first of several anthologies co-edited by Ruether. It opens with an introductory discussion of the historical and often charismatically based leadership of women in Christianity, and it presents 13 discussions beginning with Elisabeth Schüssler Fiorenza's "Word, Spirit and Power: Women in Early Christian Communities" [402]. The latter surveys women "founders and leaders" of Christian congregations and women leaders in New Testament and Gnostic communities. Ruether and McLaughlin then treat in turn, ascetic women and women in medieval Christianity, with Ruether describing the lives of selected fourth century ascetic women and their specific women's communities [318], and McLaughlin the roles of women in medieval mysticism and the development of Marian traditions. Ruth Lieberwitz then describes "The Dispute over an Active Apostolate for Women during the Counter Reformation" and Elaine C. Huber addresses "Quaker Women in the English Left Wing." The poetic, feminist mysticism of 17th century Jane Lead is then surveyed by Catherine F. Smith, and Barbara Brown Zikmund traces the reformist parallels between 19th century feminism and sectarian Christianity. Similarly, Nancy Hardesty,

Lucille Sider Dayton and Donald Dayton describe "women in holiness traditions" to indicate the cultural and structural freedom of these women from traditional gender and gender-familial responsibilities. Contemporary themes are addressed by Mary Ewens ("Removing the Veil: The Liberated American Nun") and Ellen Umansky ("Women in Judaism: From the Reform Movement to Contemporary Jewish Religious Feminism" [957]), and the social history of American Protestant women and their paths to ordination are traced by Dorothy Bass [664] and Virginia Brereton and Christa Klein [675]. Norene Carter [677] and Ruether complete the text with essays on Episcopal and Catholic ordination issues.

[210] Russell, Letty M., ed. *Feminist Interpretation of the Bible*. Philadelphia: Fortress, 1985.
This anthology of eleven essays by major contributors to the feminist theological literature is one of the most well known of feminist theological readers. It is divided into three parts, with contributors coming from various traditions and denominations. Part I addresses "feminist critical consciousness." It includes entries on the history and development of feminist and womanist critical consciousness (by, respectively, Barbara Brown Zikmund and Katie G. Cannon [612]), and an entry by Margaret Farley on the ethical bases of feminist consciousness [364]. Part II surveys "Feminists at Work," and included here are entries by Katharine Doob Sakenfeld on "Feminist Uses of the Bible" and a series of interpretive studies detailing selected images of women in the Bible (cf. Setel [384] and Thistlethwaite [870]). The final section of the reader addresses "Feminist Critical Perspectives" and includes Ruether on feminist biblical interpretation as the process of correlating biblical prophetic tradition with contemporary women's experience [366]; Schüssler Fiorenza on the function of women-church as a critique of androcentrism [370], and Russell's own synthesis of [biblical] "Authority and the Challenge of Feminist Interpretation" [367]. A postscript by Phyllis Trible closes the volume.

[211] Schüssler Fiorenza, Elisabeth, and Mary Collins, eds. *Women: Invisible in Church and Theology*. Edinburgh: T. & T. Clark, 1985.
Each of the eleven articles of this reader addresses the theological significance of women as "invisible members in a publicly male church," with Catholicism being the primary focus. Articles by Schüssler Fiorenza, Mary Boys and Iris Miller address women's invisibility in theology: first, ideologically through a critique of patriarchy (Schüssler Fiorenza) and then structurally through a study of women's theological education in Germany (Miller), the United States and Canada (Boys). Canonical issues of invisibility are addressed by Marie Zimmermann and Margaret Brennan, respectively; Zimmermann highlights the increased marginalization of women in the 1983 revised Code of Canon Law (*viz.*, women are "neither clergy nor laity"), and Brennan details the history and current significance of "enclosure," the institutionalized segregation of women in Catholic religious life. Majorie Procter-Smith and Mary Collins address the liturgical invisibility of women: Procter-Smith through a quantitative survey of "significant" and "peripheral" references to women in the Common Lectionary (with significance determined by feminist biblical and women-church criteria) and Collins through a discussion of Teresa Kane who "breached [the] role expectations" of obedience as established by three other Catholic Teresas (Teresa of Avila, Therese of Lisieux, and Mother Theresa of Calcutta). In turn, Marga Buhrig [652] examines the role of women, and especially ordained women, in the ecumenical dialogue (i.e., although small in number they are theologically significant for they represent potential obstacles to [male] ecumenical endeavors), and Kari Vogt [320] and Adriana Valero focus on sex role norms placed upon women in church history. Last, Mary Hunt provides a relational methodology for women in Christian ethics [479]. NOTE: This reader is Volume 182 of the *Concilium* series. For related volumes also from the *Concilium* series, see Schüssler Fiorenza and Copeland [275, 869] and Schüssler Fiorenza and Carr [493].

[212] Swidler, Arlene, and Walter E. Conn, eds. *Mainstreaming: Feminist Research for Teaching Religious Studies*. Lanham, MD: Univ. Press of America, 1985.
Mainstreaming is one of several bibliographic and teaching resources published by the College Theology Society [CTS] through Villanova University. It is intended for college theology teachers seeking discussion and sources for a given theological topic, in this case feminist theology. Thus, each of the eight essays presented here provides: (a) a summary of major issues attached to the author's particular area of specialization as it relates to feminist theology; (b) a description of "core" and specialized bibliographies connecting the author's area and feminist theology; (c) separate listings of topics and books suitable for student papers and reports; and (d) an evaluation of "current texts" important to the author's area and feminist theology. Titles included in this *Mainstreaming* publication are: "How to Mainstream Feminist Studies by Raising Questions: The

Case of the Introductory Course" (June O'Connor); "Feminism and World Religions" (Denise L. Carmody); "To Set the Record Straight: Biblical Women's Studies" (Elisabeth Schüssler Fiorenza [817]); "Recovering Women's History: Early Christianity" (Rosemary Rader [816]); "Women in American Catholic History" (Arlene Swidler); "Feminist Thought and Systematic Theology" (Paula Turner and Bernard Cooke [221]); "Feminist Ethics in the Christian Ethics Curriculum" (Margaret Farley [471]); and "The Feminist Turn in Social Ethics" (Daniel Maguire [481]).

[213] Weidman, Judith, ed. *Christian Feminism: Visions of New Humanity*. San Francisco: Harper & Row, 1984.

This text presents eight essays variously addressing the circumstance, that "The more one becomes a feminist, the more difficult it becomes to go to church" (p. 1). While conscious of the feminist-Christian tension, the contributors to this anthology nonetheless feel that it is necessary to work within "the institutional church," and their varying essays reflect this concern. "Feminist Theology and Spirituality" are taken up by Rosemary Radford Ruether [545]. Elisabeth Schüssler Fiorenza takes up "Emerging Issues in Feminist Biblical Interpretation" [369] and Rita Nakashima Brock describes "The Feminist Redemption of Christ," a redemption that must address frankly the connections between Christianity, patriarchy, sexual violence and physical abuse to women. Letty Russell [656] examines the changing shape of religious authority in "Women and Ministry: Problem or Possibility?" in which she offers a relationally based understanding of authority for feminist and non-feminist perspectives. Remaining essays include "American Women and Life-Style Change," a discussion of feminism, Christianity and reproductive questions by Nanette M. Roberts; "Liberating Work," an analysis of gender work by Clare B. Fischer [490]; "Human Sexuality and Mutuality" by Beverly Wildung Harrison [497] and Constance F. Parvey's description of the potential of women's solidarity world-wide, "Re-membering: A Global Perspective on Women" [923].

NOTE: For additional edited collections see Ruether and Keller [132, 133, 134, 135], Clark and Richardson [186], Andolsen, Gudorf, and Pellauer [468] and "The Mud Flower Collective" [807].

B. Overviews and Critical Assessments: 1980-1986

1. Literature Reviews and Internal Critiques

[214] Grant, Jacquelyn. "A Black Response to Feminist Theology." In *Women's Spirit Bonding*, edited by Janet Kalven and Mary Buckley, 117-124. New York: Pilgrim, 1984.

In an earlier essay [635] Grant has criticized Black liberation theology for its male centered perspective. Here she takes feminist theology to task for its assumptions borne of race-privilege. These include: (1) that white feminists assume sisterhood with Black women while ignoring the long history of superordinate/subordinate relationships between white and Black women; (2) that like white male theologians, white feminist theologians also take "one experience, that of the white middle class woman and make that the norm;" and that consequently, (3) white feminists tend to tell Black women what their roles, needs and aspirations may and/or ought to be within the feminist movement. To these circumstances Grant responds that while feminism "is on to something," it is too tied to its own class/race roots, and thereby either unwilling or unable to include participation by Women of Color. Grant calls attention to the need for Black women's participation in feminist agenda-planning and the capacity of Black women to know they can be "actively engaged in something else" (p. 124). Grant's essay is brief, powerful and pointed. It challenges white feminists to rethink the scope and concerns of inclusivity and the scope of feminism's commitment to achieve a theology that reflects the experience of all women, rather than white women of privilege only. NOTE: Also by Grant are [254] and [636]; and for responses, see Thistlethwaite [252] and Russell [250].

[215] Halkes, Catharina. "Feminist Theology: An Interim Assessment." In *Women in a Men's Church*, edited by Virgil Elizondo and Norbert Greinacher, 110-123. Edinburgh: T. and T. Clark, 1980.

This discussion by Halkes synthesizes four emphases evident in the feminist theological literature through 1979: (1) the various ways in which feminist theology may be defined; (2) some of its characteristic concerns; (3) its relationship to scripture; and (4) the necessity for dialogue between feminist theologians, other liberation theologians, and theologians "for whom the understanding of the faith lies in the world-situation and the actual condition of the Churches" (p. 120). With respect to definitions of feminist theology, Halkes cites several and identifies herself largely with Schüssler Fiorenza's now classic 1975 *Theological Studies* discussion [175]. Similarly, as she identifies characteristic concerns, Halkes points to methodological issues, concepts and images of God, language and symbol development, pneumatology, Christology, theological anthropology and ethics. Last, as she addresses feminist theology and scripture, she highlights the need for "open-minded, critical, and challenging" (feminist theological) approaches that distinguish between patriarchal and liberating texts, rejecting the former and holding the latter. In turn, she calls for dialogue that is open-minded and pluralistically based so that the larger ends of reconciliation, peace and liberation may be served. This dialogue is largely established in *New Creation: Christian Feminism and the Renewal of the Earth*. Louisville, KY: Westminster/John Knox, 1991. See the closing "NOTE" to Chapter 14.

[216] Heyward, Carter. "An Unfinished Symphony of Liberation: The Radicalization of White U.S. Women." *Journal of Feminist Studies in Religion* 1, no. 1 (1985): 95-118.
This essay reviews Elisabeth Schüssler Fiorenza's *In Memory of Her* [195], Virginia Mollenkott's *The Divine Feminine* [201], Rosemary Ruether's *Sexism and God-Talk* [190], and Majorie Suchocki's *God, Christ, Church*. The review is situated within the frank recognition that white feminist theologians must become more conversant with the experience and writings of feminists of color, and each of the four theological texts is examined in terms of its potential for dialogue beyond the privilege of white academia. Alice Walker's *The Color Purple* is skillfully utilized as the backdrop of the review, and the topics of "racism" and "Christocentrism" are identified as "stumbling blocks" in the efforts of women to achieve a stronger solidarity. The scope of these stumbling blocks becomes visible as Heyward reviews her four texts. Thus a principal weakness of Mollenkott's text is its uncritically held Christ/Church equation, for the latter sets up "barriers to the possibility of any real solidarity with most people of the world" (p. 116). Similarly, although Ruether's experience and social constructionist based liberation emphasis is lauded, she too falls short, for in Heyward's judgment *Sexism and God-Talk* does not take racism seriously enough as a theological issue. Also admired, but nonetheless faulted, is Suchocki's process theology: its strength is an attempt at inclusivity via process thought, but its weakness is its inadequate response to conflict and dissonance as they impinge upon that which is being "unified and identified as being in Christ." Finally, Schüssler Fiorenza's work is admired for its liberation efforts and their significance for solidarity in the present. For Heyward's other work, see [179], [198], [217], [242], Davis's editing of Heyward's sermons in [435], and see [437], [555] and [867].

[217] Heyward, Carter, and Mary E. Hunt et al. "Lesbianism and Feminist Theology." *Journal for Feminist Study in Religion* 2, no. 2 (1986): 95-106.
In the opening portion of this "Roundtable" discussion, co-authors Heyward and Hunt call feminist theory to task for not taking the experience of lesbian women seriously in the analysis of women's oppression. They note both the symbolic significance of lesbian experience for the full autonomy of women and point specifically to liberation as including sexual liberation as well. Finally, they call attention to the legitimating role Christianity has played in maintaining both sexist and heterosexist ideology, and they indicate four questions that should inform the development of feminist theology. These are: (1) "How is women's embodied power veiled...by the sanctions of heterosexist patriarchy?" (p. 97); (2) What is revealed "about the politics of [women's] lives by looking honestly at the virulent reactions of civil and religious institutions to lesbian love?" (p.98); (3) "What might lesbian experience teach about female experience?" (p. 98); and (4) "On what constructive theological and moral grounds can [one] radically affirm the goodness of female sexuality?" (p. 98). Responses to their discussion include those by New Testament scholar Bernadette Brooten, womanist theologian Delores Williams, ethicist Claire B. Fischer and Jewish lesbian feminist, Evelyn Torton Beck. Brooten examines the asymmetrical understanding of marriage in key New Testament texts (I Thess. 4:4, Rom. 7:2-4 and Eph. 5:21-33) to indicate historical sexist and heterosexist implications for Christian ecclesiology and theology. Fischer examines the ideological risks of discussing lesbian sexual experience openly; Williams calls for an inclusive hetero- and lesbian sexual ethic that critiques racial privilege, and Beck reiterates this call with attention to the anti-Semitic bias of Christian women, both lesbian and straight. See [216] above for Heyward's other works.

[218] Ignatius, L. Faye, ed. *Foundations* 24 (1981): 197-286.
Six articles, an annotated bibliography [222], and extended reviews of selected women/religion texts comprise this (untitled) "feminism" issue of *Foundations*, a quarterly publication of the

American Baptist Churches of the United States of America [ABC/USA]. The first articles here are biblical, and with varying levels of exegetical sophistication, they address the equality of women and men in scripture. Remaining articles address denominational concerns about women's vocations within the ABC/USA and include: (1) a "Timeline" on ABC women indicating the dates, committees, resolutions and efforts of the ABC on behalf of women's vocations from 1968-1981; (2) a summary of Lehman's early (sociological) research on "resistance to women in ministry" [695]; and (3) a discussion on the task of implementing egalitarian church structures. These articles balance the biblical entries and introduce readers to the experiences of ABC women. Finally, among the issue's selected reviews are early sources on feminism and Asian women's experience.

[219] Kwok, Pui-Lan. "The Feminist Hermeneutics of Elisabeth Schüssler Fiorenza: An Asian Feminist Response." *East Asia Journal of Theology* 3 (1985): 147-153.
This article examines the implications of Elisabeth Schüssler Fiorenza's feminist hermeneutics for Asian women. It summarizes four emphases of Schüssler Fiorenza's feminist hermeneutics and raises several questions about the latter's potential racial and class biases. The four emphases of Schüssler Fiorenza's work addressed here include: (1) Schüssler Fiorenza's dialogical-hermeneutical approach to biblical theology; (2) her use of patriarchy as a key interpretive concept in analyzing Christian tradition and experience; (3) her recovery of "women history" in *In Memory of Her* [195]; and (4) her vision of the church as a community borne of the "discipleship of equals." The values of these emphases for Asian women are that: (1) they dislodge the authoritative value of proof-texting as a form of theologizing within the Asian-Christian culture; (2) they direct one to women's experience as a normative source of understanding the revelation of the Bible; (3) they render women visible within the biblical (NT) texts; and (4) they invite all women to join in the critique of patriarchy. As she develops these last two points, Kwok also assesses Schüssler Fiorenza's discussion of "women's leadership" in the Pauline churches and the relationship of this leadership to the circumstances of women in poverty. Her discussion suggests the possibility of a white middle class bias in Schüssler Fiorenza's work as evidenced by Schüssler Fiorenza's failure to adequately link the wealthy (NT) house church leaders with the poor women of the discipleship of equals. Second, as she applies the "call to join the community of equals" to the context of contemporary Asian women, Kwok notes the possible conflict for Asian women: namely, as they leave their "father's family" to pursue either feminism or Christian experience, Asian women may find that this extinguishes (rather than empowers) their cultural heritage. Kwok closes by noting the importance of Schüssler Fiorenza's work, and she invites her Asian sisters to "solidarity" with the "poorest women at the lowest bottom of the hierarchical pyramid" (p. 153).

[220] Ruether, Rosemary Radford. "Feminism and Religious Faith: Renewal or New Creation?" *Religion and Intellectual Life* 3 (1986): 7-20.
This tightly argued essay continues several themes identified in Ruether's earlier works ([172], [192], [326] and [365]) and later expanded in *Gaia & God* [235]. It begins with an introduction describing the pervasiveness of androcentric religion in biblical and non-biblical traditions and it asks how feminists might translate androcentric symbols and stories from their "androcentric context into a context...interpreted from the side of female experience...[to empower]...women as subjects of their own histories" (p. 10). It poses the task in terms of four specific questions: (1) How can women's spirituality "enhance liberationist transformation of history rather than sacralization of male dominance?" (2) How actually can symbols/stories be translated? (3) At what point should new stories be generated (and by what norms)? and (4) Need feminists of faith follow the past divisions of male religious culture, or might not a new synthesis begin? To address these questions Ruether identifies the prophetic paradigm of Hebrew Scripture as a critical starting point in that it critiques "unjust and oppressive power" and "the use of religion to sacralize such oppressive power" (p. 12). Similarly, because feminism names patriarchy as a human, male construct of unjust power relations that can and should be changed (p. 13), it can appropriate the Bible's prophetic paradigm and become a form of midrash, i.e., an analogical retelling of a story (or symbol) toward a different and better ending. (Hence, the distinctiveness of feminist hermeneutics as midrash rather than exegesis.) Following this part of her discussion, Ruether turns to question #4: the potentials of a feminist religious synthesis (as contrasted with a re-patterning of traditional male religious divisions). She notes the presence of the women-church movement, "pagan" or Wiccan communities, and feminist minyans (p. 17), and she suggests that in spite of multiple historical conflicts, these communities can aid women in becoming "genuinely accountable to the past, to each other, and to a just and sustainable future for all of earth's beings in this project" (p. 20).

[221] Turner, Pauline, and Bernard Cooke. "Feminist Thought and Systematic Theology." *Horizons* 11 (1984): 125-137.
Also published in Swidler and Conn [212], this essay reflects the early difficulties of connecting *feminist* theological work with traditional systematic-theological concerns: both substantively in terms of specific doctrinal areas and pedagogically in terms of teaching college level theology classes. The authors begin with a brief statement of their rationale and the significance of feminist theology for teaching systematics: namely, one must re-examine the presuppositions and methodology (including the sources) of theology itself. Second, the authors consider a range of topics within which feminist theology had (by the early 1980s) made specific inroads (i.e., theological anthropology, Christology, ecclesiology and Godtalk), and they highlight key bibliographic sources for those topics. Third, the authors note the pedagogical and moral responsibility of college theology professors to teach feminist work, i.e., that students may come to know both the dynamics of such institutionalized evils as sexism and their personal responsibility to work against such evil(s). Last, the authors list additional bibliography for the doctrines they examine.

NOTE: For additional responses to the literature through the early 1980s, see Keightley [292], Elizondo [746] and Weaver [762].

2. Bibliography and Review Symposia

[222] Ignatius, L. Faye. "Feminism Bibliography." *Foundations* 24 (1981): 264-275.
This annotated bibliography contains 110 entries spread over twelve categories of feminist concern as identified by Faye. These are: women and the Bible, the church, feminist theology, women and society, inclusive worship, inclusive language, materials both "about and for women" and "about and for men," male/female relationships, films, study guides, and women's groups. Approximately half of all entries fall in the first four groups, and an additional third are resource materials for use in worship and/or workshop contexts. Entry descriptions are brief and geared primarily to individuals seeking an introduction to feminist issues. Texts not using inclusive language are so designated.

[223] Knutsen, Mary, and June O'Connor. "Review Essays: Recent Works in Feminist Theology." *Religious Studies Review* 12 (1986): 1-9.
In this review article, Lutheran theologian Mary Knutsen reviews Elisabeth Schüssler Fiorenza's *Bread Not Stone* [196] and Patricia Wilson-Kastner's *Faith, Feminism and the Christ.* Subsequently, June O'Connor (cf. [184]) reviews Rosemary Radford Ruether's *Sexism and Godtalk* [190], Sally McFague's Metaphorical *Theology* [200], and Kathryn Allen Rabuzzi's, *The Sacred and the Feminine: Toward a Theology of Housework.* [New York: Seabury Press, 1982].

[224] Perkins, Pheme, John Koenig, Rosemary Radford Ruether, and Beverly Harrison."Review Symposium: Elisabeth Schüssler Fiorenza, *In Memory of Her: A Feminist Theological Reconstruction of Christian Origins.* Four Perspectives." *Horizons* 11 (1984): 142-157.
Three of the four contributors to this symposium on *In Memory of Her* [195] (hereafter, *IMH*) focus on the formally hermeneutical dimensions of Schüssler Fiorenza's work, and the fourth, Beverly Harrison, the implications of *IMH* for the discipline of Christian ethics. Of the contributors, Harrison's response is--from the perspective of much mainline and critical sociology-- the most significant. Harrison argues that because the legitimacy of Christianity's critique of cultural political movements against status-quo conditions has traditionally been grounded in the assumption of Christianity's eschatological horizon, no one has questioned Christianity's legitimacy to judge the normative authority of social movements outside itself, which *also* may be critical of status quo conditions. Schüssler Fiorenza's model of the New Testament as a formative prototype for Christian experience, together with her plausibly developed arguments concerning the moral ambiguity of the early Christian community and its liberation directed praxis, however, all suggest a modified framework for Christian ethics. Namely, one which does not, ipso facto, have a "moral lock" on judging the moral legitimacy of praxis-based liberation movements outside Christianity's institutional pale. Harrison's review calls strong attention to this fact and expands on its implications. **NOTE:** For two additional important reviews of *IMH* (not abstracted here) see Cornell West and Ross Kraemer, "Review Essays: Elisabeth Schüssler Fiorenza, *In Memory of Her: A Feminist Theological Reconstruction of Christian Origins.*" *Religious Studies Review* 11 (1985): 1-9.

C. Feminist Theological Journals

[225] *Daughters of Sarah.*   Garrett Evangelical Seminary, 2121 Sheridan Road, Evanston, IL 60201, 1974-.
Daughters of Sarah (or *DOS*) is an evangelical feminist theological quarterly that regularly features brief articles, biblical reflections, poetry, selected book reviews, and a variety of practical resources focused around a theme specific to each issue. For examples see [279] and [498].

[226] *Journal of Feminist Studies in Religion.* Scholars Press, Atlanta, GA. 1985-.
JFSR is published twice yearly and typically features a variety of scholarly articles addressing issues related to the feminist study of religion. Additionally, it features a seminar-like formatted "Roundtable" discussion of cutting edge topics (cf., e.g., [335], [630]) and a "Reports/Living it Out" discussion featuring first person descriptions of feminist theological advocacy and/or activity (cf., e.g., [874]). Co-founded by Judith Plaskow and Elisabeth Schüssler Fiorenza and co-edited by the same through 1995, *JFSR* is now co-edited by Schüssler Fiorenza and womanist ethicist Emily Townes.

[227] *Journal of Women and Religion.* Graduate Theological Union, San Francisco, CA: 1981-.
Published initially as a semi-annual by the women faculty and students at GTU, this journal is now issued annually and features scholarly papers, reflective essays, poems, and anecdotal writings on inclusivity in ecumenical and multicultural settings.

[228] *Lilith.* 250 W. 57th St., Suite 2432, New York, NY 10107. 1977-.
Lilith is a Jewish feminist quarterly featuring various types of articles, feminist connections and resources, with frequent contributions addressing topics in religion, theology and feminist spirituality. Although not indexed in the standard Christian sources, it is an important resource for Christian feminists working either within or in dialogue with Jewish feminist spirituality.

NOTE: Two other journals--New York's *Union Seminary Quarterly Review* and *Horizons*, the quarterly journal for the College Theology Society (published through Villanova University) also feature feminist theological work, although neither is directed exclusively to the feminist study of religion. Similarly, although *The Journal of Religious Thought* (published semi-annually through the Howard University School of Divinity in Washington, DC) regularly features womanist theological work, it is directed to African American theology and church life generally, not womanist theology specifically. Likewise, the biblical journal *Semeia* (from Scholars Press in Atlanta) also features feminist work (cf., e.g., [372]), but its focus is toward creative biblical research generally, not feminist biblical research specifically. Obviously, as the many journal entries in the present bibliography indicate, several long standing sources regularly feature feminist articles, although only a few do so on a per issue basis.

7

Recent and Current Literature
(1986–1996)

The feminist theological literature published since the mid-1980s reflects an increasing differentiation of feminist theological concerns and falls almost into two distinct categories: sources published from 1986 through 1993, and those published from 1994 on, with several feminist Christian writers continuing to "defect in place" (cf. Winter, Lummis and Stokes [153]), as additional and more globally based voices enter the discussion. Overall, four trends characterize the literature.

First, there is a movement away from the critique of patriarchy as a broad and generalized phenomenon, and there is, in its place, a more directed critique of the specific values, structures and symbols (both religious and social) that sustain patriarchy; a shift, as it were, from superstructure to infrastructure. Schüssler Fiorenza's mid-90s works analyzing the assumptions of "kyriarchy" (i.e., theologically based "relations of ruling") evidence this shift [236, 238], as do specific works addressing particular aspects of "patriarchy" and its symbols (e.g., Gray [241], Johnson [232], McFague [244], Plaskow [262], Ruether [235] and Townes [258]).

Second, there is an increased attention to the many pluralisms that characterize "women's experience." That is, there is a heightened attention to the racial/ethnic, socioeconomic, demographic, sexual, religious, denominational and cultural differences that identify the experiences of women, as global, evangelical, womanist, *Mujerista*, Jewish, liberationist, and other critical voices also become "established" and core sources. Thistlethwaite and Engel [276] provide a synthesizing introduction to this literature, while the growing number of: (1) "definitions" of feminist theology (e.g., [264] and [272]), (2) critical reviews (e.g., [277] and [281]), and (3) partial syntheses (e.g., [265] and [269]) trace the development of pluralism and multicultural impacts.

Third, in the feminist theological literature published since the mid-80s one finds a distinctively *self-critical* posture--both in terms of the biases attached to "difference" as an axis of theological analysis and identification [278], and, in the literature published after 1993 specifically, the expectations attached to feminist theology as an academic discipline (cf. [238], [239], [251], [252], [254], [259], and [262]). This last characteristic of the literature is in part a carryover of the heightened attention to "difference" in the theologizing process, and as well, an effect of postmodernism on the literature of "feminism and Christian tradition." Hence the debate over feminist methodology (cf., e.g., Eriksson [240] and Jones [267], and see [330, 327] in Chapter 9), as well as the growing reactionary literature, e.g., [287] and [289].

Finally, without question, the literature in Jewish feminist theology [260-263] bursts forth in the mid to late 1990s, with its very presence clearly challenging the conventional assumption that "feminist theology" is a primarily Christian phenomenon. While that latter may be true *statistically*-- given the scope of Christian educational institutions in North America--it is with the rise of feminist theologies distinct from those of Christianity that history's wide, inter-religious questions (such as "redemption") can now, at least initially, be addressed.

Given the scope of the literature through the mid-1990s, readers may wish to scan several article length overviews as anchoring introductions. Among the most helpful for American sources are Graff [280], Schüssler Fiorenza [283], and Finger [279]. Alternatively, see Kwok [281] and Ross [268] for various international sources. Likewise, for more extended and/or book length introductions, see Carr [229], Loades [274], Schüssler Fiorenza and Copeland [275], and Russell and Clarkson [272]. Among the latter, Carr presents a generalized perspective situated within mainline (American) Roman Catholic thought, while British Anglican, Loades, presents an ongoing commentary situated within European and American Protestant and Catholic sources critical of Christian "Tradition" per se. In turn, Schüssler Fiorenza and Copeland present a series of sixteen summary essays reflecting literatures from different geographical, religious and theoretical "sites of feminist struggle," while Russell and Clarkson provide more than 450 article entries.

One further reminder about the structuring of material in this bibliography. While key sources for the diverse voices of feminist theology are presented in this chapter, more detailed listings are presented in subsequent sections of the bibliography. Hence, see Section IV for the wider literature on Womanism and Womanist theology, Chapter 22 for additional literature on global and international voices, and Chapter 23 for the wider literature on Judaism and Feminist Theology.

A. Works by Feminist Theologians

1. Roman Catholic Authors

[229] Carr, Anne. *Transforming Grace: Christian Tradition and Women's Experience.* San Francisco: Harper & Row, 1988.
This book synthesizes several of Carr's previously published essays and locates them within the wider context of "the women's ordination movement and the churches." It traces briefly the 19th century women's movement, indicating its demise after its Suffrage based one-issue platform of "the vote", and it contrasts this one issue emphasis with the potentially single issue horizon of many Catholic women seeking ordination within Catholicism. It views the wider context of the women's movement in terms of justice issues (both within and beyond the church), and it argues forcefully that "the experience of women is prophetically calling the church to itself to embody and institutionalize what it at its best has preached for centuries: that the heart of [Christian] tradition as radical faith, hope and love...is a message about personhood before God" (p. 59). Carr's expression of this point is consistent and thorough-going. She seeks—and accomplishes—a re-symbolization of several Christian motifs (e.g., spirituality, Christological and Mariological symbols), and she coordinates this resymbolization from within both feminist and traditional theological sources. Her slightly modified and previously published works presented here include "the possibility of a Christian feminist theology," **[324]** "theological anthropology and the experience of women" **[290]**, and "Christian feminist spirituality" **[549]**. Extended chapter notes, a twenty-one page "Selective Bibliography," and a helpful author-subject index close the volume. **NOTE**: Also by Carr (but not abstracted here) is her essay overview, "Feminism," in *Dictionary of Fundamental Theology*, edited by Rene Latourelle, 315-318. NY: Crossroad, 1994.

[230] Hunt, Mary E. *Fierce Tenderness: A Feminist Theology of Friendship.* New York: Crossroad, 1991.
This text examines several examples of women's friendships to develop an egalitarian theoretical framework for understanding and articulating theological realities. Its primary focus is the critique of heterosexist social organization, and specifically, the assumption of heterosexual "coupling" as the ethical exemplar of Christian (or other) relational forms. Its distinguishing feature, however, is its spiraling methodology, *viz.*, Hunt's descriptive disclosure of the values evident in women's friendships (including the possibility of sexual friendships), with the values of "attention," "generativity," and "community" all converging on "justice" as the matrix and face of "right relationship." Hunt begins by describing four sets of women's friendships to disclose the characteristics they exhibit. From these she develops a friendship model that emphasizes embodiment, love, power and spirituality as the key features of "fierce tenderness," her name for the relational posture that women's ways of befriending take. In turn, she reflects on "The Limits of Friendship in Loss and Celebration," on "Justice-seeking Friends in Unlikely Coalitions," and "Fierce Tenderness in Deed," her descriptions of "divine," "human," and "world" relatings as they emerge from the insights first detailed in the women's friendships she has earlier described. These chapters are rich. They unfold the mix of her model with the four values of attention, generativity, justice and community, and as with earlier portions of the text, they are peppered with attentive

responses to other feminist theological works on friendship, and Hunt's ongoing critique of Aristotelian logic and its coupled male-female exemplar of commitment, fidelity and purpose. This is an important--and brilliant--book. Less because it takes "established" religious symbols and reconstructs them formally in the traditional but now changing categories of a specific theological subdiscipline (e.g., the writing of a feminist christology), for it does this only minimally. Rather, its importance--and its brilliance--is its different horizon: its perspective of lesbian insight grounded in Catholic sacramentality and the humble courage this combination creates. Hunt is very clear in her opening chapters that the text is not an apologia for same-sex relations, although well it might be. Instead, as the winner of the "1990 Crossroad/Continuum Women Studies Award,"it is about widening the framework of relational thinking across the board, i.e., the decentering of heterosexist coupling as the norm and exemplar for ethical reasoning, sexual or else wise. NOTE: Also by Hunt are [479], [556], [571], [789], [918], and with Carter Heyward [217].

[231] Johnson, Elizabeth A. *Consider Jesus: Waves of Renewal in Christology*. New York: Crossroad, 1990.
Taking as her point of departure the question, "Who Is Jesus?", Johnson synthesizes various literatures to portray the many answers that Christian tradition has presented to this question. Her discussion is rooted in the assumptions of ecclesial and theological renewal particular to Catholicism since Vatican II, and her nine chapter-length discussions address various traditional and contemporary issues implicit in the "Who Is Jesus?" question: Examples of traditional issues include Jesus' "self-knowledge," and the meaning of suffering, death and resurrection. In turn, contemporary issues are the relationship of Christology to liberation and justice, including liberationist and feminist Christologies. Overall, Johnson's chapters are thorough, succinct, and grounded by ecumenical and institutionally based theological perspectives. Further, Johnson comments briefly on additional and related literature at the close of each chapter. Her discussion of feminist Christology is decidedly nuanced, i.e., she parallels feminist Christology with liberationist Christology to address the invisibility and marginalization of women--and among other things--the questions of God language and the [in]significance of the maleness of Jesus. Her key authors are Ruether, Schüssler Fiorenza and McFague, and as with other chapters, she comments briefly on the literature. Ever ecumenical, Johnson's is a solid synthesis of current Christology with feminist Christology but one of many options. NOTE: See [232] for Johnson's other works.

[232] Johnson, Elizabeth A. *She Who Is: The Mystery of God in Feminist Theological Discourse*. New York: Crossroad, 1992.
This is one of the most widely used feminist texts in contemporary theological education (cf. [417: 2-3]), and as co-winner of the 1992 Crossroad Women's Studies Award, it has received sustained attention by reviewers from various traditions and journals, a sampling of which is listed below. Overall, Johnson synthesizes a wide range of classical Christian, Jewish and feminist theological sources to demonstrate the joy and cogency of embracing feminist metaphors for God, but principally that of Ex. 3:14 , cast now as "She Who Is." But it is en route to the latter that Johnson virtually dazzles the reader. In brief, she reviews feminism's critiques of patriarchy and ecclesial androcentrism, the role of "women's experience" in the theologizing process, the meeting of biblical, feminist, and classical Christological· and trinitarian theologies, the ties between spirituality, panentheism and the earth as Sophia's own, and in her closing section, the often unaddressed and androcentric assumptions attached to "theodicy," *viz.*, the theologies of suffering theism offers as the soul's balm. Rather, Johnson suggests, there is an alternative, the possibility of a suffering Sophia-God, who renews, empowers, revitalizes, and bears one up, albeit always "under the rule of darkness and broken words." This is an elegantly written text that well meets its goal of "braid[ing] a footbridge between the ledges of classical and feminist Christian wisdom" (p. 12). To be sure, some may find Johnson's classical heritage insufficient for the immediate needs of various American denominations, but few broker the past and its possibilities for and within "women's flourishing" as well as Johnson in this text. Quite clearly, it surpasses and will long outlive her earlier and more compactly stated insights which find their poetics here. (Cf. [421], [422], [438].) NOTE: Johnson's related works also include [233], [446], and [447]. Additionally, for helpful reviews of this work, see the following: Mary E. Hines, Mary R. D'Angelo, John Carmody, and Elizabeth Johnson, "Review Symposium: Elizabeth A. Johnson's *She Who Is: The Mystery of God...*" *Horizons* 20(1993): 324-344; Mary Aquin O'Neill and Mary McClintock Fulkerson, "Reviews of *She Who Is: The Mystery of God...*" by Elizabeth Johnson." *Religious Studies Review* 21 (Jan., 1995): 19-25; and Amy Plantinga Pauw, "Braiding a New Footbridge: Christian Wisdom, Classic and Feminist." A Review of *She Who Is: The Mystery of God...*" by Elizabeth Johnson. *The Christian Century* 110(1993): 1159-1162. NOTE: See [233], [446] and [447].

[233] Johnson, Elizabeth A. *Women, Earth, and Creator Spirit.* Mahwah, NJ: Paulist, 1993.
This brief text is the 1993 Madeleva lecture in Spirituality at St. Mary's College, Notre Dame, Indiana. In it Johnson synthesizes ecofeminist and biblical feminist insights to critique hierarchical dualism as the linchpin of today's ecological crisis. She examines and assesses "kingship," "stewardship" and "*kin*ship" as images for focusing humanity's response to contemporary earth-ethical thinking, and she grounds her adoption of the kinship model in a recasting of "Spirit" theology. Her biblical images include several from the Hebrew and Christian scriptures (e.g., wind, breath, fire, and Wisdom's Presence), and these are, in turn, anchored in the relationality of God in trinitarian theology. This is a packed essay, and it evidences Johnson's enormous and established ability to synthesize clearly and creatively from the edges of several theological perspectives.

[234] LaCugna, Catherine Mowry. *God For Us: The Trinity and Christian Life.* New York: HarperSanFrancisco, 1991.
This is LaCugna's major work on Christianity's doctrine of the Trinity, and although its key points are helpfully summarized in various other publications (cf., e.g., **[458]** and **[459]**), this text provides LaCugna's detailed argument that "...Christian theology must begin from the premise that because the mystery of God is revealed in the mystery of salvation, statements about the nature of God must be rooted in the reality of salvation history" (p. 4). The discussion develops in two parts. First, in a series of chapters that lay her methodological groundwork, LaCugna traces the history of trinitarian doctrine to indicate both the connections between trinitarian theology and salvation history and the varying theologies through which the connections were initially affirmed, later separated, and finally marginalized and abandoned as central to Christian life and faith. Part II of her text then retrieves the trinitarian/salvation history connection. Namely, that relationality grounds all activity on the part of God for humanity, and that as the ground swell of salvation, this relational "God for us" is the basis for all Christian life, teaching and behavior. This is a detailed and thoughtfully written text. It builds heavily on the work of Karl Rahner and other mid-century Catholic theologians, and it leaves few stones unturned in its overview of Trinitarian doctrine and theological reflection. **NOTE:** While professional theologians will appreciate LaCugna's comprehensive discussion (cf. Susan Wood, Roger Haight, Mary Ann Donavan, Barbara A. Finan, and Catherine Mowry LaCugna. *"Review Symposium: Catherine Mowry LaCugna's The Trinity and Christian Life.* Four Perspectives." *Horizons* 20 (1993): 127-142]), those seeking a more summary level approach will perhaps prefer LaCugna's article length works on feminism and the Trinity indicated above. Additionally, because of the extended backlash against the feminist appropriation of this doctrine (e.g., Kimmel **[840]**), readers should also see LaCugna's edited text **[273]** together with Suchocki **[427]** and sources in Chapter 11.

[235] Ruether, Rosemary Radford. *Gaia & God: An Ecofeminist Theology of Earth Healing.* New York: HarperSanFrancisco, 1992.
On the book jacket blurb to this text, Harvey Cox describes it as "theology that really matters." It is at least that, although readers unfamiliar the history of societal tranformations and current ecological and environmental theories may find it slow going at points. In brief, Ruether summarizes several detailed and important historical and social theories to shed light on the development of those ethics, philosophies, mythologies, spiritualities, doctrinal syntheses and social policies, which, through the medium of Christianity (and its secular off shoots), have either contributed to or permitted lifestyles and ideologies which work *against* "biophilia" and *for* the consumption of the earth and its regularly energized life forms. But Ruether's text here is more than an ideology critique and more than an extension of several earlier and similarly sensitive works (e.g., **[192]**, **[220]** and **[567]**). Rather, as is her methodological wont, it is Ruether's synthesis of the streams of earth destruction (including among others--dualist cosmologies and philosophies, "food surplus" as a factor of social transformation, militarist and patriarchal ideologies, apocalyptic ethics and world views, denials of mortality and flawed doctrines of earth stewardship), and it is her search for alternative possibilities, which she finds first in the covenantial and jubilee traditions of the Bible and later in Christianity's sacramental and material wisdom(s). This is no small text, and the literatures Ruether summarizes all press her to address issues of environmental ethics, ecological absolutes, and the economic factors of energy, fertility and poverty that--via the food chain--tie third world populations to first world societies, who in a hundred years have surpassed the resources of millennia unimaginable. Further, it is a text that in the end also poses a transformation of religious imagery from the absolutes of detached agency and "moral monism" to the relational becomings of *Gaia*, our Mother. And all this, so that *Gaia*, the earth's marvelous balance, can be

sustained, supported and partnered with a thinking species that knows and lives within its boundaries, while yet becoming increasingly attentive to its interspecies connections and responsibilities. NOTE: For a detailed and helpful review of this text, see Christina Traina, "An Argument for Christian Ecofeminism." A Review of *Gaia and God: An Ecofeminist Theology* by Rosemary Radford Ruether. *The Christian Century* 110 (June 2-9, 1993): 600-603. Additionally, see the Index for Ruether's other works.

[236] Schüssler Fiorenza, Elisabeth. *But She Said: Feminist Practices of Biblical Interpretation.* Boston: Beacon Press, 1992.

This is Schüssler Fiorenza's most substantive discussion of feminist hermeneutics through 1993. Its overriding purpose is to create a "space" for feminist critical hermeneutical work, but here within the context of feminist theory itself, rather than the professional (i.e., academic) biblical establishment as was the case in *Bread Not Stone.* Schüssler Fiorenza begins with an overview of the feminist biblical interpretation literature. She reviews nine frameworks comprising the methods, sources, assumptions and strategies of feminist biblical hermeneutics as developed through the early 1990s, and she provides a summary of her own work, calling it a "...tenth approach...a rhetorical model of a critical feminist interpretive process for transformation." She then uses the model to demonstrate the various ways in which the experience(s) of biblical and contemporary women can be re-surfaced and reconstructed, and in each of her "space" creating chapters, she focuses on a woman of biblical significance: first, Miriam, who "leads the dance" (Schüssler Fiorenza's metaphor for the reconstructive process as a whole); second, Arachne, the weaver--an image to identify the textured quality of biblical texts and here specifically, the suppressed leadership and false opposition of Mary and Martha in Luke 10:38-42; third, Mary of Magdela--an image of feminist truth telling and a reconsideration of the Markan story of the Syro-Phoenician woman; and last, Justa, Sophia, Prisca and Sheba--images respectively, of reconstructing and redefining the capitalist patriarchy interface, the dynamics of a feminist canonical hermeneutics, the role of feminist scholars in theological education, and last, a critical feminist reading of Luke 13:10-17. Poetry by African American and womanist authors frames most of the chapters, with excerpts from Maya Angelou's "Still I Rise" prefacing Schüssler Fiorenza's final essay. Expert textual analysis, helpful diagrams, ecumenical sensitivities, and an attention to "Kyriarchy" (Schüssler Fiorenza's term for male elite relations of ruling as described, for example, by feminist sociologist Dorothy Smith [114]) all mark this volume as difficult but especially important reading.

[237] Schüssler Fiorenza, Elisabeth. *Discipleship of Equals: A Critical Feminist Ekklesia-logy of Liberation.* New York: Crossroad, 1993.

All but a handful of the 25 articles and essays collected for this volume have appeared earlier within Schüssler Fiorenza's career, but their consolidation here presents a collection organized by Schüssler Fiorenza's own reflections on her nearly thirty year long career in biblical and later feminist theological studies. The entries here include sections from her 1964 Licentiate thesis, as well as many of her early essays on feminism and the Bible and feminism and feminist theology. What makes the collection valuable, however, is not only that so many of her important essays are now published in one source, but that each is prefaced with a "contextualization" statement: Schüssler Fiorenza's own reflections on the entry at hand and her perception of how it fits within her long career in biblical-feminist theological work. New essays include Schüssler Fiorenza's reflections on ministry, the women-church movement and Roman Catholicism, and her long standing commitment to the task of helping women name the spiritual realities wrested from them by the androcentric traditioning process begun early in Christian history. This is a *wonderful* volume for understanding the sweep of Schüssler Fiorenza's thought, the scope of her professional impact, and the possibilities of biblical studies generally when interpreted in the light of feminism and its significance for Christianity. It serves synthesizing and introductory needs, and these across theological and sociological audiences.

[238] Schüssler Fiorenza, Elisabeth. *Jesus: Miriam's Child, Sophia's Prophet. Critical Issues in Feminist Christology.* New York: Continuum, 1994.

In earlier works ([236, 238]), Schüssler Fiorenza has coined the term "kyriarchy" to indicate the cumulative and multiplicative effects of androcentrism, patriarchy and patrimony as frameworks of social and normative scope, in that they define the patterns and processes of society's ascribed statuses (sex, age, race/ethnicity, and sexual orientation) and their prescribed role relations. Here she presents six essays addressing: (1) the various ways kyriarchy is regularly "reinscribed" into church and society--and more widely, American and Western cultures; (2) the social actors who continue the reinscription process; (3) Christological motifs that configure this process; and (4) the responses feminist theology must make to it all. By and large, the reinscription process happens (and continues) because the power relationships implicit in selected Christological doctrines go undetected and unthwarted by those most involved with them, *viz.*, society's professional cadre of elite, male, biblical scholars. Thus the power relationships embedded in Christological doctrines are embodied in the structures, images and assumptions of biblical exegesis, methodology, *and education,* and to the extent that the real-world population of contemporary biblical scholars maintains the present system, "reinscription" (or socialization to patriarchy) occurs. What is needed, therefore, is a shift in the analytical orientation of biblical scholars (towards a rhetorical critical paradigm of interpretation) so that readers of the biblical text may once again control the images attached to the biblical text. Cast in terms of feminist theology, then, feminist theologians must realize that Christology is not simply an evolving set of doctrines, but a series of "contesting discursive frameworks" yet grounded in and geared to "kyriarchal" (i.e., power driven and stratification directed) outcomes. The topics by which Schüssler Fiorenza unfolds this overall discussion include "Christian anti-Judaism" (in biblical exegetical studies), soteriology (and specifically its motifs of 'divine child abuse'), wisdom theology, and Mariology. And for each, Schüssler Fiorenza reviews both the androcentric and feminist literatures, with the latter now redefined in terms of "feminist apologetical" literature (i.e., feminist theology that carries over internalized kyriarchal patterns) and feminist critical liberation literature, or those studies that transcend the sex/gender assumptions of kyriarchy and move to more inclusive horizons. Last, in each of the essays, Schüssler Fiorenza unfolds the ecclesia of women as the feminist hermeneutical space of discursive action, including its experiential and basileia qualities. This is a challenging and difficult text, best read as a series of discussions following the entries noted above, and with the discussion of anti-Judaism accompanied by Plaskow **[970-971]**). Additionally, see D'Angelo on anti-Judaism in New Testament work **[433]** and **[397]**.

NOTE: For additional material by Catholic feminist theologians see the listings in Chapters 5 and 6; see the topical literatures in Chapters 8-15 (passim), and see Chapter 19.

2. Protestant and Evangelical Feminist Authors

[239] Chopp, Rebecca S. *The Power to Speak: Feminism, Language, God.* New York: Crossroad, 1989.
Describing the work of her text as a "logological" and theological effort to "encourage words about Word and to envision Word for and with words," Chopp presents a brilliant (albeit thickly written) exposition of feminist theology as the task of "emancipatory proclamation," as rooted in the new ecclesia of women-church. Her discussion develops in four chapters, with the first ("Proclamation, Women and the Word") addressing the need to recognize feminist discourse as positioned at the margins of women's experience "of Word" and appropriating it as a "perfectly open sign" that configures a new symbolic-order, i.e., new significatory discourse(s). In effect, this first chapter retrieves the legitimacy of women speaking from and out of a text that largely defines them as "other," but the text is not to be jettisoned for that fact, because it is [God's] "Word." Chapter 2 ("The Power of Freedom") then illustrates Schüssler Fiorenza's characterization of the biblical text as a "prototype" of revelatory and emancipatory experience (cf. **[369]**), with Luke 4:21-30 serving as the exemplar text. In turn, Chapter 3 ("The Community of Emancipatory Transformation") connects the proclamation of freedom with the "new ecclesia" of women-church (women speaking Word from the margins), while Chapter 4 ("Proclamation as the Word for the World") sets forth a nascent feminist systematics by contrasting feminist and "patriarchal-monotheistic" orderings of language, subjectivity and politics in a manner both similar and dissimilar to McFague's early **[200]** work: similar in that it expands McFague's process of "thought experiments," and dissimilar in that it moves fully beyond such experiments to reconfigure Christian significations in the "crisis of modernity." This is an important text. Its breadth connects several differently grounded traditional Protestant and contemporary feminist theological perspectives, and its methodology transitions one from Barthian "neo-orthodoxy" to feminist proclamation for the Protestant tradition overall. **NOTE**: Also by Chopp are **[811-812]**, and for an alternative view of "feminist proclamation," see Procter-Smith **[522]** and **[533]**.

[240] Eriksson, Anne-Louise. *The Meaning of Gender in Theology; Problems and Possibilities.* Stockholm: Almquist & Wiksell International, 1995.
This text is Eirksson's doctoral dissertation from Uppsala, and its main focus is the search for a feminist theology of gender sufficient to dislodge the gender defining power of the (revised) Holy Communion Service in Swedish Lutheranism. The search entails four stages: a summary of

conceptual and methodological issues, a contrast between the text of the Holy Communion Service and its gender defining impacts when enacted as liturgy, a critique of selected works by Ruether and Schüssler Fiorenza to see how "gender works" in their theologies and if those workings can transcend the genderizing process enacted within and acted out in the Communion Service itself, and last, Eriksson's conclusions that: (1) the theologies fail and (2) women priests in Sweden must, in effect, stand fast, as it were, as the Communion Services takes place, because over time, that posture will eventually change the patriarchal theology of the Church to make it more gender inclusive. Hence in contrast to the definitions of gender posed by Ruether and Schüssler Fiorenza (*viz.*, the depictions of women as "marginalized" or "non-persons"), Eriksson's definition of gender is "Resisto, ergo sum," and it is presented as a de facto reality as women priests celebrate the Communion. This is a provocative and *very* demanding text. Its methodological chapters challenge traditional biological and social constructionist distinctions between sex and gender and attempt a more nuanced (but not necessarily more clearly identified) reality named "physical gender." Its critique of feminism is shallow--save to say standpoint epistemologies are inadequate given the nihilism of post-modernism, and the analysis of Ruether and Schüssler Fiorenza, while succinct and at points accurate, is misdirected given that the desired task for those theologies is to outperform the theology of the Service itself as it is in process. These criticisms notwithstanding, Eriksson's analysis of the gender framing dynamics of liturgy is, itself, clear and on the mark: the theology of the Service *text* defines two realms--Divine and human, that parallel male and female gender norms and define participants accordingly as the Service *is enacted*. Dissonance is introduced when the priest is female, because as with male priests, she (qua priest) also is defined during and by the Service as "male." While one may criticize various aspects of Eriksson's discussion--e.g., Can texts alone undercut liturgical process? Isn't a more apt comparison one between the Service and a women-church liturgy? And is it reasonable to ignore the sacralization of male clericalism within the Service?--while one may raise such questions, Eriksson's analysis of the patriarchalizing power of the Service remains clear, and it is an indisputable challenge for the Church of Sweden--any by extension, other Christian theologies that sacralize the priestly role. **NOTE**: For an early history of the ordination of women in Sweden, see Brita Stendahl, *The Force of Tradition: A Case Study of Women Priests in Sweden.* [Philadelphia: Fortress, 1985].

[241] Gray, Elizabeth Dodson. *Sunday School Manifesto: In the Image of Her?* Wellesley, MA: Roundtable Press, 1994.
Together with what is now an increasing number of feminist evangelical voices **[246-247, 251]**, Gray's "manifesto" rigorously demands an accountability *from church pulpits* on Christianity's long history of misogynous teaching about women and the violence prone implications of that teaching--that incest, spousal abuse and spousal obedience are the witnesses against patriarchal "Christian forgiveness," and that if Christianity is to survive, it must undergo an entirely new reformation: *viz.*, a feminist reformation that should be built into Christianity's systemic preaching *and* educational institutions. Gray is a Christian educator whose principle works are designed largely for seminars and adult educational workshops. (Cf. her popular *Patriarchy as a Conceptual Trap*, Wellesley, MA Roundtable Press, 1982, and her 1988 edited reader, *Sacred Dimensions of Women's Experience*, also from Roundtable Press.) This text, however, surpasses her earlier work and passionately, adamantly, and ecumenically lays out a single hermeneutical principle for Christian preaching and the "reimagining" of Christianity. Says Grey, "You cannot have a children-friendly tradition until you have a woman-respecting tradition. You cannot affirm life, without affirming women...[and]...it hurts children when Christian theology, ritual and praxis denigrate and abuse their mothers--just as it hurts children to watch battering husband/fathers beating their mothers" (p. 72). Her authorities here (among others cited elsewhere in her text) are Mark 10:14 and Matthew 18:6, and it is physical and sexual violence to women and children that are here identified as the "stumbling block" to the basileia of God.

[242] Heyward, Carter. *Touching Our Strength: The Erotic as Power and the Love of God.* San Francisco: Harper & Row, 1989.
This text is a collection of seven essays that discuss sensuality and embodiment as sources of theological insight for the development of Christian ethical and feminist ethical reflection. It is exploratory (rather than formally systematic) and structured almost as if a series of meditations. The key to the essays is Heyward's critique of "erotophobia" as institutionalized by the Council of Elvira (c. 309 C.E.) on the "eve of the Constantinian settlement." The latter, she argues, was the vehicle through which Christianity "lost a major portion of its identity...[as]...a body of resistance to oppressive power relations" (p. 42), and thus, in the absence of this resistance like character-- and *in the presence* of Elvira's codified antisexual laws--the church became an agent of clericalized social-sexual control: an organization grounded in erotophobia and geared particularly to the

suppression of sensual spontaneity as a force on behalf of life and its wonder. What is more, as its ascetically defined male leadership gained ascendance, the church spawned norms and nuances which became the staple and support of such ideologies as sexism, heterosexism, violence and sadomasochism (eroticized violence), and a framework of social organization in which sexuality and particularly the sexuality of gay men and lesbian women was defined as shamefully evil. This is a difficult text, with essays of varying sophistication. The first addresses issues of coming out, the second Elvira's legacy. Essays #3 and #4 summarize heterosexism as a vehicle of "white male supremacy" and liberal Christianity's moral bankruptcy, respectively, with the latter presented more systematically in [570]. Essay #5 examines scripture as a resource on behalf of justice-making relationality, and the remaining two essays synthesize various aspects of Heyward's feminist ethics. All, however, are grounded in her critique of erotophobia and tied almost throughout by her initial work with the Stone Foundation and its psychological theory. Last, the almost meditation like quality of her writing here well attests her commitment to (and struggles with) "mutual relation" as both an energizing and justice-making force which , in turn, bears its own reward and playful revelation. **NOTE:** See [199] for a listing of Heyward's related works.

[243] Hopkins, Julie M. *Towards a Feminist Christology.* Grand Rapids, MI: William B. Eerdmans, 1995.
In seven clearly written chapters Hopkins summarizes much current biblical, exegetical and feminist theological work to discuss the three key Christological doctrines regularly problematic from feminist perspectives: the Cross, the Resurrection and the Chalcedonian doctrine of the Incarnation. Chapter I sets the framework for the discussion with a brief review of recent European history (the Holocaust, technology and secularization), theology's cultural pluralism, and the pastoral nemesis of Christianity's "pietistically" grounded and religiously gendered, Jesus/women "servant" role. A methodological chapter provides the Gospel of Mark as a grounding source for Jesus' life and death, and three subsequent chapters survey the doctrines noted above. Hopkins' closing chapter then locates Christology and spirituality within the broad framework of personal identity, cultural change and social relativity. At a superficial level, this text reads almost as if a response to Daphne Hampson's work, for Hopkins (a British Baptist minister) regularly responds to Hampson's post-modernist critique of Christian doctrine ([286]). A more substantive reading, however, underscores the vision of Hopkins' title: as she easily summarizes technical and difficult discussions within malestream and American feminist theologies, Hopkins' effort is not the redemption of past doctrine, but the empowerment of *other women also coming to subjectivity, but now in the face of such doctrine.* Thus her synthesis is towards that empowerment, and not a shoring up of traditional teaching. This is an engaging and pastorally directed text that introduces a vision of women and Christology with implications, overall, for feminist theology and young, culturally unrooted religious women.

[244] McFague, Sallie. *Models of God: Theology for an Ecological, Nuclear Age.* Philadelphia: Fortress Press, 1987.
This text is the bridge piece between McFague's earlier methodological work [200] and her more fully developed ecofeminist work [245]. In it she argues persuasively for the adoption of a "new sensibility," i.e., a new normative framework which recognizes the relational rather than atomistic character of all reality and the very real possibility that humans can bring about nuclear--and thereby species--destruction. Hence, McFague argues that this sensibility requires a *major* change in the constructive and culture defining efforts of theology. This change would entail a shift from the construction and use of metaphors, models and images that alienate, isolate and bifurcate human and divine interaction, to the construction and use of metaphors, models and images that lift up the interdependent, relational and fully ecological character of reality, including human and divine interaction. To make her case, McFague reviews various literatures on metaphors and models, and on the role and use of Scripture, "Tradition" and human experience in the theologizing process, and finally, the necessary elements of "Christian tradition" which must figure into the theologizing process. In turn, she contrasts four specific models that depict divine and human presence and interaction. These include the models of: (i) God as a monarch ruling over the earth (the traditional biblical, medieval, reformational model for divine human presence and interaction); (ii) God as a *Mother* caring for her children; (iii) God as a *Lover* with all humanity; and (iv) the model of God as a *Friend* to all humanity, in the fullest sense of the word "philia" and its implications. In her conclusions, McFague suggests that while none one of these models is fully adequate to describe and evoke the reality of God's presence to humanity, each moves humanity closer to a posture of respectful and ecologically responsible caring for the whole of creation, so that nuclear destruction can be averted. Her subsequent work [245] below, then continues the need for ecologically sensitive models. This is an important work. First, it decenters hierarchical models in favor more

relational and lateral or dialogical models. Second, it provides a framework that speaks to both feminists and traditional theologians. Third, while controversial when first published, this text has sustained and generated much subsequent feminist theological work. **NOTE**: For related literature, see Sheila Greeve Davaney and John B. Cobb, "Reviews of *Models of God: Theology for an Ecological, Nuclear Age*, by Sally McFague." *Religious Studies Review* 16 (1990): 136-42.

[245] McFague, Sally. *The Body of God*. Minneapolis, MN: Fortress, 1993.
This text continues the imaginative lines begun in McFague's earlier works (**[200]** and **[244]**) and it is her most significant book through the mid 1990s. It identifies and clearly lays out: (1) the ecological crisis facing contemporary society, (2) the imaginative needs required by a theological response to this crisis, and (3) specific theological reconstructions that arise by imagining "bodiliness" as a "model for God." McFague begins by noting the scope of the ecological crisis: it is a planetary-wide crisis, and unlike the potentials of a nuclear war (which could engender a sudden species destruction), this crisis more subtle and thus more difficult to overcome. This is because one species, i.e., humans--and particularly those of highly industrialized nations, are literally using up the resources of the earth while neither replenishing its resources nor making provisions for its continued sustenance; and all at a rate that has far outpaced the development of the earth's organic life and wholeness. Given this circumstance then, *and* given the incarnational character of Christian faith, McFague suggests an imaginative theological process, *viz.*, that of seeing the earth itself as God's "body," and this with all it can imply. And it implies is quite a bit: (a) a depiction of sin as humanity's refusal to see its [ecological] place in the wider scheme of things; (b) a meditation on Ex 33:23b (that we shall see God's back but not God's face); (c) a panentheistic theology of nature; (d) an attention to the destabalizing power of selected parables capable healing and feeding of the earth; (e) an identification with the earth's own oppression; (f) an attention to the full significance of "breath" as enlivening the earth; (g) an attention to the cosmic Christ and God's own relation to the Body; and last, an awareness of the church as Christ's body in a spatially rather than historically directed eschatology and ethic. It is a profound discussion, a wide vision, and the best yet of McFague's "thought experiments," where readers are asked to *"Just imagine..."*

[246] Mollenkott, Virginia Ramey. *Godding: Human Responsibility and the Bible*. New York: Crossroad, 1988.
Mollenkott's thesis in this brief volume is that "...human responsibility in its deepest and fullest dimension , entails *godding*, an embodiment or incarnation of God's love in human flesh, with the goal of co-creating with God a just and loving human society" (p. 2). The argument is fleshed out with evangelically grounded descriptions of mutuality, relationality and inclusivity, and readers are asked, for example, to "yield up" "us vs. them" attitudes as expressed in nationalism, denominationalism and local congregations. Mollenkott's biblical grounding is the character of Job, as cast by the provocative question, "Of what can a perfect person repent?" and her closing chapters excerpt selections from poets Audre Lorde, Adrienne Rich, Charlotte Brontë and Alice Walker, to name but four. Examples from her earlier work on feminine language for God **[201]**, discussions about godding and "darkness," godding and sexual identity, and godding and peacemaking all receive chapter length treatment, and an appendix, "Some Biblical Passages That Imply Godding," closes the volume. **NOTE**: Also by Mollenkott are **[247]** and **[574]**, co-authored with Letha Scanzoni.

[247] Mollenkott, Virginia Ramey. *Sensuous Spirituality: Out from Fundamentalism*. New York: Crossroad, 1992.
Working with evangelical, psychological and biblical sources, Mollenkott here advances the thesis that "sensuous spirituality" or "living out of the pure and eternal core of one's being," as she also calls it "breeds concern for the well being of...people and all...other creatures...on this planet...and for the planet itself..." (p. 21). It is a somewhat diffuse thesis (at least to one not reared in the intensity of fundamentalist faith), but as one moves through the text, her understanding of sensuous spirituality becomes clear. It is a joyous and embodied appropriation of one's own integrity and the utter delight one has at knowing that true selves need neither to be saved nor ransomed, but accepted, embraced and revered. Mollenkott begins by identifying the lynch-pin problem of her fundamentalist socialization: namely, that "the very core of [her] personhood...could be redeemed and controlled only by the installation of a totally-other Christ-nature..." (p. 15). She then moves quickly to the heart of her text, a critique of "heteropatriarchy" as a religious-social ideology premised on various hierarchies of "power-over," but especially those defined in terms of gender and sexual orientation. It is a strong discussion set provocatively in a reading of Luke's Magnificat as contrasted with Margaret Atwood's *The Handmaid's Tale*. Mollenkott's discussion, "Midwifing

Justice as the Wisdom of God Herself," then follows, and in this and subsequent chapters she sets forth the rationale(s) for empowering other fundamentalists to embrace diversity, pluralism and social justice, and at all points of the conversation, the full humanity of bi-sexual, lesbian and gay persons--with the latter specifically so because it is her community of accountability as a lesbian, "out from fundamentalism." This is a warm, wonderful, and loving text which casts a wide net of kindness to those less so. It addresses--among other things--sexuality, passing, outing, social transformation, the characteristics of functional and dysfunctional church families, and a variety of strategies for helping groups to move from the latter to the former. Two appendices close the text, "Milton's Use of the Bible To Defend Divorce for Incompatibility" and "Diverse Forms of Family Mentioned or Implied in the Hebrew and Christian Scriptures." **NOTE**: For related literature see **[217]**, **[230]**, **[556]** and **[627]**, and the entries in Chapter 15.

[248] Moltmann-Wendel, Elisabeth. *A Land Flowing with Milk and Honey: Perspectives on Feminist Theology*. New York: Crossroad, 1988.
This text was first published in Germany in 1985, and its well translated version provides a reflective summary of the American and European feminist theological literature published through the mid-1980s and as organized through the three categories of "Self-Discovery," "Critical Theology" and "A New Perspective on the Stories about Jesus and Women." By way of specifics, Moltmann-Wendel examines the history of patriarchy, the rediscovery of goddess religion, and various issues in feminist theology, including mother and father language for God, Sophia imagery, feminist christology, mutuality, and the effects of patriarchy on biblical redactions and translations. By way of purpose, she seeks to unfold the feminist theological search for the "invisibility of women" in Christian history and tradition, and within this, the "invisibility of a non-patriarchal God" who, by implication, can also be rediscovered and held forth (p. 6). Seen thus, Moltmann-Wendel proposes no new theological syntheses, but seeks, instead, those images overlaid with patriarchy, that are present and available if one but digs deeply enough. Her search is at points provocative. As she aligns selected feminist theological emphases with elements of depth psychology and the history of Christian art, Moltmann-Wendel demonstrates several potentials for feminist theological reconstruction. (See, e.g., her reproduction on page 104 of "Kether, Hokmah and Binah, three feminine images of the Trinity" dating from 1673.) **NOTE**: This is primarily a desciptive and summary text, but beginning readers seeking an informative and empowering overview will find helpful and engaging.

[249] Russell, Letty M. *Household of Freedom: Authority in Feminist Theology*. Philadelphia: Westminster, 1987.
In a 1984 discussion on women in ministry (see **[656]**) Russell has identified the patterns of domination and partnership as paradigms of authority distinguishing traditional and feminist understandings of Christian ministry. Here she widens that discussion to detail how the paradigm of partnership can highlight and transform various theological metaphors, but particularly church and kingdom metaphors, from exclusive to inclusive perspectives. Her discussion develops in six chapters that address, respectively: (1) the definitions and types of authority available for theological reflection; (2) the hierarchical and relational assumptions grounding "domination" and "partnership" paradigms specifically (and the role of paradigms in generating or closing off theological insight); (3) the authority of feminists to reinterpret scripture, its symbols and historical extensions (i.e., it is an authority borne of hope and rooted in both God's promises and the practice of scripture itself--hence, the potential of viewing God as a "householder"); (4) the ecclesiological implications of a partnership paradigm, i.e., a listening from the "underside" (cf. **[276]**) and a search for the ways and space [or "new household"] within which to do that; (5) the implications of partnership for an inclusive understanding of "the kingdom of God" (it becomes God's household open to all); and (6) a survey of the theological norms and practical strategies--the good housekeeping--women and men of the church need to do to combat the patrimony and patriarchy yet alive in local congregations. A transition and almost a first draft to **[250]** below, this text well exhibits Russell's ecumenical and biblical commitments and her consistent efforts to release Christianity from its patriarchal frames.

[250] Russell, Letty M. *Church in the Round: A Feminist Interpretation of the Church*. Louisville, KY: Westminster/John Knox, 1993.
This text continues and refines the "household" ecclesiology developed by Russell in **[249]**, but with key additions and nuances, including: (1) an understanding of Christian "traditioning" in terms of both its patriarchal history *and* its potential feminist future; (2) an integrated focus on feminist spirituality as the process of "staying connected"; and (3) a variety of images--church in the round, table partnership, women's quilting, "sister choice," and others--which connect the inclusive

dimensions of feminist theology to the needs of white mainline churches and their members. It is a comprehensive discussion, cast in Russell's ever readable clear expository style. Thus, Russell first notes the need for feminists--and particularly white feminists of varying privilege(s)--to connect with women (and men) who live at the margins (whether the latter are racial, social, sexual, ecclesial, economic or political). Second, she grounds Christian mission in the need for liberation directed praxis at the local, self and church organizational levels, and in a very helpful analysis of "election" and privilege, she examines the "church-dividing issue" of white racism and its implications of "hospitality" to "outsiders." Third, as she unfolds her theme of connectedness as the basis of feminist spirituality, Russell focuses on the needs and risks of coalitions, community building, self affirmation and the work of tradition choosing, as women seek "safe space" for feminist coming together. Finally, as she unfolds the main lines of her ever widening but "staying-connected-to-the margins" framework, she illustrates her discussion with two case study congregations in particular: the "Rainbow Church" of the Rev. Hanna Hen (who ministers to Korean women now Americanized through marriage as GI war brides), and a local Lutheran church as pastored by the Rev. Gladys Moore who has worked to undo the structural racism of her mixed New Jersey congregation. This is a packed and pastorally directed text that well models its message of inclusivity and partnership as the marks of a feminist ecclesiology. And, as with all of her work, it connects Russell's feminism with her initial and deepest commitments to Scripture and its promises of grace and redemption. An extended bibliography together with Scriptural, subject, and name indices completes the volume.

[251] Scanzoni, Letha D., and Nancy A. Hardesty. *All Were Meant To Be: Biblical Feminism for Today.* 3d ed. Nashville, TN: Abingdon, 1992.
Now in its third edition, this text continues to affirm the links between feminist and evangelical perspectives, as its fifteen chapters examine such issues as biblical revelation, egalitarian gender roles, sexuality, reproduction, same-sex relationships, single women, discrimination within the churches (i.e., how churches "waste" women's gifts), conflicts between work and family obligations, and in a chapter updated from each of its preceding editions ("Where Do We Go From Here--Again?") the contemporary issues of backlash, "women's health needs," domestic violence, sexual abuse, women's overload as caregivers, "The Mommy Track Debate," care for aging parents, and last, "transitions" (*viz.*, divorce and uncoupling). This is a strong and clearly written text, well within the parameters of evangelical hermeneutics (i.e., no proof-texting, but several texts cited in support of specific practices), and complete with a closing "Study Guide" that walks the reader back through chapters and issues by way of goal directed and horizon widening questions. Last, its topically arranged "Further Resources" bibliography is thorough and current through 1990. Two indices (name/subject and biblical references) close the volume. **NOTE:** Also by Scanzoni are **[574]** and **[673]**, while for other important feminist evangelical works see **[241]**, **[243]**, **[246]**, **[247]**, and **[431]**. Additionally, see **[474]**.

[252] Thistlethwaite, Susan Brooks. *Sex, Race, and God: Christian Feminism in Black and White.* New York: Crossroad, 1989.
This text examines the "difference race makes" in the theologizing process, as Thistlethwaite attempts self-consciously as a "white feminist theologian" to theologize from within a knowledge of African American women's history and the different understandings this knowledge sheds on her own and the dominant culture's casting of historic Christian symbols. The discussion develops in three movements. First, in chapters 1-2, Thistlethwaite begins with a recognition of the argument made by many African American women, that the phrase "women's experience" is a false universal, because as used by most feminists, it typically presumes the experiences of white, middle and upper middle class women (professional or not), but not the experiences of women from differing race/class backgrounds. In turn, and through a wrenching description of white and black women's experiences in American slavery, Thistlethwaite poses her question: i.e., what difference might it make if one [who is white] were to take the experiences of African American women--and not those of white women--as normative for one's theology. Thistlethwaite then begins this process, and in chapters 3-7, she examines several historic Christian symbols (Creation, the Fall, Sin, Jesus, and the Fatherhood of God) with aspects of each challenged by the insights and articulation of pain as presented by women who lack access to majority privilege (e.g., many African American women, Holocaust survivors and survivors of sexual and domestic violence). Last, Thistlethwaite synthesizes her entire discussion in terms of (1) sexual and domestic violence against women as a reality transcending class and race differences (an emphasis she has held as counterpoint throughout), (2) the ways in which white women have been complicit in the physical and economic violence done historically to African American women, and (3) the continuing tensions such a shared defined history produces for both white and black women (not least of

which are "white guilt" as [white] women come to terms with this history) and, from an analytical perspective, the need to incorporate evil within feminist anthropologies. This is a strong, albeit repetitive and at points unclearly written text. Nevertheless, its general thesis stands: To examine one's theological grounds rigorously from within the horizons of non-dominance as Thistlethwaite does here, is instructive *and* chastening, *and*, given the many particulars of her analysis, a major contribution. **NOTE**: For Thistlewaithe's subsequent work, see **[276]**.

NOTE: For additional, related material, see earlier chapters and see Section III and Chapter 18.

3. Womanist and *Mujerista* Authors

[253] Cannon, Katie G. *Black Womanist Ethics*. Atlanta, GA: Scholars Press, 1988.
This text is Cannon's doctoral thesis and it remains the classic "first source" for womanist theology generally and womanist ethics in particular. Overall, it introduces: (1) the need and methodology for womanist ethics, together with Cannon's reasons for writing; (2) the history of "The Black Women's Moral Situation..." (two chapters covering 1619-1900 and "the twentieth century"); (3) "The Black Woman's Literary Tradition as a Source for Ethics" (a summary of oral tradition as an historical medium in Black women's history); (4) "Resources for a Constructive Ethic in the Life [and then Work] of Zora Neal Hurston" (two chapters); and (5) a contrast between identified womanist themes and themes drawn from the writings of Howard Thurman and Martin Luther King. While compelling enough if read only for the broad sweep of its grounding literatures, Cannon's identification of such womanist themes of "invisible dignity," "quiet grace," and "unshouted courage" provides not only a study in "womanist ethics" (as drawn from Hurston's work), but also, a grounding methodological text in womanist anthropology. Put differently, in identifying the "moral agency" of African American women, Cannon's analysis of Hurston's life and work parallels Plaskow's early "women's studies" methodology **[203]**, and it exposes the cultural bias of much early women's studies work. Second, as it lifts up the social movement and "communal ethic" themes of African American theology, it provides a contrast to early Catholic and (dominant) Protestant feminist theological anthropologies (i.e., the resymbolization of women as also "Imago Dei" and the critique of misogyny and androcentrism within biblical, patristic and other theological traditions. See, e.g., Farley **[167]**, Clark and Richardson **[186]**, and entries in Ruether and McLaughlin **[209]**). **NOTE**: Also by Cannon are **[612]**, **[625]** and **[532]**.

[254] Grant, Jacquelyn. *White Women's Christ and Black Women's Jesus: Feminist Christology and Womanist Response*. Atlanta, GA: Scholar's Press, 1989.
This work builds upon Grant's early essays and presents a critique of feminist theology and Christology published through the mid-1980s. In particular, Grant examines the early writings of evangelical theologians Virginia Mollenkott and Paul Jewett, Roman Catholics Leanard Swidler, Rosemary Radford Ruether and Mary Daly, and Presbyterian Letty Russell. Grant's discussion is cast through a typology of "Biblical, Liberationist and Rejectionist" feminists, with the first two categories serving as an expansion of Carol Christ's "reformist/revolutionary" dichotomy **[177]**. In brief, Grant identifies not only issues of theological methodology (e.g., the relative weights of the Bible and women's experience in the task of theologizing), but as well, issues of race and class bias within the works she surveys. Grant's primary criticism of feminist theology and Christology is that it is white--not only (or even primarily) in terms of the race of the writers, but more pointedly in terms of their cultural assumptions, intellectual traditions and academic resources. Hence while the Christological concerns of these writers vary, they are essentially uniform in that they make white women's experience normative and do not utilize the experience of Black women (or for that matter, the experiences of other ethnic women of color) as a source for theology. That a tradition of Black women's experience is available as a theological resource, however, is clear. Sources exist in contemporary Black women's literature and the surviving materials of Black slavewomen, in the experiences of Black churchwomen, Black clubwomen and the "servant caste" of domestics who have survived at the hands of white society--both male and female. Moreover, Grant argues,the experiences within this tradition bespeak an altogether different resource for theology and Christology: specifically, one concerned with the physical, emotional, economic and spiritual survival of Black women, and the survival of their families and their history. That this tradition is *not* part of the mainstream feminist theological and christological literature evidences the racial and class biases of this literature, and with these, the ongoing conflict between Black and white women theologians. That this tradition *should* be part of the feminist theological literature is, for Grant, quite clear, and it bespeaks the emerging womanist theological endeavor. Grant's book is powerfully written and well-documented. Its literature is current through the mid-1980s, and its early chapters address feminist theology from both theological and denominationally based sources.

Last, its discussion and bibliography on womanism (chapter 7) is especially valuable. **NOTE**: Also by Grant are **[214]**, **[635]** and **[636]**.

[255] Isasi-Diaz, Ada Maria, and Yolanda Tarango. *Hispanic Women: Prophetic Voice in the Church*. San Francisco: Harper & Row, 1988.
This brief, bi-lingual volume addresses the sources, expectations and methodologies of Hispanic Women's Liberation Theology. It identifies the grounding features of this theology--its communally based orthopraxis on behalf of liberation (as contrasted with equality or assimilation), and it clarifies the distinctiveness of this theological perspective, *viz.*, the normative authority of Hispanic Women's lived experience (in the *familia* and *barriada*); the significant weight of Hispanic Women's enculturated values, feelings and justice-directed aspirations; and the open-ended methodology of reflection upon, analysis and ritualization of Hispanic Women's lived experience. Last, the book notes regularly that the Christian ethos of Hispanic Women's Liberation Theology is one borne of Hispanic Women's "lived experience" and thus its primary concerns are de facto not those of "official Christianity," since for Hispanic Women the latter was an enculturation of *conquistadores* values. This is an important work that signals the powerful role of "culture" in the shaping of gender, religious identity, and authority, and it provocatively illustrates the concept of "social location" in feminist theology. **NOTE**: Also by Isasi-Diaz are **[256]** and **[927-929]**.

[256] Isasi-Diaz, Ada Maria. *Mujerista Theology: A Theology for the Twenty-First Century*. Maryknoll, NY: Orbis, 1996.
This brief collection brings together ten essays that evidence the grounding and range of Isasi-Diaz's "*Mujerista*" perspective. The first three essays detail "Locating the Self in *Mujerista* Theology" and they variously review: (1) Isasi-Diaz's initial move from Cuba to the United States in the 1960s and her crystallized awareness of the significance of this move in 1987; (2) her initial recognition of ecclesiastical sexism at the 1975 (U.S.) Women's Ordination Conference and her struggle against the perceived biases of Christian Euro-American feminists of the mid-70s and 1980s; and (3) her growing commitment to a justice directed framework dissociated from sexism, classism and religious clericalism, but not Latina faith. Remaining essays then synthesize various aspects of that Latina faith under the rubric of "Doing *Mujerista* Theology," and here the emphases widen to include the struggles of Latina women to find voice within the women's movement in both church and society, Isasi-Diaz's analysis of the types of oppression Latinas regularly experience, the role of various religious and social factors in *Mujerista* theology (including the *daily lived experience* of Latina women), and, in her discussion of *Mujerista* theology as a "challenge to traditional theology," Isasi-Diaz's helpful overview of the role of enculturation in Latina experience and *Mujerista* theology. Most of these essays have appeared in previously published collections, but their synthesis here introduces the reader to the growing solidification of Isasi-Diaz's own developing *Mujerista* perspective. **NOTE**: Also by Isasi-Diaz is **[255]** and the entries cited there.

[257] Riggs, Marcia Y. *Awake, Arise and Act: A Womanist Call for Black Liberation*. Cleveland, OH: Pilgrim Press, 1995.
As a womanist ethicist known widely for her work on the interstructuring of race, gender and class bias (cf. **[508]** and **[628]**), Riggs argues here that "stratification" within the black community has created an ethical dilemma for African Americans. Namely, that as individual African Americans experience upward mobility, they become caught in the competitive demands of the dominant society, and reach, almost inevitably, a point of "sympathy without empathy" for the needs of the community as a whole. In turn, the development of such a consciousness erodes the need for a community based liberation perspective, and with it, the process of liberation itself. As a response to this dilemma, Riggs argues for a "mediating ethic" as patterned after the 19th century black women's Club Movement, and as grounded theologically in Niebuhr's relational theory of the "responsible self." The women of the Club Movement, she argues, struck a right balance between communal commitment and self transcendence, *and* their critique of the community on behalf its own self. Thus, the Club Movement ethic "lifting as we climb" permitted a widening inclusivity *within* the African American community, while judging--on religious grounds--the competitive ethic of the wider world. This is tightly argued text that requires close reading. Its opening pages on the "race versus class debate" frame Riggs' wider discussion, and its closing "sermonic fragment" movingly attests the depth of Riggs' own commitment to the community and its needs.

[258] Townes, Emilie M. *In a Blaze of Glory: Womanist Spirituality As Social Witness*. Nashville, TN: Abingdon, 1995.
This text unfolds the social and communal dimensions of womanist spirituality by connecting various historical and literary Black church and womanist resources with the ethical needs of the

contemporary African American community. It begins by synthesizing the antecedents of womanist spirituality, *viz.*, the motifs of African cosmography, the history of the "ring shout," and the ethics of the Club Women's movement. It then analyzes selected ethical issues facing contemporary African Americans (including forms of "historical and contemporary lynching," "issues gender and sexuality," and "identity and colorism in Black life"), and it closes with a four point agenda for the Black church, designed to evoke the traditional liberation ethic of Black religion as a communal and politically uplifting force within the community as a whole. Readers unfamiliar with the nuances of African "survivals" and 19th century African American evangelicalism will find the first chapter instructive, and those familiar with the literary sources of womanism will be further instructed by Townes' brilliant ability to utilize womanist literature in ethical analysis. Thus, images and excerpts from Toni Morrison's *Beloved*, Alice Walker's *The Color Purple* and Paule Marshall's *Praisesong for the Widow* unfold various ethical issues, including: the disproportionate location of toxic waste sites in or at the edge of economically poor Black communities (a "contemporary [form of] lynching"); the need for sexual self-care in the era of AIDS—and the related need to end Black heterosexism; the necessity to undo "colorism" by seeing its real roots in miscegenation and the internalization of racistly defined Black self-understandings; and last, the economics of America's structurally sustained (and now visible) "black underclass", and, with this, the communal impacts of "African American Neoconservative" politics and ideology. This is a strong and movingly written text, and it well lives up to its title to see womanist spirituality as *social witness* capable of bringing *glory* to the community and its needs. NOTE: In 1996 Townes assumed co-editorship the *Journal of Feminist Studies in Religion*. Her other works include [633] and [638].

[259] Williams, Delores. *Sisters in the Wilderness: The Challenge of Womanist God-Talk*. Maryknoll, NY: Orbis Books, 1993.
With the biblical story of Hagar [Gen. 16, 21] as her grounding theological image, this enormously important text identifies the motifs and implications of womanist theology for interpreting both America's historical "slavocracy" and the post-bellum experiences of African American women. These motifs and implications are fourfold, and they include the following: (1) the "tensions" of "forced" motherhood (as experienced by African American women during slavocracy and the "free" post-bellum period); (2) the "social role of surrogacy" (as defined by the "Mammy" role assigned to African American women in slavocracy, the post-bellum period and more recently in the potential of surrogate birth economies); (3) color symbolism or the "problem of ethnicity" as experienced by African American women (*viz.*, the wider society's pathological pattern of "white racial narcissism" which identifies white as normative and black as inferior and/or evil); and last, (4) the "wilderness" experience of both Hagar and African American women, i.e., the social circumstance of isolation and hostility which, on the one hand, connects all African American women as outsiders within the wider society, and on the other, solidifies sisters across various religious and social lines. These four issues, suggests Williams, are the framework for a Hagar/African American woman's story, and each is, as well, a critical challenge to the various theological frameworks (Black church, Black liberationist and feminist) that have sought to define Christian theology as inclusive--or at least assimilative--of African American women. Closing chapters then highlight points of conflict and consensus within these frameworks and womanist theology. This is a strong, tightly written, courageous and theologically honest, comprehensive text: it synthesizes several biblical, womanist, ethical and African American literatures, it provides a clear description of the womanist framework as a "survival/quality of life" tradition that speaks to past and present African American women's experience (including the contemporary issues of motherhood and surrogacy); it provides constructive and substantive contrasts between womanist, liberationist and feminist theological perspectives; it seeks to establish the visibility of African American women's leadership within the Black Church and its community wide denominational structures; and last, it seeks a socially empowering role for Black churches, as the latter are challenged to pool their resources on behalf of the social and ethical needs facing African American communities across the board. NOTE: Also by Williams are [341], [632], [639].

NOTE: For the wider literature on Womanist theology see Section IV. Additionally, for works by *Mujerista* theologians, Native American and Asian feminist theologians, see Chapter 23.

4. Jewish Feminist Authors

[260] Falk, Marcia. *A Book of Blessings: New Jewish Prayers for Daily Life, the Sabbath, and the New Moon Festival*. HarperSanFrancisco, 1996.
Written, according to Falk, for "those who are in the habit of praying, and for those who are not" (p. xxi), this text synthesizes traditional and contemporary Jewish pieties to provide an elegant,

deeply reflective and beautifully formatted book of prayers, blessings, and meditations for both personal and communal use. Its traditional dimensions include Falk's obvious love for the Hebrew language together with her sensitive attention to Torah, rabbinic, and liturgical insights, and her keen awareness that blessings are for celebrations in the midst of life's ordinary--and thereby-- profoundly creative moments. Additionally, for its contemporary hues, Falk writes as a feminist sensitive to the need for collaborative and empowering attitudes towards such celebrations and from an ethical framework that bespeaks a fully familiar feel for creation and covenanted spirituality. Hence, she writes theologically from immanent rather than transcendent motifs, and with speech about God that is at once is grateful for the insights of her mentors, but differentiated from them. (Cf. pp. 417-423). But there is more, for this is a fully *beautiful* text. At the level of concept and design, it presents a richness of daily, Sabbath, and new moon texts, all composed of blessings, poems and prayers--and as wanted, non-intrusive commentary cross references. Moreover, at the level of format, it provides English and Hebrew texts fully mirrored to one another, with transliterated text bridging them both, and spacious, gentle fonts that invite lingered reflection or simply time with one's text. Last, the "commentary" is itself tellingly presented at the *end* of the blessings. Falk's comprehensive index (complete with transliterations for both old and new prayers) closes the volume. For those who are, as Falk says in her introduction, either "immersed" in Judaism or simply standing yet "at the gate," this is, in a word, gold. It is brilliant, inviting, *very* user-friendly, and intended for life. NOTE: Also by Falk is [960].

[261] Gottlieb, Lynn. *She Who Dwells Within: A Feminist Vision of a Renewed Judaism.* HarperSanFrancisco, 1995.
Following the fourfold framework of "Theology," "Story," "Ceremony," and "Community," Gottlieb retrieves the image of the *Shekihnah*, Judaism's historical image of feminine Presence of God, to link it with contemporary midrash in an effort to end the "exile" of women in Judaism. Gottlieb begins with her first awareness of the need for a Jewish feminist theological voice: as she studied in preparation for the rabbinate, she found no exegetical works on women and was forced to confront the sexism of her tradition. Her awareness and in-class dialogues then compelled her to search for the *Shekihnah* Presence of God and "Her" poetic integration within the historical and mythical images of Jewish women's experience throughout history. Gottlieb's efforts, as presented here, provide is a weave of biblical meditations on justice, the power of Kabbalistic prayer, the meaning of the *Sch'ma*, and an "Honoring of the Oral Traditions of Jewish Women as Torah." The text is comprised largely of poetic presentations she has herself authored, and it blends reflections, hope, rituals, wisdom and a variety of practical applications drawn from Gottlieb's "feminist vision for a renewed Judaism". It is intended for use by women in local congregations, and it taps theology and memory to address such diverging concerns as Jewish community life, ecology, the Holocaust, gender conflict and domestic violence. And all these for a world at once faithful to custom, yet empowered to its feminist revision.

[262] Plaskow, Judith. *Standing Again At Sinai: Judaism from a Feminist Perspective.* San Francisco: Harper & Row, 1990.
This text is Plaskow's central theological work. It synthesizes several of her earlier, essay length methodological pieces (cf. [953-954]), and it casts them here as a discussion that accomplishes three things: (1) a feminist re-visioning of Judaism and its grounding symbols of Torah, Israel, and God (with this revisioning moving from the motifs of "dominance" and "power over" to those of mutuality and relationality as based on McFague's model of God as "friend"); (2) a subsequent, "new" theology of sexuality (which builds on themes of mutuality to critique the biblical and later rabbinic construction of women's sexuality "...as a locus of both Otherness and social control..."); and (3) a feminist theology of redemption as "tikkun olam," (i.e., the repair of the world, as grounded in categories of justice to critique and transform racial, class-based and sexual structures of oppression). Plaskow begins by acknowledging the challenges posed by two fundamental contradictions: (a) the Torah based assumption that women were actually absent at the giving of the Mosaic covenant at Sinai, and (b) the contemporary expectation that given such absence, women must ultimately choose between Jewish and feminist commitments and/or identities. For Plaskow, the first assumption is simply wrong, for it is untrue, and it suggests an impoverished history, as the reflections of at least some rabbis later imply. Second, the expectation of a forced Judaism/gender choice is also erroneous--and unfair--both because women were, in fact, at Sinai-- and because while subsequently excluded from Jewish theology and religious thinking, Jewish women today constitute the potential for a full (rather than "half") Judaism, as feminism and faith recover the presence, experience and power of women *at* Sinai. Thus as Plaskow has so frequently argued, the right questions are theological, and the answers are equally so. First, feminist midrash works to reconstruct the history and teaching of a male identified Torah. Second, the autonomy of

Jewish women's experience and presence (group wise) redefines the meaning of community for Israel. Third, and following McFague, the models of "friend" and "lover" replace those of "male" and dominant other" in Jewish theology and "God language." Plasow's discussions of sexuality and redemption then follow, as she removes "the erotic" from narrow conceptions of sexuality to its place as a grounding for feminist efforts on behalf of justice and the ending of racial, class-based and sexual oppressions. Detailed notes, a helpful glossary of Hebrew terms, and two indices (one general, the other biblical) then close the volume. NOTE: It is difficult to describe briefly the many facets of Plaskow's work here, including its manifold significance for Judaism and its openness to both women's religious studies and Christian ecumenism. Suffice it to say, that, as with all of her work (cf. the index), this text stands at the meeting of many disciplines with its honest, courageous, and bone-deep insights as Plaskow moves to her more directed and major points. Hence for challenging reviews, see Joanne Carlson Brown and Laura S. Levitt. "Reviews of *Standing Again at Sinai* by Judith Plaskow." *Religious Studies Review* 20 (1994): 13-20.

[263] Umansky, Ellen M., and Dianne Ashton, eds. *Four Centuries of Jewish Women's Spirituality: A Sourcebook*. Boston: Beacon, 1992.
This volume chronicles the history of Jewish women's spirituality from the mid-16th century through the late the 20th century, with documentary excerpts from numerous religious writings, women's prayers, poetry, sermons, liturgical materials, rituals, diary writings, sisterhood minutes, committee reports and other expressions of piety among Jewish women in (largely) Western Jewish experience. An extended preface co-authored by the editors indicates that the sources involve materials from 100 different Jewish women's experiences, and the volume's introductory, historical essay by Umansky locates the four-fold division of the writings: sources reflecting "Traditional Voices" (i.e., sources dating from c. 1560 to 1800); sources from "Stronger Voices" (1800-1980); sources from "Urgent Voices" (1890-1960); and sources from "Contemporary Voices" (1960-1990). Thorough introductions preface all sections, and the editors note that they have deliberately included examples of Orthodox, Conservative, Reform and Reconstructionist spiritualities. Hence readers should not expect a consistently feminist perspective throughout the text, but rather, what the authors intend: an historical presentation attesting four centuries of Jewish women's spirituality, spoken now on behalf those "earlier generations of women...[unable to]...articulate or record their own" voice and vision. This is a strong collection with "urgent" and "contemporary" voices comprising most of the text, and it clearly reflects the editors' care for the women for whom they speak.

NOTE: For the wider literature on Jewish feminist theology see Chapter 24.

5. Edited and Multiple Authored Works

The majority of edited and multi-authored works published by feminist theologians since 1985 have their particular relevance within the many topical literatures presented in Section III. Hence they are abstracted there. Particularly noted works include the following (as listed alphabetically): Cannon and Schüssler Fiorenza [348], Collins [349], Carr and Schüssler Fiorenza [321], Cooey, Farmer and Ross [495], Graff [322], King [908], Kolbenschlag [756], Plaskow and Christ [544], Procter-Smith and Walton [526], Ruether and Keller [135], Russell et al. [910], Sanders [637], Segovia and Tolbert [912], Stevens [442], and Townes [638].

B. Works About Feminist Theology

1. Definitions and Literature Overviews

[264] Chopp, Rebecca S. "Feminist Theology." In *A New Handbook of Christian Theology*, edited by Donald W. Musser and Joseph L. Price, 185-191. Nashville: Abingdon, 1992.
This article provides a broad sweep of the key emphases and basic topics in American feminist theology, with the elements of womanist theology detailed separately by Toinette Eugene [266]. For its grounding emphases, Chopp describes feminist theology's critique of patriarchy, "the speaking of women's experience," and the "transformative discourse" that feminist theology seeks within Christianity and culture. She details four topics germane to feminist theology (scripture and tradition, anthropology, symbols and ethics), and her closing comments suggest four "types" of feminist theology, with each patterned after paralleling descriptions of "secular" feminist theory (*viz.*, liberal egalitarianism, romantic expressivism, sectarian separatism and a "radical

transformist" perspective). Chopp's conclusions stress the power of feminist theology as a force of renewal and hope for contemporary culture. Her discussion is clear and informative, and it identifies various continuities between current feminist theologies and 19th century, suffrage theology. **NOTE**: For Chopp's additional work see [239] and the entries listed there, and see the note to [265] below.

[265] Copeland, M. Shawn. "Black, Hispanic/Latino, and Native American Theologies." In *The Modern Theologians*, edited by David F. Ford, 357-388. Cambridge, MA: Blackwell, 1997.
This essay provides one of the best available summaries of the three theological movements it surveys. In particular, it highlights the many ways in which these movements evidence or instantiate the wider changes in theological method and perspective typical to the 20th century, the commonalties they share, and then, following a pattern set for the volume as a whole, a concise and comprehensive summary of each movement's historical development, main issues, themes and spokespersons, and last, its achievements, yet to completed tasks and current agendas. Extended notes and bibliography then complete the entry. This is a packed and brilliantly developed discussion, and readers seeking both the theological and organization histories to the three movements it surveys will be amply rewarded. **NOTE**: Also from the same volume are "Feminist and Womanist Theologies" by Rebecca Chopp and an entry on "Feminist Theology" by Ann Loades. These latter entries are informative: Chopp addresses themes and linkages between secular and religious feminism and the works of Daly, Ruether, Schüssler Fiorenza and Delores Williams, while Loades surveys international sources in feminist theology. Neither, however, provides the detailed bibliography, organizational histories and range of issues, as does the Copeland entry here.

[266] Eugene, Toinette M. "Womanist Theology." In *A New Handbook of Christian Theology*, edited by Donald W. Musser and Joseph L. Price, 510-512. Nashville: Abingdon Press, 1992.
Although brief, this statement provides readers with a succinct overview of womanist theology and its salient features: (a) the roots of the term "womanist" in Alice Walker's poetry; (b) a definition that focuses "womanist theology" as a "signification...that permits African American women to define themselves, to embrace and consciously affirm their cultural and religious traditions, and their own embodiment" (p. 511); (c) an affirmation of womanist theology's triple critique of racism, sexism and classism; and (d) its dual focus on biblical liberation hermeneutics and an "egalitarian" Christology. For additional descriptions of womanism by Eugene see [626] and see her discussion in [906] which highlights contrast between womanist and feminist perspectives.

[267] Jones, Serene. "Women's Experience: Between a Rock and a Hard Place: Feminist Womanist and *Mujerista* Theologies in North America." *Religious Studies Review* 21 (1995): 171-179.
This compact and insightful review examines nine texts rooted in "women's experience" as a source for the theologizing process. It seeks to demonstrate (a) the various methodological assumptions attached to "women's experience" as a theological locus, and (b) the strengths and weaknesses of those assumptions on behalf of (c) the accomplishment of such specific theological goals as women's empowerment, the recasting of tradition, and the dismantlement of patriarchy. Jones begins by noting that each of her selected authors (see below) rejects "essentialist" understandings of [women's] "experience," but that some continue to use "universal" and "ahistorical" categories or frameworks (such as phenomenology or process thought) which continue to signal the disposition of a work as "solid, foundational, comprehensive in scope and generalizable in character" (p. 171). Alternatively, other writers "self consciously avoid universalizing gestures and opt instead for descriptions of experience that are historically localized and culturally specific..." (e.g., cultural anthropology and post-structuralism) and which, thereby, "challenge normative frameworks...and the undecided fate of 'truth' and its relation to doctrine" (p. 172). Thus she reviews her varoious texts and locates them in either the "rock" (group #1) or the "hard place" (group #2) category. For her own part, Jones seeks a place "between the rock and the hard place," and while she personally prefers the solidity of "rock" writers, her methodological work pushes her to the "hard place." This said, she acknowledges that neither perspective is sufficient. Texts Jones engagingly reviews include Johnson's *She Who Is* [232], Brock's *Journeys by Heart* [432], LaCugna's *God for Us* [234], Williams' *Sisters in the Wilderness* [259], McFague's *Body of God* [245], Chopp's *The Power to Speak* [239], Catherine Keller's *From a Broken Web* (Boston: Beacon Press, 1986), and Kathryn Tanner's *The Politics of God*, and Maria Isasi-Diaz's *En La Lucha*, each from Fortress, 1992 and 1993 respectively.

[268] Ross, Susan A., and Mary Catherine Hilkert. "Feminist Theology: A Review of the Literature." *Theological Studies* 56 (1995): 327-352.
This article reviews the literature of feminist theology published between 1960 (Saiving's essay [163]) and 1993, with brief mention of selected essays published in 1994. Its primary focus is the literature from the late eighties and early 1990s, which the authors characterize as grounded in a "diversity" that overrides the "reformist/revolutionary" publications of the 1970s and 1980s. Additionally, the authors note the development of the literature in terms of the six tasks of women's studies/feminist scholarship as identified by Weaver [762, pp. 154-155] (including the recovery of women's history and experience, the identification of lost traditions etc.), and they seek to illustrate the diversity needed for this task. Virtually all topics and authors are included, although given the scope of the literature none is addressed in great detail. Ross authors Part I of the essay ("The Physical and Social Context of Feminist Theology and Spirituality") and synthesizes therein, Feminist, Womanist, *Mujerista*, Asian and African sources around the themes of "embodiment," "mutuality and friendship," "social location," and "ecofeminism." Hilkert authors Part II ("Key Religious Symbols: God and Christ") and synthesizes the literature around "christology and soteriology" and "the mystery of God." A strong source for bibliography, this review should be followed with more issue oriented overviews that permit a comparative unpacking of key sources and authors, e.g., [217], [219], [220], [277], [279], [285], [340], [358]. NOTE: While not abstracted in this volume, Agnes Cunningham's "Feminist Spirituality: The State of the Question," [*Chicago Studies* 35 (1996): 141-155] draws heavily from this article. Indeed, as organized around the theme *Women--Theology and Ministry*, this journal issue addresses several topics. See [782].

NOTE: For additional literature see O'Neill [333].

2. Bibliographies and General References

[269] Finson, Shelley Davis, comp. *Women and Religion: A Bibliographic Guide to Christian Feminist Liberation Theology*. Toronto: Univ. of Toronto Press, 1991.
This guide provides a comprehensive synthesis of feminist theological literature as comprised by "books, anthologies, journal articles, special issues of journals, dissertations, newsletters, reports, study kits and other resources published during the years 1975-1988" (p. x), and as drawn from sources indexed in selected Canadian computer based networks (NOVANET and DORBIS) and hard copy indices published by the American Theological Library Association. The entries are arranged alphabetically within subtopics of the volume's eleven chapter length categories, and the compiler provides a brief description of the general contents of each chapter. Two additional features of the bibliography are its ecumenical and dialogical scope, as evidenced by its extensive chapter on Jewish feminist theology, and its appendix of "bibliographies, journals and newsletters." While not annotated, this bibliography is nonetheless invaluable for its listing of reference materials. An author index closes the volume.

[270] Musto, Ronald. *Liberation Theologies: A Research Guide*. New York: Garland, 1991.
This guide presents 1,295 entries organized topically into nine chapters that deal, variously with the biblical roots of liberation theology; early writings; papal and conciliar contributions to liberation theology; European, African, Asian, Latin American, and North American liberation theologies; and in a final chapter, "Feminist Theology." While several entries are simply listed and characterized as "not seen," the majority are either annotated by Musto or cross-referenced to annotations in other bibliographies. Both print and "near print" sources are cited, and an introductory essay spells out Musto's criteria for inclusion. Topics covered in the section on "feminist theology" include: "bibliographies," "women and the Goddess," "biblical reinterpretation," "women and the churches," "women as priests," "third world feminist theology" and "feminist theology in the first world." Catholic social teaching and the assumptions of Latin American liberation theology figure prominently in Musto's grounding criteria, and his sources for feminist theology cover Christian and Jewish writers. Title and author indices close the volume. This is an especially helpful source for contrasting feminist and other liberation theologies.

[271] Pellauer, Mary D. *Toward a Tradition of Feminist Theology*. Brooklyn: Carlson Press, 1991.
This text is Pellauer's doctoral thesis in social ethics (as co-advised by James Gustafson and Martin Marty), and it is the concept of justice in the works of Elizabeth Cady Stanton, Susan Brownell Anthony, and Anna Howard Shaw that marks Pellauer's analysis. For each of these early feminists

Pellauer traces historical contexts, each woman's selected and critical social issue, the role of religion within that issue, and the ethical horizon it portends, which in all cases, is "justice." For Elizabeth Cady Stanton this translates to the need for a rational and religiously based justice for women, apart from the churches and within the necessity of society's acknowledgment of women's right to think religiously for themselves. It is a "civil religious justice" as Pellauer terms it. For Susan B. Anthony it was a "looking up the needs of the oppressed" and particularly, women's dependence in order to fight the social, educational and economic conditions sustaining it. Last, for Anna Howard Shaw, the horizon of justice entailed the right to vote per se, or the glaring inconsistency between American theory and practice, democracy and the disenfranchisement of women, howsoever idealistically Shaw conceived it apart from other political realities. In her discussion of these women and their social-religious visions, Pellauer employs the theoretical writings of sociologist-anthropologist Clifford Geertz, ethicist Chiam Perelman, philosophers Michael Polanyi and Paul Ricoeur, and last but not least, feminist theologian Mary Daly. Her "Epilogue" locates the focus of the work's title--these three women *are* the beginnings of a feminist theological tradition--and it unfolds Pellauer's own testimony as to the necessity and validity of tradition within feminist theory and theologizing. This is a monumental work, and while it focuses the "justice" in the feminists it studies, it is not unmindful of the differences and conflicts between 19th and 20th century feminist causes and theoretical perspectives, which for Pellauer, fall to the *very* widened spheres of symbolism, subsistence and sexuality (including domestic violence). It merits careful reading and will no doubt be replicated (at least methodologically) in terms of other early feminist "ethicists" making up the recent history of the American feminist movement.

[272] Russell, Letty M., and J. Shannon Clarkson, eds. *Dictionary of Feminist Theologies.* Louisville: Westminster/John Knox, 1996.
As described by its editors, "this *Dictionary of Feminist Theologies* seeks to provide guidance to readers who are interested in all areas of Christian theology as they relate to feminism, as well as in theologies of other religions as developed by feminists" (p. ix). It does this and more. As the only work of its kind, its several hundred contributors provide brief but substantive summaries of virtually anything one can imagine vis a vis feminist theology in its multiple social locations. Moreover, although each of its entries is only a page or so in length, each provides two to three "these-will-get-you-going" key references, with the volume's full bibliography provided as the closing item of the text. This text invites--and supports--individual browsing and study, group discussion, and most obviously, ready reference use. Second, its introduction provides an alphabetized listing of all contributors, their entries, professional titles and institutional affiliations, and thus it provides accessibility to the field, and a "Who's Who" of feminist theology. Last the alphabetized entries of the text (but not author addresses) are fully on-line as the "Index of Feminist Theologies" at www.yale.edu/adhoc/research_resources/dictionary/limited.

NOTE: For biblical reference works see [343], [344] and [345]. For reference works in other areas see the topical listings in Section III.

3. Edited Collections

[273] LaCugna, Catherine Mowry, ed. *Freeing Theology: The Essentials of Theology in Feminist Perspective.* San Francisco: HarperSanFrancisco, 1993.
Ten extended essays, each on a topic important to Christian tradition and all by Roman Catholic feminist theologians, make up this informative volume of "the essentials of theology in feminist perspective." Not surprisingly, LaCugna's own entry surveys the theological issues attached to discussing the Trinity from a feminist theological perspective, while other contributors include Anne Carr on "method", Sandra Schneiders on "biblical theology", Mary Catherine Hilkert on "revelation", Elizabeth Johnson on "Christology", Mary Aquin O'Neill on [theological] "anthropology", Mary E. Hines on "church", Susan Ross on "sacraments", Lisa Cahill on "moral theology", and Joann Wolski Conn on "spirituality." These are strong contributors and each essay lucidly synthesizes relevant issues. A clear norm underlying both the collection and its entries is LaCugna's expectation that essays will highlight not only the feminist critique of Christian tradition (i.e., its critique of patriarchy and the "ideology of projecting onto God false dualisms or hierarchical arrangements between men and women") but, too, those "...liberating elements within the tradition" that are available for feminist use, as and to the extent that writers identify specifics within the tradition as "normative" (p. 3). Similarly, LaCugna notes that these essays are not meant to present "*the* feminist theology of topic *x,*" and that not all topics are equally developed within the literature. These are important qualifications, and they are evident throughout the text. This is a solid collection suitable for personal reading, group discussion, and/or academic use at both upper

division and early graduate levels. Its limitations, however, are those attached to its gifts: as it searches "the tradition" both to critique and liberate, its does so from within the tradition's own centrist and hegemenous contours. Hence a number of salient and methodologically important issues such as womanism and women's ordination await a further volumes. Endnotes and briefly annotated bibliographies follow each discussion, and a detailed index closes the text.

[274] Loades, Ann, ed. *Feminist Theology: A Reader.* Louisville: Westminster/John Knox, 1990.

Twenty-two entries by American and British feminist theologians--together with extensive editorial introductions and running textual comments--make up this near excellent, feminist theology reader. In fact, its only limitation is its lack of womanist material, an omission editor Loades readily and substantively acknowledges in both her extended introduction and the detailed bibliographic material within chapter notes. The volume is divided into three parts: "Biblical Tradition and Interpretation" (seven essays); "Christian History and Tradition" (eight entries); and "Practical Consequences" (again, seven entries), with material drawn exclusively from either major journals or chapter length discussions in books, and with all but one of the entries published since 1980. Indeed, 17 of the 22 essays were published between 1985-1989. Nor are the contributors unknown: Trible, Schüssler Fiorenza, Craven, Ringe, Lloyd, McLaughlin, Ruether, Daly, Harrison, McFague, Russell, Maitland, Ramshaw-Schmidt, and Farley stem from the American literature and Page, Slee, Wiesner, Hampson and King come from British sources. Loades' introduction sets the book's selections within three contexts: the history of the women's movement, the expansive area of women's studies, and issues facing women today: Tying all these together, she argues, is the fact that "Christian tradition" has theologically (as contrasted with the*a*logically) played out and enhanced society's sexist and gender-based institutions, while it has at the same time invited women to work for its [the tradition's] betterment. This, she argues, has created an ambivalence for women, and the present difficulty is that "whatever function they [the constructs of Christian tradition] may possibly once usefully have served, we are [now] increasingly conscious of the damage they do, and of our responsibility to do something about it." The entire volume--with its essays, editorial comments, extremely detailed footnotes, twenty-one page bibliography, and "Select Index of Names," moves to that end.

[275] Schüssler Fiorenza, Elisabeth, and M. Shawn Copeland, eds. *Feminist Theology: in Different Contexts.* Maryknoll, NY: Orbis, 1996.

The sixteen essays comprising this edited collection present differing "geographical," "religious" and "theoretical...sites of [feminist] struggle," and as such, evidence the wide pluralism of contemporary feminist theological work. More concretely, as Schüssler Fiorenza notes in her Introduction, "...this issue of *Concilium* aims to create a rhetorical space or an 'imaginary round-table' for the discussion of feminist theology in its manifold forms and articulations." Included, therefore, are feminist Latin American [Maria Jose F. Rosado Nunes], Australian [Elaine Wainwright], African [Teresia M. Hinga], European [Monica Jacobs], and American [Mary E. Hunt] perspectives, as well as feminist Muslim [Ghazala Anwar], Buddhist [Chatsumarn Kabilsingh], Jewish [Adel Reinhartz], and Christian perspectives [Aruna Gnanadason, Jaqueline Field-Bibb, and a "Concilium Round Table" of Roman Catholic theologians]. Last, social location and epistemology meet in a variety of theoretical discussions, by respectively, Gabriele Dietrich, Rebecca Chopp, Elizabeth E. Green, Marcella Althaus-Reid and M. Shawn Copeland. Contributors to the "geographic" and "religious" sites provide summary overviews of feminist effort and activities at their "site," while the theoretical essays are more interpretive.

[276] Thistlethwaite, Susan Brooks, and Mary Potter Engel, eds. *Lift Every Voice: Constructing Christian Theologies from the Underside.* San Francisco: Harper & Row, 1990.

Susan Thistlethwaite's work is regularly characterized by a respect for the pluralisms and particularities of personal and social experience, and this volume co-edited with Engel, a Professor of Historical Theology at the United Theological Seminary of the Twin Cities, is no exception. In it, that respect is exploited thoroughly on behalf of presenting liberation theology as a communally based, systematic and socially located enterprise. The volume has the appearance of an anthology-- its twenty essays reflect Asian, African, Latin American, African-American, Native American, Womanist, Gay and Lesbian, and Feminist Liberation theologies--but the editors state adamantly that it is not an anthology. Rather, it is an attempt to provide an initial systematic liberation theology borne of specific theologies of liberation. Thus, questions of method and commitment precede those of God and eschatology, and questions of grace and healing those of Christology, the church, its ministry, spirituality and scriptures. Some important features of liberation theology include the following: an attempt to speak with and on behalf of one's social community (rather than to or for it); a responsibility to dialogue with those beyond one's socially located experience (a task that requires one to hear and appreciate the experience of others); and a thorough-going recognition of "social location or context" as itself a theological locus. Thus a grounding question for all liberation theology is not where does experience fit with the tradition, but rather, "Whose experience is it you appeal to in the construction of your theology?" (p. 294). Contributors to the volume include Asian liberation theologian, C. S. Song; Korean, Japanese and Chinese liberationists, Young-chan Ro, Robert Fukada and Kwok Pui-lan; Latin American liberationist, Vitor Westhelle; Native American theologians Steve Charleston and George Tinker; Black liberationist, James Cone; Womanist Jacqueline Grant; *Mujerista* theologian, Ada Maria Isasi-Diaz; African theologians Bonganjolo Goba and Mercy Amba Oduyoye; Lesbian and Gay Ministry Associates Anita C. Hill and Leo Treadway; and American feminists, Rosemary Radford Ruether, Carter Heyward, Sharon Ringe and Mary D. Pellauer. Endnotes and a detailed subject/name index close the volume.

Additionally, see Graff [322] and Hinsdale and Kaminski [323] and see Ramshaw [523].

4. Overviews and Critical Assessments

a. Theological Perspectives

[277] Brock, Rita Nakashima et al. "Asian Women Theologians Respond to American Feminism." *Journal of Feminist Studies in Religion* 3, no. 2 (1987): 103-134.
This "special section" of *JFSR* presents papers from the Asian Women's Theologians' panel discussion held at the 1985 meeting of the AAR. The papers examine issues related to women, feminism, and religion in Japan, the Philippines, China, and Korea, and contributors include Yasuka Morihara Grosjean, Patria C. Agustin, Kwok Pui-Lan, and Soon Hwa Sun. Two themes run consistently through the papers: (a) that for these feminist women, the Bible is a book of liberation rather than oppression; and (b) the interactive patterns of Asian and white American and/or European scholars are yet strained by the implicit racism based in the class assumptions of American and Eurocentric scholarship. A closing statement by panel moderators Naomi Southard and Rita Nakashima Brock highlights these themes, as the latter express the felt needs of Asian-American scholars through such categories as "multiculturalism," "relationships and the meaning of suffering," and, last, the "need for healing" across cultural and racial barriers that yet exist for Asian-American women and women from dominant social and educational contexts. **NOTE**: See Chapter 23 for the developing literature by Asian and Asian-American feminists.

[278] Copeland, M. Shawn. "Toward a Critical Christian Feminist Theology of Solidarity." In *Women and Theology: Annual Publication of the College Theology Society, Volume 40*, edited by Mary Ann Hinsdale and Phyllis H. Kaminski, 3-38. Maryknoll, NY: Orbis Books and College Theology Society, 1995.
This article presents a tightly argued discussion for pressing feminist theology into an envisioned "fourth stage" of development, *viz.*, that of "unity within diversity." After summarizing the shifting nuances of race and ethnicity within the history of American feminist theology from the late '60s to the early 1990s, Copeland describes the conditions for the possibility of genuine solidarity between red, brown, yellow, black and white women. First (and by a process of elimination), a clarity about the nature of "solidarity" is needed, and the conventional understanding of "sisterhood" (or even common statuses of victiminzation) is insufficient for this point. Rather, "solidarity" is a communal phenomenon, borne of common and/or complimentary experience(s), shared understandings, judgments, and commitments. Put differently, the possibility of dialogue and conversion (intellectual, moral or religious) must exist among persons who would be in solidarity, for without these, persons do not transcend the conventional rhetoric. Second, the theological dimensions of solidarity need to be clear: i.e., *methodologically* in the recognition of interconnected socio-political oppressions, *anthropologically* in the moral obligation of speech (to do and become what one says one is), *communally* in the Spirit to resist domination, and (for Christians at least) *sacramentally* in terms of a common ground, as comprised by the search for and service to those marginalized by the suppression of human and political rights. As an analysis of "racially gendered difference" and the building of solidarity across differently empowered communities of Christian women, this discussion is one of the most incisive in the essay length literature, with implications for differences across religious traditions hopefully to follow. This

limitation notwithstanding, it bears comparison with Kanter's discussion **[728]** of tokenism and marginalization.

[279] Finger, Reta. "Look to the Future and Celebrate the Past: Celebrating 20 Years of Christian Feminism." *Daughters of Sarah* 20, no. 4 (1994): 4-62.
As with all issues of *DOS*, this one also presents several articles guided by the issue's selected theme, together with numerous book reviews, conference plans and resource listings. Distinctive to this issue, however, are three things: First, its attention to the November 1994 "Re-Imagining Conference" held in Minnesota "to celebrate the mid-point of the Ecumenical Decade of Churches in Solidarity with Women." Both participants and non-participants voice perspectives and overviews, with competing perspectives frankly acknowledged. Second, this issue announces a change in *DOS* editorship, with Reta Finger leaving that position after her 18 years of developing this very fine journal. Last, the issue once again focuses--as it so often does--the reality of violence to girls and women, both nationally and internationally. Finger and Sandra Volentine summarize various aspects of the "re-imagining" conference, and each announces her geographic move and subsequent editorial retirement. Letha Dawn Scanzoni provides an overview of evangelical women's feminist theology 1974-1994, and last, various authors document the abuse of girls and women both globally and nationally, with the former in terms of village violence, and the latter, women's repressed memories of domestic sexual abuse.

[280] Graff, Ann O'Hara. "Catholic Feminist Theologians on Catholic Women in the Church." *New Theology Review* 6, no. 2 (1993): 6-18.
This very readable article highlights several key developments in Catholic feminist theology since the 1968 publication of Mary Daly's *The Church and the Second Sex* **[157]**. Graff locates these developments in three broadly based categories. The first is "critical work" (including "critical work on ordination"), and here Graff cites Daly's *Church and the Second Sex*, Ruether's early anthology **[171]** and the Swidler volume prepared in response to the Vatican ban on women's ordination **[781]**. Second is "constructive work," both in terms of constructive biblical and tradition retrievals (e.g., Schüssler Fiorenza's *In Memory of Her* **[195]**) and constructive theological efforts such as by Carr **[229]** and Schneiders **[761]**. Graff's final category is "constructive proposals," and here she summarizes Ruether on women-church spirituality **[193]**, Schüssler Fiorenza on the differences gender makes in assumptions about women and "service" to the Church (see "Feminist Ministry in the Discipleship of Equals" in **[237]**), and finally, a series of five principles for democratic leadership in the [Catholic] Church, as developed by Ruether and Bianchi in their 1993 reader, *A Democratic Catholic Church* **[733]**.

[281] Kwok, Pui-Lan. "The Future of Feminist Theology: An Asian Perspective." *The Auburn News* (Fall, 1992).
This article discusses four value conflicts that condition the use and appropriation of American feminist theology by Asian women theologians and that can hinder the future development of contemporary feminist theology. The first of these conflicts is the felt tension between (a) a normative and theological commitment to "cultural and racial diversity" in the feminist theological community, and (b) the perceived reality of a class and cultural bias operative in the direction of white western women, as if their experience were normative for all. Thus, the author says, "...with other women of color, Asian women have challenged white women to stop using a 'universal' language as if they represent us." Conflict #2 stems from the facts of religious pluralism. On the one hand, Asian women must combat the "exclusivistic" attitudes of Christian missionaries (and contemporaries) who condemn the religious pluralism of Asian culture and ignore the sexism in Christianity while suggesting that "Islam, Shintoism, and Buddhism must be more patriarchal than the Christian religion." At the same, Asians (and particularly Asian women) must confront an "inclusivistic" almost patronizing perspective, which suggests that Christianity is somehow the true apex of all religions. Thus Kwok critiques theologies that presume "anonymous Christians," and she indicates that "feminist theologians must collectively begin to redefine our Christian identity without such expressions as 'uniqueness,' 'special revelation,'" etc. Third, she suggests that both Third world women theologians and American Jewish theologians must dialogue on behalf of justice and move therefore beyond their own histories of pain. Last, Kwok criticizes the feminist theological use of eroticism as a vehicle for talking about God, for this is insensitive to both the cultural norms governing Asian women's speech and the abuse of Asian women in the "international flesh trade" that grounds "so-called economic 'development.'" To close, Kwok calls for "more awareness of the contextual and embodied nature of God-talk" and the necessity for a "multi-cultural and multi-religious" framework for the doing of feminist theology. **NOTE**: For Kwok's analysis of the varying impacts of missionary Christianity on Chinese women, together

with her assessment of Chinese feminism and feminism's potentials within Christianity see her *Chinese Women and Christianity: 1860-1927*. Atlanta, GA: Scholar's Press, 1992.

[282] Ruether, Rosemary Radford. "Is Feminism the End of Christianity? A Critique of Daphne Hampson's *Theology and Feminism*." *Scottish Journal of Theology* 43 (1990): 390-400.
This essay is an extended review of Daphne Hampson's text, *Theology and Feminism* [286], in which Hampson argues that feminism and Christianity are essentially incompatible given: (1) the consistency of Christianity's male characterization of God (in the Bible, theology and worship); (2) the secular critique of Christianity stemming from the Enlightenment and of which feminism is a recent part; and (3) the absence of any change based mechanism within Christianity, given the historical character of its revelation. By way of response, Ruether summarizes Hampson's discussion and then addresses the core and periphery of her arguments. At the core of Hampson's critique of feminist theology is the assumption that Christianity is historical in its revelation and that it sees itself as uniquely so. It thereby has no mechanisms for change without an abandonment of its own integrity. Second, given the advent of modern science, Christianity is effectively on its way out and thus feminism should be concerned with bigger and better things, e.g., spirituality and a wider commitment to women. To respond, Ruether provides one of her most tradition grounded statements of feminist faith: an exposition of Christianity as an historical community of faith, which continues to make changes where none prior were thought possible, and in terms of feminist faith specifically, the painful awareness of patriarchy's long grip and the necessity of women to respect one another's choices in the face of its reach. She uses the image of the emmigre who moves away but must yet honor those who choose to stay in the "old country." By way of formal theological issues, Ruether capably exposes the Barthian reification of Christian revelation that permeates Hampson's argument, and she reaffirms the legitimacy of feminist work from several sources to challenge, respond to, and rework the tradition on behalf of its best possibilities.

[283] Schüssler Fiorenza, Elisabeth. "Changing the Paradigms." *The Christian Century* 107 (1990): 796-800.
In this brief article Schüssler Fiorenza examines her own work from the years 1964 through 1990 to indicate both the major influences on her conceptual development and the elements of change and expansion that have come to characterize her work overall. Of notable importance are: (1) her descriptions of feminism as "a movement for transforming patriarchal structures and relations of dominance" (p. 796) and patriarchy as "a sociopolitical graduated male pyramid of systemic dominations and subordinations that found its classical articulation in Aristotelian philosophy" (p. 799); and (2) her reflections on the uniqueness of the women-church symbol as a liberating and socially based hermeneutic (i.e., interpretive framework) for women within Christianity. The importance of this symbol, as described here is twofold: (a) it presents an alternative to the "exodus" symbol as a defining motif for women in organized Christianity, and (b) it permits the initial awareness of both patriarchal and egalitarian emphases within early Christian community and history. Also important in this article (but more developed elsewhere [395]) is Schüssler Fiorenza's identification of "rhetorical analysis" as a feminist based paradigm alternative to the current androcentric paradigm within biblical studies. **NOTE**: For Schüssler Fiorenza's more detailed description of patriarchy as a sex/gender system, see chapter 4 ["Justa--Seeking Common Ground: To Speak in Public: A Feminist Political Hermeneutics"] in *But She Said* [236].

[284] Tolbert, Mary Ann. "Protestant Feminists and the Bible: On the Horns of a Dilemma." *Union Seminary Quarterly Review* 43 (1989): 1-17.
Occasioned by the awareness that her students could appreciate the conceptual but not the existential, praxis dimensions of Schüssler Fiorenza's concept, women-church, Tolbert presents (1) an overview of three barriers Protestant women face in their efforts to appropriate biblically directed feminism and (2) a discussion of two "responses" Protestant women may make to the thoroughly androcentric nature of biblical writing. The barriers Protestant women face in appropriating feminism and scripture are threefold. First is the traditional "primacy of scripture," a Protestant emphasis that challenges all other approaches to the Bible, including, e.g., an 'historical reconstruction of Christian origins.' Second is the "diversity" of Protestantism, a denominational liturgical, organizational and clerical fact that fragments and isolates the power base of feminist Protestant women. Third is the individualistic emphasis of Protestantism and the familistic ethic it engenders. The barrier here is that such an ethic inhibits bonding with other women and in contrast to more communal perspectives (e.g., Catholic and womanist traditions) it can blind one to the systemic nature of misogynist oppression. In the light of these barriers, Tolbert then discusses how the Bible is, has been, and may be authoritative for Protestant feminists. Her discussion notes

the advantages and disadvantages of a re-constructionist approach to biblical androcentrism, and it then turns to a second, *supplemental approach*, that of gender itself as a hermeneutical category. Here, Tolbert employs concepts drawn from the "implied-reader/implied-writer" discussion within feminist literature, and she argues for an alternative reading of biblical literature so that gender/text conflicts may be understood and avoided. Tolbert's essay ultimately addresses the question, "Can one be both a feminist and a Christian?" and in keeping with her earlier work [372] the answer is yes, but now with explicit rationale(s). An insightful essay, this discussion is ecumenical in scope and substance, and it represents a significant advance over the largely reaactionary essays presented in the 1988 *Interpretation* discussion of feminism and biblical literature (e.g., [838] and [844]).

NOTE: For additional and related critical literature published through the early 1990s, see the sources on feminist theological anthropology in Chapter 8 and see the various methodology pieces in Chapters 9 and 10.

b. Sociological perspectives

[285] Katzenstein, Mary Fainsod. "Discursive Politics and Feminist Activism in the Catholic Church." In *Feminist Organizations: Harvest of the New Women's Movement*, edited by Myra Marx Ferree and Patricia Yancey Martin, 35-52. Philadelphia: Temple Univ. Press, 1995.
This article identifies discursive politics as "...the politics of meaning making," or more generally, the task of reinterpreting and reconceptualizing the norms of a given group, here the American Catholic Church and its hierarchy. This reconceptualizing is a largely cognitive task, in that its process entails the self-directed social redefinition of one's place within a specific system, and in the case of American Catholic feminists, it is almost the only available option, given the separation of church and state within the wider American system. But for Catholic feminists, argues Katzenstein, it has worked quite well. Katzenstein begins with a brief overview of both her concepts and the activities of American Catholic feminists. She then presents the Catholic "women-church movement" and the Leadership Conference of Women Religious (LCWR) as two examples of discursive politics, and in a closing section, she indicates the effects of such politics. While not institutionally effective in terms of changing the Church's policy on women and ordination, the "discursive politics" of women-church and LCWR Catholic feminists has had three effects: (1) this "narrative" and "expressive" process has empowered women religious; (2) it has raised consciousness on gender issues throughout the American Church; and (3) it has exerted enormous influence over the agenda of Catholic bishops in their annual meetings. Tucked as it is in an extended women's organizational reader [119], Katzenstein's discussion synthesizes much literature on the women-church movement and the LCWR's dialogs with Rome (cf. [800]), and while brief, it is provocative and should be read with her other work, [107].

NOTE: For additional sociological literature see Chapter 4, particularly Briggs [137], Neal [145-147], and Winter, Lummis and Stokes [153]; also, see Lummis and Stokes [742] on the sociology of Catholic feminist spirituality in Chapter 14.

5. Post-Christian and Reactionary Perspectives

[286] Hampson, Daphne. *Theology and Feminism*. Oxford, UK: Basil Blackwell, 1990.
This text is a post-feminist critique of the American feminist theological literature through the mid-1980s and particularly the works by Rosemary Radford Ruether, Elisabeth Schüssler Fiorenza, Sally McFague, and Phyllis Trible, and with respect to doctrines of sin and women's experience, early works by Judith Plaskow. In her text, Hampson argues that the only reasonable response of feminism to Christianity is its abandonment, for Christianity is rigorously patriarchal in its understanding of God and its assumptions about women; moreover, it is historically defunct given the advent of science and its norms for truth. Put differently, it is not only that feminism is incompatible with historical Christianity--with its biblical male God, its incarnate male God, its intra-male trinitarian theology, its male clerical hierarchy and its consistent concept of revelation as historical and historically unique. In addition, the questions and efforts of feminism vis a vis Christianity are irrelevant, given modern science. Thus, one must ask: 'Why would anyone want to be *compatible* with any of this?' Rather, Hampson suggests, feminism can be fully spiritual without being Christian. That is to say, religious feminism can be and is "post-Christian," and those who attempt a feminist reformation of Christianity are, in fact, post-Christian and should admit it. This is a strong text. It cuts to the bone, and (at the very least) shows what the absence of

hope for a tradition can look like. For other work by Hampson see **[478]**, and for Ruether's review of this text, see **[282]**. **NOTE**: Also by Hampson, but not abstracted here is *After Christianity*, London: Trinity Press International, 1997.

[287] Hogan, Linda. *From Women's Experience to Feminist Theology*. Sheffield: Sheffield Academic Press, 1995.
Working from her analysis of selected feminist, womanist and the*a*logical texts published through the mid-1980s, Hogan argues for both a more "difference" based hermeneutic in feminist theology and a recognition that neither nihilism nor pure relativism need to prevail if feminist theology recognizes its lack of an essentialist or ontological base. Rather, with this recognition, feminists, womanists and thealogians will demonstrate the truly "prototypical" rather than "architypical" character of feminist theology, and develop a truly standpoint-based epistemology. Hogan develops her discussion in three basic movements. For her groundwork, she reviews the rise of political and liberation theologies with their emphases on the legitimacy of experience and victimhood as constituting privileged theological places. She then surveys selected mid-1980s works by feminists Ruether and Schüssler Fiorenza, womanists Katie Cannon and Delores Williams, and the*a*logians Carol Christ and early Plaskow (among others) to demonstrate the various ways in which "women's experience" and "praxis" are used as a base of theological insight an*d*/or revelation, with each writer chronicled in terms of her methodological emphases. For her closing points Hogan draws from the Davaney/Christ debate (see **[330]** and **[327]**) to indicate the two needs listed above (i.e., for difference and true standpoint recognition) *sans the nihilism* so clear from Davaney's discussion. Although partially valid in terms of its main point, i.e., much feminist literature of the mid-80's did not sufficiently recognize the significance of pluralism in its methodological abstractions, Hogan's discussion is nonetheless sketchy (given the many authors she has chosen to review) and, in effect, somewhat belated, given that so much literature stands between it and its final publication (her singular reference to Schüssler Fiorenza's *But She Said* **[236]** notwithstanding). A closer attention to (1) the nuances of various authors' works, (2) an examination of "pluralism" in the early literature of feminist theology, and (3) the literature's recognition of standpoint epistemology (in perhaps an appendix discussion) would certainly have been helpful.

[288] von Kellenbach, Katharina. *Anti-Judaism in Feminist Religious Writings*. Atlanta: Scholars Press [AAR Cultural Criticism Series, No. 1], 1994.
The purpose of this text is "...to prove that anti-Judaism is a coherent belief system...[that it]...is not a minor lapse or misunderstanding among individual scholars but that each slight distortion in the presentation of Judaism contributes to a larger religious and cultural teaching of contempt" (p. vix). The discussion develops in three main movements. First, by applying Foucault's concept of "formation rules" to several themes evident in previously published discussions of anti-Judaism in Christian theology, notably **[967]** and **[299]**, von Kellenbach identifies the *antithesis, scapegoat,* and *prologue* norms governing various Christian (and secular) feminist writings about biblical and historical Judaism. Further, she details the objectivizing processes that play into and support these themes, i.e., the dynamics of making Jewish people "other," "responsible for evil," and "invisible." Second, von Kellenbach provides Christian (German and American) feminist theological examples of these dynamics, together their anti-Jewish outcomes: (1) the blaming of Judaism for both patriarchy and the death of the Goddess, (2) the denial and/or non-recognition of Jesus' Jewish heritage and insights, and (3) the ignoring and disrespecting of differences between Jewish and Christian (religious) teachings and experience. Last, after summarizing her work as a whole, von Kellenbach advocates the teaching of respect as an antidote to this circumstance, and she notes the differences in intensity between the American and German Christian anti-Jewish sources. This is an intense and arresting text, that to the novice reader, may appear (at least) choppy and at points hastily prepared, as sentences, phrases, words and/or possible interpretations of words are presented prima facie to make the threefold antithesis, scapegoat, and prologue case. But seasoned readers may also find this text difficult, for its arguments would have been better served if either (a) drawn from a *systematic* critique of specific theologians' works (rather than the critique of isolated phrases or sentences); or (b) stated more clearly as *the two-fold task of defining and documenting anti-Judaism in Christian feminist texts*. For in the absence of the latter, the discussion seems uncontrolled--or more accurately, controlled only by an undisciplined and ruthless search for the demons it would expose. Further, while none can deny that "each slight distortion in the presentation of Judaism contributes to a larger religious and cultural teaching of contempt," the absence of a clearly focused purpose leaves the text powerless to help readers become else than what they are judged to be: *viz.*, unless Jewish, then consciously or unconsciously *anti*-Jewish. This is a strong condemnation, and von Kellenbach's strategy seems to

be one of shaming or brow-beating Christians into an obeisance for all things Jewish, rather than either (a) legitimately demanding an accountability for past/present anti-Semitism, or (b) further explicating what it means to teach respect *to and within* a generation that seeks but often lacks--and at worst attempts a revision of--historical memory. While the text delivers authoritative insights (e.g., pp. 11-12 and the threefold rules), further editing might have diffused its various sweeping (e.g., pp. 30, 74, 106, 126), unqualified (e.g., pp. 18, 22, 92), judgmental (pp. 106, 126) and, in this writer's mind, at times deeply insensitive (e.g., pp. 12-13, 32) statements. Last, such editing might also have strengthened von Kellenbach's seemingly scattered and innuendo based (e.g., pp. 91, 136, 139) efforts at exposition. As an alternative, see Plaskow's adaptation **[971]**.

[289] Young, Pamela Dickey. *Feminist Theology/Christian Theology: In Search of Method*. Minneapolis: Augsburg-Fortress Press, 1990.
This text examines selected works (from the mid-80s) by Catholics Ruether and Schüssler Fiorenza and Protestant Letty Russell to identify and critique "theological method" as used in feminist theology. Following her summary introduction, Young provides chapter length overviews of each theologian's "method," a statement of her criteria for the categories tradition and Christian, her general critique of the selected authors, a summary of positions "credible" to Christian feminist theology, and an epilogue detailing her personal positions as a feminist. Overall, Young's guiding premise is that while all theologians may have various "sources" and "norms" for their theology, (1) the sources and norms for Christian theology are one and the same [they are the person of Christ as attested to by the tradition] and (2) it is this point that feminist theology ultimately ignores, for feminist theology makes women's experience both a source and a norm, and for Young, *the* source/norm-- and all at the expense of Christ as the norm. Young's discussion is provocative, but it is itself methodologically weak and for the most part reactionary. First, its critique of Russell remains unfinished and stops midway through the text. Second, the critique of Ruether and Schüssler Fiorenza become *the* critique of feminist theology, with the central issues being the maleness of Christ (and thus the Vatican's pronouncement against ordination--the apparent issue for Ruether), and alternatively, an antipathy to the Vatican Magisterium and its ultimate exclusion of women from positions of leadership and authority, the apparent problem for Schüssler Fiorenza. (Hence, according to Young, Ruether's recognition of other sources for women's theology, Schüssler Fiorenza's "magisterium of women's experience," and both theologians' involvement in the women-church movement.) Third, Young's main argument, i.e., the authority of the tradition, is essentially dogmatic; for by way of response, Young re-affirms the established biblical tradition (as based on Schubert Ogden's 'canon before a canon'), and she argues that (a) Christ's maleness is not relevant, for God could have chosen a woman for the Incarnation, and (b) for her as a Protestant, no magisterium--either Rome's or that women's experience--is acceptable. Last, and most profoundly, while Young affirms many positions consistent with the feminist theology she would critique, she leaves unaddressed the fundamental issue of who determines the criteria of equality in religious and ecclesial life. She thus misses a primary point of the feminist critique itself. A closing note: While not visibly malicious as is much anti-feminist literature (cf., e.g., **[844]**), the tone in this text is very uneven, and especially so in its closing section.. Hence, if nothing else, it illustrates the tensions and powers of denominational hermeneutics in the '90s, and the ways patriarchies of ownership--whether scriptural, ecclesial and dogmatic--can yet divide women in Christian/theological studies.

C. Dialogues within the Literature

As the scope of Protestant and Catholic feminist theological literature has developed, perspectives grounded in traditions marginalized or else wise distinct from these sources have also developed, and generated, thereby, additional feminist theological literatures. Among others, these additional literatures include Womanist and *Mujerista* theologies, Asian and Asian-American feminist theologies, and from Jewish feminists, a feminist theology which suggests the possibility of a Women's Torah as based upon the recovery of women's experience at Sinai. While the classical book-length discussions from these literatures (e.g., Cannon **[253]**, Grant **[254]**, Plaskow **[262]** and Williams **[259]**) have been included in the entries reviewed in this chapter, the more extended listings from these dialogues are presented in Sections IV and VI respectively.

III

Topical Literatures in Feminist Theology

This section of the bibliography surveys literatures attached to eight topics important to feminist theology. These topics have grounded feminist theology since its beginnings, and in terms of their organization and order of presentation, they include:

(1) Feminist Theological Anthropology

(2) Feminist Theological Method

(3) Feminist Biblical Studies

(4) Feminist Theology and Historic Christian Symbols

(5) Feminist Theological Ethics

(6) Feminist Worship

(7) Feminist Spirituality, and

(8) Feminist Theology and the Critique of Heterosexism.

These literatures might have been ordered differently, but since the goal of this section is to supplement the literature of Section II, the pattern adopted here attempts to parallel the genesis of the literature itself, with the awareness of Christianity's misogyny and androcentrism coming first to the fore (cf. Saiving [163] and Daly [161]), and followed in turn, by the growing awareness that the tradition itself must be reconstructed (cf. Hageman [168] and Ruether [172]). Hence, the section begins with a review of the literature on feminist theological anthropology as the effort, initially, to overcome patriarchy, dualism and misogyny, and as more recently, the effort to incorporate pluralism and diversity within the wide range of women's presence, as also the Image of God. Subsequent topics then move in and around a reconstruction of the tradition itself, toward finally, a recognition (present also in the literature's beginnings), that the tradition is not only sexist, but heterosexist as well. A final point needs to be kept in mind as the reader moves through this section: namely, the sources here intend a *supplemental* role in fleshing out literature presented earlier in Chapters 5-7. Thus, the topical literatures of this section are by no means exhaustive. This is especially important in terms of the feminist biblical literature, because since the beginnings of the feminist theological movement, the biblical sources, especially, have become almost uncountable. Hence, the biblical chapter here stresses grounding and formative sources with additional bibliography often embedded in specific abstracts. The topical chapters now follow, with each prefaced by an overview of key sources, authors and texts.

8

Feminist Theological Anthropology

Because the assumptions one makes about human nature cut across all considerations of social interaction, the feminist critique of Christian tradition has focused heavily on the analysis of "theological anthropology," or those assumptions that make up theological definitions of human nature. Hence the nomenclature of *"feminist* theological anthropology," and its critique of patriarchal and misogynous images and assumptions held historically within Christian tradition. These images and assumptions include the following: First, the "dualisms" of Christian tradition: the many binary-like frameworks that historically have been thought to reflect "gendered" or male/female patterns of reality, such as the association of maleness with rationality, soul, spirit, and tendencies toward the good--and, for women, the association of femaleness with emotions, body, carnality, and temptations toward evil.

Second, the patriarchal and misogynous images and assumptions embedded in Christian tradition have presumed theories of both sexual hierarchy and sexual "complimentarity." That is, they have presumed that women are created to be subordinate to men and to be defined as whole only in relation to men, whether that relationship is understood in sexual, social or political terms. Thus women are created to be auxiliaries to males and to serve as vehicles of male sexual fulfillment and/or reproductive needs.

Last, Christianity's patriarchal and misogynous images have generally assumed (and/or been supported by) various "correlates" of dualism, i.e., those social and formal organizational patterns that carry racial, economic, religious and sexual elements of in-group/out-group identity, and form, thereby, the milieux of doctrinal reflection.

Virtually all entries in this chapter challenge the patriarchal and misogynous images carried and held by Christianity and its bedrock of tradition. Sources vary, however, in the degree to which they are formally feminist and critical of Christianity's embedded misogyny. For example, theologian Rosemary Ruether [319] differs radically from social historian Elizabeth Clark [296] in her assessment of the "ambivalence" attributed to patristic theologies of gender, just as feminist historian Jane Dempsey Douglas [311] differs dramatically from Lutheran historian Roland Bainton [303] in his assessment of women and the Reformation.

This is a difficult literature, and especially for readers unaccustomed to the nuances of patristic and medieval philosophies. For these reasons then, the literature here is divided into four categories. The first category is "General and Introductory Overviews," a series of brief essays that acquaint the reader with the early efforts of feminist theologians to transcend the subordinating assumptions of traditional theological anthropology. Additionally, Edwin Schurr's sociological discussion on labeling, stigmatization and social control is also included among these introductory discussions.

Category #2 is "Bibliographies and General Reference Works," a listing of entries that highlight historical and documentary sources, and among these, sources indicating the theological frameworks governing Christianity's traditional patriarchal, misogynist and "triumphant" social norms. These sources are especially comprehensive, and each provides outstanding overviews and additional bibliographic sources.

Grouping #3 encompasses "Related Historical and Theological Sources," with entries by Briggs [306], Clark ([307], [308], [309], [310]), and Klein [312] drawing out several particulars embedded in the traditional Christian milieux. In particular, these works provide clear evidence of Christianity's historical misogyny--and Clark's assessment notwithstanding--its links to racism, anti-Semitism, theories of complimentarity, and ultimately heterosexism (cf. the literature in Chapter 15). Finally, three recently published readers close the chapter with an overview of the issues, emphases and debates salient to "feminist theological anthropology" in the mid-1990s.

Two further points should be noted here. First, in spite of the many efforts of feminist theology's early writers to break the parochial holds of traditional Christian anthropology, various other writers have critiqued early and core sources, and argued that these sources carry uncritically held racial, class, religious and/or sexual biases into the discussion of feminist Christian anthropology. Thus early works by Grant [214], Plaskow [968] and others (e.g., Cannon [625], and Heyward and Hunt [217]) have challenged the literature of this chapter, as have more recent sources addressing *Mujerista* [927] and Asian or Asian American [277] feminist concerns.

These critiques notwithstanding, the literature of feminist Christian anthropology is, as of the mid and late 1990s, cognizant of the diverse and multiple commitments of women contributing to the feminist theological corpus, and it reflects the detailed efforts of many working to find a framework wide enough to empower the needs of women worldwide (cf. [265], [272], [275], [911], [918], [919]).

Second, while the sources in this chapter clearly highlight the early and contemporary literature on "feminist theological anthropology," several sources abstracted elsewhere in the bibliography could easily be presented here. As they have emerged chronologically, noted sources include Saiving [163], Farley [167], Plaskow [203], Borresen [189], Carr [324], Cannon [612], Farley [568], and Copeland [278], and they should be read in conjunction with the entries below.

A. Feminism and Theological Anthropology: Introductory Overviews (1975-1990)

[290] Carr, Anne. "Theological Anthropology and the Experience of Women." *Chicago Studies* 19 (1980): 113-128.
After noting both the emphasis of contemporary theology on human experience and the pluralistic character of women's experience, Carr "critically correlates" three feminist analyses of the "causes and remedies" of sexism with "normative emphases" in Christian tradition. Of principal importance in this process are three "anthropological models" (i.e., three general ideas about humanness) that inform this correlation. These include: (1) past Christian emphases on "complementarity" (i.e., the idea that females and males complete each other); (2) a more androgynous or "individualized" model; and (3) a socially contexted "transformative" model that is future oriented, and structurally directed toward change in both church and society. In Carr's judgment it is the last of these models that offers the strongest hope for changing the sexist condition of women in church and society. This is because the "transformative" model holds in balance both the feminist awareness that culture structures "women's self-understanding and range of choices" (p. 125) and the Christian theological awareness that human freedom is always historical and open to transcendence. Thus, the model permits an interactive form of social critique: a gospel critique of culture that can aid "the authentic discovery of self and God in culture" and a cultural critique of the church that can help it "see that its own institutional life offers opportunity for full participation as well" (pp. 125-126).

[291] Coyle, Kathleen. "Tradition, Theology and Women in the Churches." *The Asia Journal of Theology* 4 (1990): 212-224.
This article summarizes the sweep of early and core feminist theological literature by expanding on the principal contribution of feminist theology generally, i.e., its recognition that while Christianity did not invent patriarchal ideology and structure, it nonetheless has functioned as its cultural carrier. To illustrate this point, Coyle describes the main lines of patriarchy (as both an ideology and a structure) and the current theological task: to indicate how women also are the image of God and how this insight necessitates a full re-construction of Christian tradition--symbolically, structurally and liturgically. Coyle's supportive literature draws heavily from the writings of many Roman Catholic feminist theologians (e.g., Farley, Ruether, and Schüssler Fiorenza), but parallels the work of Protestant evangelicals publishing in the late eighties and early nineties (e.g., Bird [360],

Russell **[249]**, and Scanzoni and Hardesty **[251]**). It is a thorough and well written summary that provides a compact conceptual overview of contemporary feminist theology--and within it--the tasks of feminist theological anthropology.

[292] Keightley, Georgia Masters. "The Challenge of Feminist Theology."*Horizons* 14 (1987): 262-282.
This article examines a range of issues attached to feminist theological anthropology. By way of overview, it argues that the feminist critique of Christianity is radical in at least two ways. First, this critique has methodically exposed that Christian theology has traditionally been cast in terms that "speak more directly [and] more meaningfully to the life and experience of men than of women" (p. 262). Second, it has increasingly appropriated the sociology of knowledge as a framework for theoretical discussion, including the discussion of Christian symbols and doctrine. By way of extension, therefore, this appropriation evidences at least three limitations in traditional Christian theological anthropology: (1) its androcentric, patriarchal and misogynist interpretation of human nature (or the idea that woman is, has been and should be subordinate to man); (2) the "long standing tendency to justify this subordination in women's "physical" inferiority; and (3) the subsequent exclusion of women and their experience from conversations generative of theological tradition. To illustrate these three limitations, Keightley discusses feminist theological literature published through the mid-1980s, with sources ranging from Saiving to Daly, Borresen, Ruether, Schüssler Fiorenza, Plaskow and Christ. Keightley's closing focus is a challenge to David Tracy's method of "critical correlation," for given the deep exposure of Christianity's misogynist and androcentrically grounded idea of "human nature," it is highly suspect that any one can speak meaningfully of a "common human experience" as Tracy does. Thus Keightley suggests that Tracy's methodology generates an "ideology of neutrality" and not a "liberation theology that conceives a self-conscious partisanship on behalf of the oppressed." This essay is a solid overview of the literature on feminist theological anthropology through the mid-1980s, and its focus on the social-theological construction of a specific ascribed status such as gender has clear implications for paralleling discussions relative to other ascribed statuses, e.g., race/ethnicity, sexual orientation, age, etc. **NOTE**: For a related sociological framework, see Schurr **[294]**.

[293] O'Neill, Mary Aquin. "Toward A Renewed Anthropology." *Theological Studies* 36 (1975): 725-736.
This early classic surveys liberal and radical feminist literature published from the mid-60s to the mid-70s to identify three "faces of feminism" and with these, three "visions of humanity" so that key feminist implications for Christian theological anthropology may be identified. O'Neill begins by noting the several challenges of feminist thinking for secular and religious spheres and she zeroes in on a "crucial issue for theology as a whole: [namely] an adequate understanding of what it is to be human" (p. 725). To focus this understanding she examines then current feminist literature to assess the "causes" of sexism (i.e., male supremacy, women's own sense of inferiority and the structuring of society in terms of male public and female domestic roles), and on the basis of these characterizations, she identifies "three basic ways of understanding the division of humanity into female and male" (p. 734). These include: (1) the traditional perspective of a sexual "polarity in which each sex embodies different possibilities of human being--possibilities that are denied the other;" (2) an androgenous perspective, in which sexual differences are "purely biological" and (3) a "unisex goal" in which one sex or another may be normative, but in which typically the male sex is. According to O'Neill, these three "visions" of what it means to be human have wide implications for theological anthropology, for they raise a variety of theological questions: viz., What is the "good life" in Christian revelation, and does it differ for women and men? Is it "a sin to prefer one way of being in the world over another," and if so, then what is the scope of the salvation begun in Christ? What does Christianity offer to women who feel "defined out of the divine-human experience"? and last, "What role does human desire play in the apprehension of God's will for... [humanity]?" (p. 736). Although her literature is dated, O'Neill's discussion provides an initial introduction to feminist issues inherent in "theological anthropology" and a clear critique of the "polarity" or complementarity perspective. Likewise, its analysis suggests application to ascribed characteristics other than those of gender and/or gender role.

[294] Schurr, Edwin. *Labeling Women Deviant: Gender, Stigma, and Social Control.* Philadelphia, PA: Temple Univ. Press, 1983.
This volume examines the numerous ways women are vulnerable to the dynamics of "deviantization," i.e., the devaluation of women through categories of negative sexual labeling. Schurr develops his discussion in three parts. Part I is a theoretical framework describing the super-

and subordinate dimensions of America's "gender system," and following Goffman, the power of "stigmas" as mechanisms of social control. Schurr then addresses "substantive applications" or the ways in which women are stigmatized for (1) being women and (2) departing in any way from traditional sex and gender norms. Thus he reviews and theoretically locates the research on "maternity controls," on sexuality and the stigmas of lesbianism, sexual harassment, rape and battering, on the "commoditization" of female sexuality via prostitution and pornography, and in an additional chapter, the power of labeling vis a vis women and mental illness and women and white collar crime. In his closing section Schurr examines several research implications of his discussion, together with practical strategies for social change. Readers already familiar with this literature will want to consult later discussions as summarized in Andersen [84], Chafetz [97], Basow [117], and Hess and Ferree [118]. Those seeking an introduction and comprehensive review of the research literature through the early eighties, however, will find this volume readable and instructive. Brief annotated "suggestions for further reading" follow each chapter and Schurr's general bibliography and extensive index close the volume. Of enormous significance for feminist theological anthropology, Schurr's discussion finds ample illustration in the literature below, but particularly in Ruether ([299] and [319]) and Briggs [306].

B.   Bibliographies and General Reference Works (1974-1995)

[295] Bullough, Vern, Brenda Shelton, and Sarah Slavin. *The Subordinate Sex: A History of Attitudes Toward Women*. Rev. ed. Athens, GA: Univ. of Georgia Press, 1988.

This revised (and now co-authored) text is a well known standard within the study of women's sex roles, for it candidly synthesizes the themes of misogyny and women's "subordination" in several cultures and religious settings: the worlds of Greco-Roman and early Christian culture, Byzantium, medieval Europe, England and Colonial America and (in this revised edition) the United States up through the mid-1980s with the defeat of the ERA and the rise of women's groups working against pornography and violence to women. Of particular interest to students of theological anthropology are Bullough's discussions on pedastalism, Christianity and sexuality, and in his closing chapter, a brief history of "biology, femininity, sex and change." A cautionary note: This text is not theological, and its orientation is towards an exposition of the assumptions grounding women's sex-defined social roles. It may seem, therefore, a bit off center for those seeking radical perspectives--and particularly by 1990s standards. This said, it remains a helpful historical source. For wider, more recent perspectives, see Clark [296], Kadel [297], Kraemer [298], and Wiesner [300] below. Additionally, for an early bibliography not abstracted here, see Leanna Goodwater. *Women in Antiquity: An Annotated Bibliography*. Metuchen, NJ: Scarecrow, 1975.

[296] Clark, Elizabeth A. *Women in the Early Church*. Wilmington, DE: Michael Glazier, 1983.

This work by Clark is Volume 13 of *Message of the Fathers of the Church*, a twenty-two volume series published under the general editorship of Thomas Halton for the purpose of acquainting wide audiences with "solid, readable translations...of the Fathers" on a variety of topics. Thus, as with other volumes in the series, Clark's contribution presents original translations interspersed with clarifying comments and/or notes locating the theme or sequence of concerns addressed by the selections presented. To organize her work, then Clark presents five general themes. First is "Paradise Lost: Creation, Fall, and Marriage" in which Clark surveys the patristic literature evidencing the subordination of women as this literature struggles with sexuality, sin and the goodness of creation. Second is "Women Endangered: The Apocryphal Acts and Martyrdom." This chapter excerpts literature evidencing both the costs and accomplishments of women seeking martyrdom. Third is "Paradise Regained: Asceticism in Theory and Practice," a series of selections that trace the patristic fascination for asceticism as a solution to the problems of dualism in creation, and which in turn, permits women's renewed, asexual exaltation. Clark's fourth thematic chapter is "Women in the Wider World," and here attention is directed to those selections that evidence the restrictions *and* opportunities for women beyond their assigned domestic sphere. Finally, in chapter five, Clark addresses "Women as Models and Mentors," a series of selections that demonstrate the "female friends, mothers and sisters of various Church Fathers" (p. 25). As with all her work, this volume by Clark is meticulously presented. The selections are extensive and include an array of excerpts from Augustine, Ambrose, Chrysostom, Irenaeus, Tertullian, Clement of Alexandria, Gregory of Nyssa, Jerome and Palladius. Similarly, the abridgments of the "Acts of Paul and Thecla," the "Acts of John" and "The Martyrdom of Perpetua and Felicitas" and the "Life of Olympias" are well-presented, and footnotes running through the volume identify all original sources for the citations. If there are any limitations to the volume they are these: (1) In keeping with the editorial policy of the series as a whole, only a brief bibliography of additional suggested readings is presented; (2) the volume lacks an index; and (3) it is Clark's stated assumption that "The most fitting word with which to describe the Church Fathers' attitude toward women is ambivalence" (p. 15). Here she alludes to (but does not address) the criticism by Ruether (whose work she recommends in her bibliography) that these same sources reflect not ambivalence, but misogyny. For the specific discussion by Ruether see [319]. For additional works by Clark see the entries below, and for her translations and work on Chrysostom specifically, including the entries below, see her *Jerome, Chrysostom and Friends: Essays and Translations*. New York & Toronto: Edwin Mellen Press, 1979.

[297] Kadel, Andrew. *Matrology: A Bibliography of Writings by Christian Women From the First to the Fifteenth Centuries*. New York: Continuum, 1995.
This very informative bibliography chronicles the writings indicated by its title and more. It provides brief "bios" of the women it cites, it locates various writings within the wider contexts of their historical eras and specific genre, it includes helpful lists of related bibliographies and translations, it provides a supplemental bibliography organized by type of writings, and its closing alphabetical and chronological indices readily identify all contributions. It is a most readable and useful resource that readily supplements the literature on feminist theological anthropology.

[298] Kraemer, Ross S. *Maenads, Martyrs, Matrons, Monastics*. Philadelphia: Fortress, 1988.
This text is a superlative collection of writings, sources, documents, inscriptions and the like "relating to women's religious activities in the various religions of Greco-Roman antiquity, including Judaism and Christianity" (p. 1). Its materials range from the fourth century B.C.E. to the early fifth century C.E., and they are grouped into six categories: (1) "Observances, Rituals, and Festivities;" (2) "Researching Real Women: Documents to, from, and by Women;" (3) "Religious Office;" (4) "New Religious Affiliation and Conversion;" (5) "Holy Pious and Exemplary Women;" and (6) "The feminine Divine." Kraemer writes as an historian of religion who explicitly disavows any theological purpose to her work (p. 5) and the thematic grouping of her 135 text/source entries permits clear comparisons across religious traditions and communities. Thus, in section one of her collection, one finds not only a description of "Women participants at a festival of Adonis," but also "Rabbinic arguments against a misogynist tradition" or again, "Women Blowing the Shofar on Rosh Hashanah" (both from the Babylonian Talmud). Two additional values to this important collection are many indices--of "sources," "personal names," and "divine names" and its supplemental discussion, "About the Authors and Sources." In the latter, Kraemer helpfully identifies all the Greek, Latin, and Hebrew names, symbols, abbreviations and textual sources from which she has compiled her collection. For additional work by Kraemer see [313] and see the following two sources (not abstracted here, but well worth the read): (a) "Women in the Religions of the Greco-Roman World." *Religious Studies Review* 9 (1983): 127-139; and (b) *Her Share of the Blessings: Women's Religions Among Pagans, Jews, and Christians in the Greco-Roman World*. [New York: Oxford Univ. Press, 1992]. The first is a bibliographic essay of early literature on religion, gender and social roles in Greco-Roman society; the second, a "gender-sensitive" adaptation of Mary Douglas's "group-grid" model to reconstruct the diversity of women's religions in the Greco-Roman world.

[299] Ruether, Rosemary Radford. *Faith and Fratricide: The Theological Roots of Anti-Semitism*. NY: Seabury Press, 1974/Eugene, OR: Wipf & Stock, 1995.
Re-released in 1995, this text remains a fundamental source for identifying the length and breadth of Christianity's historical and theologically indigenous anti-Semitism--or as Ruether later so succinctly puts it, the fact that "theologically, anti-Judaism developed as the left hand of Christology" (cf. [440:31]). This is a meticulously documented text, and its five chapters detail the Christological developments that engendered: (a) the rise of New Testament anti-Judaism and its negation of the Mosaic and Yawistic covenants (chapters 1-2); (b) the patristic transformation of New Testament anti-Judaism into a full blown *Adversos Judaeos tradition* (chapter 3); (c) the fourth century codification of this tradition into religiously grounded discriminatory social policies (chapter 4); and in the same chapter, (d) the application and adaptation of these policies from their early fourth century establishment under Constantinian Christianity to the Nazi-driven Holocaust of the 20th century. A closing chapter assesses the theological dimensions of this history in terms of the three grounding motifs that continue to sustain Christianity's theological anti-Judaism, and by extension, its status as a host culture for anti-Semitism ([440]). Additionally, this chapter includes Ruether's formal suggestions to the American Theological Association for modifying theological curricula to avoid the continuation of Christian anti-Judaism within seminary education and

formation. This is an *arresting* text: it is clear, systematic and unflinching, and it fully delivers on Ruether's hope that "...for the Christian for whom Jewish history since 70 C.E. is a blank, it may give some guidelines for understanding the links between Christian anti-Judaism and modern anti-Semitism" (p. 184). Second, although Ruether synthesizes hundreds of related and supportive sources, the unique character of her text comes thorough: this history belongs not only to the Christian past, but to Christianity's *present* as well, and it will continue to belong until the judgment/promise, particularism/universalism and letter/spirit motifs of Christianity's anti-Judaic myth are rejected or redefined from within a christology that does not sabotage Judaism as its theological enemy. These last points are important, for while contemporary readers may experience anger and/or ambiguity at the almost naive tone of the book's preface (as written in 1974 by Catholic ecumenist, Gregory Baum) they will experience no such feeling from the text itself. Pure and simple, its discomforting thesis remains decades after its publication: Anti-Judaism is the "left hand of Christology," and it was the early church's perception that to survive it had, virtually, to demonize Judaism and its people. **NOTE:** For a more recent but similar assessment, see John Pawlikowski, "Christology, Anti-Semitism, and Christian-Jewish Bonding," in *Reconstructing Christian Theology*, edited by Rebecca S. Chopp and Mark L. Taylor, 245-268, Minneapolis: Fortress, 1994.

[300] Wiesner, Merry E. *Women and Gender in Early Modern Europe*. Cambridge:
 • Cambridge Univ. Press, 1993.
The author of this informative and elegantly written text is an Associate Professor of History and Director of the Women's Studies Program at the U. of Wisconsin. Hence, her text could have as easily been included as an historical reference for the Women's Studies literature in Chapter I-2; it is presented here, however, because of its general scope and readability and, additionally, its attention to the role of Western Christianity as a major (but not the exclusive) force shaping social and cultural attitudes toward women. Wiesner's eight chapter text begins with an overview of the "inherited traditions" of "ideas and laws regarding women" in Western Europe. It then continues with histories of gender and "the female life-cycle," the conceptualization of "work," "literacy," "the creation of culture," "religion," "witchcraft," and in a closing chapter, the various connections between domestic and organizational power, and sexuality and honor. Each of its chapters is thorough and very readable, and students of feminist theological anthropology will find its chapters on religion and witchcraft rewarding. Additionally, each of its eight chapters is followed by a detailed bibliographic essay highlighting both standard and controversial sources for the chapter topic. A general index closes the volume.

[301] Wilson, Katharina, ed. *Medieval Women Writers*. Athens, GA: Univ. of Georgia
       Press, 1984.
Intended as a volume to "introduce the reader to some of the outstanding women writers of the Middle Ages," this anthology of fifteen selections "spans seven centuries (the ninth through the fifteenth), eight languages...and ten regions or nationalities" (p. vii). Not surprisingly, its selections reflect a primarily religious content, for as editor Wilson notes in her extensive introduction, the two conditions of "opportunity for education" and "freedom from pregnancies and family responsibilities" were realized largely by women in convents, although occasionally in aristocratic families as well. Several features recommend this volume to those seeking access to women writers of the Middle Ages. First, the selection is wide and representative of religious and secular women, although as noted, religious writers play the major role. Thus the women selected include: "The Frankish Mother: Dhouda," whose entries reflect her concern for her son's religious upbringing and her own fascination with the religious significance of number and verbal images; the "Saxon Caraness: Hrotsvits of Gandersheim"; French Country Poet, Marie de France; "The French Scholar-Lover: Heloise"; "The German Visionary: Hildegard of Bingen"; "The Provencal *Trobairitz*: Castelloza"; German and Brabant Mystics, Mechthild and Hadewijch; the Swedish and Tucson visionaries, St. Bridget and St. Catherine of Siena, English mystics Julien of Norwich and Margery Kempe, the "Spanish Love Poet: Florencia Pinar"; and the "Franco-Italien Professional Writer: Christine de Pizan." A second strong feature of this volume is that each of the introductory essays to these women is well-done. The volumes contributors' provide ample historical data on their subjects, they contrast them with other writers from the same period and they provide helpful bibliography for primary and secondary sources. Third, the editor's general introduction is especially strong. It not only details the long seven century sweep of these women's contributions, but it indicates the variety of reasons that have precluded general access to these women's writings. This is an excellent introduction to the women writers of the Middle Ages and it can be used to supplement more formally theological sources. It is well-written, well-documented, and overall, a pleasure to read.

[302] Wilson-Kastner, Patricia, et al., eds. *A Lost Tradition: Women Writers of the Early Church*. Lanham, MD: Univ. of America Press, 1981.
This text is an edited collection of writings stemming from four Christian women who wrote during the first five centuries of Christianity. These women writers include: Perpetua, a woman martyred during the first years of the second century and who wrote in anticipation of her impending martyrdom; Proba, a Christian convert and poet writing during the middle of the fourth century (c. 351 C.E.); "Egeria," a Christian pilgrim whose name and precise dates for the writing of her pilgrimage are not clearly known--but about whom it is hypothesized that her work stems from the period 404-717; and last, Eudokia, a writer from the middle of the fifth century C.E. and author of (among other things) "The Life of St. Cyprian of Antioch" (c. 440 C.E.) also presented in this collection. Extended introductory essays precede each of the selections presented in this collection, and each introduction reviews the history and exegesis of the selection presented. By way of authorship, Rosemary Rader introduces Perpetua and translates the account of her Martyrdom; Ronald Kastner and Ann Miliam introduce Proba and present Jeremiah Reedy's translation of her "Cento;" Patricia Kastner-Wilson introduces Egeria and translates the account of her pilgrimage; and last, Ronald Kastner introduces and translates Eudokia's "Life of St. Cyprian." A general introduction by Patricia Wilson-Kastner opens the text and a selected bibliography by Ronald Kastner closes it. For related material see Ruether and Clark below and the sources they cite.

NOTE: For related historical sources see Lerner ([68], [35] and [69]) and Ruether [192], while for biblical sources see Higgins [378], Schüssler Fiorenza [380], Trible [164], [165], [385] and Bellis [381].

C. Related Historical and Theological Studies (1971-1989)

[303] Bainton, Roland. *Women of the Reformation in Germany and Italy*. Minneapolis: Augsburg, 1971.
This is the first of three volumes by Bainton on 'women of the reformation.' The second and third are also published through Augsburg and are *Women of the Reformation in France and England*, published in 1973 and *Women of the Reformation, from Spain to Scandinavia*, published in 1977. In each, Bainton synthesizes historical and personal sources (most of which are not available in English) to describe the lives and experience of women attached to men of the reformation. Bainton's purposes in developing the three volumes are to (1) acknowledge "those who have not had their due;" (2) "assess the dissemination of the Reformation"; and (3) assess "the impact of the Reformation on the social order," and especially its impact on the institutions of marriage and the family. Bainton only partially reaches these goals, for his assessments are scattered intermittently in each of the volumes and without extended or chapter length discussions. Similarly, where supporting materials such as maps, chronological charts, and relevant introductory discussions of the reformation are presented in the first two volumes, they are largely omitted in the third. Overall, each volume presents a wealth of information about "women of the reformation," and to this extent the volumes are helpful. However, they are not as helpful as one might immediately expect: First, tone in each volume is frequently patronizing. Second, while Bainton intimates that the status of women in the Reformation period is "ambiguous," he nowhere critically examines sexism, misogyny, or structured superordinate and subordinate gender relations as factors in the history of the women discussed. Hence, this series is not recommended. Alternatively, see Douglass [311].

[304] Barnhouse, Ruth, and Urban T. Holmes III, eds. *Male and Female: Christian Approaches to Sexuality*. New York: Seabury, 1976.
This anthology of 22 essays on gender and sexuality is now largely dated in terms of its scholarship, grounding assumptions, and discussion of relevant issues. Four entries, on sexuality, however, remain relevant. (1) Alan Bell's, "Homosexuality: An Overview;" (2) Norman Pittenger's, "A Theological Approach to Homosexuality;" (3) Charles W. Socarides', "Homosexuality is Not Just an Alternative Lifestyle," and (4) Frank Patton, Jr.'s, "Sexuality and the Law." Bell describes the many social, cultural, and psychological variables conditioning the study of homosexuality and thus, the subsequent need to conceptualize homosexuality in plural rather than single terms. In turn, Pittenger argues against the condemnation of homosexual relations on the grounds that: (a) the task of becoming human is one of becoming a loving human being--whether heterosexually or homosexually, and (b) it is God who has created all persons and apart from a fundamentalist perspective, one cannot argue exclusively against the reality of homosexual love. The entry by Socarides contrasts sharply with the Bell and Pittenger pieces: it maintains that homosexuality is a pathology. Thus it argues against the 1973 decision of the American Psychological Association to remove homosexuality from its list of pathological disorders, and

from its "pathology" perspective, it pre-sages Socarides' late 1990s efforts at "curing" homosexuality. Finally, in spite of its dated material, Patton's essay continues to raise questions about the role of law vis a vis the right to privacy, and for that fact, it bears continued reading. The remaining essays of this volume contribute no new knowledge to the study of gender and sexuality and have been surpassed by several theoretical works, e.g., Blumenfeld and Raymond [576], Andersen [84] Freeman [88], Collins [99], Chafetz, [97] and Andersen and Collins [85].

[305] Bianchi, Eugene, and Rosemary Radford Ruether. *From Machismo to Mutuality:*
      Essays on Sexism and Women-Men Liberation. New York: Paulist, 1976.
Eight essays--four each by Bianchi and Ruether--comprise this volume. Some of the material will be familiar to those who know Ruether's work, for in "Sexism and Liberation: The Historical Experience," Ruether provides an overview of both the economic status of women in history and the significance of Christianity (and specifically the role of asceticism) for women's gender roles. This is an important essay for it identifies both racism and sexism as ideologies from which women need liberation. Other subjects addressed by Ruether may be less familiar. In "The Cult of True Womanhood and Industrial Society" Ruether addresses not only marriage and women's suffrage, but also the varying impacts of related Christological and Mariological images upon marriage and women's suffrage. Further, in "The Personalization of Sexuality" Ruether focuses on (a) the effects of privatization on marriage as an institution and (b) the implications of privatization for rethinking understandings of sexuality, including same-sex orientations. Finally, in "Sexism and the Liberated Woman," Ruether reexamines the American "sexual revolution" vis a vis the larger issues of social class, power and dependency roles, and the necessity for a more communitarian ethic. In contrast to Ruether's essays, Bianchi's entries here are more personalized. In "Growing Up Male: A Personal Experience" Bianchi recounts his own socialization to America's white middle-class norms of the 1940s and 1950s. He continues this discussion and augments it with reflections on power, capitalism and violence in "The Super-Bowl Culture of Male Violence," and in "Psychic Celibacy and the Quest for Mutuality," he responds to Ruether's "Personalization" essay by describing the differing perceptions of intimacy that exist for women and men as structurally channeled through society's aggressive/submissive gender expectations. Finally, in "From Machismo to Mutuality" Bianchi reflects on the costs and benefits of his own journey to mutuality, and he offers his reflections as insights for others. An epilogue by Ruether balances Bianchi's introduction, and a series of chapter directed study questions close this readable, still relevant text.

[306] Briggs, Sheila. "Images of Women and Jews in Nineteenth- and Twentieth-Century
      German Theology." In *Immaculate and Powerful: The Female in Sacred Image and*
      Social Reality, edited by Clarisa W. Atkinson, Constance H. Buchanan and
      Margaret R. Miles, 226-259. Boston: Beacon Press, 1985.
This extended and detailed essay painstakingly documents the interlocking grounds of anti-Semitism and sexism in German theology (and particularly German Catholicism and Lutheranism) during the 19th and early 20th centuries. It examines the gender assumptions tied to 'theologies of marriage,' the social assumptions of property and 'orders' within creation, and the ties of these all to Germany's social order prior to the rise of Hitler. Briggs demonstrates the 'feminization of Judaism' and the social consequences of both Germany's gender and racial assumptions about women and Jews: i.e., women, unless Jewish, were defined to be of some use and thus, not immediately dispensable. Readers familiar with Briggs' other works will find her tight and comprehensive writing style as evident here as elsewhere, and to some extent this may deter readers. Be that as it may. This is an especially important paper for demonstrating the ideological power of "creation" and "natural law" arguments in the service of social control and extermination policies, and one clear implication of it is that it is time only that marks the difference between the Nazi use of such arguments and their use by anti-semitic and homophobic religious and hate groups of the mid-1990s. For related studies see Ruether [299], Klein [312], and Ringelheim [966], and see the Jewish critique of Christian feminist anti-Judaism in Chapter 24.

[307] Clark, Elizabeth A. "John Chrysostom and the Subintroductae." *Church History* 46
      (1977): 171-185.
Following Hans Achelis' description of the *subintroductae* as "female Christian ascetics who lived together with men, although both parties had taken the vow of continence and were animated with the earnest desire to keep it" [Achelis, "Agapetae," *Encyclopedia of Religion and Ethics,* ed James Hasting (N.Y: 1926),1:177], Clark demonstrates: (a) the widespread acknowledgment of this practice; (b) Chrysostom's multiple arguments against it; and (c) its possible roots in the desire of women and men ascetics for egalitarian and philia-like friendships. As with all of Clark's work, this discussion is clearly written, meticulously detailed and highly recommended. Its focus on

Chrysostom provides an ample portrait of his gender-role assumptions and Clark presents them vividly and comprehensively.

[308] Clark, Elizabeth A. "Sexual Politics in the Writings of John Chrysostom." *Anglican Theological Review* 59 (1977). 3-20.

Borrowing the metaphor of 'sexual politics' from Kate Millet, Clark details the two principal gender assumptions of Chrysostom's work: First, an original (and for Chrysostom a natural) preeminence and authority of males over females; second, a subsequent 'natural spheres of activity' pertinent to marriage and family, i.e., that females are for service to their husbands and children, while males are to participate in the public domain. Chrysostom's assumptions of these male/female, super/subordinate relations are abandoned only when virginity and martyrdom are discussed, for these are statuses that attest the angelic or eschatological equality of women and men. In the temporal world, however, no such equality pertains. Clark also notes that in some writings Chrysostom seems to have had some ambivalence concerning gender, for he recognizes an actual male and female equality during the early period of the church. Further, he seems unsure of exactly when women received their subordination to men: whether before or after "the fall." Clark defends her conclusion of an "original male preeminence" [for Chrysostom], however, through a discussion of his exegesis of Gen. 1:27, Gen. 2-3, and his ongoing critique of Plato's Republic and the gender assumptions *it* presumed.

[309] Clark, Elizabeth A. "Ascetic Renunciation and Feminine Advancement: A Paradox of Late Ancient Christianity." *Anglican Theological Review* 63 (1981): 240-257.

This article exposes the ideological conflicts attendant on the adoption of an ascetic lifestyle by male and female Christian aristocrats during the fourth and fifth centuries. In terms of its social consequences the adoption of such a lifestyle meant three things: (1) a loss of inheritance and/or the continuation of family wealth; (2) the adoption of a garb clearly symbolizing a loss of social rank; and (3) a loss of women to serve as the "social cement binding noble families in marriage" (p. 241). In her discussion Clark calls attention to Jerome's own reporting that Roman nobles considered the ascetic life as "strange, ignominious and debasing" (p. 241), and she indicates the two strategies undertaken by churchmen to combat such perceptions: (1) that individuals should break completely with families as they assume an ascetic lifestyle (lest the church suffer the charge of robbing nobles of their inheritance) and (2) an emphasis on the teaching that adopting such a lifestyle would, in fact, only enhance the already noble standing of such individuals. By way of closure, Clark highlights the characteristic features of ascetic Christian life and she draws out their implications for women--the extra-domestic freedoms attained by women who became ascetics: the freedom to travel, to become educated, to receive and distribute monies and valuables on behalf of others, and, last, the freedom to exercise the class power retained from one's original social status.

[310] Clark, Elizabeth A. "Theory and Practice in Late Ancient Asceticism: Jerome, Chrysostom, and Augustine." *Journal of Feminist Studies in Religion* 5, no. 2 (1989): 25-46.

Students of Clark's work know that one of her central efforts has been to explain an apparent theory/practice paradox in the lives and writings of fourth century fathers Jerome and John Chrysostom. On the one hand, each of these men has written extensively on: (a) the natural subordination of women to men; (b) the distasteful, negative realities of marriage; and (c) the superiority of virginity over the married state. On the other hand, each has maintained (in his own personal life) long-standing and near egalitarian relationships with women ascetics whose lives each has praised and extolled. In this essay, Clark reviews her past explanations of this apparent paradox and attempts to explain a further paradox: that of Augustine, who in contrast to Jerome and Chrysostom *lacked* personal friendships with ascetic women in his mature years and in at least some writings held the view that marriage--prior to the fall, could and might have been a harmonious, companionable state (p. 33). To explain this paradox, however, past explanations (e.g., that asceticism is a social-sexual leveler providing opportunities for intellectual friendships) will not do. Instead, other social and theological factors must be examined. Clark finds two important differences between Augustine and Jerome and Chrysostom. First, in contrast to Jerome and Chrysostom, Augustine's relations with formerly wealthy ascetic women were instituted *after* he had become bishop and was, thereby, in a position to benefit from their financial divestiture upon choosing this new state of life. In Clark's judgment, this fact created a climate of suspicion (and in some cases open conflicts) between Augustine, these ascetic women and their families. Second, Augustine sought *unsuccessfully* (as bishop) to curtail all relationships between these women and their doctrinally different friends, e.g., Palagius and/or his advocates. This doctrinal strain contrasts with "Jerome's triumphant enlistment of *his* women friends in the anti-Originist campaign and to Chrysostom's ability to attract wealthy women...to support his cause in Rome" (pp. 43-44). Finally, as Clark also notes, Augustine's understandings of gender, marriage and marital roles were tied to his long-standing concerns with grace and original sin, and thus when advising women about their obligations to their husbands (e.g., Ecdicia), he was often harsh. According to Clark, these factors all cemented Augustine's isolation from ascetic women in his advanced years and help explain some of the differences between him, Jerome and Chrysostom in their respective theory /practice gaps. This essay is quintessential Clark: well-written, well argued, amply illustrated and documented to the most specific detail.

[311] Douglass, Jane Dempsey. "Women and the Continental Reformation." In *Religion and Sexism: Images of Woman in the Jewish and Christian Traditions*, edited by Rosemary Radford Ruether, 292-318. New York: Simon and Schuster, 1974.

This essay describes the impact of the Protestant reformation on the religious and social roles of Catholic (and then subsequently Protestant) women in 16th century European society. Its particular attention is directed to the "new theology of marriage" that emerged as a result of the Protestant Reformation, but in a closing portion it examines the diary entries of a Roman Catholic nun, Sr. Jean de Jussie, for insights into the experiences of self perceptions of Catholic lay and vowed women during the Protestant Reformation. By way of overview, Douglass chronicles the Lutheran and Reformed teachings of marriage together with the rise of the marital role, "pastor's wife." Additionally, and in an ecumenical tone, she notes the religious values of Lutheran and Reformed teaching and the gains they represented for women socially: e.g., the theoretical--albeit rare-- possibilities for women to receive divorces, as in the case of near-death physical abuse. At the same time, she notes the continuation of patriarchal patterns within the marital sphere, including the more typical circumstance of non-divorce (viz., women were expected to remain in abusive situations) and relatedly, the familistic role of women as transmitters of patriarchal faith, given that (at least in the Lutheran circumstance), the family was viewed as "the school of faith." NOTE: The literature on clergy marriages is sparse, but for helpful beginning sources see Carroll, Hargrove and Lummis [657], Taves [875], Deming and Stubbs [721], McKiernan-Allen and Allen [722], Hartley and Taylor [726], and Scanzoni [731]. Then see Nesbitt ([723] and [661]), Zikmund, Lummis and Chang [663], the sources on Christianity and abuse (Chapter 22), and see Potter [317] below.

[312] Klein, Charlotte. *AntiJudaism in Christian Theology*. Trans. by Edward Quinn. Philadelphia: Fortress Press, 1978.

Like Ruether's text, *Faith and Fratricide* [299], Klein's discussion also documents anti-Jewish themes in Christian theology, but here with a focus specifically on German Christian theology published from 1945 through 1971. Klein's study is a "thematic analysis" that "pushes back" to earlier sources, and it was occasioned by her acknowledged frustrations as a professor of New Testament, teaching upper division seminarians. In particular, as a Jewish convert to Catholicism and a strong supporter of Vatican II teaching, Klein spent several lecture hours of her course working to dispel anti-Jewish attitudes her students might bring to their New Testament studies. She found, however, that her students' semester papers consistently reflected the biases she had informed against, and as she examined their notes and documenting sources, she decided to trace out the biases that her students' work had carried over from various scholars. Hence her thematic analysis of several sources exhibiting specifically anti-Jewish attitudes that can be clustered around four key themes: (1) the [post-exilic] Jewish community as one called to witness religiously in non-nationalistic terms--this makes for expulsion not freedom; (2) an opposition between the "prophetic" faith of pre-exilic Judaism and the post-exilic Judaism that presumably "rejected" this prophetic faith in favor of "Jewish law;" (3) a stereotyping of Pharisees and Jewish teachers around issues of legalism not necessarily present in Jesus' own time; and (4) Jewish guilt in the death of Jesus. All are attitudes Klein finds variously in such noted New Testament theologians as Grundmann, Dibelius, Noth, Bultmann, Bornkamm, Schmaus, Jeremias, Guardini and Benoit, and all are attitudes that carry themselves culturally in the study of these theologians, regardless of one's otherwise experience of Jewish people. This is an important book, albeit for formatting reasons at points difficult to follow--e.g., quotes are not always set off within the text and at times one seems to run into another. This notwithstanding, the text is a passionate and humbling presentation both for what it says and what it illustrates: that theological education has cultural or legacy-like effects both in print and in the "formation" of Christian religious leaders, with the latter happening directly through the former, and in addition to what sociologists describe as the "structural effects" of seminary education. NOTE: For work on anti-Judaism as it has been critiqued in Christian feminist theology and developed as an element of feminist theological dialogue, see Plaskow [970-971].

[313] Kraemer, Ross S. "The Conversion of Women to Ascetic Forms of Christianity." *Signs* 6 (1980): 298-307.

The purpose of this essay is to examine the legends of the apocryphal "Acts of the Apostles" to determine the pattern of conversion they evidence for women so that the functions of asceticism for women in the first centuries of Christianity may be better illuminated. Kraemer begins with the recognition that she is working with admittedly difficult, legendary material, but she nonetheless finds a four-step pattern characteristic of women's conversions in the apocryphal Acts. First the women converted are those whose principal male support is high in social status. Typically this is a husband, but fathers are also included. Second, upon meeting and being swayed by an apostle and his [sic] preaching, the converted women adopt a celibate lifestyle, which, third, either angers the woman's spouse or endangers her potential marital status. Fourth, either the woman alone or both the woman and the apostle are punished (usually jailed), with the woman experiencing the more severe punishment, usually death. To determine the significance of celibacy for these converted women (given its possible end-point), Kraemer cites research on marginalized African women experiencing status change and their subsequent likelihood of joining sects. She acknowledges that the conversion of women within the apocryphal legend literature does not completely fit this theoretical model, but she nonetheless argues for the relevance of this related research. Thus, in a third step, she argues that marriage and motherhood were the only socially acceptable roles for women in the early centuries of Christianity and that the power of celibacy was a freeing of women from these roles. She then notes the differential impact of sexual renunciation for women and men and concludes that "Religious systems which legitimize the rejection of the established sociosexual standards as did ascetic Christianity, are likely to attract large numbers of discontented and marginal women and to propound stands of worth and redemption more consonant with their circumstances." (pp. 305-306).

[314] McLaughlin, Eleanor. "Equality of Souls, Inequality of Sexes: Women in Medieval Theology." In *Religion and Sexism: Images of Woman in the Jewish and Christian Traditions*, edited by Rosemary Radford Ruether, 213-266. New York: Simon and Schuster, 1974.

This detailed and clearly written survey of the theological assumptions attached to gender during the medieval period begins with an overview of Thomistic teaching to evidence both Thomas' absorption of Aristotelian philosophy and his continued dependence on Augustinian teaching. Thus, McLaughlin details the now well known biology of women as deformed sperm and instruments of procreation, together with Thomas' theology of gender and the fall, and the main medieval problematic that women were equal to men by virtue of their souls, but absolutely unable to move beyond their inferiority given that their physical existence incarnated that inferiority. Following her summary of Thomas, McLaughlin examines the role options facing women as defined by the "goods" of marriage--i.e., that marriage (in the medieval period) constituted first, the context of procreation, second, a remedy for sin, and last, a sacrament. It is a detailed overview that takes up the patristic and medieval teachings and the related assumptions underlying contemporary Catholic teachings on birth control and procreation. Virginity, devotion to Mary, and the assumptions of public piety as expressed in sermons and local literature of the time close out McLaughlin's discussion, with both the positive and negative dimensions of historical theological anthropology clear: while the medieval perspective did not permit women to transcend the "problem" they were, their spiritual equality as evidenced by virginity--or in some cases continent widowhood, allowed them choices beyond father and husband and thus, some measure of independence in the social sphere. Important both for its social and historical observations, McLaughlin's is one of the few discussions that combines such observations with a detailed and rounded knowledge of medieval theology and its linkages to the modern period. **NOTE:** Also by McLaughlin are **[439]**, a most provocative entry in Stevens **[442]** and, as co-edited with Ruether, **[209]**. *And*, for a contemporary perspective yet rooted in the misogynist theology McLaughlin details, see Slusser **[784]**.

[315] McNamara, Jo Ann. "Sexual Equality and the Cult of Virginity in Early Christian Thought." *Feminist Studies* 3 (1976): 145-158.

This discussion develops the thesis that the patristic literature evidences an understanding of virginity espousing the latter as a vehicle for religious commitment, *not* an anti-sexual attitude toward women. The argument is developed in terms of two assumptions McNamara traces through the patristic literature: first that celibacy was favored over marriage for both women and men; and second, that the literature defines women (and men) in terms of their socially ascribed gender roles, which in the case of women were limited to wife and mother and could be transcended through a commitment to celibacy. To demonstrate these assumptions McNamara cites from several of the

Fathers: Palladius, Chrysostom, Clement of Alexandria, Tertullian, Jerome, Ambrose, Justin Martyr, Gregory of Nyssa and, of course, Augustine. McNamara is not unmindful that the language of many patristic writers "betrays a deep-seated tendency to despise the nature of women" (p. 153). She assigns this, however, to the prejudice of their times. Nor is she unaware that piety of the period implied that "pious folk... believed that holy women might choose to become men and that God would bless them for it" (p. 153). She concludes, however, that "it was certainly not the object of the fathers to turn women into men through the virgin life. Rather they were seeking to express the absolute equality which the two sexes enjoyed outside the limitations of marriage" (p. 153). This article and its arguments are carefully developed and reasonably documented, although McNamara's general conclusion is, in fact, one of the disputed points about women in the patristic period. For her subsequent discussion see her book (not abstracted here) *A New Song: Celibate Women in the First Three Christian Centuries.* New York: Haworth Press, 1983.

[316] Nelson, Mary. "Why Witches Were Women." In *Women: A Feminist Perspective,* edited by Jo Freeman, 451-468. Palo Alto, CA: Mayfield, 1979.
"Between 1400 and 1700 approximately half a million people, most of them women, were burned as witches" (p. 336). Nelson's essay maps the contours of this horror-filled observation: (1) the efforts of both Dominicans and Inquisitors to identify sorcerers as a specific category--a task finally given ecclesiastical approval in 1326 by Pope John XXII after extended 'lobbying' efforts on the part of the Inquisitors; (2) the mid-15th century development and publication of *Malleus Maleficarum* (see excerpts in Clark and Richardson **[186]**); (3) the eventual expulsion of Inquisitors from various parts of Europe in the late 1490's; (4) the continued persecution of witches by church leaders (Protestant and Catholic) during the Reformation and Counter-Reformation periods; and (5) the secular adoption of this persecution when the church was perceived as having too much power. Nelson also offers a multi-faceted hypothesis as to why witches were women and not men. In brief, the coalition of religiously based misogyny with the economic forces of an industrializing Europe left women in the position of being perceived as those who had stolen men's reproductive powers. The industrializing factors contributing to this perception were: (a) the movement of women and men to cities with women still needing marriage for support but with men constrained by either poverty or labor-guild requirements and (b) the lowered birth rates of urban life and the decline of the feudal family structure. The thematic emphasis of these circumstances around birth and reproduction together with the religious misogyny of the time seemed sufficient for religious authorities to consider women as those who had had consort with the Devil, burned infants and the like. Hence their charge of witchcraft and the need to punish and obliterate them. **NOTE**: For an alternative interpretation of factors affecting the identification of women as witches (and rooted in the anthropological study of witchcraft, sexuality and marginalization of women from "village authorities") see Clarke Garrett, "Women and Witches: Patterns and Analysis." *Signs* 3 (1977): 461-470.

[317] Potter, Mary. "Gender Equality and Gender Hierarchy in Calvin's Theology." *Signs* 11 (1986): 725-739.
This study documents the deep gender conflicts of John Calvin's theology as they reflect his "cognitio dei" and "cognitio humanis" perspectives. The first perspective reflects a spiritual equality that translates clearly to several existential equalities: Calvin's recognition that from the perspective of God, women and men are fully equal in terms of their creation, their responsibilities for personal sin, the duties and rights in marriage and their redeemed status. The second perspective, however, reflects the social and historical world and Calvin's inheritance of its misogynist assumptions: that in spite of his thinking that women and men are created equal, women are, in fact, inferior and created to supplement men; that women are, in fact, a source of evil and that it is a woman's duty to submit to her husband even in the face of beatings and abuse unless her life is at stake. A contrast with women's writings of the time (e.g., Christine de Pizan) permits Potter to summarize the enormous ambiguity of Calvin's thought and its continued need for correctives to affirm women's equality and particularly with respect to issues of abuse and domestic violence. **NOTE**: See also the literature on violence to women in Section VI-2.

[318] Ruether, Rosemary Radford. "Mothers of the Church: Ascetic Women in the Late Patristic Age." In *Women of Spirit: Female Leadership in the Jewish and Christian Traditions,* edited by Rosemary Ruether and Eleanor McLaughlin, 72-98. New York: Simon and Schuster, 1979.
In contrast to sources that provide a centuries-wide historical sweep over the philosophical or theological assumptions made about women in patristic and/or medieval cultures (including much of Ruether's own work), this brief essay does two things: First, it identifies the potentially positive

functions of fourth century asceticism for Christian women of wealth in Roman society during the mid to late 300s. Second, it provides a detailed picture of two women crucial to the development of fourth century asceticism and the communal groups it spawned as a result of their efforts. These women were Paula and Melania. They were women of Roman wealth and standing who rejected society's marital and familial roles to establish communities of mortification and study with like minded women. Moreover, it was through their efforts and the efforts of their name sake granddaughters ('Little Paula' and 'Melania the Younger') that such communities continued and in settings largely autonomous from male control. Ruether is clear about the negative aspects of their experience: these communities entailed difficult and sacrificial living, and at many points, collaboration and collusion with the powers of patriarchy in order for women to learn Scripture and its original languages. This said, the positive benefits of ascetism were independence from most male controls, and for many women an avoidance of marital obligations arranged as early as age 14 to solidify family fortunes, lineage and the like. This is an interestingly cast essay, with Ruether's narrative as if of friends, relatives and neighbors about whom one had at some point simply lost track, but with whom one has now happily reconnected.

[319] Ruether, Rosemary Radford. "Misogynism and Virginal Feminism in the Fathers of the Church." In *Religion and Sexism: Images of Woman in the Jewish and Christian Traditions*, edited by Rosemary Radford Ruether, 150-183. New York: Simon and Schuster, 1974.

This is an exceptionally important but *densely* written classical source in the early literature of feminist theology, and thus it is helpful to begin with the problem it addresses. This problem is the obvious conundrum in the writings of the "Church fathers" during the first few centuries of the Christianity--that the "fathers" are ambivalent in their understanding of women. Women are, on the one hand, inferior, evil, and a source of sexual temptation. On the other hand, they are virtual saints, provided they are virginal, ascetic or else wise asexual--a point that culminates in the veneration of Mary as the Virgin Mother of God. Some historians (e.g., Clark [296]) would argue that this apparent ambiguity with its "good/bad," "both/and" perspective is, in essence, a fact of history and to be accepted as such, without additional commentary. But Ruether's discussion here challenges the randomness of patristic ambivalence and argues instead, that not only is one perspective (the good or the bad) not more characteristic than the other, but in fact, "both stand as the two sides of a dualistic psychology that was the basis of the patristic doctrine of man" (p. 150). Her discussion develops in four points. First, Ruether notes the historical and other-worldly tensions that characterized Christianity in its foundational moments and the import of this tension as it conditioned patristic reflection on Gen. 1:27 ("God made man in his own image...male and female he created them"). Second, she details the differing expositions of this text by Eastern and Western writers, with Gregory Nyssa and Augustine as exemplars. Thus, in the East, otherworldliness and the spiritual were attached to the first part of the Genesis statement, with the physical world exemplifying the second part, while for Augustine and Western theology, rationality constituted "man's" God-likeness, with femaleness constituting the worldly and inferior portion of creation. Third, an essentially misogynous doctrine of marriage (as based on an enormous fear of sexual spontaneity and its presumed evil character) provided the basis for Augustine's ultimate understandings of gender, and these both his sacralized androcentrism and elevation of virginity (and continence) as the equivalent of male spirituality. Last, a series of ameliorating perspectives (i.e., Jerome's less encompassing misogyny and Nyssa's own marital experience) continued to elevate marital continence as a religious norm, and these, together with selected spiritual images of women, laid the groundwork for a developed Mariology as the Virgin Mother of God. Well documented--and in the end well argued, this essay highlights both the range of dualistic perceptions grounding historical theological anthropology, and the premises of those perceptions as the sacralized ideology supporting celibate, male ordination.

[320] Vogt, Kari. "'Becoming Male': One Aspect of an Early Christian Anthropology." In *Women: Invisible in Church and Theology*, edited by Elisabeth Schüssler Fiorenza and Mary Collins, 72-83. Edinburgh: T. & T. Clark, 1985.

This essay compactly surveys the usage of the phrase "becoming male" in the writings of Clement of Alexandria and Origin (and then selected monastic literature) to show its links to both (a) such key biblical texts as Eph. 4:13, 5:28-29 and Gen. 1:26-27; and (b) the "secular" or Koine usage of the phrase, i.e., that, "There is a common scale of values of which masculine and feminine contrast and the term 'becoming male' refers without exception to development from a lower to a higher state of moral and spiritual perfection" (p. 72). In her discussion Vogt distinguishes the eschatological assumptions attached to this phrase, and she points to the symbolic nexus it accomplished for its users: a unity of doctrinal, cultural and social expectations. That is, just as women could in their spiritual journey transcend their biological sex and 'become male,' so too could men fail and 'become female.' Although brief, the discussion is well documented from primary sources, and given its focus on achievement within the spiritual (or normatively male) realm, it bears haunting parallels to the current sociological discussion of work in gendered organizations that seek to desexualize (and/or "degenderize") work roles into bureaucratically rational tasks devoid of actual workers--and this, after the pattern of the public male achiever, with issues of family and child care ideologically glossed over. For a discussion of the latter, see Hearn et al. [727], and the entry by Acker in Lorber and Farrell [92]. For more extensive material on the moral hierarchy of sex and gender roles in patristic literature, see Ruether [319]

NOTE: For additional related literature see the reader edited by Clark and Richardson [186] and see Johnson's work on Mariology ([446], [447], [422]).

D. Feminist Theological Anthropology (1991-1995)

[321] Carr, Anne, and Elisabeth Schüssler Fiorenza, eds. *The Special Nature of Women?* London: SCM Press, 1991.
In the light of its renewed political and ecclesial salience, this issue of *Concilium* examines the concept, "the special nature of women" from within three focusing frameworks: "Women's Difference in Political, Social and Ecclesial Structures," "Feminist Analyses of How Women's Difference is Constructed," and last, "Critical Feminist Theological Exploration." Many traditional dimensions of this topic are reviewed here, e.g., Catholicism's enduring use of the complementarity principle to order ecclesiastical polity [Ruether], the numerous philosophical sources typically cited in support of such a principle [Maloney], and the "construction of women's difference in the Christian theological tradition" [Gossmann]. But new and developing international perspectives also give this text its breadth. For example, "Gender and Moral Precepts in Ancient Mexico..." are discussed by Sylvia Marcos as are "Gender and Race in Christian Mission" by Kwok Pui-Lan. Likewise, Katherine Zappone briefly addresses sociobiology, feminist and theological anthropologies in search of women's elusive "special nature," while Sarah Coakley contrasts the gender emphases of enlightenment and romantic philosophies. Finally Elizabeth Johnson critiques androcentric theology and church practice from within the awareness of women as *Imago Christi*, as she addresses the question: "Can a male savior save women?" Other discussions include differences between "feminine" and "feminist" socialization and "the eternal woman and the feminine face of God." Substantive notes follow each article, but indices and supplemental bibliographies are lacking.

[322] Graff, Ann O'Hara, ed. *In the Embrace of God: Feminist Approaches to Theological Anthropology.* Maryknoll, NY: Orbis, 1995.
Divided into four sections which variously address how life is held "in the embrace of God," this expertly edited text presents twelve essays that introduce and/or summarize the historical, methodological and theologically specific issues that make up "feminist approaches to theological anthropology." Part I provides "The Framework," with Mary Ann Zimmer summarizing "Stepping Stones in Feminist Theory." While brief, it is on the mark for readers seeking a theologically directed introduction. Second, Mary Ann Hinsdale provides a *sterling* overview of the theological literature in feminist theological anthropology, with her essay matched only by the extensive notes and bibliography provided throughout her discussion. Parts II and III of this reader then address "Foundations..." and "Explorations in Experience," as issues of diversity, ethnicity (Latina and *Mujerista* perspectives), sexuality, psychology, and suffering are examined, respectively, by Graff [71], Maria Pinar Aquino and Ada Maria Isasi Diaz, among others. Finally, in Part IV, "Experience and Specific Theological Issues," Sally Ann McRenyolds and Graff together examine "Sin: When Women are the Context," and Ann Clifford and Mary Catherine Hilkert present "...An Ecofeminist Proposal for Solidarity" and "Cry Beloved Image: Rethinking the Image of God." Peter Phan's "Women and the Last Things: A Feminist Eschatology" completes the listing. These essays provide helpful notes and bibliography, they are well crafted and existentially directed, and each is mindful that difference, suffering and pain are loci for feminist reflection. The contributors' work notwithstanding, this collection bears Graff's consistent talent for pastoral care, and it remains an abiding testimony to her work. A useful Index closes the volume.

[323] Hinsdale, Mary Ann, and Phyllis H. Kaminski, eds. *Women and Theology.* Maryknoll, NY: Orbis, 1995.
This text is volume 40 of the *Annual Publication of the College Theology Society*, and together with Graff above [322], it provides a solid overview of the Catholic literature on feminist

theological anthropology; but here from a more systemic and methodological perspective, with entries characterized by their social or organizational analytical levels. Kaminski's introduction, "Theology as Conversation," highlights this emphasis: "If theological conversation is to thrive, then it must be fully opened to women and it must be cured of its systemic biases" (p. x). Sixteen essays grouped as "Entering the Conversation," "Adding Voices," and "Changing the Terms" then follow, with Joan Leonard's "Presidential Address" closing the volume. To "enter the conversation," M. Shawn Copeland [278] addresses "difference" as a methodological premise, as Caritas McCarthy, Dana Greene, and Helen Ciernick illuminate 19th and 20th century Catholic voices, including "...Women at the Second Vatican Council" (Ciernick). "Adding Voices" widens the conversation, with international (Kwok Pui-lan and Maria Pinar Aquino), theological-liturgical (Mary Rose D'Angelo and Regina Boisclair) and religious-organizational (Ann Patrick and Susan Maloney) voices citing exclusionary patterns and inclusive needs. Also here is Mary Rattigan's informative review, "Korean Women Theologians: An Observer's Appreciation." Closing essays then survey methodological and theological-symbolic issues (see Hinsdale's "...Women's Studies and Religious Studies," Linda Moody's "...Feminist Theory Meets Feminist Theology," Leonard's "Presidential Address") and essays by Kaminski, Jane Kopas and Ann O'Hara Graff.

NOTE: Because the writing of theological anthropology engages the tasks of social construction at their most fundamental level, entries throughout the bibliography are useful resources for feminist theological anthropology. Among others, these include (as listed here alphabetically): Andersen and Collins [85], Blumenfeld and Raymond [576], Coleman [581], Collins [99], Crawford and Maracek [121], Davies and Haney [496], Giddings [614], Lengermann and Wallace [91], Lerner [69], Mankiller et al. [52], Pharr [588], Wade-Gayles [609], and Williams [341].

9

Feminist Theological Method

Since the beginnings of the feminist theological movement, the question(s) of feminist theological method has always been prominent. On the one hand, several of the most formative methodological discussions in feminist theology were developed during the years 1978-1985. These discussions focused largely on the ideas of patriarchy, misogyny and women's marginalization within Christian tradition, and from a methodological standpoint they accomplished three things: They revealed the scope of women's marginalization within Christian experience and theology, they emphasized the retrieval of women's experience from patriarchally defined historical perspectives, and third, they stressed the use of women's experience as a means of revelatory insight for women, both within and beyond formal organized religion. In the light of these emphases, then, "feminist theological method" was initially identified with at least three facets of feminist theological endeavor: (a) the critique of patriarchy, (b) the retrieval of women's experience within the tradition and, for many, (c) the "telling of tales...in memoriam" as a way of "redeeming the time." (See Trible [356].) More summarily, until the mid-1980s, the issues of feminist theological method were cast largely as the doing of theology from within the awareness of women's experience *as an experience revelatory of God,* and as thereby, an experience which is central, rather than marginal, to the tradition.

This approach, however, was not without its tensions. First, the identification of women's experience was at times problematic. This is because the pluralism of women's experience was (within the world of feminist theology) neither widely visible nor well developed theologically until the mid-1980s, although a few writers did recognize both the plurality of women's experience and its significance. (See, e.g., the 1974 collection by Hageman [168] and the 1975 discussions by Plaskow [170] and Ruether [172]). Moreover, when this pluralism did become widely visible-- and then theologically developed--it did so as a struggle with the social assumptions that peoples and cultures carry unreflectively, and thus as points of conflict rather than consensus within a seemingly commonly held tradition. Hence the rise of womanist theology as, in part, a critique of "white feminist theology," and in a related manner, the rise of several communally based feminist theologies (e.g., *Mujerista* and Asian feminist theologies) as discussions of conflict and consensus with a tradition historically dominant, but now recognized in terms of its multiple social worlds.

A second methodological tension arising in the mid-1980s stemmed also from the constructs of "Christian tradition," but here from the perspectives of established and confessionally based loyalties. In particular, although the 1980s witnessed the growing awareness of multiculturalism and its theological implications, these years also witnessed the challenge of confessional moorings, for Protestant and Catholic feminist theologians accorded differing weights to the authority of the Bible and its manner of entree into the theologizing process. More generally, for many Protestant feminist theologians (cf., e.g., Sakenfeld [410]), the Bible was and is an external source of religious authority against which women's experience (or any other experience for that matter) is to be fitted, and it is an authority which has its own self-evident and self-norming emphases. In contrast, the assumptions of many Catholic feminist theologians were (and are) more diffuse, in that while the Bible is obviously a text of "revelation," it is one embedded within the socially constructed nature of all human understanding, and thus if its words are to be designated as "salvific," they must be so in manners unequivocally clear to its hearers, in this case women. More directly, "revelation," (or its constructs) must enhance the fullness of women and women's experience and not fit women into a preconceived set of patriarchal and/or androcentric teachings, such as those of the biblical framework.

This is an enormously complex point of discussion with several side issues close to the fore. Generally speaking, however, among Roman Catholic feminists (e.g., Collins [517, 518], D'Angelo [397, 398], Ruether [366], Schneiders [391]) the tendency is toward an approach to the Bible which stresses (a) its cultural and socially constructed historical character and (b) the primacy of human experience (and here specifically women's experience) as itself the norming context for revelatory or redemptive proclamation. And, what is more, this perception is *not* seen by Roman Catholic women as a violation of the primacy of the biblical text as a revelatory document. Rather--and at the risk of seeming quite simplistic--the perspective here is more that of a text speaking through a community, instead of from above or beyond that community. (Nor, one should add, does this perspective contradict general Catholic theological thinking subsequent to Vatican II. For a general discussion of this point see Richard McBrien, *The National Catholic Reporter*, 2/26/95, pp. 5-6, as well as any of the "theology of revelation" literature published within Roman Catholicism following the close of Vatican II.)

A third issue swirling about the feminist methodology literature is that of "feminist hermeneutics and 'biblical theology.'" (Cf. Trible [205] and Schüssler Fiorenza [195, 196]). This third issue brings together the long standing tensions existing between biblical studies as an academic discipline and the feminist analysis of the Bible as a church-directed and normatively significant document. Most directly, where academically rooted biblical theologians have deemed their work consistently ecumenical and enlightened over the last several decades--in that academic biblical theologians generally have battled against fundamentalism and/or other non-rationally based approaches to biblical interpretation, these same scholars (who historically, have always been male) now face the challenges of *feminist* biblical work: *viz.*, the challenge that their own work has been governed by androcentric or 'male traditioning' tendencies, and that these emphases feed the patriarchal culture of Christian tradition itself. On the one hand this issue has seemed to many to be the contrast between an "academic" and an "ideological" reading of the Bible, a debate over exegesis vs. eisegesis (cf. Witherington [846]). At the same time, it is perceived by feminist biblical scholars to be less an "academic vs. ideology" debate, and more *the choice* of one's hermeneutic: that is, the choice for a "feminist" rather than androcentric hermeneutic, or the choice for an acknowledged rather than hidden perspective, given that the "academic" character of biblical studies has developed concomitantly with its male dominant, male defined, and male identified [i.e., androcentric] population of scholars. At present, this tension is yet debated, and given various factors, one can expect it to continue in both biblical and other theological subdisciplines.

Finally, a fourth issue returns one to the original themes of pluralism, experience, and social construction, and within these, the formally *epistemological* issues of women's experience (as contrasted with the *salience* of women's experience) relative to what can be said and known theologically. In particular, as the dimensions of feminist theology have attained global voice (cf., Chapter 22), the role of "social location" within the theologizing process has become significant for all aspects of feminist theology, and questions of method have returned to discussions of women's experience and the insights of feminist theological anthropology. But now with significant differences: for here, attention is directed, on the one hand, to the "epistemologies" of women across the globe (and particularly women in countries where Christians are "in the minority"), while on the other hand, attention is directed both to the "epistemologies" of heterosexist cultures and theologies, and, alternatively, the insights of same-sex spiritualities (lesbian and gay) for the critique of patriarchy and misogyny in Christian tradition. Indeed, as the global and "out" voices of women (and men) rise, the significance of "social location" becomes more salient and requires increased methodological reflection.

These four issues--the necessity for a visible theological pluralism, the role of women's experience as a source of revelatory authority, the conflict between androcentric and feminist biblical horizons, and the widening of the pluralism-experience discussion to include globalism and same-sex spiritualities--all permeate the literature of feminist theological method--and by extension-- feminist theology across the board.

How then, might the "feminist theological methodological literature" be synthesized? Because these four issues are expressed variously throughout the full literature of this bibliography, it is virtually impossible to synthesize them into one chapter overview. As a grounding framework, then, this chapter samples early and recent essay publications addressing: (1) the nature and naming of women's experience and its implications for [feminist/womanist] theological method (Graff [331], O'Neill [333] and Williams [341]); (2) women's experience as a specific revelatory source (Carr [324], Ruether [326], Davaney [330], Christ [327], Culpepper [329], and

Peskowitz et al. [339]); (3) the global character of women's experience and the theologizing process (King [338]); and (4) women's experience and other academic frameworks depicting women's experience and 'revelation' (Plaskow [340] and Christ [337]).

Given the limitations of this chapter, then, the following list is offered for those seeking more "issue-specific" sources. Thus, for the early and general studies on pluralism and theological method, see Driver [178], Murray [181], Plaskow [170] and Ruether [172]. For contrasting perceptions of how women's experience may be utilized theologically, see the overview by Jones [267], and see the literature in Chapter 6. For the literature on feminist theological method and biblical hermeneutics (among Christian writers) see Castelli [363, 358], Farley [364], Martin [374] and Cannon and Schüssler Fiorenza [348], and the contrasting perspectives of Trible [359] and Schüssler Fiorenza [236]—all but the last in Chapter 10. In addition, see the discussion by Tolbert [284] which addresses broadly based [Christian] denominational emphases in feminist biblical studies, while for more reactionary perspectives, see Pamela Dickey Young [289] and Elizabeth Achtemeier [838] in Chapters 7 and 22, respectively. Fourth, for the widening implications of pluralism, women's experience and social construction in the articulation of theological understanding, see Grant [636], Hunt [230], Townes [258] and Thistlethwaite and Engel [276], and in Section VI, see the related but differently contexted literatures on women's ecumenism, social location and theological method, e.g., Benavides [914], Fabella and Park [933], King [908], Chung Hyun Kyung [935], Plaskow [970] and Siegele-Wenschkewitz [972]. Finally, for relevant literature mentioned earlier in the bibliography, see Chapter 6, passim. A sampling of the literature on feminist theological method now follows.

Specific Literatures

A. Early Sources: 1977-1982

[324] Carr, Anne. "Is a Christian Feminist Theology Possible?" *Theological Studies* 43 (1982): 279-297.

At its widest berth, this deeply reflective essay accomplishes four things. First, it sets the criteria for a Christian feminist theology--and ecumenically so: not by exclusion, i.e., after the manner of established androcentric thought which distinguishes Christians and non-Christians by adherence to specific tenets, but, rather, by acknowledging the commonalities of all religious feminists and then by noting within this the range of differences among self-identified Christian feminists as articulated by the Carol Christ's "reformist/revolutionary" [177] synthesis of the early literature. Second, after identifying what she sees as three important criteria, Carr describes several recent developments in the literature that illustrate those criteria. Hence she summarizes early works by Ruether, Trible and Schüssler Fiorenza. Her summaries evidence the range of tradition-entrenched sexism as perceived by these theologians, and with this, their perception of "something more," the ambiguity within the tradition that permits an alternative reading of it. Thus, as her third point, Carr suggests the possibility for a Christian feminist theology. Fourth and last, she considers concretely what some of the tasks, questions, and projections of feminist theology might be given the criteria she has developed. For the beginning student, this is a difficult but worthwhile text, for it aligns issues of hermeneutics, feminist critique and theological reconstruction with the multiple tasks needed for a response to Daly's *Beyond God the Father* [161]. Additionally, it presents [Christian] feminist theology's methodological issues during the early 1980s, and with them, the problems then yet to be addressed. For Carr's longer discussion, see [229].

[325] Raitt, Jill. "Strictures and Structures: Relational Theology and a Woman's Contribution to Theological Conversation." *Journal of the American Academy of Religion* 50 (1982): 3-17.

This 1981 presidential address to the AAR develops a "theology of relation" from within the context of two conflicting perspectives acknowledged by the author: her professional identity as an historical theologian working primarily out of the area of sixteenth century theology and her personal religious identity as a Roman Catholic mindful of the feminist critique of Christianity. The perspectives converge in the category of relation, understood from historical sources as a form of "bonding" frequently intentional in nature but imaged hierarchically, and from feminist sources as a form of mutuality, almost always intentional in nature, and imaged inclusively and in terms of egalitarian patterns. The link here is "intentionality" and for Raitt relationality becomes non-hierarchical intentional bonding. This understood, Raitt moves to a consideration of several theological subjects. Most fundamental is the eucharist as bodily relation, but also important are baptism, ministry, justification and sanctification, grace, soteriology, Christology, trinity and God. As her title indicates, Raitt wishes to move from structures (primarily linguistic, but also institutional) that have become strictures, to a framework grounded in relationality and the possibilities it offers for thematizing Christian experience. A brief description of the above topics from the perspective of persons engaged in intentional bonding provides that re-thematization. By way of assessments, this piece assumes an almost footnote like status when judged by the categories of Catholic feminist theology of the mid-eighties and beyond. Its strength, however, is its ecumenical potential: First, it recognizes the constructed symbolic quality of all religious language (including trinitarian and God language). Second, the relational ecclesiology presumed by its description of eucharist, baptism, and ministry does not differ dramatically from discussions often made by church officials and policy makers. Finally, its prophetic quality is clear: "Some years ago," writes Raitt, "I wrote that the recognition of woman as a full human being would have more impact on Christian theology than any other event since the Incarnation itself" (p. 15). That in mind, Raitt enumerates three benefits of women's recognition that "shake the patriarchal pillars": (1) the reminder that God has no gender, (2) the recognition that no one image suffices to bear the presence of God and (3) the recognition that the establishment of religion on a written, revealed scripture is inherently problematic, as religious faith "must be communicated in a comprehensible idiom" (p. 16) not the patriarchal strictures of normative, creedal and/or revealed statements.

[326] Ruether, Rosemary Radford. "The Feminist Critique in Religious Studies." *Soundings* 64 (1981): 388-402.
As with Ruether's other early work in feminist theology and religious studies (cf. [171]), this essay also seeks to mark the terrain and significance of women's exclusion from religious leadership, and here specifically in Jewish and Christian traditions. The discussion is in four parts. Part I is a description of the "sociological and historical context for women's studies in religion." This description details the exclusion of women from the leadership of Judaism and Christianity and the subsequent institutional participation of women in Jewish and Christian teaching and educational activities. Part II then chronicles the "effects of women's exclusion on [Jewish and Christian] theological culture," and in particular, three principal effects: the elimination of women as "shapers of theological culture," the definition of women as inferior to men, and the theological legitimation of this inferiority by virtue of men's association with concepts of God, rationality and goodness and the association of women with concepts of sin, irrationality and evil. Part III of Ruether's discussion then identifies the needed "tasks of feminism in religious studies." These include (1) the systematic documentation of bias against women in Jewish and Christian histories and (2) the development of an alternative history both through the discovery of overlooked evidences of women's autonomy within scriptural and historical texts and the examination of counter-cultural literatures contemporaneous with Jewish and Christian history. Last, Ruether discusses the "translation of women's studies in religion into educational praxis" via the hiring of feminist faculty in theological seminaries and schools and the establishment of feminist religious studies within theological curricula. This discussion provides a clear overview of (1) Ruether's position on the need for feminist studies in religion, (2) the tensions existing between goddess religion and possible feminist Jewish/Christian syntheses, and (3) Ruether's own predictions and projections on the incorporation of women and feminist studies within religious/theological curricula. Ruether's own work in feminist religious studies touches several areas: biblical studies and feminist hermeneutics [366]; women in American religion (with Rosemary Skinner Keller) [132-135]; Catholicism and the women-church movement [759, 760, 193, 449]; the critique of anti-Semitism [299], feminist theological method [190, 191], issues of redemption and soteriology [191, 465], and feminist ecology and spirituality [220, 235].

B. Recent and Current Literature: 1985-1995

1. Feminist Theological Method

[327] Christ, Carol P. "Embodied Thinking: Reflections on Feminist Theological Method." *Journal of Feminist Studies in Religion* 5, no. 1 (1989): 7-16.
This article is a response to the argument presented by Davaney [330] that feminist theological method (as exemplified in the writings of Schüssler Fiorenza, Ruether and Daly) is insufficiently attentive to the implications of historical consciousness in that (1) feminist theological method does

not accept the nihilism implicit in historical consciousness (by virtue of the latter's radical relativising of all knowledge); and (2) feminist theological method *should* accept this nihilism and devise a more pragmatic approach to truth, together with a projection based understanding of religious symbols. To counter this charge Christ examines Schüssler Fiorenza's work and argues that while some methodological ambiguity exists within it, Schüssler Fiorenza is legitimate in arguing for her feminist criterion of truth as validated by selected biblical texts. First, Schüssler Fiorenza does not make universal truth claims on the basis of her feminist criterion, but speaks to and from a communal [women-church] faith experience. Second, she presents a vision and expectation that is more reflective of and conducive to women's reality than is patriarchy. Last, she presents a vision and expectation rooted in embodied experience, and while this is not necessarily devoid of the 'will to power' elements attached to race, gender and class, it is at the same time more accurate and productive for women than is the embrace of nihilism implicit in historical relativism. The particulars of Christ's argument stem from an examination of Gordon Kaufmann's work on the need for theologians and other academics to have cross-disciplinary conversation, and Christ suggests that assumptions from Kaufmann's work have clouded Davaney's reading of feminist theological method. NOTE: See Davaney [330], and for the "reformist-revolutionary" casting of feminist theology from within which both Davaney and Christ write see Christ [177]. Additionally, see the remaining articles within *JFSR* issue in which Christ's discussion appears and see Day [382].

[328] Conn, Joann Wolski. "New Vitality: The Challenge from Feminist Theology."
    America 165 (1991): 217-219.
This brief article accomplishes several things: First, it defines feminist theology as "the critical evaluation of the experienced patriarchal world." Second, it distinguishes "relationalist" and "individualist" feminist theologies, with the former characterized as theologies roughly comparable to the position of Carol Gilligan and the latter those akin to political liberalism. Third, it identifies six tasks that mark the feminist theological program. Fourth, it likens contemporary Christianity's symbolic ambiguity to the 'dark night of the spirit' as described by John of the Cross, with the further implication spelled out that John's 'intellect in darkness' is comparable to the experienced need for today's theologians to abandon male centered theology. The analogy is interesting but the heart of the essay lies with point #3, the "five tasks" of feminist theology: the *documentation* and *demonstration* of misogyny in traditional biblical and theological sources, (tasks #1 and #2); the *revisioning* of such texts and sources (task #3); their *re-definition* through re-organized textual and canonical boundaries (task #4); and consequently, a discipline-wide integration of feminist insights and praxis (task #5).

[329] Culpepper, Emily. "New Tools for Theology: Writings by Women of Color."
    Journal of Feminist Studies in Religion 4, no. 2 (1988): 39-50.
This paper chronicles Culpepper's own struggles to divest herself from "patriarchal consciousness" as a backdrop for academic research. It begins with the recognition that writings by women of color are a new source for reflection for white feminists as they consider the notion of "theory" in women studies, and it unfolds the primary values Culpepper has received from her dialogue with these writings. First, a clear recognition that such writings and the experiences they embody provide an alternative understanding of "theory," namely, that "theory" is not always (or even necessarily) best understood as a logically and linearly based process of articulation. Second, Culpepper's dialogue with writings by women of color indicates to her that one can be opened to the awareness that differences and diversity are strengths and resources for discussion, borne of other's own integrity. They are *not* problems to be resolved, nor are they less important emphases to be incorporated into a homogenized (or hierarchalized) "theory" that demands conformity to an idealized or other "theoretical" norm.

[330] Davaney, Sheila Greeve. "Problems with Feminist Theory: Historicity and the
    Search for Sure Foundations." In *Embodied Love: Sensuality and Relationship as
    Feminist Values*, edited by Paula M. Cooey, Sharon A. Farmer and Mary Ellen
    Ross, 79-96. San Francisco: Harper & Row, 1987.
The foil for this discussion is the "reformist-revolutionary" schema developed by Christ [177] to indicate the extent to which early feminist theological perspectives were 'in' or 'out' of patriarchal church traditions. Davaney's main point here is that this schema masks similarities that are themselves problematic within feminist theological method. Thus she argues that while feminist theological perspectives vary in terms of both content and range of "radicality," they nonetheless labor--like all theology--under the weight of an Enlightenment problematic in the search for truth, and this point should be acknowledged so that feminist theologians can move to a more pragmatic

and differently based understanding of religious symbolization. The argument develops in three parts. First, Davaney summarizes the modern critique of quests for truth from the Enlightenment's 'correspondence theory' to Foucault's nihilistic affirmation that all perceptions as equally invalid, but differentially valued to the extent that some have more power than others. Second, she reviews the writings of Ruether, Schüssler Fiorenza and Mary Daly to indicate their respective rejections of patriarchy and their claims that feminism is in some way tied to ontological authority. (For Ruether, suggests Davaney, this tie is via the prophetic principle of the Old Testament; for Schüssler Fiorenza it is through the egalitarian inclusivity of the Jesus community, and for Daly it is through feminism's tie to Elemental Reason.) Third, Davaney notes that none of these authors fully acknowledges the radical relativism of these ontological ties, and she suggests that if feminist theology were to accept this relativism--or more specifically, the nihilism implied within it--it could and should: (1) seek a theological pragmatism with respect to its own revisioning of Christianity and its power; and (2) give up its "referential theory" of religious symbolization in favor of a fully "projectional" theory of religious symbolization. Davaney does not speculate further on what either of these outcomes might look like. Rather, she concludes that her case against the masking capacities of the reformist-revolutionary framework is made, and that the similarities she has unfolded must be addressed. **NOTE**: For varying responses to this line of argument, see Christ **[327]** and see Day **[382]**, whose introductory essay refocuses the use of "experience" in historical analysis. Additionally, for a "pre-feminist" discussion of religious symbolism, see Lonnie Kliever, "Alternative Conceptions of Religion as a Symbol System," *USQR* 27(1972):91-102.

[331] Graff, Ann O'Hara. "The Struggle to Name Women's Experience: Assessment and Implications for Theological Construction." *Horizons* 20 (1993): 215-233.
This exceptionally well written and comprehensively based discussion surveys several approaches to the social construction of gender, and specifically "women's experience," as the latter may be interpreted from within the context of "...social location, language and the quest for human wholeness" (p. 230). This is a strong essay and it accomplishes three things. First, Graff identifies the "problem": it is how to name women's experience given the multiplicity of its dimensions, their social constructions and the gap between experience and its named realit[ies]. And here, richness and variation rather than singularity prevail. Second, Graff suggests three areas in which women's experience "informs and recreates" theology. Last, she provides a discussion of each from within the context of an obvious and skilled sensitivity to both women's experience and its rooted and distorted bearings within the panoply of much Western religious tradition. By way of particulars, the theological areas to be informed and recreated by women's experience are: (1) "revelation" (which may and should be touched by the apprehension of women's experience as a search for truth--an exploration for God); (2) the "implications" of this search for "practical and prophetic human transformation" (i.e., the necessity of engaging the search for justice, community, and new models of inclusivity); and (3) the significance of women's experience as a vehicle for disclosing "mystical encounter with God" as new images and visions (borne of that experience) allow prayer, liturgy and ritual to work as intended (*viz.*, as revelatory phenomena). This essay evidences the creativity of feminist theological reconstruction, and it pulls together social and religious visions of "women's experience" presently unsynthesized in the literature, but now available for synthesis in that "the work of criticism has cleared enough space to be able to re-engage the interpretation of major theological symbols" (p. 230).

[332] Malone, Nancy, ed. "The Knowledge of God and the Knowledge of the World." *Religion and Intellectual Life* 5 (1988): 3-44.
This entry brings together five papers delivered at the 1987 American Academy of Religion meeting as responses to Sally McFague's *Models of God* **[244]**. An introductory piece by Mary Jo Weaver locates *Models* with McFague's earlier work and introduces the panelists. First is Gordon Kaufmann who receives McFague's work positively as possibly a new form of systematic theology, but who nonetheless questions the personalized qualities of McFague's mother/lover/friend models and indicates a preference for structural models given the needs of an eco-nuclear age. Second is Rosemary Radford Ruether who challenges McFague's concept of "appropriateness" as a principle of methodological strategy, for if patriarchy is as evil as McFague's discussion suggests, then its evil quality has always been the case and should be recognized as such, not considered merely "inappropriate" for the current time. Third is David Tracy's response which requests stronger clarification of the difference between "heuristics" and "hermeneutics." Fourth is James Hart's introduction of "evangel-logic" as a perspective for assessing McFague's work. This evangel-logic is a principle that stresses (1) the development of a "poetics" between a "reflector...(the creaturely human)" and "that which is reflected upon...(God or the Divine)" and (2) the usefulness of the poetics for enabling the "determination" of each pole within such a

framework. The final entry in the discussion is McFague's response to the papers: an affirmation and clarification of her use of personal models, a recognition of patriarchy's evil qualities (but the acknowledgment that she did not want an emphasis on this to deflect critics' attention from her primary point of restructuring such imagery), an affirmation of the necessity for praxis-based critiques of theological models, and an acknowledgment to Hart for his new, but yet underdeveloped discussion. **NOTE**: For additional discussions contemporary to McFague's work, see the reviews of *Models of God* by Sheila Greeve Davaney and John B. Cobb in *Religious Studies Review* 16 (1990): 36-42.

[333] O'Neill, Mary Aquin. "The Nature of Women and the Method of Theology." *Theological Studies* 56 (1995): 730-742.
With a brief allusion to her 1975 essay on feminist theological anthropology **[293]**, and an obvious bent to the experience of Roman Catholic feminists, O'Neill notes the beginnings of feminist theology in the critique of Christianity's traditional theological anthropology, and not the issue of "method" per se. She then identifies three "vectors" (or orientations) within the current literature. The first is the mainstream framework as illustrated by E. Johnson, and particularly her emphasis of the reality of a single rather than binary view of human nature. Trend #2 is the feminist theology borne of complimentarity-based reactionary critiques of mainstream writers (e.g., Frances Martin's critique, *The Feminist Question*, Grand Rapids: Eerdmans, 1994). Trend #3 is a perspective O'Neill has herself developed (e.g., her essay in LaCugna **[273]**). Important to each, argues O'Neill, is the Christology underlying it, and the subsequent potential the latter offers the life of women in the church--both theological and sociological. In turn, O'Neill uses each of the perspectives as her entree into the topic of feminist theological methodology, for each highlights key aspects of feminist theological method: its initial roots in the suspicion of texts, its related suspicion of hierarchies, and third, its attention to "women's experience," with the latter clearly rooted in the pluralisms of an embodied world. To close, O'Neill notes her own discomfort at "how hard it is to shake off the old patterns, to write theology in a new way" (p. 742). Discomfort or not, O'Neill's insights attest the power of internalized negative self norms as described by Lorde **[78]**, from whom O'Neill draws (p. 740) to indicate the cooperative rather than combative nature of feminist theological method. **NOTE**: For a sociological variation on the power of internalization (as described above), see Lewis Coser, *Greedy Institutions*, NY: Free Press, 1974.

[334] Ruether, Rosemary Radford. "The Development of My Theology." *Religious Studies Review* 15 (1989): 1-4.
This summary by Ruether locates the beginnings of her career in the change directed elements of the American Civil Rights movement and the Second Vatican Council. By way of overview Ruether notes her initial interest in identifying the links between theological ideas and social practice and the methodology necessary to this task: first a search for the "ideological patterns in Christian thought which justify violence and oppression" and second, a search for those patterns [within the tradition] which "would critique this ideology and point to its transformation." Her discussion then details how religious powers become sacralized and their victims demonized, and she illustrates her discussion with several examples from her long career. Her principal and organizing example, however, is that of feminism and the women church movement and the correlation of feminism with the prophetic and messianic principles found in the Hebrew and Christian traditions. Her discussion here is brief but clear. The female and male prophetic voices of the Hebrew Bible cause a "shift in the social location of religion...[which moves it from the side of the]...ruling class, race and gender...[to the]... side of the poor and marginalized of society." In turn, in the New Testament, "this critical transformative vision is extended to categories of social contradiction not previously considered in Hebrew Scripture," namely "a universal redemptive community not bound by an ethnic concept of divine election" (p. 3.), *or*, given her first methodological premise, its own sacralization. **NOTE**: Respondents are Katharine Rabuzzi and Rebecca Chopp.

[335] Schüssler Fiorenza, Elisabeth, Karen McCarthy Brown, Anne Llewellyn Barstow, Cheryl Townsend Gilkes and Mary E. Hunt. "On Feminist Methodology." *Journal of Feminist Studies in Religion* 1, no. 2 (1985): 73-88.
This article is a "roundtable" discussion of feminist methodology featuring contributions by *JFSR* editor and New Testament scholar Schüssler Fiorenza, anthropologist Karen McCarthy Brown, historian Anne Llewellyn Barstow, sociologist Cheryl Townsend Gilkes, and *WATER* Director and feminist theologian, Mary Hunt. Schüssler Fiorenza leads off the discussion with a statement of methodological need: feminist theology needs to coordinate both scholarship and praxis into one model so that the desired development of a feminist paradigm may occur. She suggests her own work in New Testament studies (e.g., **[195]**) serves as an illustration of what such action based

research might look like, and she details her arguments with writings from German feminist sociology. Similarly, Brown and Gilkes both note the value of participant observation research, and each fleshes her discussion out with illustrations: Brown from her research on Haitian Voodoo and Cheryl Gilkes from her research on *Black* community and family life. WATER (Women's Alliance for Theology, Ethics and Ritual) director Mary Hunt highlights the use of the WATER organization for grass roots community building and connecting with academia. Finally, historian Barstow suggests *JFSR* as a forum for documenting academic and ecclesiastical injustices to women, and debates acrossof class, race, gender and confessional issues.

[336] Schüssler Fiorenza, Elisabeth. "The Bible, The Global Context and the Discipleship of Equals." In *Reconstructing Christian Theology*, edited by Rebecca S. Chopp and Mark Lewis Taylor, 79-98. Minneapolis, MN: Fortress, 1994.
While this essay could also be listed with feminist biblical studies in Chapter 10 it is included here because of its breadth and synthetic character. Overall, Schüssler Fiorenza makes three points in this discussion. First, she notes the need for a critical feminist interpretation of the Bible: because the world is now an electronic global village defined increasingly by the disparity of economic difference between the "haves" and "have-nots," the ultimate shape of its leadership can go either of two ways--that of patriarchal fundamentalism or, alternatively, that of democracy, human rights and the economic well being of all peoples. Second--and in the light of this possibility, Schüssler Fiorenza details the "dominant" forms of biblical interpretation: *viz.*, those of fundamentalism (which, in the case of Christians, reads the Bible as a privatized, otherworldly, individualized and literally inspired document) and alternatively, scientific or positivistic biblical studies, which in the case of Christian academics, views the Bible as either a document of antiquity to be studied by experts, or one whose past meaning must be translated or applied to contemporary experience, albeit apolitically. Neither approach to the Bible is sufficient, though, because neither takes seriously the social, political and economic well being of all peoples and within this commitment the full subjectivity of women. Hence, her third point, the need for a "critical feminist biblical interpretation for liberation," which includes a fourfold hermeneutics of suspicion, historical remembrance and reconstruction, proclamation (or ethical and theological evaluation) and, last, creative imagination. The remainder of the discussion then details Schüssler Fiorenza's "rhetorical" use of the Bible as a root metaphor for change and the ekklesia of equals--as described in several other sources (e.g., **[369]** and **[414]**).

2.   Method in Feminist Religious Studies

[337] Christ, Carol P. "Mircea Eliade and the Feminist Paradigm Shift." *Journal of Feminist Studies in Religion* 7, no. 2 (1991): 75-94.
This essay examines Mircea Eliade's discussion of female religious symbolism in Paleolithic and Neolithic religions to demonstrate the need for a critical feminist revision of the androcentrism within "History of Religion" studies generally, and here, specifically, in Eliade's work.

[338] King, Ursula. "Voices of Protest and Promise: Women's Studies in Religion, the Impact of the Feminist Critique on the Study of Religion." *Studies in Religion* 23, no. 3 (1994): 315-329.
This article examines the status of women's studies in religion--or as King terms it, women's studies *of* religion. The literature reviewed ranges from the mid-1980s through the mid-1990s, and for King it indicates both a protest and a promise. By way of protest, the literature evidences a critique of misogyny and misogynous authority. By way of promise, it suggests the hope of a feminist theology with particular attention to the globalization of theology. A key emphasis for King is the concept "paradigm change," which she uses to depict the reality of women's studies "in" and "of" religion. Sociologists may find her use of this term a bit broad, but her argument that "feminist religious studies" as a specific paradigm in competition with that of androcentric religious studies is well documented and strong. Additionally, her review of British and Canadian sources here is an obvious plus for American readers. NOTE: Also by King is **[908]**.

[339] Peskowitz, Miriam, Maria Pilar Aquino, Sheila Greeve Davaney, Nantawan Boonprasat Lewis, Emilie M. Townes, and Judith Plaskow "What's In a Name: Exploring the Dimensions of What 'Feminist Studies in Religion' Means." *Journal of Feminist Studies in Religion* 11 (1995): 111-136.
This "Roundtable" discussion appears in the first issue of the *Journal's* second decade and is presented in part to honor Judith Plaskow's completed ten years of co-editorship. As such, it

provides five perspectives on the meaning of the journal's name, "feminist studies in religion." All contributors include the reality of "diversity" in "feminist studies in religion," and their particular discussions are as follows. First, Jewish feminist Miriam Peskowitz revisits the image of "Penelope the Weaver" to detail how feminist projected images may be coopted and assimilated into patriarchal frameworks. Second, Latin American feminist liberationist Maria Pilar Aquino states clearly that feminist studies in religion need stronger analyses of women and economic injustice. Third, feminist theologian/process philosopher Shiela Davaney examines selected postmodern implications of women as historical subjects. Fourth, Thai feminist Nantawan Boonprasat Lewis delineates the "binary," "ethnic," and "multicultural" approaches to "feminist studies in religion," and last, Plaskow's editorial successor, womanist Emily Townes critiques what she sees as the tendency of some younger feminist theologians to ignore the implications of social location on their own perspectives and work. Plaskow responds in detail to each presenter and describes her own grounding in the Jewish imperative to "be kind to strangers…" and its contemporary translation for the pluralized circumstance of scholars existing in both oppressor and oppressed relationships: namely, that one's own oppression can and should be used to gain insight into the oppression of others. Last, she notes the tremendous backlash facing women scholars and feminist studies in religion, and the difficulty of maintaining commitments to "speak to a broad audience about issues that make a difference in ordinary people's lives" (p. 136). Among other things, this "Roundtable" illustrates the growing need for sociological perspectives within feminist studies in religion.

[340] Plaskow, Judith. "We Are Also Your Sisters." *Women's Studies Quarterly* 21, nos. 1-2 (1993): 9-21.
This exceptionally readable essay by Plaskow accomplishes two things: First it identifies the need for greater conversation between scholars working in the fields of women's studies generally and women's studies in religion particularly. This conversation is needed, says Plaskow, because not only has religion played an important role in the subjugation and liberation of women (and thus it is important to know its gender dynamics), but in addition, women's studies in religion is an established, vital and exciting field. Further, it is an academic study with strong links to women in non-academic settings, and thus it is eminently oriented to praxis. Plaskow's second accomplishment here is her expansion of these points through an overview of the key sources and developments within women's studies in religion, beginning with Daly's *Church and the Second Sex* **[157]** and continuing to the literature of the early 1990s. In effect, Plaskow traces the critical, recovery, and constructionist phases of the feminist/womanist/*Mujerista* and Asian feminist theological sources, and she demonstrates, thereby, some of the genuinely dramatic implications of women's studies in religion for both students new to the discipline, *and* society at large. This discussion is a solid and "user-friendly" overview of the main sources. For Plaskow's earlier methodological work see **[170]** and **[203]**, and for her formally theological work see **[262]** and her entries in Chapter 4. Last, for related overviews, see the essays specifically by Hinsdale and Moody as indicated in **[323]**.

3. Method in Womanist Theology

[341] Williams, Delores. "Black Women's Literature and the Task of Feminist Theology." In *Immaculate and Powerful: The Female in Sacred Image and Social Reality*, edited by Clarissa W. Atkinson, Constance H. Buchanan and Margaret R. Miles, 88-110. Cambridge, MA: Harvard Women's Studies in Religion Series, 1985.
Womanist theology draws heavily from the literature of African-American novels for the images, themes, and characterizations that can illuminate the wider experience of African American and white women. This essay focuses that task both for womanist and [white] feminist theology. Williams develops her discussion in three parts. First, she describes three images (or "models") of Black women's experience as depicted in (respectively): Margaret Walker's *Jubilee,* Zora Neal Hurston's *Jonah's Gourd Vine,* and Alice Walker's *The Color Purple.* Williams then indicates three assumptions crucial to each of the models, and to close her discussion, she draws out three tasks necessary for the development of feminist theology by white and black feminist and womanist theologians. Williams' models are, respectively, those of the Black woman as (a) a "communal life-support person," (b) a "tragic victim," and (c) a "catalyst moral-agent." The first depicts the "survival intelligence" developed and used by Black women in the face of slavery both on behalf of their families and their communities at large, whether black or white. The second portrays the devastation of Black women when caught within the web of a "self-denying love for a single male partner." Model #3 presents the empowering, educative capacities of Black women "loving others into their own self-assertion and affirmation." Central to each of these models, says Williams, are

the assumptions that (1) a racial history (along with a gender history) determines the character of Afro-American women's experience..."; (2) that "black female and black family liberation are inseparable" and (3) that Afro-American and white attitudes towards the black woman's sexuality affect her struggle to survive and change" (p. 101). In turn, these themes suggest three tasks for feminist theology. That is, feminist theology should: (i) develop a critical hermeneutic for biblical interpretation that can *simultaneously* liberate white and black women, their families and communities; (ii) address the question of "God's liberating power to black women and black families struggling with oppression"; and (iii) explore questions of sexuality from within the perspective of "oppressed women confronting white male conceptions that lead to the subjugation, exploitation and abuse of women's bodies" (pp. 105-107). Williams concludes that the development of a methodology incorporating these tasks will be especially valuable, for it can serve as a concrete response to the tensions existing between white and Black women, and it can thus indicate a "real" or genuine inclusivity (p. 107). For her own part, her expanded work in *Sisters...* [259] addresses several issues she details here, although at a wider, more synthesizing level, i.e., in terms of womanist theology as a "survival/quality of life" theology, which in turn, frames African American women's experience(s) dialogically vis a vis the African American social, theological and denominational communities, and the increasingly multicultural community of professional feminist theologians.

NOTE: Also by Williams is "Womanist Theology: Black Women's Voices" (pp. 179-186 in Plaskow and Christ [544]), and see Grant [254] and the Womanist literature in Chapter 17. Additionally, see the literature on global feminist theology in Chapter 18 and particularly Toinette Eugene's discussion of pluralism and difference [906].

10

Feminist Biblical Studies

Perhaps one of the most developed of the feminist theological literatures, the sources in feminist biblical studies are, for all intents and purposes, limitless. This chapter samples the feminist biblical literature with early studies reflecting both the critique of patriarchy and the recovery of women's experience within the biblical texts (e.g., Trible's early work [356]), and selected recent studies reflecting various strategies both to disclose feminist biblical insight (e.g., [372], [375], [383], [385], [398]) and challenge established androcentric scholarship, whether fundamentalist [401] or symbolic [414]. By way of chapter overview, reference works are presented first, with topical literatures then following and including: (1) feminist and womanist hermeneutical literatures; (2) selected feminist works in "Old" and "New" Testament perspectives; and last, the literature highlighting tensions between "biblical theology" generally and feminist biblical theology specifically. Among the more quoted sources here are: (1) Rosemary Radford Ruether's discussion of biblical hermeneutics as a process of creative interaction between traditional biblical prophetic and contemporary feminist perspectives [366] and Elisabeth Schüssler Fiorenza's discussion of "women-church" as a hermeneutical center for biblical interpretation [369]. Other noted sources (as well as helpful overviews) are indicated throughout the chapter. Two final notes: First, it cannot be stressed strongly enough that the entries of this chapter focus on grounding and exemplary works defining the scope and frameworks of feminist biblical studies. Second, it must be noted that while feminist biblical studies is perhaps one of the most productive of the feminist theological literatures (across vitually all denominaions), it has not been without its critics, and especially so in the light of society's backlash against the feminist movement. See Faludi [822] for the discussion of this backlash and see Achtemeier [838], Stroup [844], and Witherington ([846, 847, 848]) as examples of the biblical antifeminism that reflects and supports it.

A. Reference and Resources

1. Reference Works and General Bibliography

[342] Gruber, Mayer L. *Women in the Biblical World: A Study Guide.* Lanham, MD: Scarecrow Press, 1995.
This is the first in a projected two volume series, and according to its author, "This *Guide* is meant to provide scholars, clergy, seminarians, college students and all other interested people access to books and articles--both technical and semi-popular--which shed light on women in antiquity in Israel and Judah and the surrounding countries, which play a role in the entire corpus of sacred literature commonly called 'The Bible.'...[Moreover]...The first volume is meant to provide access to books and articles, which shed light on women in the world of Hebrew Scripture, which is commonly called 'The Old Testament'...[while the second volume will shed]...light on women in

the world of the Apocrypha and the New Testament." (p. vii). In all, Gruber lists 2964 sources grouped into 18 chapters, with an introductory overview indicating the history and organization of his bibliography. The introduction is helpful, but directed mainly to scholars fully grounded in the nuances of established biblical studies, including exegesis, languages, geography and the like. This is not a beginner's text. Nor is it particularly directed to feminist or women's studies scholars, although those with an academic biblical background will find its wide listing helpful. Also helpful is that Gruber lists the language of each entry when it is not in English. Most helpful, however, are Gruber's indices, four in all: author and subject indices, an index of biblical references, and one for Hebrew and Akkadian terms.

[343] Newsom, Carol A., and Sharon Ringe, eds. *The Women's Bible Commentary*. Louisville, KY: Westminster/John Knox, 1992.
This commentary presents more than 60 essays that synthesize feminist research on both (a) the full range of books comprising the Hebrew and Christian canons (including the apocryphal literature) and (b) such related, specialized topics as "hermeneutical issues," the "everyday life of women in the period[s] of the Hebrew Bible and the New Testament," and last, the status and experience of women in "Early Extracanonical Writings." A general "Introduction" co-authored by the editors locates the history and development of the commentary and indicates many of its features: First, that while a casual reading of its title might suggest it as a commentary on Elizabeth Cady Stanton's *The Woman's Bible* **[346]**, it is not that, although it intends to honor her pioneering, if in many ways now criticized work. Second, that a range of feminist perspectives is presented, with Jewish and Christian authors represented, and with each author setting the parameters (and particular textual emphases) of her discussion. Third, that the commentaries on specific books are presented with both academic and lay audiences in mind, and fourth, that the embedded bibliographies throughout the volume pull together sources not elsewhere synthesized and/or frequently unavailable in major and more well known feminist biblical discussions. This is a landmark text, with the goal of communicating recent research clearly in mind. For a contrasting approach (which stresses the additional and related research on "social location" as a factor in feminist biblical work), see Schüssler Fiorenza below **[344-345]**.

[344] Schüssler Fiorenza, Elisabeth, ed., with the assistance of Shelly Matthews. *Searching the Scriptures: Volume I: A Feminist Introduction*. New York: Crossroad, 1993.
Together with entries **[345]** below, this volume provides one of the most comprehensive overviews of feminist work in biblical and extrabiblical studies, with Volume I addressing methodological and hermeneutical issues and Volume II specific NT books and related extracanonical texts. By way of overview, Volume I presents 24 essays that address four issues. Issue #1 is the influence of social location on methods of interpretation, with exemplary discussions including Elisabeth Gössmann's "History of Biblical Interpretation by European Women" and Teresa Okure's "Feminist Interpretations in Africa." Issue #2 is the task of "Changing Patriarchal Blueprints" (or "Creating Feminist Frames of Meaning") and here Kwok Pui-Lan's essay ("Racism and Ethnocentrism in Feminist Biblical Interpretation") and Carol Devens Green's "Native American Women, Missionaries and Scriptures" serve to illustrate. "Rethinking Critical Methods" and "Transforming the Master's House..." are the third and fourth organizing issues for the volume's several entries, and here such discussions as "Toward a MultiCultural Ecumenical History of Women in the First Century/ies, C.E." (by Barbara H. Geller Nathanson) and Allison Cheek's "Shifting the Paradigm: Feminist Bible Study" illustrate the practices of feminist communication presented by these respective category emphases. It should be noted that each of the volumes honors a "foremother" in feminist biblical studies. In Volume I the "foremother" is African American biblical scholar Anna Julia Cooper (author of *A Voice from the South* **[641]**). In Volume II it is Elizabeth Cady Stanton, author of *The Woman's Bible* **[346]**. Notes, embedded bibliography, a general index and clearly written discussions mark the volume.

[345] Schüssler Fiorenza, Elisabeth, ed., with the assistance of Ann Brock and Shelly Matthews. *Searching the Scriptures: Volume II: A Feminist Commentary*. New York: Crossroad, 1994.
In contrast to Newsom and Ringe **[343]** who present a near women's studies analog to the *Interpreter's Dictionary of the Bible*, the forty entries in Schüssler Fiorenza's commentary are, first of all, differently organized and second, self-consciously feminist and "transgressive" in orientation. The organizing principle for the volume is that of Sophia, the First and Second Testament female image of God, and the volume's entries are grouped into three sections: (1) "Revelatory Discourses: Manifestations of Sophia;" (2) "Epistulatory Discourses: Submerged

Traditions of Sophia;" and (3) "Biographical Discourses: Envoys of Sophia." For each category numerous authors address various "canonical" and extracanonical texts to hold forth the experiences and reality of women within the texts and their interpretation, and the effects of history's "patriarchalizing" canonical process. In her brief and readable introduction Schüssler Fiorenza indicates several orienting points. First, this volume is not the presentation of a "feminist canon," as she indicates that Ruether's *Womanguides* [192] is (although see Ruether's introduction to the latter). Rather, it is a "transgressive" collection, an effort at pushing the boundaries and deconstructing the infrastructure of history's "kyriarchal" canon (cf. [236 and 238]). Second, this volume is in honor of Elizabeth Cady Stanton's *Woman's Bible*, but unlike the latter, it deals with whole texts not fragments, and it is multicultural and cross traditional in approach, contra the class and anti-Semitic assumptions of Stanton's original text and in acknowledgment of the general white and European axis within 20th century feminist biblical studies. Third, this volume seeks specifically to expand the imaginative religious-communal vision of historical/exegetical studies, for it seeks to combat the "orthodoxy heresy" framework established early in the history of Christianity and supported theologically up to and through the present time. Silvia Schroer opens with an overview on "The Book of Sophia" and the remaining discussions follow. Noted American and international Jewish, Protestant and Catholic authors are included, and contributors are helpfully identified. Notes and bibliography follow each essay, but the volume lacks an index.

[346] Stanton, Elizabeth Cady. *The Woman's Bible*. Forward by Maureen Fitzgerald. Boston, MA: Northeastern Univ. Press, 1993. [First published: New York: European Pub. Co., 1895/1898].

Originally published in two volumes, this reprint of Stanton's *The Woman's Bible* includes Parts I and II, together with all the introductory and prefatory notes Stanton and her co-authors prepared for specific sections and books within the "Old" and "New" Testaments, including Stanton's statement of the need for a "Woman's Bible," the significance she hoped it would have, and (in an appendix) copies of letters and correspondence indicating various responses to the project. As a series of comments and judgments on the misogynous writings of several biblical texts, Stanton's *Woman's Bible* needs little secondary introduction, for Stanton's own introduction indicates the ideological uses to which various biblical texts about women have been put. Further, because Stanton's *Woman's Bible* is about *texts concerning women*, it is a collection of comments and commentaries on selected texts rather than full biblical books as a whole. Moreover, because its initial political direction was towards the emancipation of women in the late 19th century, it bears several of the century's prejudices within it, and particularly: (1) an ignorance of segregation and racial prejudice as also biblical issues and as also a part of the social fabric needing emancipation and critique; and (2) a limited view of gender as a population defining category, with (male) Protestant clergy and social leadership bearing the bulk of the book's criticisms, and with other contemporary Christian and Jewish women seemingly marginal to the project as a whole. These (and other) limitations notwithstanding, the book remains an historical witness to the work of women struggling towards empowerment in the face of ignorance, personal difficulties and the dynamics of institutionalized bigotry that so often thwart attempts at the empowerment of groups marginalized from mainstream lines of power. A final note: Fitzgerald's clear, extensive introductory discussion helpfully acquaints the reader with the history and tensions of Stanton's work relative to other women suffragists from Seneca Falls on. For related literature see the articles by Carolyn DeSwarte Gifford in the following collections: Ruether and Keller [132], Collins [349], and Schüssler Fiorenza [345].

NOTE: For related materials, see the reference works cited in Chapter 8 under "Feminist Theology and Theological Anthropology."

[347] Deen, Edith. *All the Women of the Bible*. 1955. Reprint, San Francisco: Harper & Row, 1983.

This is a re-released and obviously pre-feminist source, but its indexical features remain a usable resource for biblical scholars. It is well-organized, and its three part division reflects the general standing of women throughout the biblical literature. Thus, some women (by Deen's count 63) stand in the *foreground* of specific texts and stories, while others--regardless of textual location--are *named*, while women of yet a third group are *nameless and identified biblically by only their role(s)*, whether as individuals (e.g., Pharaoh's daughter) or as a group of individuals within a given role (e.g., Lot's Daughters). A cautionary note: In Part I Deen presents meditations and reflections on the experiences of women in the "foreground" of texts and stories. These reflections exemplify the cultural ethos of American race-gender norms through the early 1950s. Hence they presume the normative character of white middle class values, and within these, the assumptions of:

(1) complementarity as the marital norm, (2) motherhood as the primary female role, and (3) passivity, dependence and "purity" as desirable traits in women. Also, because the text is reprinted but not edited, Deen's bibliography extends only through the 1950s. In spite of these limitations, the text remains a useful reference with the experiences of *named* women well indexed and cross-referenced to all appropriate biblical texts. For *contemporary* readings of the same sources, see Bellis [381] and Winter [531].

2. Feminist Collections and Journal Issues

[348] Cannon, Katie G., and Elisabeth Schüssler Fiorenza, eds. "Interpretation for Liberation." *Semeia* 47 (1989): 1-153.
This issue of *Semeia* (also published separately through Scholar's Press in Atlanta, GA) includes seven essays by scholars who "seek to fashion new models and approaches for a Christian biblical interpretation that could support people's struggle for justice, self-determination and freedom" (p. 1). The contributors include womanist ethicists Katie Cannon and Shiela Briggs, pastor-sociologist Cheryl Townsend Gilkes, and biblical scholars Kwok Pui-Lan, Renita Weems, Clarice J. Martin, and Vincent Wimbush. Generally speaking, each essay focuses on the function of power in (or relative to) the Bible and its liberating capacities for freedom, or alternatively, the ways that capacity has been ideologically distorted. Thus in "Slave Ideology and Biblical Interpretation" Cannon identifies three "myths" used to support slavery throughout American church history, and in "Discovering the Bible in a Non-Biblical World" Kwok surveys alternatives to Western Christian parochialism. Similarly, Wimbush advocates the African American adoption of historical and critical cultural hermeneutics so that confessionally based ideologies may be evaluated and alternative, effective symbolic perspectives selected. In the remaining articles, Gilkes presents an Afrocentric reading of the "father to the fatherless" theme of Ps. 68 which identifies its long standing Black church parallel of God as "a mother to the motherless." Similarly, Martin examines the "politics of omission" practiced in biblical scholarship relative to Acts 8:26-40, and Weems details the potentials for sexual violence presented in the marriage metaphor employed by Hosea in 2:4-25. Last, Briggs asks: "Can an Enslaved God Liberate?: Reflections on Philippians 2:6-11." Overall, these last three essays are the longest and arguably the strongest, with Briggs's entry especially so. A powerful collection, this volume should be read in conjunction with Thistlethwaite [252], Russell [367], Ruether [190], Collins [517] and the hermeneutical literature generally, and with such sociological sources as Andersen [84], Andersen and Collins [85], Ladner [597], Collins [99] and Feagin and Feagin [122-123].

[349] Collins, Adela Y. *Feminist Perspectives on Biblical Scholarship.* Chico, CA: Scholars Press, 1985.
This collection of nine well chosen papers represents the gradual recognition of feminist biblical scholarship in 1980 by the Centennial Publications Program of the Society of Biblical Literature (SBL). Collins introduces the volume by tracing the history of this acknowledgment together with the history of feminist scholarship in the SBL, and she highlights both her assumptions grounding the selection of specific papers and the key points of the papers themselves. The resulting essays "show clearly," says Collins, that "historical-critical scholarship and feminism are not exclusive alternatives" but perspectives that exist in "creative tension" (p. 9). The entries well evidence this point. All focus on feminism, hermeneutics and historical-critical method and indicate among other things: (1) *the contrasts and similarities between 19th and 20th century feminist hermeneutics* (e.g., Carolyn de Swarte Gifford's "American Women and the Bible: The Nature of Women as Hermeneutical Issue" and Carolyn Osiek's "The Feminist and the Bible: Hermeneutical Alternatives" [354]); (2) *specific philosophical and theological questions concerning feminism, method and interpretation* (Schüssler Fiorenza's "Remembering the Past in Creating the Future" [412], Drorah Setel's "Feminist Insights and the Question of Method" and Bernadette Brooten's "Early Christian Women and Their Cultural Contexts: Issues of Method in Their Historical Reconstruction"); and (3) *literary and exegetical issues attached to interpretive efforts* (Nelly Furman's "His Story Versus Her Story: Male Genealogy and Female Strategy in the Jacob Cycle" and Esther Fuchs', "The Literary Characterization of Mothers and Sexual Politics in the Hebrew Bible" and "Who Is Hiding the Truth? Deceptive Women and Biblical Androcentrism" [383]).

[350] Tolbert, Mary Ann, ed. "The Bible and Feminist Hermeneutics." *Semeia* 28 (1983): 1-126.
Editor Tolbert suggests that the seven essays of the *Semeia* issue "should be seen as part of a growing dialogue between liberation movements and biblical scholarship, that is calling into question past assumptions and posing difficult unavoidable hermeneutical issues" (p. 1). Tolbert's

own essay [372] highlights these issues as she links the questions of feminist biblical hermeneutics with the more traditional hermeneutical literature, i.e., that of Rudolf Bultmann. The remaining articles deal with the more specialized concerns of both biblical and feminist studies: the potential of gender for the implied readership of Matthew's Gospel (see Janice Capel Anderson's "Matthew: Gender and Reading"); the use of women as symbols of discipleship in Mark's Gospel (E. S. Malbon's "Fallible Followers. Woman and Men in the Gospel of Mark"); the canonical status of women as interpreters of tradition and covenant in the Old Testament (see Toni Craven's "Tradition and Conviction in the Book of Judith"); and the exegesis specific texts that illustrate the resistance/praxis of biblical women: "'You Shall Let Every Daughter Live': A Study of Exodus 1:98-2:10" by J. Cheryl Exum and "Luke 9:28-36: the Beginnings of an Exodus." by Sharon Ringe. Finally, a more synthetic essay, William Walker's, "The 'Theology of Woman's Place' and the 'Paulinist' Tradition" addresses the gender tensions in the Pauline corpus and suggests that a "Paulinist reactionary party" developed *during the apostolic period* to counter "the egalitarianism of Paul's thought "by interpolating specific Pauline and Deutero-Pauline texts.

[351] Trible, Phyllis, ed. "The Effects of Woman's Studies on Biblical Studies." *Journal for the Study of the Old Testament* 22 (1982): 3-71.
Eight articles (including Trible's editorial introduction) comprise this special *JSOT* issue. The articles include the following, with most abstracted separately in this volume: Trible's own introduction, "The Effects of Women's Studies on Biblical Studies" [357]; "Women's Studies and Biblical Studies An Historical Perspective" by Dorothy C. Bass [352]; "Old Testament Perspectives: Methodological Issues" by Katharine Doob Sakenfeld [379]; "Sacred Marriage" by Mary Wakeman; "Feminist Theology and New Testament Interpretation" by Elisabeth Schüssler Fiorenza [368]; "New Testament Perspectives: The Gospel of John" by Adela Yarbro Collins [390]; "Feminism and Patriarchal Religion: Principles of Ideological Critique of the Bible" by Rosemary Radford Ruether [365]; "Feminist Critique: Opportunity for Cooperation" by Letty Russell.

NOTE: For related literature, see the collections edited by Russell ([174 and 210]) and see Schüssler Fiorenza ([196 and 236]).

3. Inclusive and Feminist Biblical Translations

For inclusive translations of the Psalms, the Gospels and the Pauline materials, see Chapter 13, "Feminist Theology and Christian Worship."

4. Critical Works by Elisabeth Schüssler Fiorenza

Elisabeth Schüssler Fiorenza is recognized as one of the foremost feminist biblical theologians writing in this century. Her published work dates from the mid-1970s and addresses a wide range of topics, including exegetical, hermeneutical, theological, and ecclesiological issues. Of significance in the biblical field, and indeed, almost standard references at this point, are her two volumes published in the mid-1980s, *In Memory of Her* [195] and *Bread Not Stone* [196]. The first is a critical exegesis of the gospels and Pauline literatures, undertaken to demonstrate both the need for and the manner in which the origins of Christianity may be re-interpreted along egalitarian (rather than traditional and patriarchal) lines. The second is a collection of critical essays indicating the hermeneutical and methodological assumptions grounding Schüssler Fiorenza's critique of such conventional approaches to the Bible as, for example, form criticism and historical criticism.

Since the mid-1980s, Schüssler Fiorenza has continued her biblical work with the 1992 publication of her essay collection, *But She Said: Feminist Practices of Biblical Interpretation* [236], and her 1993-1994 two volume edited work, *Searching the Scriptures* ([344-345]). Additionally, she has published extensively in the area of feminist theological methodology, and always with an eye to the role of scripture as a vehicle yet available to the salvation of women. Because of their significance for the development of the literature, Schüssler Fiorenza's two early volumes (*In Memory of Her* and *Bread Not Stone*) are abstracted in Section II of the bibliography. Alternatively, her more recent biblical works are abstracted in the present chapter.

Schüssler Fiorenza is a brilliant, but complex writer whose work is often difficult to read and not always clear to beginning students. Moreover, because she has published so widely in so many areas, it is not always easy to map one's way through her many publications. For this reason, then, the following sequence is suggested for those seeking a preliminary and chronological excursion through her work. In all, five sources are listed, and if read carefully they will prepare one for Schüssler Fiorenza's 1983 classic, *In Memory of Her,* and her subsequent women-church hermeneutics. The first of these five essays is Schüssler Fiorenza's, "Interpreting Patriarchal Traditions" **[380]**. This essay identifies key issues that Schüssler Fiorenza's subsequent publications spell out in increasingly detailed discussions. Text #2 is **[175]**; it ties Schüssler Fiorenza's biblical work to the questions of doctrine and (androcentric) theology, while text #3 **[368]** returns one to the area of biblical hermeneutics and the role of social location in biblical exegesis. The remaining two texts (**[194]** and **[411]**) synthesize Schüssler Fiorenza's methodological work from within the widening horizon of her "critical liberationist" framework. Through various means (e.g., a listing of the criteria for identifying sexist language in biblical texts) these essays set the ground for Schüssler Fiorenza's understanding of gender as a dimension of theological hermeneutics and the reality of "women-church" as an interpretive theological framework. Schüssler Fiorenza's subsequent work--including *In Memory of Her*--then becomes an expansion of these themes as she amplifies the critical range of her earliest visions and extends them to the areas of biblical methodology per se (the commentaries), methodological issues embedded in global feminist development **[336]**, Christology and Jewish Christian feminist theological dialogue **[238]**, diversity and multiculturalism **[275]** and the feminist theological critique of violence against women **[869]**.

B. Topical Literatures within Feminist Biblical Scholarship

1. Feminism, Womanism, and Biblical Interpretation

a. Early Literature

[352] Bass, Dorothy C. "Women's Studies and Biblical Studies: An Historical Perspective." *Journal for the Study of the Old Testament* 22 (1982): 6-12.
This essay details the distribution of women members in the Society of Biblical Literature [SBL] from its inception to 1980. It is cast against the historical backdrop of the developing nineteenth century American feminist movement, and it argues that three barriers needed to be overcome for women to become full participating members of the SBL: (1) attendance at meetings; (2) presentation of papers; and (3) publication of papers. A content analysis of the decennial SBL membership lists through 1970 indicates clear parallels with the salience of American feminism. The number of women in the SBL peaked at approximately 10% between 1910 and 1920, but by 1970 it had dropped to 3.5% Similarly, publications from the period 1921-1980 indicate only 51 articles and these by only 37 women. (Comparable male data permitting percentage comparisons on both authorship and articles published are not presented.) Bass calls attention to the historical estrangement between feminist thinking and professional biblical scholarship as evidenced, e.g., in the development of *The Woman's Bible* between 1895 and 1898. She suggests that if this estrangement is to be overcome, then (a) the SBL must experience a different gender configuration and (b) press questions such as those exemplified by the writers of *The Woman's Bible*.

[353] Johnson, Elizabeth A. "Feminist Hermeneutics." *Chicago Studies* 27 (1988): 123-135.
Defining feminist hermeneutics as the "interpretation of scripture done from the perspective which prizes and advocates the full human dignity of women, in contrast to those perspectives which ignore or even oppose the full humanity of women" (p. 124), Johnson introduces the reader to the "historical background" and "various models" constituting this field. The positions she surveys are those described by Osiek **[354]**, i.e., the "rejectionist," "loyalist," "revisionist," "sublimationist" and "liberationist" models. Johnson's own grounding is in the liberationist model, and it provides her the framework for assessing models #1-4. Her final criterion for the assessment, however, is the Bible, and especially as interpreted by Vatican II's teaching on revelation [*Dei Verbum*]. For Johnson, paragraph 311 of the latter affirms that "things which do not affect salvation do not belong to inspiration" (p. 134). This article is written as an introduction for those unfamiliar with the literature, and it succeeds admirably. It is substantive, pastoral, and although lacking endnotes, informed by the principal feminist hermeneutical authors.

[354] Osiek, Carolyn. "The Feminist and the Bible: Hermeneutical Alternatives." In *Feminist Perspectives on Biblical Scholarship*, edited by A. Yabro Collins, 93-105. Chico, CA: Scholars Press, 1985.
This essay synthesizes several issues and perspectives to provide a grounding for interpreting the Bible from a feminist liberation perspective. It begins with Osiek's own recognition of the contexts within which she stands. She belongs to a "large institutional church with an amazing amount of diversity in its membership and a firmly entrenched patriarchal leadership..."; she views the Bible

as part of her "own *living* history" and as something "worth salvaging;" she asserts the need for "nuances" for issues of biblical authority, inerrancy and the like, and last, she sees "tradition" as "the all-encompassing movement that contains within itself the biblical text and the factors leading to its production" (pp. 93-94). Second, Osiek reviews various early feminist hermeneutical studies to derive a five fold typology that indicates the ways women can "respond and adjust" to the situation of religious [here Christian] patriarchy. These include the extreme rejectionist and loyalist positions (where the text is either thrown out or simply obeyed), the revisionist perspective (which seeks out neglected information about women's biblical or religious history), the sublimationist perspective--a kind of 'romantic' feminism, and last, a liberationist perspective that fosters a justice directed advocacy theology. The latter, for reasons she details in terms of gospel values, is her preferred option. An illustration of feminist history, Osiek's discussion well illustrates the capacity of traditions and their members to find mechanisms of change for wider and more open perspectives. **NOTE**: For a sampling of Osiek's more recent work see her commentaries on "Galatians" and "Philippians" in *The Women's Biblical Commentary* **[343]** and *Searching the Scriptures* **[345]**, respectively.

[355] Throckmorton, Burton H., Jr. "Some Contributions of Feminist Biblical Scholars." *Union Seminary Quarterly Review* 42 (1988): 87-88.
Presented in a panel discussion on feminist biblical scholarship and the role played by context in theological interpretation, Throckmorton's compact essay describes six contributions of feminist biblical theologians to the world of New Testament studies. First, feminist biblical scholars have exposed the androcentric (male-centered) world of the whole Bible, including the synoptic gospels. Second, feminist biblical scholars have demonstrated that patriarchal assumptions have "dominated" the field of biblical studies and continue to do so. Third, feminist biblical scholars have uncovered the "systematic silencing of women's voices...names, words and activities" within the tradition of the church's New Testament study, and they have exposed, thereby, "that our New testament histories are to that extent falsified" (p. 87). Fifth, these scholars have generated an important and necessary "hermeneutics of suspicion" which in turn, has challenged the "value free" assumptions of the historical literary traditions of biblical scholarship. Finally, the work of these feminist biblical scholars has pressed male scholars "to listen and [to] help a new mutuality in...critical theological work" (p. 88). **NOTE**: For additional work by Throckmorton see **[530]** in Section III-6.

[356] Trible, Phyllis. "Feminist Hermeneutics and Biblical Studies." *The Christian Century* 99 (1982): 116-118.
Trible's brief essay compactly identifies three types and/or stages within the emergence of feminist biblical hermeneutics: (1) a prophetic documentation of patriarchy and misogynist history; (2) the recovery of forgotten biblical passages that themselves critique patriarchy; and (3) the telling of biblical tales "*in memoriam*...to redeem the [present] time." The first type "has uncovered abundant evidence for the inferiority, subordination and abuse of women in Scripture" (p. 116). It is based primarily in narrative and legal biblical sources. The second type identifies a biblical critique against patriarchy. This critique is evident in neglected and underdeveloped passages attesting to female imagery of God, the courageous acts of biblical women, and the reinterpretation of key passages used historically to oppress women (e.g., Gen 2-3). The third approach memorializes the experience of abused women. It entails reading the Scriptural stories of abused women with sympathy, patience, and a hope of "redeeming the time." All three approaches--documentation, textual recovery and the telling of tales "in memoriam," are approaches that Trible herself uses throughout her work. For illustrations see **[385]**. Additionally, see her early works **[164-165]**, **[176]** and her grounding text, *God and the Rhetoric of Sexuality* **[205]**.

[357] Trible, Phyllis, ed. "The Effects of Woman's Studies on Biblical Studies." *Journal for the Study of the Old Testament* 22 (1982): 3-5.
Trible's introduction to the *JSOT* special issue "The Effects of Woman's Studies on Biblical Studies" **[351]** highlights the historical occasioning of this special issue: Conference planners of the SBL's centennial meeting requested a session on "Women and the Bible" (under the rubric of 'the history and sociology of the Bible.') as one aspect of the society's centennial celebration. Noting that women's scholarship was neither acknowledged in the preliminary conference literature, nor proposed in discussions of future scholarship, Trible indicates that female SBL members thereby utilized the session to speak prophetically about the sin of patriarchy, both within and beyond the Bible and the SBL. The subsequent articles present aspects of the discussion. **NOTE**: For recent literature on the interchange between women's studies and biblical studies, see

the "Introduction" to Newsom and Ringe [343] and see Volume I of *Searching the Scriptures* [344] passim.

b. Recent Overviews

[358] Castelli, Elizabeth. "Heteroglossia, Hermeneutics and History: A Review Essay of Recent Feminist Studies of Early Christianity." *Journal of Feminist Studies in Religion* 10, no. 2 (1994): 73-98.
This article introduces one to the "discursive diversity...characterizing the world of feminist studies of the first several Christian centuries" (pp. 74-75), but it is not for that fact an "introductory" discussion. Rather, through a close reading of several representative sources--and a detailed summary of the variously nuanced issues surrounding the study of feminism, women, gender and "biblical" experience--Castelli highlights the theoretical and methodological pluralism surrounding women, culture and religion in the first few centuries of the Common Era. The concept "heteroglossia" is taken as the grounding image for the maze of pluralism now characteristic of feminist biblical studies. It is drawn from the characterization of womanist pluralism as the ability to speak several languages ("public, differentiated, social, mediated dialogic discourse..." cf. p.74), and it intends a similar "discursive diversity" in what is more summarily, but often uncritically, known as feminist biblical studies. The range of topics, the terminological nuances of "feminism," "gender," and "woman," the detailed differences between "theological" and "non-theological" [feminist biblical] scholarship, the notable contributions of [biblical] historical reconstruction, and the genuinely informative footnotes to this article all mark it as a superlative overview for the seasoned--or even initiated--reader. This noted, students less fluent in the literature will find this essay difficult, albeit worthwhile after the first few tries. NOTE: Also by Castelli is [363], and for her biblical work see her essay on "Romans" in *Searching the Scriptures* [345] and her *Imitating Paul: A Discourse on Power* [Louisville: Westminster/John Knox, 1990]. Although the latter is not abstracted here, it is a solid study of "mimesis" in Paul ("be imitators of me") via Foucault and the role of ideology in sustaining socialization to imitation, and thus, to obedience.

[359] Trible, Phyllis. "Five Loaves and Two Fishes: Feminist Hermeneutics and Biblical Theology." *Theological Studies* 50 (1989): 279-295.
Trible's essay is one of seven entries in the scripture issue of the 50th anniversary volume of *Theological Studies*. As such, it is intended to illustrate both the literature and scope of feminist hermeneutics and its place within the larger context of biblical theology. The essay accomplishes both tasks, but only in terms of the Hebrew, not the Christian scriptures. In addition, it serves as a clear summary of Trible's own work. The essay is in three parts. First is a brief "overview of feminism" describing the latter as a "hermeneutic of existence" that exposes both patriarchy and sexism and calls prophetically for repentance on the part of all who are engaged in such. Part II is "a sketch of biblical theology" that reveals it as a methodologically pluriform endeavor, caught between the tensions of identifying itself as either an historical and descriptive enterprise or a normative and theological task. A third portion of the essay comes to the heart of things, but not without acknowledging key limitations within biblical (read: Old Testament) theology: its practitioners have been white Christian males of European or North American ancestry, their interpretations have consistently been tilted in the direction of patriarchy, and the field as a whole has ignored virtually all current issue-related elements of biblical hermeneutics. Hence, for part III, Trible links the "overview" and the "sketch" to indicate (a) the "perspective and methods" of feminist biblical theology (an encompassing review of literature published through 1988); and (b) its "contours and contents," i.e., a description of what yet must be accomplished in feminist biblical hermeneutics. Although the literature cited by Trible is extensive, it is organized around her own work and unintegrated with publications of feminist biblical method in NT studies. An expanded version of this article published under the same title and incorporating recent New Testament literature is found in *The Promise and Practice of Biblical Theology*, edited by John Reumann, 51-71. Minneapolis: Fortress Press, 1991.

c. Principles of Feminist Biblical Interpretation

[360] Bird, Phyllis. "Translating Sexist Language as a Theological and Cultural Problem." *Union Seminary Quarterly Review* 42 (1988): 89-95.
This article focuses the question of translating sexist language in the Bible from within the framework of a translator's obligations to any ancient text, i.e., the obligation to render the text speakers' works in a "receptor" language which will convey their full meaning as clearly and comprehensively as is possible. Two assumptions ground the discussion: First, that sexist

language in scripture is "but one instance of...[the]...more general problem of transcultural communication" (p. 90); second, that in rendering the speakers' words, it is the translator's responsibility to permit the current audience to "overhear" what scripture is saying, rather than convert it to what scripture is saying. (The latter, Bird suggests, is a task reserved for varying levels of organized interpreters e.g, homileticians, liturgists). In the light of these assumptions Bird argues that biblical sexist language should be permittted to stand in translation so that its exposure may be clear. She acknowledges that not all male language is sexist, and she offers illustrations that intend inclusive reception. She argues for a sensitivity to contextual language on the part of the text and closes with the suggestion that only by an exposure of the "patriarchal and androcentric nature of the biblical text and its world can one begin to understand how revelation can be conveyed through such flawed vehicles of graces as our Hebrew ancestors and our own prophets and teachers" (p. 94). Bird's discussion is in many ways similar to those presented by Schüssler Fiorenza, although Schüssler Fiorenza also addresses the role of theologians (and specifically biblical theologians) in such a process. For early work by Bird, see [377]. For more recent material on women in the Old Testament see Trible [359] and Bellis [381]. For discussions of feminist and womanist biblical interpretation see the Newsom/Ringe [343] and Schüssler Fiorenza [344-345] volumes above and see the entries below, through [376].

[361] Brooten, Bernadette. "Feminist Perspectives in New Testament Exegesis." In *Conflicting Ways of Interpreting the Bible*, edited by Hans Kung, 55-61. New York: Seabury, 1980.
This early article synthesizes feminist New Testament exegesis as evidenced by feminist biblical scholarship published through the late 1970s. Its principal emphases, therefore, are on 'women in Paul,' the scope of patriarchal influence within the New Testament (e.g., the themes of the maleness of God and the male savior image), and last, 'the woman question' [sic] within and beyond the traditional canon and Deutero-Pauline literature. Brooten's style is readable and the essay provides initial entree into important key NT passages on women. Issues characteristic of later feminist biblical scholarship, e.g., the multiple dimensions of patriarchy as a gender-class structure and the significance of the Sophia literature, are obviously absent. NOTE: For subsequent work by Brooten, see her essay, "Early Christian Women and Their Cultural Context: Issues of Method in Historical Reconstruction," in Collins [349].

[362] Camp, Claudia. "Feminist Theological Hermeneutics: Canon and Christian Identity." In *Searching the Scriptures: Volume I: A Feminist Introduction*, edited by Elisabeth Schüssler Fiorenza, 154-171. New York: Crossroad, 1993.
Given the task of writing for an almost encyclopedic volume directed equally to scholars and lay readers, Camp's discussion covers the issues well, with additional readings serving to unfold the deep grounds on which her discussion rests. She begins with a preliminary definition of her title's terms--feminist, theological etc., and these definitions both inform and raise the questions and issues she will address, *viz.*, her fundamental conviction that the authority of the biblical text (for believing Christian women) *is* what is at stake in the title of her article entry and her succinct reviews of (a) Osiek's five fold hermeneutical typology (see below); (b) Schüssler Fiorenza's place within it and her main hermeneutical arguments; (c) Schüssler Fiorenza's differences with Ruether, Russell and Trible; (d) Camp's recognition of the realism needed by and for women in local congregations, and finally, (e) Camp's own three fold vision of the ways women might connect with scriptures and their authority, i.e., (1) a dialogical model engaging the text's persuasive power for individuals; (2) a metaphorical model (based largely but not exclusively on McFague's work); and (3) her own "trickster" model. The latter walks the line of reality's ambiguities of good and evil and the power of women to appropriate the paradox of "Woman Wisdom" and the "Strange Woman" of Proverbs, as women today read the text for guidance, empowerment and their own hermeneutical ground. There is a subtlety to Camp's discussion, and it echoes with virtual *layers* of insight as it is read-- again, again and again. NOTE: For additional work by Camp, see her essays "Female Voice, Written Word: Women and Authority in Hebrew Scripture" in Cooey et al. [495] and "Metaphor in Feminist Biblical Interpretation: Theoretical Perspectives," *Semeia* 61 (1993): 3-38.

[363] Castelli, Elizabeth. "*Les belles infedeles:* Fidelity or Feminism? The Meaning of Feminist Biblical Translation." *Journal of Feminist Studies in Religion* 6, no. 2 (1990): 25-40.
Many feminist biblical scholars approach the issue of textual translation from within either a quest for "non-sexist" inclusive language or, alternatively, a developed set of hermeneutical assumptions that can guide both textual translation and an interpretive recovery of the text. While not eschewing

either of these approaches, Castelli moves the discussion of feminist translation to the context of translational theory itself, suggesting five questions which, she says, a "feminist theory of translation" should address. First, to what extent and by what criteria should a feminist translation of biblical texts accept both (a) the "authority" of biblical texts and (b) the traditional boundaries of the textual canon? The first issue asks, in fact, "what does the phrase 'word of God' mean in feminist translation theory," and part (b) raises directly the issue of the authority of feminist translation itself relative to traditionally held extra-canonical texts. Castelli's second question is "what 'philosophy of language' should govern the project of feminist biblical translation?" This question is tied to the recognition that androcentrism is not only a recognized dimension of the biblical world view, but also an ideology encased through socially constructed terms. Third, "How shall feminist translators handle the gendered quality of contemporary translational theory," or its frequently held tacit assumption that texts are like "women who need to be tamed and/or corralled before giving up their true meaning to the meaning seekers?" Fourth, what, in fact, does a feminist fidelity to the text mean, i.e., "to whom is [feminist] virtue promised... [and]... is there a double standard in the demands for fidelity in this context as ... in other arenas where women's fidelity is compared with men's?" (p. 34). Last, how shall feminist translation theory handle the difficult issue of a text's political origins and their ongoing effects--or the presence of politically harmful teachings uncritiqued by the assumptions of modern translational theory, given that "it is within the capacity of languages to evoke equivalent responses in two historically and culturally divergent contexts, and that the purpose of translation is to cause the reader in the second setting to respond as the reader in the first setting would have" (p. 36). Castelli's essay is foundational in every sense of the word: its discussion is well-grounded in contemporary translational theory and its questions are obviously important. A companion piece to [374], see also Tolbert [372], Schüssler Fiorenza [414] and Bird [360], and for Castelli's other work, see [358].

[364] Farley, Margaret A. "Feminist Consciousness and the Interpretation of Scripture."
        In *Feminist Interpretation of the Bible*, edited by Letty Russell, 41-51. Philadelphia:
        Westminster, 1985.
Beginning with the text from Luke's gospel (24:9-11), which indicates the trivializing disbelief of the disciples towards the resurrection testimony of the women coming from Jesus' tomb, this brief essay seeks to "probe the consequences of feminist consciousness for the interpretation of sacred scripture." Antecedent to that probing, however, is the need to list at least some of the elements of feminist consciousness so that the hermeneutical principles they imply might, in turn, be identified. Farley begins, then, with an analysis of how feminist consciousness ("like any other consciousness") influences the task of interpretation: namely, by providing a kind of "negative limit," or a level of conviction "...so basic to a person's self-understanding that a contradictory witness cannot be believed without doing violence to one's self" (p. 43). She then identifies three elements of feminist consciousness she sees as that basic, and thereby grounding of a feminist biblical hermeneutic. While neither exhaustive nor necessarily comprehensive of all groups of women, these elements of feminist consciousness are believed by large groups of women and include: (1) "the conviction that women are fully human and are to be valued as such;" (2) the specification of this belief "by the principles of mutuality;" and (3) the recognition of "the importance of women's own experience as a way to understanding" (p. 44). In turn, these elements of feminist consciousness suggest three feminist hermeneutical principles for interpreting scripture: (1) the principle of "equality," (i.e., the recognition that women "must always be respected as 'ends,' not as mere 'means'"); (2) the principle of "equitable sharing," or the recognition that the principle of equality includes the "claim by all to an equitable share in the goods and services necessary to human life and basic happiness" (p. 46), and (3) the principle of "mutuality," i.e., the recognition that "autonomy as the sole basis of human dignity... and social arrangements" is atomizing and competition directed. Farley further describes these principles and then returns to the task of "probing" what they might mean to the process of interpreting sacred scripture, both as an "authoritative" text and one that has, without question, proved destructive to women. Her conclusions are consistent with other Roman Catholic feminist perspectives (e.g., Ruether and Schüssler Fiorenza) and her discussion stands as the ground for both a biblical and feminist ethical interpretive framework. **NOTE**: Also by Farley [166], [167], [471], [475], and [568].

[365] Ruether, Rosemary Radford. "Feminism and Patriarchal Religion: Some Principles
        of Ideological Critique of the Bible." *Journal for the Study of the Old Testament* 22
        (1982): 54-66.
Ruether's purpose here is to show the biblical bases by which to "ground" a critique of patriarchy. The principal basis is that biblical religion (in both the Old and New Testaments) carries within it two "threads": a tendency to reflect institutionalized sacred canopies as legitimate religious realities,

and alternatively, a prophetic critique of such [false] sacred canopies. In the biblical texts, such sacred canopies include both (1) androcentric religion--symbolized pre-eminently by the father-male image of God (which is, in turn, used to delegitimate women's experiences as also of God); and (2) the hierarchical pattern of domination and subordination that flows from the predominance of the 'father' image. As a critique of this religiously false sacred canopy, the Bible evidences a "prophetic-messianic principle" that seeks the disestablishment of oppressive economic and political power. In this context God is the advocate of the oppressed: first in the classical prophetic literature of the Old Testament and second, in the New Testament, where Jesus reinterprets messianism to mean servanthood, rather than royal kingship. In turn, this re-interpretation establishes *shalom* (and not dominance) as the ground of all reality, and it indicates mutuality and empowerment as characteristic elements of Christian communal life. These two elements--the prophetic critique of 'sacred canopies' and the messianic movement to service, empowerment and mutuality--constitute the principal biblical bases by which to ground the critique of patriarchy and they should be appropriated by feminists in the current period, for oppression itself is contextual. Moreover, by taking up these two elements as the basis for critiquing sexism, the Bible's own sexism can be critiqued and the prophetic faith further expressed.

[366] Ruether, Rosemary Radford. "Feminist Interpretation: A Method of Correlation." In *Feminist Interpretation of the Bible*, edited by Letty Russell, 111-124. Philadelphia: Westminster, 1985.

This article presents one of the most succinct, comprehensive statements by Ruether on feminist biblical interpretation. It addresses the role of experience in theology, the nature and significance of women's experience in theology, the necessity for correlating feminist and biblical principles of interpretation vis a vis the Bible and its theology, and in a closing section, the yet to be addressed tasks of feminist theology. The article may be summarized in terms of ten points. First, it is of the nature of theological methodology to interpret or symbolize moments of disclosure found in human experience so that these symbols may enhance further revelatory disclosure within the believing community. Second, a distinctive feature of feminist theology is that it uses women's experience (and not a received androcentric reification of others' experience) as such a source. Third, while women's experience may be identified in terms of women's biological possibilities—and while Ruether does not deny the potential of this fact for theology—her own definition of women's experience is that it is "women's experience as created by the social and cultural appropriation of biological differences in a male dominated society" (p. 133). Fourth, as women come to know this experience (i.e., raise it to consciousness), they recognize the socio-cultural denial, trivialization and/or negation of themselves as a class, and they can begin to fashion an alternative self-understanding. (Ruether notes that this is similar to a conversion experience, and that many women describe it as grace.) Fifth, it is precisely because of this raised consciousness (or conversion experience) that feminist and biblical principles may (and methodologically must) be correlated, because (a) feminism affirms and works toward the full humanity of women and (b) the prophetic messianic principle of the Bible affirms and works for the overthrow of oppressive institutions. Ruether's sixth point is that the prophetic messianic principle did not include sexism as a fact of historical and contextual reality, but that this omission should not preclude women from appropriating the prophetic messianic principle themselves. Seventh, a *theological* reading of feminism's affirmation of women suggests that what affirms women is of the divine and negatively, that what does not, is not. Eighth, it is this theological reading of the feminist principle that can correlate with the biblical prophetic messianic principle to bear the word of salvation to women. Ninth, the newness here is *not* in the method of correlating two such principles, for the Christological principle of correlating original and authentic images of human nature has always been a structure within theological discourse (viz., the *Imago Dei*/Christ parallels). Rather, what is new here is not the method of correlating original and authentic or biblical and [theologically read] feminist parallels, but instead, that *as also Imago Dei*, women have appropriated their experience(s) as a revelatory source. Tenth, and finally, the tasks of feminist theology are to institutionalize these hermeneutical principles in the church and its ministries so that the past will not be repeated. This is a provocative, powerful article that is often quoted out of context. For related discussions by Ruether, see **[365]** and Chapter I in *Sexism andGod-Talk* **[190]**.

[367] Russell, Letty M. "Authority and the Challenge of Feminist Biblical Interpretation." In *Feminist Interpretation of the Bible*, edited by Letty Russell, 137-146. Philadelphia: Fortress, 1985.

This essay is Russell's closing discussion of her edited anthology, *Feminist Interpretation of the Bible*. In it Russell notes the recurring observation of the anthology's contributors, i.e., that feminist criticism seriously challenges the authority of the Bible as an interpretive source for

Christian experience. Following a description of the concept, theological paradigm, as presented in McFague's *Metaphorical Theology* [200], Russell generates a description of authority suitable for use by feminists seeking to retain the Bible as an authoritative document. The image of authority underlying much biblical interpretation and church experience, notes Russell, is that of *domination*. It is an image of authority premised on superordinate and subordinate roles, and it is inadequate to the task of feminist theology for two reasons. First, it does not take into account either the Bible's prophetic promise of messianism, i.e., "the promise of God's welcome to all outsiders" (p. 144) or the cultural pluralism of today's global experience. Second, it is a model that is competitive in tone and spirit, for it views discussion as a competition of ideas with specific winners and consequent losers. As an alternative, feminist criticism suggests a more participatory paradigm for authority, i.e., an image of authority that suggests cooperation, inclusivity, non-competition and responsiveness to the experience of women and others struggling to participate in the Christian tradition. The values of this paradigm are that women would no longer need to "divide feminist experience and biblical witness," nor "face the dilemma of [a] choice between faithfulness to the teaching of Scripture and [their] own integrity as human beings" (p. 146).

[368] Schüssler Fiorenza, Elisabeth. "Feminist Theology and New Testament Interpretation." *Journal for the Study of the Old Testament* 22 (1982): 32-46.
As with entry [380], this early article describes the principal assumptions of Schüssler Fiorenza's feminist theology and her exegetical-hermeneutical framework. Four general premises are detailed: the androcentric nature of scholarly pre-understandings and frameworks, the androcentric nature of texts, translations, sources and traditions, the patriarchal nature of the biblical canonization process and lastly, the authority of the Bible and feminist hermeneutics. Schüssler Fiorenza begins by noting the constructed nature of all social worlds and the impact of feminism and women's studies on religious and biblical scholarship, i.e., the fact that, feminism has "shattered [the] unreflective assumption that the universe is androcentric" (p. 32). She then notes the potential of a feminist theology of liberation for religious scholarship, *viz.*, its challenge to the stance of value neutrality in scholarship generally and the implications of androcentrism within religious/biblical scholarship particularly. Thus, as she notes that women's studies utilizes "women's agency" as a reflective starting point for analysis, she highlights the differential effect of androcentrism in biblical texts and translations--i.e., the fact that while *generic* terms presume the presence and experience of both women and men, typical translations and discussions of leadership roles do not; rather, they presume the leadership of males, not females. Schüssler Fiorenza also addresses the conventional assumption that women are and have been marginal within the New Testament experience and tradition, but she rejects this hypothesis on methodological grounds, for as it is presented in popular and ecclesiastical thinking, it presumes a literalist reading of the New Testament uninformed by critical methods of biblical study. Further, she calls attention to the recognized cultural deviance of Christianity, and she poses the question of women's presence and agency within it to find that various texts lend plausibility to the leadership of women within Christianity as a specific counter-cultural movement. This counter-cultural movement and specifically the presence of women within it was, however, suppressed as Christianity began its structural and normative accommodation to Roman society and authority. The net effect of this accommodation was a gradual patriarchalizing process (formally established with the Bible's canonization) that eventually eclipsed (but did not completely erase) the presence of women's religious, communal leadership. Schüssler Fiorenza closes her discussion with the recognition of the Bible's two-fold quality as a text of both patriarchy *and* the presence of women, and she argues that only those texts that transcend their patriarchal location can function as liberating good news for women. A feminist, critical hermeneutics of liberation attends, she argues, to the interplay of misogynist theology and patriarchal church structure that seeks to "marginalize...[and]...displace women as ecclesial and theological subjects" (p. 44). Hence a feminist theology of liberation must reconstruct the history of women's oppression into a history of liberation.

[369] Schüssler Fiorenza, Elisabeth. "Women-Church: The Hermeneutical Center of Feminist Biblical Interpretation." In *Bread Not Stone: The Challenge of Feminist Biblical Interpretation*, 1-22. Boston: Beacon Press, 1984. [Also published as "Emerging Issues in Feminist Biblical Interpretation." In *Christian Feminism: Visions of a New Humanity*, edited by Judith Weidman, 33-54. San Francisco: Harper & Row, 1984.]
The term "women-church" is both a theological symbol and the name of a movement. As the former, it suggests Christian community grounded in a discipleship of equals; as the latter, it refers not to a separatist strategy, but rather to the efforts of women to underline their "invisibility...in biblical religion and to safeguard [their] freedom from spiritual male control." Two developments

have preceded and contributed to the development of this symbol and movement. The first is the shift from an "androcentric" to a "feminist" model of scholarship. In the androcentric model patriarchy and the structures of white male experience are normative for both popular and professional understandings. In the feminist model, however, inclusivity, diversity and non-hierarchical thinking are key. This shift has been important for it has generated the framework for a *feminist liberation* theology, i.e., a theology that highlights the equality of women as both *receivers* and *bearers* of God's word. Development #2 has been the shift from an "apologetic focus on biblical authority" to "the feminist articulation of contemporary women's experience and struggle against the patriarchy of biblical religion." The significance of this second shift has been manifold. First, because this shift has exposed the oppression of women within the Bible, it has legitimated the *experience* of women as a hermeneutic or norm for biblical interpretation. Second, it has relativized the authority of other interpretive models, e.g., doctrine or the search for a 'canon within the canon.' Third, this development has strengthened women's recovery of their previously invisible biblical heritage. When taken together these two shifts have generated a four-fold feminist model for biblical interpretation--Schüssler Fiorenza's *hermeneutics of suspicion, proclamation, remembrance and creative actualization*--which, in turn, provide the criteria for identifying patriarchy in theology, language and liturgy. (Cf., e.g., pp. 15-22 in *Bread Not Stone* and see [370] below.)

[370] Schüssler Fiorenza, Elisabeth. "The Will to Choose or Reject: Continuing Our Critical Work." In *Feminist Interpretation of the Bible*, edited by Letty M. Russell, 125-136. Philadelphia: Fortress, 1985.
In several sources Schüssler Fiorenza has described the women-church movement and symbol (cf. [369]) together with the feminist critical hermeneutics it both presumes and engenders. In this essay she synthesizes and refines these concerns and contrasts her methodology of feminist critical hermeneutics with those of other feminist and non-feminist writers. The essay is powerful, provocative and frequently cited by critics of Schüssler Fiorenza's feminist theological methodology (cf., e.g., [844]). It may be summarized in terms of seven general points and an additional five criteria that she develops for her "feminist interpretive model of critical evaluation." First, with Carol Christ [558] Schüssler Fiorenza affirms that it is "the question for women's self-affirmation, survival, power, and self-determination" that constitutes the "central spiritual and religious feminist question." Second, this quest is undertaken in various ways in an analysis of constructs tied to social identities, including those of Christianity's communal historical identity. Therefore, third, Christian (and for her Roman Catholic) feminists do not relinquish their biblical heritage. Rather, as "the *ekklesia* of women [they] claim the center of Christian faith and community in a feminist process of transformation" (p. 126). Fourth, because the oppression of all women roots from the social structural nature of patriarchy as a "pyramid of male privilege" that specifies racial and gender stratifications (with women thus interspersed within this pyramid and with third world women at its bottom), "feminist theology must articulate its advocacy position not as an option for the oppressed, but as the self-identification of women in patriarchal society and religion, since all women are socialized to identify with men" (p. 128). Thus, fifth, the locus of grace or revelation is not merely "the experience of women" but the "*ekklesia* of women," that is, "the experience of women...struggling for liberation from patriarchal oppression." This means, sixth, that feminist theology must be political in nature, since the Bible has been both a source of strength and subordination for women--the latter in that it has been used in various ways to maintain patriarchy. Hence, seventh, an *interpretive* framework for biblical theology and analysis is needed, and this framework must respect the previously enumerated points. Thus this framework must have built within it (a) a "hermeneutics of suspicion," i.e., an acknowledged awareness of patriarchy and androcentrism as possible dimensions of any biblical text; (b) a theological interpretive principle for feminist critical evaluation, rather than (contra Ruether) an interpretive principle and a method of correlation--that is, it must have a principle or means by which specific texts can be sorted for patriarchal "content and function" rather than a theological principle and an alignment of feminist and biblical insights; (c) a developed "hermeneutics of proclamation, i.e., a principle that permits the condemnation of patriarchal texts as oppressive and thus not proclaimable as a Word of God; (d) a "hermeneutics of remembrance" or a strategy that permits the feminist reconstruction and (thereby) reclaiming of oppressive texts; and (e) a "hermeneutics of creative ritualization," or a means by which women struggling for liberation actually reclaim their reconstructed texts. By way of background for the reader, Schüssler Fiorenza's first criterion has effectively been realized by the bulk of feminist biblical literature. Point (b) is her own methodological strategy as contrasted with others, i.e., those of Russell, Ruether, and strategies based on David Tracy's 'method of correlation.' Point (c) actualizes point (b), and point (d) reclaims the inclusive character of the Bible's androcentric leadership-language

about women--and thereby redeems the source of Christianity's patriarchal quality: "the tension between patriarchal society and ecclesial structures and the vision and praxis of the discipleship of equals" (p. 134). Finally, point (e) evidences the *"ekklesia* of women" after the model of the Bible itself as an open-ended structural prototype rather than an archetype abstracted from time. Taken together these five criteria link past and present experiences of women struggling for liberation from patriarchy, and they evidence the *ekklesia* of women as a redemptive and liberating church community.

[371] Schüssler Fiorenza, Elisabeth. "Biblical Interpretation in the Context of Church and Ministry." *Word and World* 10 (1990): 317-323.
When asked by the editors of *Word and World* to indicate how her exegetical-historical work has been done within the context of the church and [its] ministry, Schüssler Fiorenza responded with a brief description of her "critical feminist theology of liberation." The latter, says Schüssler Fiorenza, is an illustration of "public ecclesial discourse" in which accountability to one's [faith] community and the academy are held in necessary and critical tension. Schüssler Fiorenza's description develops in terms of two points: her biographical recollections concerning the contrast between German and American universities and her critique of Krister Stendahl's two-fold task of biblical interpretation: namely, that the biblical scholar "recovers" the "meaning meant" (by a text) so that others may apply it to current situations. For the first point, Schüssler Fiorenza recalls the church relatedness of German universities. This stands in sharp contrast to the secular-objective character of American university programs in biblical studies. For the second point--her critique of Stendahl, she highlights the contextual quality of all meanings and the ethical necessity of biblical scholars to draw out the liberating capacities of biblical texts. In turn, these emphases become the vehicles by which Schüssler Fiorenza unfolds her understanding of the Bible as a "root metaphor of the church" and her description of biblical interpretation as a task rooted in what she has elsewhere termed the "pastoral theological paradigm" (see [411]). This is a brief, but clear exposition of Schüssler Fiorenza's critical hermeneutical method and should be read in conjunction with [369].

[372] Tolbert, Mary Ann. "Defining the Problem: The Bible and Feminist Hermeneutics." *Semeia* 28 (1983): 113-126.
In fourteen informative and clearly written pages Tolbert summarizes not only the "radical and reformist" feminist positions on the Bible and its relevance, but as well, the principal writings of feminist biblical scholars through 1983. She then turns to the subject of feminist biblical hermeneutics per se, and in an analogy to Bultmann's work she identifies the issue: "The problem Bultmann squarely faced was how a pervasively mythological and Hellenistic document could continue to communicate anything of value to a scientific age which saw the universe in utterly different terms. Analogously, we are faced with the issue of how a pervasively patriarchal document can continue to communicate any thing of value to those who reject all such oppression...[Thus]...the hermeneutical and theological dilemma...still remains: how does one deal with a biblical text that is so completely saturated in an unacceptable perspective?" (p. 125). Tolbert does not answer this question, although generally speaking the answer lies with a feminist hermeneutic in biblical and especially New Testament studies. Tolbert notes clearly, however, that Bultmann's method of "separating" the concept from its expression is inadequate and that given this inadequacy, the challenge of feminist hermeneutics is especially pressing. "Indeed, if New Testament theology has a future," Tolbert suggests "it may well be with feminism." Beyond this, she implies, there is little to be said, save to participate in the dialogue.

NOTE: For related literature, see Trible's text, *God and the Rhetoric of Sexuality* [205] and Schüssler Fiorenza [483].

d. Principles of Womanist Biblical Interpretation

[373] Baker-Fletcher, Karen. "Anna Julia Cooper and Sojourner Truth: Two Nineteenth Century Black Feminist Interpreters of Scripture." In *Searching the Scriptures: Volume I: A Feminist Introduction*, edited by Elisabeth Schussler Fiorenza, 41-51. New York: Crossroad, 1993.
This brief discussion contrasts the approaches, emphases and biblical styles of Cooper and Truth as African American women interpreters of the Bible, and as women separated first, by the 80 year difference in their generations, and second, the realities of education (Cooper's) and mystical vision (Truth's). These differences notwithstanding, each interpreted the Bible in terms of freedom and liberation themes, with Cooper's "liberalism" and social gospel challenging white society on behalf of impoverished and segregated African Americans, and Truth's prophetic and theophanous

"hearing" of scripture challenging the slave owners' literalist and racist readings of scripture. This text documents the historical presence of African American women engaged in biblical interpretation and social applications, and as such it highlights not only African American feminist and womanist history, but the (albeit underdeveloped) implications of both for African American civil religion. NOTE: For additional work by Baker-Fletcher, see her essay length introduction to Cooper's *A Voice from the South* in Townes **[641]** and see her doctoral dissertation, *A Singing Something: Womanist Reflections on Anna Julia Cooper*. [New York: Crossroad] 1994.

[374] Martin, Clarice J. "Womanist Interpretation of the New Testament: The Quest for Holistic and Inclusive Translation and Interpretation." *Journal of Feminist Studies in Religion* 6, no. 2 (1990): 41-61.
The second in a two part discussion of feminist and womanist issues in biblical translation and interpretation (cf. **[363]**), Martin's essay surveys two ways in which womanist perceptions and experience influence biblical translation and interpretation. The first is an extended description of the term "doulos" with respect to both its literal and euphemistic translations (i.e., slave and servant) and its current significance for interpreting the kenosis text in Phil. 2:7. Overall, Martin acknowledges that all instances of "doulos" must be translated within their particular literary and social historical contexts (to determine the author's precise meaning), but she argues *against* euphemistic translations of "doulos," since these can lose both the etymological nuances of doulos and its psychosocial import. To make her case, she cites several social descriptions of slavery to indicate its power based control and alienating dynamics, and its dishonoring, dehumanizing characteristics. Martin's second point of emphasis is the manner in which the doulos paradigm has functioned historically as a vehicle of social control, and particularly in terms of its legitimation of American chattel slavery. Hence, she details a "hermeneutics of domination" within the process of "traditioning," and she highlights several specific critical translational and interpretive tasks incumbent upon womanist biblical scholars. Essay respondents include Johanna Dewey, Peggy Hutaff and Jane Schaberg, with all addressing both Martin's piece and its companion discussion by Castelli **[363]**.

[375] Martin, Clarice J. "The *Haustafeln* (Household Codes) in African American Biblical Interpretation: 'Free Slaves' and 'Subordinate Women.'" In *Stony the Road We Trod: African American Biblical Interpretation*, edited by Cain Hope Felder, 206-231. Minneapolis: Fortress Press, 1991.
This powerfully written essay reviews historical and contemporary exegesis on three New Testament texts (the "domestic codes" of Colossians 3:18-4:1, Ephesians 5:21-6:9 and I Peter 2:18-3:7) to demonstrate (a) the presence of an African American "liberationist" hermeneutic that has historically critiqued the master-slave relationship within these texts (i.e., their interpretation from within a "literalist" hermeneutic as was the case with pro-slavery literature) and (b) the paradoxical absence of a similar critique of the woman-wife-husband relationship within these texts. Martin offers two reasons for the absence of an African American liberationist critique regarding these texts with respect to gender and marital relations. First, interpretive activity within the Black religious community has largely been drawn to language which explicitly attests the liberating acts of God (e.g., the Exodus text); second, the African American community has uncritically adopted a pattern of gender socialization that "tolerates and accepts the patriarchal model of male control and supremacy...[as typified]...in Eurocentric, Western Protestant tradition..." (p. 227). As an antidote to this absent liberationist tradition with respect to women and wives, Martin cites the growing literature of womanist theology (and especially the writings of Jacqueline Grant and Katie Cannon) to argue that African American biblical interpretation must take a pro-active position on women's equality within the leadership of Black churches. Thus, she calls for increased efforts at African American women's theological education, including the social, financial and organization support necessary for their incorporation into ecclesiastical positions of leadership. This forthright essay synthesizes an extensive body of womanist, feminist, and sociological literatures and is highly recommended for those seeking a discussion and resources on the interaction of race and gender as factors in the tensions and development of contemporary women's religious leadership. NOTE: For additional work by Martin, see her commentary on "The Acts of the Apostles" in Schüssler Fiorenza **[345]**.

[376] Weems, Renita J. "Reading *Her Way* through the Struggle: African-American Women and the Bible." In *Stony the Road We Trod: African American Biblical Interpretation*, edited by Cain Hope Felder, 57-77. Minneapolis: Fortress, 1991.
This essay addresses the questions of "how and why modern readers from marginalized communities...[here, specifically African American women]...continue to regard the Bible as a

meaningful resource for shaping modern existence" (p. 57). To answer these questions Weems presents an analysis of the social circumstances conditioning African American women's varying possible responses to the Bible and an analysis of reader-response criticism as a theoretical framework for describing those possible responses. In brief, Weems argues that African American women find analogues to their own gender, racial and ethnic oppressions in specific texts that have survived the ideological dimension of the canonization process; further, she argues, such analogues are both empowering and legitimating of African American women's current struggles for affirmation and full acceptance in contemporary society. This is a well developed theoretical piece, which together with the 1989 *Semeia* issue upon which it builds, is one of the most important writings within the womanist theological literature. It signals the development of a critical *womanist* liberation perspective (similar to Schüssler Fiorenza's critical *feminist* liberation perspective), and it highlights the substantive difference between these two perspectives: i.e., that a "critical womanist liberation perspective" both accounts for and is accountable to (a) the experience of African American women, and (b) the interactive effects of race, gender, class and ethnic oppressions. **NOTE:** See also **[642]**.

NOTE: For additional, related literature see Cannon **[532]**, in Section III-6 see the entry by Briggs in Cannon and Schüssler Fiorenza **[348]**.

3. Feminist Biblical Scholarship and the Old Testament

a. Early Method and Interpretation

[377] Bird, Phyllis. "Images of Women in the Old Testament." In *Religion and Sexism: Images of Woman in the Jewish and Christian Traditions,* edited by Rosemary Radford Ruether, 41-88. New York: Simon and Schuster, 1974.
This early essay surveys "Old Testament" laws, the book of Proverbs, the historical books of I, II Kings and I, II Samuel, and the creation texts in Genesis to identify the various images of women these sources exhibit. It calls attention to (1) the plurality of women's images in the Old Testament (in that women were both property *and* on occasion leaders); (2) the differential sexual mores which accompanied property assumptions relative to women; (3) the auxiliary and supportive roles played by women within the essentially male story of the historical books; (4) the fully intended equivalence of Gen 1:23; and (5) the *descriptive* (rather than prescriptive) nature of the gender assumptions within the aetiological myths of Genesis 2-3. The endnotes and bibliography for Bird's discussion are extensive but obviously limited to early sources. Further, the discussion is "documentary" and pre-dates what feminist biblical literature of the mid-eighties would consider "critical" and/or "liberationist" in perspective. For more recent material on women in the First Testament see Bellis' **[381]** and various entries by Trible.

[378] Higgins, Jean. "The Myth of Eve: The Temptress." *Journal of the American Academy of Religion* 44 (1976): 639-647.
After examining several interpretations of Gen. 3:6b drawn variously from patristic, medieval and modern writers, Higgins concludes that the characterization of Eve as "temptress" is not sustained by the text. Rather, as efforts have been made to explain Adam's activities in the serpent story (or his lack of activity), the assumptions and perceptions of commentators have been subtly read back into the text. Higgins' description of the exegetical possibilities appropriate to Gen. 3:6b is succinct yet comprehensive, encompassing literature through 1975. Her several arguments persuade clearly that "Eve the temptress never performs in this text...[but that instead]...all attempts to explain concretely how Adam came to disobey God's explicit command...have been reconstructed from between the lines of the original text...[and are]...expressions of imagination, drawn mainly from each commentator's own presuppositions and cultural expectations" (p. 647).

[379] Sakenfeld, Katharine D. "Old Testament Perspectives: Methodological Issues." *Journal for the Study of the Old Testament* 22 (1982): 13-20.
This early essay by Sakenfeld describes the uneven impact of women's studies on the field of biblical theology as of 1982. On the one hand, suggests Sakenfeld, the influence of women's studies on biblical theology has been minimal, for although an attention to gender has generated an extensive literature, the field of biblical studies has remained essentially unchanged for this fact. At the same time, there are five indicators that suggest the increasing influence of women's studies in biblical theology--at least in the area of Old Testament. These include: (1) a "more systematic inquiry into the status and role of women in ancient Israelite culture"; (2) the "rediscovery of long over-looked traditions...[and]...the assessment of their contribution to a more balanced picture of

Old Testament subject matter"; (3) a "reassessment of the meaning and message of some...very famous Old Testament passages dealing with women;" (4) a "fresh and systematic attention to a number of feminine metaphors for God scattered throughout the Old Testament;" and (5) an extended attention to issues of translation and inclusivity beyond the usual boundaries of a "few specialists" and the gulf between "the guild and [the] culture/church [context]." By way of closure Sakenfeld cites Ruether's observation that sexism alone is not the problem facing feminists in biblical studies, but rather, that it is the interstructuring of sexism with racism and classism that constitutes the ultimate problem facing feminists in biblical studies. Lamentably, suggests Sakenfeld, the field of biblical studies does not yet recognize this interstructuring for it treats these three "isms" as separate problems on separate tracks. **NOTE:** Also by Sakenfeld is **[410]**.

[380] Schüssler Fiorenza, Elisabeth. "Interpreting Patriarchal Traditions." In *The Liberating Word: A Guide to Non-Sexist Interpretation of the Bible*, pp. 39-61, edited by Letty Russell. Philadelphia: Westminster, 1976.

This early essay by Schüssler Fiorenza introduces several of the concerns that will occupy her work and be spelled out in increasingly refined terms through the 1980s and 1990s. Additionally, it readily identifies many of the biblical texts feminists have found problematic since the early and transitional years of the feminist theological movement. Hence it serves as an almost classic introduction for students just beginning their study of either Schüssler Fiorenza's work or feminist biblical studies generally. Among the issues developed here are: (a) Schüssler Fiorenza's grounding concern to delegitimate sexism in biblical language so that 'salvific' texts can come through to the text's hearer/reader; (b) her observation that androcentric assumptions have governed not only the writing and editing of biblical texts, but their historical translations, ecclesiastical interpretations and standard exegesis as well; (c) her identification of several such texts and translations; (d) her initial hypothesis that a "traditioning" process (i.e., a process of patriarchalization) has governed the history of both biblical scholarship and ecclesiastical development; and (e) her summary of "insights and guidelines" (later to be called "hermeneutical principles") for handling and interpreting difficult, androcentric biblical texts. **NOTE:** For related early material see Trible **[164-165]**.

b. General Literature

[381] Bellis, Alice Ogden. *Helpmates, Harlots, Heroes: Women's Stories in the Hebrew Bible*. Louisville: Westminster/John Knox Press 1994.

This is by far the premier source for an immediate overview of feminist research on women in the Hebrew Bible. First, it is exceptionally clear and unencumbered in its development, delivery and writing style. Second, it is thoroughly respectful of ecumenism, difference and dialogue as it synthesizes works by Christian and Jewish scholars, and feminist and womanist perspectives. Its extended introduction fully reviews the history of feminist and womanist biblical scholarship--and specifically scholarship on the First Testament, with concise overviews of key authors and their works. Last, this text synthesizes not only the highlights of research, key authors and their publications, but--as its subtitle indicates--all of the relevant stories of women in the Hebrew Bible, and these by way of chapter overviews: e.g., "The Story of Eve;" "The Women of Genesis;" "The Women of Exodus and Numbers;" "The Women of Joshua and Judges," etc. Bellis' cited bibliographies here are more than impressive, beginning with her 12 page and well categorized synthesis of feminist biblical works, theory, theology and spirituality at the close of her introductory chapter, and continuing through each of her remaining ten chapters. Finally, her notes for religious educational classes in churches and synagogues and her biblical, author and "women in the Bible" indices close out the text. This is a text to be replicated (format-wise) for virtually all topics of the feminist-womanist theological literature, as it synthesizes its particulars and provides the reader *very* readable access.

[382] Day, Peggy L., ed. *Gender and Difference in Ancient Israel*. Minneapolis: Fortress, 1989.

This collection of twelve essays on various texts about women in "ancient Israel" is premised upon the assumption that "women's experience" may be viewed here in social scientific terms (rather than theological terms) and that, as such, a body of knowledge about "gender related roles and statuses" within the biblical world may be established. Day is emphatic about the non-theological character of the essays she presents, and she spends the first half of her opening introduction describing theological and feminist historical uses of women's experience--and, within the latter--the nuances attached to various rejections of "objectivity" in historical and social science. Her authority here is historian Linda Gordon, who is worth citing: "It is wrong to conclude as some have, that because there may be no objective truth possible, there are no objective lies..." Beyond this, Day's many contributors address gender asymmetries within various First Testament texts, and with erudition and detailed, if relatively "objective," exegesis. Some cautionary notes: First, for all of Day's insistence about non-theological interpretations, all but three of her 12 contributors are doctoral students or professors of religion in academic or seminary settings. Second, given the criterion of non-theological social scientific analyses, many of the essays' several insights remain tied to "ancient" texts and are thus unavailable for contemporary use—*and*, lack the benefit of insight from contemporary experiences of women. (Cf. Phyllis Bird's discussion of Hosea with that by Setel below [384].) Among the more noted of Day's contributors are Phyllis Bird, Susan Niditch and Carol Newsom. A bibliography of author sources is included and an index closes the volume. This is a mixed bag: its essays are exegetically erudite and informed. At the same time, they seem separate from the foray of how biblical language can, may·be, and has been used historically to uphold various "interlocked" and "interstructured" oppressions.

[383] Fuchs, Esther. "The Literary Characteristics of Mothers and Sexual Politics in the Hebrew Bible" In *Feminist Perspectives on Biblical Scholarship*, edited by Adela Yarbro Collins, 117-144. Chico, CA: Scholars Press, 1985.
Drawing upon Robert Alter's discussion of the "annunciation-type" scene within the Hebrew Bible [*The Art of Biblical Narrative*, NY: Basic Books, 1981) in which barren women are promised fertility and then given sons, Fuchs examines six "annunciation-type" scenes to expose the Bible's patriarchal control over the institution of motherhood. The annunciation scenes include the stories of Sarah, Rebekah, Rachel, the wife of Manoah, Hannah, and the Shunammite woman, and the discussion develops in three parts. First, Fuchs notes the gradual process of mother uplifting that occurs from annunciation scene #1 (Gen. 17, in which Sarah is completely marginalized from participation--save that of laughing--as Yahweh promises Abraham a son), to annunciation scene #6 (II Kings 4) in which a nameless Shunammite woman is directly rewarded with a son for her "upright conduct." Second, Fuchs draws out the ideological significance of this uplifting process: That is, that it places the biblical role of mother directly under Yahwistic control and thus at the service of male lineage and glory. Last, Fuchs contrasts the various parenting activities for women and men within these (and other) biblical stories to note the wide and complex range of relationships fathers have with and/or on behalf of their sons and, alternatively, the narrow and subservient (albeit caring) relationships to which mothers are restricted by virtue of their subordinate place within the patriarchal family. In a companion discussion in the same volume ("Who is Hiding the Truth? Deceptive Women and Biblical Androcentrism," pp. 136-144) Fuchs continues her analysis of biblical androcentrism by examining several stories of women's deceitfulness, *viz.*, those of Rebekah (Gen 27), Rachel (Gen. 31), Tamar (Gen. 38), Potiphar's wife (Gen. 39), Achseh (Josh. 15), Rahab (Josh. 2), Jael (Judges 5), Delilah (Judges 16) Michal (I Sam. 19), and Jezebel (II Kgs 9) to expose the two "strategies" by which the Bible discriminates against (deceitful) women: First, its silence as to their *necessary* motivation--they are powerless within the patriarchal system; and second, the consistently negative presentation of women who "deceive for causes not meant to enhance male power" (p. 142). **NOTE**: For additional literature on mothers in the Hebrew Bible, see J. Cheryl Exum's "'Mother in Israel': A Familiar Story Reconsidered," in [210] edited by Russell, but not abstracted here.

[384] Setel, T. Drorah "Prophets and Pornography: Female Sexual Imagery in Hosea." In *Feminist Interpretation of the Bible*, edited by Letty Russell, 86-96. Philadelphia: Westminster, 1985.
This compact, informative essay examines the objectification of female sexuality in the book of Hosea, to illustrate the identification of women's sexuality with evil--an identification not visible prior to the literature of the so called "Latter Prophets" of the Hebrew Bible (i.e., Isaiah, Jeremiah, Ezekiel and the twelve Minor Prophets). Setel roots her discussion in a contrast between the images of female sexuality evident within biblical teaching prior to the latter prophets (i.e., the perception of female sexuality as a phenomenon of property owned by males) and the specific framing of female sexuality within the Yahweh-Israel, male-female, fidelity/infidelity, marriage/salvation metaphors in Hosea. She notes the functioning of the harlotry image relative to gender and promiscuity (i.e., that while both males and females may be promiscuous or may 'act the harlot,' only females *are* harlots) and she draws out the implications of Hosea's salvific efforts on behalf of his wife Gomer, and by extension, those of Yahweh for Israel. Among others, these implications include the ownership and the power to punish evil and the parallels of these implications with pornography as a phenomenon of male control and dominance over women in contemporary society. Setel also considers the liturgical implications of the Hosea text, that its function as a text of control may for some preclude its public proclamation as the Word of God. A

tightly woven discussion, this brief essay exemplifies the difficult task of examining both holiness and separation motifs and the pre-biblical patriarchal motifs carried but not created by Hebrew scripture (cf. Lerner [68]). NOTE: For Setel's more recent work, see [956] and see her commentary on "Exodus" in *The Women's Biblical Commentary* [343].

[385] Trible, Phyllis. *Texts of Terror: Literary-Feminist Readings of Biblical Narratives.* Philadelphia: Fortress, 1984.
The tragic, undeniable stories of four Old Testament women--Hagar (Gen. 16:1-16; 21:9-21), Tamar (2 Samuel 13:1-22), an unnamed woman (Judges 19:1-30), and the daughter of Jephthah (Judges 11:29-40) are retold here through Trible's skillful use of rhetorical criticism and a feminist "hermeneutic of remembrance". Elsewhere [356] Trible has distinguished three stages of feminist hermeneutics: (1) the prophetic documentation of patriarchy and misogynist history (2) the recovery of forgotten biblical passages which themselves critique patriarchy and (3) the telling of biblical tales *"in memoriam...* to redeem the [present] time." *Texts of Terror* exhibits this third stage of feminist hermeneutic and exposes the androcentric and inadequate nature of traditional biblical exegesis. Of particular salience is Trible's clear capacity to expose patterns of female invisibility long unmentioned in conventional exegesis and, further, her ability to link these patterns with contemporary issues and experience. Extensive indices on authors and editors, Hebrew words, scriptural references and subjects--together with copious chapter endnotes--provide a running commentary on the range of exegetical and methodological sources in Old Testament studies.

NOTE: For additional sources, see Trible [165, 205] and Gruber [342], see Schüssler Fiorenza [412-413],and see Baskin [948] and Davidman and Tenenbaum [949].

3. Feminist Biblical Scholarship and the New Testament

NOTE: While the bulk of feminist New Testament scholarship is well represented by the entries in both *The Women's Bible Commentary* [343] and *Searching the Scriptures* [344-345], the entries below illustrate historical touchstones in feminist New Testament work: touchstones for the Synoptic Gospels because these studies indicate early (Munroe), recent (Schüssler Fiorenza) and current (Schaberg) turning point discussions, and touchstones for John and the Epistles because they highlight classical exegetical (e.g. [391]) and theological (e.g. [394]) issues attached to feminist biblical research.

a. The Synoptic Gospels

[386] Munro, Winsome. "Women Disciples in Mark." *Catholic Biblical Quarterly* 44 (1982): 225-241.
An early feminist exegetical source, this essay addresses the relative invisibility of women in Mark's gospel prior to their dramatic appearance in 15:40-16:8, the period of Jesus' death and the early preaching of the resurrection. While Mark's androcentric culture may explain a part of this early invisibility, it is not a sufficient explanation of the distinctiveness of the women in the closing verses of this gospel. Rather, as Munro hypothesizes and demonstrates, a redactional effort is at work, controlling and minimizing the appearances of women throughout the text. Thus, although women are members of the crowds, they are not part of Jesus' public ministry. Similarly, although women are members of Jesus' inner circle of disciples, they are not among the twelve, nor are they named (sufficiently) to become acknowledged tellers of the tradition. That Mark has more mentions of actual women than do the other gospels (the preponderance of his narrative material notwithstanding) is established by Munro by a comparative frequency count of named and unnamed male and female characters in the gospel sources (Mark, 'M', 'L', 'Q' and John). Additionally, that some women were of high leadership standing in the early Christian community is evidenced both by the "...in memory of her...' comment (now memorialized by Elisabeth Schüssler Fiorenza) and Mark's contrast of the women in 15:40 with the twelve: where the latter fled, the women did not, and the reconvening and authority of the twelve depended on the women's testimony. Finally, that Mark denies the proclaimer role to the two Marys and to Salome--but not to other nameless women--is of strong significance for Munro, for it suggests the potentially competitive standing of these women among Christian leaders and lends credibility to the extra-canonical traditions of Mary Magdeline as "an apostle of the apostles" whose leadership conflicted frequently with that of Peter. (Similarly, see Brown [389] and see Clark [296].) NOTE: Munro's essay is recognized by many as a groundbreaker in feminist biblical studies and it has influenced much feminist biblical scholarship. See Schüssler Fiorenza's *In Memory of Her* [195] and see Mary Ann Tolbert's commentary on "Mark," pp. 263-274 in *The Women's Bible Commentary* [343].

[387] Schaberg, Jane. "Feminist Interpretations of the Infancy Narrative in Matthew."
Journal of Feminist Studies in Religion 13, no. 1 (Spring, 1997): 35-62.
This article examines two "different categories of feminist interpretation of one chapter of the
infancy narrative, Matthew 1" (p. 36). It presents an admittedly controversial and multi-layered
thesis, and it argues the plausibility of the thesis through an introduction of the category of
"struggle" as a vehicle for reading the text. The discussion develops in three stages. Schaberg
begins with a general statement of her thesis and its interpretive ramifications. She suggests that
this particular text can be read "persuasively as a communication of the tradition not of a
miraculous, virginal conception, but of a biologically normal illegitimate conception," and she
acknowledges that given the need to summarize elements "in the text" that support her contention,
she must ask, in effect, what the phrase "in the text" in fact means. Second, she reviews pertinent
feminist theological and exegetical sources and she synthesizes them through five questions that
highlight issues of interpretation (see p. 48) but do not address either the "allusions in Matthew 1 to
Dt. 22:23-27" or the possibility of thinking about the conception of Jesus as illegitimate. She then
presents her thesis in the framework of "struggle" (as developed by Itumeleng Mosala in *Biblical
Hermeneutics and Black Theology in South Africa* [Eerdmanns, 1989]), and she completes her
discussion through the characterization of Matthew's problem as having to "make theological sense
of the tradition concerning an illegitimate pregnancy." Schaberg then reviews "non-feminist
critical" responses to her work to document their acrimony and hostility. Schaberg's is a
demanding but scholarly and persuasive discussion. Hence beginning readers may wish to review
her less complex presentation, "The Foremothers and the Mother of Jesus" in **[418]**. Additionally,
readers should see Schaberg's work cited below in both **[388]** and **[873]**.

[388] Schüssler Fiorenza, Elisabeth. "Theological Criteria and Historical Reconstruction:
Martha and Mary: Luke 10:38-42." In *Protocol of the Colloquy of the Center for
Hermeneutical Studies in Hellenistic and Modern Culture*, 1-63. Berkeley, CA:
Center for Hermeneutical Studies, 1987.
This essay, which is substantially and *fruitfully revised* in **[236]** analyzes the Mary and Martha
story from Luke's gospel to indicate the methodological dynamics of Schüssler Fiorenza's four
fold, critical feminist hermeneutical interpretation of biblical texts. Schüssler Fiorenza's starting
premise here is the linguistically grounded androcentric character of the Bible and the subsequent
hermeneutical need for 'suspicion,' feminist reconstruction and proclamation and, last, a feminist
hermeneutics of actualization and remembrance. As applied, her discussion unfolds past
androcentric interpretations of the Lukan text: e.g., its abstraction as an example of two theological
principles, its confessional use as a rationalization of specific gender roles, and its character as a
text pitting the experience of one woman against another. Second, her discussion permits a critique
of the practice of uncritically importing other frames of reference (such as social scientific
perspectives) into biblical studies, because as evidenced here, the androcentric frames of other
perspectives can equally mask the experiences of women suppressed within the text (here, e.g., the
leadership roles of women in house churches). Apart from its exegesis, what distinguishes this
particular essay, however, is its colloquy status; for with it Schüssler Fiorenza is the first woman
biblical scholar to address the Center for Hermeneutical Studies. Hence the paper receives several
responses from a variety of biblical and other scholars, as well as general discussion by center
participants, students and visiting faculty. The participants are too numerous to list here, but many
of these comments are incorporated into the greatly expanded and revised version presented in *But
She Said* **[237]**, with the latter the preferred and more clearly presented discussion. **NOTE:** For
additional feminist exegetical literature on Luke and Luke-Acts, see the following sources, not
abstracted here, but which, together with Schüssler Fiorenza, provide a solid grounding for
feminist work on Luke. See Mary Rose D'Angelo, "Women in Luke-Acts: A Redactional View,"
Journal of Biblical Literature 109 (1990): 441-461; see Turid Karlsen Seim, "The Gospel of Luke,"
pp. 728-762 in Volume II of *Searching the Scriptures* **[345]**; see Jane Schaberg, "Luke," pp. 275-
292 in *The Women's Bible Commentary* **[343]**; see Clarice Martin's commentary on "The Book of
Acts," pp. 763-799 in Volume II of *Searching the Scriptures* **[345]**, and see Barbara E. Reid's
Choosing the Better Part? Women in the Gospel of Luke. Collegeville, MN: Liturgical Press, 1996.

b. The Gospel of John

[389] Brown, Raymond. "Roles of Women in the Fourth Gospel." *Theological Studies*
36 (1975): 688-699.
This essay identifies four women--Mary Magdalene, the "Samaritan woman," Martha, (sister of
Lazarus) and Mary, Jesus' mother--who in Brown's judgment are deliberately distinguished by the
author of this Gospel as disciples of Jesus in the fullest theological sense of that word. Further,

because they are thus distinguished, and because the meaning of discipleship (and not formal membership in the early church) is the crucial aspect of this Gospel writer's own ecclesiology, their status and distinctive roles have near unprecedented authority in the Christian community of the late first century and by extension, theological significance for the present time. After an extended discussion of interpretive and methodological issues, Brown works with several texts, but chief are these: (a) 4:39, 42 (which evidences the evangelical missionary significance of the Samaritan woman whose testimony on behalf of Jesus caused others to believe); (b) 20:2-10 and 20:17-18, which evidence, respectively, the appearance of the risen Christ to Mary Magdalene (but not Peter and the Beloved Disciple) and the concomitant command to her to go and tell the others; (c) 11:27 in which Martha (sister of Lazarus) 'confesses' the messiahship of Jesus (a confession made by Peter in Matthew's gospel); (d) 20:16 in which the risen Christ addresses Mary by name in a manner suggestive of the shepherd who knows his sheep; and finally (e) 19:25-27, which depicts the involvement of Mary, Christ's mother in the marriage at Cana. In each text Brown highlights the contrast made by the Gospel writer with other leadership figures of the early church: Mary Magdeline and Martha with Peter and the Beloved Disciple, Mary Magdalene and the disciples at the last supper, and Martha and Lazarus, the only man directly named by the Gospel author as the "beloved" of Jesus. These contrasts are deliberate, Brown argues, and they indicate the "first-class" status of the women as disciples in the early church--and by extension--in the church of the "current" time (1975). **NOTE**: For additional material on women in John's gospel, see Collins [390] and Schneiders [391] below, Newsom and Ringe [343] and Schüssler Fiorenza [195].

[390] Collins, Adela Y. "New Testament Perspectives: The Gospel of John." *Journal for the Study of the Old Testament* 22 (1982): 47-53.
Presented as a contribution to SBL seminar discussion "The Effects of Women Studies on Biblical Studies" [352], this paper indicates that the rise of women's studies in the 1970s had at least four avenues of impact on biblical studies: through (1) the post-Jewish and post Christian critique of Bible traditions; (2) the feminist critique of patriarchy within the Christian church; (3) the development of new and distinctive religious symbols, and finally, (4) the raised consciousness of individuals at the church's "grass roots" levels. Further, author Collins argues that these critiques--and especially those pointing to the patriarchy of the Bible--cannot be ignored; however, she also suggests that the Bible contains within itself the seeds of its own correction for it has foundational images such as the exodus and the egalitarianism of the early church that serve as anchors for beginning and end points in church and society (p. 49). She thus articulates a hermeneutical principle for biblical study, i.e., that "symbols which express what ought to be both in terms of an ideal time of origins and of the ideal future... can and should be used to criticize what was deflected in many biblical texts and what is today in society and church" (p. 49). Collins then illustrates both the principle and its feminist value through a review of several symbols evident in the gospel of John, including the Logos-Sophia symbol (which evidences the femininity of God) and the ecclesiological symbols of the "shepherd and his sheep" and the "vine and its branches." For Collins, these symbols evidence mutuality and non-hierarchical community living, all values consistent with feminist emphases. Also by Collins is [349].

[391] Schneiders, Sandra M. "Women in the Fourth Gospel and the Role of Women in the Contemporary Church." *Biblical Theology Bulletin* 12 (1982): 35-45.
Schneiders' purpose here is to explore the roles, activities and standing of women in the Fourth Gospel. It is not, she argues, to provide a theological or exegetical base from which to argue the legitimacy of women's ministries within Roman Catholicism. That, in Schneiders' judgment is not necessary, since the "repressive treatment of women was *never* based on Scripture," and does not, therefore, need to be addressed by Scripture (p. 35). Schneiders' exploration is fruitful. It finds women to be autonomous individuals in important relationships with Jesus and enacting unusual roles in that relationship. These latter include the roles of (1) apostleship (e.g., the Samaritan woman); (2) representative for the faith community (i.e., Martha's confession of faith); (3) anointing disciple (Mary): and (4) primary witness to the resurrection (Mary Magdalene). Schneiders' conclusion focuses her purpose: If this investigation exposes the character of women as disciples and ministers within the Fourth Gospel, then it shows the extent to which women and men may be "called to full discipleship and ministry in the Christian community" (p. 44). The bibliography of this essay extends through 1982, but the discussion remains relevant and comprehensive both in terms of its initial purpose *and* its theoretically unnecessary but nonetheless clear relevance to the discussion of women's ministries in Roman Catholicism. **NOTE**: For additional and subsequent work by Schneiders on the Gospel of John (which also provides an excellent introduction to feminist critical hermeneutics), see "A Case Study: A Feminist Interpretation of John 4:1-4a" pp. 180-199 in Schneiders, *The Revelatory Text: Interpreting the*

New Testament as Sacred Scripture [HarperSanFrancisco, 1991]. Additionally, see Gail O'Day's commentaries on John and 1, 2, and 3 John in *The Women's Bible Commentary* **[342]**.

c. The Pauline Epistles

[392] Boucher, Madeleine. "Some Unexplored Parallels to I Cor. 11:11-12 and Gal. 3:28: The NT on the Role of Women." *Catholic Biblical Quarterly* 31 (1961): 50-58.

An early exegetical discussion of the Pauline (and Deutero-Pauline) texts dealing with women's social and religious roles (i.e., Col. 3:18; I Peter 3:1-6; Titus 2:4-5; Ephesians 5: 22-24; I Cor. 11:3-16, 14:33-35 and I Timothy 2:11-15), Boucher's discussion is developed in four parts. An introductory section sets the framework: *viz.*, the New Testament exhibits arguments for both the equality and the subordination of women, and as Boucher's background research suggests, these positions are in tension because the Pauline "breakthrough" of Gal. 3:28 requires social implementation in addition to theological (or "eschatological") affirmation. Part I then examines the sources of Jewish and Christian subordinationist and egalitarian positions, and here Boucher hypothesizes that both perspectives were present in pre-Christian, rabbinical understanding. Clear rabbinic parallels to the epistle texts are cited, but because they cannot be unequivocally dated, the hypothesis is neither confirmed nor sustained, but rather, discussed in Part II. Thus Boucher considers the meaning of subordinationist/equality theories in the biblical texts, and she argues that Galatians text 3:28 is in fact an "ecclesiological/baptismal" text intended to deal with the "gentile problem," not the equality of women. Boucher concludes in Part III that the subordinationist/equality texts are in tension, but in terms of the contemporary mindset only. In the biblical texts there is no tension between an eschatological or theological equality ["coram Deum"] and an inequality that is social in nature. **NOTE:** For more recent literature on the Galatians text, see Schüssler Fiorenza **[195]** and see the commentaries on "Galatians" by Carol Oseik and Sheila Briggs, respectively, in *The Women's Bible Commentary* **[343]** and *Searching the Scriptures* **[345]**. Additionally, see Cannon and Schüssler Fiorenza **[348]** and see entry by Catherine Keller on "Eschatology" in Russell and Clarkson **[272]**.

[393] Gillman, Florence M. *Women Who Knew Paul.* Collegeville, MN: The Liturgical Press, 1992.

This brief discussion distills and summarizes much of the feminist literature on Pauline texts through the early 1990s and particularly the work of Schüssler Fiorenza. It is a very readable overview, with college theology students (and faculty) obviously in mind as the intended audience. Moreover, its clarity and sensitivity recommend it for wider uses including those of women's spirituality groups in either parish or women-church settings.

[394] Schüssler Fiorenza, Elisabeth. "Women in the Pre-Pauline and Pauline Churches." *Union Seminary Quarterly Review* 33 (1978): 153-166.

Two biblical texts historically problematic for women are I Corinthians 11:2-16 and I Corinthians 14: 33-36, which advance the so-called "Pauline teaching" on "headship" and "women's silence," respectively. In this early discussion Schüssler Fiorenza addresses these texts from within a three staged argument: (1) a critique of the revisionist and early feminist perspectives precluding a clear reconstruction of the androcentric nature of early New Testament Christianity; (2) a supplemental summary of women's activities within early Christianity as evidenced across the Pauline literature as a whole; and (c) a statement of conclusions and implications that unfold the role of feminist theology for contemporary Christian and church experience. Schüssler Fiorenza begins by exposing the fallacies of the revisionist and (secular) feminist arguments against these Pauline texts. These texts are neither simply chauvinistic nor essentially liberationist as much literature would suggest (cf. **[407]**). Rather, they are texts embedded within and articulated in the light of Western society's general androcentric image of humanity (i.e., that the male is norm and the female an auxiliary or marginalized other). Hence, the methodological problem facing the exegete here is that neither the revisionist (liberationist) *nor* the early feminist ("Paul was a chauvinist") approach dismantles society's androcentric framework, for each is too busy protecting the Pauline text. Social theory, however, and especially the sociology of knowledge push one to challenge the androcentric model and develop alternatively, a model more faithful to the Pauline literature. In turn, this becomes Schüssler Fiorenza's task in the second portion of the essay, as she highlights the many ways in which androcentrism has masked the leadership experiences of women in early Christianity and the inclusive elements within Pauline writing. Her conclusions then locate the interpretation of these two texts within the wider context of these issues and her critique of the "love patriarchalism" as a model for interpreting New Testament data. While well surpassed by such later works as [194] and [395], this early piece evidences the initial struggles of biblical feminist scholars to gain legitimacy for their perspectives and work.

[395] Schüssler Fiorenza, Elisabeth. "Rhetorical Situation and Historical Reconstruction in I Corinthians." *New Testament Studies* 33 (1987). 386-403.
This article identifies the need for an analytical and critical interpretive biblical methodology--beyond the scope of standard exegesis--to break through the taken for granted dogmatic readings of Pauline texts depicting women, their roles, experience, and social location within the early Christian community. Second, it identifies 'rhetorical criticism' as a methodology appropriate to this need, for rhetorical criticism acknowledges that texts are premised on an author's desire for a specific effect among real or perceived "implied" readers. The methodology here is not unique to Schüssler Fiorenza, but her analysis of the types of "rhetorical discourse" that can be employed by speakers/writers (here Paul) suggests that Paul's words to and about women here are elements of "deliberative" and not "forensic" or "juridical" discourse. The net effect of Paul's words, then--and particularly with respect to the so-called "women's passages," is that they are directed toward educated and class level peers who, in turn, will conclude to Paul's authority and thus support his positions about the women of Corinth--who, by definition, are not a part of the deliberating hearers Paul wishes to sway. This is sophisticated discussion that radically displaces early research on women in I Corinthians (e.g, Parvey [399]). It is on target, well documented, and technicalities notwithstanding, well-argued. NOTE: For related material on rhetorical criticism and I Corinthians, see Wire's commentary on "I Corinthians" in *Searching the Scriptures* [345], and see her own text (not reviewed here) *The Corinthian Women Prophets: A Reconstruction through Paul's Rhetoric* [Minneapolis, MN: Fortress, 1990].

[396] Whelan, Caroline F. "Amica Pauli: The Role of Pheobe in the Early Church." *Journal for the Study of the New Testament* 49 (1993): 67-85.
This article reviews the arguments for and against the depiction of Phoebe as a woman of authority within the early church and specifically within the context of Pauline Christianity. The author demonstrates that the terms *diakonos* and *prostatis* each require interpretation apart from the androcentric assumptions embedded in conventional translations and biblical scholarship, and she argues convincingly that Paul regarded Phoebe as an effective peer upon whom he could count for financial and personal support while traveling in his mission work. The key to Whelan's argument turns on her reading of Romans 16 and the frequently overlooked significance of the stratification patterns indicated by "letters of reference" and introduction in Roman society, which in this case indicate that where Phoebe supported Paul financially and socially as he traveled, Paul provided Phoebe with "an entire network of people who would be more than grateful to extend their hospitality to a wealthy patron" (p. 85).

d. Women's Leadership in the Early Christian Community

[397] D'Angelo, Mary Rose. "Re-membering Jesus: Women, Prophecy, and Resistance in the Memory of the Early Churches." *Horizons* 19 (1992): 199-218.
This essay discusses women, prophecy and resistance "in the memory of the early churches" from the perspective of "re-membering," a term D'Angelo defines from within the works of Trible [356] and others. In brief, "re-membering" is intended to convey three ideas: (1) "bringing what has been hidden out of the shadows of history" (2) "putting together what has been dismembered" and (3) "making someone a member of oneself...[or]...of the community in a new way" (p. 202). Thus, "re-membering" is a strategic task, and for D'Angelo it aids in refocusing two topics significant to feminist biblical reconstruction. First, "re-membering" aids in refocusing 'the locus' of the Spirit of God. Thus, in contrast to perspectives that see the Spirit of God as located pre-eminently within Jesus, D'Angelo presents a framework that--by bringing various hidden or background factors into the foreground--locates God's spirit as present to and within the *"reign of God" movement as a whole*, and not only one individual. Hence, in the early Christian community, God's spirit was present to a communal group within which Jesus (and others) acted. Second, "re-membering" permits an alternative understanding of the object of Jesus' preaching: *viz.*, its perception and recognition as a critique of Roman imperialism and not a critique of the teachings of the scribes and Pharisees. The values of such "re-memberings" (or intellectual "shifts" as D'Angelo also terms them) are many. Among others, they suggest a "spirit Christology" that can serve feminist theology without falling into various intellectual traps, including (for D'Angelo) the question posed by Ruether (i.e., "Can a male savior save women?"). Additionally, they can open the biblical literature widely across denominational and feminist Jewish-Christian, ecumenical lines. NOTE: Also by D'Angelo are [398] and [433] and for her additional biblical work, see her commentary

on "Hebrews" in *The Women's Bible Commentary* [343] and on "Colossians" in *Searching the Scriptures* [345].

[398] D'Angelo, Mary Rose. "Women Partners in the New Testament." *Journal of Feminist Studies in Religion* 6, no. 1 (1990): 65-86.

This essay examines the participation of women "in the early Christian practice of missionary couples..." and specifically the missionary couples of Tryphaena and Tryphasa as named in Romans 16:12, Evodia and Syntyche as named in Phil. 4:1, and Mary and Martha as described in Luke 10:38-42 and John 11:1-12, 19. D'Angelo focuses her discussion on the missionary work of these women pairs both to the early church and to each other, and she speculates on the possibility that such pairs represent an experience of the lesbian continuum identified by Rich [589]. Her discussion is provocative, scholarly, and cogently argued. By way of conclusion D'Angelo suggests that these few instances might be regarded as "the tip of a very deeply submerged iceberg..." which in all likelihood reaches to the literature of the patristic period as the pairing of Perpetua and Felicity could augur. NOTE: See [397] for D'Angelo's additional works.

[399] Parvey, Constance F. "The Theology and Leadership of Women in the New Testament." In *Religion and Sexism: Images of Woman in the Jewish and Christian Traditions*, edited by Rosemary Radford Ruether, 117-149. New York: Simon and Schuster, 1974.

One of the earliest contemporary essays surveying the status of women in the New Testament, Parvey's discussion is fourfold. It begins with an overview of the comparative social standing of first century Jewish and Greco-Roman women, turns subsequently to an analysis of I Cor 11, 14 and Eph. 3:28, and then presents a brief summary of women in the pastoral epistles. It closes with a summary of the male/female pairing parables in Luke and a description of prominent women in Acts. Parvey's discussion of the Corinthian texts is conditioned by her reading of I Cor 12:26-27, which affirms the egalitarian quality of all the 'members of the body,' and it is this text and not Gal 3:28 which Parvey cites as the basis for her judgment that Paul is one whose theology and social thought are in conflict. The conflict is evident in both I Cor. 11 and 14 where it is custom rather than Paul's new (and radical) theology that reigns. By way of contrast, however, it is Paul's new theology (i.e., his end-time ethic) that governs Gal. 3:28, but that is lost again (to custom and social pressure) in the pastoral epistles. "The dicta of Paul in I Cor., intended as temporary measures," says Parvey, "become frozen and transmitted as carbon copy guidelines for use in later churches." This is an important point, for Parvey concludes that the later churches "inherited" two "widely divergent messages: the theology of equivalence in Christ [and] the practice of women's subordination" (p. 146). By way of closure she suggests that these dual messages have generated a "spiritual dualism" and the "social negation of women" (pp. 146-147) that the present church must abandon in favor of Paul's original "in Christ" emphasis. NOTE: Parvey's essay was critical in early feminist biblical work, but it has since been surpassed by such discussions as Schüssler Fiorenza [395] and Wire's commentary on "I Corinthians" in *Searching the Scriptures* [345].

[400] Pippin, Tina. "The Heroine and the Whore: Fantasy and the Female in the Apocalypse of John." *Semeia* 60 (1992): 67-90.

Using insights and observations drawn from fantasy and science fiction theory, Pippin examines the "Heroine" and "Whore" images in the "Apocalypse of John" to assess the gender codes implicit in the Apocalypse text. In particular, Pippin draws attention to the Lamb/innocence motifs, the Church/Bride and Evil/Whore motifs and the marginalization and silencing of women in the text and, in the light of science fiction and fantasy theory, the eventual exclusion of women from utopia for purposes other than reproduction, male eroticism and/or the use of women as objects of violence. By way of methodology, Pippin's discussion is synthetic rather than exegetical, but sci-fi and fantasy parallels support her plausible if painful conclusion. Namely, that the "Apocalypse of John" exhibits an extreme level of misogyny and is *not* empowering of women. In the same journal issue, Johanna Dewey's response to Pippin provides a helpful overview of both Pippin's essay and from a different perspective, the dynamics of gender encoding in contemporary biblical commentary. Absent from both, however, are the parallels to be drawn between the misogyny of the Apocalypse and contemporary backlash and antifeminism in the New Right, although the discussions by Faludi [822] and Kinnard [823] provide preliminary sources. NOTE: For Pippin's more formal work, see her commentary on "The Revelation to John" in Schüssler Fiorenza [345]. Additionally, see Schüssler Fiorenza's own initial exegesis on "The Revelation to John" (not abstracted here) *The Book of Revelation: Justice and Judgment*. [Minneapolis: Augsburg, 1991].

[401] Schüssler Fiorenza, Elisabeth. "The Apostleship of Women in Early Christianity." In *Women Priests: A Catholic Commentary on the Vatican Declaration*, edited by Leanard Swidler and Arlene Swidler, 135-140. New York: Paulist, 1977.

In a separate exegetical discussion in the same volume Schüssler Fiorenza has clarified that the terms "the apostles" and "the Twelve" do not designate--in early New Testament traditions--a simple one to one, paralleling, co-extensive group, but rather two distinct circles of leadership who "only partly overlapped." In this exegetical note she asks, therefore, whether women might have received the apostolic charge, even though they were not [named] among the Twelve" (p. 135). The bulk of the New Testament evidence provides an affirmative answer, and this, in spite of the varying understandings of apostleship evidenced in the New Testament. To make her point Schüssler Fiorenza unfolds four definitions of the term "apostle" as used in the New Testament (including the Lukan specification that "replacement" apostles must be male), and she specifically notes the curious absence of an historical foundation for this Apostles/twelve equation, since the Pauline letters indicate a much wider circle of apostles (including women) in Christianity.

[402] Schüssler Fiorenza, Elisabeth. "Word, Spirit and Power: Women in Early Christian Communities." In *Women of Spirit: Female Leadership in Jewish and Christian Traditions*, edited by Rosemary Radford Ruether and Eleanor McLaughlin, 29-70. New York: Simon and Schuster, 1979.

As with several of her early writings **[401]**, this essay documents two aspects of early Christian community life: the leadership roles of women within the early Christian community and their gradual displacement by male leadership through a process of "patriarchalization" that emerged as Christianity accommodated itself to its surrounding Roman culture. Schüssler Fiorenza begins here by noting that traditional treatments of leadership within the early Christian community *assume* rather than demonstrate the marginality of women in leadership roles, and that much recent scholarship challenges this assumption. She then examines current scholarship to detail the activities and status of women as founders and leaders of Christian congregations and as prophets in early Christianity. Following this documentary portion of her discussion, she surveys "women and the divine feminine principle in Gnostic religious communities" and "the theological justification for rejection of women's leadership" to demonstrate the context and process of Christianity's patriarchalizing process. She notes the similarities and conflicts evident in canonical and non-canonical sources, as they, in turn, reflect leadership disputes, and she highlights the growing stigmatization of women within the Christian church's early centuries. Schüssler Fiorenza concludes that such conflicts (which are evident well into the third century literature) provide strong support for her initial thesis, i.e., that women were not marginal to Christianity's early leadership, but, rather, gradually suppressed and displaced. For paralleling discussions by Schüssler Fiorenza see the following (not abstracted in this volume): "The Study of Women in Early Christianity: Some Methodological Considerations." In *Critical History and Biblical Faith: New Testament Perspectives*, edited by Thomas J. Ryan, 30-58. Villanova, Pa.: Catholic Theological Society, Villanova University, 1979 and "Women in the Early Christian Movement." In *Womanspirit Rising: A Feminist Reader in Religion*, edited by Carol Christ and Judith Plaskow, 84-92. New York: Harper & Row, 1979 (see **[206]**).

5. Supplemental Sources

[403] Balch, David L. *Let Wives Be Submissive: The Domestic Code in I Peter*. Chico, CA: Scholars Press, 1981.

This exegetically detailed monograph examines the "household codes" in I Peter in the light of two principal factors: their philosophical parallels in Platonic and Aristotelian thought, and second, the *apologetic* potential these parallels provided as a means of countering the perception (by Romans) that female and slave converts to Christianity were disrupting the social order by refusing to worship either the household gods of one's husband (the case of women converts) or the household gods of one's master (the case of slaves converted to Christianity). According to Balch, "the author of I Peter encouraged [converted] slaves and wives to play the social roles which Aristotle had outlined" so that persons "reviling" the members of this "new" and "despised" religion would be shamed and (in the case of non-Christian husbands) perhaps converted (p. 109). Thus, in Balch's judgment the household codes were not developed in response to an attempt to make Gal 3:28 a social reality, nor were they written as a means of converting additional members to Christianity, except for those men already married to women converts. For a more readable discussion that first builds upon and then moves beyond Balch's work, see the discussion of "household codes" presented by Schüssler Fiorenza in Part III of *In Memory of Her* **[195]**.

Additionally, for reviews of Balch and other literature, see Antoinette Wire's review essay in *Religious Studies Review* 10 (1984): 209-216.

[404] Bartchy, S. Scott. "Power, Submission and Sexual Identity among the Early Christians." In *Essays on New Testament Christianity*, edited by C. Robert Wetzel, 50-80. Cincinnati, OH: Standard Publications, 1978.
In an effort to challenge the reader's own experience of gender socialization (with the latter understood as the internalization of traditional, stereo-typed male/female roles), Bartchy argues that it is ultimately Christ who is the norm for adult identity, and that this norm presumes an egalitarian framework for interpreting male/female interaction. To make his case Bartchy examines the Pauline corpus to address several texts and/or groups of texts that delineate roles of women. He groups these texts into *normative, descriptive,* and *problematic* categories. Normative texts are those "which 'declare the ways things are to be' in the New Covenant." These include Acts 2:17-18, I Cor. 7-4-5. Gal. 3:28, I Cor. 7:7 and I Cor. 11:11-12. Descriptive texts "report the activities of Christian women, without making any comment for or against these activities." These include (as a block) Mt. 28:9-10, Mark 16:7, 9-11, Luke 24:10-11 and John 20: 14-18. Also descriptive are I Cor 11:4-5, Acts 21:8-9, Phil. 4:2-3, Rm 16:1-4. Problematic texts are I Cor 14:34-34 and I Tim. 2:11-15. Bartchy's strategy is to present, summarize and discuss each of these texts. Principal elements in the problematic texts include (1) the reconsideration of 'authentein' as a form of malicious or malevolent control (as contrasted with mere authority); (2) the questionableness of anachronistically identifying "authority" and "teaching office" within the early church; and in his closing section (3) the 'kephale' text of Eph. 5:22. Bartchy's discussion is clear and to the point. His evangelical perspective requires that each text be thoroughly addressed, and although he recognizes neither the culturally based asymmetry of the texts' marital and male/female roles (nor the exegetically relevant 'household codes'), he nonetheless concludes that "any teaching that gives male Christians permission or encouragement to continue to talk and act like 'masters' and 'bosses' as their culture has taught them...clearly would be opposed to all that Jesus said and did" (p. 78).

[405] Graham, Ronald W. "Women in the Pauline Churches: A Review Article." *Lexington Theological Quarterly* 11 (1976): 25-34.
Six studies, published respectively, in 1893, 1950, 1963-1964, 1971-1972, and 1972 (two essasy) are reviewed here by Graham. By far, the essays under review address the "Pauline" (I Cor 7; Gal. 3:28), the "questionable" (I Cor. 11:3-16; 14:34-35) and/or the "pseudonymous" texts (I Tim 2:11-15; 5:3-16 and Titus 2:3-5) that have traditionally been used to define the religious and social roles of women, although the 1893 piece discusses also the presence and activities of women in Acts. After summarizing the main points of each essay, Graham presents four conclusions: First, "what is clear and unequivocal...should be the norm" e.g., Gal. 3:28. Second, "a distinction can and should be drawn between what is of the everlasting order of things, e.g., 'male and female' [Gal 3:28] and what is a product of history" and thereby changeable. Third, "the widespread and taken for granted should be given more weight than two exceptions." Fourth and finally, "what is contradictory to or a declension from the 'norm' may, by that very token, be dismissed as non-Pauline" (p. 34). This is an informative piece that introduces the reader to traditional sources frequently cited in feminist readings of Paul. For later and more current literature see the relevant entries in the Newsom and Ringe **[343]** and Schüssler Fiorenza commentaries **[345]**. Additionally, for a very readable and helpful essay on what is and is not "Pauline" in authorship, see William O. Walker, Jr. "The 'Theology of Woman's Place' and the 'Paulinist' Tradition," *Semeia* 28 (1983): 101-112 (not abstracted here).

[406] Meeks, Wayne. "The Image of the Androgyne: Some Uses of a Symbol in Earliest Christianity." *History of Religions* 13 (1974): 165-208.
This classic, highly technical exegetical discussion examines the androgyne symbol in several Hellenistic Greek and Roman sources (e.g., cultic associations, philosophical schools and various rabbinical writings) to illustrate the distinctive usage of this symbol by Paul in Gal. 3:28. The author argues that Paul's use of this symbol was socially supported by female and male religious leadership within the early Christian community and that the radicality of Paul's usage reflects a clear sense of a realized eschatology. In addition, the author acknowledges and identifies a multiplicity of religious and social factors that functioned to diminish the radicality of Paul's usage, and he concludes to an affirmation of a realized eschatology that was later "spiritualized" at the expense of egalitarian social-religious roles within the Christian community. This is an important source in the identification of the "discipleship of equals" as developed by Schüssler Fiorenza, and its foundation to the development of her imaging of the "*ekklesia* of women." For her work on both of these points, see *In Memory of Her* **[195]** and her related text **[236]**.

[407] Scroggs, Robin A. "Paul and the Eschatological Woman." *Journal of the American Academy of Religion* 40 (1972): 283-303.

This article is frequently cited as *the* source that details the eschatological equality of women and men, but not their social equality as established by an ascetically rooted obliteration of sexual differences. It is a tightly organized paper and develops in five parts. The first is a series of introductory comments in which "supporters of women's lib" are chastised for their ignorance of Paul, and the major question of the article is raised: "Is Paul really one of the great all-time male chauvinists, as women's lib would have it?" (p. 283). The second and third parts discuss the theological and social contexts that inform Gal 3:28, and a fourth part discusses this text and others related to women's activities (i.e., Phil 4:2f, Rm 16, I Cor. 7 and I Cor. 11:2-16). A final section presents Scroggs' conclusions. For theological factors conditioning Paul's thought, Scroggs cites Paul's critique of the Law, his Christological model of the eschatological Adam, and with this, the eschatological community of the baptized. For social factors, he cites the tension between paganism and Judaism that "become for the Christian Paul, a cross fire between his Hellenistic Judaism and his basic Christian theological stance (p. 291). These tensions (together with the eschatological reality of the 'Last Adam') are exposed in Gal 3:27f where social characteristics are denied at the eschatological level, but not (for that fact) at the historical level. Rather, according to Scroggs, Paul's perspective on Gal 3:28 is really found in I Cor. 7:17-27. Here, the "marks of circumcision or uncircumcision are left unchanged; the slave should accept his servitude [and] the marriage relation should remain as it is." According to Scroggs, "within the community female and female are equal...[but Paul]...in no way wishes to eliminate the sexual relationship between male and female" (p. 293). Scroggs expands these points by means of other texts, and in his conclusion he notes that Paul is "not the all-time male chauvinist," but in fact, "the one clear voice in the New Testament asserting the freedom and equality of women in the eschatological community" (p. 302). In a rejoinder to his critics ["Paul and the Eschatological Woman Revisited." *Journal of the American Academy of Religion* 42 (1974): 532-537], with the bulk of his discussion directed to Mary Daly's comments in *Beyond God the Father* [163] Scroggs argues for: (1) the necessity of separating Pauline and non-Pauline literature (because only one characteristic text is actually Pauline [I Cor 14:33b-36]); (2) that because Gal 3:28 is part of an early baptismal formula, it is the church (not Paul) who has proclaimed "the complete equality within the community of all people and groups;" and therefore (3) "Distinctions between groups remain...[but]...Values and roles built on such distinctions are destroyed" (p. 533). Last, Scroggs argues that only two passages [I Cor. 7 and I Cor. 11:2-16] can be claimed as grounds for calling Paul a chauvinist. However, they shouldn't be, because in the first, Paul affirms the legitimacy of marriage and the equality of sexual rights and responsibilities of women and men in marriage; and in the second, data are lacking for a full judgment concerning the meaning of *kephale*. The text, he suggests--and especially v. 3, "...is in all likelihood a Christian midrash on Gen 2 [focusing on "source" and not "head"] and [thus it] does not assert male dominance" (p. 534). In sum, for Scroggs, Paul has "...a history of liberation, a baptism of liberation, and a practice of liberation" (p. 535). **NOTE:** For a particularly perceptive critique of Scroggs' work see Elaine Pagels, "Paul and Women: A Response to Recent Discussion," *Journal of the American Academy of Religion* 42 (1974): 538-549.

C. Works about Feminist Biblical Scholarship

1. General Discussions

[408] Moltmann-Wendel, Elisabeth. *The Women Around Jesus*. New York: Crossroad, 1982.

This book presents a series of studied reflections on the "women around Jesus:" "Martha," who most likely served at table (Luke 10:38-42) and as well, confessed the messiahship of Christ (John 11:1-44); "Mary of Bethany," her sister; "Mary Magdalene," the apostle of the apostles; the unknown woman who anointed Jesus (Mark 14:3-9); "The Group of Women in Mark," who remained faithful as others fled; the "Mothers" in Matthew's gospel; and "Joanna, a Lucan Lady." For each, Moltmann-Wendel exposes strength, the capacity to function in self-identified terms and a model of integrity in the androcentric world of biblical writing and historical commentary. In the authors words, "This book attempts to remove the burden of the patriarchal past from a small section of the New Testament" (p. 11). It seeks to re-imagine these women's stories apart from both the sexist assumptions that suppress women within the text (p. 8-9) and also within its hearing in the contemporary moment. Methodologically, it is an expression of imaginative re-construction that opens out the circumstances of the women in their stories by re-configuring the artistic, historical, and cultural-theological motifs that have shrouded and muffled their presence. It is a readable text grounded largely in German feminist biblical scholarship through the late seventies, but formatted for general readership. Thus, it can serve as an introductory text on women and religion, a meditative source, or a primer on women-centered reconstruction of patriarchal texts.

[409] Perkins, Pheme. "New Testament Ethics: Questions and Contexts." *Religious Studies Review* 10 (1984): 321-327.
The question of "method" is the principal issue addressed by Perkins in this review of 78 New Testament/Ethics sources published between 1978-1983, and by "method" Perkins assumes (at least) the "search" for an adequate understanding of the context(s) of New Testament writings and an interpretive and/or theological framework that permits dialogue between the New Testament contexts and those of today. The question is important: First because of the diversity of the New Testament paraenesis, and second, because contemporary studies continue to shed light on the world of first century C.E. and within it the forms of ethical reflection evident in non-biblical sources. Given these observations, Perkins organizes her review topically in terms of "phenomenological and personalist" approaches to the ethics and the New Testament, several "politically based hermeneutics," and "the feminist critique" of New Testament writings. She notes the significance of 'kingdom ethics,' 'wealth and material possessions,' the lack of an ethics/social change equation in the New Testament literature, and lastly the importance of the feminist critique. While the latter is viewed by some as an alternative political hermeneutic, it is more than this: with the distinction between archetype and prototype as made by Schüssler Fiorenza (cf. [411, 385]), all discussions about the "interrelationship between...experiences of the demands of justice and love...and the exhortations of the Bible must be re-thought" (p. 325). Perkins closes with the recognition that although church language focuses on eschatological values, "...we continue to live with a moral vision that is little more than [the] legitimation of our particular, cultural horizon" (p. 325). For material on Schüssler Fiorenza's discussion of the Bible as archetype or prototype, see [411]. Briefly, Schüssler Fiorenza distinguishes between approaches that see the Bible as an archetype or set blueprint for human experience, and those that focus it as a prototype, or a plurality of images that can propel human experiences into motion and structural transformation. NOTE: For a more general discussion by Perkins (and presented amidst several anti-feminist perspectives) see her essay, "Women in the Bible and Its World." *Interpretation* 42 (1988): 33-44. Also, see her commentary on "The Gospel of Thomas" in *Searching the Scriptures* [345])

[410] Sakenfeld, Katharine D. "Feminist Perspectives on Bible and Theology: An Introduction to Selected Issues and Literature." *Interpretation* 42 (1988): 5-18.
In this frequently cited discussion, Sakenfeld addresses four issues that have assumed increasing importance in feminist theological literature. For Sakenfeld, these issues are "...the place of experience in coming to grips with Scripture; ways of using the Bible in feminist theologies; special problems of method in feminist biblical scholarship; and language about God" (p. 6). Of these issues the first is the most developed by Sakenfeld and the third, the least. To get at the first issue Sakenfeld surveys the principal writings of feminist biblical theologians E. Schüssler Fiorenza, Letty Russell and co-authors Nancy Hardesty and Letha Scanzoni. The writings of these women imply a continuum, at one end of which is Schüssler Fiorenza's presumption that "the context of the feminist struggles to overcome oppression provides the experience by which biblical facts may be evaluated" (p. 7). At the opposite end of the continuum is an evangelical emphasis (e.g., Hardesty and Scanzoni) that "formally" subordinates the role of experience to Scripture and sees experience in terms other than the struggle for liberation. Finding a middle ground is Russell who follows a biblical emphasis on an "authority for the future," itself a possibility compatible, indicates Sakenfeld, with the womanist ethics of Katie Cannon (p. 9). Issue #2 entails the use of the Bible as a feminist theological resource and here three uses are described: textual reinterpretation (e.g., Trible's work [164-165] and [356]); the recognition of biblical themes that criticize patriarchy (e.g., Ruether's writings [365-366]); and the reading of texts "in memoriam" (Trible, [356]) or through a "hermeneutics of remembrance" (Schüssler Fiorenza [369]). These uses, however, all presume something of both experience and the text's authority, although Sakenfeld does not specify what exactly is presumed. Issues #3 and #4 are method and language and here Sakenfeld briefly describes (but does not discuss) Schüssler Fiorenza [368] and [395] and discussions of Tennis' [429] and Achtemeier's [838] affirmation of father language for God. A frequently cited introduction to feminist interpretive issues, this entry should be followed by the more substantive literature (e.g., Tolbert [372], Bird [360], Schüssler Fiorenza [236], and Trible [359]). Sakenfeld has frequently synthesized issues of feminist biblical theological method. See [379], see "Feminist Uses of Biblical Materials" in Russell [210], and see "Feminist Biblical Interpretation" *Theology Today* 46 (1989): 154-168. The *Interpretation* entry, however, is her most thorough.

NOTE: For additional, related sources, see Kwok Pui-Lan [219] and Tolbert [284].

2. Feminism and the Critique of "Historical Critical Method"

As part of her feminist biblical work, Schüssler Fiorenza has consistently challenged the "traditioning" or androcentrizing dynamics at work in the academic world of biblical scholarship, and particularly as these dynamics have been evident in contemporary exegesis and biblical theology. This challenge has taken three basic forms. First, Schüssler Fiorenza has regularly identified what she sees as the key assumptions and androcentric models of academic biblical scholarship (cf. [411]). Second, she has clarified the distinguishing assumptions of feminist biblical scholarship (cf. [413]). Last, she has challenged the normative assumptions of all denominationally identified biblical scholarship, in that the latter is specifically religious scholarship directed to the needs of believers in faith communities, and directed thereby, to the salvific needs of women (cf., e.g., [415]). The entries below illustrate her concern with the biases of academic "traditioning," or what in sociological terms are the dynamics of "sex-typing" within professional organizations. (Cf. Hearn et al. [727], Skevington [113], and Smith [114], as well as the sociological literature in Chapter 3.)

[411] Schüssler Fiorenza, Elisabeth. "'For the Sake of Our Salvation…': Biblical Interpretation and the Community of Faith." In *Bread Not Stone: The Challenge of Feminist Biblical Interpretation*, pp. 23-42, edited by Elisabeth Schüssler Fiorenza. Boston: Beacon, 1984. [First published as "'For the Sake of Our Salvation…' Biblical Interpretation as Theological Task." In *Sin, Salvation, and the Spirit*, edited by D. Durkin, 21-39. Collegeville, MN: Liturgical Press, 1979.]
First published in 1979 this discussion addresses two questions: First, 'how can the academic biblical community be relevant to the wider faith community in its search for the meaning of faith?' And second, 'how can the academic biblical community do so without reifying biblical language, thought and text(s)?' The questions arise both from the contemporary search for meaningful faith and the fact that the academic community has isolated the biblical text in all its historicity as it has sought to establish (through various critical methodologies) the exact original meaning(s) of the biblical text(s). To address these questions and thereby redress the academic community's isolation of the biblical text, Schüssler Fiorenza describes two paradigms that have governed biblical discussion and its relevance: these are the "doctrinal" paradigm and the "historical paradigm." As described by Schüssler Fiorenza, "the doctrinal paradigm" is an image of the Bible as literally, "the Word of God." It is revelation to be accepted without question and its defense (when challenged) is through "proof-texting" whether such proof-texting entails allegorizing, psychological or liturgical affirmations. Schüssler Fiorenza argues that this type of paradigm is theologically dangerous, for it sets the Bible up as an ideological justification of church doctrine, and this, in turn, permits a similar proof-texting approach to church dogmatics. Paradigm #2 is the "Historical Paradigm," and according to Schüssler Fiorenza, paradigm #2 views the Bible as a "book of the past" to be examined "objectively," so that its actual, original and timeless meanings may be discerned. This is an important paradigm, and although recent hermeneutical literature has discredited its epistemological bases, it continues to govern the bulk of contemporary exegesis. Its best use, however, is in service of a new and emerging paradigm, i.e., the "pastoral-theological" paradigm, which Schüssler Fiorenza suggests as a corrective to both the doctrinal and historical paradigms. This new paradigm recognizes that the Bible is a living document responding to its own questions and milieux, and that it thereby, models its own usage for later time. This said, the adoption of this newly emerging paradigm presumes several things. These include: (1) that it is the community of faith and not an academic community only that brings questions to the Bible; (2) it is the faith community's questions themselves that form the basis for interpreting the Bible; (3) the academic community is accountable to the community of faith; and (4) that if church teaching is correct in proclaiming the Bible as *revelation*, differing populations within the faith community will need to utilize what is revelatory for them and prescind from what is not. According to Schüssler Fiorenza, the implications for women's revelatory needs here are clear: only those texts that are "non-sexist…present biblical revelation, if the Bible is not to become a tool for the further oppression of women" (p. 41). NOTE: In a subsequent and similar discussion first published as "Toward a Feminist Biblical Hermeneutics: Biblical Interpretation and Liberation Theology" in *The Challenge of Liberation Theology: A First World Response*, [edited by Brian Mahan and L. Dale Richesin, 91-112. New York: Orbis Books, 1981, but reprinted in *Bread Not Stone* (pp. 43-63) as "The Function of Scripture in the Liberation Struggle"] Schüssler Fiorenza continues to argue that only non-sexist and non-androcentric texts can or should have revelatory authority. Additionally, she argues that a new paradigm of "emancipatory praxis" needs to be established and that biblical scholars and theologians should be accountable to the advocacy principle inherent in such a praxis. More pointedly, biblical scholars and theologians should acknowledge "their own presuppositions,

allegiances and functions within a theological political context...[in order to]...scrutinize not only the content and 'traditioning' process within the Bible, but also the entire Christian tradition, and determine whether or not it serves to oppress or liberate people" (p. 62). Further, it is also in this article that Schüssler Fiorenza begins a fairly sustained description of the Bible as a "prototype" rather than an "archetype" for revelation, although the discussion does not reach its most clear statement until her work in the mid-1980s (cf., e.g., [370]).

[412] Schüssler Fiorenza, Elisabeth. "Remembering the Past in Creating the Future: Historical Critical Scholarship and Feminist Biblical Interpretation." In *Bread Not Stone: The Challenge of Feminist Biblical Interpretation*, 93-116. Boston: Beacon, 1984. [Also published in *Feminist Perspectives on Biblical Scholarship*, ed. by Adela Yarbro Collins, 43-63. Chico, CA: Scholars Press, 1985.]

This discussion is in many ways a bridge point between [411] and [413], and its general discussion entails a summary of "male scholarly rhetoric [as measured] against...feminist critical biblical interpretation..." Overall, Schüssler Fiorenza briefly reviews the Rankean perception of history and the dispassionate value free professional exegetical role it engenders. Second, she critiques this perspective in the light of hermeneutical literature that demonstrates the fallacy of arguing that biblical interpretation is a value free enterprise involving the historically neutral reconstruction of texts and their initially intended meanings (for their past communities). Rather, she notes, contemporary literatures and philosophies point to the need for public discussion of one's methodological, cultural, and social interpretive assumptions, and particularly so with respect to one's socio-political assumptions, for life worlds influence interpretation. To continue her discussion, she aligns a summary of feminist critical theory with these first two points to indicate the necessity for a critical feminist biblical interpretation. In particular, she calls attention to not only the *partial* quality of androcentric scholarship (in that it assumes the male as normative), but as well, its subsequent and encompassing bias in that "its intellectual discourse and scholarly frameworks are determined only by male perspectives [and] primarily of the dominant classes" (p. 107). Finally, she illustrates her discussion through the variety of implications it has for biblical studies and the portrayal of women within early Christianity. This is a general and theoretical discussion and it is helpfully read in conjunction with her early exegetical discussions, e.g., [368, 380, 401, 402], and of course, *In Memory of Her* [195].

[413] Schüssler Fiorenza, Elisabeth. "Toward a Critical Self-Understanding of Biblical Scholarship." In *Bread Not Stone: The Challenge of Feminist Biblical Interpretation*, 117-149. Boston: Beacon, 1984.

Four general points govern this discussion of methodology in biblical scholarship. First, Schüssler Fiorenza identifies the general problem in contemporary biblical scholarship: namely that various groups, but particularly liberation and feminist theologians are (for different reasons) dissatisfied with the assumption of biblical scholarship as a "value free" enterprise. Second, this means that from a feminist perspective, the "task of biblical scholarship must be to develop a critical method that does not 'render God' as a god of patriarchal oppression." Third, and relatedly, this means that rather than eliminating "assumptions and presuppositions," they should be made "conscious in a public critical discussion and interpretation" (p. 135). Last, this consciously developed and public critical process should engender an "advocacy stance" for biblical scholarship, because biblical scholarship is scholarship on behalf of believing communities--past and present--and thus it must engender historical solidarity with these communities by becoming "a critical memory and theological-prophetic challenge to establishment society and church" (p. 149). This is an exceptionally detailed and thickly argued discussion with Schüssler Fiorenza's (typically) vast knowledge of biblical scholarship filling in the pages between main points. Hence, to demonstrate the difficulties inherent in contemporary biblical scholarship Schüssler Fiorenza first summarizes and critiques the main arguments and literatures that support the traditional exegesis/interpretation division of labor within biblical scholarship, with key authors named and examined (Barr, Stendahl, Bultmann, Gadamer, the New Hermeneutic school, etc.). Second, she critically summarizes the main lines of Juan Segundo's liberation theology and particularly its assumptions of God's preferential option for the poor, and--catechetically--that one "learns to learn" [faith] by "entrusting...[one's]...life and meaning to the historical process that is reflected...and embodied... in the tradition" (p. 139). Neither assumption works immediately for women, she argues, because (1) the Bible exhibits mixed messages to women; (2) Segundo's discussion of the faith educational process too cleanly splits content and method a la the exegetical-interpretive division of labor within biblical scholarship generally, and (3) it remains entrapped in the assumptions of androcentric scholarship. Hence it cannot exercise the full critical power of an advocacy stance so as to "not 'render God' as the god of patriarchal oppression. Given these arguments, Schüssler Fiorenza suggests that a critical (and subsequently evaluative) hermeneutics (see [483]) must be developed, i.e., a "hermeneutics of suspicion" that works within and on behalf of the believing community to generate an interpretive work that can critically liberate the community.

[414] Schüssler Fiorenza, Elisabeth. "The Ethics of Interpretation: Decentering Biblical Scholarship." *Journal of Biblical Literature* 107 (1988): 3-17.
This article is Schüssler Fiorenza's Presidential Society for Biblical Literature (SBL) address, delivered at the annual SBL meeting in Boston, Dec. 5, 1987. After an extended introduction that sets her purpose as that of identifying and introducing a new paradigm for biblical scholarship, i.e., that which she describes as the "rhetorical paradigm," Schüssler Fiorenza develops her address in terms of three main concerns. The first is an historical overview of the role of women in the SBL for it illustrates the crucial factor of "standpoint" or "social location" as a starting point for theology. Here, she follows Bass' discussion of the history of female membership in the SBL [352], but she augments Bass's study with the observation that *contemporary* feminist biblical scholarship arises directly from the experience of feminism, and in contrast to the first wave of feminism (that of Stanton's *Women's Bible*), this second wave *does* engage women biblical scholars. The question, therefore, is how women and women's scholarship can be increased and augmented in the society, or: "What kind of ethos, ethics and politics of the community of biblical scholars would allow us to move our work done in 'the interest of women' from the margins to the center of biblical studies?" (p. 8). This question generates the second element of her presidential address, a review and critique of the "scientistic paradigm" that has grounded biblical scholarship since its initial break with the religious dogmatism. The weakness of this scientistic perspective, argues Schüssler Fiorenza, is its detached and apolitical nature, for these values mask the fact that scholarship always has consequences and that scholars have a responsibility to attend to this fact. To illustrate possible SBL precedents for the "decentering" of the scientistic perspective, then, Schüssler Fiorenza examines past SBL presidential addresses, and she finds that at least three former SBL presidents have called for a value-directed approach to biblical scholarship. Her final point of discussion becomes, therefore, a description of the rhetorical paradigm with its implications for the organizational structuring and doing of biblical scholarship. In brief, because this paradigm understands historical sources and data "as perspectival discourse constructing...worlds and symbolic universes," (and thus constructing *meaning*), it raises the question of power as a dimension of scholarly activity, and it requires a process of "double ethics" from scholars. The first of these ethics is an "ethics of historical reading," which asks: 'what kind of readings can do justice to the text in its historical contexts?". The second ethic is an "ethics of accountability" or the assumption that scholars should be responsible for both "the choice of their theoretical interpretive models...[and for]...the ethical consequences of the biblical text and its meanings" (p. 15). Overall, this means that scholars must be responsible for identifying what the text does "to a reader who submits to its world of vision," both in past and current usage and in social and ecclesial settings. This discussion refines Schüssler Fiorenza's early works on biblical paradigms and feminist evaluative hermeneutics [483], and it parallels her recent work on "biblical interpretation and critical commitment" [415].

[415] Schüssler Fiorenza, Elisabeth. "Biblical Interpretation and Critical Commitment." *Studia Theologica* 43 (1989): 5-18.
As with much of her critical biblical work, this essay by Schüssler Fiorenza also addresses the questions: "Is it possible for biblical scholarship to be value-neutral [and] objective or [even] should it be?" and "How does the commitment to a particular community, theoretical perspective, and historical struggle impinge on or foster critical inquiry and biblical scholarship?" (p. 5). In her earlier work (e.g., *Bread Not Stone*, [196]), she has addressed these questions through (1) a discussion of the need for biblical theology to become more self-critical of its androcentric assumptions and (2) a description of various paradigmatic images governing the possibilities of biblical scholarship. Here the emphasis on self-criticism continues as does the strategy of identifying paradigmatic assumptions within biblical scholarship. New to the discussion, however, is her integration of rhetorical criticism as a possible paradigm for biblical studies and its application to the issue of anti-Semitism within the gospel of John. Her argument may be summarized in five points. First, the currently regnant "empiricist paradigm of biblical studies" is itself not value-free, for although it emerged historically in an attempt to be free of dogmatic and ideological assumptions, it itself masks its own "masculine embodiment." Further, it maintains this status quo by perjoratively defining the conceptualized frameworks of marginalized "Others" as ideology not scholarship. This is inaccurate and a "truncation" of the Enlightenment ethos that sought knowledge on behalf of a just, free society. Thus, second, it is the task of marginalized Others to name their own subjectivity, and one strategy for this within biblical studies is through the adoption

of a "rhetorical" paradigm for biblical studies. The elements of this paradigm include the recognition and use of critical biblical skills, but on behalf of indicating (a) how the text itself worked in its own time to elicit responses from readers so that (b) its potential for ideological distortion is both minimized and corrected in the context of present readers/listeners. This, of course, requires radical self criticism on the part of biblical scholars. Thus, the third point of Schüssler Fiorenza's argument is the adoption of this paradigm with its "double ethics:... an ethic of historical reading" (showing how the text worked in its own day) and an "ethics of accountability," indicating its praxis-based correction in the present. Fourth, the illustrative case for this task is the anti-Semitism in John's gospel and Schüssler Fiorenza follows this through by showing how the expulsion of Christians from the synagogue was used as a communicative point to enhance the distinction between Christianity's community of origin and the then contemporary Jewish community. In Schüssler Fiorenza's analysis this communicative strategy became identified with historical fact which, in turn, fed anti-Semitic threads throughout history. Schüssler Fiorenza thus concludes (point five) that "biblical scholarship has the responsibility not only to elaborate the historical-religious meanings of the biblical texts but also to reflect critically on the Christian identity formations they produce" (p. 15). As with all her work, the notes here contain extensive bibliography and further discussion.

[416] Schüssler Fiorenza, Elisabeth. "Text and Reality-Reality as Text: The Problem of a Feminist Historical and Social Reconstruction Based on Texts." *Studia Theologica* 43 (1989): 19-34.

This article unfolds the significance of the term, "feminist," as a qualifier of the terms, "historical and social reconstruction" as applied to biblical texts. It echoes the two major emphases of Schüssler Fiorenza's earlier methodological pieces, i.e., her critique of the exegetical-scientistic or objectivistic approach to biblical studies [412] and her continually expanding search for a "paradigm" that expresses the breadth of concerns she sees at stake in feminist biblical studies ([411] and [395]). New to this methodological discussion, however, is her emphasis on "rhetorical criticism" as the model (or "paradigm") to indicate the full scope of the meaning of "feminist" biblical studies. The argument develops in four points. First, there is the problem: There is a dualistic epistemology that presumes the legitimacy of "historical social reconstruction on the basis of texts without reference to the inquiring subject" (p. 19). Further, this is problematic because it ignores a complex (three-way) communication process between the text, the interpreter and the reader. Point #2 is Schüssler Fiorenza's (here expanded) critique of the scientistic approach to biblical studies: its assumption of a clean break between past and present and its subsequent requirement that the interpreter presume a value-neutral stance so that the historical facts of the text can be retrieved. For Schüssler Fiorenza, not only is history not so cleanly divided, but such neutrality ignores the reality structuring capacity of language and the ability of a text to engage and subsume an unengaging (uncritical) reader. Schüssler Fiorenza's third point is her contrast between poststructuralist thought and feminist critical thought. While detailed, this contrast basically emerges as one that evidences feminism's recognition that texts are ideologically scripted (p. 26), that feminist scholars seek to present a *different* history, and that to do that, *feminist* historical reconstruction requires (1) the exposing of ideologically negative scripting and with this, the near simultaneous presentation of once subordinated Others as subjects of their own history. Last, Schüssler Fiorenza points out that while feminism rejects the enlightenment emphasis on "Man" (and with it the subordination of Others), it nonetheless accepts the democratic principles of the Enlightenment. As her fourth and last main point, Schüssler Fiorenza applies the entire discussion to her own assessment of what she tried to accomplish in *In Memory of Her* [195], and here, the "rhetorical approach" to reconstruction becomes clear. Because it is a sign of oppression not to have a written history, and because feminism supports a rhetorical reading of the text (i.e., a reading that opens out a writer's intentions and structuring of words to that end), *In Memory of Her* focused on both a critique of androcentric language with its marginalization of women *and* a critical reading of scripture in terms of an ideological critique of "patriarchy" as the prevailing social system model evident in the text(s). Thus, *In Memory of Her* evidences a "deconstruction of the patriarchal 'rhetoric of otherness' as well as [a] reconstruction of the reality and voice of the silenced others..."(p. 31). And in doing this it exposes the poverty of the scientistic model and the wealth of the "rhetorical-emancipatory" paradigm that empowers women of today, from and through the voices of women who lived in the past, but followed the Spirit of God.

D.   Teaching about Feminist Biblical Studies

See Chapter 20, "Feminist Theology, the Academy and Theological Education."

11

Feminist Theology and Historic Christian Symbols

This chapter presents literature on six historic Christian symbols. These are the symbols, *God, Christ, Mary, the Church, the Trinity*, and *Redemption*, with the latter taken here as the symbolic nexus of *Sin/Salvation/Eschatology*. These symbols are foundational to Christian theology. Moreover, because the theological casting of these symbols has generally presumed a gendered and hierarchical patterning of social and formal organizations in which the *cultural and social norms* of "Christendom" have been deemed superior to those of all others, each of these symbols is not only a specifically "religious" symbol, but a symbol of social and political consequence as well. Indeed, as one reads the literature, it is as if each of these symbols were a vast hologram now being carefully turned because of its extensive detail, and met--because of that same detail--with a continuing range of feelings, expectations, religious sensitivities, socio-political analyses, and last, all possible ethical challenges and affirmations. Viewed in this light, a helpful overview to these topics is LaCugna's recent collection, *Freeing Theology: The Essentials of Theology in Feminist Perspective* [273]. Likewise, for article length overviews the reader should see the following: First, for early overviews of the feminist literature on "God" see Halkes [420] and Johnson [421]; second, for an overview of feminist Christology through the mid '80s see Darling-Smith [434], and see the reader by Stevens [442] for literature through the early '90s; third, for feminist Mariological literature see Borresen [444] and Johnson [446, 447]; fourth, for feminist theological literature on "the church" see Ruether [449]. Last, for an overview of the literature on sin and redemption in feminist theology see Smith [466]. It is important to note that as feminist theologians rethink and reconstruct various Christian symbols, the task at hand is literally to reweave them from within imageries that express women as also created in the image of God, *with all the autonomous and relational dimensions that may imply,* and to disclose, thereby, the salvific power of these symbols as specifically available to women (although not to women only).

Some chapter caveats: Because the discussion of these symbols has increased so dramatically since the mid-1980s, many sources relevant to this chapter have already been indicated in the literature in Section II. Hence the entries below are heavily cross referenced back to earlier abstracts. Additionally, because of the extensive interweave of these materials, the literatures below are typically prefaced with introductory notes and related cross references. The feminist literature on "Godtalk" is presented first, with literature on Christology, Mariology, ecclesiology, the Trinity and redemption [sin/salvation/eschatology] to follow.

A. Feminist Approaches to the Doctrine of God

Limited space precludes a full description of the feminist appropriation of "God language" following feminist theology's initial critique of religious patriarchy during the mid and late 1960s. Nor is it feasible to amass into one chapter all of the related topics--liturgy, christology, the Trinity, homiletics, spirituality, biblical studies, ethics etc., *and* the numerous appropriations and/or extensions of feminist theology by various women's communities since the mid-80s--which also reflect the ways in which feminist theologians speak about God. Rather, what must be said is that in spite of the enormous pluralism of feminist theological "Godtalk," the overarching concern of feminist theologians is that "Godtalk" *not legitimate* the normativeness of male experience for either religious or social reality, and that Godtalk *not legitimate* the use of hierarchical patterns for institutional and interpersonal interactions. Rather, "Godtalk" should empower people, with the norms of mutuality, relationality, respect, and justice coming to ground the patterns of both institutional and personal interaction(s). This is evident in virtually every major feminist, womanist, Asian, evangelical, goddess, Jewish, lesbian, and *Mujerista*, [feminist] theological perspective, and it is what unites the literature in the face of its extended and multiple diversities.

The entries below reflect these varied perspectives. Hence, by way of chapter guideposts, Ruether's early essay **[425]** identifies grounding issues for the feminist appropriation of God-language within Catholic feminism, while Kelly Brown Douglas's discussion **[419]** indicates womanist issues grounding the appropriation of "Godtalk." In turn, the entries by Halkes **[420]** and Johnson **[421]** evidence early thematic and methodological overviews. Third, the reader by Carr and Schüssler Fiorenza **[418]** excerpts various sources published through 1988--and particularly those presenting feminist mother and friend images for God. Fourth, Suchocki's **[427]** discussion demonstrates the role of ideology in "classical" trinitarian Godtalk, while yet other sources (e.g., Metz/Schillebeeckx **[423]**, Moltmann-Wendel/Moltmann **[424]**, and Solle **[426]**) illustrate various institutional and liberationist perspectives. Fifth, Tennis **[429]** and Thistlethwaite **[430]** well illustrate the *range* of problems inherent in androcentric and patriarchal God language, while Johanna Bos's text **[427]** presents the case for "reimagining God" given the diversity expressed in Scripture.

Two final notes: First, it cannot be stressed strongly enough that several previously abstracted sources are equally relevant to the literature presented below as examples of feminist and womanist Godtalk. As listed alphabetically, these include: Rebecca Chopp's *The Power to Speak: Feminism, Language, God* **[239]**, Mary Daly's *Beyond God the Father* **[161]**, Carter Heyward's *Touching Our Strength* **[242]**, Elizabeth Johnson's *She Who Is* **[232]**, Sally McFague's *Models of God* **[244]**, Judith Plaskow's *Standing Again at Sinai* **[262]**, Rosemary Ruether's *Sexism and God-Talk* **[190]**, her *Gaia & God* **[235]**, Susan Thistlethwaite's *Sex Race and God* **[252]** and Delores Williams' *Sisters in the Wilderness: The Challenge of Womanist God-Talk* **[259]**.

Second, because the feminist discussion of God has occurred in conjunction with the discussions of "inclusive" language and trinitarian theology, the sources below should be read in conjunction with the trinitarian and worship literatures presented later in this section. The alphabetized entries now follow.

[417] Bos, Johanna W. H. van Wijk *Reimagining God: The Case for Scriptural Diversity*. Louisville, KY: Westminster/John Knox, 1995.
Written partly in supportive response to Elizabeth Johnson's *She Who Is* **[232]** and partly in response to the negative press attached to the November 1993 Minneapolis "Re-Imagining Conference," this text provides a clear summary of the standard exegetical literature evidencing the diversity of biblical names for God in the First and Second Testaments. While it covers little new ground, it reviews various scriptural images for God ("Warrior," "King," "Lord," "Teacher," "Father," "Rock" and "Maker"), the literature and issues identified with calling God "Maker," "Mother," "Eagle," "Spirit," "Sophia" and "YHWH," and in a closing chapter, the empowering implications of using such language. Throughout, Bos is attentive to the recognition that no one name or title for God is sufficient, and that for every title or name, one must be able to say it both "is and is not." Second, Bos' principal metaphor for the need of such diversity is Israel's period of Exile--to which she likens the power of patriarchal language. While one might wish (for various reasons) for a different metaphor, Bos' text remains a helpful survey of the scriptural diversity of which she writes, and it is easily adaptable to adult education and seminary audiences alike.

[418] Carr, Anne, and Elisabeth Schüssler Fiorenza, eds. *Motherhood: Experience, Institution and Theology*. Edinburgh: T. & T. Clark, 1989.
In other volumes of the *Concilium* series Carr and Schüssler Fiorenza present collections on work and poverty in women's lives **[493]** and the impact of theology as a factor defining women as beings with a "special nature" **[321]**. Here, they present fourteen essays exploring motherhood as both "a theological concept" and a "social, cultural and religious institution and ideology" (p. 3.) Overall, the essays are relevant to several feminist theological concerns (e.g., ethics, peace, and anthropology). But salient here are the five essays in Part III on "Motherhood in Religious Language and Symbolism." These essays survey the biblical motifs of "God as Mother" in the book of Hosea (by the German feminist theologian, Marie-Theres Wacker); the genealogy of Jesus (*viz.*, "The Foremothers and the Mother of Jesus" by New Testament scholar, Jane Schaberg, cf.

[387]); a second essay on Mary--here, "Maternal Friend or Virgin Mother?" (by Els Maeckelberghe from the University of Groningen in the Netherlands); and finally, two further essays on God: "The Divine as Mother" by Ursula King and "Mother God" by Sally McFague--the latter largely a synopsis of *Models of God...*" [244]).

[419] Douglas, Kelly Brown. "To Reflect the Image of God: A Womanist Perspective on Right Relationship." In *Living the Intersections: Womanism and Afrocentrism in Theology*, edited by Cheryl Sanders, 67-77. Minneapolis, MN: Fortress, 1994.
This essay examines womanist care (or the "womanist way of relating") as a series of four values that can serve African Americans in the search for empowering and salvific religious images. These values stem from the "culture of resistance" African American women have experienced historically--from African women enslaved in America, and they include the following: (1) a community wide framework of familism in which the community is one's family and one's family is part and parcel of the community; (2) the value of developing individual identities, (including those of same-sex orientation); (3) the related value of African Americans to "free [local] communities from restrictive ideologies about the nature of households and who [within them] can raise children;" and (4) the need to model the mutuality and reciprocity so characteristic of enslaved women's relationships and "especially those with their men." By way of application, Douglas examines the implications of these values for African Americans who would "seek to be in the true image of God" and she concludes to the "duty...[of]...African American women and men doing theology to help to forge a new 'culture of resistance' that will promote life and wholeness for the entire community...[and thus reflect]...the image of God who is life and wholeness."

[420] Halkes, Catharina. "The Themes of Protest in Feminist Theology against God the Father." In *God as Father?* (Concilium 143), edited by Johannes-Baptist Metz and Edward Schillebeeckx, 103-112. Edinburgh: T. and T. Clark, 1981.
This discussion succinctly surveys the early feminist theological literature by Daly, Ruether, Goldenberg, and Christ and Plaskow to identify feminist objections to the use of "father" language for God and to formulate Halkes' own position toward this literature. By way of overview, Halkes organizes the early literature along a continuum of objections that in many ways parallels Carol Christ's 'reformist/revolution' distinction [177]. Thus, she notes that for some feminists the need seems to be one of rethinking Christianity's androcentric symbols, while for others it is to reject Christianity altogether in favor of Goddess religion and/or "worship of the goddess." Where Halkes differs from Christ, however, is in her starting point and perceived audience. In contrast to Christ's attention to religious and women studies generally, Halkes writes as a "feminist theologian" and her concern is for a more specific population, *viz.*, feminist Roman Catholic theologians who are seeking to give their religiosity a different form, given the pain that patriarchal excess historically has caused. Halkes' efforts, therefore, are toward the empowerment of this group as "internal reformers" of biblical exegesis, church dogma and church custom, and particularly women's ordination. To close her discussion (and still paralleling Christ's typology), Halkes notes the re-interpretive and rejectionist possibilities facing Catholic women, and she identifies herself with positions then currently held by Catholics Ruether and Schüssler Fiorenza, and Protestant evangelicalist Virginia Mollenkott.

[421] Johnson, Elizabeth A. "The Incomprehensibility of God and the Image of God as Male and Female." *Theological Studies* 45 (1984): 441-465.
Readers seeking a compact, comprehensive introduction into the ways in which theologians currently use female language for God will find this essay particularly helpful, for in it Johnson does four things. First, she affirms and reviews the classical doctrine of God's incomprehensibility: the teaching that "it is proper to God as God to transcend all direct similarity to creatures and thus never to be known comprehensively or essentially as God" (p. 441). Second, she highlights the linguistic premise of this teaching: i.e., that all language for God is analogical. Third, she juxtaposes this premise with the charge of "many women theologians" that an exclusive use of masculine language for God is, in fact, idolatrous, and she exposes both the necessity and legitimacy of using both feminine and masculine language for God. Last, Johnson surveys three principal ways in which the literature attests the current usage of feminine language for God. These include: (1) the application of such "feminine traits" as nurture, gentleness and mothering to God--a strategy that feminizes God and "evens out" the masculine emphasis of God the Father; (2) the acknowledgment of an actual feminine dimension within the Divine--a strategy that identifies femininity within the Holy Spirit in terms of the Spirit's identification with love and gentleness; and (3) the full blown and independent use of masculine and feminine language for all that is or can be said about God--a strategy that preserves the legitimacy of female language and experience as a

potential imaging of God, as grounded in the teaching of Genesis 1. By way of value, Johnson judges the first two strategies yet androcentric in quality, for in each, traditionally based superordinate and subordinate gender assumptions remain in tact, and feminine language for God does not attain the footing held by masculine language. In the third strategy, however, both feminine and masculine images are recognized as equally and independently valid as language for God (and via the principle of analogy, equally and independently invalid), and this is Johnson's preferred strategy. For related material see Johnson [422] and Farley [166-167].

[422] Johnson, Elizabeth A. "Mary and the Female Face of God." *Theological Studies* 50 (1989): 500-526.
Among other things--its comprehensive review of the Mariological literature, the clarity of its ordered presentation, its clear statement of purpose, premises and limitations, and the obvious depth of Johnson's own faith--among these things, Johnson's article also moves one comfortably into fully feminist metaphors for God, without engaging in what is (in effect) an "add-a-trait" methodology (see Mary McClintock Fulkerson, *Changing the Subject*, Fortress Press, 1994, p. 37) a style Johnson herself has, over the years, fully disavowed. Johnson's fullest treatment of "the mystery of God in feminist theological discourse" is her book, *She Who Is* [232], with the last quoted words as its subtitle. But here, in this precursor article, she demonstrates brilliantly how female images of God may be retrieved and "returned" to God, without presuming that the latter are either parts or dimensions of God after the manner of a gender dualism, or elements of the feminine divine to be aligned with God's masculine or more "male" imaged side. Johnson begins with her purpose and premises: a theological discussion that considers the possibility of retrieving female images of God as drawn from the history of language and religious affect about Mary, but as possibly transferred from God to Mary as a consequence of patriarchal distortion. She states her criteria for recognizing transferred imagery (p. 504) and with a review of historical devotional and theological literature done nicely as a synthesis of ten general perspectives, she finds various clues for using Mariological expectations as sources for God-metaphors. It is a detailed discussion, but five elements of imagery to be returned as feminist metaphors for God emerge: God's maternal countenance, Her divine compassion, Her power and Her might, Her immanence and Her creative energy. By way of conclusion, Johnson notes that neither these nor other images based on the experience of women exhaust the possibilities for God language--nor is God language limited to only these images, for others (such as "friend") are not easily retrievable from the Marian tradition. This said, her hypothesis of retrieval and return is confirmed, with little to quibble with in the lines between. **NOTE**: See [232] for Johnson's additional work.

[423] Metz, Johannes-Baptist, and Edward Schillebeeckx, eds. *God as Father?* Edinburgh: T. and T. Clark, 1981.
This 1981 issue of the Concilium series provides an accurate index of mainline Catholic and Protestant responses to the early years of the feminist theological movement. Its 17 articles address the use of "father language" for God in terms of such traditional historical and theological issues as the significance of father imagery for prayer, trinitarian theology and the "proper" naming of God, and the editors' introduction reflects the struggle of androcentric theologians faced with both feminist perspectives *and* the experience of women throughout Christianity. Namely, that "...The handling of [the volume's] theme has remained selective, and marked and limited by accidental factors." This noted, the editors hope the volume will "...help the reader to find his [sic] bearings..." (p. vii). Entries by feminist theologians include Halkes [420] and Ruether [425], as well as two early essays not abstracted here, but well worth the read: Dorothee Sölle's "Paternalistic Religion as Experienced by Woman" and Arlene Swidler's "The Image of Women in a Father-Oriented Religion."

[424] Moltmann-Wendel, Elisabeth, and Jürgen Moltmann. *God--His and Hers*. New York: Crossroad, 1991.
Six essays make up this collaborative collection on theology, Christology and the gendered patterns of thinking to which traditional theology is subject and about which feminist theology is critical. The entries vary in both scope and substance, with all but the last previously published or presented elsewhere during the period 1981-1989. Essay #1 is an ecumenically directed lecture, presented jointly by the authors to an audience in Sheffield England and advocating a wholeness of theology based on the shared insights of women and men theologians. Subsequent entries follow the model of "joint presentation," and address selected issues of gender and theology, including: (1) the ways gender can affect meanings of oppression and emancipation; (2) the need for and the ability to use and 'mother' and 'father' language for God; and (3) the perceptions of salvific titles for Jesus in biblical exegesis. Most notable in this brief volume, however, is the closing chapter on "The

Theology of the Cross," where Jurgen Moltmann summarizes his more extensive work on the "Cross" as symbolic of the suffering of God, and where Elisabeth Moltmann Wendel asks: "Is There a Feminist Theology of the Cross?" The emphases in these two essays vary. The first stresses pathos and the second, relationality. Both, however, agree that scripture is the starting point for theologizing about the Cross and its meaning as the reality of redemption by the power of God, and thus both remain tradition directed, albeit with acknowledged accommodations to the needs of contemporary women and men.

[425] Ruether, Rosemary Radford. "The Female Nature of God: A Problem in Contemporary Religious Life." In *God as Father?*, edited by Johannes-Baptist Metz and Edward Schillebeeckx, 61-66. Edinburgh: T. and T. Clark, 1981.
In a clear and tightly written essay Ruether summarizes the feminist critique of patriarchal God imagery as developed by the early 1980s: "When God is projected in the image of one sex, rather than both sexes, and in the image of the ruling class of this sex, then this class of males is seen as consisting in the ones who possess the image of God primarily...[with] all other groups addressed by God only through the mediation of the patriarchal class" (p. 61). In her discussion Ruether examines the "suppressed feminine in patriarchal theology," "goddess religion," and the criteria for Christianity's reconstruction of Godd(ess) imagery as creativity working for an as yet unrealized humanity.

[426] Sölle, Dorothee. *Thinking about God: An Introduction to Theology*. London and Philadelphia: SCM Press and Trinity Press International, 1990.
This is the most systemically developed of Sölle's recent works, and its distinctiveness is that it is a sustained commentary on the task(s) of systematic and liberation theology, with the latter understood as the movement from lived praxis to sustained reflection, and from such reflection back to lived praxis. It is a text grounded in liberationist expectations and commitments, but in contrast to liberation theologies that challenge either denominational structures or particular spiritualities, this text focuses on the historical movement from liberalism to liberationist thinking. Thus, as one moves through Sölle's discussion, one finds not only her "invitation to know the joy of doing theology," but as well, her historical charting of [Christian] orthodox, liberal, and liberationist theologies, images and symbols--and these from within their first, second and third world constituencies. It is a lucidly written text (drafted from lectures delivered to non-theological audiences), it is clearly mindful of feminist theology's critique of "domination" as an illegitimate motif of 'God-Language,' and it carefully grounds the emphases and contextual bases of Reformation, Continental, feminist and African-American theologians. Last, its closing chapter synthesizes the entire discussion in a feminist reading of Martin Buber's *I and Thou* philosophy, so that chapter length discussions of central Christian symbols (creation, sin, redemption, Christology, the kingdom of God and the church, peace, theism and God) all come together in a philosophy of dialogue rather than domination, and in an intersubjectivity that cuts across generations and traditions. A bibliography directed to each chapter topic and an index of biblical references close this versatile, evocative and insightful volume. Also by Sölle is **[557]**, and for her earliest feminist theological reflection see her text (not reviewed here) *To Work and To Love: A Theology of Creation*, co-authored with Shirley Cloyes [Philadelphia: Fortress, 1984].

[427] Suchocki, Majorie. "God, Sexism and Transformation." In *Reconstructing Christian Theology*, edited by Rebecca Chopp and Mark Lewis Taylor, 25-48. Minneapolis, MN: Fortress, 1994.
In an earlier discussion **[453]** Suchocki has demonstrated the male character of trinitarian language and argued for its removal. Here she demonstrates the potential of feminist theology for the redevelopment of trinitarian theology. The discussion develops in four parts. First, Suchocki presents an overview of classical trinitarian theology cast as a response to "the idea of evil," with the latter understood as "lust, ignorance, and death" resulting from the mis-use of the will by finite human beings. She details how various aspects of trinitarian doctrine emerged in response to this particular understanding of evil, and she identifies the idea of God's "immutability" as a key feature within the trinitarian synthesis. Second, Suchocki notes how, ideologically, this particular "idea of evil" both supported and reflected Western patriarchal culture, and how, in turn it was supported by classical Christianity. Third, and by way of transition, she notes how such ideas can (under changed conditions) lose their resonance with human experience, and in this light, she asks whether and how trinitarian theology might be "stretched" to incorporate a more contemporary understanding of evil: namely, the idea of evil as structured oppression, whether of "race, gender, sexual orientation, handicapping conditions, class or the environment" (p. 27). The recognition of evil as structured oppression is pre-eminent in feminist theology, and in Suchocki's hands it

permits her last and closing points: Namely, a synthesis of several feminist theological emphases that demonstrate (among other things): (1) the value of relationality over immutability, (2) the feminist theological emphasis on immanence rather than transcendence, (3) the idea of liberation through empowerment, and overall, the ways in which feminist diversity can be brought to bear upon culture wide questions involving religious symbols, doctrines and social structure. This is an important article. First, it evidences the ideological connections between theological, theological anthropological, ethical, and formally soteriological concepts. Second, it exhibits the widening range of feminist resources available for the *re*developing Christian doctrine. **NOTE**: For additional discussions of ideology and its role in the development of Christian doctrine see various works by Ruether (e.g., **[172]**, **[299]**, **[326]** and **[465]**), and see the literatures on feminist ethics and sin/salvation and eschatology.

[428] Santmire, H. Paul. "Retranslating 'Our Father': The Urgency and the Possibility."
      Dialog 16 (1977): 101-106.
This article reviews the "translational history" of the term, "abba," to indicate the theological and pastoral justifications of using the phrase "Our Parent" (rather than Our Father) as the term of address in praying "The Lord's Prayer." The theological discussion roots in Tillichian personalism coupled with feminist biblical exegesis through the mid 1970s and the author's preference for the "Our Parent" phrase (rather than Father-Mother) language rests with the decision to avoid language that might imply sexual dualism in God. **NOTE**: For an important assessment of the literature associated with the ABBA argument(s), see **[433]**. The latter surveys the wide range of New Testament scholarship that no longer holds to "abba" statements as indicative of a uniquely special relation between Jesus and God, and it highlights several implications of this fact. Additionally, see von Kellenbach **[288]**.

[429] Tennis, Diane. *Is God the Only Reliable Father?* Philadelphia: Fortress, 1985.
In response to feminist perspectives that argue *against* the use of masculine language for God, this text argues forthrightly for retaining the masculine symbol "Father" as a primary designation for God. Tennis's argument is based on a reversal of mainline feminist logic. Where feminism largely sees male symbolization as disempowering to women in that it values men while devaluing women and/or reflects and supports the abuse of women, Tennis suggests that the goodness of the biblical God, as Father, can be redemptive of the negative symbol itself, and that the redeemed symbol can then stand again as a model for women and men. Tennis describes the power of Jesus as a Servant on behalf of women (and thus as a challenge to male privilege) and she invites all women to recognize the value of Jesus' maleness precisely as servant: namely that in contrast to women, he did not have to assume the role of servant, but did so willingly and thus can be held up as one who exposes male privilege rather than as one who supports it. She concludes, therefore, that there are advantages to having a male savior and that (among others) one is his capacity to be a model for men. This is an ambiguous text: on the one hand it evidences an obvious dialogue with the core feminist literature of the mid-1980s, with the names Saiving, Plaskow, Ruether and Schüssler Fiorenza peppering its specific chapters. At the same time it looks down on "mother" language for God while it indicates that in joining "the underclass of women and other servants" Jesus's maleness was and is an asset, and that it is this dynamic that seems to be salvific for women. Missing throughout, however, is an assessment or response to the core argument as first presented by Daly **[161]**, i.e., that "when God is male, male is god."

[430] Thistlethwaite, Susan Brooks. "God and Her Survival in a Nuclear Age." *Journal*
      of Feminist Studies in Religion 4, no. 1 (1988): 73-88.
Writing in response to the growing power of the American "Religious Right" and the perception of some within it that "nuclearism" represents God's final judgment for the United States, Thistlethwaite suggests that this perception "eviscerates" the doctrine of God and that the sources for a renewed doctrine lie in the study of Black women's experience(s) of survival and their religious thematization. For her argument, Thistlethwaite critiques both liberal and feminist theologies, but specifically the works of Gordon Kaufmann, Paul Tillich, and Mary Daly. For her analysis of Black women's experience she draws variously upon the writings of Audre Lorde **[78]**, Alice Walker, and Toni Cade Bambera: first to indicate the differing perspectives of survival embedded in liberal theology, "white feminist" theology and the experience of African American women, and second to highlight that survival entails more than mere continuity in being, and more than material progress across time. Rather, what is to be learned from the survival experience of African American women is that survival requires a spirituality different from that of Western linear thought, and one rooted deeply in the sacredness of the earth itself. **NOTE**: Although now largely surpassed by the enormous expanse of literature within womanist theology and spirituality,

Thistlethwaite's essay clearly illustrates the painful impact of "race" as an unspoken variable within the theologizing process.

B. Feminist Christologies

Feminist theologians seek understandings of Jesus that are empowering rather than debilitating to women. For some feminist theologians (e.g., Carol Christ and Mary Daly) this means an abandonment of any discussion about Jesus per se, and the taking up of a new perspective such as goddess religion (Christ [558]) and/or feminism itself (cf. the introduction to Daly's 1978 edition of [157]). For other feminist theologians, however, this empowerment entails various modifications and/or re-conceptualizations of classically stated "christologies" (i.e., understandings about who Jesus is): e.g., Brock [432], McLaughlin [439] and the sources identified by Darling Smith [434]. Third, for others yet (e.g., Carter Heyward [435] and Rosemary Radford Ruether [440, 441]) the feminist reconstruction of Christology entails *both* an abandonment of the triumphalism and ethnocentrism frequently found in Christological writing and symbolization *and* a corresponding use of Christological symbols as bridges--rather than barriers--to communication in a pluralistically grounded and ecumenically based dialogue. Finally, for several feminist theologians writing in the early to mid 1990s, the feminist reconstruction of Christology entails an appropriation of the Sophia/Wisdom tradition for Jesus and a corresponding spirituality and re-imagining of Jesus as the [feminist] Wisdom of God (cf. Aldredge-Clanton [432] and Johnson [438]). Sources developing these many perspectives are listed below, and together they evidence the enormous diversity in feminist Christology.

One further point is important here. Two emphases often ignored within the literature are those of the racist and anti-Semitic biases carried culturally by conventional Christological images (although see Ruether's early work ([172] and [440]) and see Heyward below [437]). Since the late 1980s, however, several sources have attempted a redress of these biases, with Jacqueline Grant's *White Women's Christ and Black Women's Jesus* [254] standing as the well known critique of racist assumptions implicit in many early feminist works, and various sources seeking to dismantle the anti-Semitism of New Testament and later biblical exegesis (see Ruether [299] and Schüssler Fiorenza [238]).

[431] Aldredge-Clanton, Jann. *In Search of the Christ-Sophia: An Inclusive Christology for Liberating Christians.* Mystic, CT: Twenty-Third Publications, 1995.
In a response to the question first posed formally by Ruether ("Can a Male Savior Save Women?" [441]) this text focuses on a resurrection based Christology with the imagery and implications of the Bible's "Wisdom" passages--its descriptions and appellations of Hokmah/Sophia--serving as the main frames for its Spirit-filled Christology. Aldredge-Clanton begins by making the case for an inclusive Christology: "Seeing Christ in exclusively male images places external and internal limits on Christ's living within and ministering through women" (p. 5), and the introduction of feminine terms such as "Sophia" and "She" for [the risen] Christ serves to rectify this problem. Aldredge-Clanton then summarizes the biblical motifs Hokmah/Sophia and the ways in which they open out a richer Christological experience. Her discussion is intended for a lay audience and for use within congregations, and to that end, she summarizes the general Christological literature, the implications of a Sophia Christology for spirituality, social justice, ecclesiology and ministry, and within these all, Christian worship. Fully two chapters provide worship resources--prayers, hymns, calls to worship etc., first for the seasons of the liturgical year and then for specific occasions such as the need for healing and renewal (for victims of violence), empowerment, birthing, and other areas of feminist, inclusive emphasis. This is a very readable text, with strong endorsements by both nationally known feminists such as Ruether and M.T. Winter, and by feminists more local to Aldredge-Clanton's own ministry, i.e., Cindy Johnson (Founder and Director of *Bread for the Journey Proclamation Ministries*) and the Rev. Carolyn Bullard-Zerweck, of the Greater Dallas Community of Churches.

[432] Brock, Rita Nakashima. *Journeys by Heart: A Christology of Erotic Power.* New York: Crossroad, 1988.
This text challenges several of the "hero-like" assumptions attached to the language of Christian soteriology, but particularly those aligned with patriarchal family motifs (as expressed in classical trinitarian language) and those aligned with the motifs of atonement and restitution, as expressed in Anselm's classical casting of redemption. As an alternative to these, Brock presents the language of "heart...[her]...metaphor for the human self and [its] capacity for intimacy" as based upon vulnerability, openness and relationality. Brock develops her discussion in five chapters. In her first two chapters she examines "patriarchal ideologies...[to show]...the cost to...society of male

dominance..." for the latter causes people to lose their "...capacity to see the true meaning of love" (p. xiv). She grounds her discussion here in the psychological framework of object relations theory, and her intent is to unfold the fully relational character of the self and its capacity for love, with the latter being the capacity for intimacy and vulnerability, as contrasted with the way of patriarchy and its character as "unilateral power." Brock's third chapter is "The Feminist Redemption of Christ," and it is here that she grounds "salvation" in the relational character of love as intimacy and vulnerability, for here, she regrounds Christianity's heroic and patriarchal (read: unilateral) images of Christ (*viz.*, his traditional depiction as the divine and atoning son of God) through the more relational imagery "of heart," or the imagery of "Christa/Community," Brock's symbol for the loving empowerment of children healed by their capacity for vulnerability and intimacy. This is a key discussion for it synthesizes her earlier analysis of patriarchy as creating "false selves" through manipulation, control, and the assumption that love entails "fusion," and it applies it to the classical doctrinal language of the Trinity and Christ's suffering for humanity and its sins--including "original sin." Brock's closing chapters then complete the discussion though an analysis of Mark's Gospel to demonstrate both the "erotic" (that is, life liberating) powers of "heart," as manifested in the gospel language of exorcism and vulnerabilities of the Christa/Community resurrection memory. **NOTE**: This is a strong and personalized reconstruction of classic Christological teaching, and while it does not spell out the wider connections of "heart" Christology to the context of social theory (cf. Ruether **[191]**, with whom Brock disagrees), it nevertheless makes a compelling case at the interpersonal level. Second, her discussion lends strong support to exegetical studies which also focus the communal rather than "hero" readings of New Testament Christology (cf. D'Angelo **[397]**).

[433] D'Angelo, Mary Rose. "ABBA and 'Father': Imperial Theology in the Jesus Traditions." *Journal of Biblical Literature* 111 (1992): 611-630.
This article presents a fully documented critique of the 1933 thesis developed by Joachim Jeremias concerning Jesus' address of God as ABBA and the supposed uniqueness of this address on the grounds that: (1) it represents a *special teaching by Jesus*; because (2) it suggests an emotional intimacy unique to Jesus and God; because, (3) it is a term of address used by Jesus and Jesus alone--that is to say, it was a practice of addressing God used in neither the early church nor in the Judaism of Jesus's time. This study is important for two reasons. First, it provides literature that argues persuasively against the thesis developed by Jeremias, and thus against its subsequent exclusionary and anti-Semitic/anti-Jewish use. Second, D'Angelo's discussion thereby challenges the authority of those who currently use the Jeremias argument as a bulwark against changes in traditional liturgical language on behalf of feminist and/or inclusive concerns. D'Angelo concludes that while the metaphor of ABBA is important to the New Testament, its presence does not preclude the use of other metaphors for God, nor the fact that many metaphors are needed. For additional work by D'Angelo see **[397-398]** and see her commentary on "Colossians" in Schüssler Fiorenza **[345]**.

[434] Darling-Smith, Barbara. "A Feminist Christological Exploration." In *One Faith, Many Cultures: Inculturation, Indigenization and Contextualization*, edited by Ruy O. Costa, 71-80. Maryknoll, NY: Orbis, 1988.
After describing her own personal shift from evangelical to mainline Protestantism and her adoption of a liberationist theological perspective, the author contrasts three specifically feminist Christologies: the "metaphorical christology" of Sally McFague, the "sacramental christology" of Carter Heyward, and the "antipatriarchal christology" of Rosemary Radford Ruether. The author indicates that she finds "empowering and liberating images of Jesus' life" in each of these christologies, and she notes their consistent roots in the literature of the synoptic Gospels, rather than other New Testament sources. She acknowledges that further feminist work is necessary to combat the Bible's frequent devaluations of women, but she finds no incompatibility between her Christianity and her feminism. This discussion is brief and insightfully presented. Further, it illustrates the ecumenical potential of both the christologies under review, and the efforts of the feminist theologians who move beyond their confessional and denominational divides. For additional literature see May **[919]**, Tolbert **[284]**, O'Neill **[922]** and, of course, the writings of McFague **[244]**, Heyward **[199]**, and Ruether **[190-191]**.

[435] Davis, Ellen, ed. *Speaking of Christ: A Lesbian Feminist Voice/Carter Heyward*. New York: Pilgrim, 1989.
Three essays and twelve sermons comprise this brief "speaking of Christ" collection of Heyward's works written between 1984-1988. The essays are Christological in focus with the first two presenting Heyward's critique of the epistemic dualism she sees so prevalent in classical

(Chalcedonian and Anselmian) christology. Her third essay--also christological in focus--presents "theological lessons from Nicaragua:" a series of affirmations about the concreteness of life as lived by those unaccustomed to privilege and for whom Heyward has regularly advocated justice and human rights. For the sermons in this collection, editor Davis has culled twelve brief and wide ranging homilies. Four are memorials, *viz.*, to a friend who has died from AIDS; to the passing of Nelle Morton; to the honor of William Stringfellow, her first theological mentor; and to the memory of J. Brooke Mosley, an Episcopal priest known widely for his human rights activism. Two other sermons offer words of affirmation: first to seminarians preparing for theological examinations; and second, for friends assuming the garb of priesthood. Additional sermons depict the struggles and joys of those living with injustice in Nicaragua, and others still offer benedictions: one for "All the Saints" martyred on behalf of "love, peace, justice courage and compassion" and another for the members and friends (i.e., supporters and visionaries) of the Philadelphia Eleven on the tenth anniversary of their ordination. As with her other work these writings also emphasize the themes of justice, right relation and the becoming of God; but here less formally so, and apart from the three christological essays, in pastoral rather than academic terms.

[436] Gibson, Joan. "Could Christ Have Been Born a Woman? A Medieval Debate." *Journal of Feminist Studies in Religion* 8, no. 1 (1992): 65-82.
First, some background: An important dimension within both the theological and Christological discussions of feminism and salvation has been the argument posed by biblical and trinitarian fundamentalists to the effect that because Jesus was male, God *is* male, because Jesus was and is the *Son* of God. Further, the general feminist theological response to this point has been the three-pronged argument posed largely by Roman Catholic feminists, that: (a) the significant factor of salvation is that God became *incarnate* (and not incarnate as a male) and that, as such--and as much current biblical theology and research attests--(b) the biblical corpus reflects the culture of its time (here an androcentric, male-dominant perspective), but (c), given a different culture and time, God could theoretically have become incarnate as a female. It is this sequence of concerns to which the above essay by Gibson speaks, for Gibson's discussion documents the question as posed and debated from the twelfth to the fifteenth centuries. In particular, Gibson examines the extant commentaries on Peter Lombard's *Sentences,* for the latter do address the question, 'could Christ have been born a woman?' Gibson's own discussion documents the unfolding of this question as it turned on such considerations as philosophical and theological anthropology, the definition of person (*homo)*, the issue of "appropriateness," and the cultural and philosophical gender assumptions grounding various other, but related doctrinal developments through the fifteenth century. The discussion is detailed and the Latin sources well-documented.

[437] Heyward, Carter. "Must 'Jesus Christ' Be a Holy Terror?--Using Christ as a Weapon Against Jews, Women, Gays and Just About Everybody Else." In *Our Passion for Justice: Images of Power, Sexuality and Liberation,* 211-221. New York: Pilgrim, 1984.
Presented in 1981 as a paper for Jewish and Christian "feminists of faith," this discussion highlights the ideological and social control functions of traditional Christology relative to the disenfranchised groups indicated in its title. In her discussion Heyward calls attention to the (then current) feminist struggle over maintaining doctrinal continuity with Christianity's historical trinitarian and Christological teaching (as developed from the early church councils of Nicea and Chalcedon), and she calls for a "discontinuity" with traditional Christology to avoid its ethnocentric and triumphalist orientations. She focuses "right relation" as the framework for interpreting Christianity's universal/particular tensions, and she closes with an affirmation of Christianity's more universal possibilities as precisely a religion of "right relation." Although now largely surpassed by current literature, Heyward's essay stands as an early and courageous witness to the efforts and struggles for inclusivity characteristic of the literature during the mid and late 1980s, *and,* despite its limitations, the forces that would yet prevail against such inclusivity.

[438] Johnson, Elizabeth A. "Jesus, the Wisdom of God: A Biblical Basis for Non-Androcentric Christology." *Ephemerides Theologicae Lovanienses* 61 (1985): 261-294.
Mindful that the "maleness of Jesus has been used to identify the humanity of male human beings as normative and exclusively capable of the representation of God" (p. 263), Johnson surveys sixty years of Sophia-Wisdom research literature to address the question of whether "there can be a full Christology which is faithful to the hard won insights of the tradition's proclamation at the same time that it breaks out of the usual androcentric pattern" (p. 263). Her answer is clearly in the affirmative, and to accomplish this Christological reconstruction she examines: (1) the imagery of

Sophia in Jewish Tradition; (2) the Wisdom Christology of the New Testament; and (3) the use of Wisdom Christology in the Post-Biblical Period. Her survey illustrates how the female imagery of Sophia was first celebrated as a positive and legitimate image of God, but was then subsumed into masculine motifs under the influence of patriarchal culture and androcentric assumptions. Her conclusions stress the potential of female wisdom imagery for Christological thinking and "the possibility of a Christology...which uses in addition to categories of Father and Son or God and His Word the categories of Sophia-God and her child, who is Sophia incarnate" (p. 293). Ecumenical in scope, this comprehensively documented study provides a Christological parallel to both Schüssler Fiorenza's reconstruction of Christian origins [195] and trinitarian discussions not premised upon a fundamentalist reading of Father-Son-Spirit as the literal name of God. For material that extends Johnson's work in psychological categories, see Rae and Marie-Daly [560]. Additionally, for Johnson's own extensions see her book length discussions [231] and [232].

[439] McLaughlin, Eleanor. "'Christ My Mother': Feminine Naming and Metaphor in Medieval Spirituality." *St. Luke's Journal* 18 (1975): 228-249.
This early essay by McLaughlin provides an immediate and simply written introductory overview to medieval spirituality and the imagery of motherhood as predicated of God. McLaughlin begins by addressing the conflict over the ordination of women in the Episcopal Church emerging during the early 1970s, and she says her purpose is two-fold: It is "to look...to the presence or role of the female... in the words and images used by medieval Christians for God, whom the priest in some way symbolizes" (p. 229) and it is to re-examine the assumption of maleness as inherent in the "Tradition's" notion of priesthood. Literature bearing on "Mary, the Mother of God" is for practical reasons omitted. Instead, early patristical references are cited, as are references from Anselm, Marguerite d'Oingt (a thirteenth century prioress of a convent of Carthusian nuns), Gertrud the Great, Mechthild of Hackeborn, Julien of Norwich, Catherine of Siena, St. Bernard and St. Francis of Assisi. For each, relevant passages are cited in full with "mother," "friend," and "lover" images detailed. To close, McLaughlin reflects upon the significance of androgenous and non gender-based language for God. She calls attention to, respectively: the medieval spirituality of God as Love; the pre-modern unsecularized world view of medieval life and its concomitant emphasis on immanence rather than transcendence; and last, the absence of sexual reductionism so prevalent in the contemporary period. Written decades ago, this essay is still relevant and informative, and pastoral in the best sense of the word. **NOTE:** For a more detailed discussion of Jesus and mother imagery in the medieval period, see Carolyn Walker Bynum, *Jesus as Mother: Studies in the Spirituality of the High Middle Ages.* Berkeley and Los Angeles, Univ. of California Press, 1982.

[440] Ruether, Rosemary Radford. "Christology and Jewish Christian Relations." In *To Change the World,* 31-43, New York: Crossroad, 1983.
Tied to her feminism through its rejection of imperialist Christology (cf. [441]), this essay summarizes the judgment/promise, particularism/universalism, and letter/spirit motifs of Christianity's historical anti-Judaic myth and the theological needs that must be met if the myth is adequately to be rejected and Christology redefined. Overall, Ruether argues that it is Christianity's understanding of "fulfilled messianism" that needs to be redefined, for it yet grounds the anti-Jewish proof texting of the patristic period and its carryover into: (1) contemporary exegesis, preaching and theology; (2) the triumphalist (as compared to universalist) elements of Christian teaching; and (3) the law/grace, spirit/letter, and old/new Adam dualisms of Christian teaching which continue Christianity's tendency to project "the shadow side of human life on to the Jews as the symbol of the fallen and unfulfilled side of human existence" (p. 41). To correct such historical prejudices and their social consequences, Christology needs to recast in terms that are proleptic and anticipatory; i.e., in terms that see Jesus as "one who announced...messianic hope, but who also died in that hope crucified on the cross of unredeemed human history" (p. 42). Similarly, Christians must recognize that "The final point of reference for the messianic advent still remains in the future," a point well acknowledged by liberation theology. Last, Christians must recognize that "...the cross and resurrection are contextual to a particular historical community...[and]...that does not mean that these are the only ways [hope] can happen; or that other people may not continue parallel struggles on different grounds...[e.g., Jews and the Exodus/Torah tradition]" (pp. 42-43). Rather, a genuine universalism must be found, one rooted in "...new possibilities of human solidarity in our differing ways of mediating hope in the midst of defeat" (p. 42).

[441] Ruether, Rosemary Radford. "Christology and Feminism: Can a Male Savior Save Women?" In *To Change the World,* 45-56, New York: Crossroad, 1983.
Ruether first sets the framework for her discussion by noting the ways in which christology has been used against women. The "anti-women use of christology is expressed most strongly in

Aquinas (although also in Augustine) where, following Aristotle, Thomas develops an ontologically based male/female hierarchy that, in turn, makes the incarnation of the Logos as male, an ontological necessity" (p. 45). Ruether then calls attention to both the application of this male christology to the question of ordination within the Catholic, Anglican and Orthodox traditions and its use for the maintenance of an all male clergy. However, in contrast to positions that view the male symbol of Christ as "hopelessly patriarchal," Ruether argues that the tradition exhibits other (albeit limited) christological images: *viz.*, those of an "androgenous Christ" and an "iconoclastic" Christ. According to Ruether, androgenous images of Christ can be seen in selected gnostic writings, in the mysticism of several medievalists, (e.g., Julien of Norwich) and in the writings of nineteenth century sectarian and utopian groups (e.g., the Shakers). These images stress the nurturing aspect of Christ, but are still androcentric in that they ultimately require women to pattern themselves (in one way or another) after males. More fruitful is the "prophetic-iconoclastic Christ," the image of Christ as the "critic," rather than the "vindicator" of the social order (p. 55). The roots of this iconoclastic image are solidly biblical and keep one attuned to the gospel emphases of Christ as the "liberator-servant" or the one who images a "new humanity of service and mutual empowerment" (p. 56). A third image in the tradition, the "imperialist" Christ, is also detailed by Ruether, but as the legitimating image of the antiwomen use of christology, it is, in Ruether's judgment, of no value. NOTE: For an overview of Ruether's work in Christology see Mary Hembrow Snyder's text (not abstracted here), *The Christology of Rosemary Radford Ruether: A Critical Introduction*. Mystic, CT: Twenty-Third Publications, 1988. Snyder clearly summarizes Ruether's work and provides helpful comparisons with several other mainline perspectives.

[442] Stevens, Maryanne, ed. *Reconstructing the Christ Symbol: Essays in Feminist Christology*. New York: The Paulist Press, 1993.
This text presents the six papers prepared for the feminist Christology symposium, "Who Do You Say That I Am," held at Creighton University in April of 1992. The contributors include keynoter Rosemary Radford Ruether, Asian-American feminist theologian Rita Nakashima Brock, womanist theologian Jacquelyn Grant, "Americanist" Marina Herrara, Catholic feminist Elizabeth A. Johnson, and medievalist scholar and Episcopal priest, Eleanor McLaughlin. Each of the presenters provided work that synthesized their main views, with Ruether's essay providing an historical overview of traditional, patriarchal Christology, and a call for perspectives that respect particularities and foster universal rather than parochial dialog. In turn, Brock and Grant synthesize their respective positions, with previous works signaling each writer's main theme, i.e., Brock's emphasis on christology and child abuse ("Losing Your Innocence, But Not Your Hope"), and Grant's identification of Christ as particularly, a co-sufferer with and liberator of African American women. Eschewing the term feminist because of its perceived limitation to sexism and insufficient attention to patriarchal class oppression, Marina Herrara describes herself as an "Americanist," whose Christology focuses Jesus as working relationally towards empowerment, rather than hierarchically for "power over." In a word, Jesus is a "linker" not a "ranker." Last, Elizabeth Johnson provides a very readable synthesis of her work on Jesus as Sophia, and McLaughlin returns to the issue of Jesus's maleness to provide a most provocative and informative discussion on how body symbolism works and why liberal feminist theological responses to the maleness of Jesus miss the mark because they are still addressing the dualism of Chalcedon (humanness and divinity) and not the dualism (maleness and femaleness) shaping today's experience and symbolic needs. Her response synthesizes medieval God-Christ-mother images and the potential of 'cross-dressing' as a hermeneutical frame for the gender issues attached to current Christ symbol needs.

[443] Young, Pamela Dickey. "Diversity in Feminist Christology." *Studies in Religion/Sciences Religieuses* 21 (1992): 81-90.
This essay surveys various feminist writings in christology to indicate the diversity of positions feminist theologians hold relative to four questions, which in the author's mind, should be asked of any feminist theologian. The questions stem ultimately, says Young, from Ruether's general question ('Can a Male Savior Save Women?' [441]) and as expanded by Young these four questions are: "(1) What understanding of salvation is operative? (2) What is the role of Jesus? (3) What is the relationship between Jesus and the Christ or christology? [and] (4) What is the significance of Jesus' maleness?" (p. 81). Prima facie, the questions appear engaging and Young suggests their power for classifying the writings of such theologians as Ruether, Grant, Brock, and Mollenkott to name but four of her eight authors. The discussion fails, however, for not only are the questions too diffusely defined at the beginning of her essay, but the theologians examined differ widely in terms of their own premises and assumptions and few of these differences are taken into account in Young's analysis. For more helpful overviews of the literature see Darling-Smith above **[434]** and the summary chapters in Johnson **[231]** and LaCugna **[273]**.

NOTE: For related literature in addition to the entries above, see Hopkins [243]; Grant [636]; and see the developing literature on Asian feminist Christology as cited by Fabella and Park [932] and Chung Hyun Kyung [935].

C. Feminist Theology and Mariology

The feminist reconstruction of Marian literature and symbolization remains underdeveloped, although as Johnson's work on the motherhood of God [422] indicates, the Marian tradition is rich with feminist metaphors for God and the women-church experience. Below are Johnson's early essays, together with entries by Borreson, Hines, and Ruether indicating the ecumenical and potential women-church significance of Marian symbolization. Aldditionally, see Jane Schberg's exegetical discussion "The Infancy of Mary of Nazareth," pp. 708-728, in Schüssler Fiorenza's *Searching the Scriptures*, Vol II [345].

[444] Borreson, Elizabeth Kari. "Mary in Catholic Theology." In *Mary in the Churches*, edited by Hans Kung and Jurgen Moltmann, 48-56. New York: Seabury, 1983.
In succinctly informative terms this article does two things. It first identifies the influence of androcentric assumptions upon three approaches to Marian thought (*viz.*, the Christological, ecclesiological and Mariological approaches to Marian thought); and second, it considers the theological and ecumenical implications of such androcentric assumptions, together with the power of sociocultural constructs for theology. Fundamentally a study directed to ecumenical questions, this piece clearly portrays the significance of androcentric assumptions for the theologizing process and its implications for women via Marian thought. By way of example, for Christological-Marian thought (i.e., Marian thought generated initially by early church questions about Christ), androcentrism has dictated the biological bases of *theotokos* and *Mater Dei* symbolism(s) that in light of contemporary gynecology "makes Mary's role far more important than is compatible with the theocentrism of the great ecumenical councils" (p. 50). Similarly, the ecclesiological symbolism of Mary as a "type" of the church (as based on the Eve-Mary parallels of patristic writing) is also grounded in androcentrist assumptions, and this symbolism is now "void" given the recognized illegitimacy of active and passive roles associated with the nuptial imagery. Third, the specifically Mariological dogmas of the Immaculate Conception and Mary's Assumption are also based "wholly on conjectural anthropological theories" (p. 51) and have as a consequence, "become literally incomprehensible" (p. 52). Borreson's discussion extends provocatively into Post-Vatican II images of Mary and should be read in conjunction with Elisabeth Johnson's work [422]. NOTE: Readers may find other entries in this *Concilium* volume helpful, although they are not reviewed here. See, e.g., Virgil Elizondo's "Mary and the Poor: A Model of Evangelizing," Catharina Halkes' "Mary and Women," and Maria Kassel's "Mary and the Human Psyche Considered in the Light of Depth Psychology."

[445] Hines, Mary E. "Mary and the Prophetic Mission of the Church." *Journal of Ecumenical Studies* 28 (1991): 281-298.
This article accomplishes three things. First, it briefly summarizes the history of Marian doctrine and its associated patterns of devotion--up to and through twentieth century church literature, including the documents of Vatican II. Second, it contrasts these "traditional" perspectives with recastings of Marian symbolization, with the latter drawn from contemporary feminist and Latin American liberationist literature, e.g., Johnson [422] and Leonard Boff (see *The Maternal Face of God: The Feminine and Its Religious Expressions*. Trans. by Robert Barr and John Diercksmeier. SanFrancisco: Harper & Row, 1987, not reviewed in this volume) Last, it locates these contrasts within the context of ecclesiastical ecumenism, with selected Catholic, Lutheran and Anglican sources synthesized as a means of potential consensus vis a vis Mary's 'prophetic' role as a symbol of the church's post-Vatican II ecclesial pilgrimage.

[446] Johnson, Elizabeth A. "The Symbolic Character of Theological Statements About Mary." *Journal of Ecumenical Studies* 22 (1985): 312-335.
Ecumenically based theological language about Mary has often proved problematic, with Roman Catholics tied clearly to specific doctrinal pronouncements and a penchant for literalism concerning biblical statements about Mary, and Protestants tied to a de-emphasis on Mary and a tendency to see all Mariological statements as ultimately Christological in character. Johnson's discussion addresses this ecumenical polarity by developing the thesis that most theological statements about Mary may be interpreted as symbolic statements about the church, with the latter understood in is full communitarian sense, i.e., as "we Christians." According to Johnson, there are only two

Mariological statements—Mary as the "Mother of Jesus" and Mary as the "Mother of God"—precluded from this strategy of ecclesial-symbolic interpretation, because such an interpretive rule cannot apply to them. Such a rule can, however, apply to other Mariological statements (e.g., the doctrines of Mary's Immaculate Conception [proclaimed by Pius IX in 1854] and her Assumption into heaven [proclaimed by Pius XII in 1950]), and as applied, this rule indicates specific implications for the Christian community. These include the theological and historical preeminence of grace over sin, the inclusive reach of a saving God, and the eschatological but pilgrim grounding of the church's present historical existence. None of these insights may be ignored, Johnson argues, and each has ecumenical value. Principally they widen the context of dialogue across theological lines while maintaining regard for Protestant and Catholic sensibilities, and they provide a balance of eschatological and historical images that (theoretically) preclude the development of triumphalist ecclesiologies and imagery. This article is obviously important to students of ecumenics, but its ties to feminist theology cannot be overlooked. When read in conjunction with Johnson's other work [447] and [422], the full potential of her symbolic language principle becomes clear in that the autonomy of women becomes an appropriate image for the adulthood of Christian community and interaction, whether personally or across denominations.

[447] Johnson, Elizabeth A. "The Marian Tradition and the Reality of Women." *Horizons* 12 (1985): 116-135.
After noting the plurality of factors affecting the development of contemporary Mariological thought since Vatican II, Johnson surveys three feminist critiques of traditional Marian teaching: First that "the Marian tradition has been intrinsically associated with the denigration of the nature of women as a group" (p. 121); second, it has "dichotomized the being and roles of women and men in the community of disciples" (p. 124); third, it "has truncated the ideal of feminine fulfillment and wholeness" (p.126) The truth of the first charge rests (Johnson argues) with Christianity's historical association of women with evil and with Mary's status as an exception to this rule, as evidenced, for example, by the classical Eve-Mary/fall-redemption contrasts of patristic literature. The truth of the second critique rests with the gender alignment of activity and passivity within human experience, with males assigned the active dimension and females the passive. This roots in and is evident from the traditional assumptions attributed to Mary's "Magnificat" in Luke when an obedient response to a male God provides imagery for normative social patterns of submission to males and an ideal of complementarity in both social and ecclesial spheres. Finally, the truth of the third critique lies with three images historically developed about Mary, i.e., her status as "handmaiden," "virgin," and "mother," with these generating submissive, women-deprecating, and self-sacrificing roles for women. To combat the effects of these three critiques, Johnson offers a critical reinterpretation of imagery on which they are based. Thus, in contrast to assumptions of Mary's exemplary, exceptional status, Johnson points to the developing recognition of Mary as an individual and real person within Jesus' life. Second, to the assumptions of active and passive gender complementarity, Johnson emphasizes Mary's independent capacity to hear and enact the Word of God. Finally, to the handmaiden, virgin and mother imagery, Johnson highlights (again) Mary's courageous discipleship, her complete autonomy from males and her self-chosen opportunity for solidarity with other women. Johnson concludes that for the re-symbolization of Mariological thought to take shape, it must be supported by the real equality of women and men in the church, for which she maintains hope.

[448] Ruether, Rosemary Radford. *Mary: The Feminine Face of the Church.* Philadelphia: Westminster, 1977.
The grounding observation of this early work on feminine religious imagery is that those churches that are most venerating of Mary are the least supportive of women's progress and humanization in the secular sphere, and thus Ruether examines the biblical motifs of Goddess religion and contrasts them with elements of Marian doctrine, devotion and spirituality. Her goal is to find a "humanizing" element within Catholicism's extensive Marian tradition and in her final chapter she briefly examines the symbol of "women as church," with an attention to the history of women's victimization in an overly masculinized theology and its structures. The discussion is clear and well documented, and it remains an initial source for studying the development of Ruether's work in feminist ecclesiology, systematics and ethics.

D. Feminist Theology and The Church

At increasing rates, feminist theologians are writing about "the church." For some, e.g., large numbers of Catholic and Protestant laywomen and professional theologians, this means an attention to the women-church movement as a space of inclusive and paracongregational, women-identified worship—cf. the women-church literature in Chapter 19, and Ruether's 1993 overview below [449]. For others, e.g., many globally based feminists, an attention to "the church" affords the opportunity to examine not only the international character of the women-church movement (cf. Hunt [918] and O'Connor [921]), but, too, the nature of "authority" in Christianity, including: (1) its hierarchical histories and current possibilities (see Russell [249] and [250]); (2) its ties to Christian mission worldwide (Russell [911]); (3) its ecumenical significance relative to the suffering of women in "third world" countries (see Benavides [914] and Oduyoye [920]); and (4) its role in legitimating violence to women, whether biblically (Dodson Gray [241]), ideologically (Copeland and Schüssler Fiorenza [869]), or congregationally (Cooper-White [865]). Because the feminist theological literature on "the church" encompasses so many facets of Christian institutional and organizational life, the sources cited here are cross referenced in terms of their relevance to other and at times quite specific discussions. Hence, for the bulk of the literature, the reader should browse titles listed in Chapter 19 under the subheading of "The Women-Church Movement," and in Chapter 22 and 23 under the headings of feminism's "Global Voices" and "The Church and Violence to Women" respectively. Absent these, Ruether's essay below provides an historical overview of the women-church movement and its general development, while Thistlethwaite's early essay [450] previews much of her subsequent work.

[449] Ruether, Rosemary Radford. "The Women-Church Movement in Contemporary Christianity." In *Women's Leadership in Marginal Religion: Explorations Outside the Mainstream*, edited by Catherine Wessinger, 196-210. Urbana, IL: University of Illinois Press, 1993.

Next to her 1985 book length discussion of the women-church phenomenon [193], this is Ruether's most synthesized statement about the women-church movement. Further, because she writes descriptively here, in an effort to chronicle the movement (rather than to break new theological ground), her essay serves as a solid introduction to the women-church movement and an especially informative overview of its main concerns. In her summary she identifies: (1) the various developments that eventuated in the American women-church movement (e.g., the rise of American feminism, the ordination movements in the American Protestant and Catholic churches generally and the temporally close histories of the American Episcopal, and Catholic Women's Ordination Conference(s) specifically); (2) the significance of clericalism within patriarchal Christianity and its replacement by the more communal norms of the women-church movement; (3) the general assumptions grounding the theological anthropology and creation based spirituality of most women-church advocates; (4) the values grounding the movement's positions on "sexuality and lifestyle"; (5) a summary of the movement's rejection of patriarchal symbols and their social and theological assumptions; and (6) a recognition that the movement yet needs clarity about its ability to span tradition and goddess religious/liturgical images. This article is strongly recommended for those seeking an initial history of the women-church movement, its main emphases and key theological assumptions.

[450] Thistlethwaite, Susan Brooks. *Metaphors for the Contemporary Church*. New York: Pilgrim, 1983.

This early volume by Thistlethwaite argues "...for a more authentic approach to the doctrine of the church for all Christians" (p. xiv), and reflects several of the themes that will eventually come to characterize Thistlethwaite's later work. Last it presents these themes from within a dialogue with traditional Christian categories, symbols and motifs. Thematic emphases important to her later work include: (1) a concern for gender inclusivity and the struggle of women to combat the detrimental effects of power-based hierarchies; (2) an attention to liberation theologies, peacemaking and an end to violence as the primary locus of theology; (3) an undeterred commitment to the ecumenical possibilities of women in all churches, despite the presence of racism within both the women's movement and the peace movement; (4) a strong commitment to the assumption that Christian symbolism must be appropriated and rethought in terms developed by varying groups currently excluded from full church participation; and (5) a relational vision that seeks to overcome "theologies of exclusion" in favor of theologies of inclusive and mutual social-theological construction. As a work written largely for a popular lay audience, this volume is well-documented and clearly written. Its tone is challenging on issues of conflict, and its self conscious attempt to use metaphors creatively in an effort to integrate liberationist and other perspectives into traditional Christian discourse is obvious. It differs from Thistlethwaite's most recent work, however, in that its challenges are yet are rooted in an attempt to integrate liberationist thinking within organized religion, rather than unfold it as a form of systematic theology directed to the establishment of an alternative community perspective. For the latter, see [276].

E. Feminist Theology and the Trinity

Of all of Christianity's core symbols, perhaps none is more intensely discussed than that of the Trinity. From within the context of feminist theology the discussion is two-fold. First, attention is directed to the social consequences of this doctrine: its sacralization of patriarchy, its evolutionary language, and its cultural capacities to image hierarchy as a divinely proscribed form of social organization. Second, attention is directed to the "recovery" and/or reconstruction of this symbol in terms of its relational and egalitarian emphases. These latter include the development of inclusive language, the use of the Trinity as a grounding icon for a renewed theological anthropology, and at the level of formal and informal organizational structures, the attempt to generate lateral and democratic patterns of interaction rather than hierarchical and patriarchal patterns.

Similarly, the discussion of the Trinity by non-feminist theologians is equally intense, and this seems to hold whether these non-feminist theologians are passively androcentric or pro-actively antifeminist. Thus in contrast to feminist discussions, the non-feminist literature presents a second range of concerns. At one end of the spectrum are discussions seemingly sympathetic to feminist argumentation, but ultimately unyielding with respect to linguistic and hierarchical trinitarian assumptions. At the other end of the spectrum are discussions clearly vituperative and punitive in nature, in that they charge not only feminist "theologies" of the Trinity, but specific feminist theologians as well, with the heretical denial and/or destruction of the Christian church and its faith. Sources illustrating the feminist reconstruction of trinitarian doctrine are presented below, but particularly relevant sources abstracted elsewhere in the bibliography include the following: (1) Catherine LaCugna's 1992 book length discussion of the Trinity [234] and her particular applications of trinitarian theology to baptism [520] and the discussion of women's ordination within Roman Catholicism [780]; (2) the early methodological pieces of feminist theology, and especially those by Farley [166] and Andolsen [467]; (3) the feminist biblical discussion of Sophia and Jesus and especially works by Johnson [438] and Schüssler Fiorenza [195]; (4) selections from the feminist literature on liturgy and worship--e.g., Collins [517], Duck [457], Procter-Smith [522], and Gail Ramshaw [523]; (5) Elizabeth Johnson's *She Who Is* [232] (and especially its closing chapters); and (6) Mary Ann Suchocki's discussion of power, the Trinity and feminist theological method [427]. NOTE: An important factor that should not be ignored in this discussion is the 1994 sociological study published by Winter, Lummis and Stokes [153]. Their research demonstrates clearly that of all the religious symbols painful to women socialized within patriarchal Christianity, it is the "power symbol" of the Trinity--as Father, Son and Holy Spirit-- that cuts most deeply. The sources below should be read in conjunction with both their data and the entries cited above.

1. Early Literature (1980-1985)

[451] Oxford-Carpenter, Rebecca. "Gender and the Trinity." *Theology Today* 41 (1984): 7-25.

This early article identifies six "solutions" to what the author describes as the "gender-Trinity" problem, or the struggle of contemporary Christians to come to grips with the late second century emergence of an "all masculine" image of God. These solutions include: (1) a re-affirmation of exclusively masculine imagery for God; 2) a complete feminization of God imagery by way of goddess religion; (3) the use of both masculine and feminine images for God (i.e., the development of an androgenous god language); (4) the addition of a specifically feminine persona to the currently reigning three personae of the Trinity; (5) a "de-sexing" of the Trinity through the use of non-sexual images; and (6) a "de-personalizing" of the Trinity via the use of nature imagery and/or abstract categories. The author notes and assess the strengths and weaknesses of each solution, and in the light of both her background as an educational psychologist and her reading of current theology, she finds only three solutions with merit: androgenous language, and the "de-sexing" and de-personalization of trinitarian language. She therefore suggests the necessity for multiple metaphors for describing religious experience and a "rejection" of the "tyranny of traditional religious language" (p. 24). Theological readers may initially be put off by the author's suggestion to "de-personalize" trinitarian language, but her actual emphasis is toward the use of philosophical and non-anthropomorphic language. Likewise, her discussion lacks a grounded critique of misogyny-- and thus critical feminist liberation theologians will be disappointed--but Oxford-Carpenter's purpose here is synthesis, not critique. Additionally, she writes as a free-lance theologian and thus the discussion is developed apart from the demands of confessional conformities. This is a thorough synthesis for its time, clearly written with literature current through the early 1980s, a "sleeper" within the then developing genre of feminist trinitarian reflection.

[452] Ramshaw-Schmidt, Gail. "Naming the Trinity: Orthodoxy and Inclusivity."
    Worship 58 (1984): 491-498.
This article attempts a balance between "orthodoxy and inclusivity" vis a vis traditional trinitarian
language through the development of an alternative and *supplemental* designation for the Trinity:
that of "God the Abba, the Servant, The Paraclete." The rationale for this supplemental formulation
is two-fold. First, the recent plethora of research on gender and God-language has generated a
consensus of six principles that both permit a re-grounding of trinitarian language and suggest at the
same time the parameters of its development. Second, an examination of the traditional formula
suggests its congruence with a soteriological image that can itself be recast, so that a supplemental
formula may be developed. At the heart of the traditional formula suggests Ramshaw-Schmidt, lies
an image of soteriology that is atonement based and articulated through the categories of sin and its
forgiveness. Without denying the legitimacy and theological affirmations of this metaphor,
however, one can also cast Christianity's soteriological emphasis in terms consonant with twentieth
century "existential chaos" (both individual and social), and one can thereby affirm God as the
"meaning" met in such suffering. The benefits of this soteriological recasting are that it permits a
synthesis of: (a) specifically biblical categories for trinitarian affirmation, i.e., those of God, the
Abba, the Servant and the Paraclete; and (b) a synthesis faithful to both the classic normative
formula and the need for an ungendered trinitarian appellation. For Ramshaw's more recent and
liturgically directed discussion, see [523].

[453] Suchocki, Majorie. "The Unmale God: Reconsidering the Trinity." *Quarterly
    Review* 3 (1983): 34-49.
Suchochi's task here is to demonstrate that the terms "Father, Son and Holy Spirit" do not always
or even necessarily need to be heard as masculine in nature. Rather, they can be released from their
historical "sexist moorings" and ultimately prove a symbol through which humanity can again "Let
God be God." Her task is accomplished in three basic steps. After demonstrating the pervasiveness
of the masculinity of Trinitarian language as a God symbol, Suchochi asks if this was always the
case, and that if not, how this circumstance came to be and might, in turn, be altered. Her answers
to these questions proceed to step two, a review of the biblical imagery of God as historically
concerned for justice in society--in both testaments--and to, in the Christian context of
evangelization, an eventual use of philosophical language to depict the biblical emphases of God's
constancy of character. The latter, however, also brought about the simultaneous effect of the
language becoming "designations for the nature of God, in and for 'himself'" (p. 43) and thus there
developed a language of God's "masculinity," as dissociated from the concern for social justice
evidenced in biblical images in both "Old" and "New" Testaments. Last, to re-infuse the initial
biblical images with their emphases of God's constancy of character as a God of justice, Suchochi
makes three suggestions: (a) an extended and deliberate attention to the metaphorical character of
all language about God--with contrasting images of God providing the means to that deliberate
attention; (b) the removal of all pronouns in speech about God (the biblical and historical precedents
for which is the substitution of the other language for the tetragrammatron of Exodus 3:14 and the
piety of Judaism's "G-d" language); and (c) the abandonment of theology's Hellenistic categories
for those more responsive to contemporary motifs and images--as found for example, in
contemporary process philosophy. This is a clear, helpful beginning point for a reconsideration of
masculine trinitarian language, but Suchochi's more substantive (and recent) argument is [427].

2.   Responses to the Early Literature

[454] Belonick, Deborah Melacky. "Revelation and Metaphors: The Significance of the
    Trinitarian Names, Father, Son and Holy Spirit." *Union Seminary Quarterly
    Review* 40 (1985): 31-42.
To demonstrate what she views as the non-convincing character of the feminist charge that
trinitarian language is both non-inclusive and a deification of maleness, Belonick reviews Eastern
patristical writings to marshal five 'point/counter-point' arguments. These arguments are as
follows. First, while it is true that some passages in the fathers are degrading to women, it is also
true that women are praised in the patristical writings. Thus, following Clark [296] one must say
that the fathers are "ambivalent" about and not condemning of women. Second, "given instances in
which the justice of the Church freed women from injustices of the neighboring culture, it becomes
contradictory to assert that the names 'Father,' 'Son' and 'Holy Spirit' are products of a church
unable to rid itself of patriarchal influences" (p. 37). Third, it is "equally unconvincing to
argue... that the traditional trinitarian doxology resulted from ignorance of the biological process of
creation," for Chrysostom knew that "by the commingling of their seeds is the child produced" (p.
37). Fourth, it seems "equally implausible that contempt for femininity caused the Church to call

God 'Father' and 'Son' rather than 'Mother' and Daughter'...since the mode of life of the Holy Spirit was associated with femininity" (pp. 37-38). Fifth, it was women themselves who (at least in the Eastern Church) were proclaimers of the Trinity and in some cases teachers of the Fathers. Belonick does not name any feminist theologians against whom she argues. Nonetheless, she draws several conclusions from her research. Chief among them are: (1) the names 'Father,' 'Son' and 'Holy Spirit' are revealed names, i.e., personal names for the Trinity rather than indicators of sexuality in God; and (2) "The historical context in which the terms 'Father, Son and Holy Spirit' were used does not support assumptions that these names were products of a male culture or hierarchy" (p. 39). In the absence of critically cited literature, Belonick's discussion appears ideologically rooted, and thus the reader is referred to LaCugna [234] and McFague [244] for more detailed materials.

[455] Bondi, Roberta C. "Some Issues Relevant to a Modern Interpretation of the Language of the Nicene Creed, With Special Reference to 'Sexist' Language." *Union Seminary Quarterly Review* 40 (1985): 21-30.
A self-acknowledged conservative who has traditionally favored "preserving the words and symbols of the early Church just as they stand," Bondi's purpose here is "to examine some of the factors relevant to the apparently patriarchal language of the Creed" (p.21). These factors include (1) a 'symbolic link between sex and death' (as evidenced by the patriarchal writings on celibacy, marriage and women); (2) the Chrysostom tradition of the 'unknowability of God and the need for metaphorical language' when speaking of God; (3) the significance of the different wordings of Nicea and I Constantinople; (4) the tension between truth affirmations per se and biblical/non-biblical language; (5) the acknowledged reality of alternative interpretations of biblical texts on both God and male/female interactions; and (6) the increasing numbers of women who are alienated from church life because of a language perceived as alien and suspect. As she examines each of these factors, Bondi builds the general argument that it was the *faith* of Nicea and not its specific "wordings" that I Constantinople affirmed. Thus, one need not be a literalist in terms of specific words and especially so if specific wordings lead people away from the gospel faith to which the Creed is directed (cf. p. 24). Further, given both the misogyny of the fathers and the fact of female images for God in both the Old Testament and the Syriac tradition, it becomes reasonable to consider the use of feminine imagery for God within the context of church worship. Thus, as regards the Creed, Bondi recommends that "we avoid all names for God that are gender linked, except for those names which refer to the Incarnation; for our insistence on the pre-eminence of masculine names hurts our witness to the very God we confess" (p. 28).

[456] Hein, S. Mark. "Gender and Creed: Confessing a Common Faith." *The Christian Century* 102 (1985): 379-381.
This article presents an admittedly selective survey of the faith/language issues surrounding a World Council of Churches proposal for establishing the Nicene-Constantinopolitan creed as a symbol of Christianity's apostolic and ecumenically diverse faith. An issue of importance to author Hein, however, is how the term "father" shall or shall not be used within such a creed, and to demonstrate his concern, he surveys two broad perspectives concerning the use of language as a vehicle for expressing faith--and these as they apply to the term "father" in the creed. One position holds that faith and its linguistic expression are indeed "separable" and thus the creedal reference to God may be expressed in non-gendered language. Alternatively, a second position holds that faith and its linguistic expression are not easily separable and that the term "father" expresses something unique within Christianity's apostolic faith and its creedal expression. Author Hein addresses this issue through recourse to Cappadocian theology and the implications of gendered language within the creed for an understanding of generativity. He concludes, however, that no immediate solution to this discussion is evident, and he expresses a hope for continued dialogue on the matter. Feminist readers will find Hein's characterization of "generativity" limiting--in that it assumes a biologically passive and temporally receptive role to women in reproduction, while readers committed to such an assumption will in all likelihood find it verified in Hein's brief reflections. For literature more feminist in approach, see Farley [166], LaCugna [234] and [458], and Duck [457].

3. Literature from 1986-1992

[457] Duck, Ruth. *Gender and the Name of God: The Trinitarian Baptismal Formula.* New York: Pilgrim, 1991.
This text is an expansion of Duck's doctoral thesis from Boston University's School of Theology. It seeks an expression of the Christian baptismal formula that is, on the one hand, fully reflective of the church's offer for new life in Jesus Christ, and on the other, freed from the grip of patriarchal

assumptions and social relations as reflected in the traditional baptismal formula. It is rooted largely in the assumptions characteristic of LaCugna's [234] work (and with whom Duck briefly studied at Notre Dame), but in contrast to LaCugna's general literature it focuses specifically on the immediate pastoral needs of pastors and parishioners in local congregations. Duck begins by noting the existential difficulties attached (for many) to the preponderance of masculine language for God and the need for an alternative metaphor that does not contradict the premises of baptism while cast, albeit within the formula of patriarchal language. She argues that "speaking of God in masculine but not feminine terms...reinforces patriarchal patterns of valuing the male and devaluing the female" and that the enormity of statistics on sexual abuse signals caution with respect to male language for God. Moreover, she makes a paralleling argument for "mother" language for God, indicating that "parenting" language per se may not be the most immediately adequate. Second, Duck challenges the church organizational assumption that baptismal agreement must precede church structural union and that the latter is, in fact, helped by the traditional formula. Her remaining chapters then detail the specifics of her argument, including her discussions of metaphor and revelation, statistics on father incest and sexual abuse, the nature of worship apart from patriarchy, the meaning of trinitarian naming, criteria for developing new baptismal formulae, and by way of closure, a review of specific suggestions for altering the standard baptismal language. For her own part she would revive the ancient practice of communal questions and answers involving commitments from and/or on behalf of the baptismal candidate and as cast (partially) in the language of God as "Source" as presented by Ruether in a women-church liturgy. The discussion is strong, pastorally directed, and well documented with both liberal and conservative sources. It is also, as Kay's review [462] indicates, fearsome to patriarchal perspectives.

[458] LaCugna, Catherine Mowry. "The Trinitarian Mystery of God." In *Systematic Theology, Volume I,* edited by Francis Schüssler Fiorenza and John P. Galvin, 149-192. Minneapolis: Fortress, 1991.

After her book length discussion [234], this essay is perhaps the best and most readable summary of LaCugna's work on the Trinity. It begins (as does her book) with her acknowledgment of trinitarian doctrine as essentially forgotten within Christian tradition or as, alternatively, a conundrum of mathematical gymnastics. It then continues with her basic arguments: first, her grounding premise that trinitarian doctrine is, in fact, the meeting of grace, redemption and the mystery of God. That in her words, "oikonomia" (the mystery of redemption) is "theologia" (the mystery of God)--and second--that, as such, trinitarian teaching is eminently practical in addressing issues of worship, ethics, spirituality and doctrine. By way of overview, LaCugna traces both the biblical roots of trinitarian language and the progression of controversies that generated it. Her discussion is sensitive to historical Latin and Greek theologies, the 'economic' and 'immanent' perspective so well developed by the late Karl Rahner, contemporary ecumenical problems dealing with such long historical issues as the "filioque" clause, and in her closing remarks, the need for a balance between female and male language when speaking of God. This is an important "bridge" discussion: religious conservatives will appreciate LaCugna's full commitment to trinitarian theology as "the" Christian doctrine of God, but in all likelihood, conservatives will balk at her skilled acknowledgment that "Father" is a synonym, equally valid to that of "Mother." Likewise, liberals will appreciate the latter, but struggle with the almost apolitical tone of her work--that at no point (at least in this particular essay) does it step into the feminist critique of abusive ecclesiastical power. For LaCugna's more "practical" applications of trinitarian theology, see [459]. Additionally, for work which draws on LaCugna, see Johnson's *She Who Is* [232] (and particularly her last chapter) and see Johnson's article, "Trinity: Let the Symbol Sing Again." *Theology Today* 54 (1997): 299-311.

[459] LaCugna, Catherine Mowry. "The Practical Trinity." *The Christian Century* 109 (1992): 678-682.

True to its title, this brief overview of trinitrian doctrine addressees the "practical" implications of the Trinity as a doctrine of *salvation,* i.e., its focus as a doctrine grounding the personal nature of God and the faith norms of believers in Christian community. LaCugna begins by describing the long history of obscurity attached to this doctrine, its retrieval by mid-20th century theologians and its specific history as a doctrine discussed primarily at the level of "substance" rather than existential impact. In brief, she argues that (1) the gains of intellectual achievement attached to this doctrine (at the height of medieval theology) were accomplished through the loss of its existential value as a statement about God's love for the believer, and (2) that it is the presence of these gains that so confuse individual believers and their appropriation of this doctrine as a living element of faith. In turn, she argues that (3) the "practical" import of this doctrine should always be held, in effect as the mirror [the icon] of the believing community, so that the church can "exist as the mystery of persons who dwell together in equality, reciprocity and mutual love" (p. 682). **NOTE:** for her fullest discussion of the history of this doctrine see *God With Us* [234] and see [458], [520] and [780] for its "practical" implications.

[460] Thistlethwaite, Susan Brooks "On the Trinity." *Interpretation* 45 (1991): 159-171. This article examines two fundamental questions within the current discussion of gender and trinitarian language: (a) is the traditional formulation of the Trinity as 'Father, Son and Holy Spirit' sexist? and (b) Is this formula a literal or metaphorical casting of God's name? To examine these questions Thistlethwaite reviews the development of trinitarian doctrine from within two sets of methodological assumptions: the assumption of language as a task (and product) of communal construction and signification; and second, the assumption of language as an expression of "performative utterance." From the first set of assumptions, Thistlethwaite calls attention to the patriarchal norms evident in biblical and patriarchal writing. Further, she highlights the "essentialist trap" inherent within the 'literal name vs. metaphor' approach to trinitarian language. From the second set of assumptions, she re-examines the long standing theological affirmations common to the "economic" and "immanent" emphases of trinitarian discourse, and she argues for a more "empancipatory" approach to trinitarian theologizing, i.e., an approach subject to a "performative criterion of truth" (p. 171). This performative criterion of truth raises the question: "Does it [the language in question] do the truth?" That is, "Does it witness to God's radical relationship to the world.... [and]... Will it *help us*? If it will not," she boldly concludes, "God help us all." Thistlethwaite's concern is for language that is capable of empowering communities in their full social, historical settings, and because "gender does not occupy a privileged position" relative to "race/ethnicity, age and class," performance language must emancipate each of these "socially significant constructs for religious experience" (p. 160). Thus, for Thistlethwaite, the important questions are not whether traditional trinitarian language is sexist, or whether it expresses an actual or metaphorical name for God. Rather, the important theological question is "how to adjudicate among competing points of reference for truth claims" (p. 160) and for Thistlethwaite, the criterion of importance is the "emancipatory" or performance character of such claims as they seek truth status.

[461] Zikmund, Barbara Brown. "The Trinity and Women's Experience." *The Christian Century* 104 (1987): 354-356.
This brief article draws on Carol Gilligan's work [476] to show the compatibility that may exist between women's experiences and the doctrine of the Trinity. Zikmund's focus is on the *perichoresis* emphasis within trinitarian theology, i.e., the inner relational activity among the persons of the Trinity, and its analogues in women's experience. Intended for popular reading, this article lacks bibliographical material and references to other feminist work on the Trinity.

4. Responses

Responses to the feminist appropriation of trinitarian language have stemmed largely from Protestant antifeminist circles in which both scripture and dogma are interpreted in literalist and anthropomorphic perspectives. Hence a chief concern in this literature has been to protect the name of God as a male name. Additionally, these responses have accused feminist theology of both heresy and the attempted destruction of Christianity. Kay's discussion below evidences the former and the antifeminist literature in Chapter 21 evidences the latter.

[462] Kay, James F. "In Whose Name? Feminism and the Trinitarian Baptismal Formula." *Theology Today* 49 (1993): 147-158.
This essay is an extended review of Duck's volume, *Gender and the Name of God: The Trinitarian Baptismal Formula* [457], and it is by James Kay, who was the key author in the development of the liberalized baptismal formula adopted by the Riverside Church in New York in 1982. It is an exceptionally negative review. It is critical of both Duck's main arguments and proposed language for an alternative to the traditional baptismal formula of baptizing "... in the name of the Father, the Son and the Holy Spirit" and it is virtually castigating of her presumed right to make such arguments. Moreover, its tone is blatantly hostile and carried by ridiculing and sarcastic statements, such that if Kay has arguments to make, they are lost in the shuffle.

NOTE: For additional reactionary responses to the feminist theological literature on the Trinity, see Chapter 21 and particularly the entries by Kimel [840] and Wainwright [845].

F. Sin, Salvation and Eschatology

As preliminaries to this literature see Saiving [163], Ruether and McLaughlin [209] and Plaskow [203]. Saiving's essay ["The Human Situation: A Feminine View"] was the first published feminist theological gender analysis of "sin," and the Ruether-McLaughlin text the first feminist theological reader to link realized and initiated eschatologies with the religious experience and leadership of women in early Christianity. In turn, Plaskow's dissertation [*Sex, Sin and Grace*] expanded Saiving's initial insight to present a sustained feminist critique of 'sin' and 'grace' in the theologies of Paul Tillich and Reinhold Niebuhr. Subsequent literature has built largely from these sources.

Generally speaking, the feminist literature on redemption (or what is here taken as the symbolic nexus of sin/salvation and eschatology) is underdeveloped. This said, current sources suggest at least four approaches to this topic. The earliest is the formal discussion of "sin," "salvation" and "eschatology" as symbols that are either dualistic or androcentric and in need of feminist critique. This approach is consistent with Berry's 1978 discussion [463], even though the latter remains grounded in androcentrist frames.

Alternatively, a number of feminist theologians approach sin, salvation and eschatology through categories addressing *institutionalized* evil, and particularly "sin" as institutionalized through racial, class and gender stratification(s). This second approach is especially salient in the literatures of feminist and womanist ethics (cf. [482] and [508]), the womanist critique of sin and suffering ([638]), and the liberationist themes of *Mujerista* theology ([928]).

A third approach, a "hermeneutics of judgment," is also present in the literature. This approach stresses both the pnuematological awareness of evil and the spirit filled judgment of women against it. Delores Williams' text, *Sisters in the Wilderness: The Challenge of Womanist God-Talk* (abstracted in [259]), is the groundbreaking discussion here, and as supported by the sociological research on African American women's religion (cf. Gilkes [615] and Collins [99]), its interdisciplinary significance is enormous.

Redemption and the seeds of Christian anti-Semitism. One further approach to the feminist literature on "sin, redemption, and eschatology" requires mention at this point. Because within the Christian framework the concepts of "sin, redemption, and eschatology" are virtually inseparable from those of Christology, the dialogue between Jewish and Christian feminists labors intensely under the weight of Christianity's historical norms of anti-Semitism: *viz.*, those theological premises that permit the social sanctioning of specifically anti-Jewish prejudice--and ultimately, Western society's history of anti-Jewish persecution. These premises include such specifically Christian ideas as history's "fulfillment" in Jesus, or the fulfillment of Judaism in Christianity, or the fulfillment of the "Old" Testament in the "New" [Testament], or the necessity for Jews to convert to Christianity to be saved. Implicit in such assumptions is the perception that redemption is a kind "zero-sum" game, i.e., a process by which Christianity is to be triumphant over all non-Christians, and within which all non-Christians, but particularly Jews, are to be punished. While ecumenical discussions within organized religion have in the last quarter of the twentieth century worked steadily to overcome such prejudices (cf. Ruether [299] and Klein [312] and the sources cited in the endnotes in the General Introduction), the discussion of "redemption" from within a framework that critiques religious ethnocentrism—while respecting religious freedom—has only just begun. Among Christian feminists it is evident in the writings of D'Angelo [433], Ruether [440], Heyward [437] and Siegele-Wenschkewitz [972]. Among Jewish feminists the most noted spokeswoman is Judith Plaskow [970-971], although as her several articles indicate, her work in many ways synthesizes lesser known sources. This discussion is especially significant: First, the discussion itself lays the groundwork for a rethinking of androcentric ecumenism and the necessity for organized religion to include feminism within its pale. Second, it suggests a refocusing of traditional theological faultlines, with images of creation, redemption and spirituality coming together in ways differently powerful for women in western (and Eastern) religion, and differently powerful for Christians and Jews across the board. Some of this discussion is already underway via the growing influence of eco-feminist work (cf. Adams [564]), but much remains to be done. The entries below provide initial overviews of the Christian feminist literature on "sin, salvation and eschatology," and the reader is referred to the discussions cited earlier in this overview for feminist, womanist, and Jewish-Christian dialogical sources.

[463] Berry, Wanda Warren. "Images of Sin and Salvation in Feminist Theology."
    Anglican Theological Review 60 (1978): 25-54.
This essay develops as a two part survey. First, it surveys the concepts of sin and salvation in the early works of Rosemary Radford Ruether, Mary Daly and Letty Russell. Second, it contrasts these concepts with five Pauline images both to show parallels between the Pauline and feminist

perspectives, and at the same time, Berry's perception that feminist theology does not sufficiently "dialogue with the tradition." By way of overview, Berry clearly identifies: (1) the "sin as dualism/salvation as mutuality" themes in Ruether; (2) Mary Daly's sin/salvation distinction between patriarchal and self naming; and (3) Russell's early emphases on as "sin as struggle and salvation as shalom." Berry then synthesizes the redemption/liberationist and enmity/reconciliation, themes in Paul, and with these, three parent-child images that evidence the overcoming of dualism, the unity of creation and the "revealing of the children of God," all themes Berry finds compatible with various emphases in the theologians she has examined. Last, she draws attention to the universalist themes found in Paul, Ruether, Daly and Russell, i.e., the yearning expressed by each of these writers of all creation for its fundamental wholeness. Where she parts company with Ruether, Russell and Daly, however, is in their lack of attention to justification and atonement--a lack that for Berry, voids the experience of guilt for sin that, in her judgment, is also constitutive of Christian tradition. This is an early and detailed essay that struggles for a feminist Pauline synthesis, and in the end, an articulation of "personal responsibility" for sin. For the latter, however, it returns to the androcentric assumptions its author first avoids, and it thus remains caught in a "blame the victim" perspective now surpassed by the work on atonement and "divine child abuse" (see Chapter 23).

[464] Finger, Reta, ed. "Sin and Grace: A Christian Feminist Perspective." *Daughters of Sarah* 16, no. 1 (1990): 4-55.
This brief issue of *DOS* presents both anecdotal and theoretical discussions of "grace" and "sin," with the anecdotal essays focusing sin and grace through an addiction/recovery framework (and largely with respect to sexual abuse), and the more theoretical pieces addressing social and systemic aspects of "sin," largely in liberationist and activist perspectives. Additionally--and as is always the case with *DOS*--this issue presents numerous extended book reviews on its thematic topic (with again, an attention here to the addiction and recovery literature), and it lists several sources and resources for women dealing with addition and abuse experiences.

[465] Ruether, Rosemary Radford. "Dualism and the Nature of Evil in Feminist Theology." *Studies in Christian Ethics* 5 (1991): 26-39.
From her earliest texts **[171, 172, 299, 190, 191, 192, 193]** Ruether has regularly identified "dualism" as a grounding problem for Christian theology. Here, her discussion both synthesizes earlier emphases and tightly weaves them into an ethical grounding borne of her feminist "relational" understanding. In her own words, Ruether wants to "explore [the] pattern of defining good and evil as an absolute dichotomy which is then connected with the mind-body dualism...[and in turn, with]...male/female dualism in either its masculinist form, which sees "'female sensuality'" as the problem, or in its feminist version that sees masculine intellectual pride as the problem" (p. 26). Thus, her discussion entails: (1) a summary of the Greek patriarchal antecedents to such dualism (i.e., the emergence of Platonic and Aristotelian gender hierarchies); (2) their patristic and medieval syntheses via Augustinian and Thomistic theologies; and (3) the social dynamics that shape these theologies and ultimately fuse them within three dimensions of human consciousness: (a) the ethical 'is/ought' dimension; (b) the existential "self-other" boundary; and (c) the felt differentiation between personal subjectivity and its object environment. In brief, Ruether demonstrates that the polarities of these distinctions became identified, respectively, with maleness and femaleness through a social constructional process based on domination and subjugation, as driven by three "stances" that dominant groups may assume toward subjugated others: *viz.*, "exploitation, demonization and idealization." Thus, for Ruether, it is the fullness of this framework--with its various nuanced assumptions--that needs deconstruction. For her part, Ruether provides this deconstruction through the specifics of her discussion. She then proceeds to "reconstruct" the notions of "evil" and "good" by unfolding "distorted" and "loving" relationality (respectively), with distinctions made for the interpersonal, social-historical and ideological-cultural dimensions of each. In turn, she closes by noting the implications of "loving relationality" for fully human community with its never completed aspects, but its openness "to receive and manifest the redemptive work of God." This is a complex discussion, best read after a familiarity with the *full range* of Ruether's work, including *Gaia & God* **[235]**, where its many ideas--as well as that full range--find invaluable expansion.

[466] Smith, Christine M. "Sin and Evil in Feminist Theology." *Theology Today* 50 (1993): 208-219.
This article provides an easily readable survey of the concepts of sin and evil as discussed or implied in the writings of Katie Cannon, Rita Nakashima Brock, Mary Potter Engel and Carter Heyward. It is particularly helpful in that it describes the key concepts of these theologians and

their respective emphases on social and personal sin. Additionally, Smith briefly describes the impact of "social location" for each of these four theologians and the effects of "white" middle class Christian values in the development of her own work on sin and evil. Her concluding comments conceptualize her own work as that of "resistance" to the "web" of oppressions that beset humanity. Additionally, she writes that because "feminist theology takes as its starting point concrete human suffering and oppression" (p. 218), it necessarily engages one in this task of resistance.

NOTE: Closely related to feminist theology's discussion of sin, salvation and eschatology is the literature on feminist spirituality as both justice-based and ecologically rooted. Hence see Ruether [235], McFague [245], and the related sources in Chapter 14. Additionally, see various sources Chapters 12 and 23 on feminist ethics and feminist ecumenism, respectively. Finally, for an alternative reading of sin and evil in feminist theology, see Kathleen Sands, *Escape from Paradise: Evil and Tragedy in Feminist Theology.* Minneapolis, MN: Fortress Press, 1994. Sands critically examines the approaches to evil presented in Judith Plaskow's early work, Carol Christ's goddess theology, Rosemary Ruether's general essays and systematic works (including *Gaia & God*), and Toni Morrison's *Beloved* to argue the inadequacies of all theology in the face of human tragedy.

12

Feminist Theological Ethics

The "praxis" assumptions of feminist theology are nowhere more evident than in the literature of feminist ethics, where the themes of egalitarianism, inclusivity, relationality and the authority of women's experience as interpretive frameworks are everywhere discussed. This section evidences the presence of those themes in literatures which present *definitions of feminist ethics, discussions of feminist ethical method,* and *discussions of key issues.*

At the level of definition, the literature ranges from feminist critiques of "agape," (e.g., Andolsen [467]) to the relationship between feminist anthropology and feminist ethics (e.g., Farley [472]), and as a consequence, the relationship of feminist ethics to feminist spirituality and feminist political action. (For examples here, see the entries in Andolsen et al. [468] and Daly [470]; and in other portions of the bibliography, see Harrison [207], Heyward [555], and Ruether [545].)

Apropos methodological issues, the literature ranges widely, but overall, three main concerns are clear: first, an early articulation of feminist hermeneutical principles by which to ground feminist ethical discussion (e.g., Farley [471], Haney [473], and Hunt [479]); second, a lingering debate over gender differences in moral reasoning (as generated by Gilligan's work [476]); and third, the need for clear political theory for combining praxis and reflection (e.g., Robb [482], Schüssler Fiorenza [483], and Legge [487]).

Last, by way of topics and specific ethical issues, the literature yet identifies the dominant culture's continued devaluation of women, women's work, women's sexuality, and women's rights to reproductive freedom as biases still to be overcome. Further, it identifies the varying and combined effects of several social statuses (race/ethnicity, sex, gender or gender role, age, social class and sexual orientation) as interactions negative for women, in that women experience "dual," "triple" or "multiple" oppressions, and in ways that the majority of American males characteristically do not. These multiple oppressions are typically described in the literature as the experience of "interstructured oppression," and they entail the combined effects of "race, gender and class," or more recently, "race, gender, class and sexual orientation." These effects, it is important to note, are interactive, not additive. Thus even though the idiom of "dual," "triple" and "multiple" oppressions suggests a sequence of injustices, it must be remembered that these oppressions are *analytically* distinct only, and that at the existential level, they are combined in impact. (Again, cf. Robb [482] and Legge [487].)

A final note. As one might expect, the literatures on sexual harassment and violence against women could also be included here. These literatures are, however, reserved for Chapter 22.

A.   Definitions of Feminist Ethics

[467] Andolsen, Barbara Hilkert. "Agape in Feminist Ethics." *Journal of Religious Ethics* 9 (1981): 69-83.
In this essay Andolsen describes two "groundings" of agape as an expression of Christian love. The first is its grounding in Christology such that agape becomes total self-sacrifice on behalf of the

other, a perspective exemplified in the writings of Nygren and Reinhold Niebuhr. An alternative approach is the grounding of agape in trinitarian doctrine, as exemplified by Margaret Farley [166]. In the latter approach agape is understood as "mutuality in relationship." Andolsen sees four benefits to this kind of re-grounding: (1) it is compatible with Saiving's [163] recognition of women's sin as the absence of self-love; (2) it dislodges agape as a basis for women's domestic roles in the private sphere by means of male-female, public-private, and/or justice-agape dualisms; (3) it promotes the necessity of rethinking the relationships among social structures, personal responsibility and concrete social conditions; and (4) its trinitarian grounding highlights both the necessity and difficulties attached to re-symbolizing trinitarian thinking through women as images of the divine. NOTE: For related works, see Farley [166] and LaCugna [459].

[468] Andolsen, Barbara Hilkert, Christine E. Gudorf, and Mary D. Pellauer, eds. *Women's Consciousness, Women's Conscience: A Reader in Feminist Ethics.* Minneapolis, MN: Winston Press, 1985.
Nineteen essays (eleven reprinted from earlier sources) make up this substantive, ecumenically based anthology in feminist ethics. The essays date from 1979 through 1985, with original contributions by editors Andolsen and Pellauer and contributors Ada Maria Isasi-Diaz, Toinette Eugene, Janice Raymond, Christine Gudorf, Ruether Smith, and Catherine Keller. Reprinted entries include essays by Nancy Bancroft, Rosemary Radford Ruether, Judith Plaskow, Bev Harrison, Elisabeth Schüssler Fiorenza, June Jordon, Carol Robb, June O'Connor and Margaret Farley. The text is divided into three parts: (1) aspects of women's experience, *viz.,* unpaid household work (Andolsen), violence (Pellauer) [868], racism and anti-Semitism (Plaskow, [968]), peace (Ruether), feminist/*feminista Hispana* tensions (Isasi-Diaz) [927], the economy (Bancroft), and the "nature/history split in feminist thought" (Griscom); (2) reproductive rights (Harrison), Schüssler Fiorenza on "discipleship and patriarchy" ([483]) womanist spirituality and sexuality (Eugene), female friendships (Raymond), parenting (Gudorf), and Jordon on "the nature of love." In Part III, Farley discusses "Feminist Theology and Bioethics" [500], and Robb, Smith, Keller and O' Connor address issues of methodology and critical reflection. Discussions are well documented, but the volume lacks indices and supplemental bibliography.

[469] Cahill, Lisa Sowle. "Feminist Ethics." *Theological Studies* 51 (1990): 49-63.
This essay reviews the periodical literature published by Christian feminist ethicists during the period 1987-1989. The bulk of the sources are Roman Catholic and given the Vatican's posture towards women's issues in the late 1980s, Cahill finds this "an opportune moment" to examine the "aims and accomplishments of Roman Catholic feminism." Her synthesizing concerns, therefore, are: (1) the definition of feminist ethics; (2) the implications of feminist ethics for understanding "recent church teaching"-- especially on the institutions of ministry and motherhood; and given the nature of feminist ethics, (3) the epistemological status of moral truth and moral reasoning. According to Cahill, the task of feminist ethics is two-fold: feminist ethics seeks to define the concept of equality between women and men and to elucidate the criteria by which to reform society "so that the full equality of women in respected" (p. 50). Christian feminist ethicists vary in their approaches to these goals but virtually all support them. Similarly, virtually all feminist ethicists address (in varying degrees) the following concerns: (1) the use of women's experience as a critical source and norm for the development of feminist ethics; (2) an awareness of the historical, perspectival nature of all theological/ethical statements; (3) an emphasis on the social and communal nature of feminist ethical theorizing; (4) an attention to the moral significance of "embodiment" as an aspect of feminist ethical thinking; and (5) the selected use of Christian resources, philosophy, and social analysis to guide the development of feminist ethical goals. As regards "recent church teaching," feminist ethics challenges both the gender bias of Catholicism's exclusively male priesthood and the ideology of gender-based asymmetry which underlies traditional religious and social notions of motherhood. With respect to moral truth and methodology, feminist ethics is obviously historical and perspectival (as are other disciplines), but committed to a truth verified by praxis "in a life [and society] which are relatively more true and more just" (p. 64). Cahill's own methodology in this essay is dialectical. She pulls together several theological and ecclesiastical sources and attempts a balance of criticism and challenge. Her discussion is well-written and well-documented (although limited given her aims), but both the discussion and the notes are a solid introduction to the issues of sexism and reproductive rights within institutionally based Catholic feminist writing. NOTE: Also by Cahill is [499], and for feminist ethical questions *not* addressed by Cahill, see Roman Catholic authors Farley [568], Hunt [479], and Maguire [505] and Protestant authors Harrison [503], Heyward [570], Davies and Haney [496] and Robb [482].

[470] Daly, Lois K., ed. *Feminist Theological Ethics*. Louisville, KY: Westminster/John Knox, 1994.

This reader presents twenty-two classic essays in feminist theological ethics to illustrate the "...struggles *and* joys that take place as voices emerge and women name themselves: feminist, womanist, mujerista" (p. xv). Its major subdivisions include "Change and Challenging Assumptions" (seven entries); "Taking on the Traditions" (five entries); and last, "Exploring Our Lives Together" (ten entries). Several of these entries are abstracted in the present volume ([467], [473], [482], [490], [500], [502], [570], [625], [626], [632], [906]). The remaining address "practical" issues and include: Clare Fischer's "Let Her Works Praise Her" (a 1975 feminist theology of work based on Proverbs 31); Janice G. Raymond's 1990 "Reproductive Gifts and Gift Giving: The Altruistic Woman" (an analysis of how altruism devalues women engaged in surrogate pregnancies); Karen Lebacqz's 1990 "Love Your Enemy: Sex, Power, and Christian Ethics" (an argument on the need for a 'role-based' morality for heterosexual women who may have been sexually abused but are now moving beyond that experience); Anne McGrew Bennett's 1975 "Overcoming the Biblical and Traditional Subordination of Women;" two entries on eco-feminism (by Catherine Keller and editor Daly, respectively); E. Bettenhausen's "The Moral Landscape of Embodiment;" Joan Griscom's well known "On Healing the Nature/History Split in Feminist Thought;" and Mary Hunt's "Medals on Our Blouses? A Feminist Theological Look at Women in Combat." The strength of the reader is its breadth of entries; its weakness, the lack of indices and supplemental bibliography.

[471] Farley, Margaret A. "Feminist Ethics in the Christian Ethics Curriculum." In *Mainstreaming*, edited by Arlene Swidler and Walter Conn, 65-76. Lanham, MD: University Press of America, 1985.

Farley's curriculum essay identifies both the pluralistic basis and the key substantive and methodological issues that typify feminist ethics in the mid-1980s. It provides introductory bibliography on both types of issues (in all, 17 references) and through a description of twenty-three supplemental bibliographic sources, it indicates how such issues may be incorporated into general curricula and standard Christian ethics courses. An additional value to Farley's essay is her suggested reading lists for specific topics related to both sexual ethics (32 entries) and medical ethics (14 entries). In all, Farley's discussion indicates 85 distinct bibliographic sources for use in the teaching of general and particular issues in feminist ethics and their introduction into more standardized courses. The cited literature is current through the mid-1980s. For helpful material published after 1985, see Cooey, Farmer and Ross [495], Davies and Haney [496], Bruland [474], Bounds [485] and the literature on womanist ethics in Chapters 16 and 17.

[472] Farley, Margaret A. "Feminist Ethics." In *The Westminster Dictionary of Christian Ethics*, edited by James F. Childress and John Macquarrie, 229-231. Philadelphia: Westminster, 1986.

Defining feminism as both a "conviction and a movement opposed to discrimination on the basis of gender...[and thus as a conviction and movement which] opposes...therefore, any ideology, belief, attitude or behavior that establishes or reinforces such discrimination," Farley identifies feminist ethics as "any ethical theory that locates its roots in feminism" (p. 229). She distinguishes varying types of feminism (i.e., liberal, socialist and radical), and she succinctly surveys the thematic emphases which cut across this pluralism: a concern for the "meaning of human embodiment...the nature of the human self...the value of the world of nature...and patterns for human relationships" (p. 230). Methodologically, feminist ethics addresses: (1) the value of women's experience as a substantive source of ethical insight; (2) the increasing importance of ecological issues; and as its grounding concern, (3) the "principle that women are fully human and are to be valued as such." This means that feminist ethics rejects "strong theories of complementarity" and focuses instead on a "positive principle of equality," with this principle "based not only on the self-protective right of each to freedom, but on the participation of all in human solidarity" (p. 230). Feminist ethics thus takes a "critical stance in relation to past theological justifications of the inferiority of women to men...[it]...challenges the association of women with evil, is opposed to religious 'pedestalism'...[and is]...concerned with the formulation of a theory of justice...[that]...will illumine more adequately every form of human and Christian relationship" (p. 231). **NOTE:** For Farley's grounding work see [166] and [167].

[473] Haney, Eleanor Humes. "What Is Feminist Ethics? A Proposal for Discussion." *Journal of Religious Ethics* 8 (1980): 115-124.

This proposal for the development of feminist ethics is rooted in the recognition that "neither what is natural nor what is revealed is necessarily the same for those in a subordinated position in a society as it is for those in a position of dominance" (p. 115). The recognition acknowledges women's marginality (both socially and historically and in the cultural variations of first and third world peoples), and it provides Haney with strong reasons for questioning both the 'natural' and 'revealed' characterizations of traditional ethics. The latter has not been informed by the experience of most of the world's peoples, she argues, and a new vision and methodology are needed. That vision and methodology are encompassed by the imaging of ethics through categories of nurture and friendship and more, through the actual *doing* of nurture and friendship. Further, this new vision and methodology must focus on non-hierarchical and interdependent ways of speaking about God, for women need presently to experience a sense of 'at-homeness' with both 'being' and 'the universe,' rather than notions and images of self-sacrifice. Indeed, for Haney, "feminist ethics is fidelity to being" (p. 124) and if this fidelity is taken together with honesty and integrity, then the values of friendship and nurture can work to transform the status quo of competitive greed, utilitarian ethics, and the absence of integrity in both personal and social interactions.

B. Feminist Ethical Method

1. Theoretical Discussions

[474] Bruland, Esther Byle. "Evangelical and Feminist Ethics: Complex Solidarities." *Journal of Religious Ethics* 17 (1989): 139-160.
This discussion synthesizes the literature on evangelical feminism through the late 1980s and summarizes the growing rapprochement between evangelical feminist and "broadly-Christian feminist" perspectives, with specific attention to feminist ethics. Overall, a "feminist ethics hybrid" is developing, with several themes common to both evangelical and "broadly-Christian" feminist perspectives. After summarizing the history of evangelical feminism to the current period (cf., e.g., Scanzoni and Hardesty [251]), Bruland notes the struggles of contemporary evangelical feminists to maintain both ties to their biblical heritage and a credibility with secular and "broadly-Christian" feminism (e.g., Trible, Russell, Schüssler Fiorenza, Ruether, Harrison and McFague). Last, Bruland details the "complex solidarities" cutting across evangelical and feminist perspectives: *viz.*, a common concern for: (1) "personal" methods of ethical theorizing (the feminist's personalized ethical journey and the evangelical's personal testimony); (2) an attention to relationships as a component of ethical value systems (e.g., Harrison's relationality and evangelicalism's emphasis on community fellowship); (3) skepticism towards rationalism as *the* basis for ethical systems (feminism's embodied reason and evangelicalism's Pentecostalism and "external word"); (4) attention to power issues (feminism's "empowerment" emphasis and evangelicalism's populism and Spirit egalitarianism); and (5) attention to social justice issues (e.g., an opposition from both groups to racism and third world poverty). Where feminist and evangelical ethics differ, however, is in their focus and methodologies, or grounding assumptions. These movements have different understandings of *personal experience* as an ethical resource (feminist psychology vs. the revealed Word), of sin (systemic injustice vs. structures and individual accountability), and of *norm derivation* (feminism's critique of dualism and social location vs. evangelicalism's otherworldly eschatology). These deeply held differences need resolution lest other questions (e.g., the legitimacy of homosexual lifestyles) continue as scapegoated reasons for splits among evangelical women's groups.

[475] Farley, Margaret A. *Personal Commitments: Beginning, Keeping, Changing*. San Francisco: Harper & Row, 1986.
This volume is Farley's most extended discussion of the nature of commitment: what it is, what works to sustain or debilitate it, how varying commitments may be in conflict (whether commitments to persons, organizations, self and/or "overarching values"), and what conditions permit one's release from or abandonment of commitment. Farley begins by defining commitment as the notion of a "claim" (that is, to commit to someone or something is to permit that other to have a claim on one's self).She then traces out the varying ways in which claims may be perceived, held and at times modified. Farley roots her discussion through an articulation of love as "the affective affirmation" of another's "full and well being," and it is this perception which in turn becomes understood as "just love," or the basis of loving both interpersonally and universally. By way of closure, she describes the biblical metaphor of covenant as the basis for grounding *equality, mutuality* and *justice* as the norms of love, and she considers the universal and social implications of her discussion. This is a highly nuanced discussion informed by wisdom, poetry, academe, feminism and biblical imagery. It leans largely (although neither exclusively nor uncritically) in the direction of "fidelity" to "doing the deeds of love" and it addresses head on the difficult questions

how self-love and other love conflict and need perceptive analysis and--for Farley--covenential grounding. **NOTE**: See Farley's other works in this chapter and see [166], [167] and [364].

[476] Gilligan, Carol. *In A Different Voice: Psychological Theory and Women's Development*. Cambridge, MA: Harvard Univ. Press, 1982.
This text is a classic in feminist ethics--albeit less so for its specific findings concerning the Kohlberg model of ethical development (cf., e.g., Lawrence Kohlberg, *The Philosophy of Moral Development: Volume I: Essays on Moral Development*. NY: Harper & Row, 1981)) and more for its characterization of gender and ethical reasoning as reflecting two distinct ethical voices: (1) the traditional voice of males, in which ethical reasoning is tied to issues of rights and responsibilities according to specific depictions of what is fair and just; and (2) a "different voice," the voice of women, in which ethical choices are seen more in terms of relationality, equitable outcomes and a minimizing of pain and exclusion. Often depicted as the contrast between an "ethics of rights" and an "ethics of care," Gilligan's discussion has at times been taken as the premise for arguing that women and men experience *genuinely different* ways of knowing and thus reflect genuinely different ways of being. Gilligan rejects such interpretations of her work but the characterization lingers. **NOTE**: For additional discussion of her work, see Larrabee [480], Grey [477] and Kerber et al. [486] below.

[477] Grey, Mary. "Claiming Power-in-Relation: Exploring the Ethics of Connection." *Journal of Feminist Studies in Religion* 7, no. 1 (1991): 7-18.
Using insights drawn from several psychological sources, but particularly Gilligan [476], Grey explores the question: "...does using an image like power-in-relation...present a liberating ethic for women or trap us further into destructive, oppressive patterns of relating?" (p. 7.) The discussion develops in two parts. The first is Grey's identification of "connectedness" as a "revelatory paradigm," i.e., a framework that can "*enable* differentiation, pluralism and diversity--whether religious, racial or sexual--in a such a way that the experience of one ethnic or faith group does not hold an exclusive position..." [relative to others] (pp. 12-13). In Part II Grey applies this perspective to several philosophical anthropological assumptions currently debated within feminist ethics, with four new goals emerging as priorities. Specifically, she argues that an 'ethics of connection' begins with (1) a "redefining of the self" as a "fluid unity of many self-moments" such that (2) the dynamics of "attachment" and "separation" (in individual life) may be re-assessed so that (3) an "environment of healing" can develop in which (4) new relational energies come to the fore on behalf of justice for women. By way of concrete application, women must therefore find their own voices(s), and women of privilege must work to empower other groups in terms of their own particularities (pp. 17-18). **NOTE**: For an alternative perspective, see Hampson [478].

[478] Hampson, Daphne. "On Power and Gender." *Modern Theology* 4 (1988): 236-250.
This discussion contrasts the varying compatibilities of three concepts--those of powerfulness, powerlessness and empowerment--with selected emphases in Christian tradition. The discussion roots in the gender orientations described by Gilligan [476], and Hampson argues six points. Namely, that: (1) the image of God's powerfulness fits well with the individualist and contractual assumptions of maleness as described by Gilligan; (2) these emphases exhibit the patriarchal notion of God found in biblical and theological sources; (3) while power*less*ness fits only when postulated of a suffering redeemer, it *also* exhibits the patriarchal notion of God found in the tradition--for here powerfulness is given up and others are asked to enter into a similar process of kenosis; (4) each of these concepts (*viz.*, powerfulness and powerlessness) is destructive to women, and (5) women, but particularly feminist women reject them in favor of *empowerment;* because (6) its relational and connectional emphases suggest the empowerment of all. To close, Hampson follows Haney [473] to suggest that the concept "friendship" illuminates feminist ethical insight because it engenders support and respect among equals and neither the judgmental nor 'power over' emphases of both powerfulness and powerlessness (the latter albeit with power abnegated). Hence Hampson argues that empowerment is incompatible with Christianity's core emphases, and for her illustrations, she describes the tensions of women's ordination in Anglicanism. **NOTE**: For an alternative view, see Grey [477].

[479] Hunt, Mary E. "Transforming Moral Theology: A Feminist Ethical Challenge." In *Women: Invisible in Church and Theology*, edited by Elisabeth Schüssler Fiorenza and Mary Collins, 84-90. Edinburgh: T. & T. Clark, 1985.
Readers familiar with Hunt's political definition of lesbianism, described in Wilson, Scanzoni, and Hunt [575], will find this theme re-articulated here as she presents "lesbian insight" as a grounding

premise for reflecting upon ethical methodology. In Hunt's work "lesbian insight" is the positive and celebrative affirmation of women's communal relationality with the latter constituting the empowering possibilities of a feminist critical ethic, since it attends to questions of economic justice and equity and the process of empowerment by inclusion. Thus for Hunt, "lesbian insight" has less to do with the sexual/genital intimacy which some women may experience, and more to do with the affirmation of women's community building capacities through justice activities. Seen in this light, Hunt's feminist ethical challenge is for the development of an ethical methodology rooted in relationality and the recognized acknowledgment of women's experience as the source of women's ethical involvement, both in terms of the questions women raise about their experience and the questions it raises for them. Hunt's position contrasts sharply with the traditional androcentric emphases of moral methodology (which emphasize abstractions about women's experience and the naming of women's sexuality from within sexist and heterosexist assumptions), and thus she emphasizes consistently, that empowerment presumes inclusion and the self-identified questions of those being included. NOTE: This essay is by no means the most clearly written of Hunt's published work, and it requires sustained reflection. For additional works by Hunt see [556] and [575]; for additional literature on lesbianism and feminist ethics, see Mollenkott [247], and Heyward [242, 570] and Hill [627].

[480] Larrabee, Mary Jeanne, ed. *An Ethic of Care: Feminist and Interdisciplinary Perspectives*. New York: Routledge, Chapman and Hall, 1993.
This reader roots in the feminist, ethical and social scientific discussions attached to Gilligan's *In A Different Voice* [476]. It presents 17 essays grouped around four thematic frameworks. These are: (1) "...Probings..." four essays that examine psychological and philosophical aspects of the 'Kohlberg-Gilligan debate'; (2) four historical and culturally directed essays that "expand the question" to examine Gilligan's work with respect to ideology, race and gender dualism; (3) a group of five essays (including two literature reviews) which "check the data" to assess Gilligan's constructs, methodology, and measurements; and last, four essays that try to move Gilligan's work to a wider understanding of "care" via discussions of liberation, contextualization, socialization, and the "separation" of 'care' from assumptions congruent with traditional gender norms. An extended introduction helpfully locates the reader within the literature, and a comprehensive listing of cited references together with a detailed index close the volume. Among journal sources represented here are *Child Development, Ethics, Signs*, and *Social Research*. NOTE: For additional literature see Cynthia S. W. Crysdale, "Gilligan and the Ethics of Care: An Update." Religious *Studies Review* 20 (1994): 21-28.

[481] Maguire, Daniel. "The Feminist Turn in Christian Ethics." In *Mainstreaming: Feminist Research for Teaching Religious Studies*, edited by Arlene Swidler and Walter Conn, 77-83. Lanham, MD: University Press of America, 1985. [First published in *Horizons* 10 (1983): 341-347.]
Maguire does not use the term 'paradigm shift' to describe this feminist turn in ethics, but well he might, for his own metaphors are of similar scope. This turn involves "the change from sexist-patriarchal to feminist and eventually inclusively humanistic thinking" and in a word it is "massive" (p. 78). For Maguire, it is of the caliber of a "conversion," a "kairos," and a quote from John 9:25: "Whereas I was blind, now I see." Five elements make up the substance of this 'feminist turn.' First is "the nature of nature" for "feminism calls us from a two-nature to a one-nature ethics" (p. 80). (Read: dualism destroys.) Second is the nature of the "person," and here the turn requires an abandonment of isolationist imagery and the adoption of relational categories. Third and fourth are the 'linkage of public and private morality' and 'technologized rationality,' and both need foundation in a theory of justice so that (among other things) economics, politics and epistemology can function for the choosing and nurturing of life, not death. A last element of the feminist turn requires reading theological sources, where a "healing supplement to male labors in this field is now arriving" via "Elisabeth Schüssler Fiorenza, Phyllis Trible, Sandra Schneiders and Elaine Pagels, to mention only a few" (p. 83). Maguire presents recommended sources for each of these areas and his discussion is supplemented by that of Margaret Farley [471].

[482] Robb, Carol S. "A Framework for Feminist Ethics." *Journal for Religious Ethics* 9 (1981): 48-68.
This article examines nine elements embedded within the task of "social ethics" reflection. It indicates how one of these elements--the analysis of oppression--can affect all others: one's starting point for reflection, the gathering of data about the historical situation, loyalties to constituencies, and theories of value to name a few. The discussion of these elements is rooted in a clarification of feminist ethics, and to that end four frameworks for feminist ethics are summarized: "Radical

Feminism," "Sex-rolism," "Marxist-Leninist Feminism" and "Socialist Feminism." After Robb summarizes each of these frameworks, she contrasts the differential implications their respective "analyses of oppression" have for other elements of feminist ethics (starting point, loyalties, etc.). She then concludes by noting the potential for such concerns for feminist and other ethicists engaged in tasks of community formation. This article is clearly written and well documented. Its grounding literature extends only through 1978, but it remains a strong and thorough introduction to issues and perspectives in feminist ethical method. For related perspectives see Haney [473] and Davies and Haney [496]. For contrasting and Roman Catholic perspectives see Cahill [469], Farley [472]; for Womanist perspectives sharing the same starting point but reflecting differing methodologies, see Cannon [253], Williams [639], and Eugene [626]. Last, for sociological literature sensitive to Robb's methodological concerns, see Andersen, [84]; Andersen and Collins [85]; Collins [99] and Lengermann and Niebrugge-Brantley [108].

[483] Schüssler Fiorenza, Elisabeth. "Discipleship and Patriarchy: Toward a Feminist Evaluative Hermeneutics." In *Bread Not Stone: The Challenge of Feminist Biblical Interpretation*, 65-92. Boston: Beacon Press, 1984.
This discussion (which appears in an abbreviated form in [468]) is Schüssler Fiorenza's summary overview of the use of the Bible as a critical and communally owned text of feminist and other liberations, and amidst her incisive observations about the Bible and the Moral majority she develops five points. First, that it is Scripture which provides normative grounding for the Christian community's ethical work, precisely because it is scripture which is proclaimed in historical remembrance within the believing community. Second, however, there is a need to establish an "evaluative" hermeneutics for the ethics/exegesis reading of Scripture, because "historical remembrance" can be "nostalgic" and thus supportive of an oppressive status quo. Thus, (point three), she proposes "a development of biblical ethics that does not presuppose the apolitical character of Scripture and assume that *all* biblical tradition and texts have the authority of Scripture and promote the 'common good' merely by reason of their inclusion in the canon." (pp.69-70.) Fourth, she uses the *Haustafeln* codes as the test case for her discussion. Last, she notes what, in fact, an evaluative critical hermeneutics does, and in doing so she distinguishes her own liberationist position from those of Letty Russell [174], Phyllis Trible [205] and Rosemary Ruether [326]. For Schüssler Fiorenza, a critical evaluative feminist hermeneutics does not seek to distinguish between "historically limited patriarchal traditions and the liberating biblical tradition" (Russell) or between the "liberative essence of a revealed text and its historical patriarchal-cultural expression" (Trible), or between the Bible's "liberating prophetic critique" and its historical cultural deformations (Ruether). All of these are backward looking and risk the establishment of texts as authoritative revelatory texts. Rather, what is needed is an evaluative hermeneutics: a forward looking process which sets the Bible as a prototype for its own and society's critique, in that the proclamation from within the community of faith--including and especially the community of the marginalized now again allows the "gospel" to be recognized as "the power of God unto salvation."

NOTE: For additional literature, see Harrison and Robb [207] and Kalven and Buckley [208].

2. Bibliography and Review Symposia

[484] Bounds, Elizabeth, ed. "Special Issue in Honor of Beverly Wildung Harrison." *Journal of Feminist Studies in Religion* 9, nos. 1-2 (1993): 1-249.
This "Special Issue" of the *Journal* to honor Beverly Harrison--her work, her vision, her accomplishments, and her extensive influence in feminist religious ethics--presents eleven articles and three bibliographic essays which demonstrate the range of her work. It is a varied testimony-- political, sexual, economic, Womanist, *Mujerista* and feminist--and written from the postures of strength she has so clearly provided her students and colleagues within the field. The contributors include Ada Maria Isasi-Diaz, Katie Cannon, Joan Martin, Pamela Brubaker, Delores Williams, Elly Haney, Marvin Ellison, Peter Paris, Barbara Hilkert Andolsen, Carol Robb, Mary Pellauer, Margaret Farley, Ruth Smith, Donna Bivens, Elizabeth Bettenhausen, Nancy Richardson, guest editor Bounds, Marilyn Legge and Christine E. Gudorf. Abstracted in the present volume are the bibliographic entries by Bounds [485] and Legge [487].

[485] Bounds, Elizabeth, ed. "Resources in Feminist Religious Ethics." *Journal of Feminist Studies in Religion* 9, nos. 1-2 (1993): 227-232.
This annotated bibliography on feminist religious ethics features a synopsis of Beverly Harrison's key works (10 entries) along with descriptions from eleven other sources addressing political, social and economic dimensions of feminist religious ethical issues. It is intended as "a 'basic

reading' list for those who wish to further explore feminist religious ethics" (p. 227), and it appears as a contribution to the special issue of the *Journal of Feminist Studies in Religion* prepared in honor of Union Seminary Professor Beverly Harrison for her work feminist religious ethics.

[486] Kerber, Linda K., Catherine Greeno, Eleanor E. Maccoby, Zella Luria, Carol B. Stack, and Carol Gilligan. "On *In a Different Voice*: An Interdisciplinary Forum." *Signs* 11(1986): 304-333.

This interdisciplinary forum presents four extended discussions of Gilligan's *In a Different Voice* **[476]**. These include: (1) "cautionary words for historians" employing Gilligan's work--in that the latter comes close to positing a 'separate spheres' framework (Kerber); (2) a methodological critique of Gilligan's reading of Kohlberg together with a substantive review of the literature and data challenging Gilligan's hypothesized 'sex differences' framework (Greeno and Maccoby); (3) an additional methodological critique suggesting more rigorous controls on Gilligan's sampling and coding techniques (Luria); and (4) a theoretical critique by Stack, who contrasts Gilligan's care/justice emphases with her own work on the cultural survival strategies of Southern African-American migrant returnees--and who exposes, thereby, an unaddressed race/class bias in Gilligan's work. In a response to her critics Gilligan argues that: (a) critics are using androcentric data and concepts to critique what is genuinely women's experience; (b) that she, Gilligan, has not been read carefully enough by her critics for she is not positing fundamental sex differences, but rather women's own read on their experience as contrasted with male constructions of it; and (c) that these particular theoretical and methodological critiques don't, in fact, hold--for various reasons, and Gilligan cites particulars in her own defense. Readers sympathetic to 'cultural' or 'soft' feminism (cf. Hess and Ferree **[118]**) will in all likelihood lean more to Gilligan's arguments than to those of her critics. Social scientists, however, will probably follow Greeno and Maccoby given their extended command of the literature and the more 'rigorous' methods they wish as standards for discussion.

[487] Legge, Marilyn J. "Visions for Power-In-Relation: A Bibliographic Survey." *Journal of Feminist Studies in Religion* 9, nos. 1-2 (1993): 233-238.

While exposing the reader to a select list of important, recent sources drawn from feminist ethics, social theory and theological reflection, this essay also details the hermeneutical axes of Beverly Harrison's long years of ethical reflection, and the significance such axes retain for feminist ethics across the board. Noting that Harrison's consistent emphasis has been the necessity for holding power accountable in all sectors of social and communal relations, Legge identifies four hermeneutical principles--four hermeneutical axes if you will--around which Harrison's' work has pivoted and from within which Legge's selected sources may be examined. These axes are the power differentials which exist relative to "...sex/gender organization...class relations and their mystification, racial/ethnic traditions and current dynamics, and sexuality and social order" (p. 233) and Legge's synopsis of their scope in Harrison's work is as succinct (and perhaps as good) as it gets. This is a *strong* essay, notable both for its nuanced framework and the selected feminist ethical sources and resources (books and articles) it reviews. **NOTE**: For a more delimited discussion on "Issues of Race in Feminist Ethics," see Christine Gudorf's review essay by that title in the same journal issue. Gudorf provides substantive summaries of five important texts together with an analysis of "difference" as an emerging category for feminist ethical analysis.

NOTE: For related literature, see the entries on feminist spirituality in Chapter 14.

C.　Issues in Feminist Ethics

Closely related to all of the literature listed under "issues in feminist ethics" are the literatures organized in Chapters 8 and 14 under the categories "Theological Anthropology" and "Feminist Spirituality." Hence, readers should cross-check the entries below with those in each of these sections.

1.　Women, Work, and Poverty

[488] Carr, Anne. "Women, Justice and the Church." *Horizons* 17 (1990): 269-279.

In a previously published volume co-edited with Schüssler Fiorenza **[493]**, Carr has presented data on the global feminization of poverty and the rising numbers of women and children victimized by this phenomenon. In this essay she reflects briefly, but pointedly on these data. Following Margaret Farley's trinitarian framework for Christian ethics **[166]**, Carr points to the theological, Christological and ecclesiological implications of the public-private split which undergirds the feminization of poverty, i.e., the assumption that women's domestic work is not really "work," since it is not wage work. At the theological level the ethical implications addressing this assumption are clear: the God who "is love" is a God of relational love and this God demands such relational love at both the personal and social levels. In turn, this requires a rethinking of the nature of justice and one's elements of commitment to it. Similarly, at the Christological level the implications addressing assumption about women's work are also clear: i.e., an imitation of Christ which requires "new understandings of human political responsibility... including transformative action" (pp. 276-277). Finally, at the ecclesial level, this assumption means a new reading of the institutional church, and from the perspective of "power-with" and power on behalf of, but not "power-over." Specifically, one must envision a church structure which is geared to the "empowerment" of those who have not power," so that the church can assume a vanguard position on behalf of justice for women, both within and beyond its institutional walls. For related literature, see: the discussion of gender stratification in Chafetz [98]; see Feinberg and Knox on the feminization of poverty [124], and see the supplemental statistical data in Ries [126], Rix [127] and Tauber [128].

[489] Chittister, Joan. *Job's Daughters. Women and Power*. New York: Paulist, 1990.
The sixth annual "Madeleva Lecture on Spirituality" presented at St. Mary's College in Notre Dame, Indiana, this highly readable and informative discussion is divided into three parts. First is "The Nature of Power." Here Chittister's social psychology background comes to the fore as she moves easily from the characterization of Job as today's woman (p. 6) to Max Weber's emphasis on the use of power, and further, to Rollo May's five fold typology of *exploitative, competitive, manipulative, nurturant* and *integrative* power. Chittister then examines the experiences women have with each of these types of power, and she applies them to Part II, "Women and Power: An International Agenda." In a thoroughly documented discussion she leaves no doubt as to the powerlessness of most women on this earth. "Without a doubt," she says, "exploitation, competition and manipulation of women are everywhere the national policy, the legal expectation, [and] the ideological ideal" (p. 69). Nor is there any doubt about the needs for the future. In Part III, Chittister notes that "like Job, women know that the inhuman and the unequal and the unfair simply cannot be the will of God" (p. 69). Thus, she sets forth a vision for peace, for development and for equality. In this section hard data and hard truth come together, and the reader is left facing both. This is a powerful "Madeleva lecture in spirituality," suitable for use as a discussion piece, a meditation, or a feminist primer on experience and theology, and the hope that can be borne from each. For additional discussion by Chittister see [754]. For Catholic social teaching see Riley [491]. Additionally see the sources on poverty cited by Feinberg and Knox [124], and see French [24], Heise [28], Fenton and Heffron [45], Morgan [9] and Neft and Levine [10] for international statistics. Last, see Ries [126], Rix [127] and Tauber [128] for U.S. statistics and see Kemp [512] below.

[490] Fischer, Clare B. "Liberating Work." In *Christian Feminism: Visions of a New Humanity*, edited by Judith Weidman, 117-140. San Francisco: Harper & Row, 1984.
This article presents three "approaches...[that] ...underpin the distortion in attitude and practice regarding women's work" (p. 123) in an effort to suggest the "resilience of prejudice against women's productive activity" (p. 124). The identified approaches include 'the sexual division of labor,' the 'separation of work and home' (as gender defined spheres) and what Fischer terms 'the division of aspiration and opportunity.' Fischer identifies the ideological assumptions of each approach and fleshes her discussion out with examples which illustrate how society maintains a devalued perspective of women's work activity; that is, how society marginalizes women by making women's work invisible and tying it to nurture activities, while linking man's work with 'world building' and dominance over nature. A concluding section highlights the 'work ethic' of Gertie Nevels, the heroine of Harriet Arnow's novel, *The Dollmaker*, as an example of what "liberated work" might look like. This essay bursts at points with insights about society's attitudes towards women's work, and it is thus very relevant to feminist theological ethics; but its discussion is at other points scattered and--while worth the effort--difficult to follow. For related sources see, Riley [491], Ruether [492] and Harrison/Robb [207].

[491] Riley, Maria. *Transforming Feminism*. New York: Sheed and Ward, 1989.
This text aligns the principal emphases of American feminism with those of Roman Catholic social teaching as identified from encyclicals and church documents published between 1891 and 1988. The alignment permits a "dialogue" between these two frameworks, and the outcome is a "feminist revision of Catholic social teaching" with implications both for feminism and Catholicism. The text

is divided into five chapters. Chapter I identifies the study's main questions: why and how such a dialogue might take place. Chapter II surveys the history of American feminism with attention to its bureaucratic, organizational and collectivist dimensions—and further, its place within global feminism during the decades of the seventies and eighties. Feminist ideological and theoretical emphases are summarized in Chapter III, and in Chapter IV the theological legitimacy of the discussion is detailed. This legitimation is rooted in Vatican II's teaching in *Gaudium et Spes* (para. 11) that the church must read the 'signs of the times' and it is in this chapter that two such signs are read and aligned: *viz.*, the experience of women and Catholic teaching on justice and personhood. The implications and results of this reading are then presented in Chapter V, where Riley notes the necessity for structural changes in both church and society and the need to abandon both androcentrism and patriarchal culture. The volume lacks subject and author indices, but two appendices containing historical charts on the material presented in the text close the volume. This is an informative, provocative, and rewarding text. It is tightly written and requires close reading; but its methodological strategy is fruitful and will, in all likelihood, find replication and/or extension by writers in other denominations.

[492] Ruether, Rosemary Radford. "Home and Work: Women's Roles and the Transformation of Values." *Theological Studies* 36 (1975): 647-659.
This early article by Ruether remains one of her most important and seminal pieces in theological ethics. First, it surveys the shape and social location of women's work within pre-industrial, industrialized and communist societies. The survey is itself succinctly illuminating both for its descriptive detail and critique of the totalizing claims of Marxist philosophy, but beyond this, it highlights the role of religion in shaping and conditioning perceptions of women's work, both biblically and in the modern period. Second, the article argues for a reorganization of value priorities which will evidence a recovery of home-based community and autonomy, and the experienced affirmation of these values via work as a framework for personal development and integration. Often overlooked, this essay intimates several emphases later to be explicit and consistently thematic in Ruether's work: her critique of religious patriarchy [171, 172] and of Christianity's misogynist perception of women [319]; the dynamics of theological methodology and symbol construction [326]; her 'iconoclastic' Christology [441]; her relational ethic, feminist spirituality and ecological commitment ([567] and [235]; and last, Ruether's theological discussions of clericalism, gender and sexuality [759], and patriarchy and abuse in Brown and Bohn [863].

[493] Schüssler Fiorenza, Elisabeth, and Anne Carr, eds. *Women, Work and Poverty*. Edinburgh: T. & T. Clark, 1987.
Sixteen essays comprise this *Concilium* reader on women, work and poverty, and Schüssler Fiorenza's editorial introduction provides the wide framework for their selection. Namely, that the essays reflect a "critical feminist theology" of how women, work and poverty are structurally and ideologically maintained, both within and beyond ecclesiastical walls. By and large, the editors argue that women, work and poverty are linked through several globally based factors, but notably: (1) the presence of domestic and extra-domestic violence; (2) the coupling of this violence with women's socialization to domesticity; and (3) the various theologies that provide ideological support to domesticity and unpaid "shadow" work, whether in and beyond church organizations. By way of specifics, Marita Estor, Hannelore Schroder and M. Shawn Copeland provide "systemic analyses," respectively, of women's unpaid labor, the inverse economics of mother/father parenting roles, and the "intersection of racism, sexism and classism in women's exploitation." In turn, several case studies document women's poverty and exploitation in international, homeless and church-wide structures, and four closing entries suggest still needed areas of feminist reflection, analysis and reconstruction. Last, Carr's editorial reflections "Sharing and Feeding the Hunger..." view the entries as a whole to press the important methodological issue of how to make women's needs *more visible* within and beyond religious and social spheres.

NOTE: For global data on women and poverty see Morgan [9] and Neft and Levine [10]; for U.S. data see Feinberg and Knox [124], Ries [126], Rix [127], and Taeuber [128].

2. Women and Sexuality

NOTE: For general bibliography on women and sexuality see Sahli [54]. Additionally, see Chapter 15 ("The Feminist Critique of Heterosexism") and Chapter 22, "Patriarchy, Violence and Sexual Harassment in the Churches."

[494] Becher, Jeanne, ed. *Women, Religion and Sexuality: Studies on the Impact of Religious Teachings on Women.* Philadelphia: Trinity Press International, 1990.
This collection of papers surveys formal and traditional teachings about women's sexuality from within several religious perspectives: Judaism (both Orthodox and Reform, by Blu Greenberg **[975]** and Pnina Levinson **[976]**, respectively); Hinduism (Vasudha Narayanan); Islam (Riffat Hassan); the tradition of Akan from Ghana (Elizabeth Amoah); Buddhism (Junko Minamato); Romanian Orthodoxy (Anca-Lucia Manolache); French Orthodoxy (Elizabeth Behr-Sigel and Nicole Maillard); Roman Catholicism (Maria-Teresa Porcile-Santiso and Rosemary Radford Ruether); and New Zealand Anglicanism (Janet Crawford). A response to the latter by Carter Heyward closes the text.

[495] Cooey, Paula M., Sharon A. Farmer, and Mary Ellen Ross, eds. *Embodied Love: Sensuality and Relationship as Feminist Values.* San Francisco: Harper & Row, 1987.
This reader in feminist ethics presents 13 original essays on embodiment and relationality, subgrouped around the ideas of: "Embodiment, Identity and Value" (four essays); "Embodiment, Communication and Ethics" (five essays); and "Embodiment, Relationship and Religious Experience" (four essays). Contributors to the first group include editor Cooey, feminist theologians Ruether and Schüssler Fiorenza and goddess thealogian, Carol Christ. All offer reflections on the ways various dualisms shape women's experience, and all offer insights toward freeing women from the oppressions borne of such dualisms. In the second set of essays, contributors Sheila Davaney **[330]**, Claudia Camp, Sharon Farmer, Linell Cady and Mary Ellen Ross variously depict the relational dimensions of communication--how communication is and ought to be understood as relational, whether the communication is biblical/theological language (Camp and Farmer), the behaviors (and ideologies) of Christian "love" (Cady), or the affirmation of individualism and autonomy as ethical issues in world hunger (Ross). In the final set of essays, attention is directed to relationality and embodiment as expressed in the gendering dynamics of religious experience. Here contributors Ellen Umansky, Terris Castaneda, Patricia Hill and Gregor Goethals address, respectively, gender roles in historically specific Jewish communities, the impact of Christian tradition on contemporary African women, the religious-gender expectations of women in Harriet Beecher Stow's writing, and the expressions of intimacy and justice in women's art. These essays reflect several feminist perspectives, including critiques of feminist theological method (cf. **[330]**); they are consistently provocative (e.g., Camp's "Female Voice, Written Word: Women and Authority in Hebrew Scripture"); and many (e.g., Cady's "Relational Love...") draw well from sociological theory--in this particular case, Geertz's "religion as a cultural system."

[496] Davies, Susan E., and Eleanor H. Haney, eds. *Redefining Sexual Ethics: A Sourcebook of Essays, Stories and Poems.* Cleveland, OH: Pilgrim, 1991.
This collection is divided into two widely based sections. The first is "The Ground We Walk On," a series of 24 poetic and reflective statements addressing the contributors' personal experiences, selected essays on "Religious Community, Theology and Sexuality" and an extended series of entries on "Social Structure and Sexuality." The contributors to this first section reflect the inclusive efforts of feminist ethics generally, with Native-American, Womanist, feminist, Asian and *Mujerista* perspectives each represented and addressing (in varying degrees) the issues of abuse, domestic violence, same-sex relationality, compulsory monogamy, and the interstructuring of American sexual, racial, gender and class norms. In Part II, "The Land We Seek," an additional 14 contributors provide visions of a changed ethical world, with the possibilities here also articulated in poetic and reflective terms. A final section (prepared by editor Davies) surveys feminist pedagogy and offers a variety of study questions which contrast and highlight emphases of topically related entries. In addition to both the range of concerns addressed by this collection and the varying genres which reflect that range, a second value to this collection is its inclusion of male sexuality--black, white, gay, and straight--as an element of the feminist discussion. Chapter notes and a list of contributors (but no indices) close the volume. This collection helpfully identifies current issues and possibilities in feminist sexual ethics and will prove useful both to those seeking a helpful undergraduate reader/text and those seeking an initial overview of the field.

[497] Harrison, Beverly W. "Human Sexuality and Mutuality." In *Christian Feminism: Visions of a New Humanity,* edited by Judith Weidman, 141-157. San Francisco: Harper & Row, 1984.
This entry by Harrison articulates "Christianity's legacy of human sexuality and gender roles," through categories drawn largely from James B. Nelsen's *Embodiment: An Approach To Sexuality and Christian Theology* [Minneapolis: Augsburg Press, 1978] to identify the values of embodied

respect and mutuality as bases for a feminist ethic of sexuality. Harrison argues that because Christianity's "traditional" ethic is premised on a hierarchy of complimentary gender roles-- with males holding power over females--sexuality is, in turn, an existential struggle for "power over" persons (or, alternatively, the giving over of one's own power to another), such that the freeing experience of genuinely encountered mutuality between equals is virtually precluded. A feminist affirmation of embodied sexuality, however, opens the possibility for a different ethic: one which discards complementarity and emphasizes instead, empowerment (rather than power over or power abrogated) and mutuality (rather than coercion or exploitation). Last, this ethic fosters a vision of justice-seeking in the making of "right relations" and it thus re-opens the consideration of personal agency before the biblical teaching of a Living God. This essay compliments Harrison's discussion of "Homophobia and Misogyny" [569] and like the latter, it bursts with implications for several considerations: an understanding of ministry freed from the negative [hetero]sexuality of "familism" whether in congregations or clergy marriages; analyses of racial and structured bigotry; and an understanding of work in industrial society as grounded in a theology of justice rather than complementarity.

[498] Lugibihl, Jan, ed. "This is My Body...A Response to Prostitution." *Daughters of Sarah* 19, no. 1 (1993): 4-41.
This issue presents several brief but informative discussions about prostitution, with the majority addressing "sex tourism" and child prostitution in Asia, and others the various dimensions of prostitution as a social reality: its frequent roots in the experiences of early childhood molestation, its violence as a pimp-controlled exploitation of poor (and not so poor) women's sexuality, and the many similarities prostitution bears to other aspects of women's lives and sexual experience. Among others, contributors include various *DOS* editorial staff (Finger, Falsani, and Volentine), anti-abuse activists Lisa Hendrickson and Sr. Joan Brown and psychologists Mary Jo Meadow and James Murphy. This is a painful issue of the journal, with statistics and ethics all too clearly in view and with its truths stated in undeniably clear terms. Various reviews and responses to the *DOS* issue on "Divine Child Abuse" [864] close out the issue.

3. Women and Reproductive Freedom

[499] Cahill, Lisa Sowle. "Catholic Sexual Ethics and the Dignity of the Person: A Double Message." *Theological Studies* 50 (1989): 120-150.
One of seven entries in the "Moral/Ethics" issue of the "Fiftieth Anniversary Volume" of *Theological Studies*, this essay summarizes the development of Catholic sexual ethics and the emergence of personalist motifs within Catholic sexual ethics from 1939 through 1989. Thus it surveys the bulk of twentieth century Catholic thought on contraception and sexuality, including the gradual personalization of natural law theory, the emergence of ethical questions attendant on same-sex relations, issues relevant to reproductive technologies and last, the significance of women's experience as a source of ethical insight. The literature on feminism is limited largely to Rosemary Radford Ruether's work since her bibliography on ethics, sexuality and feminism spans more than 25 years of published work within the Catholic theological setting. Strong points of Cahill's discussion include: (1) the historical framework it provides; (2) its clear summary of the factors precipitating the development of personalist-traditionalist tensions in Catholic ethical literature; (3) its bibliography on Ruether; and (4) the challenging conclusions it presents for traditionalist Catholic ethics. It is a solid bibliographic source for Catholic natural law (*and* its limitations) and for the early sources of personalism in mainstream Catholic sexual ethics.

[500] Farley, Margaret A. "Feminist Theology and Bioethics." In *Women's Consciousness, Women's Conscience: A Reader in Feminist Ethics*, edited by Barbara Hilkert Andolsen, Christine E. Gudorf and Mary D. Pellauer, 285-305. Minneapolis, MN: Winston Press, 1985.[Also published in *Feminist Theological Ethics*, edited by Lois K. Daly. Louisville: Westminster John Knox Press, 1994.]
In a manner similar to her discussion of feminist consciousness and the interpretation of biblical texts [364] Farley here explores three feminist theological themes--relationality, embodiment and nature--to identify their "connections to issues in the field of bioethics" (p. 285). Theme #1, relationality, is grounded in the need to overturn historically distorted super- and subordinate perceptions of gender roles as generated historically by patriarchal religion. Embodiment, or theme #2 also stems from the critique of patriarchal Christianity, and it seeks to redress Christianity's association of women's bodies with evil and/or idealized perfection. Last, the feminist theological assessment of "nature" redresses the "predatory hierarchical" God-creation pattern presumed by patriarchal religion--and acknowledges limits to what is ethically possible and permissible within

creation, given the embodiment of human persons. Following her summary of these themes, Farley presents selected elements of feminist methodology, but notably the feminist hermeneutical principle that "what diminishes or denies the full humanity of women must be presumed not to reflect the divine..." (cf. Ruether [365, 366]), and she examines *in vitro* fertilization as one "bioethics issue." Her discussion details the implications of both the principles and the hermeneutic she has unfolded, as she addresses issues of women's empowerment and agency in the decision to bear *and rear* children and the role of distributive justice as the grounding norm of such decisions when other "basic human needs place legitimate prior claims on the recourses involved" (p. 304). Her closing comments sum the discussion and consider further avenues of analysis. **NOTE**: For additional (Catholic) sources on bioethics and women's sexuality as discussed through the early 1990s, see the essays by Gudorf, Ryan and Lauritzen in Curran, Farley and McCormick [755].

[501] Finger, Reta, ed. "Christian Feminist Perspectives on Birth, Abortion, and Adoption." *Daughters of Sarah* 18, no. 4 (1992): 4-55.
The plural character of the noun "perspectives" in this thematic issue of DOS intimates its breadth; for in addition to "A Christian Feminist Dialogue on Abortion" (with well developed arguments pro and con) the issue's usual array of brief but pointed articles addresses several "perspectives" on birth, abortion and adoption. These include feminist and evangelical reflections on infertility, surrogacy, adoption, birthing, sexuality, and the grief(s) of miscarriage and children lost. In addition (and as regular *DOS* features) the issue presents a variety of topically related reviews and numerous listings of "books in brief," personal and organizational resources.

[502] Harrison, Beverly. "Theology and Morality of Procreative Choice." In Beverly Harrison, *Making the Connections: Essays in Feminist Social Ethics*, edited by Carol S. Robb, 115-134. Boston: Beacon, 1985.
First published in 1981, but significantly revised for inclusion in this reader, Harrison's discussion here identifies both the general sources of acrimony separating "pro-life" and "pro-choice" positions on the issue of abortion and the moral principles which support the pro-choice position. Important points include (but are not limited to) the following: First, Harrison begins by noting the significance of procreation as an indicator of divine blessing and its concomitant sacralization via the rise of patriarchy. Second, as she reviews general Catholic and Protestant perspectives on abortion, she notes the essentially singular position of Protestant theologians and Catholic hierarchy on this issue, *viz.*, that Catholic hierarchical leadership does not recognize women's moral agency-- women's choice--in matters of sexuality and procreation, and that, in effect, Protestant theologians do not either, since the latter call upon either Catholic natural law (or biblicist anti-intellectualism) to bolster their opposition to women's choice. Third, Harrison notes the paucity of theological references to abortion prior to the 19th century. That is, although medievalists had understood abortion as the termination of life after its "quickening" in the womb, theology did not hold the current pro-life perspective of seeing fetal life at conception as equal with full human development. (Nor, she notes, were Protestant clergy particularly vocal about abortion prior to 19th century American anti-immigration perspectives seeking Protestant clergy support.) Fourth, Harrison identifies several moral principles which should ground the anti-abortion/pro-choice discussion, and paramount among them is the need to develop theory in the light of an accurate rendering of the experience of the agent facing the specific moral decision--here, females faced with the possibility of legalized involuntary pregnancy as resulting (variously) from sexual violence, a lack of reproductive knowledge, contraceptive failure etc. All of these factors--and the several years of commitment entailed in child rearing--must be weighed against the reality of rhetoric which equates abortion with murder and in a society which has yet to protect the full rights of the women who would be forced to experience involuntary pregnancy. Fifth, and relatedly, Harrison reviews the wisdom and necessity for safe choice-supported social policy regardless of individuals' positions on abortion, and last, she argues strongly for a theological exposition of women's right to bodily integrity and the rejection of morally objectionable economic or racist arguments in support of pro-choice perspectives. Harrison's discussion here is prepared in conjunction with Shirley Cloyes, with Harrison's more developed arguments appearing in *Our Right to Choose* [Boston: Beacon, 1984]. Her bottom line for both texts, however, is that it is the right of choice which is the moral right women are now denied, and it is the establishment of this right which will evidence society's justice for all.

[503] Harrison, Beverly W. "Situating the Dilemma of Abortion Historically." *Conscience* 11 (1990): 15-20.
This discussion was presented at the 1989 *Catholics For a Free Choice* conference, "Future Shock: New Challenges in Ethics and Reproductive Health," and it is a readable, succinct statement of

Harrison's procreative "choice" position. Following her preliminary comments on the purpose of the conference and the development of her own feminist thinking, Harrison begins with her classic insight that feminist ethical methodology must start with a demystification of the power relations surrounding any given problem, and here specifically, the issue of women's choices about childbearing and reproduction. These power relations continue the growing "pauperization of women" or the continued control of women, but particularly women's work and reproductive rights, through the global structures of sexism, classism, and racism. They are worldwide and, among other things, they are the continuing indicator that women are not taken seriously as moral agents. Second, Harrison addresses the relationship between moral and political rights, and the necessity for feminists to communicate *politically* the idea that it is women's *moral right to bodily integrity* which grounds choice and reproductive rights, and not vice versa. Third, Harrison considers the range of effort needed to institutionalize such thinking, and it is vast. She notes the use of torture and violence as mechanisms of social control, and she characterizes the current assault on legal abortion as a "form of low-intensity warfare against women." Last, she calls for the construction of an ethic which recognizes "deep *revulsion against* bodily violations," including that of "enforced pregnancy" (p. 20). As with her wider discussion of abortion [*Our Right to Choose, Toward a New Ethic of Abortion*. Boston: Beacon, 1984] and her related work, this piece also reflects both (a) Harrison's deep care for the fate of women and the children they bear--which as she notes at the beginning of her remarks is a care for "the well-being of everybody;" and (b) her consistently keen sense of social dynamics and the real political needs for the success of feminist efforts--here the decentering of choice as enshrined in the "liberal" rights of the private sphere--and its *recentering* in the public, i.e., moral (human and civil) sphere.

[504] Hume, Maggie. "Contraception in Catholic Doctrine: The Evolution of an Earthly Code." *Conscience* 13 (1992-1993): 5-22.

This clearly written and highly readable discussion presents an historical overview and analysis of Vatican teaching on birth control, as the latter stems from papal readings of biblical, patristic, medieval, and post-reformational sources and carries through to the Second Vatican Council, *Humanae Vitae* and current discussions of feminism, sexuality and American church involvement in the anti-abortion movement. The author demonstrates the historically fluid, evolving norms grounding the Vatican discussion of sexuality and contraception, and she attends consistently to the impact of demographic, economic and nationally localized issues on ecclesiastical, canonical, theological and ethical discussion. Her analysis includes an extended discussion of the role of dissent from non-infallible teaching, and she closes with the observation that current Vatican discussion reflects less a concern about sexuality and contraception, and more an engulfing power play between the Vatican and the rights and opportunities of Catholic theologians to question and discuss non-infallible teachings. This is an informative overview: it synthesizes information from several sources and provides the reader with a ready access to both the literature and current issues. **NOTE:** For related literature see Hofman [511], Mills [513], and Maguire [505] below. Additionally, see Chapter 8 and the Subject Index for sources on misogyny and sexuality.

[505] Maguire, Majorie Riley. "Pluralism on Abortion in the Theological Community: The Controversy Continues." *Conscience* 7 (1986): 1-10.

This article was occasioned by a critique of *Catholics For a Free Choice* (CFFC) presented by Richard Doeflinger in the 11/16/85 issue of the Jesuit weekly, *America*. In the latter, Doeflinger had been strongly critical of both the organization, CFFC, as well as Daniel Maguire, a widely published Catholic ethicist, who together with 96 other Catholic ethicists and theologians had signed a *New York Times* ad (10/7/84) signaling the presence of pluralism within the Catholic community (on the issue of abortion), and additionally, the possibility of "legitimate dissent" from the hierarchical teaching of Rome on this issue. In response, then, Marjorie Maguire presented this discussion as a defense of both CFFC and Daniel Maguire, who had been singled out in the *America* article for specific mention. Maguire's response is developed in two parts. First, she presents a summary of the NY Times ad, its signers and Doeflinger's erroneous assumptions and statements about it. Second, she presents a review of the then current literature evidencing the plurality of Catholic theological opinions addressing the issue of abortion and the responses one might make to the Catholic hierarchy's position that the "termination of all pre-natal life is morally wrong in all cases." Her review cites ethical, theological and canonical sources and summarizes the doctrine of probabilism, the debates about personhood and ensoulment, and the widening base of insights constituting the theological horizons of Catholic theologians generally. **NOTE:** For publications by Roman Catholic authors holding to the historical pluralism of abortion perspectives in Catholic theology, see the semi-annual publications of *Conscience*, "a news journal of prochoice

Catholic opinion" published by Catholics for a Free Choice, 2008 17th St., NW Washington, DC, 20009.

4. Interstructured Oppression

[506] Andolsen, Barbara Hilkert. "Gender and Sex Roles in Recent Religious Ethics Literature." *Religious Studies Review* 11 (1985): 217-223.
This discussion examines "religious ethics literature" current through 1983 to assay its responses to the questions: "Are there differences between the sexes (beyond reproductive differences) which we have a moral obligation to respect? [and] Should human beings shape culture to enhance or minimize sexual differences? In her review Andolsen observes that religious ethicists need greater attention to empirical data and that gender is typically understood from within the heterosexual framework of complementarity. By way of literature topics, she notes that the literature is undecided on whether women have an "innate moral superiority" over men and whether culture socializes males to "distorted [gender] expectations." As a last point she indicates that the literature evidences a "deepening critique of the feminine" (actually she is referring to Harrison's ideological critique of femininity as the 'hook' for women's gender compliance), and she calls for a more empirically sensitive ethical reflection, for greater attention to the socio-historical construction of gender and 'embodiment,' and 'further clarification of a vision of full human personhood as male and 'female." The essay lacks a clear feminist focus, and it is not recommended as one of Andolsen's better pieces. Rather, the reader is referred to Andolsen et al. **[468]**. Similarly, a companion piece in the same journal is also not recommended. In "Social Science of Gender Differences: Ideological Battleground" [*Religious Studies Review* 11(1985): 223-228] author Richard Kahoe reviews much literature drawn from *Psychological Abstracts*. Kahoe's discussion, however, is at points blatantly sexist (e.g., p. 227), unmindful of social structure as a factor in power relations, and is unnecessarily obscure in both tone and approach. For more readable and "user friendly" sources, the reader is referred to the theoretical and supplemental listings on gender and sex roles presented in Section I of this bibliography.

[507] Collins, Patricia Hill. "Third World Women in America" In *The Women's Annual: 1980; The Year in Review*, edited by Barbara Haber, 87-116. Boston: G. K. Hall, 1981.
This early essay by Collins provides an introductory overview of the sociological issues attached to "race, sex and social class," with discussion and data on Black women, Mexican American women, Puerto Rican, Native-American and Asian-American women. Collins' data here need obvious updating from subsequently published sources, but her discussion and bibliography are helpful early sources. Last, her listing of agencies and supportive organizations for Women of Color is also helpful, for it provides full mailing addresses and brief organizational histories. For Collins' principal work see **[99]**.

[508] Riggs, Marcia Y. "The Logic of Interstructured Oppression: A Black Womanist Perspective." In *Redefining Sexual Ethics: A Sourcebook of Essays, Stories, and Poems*, edited by Susan E. Davies and Eleanor H. Haney, 97-192. Cleveland, OH: Pilgrim, 1991.
This discussion synthesizes several emphases which provide the basis for Riggs' analysis of the concept, *interstructured oppression*. These include: (1) Riggs' highly nuanced understanding of womanism and its relation to black people generally; (2) her critique of the concept, "relationality," as open to "weak" and "strong" ethical usage; and (3) her synthesis of womanist, feminist and biblical insights as dimensions of a liberative social ethic that can direct the pattern of ethical expectations among white feminists and black womanists within the academy. According to Riggs, the womanist vision is "inextricably bound up with the struggle of Black people for liberation from race, gender and class oppression" (p. 98), but because the latter is often heard in terms of two readings of relationality--the one biological and the other sociohistorical, ambivalent expectations exist between and among feminist and womanist scholars. In particular, a 'biological' reading of relationality seeks to bond women in terms of women's generic biological status as women, and not in terms of their differing historical experiences, *viz.*, the idealization and conflation of genteelness with white women's experience on the one hand, and the denial of personhood and the enslavement of Black women on the other. Thus, a biological reading of relationality can engender a "weak" ethical posture vis a vis the relations of black and white women, because the socio-historical fact of depersonalization via slavery is missing from white women's consciousness. Alternatively, a socio-historical reading of relationality can engender a "strong" ethical response (vis a vis the relations of black and white women), precisely because it recognizes and includes an awareness of

the historical and sociocultural evil done (by whites) to black women. It is Riggs' hope that the sociohistorical reading of relationality will come to prevail, for when read in the light of biblical liberation emphases, it can provide a normative framework for ethical decision making by white and black women within the academy about issues tied to "racial privilege."

NOTE: For related literature, Thistlethwaite [252], Thistlethwaite and Engel [276], Opotow [514] and Reid and Clayton [516] below.

D. Supplemental Sources

[509] Collins, Randall and Scott Coltrane. *Sociology of Marriage and the Family: Gender, Love, and Property.* 4th ed. Chicago: Nelsen Hall, 1995.
A standard introductory "sociology of marriage and the family" this text incorporates feminist insights and critiques of patriarchy, sexism and androcentrism into the majority of its discussions. It approaches "marriage and family" from the usual sociological division of concerns, e.g., definitions of marriage and types of family structure, the impact of racial and economic stratification systems, male and female statistics on the emotional, sexual, marital, divorce and re-marital status of Americans, questions of childbearing, sexual rituals, the future of marriage and the like. The discussion of marital/extramarital violence is clear, well-documented and informative to those unfamiliar with the literature, although specific texts in this area should be also consulted. The text is directed to a general audience, albeit with asides to the young college-aged student, its presumed audience. The overall orientation is a conflict rather than a functionalist perspective, and the book's general formatting makes it readable and easy to use. Its data are inclusive through the publication year, and while this abstract is based on the 1995 edition, a 1997 text is available. For updating data on marriage, family size, divorce, and related racial and economic factors, readers should consult the well-indexed, annual publication, *Statistical Abstracts of the United States.* Additionally, for a text that seeks to address both conflict and functionalist perspectives while being sensitive to "liberal" and "evangelical" theologies, see the regularly revised, *Men, Women and Change: A Sociology of Marriage and Family,* Letha Dawn Scanzoni and John Scanzoni. [New York: McGraw-Hill.] Although not reviewed in this volume, it is a highly readable college level introductory discussion, self-consciously aware of evangelical Christian values, and theoretically open to a plurality of perspectives. Additionally, see Chapter 21 for sources on violence in families and see Chapter 16 for the literature on African American women.

[510] Freeman, Jo. "The Revolution for Women in Law and Public Policy" In *Women: A Feminist Reader* edited by Jo Freeman, 365-404. 5th ed. Mountain View, CA: Mayfield, 1995.
This comprehensive discussion focuses the "revolution" in law and public policy for women in terms of four topics: (1) a review of family law, protective labor legislation and the civil and political rights of women to identify the "tradition of internalized dependency" to which women have historically been socialized in English and American society; (2) an overview of Supreme Court decisions concerning women, work, education, the military, pregnancy and parenthood issues; (3) the "legislative gains" women have made in terms of equal pay, Title VII and EEOC, the early history of the ERA, and the "family leave act;" and (4) the "Challenges Ahead," *viz.*, the need for a social reorganization which, among other things: (a) "abolishes institutionalized sex role differences and the concept of adult dependency," (b) "recognizes the individual as the principal economic unit," and (c) "provide[s]...necessary services for individuals to support themselves and help support their children." Additionally, other newly disclosed problems that also need legal redress include: "glass ceilings," the prevalence of violence, degradation and pornography in work and society--and in the home, incest, sexual abuse and domestic violence. While current only through 1993, this text provides a detailed review of cases and legislative history. **NOTE:** For a more expanded discussion (not abstracted here), see Joan Huff, *Unequal Before the Law: A Legal History of U.S. Women.* NY: New York Univ. Press, 1991.

[511] Hofman, Brenda. "Political Theology: The Role of Organized Religion in the Anti-Abortion Movement." *Journal of Church and State* 26 (1986): 225-248.
This article surveys the political activity of conservative religious groups—but notably the National Conference of Catholic Bishops [NCCB]—in their efforts to overturn the 1973 Supreme Court decision, Roe v. Wade, and secure, in addition, the passage of a constitutional amendment prohibiting abortion. By way of background the author notes several distinctions between public and private issues, and she surveys the plurality of positions that various religious groups hold about abortion. These include a range of theological options about the 'ethics' of abortion and the

specific theological issues it engenders: when conception begins, what quality of life factors can or may affect decisions about abortion and the question of privacy in such decisions. Hofman then examines the literature and lobbying efforts of the NCCB from within this framework and she identifies the many nuanced definitions grounding the NCCB's efforts to influence the political process. Similar efforts by conservative Protestant groups are also identified, but attention is directly mostly towards the NCCB. This is an informative and clearly written article which quickly introduces the reader to the main lines of American Catholicism's political efforts at undoing Roe v. Wade. For general literature on the history of American bishops vis a vis women see Iadorola [747]. For two critical reviews of the theological perspectives underlying the NCCB's political efforts, see Hume [504]. and Maguire [505], while for a history of the "Religious Coalition for Abortion Rights" (which indicates that a pro-choice position can also be religiously grounded) see Mills [513].

[512] Kemp, Alice Abel. "Poverty and Welfare for Women." In *Women: A Feminist Reader* edited by Jo Freeman, 448-480. 5th ed. Mountain View, CA: Mayfield, 1995.
Students of feminist ethics will find this article helpful in several ways. First, students unfamiliar with sociological discussions of U.S. poverty will find this article's concepts and statistics (e.g., definitions of poverty and the poverty rate and basic poverty trends for persons, families and children) clearly defined, well graphed and easily readable. Second, students more experienced with the literature will appreciate Kemp's general overview, her summary of the "feminization of poverty" (i.e., in 1992 women comprised 57.4% of the poverty population), and her general discussion of theories of why women are poor. With census and other data current through 1992, the detailed notes and extended bibliography completing this discussion make it a most useful introductory source.

[513] Mills, Samuel A. "Abortion and Religious Freedom: The Religious Coalition for Abortion Rights (RCAR) and the Pro-Choice Movement, 1973-1989." *Journal of Church and State* 33 (1991): 569-594.
This article surveys the history and development of the *Religious Coalition for Abortion Rights* (RCAR) from its inception in 1973 to its protest against the Bush administration's request that the Supreme Court use Webster v. Reproductive Health Services to overturn Roe v. Wade in April of 1989. Overall, the author focuses this history around (1) the efforts by the RCAR to combat conservative attempts to overturn Roe and establish a constitutional amendment prohibiting abortion and (2) the manner and means through which RCAR attained media exposure and visibility during the mid and late 1980s. With respect to its efforts to combat conservative forces, Mills notes that the RCAR spent most of its energies from 1973 to the mid-80s on the attempt "to convince Conree that the abortion decision was inextricably related to religious considerations on which no consensus existed" (p. 572). The substance of this effort was tied to the range of time frames and the plurality of perspectives held by various religious groups concerning the concept of fetal personhood, and according to Mills, the RCAR was successful in communicating that "the pro-choice position can be and frequently is a deeply religious one" (p. 591). Second, by way of increasing its visibility and effectiveness as an advocacy group, the RCAR gained heightened exposure and credibility when its exposure of 'bogus abortion clinics' was publicized by nationally syndicated media such as the *New York Times*. RCAR's least successful efforts, suggests Mills, have been in the attempt to secure public funding for abortions and in combating of the power of the Hyde amendment.

[514] Opotow, Susan, ed. "Moral Exclusion and Injustice." *Journal of Social Issues* 46 (1990): 1-182.
This thematic issue of *JSI* examines the subject of "moral exclusion and injustice" from a variety of perspectives, including theory, research, and practical philosophical questions. Editor Opotow's opening essay sets the framework by noting that "moral exclusion occurs when individuals or groups are perceived as outside the boundary in which moral values, rules and considerations of fairness apply" (p. 1). She then continues with an exploration of the conditions and variables that enhance and inhibit "the scope of justice" as perceived by individuals and groups. Subsequent essays amplify theories and research questions attendant on the development of individuals' exclusionary attitudes (and behaviors) and those of social groups and organizations. Psychological theories (e.g., "splitting" and "object relations theory"), mechanisms by which individuals (and social groups) disengage from moral responsibility, racial/ethnic, occupational and philosophical questions all receive attention in this journal issue, and as both the editor and individual contributors note, while justice research in the social science literature is by no means cohesive, certain

contributing factors can be identified and used as bases for additional research. Theologians and ethicists will find this a readable and *very* informative journal issue (with technical statistical material kept to a minimum) and sociologists will find it helpful in conceptualizing problems common to both fields.

[515] Parrillo, Vincent N., ed. "Multiculturalism and Diversity." *Sociological Forum* 9 (1994): 519-640.
This special issue of the *Forum* presents five essays addressing various aspects of multiculturalism in the United States. Parrillo's "Diversity in America: A Sociohistorical Analysis," provides the introductory overview and is followed by Martin Spencer's "Multiculturalism, 'Political Correctness,' and the Politics of Identity," which details the history of nativistic and cosmopolitan perspectives. Third is "Diversity and Equality: Race and Class in America," by Walda Katz-Fishman and Jerome Scott, who examine the economic and political polarizations borne of the electronic revolution and, alternatively, the latter's democracy producing possibilities. Fourth, Ruben G. Rumbaut updates immigration statistics together with the economic and settlement patterns of the 'new diversity' from World War II through the 1990 census, while, Harald Runblom's "Swedish Multiculturalism in a Comparative European Perspective" closes out the issue. All essays are well-documented and easily readable by non-technical audiences. NOTE: For international sources as well as several culturally specific bibliographies, see *Multiculturalism and the Canon of American Culture*, edited by Hans Bak. VU Univ. Press, Amsterdam, 1993.

[516] Reid, Pamela Trotman, and Susan Clayton. "Racism and Sexism at Work." *Social Justice Research* 5 (1992): 249-268.
Presented as one of several articles within a thematic issue addressing "Affirmative Action and Social Justice" [see *Social Justice Research* 5(1992): 219-341, edited by Susan Opotow], this article describes racism and sexism as prejudices which engender discrimination, but from within the contrasting 'social' and 'individual' assumptions which condition: (a) the definitions of racism and sexism; their singular ("main") and combined ("interactive") effects; and (c) the ways in which perceptions about racism and sexism condition affirmative action programs and, last, the subsequent perceptions recipients and audiences have about such programs. The authors draw out several practical and research based implications, and the discussion is particularly strong in its analysis of the *non-paralleling* effects which these two prejudices have both socially and institutionally, and the ways in which these non-paralleling effects victimize women of color.

NOTE: For current data on the changing status and statistics of American families beyond that provided in Collins [509], see the discussions provided in such regularly updated introductory sociology texts as those indicated in the "General Introduction" to the bibliography.

13

Feminist Theology and Christian Worship

The literature gathered under the heading, "Feminist Theology and Christian Worship" is multi-dimensional and reflects the many ways in which controversy can come to surround religious symbols. On the one hand, it is a literature which celebrates the role of women in rites and rituals, with clear attention to the prophetic power of religious language as a vehicle of social change. At the same time, it is a literature often reduced--and almost mockingly so--to "debates about inclusive language," as antifeminists trivialize feminist efforts to mirror the fullness of historical and denominationally grounded communities of worship (cf. Stroup [844]).

Overall, two issues continue to be in conflict. The first is the ongoing question of liturgical language and its "gendered" theological width. That is, should language, as a medium for speech about God, be used minimalistically? That is, should liturgical language be geared only to the use of "non-sexist" or "non-androcentric" theological constructs and images? Or alternatively, might it not also be focused to its maximal potential, through the use of "female," and ultimately "feminist," language for God: *viz.*, the use of female nouns and pronouns such as "Mother" and "She," and in the long run, such specifically feminist biblical appropriations as "Sophia" and "Holy Wisdom." While much current theology supports and indeed advocates such a maximal linguistic usage, there are few churches able to sustain such a vision and move comfortably to its social—and sociological—implications. Hence the absence of denominationally published congregational resources.

The second issue at play in the feminist liturgical literature is the driving issue of power: both in the conventional sense of "Who shall control the language of the liturgy?" and more widely, the institutional sense of "How can communities become more empowered toward inclusive belonging?" This is an obviously important issue, for given that churches typically require theological rationales to make changes in their organizational and liturgical structures, power here is tied to a variety of methodological, doctrinal, and other symbolic issues, including those of trinitarian and Christological reflection, the significance of ordained women, and last but by no means least, the communal experiences of "women-church" and women's spirituality groups. Hence, the potential for controversy surrounding the role of women in rites and rituals and the attempts of antifeminists to reduce feminist liturgiology to a seemingly trivialized "debate about inclusive language."

In the literature below Collins ([517], [518]) and Procter-Smith ([521], [522]) consistently present cutting edge discussions on the prophetic and performative capacities of feminist language and liturgy, while early sources (e.g., Neufer-Emswiler and Neufer-Emswiler [525] and Swidler [529]) illustrate the gradual incorporation of women's experience into congregationally rooted worship settings. In turn, various resources indicate the media of transformation in church liturgical organization (e.g., *The Inclusive Language Lectionary* [524], Schaffran and Kozak [527], Throckmorton [530] and Winter [531]) while the chapter's closing entries evidence both the institutionalization of womanist and feminist homiletics (cf., Cannon [532], and Procter-Smith [533] and Smith [534], respectively) and a selection of sermon collections ([535[, [536], [537]) published early in the development of the literature.

A few final notes: First, it is obvious that the literature of this chapter should be read in conjunction with sources for other sections, but particularly the general literatures in Section II and the entries in Chapter III-4 on "Historical Christian Symbols." Second, because most of the "early literature" on inclusive worship was experimental in nature and done through the editing and xeroxing of older hymns and service texts revised for specific groups and/or liturgical occasions, the published literature here is sparse, although the Swidler and Watkins texts are good indicators of the construction and revision of existing materials for early feminist use--and in Watkins's case, the attempt to understand the place of feminist materials vis a vis established and socially settled theologies of congregational worship. Likewise, because of the rapid and very fluid development of feminist liturgies per se, readers should consult current periodical indices for denominationally rooted feminist and womanist worship resources, and WATER (the Women's Alliance for Theology Ethics and Ritual) located in Silver Spring, MD (cf., e.g., [789]) for ecumenical sources.

Last, there are at least two sources which are not abstracted here, but which might still be of use for many. These are *Image-breaking/Image-building: A Handbook for Creative Worship with Women of Christian Tradition* by Linda Clark, Marian Ronan and Eleanor Walker and *Bread for the Journey: Resources for Worship*, edited by Ruth Duck. Both were published through Pilgrim Press in 1981 and both contain materials still helpful for many local congregations.

A. Worship and Inclusive Language

1. Theological Sources

[517] Collins, Mary. "Naming God in Public Prayer." *Worship* 59 (1985): 291-305.
The purpose of this article is two-fold: it seeks first to place before the North American Academy of Liturgy the question, "How shall we address God in public prayer?" and second, it seeks subsequently to synthesize and critically review the various arguments (pro and con) for using either dimorphic (Mother/Father) language for God, or gender specific referents for God (e.g., he/she). The discussion is nuanced and no final specific names for God are presented, save that of the biblical name, YHWH. Among Collins' important observations, however, are the following: First, the pre-eminence of exclusively masculine or Father language for God cannot be sustained in the light of much current New Testament research which challenges the long standing "Abba" research provided by Joachim Jeremias (cf. D'Angelo [433]). Second, the use of medieval mysticism cannot be used to legitimate the exclusive use of "Mother" language for God--since as Bynum's *Jesus as Mother: Studies in the Spirituality of the High Middle Ages* [Berkeley: UCLA Press, 1982] shows, "mother" is but one of many medieval images used for God. Third, "an uncritical cherishing of androcentric images for God in public prayer at the end of the late twentieth century is self-indulgent" whether men or women do the cherishing. Rather, in the face of a contemporary linguistic poverty, "carefully crafted adjective and clauses" will, for the present, have to serve as vehicles of addressing the ineffable. By way of closing her discussion, Collins juxtaposes two deeply profound observations: first, the English language suffers from an ongoing "androcentric undertow," *and* the possibility of heresy that it engenders. Second, she notes that "in the present era we are increasingly aware of women all over the world who have been...confronting structures of violence and calling men and nations to justice and reconciliation...[i.e., doing activities which are themselves]...characteristics of the one ineffable God YHWH..." (p. 303). NOTE: Also by Collins are **[518]** and **[211]** co-edited with Elisabeth Schüssler Fiorenza.

[518] Collins, Mary. "Principles of Feminist Liturgy." In *Women at Worship: Interpretations of North American Diversity,* edited by Marjorie Procter-Smith and Janet R. Walton, 9-26 Louisville, KY: Westminster/John Knox, 1993.
Like **[517]** above, this discussion also reflects Collins' solid grasp of the differences between traditional and feminist perspectives. It is a "theoretical account of implicit principles of liturgical order that are in tension whenever feminist consciousness and traditional consciousness meet" (p. 10), and it describes five principles of feminist liturgical practice. After an introduction detailing the occasion of her reflections, Collins notes that feminist liturgy: (1) ritualizes relationships that emancipate and empower women; (2) are a product of a community of worshippers; (3) are critical of patriarchal liturgies (and especially their phallocentric symbols and matter/spirit dualisms); (4) are now constituted by a distinctive repertoire of symbols and strategies; and (5) are liturgical events which engender additional liturgical events but not feminist liturgical texts. As a portion of her discussion, Collins reflects upon the differences between describing feminist worship as feminist "ritual" rather than feminist "liturgy." She finds insights in each characterization and while neither fully satisfies for the breadth of her topic, she skillfully draws on the traditional notion of

"leitourgia" as an act of "good order" to indicate that howsoever it is named, "...wherever feminist consciousness is emerging, people are gathering to explore ritually and then to embody fully a future of relationships different from what has long been believed to be the truth of things" (p. 24). Well documented, fully ecumenical and clearly thought provoking.

|519| Hardesty, Nancy A. *Inclusive Language in the Church*. Atlanta, GA: John Knox, 1987.
This brief, practically directed volume describes the "confusion" and "rage" pastors and parishioners often experience over "inclusive language" in local worship. Its purpose is to demonstrate that the language of worship may be expanded rather than restricted (p. 14), and its succinct discussions of theological issues and concrete needs mark it as one of the best pastorally directed discussions available. Its chapters are brief but thorough, undergirded by contemporary scholarship, and mindful of parishioners' needs for a balance between congregational stability and new theological perspectives. Bibliography through 1984, study questions, subject and Scripture indices, and a listing of worship, prayer, proclamation and hymnal resources close the volume.

[520] LaCugna, Catherine Mowry. "The Baptismal Formula, Feminist Objections, and Trinitarian Theology." *Journal of Ecumenical Studies* 26 (1989): 235-250.
As abstracted by the author [p. 235]. . . "Some churches in the U.S.A. and Canada have recently undertaken study of the baptismal formula, occasioned by various liturgical experiments that dispense with the traditional formula of Mt. 28:19. In most cases the liturgical variations are motivated by the concern for sex-inclusive language; however, discarding one of the few practices that the churches have in common creates a difficult ecumenical situation. This article begins by examining feminist objections to the baptismal formula; then, from the standpoint of trinitarian theology, it examines whether the language of 'Father, Son and Spirit' really supports a masculine view of God. The thesis of the article is that, while the trinitarian tradition, like the Bible is *both* the source of revelatory truth about God *and* a powerful resource for patriarchal culture, it is unnecessary to repudiate the baptismal formula as inherently sexist and patriarchal. It concludes with a theology of baptism in which baptism is understood, first of all, as creating the possibility of living right relationship and, second, as being the source of power by which the people of God can become an inclusive community." The extensive bibliography, comprehensive and provocative discussion all recommend this article for serious study. **NOTE**: Also by LaCugna are **[234]**, **[273]**, **[458]**, **[459]**, and **[780]**.

[521] Procter-Smith, Majorie. *In Her Own Rite: Constructing Feminist Liturgical Tradition*. Nashville: Abingdon, 1990.
As the literatures of feminist theology, ethics, ritual and spirituality have expanded during the period of the late 1980s, few sources have systematically addressed the construction of a feminist (and Christian) liturgical *tradition* from within a consistently radical feminist perspective. Rather, sources have either indicated the grounding assumptions of situation specific liturgical rituals (e.g., Collins **[518]**) or alternatively, the assimilation of women's ritual and liturgy within the context of confessionally based denominational frameworks (cf., e.g., Swidler **[529]**). Procter-Smith's book moves beyond both of these tasks to provide a critical theological and feminist grounding for feminist liturgical *tradition*. The author's discussion parallels the four-fold hermeneutical task identified by Schüssler Fiorenza, i.e., a "hermeneutics of suspicion," "remembrance," "proclamation" and "creative actualization" (cf., e.g., **[195, 369]**), and it grounds this task in the wider context of "feminist anamnesis," i.e., feminist memory and imagination. By way of organization, Procter-Smith contrasts emphases of feminist liturgical need with the emphases of the more established liturgical movement to highlight both the nature and function--and androcentrizing of Christian liturgical activity. She thus incorporates the issues of language, God-talk, leadership and authority and established Christianity's liturgical disobedience to the gospel within her discussion, and her volume is by far, the most theoretically strong and nuanced of the literature through 1990. A well-written, well-documented and thoroughly ecumenical feminist volume, this work will in all likelihood become a classic. It is highly recommended to those seeking a foundational discussion of feminist liturgical thinking and activity and to those seeking a recovery of lost imagination and the hope for an embodied community of prayer. Although the text lacks indices and supplemental bibliography, chapter notes provide practical and theoretical references.

[522] Procter-Smith, Marjorie. "Lectionaries--Principles and Problems: Alternative Perspectives." *Studia Liturgica* 22 (1992): 84-99.
The purpose of this article is two-fold. Procter-Smith seeks first, to survey varying responses to recently published feminist/inclusivist lectionaries, and second, to respond to the questions and

concerns raised and/or implicit in these responses. Her discussion thus entails an identification of (1) the translational and canonical dissatisfactions which various groups have with such lectionaries, (2) an overview of alternatives available in the light of those dissatisfactions, and (3) a consideration of the feminist and liberationist theological hermeneutic(s) which presently govern efforts toward inclusive and pastorally sensitive worship materials. As with her earlier work [521], this essay is marked by the breadth of its vision, analysis and insight, and Procter-Smith's ability to cut cleanly to the issue(s) at hand: and here particularly, to the authority of the Bible in the context of the worshipping community and the ways in which that authority might be understood, appropriated and effected. This is an important article--both for its analysis and the literature it reviews--and it will prove a grounding source in the long term discussion of language, feminist theology, spirituality and worship.

[523] Ramshaw, Gail. *God Beyond Gender: Feminist Christian God-Language.*
    Minneapolis, MN: Fortress, 1994.
This text analyses "feminist Christian God-language" from the perspective of Lutheran theology and worship. It summarizes various biblical and feminist theological discussions, and working largely from LaCugna's work in trinitarian theology (see the listings in [520] above), it makes the case for a "reform of God-language" which is faithful to both a Lutheran commitment to the Triune God and an openness to non-fundamentalist [trinitarian] doctrine (cf., Kimel [840]). It examines issues of inclusive language, hymnody and congregational worship, "the language of trinitarian doctrine," anthropomorphic metaphors for God, and at its close, the need for a "continual and faithful reformation" within Lutheran liturgy and theology. It is not--by several standards--a radical text, for (among other things) it leaves open the linkages between clericalism, Trinitarian theology and "the Christian God." At the same time, it is a courageous text for it seeks a balanced walk between much of feminism that is potentially radical and what Ramshaw understands as previously held fundamentalist doctrine. For Ramshaw's earlier work see [452].

2. Lectionaries and Worship Resources

[524] *An Inclusive Language Lectionary: Readings for Year A.* New York: Pilgrim,
    1983. *An Inclusive Language Lectionary: Readings for Year B.* New York:
    Pilgrim, 1984. *An Inclusive Language Lectionary: Readings for Year C.* New
    York: Pilgrim, 1985.
The three year cycle of readings presented in these volumes is the same as that practiced by "Anglican, Protestant and Roman Catholic" English speaking churches, but the uniqueness of the series is its use of inclusive language for human beings, God, and the person of Christ. Texts themselves are based on the Revised Standard Version of the Bible, and in all cases of translation, the original RSV text is placed in brackets after the inclusive adaptation. Thus, the first verse of Psalm 71 (as presented on page 4 of year C) reads: "In you O God [or Lord] do I take refuge..." with the bracketed text "[or Lord]" indicating the original RSV translation. Three principles ground the adaptations undertaken in this lectionary. First, "all readings have been recast so that no masculine word pretends to include a woman" (Year C, p. 11). Thus, "brothers" e.g., becomes "brothers and sisters." Second, because it is theologically the concept of a divine *incarnation* (and not the incarnation of the divine into a male body) which is crucial, language about Jesus takes his maleness for granted. Thus he is spoken of as "the Human One," "Child," or "Child of God." Finally, because biblical translators recognize that the attributes, "gender, race and color" are all metaphorical when used of God, translators in these volumes use different, less exclusivizing metaphors for God. These include female images which can "balance" male images (*viz.*, God as mother, midwife and bakerwoman) and impersonal metaphors which seek to transcend either racial or ethnic particularities: e.g., the imaging of God as "love, rock and light." Each of the three volumes contains a brief introduction and discussion of how to use a lectionary, and "Years B" and "C" extend that introduction to include points summarized here. Finally while "Year A" presents only lessons and gospel texts, "Year B" and "Year C" also include psalms.

[525] Neufer-Emswiler, Sharon, and Thomas Neufer-Emswiler. *Women and Worship:*
    A Guide to Non-Sexist Hymns, Prayers, and Liturgies. San Francisco: Harper &
    Row, 1984.
An updated version of their 1974 volume, this guide provides a series of non-sexist hymns, prayers and liturgies, with hymnal and liturgical resources drawn from Baptist, Christian, Methodist, UCC, Lutheran and Presbyterian sources. An additional introductory chapter briefly surveys the "importance of language" from theological, psychological, sociological and linguistic sources and an additional appendix new to this revised edition provides "guidelines for non-sexist use of

language in worship." The volume closes with a listing of worship resources available through 1983, including films, books, articles, and congregationally based materials. This is a readable and helpful resource which can be used by professional and lay church workers at both introductory and advanced levels.

[526] Procter-Smith, Marjorie and Janet R. Walton, eds, *Women at Worship: Interpretations of North American Diversity*. Louisville, KY: Westminster/John Knox, 1993.
This collection of fourteen essays brings together *Mujerista*, Feminist, Womanist, Pagan, erotic, and Jewish discussions of women's ways of worshipping to provide descriptive and analytical accounts of specific worship experiences the authors have participated in. It is an informative collection, and while it presumes a working knowledge of the religious and theological perspectives it presents, it is true to its task of presenting diversity, and thus the wide sweep of women's worshipping possibilities. Although it lacks an index, it can easily serve as a secondary reader in undergraduate courses in women's studies and as a general reader for those acquainted with the religious and theological perspectives it represents. For entries abstracted from this reader, see **[517, 959, 963]** and see additional cross references cited in Neu **[790]**, Williams **[632]**, and Brown and Bohn **[863]**.

[527] Schaffran, Janet and Pat Kozak, eds. *More Than Words: Prayer and Ritual for Inclusive Communities*. 2d ed. Oak Park, IL: Meyer Stone Books, 1988.
This rich and elegantly written collection of worship services and resources is grounded in the consistent expression of inclusivity as a philosophical and liturgical norm. The authors begin by noting that the "prevailing 'current' in our society and church encompasses racism, sexism and ageism..." and that their purpose is to invite others to "paddle upstream" with them against such a current (pp. 1-2). They are less concerned with assigning blame and/or calculating which bigotry constitutes a worse evil, and more concerned with worship services that point people in a different direction and keep them focused to that. Their text includes, therefore, five extensive beginning chapters which address and illustrate the issues or, in their words, the "Concepts and Values" attached to 'inclusive language,' 'symbols and rituals,' 'images of God,' and 'cultural pluralism.' The text then continues with "guidelines for developing prayer services," with prayers and several specific services, and with a listing of resources--bibliographic and musical--incorporating the concepts and values described in the beginning chapters. It is a well put together book, a carefully written and well formatted book, and a book that lends itself to various groups, liturgical and otherwise, including educational groups, spirituality and/or women's parish groups, and clergy groups wanting to learn about gender and worship.

[528] Schreck, Nancy and Maureen Leach, eds. *Psalms Anew: In Inclusive Language*. Winona, MN: Saint Mary's Press, 1986.
This is a four week Psalter for Morning and Evening Prayer: the Benedictus, Magnificat, Doxology and the Psalms, all cast in inclusive language. The format is designed for those who wish to pray the psalms without the encumbering linguistic modifications evidenced in the *Inclusive Language Lectionary* **[524]** by means of its contrasting use of inclusive and androcentric linguistic expressions. This Psalter is highly recommended, and is of the caliber of *Womanword* **[531]** in terms of format, clarity and ease of use.

[529] Swidler, Arlene, ed. *Sistercelebrations*. Philadelphia: Fortress, 1974.
This brief volume exemplifies feminist worship during the mid 1970s. It presents nine worship services developed by Protestant, Catholic and Jewish authors, with brief introductory statements preceding each service. Two of the services were planned for specific occasions and would need extensive revision if adopted for different contexts. The remaining services can be adapted or used "as is" in congregational, home or educational settings. The use of inclusive language varies with each service and users may wish to adapt specific benedictions and invocations. For more recent sources--although largely Christian, see Schaffran and Kozak **[527]**, Proctor-Smith and Walton **[526]**, and Winter **[531]**.

[530] Throckmorton, Burton H. Jr., trans. and ed. *The Gospels and the Letters of Paul. An Inclusive-Language Edition*. Cleveland, OH: Pilgrim, 1992.
This translation of the four Gospels and the letters of Paul (exclusive of the pastoral epistles) pulls together many of the translations long available in the more widely known *Inclusive Language Lectionary (ILL)* **[524]**, but gathered here into one source not three, as dictated by the three year

cycle of the *ILL*. A brief introduction chronicles the history of the *ILL*, and the volume closes with an appendix describing various issues and emphases governing the use of inclusive language.

[531] Winter, Miriam Therese. *Womanword: A Feminist Lectionary and Psalter; Women of the New Testament*. New York: Crossroad, 1990.
M. T. Winter is an internationally know Catholic liturgist-musician, and here she presents a systematic identification of women in the New Testament, together with a series of feminist renditions of psalms telling the stories of these women. The text is divided into three sections: (1) "Women and Shaddai in the Spirit of Jesus," the stories of Elisabeth and Mary; (2) "Women and Jesus in the Spirit of Shaddai," the stories of women throughout the gospels; and (3) "Women and the Spirit of Jesus and Shaddai," the stories of women in the early church, as drawn from Acts and the epistles. In each section Winter presents both brief biographies of the women and a description of the scriptural context in which the woman (or group of women) is named. She then renders the women's stories through a feminist lectionary reading, scripted when necessary to include both a narrator and contemporary women's involvements. In addition, each woman's entry includes questions for personal and group reflection, and finally a feminist psalm in keeping with the entry described. Four "songs" of women's strength then close the volume. Although the grounding emphases of this lectionary/psalter are those of the Catholic women-church movement, its spirit transcends denominational divisions, and it can be used by women from various backgrounds. It is elegantly illustrated, helpfully formatted, and it can serve as an ongoing book of worship for women's spiritual communities. NOTE: Several of Winter's subsequent volumes (not abstracted here) follow a similar pattern and format. See, e.g., *WomenWisdom: A Feminist Lectionary and Psalter: Women of the Hebrew Scriptures, Part One* (NY: Crossroad, 1991); *WomenWisdom: A Feminist Lectionary and Psalter: Women of the Hebrew Scriptures, Part II* (Crossroad, 1992); and *The Gospel According to Mary: A New Testament for Women* (Crossroad, 1993). Also, for related sources see Ruether [192], Neu [795], and Keene [903].

NOTE: For additional references on worship resources, inclusive language and liturgical patterns, see Teresa Berger, "Women and Worship: A Bibliography Continued," *Studia Liturgica* 25 (1995): 103-117. The resources gathered there by Berger are chronicled by year of publication from 1988-1995, and include most of the entries listed in the present chapter on "Feminist Theology and Christian Worship," as well as several European and non-English sources. Second, they span writers from several mainline denominations and include sources on inclusive language in conservative denominiations, (although they are not annotated). Third, in her brief, opening discussion Berger indicates two other bibliographic sources, which I have not reviewed, *viz.*, an earlier bibliograpy prepared by Berger for *Studia Liturgica* in 1989 [see *Studia Liturgica* 19 (1989): 96-110] and in *Liturgy Digest*, an "…annotated bibliography of (mainly North American) women *authors* on liturgical subjects or subjects of liturgical relevance" (p. 103). [See *Liturgy Digest* 1, no. 2 (1994): 106-185.] Finally, in the 1995 bibliography indicated above, Berger provides an "addendum" to her own earlier work to include sources published prior to 1988.

B. Womanist and Feminist Preaching, Sermon Collections

1. Womanist and Feminist Preaching

[532] Cannon, Katie G. "Womanist Interpretation and Preaching in the Black Church." In *Searching the Scriptures: Volume I: A Feminist Introduction*, edited by Elisabeth Schüssler Fiorenza, 326-337. New York: Crossroad, 1993.
This essay examines the "redactional processes" of preaching in the Black church as an expression of womanist hermeneutics. It draws theoretically from both the feminist liberationist work of Elisabeth Schüssler Fiorenza and the homiletic "explorations" of Isaac R. Clark. By way of overview, Cannon describes the task of womanist interpretation as that of identifying--both in preparation and in the preaching moment--the ways Black women have historically been--and must continue to be--"complex moral agents." Cannon develops her discussion in terms of three points. First, she describes the vision of Black preaching as understood by her former professor, Isaac Clark: it is a proclaimed word of God as evidenced in the behavior of Jesus and as now linked imaginatively to the experience and needs of contemporary African Americans. Second, Cannon challenges the linguistic sexism and negative female imagery she has experienced within African American preaching, and she holds forth the contrasting "ethic of resistance" as practiced historically by African American women and as emphasized by her characterization of African American women as "complex moral agents." Third, Cannon raises the many theoretical and programmatic questions such a contrast engenders for the role of the "womanist preacher," i.e., the

womanist interpreter who proclaims a liberating word. This is a significant essay for womanist preaching and interpretation, not only because it highlights the womanist philosophical anthropology of Cannon's earlier work [253], but also because through its notes and discussion, it creatively links three previously disparate literatures, viz., those of womanism, feminist theology and African American homiletics.

[533] Procter-Smith, Majorie. "Feminist Interpretation and Liturgical Preaching." In *Searching the Scriptures: Volume I: A Feminist Introduction*, edited by Elisabeth Schüssler Fiorenza, 313-325. New York: Crossroad, 1993.
In earlier works [521, 522] Procter-Smith has identified the androcentric and patriarchal character of liturgical practice(s) and milieux. Here, she brilliantly continues these emphases, but now in the light of Chopp's idea of feminist preaching as "emancipatory preaching" (cf. Chopp [239:49]). Procter-Smith begins by noting that the liturgical setting of preaching *de facto* reinterprets the proclamation of the biblical text by virtue of various social variables. In turn, she identifies both: (a) the specific needs which define emancipatory preaching--that women must speak authoritatively and on behalf of women; and (b) the four problems faced by feminists preaching within liturgical settings. The latter include (i) appropriating the authority of the Bible while yet decentering its socially imposed patterns of androcentric authority; (ii) decentering the androcentrism of lectionary structures by selecting and using texts carefully on behalf of women; (iii) combating the androcentrism and patriarchy inherent in specific preaching models; and (iv) opposing the androcentrism and patriarchy imposed by lectionary-based juxtapositions of texts in terms of seasonal, sanctoral or other liturgical concerns. As resources for dealing with these problems, Procter-Smith highlights feminist textual typologies, biblical translations, and amplifications. The latter are words and gestures which recognize that women have been silenced or else wise subverted, but which open, thereby, the possibilities for using texts as vehicles of lament, exorcism and repentance. As with her earlier work, this essay is ecumenical, dialogical and communal in character, and committed to the same as principles of emancipatory proclamation.

[534] Smith, Christine M. *Weaving the Sermon: Preaching in a Feminist Perspective.* Louisville, KY: Westminster/JohnKnox, 1989.
Using imagery drawn from the craft of weaving, Smith presents a theoretical overview she describes as feminist approaches to preaching. It is a perspective informed by a consistent attention to women's lives--as evidenced in feminist exegesis, theology and methodology--and it opens out several lines of connection between more traditional homiletical perspectives (e.g., Fred Craddock's work). The imagery of the weaving *craft* is important, here, for Smith is not simply describing a metaphor. Rather, each chapter is prefaced with specific texts from a weaving instructional discussion, and the parallels of the craft itself are drawn for feminist preaching. Hence, the weave is made up of the overall "web," with specific emphases (e.g., elements of feminist ethics, critique of misogyny, patriarchy etc.) making up the strands of the "weft." A clearly presented discussion, this connects various elements of cultural feminism, a Gilligan/Choderow framework of socialization, and a global orientation with strong leanings to ecofeminist theory and ethic. It is mindful of its own limitations in that it recognizes both the methodological and substantive difficulties of the weaving imagery, and its literature is current through the mid-1980s.

2. Sermon Collections

[535] Crotwell, Helen Gray, ed. *Women and the Word: Sermons*. Philadelphia: Fortress, 1978.
This early collection of twenty-one sermons by women was compiled by Crotwell to illustrate both the range of women's preaching styles and the variety of theological assumptions women bring to their task. The contributors represent a variety of denominational traditions, and several present important, early perspectives in feminist theology and/or ethics--e.g., Letty Russell, Nadine Foley, Phyllis Trible, Carter Heyward, Rosemary Radford Ruether and Dorothy Soelle among others. While feminist exegesis, theological reconstruction and homiletical theory have developed significantly since the publication of this collection, its entries serve as an historical benchmark for comparative preaching styles, women's ecumenisms and the questions women preachers yet face as they enter pulpits unaccustomed to their presence.

[536] Farmer, David and Edwina Hunter, eds. *And Blessed Is She: Sermons by Women.* San Francisco: Harper & Row, 1990.
This book of 'sermons by women' was prepared by the editors to provide a series of "role models" for women preachers. In all, twenty-two sermons are presented: seven in Part I ("Women

Preachers of the Past") and fifteen for Part II ("Contemporary Women Preachers"). Editor Farmer handles the historical section, and after an initial survey of women's preaching and homiletical experiences, he introduces each of the sermon entries with a brief biography of the sermon's author. In turn, Hunter handles the contemporary sermons, but in a differently styled format, including (1) a brief *auto*biographical statement by the preacher in question; (2) the sermon itself; and (3) a brief description of the occasion and hermeneutical principles undergirding the sermon development. Overall, the selections are strong and the reflections informative and instructive. A weakness in Part I is the absence of historical womanist preachers (cf. **[615]** and **[646]**), but contemporary womanist preachers are included in Part II.

[537] *Spinning a Sacred Yarn: Women Speak from the Pulpit.* New York: Pilgrim, 1982.
This volume is a collection of sermons by thirty-six women--lay, ordained, Jewish and Christian-- active in the feminist theological movement during the 1972 and early 1980s. Some of the contributors are now known for their early and consistent emphasis on particular issues (e.g., Marie Fortune and the necessity for ministry to abused women), while others (e.g., Ruether) were well established at the publication of the collection. The sermons themselves provide an overview of many feminist theological issues (whether then emerging or already established during the early 1980s), but the collection is severely limited by the absence of any index, bibliography, editorial comment, or even a statement by the publishers as to criteria for sermon selections. Rather, this is a collection pure and simple: a series of sermons, with each prefaced by the text on which the sermon is based.

NOTE: For related and additional literature, see Robert R. Howard, "Women and Preaching: A Bibliography." *Homiletic* 17, no. 2 (1992): 7-10, and see Carter Heyward's sermons in both **[199]** and **[435]**, with the latter as collected by Davis. Also, for Womanist literature in addition to Cannon and the enties cited above, see Dodson and Gilkes **[613]**, Webb **[620]**, Riggs **[628]**, Baer **[643]**, and Sanders **[647]**. Last, for sources on Jewish feminist worship see Elwell **[959]**, Falk (**[260]** and **[960]**) and Wenig **[963]**.

14

Feminist Spirituality

Since its beginnings in the late sixties and early 1970s, the literature on feminist spirituality has grown enormously, with three themes becoming most prominent. Theme #1 is the rise of a very broadened understanding of the term spirituality itself, with one focus of the literature addressing the differentiation of "spirituality" from its church based "dogmatic" and "moral theological" sources, and a second focus addressing "post-Christian" manifestations of feminist spirituality. Schneiders' discussion [547] documents this first theme, as she highlights the differentiation of "spirituality" from its doctrinal moorings (and particularly with respect to [feminist] Roman Catholic work on spirituality), while Eller's [542] discussion traces "post-Christian" feminist spirituality. Likewise, additional literature within this first theme addresses a variety of "goddess" based spiritualities, with illustrative sources including Carson [538], Christ ([558] and [559]), and Rae and Daly [560].

A second theme in the literature has been the consistent association between spirituality and issues of social justice, and here both "goddess" and "religious" sources interweave. For examples here, see Spretnak [4] from Section I-1, Hunt [556], and Heyward [555], and much of the literature cited by MacNichol and Walsh [539]. This perspective is communal in the widest sense of the word in that it eschews both the parochialism and ethnocentrism of much Christian experience and theology. Moreover, its reach is historical and fully ecumenical in that it demands an accountability on behalf of women globally, whether in "first" or "third" world countries. (See the literature on women's ecumenism in Section VI-3 and especially Benavides [914], Gnanadason [916] and Hunt [918]).

A third important emphasis in feminist spirituality has been the rising consciousness of ecofeminism, an amalgam of "deep" ecological ethics and the nuances of cultural and (often) socialist feminism. See, e.g., Adams [564], Coyle [565], Hinsdale [566] and Ruether [567], and see McFague [245], Johnson [233] and Ruether [235] from Section II-3. This third emphasis also brings together much of the feminist theological research on the Sophia (or female wisdom) symbol within Hebrew and Christian Testaments, and thus it approximates several of the motifs present in "creation spirituality," although as Johnson's work [233] indicates, it is at times developed in contradistinction to creation spirituality.

Two additional emphases within the literature are those of womanist spirituality and the discussion of feminist spirituality within Judaism. Womanist spirituality entails a "survivalist" perspective tied to family and community commitment within the context of African American experience--before, during and after the period of American slavery (cf. Cannon [612] and Williams [639]). Additionally, it is a perspective tied closely to the class analysis of mainline Christologies (cf., e.g., Sanders [631] and Grant [636]), and, further, the soteriological (or "savior") imagery of traditional Christian belief (cf. Kelly-Brown [634] and Townes [638]). While an obviously fourth focus within the literature on feminism and spirituality, its key sources are presented in Section IV-2, where the wider womanist and womanist theological sources are detailed.

Similarly, the discussion of feminist spirituality within Judaism is also presently developing and here the emphases are two-fold. One emphasis (and currently the predominant emphasis) is defined by the commitments inhering in the image, "tikkun olam" or "the repair of the world." Its representative authors include Plaskow [262] and Ackelsberg [958], and like the justice spiritualities listed in this chapter, this perspective, too, seeks an accountability from history, but here from within the tensions of Torah and Tradition and the grounding each has historically provided Judaism as a faith tradition.

A second emphasis in feminist Jewish spirituality is descriptive, with attention directed largely to the piety and religious dignity of Jewish women, and particularly the survival skills and social contributions such piety and dignity have historically engendered during times of persecution. This effort has been developed largely by Ellen Umansky [263] and it is in many ways methodologically similar to the Ruether and Keller series on women and religion in the United States. It is not, however, exclusive to Umansky, as the developing sources on feminist Judaism ([960], [260] and [261]) and Jewish women's history [948] indicate, and as more recently, the Holocaust Survivors' literature well attests (Goldenberg [964] and [965]).

Although these five dimensions of feminist spirituality (its differentiation from historical theology, its anti-patriarchal and goddess emphases, its justice and ecofeminist emphases, and its womanist and Jewish expressions) all seem different from one another--and indeed, in many ways are different from one another--they nonetheless share a common factor: Namely, that as Schneiders, Eller and others (e.g., Winter, Lummis and Stokes [153]) have pointed out, "spirituality" is no longer the property of institutionalized religion, nor is it the property of patriarchal revelation. Rather, it is the energizing dimension of varying feminist communities and commitments, and thus a potential bond across which and beyond which patriarchally divisive concerns can be bridged.

One further note: Clearly the literatures on lesbian spirituality and a number of globally directed spiritualities (e.g., [914] and [916]) might also be included within this chapter. However, like those of Womanism and Jewish feminism these spiritualities are also currently developing and they are located in their respective sections of the bibliography. See Chapter III-8 ("The Feminist Critique of Heterosexism") and see Chapter VI-3 ("Feminist Theology's Global Voices.").

A. General and Introductory Works

1. Bibliographies

[538] Carson, Anne. *Feminist Spirituality and the Feminine Divine: An Annotated Bibliography*. Trumansburg, NY: Crossing, 1986.
Seven hundred thirty-nine (739) entries dealing with goddess religion form the principal focus of this bibliography, but entries on 'women and Christianity' and 'the Bible' are also included. All entries are alphabetized, sequenced numerically, and listed by number in the subject index. The volume contains neither topical subdivisions nor a separate author index, but entries are generally accessible and quite readable. An introductory essay by Carson focuses the range of materials, and the literature is current through 1985.

[539] MacNichol, Sally Noland, and Mary Elizabeth Walsh. "Feminist Theology and Spirituality: An Annotated Bibliography." *Women Studies Quarterly* 21 (1993): 177-196.
This bibliography presents 174 briefly annotated items grouped into 13 categories. As identified by their authors these are: "women's spirituality," "Goddess and pagan material", "Native American" [spirituality], "lesbian theory" [and spirituality], "Jewish" [spirituality], "Muslim, Buddhist, and Hindu" [spiritualities], and "Christian theology." Also listed are "Womanist and Mujerista theology and ethics;" "Christian Women in Africa, Asia and Latin America;" "Christian ethics, history, and biblical studies," and last, "anthologies." On average, each category contains 10-15 entries with "Goddess and pagan material" and "Christian theology" comprising the two largest groups with approximately two dozen entries each. The authors are graduate students at New York's Union Theological Seminary, and by their decision, books only (and not journal articles) are presented. The range of entries is thorough and presumes spirituality at its widest berth, i.e., that of self-transcendence and personal development.

2. General Introductions

[540] Cady, Susan, Marian Ronan, and Hal Taussig. *Sophia: The Future of Feminist Spirituality.* San Francisco: Harper & Row, 1986.
Characterizing spirituality as a "major feminist development of the 1980s" these authors define spirituality as "the actualizing of the human capacity for self-transcendence" (p. 2), and they trace the development of the Sophia-Wisdom symbol through its Hebrew, Christian and Post-biblical sources. These topical divisions are standard within the Sophia-Wisdom research literature (cf. e.g., Johnson [438]), and their chapter-length discussions here provide the lay reader with a ready access to the more technical sources. Two closing chapters chart the potentials of a Sophia-based spirituality in terms of opposition to patriarchy, domination, and race and class differences among women, and the linkages which can be made between a Sophia-based spirituality and the more traditional Christian affirmations of incarnation, suffering, and death. Further, these linkages are spelled out in terms of the experience by women of invisibility, marginality, suffering and oppression. This is a readable and informative book. Although it lacks an index and supplemental bibliography, it nonetheless serves several ends: theologically oriented readers will find it a stimulating source for the development of inclusive theological language, while sociologists will find it a "mother-lode" of those elements that generate religion as "a cultural system."

[541] Conn, Joann Wolski. *Women's Spirituality: Resources for Development.* New York: Paulist, 1986/1996.
This collection of "resources" for developing women's spirituality within a Catholic Christian framework is divided into four sections. The first is "Issues in Women's Spirituality," a series of summary discussions that describe and survey what women's spirituality is, what supports it and, equally important, what doesn't. Part II then examines "Women's Psychological Development," with essays here focusing on theories of self, ethics, "the construction of femininity," and such specific topics as conflict and anger. A feminist appropriation of historical resources characterizes Part III ("Characteristics of Religious Development") and specific examples of feminist reconstruction inform part IV, "Revisoining the Tradition of Christian Spirituality." This is an excellent collection and while limited to issues attached primarily to the history of European Catholic spirituality, it well models how feminists within a single denomination can find what is valuable and distill it from what is not. Second, as the *revised* edition of an alrady good collection, the text demonstrates the process of "sifting" currently happening to women within the context of Catholic spirituality as transformed by wider perspectives. Notable pieces culled from the *first* edition include Conn's own discussion of the ways in which women's spirituality is restricted [551]; an entry by Sandra Schneiders ("The Effects of Women's Experience on their Spirituality") detailing the negative effects of theology and socialization on women's abilities to minister, Anne Carr's discussion of spirituality as embodied in the notion of friendship [549], Elizabeth Johnson ("The Incomprehensibility of God..." [421]), and Elisabeth Schüssler Fiorenza ("The Sophia God of Jesus and the Discipleship of Women"). Likewise, from the second edition, noteable pieces include (but are not abstracted here): Mary Jo Weaver's "Cancer in the "Body of Christ," a statement of the pain and ecclesial disppointments women have experienced since Weaver first wrote *New Catholic Women* [762] and" Jesuits and the Situation of Women in Church and Civil Society," a 1995 statement by the Jesuit General Congregation. Feminist appropriations of Ignatian, Carmelite, Salesian are also carried over from the first editio and augmented in the second.

[542] Eller, Cynthia. "Twentieth Century Women's Religion as Seen in the Feminist Spirituality Movement." In *Women's Leadership in Marginal Religions: Explorations Outside the Mainstream,* edited by Catherine Wessenger, 172-195. Urbana: University of Illinois Press, 1993.
This exceptionally informative and clear discussion by Eller accomplishes several things: First, it identifies and details three historical factors important to the development of "post-Christian" feminist spirituality. These are "the radical feminism of the 1960s, increas[ed] frustration among feminists within traditional religions, and an ongoing concern with alternative worlds of meaning (p. 173)." Second, it synthesizes "central elements of feminist spirituality" and third, it reflects on the substantive dimensions of feminist spirituality as "women's religion." By way of synthesis, Eller suggests that the contemporary feminist spirituality movement has developed beyond its initial roots in politics, feminism and gentle 'witchcraft,' and is now characterized by: (1) a sense of trust with goddess religion and goddess presence; (2) specified patterns of sacred history; (3) seasonally grounded and self-empowering ritual(s); and (4) "magic" as the expressive, energizing and focusing dimensions of such ritual. For closure, Eller examines the positive and negative ways in which the association of women with nature can be thematized, and the subsequent strategies

available to women for recouping the symbolic assumptions of this association. **NOTE**: This essay *far surpasses* Eller's related discussion in *Continuum* 2, nos. 2 and 3 (1993): 77-102 (not abstracted in this volume). Additionally, it is expanded and supplemented with helpful interview data from an availability sample of 32 feminist spiritualists (identified pseudonymously) in *Living in the Lap of the Goddess: The Feminist Spirituality Movement in America*, [New York: Crossroad, 1993]. Although not abstracted here, the latter addresses the history, sociology and current experience of ("secular") spiritual feminists vis a vis women's empowerment, ritual, magic and nature, goddess experience, politics and feminist spirituality, and the 'gifts' of feminist spirituality itself--and all in clear and readable terms.

[543] Gillikin, Jo, and Anne Barstow, eds. "Spirituality and Religions." *Women's Studies Quarterly* 21 (1993): 4-219.
This double issue of *Women's Studies Quarterly* synthesizes several important discussions and presentations under its four thematic divisions of "teaching about women and religion;" "scholarly witness," "spiritual witness" and "resources." Of particular note are: (1) Judith Plaskow's lead essay, "We Are Also Your Sisters: The Development of Women's Studies in Religion" **[340]**; (2) Delores Williams' "Inner Voices, Apparitions and Defiance in Nineteenth-Century Black Women's Narratives," (a theme regular to Williams' work and amplified in her book *Sisters in the Wilderness* **[259]**), and from the category of "resources," (3) an extended, annotated bibliography on "Feminist Theology and Spirituality" **[539]** by Sally Noland MacNichol and Mary Elizabeth Walsh. Other contributions from this double issue include specific discussions of goddess religion and spirituality, and two course syllabi: "Hunger for Justice" and "Women Mystics" prepared (respectively) by Michele James Deramo and S. Shawn Madigan.

[544] Plaskow, Judith, and Carol P. Christ, eds. *Weaving the Visions: New Patterns in Feminist Spirituality*. HarperSanFrancisco, 1989.
This collection presents 33 essays reprinted from various sources and organized thematically around (1) the empowering dimensions of women's various symbolic heritages; (2) the ways in which women "name" the sacred; (3) concepts of the "self in relation," and (4) the ways in which feminist theologians seek a "transforming [of] the world." It is a continuation of the dialogues begun in the editors' first co-edited volume **[206]**, but here with an attention to the insights gained in a decade of feminist work: a recognition of diversity--and divisions--current in feminist theory and theology; an abandonment of the editors' initial "reformist/revolutionary" classificatory framework (as expressed in Womanspirit Rising) and the recognition of transformation as key to much feminist/women's religious literature; and a concrete attempt to move beyond the "institutionally reinforced separations" which the editors note, "feed into patriarchal boundary making and methods of control" (p. 8). Contributors include religious feminists working both apart from and in the light of traditional and non-traditional [religious] perspectives (e.g., McFague's "God as Mother," Ruether's "Sexism and God-Language," Christine Downing's "Artemis" and Carol Sanchez's "New World Tribal Communities") and the editors' overall purpose is "to do theology...in a different voice." The editors provide a helpful preface and general introduction, and specific overviews for each of the volume's thematic sections.

[545] Ruether, Rosemary Radford. "Feminist Theology and Spirituality." In *Christian Feminism: Visions of a New Humanity*, edited by Judith Weidman, 9-32. San Francisco: Harper & Row, 1984.
This compact and clearly written essay introduces the reader to the four main lines of Ruether's feminist theological work: (1) the need for feminist theological work, (2) the tasks and difficulties facing feminist theology (3) patterns of feminist (and patriarchal) spirituality and (4) "directions for the feminist reconstruction of Christian symbols." Stated briefly, it is Ruether's contention that the need for a feminist theology arises from the historical (and present) impact of sexism: i.e., its marginalization of women and their subsequent religious, cultural, and structural depiction as beings less able than men to image God. Against such depictions, says Ruether, is Christianity's proclamation that the incarnation assumes all humanity and thus women, too, are the "imago dei." Feminist theology holds Christianity to its proclamation, and hence the primary tasks of feminist theology become both a critique of Christianity's patriarchal/misogynist history and a reconstruction of theological traditions from within the feminist appropriation of women as also the image of God. This means that feminist spirituality will need to focus on ethical-political concerns (rather than privatized faith and/or goddess religion), and that patterns of Christian symbolization (i.e., God-language and language about cosmology, creation, Christology, theological anthropology, redemption, community, church leadership, ritual, cult action, praxis and the like) will all need to be rewritten from the ground up. Ruether then offers suggestions for this re-thinking and in spite

of the acknowledged difficulty of the task, she illustrates the scope of feminist theology, from analogical language about God to the "marks of the church," the latter by way of feminist base communities.

[546] Schneiders, Sandra M. *Women and the Word: The Gender of God in the New Testament and the Spirituality of Women.* New York: Paulist, 1986.

From its recognition on page 1 that the "gender of God" is a thoroughly modern question, to its ordered conclusions on pages 67-71, this brief volume explodes with insights suitable to its subtitle: that the question of God's gender and its attendant issues are primarily concerns about women's spirituality, that is, issues of how women "can find a creative and liberating understanding of God and of Jesus...which does not glorify masculinity at the expense of femininity and does not justify the oppression of women by men..." (p. 7). In the light of the question raised by so many (*viz.*, "Can one be both a feminist and a Christian?" **[178]**) Schneiders first describes the impact of patriarchal language and the various names and metaphors used for God both by the Old Testament and in Jesus' presentation of God. She then examines those feminine qualities typically viewed as the inferior characteristics of women, and following along the lines of Mollenkott, Trible and McFague, she redefines these characteristics along salvific lines. As her backdrop for all this, Schneiders skillfully addresses the issues attached to symbolic language for God, both Trinitarian and Incarnational. Her discussion here is solid, although a sociologically informed reader might wish a further exposition along critical structural and/or political lines. This is a readable and highly informed discussion which presents biblical exegesis and its implications for readers of almost any level. It is a reasoned, introductory text for those seeking mainstream feminist New Testament sources which speak to the past and future possibilities of women's religious experience. It carries the reader comfortably through feminist work published through the mid-80s and is highly recommended.

[547] Schneiders, Sandra M. "Spirituality in the Academy." *Theological Studies* 50 (1989): 676-697.

This article explores the history and use of the term "spirituality" in order to note the broadening use of this term--ultimately its differentiation from the normative fields of dogmatic and moral theology--and, relatedly, its significance as a name for both an academic discipline *and* the experience that such a discipline studies. Schneiders' frame of reference here is Roman Catholicism, but her discussion is not limited to Roman Catholic sources or experience. Rather, her Catholic framework permits pre- and post (Vatican II) contrasts in the assumptions Christians have made about what constitutes (1) spirituality, (2) the experiences which nurture and ground it, and (3) the theological discipline(s) which study it. For her own position, Schneiders develops several reasons for adopting an "emergent" (rather than "dogmatic") definition of spirituality, and like other spirituality writers (e.g., Carr **[549]**) she defines spirituality as "the experience of constantly striving to integrate one's life in terms not of isolation and self-absorption but of self-transcendence toward the ultimate value one perceives." (p. 684). Additionally, in contrast to those who argue that the study of spirituality should be identified as either a subdiscipline of dogmatic or moral theology (or a form of "spiritual theology" per se), Schneiders argues that the spirituality/theology interface is a partnership: a task of mutual illumination akin to that of the theology/biblical studies interface, where one set of studies aids and nourishes the other but remains autonomous from it. Seen thus, the academic discipline of "Spirituality" is that "...*field of study which attempts to investigate in an interdisciplinary way spiritual experience as such,* i.e., as spiritual and as experience" (p. 692). Her purpose here is to include not only religious experience in the technical sense, "but [also] those analogous experiences of ultimate meaning and value which have transcendent and life-integrating power for individuals and groups." (*Ibid.*) Further, such a description of the field permits a clarification of its general characteristics as (1) an interdisciplinary, "descriptive-critical" rather than "prescriptive-normative" discipline, and (2) an ecumenical, interreligious, cross-cultural and holistic endeavor (cf., e.g., **[548]**). **NOTE**: Also by Schneiders but not abstracted here is her essay, "Feminist Spirituality" in *The New Dictionary of Spirituality*, edited by Michael Downey, 394-406 [Collegeville, MN: Liturgical Press, 1993], in which she summarizes both secular and religious feminist spiritualities, as well as her particular focus on "Christian (Catholic) feminist spirituality."

[548] Zappone, Catherine. *The Hope for Wholeness: A Spirituality for Feminists.* Mystic, CT: Twenty-Third Publications, 1991.

Working from a wide range of religious, philosophical and psychological sources that help to focus feminist spirituality as a process of *hoping for wholeness* (within one's self, with the members of one's social world, with the Sacred, and ultimately with the earth itself), Zappone provides the novice reader with a nuanced discussion that addresses both academic and deeply personal questions, just as it simultaneously seeks to empower the reader in her own "hope for wholeness." This is a delicate and gentle text. Its focus is reader empowerment (as opposed to structured argument) and Zappone's background as a teacher and editor of the *Irish Journal of Feminist Spirituality* is clear as she carefully leads those seeking a grounding for their own development and work. Virtually all key sources from the mid-sixties on (including both Daly and *Womanspirit Rising)* are woven into this text, and issues of mutuality, justice-making, "symbol systems," sexuality, and dialogue across social and religious differences are all addressed. The primary focus is Christian and rooted in Zappone's own Catholic heritage; but the vision is to "make the connections" across personal, social, religious and ecological ties. This is a helpful synthesis and particularly suited for those seeking a first framework for their own journey to wholeness.

3.   Early Literature

[549] Carr, Anne. "On Feminist Spirituality." *Horizons* 9 (1982): 96-103.
In this essay Carr develops an understanding of feminist spirituality by critically correlating elements of feminist consciousness with key assumptions of Christian spirituality. For the former she draws upon two insights of feminist consciousness raising: first, that autonomy and self-transcendence are legitimate goals for women, and second, that feminism must be concerned with the liberation of all oppressed peoples (p. 99). For themes in Christian spirituality Carr notes that: (1) spirituality involves the "whole of [one's] deepest religious beliefs, convictions, and patterns of thought, emotion and behavior in respect to what is ultimate..." (p. 98); (2) this range of phenomena may or may not be "reflective;" (3) spirituality is culturally conditioned, but nonetheless "unique" to each individual; and (4) it is steeped in questions of ultimate worth and value (p. 97). The outcome of Carr's correlation is an understanding of feminist spirituality as that spirituality which stresses "female bonding in sisterhood, affirmation of the self-actualization and the self transcendence of women..." and efforts to combat the "interrelationships among sexism, racism, and classism..." (p. 101). Finally, as an added benefit of this developed correlation, Carr notes that one can discern not only the outlines of women's spirituality in general, but also men's spirituality, and the primacy of friendship as a metaphor or model for describing the divine-human relationship. **NOTE**: For key discussions of friendship as a model for divine-human relations, see McFague **[244]** and Plaskow **[262]**.

[550] Conn, Joann Wolski. "Horizons on Contemporary Spirituality." *Horizons* 9 (1982): 60-73.
In this brief essay Conn reviews twelve books on spirituality published in 1980 and 1981. The review takes up familiar themes: the "principal sources or methods for understanding and describing Christian Spirituality," the relationship between "human development and spiritual development," the "controlling models" of both holiness and spiritual growth, "central images of God," and "the role of social concern...[and]...action for justice" (p. 60). As she examines her selected texts, Conn finds five trends: a focus on experience as the starting point for both reflection upon and the development of spirituality, the centrality of the 'self' (whether as dependent on God or discovered through spiritual growth), "the value of classical sources for current questions, a concern for the link between prayer and social justice," and "an emerging attention to women's issues" (p. 71). Authors reviewed by Conn include Robert Faricy, Matthew Fox, Urban Homes, Thomas Keating, Morton Kelsey, Kenneth Leech, Henri Nouwen, William Shannon, Ann Ulanov and Rowan Williams. Writings are grouped accordingly as introductions, histories or studies on specific persons and/or perspectives.

[551] Conn, Joann Wolski. "Women's Spirituality: Restriction and Reconstruction." In *Women's Spirituality: Resources for Christian Development,* edited by Joann Wolski Conn, 9-30. New York: Paulist, 1986. [First published in *Cross Currents* 30 (1980): 293-308]
This article examines the "problematic nature" of spirituality vis a vis women's experience. It then identifies three ways in which that problematic nature is being addressed and "reconstructed." Conn begins by defining spirituality as "the experience and/or study of the actualization of human self-transcendence by the Holy, [or] by Ultimate Concern--that is, by what is acknowledged as 'religious'" (p. 9). In the Christian context this is understood as "the actualization of this human capacity through the experience of God, in Jesus Christ, through the gift of the Spirit" (pp. 9-10). What makes this experience problematic for women, however, are three things: First, that models of development for women have typically been "restricted;" that is, they have been limited to service roles without self-actualization. Second "Christian teaching and practice have significantly contributed to this "restriction" in that Christianity has often equated women's religious role with

domestic service and obedience, and at the same time supported this equation with alienating, masculine images of God. Finally, as a consequence, many women feel that the only path to self-actualization is the abandonment of Christian experience and with this the rejection of spirituality and its actualizing possibilities. To counter these problematic aspects Conn reviews research by Gilligan and Sasson ["Success Anxiety in Woman: A Constructivist Interpretation of Its Source and Significance," *Harvard Educational Review* 50 (1980): 13-24] to identify the relational strengths which typify many women's experience. She then links these to traditional and recent literature on women's religious leadership and inclusive biblical exegesis (as drawn from such varied sources as Teresa of Avila and the biblical resources provided by Schüssler Fiorenza and Trible) to indicate the possible lines of a reconstructed spirituality for women.

[552] McLaughlin, Eleanor. "The Christian Past: Does It Hold a Future for Women?" In
    Womanspirit Rising: A Feminist Reader in Religion, edited by Carol Christ and
    Judith Plaskow, 93-106. New York: Harper & Row, 1979.
This essay examines the writings of two medieval women--Christina of Markyate and Julien of Norwich--to illustrate the thesis that "Christian faith and Christian institutions have been in certain times and under certain conditions radically supportive of women and informed by women's experience" (p. 96); and further, that as such, they have countered some of the more stereotypical images of women evident in Christian history and tradition. By way of particulars, the "life of Christina" reflects a woman capable of renaming herself and transcending the ecclesiastical and social forces that would have precluded her choice for a celibate and communal commitment. Similarly, Julien's work reflects that of a women "doing theology:" i.e., a woman reflecting on the nature and activity of God, but specifically through the images motherhood and nurture as applied to Christ. McLaughlin's discussion permits her three concluding observations. First, while medieval Christianity produced a hierarchical order defined according to "dignity and function," the opportunity for holiness was neither limited to nor precluded by the all male clerical bureaucracy of the church. Rather, women as well as men could be saints. Second, because the pre-industrialized experience of family life with its birthing and nurturing dimensions was the normative model for women's physical and spiritual realities in the Middle Ages, "the theological language...[of]...popular piety often reflected the real-life experiences of women in a way that is not the case today." Thus, one can ask how the experience of women might today be lifted up and reflected in religious language. Third, because the examples she describes in her essay indicate a theological language that often broke through the androcentrism and patriarchy of its time to give dignity to the experience of women, they permit the question: "Could this happen once again?" Could this "...other *persona*, the seeker after God, model of human holiness and divine action, wholly equal with her brother in the pursuit of Christian perfection...function as a generator of questions and challenges" (p. 105) as women (and men) today seek empowering illustrations of their current faith and tradition experience?

[553] Ochs, Carol. *Women and Spirituality*. Totowa, NJ: Rowman and Allanheld, 1983.
In an attempt to present a description of spirituality patterned after women's experience of mothering and not what Ochs describes as the traditional male model of individualism (p. 2), Ochs focuses attention on the significance of nurturing as the guiding concept of spirituality. The value of this concept is that it points to relationships rather than individualism and isolation (whether with God or Being) as the "goal" of spirituality. Further, it directs one to the possibility of ecstasies within daily, ordinary life, not a life beyond the sphere of human interaction. The "letting go" of self which happens in the experience of nurturing a child from birth is crucial for Ochs. This experience opens up the themes of relationship, connectedness and personal experience as sources for thinking about spirituality, and as she develops her discussion she addresses conflict, suffering, guilt, death and joy. Och's discussion is practically oriented and with but a few exceptions easily readable. It presumes little or no theological background, and it is intended for both women and men for it is Ochs' conviction that mothering is something all people can do--either because they have in fact borne and raised children, or alternatively, have learned from having been mothered. Her conviction here is moot. In her text she gives no attention to the fact that mothering per se is not a universal experience (i.e., doing and remembering are not synonymous), nor is it always well done. Finally, Och ignores the fact that the economic dependency of women (by virtue of mothering) is in many cases unchosen, and that in cultures less privileged than America's comfortable classes, it may not begin to approach the possibilities she details here.

NOTE: For additional early literature see Goldenberg [139], Morton [202] and Gillikin and Barstow [543]. Also, for a helpful synthesis of early Catholic feminist spirituality, see Weaver [762].

B. Expressions of Feminist Spirituality

1. Justice and Feminist Spirituality

[554] Finley, Nancy J. "Political Activism and Feminist Spirituality." *Sociological Analysis* 52 (1991): 349-362.

Feminist theologians generally suggest that feminist spirituality is both politically empowering and justice directed. This exploratory study summarizes data supportive of such a perspective, but with observations drawn from a study of Dianic Wiccan feminists, members of a 'new religious movement' (NRM) feminist witchcraft group. The key question in Finley's study is whether and under what conditions participation in NRMs (here Dianic Wicca) facilitates a transformation of self in the direction of political activism, and how specifically this happens for women, who are de facto, at a structural disadvantage in American society. Finley's answer is the variable of "efficacy" (or the sense that one can modify one's environment), and her questionnaire data from a sample of 35 Wiccan feminists suggest that efficacy is enhanced when the religious group's teachings "contain an ideological component that challenges the systemic link of self evaluation and power." Finley's discussion of her data incorporates observations about the non-hierarchical religious organization of Dianic Wicca, the ideological/cosmological teaching of Wicca on the connectedness of all things, and the potential influence of Wiccan chants stressing the "oneness" of all things. She concludes that efficacy can indeed be enhanced by the ideological teachings of NRMs (if they challenge the systemic link between self evaluation and power) and she suggests several specifics for follow-up research. NOTE: For related literature see Lummis and Stokes [742].

[555] Heyward, Carter. "Is a Self-Respecting Christian Woman an Oxymoron? Reflections on a Feminist Spirituality for Justice." *Religion and Intellectual Life* 3 (1986): 45-62.

Justice-making, right-relations, self-respect and a commitment to honest dialogue are themes regularly addressed in Carter Heyward's writings. Here they receive fresh expression vis a vis the role of society in fostering both self-respect and respect from others. Heyward begins by noting the basic conditions of justice to which all persons are entitled: "ready access to food, shelter, medicine, education, work, and leisure time" (p. 47). She notes, however, the difference gender can make in the pursuit of such entitlements, for society supports the pursuit and establishment of such rights for men, but not for women. Rather, women are encouraged to work for such rights on behalf of others but *not* for themselves. The climate for such a double standard, Heyward argues, is that of privatized Christianity (by way of liberal Protestantism) and its consequences are enormous: efforts at justice-making are thwarted or neutralized, and pride (rather than women's lack of it) remains the chief understanding of sin. The paradox, however, is that as an historical agency, the church has taught justice-making in spite of its institutional sin(s). Thus, as one steps into doing justice, one steps into the real power of Christian experience. Ultimately this means a re-creation of the church(es) from within an accountability to God's world: viz., a commitment of self and institutional resources to the needs of those marginalized, an awareness of God's name as Justice, and a commitment to speak the truth radically and consistently in all political and social life. NOTE: Also by Heyward are [179], [198], [216], [217], [242], [437] and [867].

[556] Hunt, Mary E. "Lovingly Lesbian: Toward a Feminist Theology of Friendship." In *A Challenge to Love*, ed. by Robert Nugent, 135-155. New York: Crossroad, 1989.

This essay examines lesbian feminism, the emerging awareness of Catholic lesbian feminists, and the qualities of lesbian friendship that can foster a restructuring of the notions of God, humanity and the world. These qualities include relationality, community, honesty, non-exclusivity, flexibility and other-directedness, and for Hunt they augur the friendship of God: a care for the creation, an indomitable optimism for justice, peace and mutuality, and the evidence of a commitment to each. Most central to Hunt's work is her regularly voiced conviction that "lesbian insight" must be freed from its heterosexist definitions so that its true character can be seen, that is, its character as the gift and ground of friendship between and among women--with or without genital intimacy, and of necessity not contingent on the latter. Hence her work emphasizes the lateral (rather than "liberal") and horizontal (rather than "hierarchical") nature of women's friendships (with women and men) and their implications for a post-heterosexist world: i.e., a vision of women's community and relationality as paradigmatic of Christian experience and tradition, or the creation of a world in which (1) the ability to love persons is present without coercion and in which (2) the normativity of love and justice are the essence of revelation and the purpose of creation.

[557] Soelle, Dorothee. *The Window of Vulnerability: A Political Spirituality.* Minneapolis, MN: Fortress, 1990.
As with all of Soelle's works, this volume too addresses the issues of militarism, totalitarianism and fascism as each impinges upon and threatens the capacity for transcendence in human consciousness. And, like Soelle's *The Strength of the Weak,* this volume too is a series of essays (seventeen in all) focused around the broad cultural shifts which now shape Christian symbolism in its European first world heritage. The essays here were written between December 12, 1979 and July 16, 1985, and they are grouped, thematically, into three sections. "Security" is the theme of Part I and here, Soelle's essays focus on Western militarism and the peace movement, the culture of disobedience, and "Christianity and Post-Marxism." Part II thematizes essays around "God, Mother of Us All" with the emphasis here on feminist theology's re-symbolization of Christianity's deepest and most far-reaching images. In Part III, "Cells of Resistance," Soelle reflects upon the work of Kierkegaard, Bultmann and Barth, on the American New Right (which she labels "Christofascism"), on "Civil Disobedience" and in a final essay, entitled, "God Is All-Sharing," the role of myth and narrative in religious and media-based language. Soelle is a powerful essayist commanding academic *and* existential attention, and the historical, global, and ecumenical dimensions of her work recommend her as a feminist of distinction.

NOTE: For related literature abstracted elsewhere in the bibliography, see Solle **[204]**, Townes **[258]**, Chittister **[754]**, Lummis and Stokes **[742]**, and Katzenstein **[285]**; and see Chapter 23 for discussions of feminist spirituality and women's global ecumenism, *viz.,* Benavides **[914]**, Gnanadason **[916]**, Fabella, Lee and Suh **[932]**, Fabella and Park **[933]**, and Talbot **[938]**.

2. The Goddess and Feminist Spirituality

[558] Christ, Carol P. "Why Women Need the Goddess: Spiritual, Psychological and Political Reflections." In *Womanspirit Rising: A Feminist Reader in Religion,* edited by Carol P. Christ and Judith Plaskow, 273-287. New York: Harper & Row, 1979.
This essay is a classic source in the discussion of "women and Goddess religion," both for its frank departure from traditional Christianity and its clear affirmation of women's experience, will, values and bondings apart from patriarchy. According to Christ, women *need* the goddess precisely because patriarchal religion has suppressed each of these facets of women's reality, and whether women perceive "the goddess" as a reality external to themselves (or internal to their experience), the goddess is a powerful symbol for women because it validates the "legitimacy of female power as a beneficent and independent power" (p. 277). Christ's emphasis here is subtle but important, and the reader is referred to the essay itself for Christ's full discussion. To be noted, however, is that according to Christ, the very question of 'is there a goddess out there' is itself patriarchal in that it mirrors the manner of theology and not *thea*logy, or as she puts it, the manner of "explanation" rather than the primacy of symbols and their power. The latter, however, is what women bring to the goddess, and what, in turn, goddess religion does for women. For in validating women's power, the goddess lifts up not only women's experience, but women's will, values and bondings—and all apart from patriarchy.

[559] Christ, Carol P. *Diving Deep and Surfacing: Women Writers on Spiritual Quest.* Boston: Beacon, 1980.
This volume is one of the "early voices" of women's spirituality as a search for women-identified values which exist apart from patriarchy or the encompassing of women's consciousness within it. Thus Christ's primary goal here is to present a description of "women's religious experience... articulated in women's own language, not forced into the structures of male theology" (p. xii). To accomplish her task, Christ draws upon the searching or quest-like themes evident in such writers as Doris Lessing, Kate Chopin, Margaret Atwood, Adrienne Rich and Ntozake Shange. She pulls them together through Mary Daly's description of women's movement from "nothingness" to "new naming." Christ begins by recounting the value of "stories" both as a genre and medium of self-expression, and she links the need for women to tell their contemporary stories with both the literature she describes and the experience of women marginalized from the conditions which would permit their own legitimation of experience. In a closing chapter Christ synthesizes the themes of her selected authors and connects them to the wider aspects of women's religious and communal experience. For Christ's other work, see Christ **[558]** Christ and Plaskow **[206]**, and Plaskow and Christ **[544]**.

[560] Rae, Eleanor, and Bernice Marie-Daly. *Created in Her Image: Models of the Feminine Divine*. New York: Crossroad, 1990.
This co-authored work integrates various psychologies of women's experience with classical Christian trinitarian symbols to present an interpretation of trinitarian thinking sensitive to the need for non-androcentric perceptions of transcendence and/or the divine. It is a generalized discussion-- differentiated from any particular denominational affiliation--but rooted largely in Roman Catholic sources. The psychological sources include Anne Wilson Schaef's *Women's Reality* (but not Schaef's later work) and selected aspects of Jungian psychology. The ethical framework derives from and is directed to ecofeminism (cf., e.g., Adams [564]) and a concern for peace and justice issues. Chapter notes and a brief index (but no supplemental bibliography) close the volume. NOTE: This work is not without its difficulties. First, describing but not naming the divine while using (at the same time) such god-language as the "feminine divine" may hinder some readers in the opening chapters. Second, those unfamiliar with the Sophia-Wisdom literature may feel the need for some background material before tackling this text. Students familiar with the the Sophia-Wisdom literature, however (e.g., Johnson's early work [438] and more recently *She Who Is* [232]) will move quickly through the text and finds its discussion provocative.

3. American Culture and Feminist Spirituality

[561] Barciauskas, Rosemary Curran, and Debra B. Hull. "Other Women's Daughters: Integrative Feminism, Public Spirituality." *Cross Currents* 38 (1988): 32-52.
This article is virtually two discussions in one. It is a summary of survey (n=158) and interview (N=40) data on the responses of an admittedly limited sample (white working professional women from West Virginia) to the competing time and energy demands of work and family-nurture roles, as influenced by the variable *agape* (the sacrifice of self for the other). It is also a reflection on the notions of "calling" and "inclusivity" as bridge concepts in the development of a feminist public spirituality patterned after needs described in Bellah's *Habits of the Heart*. [NY: Harper & Row, 1985]. Does agape reduce the stress of the competing demands of work and family life? Barciauskas and Hull's data suggest no association between agape and the resolution of competing work and family demands, but their data do indicate two perspectives respondents have about this conflict: (1) an "individualistic" perspective (which argues that it is the worker's own responsibility to handle the conflict); and (2) a "relationalist" perspective (which says the workplace should accommodate family needs). What distinguishes these perspectives is the respondent's having already sacrificed a part of her career progress because of family needs, (typically the reduction of one's work schedule from approximately 60-75 hours per week to 40 hours per week). On the basis of these data Barciauskas and Hull suggest that the emphases of the relationalist perspective can be coordinated through the notions of "calling" and "inclusivity" to generate a feminist public spirituality which balances self-giving and other-giving in both the home and the work-place. Such emphases, they argue, (and particularly the capacity of women for nurture) can counter the ideologies of individualism and careerism and serve to make an independent statement of women's self-affirmation (p. 47). Although rooted in empirical research and directed to an important philosophical question, this study is limited. First, its measures and variable relations are not clearly stated; second, because it opens a dual ethical possibility for the working woman--but not the working man, i.e., the humanization of both the home and the work-place, it seems to legitimate and extend rather than to remove the abusive potential of "calling" and "agape" for women with dual commitments.

[562] Porterfield, Amanda. *Feminine Spirituality in America: From Sarah Edwards to Martha Graham*. Philadelphia: Temple Univ. Press, 1980.
In contrast to discussions of spirituality which focus the spirituality of women from within either denominationally rooted sources (e.g., confessional or historic symbols) or alternatively from within extra-denominational sources (e.g., goddess religion), Porterfield's discussion focuses women's spirituality in terms of two culturally specific American emphases: the gender assumptions within American Puritan thinking and their expression in women's novels, poetry and personal spiritual literature. This is an elegantly written and richly detailed book. It highlights the gender expectations available to privileged New England women from the dawn of Puritanism through the nineteenth century. Thus it highlights that white, educated, and economically secure women were expected to (and did) receive graciously the moral authority awarded them by church and society as they were assigned their "place," and they thus were able to function powerfully in the development of art, literature, social work and family life. Porterfield's chapter on Emily Dickinson is especially rewarding, as is her chapter on the "domestication of theology, i.e., its transfer of teaching authority from the church to the home via Horace Bushnell's theories of

Christian education." These values noted, Porterfield's discussion is dated, in that its principal emphases reflect a sustained concern with upper-strata Puritan women only. Hence, for images drawn from other social worlds and other spiritualities of the same time period, see, for example, the literature cited by Lerner [77], Grant [254], and Cannon [253].

[563] Yates, Gayle Graham. "Spirituality and the American Feminist Experience." *Signs* 9 (1983): 59-72.
This review examines a "selected list of scholarly works that have arisen out of an articulated feminist religious position" (p.61) during the period 1976-1981. The author's purpose is to indicate the varying ways in which "women's experience" has been normative for scholarship in four areas: (1) "theology and cognitive theory;" (2) "historical and cultural studies;" (3) studies on women's "practices and reflection;" and (4) studies on women's "literature and spirituality." The first and third of these topics receive the most thorough discussion and the author ably contrasts the feminist-theological and "goddess" traditions exemplified in each. Additionally, she incorporates early womanist writings within her discussion of women's literature and spirituality. This review serves as an indicator of the early emphases and questions addressed by women scholars in the area of feminist spirituality. Its notes are extensive and its discussion is undertaken from within the assumptions of women's studies generally rather than feminist theological concerns particularly. It is a solid introductory essay and should be followed up with later feminist spirituality literature.

4. Ecology and Feminist Spirituality

[564] Adams, Carol J., ed. *Ecofeminism and the Sacred.* New York: Continuum, 1995.
This text brings together twenty essays by prominent religious and secular feminists in order to indicate the many ways that feminist spiritualities work to combat environmental exploitation. Religious and theological critiques comprise the first group of essays, with contributions by Ruether, Delores Williams, Catherine Keller, Stephanie Kaza, Judith Plaskow, Sallie McFague and Lina Gupta providing analyses of dualism and women/earth domination (and/or pollution) across several historic traditions. Particular (and often more secularly cast) perspectives make up Part 2 of Adams' reader, with contributors here addressing "specific aspects of ecofeminist spirituality to determine whether they advance or impede the ecofeminist project" (p. 6). And here, contributors include Karen J. Warren, L. Teal Willoughby, Ellen Cronan Rose, Andy Smith, Gloria Orenstein and Shamara Shantu Riley. Finally, in Part 3 ("Embodying Ecofeminist Spiritualities"), Adams presents several essays which, together, detail the political and activist connections between "animal, vegetable and mineral." While many of the selections synthesized by Adams transcend formal theological perspectives, they come together in their commitment to challenge the activities, images and economies that sustain environmental exploitation and undercut the "...simple formula for environmental change..." that Adams presents: namely, "Anything the absence of which would cause daily discomfort probably presents something that is environmentally exploitative" (p. 8).

[565] Coyle, Kathleen. "Renewing the Face of the Earth." *Asian Journal of Theology* 7 (1993): 114-127.
This article lays out the broad implications of ecofeminism for Christian spirituality. It begins with a summary of the social, economic and patriarchal assumptions attached to the 'mechanistic' model undergirding Western society and its development, and it moves through various theological and ecological themes which can fruitfully be used--in Coyle's judgment--to (literally) save the earth. It is an informative and deeply moving discussion which highlights the pluriform understandings which can be attached to the notion of "creation spirituality."

[566] Hinsdale, Mary Ann. "Ecology, Feminism, and Theology." *Word and World* 11 (1991): 156-164.
This essay examines salient emphases within both feminist and ecological literature to disclose (1) their possibilities of dialogue with select feminist and process theological emphases so that (2) the implications of such a dialogue for a theology of creation may be described. The discussion develops in four parts. First is a review of the "reformist" and "revolutionary" perspectives within the ecological literature. These reflect (respectively) "environmentalist" (or utilitarian) and "deep ecological" (or egalitarian) attitudes about both nature the role of humanity in and within nature. Section II reviews the "liberal," "cultural," and "socialist," perspectives of [eco-] feminism to detail the earth ethic(s) within them and the consistency of these ethic(s) with liberal, cultural and socialist feminist solutions to sexism and patriarchy. A third discussion briefly reviews selective affirmations within feminist and process theological writings to show their openness to an ecologically based understanding of creation, and in a final section, Hinsdale describes the

implications of her research: the possible reinterpretation of Gen. 1:26-28 to stress the *ecocentric* interdependence of all life forms; a corresponding focus on the concept of relationship so that intrinsic differences in life forms could be affirmed; the necessity to deal with "Evil" and human responsibility within such a framework, and last, a recognition that such a task could eventuate in an affirmation of "the hermeneutical privilege of nature [and/or] the earth." Hinsdale's discussion is informative and provocative. Its strongest emphasis is in introducing the reader to the literature of ecofeminism and its implications for androcentric theology. Its weakest point is the near equation of feminist theology with ecology and goddess theology, and not the wider literature of feminist Christian spirituality readily available in the journal literature. NOTE: See also McFague [245].

[567]   Ruether, Rosemary Radford. "Ecology and Human Liberation: A Conflict between the Theology of History and the Theology of Nature?" In Rosemary Radford Ruether, *To Change the World*, 57-70. New York: Crossroad, 1983.

This compact statement by Ruether advances a five part thesis. First, at the heart of today's global ecological problems is *not* the nemesis of increased technology, but rather, its profit driven pattern of social domination which neither respects nor is required to respect the rights of workers and human beings in (primarily) third world countries. Second, there is an illegitimate theological grounding of this dominative pattern, i.e., a presumed Judeo-Christian tradition favoring the "subordination of nature and 'man's' [sic] domination over it" (p. 59). Third, while liberal, Marxist and romantic responses have each attempted to alter the pattern of scientific and industrial domination, each in its own way has failed, for none fully respects the victims it would redeem (pp. 63-66). Fourth, as an alternative world view, a conversion to a "new culture of acceptance of finitude and limits" (p. 66) is necessary. Fifth and last, this conversion process is consistent with biblical and ecologically directed norms. That is, to convert to a perspective of finitude and limits is to recognize the necessity for balance and harmony with and within nature, and it is to abandon the purely linear reading of human history as directed to either one final or one supra-historical goal. Neither of these conversion needs is incompatible with biblical images, argues Ruether, but they do require an eschatology that rejects the traditional dichotomy of "Hebrew" and "Greek" thinking, and which recognizes, alternatively, the biblical connections between covenant and Shalom, and the Jubilee requirement for a regular (i.e., "cyclical") rest and replenishment of the earth.

NOTE: For related literature see Ruether's essay [220] and see her *Gaia & God* [235]. Also, for an additional theological critique of the social and cultural images sustaining the sacralization of domination and the association of women and nature imagery, see Catharina J. M. Halkes, *New Creation: Christian Feminism and the Renewal of the Earth*. Louisville, KY: Westminster/John Knox, 1991. Although not abstracted here, Halkes' text critically summarizes the historical development of earth, nature, and domination imagery in Christian theology. Second, it recasts the themes of covenant and creation in terms compatible with Jurgen Moltmann's *The Trinity and the Kingdom of God* [London: SCM, 1981] and his *God and Creation* [London: SCM, 1985].

15

Feminist Theology and the Critique of Heterosexism

Tied to the assumptions of patriarchy, androcentrism and misogyny is a fourth gender norm, that of *heterosexism* or *heterosexist ideology*, as it is also called. This chapter presents the feminist theological literature that critiques this ideology.

This literature has been developing strongly since the mid-1980s and most (but not all) of its sources stem from that period. It is a compact literature in that its key sources are few in number. At the same time, it is a dispersed literature, for much of feminist theology's critique of heterosexism occurs as assumptions embedded within wider discussions (cf., e.g., the literatures on feminist spirituality and/or feminist theological education in Sections III-7 and V-3 respectively). In the entries below, attention is directed both to the key sources published by major feminist theologians during the years 1978-1994 and a variety of supplemental sources reflecting related pastoral, theological and sociological perspectives. As a grounding to these sources, however, some background on the meaning of heterosexism, itself, is helpful.

As it is generally understood, heterosexism is an ideology--or cluster of role defining values-- that affirms four things. First, heterosexism affirms that sexuality and its attracting aspects are best understood and thematized around concepts of sexuality that image the latter as an attraction of dissimilar or differently sexed and differently gendered forces: for example, women and men, maleness and femaleness. Second, heterosexism affirms the idea that *complementarity* is the norm for understanding such dissimilar or differently sex-gendered forces. That is, these differently directed forces are to be understood as elements which *complete* each other and make, thereby, a realized whole. Third, and relatedly, heterosexism typically presumes some form of sexual hierarchy, or the assumption that the dissimilarly directed aspects of sexuality are ordered in a pattern of superordinate and subordinate relations, with masculinity and maleness having priorities over femininity and femaleness. Finally, heterosexism affirms that given the "normativeness" of both complementarity and "sexual hierarchy," all other understandings, experiences or expressions of sexuality are to be judged as abnormal, and specifically so to the extent that they depart from heterosexist understandings of "male-female complementarity." Hence, sexuality is to be understood (and judged) in the light of heterosexism itself, as a moral, and thereby, social and political norm. These four elements--that sexuality is comprised by the attraction of dissimilar or differently sexed and differently gendered forces that are complimentary to each other and hierarchically arranged--and that this is as it should be--are the heart of heterosexist ideology.

In effect, it is this last element of the heterosexist value set, i.e., the idea that 'this is the way things should be,' that secures heterosexism *as* primarily a value structure, and thus as a cultural norm to be internalized, at least within the wide contours of Western religious experience. Moreover, because the components of heterosexism are tied deeply to traditional Christian understandings of creation and theological anthropology--*and* because these components receive common sense verifications through established patterns of gender socialization, there is often little to challenge the sense of normativeness attached to heterosexism, or more specifically, its status as a cultural norm to be internalized.

In contrast to all of this, however, is the feminist and here specifically, the feminist theological critique of heterosexism, for as feminist theologians examine heterosexism, they have emphasized two points: First, that heterosexism is, as a normative framework, inadequate to the moral needs of human beings as such; second, that this moral inadequacy stems from the very assumptions upon which heterosexism rests (i.e., the gender norms attached to patriarchy, misogyny and androcentrism) *and* the subsequent role relations these values engender (*viz.*, male dominant sexual hierarchies and a contempt for women and women's sexuality).

In particular, the literature points out that heterosexism affirms or takes as legitimate those features of androcentrism and patriarchy which are, in fact, most destructive to women. That is to say, heterosexism takes for granted the assumptions that male normativeness, sexual hierarchy, complimentarity and misogyny *are* and *should be* normative. In turn, these latter affirmations support the idea that human beings may legitimately be ranked--that is, valued as worthwhile--in either of two ways: either as (1) objects subject to the norms of ownership and male authority--a benign pattern, or alternatively, (2) as objects subject to the norms of ownership and male misogyny.

In the first case the governing norm is that of the ownership and/or the authority of males over all things *not* male, and thus it is assumed that human beings may be judged--that is, ranked or identified--in terms of the extent to which they approach or approximate "maleness." This is generally an androcentric norm (and within this, a patriarchal norm) in which males own or have hereditary authority over all properties (i.e., all women, children, things and animals) until younger males (i.e., sons) can grow to adulthood to assume *their* position of ownership and/or authority.

Alternatively, the misogynous variant of heterosexism assumes a different grounding for ranking and identifying human beings. In particular, the misogynous variant of heterosexism presumes that it is legitimate to rank or identify human beings in terms of the extent to which they *lack* maleness, and are thus viewable as "non-male" or "female," i.e., a lower life form created for male use, pleasure and/or contentment.

It is precisely this barbarous understanding of human nature--in both its androcentric and misogynous forms--that feminist theology critiques as evil and rejects as the basis of sexuality. Instead, feminist theology affirms a relational and egalitarian sexual ethic appropriate to both same and differently sexed orientations and relationships. Moreover, as it articulates this affirmation theologically, feminist theology notes that it is both females (and males) who are the image of God, and that it is the "Imago Dei" status of being human--and neither the sexual expression, orientation or affectional preference of persons--which constitutes the dignity of being a created person. Further, and quite significantly, feminist theologians note that these affirmations are underscored by the values of mutuality and respect, relationality and justice, and reciprocity and dialogue, as rooted in the classical understanding of the Trinity as the "Icon" of God, and as grounded, thereby, in the Christian doctrine of Creation. Finally, the feminist theological critique of heterosexism points out that heterosexism is not simply an "opinion" among others that can stand in the marketplace of ideas. Rather, it is a value structure of enormous consequence, for it fosters and permits bigotry, hate, and all too frequently, violence against gay and lesbian persons, since neither gay nor lesbian persons can be included in the definition of 'female' and 'male' as presumed by the heterosexist framework.

Put in terms of its widest emphases, then, the feminist theological critique of heterosexism points out that heterosexism affirms subtle and destructive assumptions about sexuality and human beings, in that it does not question the merging of misogyny (literally: the hatred of women) and male dominance (literally: the notions of sexual hierarchy and the legitimacy of male empowered ownership across social and sexual dimensions), which when experienced together, translate first to homophobia (the fear of same-sex oriented persons); second, to same-sex prejudice against gay and lesbian persons; and third, to concrete and often physically violent discrimination against gay and lesbian persons.

The elements of this critique are evident throughout the entries abstracted below, with the essays by Harrison [569], Heyward [570], Hunt [571] and Ruether [573] all indicating feminist theology's long-standing recognition of the social, physical, and emotional violence engendered by heterosexist thinking. Additionally, the early text by Scanzoni and Mollenkott [574] evidences the feminist critique from evangelical sources, while the ecumenical volume by Roman Catholic Patricia Jung and Lutheran Ralph Smith [572] provides a detailed—if at times difficult to read—critique of much mainline theology that needs correction and updating in the domain of individual denominations. Last, a variety of sources scattered throughout the bibliography are cross-referenced within the entries below.

As already noted, this literature assumed prominence in the mid to late 1980s. Its several implications, however, remain underresearched and include (among others) the need to investigate: (i) the conceptual and empirical linkages between familism, religion and heterosexist prejudice (although see Harrison's early work [497]); (ii) the linkages between familism, heterosexism and political and religious organization--and especially the social political question of who controls violence as a social sanction (cf. [588]); (iii) the dynamics of "passing," both in progressive and reactionary eras and across other contexts of stigmatization, including racial (e.g., Lorde [78], Collins [99]) and religious (Plaskow [968]); (iv) the functions of religious support groups for gay and lesbian persons within the frameworks of denominational structures and more pluralized theologies (cf. [572] and [587], and (v) the growing role of backlash as mainline churches address ordination and sexual orientation, and as churches of the Right attempt reparative therapies and "transformational" ministries against gay and lesbian persons.

A. Theological Critiques of Heterosexism

[568] Farley, Margaret A. "An Ethic for Same-Sex Relations." In *A Challenge to Love: Gay and Lesbian Catholics in the Church*, edited by Robert Nugent, 93-106. New York: Crossroad, 1989.
In an attempt to move beyond the question of whether "homosexuality offers one of the possible ways for Christians to live out the sexual dimension of their lives," Farley addresses instead, the question: "What norms should govern same-sex relations and activity?" (p. 93). Her task requires, however, that she review the wider question of the moral status of homosexual relations and activity generally, and to that end, she examines current findings and information from four sources for ethical reasoning: scripture, tradition, other disciplines of knowledge, and current human experience. Her reviews in each of these areas suggest neither an absolute prohibition of same-sex relations and activity, nor its unqualified acceptance. With that observation at hand, Farley attends to the business of ethical analysis proper and indicates a justice ethic for same-sex relations and activity. This ethic requires a respect for persons as ends in themselves, the autonomy of choice in same-sex relations and activity, and the recognition of relationality as an axis of interaction. The ethic is carefully developed and qualified in terms of the equivalence of justice for both hetero- and same-sex relations, and as with all her work, it precludes the assumption of superordinate and subordinate relations between human beings. It is well argued, clearly written, free of heterosexist bias, and recommended for those seeking an illuminating overview discussion.

[569] Harrison, Beverly W. "Misogyny and Homophobia: The Unexplored Connections." In Beverly W. Harrison and Carol S. Robb, ed. *Making the Connections: Essays in Feminist Social Ethics*, 135-151. Boston: Beacon, 1985.
In a discussion first published in 1981, but revised and edited here with Carol Robb, Harrison describes several "unexplored connections" between homophobia (prejudicial fear of same-sex oriented persons) and misogyny, the contempt for and/or hatred of women. These connections are the common roots of each in "mind/body" and "nature/spirit" dualisms, their institutionalization through economically grounded and religiously sanctioned heterosexism, the possibility of their exploitation by conservative American religion (via the argument that liberalism represents the destruction of "family values," and, last, the need for feminist historical analyses of homophobia and misogyny--and particularly, the analysis of sexuality, gender and those socialization patterns that foster the internalization of misogyny as a cultural value. Harrison's discussion is both analytical and theoretical. After noting that misogyny is a "far more consistent trend within Christian history than [is] homophobia" (p. 140), Harrison exposes the grounding assumption of homophobia, i.e., the assumption of male/female super- and subordinate sexual complementarity as evidenced in the stereotypical assumption that in male same-sex relations one male necessarily takes on and enacts the [subordinate] female sexual role. Further, Harrison notes that while much research has discredited this historical stereotype, it still remains and is bolstered by conventional Christian teachings about marriage and sexuality. To close her discussioin, Harrison examines selected implications of Christianity's ethic of sexuality. In particular, she notes that because Christianity maintains the misogynist basis of hierarchical complementarity in sex and gender roles, it misses the true meaning of sexuality in terms of mutuality and respect between equals (the precondition for genuine and joyous eroticism), and it is ideologically compatible with perspectives which support abuse, compliance with exploitative sex, doctrines of racial superiority, and conventional patterns of social-sexual control. While much subsequent literature expands upon the themes developed here by Harrison, this essay remains a classic.

[570] Heyward, Carter. "Heterosexist Theology: Being Above It All." *Journal for Feminist Study in Religion* 3, no. 1 (1987): 29-38.
Heyward's thesis here is that "liberal Christianity is morally bankrupt in relation to women and all homosexual persons." She argues that liberalism is "not only set against collective advocacy as a

primary mode of Christian witness...[but it is]...contemptuous of the particular claims of feminist and all openly gay/lesbian people" (p. 31). The critique is in two parts. Part I exposes the ideological key to Paul Tillich's theology, its capacity to keep role relations in place, as it were, through God's "non-involvement" in creation and the individuality that such non-involvement engenders. Such theology neutralizes collective efforts for just relations in society, and it deceives individual hopes for justice, for it ignores that "freedom is itself not value-free... but the power of personal agency in the context of just social relations" (p. 35). Part II of the critique addresses the power of liberal theology to transform women and openly gay/lesbian lifestyles. That is, while conventional wisdom suggests that liberalism is permissive with respect to gender and life-style concerns, Heyward argues that it is so *only to the extent* that women and gay/lesbian people maintain *public* conformity to patriarchal norms. When such norms are publicly transgressed, however, the moral bankruptcy of liberalism becomes clear, for liberalism cannot and does not embrace the legitimate demands of women and gay/lesbian persons for recognition and inclusion within the human community. By way of conclusion, Heyward suggests that liberal religion is itself "under threat," but "at stake this time," she says, "are not the bodies of witches and faggots, but the nature and destiny of God" (p. 38).

[**571**] Hunt, Mary E. "Political Oppression and Creative Survival." In *Women's Spirit Bonding*, edited by Janet Kalven and Mary Buckley, 249-254. New York: Pilgrim, 1984. (See entry [**575**] below.)

[**572**] Jung, Patricia Beattie, and Ralph F. Smith. *Heterosexism: An Ethical Challenge.* Albany: SUNY Press, 1993.
This text is a sustained critique of heterosexism in the theology and ethos of American mainline Christianity, with particular attention to the theology, practices and current experience of the Evangelical Lutheran Church in America (ELCA). The authors are a lay Roman Catholic theologian (Jung) and an ordained Lutheran pastor (Smith) and at the time of their writing, each was a professor at Wartburg Theological [Lutheran] Seminary. Hence, as they write, they do so"...as Christians [writing] to Christians in order to call the Christian community to a reform that can in turn inform the larger society" about its heterosexist bias, i.e., its assumption that different sex attractions are better than same-sex attractions. Their discussion develops in seven chapters. Chapters 1-2 set the grounds and parameters for their work: Because heterosexism is a "reasoned system of prejudice" to the majority of people in both churches and society, (that it, it is a ranking of sexual orientations that makes sense to large social and religious majorities), their task is to demonstrate that heterosexism is a "noncredible tradition" (i.e., a faulty constellation of cognitions about sexuality), so that, with this established, fears about homosexuality may be addressed and an egalitarian sexual ethic developed. To that end, then, they identify five "moral positions regarding homosexuality," with each laid out in terms of its theological anthropology, ethical axioms and subsequent moral rules. (These positions range, respectively, from the idea of homosexuality as total sinfulness to its conceptualization as random variation akin to the circumstance of left-handedness, with "conservative but compassionate positions" falling between these two poles). Chapter 3 then reviews the biblical literature and exegesis addressing same-sex relations, while chapter 4 summarizes the "costs" of heterosexism, and chapters 5-7 the tasks of "confronting," "dismantling" and "moving beyond heterosexism." Space precludes a full summary of Jung and Smith's discussion, but key points include an excellent overview of biblical work grounding key texts thought traditionally to unequivocally condemn same-sex relations, a clear summary of the fears society (and churches) have of same-sex attractions, two specific examples of how church policies may be reformed to address those fears (i.e., detailed discussions of why and how churches can incorporate same-sex marriages and the ordination of lesbian and gay persons), and last, a closing postscript that highlights the value of a pluriform rather than uniform understanding of sexuality in a world created by God and geared expressively to the fullness of species diversity. Detailed endnotes, useful bibliography and a general index close the volume. This is a courageous, prophetic and well documented text. It succeeds in exposing the "nonrational" quality of heterosexism, and while it does so on specifically Lutheran biblical-theological grounds, its arguments may be extended to most mainline denominations. Portions of the text (e.g., chapters 1-2) are difficult and demanding, but its intensity engages one from the biblical material onward. Second, while some of its initially stated assumptions might stun persons victimized by the New Right (e.g., "heterosexism is not the result of evil actions perpetrated by malevolent people..." p. 10), its wider discussion rings true: to deny non-heterosexist love the opportunity for fidelity, joy and the wonder of God is, in a word, anti-Christ.

[573] Ruether, Rosemary Radford. "Homophobia, Heterosexism, and Pastoral Practice." In *Homosexuality in the Priesthood and the Religious Life,* edited by Jeannine Gramick, 21-35. New York: Crossroad, 1989.

This discussion by Ruether accomplishes several things. First, it critically examines "three interlocking views of homosexuality," i.e., its characterization as "sin, crime and disease, so that the conceptual linkages across these characterizations may be exposed. Ruether then identifies this linkage and its components. It is the ideology of patriarchal heterosexism and it links misogyny and homophobia through a sexual debasement of women and through (male) society's fears of this debasement within themselves given the possibility of same-sex genital relations among men. Second, this article presents an alternative ethical framework for examining same-sex relations. This framework is a perspective Ruether terms "relational" morality, and it is based on the findings and implications of a 1977 Catholic Theological Society of America (CTSA) report on homosexuality [*viz.,* Kosnik et al., *Human Sexuality: New Directions in American Catholic Thought,* New York: Paulist Press, 1977]. As reported by Ruether, the premises of this report include the following: (1) a view of human experience which is both wholistic and sexually diverse--that is, a view of human experience that includes sexuality but does not make biological "complementarity" normative for sexual expression; (2) an acknowledgment of mutuality, equality and respect as the basic values and norms for interpreting all interpersonal and ethical interaction; and (3) an awareness of the provisional nature of ethical judgments given the variations which can and do occur within socialization and social control processes engendered by society In turn, Ruether notes that the CTSA report concludes that same-sex relations are a "natural sexual orientation of a 'normal' minority of persons." By way of expanding upon the CTSA report, Ruether notes several questions which may be raised about sexuality, socialization and social control, and she closes with the suggestion for ritualizing same-sex relations, so that open and committed relationships may develop as freely chosen ways to express human authenticity. Ruether's is a strong and important response to the Catholic literature on this topic.

[574] Scanzoni, Letha, and Virginia Ramey Mollenkott. *Is the Homosexual My Neighbor? Another Christian View.* San Francisco: Harper & Row, 1978/1994.

The first edition of this text was written prior to the public rise of the New Right in American society and politics during the early and mid 1980s. This first edition addressed biblical and exegetical materials on homosexuality, literature from the social and behavioral sciences, and specific ecclesiastical texts indicating both supportive and non-supportive perspectives on gay and lesbian experience. Last, it closed with a consideration of possible Christian ethic(s) concerning same-sex experience. The revised edition repeats these themes and argues for full sexual inclusivity within Christianity. It also updates exegetical and other sources, and particularly the annotated bibliography of the first edition. This is a classic and very readable text. It presents the full spectrum of issues attached to same-sex relations and Christianity, and it is strongly recommended for both congregational use and use by those either those beginning their exploration of the literature or seeking a more differentiated understanding of the relationships between homophobia, misogyny, and Christianity--and prejudice towards those of same-sex affectional orientations.

[575] Wilson, Lynn, Letha D. Scanzoni, and Mary E. Hunt. "Lesbianism and Homophobia." In *Women's Spirit Bonding,* edited by Janet Kalven and Mary Buckley, 239-262. New York: Pilgrim, 1984.

A portion of the materials presented in *Women's Spirit Bonding,* this chapter-length discussion includes (1) a presentation on the fears and angers of lesbian women by Lynn Wilson; (2) a reflection by Letha Scanzoni on Christianity's enormous difficulties with same-sex oriented persons and same-sex relationality; (3) a political definition of lesbianism by Mary Hunt; and (4) a panel response to the issues raised by the presenters. Each of the presentations bears reading on its own, but Hunt's ethically insightful and politically strong approach to defining lesbianism ("Political Oppression and Creative Survival") together with the panel discussion it generated merits particular mention. In brief, it exemplifies many of the elements now current in the feminist critique of heterosexism, including (1) an identification of the homophobic connections between sexism and heterosexism; (2) the affirmation of relationality apart from gender-dependent role definitions, and (3) the affirmation of women's sexuality as defined by relational and community creating capacities rather than genital intimacy, which while not precluded, is nonetheless personal and incidental to social questions of justice and community empowerment.

NOTE: For additional entries by evangelical, womanist, and various Roman Catholic authors see Mollenkott **[247]**, Hill **[627]**, and Zanotti **[752]**, respectively. Additionally, see The Mud Flower Collective **[807]** and Heyward and Hunt **[217]**.

B. Related Pastoral, Theological, and Social-scientific perspectives

[576] Blumenfeld, Warren J., and Diane Raymond. *Looking at Gay and Lesbian Life*.
      Boston: Beacon, 1988.
This nine chapter volume is designed for readership by both gay and straight audiences. It is
clearly written and its scholarship ranks with that of John Boswell's *Christianity, Social Tolerance
and Homosexuality: Gay People in Western Europe from the Beginning of the Christian Era to the
Fourteenth Century*. However, where Boswell's discussion is historical and focuses primarily on
homosexual (or male) same-sex experience, this text addresses contemporary social scientific
research about both gay *and* lesbian life. Specific chapter headings convey the breadth of this work.
Thus, "Socialization and Gender Roles," "Sexuality," and "What Causes Homosexuality" comprise
the first three chapters and "Sexuality and the Heritage of Western Religion," "Prejudice and
Discrimination," and the "History of Lesbian and Gay Liberation Politics" comprise chapters 4-6.
Remaining chapters include: "AIDS: Politics and Precautions," "Life-styles and Cultures," and
"Literature." Readers seeking material current through 1988 with clear discussions of liberal and
conservative perspectives will find this book informative, helpful, and readable. Further, its
extensive chapter bibliographies and detailed index make it an invaluable research tool and/or
benchmark text suitable for use by graduate and undergraduate students, laity, and church leaders.

[577] Blumenfeld, Warren J., ed. *Homophobia: How We All Pay the Price*. Boston:
      Beacon, 1992.
This highly readable and informative volume is a collection of seventeen essays by a variety of gay
and lesbian, bi-sexual and straight professionals, activists, artists and clergy, all largely from the
Boston area. The collection is divided into four sections. First is "Definitions and Origins:
Homophobia and Other Oppressions," a topical division which includes discussions of gender,
homophobia, racism, power and moving beyond 'binary' thinking. Discussions of gay and lesbian
teenage suicide rates, parenting issues and gay/straight marriages make up Section II ("Children,
Family and Homophobia"), and essays addressing such topics as lesbians in the military, and the
impact of religion, AIDS and censorship on gay-lesbian and bisexual experience make up Section
III, "Other Societal Manifestations of Homophobia." A last section, "Breaking Free" works to
identify benefits of living in a non-homophobic society. Blumenfeld's grounding assumption in the
organization of this reader is that homophobia affects all members of society, and that while no one
member is responsible for the creation of homophobia, all members are responsible for its
eradication. To that end he closes the volume with a sample workshop designed to sensitize lesbian
and gay, bisexual and heterosexual persons to their own homophobic realities, such that they can
work on eradicating homophobia from their personal and professional experience. Persons
unfamiliar with the concept of homophobia will find this text helpful and enlightening. Readers
seeking enhanced literature, research and knowledge will also find it helpful, and virtually all
readers will find its straightforward and clear style adaptable to a variety of needs, contexts and
audiences. Also by Blumenfeld is [576].

[578] Blumstein, Philip, and Pepper Schwartz. "Intimate Relationships and the Creation
      of Sexuality." In *The Sociology of Gender: A Text-Reader*, edited by Laura
      Kramer, 173-187. New York: St. Martin's Press, 1991.
The "nature-nurture," "environmentalist-essentialist" debate over the genesis of sexual orientation is
re-examined by these authors on the basis of extensive interview and survey data with heterosexual
and same-sex couples. The authors' purpose is to illustrate the fruitfulness of approaching sexuality
as a *variable* within human experience, dependent--in large part--upon the opportunity for entering
into relationships which can be expressed sexually as well as socially. Overall, they review both
the heuristic and substantive values of the Kinsey scale and they point to its limitations as a
categorizing tool. Rather, the authors suggest, to the extent that opportunities for entering into
relationships exist, sexuality may be (and is) expressed in various ways, with individuals making
choices on the basis of several factors (including norms, structures and personal values), and this
empirical "fact" suggests the necessity for a thorough re-conceptualization of sexuality: both
theoretically and empirically, and in terms of which transcend the Kinsey continuum.

[579] Boswell, John. *Christianity, Social Tolerance and Homosexuality: Gay People in
      Western Europe from the Beginning of the Christian Era to the Fourteenth Century*.
      Chicago: University of Chicago Press, 1980.
This text provides an historical study of intolerance with homosexuality as its illustrative case.
Boswell's introduction sets the parameters and expectations: The study is "offered as a contribution

to [a] better understanding of both the social history of Europe in the Middle Ages and intolerance as a historical force" (p. 4) and homosexuality is taken as the illustrative case for several reasons, not the least of which is that "hostility to gay people provides singularly revealing examples of the confusion of religious beliefs with personal prejudice" (pp. 5-6). Subsequent chapters then clearly detail definitional issues, the "tolerance" of homosexuality within the ancient Roman world, biblical, patristic and medieval 'beliefs' about homosexuality and the emergence in the Middle Ages of social, religious and canonical constraints against gay persons. Two appendices ["Lexicography and St. Paul" and "Texts and Translations"], a bibliography of "Frequently Cited Works," and an "Index of Greek Terms" together with a "General [name-subject] Index" complete the volume. Numerous bibliographic citations and additional insights and observations appear in the extensive footnotes running throughout the text.

[580] Boswell, John. "Homosexuality and Religious Life: A Historical Approach." In *Homosexuality in the Priesthood and the Religious Life*, edited by Jeannine Gramick, 3-20. New York: Crossroad, 1989.
This essay provides a brief overview of homosexuality in religious life with the use of an "insider-outsider" framework to describe the "pervasive invisibility" of gay and lesbian persons in celibate communities and the secular medieval priesthood. By way of specifics, Boswell succinctly addresses the implications of "normality" vis a vis heterosexual and same-sex relations, the structural opportunities offered by celibacy and religious life, and the medieval experience of romantic love in celibate communities. He illustrates the latter with examples of medieval monastic and love poetry, and he closes his discussion with the rise of hostility toward gay and lesbian persons evident initially in the middle of the 13th century: For Boswell's more detailed discussion see [579] and the literature cited there.

[581] Coleman, John. "The Homosexual Revolution and Hermeneutics." In *The Sexual Revolution*, edited by Gregory Baum and John Coleman, 55-64. Edinburgh: T. & T. Clark, 1984.
This article accomplishes two things. First, it discusses briefly the three sociological pre-conditions that have contributed to the development of homosexuality as a socially visible phenomenon. These conditions are those of developed capitalism, urbanization and the norm of individualism engendered in historic Protestant cultures. Second, this essay describes the varying communal values that typify homosexuality as a socially visible phenomenon, and it summarizes the hermeneutical or interpretive power of these values for gay and lesbian persons vis a vis established mainline religion. Thus, according to Coleman, as homosexuality has increasingly become viewed as a life-style embedded within a supportive and nurturing communal network--and less as the behaviors of sick and/or immoral individuals, gay and lesbian people have developed a "hermeneutics of suspicion" with respect to the "traditional Christian condemnation of *all* same sex experience of genital love" (p. 60). Further, the general lines of this hermeneutic involve an "awareness of systematic distortion in communication about homosexuality in Western culture" and an awareness that, as Christians, gay and lesbian persons must also tell "their religious stories" so that the "church's social imagination" may be enriched. Coleman concludes that because the gay and lesbian community is no longer marginalized by invisibility, it will be difficult to bypass the experience of gay Christianity as it attempts a fuller articulation of its theological claims and their correlation(s) with human experience.

[582] Gramick, Jeannine, ed. *Homosexuality in the Priesthood and the Religious Life.* New York: Crossroad, 1989.
The twenty-two essays in this anthology are grouped into "ecclesial," "personal," and "ministerial" perspectives. Among the ecclesial perspectives John Boswell's historical discussion, "Homosexuality and Religious Life" [580] is especially informative. In brief, it describes the significance of homosexuality as an ascribed status, the value of celibacy as a mechanism of achievement apart from traditional gender roles, and last, the presence of romantic and sexual liaisons among noted medieval religious figures. Also important in the ecclesial section are R. R. Ruether's "Homophobia, Heterosexism, and Pastoral Practice" [573] and Daniel Maguire's "The Shadowy Side of the Homosexual Debate." The former exposes the misogynist and heterosexist assumptions underlying homophobia, while the latter details homosexuality as a front for such unresolved Catholic issues as authority in Church practice, a failing theology of celibacy, a tabu-based sexual ethics and the absence of friendship and community as the bases of sexual ethics. The text's "personal perspectives" are individual (and often pseudonymous) essays by gay and lesbian clergy and/or religious. These essays deal primarily with the trials and pain of closeted marginality. "Ministerial Perspectives" deals primarily with issues of coming out, counseling and support, and

in this section, Nugent's article, "Homosexuals and Seminary Candidates" is a "must read" by those interested in theological education. Endnotes follow each essay and a supplemental bibliography of selected literature from 1962-1989 closes the text. The text contains no index, nor is it presented as a companion reader to [583], although it easily can function as such.

[583] Gramick, Jeannine, and Pat Furey, eds. *The Vatican and Homosexuality: Reactions to the "Letter to the Bishops of the Catholic Church on the Pastoral Care of Homosexual Persons."* New York: Crossroad, 1989.
Twenty-five essays grouped into three categories comprise this response to the CDF's October, 1986 "Letter to the Bishops of the Catholic Church on the Pastoral Care of Homosexual Persons." Following a reprint of the letter in the text's introduction, Part I presents nine essays which generally discuss and critique the letter by raising questions of definition, data manipulation, and the legal rights of gay and lesbian persons. Part II presents personal and pastoral responses to the letter including judgments concerning the scope of Rome's authority and the judgments of several Catholic leaders concerning the worth and application of the letter's teaching. Part III, "The Future: Debate and Developments," closes the volume with seven essays addressing cultural and ethical issues *unaddressed* by the letter, but associated with it: e.g., the relation between speech, self, and sexual expression; the ethics of imposing a "tabu ethic;" and by Giles Milhaven, "How the Church Can Learn from Gay and Lesbian Experience." The essays are brief, informative and challenging, and endnotes follow each. Lacking, however, are indices and supplemental bibliography.

[584] Greenberg, David F., and Marcia H. Bystryn. "Christian Intolerance of Homosexuality." *American Journal of Sociology* 88 (1982): 515-548.
This entry both challenges and expands Boswell's work **[579]**, for it locates the roots of Christianity's intolerance for homosexuality in two historical developments: the advent of enforced celibacy within the Roman church in its "Gregorian reforms" from the late 11th to the mid-13th century and the concomitant class conflict which emerged in the 11th and 12th centuries between "bourgeoisie and aristocracy" among the laity. In brief, Greenberg and Bystryn argue the following. First, the question to be addressed is why Judaism and Christianity (and specifically Christianity) but not other religions of the ancient world came to abhor homosexuality. The question is important, the authors argue, for with but a few exceptions in "pagan" literature, homosexuality was either tolerated or viewed as a non-problem. Second, although homosexuality was intermittently condemned by patristical writers, the main focus of such patristical thought was against sexuality per se and not homosexuality in particular. (Although John Chrysostom is cited as an exception to this generalization.) Thus, third, it is the intolerance which arises by the 13th century which must be explained, and the two key factors are (a) the Gregorian reforms, which for financial and political reasons included the dissolving of priests' marriages and the incorporation of celibacy as a clerical norm; and (b) the emerging association of homosexuality (and sodomy) as elements of an elite, courtly life-style (as contrasted with the industriousness of self-reliant bourgeoisie). According to Greenberg and Bystryn, the foreclosure of clergy marriages generated the possibility (and eventuality) of homosexuality within the clergy as a compensation for sexual loss. In turn, the "feminization" of courtly dress, hair styles and the like contrasted sharply with the gender norms of most laity. Thus the seeds for intolerance were laid, and as such, they precipitated a climate for psychological projection and eventually, the intolerance itself.

[585] Maguire, Daniel. "The Morality of Homosexual Marriage." In *A Challenge to Love: Gay and Lesbian Catholics in the Church*, edited by Robert Nugent, 118-134. New York: Crossroad, 1989.
This essay was first prepared in the early 1980s, but bears obvious relevance in the light of recent developments in both American military policy and similarly cast Vatican publications. An ethicist whose career spans nearly 30 years of teaching and publications, Maguire considers four points as he addresses the "morality" of homosexual marriage. These include: (1) the moral reasonableness of homosexuality as a variation in sexual orientation (as contrasted with either a pathology or circumstance of sinfulness); (2) the actual notion that marriage can be an option for same-sex oriented persons; (3) the two possible objections which might be raised against marriages between persons of a same-sex, and (4) the legitimacy of "probabalism" as a framework for holding to the morality of same-sex marriages when other authorities hold an opposing perspective. Maguire's analysis stems from Catholic moral theology and readers unfamiliar with the latter may find its possibilities for pluralism surprising. In particular, Maguire argues that the burden of proof for dismissing homosexuality as either sick or sinful lies with those who consider it as such, and that for either position, the harm done must be demonstrated, not assumed. Similarly, Maguire argues against the "be-but-don't-do" perspective of mandatory celibacy by noting that (a) celibacy is a

charism requiring intense communal support--even for heterosexuals, and that (b) Catholic moral theology does not require anyone to do the impossible. As regards the possibilities of same-sex marriages, Maguire discusses the "indispensable goods" of marriage and the evidence from Vatican II and elsewhere that procreation is no longer considered the only good of marriage. Further, because his perspective departs radically from that of the hierarchical magisterium, Maguire closes his discussion with a description of "moral probabalism" to illustrate both that a legitimate plurality of opinions *can* exist on a given subject, and that under certain conditions, one may legitimately dissent from the (non-infallible) teachings (of the hierarchical magisterium) on such subjects: in this case, the circumstance of homosexuality and the possibility of homosexual marriages.

[586] Nugent, Robert, ed. *A Challenge to Love*. New York: Crossroad, 1989.
First published as a collection of essays for "New Ways Ministries" located in Hyattsville, MD in 1983, this volume has been expanded and revised to include 18 essays addressing "societal," "biblical-theological," "pastoral" and "vocational" perspectives relevant to the experience of gay and lesbian Catholics, lay and ordained. Discussions of societal perspectives examine issues of prejudice and definition, political responsibility and "the creative role of the gay community in building a more humane society" with contributors including Jeannine Gramick, James Zullo, James Whitehead, Gregory Baum and John McNeill. Authors addressing biblical-theological perspectives include Michael Guinan, Lisa Cahill, Margaret Farley, Edward Malloy, Daniel Maguire and Mary Hunt. The section on pastoral perspectives includes discussions by Gabrial Moran (on education) and Matthew Fox (on spirituality), by James and Evelyn Whitehead on "maturity" and Bruce Williams on "gay Catholics and Eucharistic communion: [the] theological parameters." "Vocational Perspectives" constitutes the last main division of Nugent's reader and here selected authors take up questions of marriage, vocational discernment, celibacy and religious life. Some of these essays reflect a "pre-AIDS" mentality" in that they do not address the relationship of homophobia and HIV infection, and all precede the Vatican's July 15, 1992 statement indicating the conditions under which the Vatican feels discrimination against gay and lesbian persons is legitimate. Because of the growing salience of gay ordinations within selected denominations, seminary personnel may wish to consult the essays by M. B. Pennington and Daniel Maguire for their observations concerning celibacy and religious vocation. Additionally readers of feminist ethics may wish to examine the entries by Farley [568], Maguire [585], and Hunt [556]. With an introduction by Walter Sullivan (then the Catholic Bishop of Richmond) this volume presents the full range of conservative to liberal Catholic thinking on homosexuality through the early 1980s, and it should be read in conjunction with Nugent's later work [587], entries by Gramick ([582, 583]) and the entries cited there. An extensive index and Catholic bibliography current through 1982 close the volume.

[587] Nugent, Robert, and Jeannine Gramick. *Building Bridges: Gay and Lesbian Reality and the Catholic Church*. Mystic, CT: Twenty-Third Publications. 1992.
Unlike their previously published works which are limited largely to edited collections on homosexuality and Roman Catholic clergy [582], this volume presents essays authored by Gramick and Nugent on four major topics relevant to Catholicism and its lesbian and gay constituencies. These topics provide the four-fold division of the book and they include "Educational and Social Concerns" (*viz.*, gay and lesbian rights, the "debunking" of "myths" and a discussion of what is "natural"); "Counseling and Pastoral Issues" (e.g., same-sex relations, sexuality and marriage); issues of import to "Clerical and Religious Life;" and in Part IV, a series of essays illustrating "Evolving Theological Perspectives." These essays reflect observations and insights drawn from the authors' twenty-year long ministry to the Catholic lesbian and gay community and their equally long study of the social scientific research on same-sex relations. Of particular importance is Section IV. With its entries on "The U.S. Hierarchy and Current Thinking" and the evolving spirituality of Catholic gay and lesbian faith, it suggests several implications for discussions of theological method, Catholic sexual ethics, and the church's role in social leadership. As a footnote to the entry on homosexuality and the hierarchy, however, it must to be said that the latter pre-dates the Vatican's July 15, 1992 statement purporting to justify discrimination against gay and lesbian persons in selected social spheres.

[588] Pharr, Suzanne. *Homophobia: A Weapon of Sexism*. Chardon Press. 1988.
This book details the enormous impact of homophobia as a tool in the suppression of women's authority to define their own experience. It is organized into five chapters that respectively: (1) define and identify homophobia as a specific *weapon* of sexism; (2) indicate the "effects of homophobia on women's liberation;" (3) provide "strategies for eliminating homophobia;" (4) identify the "common elements of oppression" cutting across gender, race, class, age and sexuality;

and (5) suggest strategies for lesbian women seeking freedom from their own internalization of homophobia as a social force. Pharr is a lesbian activist who conducts workshops for lesbian women and straight women and men who wish to overcome their own internalized homophobia. Hence her discussion is both theoretical and practical. At the theoretical level, because homophobia is a *weapon* of sexism, it links violence, heterosexism and women's economic dependence into a mantle that serves to threaten women's physical safety, their opportunities for work, the custody of their children, and more generally, the civil and human rights the vast majority of American society takes for granted. Further, and of particular importance to both sociologists and theologians, Pharr describes the experiences of an exceedingly, invisible abuse problem, i.e., that of abuse within the lesbian community itself (although cf. [853]). This is a powerful and lucidly written text that details policy, organizational and ethical considerations, and it should be read by all parties interested in abuse, sexuality, sexual orientation and feminism's critique of heterosexism--in both church and society.

[589] Rich, Adrienne. "On Compulsory Heterosexuality and Lesbian Existence." *Signs* 5 (1980): 631-661.
This now classic essay seeks to detail how the bias of *compulsory heterosexuality* has not only conditioned feminist theory, but undercuts it as well. The discussion is in four parts. First, Rich seeks to expose compulsory heterosexuality as a bias institutionalized in virtually all elements of both society's (and feminism's) understanding of women. Rich does this through a review of key feminist writings through 1980, and in none of these, says Rich, is "the question of lesbianism" ever raised: i.e., the question of "...whether in a different context or other things being equal, women *would* [in fact] choose heterosexual coupling and marriage... .[Rather]...heterosexuality is presumed as a 'sexual preference' of 'most women,' either implicitly or explicitly" (p. 633). Hence its conditioning of feminist theory. Having exposed the heterosexual bias, Rich then examines the political dimensions of heterosexuality by describing (and vividly illustrating) seven characteristics of male power. These characteristics are taken from a discussion which exposes them as the means for establishing unequal power between males and females, and for Rich they betray the assumption of a requirement toward heterosexuality because they regularly "wrench women's emotional and erotic energies away from themselves and other women and from women identified values" (p. 658). Finally, to indicate her understanding of lesbianism, Rich contrasts the two concepts, "lesbian existence" and "a lesbian continuum." The former is the historical presence of lesbians and their continuing creation of meaning in their experience; the latter, a range of woman-identified experiences that may include, but are not limited to, same-sex genital activity or desire. A closing summary indicates the social and emotional costs of heterosexist bias and the further implications of its presence as an institutionalized ideology.

NOTE: For related literature see Chapter 12 on "Feminist Theological Ethics" and particularly Susan Opotow's essay, "Moral Exclusion and Injustice" [514].

IV

Feminism and Womanist Theology

With the advent of a distinct feminism within the African American community (cf., hooks [29-30], Hill-Collins [99] and Dill [602, 622]), black women writers and theologians have begun to describe an orientation to black community life which focuses on both survival and familism, and a combination of universalism and racial pride as experienced and evidenced by African American women throughout American history. This orientation is called "womanism," and while the name of this orientation stems from Alice Walker's 1983 volume, *In Search of Our Mothers' Gardens: Womanist Prose* [San Diego: Harcourt Brace Jovanovich], its referents are deeply historical. They are the two-hundred and fifty-six year long period of American chattel slavery and the profound survival and support commitments of African American women during not only this period, but as Cannon [612], Williams [632] and others [592] note, the periods of reconstruction, segregation, integration, and more recently, the "new" racism which have all followed chattel slavery. This section of the bibliography presents literature that grounds both the womanist orientation and its theological development. By way of overview, the section is divided into two chapters. The first presents reference works and introductory sources that provide a framework for understanding the development of womanist thinking. Chapter 17 then presents literature on the development of womanist consciousness, together with an identification of key topical literatures in womanist theology.

For readers unfamiliar with the history of African Americans, the overview by Franklin and Moss [594] remains classic and especially if read back to back with Loewenberg and Bogin [606], Dill [602], Giddings [614], Wade-Gayles [609], and the sociological entries by Ladner [597], Gilkes [603], and Terrelonge [624]. Second, several entries from Section I are also important here, and particularly the Hull, Scott, and Smith volume on Black Women's Studies [49], the historical works by Gerda Lerner [77], Elizabeth Fox-Genovese [75], and Jacqueline Jones [76], and for the study of racial and ethnic relations, the texts by Benokraitis and Feagin [86], Feagin and Feagin [122-123], and Zinn and Dill [83].

An important feature of the womanist perspective is its evolving character. Through the mid-1990s, womanism has evolved to include: (1) an orientation to black women's survivalism throughout the social history of African Americans in the United States (cf. Cannon's early work in womanist ethics [612] and see Weems [642] and Williams [639]); (2) a framework for interpreting the role of the Black church vis a vis social stratification and the "interstructuring" of race, gender and class issues (cf. Sanders [631]); (3) a model for African American women's organizational strength against racism in American society (cf. Riggs [257, 628]); and, (4) a justice based spirituality which synthesizes each of these frameworks to address policy issues affecting African Americans across the board (e.g., Townes [633, 258]).

A final caveat: At no point should the reader conceive of womanism as merely a form of "feminism-in-black," as if the differences between womanist and feminist thinking were analogous, but for whatever reasons, presently separated or segregated. Rather, womanism is a cultural consciousness that stems from the commitments of black women to black family and community life and *within these* to gender and "women's experience." For this reason, therefore, the development of womanist theology is characterized here as the development of an alternative core literature, *viz.*, a literature that stresses: (a) the social, sexual, familial, and occupational experiences of African American women--both within and beyond the Black community and within and beyond the varying structures of black family life; (b) the existential, biblical and theological images which this survivalism can and has engendered; and (c) the various resources such images engender for womanist theological, womanist/feminist, and womanist/Black church applications.

16

Womanism and Womanist Theology—
The Background Literature

A. Bibliographies and Preliminary Reference Materials

[590] Baer, Hans A. "Bibliography of Social Science Literature on Afro-American Religion in the United States." *Review of Religious Research* 29 (1988): 413-430.
This bibliography is "aimed primarily at social scientists who are interested in various dimensions of Black religion during the twentieth century" (p. 413). The literature is current through 1985 and covers six categories: (1) "Overviews of Black Religion," (2) "Studies of Black Churches in Specific Locales (Rural and Urban)," (3) "Community Studies with Extensive Discussions of Black Religion," (4) "Studies of Black Churches in Specific Locales (Rural and Urban)," (5) "Dimensions of Black Religiosity; White Churches, Racism and Black Americans," and (6) "The Occult Among Black Americans: Voodoo, Hoodoo, and Magic." Section 5 is the most comprehensive with 172 entries and Section 4 the least, with four entries. In all, Baer lists 336 items with numerous sectional subdivisions to guide the user. Missing, however, is research on women in Black religion.

[591] Cone, James H., and Gayraud S. Wilmore, eds. *Black Theology: A Documentary History: Volume Two: 1980-1992*. Maryknoll, NY: Orbis Books, 1993.
With its emphases on: (a) the "second generation" of African American theologians and their literature; (b) the necessity and work of a clear dialogue between black theological reflection and black congregational life; (c) the developing literature in African American hermeneutics and biblical studies; (d) womanist theology; and (e) the "global context" of African American theology, this second anthology in the Black Theology Documentary History series is distinctively and self-consciously different from the first. In the first volume, attention was directed to the history and prophetic development of African American theology, and particularly its roots in the black power movement and the social conditions of African Americans. Here, while empowerment concerns still ground African American theological reflection, attention is more directed to the questions of *how* African American theology fits against other perspectives, and especially those of the theologizing task itself. Hence, Volume II presents 33 essays reflecting the positions of Black theologians in the above five areas. Editorial introductions well preview each section, notes follow all entries and a 53 item annotated bibliography and comprehensive subject index close the volume. Last, and of special note, is Cone's characaterization of womanist theology as "the most creative development to emerge out of the Black theology movement during the 1980s and 1990s" (p. 257).

[592] Dudley, William, and Charles Cozic, eds. *Racism in America: Opposing Viewpoints*. San Diego, CA: Greenhaven Press, 1991.
This text is a volume within the *Opposing Viewpoint Series*, a resource for teaching undergraduate sociology; as such, it presents essays of contrasting perspectives on a number of questions relevant to any given topic, here that of racism. While not generated from within a consciously feminist perspective, its questions and bibliography are useful to both womanist and feminist theologians. With an average of 6-7 articles per question the text compactly addresses such questions as: "How serious is the problem of racism in America?" "Is racism responsible for minority poverty?" "Does affirmative action alleviate discrimination?" "Should minorities emphasize their ethnicity?" and

"How can racism be stopped?" Further, the editors provide additional journal bibliography at the close of each chapter, along with exercises designed to heighten consciousness on issues. Last, a list of issue-related organizations together with an extended bibliography and subject-author index close the volume. This is a helpful teaching resource: it provides an overview of racism in the '90s and can be used effectively with literature from several theological perspectives. **NOTE**: Also from the same series is the 1997 volume, *Discrimination*, edited by David Bender et al., which addresses issues about the scope, causes, interpretations of and potential solutions to discrimination as based on race, ethnicity, sex, and sexual orientation.

[593] Evans, James H. Jr., comp. and G. E. Gorman, advisory editor. *Black Theology: A Critical Assessment and Annotated Bibliography*. Westport, CT: Greenwood Press, 1987.
Readers seeking familiarity with the wide range of issues falling under the umbrella, Black Theology, will find this reference extremely helpful. In it Evans synthesizes more than 450 sources from the American and international Black theological literature to demonstrate: (a) the "Origin and Development" of American Black Theology from 1968 on (268 entries); (b) the emphases of "Liberation, Feminism and Marxism" within American Black theology (65 entries)--including womanist sources through 1986; and in terms of its widest dimensions, (c) Black theology's "Cultural and Global Discourse" (129 entries). A brief "critical introduction" highlights (among other things) Evans' distinction between "church theology and folk theology" as well as the early tensions grounding black, feminist and womanist theologies. The volume closes with cross-referenced author, title and subject indices. All entries are annotated and alphabetized within each section, and their chronological numbering serves to indicate cross-references throughout the text and its indices. This is an exceptionally fine bibliography for the historical and global literature within Black theology, and while its womanist literature is understandably sparse, important early sources are included. **NOTE**: For literature published subsequent to Evans' bibliography see the bibliography in Cone and Wilmore **[591]**. Also, for Evans' own theological work, see *We Have Been Believers: An African-American Systematic Theology* [Minneapolis: Fortress Press, 1992]. While not abstracted here, it powerfully addresses African American history, suffering, and church life in terms of hermeneutical and narrative theological method, current liberationist (e.g., Cone), womanist (e.g., Grant and Brown) and African perspectives, and always with an eye to the impact of racism on both traditional Christian symbols and such formal theological questions as anthropology, theodicy, etc.

[594] Franklin, John Hope, and Alfred A. Moss, Jr. *From Slavery to Freedom: A History of Negro Americans*. 6th ed. New York: McGraw-Hill, 1988.
This text remains the classic standard on the history of African Americans in the United States from the arrival of twenty free African indentured servants at Jamestown in 1619 to the leadership of American civil rights activists in the American anti-apartheid movement of the early 1980s. It is a text as mammoth in scope in its sixth edition as it was in its first and subsequent editions, and its ongoing and now co-authored revision reflects the impact of interdisciplinary and updated historical scholarship. Like earlier editions, this one also locates the history of African Americans *in* Africa with opening chapters describing African culture, economics and society, and the widening scope of European slave-trading from Africa to the New World. Subsequent chapters detail the history of African Americans during colonial slavery, the Civil War and Reconstruction, the period of legalized segregation, and the multitude of experiences conditioning the African American experience during most of the twentieth century: *viz.*, America's wars, the "Great Depression," the 20th century struggles of African Americans for inclusion in the social system, the American civil rights movement, and the achievements of African American in politics, the arts, education, the economy, and professional and para-professional spheres. Detailed discussions ground all chapters, and the authors' closing chapter returns, again, to Africa and the anti-apartheid movement. An especially valuable aspect of this text are the supplemental bibliographic essays that provide extensive source materials for each of the separate chapter topics. A well prepared index closes the volume.

[595] Gilton, Donna. "Afro-American Womanist Theology." *The Woman's Pulpit* 69 (April-June, 1991): 4-6.
This article locates the rise of womanist theology vis a vis American Black theology. It details the differences between womanist and Black theology, womanist and feminist theology and womanist and (Latin American) liberation theology. It identifies several sources from womanist theology and introduces the "multi-faceted analysis" (p. 5) womanist theology envisions if it is to develop its critique of race, class and gender discrimination. The literature cited is current through 1987 and

although the article is itself brief, it is an informative introduction to the literature of womanism and theology. For additional sources on womanist theology, see Grant **[254]**, Copland **[265]** and **[640]**.

[596] Jones, Lawrence J. "The Organized Church: Its Historic Significance and Changing Role in Contemporary African American Experience." In *Directory of African American Religious Bodies: A Compendium by the Howard University School of Divinity*, edited by Wardell Payne, 1-20. Washington, DC: Howard Univ. Press, 1991.
This essay introduces the Howard University Divinity School's compendium on African American religious bodies and organizations **[599]**. The essay itself is an edited version of a piece prepared by Jones for the ALA in 1975 and its revised inclusion within the compendium virtually guarantees it a wider and perhaps more theologically directed readership. By way of overview, Jones surveys the development of African American religious organizations from the early and enforced Christianization of slaves during the 17th century to the development of Black churches in the early and mid-18th century and the denominational structuring and restructuring of African American religion in the 19th and 20th centuries. To frame his discussion, Jones draws upon the historical experience of African Americans: an ongoing affirmation of African American humanity in the face of slavery, a variety of experiences borne of modern social forces (e.g., the migration of African Americans to Northern and industrialized economies during the 1930s through the 1960s, the subsequent activist and engaged ministries of African American clergy and academic theologians), and last, the differentiation of African American religious activity beyond traditional groupings to the teachings of Marcus Garvey, the Nation of Islam and the somewhat separate histories of African Americans in Judaism and Roman Catholicism. This is an informative essay, but with two unexplainable limitations. First, there is no discussion of the religious organizational contributions made by African American women to African American religion, including the development of American womanist theology. Second, as he describes the distribution of African Americans within Judaism, Jones does so uncritically from within the hegemony of a Christian theology that views Judaism as "essentially an ethnic and cultural religion invested in the popular mind with social, economic, and especially political interests." Both are incongruous in the light of literature contemporary with the publication of this essay, and the latter is "insensitive," to say the very least.

[597] Ladner, Joyce, ed. *The Death of White Sociology*. New York: Random House, 1973.
Twenty-six essays grouped into eight sections ranging from "The Socialization of Black Sociologists" to the development and study of "Black Sociology," "Black Psychology," and "Institutional Racism" make up this collection of theoretical, historical and case study discussions on the effects and significance of "race" for social science. Ladner traces the history of 'Black sociology' through the rise of the Black academic caucuses in a variety of disciplines during the late 1960s and early 1970s. She highlights the necessity of theories and constructs that acknowledge the involuntary aspects of African American experience, critique and challenge mainstream sociology's characterization of Black experience as deviant, and last, offer alternative priorities, possibilities and directions for future research. Although now dated when viewed against much current sociological work (e.g., Andersen **[84]**, Collins **[99]** and their co-authored text **[85]**), this is an important historical source, with contributions from E. Franklin Frazier, Kenneth Clark, Dennis Forsythe, Ethel Sawyer and Andrew Billingsly. **NOTE**: For more current literature on racial and ethnic relations see Feagin and Feagin **[123]**.

[598] Lincoln, C. Eric, and Lawrence H. Mamiya. *The Black Church in the African American Experience*. Durham, NC: Duke Univ. Press, 1990.
Using a variety of historical, theological and interdisciplinary sources, together with survey data from a national sample of African American clergy (n=2150), Lincoln and Mamiya provide a comprehensive description of the Black Church in America. Their discussion seeks to identify the concrete elements of a "black sacred cosmos," and to this end the authors present thirteen chapters detailing the following: (1) the history and demography of Black America's seven "totally controlled black denominations"; (2) the distinctive emphases of rural and urban Black churches; (3) the plethora of economic, political, and demographic concerns facing contemporary African American religious leadership--including the connections between Black churches, black families and the problems facing young African Americans; (4) the status and role(s) of women in contemporary African American religious leadership (see **[141]**); (5) the sociology of music ("the performed word") in the Black Church; and last, (6) a summary of the issues facing Black clergy and the Black Church as the 21st century approaches. Among its many values, the text permits

extensive study and perusal--with each chapter sufficiently readable to stand alone. Notes, an extensive bibliography, and a thorough index close the text.

[599] Payne, Wardell, ed. *Directory of African American Religious Bodies: A Compendium by the Howard University School of Divinity.* Washington, DC: Howard Univ. Press, 1991.
This volume is the most comprehensive directory on African American religious organizations currently available and it provides a wealth of information as edited by Payne, a sociologist who is also a minister in the Washington D.C. area. The directory is divided into nine sections. These present, respectively: (a) an introductory essay on the history of the Black church in America through the late 1970s **[596]** by Lawrence Jones, Dean Emeritus from Howard University's Divinity School; (b) three separate sections describing a variety of African American religious bodies, councils, ecumenical and educational organizations; (c) a "selective" (but extensive) listing of African American religious scholars (including womanist and black feminist scholars); (d) summary data on African American membership in mainline white churches; and (e) selected historical essays on such African American religious traditions as, e.g., "African American Baptists," (by C. G. Newsome, Dean of Howard Divinity) and the "History of the African American Roman Catholic Church in the United States" (by Cyprian Davis, OSB). Extensive appendices, bibliographies, and indices--each with countless cross references--close the volume.

[600] Wilmore, Gayraud S., and James H. Cone, eds. *Black Theology: A Documentary History 1966-1979.* Maryknoll, NY: Orbis Books, 1979.
Divided into six sections, this volume presents a series of 56 essays and/or historical documents that address the following areas: (I) "The End of an Era: Civil Rights to Black Power [6 essays];" (II) "The Attack on White Religion [7 essays];" (III) "Black Theology and the Response of White Theologians" [6 essays]; (IV) "Black Theology and the Black Church" [16 essays]; (V) "Black Theology and Black Women" [6 essays]; (VI) "Black Theology and Third World Theologies" [15 essays]. Editor Wilmore introduces sections I, II and IV, while Cone introduces sections III, V and VI. The section on "Black Theology and Black Women" includes entries by Frances Beale **[610]**, Theresa Hoover **[618]**, Jacqueline Grant **[635]**, Pauli Murray **[181]**, James Cone and Alice Walker. A thirteen page annotated bibliography on Black theology prepared by Vaughn T. Eason lists 43 book entries published between 1964 and 1977 and 106 articles entries published between 1963 and 1979. An 18 page subject/author index (with entry titles included under author names) closes the volume and marks it as an especially helpful reference tool.

NOTE: For additional bibliographies see Mankiller et al. **[52]**, Redfern **[53]** and Hull, Scott and Smith **[49]**; for general literature see Davis **[72]**, Fox-Genovese **[75]**, Jones **[76]**, Lerner **[77]**, and Malson et al. **[79]**. Last, for literature on the development of global racism, see Feagin and Feagin **[123]**.

B. Black Women/Black Families

[601] Cheatham, Harold E., and James B. Stewart, eds. *Black Families: Interdisciplinary Perspectives.* New Brunswick, NJ: Transaction Publishers, 1990.
This book "resurrects" the theoretical perspectives of W. E. B. DuBois and E. F. Frazier as grounds for an Afrocentric framework for the study of black families. The authors are mindful of the limitations conditioning the works of these early African American sociologists, but through an analysis of their writings, key meta-theoretical emphases come to the fore to support: (1) an ecologically based framework for studying black family experience (i.e., an analysis of how black families interact with other external social systems such as the Black church, hospitals, the federal government etc.); (2) an analysis of the internal dynamics in black family experience (e.g., value differences and value transmission, gender perceptions); and (3) a pluralized perception of black family experience sensitive both to the impact of cross cultural settings and the necessity for various intervention strategies within selected topics of importance. The outcome of these theoretical and meta-theoretical investigations is an 18 entry anthology focused on the ecological and interactive issues mentioned above. The grounding premise of the anthology is that the study of [American] Black families has been conducted in terms of stereotypes and/or "the evolution of stereotype[s] through successive theoretical formulations from *pathological* to *culturally deficient* to *culturally different"* (p. 396), and Cheatham and Stewart seek a corrective that attends to the cultural specificity of Black families in their own right, rather than the ideological presuppositions of a dominant theoretical framework. **NOTE:** For related literature see McAdoo **[607]**.

[602] Dill, Bonnie Thornton. "The Dialectics of Black Womanhood." *Signs* 4 (1979): 543-555.

Following Frazier's 1965 analysis, *The Negro Family in the United States,* and the 1965 U.S. Department of Labor report, *The Negro Family: the Case for National Action* (often termed simply "the Moynihan Report"), American social science has often assumed that matriarchy is an appropriate model for interpreting the position and roles of black American women during both slavery and the contemporary period. Sociologist Dill challenges this research tradition. She argues for a more dialectical and less linear approach to the study of Black American women, and she shows that the work experience of African American women has engendered "alternative notions of womanhood contradictory to those that have been traditional in American society" (p. 543). The argument has four points. First, the Frazier and Moynihan studies are inadequate: Frazier's because it is based on insufficient data and Moynihan's because it uncritically links the high labor force participation rate of black women with matriarchy and the "psychological emasculation of black men" (p. 548). This, according to Dill, "blames the victim" and makes black women responsible for the "failure of the black community to gain [economic] parity with the white community" (p. 548). Second, traditional social science has assumed a "monolithic whole" relative to black family research and ignored, thereby, the interactive forces of race and social class. "Afro-American culture...[does not]...disappear," argues Dill, as "black Americans gain middle class status." Rather, ethnicity and social class are distinct variables, referring, respectively, to "historical identification" and "behavioral similarities" (p. 551). Third, to generate an appropriate or dialectical framework for understanding black women's work role and social identity, one must understand racial oppression and economic exploitation, for these, together with ethnicity and class provide the necessary variables to interpret the black woman's high level of work experience. Specifically, these variables call attention to the fact that black *women* also were slaves--also "beasts of burden," and thus were women who were never to have the "benefit" of America's traditional gender assumptions (i.e., psychological weakness, passivity, dependence etc.). Fourth, these observations have implications for understanding the experience of contemporary black women: (a) they help explain the lack of black women's identification with the American feminist movement, for while working for pay outside the home is and has been a *goal* of the women's movement, it is and always has been a *necessity* for black women; (b) if the slave or "beasts of burden" image is historically more accurate than that of the matriarch, then the survival and cultural values learned by black women can open one to other images which suggest "possibilities of a new definition of femininity for *all* American women" (p. 555). NOTE: also by Dill is **[622]** and (with Zinn) **[83]**.

[603] Gilkes, Cheryl Townsend. "Dual Heroism and Double Burdens: Interpreting Afro-American Women's Experience and History." [A Review Essay] *Feminist Studies* 15 (1989): 573-590.

This extended review analyzes four mid-1980s interpretations of "Afro-American women's experience and history." These include: Giddings' *When and Where I Enter: The Impact of Black Women on Race and Sex in America* **[614]**; Jaqueline Jones' *Labor of Love, Labor of Sorrow: Black Women, Work and Family, from Slavery to the Present* **[76]**; *We Are Your Sisters: Black Women in the Nineteenth Century,* edited by Dorothy Sterling [NY: Norton, 1984]; and last, *Ar'n't I a Woman: Female Slaves in the Plantation South.* by Deborah Gray White [NY: Norton, 1985]. Giddings' volume is commended for its excellent analysis of race and sex in the development of historical attitudes now conflictual between white and black women. Jones' encyclopedic knowledge is equally commended, but the text as a whole is limited, says Gilkes, by an ongoing assumption of women's history as "white women's history" and Jones' subsequent inability to read black women's history from any other point of view. In contrast, Gilkes attests the "instant classic" quality of Dorothy Sterling's work, a sourcebook "in the tradition of Gerda Lerna's *Black Women in White America*" **[77]**. Last, Deborah White's analysis of slave women's experience suggests several new research possibilities, not the least of which is the "more rigorous discussion on women's solidarity within black institutions, especially patriarchal black churches with their paradox of female independence and collectivism within a framework of male leadership" (p. 587).

[604] Ihle, Elizabeth, ed. *Black Women in Higher Education: An Anthology of Essays, Studies, and Documents.* New York: Garland, 1992.

This anthology reproduces various "essays, studies and documents" that attest to the "...dreams, obstacles, disappointments and achievements [of African American women] in the history of African American women's higher education" (p. xxxvi). In all, fifty-four primary sources are presented and grouped historically in terms of: (1) "The Beginning: Late Nineteenth Century" (eleven entries); (2) "A New Century Opens: Rules and Policies" (seventeen entries); (3) "Mid-Century: Discrimination by Race and Sex (seventeen entries); and (4) "Breaking Away: Higher

Education in the 60s and Beyond" (nine entries). An extended introduction by editor Ihle locates each of these historical divisions and provides a synopsis of each entry within the divisions. Additionally, it identifies the many key leaders in African American women's higher education (e.g., Mary Church Terrell, Mary McLeod Bethune, and Florence Read), and by its descriptive detail of the varying settings and contents of its entries, it stands as a major contribution to African American Women's Studies and Women's Studies generally. Sociologists interested in the history of African American women's sororities will find this a valuable primary source, as will users interested in issues of race and single sex education. A limitation to the work, however, is its "reproduction" quality: with several different genres represented, including aged photographs, the print size and quality of entries vary enormously.

[605] Jones, Jacqueline. *The Dispossessed: America's Underclass from the Civil War to the Present.* New York: Basic, 1992.
In an earlier work [76] Jones has detailed what she describes as the "stubbornness of a mother's love" within the African-American community. Here she examines "American's underclass from the Civil War to the present," i.e., through 1990. Her purpose is to challenge the culture of poverty theory which undergirds much political rhetoric about America's underclass and the role of Blacks within it, and her discussion of late twentieth century American poverty, crime, drug abuse and racial pluralism is persuasive. There are many--and new--underclasses, she argues, and the key to understanding them is not the political rhetoric of welfare fraud or the ghettoization of American black experience. Rather, it is the labor mobility and the migratory patterns of rural American families, together with the settling of new immigrant groups into a post-industrial economy. Informative end-notes, an extended bibliography, and a general index close the volume.

[606] Loewenberg, Bert James, and Ruth Bogin, eds. *Black Women in Nineteenth Century American Life.* University Park, PA: The Pennsylvania State Univ. Press, 1976.
While this collection of writings by African American women predates the self-conscious articulation of womanist literature within the theological-academic context, it nonetheless presents an informative and useful series of source writings by twenty-four African American women--ten free and fourteen born to slavery--but "all born before the Civil War or during it" (p. x). The sources include excerpts from diaries, letters and articles, and among the contributors are such notables as Jarena Lee, Harriet Tubman, Sojourner Truth, and Ida Wells-Barnett. Contributors perhaps less well known to a generalized white audience include memoir writer Annie Louise Burton, educator Ann Plato, and lecturer-abolitionist Nancy Prince to name but three. In all, sources are grouped into four thematic sections: family and kinship, religion, social inclusion, and education, with each prefaced by an editorial introduction indicating important historic events, time-frames and biographic details of the writers' lives. The editors' introductory chapter ("Selves and Society") highlights particular and universal themes evident in the sources synthesized for review, and a bibliography and general index close the volume. The bibliography is especially helpful: it lists additional writings by the 24 women the authors survey, it provides a guide to additional sources, and it lists reference works from mid-nineteenth century through the early 1970s.

[607] McAdoo, Harriette Pipes, ed. *Black Families.* 2d ed. Newbury Park, CA: Sage, 1988.
This second edition of McAdoo's reader on Black families continues the first edition's emphasis on the internal diversity within Black family structure and experience, but with earlier essays updated to include research through 1987. Similarly, McAdoo's preface to the first edition is reprinted with its clear summary of both the primary conceptualizations of Black family life and its overview of key historical and scholarly resources. Overall, McAdoo organizes the volume's twenty-one essays into five categories, with each helpfully introduced by a summary of issues and author concerns. McAdoo's categories include: (1) [the] "History and Theoretical Conceptualizations of African-American Families"; (2) "Demographic, Economic, Mobility and Educational Patterns"; (3) "Male-Female Relationships in African-American Communities"; (4) "Socialization within African-American Families"; and (5) "Family Policies and Advocacy for Black Families." While sociologists may already know this volume, womanist and feminist writers will find its discussions informative and helpful.

[608] Staples, Robert, ed. *The Black Family: Essays and Studies.* 4th ed. Belmont, CA: Wadsworth, 1991.
This anthology of thirty-three essays on Black family life is a standard and regularly updated sociological collection that addresses family roles, social and economic aspects of Black family life,

sex roles and male-female relationships, health issues--and in this fourth edition--alternative lifestyles, to name but a few of its important topics. The bulk of the literature dates largely from the period 1984-1990, although selected pieces published prior to 1984--including an excerpt from E. Genovese' *Roll, Jordon Roll: The World the Slaves Made* [Pantheon Books, 1974]--are also included. NOTE: In [614] Giddings strongly criticizes Staples' early work for its uncritical acceptance of the "Moynihan Report" and his subsequent inattention to issues of gender discrimination among African American women. Her criticism is on the mark, although it should be noted that in this anthology Staples nonetheless modifies his initial position with a greater attention to the socioeconomic structures affecting Black family life and the interaction of race and gender within the experience of Black women--and men. Additionally, his attention to the experience of Black lesbian and gay issues highlights a widened perspective in the sociology of Black family research. For additional literature on Black families, see McAdoo, [607] and see the literature cited by Benokraitis and Feagin [86].

[609] Wade-Gayles, Gloria. *Crystal Stair: Visions of Race and Sex in Black Women's Fiction*. New York: Pilgrim, 1984.
Readers interested in understanding the interplay of race and sex/gender as factors in the development of black and white feminist perspectives will find this discussion informative, compelling, and in the deepest sense of the word, *instructive*, for its focus is two-fold. It faces head on the history and variety of racial gender assumptions conditioning black and white women's interaction both within and beyond the "feminist" movement, and it unfolds the varying impacts of sex and race on the identities of Black American women as exemplified in Black women's literature. The discussion develops in seven chapters. After a strong introduction that presents the rationale for her work, Wade-Gayles identifies and describes the salient events and race-gender perceptions prevalent during the period, 1946-1976: the rise of the Civil Rights movement, the impact of media on race perceptions, the beginnings of the [white] feminist movement, the struggle of race vs. gender as the locus of black women's commitment, and her own posture as a Southern, African American feminist. Her subsequent chapters then depict the racially and sexually defined social and gender roles that have defined the range of experiences open to Black women in American society: *viz.*, those of "mother" and sometimes "wife;" those of women overburdened by race, sex and social class, those caught between the awareness of anger and the absence of resources, and those who in spite of it all arise to self-transcendence. The final chapter returns to the tensions between feminism and the "double jeopardy" of African American women, *and* the hopes that Wade-Gayles sees for the "narrow space" in which Black women find themselves as *Black women*, i.e., as persons defined by the assumptions of neither race nor gender only, but by themselves in their possibilities for wholeness. This is a moving and ethically demanding text. It echoes much of the womanist theological literature and instructs the reader well on the intersection of race and gender in African American women's literary (and real) experience. Extended endnotes and a helpful bibliography round out the text.

17

Womanist Theology, Biblical Studies and Ethics

A. Womanism, The Black Church and Black Feminism

1. The Development of Womanist Consciousness

[610] Beale, Frances. "Double Jeopardy: To Be Black and Female." In *Black Theology: A Documentary History, 1966-1979*, edited by Gayraud Wilmore and James H. Cone, 368-376. Maryknoll, NY: Orbis, 1979.
Theologian James Cone credits this article with his own coming to consciousness of black feminism. Written prior to both *Roe v. Wade* and the American anti-apartheid movement of the mid and late 80s, this discussion (which was first published in 1970) calls attention to: (1) the systemic economic impact of racism on black men *and women* (both in the U.S. and South Africa); (2) ideological splits between black men and women that portray black men as weak and black women as strong (*both* are strong); (3) "bedroom politics," (i.e., the powerlessness of economically impoverished women of color before America's national and international efforts at sterilization policies); and (4) the differences between black and white women's feminism and the conditions of interracial feminist bonding: i.e., the recognition by white feminists that capitalism and racism are *all* women's enemies.

[611] Brown, Elsa Barkley. "Womanist Consciousness: Maggie Lena Walker and the Independent Order of Saint Luke." *Signs* 14 (1989): 610-633.
Defining womanism as a "…philosophy…that concerns itself both with sexual equality in the black community and 'with the world power structure that subjugates' both blacks and women" (p. 613-614), Brown examines the career and accomplishments of Maggie Lena Walker in her role as the Grand Worthy Secretary of the Independent Order (I.O.) of St. Luke from 1899 to 1934. The I. O. of St. Luke was a mutual aid society formed for the benefit of African American women shortly after the Civil War. It became non-exclusionary in membership in the 1880s, and as Brown's case study demonstrates, it flourished under Walker's leadership with membership levels exceeding more than 100,000 in 28 states. Brown's discussion details Walker's many accomplishments, and in the process lifts up womanist values evident from the history of organization: a substantive and practical recognition of the interlaced nature of race and sex discrimination; a commitment to the strength and employment of the whole African American community; an awareness and political use of the overlapping family, church and other networks within the African American community; and as a last example, a clear perception of the strength borne from the mutual rather than antagonistic (economic) efforts of black women and men. Brown's discussion details these and more and (as with all *Signs* publications) provides extensive primary and secondary bibliography.

[612] Cannon, Katie G. "The Emergence of Black Feminist Consciousness." In *Feminist Interpretation of the Bible*, edited by Letty Russell, 30-40. Philadelphia: Westminster Press, 1985.
In this, her first article on womanist ethics, Cannon develops the thesis that to gain insight into the feminist consciousness of African American women, one must first understand the "historical context in which Black women have found themselves as moral agents" (p. 30). This context is the

experience of African American women in the Black church from the period of slavery through the late 20th century, and it has enabled Black women to combat three struggles: (1) "the struggle for human dignity;" (2) "the struggle against white hypocrisy;" and (3) "the struggle for justice." Cannon cites various ways the Black church has strengthened Black women throughout these struggles. First, the Black church has strengthened women in the "struggle for dignity" during the period of slavery because its emphasis on the power and leadership of a sovereign God sustained Black women (and men) through two centuries of experience that generated the question of whether Black people "were human beings or...property and [thereby] something less than human" (p. 33). Similarly, in the "struggle against white hypocrisy" the Black church provided a context of support during the period of segregation, as it was the only totally Black controlled institution during this period and able, thereby, to generate self-affirmation, respect, and survival. Finally, in the "struggle for justice" during the period between the two world wars, the Black church continued its supportive and then emerging political role, because as churchwomen, Black women worked to raise the "question of color" as "*the* single most determining factor of Black existence in America" (p. 39). In the present period, poverty, hunger and unemployment continue to be the context of Black women's struggle as they combat "race/class/gender oppression" (p. 39). And in *this* struggle, Black women are contemporary prophets to one another, sharing a consciousness that is, in Alice Walker's terms, "Black womanist consciousness:" a strength that enables Black women to "dispel the threat of death in order to seize the present life" (p. 40). Also by Cannon are [253], [348], [532], [625] and [810].

[613] Dodson, Jualyne, and Cheryl Townsend Gilkes. "Something Within: Social Change and Collective Endurance in the Sacred World of Black Christian Women." In *Women and Religion in America, Volume 3: 1900-1968, A Documentary History*, edited by Rosemary Radford Ruether and Rosemary Skinner Keller, 80-130. San Francisco: Harper & Row, 1986.
This article previews and introduces several grounding documents that illustrate the pro-active roles Black women played in African American culture and community during the early and mid-twentieth century. First, within the Black culture at large, African American women served as evangelists, hymn-writers and founders of such organizations as the "National Association of Colored Women's Clubs" and the "National League for the Protection of Colored Women," both of which were formed to fight the effects of segregation imposed by white society. Second, within Black religion, Black women served as the life-blood and cultural carriers of the Sanctified Church, and as the moral (if not ordained) leaders (together with black male clergy) of the Baptist and other churches. Further, Black women of the twentieth century founded and organized the annual celebration of "Women's Day" within Black churches, including those Black congregations affiliated with predominantly white denominations. The documents evidencing such leadership include hymns, biographical writings, and various organizational documents. Author Dodson is an historian (cf. [646]) and Gilkes an ordained minister and sociologist ([603], [615] and [616]).

[614] Giddings, Paula. *When and Where I Enter: The Impact of Black Women on Race and Sex in America*. New York: William Morrow and Company Inc., 1984.
This text introduces the reader to the history of African American women in the United States. It begins with the brutal lynching of Stephen Moss in Memphis, Tennessee on March 9, 1882, and it uses this experience to illustrate both the racial and gender stereotypes held by whites about Blacks in the late 1800s. It then details the subsequent anti-lynching campaigns led politically and socially by Mary Church Terrell and Ida B. Wells, and following this powerful text-wide introduction, it turns to the circumstances and resistance history of African American women from 1609 to the 1980s and the American "women's movement," a century and more after Moss's horrific and barbaric murder. This is a strong, dramatic and engaging text in which slave women, free women of the North, women in Reconstruction, the Club Movement, the various organizations of the Civil Rights Movement, the feminist movement, *and* Shirley Chisholm's candidacy for President of the United States, all speak to illustrate the strengths and challenges of African American women to race and gender dehumanization and discrimination. As an historical overview, it fully transcends a simple chronology, and it offers, instead, what Giddings says is her mission to "tell a story largely untold." And tell it, she does. While readers will want to see the general literature for historical material beyond the 1980s (e.g., Benokraitis and Feagin [86], Collins [99], Mankiller et al. [52], Gilkes [603], Barnet [621], Dill [622], and Terrelonge [624]). Giddings' text remains an unparalleled classic on African American women's history and the interaction of race and gender within American anti-Black prejudice, violence and discrimination. **NOTE**: For related literature, see Frances Smith Foster's *Written by Herself: Literary Production by African American Women*,

1746-1892. [Bloomingdale: Indiana Univ. Press, 1993]. While not abstracted here, it is a helpful supplement to Giddings' early chapters.

[615] Gilkes, Cheryl Townsend. "Together and in Harness: Women's Traditions in the Sanctified Church." *Signs* 10 (1985): 678-699.

This article summarizes the manifold significance of the Sanctified Church for the leadership strengths and skills of African American women. By way of background, The Sanctified Church is a collection of churches and denominations that arose during the post-Reconstruction South as an expressive framework for changes occurring in Black worship experience. It is an ethnically rooted tradition with pentecostal leanings and a highly personalized, expressive and Spirit filled religious experience. And, according to Gilkes, it is also an institutional setting that fostered the leadership skill(s) of African American women by at least four principal means. First, the Church generated and supported the education of African American women, and particularly for the sake of "uplifting the race." In turn this countered the wider society's regular devaluing of African American women through the vehicles of racism and sexism. Second and third, the Church provided a learning ground for African American women's economic and political development and empowerment, in that it provided a number of networks in and through which African American women organized to nurture and develop church community life. Finally, although layered with religious sexism (ranging from women's ordination to women's subordination), the Sanctified Church provided African American women with strengths for combating its religiously grounded sexism--and the racism that has fostered it in African American males. This is a strong and informative article. It introduces readers to religious traditions and experiences frequently overlooked within the sociology of religion, and frequently unavailable within the research agendas of women's leadership in Christian tradition prior to the 1990s.

[616] Gilkes, Cheryl Townsend. "The Role of Church and Community Mothers: Ambivalent American Sexism or Fragmented African Familyhood?" *Journal of Feminist Studies in Religion* 2, no. 1 (1986): 41-59.

Following her discussion above **[615]**, Gilkes here describes the "ethic of familyhood" that prevails within the social and religious worlds of Black Church and Community life. She describes the authoritative status of "church and community mothers," i.e., women who are typically the older and active members of a given church community--and who are filled with care for the community and its members--and she traces this role to the "West African legacy of independent women." Her discussion cuts across several churches within the Sanctified tradition, and it focuses the power of women's networks within the Sanctified churches. In her closing observations, Gilkes identifies the two-fold significance of these community mothers: On the one hand, they are the source of women's strength in the churches--whether those churches ordain women to pastor and preaching roles, or alternatively are under the authority of bishops who will not ordain women. At the same time--and even in those churches where religious sexism bars women from pastoring and preaching, these same strong women's worlds are a strength *against the sexism and racism from the wider society* that seeks generally to engage male religious leadership on issues of social change while ignoring (or trivializing) the possibilities of women's religious leadership. Hence the "ambivalence" in Gilkes' title, but the now documented and published visibility of these women.

[617] Goldsmith, Peter. "A Woman's Place is in the Church: Black Pentecostalism on the Georgia Coast." *The Journal of Religious Thought* 46 (1989-1990): 53-69.

This essay attempts to "give a new twist to a very old scientific puzzle: how to account for the numerical superiority of women in religions of the politically and economically disenfranchised?" (p. 53). More commonly, Goldsmith attempts an explanation of the preponderance of women (as compared with men) in Pentecostal churches. As an anthropologist, Goldsmith recognizes but eschews traditional explanations positing an immediate link between social deprivation and opportunities for compensation--whether these theories are directed to exposing the capacity of such compensation for maintaining the status quo or, alternatively, providing opportunities for strength and hope in the face of adversity (cf. Gilkes **[615]** and **[616]**). Rather, Goldsmith posits an analysis of women in black Pentecostal churches through the framework of traditionally understood public/private, instrumental/expressive gender roles, with women assigned (by church leadership) to the tasks of "reproducing" the church through the nurture of the "saints" (p. 58). Goldsmith develops this hypothesis through a description of: (1) the nurture and witness activities assigned to churchwomen, (2) the prohibition against their preaching, and (3) the familial quality of the Pentecostal church. Additionally, he notes that men's religious roles are played out largely beyond the church sphere (e.g., singing in a gospel quartet) but they nonetheless contribute to the financial well-being of the church and most importantly, in a manner that maintains the autonomy and authority of the male pastor. Males, he says, retain their autonomy and authority, while females "reproduce" the church. While provocative, Goldsmith's argument is limited in at least two ways. First, it is rooted in the assumptions of an instrumental-expressive gender orientation, and thus it is itself ideologically cast. Second, it ignores the empirically interesting hypothesis suggested by Sanders [629] and Cannon [612], that it is the extensive participation of women in the black churches (Pentecostal or otherwise) that has fostered the development of black womanist ethics.

[618] Hoover, Theresa. "Black Women and the Churches: Triple Jeopardy." In *Black Theology: A Documentary History, 1966-1979*, edited by Gayraud Wilmore and Jones H. Cone, 377-388. Maryknoll, NY: Orbis, 1979.
The effects of race and gender and the presence of male dominated clerical leadership within the black churches are the three elements of "jeopardy" Hoover describes, although her primary emphasis is on detailing the activities of black church*women*, since within the institutionalized print media they have been invisible from both black and white view. Hard data alone do not tell the story, but well they might. Hoover cites five major blackwomen's "mission" organizations, each ranging in size "from two thousand to thirty-thousand local units in the United States with a combined membership in the millions" (p. 382). In addition, Hoover notes the participation of black churchwomen in ethnic groups, ecumenical groups and denominational caucuses, the latter being an organizational experience that has heightened black women's awareness of racial-gender ideologies. Hoover also describes the "strengthening" of black women in faith, and illustrates keenly what Cannon and others have (ten years later) described as the tradition of "womanism" in black churches. (See e.g., Hoover's description of black women in (p. 387) and see Cannon [253]). Finally, like Dill [602], Hoover notes the dual standard of racial pedestalism, i.e., the cultural assumption applied to white but not black women, that women should be "above the fray, protected, adored, and excluded" (p. 387). For whatever this has meant to white women (and Hoover does not speculate), it has meant strength and a prophetic role for black women within the historic black church and a distinctive contribution to these churches by black women as *black women*. A powerfully written article, this should be read in conjunction with essays by Carpenter [644-645], Cannon [612, 625], Grant [214, 635, 254, 636] and Williams [341, 259].

[619] Sawyer, Mary R. "Black Religion and Social Change: Women in Leadership Roles." *The Journal of Religious Thought* 47 (1990-1991): 16-29.
Written as a supplement to D. Carpenter's study on black women in religious institutions [645], Sawyer's discussion traces the contributions of black women involved in religiously based social change activities from the period of slavery to that of the late 1980s. She identifies the contributions of black women during the ante-bellum period, a period of "transitions" (i.e., the 1940s through the 1960s), and the involvements of black women in the ecumenical movement of the mid and late 20th century. In all Sawyer identifies more than forty women who serve as role models for those concerned with justice for women "whatever their point of origin" (p. 18). The names of these women range from the historically famous (e.g., Maria Stewart, Harriet Tubman and Sojourner Truth) to those less well known--at least among white feminist scholars and again, to those currently known and famous (e.g., Shirley Chisolm, retired United Methodist Bishop Leontyne Kelley and current Episcopal Bishop Barbara Harris). Among the perhaps lesser well known names of black women identified by Sawyer are: Dorothy Height, the Director of the District Action Program on Integration for the national staff of the YWCA from 1944-1977; Bell Hendon and Ida Mae Myller--both original members of the Executive Committee of the Fraternal Council of Negro Churches organized in 1934; Burma Whitted, Dorothy Ferebee and Jane Spaulding--co-chairs of major committees organizing the Prayer Pilgrimage to Washington following the 1954 Brown vs. Board of Education Supreme Court decision; and Ella Baker, who is now credited with the founding of "Student Nonviolent Coordinating Committee" (SNCC). Written by a white feminist who acknowledges the "womanist...holistic agenda of liberation [that seeks] to address issues of sexism without excluding the distinctive experiences of black women and without ignoring the realities of racism" (p.18), this piece is as provocative as it is informative. As one begins to appreciate the extensive contribution of religious black women in the political/secular arena, its discussion opens the possibility of an entirely new reading of American Civil Religion.

[620] Webb, Lillian Ashcraft. "Black Women and Religion in the Colonial Period." In *Women and Religion in America--Volume 2: The Colonial and Revolutionary Periods*, edited by Rosemary Radford Ruether and Rosemary Skinner Keller, 233-259. San Francisco: Harper & Row, 1983.
This volume II entry in the Ruether-Skinner three-volume series of *Women and Religion in America* highlights the experience of African American women slaves vis a vis Colonial

Christianity's long standing ambivalence concerning Christian freedom and chattel slavery. To articulate this ambivalence and its experience by African American women held in bondage, Webb notes the partial economic independence of African women prior to slavery, their social standing under locally based tribal, Levarite-like marriage laws and their subsequent struggles with Virginian Anglicanism, New England Puritanism, Methodism and the conversions of the Great Awakening Period, and the reluctance of late 18th century Quakers to admit black women into Friends' membership. Webb calls attention to the differential application of church standards to African and African American women held in slavery, and she underscores the contributions of several African American women who exhibited fervor and zeal on behalf of other enslaved women. The entry closes with fourteen documents exhibiting the trends and events she describes.

2. Womanism and Black Feminism

[621] Barnet, Bernice McNair. "Black Women's Collectivist Movement Organizations: Their Struggles during the 'Doldrums.' " In *Feminist Organizations: Harvest of the New Women's Movement*, edited by Myra Marx Ferree and Patricia Yancey Martin, 199-219. Philadelphia: Temple Univ. Press, 1995.
Drawing upon both archival data and data from a series of 16 in-depth interviews with civil rights' activists of the 1950s (with all data collected in the mid to late 1980s), Barnet describes the history and makeup of two Black women's "collectivist" organizations: the Women's Political Counsel, a professional group of Black middle class women (mostly academics) formed in 1946 to combat racism in Montgomery Alabama, and the "Club from Nowhere," a grass roots organization formed also in Montgomery, but during and in support of the 1956 Montgomery bus boycott in Montgomery. Barnet's purpose is two-fold. She seeks to show that the period of feminist history frequently considered the "doldrums" by dominant feminist historiographers was not that--at least not if the experience of Black women is counted; and second, that although "gender oppression" was not (and is not) the only or main political target of much Black women's organizational activity, the latter is nonetheless "feminist" activity, albeit from the point of view of Black women's different and triply rooted history of race, gender and class oppression. The discussion is strong, clear and persuasive, and its nuanced character is instructive. By detailing what are now considered the organizational dimensions and motifs of "feminist" organizational activity, Barnet demonstrates how the civil rights political activity of Black women was (and is) the functional equivalent of much contemporary feminism. Further, this equivalency is drawn out in terms of the gendered activity of Black women working as women in contrast to the male dominant leadership of the civil rights movement. Barnet's discussion stands therefore, as both an independent contribution to the literature and a corrective critique of much feminist history and historiography.

[622] Dill, Bonnie Thornton. "Race, Class, Gender: Prospects for an All-Inclusive Sisterhood." *Feminist Studies* 9 (1983): 131-150.
Building on Fox-Genovese's political critique of the feminist concept of sisterhood, which (as cited by Dill) distinguishes between the "bourgeois individualism" of women's personal choices and the more progressive understanding of bonding towards political and economic change on behalf of women's shared needs and experiences, Dill first describes reasons why African American women do not identify with either definition, and she subsequently develops a framework for re-thinking relations between white feminist and racial ethnic women. There are basically three reasons why Black women do not identify with white feminist goals: the first is the perception that the women's movement is a white middle class movement; second, Black women fear the abandonment of white feminist efforts against racism once feminist goals are achieved (as exemplified in first wave feminism); third, Black women have a different experience of sisterhood among themselves, borne of racist oppression and committed at base to an "improvement" (p. 134) of the race, and within this the eradication of sex discrimination. In the light of these observations, Dill's framework becomes one of analyzing Black women's self-perceptions as structured by the world(s) in which Black women live, and thus she identifies Black women's domestic work as a locus of investigation. Dill supports her discussion with data comparing white female immigrant and Black female domestic workers over several decades, and she draws out the class, gender, and racial implications of such an analysis. She then argues for an abandonment of the concept 'sisterhood' and the adoption of politically pluralized coalitions directed to tasks that support *all* women (and working class women particularly), and she identifies structural avenues for redirected feminist goals. Crucial to her discussion is the emphasis on Black women's self perceptions as defined by their experience in Black society, for this emphasis acknowledges the realities of institutionalized racism as an intervening and mediating variable in Black feminist and community activities.

[623] Hayes, Diana L. *Hagar's Daughters: Womanist Ways of Being in the World.* NY:
Paulist Press, 1995.
This text is the 1995 Madeleva Lecture in Spirituality, sponsored by the Center for Spirituality at
St. Mary's College, Notre Dame Indiana. Its focus is womanist spirituality and the enormous
strength of African American women finding and giving voice to the tasks of community survival.
Hayes begins with an overview of "womanism" as described by Walker's now famous description
(cf., e.g., **[630]**), and she supplements Walker's imagery with those of other writers. She then
presents three stories of womanist strength: Celie's in Alice Walker's *The Color Purple*, [NY:
Pocket, Books, 1962], that of Baby Suggs in Toni Morrison's *Beloved*, [NY: Alfred A. Knopf,
1987], and third, her own, as Black Catholic theologian struggling against the racial, gender and
religious stereotypes that have objectivated her and muted her own religious, womanist voice. This
is a strong text. It uses the imagery of Hagar to synthesize the historical, communal/other-
mothering role of African American women who have held and borne African American culture in
the face of all efforts to destroy it, and it calls upon contemporary African American women to
reclaim and re-vision the Black community's values in the face of America's materialist ethic of
privatization. NOTE: Also from the Madeleva series are **[489]**, **[546]**, and **[233]**.

[624] Terrelonge, Pauline. "Feminist Consciousness and Black Women." In *Women: A
Feminist Perspective*, edited by Jo Freeman, 607-616. 5th ed. Mountain View, CA:
Mayfield, 1995. [First published in *Women: A Feminist Perspective*, edited by Jo
Freeman, 556-566. 4th ed. Mountain View, CA: Mayfield, 1989.]
This discussion challenges the view that sexism is a factor of "minimal importance in the overall
oppression of the black woman" (p. 607), and that, by implication, it is racism alone that accounts
for the "unequal condition" black women's experience. Rather, suggests Terrelonge, it is the
interface of both racism *and* sexism that accounts for the overall oppression of black women, and
specifically as these factors intersect in a market economy that has corporate profit as its sole and
"superordinate" goal. Terrelonge develops her discussion by documenting: (1) the rise of
America's occupationally segregated labor market and the role that racial and gender norms play in
support of a profit making economy; and (2) the ways in which various social myths about black
women are used to deflect attention from sexism as a problem within the African American
community. Third, Terrelonge identifies and critically responds to five reasons why black women
might distrust the development of a black feminist consciousness, and she highlights the benefits of
black feminist consciousness to black women and men alike. Published initially in 1989, the
strength of Terrelonge's discussion is its clear analysis of race and gender as factors supporting the
economics of corporate profit, and the challenge that exposing this fact makes to a "racism only"
hypothesis of black women's oppression.

B. Womanist Ethics, Theology and Biblical Studies

1. Womanist Ethics

[625] Cannon, Katie G. "Hitting a Straight Lick with a Crooked Stick: The Womanist
Dilemma in the Development of a Black Liberation Ethic." *The Annual of the
Society of Christian Ethics* (1987): 165-177.
Mindful of the competing expectations inherent in her roles as both a Christian social ethicist and a
womanist liberationist ethicist, Cannon addresses the question: "What importance do race and
gender have as meaningful categories in the development of a Black liberationist ethic?" (p. 165).
To answer this question Cannon re-examines the implications of her two professional roles. First,
as a Christian social ethicist, Cannon is expected "to discount the particularities of her lived
experience." For the ethicist who is also a womanist scholar, however, this means transcending
one's Blackness and risking marginalization, professional invisibility, and/or trivialization, and the
possibility of "succumbing to the temptation of only mastering the historically specified perspective
of the Euro-American masculine preserve" (p. 166). Second, because her role as a womanist
scholar requires "describing, documenting and analyzing the ideology, theologies and systems of
value that perpetuate the subjugation of Black women" (p.170), the Black womanist scholar must
work "in opposition to the academic establishment, [while] yet building upon it" (p. 168). Thus the
womanist scholar must identify the white male biases present within the discipline, while yet
unearthing the experiences of Black women as subjects worthy of study. The risk here is that of
being "misunderstood, misinterpreted, and frequently devalued as a second class scholar
specializing in Jim Crow subject matter" (p. 166). These competing expectations highlight race and
gender as categories of ethical thought for they press the womanist scholar to address the

inadequacies of not only traditional ethical work, but also the writings of feminist [white] scholarship and [male] Black theology, since each of the these literatures ignores the experience of Black women. Last, because the requirements of womanist scholarship press one to examine such distinctive concerns of as, e.g., Black women's institutions, clubs, organizations, magazines and literature, one is pressed to identify the role(s) of Black churchwomen as "active subjects," not subjects who have been "objectified" and "degraded" in Black church life. **NOTE**: See also [612].

[626] Eugene, Toinette. "Moral Values and Black Womanists." *Journal of Religious Thought* 44 (1988): 23-34.
This rich and nuanced essay accomplishes three things: First, it identifies the historically developed feminist values African American women have traditionally lived by. Second, it traces the development of these values from both their roots in the historic Black Church and the communal experience of black women through the 20th century. Third, it indicates the many points of dialogue necessary between black and white feminists (and between Womanist and feminist theologians) if true liberation is to occur. The values characteristic of black feminism (or Womanism) are those of "public activism and private endurance" and the moral care of black women for all members of the black community: women, men, children, and the black family as a social unit. This activist care has been expressed variously throughout black women's history, and it evidences the ability of black women for moral resistance and survival. Additionally, it is this particular capacity for care which undergirds the awareness by black women that--in contrast to white feminist separatists--oppression is not sexual only, but racial, sexual, and economic. Thus, according to Eugene, "White feminists have a responsibility to learn about black women's perspectives on women's issues, to analyze how racist structures may distort the impact of white feminist proposals, and to support black women in their self-defined struggle for liberation" (p. 27). Eugene's essay solidly synthesizes the moral and *historically communal* nature of womanist thinking, and thus implies a key differences between womanism and white feminism, i.e., that womanism is an oral and community carried tradition, whereas feminism has been a class-based and politically (but not necessarily communally) sustained social movement. **NOTE**: Also by Eugene are [266] and [906].

[627] Hill, Renee. "Who Are We For Each Other?: Sexism, Sexuality and Womanist Theology." In *Black Theology: A Documentary History, Volume II: 1980-1992*, edited by James Cone and Gayraud Wilmore, 345-351. Maryknoll, NY: Orbis, 1993.
In contrast to much womanist theological literature, this article focuses directly on the need to address lesbianism within the womanist theological community and accord it the positive reality Walker's original definition of womanism implies. Hill's discussion develops i four points. First, Hill reviews Walker's definition of a womanist (which includes "a woman who loves other woman sexually and/or nonsexually"). Second, she notes the relative lack of discussion about lesbianism among womanist theologians, and she considers two possible explanations for this, *viz.*, (a) womanist theologians have addressed racism within the Black community (not sexism); and (b) sexuality issues are largely the concern of white feminists. Third, Hill challenges Delores Williams' limitation of womanism (in a companion essay in the same volume) to community and survival issues rather than community, survival, and sexuality issues. Last, after providing several illustrations of womanist spirituality and womanist acts of relation, Hill affirms the legitimate place of sexuality as a womanist theological concern. Christian womanists, she argaues, must address sexuality and affirm lesbian women and gay men specifically, because womanism opposes the multiple oppressions of women and affirms the full, inclusive love of Christ for all (p. 250).

[628] Riggs, Marcia Y. "The Socio-Religious Ethical Tradition of Black Women: Implications for the Black Church's Role in Black Liberation." *Union Seminary Quarterly Review* 43 (1989): 119-132.
The title of Riggs' essay suggests its main divisions. After locating her discussion in the literature of black womanist ethics and theology, Riggs presents an exposition of the socio-religious tradition of black women and a statement of its implications for black churches seeking a role in the liberation of Black Americans. To identify the elements of this socio-religious tradition, Riggs draws upon the writings of six 19th and early 20th century black women who exercised leadership both within and beyond the boundaries of the black church. Writing (for the most part) independently of one another, these women nonetheless converged on a number of value affirmations: e.g., that there is a clear link between capitalism and slavery, that gender is a distinctive factor in both the intents and experience of racism, that the justice of black people cannot

be separated from considerations of the biblical ideas about the justice of God, and that black women have been and are committed to the "elevation" of Black people as a whole, including their moral and political advance (p. 125-126). Riggs suggests that as the core of black women's socio-religious tradition, these values have at least three implications for the black church as a community of moral discourse. First, they direct the church to consider the adequacy of the character traits it nurtures in its members. Second, they press the church to develop a more community based covenant ethic, which not only supports the experience of black liberation, but simultaneously questions the gender discrimination within the black church regarding women's leadership roles, including ordination. Third, they foster moral discussions of race, class and gender issues as a whole and they imply that historically black churches "should not be abandoned too quickly in favor of alternative, integrated institutions" (p. 130). For Riggs, this means that Blacks "must not be afraid to embrace some form of separatism as positive, normative strategy in the struggle for black liberation" (p. 130). Also by Riggs are [257], [508] and [648].

[629] Sanders, Cheryl. "Ethics and the Educational Achievements of Black Women." *Religion and Intellectual Life* 5 (1988): 7-16.
This article seeks to explain the differing educational and occupational achievement levels of black women and men through a discussion of black womanist ethics. A professor of Christian ethics at Howard University Divinity School, Sanders first notes the rise of black women (but not black men) in the teaching profession following the periods of slavery and reconstruction. This rise did not threaten white males, nor did it take professional positions desired by black men. Sanders' question, therefore, is: how can one explain this and with it, the emergence of black women (but not black men) in professions other than teaching? One hypothesis, suggests Sanders, is the increased exposure of black women to the womanist values of autonomy, commitment and love that black women have by virtue of their relatively higher participation in black churches. These are important values with implications for (a) black family life; (b) the socialization of youth towards educational goals; and (c) an enhanced vision of the black professional woman as one who, like her sisters before her, is concerned with "uplifting" not only herself, but the community as a whole (p. 15). Sanders closes with reference to ethicist Preston Williams' emphasis on the "mastery of self understanding" as a first step in a black ethic of achievement [Preston Williams, "Ethics and Ethos in the Black Experience," *Christianity and Crisis* 31 (1971): 109] and she applies Williams' discussion to the race-gender experience of black women.

[630] Sanders, Cheryl, Katie G. Cannon, Emilie M. Townes, M. Shawn Copeland, bell hooks, and Cheryl Townsend Gilkes. "Christian Ethics and Theology in Womanist Perspective." *Journal of Feminist Studies in Religion* 5, no. 2 (1989): 83-112.
Cheryl Sanders presents the lead paper in this "roundtable" discussion, with the remaining authors serving as respondents to her piece. It is an intense and engaging discussion for at this point in her thinking, Sanders is critical of using either the term, image and/or concept of "womanist" as a framework for ethics and theological discourse by and on behalf of African American women. After a detailed analysis of Walker's term, Sanders indicates that "The necessary and sufficient condition for doing womanist scholarship has to be adherence to the context, criteria and claims inherent in Walker's definition..." (p. 87) and in Sanders' view, these are not met by current usage. In particular, for Sanders, the term is secular not religious, and too frequently tied to issues of lesbianism, which, for Sanders, is not helpful given the need for the solidity of Black families in the African American community. Sanders' discussion is substantive and challenging, and each of the respondents takes vigorous issue with its varying elements, with debates ranging from the role of feminism in the black community (hooks and Gilkes) to the distinction between "secular womanists and Christian womanists" (Phelps), to issues of theological method generally (virtually all respondents pick up on this), and in some cases the role of homophobia in the black [theological] community (cf. e.g., Hill [627] and see Townes [258]).

[631] Sanders, Cheryl. *Empowerment Ethics for a Liberated People*. Philadelphia: Fortress Press, 1995.
As Sander's earlier works indicate, she has consistently favored an interpretation of womanism that places it within the wider framework of Church-related social ethics and the ethical needs of the African American community. It is a perspective that emerges clearly in this text as womanist thinking becomes one of the many resources Sanders draws upon to consider "...African American notions of moral progress from the nineteenth to the twentieth century" (p. ix). This is a profound and carefully nuanced text. Its central question is how African Americans with social and economic resources can help victimized African Americans become empowered and eventually re-moralized, and thus contributors to the social justice streams of African American ethics and religion. By way

of setting the question, Sanders critically examines Black Liberation theology, which she determines is a necessary but not sufficient condition for an "ethics of empowerment." For resources, then, she turns to seven images of empowerment drawn from 19th and 20th century African American experience, and for each, she identifies a setting and historical spokespersons, and in a final chapter, the constellation of all seven images as community directed possibilities within the ministry and service of the Black Church. Each image is, therefore, an empowering icon for moving victimized Black Americans (and particularly African American males) beyond victimization and into restoration or "remoralization" within the African American community. Testimony, protest, uplift, cooperation, achievement, remoralization and ministry are the key images described, with womanism finding its place in the description of achievement. *This is an important book.* It addresses ethical responsibilities across race, gender, and class levels, and *towards* the concrete audiences of local African American (and one might ask: why not all) congregations. Last, its specific questions, as identified in the introductory chapter (pp. 1-2) pose a translational challenge for other womanist and feminist perspectives.

[632] Williams, Delores. "The Color of Feminism: Or Speaking the Black Woman's Tongue." *Journal of Religious Thought* 43 (1986): 42-58.

The relatively low level of involvement by female African Americans in the American feminist movement has been documented in several sources, e.g., [624]. In this essay Williams first discusses some of the reasons for this low level of involvement, and she then indicates ways in which feminism must change if it is to "fit" the experience of American black women. Why have black women assumed such a low level of involvement in American feminism? Two answers are that: (a) 19th century feminism was premised largely on racist and classist ideologies and (b) 20th century feminism has assumed "patriarchy" as the sole (and adequate) explanation of all women's oppression in church and society. And it is the latter, Williams argues, which simply is not true. Williams' argument here is two fold. First, black women do not experience patriarchy (i.e., the control of their lives by men) but rather, *demonarchy*, or the control of their lives by white institutionalized realities that have permitted slavery, discrimination, suffering, and the suppression of black creativity. Second, by focusing on "patriarchy," feminism has ignored the involvement of white women in the oppression of black *people*, i.e., the oppression of black women, black men, and black children. Further, feminism has assumed that patriarchy views all women as equals, but in fact, in society's eyes, patriarchy does not. Instead, white women benefit intergenerationally in terms of both their own access to society's resources and their children's access to such resources. Williams argues that if feminism is to be "colorized," (or adapted to "fit" the black women's experience) it must take into account the strong tradition of the black family, and focus accordingly on the physical and spiritual survival(s) of black women and their efforts simultaneously to free all black people, *viz.*, black women, black men and black children. To close, Williams notes that if "patriarchy" has any implications for black women's experience it is in the context of "some black churches," and she draws out the ecclesiological implications of this point. **NOTE**: For a succinct description of womanist and feminist theologies based largely on this article, see "Womanist Theology/Feminist Theology: A Dialogue," *Daughters of Sarah* 15, no. 2 (1989): 6-7, and of course, see Williams, [259]. Additionally, see Williams' essay, "Rituals of Resistance in Womanist Worship," pp. 215-223 in Procter-Smith's *Women at Worship* [526].

[633] Townes, Emilie M. *Womanist Justice, Womanist Hope.* Atlanta, GA: Scholar's Press, 1993.

Originally Townes' Ph.D. dissertation, this concentrated and compelling study accomplishes five things: First, it familiarizes the reader with selected dimensions of Ida B. Wells-Barnett's life and work, but particularly her intense campaign against the lynchings of Black Americans during the late 19th and early 20th centuries. Second, it identifies several of Wells-Barnett's religious and ethical beliefs, and these against the cultural backdrop of racially grounded gender and class assumptions of the 19th century and the violence they presumed. Third, it examines and assesses several theological implications discernible within the prophetic and individualized leadership style evidenced by Wells-Barnett. Fourth, it demonstrates how the careful use of biographical and related materials can open out models of religious leadership for traditions in transition. Finally, it evidences a respect for the realism so necessary to change-directed efforts, and this without the sacrifice of either individual integrity or prophetic edge. This is an important, tightly written work, and it requires close reading. Moreover, its closing "pastoral/priestly" focus places it squarely within the current milieux of not only womanist, but African American theology generally and the current need to link theological and congregational reflections within African American theology. Last, it echoes loudly the ongoing question its discussion of nineteenth century gender/class norms raised: Namely, how and in what ways do the cultural norms of class and gender produce violence for their continuing but ideologically masked support? **NOTE:** Also by Townes are [638] and [258] and for related literature see Cannon [253] and Riggs [508]

2. Womanist Theology

[634] Brown, Kelly Delaine. "God Is As Christ Does: Toward a Womanist Theology." *Journal of Religious Thought* 46 (Summer-Fall, 1989): 7-16.
The purpose of this essay is to clarify the meaning of the term "womanist" and to indicate its relevance and significance for Christian theology. Brown begins by citing the now classic definition offered by Walker, i.e., the derivation of this term from the phrase "acting womanish...[which suggests]...outrageous, audacious and willful behavior." Brown then highlights the power of this term as a two-fold symbol for black women. On the one hand, "womanist" counter-effects the comparison of black with white women and indicates an autonomous tradition of survival for black women. At the same time it counter-effects the sexism of black males by indicating the survival of black *women*. The theological significance of this term is also two-fold. First, the term "womanist" sensitizes black women theologians to the need for the concrete application of biblical insights--and specifically the concrete application of Christological statements, such that the latter become neither a tool of gender oppression in black churches (by virtue of Christ's maleness), nor a tool of mollification vis a vis black racial oppression by whites. Second, the term "womanist" signals that such concrete statements about Jesus should be "liberation" statements, or statements that aid the materially oppressed and strengthen black women specifically. In formal categories, therefore, the term womanist in relation to theology means (according to Brown) "...utilizing black women's distinct struggle against sexism and racism as the prism from which to determine the importance of God and Jesus Christ for the black community" (p. 16). This article is a clear expression of the "Womanist" symbol in process, and its notes and discussion indicate the power of the symbol as one of strength against "multidimensional oppression." For Brown's more extended work in womanist Christology, see Kelly Brown Douglas, *The Black Christ*. Maryknoll, NY: Orbis Books, 1994.

[635] Grant, Jacquelyn. "Black Theology and the Black Woman." In *Black Theology: A Documentary History, 1966-1979*, edited by Gayraud Wilmore and Jones H. Cone, 418-433. Maryknoll, NY: Orbis, 1979.
This early essay by Grant (written while she was still in graduate school) identifies the problem of Black women's invisibility within Black theology and church life. Grant begins by noting the overlap of several types of oppression (racism, sexism and classism), and she calls attention to the perspectival nature of many liberation theologies. She then directs her attention to Black theology specifically and following James Cone's criteria for Black liberation theology, she demonstrates its own exclusively male focus. Additionally she details the invisibility of women in Black churches (an important irony in that Black women are the moral and statistical [70%] backbone of the Black church), and she highlights the difficulties experienced by Black women seeking ordination and positions of church leadership--both past and present. By way of closure Grant argues that the lived experience of poor Black women must become the grist for Black liberation theology or the latter must recognize itself as striving for (and having attained) parity with White Theology. Moreover, she refuses to be intimidated by the argument that sexism and racism are separate problems and/or that Black theology must bring itself to solve the latter but not the former. Quoting from Sojourner Truth, she highlights their connectedness and with Sojourner Truth, she affirms that she also wants to "keep things going while things are stirring...." (p. 431). This is a strong and informative essay, both for its narrative discussion on the ecclesial and theological invisibility of Black women and its extensive notes and source materials on the history of Black women's entry into the ordained ministry. It is highly recommended. For related material see Carpenter [644].

[636] Grant, Jacquelyn. "Subjectification as a Requirement for Christological Construction." In *Lift Every Voice: Constructing Christian Theologies from the Underside*, edited by Susan B. Thistlethwaite and Mary Potter Engel, 201-214. San Francisco: Harper & Row, 1991.
To speak about "subjectification" as a requirement for Christological construction is to recognize that hearers of the gospel and/or of Christian tradition are themselves to be recognized as potential speakers of the gospel (or Christian tradition) and speakers from within their own experience and social location. It is to recognize that past theological literature has largely presumed that "non-whites" [sic] and women were deemed "objects" or passive recipients of religious language, rather than "subjects" or voices who also might speak and shape such language. With respect to African American women, therefore, such subjectification (or the becoming of voices) requires first, an

identification of the social experience and historical location of African American women; and second, an answer to the question posed by Jesus: "Who do you say that I am?" To illustrate this process, Grant briefly describes the social history of African American women, and after noting their "most oppressed of the oppressed" status, she describes Jesus as both a companion to the "little people" and as an affirming and empowering presence on behalf of Black women's liberation from racist, sexist and classist oppression. In her discussion Grant addresses Ruether's work on the question, "Can a male savior save women?" and as in her book [254] she charges Ruether's work with class and racial bias. She then affirms the proposition that it is Jesus' humanity and not his maleness that is significant for liberation. NOTE: As an orientation to this article the reader should consult the introductory section to the anthology entry for it describes the methodological assumptions within the entry. Additionally, one should read Grant's early critique of feminist theology [635] and relevant sections from her book [254].

[637] Sanders, Cheryl, ed. *Living the Intersection: Womanism and Afrocentrism in Theology.* Minneapolis, MN: Fortress, 1994.
Nine essays--each by a noted womanist theologian or scholar, make up this brief reader on the differences, similarities and tensions existing between womanism and Afrocentrism as frameworks for interpreting the religious and social history of African Americans. For openers, Cheryl Gilkes's contribution, "We have a Beautiful Mother: Womanist Musings on the Afrocentric Idea," acknowledges the ideological "straightjackets" that can arise from Afrocentrism. This said, it also highlights the wider perspectives of Afrocentrism and their congruence with elements of womanism. Essay #2 (by Delores Williams) critiques the gender assumptions implicit in Afrocentrism, and particularly their significance for African American churches. Other contributors (e.g., Lorine Cummings, Deborah E. McDowell, and Youtha C. Hardman-Cromwell) focus more on unfolding specific aspects of womanist history and insight, while still others (e.g., Kelly Brown Douglass [419]) address the meaning of womanism for particular religious symbols. Finally, Douglass and Cheryl Sanders each examine the distinctiveness of womanism and Afrocentrism for theological education and its role within the African American community. For related literature, see Sanders [809].

[638] Townes, Emilie M., ed. *A Troubling In My Soul: Womanist Perspectives on Evil and Suffering.* Maryknoll, NY: Orbis, 1993.
Fourteen essays comprise this reader on womanist ethics, theology and theodicy, with the full range of Black women's suffering and strength pressing for inclusion. Several essays, but notably those by Marcia Riggs, Rosita deAnn Mathews, Emilie Townes and Jamie Phelps address structured evil, with Phelps's discussion focusing specifically on racism within Roman Catholicism, even as--and especially in the light of--the American hierarchy's published recognition that racism is a sin. Other entries (e.g., those by Cheryl T. Gilkes, M. Shawn Copeland and Katie Cannon) recount stories of recent and historical suffering (i.e., womanist survival and resistance), while yet a third group of essays (by Clarice Martin and Frances Wood) provide an intense and clear voice asking "Why?" Finally, a fourth group of papers addresses the power of "womanist voice" on sin and salvation. In particular, Delores Williams provides a content analysis of several womanist narratives and sources to articulate perceptions of sin prevalent in enslaved women's experiences and Karen Baker-Fletcher provides a studied--and engaging--overview to Anna Julia Cooper's *A Voice from the South.* Also by Townes are [633] and [258].

[639] Williams, Delores. "Women's Oppression and Life-Line Politics in Black Women's Religious Narratives." *Journal of Feminist Studies in Religion* 1, no. 2 (1985): 59-71.
This article describes a fourfold "multi-dimensional assault" on black women together with the various survival strategies or "life-line politics" black women have used to survive such assaults. These assaults include: an assault on black women's reproductive and nurturing capacities (an assault perpetrated on to black women by white men and white women respectively); an assault on black women's self-esteem (via an illegitimate aesthetic of white beauty); and last, an assault on black women's "independent right to choose and maintain positive, fulfilling and productive relationships" (p. 60), an assault to black women from white society generally and, at times, black males particularly. These assaults are described through the literature of Zora Neal Hurston, Margaret Walker and Alice Walker and to combat these assaults, the characters of black women described by these authors have developed three principal strategies: (a) forging strong relations with other black women (and men); (b) removing themselves from the sources of their oppression; and (c) "changing their consciousness about the meaning of values... fundamental to black women's early conditioning and to the ethical, moral, and religious foundations of the Afro-American

community" (p. 66). A theological awareness and reflection upon these assaults--and the strategies used to combat them--suggest four tasks that can broaden the boundaries of [white] feminist theology. These tasks are: (1) the development of concepts that describe women's oppression of women; (2) the development of a feminist critical hermeneutic that extends the concept "women's experience" beyond that of Anglo-American middle-class women; (3) the incorporation of black folk tradition (and other differing cultural data) into feminist theological work; and (4) the development (by black and white women) of theological perspectives that stand in "deadly conflict with notions of good, beauty, God, right and wrong based on white supremacy and male superiority" (p. 71).

[640] "Womanist Theology." Part IV of *Black Theology: A Documentary History, Volume II: 1980-1992*, edited by James Cone and Gayraud S. Wilmore, 257-351 Maryknoll, NY: Orbis, 1993.
Nine essays by contemporary womanist theologians comprise this well grounded portion of the Cone/Wilmore reader **[591]**, and what distinguishes their presentation is not only Cone's assessment that "Womanist theology is the most creative development to emerge out of the Black Theology movement during the 1980s and 1990s" (p. 257). Also significant is their location in one source. Of these essays, four are abstracted in the present volume; those by Toinette Eugene **[626]**, Katie Cannon **[625]**, Cheryl Sanders **[630]**, and Renee Hill **[627]**. Entries not abstracted in the present volume include Delores Williams' "Womanist Theology: Black Women's Voices;" Kelly D. Brown-Douglass' essay, "Womanist Theology: What Is Its Relationship to Black Theology?" (although see **[634]**); Cheryl Gilkes' discussion, "Womanist Ways of Seeing;" Diana Hayes' "Feminist Theology, Womanist Theology: A Black Catholic Perspective" (although see **[623]**). An additional entry by Jackie Grant synthesizes much of her womanist Christological reflection. Cone's editorial overview details the issues and developments in each entry, and provides background on each of the writers. Other womanist sources not included in the Cone-Wilmore volume are Martin **[374]** and Renita Weems, "Womanist Reflections on Biblical Heremeneutics," not abstracted here, although see **[376]**.

NOTE: See also Williams **[259]** and Williams **[341]**.

3. Womanist Biblical Studies

[641] Cooper, Anna Julia. *A Voice from the South.* [With an Introduction by Mary Helen Washington.] New York: Oxford Univ. Press, 1988.
Published through *The Schomberg Library of Nineteenth Century Black Women Writers*, this text reprints a series of eight essays addressing various aspects of race-gender prejudice, the role of African American intellectuals, and the roles of African American women in the movement to "uplift the race" following the periods of Emancipation and Reconstruction in the American South. The essays are powerful and pointed, and reflect the "voice" of African American women as (to use Katie Cannon's terms) "complex moral agents," with Cooper's "Voice" standing as the voice for all. The essays detail Cooper's frustrations with and challenges to white feminists of her day, prejudice towards American Indians, her aspirations for African American achievement (cast in a rhetorical reversal of American racist values) and the expectations she has for Black American achievement across the board, with women's roles as recognized and central. The detailed "Introduction" by Mary Helen Washington provides an overview of Cooper's life and many achievements--as a teacher, a prominent scholar and leading critic of racism and sexism in American society, and as a major contributor to African American culture and education until her death in 1964 (at age 105!)--and a "Forward" to the volume by Henry Louis Gates, Jr. introduces and chronicles the development of the Schomberg Series. Deeply prophetic, this is African American women's history that should be required reading for all. NOTE: For a discussion of the womanist hermeneutical implications of Cooper's work, see Baker-Fetcher **[373]**, and see Baker-Fletcher's essay in Townes **[638]**. Although not abstracted here, the Townes entry synthesizes the deep (and theologically) musical motifs of Cooper's writing, together with her use of the metaphor "voice."

[642] Weems, Renita J. *Just a Sister Away: A Womanist Vision of Women's Relationships in the Bible.* San Diego, CA: Lura Media, 1988.
Among the most frequently cited characteristics of womanist thinking are that womanism entails "private pain" but "public survival" and a love for all people in the womanist's community: families, children, black men and women and even those beyond the barriers of America's racist thinking. This text exemplifies all of these values and provides an empowering vision of women's

strength through biblical generations into the present time. In particular, Weems deals with concrete experiences of women's marginality and invisibility: e.g., being the wife of a public person; keeping faith with past fallen leaders; resisting the temptation to exploit another woman for personal gain; learning to weep for one's self and all women; finding strength in women. To unfold these womanist values, Weems empathically narrates the stories of women contained in nine biblical passages (Gen 16:1-16, 21:1-21; The Book of Ruth; Luke 10:38-42; Judges 11:1-40; Numbers 12:1-16; Luke 8:1-3; Esther 1:1-2:4; Luke 1:5-56 and Gen 19.). She lifts up the empowering elements in each of the stories and without bowing to the misogyny in each, she finds the strength of women to be sisters to one another. Her book is neither a set of sermons, although each narrative entry has a compelling element to it; nor is it a series of exegetical surveys with contemporary application, although exegesis has obviously informed each narrative. Rather, Weem's volume is the telling of tales not as "texts of terror" (cf. Trible [385]), but as texts of women's witness and empowerment. It is thoroughly womanist (read: thoroughly empowering and insightfully compelling) and given its provocative chapter based study questions, recommended for both lay and academic groups. NOTE: For Weems' formal exegetical and hermeneutical work, see [376].

NOTE: For additional womanist biblical/theological literature see Baker-Fletcher [373], Martin [374-375], Weems [376], and Cannon and Schüssler Fiorenza [348], and see Cannon's essay on womanist homiletics [532].

C. Womanism, Ministry and African American Churches

[643] Baer, Hans A. "The Limited Empowerment of Women in Black Spiritual Churches: An Alternative Vehicle to Religious Leadership." *Sociology of Religion* 54 (1993): 65-82.
This discussion draws upon the author's ten year long history of ethnographic research into 42 spiritualist congregations (from the years 1978-1987) to describe both the history and geographic distribution of those congregations and further, their empowering dimensions for women. Baer's focus is the difference between personal and structural empowerment, and he argues that Spiritualism has proved personally but not structurally empowering for African American women. Although rich in detail, this article is not the best source for understanding spiritualism and its empowering dimensions for African American women. Rather, Baer's argument appears somewhat forced, as if constrained to fit within the context of a larger research agenda, such as the development of a general typology for studying black spiritualist experience. Hence for literature more focused on the experience and specifically leadership-based roles of women in spiritualist churches, the reader is referred to Gilkes [615-616].

[644] Carpenter, Delores. "The Professionalization of the Ministry by Women." *The Journal of Religious Thought* 43 (Spring-Summer, 1986): 59-75.
This important and pioneering essay reports employment and professionalization data from a national sample of black clergywomen (N=121) who received their Master of Divinity degrees during the period 1972-1984. The sample represents a 45% response rate from 269 identified graduates. The purpose of the study was two-fold. First, Carpenter wished to establish a baseline of black clergywomen data so that comparisons might be made with data reported by Carroll, Hargrove and Lummis [657]. Second, Carpenter wished to identify factors that aid or impede the professionalization of black women clergy. Ministerial position (both by parish/non-parish titles), church size, income levels, and career goals at seminary entrance and completion are some of the descriptive variables Carpenter presents. For her professionalization variable, Carpenter follows J. Carroll's characterization of the minister as a "reflective practitioner [Carroll, "The Professional Model of Ministry—Is It Worth Saving?" in *Theological Education* 21 (1985)]. Factors inhibiting black clergywomen's professional development include sexism (e.g., sex-role stereotyping) and for approximately one in five respondents, clergy and structural factors. As compared with Carroll, Hargrove and Lummis, Carpenter's data identify: (1) both parish and non-parish roles within professionalization; (2) a larger proportion of respondents serving churches with memberships under 100; (3) a paralleling impact of seminary on the decision for parish rather than specialized ministries; and (4) a disproportionately higher percentage of black women attending university-related seminaries. Because quantitative data on black women clergy are sparse, Carpenter's research is especially important, with future research currently in process. (See Barbara B. Zikmund, Adair Lummis, Patricia M. Y. Chang, *Women Clergy: An Uphill Calling*. Louisville: Westminster/John Knox Press, 1998, [663] for clergywomen data available through 1994.)

[645] Carpenter, Delores. "Black Women in Religious Institutions: A Historical Summary from Slavery to the 1960s." *The Journal of Religious Thought* 46 (Winter-Spring, 1989-1990): 7-27.

Readers seeking a discussion of black women in religious institutions from within the context of the ministry as a changing institution will want to refer to Carpenter's essay, "The Professionalization of the Ministry by Women" **[644]** and to the data cited by Lincoln and Mamiya **[141]**. Readers seeking an informative survey of individual black women functioning within (and beyond) religious institutions, however, should consult this essay, for after detailing the growing number of publications now emerging on "black women and religion," Carpenter introduces the reader to specific individuals who have ministered to the black community through its long history. Nationally famous individuals (e.g., Harriet Tubman, Sojourner Truth and the Grimke sisters) need little or no introduction, but readers unfamiliar with black history will find Carpenter's identification of black women preachers during the period of slavery (e.g., Mother Suma and Aunt Hester) and throughout the 19th century (e.g., Maria Stewart, Jarena Lee, Charlotte Fortner and Amanda Smith) helpful. Likewise, readers will learn of black women's missionary efforts in Africa, the 20th century black women of the 'club movement,' the establishment of "women's day" in black churches, black women in Christian educational and professional church leadership roles, and lastly, factors that militate against many black women becoming ordained within their churches. Data from the author's doctoral thesis on black women seminarians together with preliminary data on black lay attitudes towards women clergy compete the discussion.

[646] Dodson, Jualyne. "Nineteenth Century A. M. E. Preaching Women: Cutting Edge of Women's Inclusion in Church Polity." In *Women in New Worlds: Historical Perspectives on the Wesleyan Tradition,* edited by Hilah Thomas and Rosemary Skinner Keller, 276-289. Nashville: Abingdon, 1981.

This article focuses on the organizational exclusion of women preachers from the status of ordained clergy in the A. M. E. Church from its official founding in 1816 through 1900, the year in which a male controlled deaconess order was established for AME women preachers. It thus stands in vivid contrast to much womanist literature that presumes this organizational exclusion but highlights instead, the moral authority and wider cultural and personal successes of nineteenth century AME women preachers. Dodson's discussion is historical and analytical. By way of history, Dodson traces the efforts of AME women preachers to gain full ministerial status from their first request for such status at the Church's 1848 quadrennial convention through a near success at the Church's 1886 convention. Her discussion is clear and richly documented from church and other records, and as she traces the history of AME women preachers, she identifies the two official roles formally created to include AME women preachers within the Church's organizational structure: *viz.,* the stewardship role created in 1868 and the deaconess role created in 1900. Analytically, Dodson then contrasts the differential expectations and lines of authority incumbent upon male and female occupants of such roles. She finds that males receive upward church mobility from such roles, whereas females do not, and that males rather than females retain jurisdictional control over entrance to such roles. This is an informative and well-written article that should be read in conjunction with other womanist literature and literature addressing the entry of women into white denominational structures, (e.g., Nesbitt **[701]**). Further, its discussion often parallels patterns identified by Katzenstein **[107]** on gender integration in both the U.S. military and the Roman Catholic Church .

[647] Sanders, Cheryl. "The Woman as Preacher." *Journal of Religious Thought.*43 (1986): 6-23.

This essay contrasts the differing emphases of male and female black preachers of varying denominations by analyzing 36 sermons drawn from three published sermon anthologies. The study is exploratory and the author identifies and examines: (1) sermon forms, (2) types of biblical texts selected, (3) sermon themes, (4) use of inclusive language, and (5) specific homiletical tasks. Sanders' findings are that: (a) women and men generally seek to accomplish the same things in their preaching, although (b) women "were reluctant to criticize the church... while the men shunned the tasks of testifying and inviting hearers to Christian commitment" (p. 21); (c) women's use of inclusive language challenges men to acknowledge and respect their presence and contribution to church life and (d) women need to "learn how to sharpen their own testimonies and call for commitment with the cutting edge of prophetic indignation" (p. 22). Although limited to the data available from published anthologies (rather than those of a more formalized sampling frame), this essay indicates how one can mine current literature to examine gender as a variable in the preaching process. Last, because it deals with sermons by black preachers, it is a discussion source from which white feminist (and other) homileticians can learn.

D. Racism, Womanist and Feminist Theologies

[648] Mercadante, Linda, Marcia Y. Riggs, Victoria Byerly, Renita J. Weems and Barbara Andolsen. "Racism in the Women's Movement." *Journal of Feminist Studies in Religion* 4, no. 1 (1988): 93-114.

This 'roundtable' addresses the subject of "racism in the women's movement" through a series of responses to Barbara Hilkert Andolsen's *Daughters of Jefferson, Daughters of Bootblacks: Racism and American Feminism* [Mercer Univ. Press: Macon GA, 1986] which traces the racial and racist parallels between nineteenth and twentieth century feminist ideology and activity. Virtually all of Andolsen's roundtable respondents attest the historical value of her work, but they vary in both the assumptions they bring to her text and the chapter-based issues they address. Thus, Mercadante focuses on the inability of white feminist thinkers to deal adequately with the concept of a powerful, liberating (and usually male named) transcendent God, and with this, a subsequent inability to deal with the social myth of "True Womanhood." Similarly, ethicist Riggs addresses the lingering covert ideology of white supremacy (which she perceives in white feminism) and the subsequent inability of white feminists to embrace a "renunciation of privilege," both racial and economic. In contrast to these perspectives, writer Byerly approaches Andolsen's discussion with a class-based analysis, and she questions the absence of attention to working class women's experience within Andolsen's work, and specifically, the stratification among white women within the women's movement and the simultaneous assumption that when inter-racial discussion takes place, "middle-class" typically is understood to mean white women's experience and "working class," black women's experiences. Byerly argues that such assumptions serve to reinforce negative stereotypes about black women's experience, while yet fostering ignorance about economically poor white women's experience. Last, biblical theologian Renita Weems criticizes the absence of a theologically rooted ethical analysis of racism in white feminism, and she calls for a vision and praxis that empowers women to stop "sinning" against women (because it is so profitable to do so) for the sake of *all* women. Andolsen's response to this roundtable is as varied as the criticisms of her work, but generally she points to the lack of methodological categories within feminism to address selected concerns of roundtable members, and she re-affirms a premise of her book: namely, that white women must learn to assert their needs for justice while respecting the autonomy of other groups of women to do the same.

[649] Monroe, Irene, ed. "The Intersection of Racism and Sexism: Theological Perspectives of African American Women." [A Special Double Issue] *Journal of Women and Religion* 9-10 (1990-1991): 3-103.

This special double issue of the *Journal* presents nine articles and seven poems that depict the experiences of African American women in several settings either adjacent to or directly within religious and theological institutions and organizations, and as grounded in the twofold experience of race/sex prejudice. Pamela Cooper-White's "Publisher's Forward" asserts clearly the need for white women to not patronize African American women (and especially so since white middle class women typically condemn white male patronization) and she states clearly that this issue of the *Journal* is "our sisters' forum." And it is. Articles by Sandra Blair Smith, Traci West, Bernadette Evans and Regina Anderson examine, respectively, the tasks of African American women's survival, the costs of internalized racism, suffering within the "Black Diaspora," and last, "Lament Reflections," Anderson's own observations about serving in prison ministry. Additionally, Linda Boston, Shoonie Hartwig and editor Monroe offer discussions of race and gender in the theologizing process, with a second offering by Monroe addressing sermon construction specifically. Finally, and of specific interest to social scientists, Methodist Pastor Dorothy Williams summarizes her findings and reflections on "the high cost of oneness" (including the stresses, expectations, socialization, preparation and after placement needs of African American clergywomen) as described from her interviews of 18 African American Methodist clergywomen serving in "cross-racial" appointments.

[650] Volentine, Sandra, ed. "Reflecting On Womanist Concerns." *Daughters of Sarah* 19, no. 3 (1993): 1-51.

As with other thematic issues of this journal, this issue provides theological overviews, extended book reviews and a variety of practical resources for the topic at hand, here the discussion of race and ethnicity as sources of religious and theological conflict and creativity, and with particular reference to womanist and feminist literatures. Among the contributors are: (1) Toinette Eugene who highlights selected elements of feminist and womanist perspectives to show dialogical possibilities; (2) Native American Andi Smith who critiques the stereotyping and trivialization of much Native American spirituality and autonomy by both "white feminists" and the "New Age

Movement;" (3) Barbara Groth and Cathi Falsani who, in separate articles, identify numerous aspects of racism within white feminist thinking and organizations; (4) Helen Fergeuson who applies the recovery model to racism to depict it as a social dysfunction; and (5) Rosalyn Weaver who skillfully combines the biblical story of Hannah with the history of several African American heroines. This issue is an excellent introduction/overview for readers unfamiliar with the nuances of feminist and womanist perspectives, and its range of standard features (biblical reflections, poetry, book reviews etc.) coordinates feminist, womanist and other racial ethnic perspectives.

NOTE: For early theological literature addressing racism in feminist theology, see Murray **[181]**, Grant **[214]**, Heyward **[216]**, and Culpepper **[329]**, while for more recent literature see Thistlethwaite **[252]**, Thistlethwaite and Engel **[276]** and Williams **[341]**.

V

The Religious Leadership of Women

This section presents literature on the religious leadership of women in American Protestant and Roman Catholic contexts. By way of overview, selected theological and statistical sources introduce the subject of women's religious leadership, with attention then directed, respectively, to the "authorized" leadership of women in American Protestantism and the history and current sociological research on women in ordained ministries. A second chapter then presents literature on the "recognized" (but presently *un*authorized) leadership of women in Roman Catholicism (e.g., the women's ordination movement, the women-church movement and the feminism of women in "vowed" communities). A third chapter then synthesizes the literature on "Women's Leadership, the Academy, and Theological Education." The distinction between the "recognized" and "authorized" leadership of women may be new to some readers. As used by Hartford Seminary President Barbara Brown Zikmund, it refers to the organizational significance of ordination. Hence, the "authorized" leadership of women entails the full institutional acceptance of women into a denomination's ordained organizational polity, while the "recognized" ministry of women entails the social or communally recognized leadership of women, but not their institutional, organizational incorporation. For Zikmund's specific comments see "Women and Ordination" in Ruether and Keller [135: 294] and see the discussion in [663].

Several themes cut across the literatures of the chapters in this section. First, although Protestant and Catholic women have experienced differing patterns of discrimination within their churches, they have each experienced marginalization from centralized roles of church organizational leadership. Further, this marginalization continues: in Roman Catholicism as women are yet banned from the status of priest and ordained minister before the People of God, and in Protestant churches--almost across the board, as women experience continued sexism, elements of religious backlash and various glass ceilings in denominational structures and organizations.

Second--and with no small amount of irony--it is these same Protestant and Catholic women who, while marginalized, are nonetheless the mainstay of "Full Time Equivalencies" for many seminary student rosters, Protestant and Catholic alike. Third, in addition to their marginalization from most positions of church leadership, these women continue to experience both traditional and contemporary forms of ecclesial discrimination, with the former constituted by differing salaries, benefits, ordination tracks, and careeer histories (cf. [663] and [701]), and the latter issues of modified misogyny cast in terms of homophobic, familistic and/or heterosexist assumptions about ministry (as exemplified by various pre-ordination commitments required of ordination candidates). Fourth--and again with some irony--these women continue to experience the impact of "clericalism" within their lives, and particularly "paternalistic clericalism." At issue here is a phenomenon described in feminist conversation as "white male ecumenism," but identifiable more formally--and more sociologically--as the ecclesial struggle to define a "theology of ordination." Put differently, should one say that ordination confers a "call to service" and is thus a process within which human and social factors are both important and malleable? Or, alternatively, should one say that ordination confers a "special charism" indicative of the recipient's divinely declared distinctiveness and set apartness? The discussion itself is a grounding condition for the stratification of religious roles in terms of lay and "clerical" states, and although the demise of clericalism in many Protestant denominations has historically opened a number of once "male only" doors to women, its presumed demise across the *full* Christian spectrum has glossed the historical sex-typing of the ministry, and thus opened *new* possibilities for women's subordination and/or containment (cf. Nesbitt [661] and see Zikmund, Lummis and Chang [663]). Moreover, that a discussion attempting a "theology of ministry" has arisen in the mid-80s and early 1990s, *that is, at a time when women's numbers in ordained ministry have dramatically increased*, suggests both (a) the possibility of a *re*-clericalizing of the ministry along sex-typed and sacralized historical roles, and (b) the "traditioning" dynamics that such clericalizing can imply: *viz.*, "the relationship of a dependent adult to a dominant adult being assimilated into that of a child to a male parent," and with this, the disempowerments clericalism can effect (Ruether [193:76]). Indeed, it is this kind of circumstance which propels some religious feminists to declare the need for a *hermeneutics of suspicion* for all theologies of ordination, and it is this kind of circumstance which makes some women at least wary about the future of women in ministry. (Cf., e.g., the conflicting perspectives expressed at the November, 1995 Women's Ordination Conference in Washington D.C., as reported in the *National Catholic Reporter*, December 1, 1995 [*NCR* 36, no. 6, pp. 9-11]. The circumstance of ordained ministry as a reclericalized phenomenon is currently *under*researched and to that extent wonting, save for Nesbitt's work noted above.

Finally, "inclusivity" is a fifth theme cutting across the leadership experiences of women in Christian tradition, and here the literature speaks both to churches and their structures of theological education, with the criteria of inclusivity going beyond gender to include race/ethnicity, sexual orientation, age and social class. Indeed, if there is yet an issue of ecumenical and interdisciplinary pre-eminence, it is the need for conceptual frameworks that respect pluralism while evidencing inclusivity at all levels of church structure and organization.

Some guideposts to the literature: For readers with no prior knowledge of the history of women's ordination within Protestant and Catholic traditions, the historical overviews presented by Zikmund ([681] and [682]), Carter [677], and Wallace [787] are good starting points, as is the essay by Boyd and Brackenridge [674] on the ordination of women in the Presbyterian tradition. Likewise, the entries by Charlton [697] and Kleinman [698] suggest the need for inclusivity in seminary and theological education, while those by The Mud Flower Collective [807], and more recently, Chopp ([811] and [812]) suggest the complexity of tasks awaiting its accomplishment.

Additional guideposts to the literature include the following: (1) the Carroll, Hargrove and Lummis [657] study of clergywomen in predominantly white, mainline denominations; (2) Carpenter ([644] and [645]) and Lincoln and Mamiya [141] for the literature on clergywomen in African American denominations; and (3) Ruth Wallace's *They Call Her Pastor* [787], for data on the "authorized" (but not ordained) leadership of women in parish administration within Roman Catholicism.

Also, for the background literature on the "traditioning" process in ministry see the early collection by Ruether and McLaughlin [209], see Zikmund [682], Ruether [759], Bianchi and Ruether [733], and Schüssler Fiorenza [411-412]. Although some of these entries are located in other sections of the bibliography, they well detail the gendered tensions cutting across the study of theology, ministry, and theological education.

Likewise, for background literature on Roman Catholicism and the dimensions of conflict over women's ordination within Roman Catholicism, see the sociological entries by Ebaugh [737], Hoge [741] and D'Antonio et al. [736]; and see the theological entries by Ashe and Morriss [745], LaCugna [780], Bianchi and Ruether [733], Swidler and Swidler [781], and Asen [763]. Additionally, see the literature in Chapter 19 on both the "women-church" movement in Catholicism and women in convent communities. Last, for current literature on the conflict between Rome and American bishops over women's ordination, see the standard periodical indices and see the independent Catholic news weekly, the *National Catholic Reporter* (115 East Armour Blvd., Kansas, MO, 64111) passim or at its web site, www.natcath.com.

In particular, see "Publisher Destroys Book on Vatican's Order," in the July 31, 1998 issue of *National Catholic Reporter* (volume 34, no. 35, pp. 3-4), published just as the final edits for this bibliography were being completed. The book referred to in the *NCR* article is *Woman At the Altar*, by Sr. Lavinia Bryne of Cambridge, England, and its remaining 1300 copies were destroyed by its publisher, the Liturgical Press of Collegeville, MN. According to the *NCR* article, "The publisher [the Liturgical Press of Collegeville, MN] was acting on a request from Bishop John F. Kinney of St. Cloud Minn., who, in turn, was acting on a directive from the Congregation for the Doctrine of the Faith..." to destroy the remaining 1300 copies of *Woman At the Altar* because the author (who is active in feminist theological work in England) holds that (Catholic) women should be ordained. The abstract for this book [765] (prepared well before the publication of the NCR article) appears in Chapter 19 of this book.

18

Feminism and Women's Leadership in American Protestant Churches

As noted in the overview to this section, this chapter provides literature on the religious leadership of women within American Protestantism. Representative theological and statistical perceptions of that leadership frame the wider literature, with the entries by Harrison [654] and Russell [656] illustating classical theological sources and Carroll, Hargrove, and Lummis [657] and Jaquet [659] the sociological classics. Several background liteatures then frame the sociological literature on women in ordained ministry, and the chapter closes with a listing of important related sources. While the main emphases of the literature have been detailed in the overview to this section, it should be noted that the recently published *Clergy Women: An Uphill Calling* by Hartford Seminary President Barbara Brown Zikmund and sociologists Adair Lummis and Patricia Chang [663] is a most important interdisciplinary work. Its comprehensive data, its clear readability, and its attention to such difficult topics as "boundary issues" make it required reading for those engaged in seminary and theological education.

A. Perceptions of Women's Religious Leadership (1983-1997)

1. Feminist Theological Perceptions

[651] Bos, Johanna W. H. van Wikj. *Reformed and Feminist: A Challenge to the Church*. Louisville, KY: Westminster/John Knox, 1991.
Although not formally about the institution of ministry per se, this discussion by a noted Presbyterian biblical scholar highlights the mainstream framework of many ordained women. In her text Bos provides an autobiographical summary of the factors leading up to her feminist commitments: her early childhood awareness of the costs of commitment to those without voice (an experience borne of seeing Jews betrayed during the Holocaust); her keen sense of the Bible as a document of living religious authority (a sense born of Calvin's 'plain sense' hermeneutic); and her gradual awareness of women as victims without power through much of the world and the requirement of Christians to speak on behalf of precisely those lacking voice and power. The discussion is in many ways an extended sermon borne of Bos's reflections on various women's stories in the Bible, including selected "texts of terror" (Judges 4:17-22 & 2 Kings 4:1-7), the books of Esther and Ruth, and genealogical stories that press readers to find the answers and responses to silence, absence and the disempowerment of women in contemporary society. A broadly based discussion, it provides a framework for envisioning women's leadership in theological educational and church contexts.

[652] Buhrig, Marga. "The Role of Women in the Ecumenical Movement." In *Women: Invisible in Church and Theology*, edited by Elisabeth Schüssler Fiorenza and Mary Collins, 91-98. Edinburgh: T. & T. Clark, 1985.
This article summarizes the emerging visibility of women in the World Council of Churches (WCC) from 1968 to 1983, with the he discussion of women's ordination and the "problem" of church

unity constituting Buhrig's primary focus. Thus, she calls attention to: (1) the presence of a "problem" of church unity existing centuries prior to the ordination of women; (2) the conflicting theological norms governing this discussion (viz., an emphasis on ecclesiology and the doctrine of ministry as "fundamentals of faith" rather than a discussion of the doctrines of creation, theological anthropology and Christology); (3) the anomaly of women's increasing visibility within the WCC and yet the continued theological marginality of women; (4) the ongoing aversion of the church universal to address--theologically--the question of sexuality and the full humanity of women; and (5) the pastoral and ambivalent circumstances of (a) women leaving institutionalized Christianity in search of other models of service to humanity and (b) the struggles of those women who remain to call the church to accountability in terms of the gifts of all members, including women.

[653] Gannett, Dulcie, ed. "Women in Ministry" *Daughters of Sarah* 19, no. 2 (1993):1-53.

This thematically directed issue of *DOS* pulls together a variety of brief articles, poems, book reviews and biblical reflections to indicate the wide variety of gifts, services, celebrations, and continuing concerns that make up the "ministry of women." Among the "continuing concerns" are those of women in ordained ministry, including professional development after first calls, the use of power on behalf of others, the difficulties of 'mutuality' in ministry, and in evangelical circles, the continued need for biblical clarity of roles, expectations and gender understanding. Additional discussions provide brief comparisons of women's service groups, (e.g., "Shaker, Mennonite and Catholic Sisters" by Sally Ann Strickler), a woman's story of adoption, research by Allison Stokes from the *Clergywomen's Interfaith Institute* in the Berkshires in western Massachusetts, and in a particularly searing discussion, the needs of "two thirds world women," viz., women in Africa and elsewhere who yet suffer the violence of misogyny and poverty, including the now rapid spread of AIDS (see Linda Tripp's "Bleeding Backs and Torn Vaginas").

[654] Harrison, Beverly W. "Keeping Faith in a Sexist Church: Not for Women Only." In *Making the Connections: Essays in Feminist Social Ethics*, 206-234. Boston: Beacon, 1985.

After describing the specific factors that led to her adoption of feminism as a framework for Christian ethical reflection--her socialization to both traditional gender roles and the necessity for higher education, her long involvement in Presbyterian church work, her acceptance and respect by male teachers and mentors, her work in campus ministry and administration, and last her pursuit of a Ph.D. and a teaching career--and within all this her gradual appropriation of the significance of gender in theological and social discourse--after describing all this, Harrison addresses directly, the task of keeping faith in a sexist church. She begins with an overview of the feminist critique of Christianity in the nineteenth century and moves to a summary of her politically based Christology of praxis. In tandem with this she describes her "this worldly" spirituality and the affirmation of justice as the ground and source of feminist spirituality. The second portion of her discussion addresses related concerns, and here Harrison identifies the three deeply problematic "Christian" emphases in need of feminist critique. These are the alienating, androcentric language of God in relation to humanity and the body-soul and nature-history dualisms grounding Christian theology. Second, she re-affirms her long standing commitment to the premise that women (and men) entering seminary (and/or theological education) must come to see the necessity of doing justice on behalf of women, and thereby on behalf of all "marginated" people. As with all Harrison's work, this piece is honest to the core, deeply moral, and keenly aware of the social forces grounding both the vision she espouses and the factors that can--and often do--work against it.

[655] Rhodes, Lynn N. *Co-Creating: A Feminist Vision of Ministry*. Philadelphia: Westminster, 1987.

Readers expecting a simple injection of feminism into the traditional structures of parish ministry will find this book disappointing, for the sum and substance of its pages are exactly what its title and subtitle suggest. It is a statement of "vision": of hope, of expectation, and of the sturdy commitment of feminist women to bring both to fruition. Four topics--authority, salvation, mission and vocation--comprise the vehicles through which Rhodes unfolds this vision, and the discussion is frank, feminist and in the best sense of the words "now out in the open." The "data" for her discussion stem from extensive conversations with fourteen mainline clergywomen--all white, all engaged in pastoral ministry--and the theological framework within which it is framed are the writings of Letty Russell, Rosemary Ruether and Beverly Harrison. Rhodes' central premise is that as women appropriate the strength and integrity of their own experience as sources of Christian "revelation," they find that they become a part of its present history and reconstructive moment, for they are able to empower both themselves and those with whom they interact. They become, in other words, co-creators. Its limited sample nothwithstanding, the focus of this text is women centered and inclusive, and it is cohesive in terms of such themes as "right relations," mutuality, "power with" and through rather than "power over." Moreover, Rhodes' depth as a pastor and seminary professor is evident in her deft ability to portray her subjects' insights. This book should be required reading by all persons in any way associated with seminary and theological education: students, administration, faculty, church leaders, sociologists of religion, laity concerned with their congregations, and funding and accrediting agencies across the board.

[656] Russell, Letty M. "Women and Ministry: Problem or Possibility?" In *Christian Feminism: Visions of a New Humanity*, edited by Judith Weidman, 75-92. San Francisco: Harper & Row, 1984.
The title to this essay is a deliberate play on both the continued resistance to women clergy as experienced in various denominations--though the mid 1980s--and the conclusion by Carroll, Hargrove and Lummis [657] that women in ordained ministry constitute a new "opportunity" for the churches. Hence Russell examines the problem, a paradigm of pyramid-like domination: a hierarchical image of Christian belonging that generates (1) a two class [clergy/laity] pattern of church membership and within this (2) super and subordinate patterns of clergy-laity relations relative to the prophetic, priestly and kingly roles of Christian ministry. The historical outcomes of this paradigm, suggests Russell, are the "one-sided" assumptions about the church's ministry: that it is (a) sufficiently enacted by a proclamation of God's word (which demands obedience), (b) a priestly work of absolution to the community, and (c) a specific group (i.e., clergy) representing the power of God in Christ and the order of life within the Church. As an alternative perspective, Russell suggests a "paradigm of doxology." This paradigm celebrates more lateral and inclusive patterns, and has as its grounding image both the rainbow pattern as promised in the Noahite covenant and those gospel parables identifying service as the Christian vocation. Hence, this paradigm is about a "ministry of service for empowerment" for the whole Christian community. After detailing both the problem (domination) and the possibility (doxology), Russell then addresses the tasks of *engendering* the possibility, and she speaks directly of strategies for bringing about changes within congregations, i.e., the efforts of parishioners and leaders to develop a synergistic process directed towards inclusivity, to challenge the "pinnacle" complex of traditional clerical leadership and to find "subversive" patterns for bringing about community identified needs for congregational change.

NOTE: See Prelinger, [685], in "The History and Sociology of Mainline Protestantism."

2. Statistical and Demographic Perceptions

[657] Carroll, Jackson, Barbara Hargrove, and Adair Lummis. *Women of the Cloth: A New Opportunity for the Churches*. New York: Harper & Row, 1983.
This text is the first empirically based interdenominational analysis of women in ordained ministry. It is rooted in Bock's discussion of clergywomen and professional marginality [692] and Lehman's work on "lay" and "organizational" resistance to women clergy ([706] and [712]), and its data are drawn from three principal sources: random samples of women and men clergy in nine mainline American denominations, laity from each of those denominations, and an availability sample of 80 women faculty teaching full-time in forty U.S. Protestant and non-denominational seminaries. *Women of the Cloth* begins by comparing the history and status of American clergywomen to women in other major professions. It then presents detailed discussions on (1) the family backgrounds of women who enter seminary (2) the motivations of women for entering seminary (3) their perceptions of colleague and lay acceptance (4) conflicts between clergy and gender roles in public and private life (5) levels of feminism among female and male clergy and (6) the comparative standing of female and male clergy on such variables as placement experiences, employment status, type of ministry position, perceived effectiveness and church stability, salary and call histories. Thirty-three data tables (together with relevant statistical tests) are presented throughout the book's nine chapters of discussion, and a study appendix presents frequencies for responses to the questionnaire items. The references in endnotes (mostly sociological, rather than theological) are clear and comprehensive, and a general index closes the volume

[658] Chang, Patricia M. Y. "Female Clergy in the Contemporary Protestant Church: A Current Assessment." *Journal for the Scientific Study of Religion* 36 (1997): 565-573.
As the lead article introducing papers from the *Society for the Scientific Study of Religion*'s 1997 "Symposium on Women and the Ministry," Chang's paper provides one of the most immediate

sources assessing the literature on women clergy through the mid-1990s. Overall, Chang focuses the literature in terms of three frameworks: its benchmark beginnings with the descriptive 1983 *Women of the Cloth* survey by Carroll, Hargrove and Lummis [657], the consolidation in the 1990s of women clergy as a secondary labor market borne of several discriminatory ecclesial labor practices, and last, the various "push" and "pull" factors driving this market and confirmed by the [in press] 1998 Zikmund, Lummis and Chang update of Carroll, Hargrove and Lummis. (See *Women Clergy: An Uphill Calling* [663]). By way of conclusions, Chang identifies four continuing research needs: (1) the need for additional comparative female and male clergy data; (2) the need for understanding how institutional factors shape individual callings; (3) studies addressing the experiences of clergywomen outside the white, Protestant "mainline;" and (4) studies on clergywomen *exits* from institutional ministry. **NOTE:** Other symposium papers here inclue: Mark Chaves and James Cavendish, "Recent Changes in Women's Ordination Conflicts: the Effects of a Social Movement on Intraorganizational Controversy"; Paula Nesbitt, "Clergy Feminization: Controlled Labor or Transformative Change?" [661]; Joy Charlton, "Clergywomen of the Pioneer Generation: A Longitudinal Study"; and Patricia Chang, "In Search of a Pulpit: Sex Differences in the Transition from Seminary Training to the First Parish Job." Briefly, Chaves and Cavendish examine a century long history of clergywomen related conflicts in various denominations while Nesbitt documents the rise of women clergy as a secondary labor market (cf. [661]), and Charlton (author of [697]) interviews women she first studied two decades earlier. Last, Chang's second paper documents several long standing trends in clergywomen research.

[659] Jaquet, Constant H. "Women Ministers in 1986 and 1977: A Ten-Year View." In *Yearbook of American and Canadian Churches: 1989*, edited by Constant H. Jaquet, 261-266. Nashville: Abingdon, 1990.
Using questionnaire data from respondents in over 300 American and Canadian denominations and institutional data published in the *Fact Book on Theological Education* for the academic years 1987-1988, Jaquet details (1) the percentage increase of women in full ministerial positions for the period 1977-1986 and (2) the percentage increase of women in American and Canadian seminaries through 1988. Overall, the proportion of women in full ministerial positions has increased by 98% for the ten year period, 1977-1986 as women are now an estimated 7.8% of the mainline clergy population. Second, their continued presence seems ensured in that women now comprise slightly more than one of five seminarians [22.5%], an overall 10 year increase of 110%. Two other sources of data cited by Jaquet are (a) an April 6, 1987 article from "The Washington Times" (presenting data on women in the rabbinate) and (b) the researches of specific denominational agencies. Within Judaism women now comprise 7.0% of Reformed rabbis, 24.5% of Reconstructionist rabbis and .4% of Conservative rabbis. Salary and other occupational data for women rabbis are not presented, but as Jaquet moves to denominationally sponsored studies, he notes both general salary patterns and patterns of clergywomen placements. Overall, data from Episcopal, American Baptist and UCC churches all suggest continued discriminatory patterns in both salary and placement figures in that women receive significantly lower salaries than do men and less desirable ministerial placements. Finally, to close the discussion, Jaquet presents sexual harassment data from UCC women and two clearly presented tables indicating the distribution of women clergy in American and Canadian denominations. (For additional data on sexual harassment, see Majka [879] and the literature in Chapter 18.) **NOTE:** In a previous article addressing clergy salaries and income levels during the early 1980s (published in the 1984 edition of the *Yearbook of American and Canadian Churches*) Jaquet summarized questionnaire data from clergy respondents in eleven denominations (including the United Church of Canada), to outline frequencies for the following: (1) clergy age and sex; (2) clergy educational levels by sex; (3) clergy median salaries, range, and means by denomination; (4) salary and age (by sex); (5) salary and present position (by sex); (6) salary and educational level; (7) mean salaries and total clergy income (in 11 denominations) and (8) salary and total family income of responding clergy. In addition, he briefly noted regional differences, the effects of inflation ,and the comparison of clergy income with other professional salaries. (See "Clergy Salaries and Incomes in 1982 in Eleven U.S. Denominations." In *Yearbook of American and Canadian Churches: 1984*, edited by Constant H. Jaquet, 265-269. Nashville: Abingdon, 1985.) Both of these papers find their data "updates' in the 1998 Zikmund, Lummis and Chang Hartford women clergy study [663] below.

[660] King, Gail Buchwalter. "Trends in Seminary Education." In *Yearbook of American and Canadian Churches: 1993*, edited by Kenneth Bedell, 261-264. Nashville: Abingdon, 1993.
As Associate Director of the Association of Theological Schools, King has compiled and briefly described data for total enrollments in member schools with breakouts by degree type and full time

equivalents. Additionally, she notes percent changes for women and Hispanic seminarians for the years 1972-1992; for African American seminarians for 1970-1992 and for Pacific/Asian seminarians for the years 1977-1992. In 1992 women comprised 30.1% of all member school seminarians; Hispanic enrollment was 2.6%, African American 8.8%, and Pacific/Asian 4.9%. Readers should note that these enrollment figures include each other at various points since the ATS data do not indicate gender/race/ethnicity breakouts. Last, King notes both the need for increased African American Ph.D.'s and the slow increase in the numbers of seminary women faculty, a slow growth she presumes is due to the slow turnover in established positions, but for which curent data are lacking.

[**661**] Nesbitt, Paula D. "Clergy Feminization: Controlled Labor or Transformative Change?" *Journal for the Scientific Study of Religion* 36 (1997): 585-598.
Working with cohort data from both Episcopal (N=1,373) and Universalist Unitarian clergy (N=196) ordained between 1920 and 1970, Nesbitt examines the general hypothesis that the rising numbers of women clergy in both denominations evidences a feminization of the clergy profession, with women clergy being "clustered into a gender segregated labor supply for subordinate positions" which, de facto, constrain the range and extent of women's authority to change the ministry profession in ways consistent with feminist agendas. Her full discussion of this process (and the multiple impacts of "clergy feminization" across several statuses linked by gender) is presented in her text, *Feminization of the Clergy in America: Occupational and Organizational Perspectives,* Oxford Univ. Press, 1997.

[**662**] Stump, Roger. "Women Clergy in the United States: A Geographic Analysis of Religious Change." *Social Science Quarterly* 67 (1986): 337-352.
Using census data from 1970 and 1980 and a measure of "static dissimilarity" developed from his wider research on innovations and geographic diversity, Stump does four things in this study. First, he maps the changed geographic distribution of American women clergy for the years 1970 and 1980. Second, he tests and confirms (via regression analysis) the hypothesis that this changed distribution is due largely to three factors--the degree of urbanization particular to given areas, the expansion of secular roles open to women in those areas, and the presence of mainline churches in those areas. Third, through his developed measure of "static dissimilarity," Stump identifies five geographically distinct areas of clergywomen increase for the period 1970-1980, with areas initially open to women clergy showing the greatest growth of receptivity to more women clergy, and thus areas of heightened regional diversity and religious innovation. Fourth and last, Stump examines the implications of clergywomen presence in those areas as specific vehicles for further religious innovation and religious diversity. Technicalities aside, Stump demonstrates that clergywomen populations grow where the growth has already occurred, and that this growth provides the opportunity for clergywomen to demonstrate different approaches to ministry in the congregations they serve, such that an increase in the ministerial diversity of specific denominations can occur. **NOTE:** See also Larson and Shopshire [**699**] and O'Neil and Murphy [**702**] below.

[**663**] Zikmund, Barbara Brown, Adair Lummis and Patricia Mei Yin Chang. *Clergy Women: An Uphill Calling.* Louisville, KY: Westminister/John Knox, 1998.
This is a comprehensive update and expansion (with data through 1994) of the 1983 Carroll, Hargrove and Lummis *Women of the Cloth* study [**657**], with clergy and laity data collected from fifteen "predominantly white Protestant denominations," including those surveyed in 1983, albeit now as members of merged churches. The authors survey "old" and "new" issues, with the latter (e.g., gender differences in career histories, career exits, marital and other conflicts, sexual orientation, singleness, burnout, boundary and health issues, and the experiences of women in non-parish ministries) now available for study given the 25-30 year history of women in mainline ministries. Further, their research draws from and supports a wealth of established research and discussion (cf., e.g., Jaquet [**659**], much of Lehman's work, and more recently, Nesbitt [**661**]), *and* it breaks new ground as they focus their findings in terms of "congregation-centered," "institution-centered," and "spirit-centered" denominations--a typology that pemits several comparisons across feminist and varied theological lines. Third, and in many ways most importantly, while the authors present a text that balances the need for quantitative data with a clarity of presentation for non-technical audiences (cf., e.g., the 28 statistical *appendices*), they also examine the *institution of ministry* itself to note that new visions of ministry are rising, and as theological re-framings distinct from, but adjacent to Nesbitt's secondary market hypothesis [**661**]. Two final points. First, the study instruments include both a twenty-nine page mailed questionnaire (completed by 2170 male and 2668 female clergy) and "short and long semistructured telephone interviews" conducted with selected male and female subsamples (each n=125) for

indepth issues. Second, while the researchers did not sample from either Catholic or historically black Protesant churches, data from ethnic minority men and women are included from the churches sampled. This is a "must read" for *all* involved in sociology and theological education, and the interpretive/analytical teaming of the authors makes it especially rewarding.

B. Key Background Literatures

1. Women's Leadership in the History of American Protestantism

A background note: For general reference and bibliographic works on women's leadership in the history of American Protestantism see Bass and Boyd [130], James [131], and Ruether and Skinner [132-135] under "Women in American Religion." Additionally, see Lindsey [142] and MacHaffie [143] for various historical sources, and see Chapter 10 for the biblical literature on women's religious leadership. Finally, see Bendroth [825] and DeBerg [828] for overviews of women and American fundamentalism, with Bendroth tracing the symbolic role of gender in the development of fundamentalist anti-feminism and DeBerg its expression and rationalization through popularized and tract level publications.

[664] Bass, Dorothy C. "'Their Prodigious Influence': Women, Religion and Reform in Antebellum America." In *Women of Spirit: Female Leadership in the Jewish and Christian Traditions*, edited by Rosemary Radford Ruether and Eleanor McLaughlin, 279-300. New York: Simon and Schuster, 1979.
This article describes several of the religious and social forces that contributed to the involvement of [white middle-class] women in the anti-slavery efforts of the early and middle nineteenth century. Among religious forces were: (1) women's involvement in the evangelical missionary efforts spawned by the period of the Second Great Awakening [1795-1835]; and (2) the eventual anti-clericalism that some women adopted during the 1840s and 1850s. Social forces included: (1) the development of the "cult of domesticity;" (2) the ideologization of women's religious activity into the nurture-based gender roles assumed by this framework; and (3) the 'reform ethic' that characterized women's religious activity during the generation after the involvement of women in evangelical activities. It is Bass' contention that while women served (and were defined) as auxiliaries to the clerical leadership of evangelistic preaching during the period of the Second Great Awakening--and thus exercised their abolitionist activities via their extra-familial role as moral guardians, their involvement in anti-slavery efforts of the late 1830s and beyond reflected a different moral authority, one more politically directed, and one borne of a moral freedom "which relied on neither clerical allies nor the special virtues of femininity for its exercise" (p. 294). By way of illustration Bass cites the differences between abolitionist activities tied to the crusade against sexual licentiousness and the work of such women as (among others) the Grimkes. This is an informative article, and its religious and social factors are fleshed out in terms of women's organizational abilities, the difference between urban and rural reform efforts etc. **NOTE:** Although Bass is mindful of the tensions between feminist and abolitionist efforts, her attention here is to the legacies of ante-bellum reform consciousness. For her further discussion see "'In Christian Firmness and Christian Meekness': Feminism and Pacifism in AnteBellum America" in *Immaculate and Powerful: The Female in Sacred Image and Social Reality*, edited by Clarissa W. Atkinson, Constance H. Buchanan and Margaret R. Miles. Cambridge, MA: Harvard Women's Studies in Religion Series, 1985. Alternatively, see Williams [341] in the same volume.

[665] Bednarowski, Mary Farrell. "Outside the Mainstream: Women's Religion and Women Religious Leaders in Nineteenth Century America." *Journal of the American Academy of Religion* 48 (1980): 207-231.
This article contrasts selected doctrinal emphases in four nineteenth century religious movements (Shakerism, Spiritualism, Christian Science and Theosophism) to indicate the avenues of religious leadership opened to nineteenth century women by means of the doctrinal emphases within these movements. In particular, the author argues that a bi-sexual or non-anthropomorphic concept of God, a denial or down playing of Christianity's doctrine of the Fall, an aversion to clerical leadership and the negation or devaluing of marriage all permitted women members of these movements the opportunity to bypass traditional gender expectations and assume roles of religious leadership within the make-up of these movements and their localized communities. The author suggests but does not develop possible parallels between these emphases and late twentieth century feminist theology and/or religious thought. Nonetheless, the article is extremely informative, well documented, and rich in implications, with several of the latter carried through by Wessenger in her 1993 anthology [136].

[666] Blauvelt, Martha Tomhave. "Women and Revivalism." In *Women and Religion in America, Volume 1: The Colonial and Revolutionary Periods,* edited by Rosemary Radford Ruether and Rosemary Skinner Keller, 1-45. San Francisco: Harper & Row, 1981.

This article examines the appeal and function of revivalism for nineteenth century women, as both members and supporters of revivalist groups and meetings. It contrasts the conversion experiences of Northern and Southern women--slave and free--and focuses the functions of revivalism through a discussion of women's gender roles as expressed in the "cult of domesticity" and the potential of revivalism to bind women together for feminist concerns. Additionally, as with other entries in the Ruether-Keller three volume series **[132-135]**, it presents source documents that ground the discussion, and here these include: (1) the autobiographical and diary accounts of the conversion experiences of Amanda Berry Smith and Evangelist Margaret ("Maggie") Newton Van Cott; (2) excerpts from the speeches/sermons of Sojourner Truth and Charles Finney; and (3) documents describing both the "ideology of feminine piety" and "southern male opposition to women's piety." **NOTE:** For related literature addressing the evangelical activities of eighteenth century Puritan and Wesleyan women as, respectively, narrowing and widening frameworks for female evangelical activity during first part of the nineteenth century, see Martha Tomhave Blauvelt and Rosemary Skinner Keller's, "Women and Revivalism: The Puritan and Wesleyan Traditions," in Volume II **[133]** of the Ruether and Keller series.

[667] Dunn, Mary Maples. "Saints and Sisters: Congregational and Quaker Women in the Early Colonial Period." In *Women in American Religion,* edited by Jane Wilson James, 27-46. Philadelphia: Univ. of Pennsylvania Press, 1980.

This essay contrasts the implications of Puritan and Quaker doctrine for women in seventeenth century colonial America to indicate the social and religious roles expected of women within these traditions and the differing outcomes such teachings had, relative to the autonomy and involvement of women in these traditions. In brief, the author details: (1) the Puritan emphasis on re-affirming women's subordination as expressed in Genesis and the teachings of Paul; (2) the defeat of women's attempt within Puritanism to interpret religious doctrine before women (and men), as exemplified in the trial of Anne Hutchinson; and (3) the efforts and impact of Puritanism's disciplining of women to silence and the acceptance of the religious role of motherhood with its emphases on the moral upbringing of children. Puritanism's location within the "new world" and especially its struggle over antinomianism within the theocracy of the Bay Colony provided the setting for such developments and these contrasted sharply with the emphases of the Society of Friends in Pennsylvania: *viz.,* the concept of lay ministry that demanded women's involvement and enactment of Society norms, the subsequent organizational involvement of women in religious activity designed to maintain those norms, and most fundamentally, an "enlightenment by the Spirit" norm for changing or adapting unwanted scriptural understandings. As a backdrop to these contrasts, Dunn also traces the clericalizing process within Puritanism (which silenced not only women, but men as well), and she highlights factors evidencing the feminization of American religion in this period. This is an especially informative article supported by extensive bibliography and historical sources.

[668] Gifford, Carolyn de Swarte. "Women in Social Reform Movements." In *Women and Religion in America, Volume 1, The Nineteenth Century: A Documentary History,* edited by Rosemary Radford Ruether and Rosemary Skinner Keller, 294-340. San Francisco: Harper & Row, 1981.

As an entry in the Ruether/Keller documentary series, Gifford's discussion is both an overview and compendium of key sources on women active in 19th century social reform movements. As an overview, it introduces main figures and summarizes the tensions and accomplishments of women active in 19th century social reform movements. Relatedly, it provides excerpts from abolitionist, feminist and temperance directed women. According to Gifford, women active in 19th century social reform faced two major issues: first, the issue of "strategy" (or whether one's efforts should be gradualist or dramatic--and especially so when grounded in religious teaching); second, precisely because they were women seeking social reform, these women faced the issue of credibility, and particularly so as they moved from "beyond their sphere" into the critique of society and its systems. For illustrative documents, Gifford includes excerpts from various reformers' letters, diaries, speeches and works on temperance; and, although not discussed in the essay, excerpts from Ida B. Wells-Barnett's Feb. 13, 1893 speech, "Lynch Law in All Its Phases." For additional work by Gifford see her essays in Collins **[349]** and Schüssler Fiorenza **[344]**. Also, see Bendroth **[825]**, DeBerg **[828]**, Giddings **[614]** and Klatch **[833]**.

[669] Irwin, Joyce. *Womanhood in Radical Protestantism: 1525-1675*. New York: Edwin Mellen Press, 1979.

Following the usage that distinguishes "magisterial Protestantism" as those Protestant developments borne of magistrates' declarations during the sixteenth century reformational period, Irwin describes "radical Protestantism" as that which dissociates itself from all secular and other authorities to follow a literal reading of the Bible and its implications for social life. She then focuses her discussion of "womanhood in radical Protestantism" to the period just prior to the development of Pietism (hence the 1525-1675 time frame) and she presents a series of primary source documents depicting "womanhood" during this time. Her purpose is to provide a synthesized access to primary sources for use by women scholars in both their teaching and research, and her sources (which are largely from male religious leaders of this period) are arranged as follows: "Women in the Bible;" "Women as Wives;" "Women and Learning;" "Women in the Church," and "Women as Preachers and Prophets." Anabaptist, Quaker and other sources are included, and Irwin prefaces each thematic set with a brief overview of issues and relevant background material. This is a specialized text directed primarily to historians already familiar with the domain assumptions of Irwin's selected time-frame and the very nuanced reformational developments preceding and running currently through it.

[670] Keller, Rosemary Skinner. "Patterns of Laywomen's Leadership in Twentieth Century Protestantism." In *Women and Religion in America, Volume 3 1900-1968: A Documentary History*, edited by Rosemary Radford Ruether and Rosemary Skinner Keller, 266-309. San Francisco: Harper & Row, 1986.

This article "lifts up...cameo" portraits of several 20th century laywomen to identify the patterns of leadership--the decisions, the conflicts and the strategies --they employed as they worked on behalf of newly found organizational acceptance and incorporation following the 19th century success of women's home and foreign missions. Individuals "lifted up" include Northern Baptist professional volunteers Helen Barret Montgomery and Lucy Waterbury Peabody, Belle Harris Bennett of the Methodist Episcopal Church, South; "applied theologian," Georgia Harkness of Garrett-Theological Seminary, and medical missionaries Anna Kugler and Ida Scudder. A variety of archival church and related documents provide the bases for the discussion. Two additional essays (Keller's "Lay Women in the Protestant Tradition" from Volume I of the Ruether and Keller series and Dorothy Jean Furnish's "Women in Religious Education: Pioneers for Women in Professional Ministry" from Volume 3 of the series) provide helpful, related discussion. The first details the success of women's missionary activity in the 19th century--a topic well documented by several sources (cf. Brereton and Klein below). The second highlights additional 'cameos:' here, African American and white women in professional religious educational ministries within congregations, and additionally, seminary faculties. This is a discussion of sources helpfully read in tandem with works by Zikmund ([681] and [682]).

[671] Kirkpatrick, Frank G. "From Shackles to Liberation: Religion, the Grimke Sisters and Dissent." In *Women, Religion and Social Change*, edited by Yvonne Y. Haddad and Ellison Banks Findly, 433-455. Albany, NY: SUNY Press, 1985.

This essay demonstrates the potentially strong correlation between evangelical religious faith and efforts at social reform. The abolitionist activities of the Grimke sisters provide a strong historical source for the argument, and Kirkpatrick develops his discussion in terms of four main points: the "emerging [anti-slavery] convictions" of the Grimke sisters as children of slave owners in South Carolina at the beginning of the 19th century; their use of "Scripture" to buttress an abolitionist perspective; their singular focus on the "centrality of the Lordship of Christ" as their grounding premise and authority; and their critiques of all power (but Christ's), together with their subsequent rejection of ecclesial and civil authorities to interpret social morality. Extensively documented, this article provides several points of contrast with feminist New Testament work currently being done today.

[672] Mitchell, Norma. "From Social to Radical Feminism: A Survey of Emerging Diversity in Methodist Women's Organizations, 1869-1974." *Methodist History* 13(1975): 21-44.

This essay is a clear and strongly developed overview of women's feminist organizational activities in the United Methodist Church (UMC) from 1869-1974, with the discussion developed in terms of four major concerns. These include: (1) A well developed description of the 19th century American feminist movement, both in terms of its "radical" mid-century feminist demands for women's equality and its subsequent "social" or "expedient and non-ideological" feminism in the late 19th century; (2) a summary of the efforts of 19th and 20th century Methodist women in the Northern and Southern churches to achieve laywomen's rights within the churches and the establishment of women as clergy; (3) a description of both the "new" (1970s) outlook of United Methodist women and the factors affecting this outlook; and (4) a contrast between the social feminism of the 19th century and the "new feminism" of Methodist women [in 1974], that involves an attention to self-affirmation rather than self-abnegation; a questioning of women's traditional gender roles, and a critique of the racist-sexist structures of the UMC and the desire of new Methodist feminists to overcome such interstructured bigotry. **NOTE**: For early British and American sources on Methodist women, see Kenneth E. Rowe, *Methodist Women: A Guide to the Literature*. Junaluska, NC: General Commission on Archives and History, United Methodist Church, 1980.

[**673**] Scanzoni, Letha Dawson, and Susan Setta. "Women in Evangelical, Holiness and Pentecostal Traditions." In *Women and Religion in America, Volume 3: 1900-1968*, edited by Rosemary Radford Ruether and Rosemary Skinner Keller, 223-265. San Francisco: Harper & Row, 1986.
This article describes the "positive" acceptance of women Pentecostal leadership during the beginning of the twentieth century, its subsequent restriction during the 1930s and 1940s, and its re-emergence during the 1960s-1970s, with reasons cited for this vacillation: the 'routinization of charisma' as argued by Barfoot and Sheppard [**691**], the initial limited equality of women in Pentecostal (and holiness) churches, the reactions of conservative evangelicals to the rising numbers of women in the work force, the "conservative evangelical penchant for order" (and within this women's place as an auxiliary to her husband), and lastly, factors associated with the sect-to-church process experienced by many Pentecostal groups, i.e., the professionalization and bureaucratization of ministry and the rise of a commitment to biblical inerrancy. This is an informative discussion with helpful documentation. For related literature see, "Women in the Holiness Movement: Feminism in the Evangelical Tradition." by Nancy Hardesty, Lucille Sider Dayton and Donald Dayton in Ruether and McLaughlin [**209**].

NOTE: For additional literature, see the following womanist sources: Carpenter [**644, 645**], Dodson [**646**], Gilkes [**615**], and Sawyer [**619**], and see Taves [**152**].

2. Histories of Women's Ordination in American Protestantism

[**674**] Boyd, Lois A., and R. Douglas Brackenridge. "Presbyterian Women Ministers: A Historical Overview and Study of the Current Status of Women Pastors." In *The Pluralistic Vision: Presbyterian and Mainstream Protestant Education and Leadership*, edited by Milton J. Coalter, John M. Mulder and Louis B. Weeks, 289-307. Louisville, KY: Westminster/John Knox, 1992.
The especially helpful notes--together with the historical sources and general framework of this discussion--make it one of the best summary essays available on the history of Presbyterian women clergy. The authors correctly recognize that "...if [ordination] is no longer a real issue within most Protestant denominations, then whether congregations are going to accept women pastors...[or not]...is a real issue," and they focus their six part discussion of Presbyterian clergywomen history around this point. They survey the "historical background" of women's ordination in Presbyterian churches, the experience of Presbyterian women clergy in "recent decades," the "evidence concerning acceptance" of Presbyterian women clergy (and the "hesitancy [of laity] to change") and last, several "areas of exploration" yet needing investigation. Their discussion incorporates the distribution and occupational characteristics of Presbyterian women clergy in local, regional, and national church structures, and in contrast to discussions that highlight the clergy surplus within Presbyterianism, these authors examine impacts of race, marital status and gender-related issues facing Presbyterian women clergy. Among important questions yet to be addressed are: How will the progress of Presbyterian women clergy be measured and tracked? What role will marginalized persons play in the congregational expectations women clergy have? And how will gender affect the status of women in both church *and* society, and the status of women clergy specifically.

[**675**] Brereton, Virginia Lieson, and Christa Ressmeyer Klein. "American Women in Ministry: A History of Protestant Beginning Points." In *Women of Spirit: Female Leadership in the Jewish and Christian Traditions*, edited by Rosemary Radford Ruether and Eleanor McLaughlin, 301-332. New York: Simon and Schuster, 1979.
With a focus on the "long history of expanding female leadership in the American Protestant churches" (p. 302), Brereton and Klein (1) call attention to the feminist exposure of the unfulfilled

possibilities of women's ministry (as evidenced by numerous gender-based occupational indicators) and (2) provide a cross-denominational, historical overview of women's leadership in American mainline churches. The overview is divided into three sections: "Women Alongside the Churches: 1861-1925;" "Women Within the Churches: Organizational Mergers, Lay Status and Professional Church Workers, 1920-1925;" and "Women in the Pulpit: Ordination, 1945-1970." The first part documents the extensive independent and financially successful efforts of women in home and foreign mission work within American Protestantism and the ultimate cooptation of this work by male clerical leadership once its financial success was clear. It is the longest portion of their overview. Part II documents the youth and educational work of women in churches and the ambiguity and precariousness of women's professional status once these types of work were formally institutionalized beyond the voluntary level. Part three briefly examines the factors leading up to the ordination of women in Presbyterian, Methodists and Lutheran traditions, with particular attention to the role of the World Council of Churches in this "long history of leadership." An epilogue followed by the authors' extensive endnotes complete the discussion.

[676] Carson, Mary Faith, and James H. Price. "The Ordination of Women and the Function of the Bible." *Journal of Presbyterian History* 59 (1981): 245-265.
In 1956 the Presbyterian Church of the United States of America (PCUSA) formally admitted women to the ordained ministry. In 1964 the Presbyterian Church of the United States (PCUS) followed suit. These two churches, known informally as the "northern" and "southern" Presbyterian churches, merged in 1983 to form the Presbyterian Church in the United States of America (PCUSA). In this entry Carson and Price trace the ecclesiastical history of women's ordination in the PCUSA and PCUS churches. What distinguishes this discussion, however, is its focus on the ways both churches used biblical texts as authoritative sources of guidance for the discussion. That is, did these churches use a "hard" view of biblical authority, i.e., a view that presumes a predisposition to the Bible's authority on a given subject, prior to discussion and/or information about that subject? Or did they use a "soft" view: a view that recognizes the Bible as one source of insight, but one to be tempered by other sources of insight such as "contemporary experience." In their analysis of Presbyterian discussions and documents, Carson and Price found that each of these churches was likely to employ a soft (rather than a hard) view of biblical authority, although they did note the presence of the hard view within the PCUS. The authors surmise that: (1) both churches were influenced by the ascendance of critical methods of biblical study that had made inroads into the seminaries by the late 1940s; and (2) neither church clearly addressed the question of exactly what makes the Bible authoritative. The authors also observe that experience was an interpretive norm more frequently than many realized at the time, and that an attention to the issue of biblical authority could have precluded much conflict over women's ordination, and in the end, aided the church itself.

[677] Carter, Norene. "Entering the Sanctuary: The Struggle for Priesthood in Contemporary Episcopalian and Roman Catholic Experience, Part I: The Episcopalian Story." In *Women of Spirit: Female Leadership in the Jewish and Christian Traditions*, edited by Rosemary Radford Ruether and Eleanor McLaughlin, 356-372. New York: Simon and Schuster, 1979.
Carter's essay chronicles the organizational struggles of women to become priests within the American Episcopal church from the "restoration of the order of deaconesses by the bishop of London in 1862" (p. 357) through the September 1976 legitimation of the ordination of the "Philadelphia eleven" (on 7/29/74) to the adoption of the "conscience clause" by Episcopal bishops in October, 1977. A second and interpretive portion of her essay reviews the theological arguments evidenced by supporters and opponents of women's ordination within Anglicanism, with particular attention to the androcentric and male-defined biological assumptions undergirding traditional notions of ministry, priesthood and God, and the threat to male sexuality such a critique engenders. Now an historical footnote within the literature given the ordination of same-sex oriented persons within the (American) Episcopal church during late '80s and early '90s and the November, 1992 decision of the Church of England to ordain women, this article remains a helpful initial overview to those beginning their study of this issue and the power of androcentrism to create bitter conflict within organized religious leadership. (Cf., e.g., Prelinger **[685]**).

[678] DeBerg, Betty A. [with Elizabeth Sherman], comp. *Women and Women's Issues in North American Lutheranism.* Philadelphia: Augsburg Fortress, 1992.
Produced under the sponsorship of the Commission for Women of the ELCA, this bibliography focuses specifically on the experiences of North American Lutheran women. Its purpose is to clarify the "contributions" of these women to the development of Lutheranism in North America

and to identify a variety of Lutheran perspectives on the religious and social roles of women. The entries are not annotated, but its format and general organization suggest an ease of use suitable for adult lay and clerical readers. The topics covered include various aspects of mission and congregational life, ecumenism, education, social issues, synods, women's ordination, feminist theology (a weak section), immigrants, organizations, scripture and "worship and preaching." Although it lacks an index, this is a useful introductory bibliography for information about Lutheran women. For DeBerg's other work see [828].

[679] Hewitt, Emily and Suzanne Hyatt. *Women Priests: Yes or No?* New York: Seabury, 1973.
This brief volume responds to various arguments and prejudices frequently voiced against wider social roles for women generally and the ordination of women within the American Episcopal church particularly. Its authors were among the first Episcopal women priests in the United States, and although much of its discussion may now appear dated, it is nonetheless an historical and first hand (written) account of the conflicts and struggles of women against sexism within the American Episcopal church during the decades of the late sixties and early 1970s. NOTE: For a related discussion (not abstracted in this volume) see Carter Heyward, *A Priest Forever* [New York: Harper & Row, 1976].

[680] Penfield, Janet Harbison. "Women and the Presbyterian Church: An Historical Overview." *Journal of Presbyterian History* 55 (1977): 107-123.
Drawing from General Assembly Minutes and other Presbyterian archival sources, Penfield traces the development of four overlapping "phases of the participation of women in the Presbyterian Church" (p. 197). These include the rise and growth of women's "cent's societies," the development of home and foreign mission boards, the activities of women in mission areas, and the efforts of Presbyterian women to gain parity with men in the context of denominational church structures. The discussion is cast against the general backdrop of American Presbyterian church history, and the author's numerous examples of individual women's efforts (together with the denomination's perceptions of these efforts) indicate both the struggles of these women and their personal and extra-denominational achievements. Penfield's essay is a helpful source on the activities of individual Presbyterian women, and her discussion of women's efforts at parity within denominational structures (and specifically the efforts of women in seminary) anticipates much of the now standard literature on clergywomen research.

[681] Zikmund, Barbara Brown. "The Struggle for the Right to Preach." In *Women and Religion in America, Volume 1: The Nineteenth Century, A Documentary History*, edited by Rosemary Radford Ruether and Rosemary Skinner Keller, 193-241. San Francisco: Harper & Row, 1981.
As with other entries in this and subsequent volumes of the Ruether-Skinner documentary history series on *Women and Religion in America*, Zikmund's essay highlights topically specific documents; here, nineteenth century literature exemplifying the arguments for and against women's right to preach in Protestant churches. Zikmund frames her survey through a theologically based liberal/conservative classification, with "liberal" understood as favoring internal church change (and thus supportive of women's preaching rights) and "conservative" understood as seeking status quo maintenance (and thus opposing women's preaching rights). With this distinction drawn, she describes four general arguments advanced in favor of women's right to preach and three against it. "Pro" arguments included: (1) a woman's call comes from the Holy Spirit and is thereby authentic; (2) the practical needs for mission demand women's preaching; (3) women are already actively ministering and should thus be acknowledged; and (4) "authoritative" scriptural prohibitions can (and need) to be re-thought. Arguments against women's preaching included: (1) the authoritative teaching of Scripture, which in several ways, prohibits women's preaching; (2) the idea of permitting women limited activity in churches, but not preaching since the latter is tied to church administration; and (3) "social and historical reasons" for women's not being permitted to preach, i.e., women's limited intelligence and specific (and some argued "salvific") vocation to motherhood and childbearing. Zikmund's essay is an informative and helpful source for getting acquainted with the literature on women's preaching in the nineteenth century. Writers represented by the documentary sources include, on the 'pro' side: Temperance leader Frances Willard; AME preacher Jarena Lee; Congregationalist and first ordained woman Antoinette Brown; and revivalist Phoebe Palmer. "Con" writers include: Disciple of Christ member, Barbara Kellison; Congregationalist C. Duren, Presbyterian Samuel Niccolls, and Lutheran Margaret Seeback. For related literature see the Zikmund's bibliography, see her entry in Ruether and McLaughlin [209], and see the literature cited by Bass and Boyd [130].

[682] Zikmund, Barbara Brown. "Winning Ordination for Women in Mainstream Protestant Churches." In *Women and Religion in America, Volume 3: 1900-1968: A Documentary History,* edited by Rosemary Radford Ruether and Rosemary Skinner Keller, 339-383. San Francisco: Harper & Row, 1986.
Readers familiar with Zikmund's earlier discussion [681] together with entries by Dodson and Gilkes [613] and Dodson [646] will be familiar with nineteenth century sources on women and their struggle towards full clergy status. In this essay Zikmund chronicles the establishment of women's ordination in the Methodist, Presbyterian, Lutheran and (American) Episcopal churches. She begins by noting both the voluntaristic character of mainline church history and experience, and the historical tie between the establishment of lay leadership in mainline churches and that of women's ordained leadership. She notes that the former virtually always precedes the latter, and that for most mainline denominations the establishment of women's full clergy status has involved practical and/or organizational rather than theological concerns, with episcopally oriented churches being the exception to this norm. She then surveys the key moments of the women's ordination process within the four denominations mentioned above. An especially helpful feature of her discussion is the careful attention she accords the numerous internal mergers that have marked these varying ecclesial groups. Source documents date from 1924-1964 and include conference and committee minutes excerpts, individual clergywomen's recollections, and examples of arguments for and against women's full clergy status. Excellent end-notes and bibliography are also provided.

3. Mainline Christianity: History and Recent Sociology

a. General Studies

[683] Hoge, Dean R., and David A. Roozen, eds. *Understanding Church Growth and Decline: 1950-1978.* New York: Pilgrim, 1979.
Several technical, chapter length specific studies addressing a myriad of factors affecting church growth and decline make up this now semi-classical text on early patterns of decline in mainline Protestant churches. The primary contributors to the volume are Dean Hoge of Catholic University, and David Roozen and William McKinney, each of Hartford Seminary in Connecticut. Together (and with selected others) they examine several social, cultural, demographic, and theological explanations (and/or perspectives) concerning changes in denominational populations, with virtually all mainline denominations examined (in greater or lesser degree). The findings here are too numerous to detail, and readers uncomfortable with rote data presentation and unimaginative data graphics will find the very clearly written Hoge/Roozen summary chapter their particular preference. Similarly, readers familiar with the "clerical" paradigm of theological education will find several of these discussions idiomatically familiar, if nonetheless disquieting. Two findings expanded in later works ([686] and [687]) are the loss of a grounding cultural center within mainline Protestantism (but see Prelinger's critique of this [685]) and a growing polarization between individualized secular and spiritualized perspectives. This is not a feminist text. Rather, it provides baseline data and discussion for several denominational issues relevant to feminist theology and its critiques of ministry as a male dominant occupation.

[684] Hunter, James Davison. *American Evangelicalism: Conservative Religion and the Quandary of Modernity.* New Brunswick, NJ: Rutger's Univ. Press, 1983.
Hunter's work on evangelism is well known in sociological circles. Here he addresses the question: "if modernization secularizes [i.e., erodes religious beliefs] and America is among the most modern societies in the world, how then is it possible that Evangelicalism survives and even thrives in contemporary America?" (p. 4). His answers focus on both the responses of evangelicalism to the loss of religious plausibility and the specific demographics of recent evangelical converts. For the former, Hunter notes a "domestication" of once fiery religious beliefs and a politicization of personal or private morality; for the latter, a young, rural, predominantly female, middle and lower income group removed from the immediacy of modernity, and attempting to keep it at bay by means of a new, competitive values framework. An insightful and well written study, its data are from a sample of Americans, ages 18 and over (N=1533) collected by the Princeton Research Center from November 1978 to February 1979 for use by the evangelical journal *The Christian Century.*

[685] Prelinger, Catherine M. *Episcopal Women: Gender, Spirituality and Commitment in an American Mainline Denomination.* New York: Oxford Univ. Press, 1992.
In contrast to most studies on American mainline churches, Prelinger's text "explores gender as a crucial organizing principle of religious life and thought in a liberal Protestant denomination" (p. 4).

Thus where other studies might examine American Protestantism's perceived loss of denominational loyalty, cultural hegemony, "moral center" without regard to gender as either an organizing ecclesial principle or even a variable of analysis (cf., e.g., **[683]**, **[684]**, **[686]**, and **[687]** respectively), Prelinger's text starts with the recognition that *churches are gendered* and thus open to an analysis from within the experience of women and men, and not solely the de facto [male] leadership patterns so regularly taken as a reflections of the entire denomination's experience. Hence her takes sociology to task for generalizing from leadership findings to denominational realities, and it takes the denomination to task for ignoring its gender defined patterns. This is a refreshing, empowering text, and its eleven interview and questionnaire based essays provide discussions on "Historical Perspectives," "Contemporary Voices" and "Images of a New Church". Contributors include Rima Lumin Schultz, Elizabeth Hayes Turner, Joan Gunderson, Mary Sudman Donovan, Joanna B. Gillespie, Majorie Nichols Farmer, Irene Q. Brown, Sandra Hughes Boyd, editor Prelinger, Constance Buchanan, Margaret Miles and Dorothy Bass, and the discussions range from historical studies of women's leadership, the "parallel" women's church among Episcopalians and the differing social history of African American women in the church, to recent and current histories and interpretations of the status of lay and ordained women, women's devotional practices, and the denomination's standing vis a vis American and Anglican experience.

[686] Roof, Wade Clark, and William McKinney, eds. *American Mainline Religion: Its Changing Shape and Future*. New Brunswick, NJ: Rutger's Univ. Press, 1987.
Using data from *The General Social Survey*, this text provides an insightful analysis of America's "fragmented mainline." It reviews the many theories and explanations attached to the keenest indicators of that fragmentation, but particularly those theories attached to the membership declines in liberal Protestant churches and the growth or stability patterns evident in other religious groupings, i.e., "Conservative" and "Moderate Protestants," "Black Protestants," "Catholics," "Jews," "Others" and those of "No Preference." The authors' principal concern is with the collapse of the "moral center" of American mainline religion (see chapter 1), and overall, they argue two main points. (1) That if one interprets this collapse only in terms of the Kelly hypothesis (i.e., that conservative churches are growing because churchgoers are looking for religious stability and not socially directed theological liberalism [Dean M. Kelly, *Why Conservative Churches Are Growing*, NY: Harper and Row, 1972]), one, in effect, misses the sociological boat, because (2) while the Kelly hypothesis has much truth to it, the bigger issues are demographic: America's liberal Protestant churches are aging, and their reproductive rates are not sufficient to replenish their membership rolls. Hence, given that age and mobility factors widely influence the social (symbolic) and communal (cultural) bases of religious belonging, interested parties need to refigure their strategies for responding to and planning/theologizing about the changes they are experiencing. The authors then suggest specific themes characteristic of the "new denominationalism," and the ways in which "communities of memory" might respond to the realities of individualism and the problems of a de-moralized public ethos. This is an important book and when first published, it was widely praised for its comprehensiveness and interpretive scope. Moreover, although many studies have subsequently addressed specific denominational circumstances (cf., e.g., Dean Hoge, Benton Johnson and Donald Ludens, *Vanishing Boundaries: The Religion of Mainline Protestant Baby Boomers*. Louisville, KY: Westminster/John Knox, 1994), none has (through the mid-1990s) supplanted Roof and McKinney in terms of an overall analysis of "mainline" religion's waning authority in the United States. This said, the text is not without its weaknesses and chief among them are the absence of any analysis of the data by race and gender breakouts (with or without controls for theological orientation). This is a serious limitation. Not because such analyses might produce a different assessment of mainline Christianity's eroded social authority (they most likely would not), but rather because such analyses might have opened a wider range of possibilities for mainline churches--in a word, a different casting of membership and leadership, similar perhaps to the possibilities offered by such studies as Carroll, Hargrove and Lummis **[657]**, Prelinger **[685]**, and Stump **[662]**, and less influenced by the androcentrism of sociology of religion's own theoretical frames.

[687] Wuthnow, Robert. *The Restructuring of American Religion: Society and Faith Since World War II*. Princeton, NJ: Princeton Univ. Press, 1988.
This text is widely acclaimed for both the breadth of its scholarship and the significance of its most noted observation: namely, that America's mainline denominations have lost their salience as specific identifying symbols for large numbers of Americans. Wuthnow's discussion is developed from a monumental synthesis of several historical and social surveys that permit the following: (1) a mapping of rising levels of education and mobility among Americans through the early 1980s,

together with the related patterns of religious switching associated with this mobility; (2) the growth of ecumenism (and the decline of several forms of religious prejudice) through the 1980s; (3) the increased rates of religious intermarriage current in mid and late 20th century religious America, and--among other factors too numerous to name in detail, (4) the tremendous "relevance" of religion for many Americans during the 1960s-1970s. This last point has some irony for many church leaders, for to the extent that Americans of the '60s and '70s found religion relevant to social issues, the social issues became avenues of religious expression, with the net effect being the loss of denominational identity as a salient symbol for many Americans. This, together with the rise of many new sects and sect-like religious movements and groups accounts (in part) for the shift in religious values--the restructuring--among mainline church-going Americans. For Wuthnow's more recent (and arguably androcentric) interpretive discussion, see [688] below. Also, for Wuthnow's work on American "civil religion" in both its traditional (Bellah-like) and reactionary (New Right) forms, see *The Struggle for America's Soul* [Grand Rapids, MI: William B. Eerdmans Pub. Co., 1989].

[688] Wuthnow, Robert. *Christianity in the Twenty-First Century: Reflections on the Challenges Ahead.* New York: Oxford Univ. Press, 1993.
Written from the perspective of the social scientist as cultural critic, this text examines a variety of factors affecting the ethos of mainline Protestantism from the period of its heyday in the 1950s through its years of membership decline and institutional malaise during the decades of the 1970s and 1980s. The factors affecting this ethos are grouped into five types of "challenges" facing "the Church," and for each, Wuthnow synthesizes both general findings attached to formal and common sense indicators and various vignettes drawn from the experiences of individual believers. Further, he regularly offers suggestions designed to address the problems as he sees them. "Liberals" identified with Protestantism's historic hegemony and seeking an insightful dose of comfort for the challenges posed by the New Right will not be disappointed by this text, nor will followers of Bellah's *Habits of the Heart*. For as understood by Wuthnow, the types of challenges facing the church are *institutional, ethical, doctrinal, political,* and *cultural,* and as addressed by him, the weave of community, congregational life, changed family structures, traditional and fundamentalist civil religion, political and other symbols, social mobility and the personal need for memory, community and belonging all come to the fore. This is an elegantly (almost pastorally) written synthesis, but not visible within it are the voices of Protestants (and others) not identified with the hegemony of America's mainline ethos, but nonetheless also touched by it and also influential in its development and change: e.g., the voices identified by Prelinger [685], Chopp [812], and Wheeler [821]. Rather, the discussion seems directed to the decline of the mainline ethos as almost a benevolent parent--indeed as almost a good father, but one oblivious to the needs, presence and accomplishments of his many and younger children.

b. Studies in Church Leadership

[689] Carroll, Jackson. "Toward 2000: Some Futures for Religious Leadership." *The Review of Religious Research* 33 (1992): 289-304.
Working with Wuthnow's concept of 'restructuring' as a re-patterning of the symbolic markers that identify social groups and categories of people [687], Carroll examines the "re-patterning" of Christianity's image of the "religious leader" to shed light on three aspects of religious authority currently undergoing change within the Christian milieu, and more, to provide some tentative suggestions as to the circumstances of Christianity for the year 2000. Carroll identifies three contexts from within which the image of the Christian leader is undergoing re-patterning. First, the *symbolism* of Christian ministry is changing as women increasingly hold positions of pastoral leadership in local congregations. Second, clericalism is waning as clergy and laity now engage one another as partners in ministry rather than as (respectively) donors and recipients of ministry. Third, the "interpretive" or truth authoritative role of ministers is changing, with more mainline clergy seeking facilitator and/or pastoral counselor roles as Christianity bumps up against the relativities of modernity. In the light of these patterns and their details, Carroll predicts continued rigidity against women's ordination in Roman Catholicism; intensified conflict in many Protestant churches as issues of clergy-laity partnership increase; and an intensification of efforts by conservatives to avoid the 'corrosive' effects of modernity for biblical and other (conservative) religious teachings. This is an insightful article that just brims over with Carroll's career long study of ministry and its patterns of authority, both historical and "reflective." But therein lies the rub: For while it is at numerous points brilliant, it is decidedly androcentric in that it ignores the implications of a changed *symbolism* (his first point) for the symbolism of ministerial leadership per se, *beyond* the organizationally obvious patterns of egalitarianism, which (in theory) do not

necessarily have anything to do with gender. For his wider, but substantively similar discussion, see *As One With Authority: Reflective Leadership in Ministry*. Louisville, KY: Westminster/John Knox, 1991.

[690] Glock, Charles Y. "The Churches and Social Change in Twentieth Century America." *The Annals* 527 (May, 1993): 67-83.

Using public opinion data collected by Gallup and others since the late 1930s, Glock first demonstrates four areas of American social change. These include the decline of Anti-Semitism and of racial prejudice and discrimination, and further, changes "in the role and status of women" and changes "in sexual practices and attitudes among Americans." Glock then discusses the ways in which these changes are significant for American churches. First, each has clear implications for the way the churches view scripture, and particularly the "openness of denominations to reinterpret scripture to accommodate change" (p. 78). In turn, the latter has affected church membership levels, with accommodating churches experiencing large membership declines and "least compromising" churches continuing the growth levels that both mainline and conservatives experienced prior to the 1960s. Finally, a third implication is how accommodation affects the ability of churches to exercise moral authority. Conservative churches cannot presume that minimal accommodations will guarantee continued success in retaining and gaining members, for as new changes occur, new needs to accommodate will also arise. However, an organizational strength of these churches, says Glock, is their ability to quietly accommodate *old* issues of changing consciousness while opposing *new* areas of change, i.e., their ability to quietly drop negative scriptural stereo-types while vigorously opposing such new concerns as abortion and homosexuality. By way of contrast, Catholic and mainline Protestant churches will need to tap older loyalties, although few supports for this strategy seem apparent. Instead, these churches may need to become "smaller and more ideologically homogeneous" to affect membership (and thus) commitment levels.

NOTE: See E. Dale Dunlap, "The Protestant Experience and Democratic Ecclesiology," pp. 207-225 in [733]. While not abstracted here, it provides a helpful overview to the theological norms governing much of American Protestant church life.

C. The Sociology of Women in Ordained Ministry

1. General Studies and Early Clergywomen Research

[691] Barfoot, Charles H., and Gerald T. Sheppard. "Prophetic vs. Priestly Religion: The Changing Role of Women in Pentecostal Clergy." *Review of Religious Research* 22 (1980): 2-17.

This article traces the "routinization of charisma" in the Assemblies of God Church from the period of its founding in 1914 to its racially white solidification in 1932 to evidence a shift from "prophetic" to "priestly" leadership, which at the organizational level entails the gradual dissolution of women's ordained leadership. The discussion is premised on Weber's observation that (as cited by the authors) while the "religion of the disprivileged classes…is characterized by a tendency to allot equality to women" this "receptivity to women" occurs only in the early moments of a religious movement's organization, and then effectively vanishes as a second process starts, i.e., one of male organization leadership (and a devaluing of female pneumatic leadership) that arises as the twofold process of the "routinization of charisma and the regimentation of interactive roles" begins. The authors demonstrate the applicability of Weber's observation by examining the initial authority of Aimee Semple McPherson in the Assemblies of God Church and the church's own organizational developments as evidenced by its General Councils held in 1917, 1923, 1927, and 1931. Over time, these Councils established licensing and credentialing policies that would exclude prophetically "called" women (such as McPherson) from "priestly" (ordained) leadership within the church, and replace them with men. The authors then speculate about the future of women clergy in mainline denominations and suggest the possibility of a similar pattern for mainline women. Absent from this discussion is a consideration of the organizational conditions (as suggested, for example, by resource mobilization theory) that can aid the maintenance of women clergy in church administrative positions *already* grounded in licensing and credentialing policies. The latter is a fruitful theme implicit in Lehman's work [706] and much literature on seminarian populations [699], and it could suggest a re-reading and test of Weber's early observations. For an historical analysis of the same phenomenon, see Scanzoni and Setta [673].

[692] Bock, Wilbur. "The Female Clergy: A Case Study of Professional Marginality."
     American Journal of Sociology 72 (1967): 531-539.
Using Census data for the decades 1900-1960, Bock tests five propositions that permit the
characterization of women clergy [from this period] as a marginal grouping within the clergy
profession. These propositions entail comparisons with males and suggest that--in contrast to male
clergy of the same periods, women clergy will evidence: (1) no major increase in population
numbers for the period 1900-1960; (2) a higher proportion of black rather than white recruits; (3)
an older rather than younger clergy population; (4) lower levels of formal education; and (5) a
population whose members are less likely to be married and living with a spouse [as clergy and
female marital roles are inherently incompatible (p. 533)]. Bock's analysis confirmed his
propositions, but largely by data from the 1950-1960 decade only. Consistently confirmed by all
decennial data was proposition #5 concerning conflict between traditionally understood gender and
clergy roles. Bock's work has proved fruitful in a number of ways. Specifically, Wallace **[696]**
has re-examined and expanded Bock's concept of marginality and tested her revised notion with
data from the 1970 Census. Similarly, Scanzoni's research **[731]** has lent strength to Bock's fifth
proposition, as have (anecdotal) data discussed in Carroll, Hargrove and Lummis **[657]**.
However, the remainder of Bock's data are now historical, given the extensive increase (cf. e.g.,
[663]) in the numbers of women clergy in mainline (but not sectarian) churches.

[693] Hale, Harry Jr., Morton King, and Doris Moreland Jones. *New Witnesses: United
     Methodist Clergywomen.* Nashville, TN: Division of Ordained Ministry [United
     Methodist Church], 1980.
Using data from a sample of 838 Methodist women clergy (collected in the late 1970s as
commissioned research for the UMC), the authors describe the personal and social characteristics of
sample members, "their career histories from call to present job," and "the satisfactions and
problems they have experienced at each stage along the way." A total of 80 data tables provide
numeric summaries (frequencies with adjusted and cumulative percents) of all variables, with
breakouts for age, call history, current position, church size, work history, compensation, types of
satisfactions and problems, theological orientation and attitudes towards feminism, to name but a
few. No hypotheses are tested, nor are comparable male data presented. Rather, the focus is
descriptive, geared to general readership and directed to a census of the then emerging UMC
clergywomen population. The findings are clearly presented and frequently parallel those of later
and more substantive comparative research (e.g., Carroll, Hargrove and Lummis **[657]**, and
Larson and Shopshire **[699]**): *viz.*, the women's *very* low compensation, a substantial number of
clergy couple spouses, service in small congregations and a clear identification with the traditional
preaching pastoral role. 'Satisfactions and problems' are presented primarily in terms of qualitative
data (a chapter on "Cries of the Heart"), but a subsequent volume [*Clergywomen: Problems and
Satisfactions.* Lima, Ohio: Fairway Press, 1985] provides frequency distributions on persons with
whom the clergywomen report difficulties at a series of five stages defining the progression from
initial call to congregational placement. Additionally, in that latter volume the authors call attention
to the two principal problems clergywomen face, i.e., marital stress in the face of institutional
demands and self doubts in the face of sexism and discrimination. The authors provide suggestions
for change in each volume, but the first volume's suggestions are by far the more structurally
directed.

[694] Jones, Arthur R., Jr., and Lee Taylor. "Differential Recruitment of Female
     Professionals: A Case Study of Clergywomen." In *The Professional Woman*,
     edited by Athena Theodore, 355-362. Cambridge, MA: Schenkman, 1971.
This early descriptive and exploratory study of women clergy uses data from an availability sample
of 61 women ministers to examine two conditions necessary for entry into any profession, *viz.*, the
presence of appropriate space for new and/or distinctive members within a given occupation, and
the presence of normative patterns that either "encourage or discourage" those entries. Overall,
with respect to these and other questions, Jones and Taylor found that among their sample
members: (1) most came from homes in which both parents were active church participants and in
which the early life of the sample members was religiously nurtured; (2) call experiences were
gradual and life-long rather than sudden and dramatic; and (3) approximately two-thirds of the
sample had to accommodate their long term vocational goals by spending extended periods of time
(and in some cases years) in a related charitable or other church-based work setting while awaiting
specific ministerial placement. In contrast, however, the remaining one third of the sample *did*
move directly into their chosen ministerial professions directly after their theological education. For
more comprehensive studies on this topic, see Lehman's early work on clergywomen placements
and his discussions of lay and organizational resistance to women clergy.

[695] Lehman, Edward. *Project S.W.I.M.: A Study of Women in Ministry.* Valley Forge, PA: Task Force on Women in Ministry of the American Baptist Churches, 1979.

This "study of women in ministry" is the first of Lehman's numerous studies on women clergy. It is based upon data collected from various American Baptist samples (American Baptist laity, female and male clergy, female and male seminary seniors, executive and area ministers, pulpit committee representatives and American Baptist lay women), and its purpose is to ascertain the various factors associated with the placement of women (and men) clergy in local congregations. Similarly, it seeks to identify factors associated with a resistance to such placement. Among his findings, Lehman notes that: (1) it is males rather than females who will experience greatest acceptance and least resistance; (2) it is older, divorced (or widowed) female clergy *not using* the denomination's placement structure who are least likely to receive placement; (3) there is the tendency (in spite of the resistance to women clergy) for individual pulpit committee members (and area ministers) to be largely accepting of women clergy on *an individual basis* (although that sense of acceptance is garnished with clear gender related preferences relative to certain ministerial tasks); and (4) there are obvious time and salary lags women clergy experience when compared to male clergy of the same status. As a result of this study, Lehman developed numerous more formalized hypotheses involving both these early Baptist samples, and then later, Presbyterian and British Anglican samples. As with all of Lehman's research, this study is clearly written, attentive to the questions and sensitivities of theological and non-statistical readers, and as a beginning study of women in ministry, a model of exploratory and ground breaking analysis. For his later work, see [707].

[696] Wallace, Ruth A. "Bringing Women In: Marginality in the Churches." *Sociological Analysis* 36 (1975): 291-303.

Following Simmel and Durkheim, sociologist Wallace describes female marginality as the circumstance of women who live at the boundaries of two worlds. The first is society's expectations of women for home and female dominated occupations; the second is that of the "male dominated world," in this case, "decision making or leadership positions in the Christian churches." Wallace notes the "change agent possibilities" of such marginality and by the use of anecdotal, historical and Census data through 1970 (cf. Bock, [692]), she details three types of marginality: *marginals in preparation* (those professionally prepared for but barred from ordained ministry--principally Roman Catholics); *marginals in transition* (women ordained but denied full entry to the ministry--at the time of her article "The Philadelphia Eleven") and *marginals in the profession* (those functioning in ordained ministry, but mindful of its sexism, seeking its change). The problems and circumstances faced by each group are described as are potential strategies for responding to and dealing with such problems.

2. Recent Clergywomen Research

a. Clergywomen Recruitment, Socialization and Placement

[697] Charlton, Joy. "Women in Seminary: A Review of Current Social Science Research." *Review of Religious Research* 28 (1987): 305-318.

As abstracted by the author [p.305]...The number and proportion of women in seminary are increasing tremendously. Yet current social science research reveals that the career choice process takes longer and is more difficult for women than for men, with women dealing with issues such as the lack of role models and personal discouragement. Personality patterns of women and men in seminary are similar, though some may be perceived as more aggressive than parishioners think they should be. Seminary environments are changing; the proportion of women on the seminary faculties is slowly growing, more courses and interest groups for women are available. The research on the experience of women in seminary, however, is contradictory. Some studies suggest that women's experiences have generally been positive, other research has found substantial dissatisfaction. Issues of legitimacy and feminism are clearly important, but significant research questions regarding integration, transformation, family, the profession and gender theory are yet to be answered. **NOTE:** See [658] for references to Charlton's recent work.

[698] Kleinman, Sherryl. "Women in Seminary: Dilemmas of Professional Socialization." *Sociology of Education* 57 (1984): 210-219.

Using participant observation, recorded interviews and field notes from a sample of fifteen female and fifteen male seminarians and a small number of faculty and administration at a midwestern, Methodist seminary, the author explores the hypothesis that a humanistically based ideology of egalitarianism both serves and *dis*-serves the professional socialization of women seminarians. According to Kleinman, this ideology works in the short run to provide a theological rationale for women entering into ministry (since *"all* [women and men alike] are called by God"), but it nonetheless masks three potential problems women seminarians and clergy in all likelihood will face. Problem #1 is the inevitable status conflict to which clergywomen will be vulnerable in local congregations, since parishioners do not hold egalitarian perspectives, but rather traditional ministerial expectations concerning the gender, expertise and [gendered] authority of clergy. Problem #2 is the difficulty in combating sexist language and/or attitudes, because the egalitarianism of the humanistic ideology requires tolerance of all genuinely different perceptions, but it does not provide criteria for assessing various perspectives. Problem #3 is an experience of "gender harassment," i.e., a questioning of the female seminarian's (or minister's) commitment to ministry, given the potential conflicts that may arise between the demands of ministry and those of marriage and family. For the last point, Kleinman argues that since female and male seminarians are *both* questioned by church committees about their current or future marital plans, women seminarians do not see any discriminatory patterns within the fact of the questioning. Rather, they feel they are being treated "equally" with male students. The humanistic ideology, however, deflects attention from the social realities of: (1) dual career marriages; (2) the continued nurturing expectations for women in wife/mother roles; and (3) the propensity of male church committee members to yet view women's marital and family roles as detriments to full professional involvement and ministerial commitment. Thus, the egalitarian ideology masks potentially discriminatory behavior from the view of women seminarians. NOTE: For an early and yet engaging theoretical discussion of the structural double-bind society generates for married professional women, see Rose Laub Coser and Gerald Rokoff, "Women in the Occupational World: Social Disruption and Conflict" in *The Family: Its Structures and Functions*, edited by Rose Laub Coser , 490-511. New York: St. Martin's Press, 1974. Additionally, see the entries in this chapter, but particularly Scanzoni [731] and Nesbitt [723].

[699] Larson, Ellis L., and James M. Shopshire. "A Profile of Contemporary Seminarians." *Theological Education* 24 (1988): 10-136.
This issue length study presents a descriptive survey of students preparing for their Master of Divinity degrees in American mainline denominations, with the authors focusing particularly on the experience and expectations of older, second career seminarians. The data stem from mailed questionnaires completed by 2,696 seminarians representing 49 accredited institutions, and the variables of age (30-39, 40 and up), sex, and denomination (Protestant, Catholic) are used to delineate (among other things) respondents' patterns of vocational choice, seminary selection, marital status, perceptions and evaluations of their seminary education, financial needs, debt levels, theological orientation, and first and subsequent call expectations. While not directed specifically to the study of women seminarians, the discussion necessarily presents gender comparisons on all reported variables. The study is geared to a general theological readership and its more than 50 data tables are clearly described. Methodological and sampling issues are reserved for appendix discussion together with the study questionnaire and a listing of the participating institutions. In all, 28 principal findings are presented and among the more salient findings are those dealing with race, gender and student finances, and theological orientation and attitudes towards social change. A bibliography (largely from applied theological sources) closes the report.

[700] Lehman, Edward. "Placement of Men and Women in the Ministry." *Review of Religious Research* 22 (1980): 18-40.
Using data from a sample of 214 male and female graduates of the American Baptist Church, Lehman examines two sets of factors that can affect a beginning minister's likelihood of successful ministerial placement. Set #1 entails "socialization" variables; these include the candidate's GPA, degree track, theological orientation, expectations about inclusive language, SES background and marital status, all variables tied to the assumption that individual achievement will engender successful placement. Set #2 entails structurally based variables such as the candidate's use of the church/seminary's placement system, letters of reference, contacts with area executives etc. These latter variables are tied to the assumption that it is the institution qua institution that allots placement to candidates or that one's placement is grounded in organizational process rather than individual achievements (the socialization model). Variables correlating with successful placements indicate that the two sets of variables work differently for women and men, with men benefiting from the natural like outcomes associated with the socialization model and women the organizational reality of the structural mode. A regression analysis confirmed this finding and in his discussion Lehman considers three implications of his data: (1) that women students have a need to use the placement system to gain the legitimacy they lack by virtue of cultural assumptions tied to ministry as a male

occupation; (2) that because of such cultural assumptions women need advocacy on the part of denominational advocates more so than men; and (3) that the factors affecting women's placement (i.e., use of denominational structures) are to some extent within women's control and can be productively engaged. For subsequent expanded work by Lehman, see his various entries in this chapter.

[701] Nesbitt, Paula D. "Dual Ordination Tracks: Differential Benefits and Costs For Men and Women Clergy." *Sociology of Religion* 54 (1993): 13-30.
Using career history data from samples of Episcopal (n=1018) and Universalist Unitarian (n=140) female and male clergy ordained between 1950 and 1985, Nesbitt first documents the rise of two ordination tracks: "a primary ordination track," i.e., an M.Div. program directed to the traditional role(s) of congregational ministry and church leadership; and a more recently developed secondary ordination track, *viz.*, the permanent diaconate within the Episcopal church and a paralleling religious educational ministry within the Universalist Unitarian community. Nesbitt then examines the career outcomes for her sample members educated within such tracks, and she notes gender differences that occur within but not across denominations: (a) a distinct sex segregation by track, with "feminization" clearly occurring in the secondary tracks; and (b) the presence of "more negative occupational effects" for women within the newer tracks, than for "males holding the traditionally normative ordained status of their denomination" (p. 24). Nesbitt discusses her data in terms of several important considerations, including the various structural and ideological functions such dual tracking can serve. That her findings hold for such diverse denominations is important, and she spells out implications for other churches developing dual ordination tracks (e.g., the UMC and the ELCA). Some readers may find statistical portions of this article difficult, but its discussion is readable and important to researchers and theologians alike. **NOTE**: For further work by Nesbitt, see ([661], [717] and [723]) and see her full text, *Feminization of the Clergy in America: Occupational and Organizational Perspectives.* [Oxford Univ. Press, 1997], where the wider implications of dual tracking are fully detailed.

[702] O'Neill, Joseph, and Richard T. Murphy. "Changing Age and Gender Profiles Among Entering Seminary Students: 1975-1989." *Ministry Research Notes: An ETS Occasional Report.* Princeton, NJ: Educational Testing Service, 1991.
Using data from a number of archival sources and cognizant of the methodological difficulties attached to the amassing of 80,000 non-uniformly collected data records on Jewish and Christian seminarians nationwide, the authors have nonetheless combined such records to examine several characteristics of the American seminary population evident in the period 1975-1989. This report is the first of several promised as forthcoming, and its primary emphases address the experiences of women seminarians and the emergence of second career students in seminaries. For women, selected study findings include the following: First, the number of women entering seminaries has increased five-fold during the period 1972-1987, with women students generally scoring significantly higher than male students on GREs, but still facing resistance in parish placement processes. Second, women have more varied marital backgrounds than do men, in that men are almost always married and women are more likely to either have never married or (in one in four cases among older women) to have experienced divorce. Third, women leave seminary with significantly higher debt loads than do men. Other findings include descriptions of the pre-seminary career and educational experiences of seminarians 30 years and older (i.e., "second career" students), selected findings for specific non-denominational divinity schools, and policy implications for pension funding that arise out of the changed age-profile of contemporary seminarians.

[703] Schrenkengost, George E. "The Effect of Latent Racist, Ethnic and Sexual Biases on Placement." *Review of Religious Research* 28 (1987): 351-366.
Drawn from the author's 1983 doctoral dissertation data, this study examines the impact of latent racial, ethnic, and gender biases on clergy placement within a twelve district-wide area of the United Methodist Church in the North Central section of the United States. An eight page questionnaire requesting several types of data was completed by a "general" sample of laity (N=933) and clergy (N=208) stratified by both gender and race/ethnicity. Of particular research interest were ten vignettes presenting hypothetical candidate data, with respondents asked to indicate their level of support for each of the ten candidates. Findings based on frequency tables, regression analysis and (an unclearly presented) factor analysis suggest both *support* for non-traditional candidates *and* patterns of latent bias, with white laity preferences still ordered in terms of (1) white males, (2) women [race/ethnicity unspecified] and (3) candidates whose race or ethic background is different from those of congregation members. Although these findings suggest the

impact of latent biases, the author notes that the candidate characteristics presented in the vignettes explain less than 5% of the variation in receptivity scores. A better indicator says, Schrenkengost, is church attendance. In his general sample "less frequent" attenders are more receptive to non-traditional candidates, although in churches served by women, those who participate *least* "were far less supportive" and "were much more negative than others in rating ethnic minority or female vignettes" when visitation was the desired pastoral priority. (p. 357). Schrenkengost does not speculate on these or other findings he cites from the ten data tables he presents in his article. Rather, he presents his findings, comments on the difficulties of 'in-house' research [he is a United Methodist minister], and lets sit several potentially important findings: e.g., potential race/gender interaction effects and the fact that of all the potentially latent biases involving women in the vignette data, divorce was stronger than gender, race or age. (See Table 7, p. 359.)

[704] Taylor, Marvin. "Trends in Seminary Enrollment." In *Yearbook of American and Canadian Churches 1984*, edited by Constant H. Jaquet, 270-272. Nashville: Abingdon, 1985.
Six data tables (drawn from institutionally reported data published through the Association of Theological Schools in the United States and Canada [ATS]) provide Taylor with descriptive materials for discussing trends in seminary enrollment for the years 1977-1983. Data include annual figures for "Autumn Enrollments of ATS Memberships--1977-1983," "Comparisons of Total and Full-time Equivalencies" and annual figures and percentage increases for women, Black, Hispanic and Pacific-Asian American students. All four of these last mentioned groups evidence regular and steady annual percentage increases within the total seminary population for the period 1972-1983, although year-to-year figures indicate decreases among women, Black and Hispanic groups for the late 1970s and early 1980s, with data for the Pacific/Asian-American group too sparse to permit generalizations.

b. Lay Attitudes of Resistance and Receptivity

[705] Jelen, Ted. "Weaker Vessels and Helpmeets: Gender Role Stereotypes and Attitudes toward Female Ordination." *Social Science Quarterly* 70 (1989): 579-585.
Using data from the NORC General Social Survey (GSS) for 1986, Jelen examines the several possibilities concerning two religious/gender stereotypes of women, *viz.*, a "weaker vessel" stereotype indicating women's inferiority to men and, second, a "helpmeet" stereotype indicating women's inequality to men, but not necessarily their inferiority. For research questions Jelen asks whether these stereotypes are empirically distinct and if so, which better predicts opposition to women's ordination across various denominational respondents (i.e., Catholic, Evangelical, and Moderate and Liberal Protestants). Data from a factor analysis of 14 GSS items indicate the presence of the two distinct stereotypes, and subsequent analysis indicates that, overall, it is the "weaker vessel" stereotype that better predicts opposition to women's ordination. The exception, however, is among Roman Catholic males, for whom the 'helpmeet' stereotype predicts opposition. Jelen suggests the possibility that a theological doctrine underlies this difference. In particular, he suggests that Catholic teaching about Mary may influence Catholic male expectations of females as religious leaders, such that while women may not be viewed as incapable of ministry, they may be viewed as doing ministry in a distinct sphere--a kind of theological separate but equal context of service. While some readers may see uncritical and ambiguous assumptions in Jelen's description of the two stereotypes, his analytic strategy is sound: it asks how specific role stereotypes may be *differently sexist,* and by extension, how they may (or may not) work for specific feminist theological goals.

[706] Lehman, Edward. "Patterns of Lay Resistance to Women in Ministry." *Sociological Analysis* 41(1980): 317-338.
The data for this study are drawn from the laity sample (N=424) of Lehman's clergywomen study for the American Baptist churches (ABC) [695]. Here Lehman seeks to examine both the extent to which laity of the ABC are receptive (or resistant) to women clergy and the factors associated with such receptivity/resistance. Receptivity is conceptualized in terms of three distinct dimensions: a perceptual dimension (the tendency to stereotype), an evaluative dimension (the preference for a male or female clergy relative to specified tasks), and a behavioral dimension (a willingness to discriminate against a female candidate for pastor). Generally speaking, lay receptivity is multidimensional and differences in lay receptivity are ordered by four sets of factors. First are differences in laypersons' theological preferences, with theological conservatives being more resistant and liberals more receptive. Second are personal traits commonly associated with prejudice in general; that is, persons who are older, who have little formal education and who are

not married tend to hold the largest number of stereotypes of clergywomen and tend to prefer men in most aspects of ministry. Third are the reference group "orientations" of the lay respondents, with laity reflecting their reference group perceptions of clergywomen candidates as either a positive or negative force for the church, regardless of their own personal opinion. Finally, church structural characteristics are a fourth factor. According to Lehman, "problem churches" (i.e., those with low membership and budget problems) are more likely to call a woman than a man, whereas "healthy" churches (i.e., those with both strong memberships and budgets etc.) are more likely to call a man than a woman. NOTE: See also [709] and [712].

[707] Lehman, Edward. *Women Clergy: Breaking Through Gender Barriers*. New Brunswick, NJ: Transaction, 1985.
This text synthesizes Lehman's clergywomen research through the early 1980s (see the articles in this portion of the bibliography), and it remains as both the grounding introduction to his work and its umbrella overview as well. It is an exceptionally clear text, in that its theoretical and empirical discussions are directed to lay readers' needs without sacrificing analytical rigor, and its chapter length discussions of resistance/receptivity, congregational stability, placement issues and the like are a model in applied research that seeks to communicate clearly and meaningfully to a non-technical audience. Additionally, its overall themes and concerns serve as Lehman's own baseline for his subsequent British and Australian research (cf. [713]), while his brief and annotated bibliographies at the close of each chapter serve to introduce the beginning student to the key literature grounding his research. In sum, it is, together with Carroll, Hargrove and Lummis [657], one of the key introductory sources to clergywomen research and an initial baseline for subsequent theoretical developments, e.g., Nesbitt's work ([661], [701], [717] and [723]) andSimon and Nadell's work contrasting clergywomen and women rabbis [719]).

[708] Lehman, Edward. "The Local/Cosmopolitan Dichotomy and Acceptance of Women Clergy: A Replication and Extension of Roof." *Journal for the Scientific Study of Religion* 25 (1986): 461-482.
Using data from his British clergywomen sample ([713]), Lehman first refined the local-cosmopolitan dichotomy as developed by Roof and then tested its power to predict receptivity to women in the four denominations examined in his British study. By way of specifics, Lehman first re-examined Roof's discussion of localism to identify two empirically distinct dimensions to this concept: a diffuse cultural dimension indicating a loyalty to *ideas and things* local (as contrasted with ideas and things extra-local) and a social-structural dimension indicating a commitment to a specific geographic *locale*, i.e., a group or place structurally similar to that of an identifiable and concrete reference group. Second, Lehman identified a religious parallel to the cultural localist dimension, a phenomenon he dubbed ecclesiological localism, with its defining emphasis being that of a commitment to local churches generally rather than to one's denomination or "wider programs dealing with world problems." Third, Lehman hypothesized the possibility of a direct effect between religious involvement and sexist attitudes, as contrasted with the potentially spurious involvement/consequences association suggested by Roof. Last, Lehman operationalized his discussion in terms of Roof's general path model to test the effects of all localist variables and religious involvement as predictors of sexist attitudes towards women clergy. Weak but significant zero-order correlations supported both religious involvement and all dimensions of the localist orientation as predictors of religious sexism, but the path analysis indicated that of these four variables, only religious involvement, cultural localism and ecclesiological localism held direct effects for sexism, while social localism (and various demographic variables) worked through cultural and ecclesiological localism to affect sexism. These findings suggest the empirical independence of the cultural and social localist orientations and the non-spurious impact of religious involvement on [sexist] attitudes towards women clergy. A follow-up study ("Localism and Sexism: A Replication and Extension." *Social Science Quarterly* 71 (1990): 184-195) confirmed these findings and identified a fourth (albeit awkwardly described) dimension of the localist orientation, *viz.*, a *social* ecclesiological localist orientation, or a congregationally specific loyalty, as contrasted with the more diffuse and culturally directed commitments of the ecclesiological localism identified in the *JSSR* study.

[709] Lehman, Edward. "Sexism, Organizational Maintenance and Localism: A Research Note." *Sociological Analysis* 48 (1987): 274-282.
Using mailed questionnaire data collected in 1984 from a sample of 1,414 British laity from four denominations (the Baptist Union, the Church of England, the Methodist Church, and the United Reform Church), Lehman tested the possibility that his previous findings on religious sexism and organizational maintenance were spurious and were, in reality, an artifact of the "local" orientation.

The British data both supported his previous findings (i.e., that religious sexism or resistance to having women clergy is related positively to members' sense that such a circumstance would constitute an organizational threat to the local congregation) and suggested that this relationship holds even when controls for localism are introduced. Lehman concludes that "organizational maintenance" and "localism" operate independently of each other, and that they "are best conceived of as separate conceptual spaces when considering modes of explaining differences in religious sexism" (p. 280). NOTE: The article appendix presents measures and reliability coefficients (alphas) for the variables of sexism, organizational threat, cultural, social, and ecclesiological localisms.

[710] Lehman, Edward. "Research on Lay Church Members' Attitudes Toward Women in Ministry: An Assessment." *Review of Religious Research* 28 (1987): 319-329.
As abstracted by the author... (p. 319) "This essay presents a review of empirical research into the receptivity lay church members display toward women clergy. The evidence to date indicates that receptivity to women in ministry has characteristics similar to attitudes toward other objects. Receptivity can be differentiated into at least three dimensions--perceptions, affect and motivations to act. These dimensions vary widely among lay church members, although the overall tendency is to be more accepting than rejecting of clergywomen. These variations are associated with other member attributes, e.g., level of sexism in general, traditional religious involvement, type of church and community, and cultural localism. After contact with women ministers, especially contact in-role, the level of receptivity tends to increase, as does the cognitive complexity of the attitude structure. While these patterns appear to recur in various studies, there is yet much we do not know about certain denominational groups and from perspectives other than sociology."

[711] Royle, Marjorie H. "Women Pastors: What Happens After Placement?" *Review of Religious Research* 24 (1982): 116-126.
This study is premised on the assumption that a congregation's dissatisfaction with the sex/gender of its new minister will be reflected in both giving and membership patterns during (at least) the first year of that minister's leadership, and that if satisfaction or acceptance of the minister occurs, losses will begin to decrease after the first year. Hence the study tests three hypotheses: first, a test for gender-based marginality (as evidenced by the disproportionate placement of women in small and financially troubled congregations); second and third, tests for the decline and then reversal of membership levels and financial giving following the first year of the new minister's placement. The data for the study include gender comparisons for women and men entering ministry since 1970 and serving in parishes through 1978, and the denominations from which the data are culled include Disciples of Christ, the Lutheran Church in America (now a part of the Evangelical Lutheran Church in America following a 1986 merger with two other Lutheran bodies) and the United Presbyterian Church. With the exception of data from the Lutheran subsample, Royle finds little evidence to support the idea that membership and giving will decline with the placement of women clergy, and she concludes that "incorporation of large numbers of women [into parishes] will be relatively smooth" (p. 12). By way of background this study was the first to test the 'contact' hypothesis in terms of clergy sex, membership and giving levels, and it should be followed with a study of Lehman's work that expands the contact theory to a number of additional variables. Additionally, the reader should consult the *Yearbook of American and Canadian Churches* for financial data on churches during the '80s and early '90s.

c. Organizational Resistance to Women in Ministry

[712] Lehman, Edward. "Organizational Resistance to Women in Ministry." *Sociological Analysis* 42 (1981): 101-118.
Drawing from data collected for his study of women in ministry for the American Baptist Churches [695]--including samples from denominational and area executives (n=117), clergywomen (n=94), clergy*men* (n=120) pulpit committee representatives (N=98) and a national sample of laity (n=424)--Lehman assesses the plausibility of an organizational maintenance norm as a framework for interpreting clergywomen placement in local churches. In all subsamples, this norm is upheld when individuals are faced with the choices of either (a) discriminating against women candidates-- as indicated by attitudinal but not behavioral measures, or (b) maintaining a commitment to local church viability. Lehman concludes that "where the values of organizational viability and equal opportunity for clergywomen are experienced as being in conflict, church members and officials will tend to act more to protect organizational viability than to comply with denominational policy concerning placement of clergywomen" (p. 116). Data for male and female national and ABC seminary enrollments for the years 1970-1971 and 1979-1980 indicating drops for men and rises

for women support this conclusion, and Lehman notes that seminaries have also opted for organizational maintenance even though the net or unintended result has been "…to help create the 'clergywomen problem' in the first place" (p. 116).

[713] Lehman, Edward. *Women Clergy in England: Sexism, Modern Consciousness and Church Visibility*. Lewiston, NY: Edward Mellen Press, 1987.
Edward Lehman is widely known for his research on both "lay…" and "organizational resistance" to women in ordained ministries (and alternatively, lay and organizational "receptivity" to women clergy), and his text here examines both, but now with English questionnaire data drawn from laity samples from four British denominations: The Baptist Union (n=360), The Church of England (n=347), The Methodist Church(n=349), and The United Reformed Church (n=358). Overall, this study extends Lehman's general portfolio of research concerns: (1) an assessment of lay attitudes toward women clergy in terms of cognitive, feeling and behavioral dimensions; (2) an analysis of the social and denomination factors affecting the acceptance and integration of women into the professional ministry; (3) an examination of the "local/cosmopolitan dimension" as applied to churches and their ecclesial cultures; (4) the impact of sexism on attitudes of receptivity and resistance to women clergy; and (5) the differential effects of sexism and "organizational maintenance" in the integration of women into the ministry profession. What distinguishes this study, however, are three things: its theoretical location in the framework of secularization theory and the application of this framework to English churches and the history of the women's ordination movement in The UK, and, last, Lehman's own background and subsequent ability to compare British and American data. Among his findings are the following: that (1) the laity of his samples generally accept women clergy, but with clear variations in the *cognitive* (tendency to stereotype), *feeling* (gender preferences for particular clergy roles or tasks), and *behavioral* (willingness to discriminate) dimensions of resistance/receptivity; and (2) that the leadership of the local minister of respondents' own churches was the single most important predictor of lay attitudes, with other factors such as level of traditional religious involvement, attachment to modern consciousness and motivation to protect the local congregation serving to explain variations in degrees of resistance/receptivity to women clergy. Thus, members with "narrow and provincial *Weltanschauungen*" were more sexist than those with broad and cosmopolitan world views" (p. 185), and congregations with "growing memberships" and budgets ahead of inflation were more likely to be resistant to women in ministry than those that are financially marginal, since the former had the resources to pick and choose leadership, while the latter did not (p. 186). In sum, Lehman found that as a set of attitudes, religious sexism worked within the cultural frames of sample members, i.e., "their specific subcultures and world views, [their] religious commitments and denominational identification, the kind of congregations they participate in and the ways in which they relate to their local church" (p. 187). NOTE: For Lehman's additional clergywomen research beyond the American setting, see his *Women in Ministry: Receptivity and Resistance* [Melbourne: The Joint Board of Christian Education, 1994], which, according to Nesbitt [*Review of Religious Research* 37 (1996): 184-185], extends the questions and strategies of his previous research to the Anglican and Uniting Churches in Australia, and finds patterns of receptivity and resistance similar to those of his earlier American and British samples.

[714] Nason-Clark, Nancy. "Ordaining Women as Priests: Religious vs. Sexist Explanations for Clerical Attitudes." *Sociological Analysis* 48 (1987): 259-273.
Using both questionnaire and interview data from a sample (n=284) of Anglican deacons, Anglican clergymen and their wives, Nason-Clark examined both theological and sex role variables to determine which more strongly predicted resistance to the ordination of women within the Church of England. While her several theological measures indicated a clear correlation between religious conservatism and resistance to women's ordination, her regression analysis of theological and sex role measures tapping support for wider social roles for women indicated that the latter were generally a stronger predictor of resistance to women's ordination. That is, clergymen who were opposed to women's ordination scored lower on the "appropriate roles for women scale," (indicating opposition to wider roles for women), while clergymen in favor of women's ordination scored higher--indicating support for wider roles for women. Similarly, as reported by Nason-Clark from previous related research, "personal and family characteristics such as age, marital status, education…[and others]…were not associated with specific opinions on the priesthood of women," but they were related to "whether or not an individual was restrictive or egalitarian in their sex role beliefs" (p. 269). Nason-Clark concluded, therefore, that the opinions of priests and their wives towards women's ordination were more strongly related to their opinions about the rights and responsibilities of women generally, but that religious variables provided a framework for rationalizing resistance to women's ordination.

d. Clergywomen and the Ministry Profession

[715] Lehman, Edward C. Jr. "Gender and Ministry Style: Things Not What They Seem." *Sociology of Religion* 54 (1993): 1-11.

This article is Lehman's 1992 Presidential Address to the Association for the Sociology of Religion, and it summarizes the key findings of his longer, book length discussion, *Gender and Work: the Case of the Clergy* [Albany: SUNY Press, 1993]. In both discussions Lehman examines nine dimensions of ministry to test the proposition that sex (or gender) predicts specific differences in the ways women and men minister. His findings indicate that sex differences exist on four of the nine dimensions, but that these differences emerge only when one controls for race/ethnicity, seminary cohort, and type of placement. A subsequent discussion then interprets both the findings and the frameworks generating them through the phenomenological philosophy of Alfred Schutz who distinguishes between social and scientific levels of discourse, i.e., first and second order constructs, and their corresponding types of validity. In brief, Lehman suggests four things: First, that much sex difference clergywomen research has, perhaps, been the test of first order constructs (propositions that function to legitimate women clergy), rather than the test of second order constructs (propositions that seek explanations of first order constructs). Second, he suggests that this explains why so many expected empirical differences turn out not to exist. Third, he cites recent feminist theory to argue that if there is a chance that strategic based discussions are detracting from the institutional equality of female and male clergy, then perhaps "antagonists will want to reconsider the importance of the entire discussion" (p. 10). Lehman's work here is subtle and requires close reading for its full appreciation. And, while it exhibits nuances with which one might well quibble, its discussion of 'first' and 'second order constructs' is valid, and it beckons a dialogue on the ways in which feminist theory might enhance the sociology of women clergy research. NOTE: Lehman's tested dimensions (with each having respective "masculine" and "feminine" possibilities) include: (1) "willingness to use coercive power," (2) "striving to empower congregations," (3) "desire for formal authority," (4) "desire for rational structure," (5) "ethical legalism," (6) "general interpersonal style," (7) "orientation to preaching" (8) "criteria of clergy status," and (9) "involvement in social issues."

[716] Nason-Clark, Nancy. "Are Women Changing the Image of Ministry? A Comparison of British and American Realities." *Review of Religious Research* 28 (1987): 330-340.

Working with findings drawn from both her own research on women clergy in England [714] and several American studies of women in ministry (e.g., Carroll, Hargrove and Lummis [657] and Lehman's early research), Nason-Clark provides a readable, benchmark summary of the main differences between (American and British) women and men clergy as of the early and mid-1980s. In particular, she notes that female and male clergy differ in terms of personal characteristics (e.g., marital status), the factors drawing them into ministry, the costs and benefits of their work in ministry and the types of obstacles women (but not men) face as they enter into and work within ministry. Overall, she concludes that (1) women *are* changing the face of the profession--largely through a more collegial/collaborative and personalized pattern of ministerial leadership--in spite of less support for entering, less financial compensation, and greater demands on their time and energy; but that, (2) women yet face strong obstacles to their desire and opportunity to minister within the church, i.e., structural obstacles within various sectors of the Christian community (e.g., Catholicism's continued official resistance to women's ordination); issues surrounding clergywomen placement, lay and clergy resistance to women in ministry, and last, "the traditional symbolism and liturgy of the church defined in exclusively masculine terms" (p. 338).

[717] Nesbitt, Paula D. "First- and Second-Career Clergy: Influences of Age and Gender on the Career-Stage Paradigm." *Journal for the Scientific Study of Religion* 34 (1995): 152-171.

Using data from Episcopal (n=1373) and Unitarian Universalist (n=196) clergy samples, Nesbitt examined factors affecting the upward mobility and career attainment of female and male clergy to test four hypotheses developed from the traditional career-stage paradigm with its five stages of *preparation, entry level positions, attainment, maintenance* and *decline*. Her analyses paid particular attention to the changing age, gender and work histories of the clergy population (i.e., the facts that seminarians *are* older at entrance and ordination, are often second career candidates, and typically include more and older women). Her hypotheses included the expectations that "upward occupational mobility and attainment of male clergy should be negatively sensitive to age;" (2) "second career clergy ordained over age 45 should experience limited attainment compared to those ordained younger;" (3) "men ordained by age 30 should experience the greatest amount of occupation advance;" and (4) "women clergy should display fewer age related effects than men, as a result of the suppressing effect of gender on their career trajectory." Several multivariate analyses confirm her hypotheses (see pp. 106-107 for her detailed results), and her data strongly support her overall conclusions that the traditional paradigm is inherently biased against women, and that while second career males can expect moderate attainment, positions of denominational influence are and will remain populated by men who (a) were socialized occupationally during their early years and (b) tend to hold "less positive attitudes toward non-traditional entrants," e.g., women and second career males. Nesbitt predicts future "occupational and organization" tensions in the light of these continuing demographic patterns. **NOTE**: Also by Nesbitt are [661], [701], and [723].

[718] Royle, Marjorie H. "Using Bifocals to Overcome Blindspots: The Impact of Women on the Military and the Ministry." *Review of Religious Research* 28 (1987): 341-350.

This article does two things. First, it clearly summarizes three areas of conflict that surface as women enter and achieve critical mass in both the military and the ministry. Second, it describes several organizational processes that also come to light as these conflict areas (or "blindspots") become visible. Royle begins by describing the decade of progress women have made in each institutional sphere. She then describes subsequent but previously overlooked areas of conflict in each institutional sphere: (1) the conflicting assumptions attached to both gender and work vis a vis each institution--that is, males have careers to which they owe 'on call' loyalty, but as women have entered the ministry and the military, family and parenting commitments have forced a modification of the professional role as an all consuming sphere; (2) the replacement of the traditionally male-centered "two person career" [729] with that of a "dual career" couple/family and its attendant placement and labor lost needs; and (3) the differences between generalists and specialists within each sphere, with questions of status, comparable worth, and promotion figuring most prominently. As a result of these now visible blindspots, typically unseen illustrations of various organizational processes have also emerged, with the latter including (a) the recognition of bureaucratic structures that facilitate equal professional opportunities; (b) new examples of the equipotentiality of means (ways of circumventing bureaucracies); and (c) examples of how structure and polity and theology and group rhetoric can serve to integrate women into these heretofore exclusively male worlds. To close, Royle notes the ongoing need for critical mass and organizational sponsorship as factors crucial to the integration of women into male dominant professions, and she identifies one last blindspot: the "pleasantness factor," the possibility that because men discover they *like* having women within the organization, they may admit but not advance women within the organization. **NOTE**: For related literature see Katzenstein [107] and [285].

[719] Simon, Rita J., Angela J. Scanlan, and Pamela S. Nadell. "Rabbis and Ministers: Women of the Book and the Cloth." *Sociology of Religion* 54 (1993): 65-82.

Using data from an availability sample of 35 women rabbis and 25 mainline Protestant women clergy, the authors survey characteristics of women's religious leadership across Jewish and Christian traditions. Their discussion is descriptive and focuses on the personal backgrounds, current professional roles and long term expectations of both the rabbis and the ministers, and the authors find extensive similarities across the samples with respect to background and leadership style characteristics, including the fact that the respondents from both groups see themselves as more 'relational' and/or more 'nurturing' than males in their profession. Important differences do, however, exist: the rabbis are younger than the clergywomen; they have more pragmatic than spiritual reasons for selecting their profession; they are more likely to preach about justice and women's issues (as contrasted with specifically "spiritual" or individualized issues); and last, the female rabbis see themselves as having a professional role unique from that of male rabbis ten years hence while the ministerial sample members see female and male experiences of ministry moving to a convergence within ten years. This is an important discussion. It contributes to the study of gender and religious leadership across Jewish and Christian traditions, and it identifies baseline questions needing empirical and systematic study. **NOTE**: See Cowan [892] on women rabbis and sexual harassment, and see the "Research Note" by Simon and Nadell, "In the Same Voice: Or Is It Different? Gender and the Clergy?" *Sociology of Religion* 56 (1995): 63-70.

[720] Stevens, Lesley. "Different Voice/Different Voices: Anglican Women in Ministry." *Review of Religious Research* 30 (1989): 262-275.

Using both anecdotal and quantitative data from a questionnaire survey of Canadian Anglican clergywomen (N=108), Stevens first illustrates the relational and interpersonal qualities of Gilligan's [different voice] "ethic of care" and then points up significant differences between radical and non-radical sample members. A final point of Stevens' discussion then considers selected pastoral and research implications of these radical/non-radical differences. An important factor in Gilligan's discussion is that women and men are socialized differently. Thus men are socialized towards accountability and institutional justice and women towards relationality and interpersonal care. Stevens does not present data on the early socialization experiences of sample members, but their reported experiences of discrimination imply at least a difference in *professional* socialization experiences. This point is implied, however, not stated, and comparable male data are lacking. To distinguish radicals from non-radicals, Stevens classifies respondents in terms of their responses to a 20 item radicalism scale with subsequent tests for age, education, location, and type of work differences. These tests (presumably 'chi-squares') indicate that radicals are younger than non-radicals, more educated, located in urban rather than non-urban settings and functioning in non-parish work settings. With respect to scale items, radicals differ from non-radicals in several areas, but primarily on sexual ethics items, with radicals more likely to support the pro-choice position on abortion and civil and human rights for gay and lesbian persons both within and beyond the church, including ordination. Radicals and non-radicals do not differ on peace and economic justice issues and Stevens notes the pastoral and research implications of this point: It provides potential links between the personal and political domains (a weakness in Gilligan's discussion) and it widens the notion of the unchurched to marginal groups, an audience radicals seek to serve. Stevens' article is both readable and provocative. Its anecdotal data provide a fresh expression of many clergywomen's experience, but the heavy anecdotal emphasis together with the lack of comparable male data limit the study. For additional material seethe entries in Section III-5 on Feminist Ethics.

NOTE: See the literature on "Womanism and Ministry" in Section IV-2 (and particularly Carpenter [644]), and see Lincoln and Mamiya [141] in Section I.

e. Clergywomen and Clergy Marriage

[721] Deming, Laura, and Jack Stubbs. "The Two-Career Marriage: Implications for Ministry." *Word and World* 4 (1984): 173-181.
This article contrasts the contemporary experience of female clergy spouses with the traditional expectations of the role, "minister's wife," to indicate (1) the conflicts inherent in the newly emerging female clergy spouse role and (2) a series of practical suggestions for handling such conflicts. The traditional image of the "minister's wife" is sketched from Leonard Sweet's *The Minister's Wife: Her Role in 19th Century America* (Philadelphia: Temple, 1983) which identifies four minister's wife roles--those of 'companion,' 'sacrificer,' 'assistant' and 'partner,' and the authors examine each as it may be affected by the condition of a full-time career on the part of a contemporary female clergy spouse. Several areas of conflicting parishioner/spouse role expectations are identified, and strategies concerning housework, meal preparation, church involvement, commuter marriage possibilities and spousal fidelity are offered. Although their discussion is supported by anecdotal data only, this essay is provocative in terms of the assumptions it evidences concerning the changing structure of the ministry profession itself. In particular, what defines the female clergy spouse's contemporary role is not support for the individual ministry of her husband (the grounding of the traditional minister's wife role), but rather, an affirmation of her own role as a lay person who supports church work generally and *through this* her husband's ministry. Thus, from a sociological perspective, this article evidences the decline of the two-person career model of ministry [729] and its secularization as a two-career marriage. Additional discussion evidences the ambiguity present within an assumption of "gender complementarity" as the basis of clergy marriage generally, and the idea of a the "minister's wife" role as itself a specific vocation.

[722] McKiernan-Allen, Linda, and Ronald J. Allen. "Colleagues in Marriage and Ministry." In *Woman Ministers: How Women Are Redefining Traditional Roles*, edited by Judith Weidman, 169-182. San Francisco: Harper & Row, 1981.
This article is a helpful summary of the person-role boundary issues facing clergy couples who serve in the same congregation. Although limited to anecdotal data, it illuminates many of the structural and reference group problems clergy couple members face, and it includes their tactical strategies for overcoming such problems. It provides a brief--and from a feminist perspective--provocative description of how clergy couples may be legitimated theologically (cf. p. 181), and it points up the difficulties faced by couple members when one feels the necessity for a new and different type of call. The literature on clergy couples is sparse but recently emerging. See, e.g., Scanzoni [731]; see relevant passages in Carroll, Hargrove and Lummis [657]; see Nesbitt [723] and see bibliography cited in Zikmund, Lmmis and Chang [663]. Also, for an older, more

conventional approach to the topic of clergy couples, see Roy Oswald, *Married to the Minister: Dilemmas, Conflicts and Joys in the Role of the Clergy Wife*. Washington, D.C.: Alban Institute, 1980 (not reviewed here); see Richard Goodling and Cheryl Smith ["Clergy Divorce: A Survey of Issues and Emerging Ecclesiastical Structures." *Journal of Pastoral Care* 37 (1983): 277-291] for an overview of the ministerial literature on clergy divorce published through the early '80s, and see E. M. Rallings and David J. Pratto, *Two Clergy Marriages: A Special Case of Dual Careers*. Lanham, MD: Univ. Press of America, 1984.

[723] Nesbitt, Paula D. "Marriage, Parenthood and the Ministry: Differential Effects of Marriage and Family on Male and Female Clergy Careers." *Sociology of Religion* 56 (1995): 397-416.
Using data from a sample of 974 male and 399 female Episcopal clergy whose careers were coded in terms of entry, mid-level and senior positions, Nesbitt examined the effects of marriage and family on career mobility for women and men clergy, as based on the conventionally understood assumptions about marriage and family within traditional clergy roles. Namely, that: (1) marriage and children would have direct effects for male upward mobility and attainment; (2) single women clergy "would have more full-time employment and higher occupational attainment" when controls for age and entry placement were used; (3) the presence of children would inversely affect full-time work and attainment for women; and (4) gender differences in occupational attainment would be more significant than differences attributed to marriage and family (p. 401). Expectation #1 was confirmed for marriage and children helped male career mobility, but not female mobility. Second and third, marital status and children had no effect on the full time employment of women clergy ("single women with no children were as likely as married women with children to work part time... and the presence of children had no effect on work status for women priests in any placement tested" (p. 404). Last, gender outweighed both marriage and children in predicting occupational attainment, with effects clearly present for men and not women. Nesbitt's research is substantive, detailed and ground breaking, and her conclusions are clear: "...the two most important resources for male clergy attainment... are their gender attribution and their having a wife--resources to which women clergy categorically cannot have access" (p. 412). Her discussion considers implications for denominations addressing issues of both celibacy *and* clergy marriage.

3. Related Studies

[724] Berk, Marc. "Pluralistic Theory and Church Policy Positions on Racial and Sexual Equality." *Sociological Analysis* 39 (1978): 338-350.
Using data from a sample of seventy denominations (with memberships made up of 85% of recorded church members in 1974), Berk examined the "influence of pluralistic theory in explaining church policy positions on racial and sexual equality." (From the author's abstract, p. 338.) Berk expected that--like political parties with heterogeneous memberships--large denominations, too, would be more likely to adopt moderate, non-extremist positions than would smaller denominations with more homogenized memberships. Thus he tested the hypothesis that size affects the type of denominational policy adopted [i.e., 'discriminatory,' 'no position,' 'liberal,' or 'activist'], with the variable size used in the absence of specific measures for heterogeneity of membership. Berk found no support for the pluralist theory. Rather, large churches were more likely than small churches to adopt extremist positions, whether discriminatory or activist. To explain this unanticipated finding, Berk tested two additional hypotheses: (1) large churches are more likely to have apathetic members and (2) churches with apathetic memberships will be more likely to adopt extremist positions. Per capita contributions were used as the measure of apathy. Both hypotheses were confirmed. The discussion was developed in the light of Michels' "iron law of oligarchy" (i.e., that an organization's few leaders *will* become insulated from the rank and file), and introducing the control variable of organizational structure [hierarchical vs. democratic] did not change the results. Both apathy and structure are thereby suggested as factors in the development of churches' extremist and non-extremist positions on racial and sexual equality.

[725] Eagly, Alice H., and Blair T. Johnson. "Gender and Leadership Style: A Meta-Analysis." *Psychological Bulletin* 108 (1990): 233-256.
This study examines 370 organizational and other studies to test the assumption that individuals socialized for and occupying similar leadership roles will not differ in their leadership styles and thus not exhibit the stereotypical assumptions of [female] interpersonal vs. [male] task oriented emphases often presumed about such roles. The hypothesis is, overall, confirmed, but the authors also find evidence of gender differences among individuals not socialized for leadership roles, but yet functioning within them: e.g., the tendency across various settings for women to exhibit more

democratic styles while males exhibit more autocratic styles. The authors discuss their findings in terms of role theory, tokenism and gender spillover in male dominant organizations. They conclude with nuanced suggestions for revisions in both management and organizational theory, and they suggest subsequent research on different styles and leadership effectiveness. This is an excellent review of the literature on gender and leadership style, but it is unquestionably directed to a social scientific rather than theological readership.

[726] Hartley, Shirley F., and Mary G. Taylor. "Religious Beliefs of Clergy Wives."
    Review of Religious Research 19 (1977): 63-73.
Using questionnaire data based on a modified version of the Glock and Stark "orthodoxy" index and obtained from a sample of 448 women married to clergy working in six mainline denominations, Hartley and Taylor examined both the distribution and correlates of liberal and conservative theological orientations among their sample members. Their principal findings included the predictable differences in liberal and conservative orientations as based on the respondent's current denominational affiliation, level of education, and participation in church or home-based religious activities. In contrast, age, region, and degree of church involvement in one's family of origin were not related to liberal and conservative orientations. An additional line of investigation examined the relationship between the respondent's theological orientation and sense of personal fulfillment as coming through her husband's ministry and work, and here Hartley and Taylor found that "traditional" (rather than "least traditional") beliefs did predict. Likewise, through Chi-square analysis, the authors found that traditional beliefs were significantly related to the idea that the minister's wife should have a calling to that status, but only moderately so (Spearman's r=.239). The follow-up study by Hartley ["Marital Satisfaction Among Clergy Wives." *Review of Religious Research* 19 (1978): 178-191] examines correlates of marital satisfaction and finds that while traditional beliefs do not predict satisfaction, the clergy wife's fulfillment through her husband's work does (Spearman's r=.224). Other significant but weak associations are noted, and Hartley's reflections on the data are almost more interesting than the study itself, given both of its own time period *and* the current literature on clergy sexual harassment. (See also Chapter 22).

[727] Hearn, Jeff, Deborah L. Sheppard, Peta Tancred-Sheriff, and Gibson Burrell, eds.
    The Sexuality of Organization. Newbury Park, CA: Sage, 1989.
An important feature in feminist sociology is the study of gender in formal organizations: e.g., the ways in which organizations use stereo-typical understandings of gender both to maintain superordinate and subordinate relations between men and women and/or the ways in which organizations ignore gender on the assumption that organizations are "gender neutral" or task efficiency oriented. (Cf. e.g., Acker in Lorber and Farrell [92].) In contrast to these perspectives, this volume explores the sexuality of *organization* per se, where the latter is itself the concept under scrutiny and understood as a process and not a series of discrete bureaucratic entities. Additionally, the discussion is undertaken by a group authorship made up of feminist [women] sociologists and pro-feminist male sociologists. This is a cutting edge work, and several of its chapter length discussions evidence this point. For example, its theoretical introduction sets the volume squarely in opposition to the standard study of organizations as agencies of production; rather, this text examines the concept of organization itself and this from within the triad of gender, sexuality and power. Second, the text includes a full literature review of standard organizational theory from within the context of gender and sexuality. Third, several chapters examine "sexuality in the work place" both in terms of its construction and differential consequences vis a vis women, men, sexual harassment and discrimination; (4) additional chapters examine "male dominance" in a variety of settings and specifically in terms of its consequences for both women and men; last, the volume evidences an important attention (and two full chapters) to sexuality and organization and these relative to traditional assumptions about sexuality and "public and private spheres." This last is particularly strong, with a chapter length discussion of the implications of disclosure for lesbians in the work place. Readers will find this volume stimulating and provocative, both for what it says and implies, and especially with respect to understanding gender, sexuality and power in the 'organization' of ministry. An extended bibliography and general index close the volume. **NOTE:** For related literature, see Smith [114].

[728] Kanter, Rosabeth Moss. "Some Effects of Proportions on Group Life: Skewed Sex
    Ratios and Responses to Token Women." *American Journal of Sociology* 82
    (1977): 965-990.
This study is a classical source for much of the early research on women clergy, with its theoretical framework continuing as a source of insight for majority/minority interaction. Kanter identifies three major interactive patterns associated with the presence of "tokens" in an organization, i.e., the

presence of group members who are in all ways like other group members, save for one specific, identifying "master" or overriding social status (e.g., gender) or, alternatively, a distinctive characteristic salient within the larger group (e.g., blindness among sighted individuals). Various perception dynamics associated with this significant characteristic highlight the individual's difference from the group and thus define the potentials available to "dominants" (other group members) for handling such difference(s). These perceptual phenomenon include: heightened *visibility*, with its subsequent performance pressures for the token to overachieve; *polarization*, or the heightening of differences between the token and the dominants, with specific consequences for token/dominant group boundaries (e.g., isolation and loyalty tests); and *assimilation*, or the circumstance of stereotyping, i.e., the token's "attributes are distorted to fit pre-existing generalizations about their social type" (p. 471). Kanter develops her argument in terms of the effects of relative proportions of individuals in groups, with tokens constituting individuals capturing not more than 15% of a group membership. Illustrations are from the experiences of women in corporations and are applicable generally to the study of women clergy. Also by Kanter (but not abstracted here) are her two related, early organizational studies: *Men and Women of the Corporation* (NY: Basic Books, 1977) and *The Change Masters* (NY: Touchstone, 1983).

[729] Papanek, Hannah. "Men, Women and Work: Reflections on the Two-Person Career." *American Journal of Sociology* 78 (1973): 852-872.
In this essay Papanek describes several "aspects of American women's 'vicarious achievement' through their husbands' jobs in a special combination of roles" that Papanek describes as the "two-person single career," or more simply, the "two-person career" (p. 852). This role combination involves the assumption that a husband's employing institution that the use of his wife's time and energies are "neither important nor productive in the economic sense of the term" (and thus they may be used to serve the husband's career [p. 856]), and it involves further, the wife's socialization to such vicarious achievement through her self-definition as an auxiliary. Thus in this role combination the wife achieves vicariously by serving her husband's career *socially* (as is the case with the diplomat's wife), *emotionally* (the military officer's wife) and/or *occupationally* (e.g., the faculty member or small businessman's wife). Papanek notes that there is a structural ambivalence in each of these cases, as the wife must perform her unpaid role skillfully--but not in a manner that surpasses the image of her husband before his peers. Thus Papanek notes the social control functions of this role combination: on the one hand it offers the wife vicarious achievement through quasi-occupational efforts and the security of family achievement. On the other, it aids the husband's status, competitive and professional edge relative to his peers and competitors. Cross-cultural implications for social change, ideology and conflict are also drawn out.

[730] Shriver, Peggy, Ann DuBoise, Suzanne Hyatt and Holly Bean. "Reactions to Women in Ministry Research." *Review of Religious Research* 28 (1987): 377-394.
This round-table like discussion provides feedback on clergywomen research to social scientist researchers who participated in the joint meeting of the Religious Research Association, the Society for the Scientific Study of Religion [SSSR] and the National Council of Churches' Commission on Women in Ministry [CoWim], held in Savannah, Georgia, in October, 1987. The presenters voice several concerns: e.g., the need for adequate sampling (as based on updated church ordination records); the desire to discuss clergy and laity policy implications of clergywomen research data; the need to tap yet unidentified historical and anecdotal data; and last, the need for respondent privacy and confidentiality--all of which are needs consistently addressed by women clergy researchers.

[731] Scanzoni, John. "Resolution of Conjugal-Occupational Conflict in Clergy Marriages." *Journal of Marriage and Family* 27 (1965): 396-402.
This study suggests that it is theologically *liberal* rather than theologically *conservative* clergy who are likely to perceive the competing time demands of clergy and family roles. Using data from a sample of 31 clergymen and their wives--couples classified as either "church-like" (i.e., liberal) or "sect-like" (i.e., conservative) in theological orientation, Scanzoni tested the hypothesis that the "...church-like clergyman [sic] would consider it more legitimate to give greater priority to conjugal roles than would his [sic] sect-like counterpart." Although tested on a small--and as regards clergy--an exclusively male sample, the hypothesis was confirmed: when faced with the conflicting time demands of clergy and family roles, clergy of a church-like or liberal theological orientation tended to let some clergy roles go unfulfilled so that time could be spent in the fulfillment of conjugal or familial roles. Alternatively, sect-like or conservative clergy tended to respond to clergy roles only, with family needs subordinated to those of ministry. NOTE: See also [722] and the literature cited there, especially [633].

[732] Stackhouse, John G., Jr. "Women in Public Ministry in 20th-century Canadian and
     American Evangelicalism: Five Models." *Studies in Religion* 17 (1988): 471-485.
After noting the three criteria by which evangelicals typically are socially and religiously identified
(i.e., commitments to biblical authority, literal exegesis, and the "straightforward application" of
biblical text(s) to faith and practice), Stackhouse identifies five models from which evangelicals
have traditionally understood "opportunities for women in public ministry." The first is that of the
"invisible majority," where women effectively practice no public ministry--at least in terms of
having authority over males within the church--although Stackhouse notes the exceptional case of
teaching in mixed Sunday School groups. At the opposite end of his typology is Model #5--that of
"equal partners in ministry," as based upon the assumption that "God gifts people for public
ministry without regard to sex." Models #2, #3 and #4 fall between these extremes. Model #2 is
the "missionary exception," (which permits women authority until indigenous male leadership can
arise) and Model #3 is the "parachurch parenthesis," or such evangelical organizations as the
Intervarsity Christian Fellowship. Last, Model #4 is the "under authority" arrangement that most
closely parallels Christian patriarchal marriage as defined by such biblical passages as I Cor. 11:3,
Eph. 5:22-24 and I Tim. 2:12. Stackhouse closes by noting the forces pulling adherents away from
such models, including (among others) the observed success of many women working in the
context of Model #5.

19

Feminism and Women's Religious Leadership in American Catholicism

This chapter surveys literature on feminism and women's leadership in American Catholicism. It locates that leadership within the wide contours of American Catholic experience since the Second Vatican Council (1962-1965), and it identifies three arenas of that leadership: the struggle of women to become ordained clergy within American Catholicism, the wider and more ecumencially based women-church movement within American Catholicism, and the variously framed organizational changes experienced by Catholic sisters (nuns) in the United States.

Overall, the social character of American Catholicism changed dramatically after the Vatican Council. First, As Hoge's research [740] suggests, American Catholics were ripe for the loosening of institutional boundaries brought about by Vatican II. Catholics were no longer ethnic enclaves only, but democratized and pluralized in their thinking and social milieux. Second, as Ebaugh [737] and contributors to Bianchi and Ruether [733] point out, the process of "revitalization" borne of the Council was theologically generated and grounded in a "People of God" ecclesiology. Hence it was and pluriform in outcome. Third, as both sociological (cf. D'Antonio [734-735], D'Antonio et al. [736], Gallup [739] and various theological sources, e.g., Swidler and O'Brien [744]) indicate, lay Catholics have assumed postures independent of unsupportive clerical leadership, and they are not likely to return to earlier patterns. Fourth and finally, as numerous other sources indicate (e.g., Lummis and Stokes [742], Ruether [743], Murphy [750], Yeaman [751] and most Catholic authors in this entire bibliography), the contemporary posture of many Catholic women is in the direction of social justice activities and spiritualities that complement Catholic heritage. These elements of ecclesisal change cut across the Catholic population, and are reflected in both the literatures of women seeking ordination and those experiencing a wider more women-church experience. Moreover, the emphasis on justice-based spiritually is a key feature of women in vowed communities, despite their aging memberships and declining numbers. (Cf. Neal [799] and Turner and Quinonez [800].

In the literature of this chapter everal sources stand out as quintessential statements of Catholic feminist faith. Among these are Ruether [759], Schneiders [761], Zanotti [752], LaCugna [780], Neu [795] and the Neal and Turner-Quinonez works noted above. A strong current in American feminist theology, the sources here should be read with those by Catholic authors in Section II. Addtionally, see [765] and the closing paragraph of p. 83.

A. General and Introductory Works

1. The Sociology of Contemporary American Catholicism

[733] Bianchi, Eugene, and Rosemary Radford Ruether, eds. *A Democratic Catholic Church: The Reconstruction of Roman Catholicism.* New York: Crossroad, 1993.
The papers collected here are intended to challenge the statement that "the church is not a democracy" by challenging the two key assumptions upon which it rests: Namely, that the church has always had a centralized, monarchical and hierarchical structure of authority, and that this form

of government was given to the church by Christ. The latter is an especially important point of discussion the editors argue, for it goes beyond the "merely" academic level and reaches into the experience (and thereby life possibilities) of Catholics everywhere. Among the volume's many contributors are feminist New Testament scholar, E. Schüssler Fiorenza, who demonstrates the biblical practice of local, egalitarian and congregational (rather than episcopal) governance; canonist John Beal who helpfully identifies several structures of church law available for democratic Catholic experience; Catholic moral theologian, Charles Curran, who advocates applying Catholic teachings on subsidiarity and justice to the church itself; Jesuit sociologist, John Coleman, who argues "Not Democracy But Democratization;" and sociologist, Marie Augusta Neal, who in [799] details democratization among American women religious. Other contributors include Hans Kung, Walter Goddijn, Phillip Berryman, Pedro A. Ribeiro De Oliveira, Jay Dolan, E. Dale Dunlap, and Bianchi and Ruether who detail the historical and theological grounds for *participation, conciliarity, pluralism, accountability*, and *dialogue* as the principles of democratization within "the church."

[734] D'Antonio, William V. "Autonomy and Community: Indicators of Change Among the American Catholic Laity." *Proceedings of the Canon Law Society of America* 54 (1992): 1-24.
This paper summarizes data from several sources (including those mentioned in [733] above) to indicate (1) the increasing degrees of personal autonomy typical of many Catholic laity since Vatican II and the publication of *Humanae Vitae* and (2) the phenomenon of "small faith communities" currently operating both within and beyond formal church organizational boundaries. D'Antonio argues persuasively that the data pose important questions for Roman Catholic episcopal leadership, both in terms of the extent to which such leadership can expect compliance with traditional church norms and expectations, and the ways in which church leadership may--and may need to--interact with small faith groups as voluntaristic associations, because the latter are reforming the church from the ground up. Supporting data tables are highly readable, and the discussion is directed to non-technical readers, with data analyses broken down in terms of "weekly," "occasional" and "seldom/never" mass attendance, age and sex groups, and a variety of attitudinal items on Catholicism's difficult and currently controversial topics (e.g., women's ordination, various definitions of Catholic identity, condoms and AIDS prevention, divorce and abortion, issues of sexuality) and the authority of the bishops for defining such.

[735] D'Antonio, William V. "Autonomy and Democracy in an Autocratic Organization: The Case of the Roman Catholic Church." *Sociology of Religion* 55 (1994): 379-398.
This 1993 Presidential address to the Association for the Sociology of Religion repeats several findings indicated in [734], but from a more formal sociological perspective. The discussion draws from several sources (historical and archival data, theological literature, various Gallup polls, and D'Antonio's own participant observation in small faith communities) to demonstrate the central premise that "...there is evidence of an emerging pluralism within the Church to accompany a personal autonomy already well documented" (p. 379). Measures of commitment to Roman Catholicism and laity responses to several items marking new (and widened) parameters of Catholic belief and practice all suggest that D'Antonio's premise is accurate, with traditional formal organizational assumptions of 'hierarchy' now genuinely challenged by more laterally directed patterns of lay interaction. Among the kinds of indicators tapped by D'Antonio are behaviors and attitudes which increasingly challenge the traditional definition of what a "good Catholic" is, as well as beliefs about who has the moral authority (church leaders? individuals? both?) to decide what is right and wrong. Finally, his data on lay attitudes towards democratic structures in the Church, along with such phenomena as Small Base Church Communities and priestless parishes all support the widened perspectives he describes, and they lend detailed credibility to his overall thesis.

[736] D'Antonio, William V., James D. Davidson, Dean R.Hoge, and Ruth A. Wallace. *American Catholic Laity in a Changing Church.* Kansas City, MO: Sheed and Ward, 1989.
Since its assimilation into the world of main-line denominations at the close of the Second Vatican Council in December, 1965, American Catholicism has publicly struggled with several issues implicit in that assimilation process: the role of individual conscience in Catholic identity, the scope (and perceived relevance) of Roman ecclesiastical authority, the organizational problem of declining personnel resources (both in terms of priests and female religious) and the changing perceptions of laity as to the indicators of Catholic identity and church/tradition commitment. In this work, which synthesizes several sources of survey data--but principally the data from a 1987 nationwide Gallup poll, the authors chart the scope of these assimilation based concerns. The persistent issue

throughout their study is that of American *Catholicism's changing perception of Church authority and the varying commitments that laity have to that authority.* The authors' conclusions highlight their eight chapter length discussions as they indicate that "the ethos of American society seems to have combined with the teachings of Vatican II to encourage greater person autonomy...[and]...laity are...[no longer]...willing to allow hierarchy to define good Catholics by traditional standards of sexual marital conduct" (p. 187). The authors suggest the necessity of a "pattern of leadership...[that is]...open, tolerant and flexible" (p. 188), and they examine future scenarios of church life given the current status of American laity and the rising numbers of Hispanic Americans now entering the American church. This is an extremely readable and informative text that addresses several issues important to both Catholic and Protestant feminist theologians, and it should be required reading by all. For an update of much of its data see the "Special Gallup Supplement" to *The National Catholic Reporter,* October 8, 1993. Additionally, see D'Antonio's 1995 article in *The Washington Post,* "Outlook" section, "A Long Way from Rome: Why U.S. Catholics Stray from the Pope's Teachings," April 9, 1995, pp. C1-C2.

[737] Ebaugh, Helen Rose Fuchs. "The Revitalization Movement in the Catholic Church: The Institutional Dilemma of Power." *Sociological Analysis* 52 (1991): 1-12.
The first "dogmatic constitution" proclaimed by the Second Vatican Council was *Lumen Gentium,* the dogmatic constitution on "the Church." It was proclaimed on 9/21/64, and it described "the Church" as the "People of God," or a body of believers bound by faith and extending beyond the confines of juridical organization only; that is, beyond the pre-Vatican II notion of the church as a hierarchical system. This central point constitutes the axis of concern around which Ebaugh focuses her 1990 Presidential Address to the Association for the Study of Religion. Thus, in this address she identifies the "dilemma" of power engendered by the expectations and unanticipated consequences of this document: (1) the perception by laity that religion was privatized in nature rather than organizational only; (2) the emergence (and especially in America) of "selective Catholicism" or the fact that Roman Catholics were becoming more discriminating in terms of their loyalties and affiliative involvements; (3) an emphasis on religion as an ethnic and cultural reality--a resource for living rather than an institutional affiliation; and (4) a "revitalization of traditional values by means of social support groups within the [local] church." Ebaugh focuses her discussion in terms of resource mobilization theory and she describes several examples of these "people of God" outcomes. Her discussion is cogent, clear, and easily readable by theological audiences. For a more detailed discussion of several aspects of Ebaugh's main thesis, see D'Antonio et al. [736]. Alternatively for an analysis of Vatican II's impact as based upon assimilation rather than conciliar teaching, see Hoge [740]. Last, for an alternative take on "revitalization" within Catholicism, see Porterfield [149].

[738] Fox, Thomas C. *Catholicism on the Web.* New York: MIS Press, 1997.
This is a valuable resource for staying current with Catholic organizational, lay and professional concerns (whether theological, historical, feminist, social or clerical), and while it is not an immediate study in the sociology of American Catholicism, it well represents what the writer of its back cover blurb notes. Namely, that the "...Web is enlarging and doubtless will continue to enlarge the very notion of the "Catholic Community" in ways we are just beginning to imagine." Fox is the editor and associate publisher of the award winning *National Catholic Reporter,* an American Catholic weekly initiated after the Vatican Council and still presenting clear, honest reporting on all issues of importance to American Catholics. His text here, then, is one drawn from a bedrock of sources and it provides an annotated listing of literally hundreds of web sites organized around eighteen topics reflecting Catholic organization, ideas, activism and transcendence. By way of illustration, the section on "Catholic Ideas" includes chapter length listings of [Catholic] History, Teachings, Education, Communications and Information. Also included are a appendix of "On Line Directories" and a clear and thorough index. While much here will interest neither feminists nor sociologists, *much will,* as URLs for libraries and bibliographic sources are clearly listed and helpfully described.

[739] "Gallup Survey of U.S. Roman Catholics." *The Gallup Poll Monthly* no. 335, (August, 1993): 21-40.
This study presents data from a national sample of adult (American) Roman Catholics (N=788) interviewed by phone August 3 though August 5, 1993. The article presents frequency distributions for 28 items addressing various aspects of Catholic beliefs, attitudes and practice, with additional tables indicating breakouts for several subgroups and various elements of trend data as drawn from past and current survey items. Moreover, virtually all variables are displayed by age groups. Important and controversial topics addressed in this survey include women priests and

married clergy, parishioner satisfaction with various aspects of the Church teaching and organizational life, respondent definitions of what makes a "good Catholic," respondent perceptions of conflict between church teaching and personal behavior, items on Catholic schools and education, the importance of religion to respondents, parishioner sermon expectations, and in a final section, six items on pedophilia within Catholicism. These last items present important descriptive data on: (a) the extent to which respondents feel that sexual abuse by priests is "widespread..." (48% think so, 45% do not and 7% have no opinion); (b) whether the Church "has done a good job or a bad job in handling the problem..." (35% say "good job," 53% say "bad job" and 12% have "no opinion"); (c) whether the church is "more concerned with its own image than in handling the problem..." (64% say "own image," 26% say "solving problems," and 10% have "no opinion"); (d) whether parishioners are "willing to accept [a rehabilitated priest] as their parish priest" (35% are "willing," 58% are not and 7% have "no opinion"); (e) whether respondents have "ever known anyone who has been sexually abused by a priest" (7% have, 93% have not); and (f) whether respondents have "ever been sexually abused by a priest" (1% say "yes," 99% say "no"). **NOTE:** See D'Antonio [734] above, and see the canonical literature in Section VI.

[740] Hoge, Dean R. "Interpreting Change in American Catholicism: The River and the Floodgate." *Review of Religious Research* 27 (1986): 289-299.
Using the image of a dam opened wide, and through which much stored up water can suddenly rush, Hoge examines the impact of the Vatican Council and its teachings when--transported to the United States--they functioned as a dam opened wide and through which the stored up effects of assimilation could rush in on American Catholic life. Hoge's discussion focuses less on the specific teachings of Vatican II and more on the bottled up receptivity awaiting it, namely, the pressures of assimilation that were being built up among American Catholics from the 1950s onward: *viz.*, a greater social and political tolerance for Catholics (as evident from the 1960 presidential election of JFK); the rising levels of education and income among Catholics during the sixties, and the attainment of income parity with Protestants in the 1970s; a subsequent convergence with Protestants on several social and political issues; and a readied anticipation among women religious (cf. Kohlmer [805]) working in Catholic educational and social institutions. Hoge's point is simple: In contrast to arguments suggesting the Council pushed American Catholicism in either a good or bad direction (depending upon one's point of view), it is more that the teachings "sold themselves" to an educated and change-comfortable audience; one already assimilated into the general assumptions of American culture, and thus amenable to religious/church change. A second portion of the essay contrasts Catholic and Protestant membership levels through the 1980s.

[741] Hoge, Dean R. *The Future of Catholic Leadership: Responses to the Priest Shortage.* Kansas City, MO: Sheed and Ward, 1987.
Using archival data and data from a variety of different surveys, Hoge examines the priest and membership trends of American Catholicism from pre-conciliar years to the mid-1980s, with projections for 2000 and beyond. His data are solid and based on numerous college student surveys he has previously undertaken, together with two sets of trend data--one for adult Catholic laity and the other for priests, with each involving then new (i.e., 1985) data designed to re-examine previously collected, NORC developed items. Hoge's findings are clear: there is a priest shortage nationwide, but yet to be felt in the "priest-rich" Northeast. By way of solution(s) Hoge offers several strategies grouped into four types. These are "options" which, respectively: (a) "reduce the need for priests;" (b) "get more priests, with existing eligibility criteria;" (c) "get more priests, with broadened eligibility criteria;" and (d) "expand the diaconate and lay ministries." Among the many features included in this study are: (1) Hoge's comparison of the priesthood problem with leadership issues in the military (and specifically, the U.S. Navy, a chapter authored by retired Lt. Com. Barbara Williams); (2) his strong analysis of celibacy as *the* major problem in priest recruitment efforts; and (3) Hoge's acknowledged bias for the "practical" and "political" elements of church change. **NOTE:** For related literature, see Katzenstein [107]. Also, see Richard A Schoenherr and Lawrence A. Young, *Full Pews Empty Altars: Demographics of the Priest Shortage in United States Catholic Dioceses.* [The University of Wisconsin Press, 1993].

[742] Lummis, Adair, and Allison Stokes. "Catholic Feminist Spirituality and Social Justice Actions." In *Research in the Social Scientific Study of Religion* 6 (1994): 103-138.
This article "addresses the question of the relationship between personal feminist spirituality and involvement in social justice activities among Catholic sisters and laywomen in comparison to women in other denominations" (p. 104). The authors draw their data from the larger Hartford study of women's spirituality [153], and by way of analysis they compare not only the

spirituality/justice involvements of Protestant and Catholic women, but Protestant lay and ordained women, Catholic lay and vowed women, and given a subsample of Hispanic women, Hispanic and non-Hispanic sisters and laywomen. Additional groups of comparison include ordained, liberal and 'unchurched,' and conservative lay Protestant women. Notable findings include: (1) women who espouse a feminist orientation are more likely to be active in social justice concerns; (2) Catholic sisters (including Hispanic sisters) are generally more feminist than Catholic laywomen (as are--in this sample--Protestant clergywomen more so than Protestant laywomen); and (3) for virtually all groups, membership in a spirituality group (as contrasted with no membership or membership in a traditional women's church group) is as important as personal feminist spirituality in predicting social justice involvements. Further analysis also indicates that "involvement in community outreach" generally and being a "joiner" of various groups are each major predictors of working for systemic change (p. 129). In turn, a closing discussion further specifies group differences on these additional predictors and the potentials of Hispanic women *leaders* for incorporating Hispanic Catholics within the American Catholic Church. This research is significant not only for its confirmation of much feminist theological work on spirituality and justice involvement, but also for its identification of the wide templates (*viz.,* community outreach and joiner activity) upon which feminist spirituality and involvement can build. Indeed, the traditional Catholic orientation to service for the "commonweal" finds nuanced grounding here, and it highlights the potential for Catholic feminist breadth in the US.

[743] Ruether, Rosemary Radford. *Contemporary Roman Catholicism: Crises and Challenges.* Kansas City, MO: Sheed and Ward, 1987.
This volume details three areas of challenge facing Roman Catholicism as it enters the 21st century. As described by Ruether, these are: (1) the challenges "posed by democratic values and human rights in the church's institutional life;" (2) "the demands of women for full participation in the church's ministry, and the crisis over the church's teachings on sexual morality;" and last, "the challenge of Third World liberation struggles and the Church's alignment with the poor in those struggles" (xvii). Ruether opens with an historical overview of Catholicism's post conciliar experience from 1965-1985. She then addresses each of these "challenges" in terms of contemporary culture and its impact on formal church teachings. A closing chapter examines options for liberal and left thinking Catholics who consider leaving Catholicism given the frustratingly slow and presently reactionary pattern of change in Catholic life. For the discussion of the "demands of women" see [759]. For Ruether's earlier article length discussion of these crises, see her, "Crises and Challenges of Catholicism Today," *America* 54 (March, 1986): 152-158.

[744] Swidler, Leonard, and Herbert O'Brien, eds. *A Catholic Bill of Rights.* Kansas City, MO: Sheed and Ward, 1988.
This collection of brief papers and introductory essays lists and expands upon 35 "rights" of Roman Catholics provided by the 1983 revision of the Code of Canon Law and synthesized here in concise detail by members of the *Association for Rights of Catholics in the Church* (ARCC). The contributors include systematic and pastoral theologians (e.g., Hans Kung, Rosemary Radford Ruether, & Margaret Brennan), canonists (James Coriden, Paul Golden), ethicists (Charles Curran, Paul Surlis) and a variety of others who, as members of the ARCC, write from the tradition of Catholic teaching on Human Rights to bring about "...substantive structural change in the Church...[including]...a collegial understanding of the church in which decision-making is shared and accountability is realized among Catholics of every kind and condition...[because of]...fundamental rights...are rooted in the humanity and baptism of all Catholics" (p. ix). This is a powerful and empowering text, with entries on conscience, access to information, sacraments, ministry, voluntary associations (the latter by Ruether), the training of church office holders, workers' rights, academic freedom, family planning, worship, and inclusive language to name but one third of the list. For sociologists, it identifies a culture often overlooked in assessments of change in Roman Catholicism since Vatican II. Additionally, for feminist and other theologians, it indicates the wide parameters of much feminist biblical and "women-church" vision.

NOTE: See also Katzenstein [107, 285] and O'Connor [921].

2. Gender and American Catholicism

[745] Ashe, Kaye, and Frank Morriss. "The Role of Women in the Catholic Church." *The Critic* 42, no. 2 (1990): 14-33.
This article is an extended 'point/counter-point' debate on the subject of women's ordination in Roman Catholicism. The debaters are authors Morriss (a conservative Catholic layman) and Ashe

(a theologically progressive Catholic nun), and although both debaters cite specific "authorities" (Morris: canon law and conciliar documents and Ashe contemporary Catholic theology and conciliar/post-conciliar emphases), the article is not intended as a scholarly piece. Rather, it reflects the polarization of Catholic thinking on women's ordination and the temperments that sustain it. The issues debated include: (1) the nature of authority and obedience (as perceived from within contrasting conservative and conciliar expectations); (2) the gratuitous nature of priestly and/or ministerial vocations (a point of agreement between the debaters); (3) the nature of religious leadership (as perceived from within contrasting clerical and communal perspectives); and (4) the nature of the church (as perceived from within hierarchical and egalitarian expectations). While not presented as an academic piece, the article quickly delivers both a feel for the topic and an immediate entree into the questions that so painfully divide many Catholics on this issue. It is readable and strongly recommended.

[746] Elizondo, Virgil, and Norbert Greinacher, eds. *Women in a Men's Church.* Edinburgh: T. & T. Clark, 1980.
As volume 134 of the *Concilium* series, this collection of essays examines a range of concerns related to gender in Roman Catholicism, with assessments of patriarchy and its effects assuming the central--but not sole--emphasis. In all, twelve authors examine a variety of topics the editors group into four generic categories such as "Historical Development," "Theological Perspectives" and the like. More accurately, the text presents such varying concerns as the development and entrenchment of (clerical) male dominance within Roman Catholicism (three entries); the scope and impact of feminist theology within Roman Catholicism (three entries); biblical images and assumptions about gender (two entries); Catholic sexual ethics (one entry); celibacy and gender (one entry); and last, gender and its role in social ethics (two entries). Worthy of particular mention are the entries by Nadine Foley and Marie Augusta Neal. Foley's discussion ("Celibacy in a Man's Church") highlights the ideological function of celibacy as a bulwark against positive perceptions of female sexuality. In turn, Neal's discussion is quintessential social ethics, providing first, an analysis of the ways in which religion (here Catholicism) "celebrates" first world privatizations rather than issues of peace and moral demography, and second, a clearly developed framework for moving in alternative directions. Also included is Catharina Halkes' bibliographic essay on feminist theology [215].

[747] Iadarola, Antoinette. "The American Catholic Bishops and Woman: From the Nineteenth Amendment to ERA." In *Women, Religion and Social Change*, edited by Yvonne Yazbeck Haddad and Ellison Banks Findly, 457-476. New York: SUNY Press, 1985.
This well detailed and stimulating essay traces the history of the American Catholic bishops' attitudes and involvements with women's rights from the suffragette movement of the 19th century to the death of the ERA in 1982. The author documents the 19th century American and traditional Roman Catholic natural law norms undergirding what she describes as the "pedestal Mary" image of women operative in 19th and early 20th century Catholic consciousness, and she counterpoints her discussion with an engaging overview of the ordination struggle of Catholic women from the 1960s through the early 1980s, when the National Council of Catholic Bishops (the NCCB) promised a pastoral on 'women in church and society.' This article is especially helpful for its ecclesiastical sources on women's ordination within Catholicism and it is strongly recommended. (Note: A first draft of "promised pastoral" was finally begun in 1988; it was sufficiently criticized by lay and religious women scholars that it was withdrawn. A second draft published in 1991 was also withdrawn, and a third draft was voted not to be released at the annual meeting of the NCCB in Washington, D.C., in November, 1992.) For related materials see the literature presented under 'canonical sources' and 'the present reality' and especially the discussions by Wallace [786, 787, 788]. Additionally, see the web sites listed by Fox [738].

[748] Getz, Lorine M. "Women Struggle for an American Catholic Identity." In *Women and Religion in America, Volume 3: 1900-1968, A Documentary History*, edited by Rosemary Radford Ruether and Rosemary Skinner, 175-222. San Francisco: Harper & Row, 1986.
This article complements Ewens [804] summary of the leadership activities of American nuns during the 19th century and should be read in conjunction with it. In brief, it is Getz's argument here that for the bulk of the 20th century, it is Catholic lay women (and not Catholic sisters) who take the lead in defining Catholic women's identity, for with: (1) the late 19th century arrival of a second wave of immigrants; (2) the development of Catholic schools as vehicles of institutional loyalty and membership retention; and (3) the 1917 Code of canon law, Catholic sisters were placed

in institutional settings which both removed them from engagement with the wider society and exhausted their energies on behalf of organizational and institutional self-maintenance. Alternatively, suggests Getz, but for the handful of sisters who generated institutions of higher learning (e.g., Sr. Madeleva), it was lay women who defined Catholic women's identity during the twentieth century, and this through their principal roles as factory workers, wives and mothers. Further, although their numbers were small, such lay activists as Mother Jones and Dorothy Day had enormous impact, suggests Getz, for they provided concrete aid to the fragmented poor of large cities and set precedents for communications networks and non-violent methods of social change. To close, Getz notes the two events completely unanticipated by Catholic women in the 1950s (i.e., the Second Vatican Council and the American Women's Movement), and she suggests that it is their coming together in the 1960s which has "...set the stage for a confrontation between Catholic women, both lay and religious, and the Vatican in the 1980s" (p. 181). Seventeen source documents evidencing Catholic lay women's labor involvement, social action and spirituality, and the activities of religious women in hospital, educational and foreign mission work support Getz's discussion.

[749] Kennelly, Karen, ed. *American Catholic Women: A Historical Exploration*. New York: Macmillan, 1989.
Published as Volume 6 of *Makers of the Catholic Community: The Bicentennial History of the Catholic Church in America Authorized by the National Conference of Catholic Bishops,* with Christopher J. Kauffman serving as General Editor, this volume, *American Catholic Women: A Historical Exploration,* surveys the contributions of Catholic women to the American Church in terms of seven independently developed chapter discussions. Editor Kennelly opens the volume with "Ideals of American Catholic Womanhood," which describes the educational commitments and teaching contributions of women's religious communities, and given the 19th century cult of domesticity, the ambivalence of Catholic women and Catholic bishops over the eventual struggle for women's rights. Mary Ewens then addresses "Women in the Convent" and traces the development of American women's religious communities. Colleen McDannell's entry focuses "Catholic Domesticity, 1860-1960" by pulling together various threads of American expansion: ethnic diversity, parish experiences, and familism and gender roles. In turn, "Catholic Women in the Labor Force, 1850-1950" by Mary J. Oates continues the ethnic emphasis and documents the presence of Catholic women in domestic work, theater and the arts, public education, Catholic college teaching and administration, the service professions of nursing and social work and the more male-dominated professions of medicine and law. Two essays deal with women and the political sphere: James Kenneally's "A Question of Equality" and Debra Campbell's "Reformers and Activists." Kenneally's piece focuses directly on the details of Catholic women for and against women's rights. The piece by Campbell surveys women's activities on behalf of social justice concerns with discussion ranging from the Temperance Movement to Dorothy Day and more contemporary figures. Finally, Rosemary Rader examines "Catholic Feminism: Its Impact on United States Catholic Women" [757] and finds (generally) the development of organized networks among women's religious communities and the now standard, classical works on feminism in Catholic theology, i.e., the writings of Mary Daly and Rosemary Radford Ruether. This is a readable and informative, but limited work. Its chief limitation is the absence of critical theoretical frameworks (whether from organizational theory, social movements theory, theology, feminism or women's studies) and thus, scholars seeking insights into the current conflicts of gender and church authority in late 20th century Catholicism will want to turn to such theological sources as Weaver [762], Riley [491], and Ruether [760] and such sociological sources as Neal [145, 146, 147], D'Antonio [734, 735] and Wallace [787], and the sociology/theology interdisciplinary work of Lummis and Stokes [742].

[750] Murphy, Margaret. *How Catholic Women Have Changed*. Kansas City, MO: Sheed and Ward, 1987.
This text presents the stories of more than three hundred Catholic women known to the author and surveyed by her through the use of a simple questionnaire surveying "reasons why Catholic women have changed."' Murphy neither pretends to nor intends statistical and sociological expertise (pp. 23-24), but in attempting to describe her own changing perceptions with Catholicism, she realized there must be others from her generation feeling the same things, and she sought to document this for herself. Her discussion portrays the experiences of white middle class, married Catholic women influenced by several factors, including Vatican II, personal friends and the women's movement, and concerned to make the church more responsive to women. Her journalistic style carries the reader easily over discussions of Catholic women's 'love-hate' relationship with the church, the religiously heightened awarenesses of Catholic laywomen and women religious, and a

host of other more "scientifically" documented observations, among which are the following. First, that sisters would have changed with or without Vatican II. Second, Catholic women (like other Catholic laity) prefer to think from their own consciences. Third, Catholic women can comfortably handle work and family obligations, as well as questions of value within society. And fourth, Catholic women are yet ambivalent about the women's movement which has done so much for them (and other women) in the decades contemporary to Vatican II and its impact.

[751] Yeaman, Patricia A. "Prophetic Voices: Differences Between Men and Women." *Review of Religious Research* 28 (1987): 367-377.
This paper utilizes the contrasting "justice/accountability" and "care/equity" emphases of the Kohlberg and Gilligan ethical frameworks to identify and interpret gender differences among members of an advocacy and change based Roman Catholic organization, the "Association for the Rights of Catholics in the Church" (ARCC, cf. [744]). The study data come from responses to three open-ended items taken from questionnaires mailed to an ARCC sample. The items of interest focus on members' "critiques of the institution," their "image of God" and their "visions of the future," with Yeaman's purpose being the identification of gender differences on these items. Because of a low response rate (25.4%), findings refer to sample members only, not the ARCC itself, and not the Catholic population at large. Generally speaking, Yeaman finds clear patterns of gender difference in the areas of God images and visions of the future, with women more likely than men to hold inclusive (i.e.,Gilligan-like) perspectives on both God and the future of the church. Findings on the item addressing "institutional critiques," however, are more nuanced. Both women and men critique the institutional reality of the church's hierarchy, but women are more likely than men to identify that hierarchy with patriarchy. Similarly, clergy and laity differ in their critique, with laity tending to include clergy *within* the hierarchy, and clergy seeing the hierarchy as distinct from themselves, i.e., beginning with the bishop level of church structure. Yeaman recognizes the tentativeness of her findings and calls for systematic, cross-cultural research. A cautionary note: this paper is generally well-written, but it contains several word processing errors. ALso, for additional sources on Gilligan, gender socialization and ethical thinking, see [480], [486], and [720].

[752] Zanotti, Barbara A., ed. *A Faith of One's Own: Explorations by Catholic Lesbians.* Trumansburg, NY: Crossing, 1986.
Five types of strength--each set in the manner of a beatitude--provide the framework and focus for this collection of 30 "explorations" by Catholic lesbian women. Of especial note is Mary Hunt's essay, "Loving Well Means Doing Justice," for it describes both her own development as a Catholic theologian and the emergence of the women-church movement. Moreover, it reflects the general purpose of the volume, which is to detail the faith of Catholic women who work *against* patriarchy and *for* "an affirmation which infuses existence with meaning and purpose" (p. xi). Thus, as editor Zanotti notes in her introduction (p. xiii), the Catholicism of these women is less that of the institutional church and more that of a "religious/cultural" background: more that of Catholicism's (American) immigrant church of the forties, fifties and early sixties, which blends a strength drawn from ethnic ties with the ability to resist (and perhaps redeem) an extreme authoritarian spirit and structure. This strength is vividly evident in each of these short (4-5 pages long) essays, and each is a powerful story of "the varieties of Catholic lesbian faith" (p. xi). Endnotes follow the essays, and a select bibliography and listing of Catholic feminist and lesbian organizations close the volume.

NOTE: For early related literature see Lee [180] and Patricca [182] in.

3 . Feminism and American Catholicism

[753] Aggeler, Maureen. *Mind Your Metaphors: A Critique of Language in the Bishops' Pastoral Letters on the Role of Women.* New York: Paulist, 1991.
This text presents an analysis of the principal metaphors and images used to describe women in twelve Catholic Bishops' Pastoral letters published between 1974 and 1987. It is a fascinating study, and while it was completed prior to the NCCB pastoral on "women and the church" [783] (and thus does not include the latter), it nonetheless provides an index of multiple insights into the workings of Catholic episcopal thinking concerning women, "the Church," "change," and the all too frequently underestimated 'power of one' [woman] to challenge the American hierarchy on behalf of all. Aggeler frames her analysis with a history of American Catholic women from the 19th century to Vatican II and then "from Vatican II until 1978." It is a brief, but helpful summary of gender and the hierarchy as based on several ecclesiastical documents, including those from

Vatican II. Aggeler's analysis then follows, as she examines the specific metaphors she finds in her selected documents. Overall, Aggeler organizes her discussion into four categories (Women and Culture, Women and the Church, Women and Men, and Conversion and Reconciliation), and for each she identifies the varying pastorals attached to issues of structure, bias, complimentarity, theological method and theological anthropology. Her closing appendices then list all metaphors by author and document. This is an excellent introduction to the episcopal assumptions attached to gender in American Catholicism, and its discussion can be adapted to Catholic lay and professional audiences, *and* other literatures on inclusivity.

[**754**] Chittister, Joan. *WomanStrength: Modern Church, Modern Women*. New York: Sheed and Ward, 1990.
This collection of sixteen essays, sermons, reflections and interviews by (and/or with) Catholic Benedictine Sister Joan Chittister is one of the clearest expressions of Catholic feminism currently in print, and particularly so, as grounded in the assumption of feminist spirituality as "justice seeking" spirituality. Moreover, the "justice" of Chittister's vision spans not only the Catholic hierarchy's need to let go of its clericalism on behalf of women's ordination, but as well, its need to let go of its clericalism on behalf of the world's poor women, their children and their families. And, as if this is not enough, Chittister's is a vision backed by the reach of her own peace making commitments, and the common cause she finds in traditions and literatures as distinct as the those by Dietrich Bonhoeffer, Sufi and Hasidic masters. None of these essays is easy reading; for the passion and dignity Chittister demands on behalf of women around the world is everywhere arresting: in her opening essay, "WomanStrength," which clears up any confusions Catholics or others may have about the full dignity of women vis a vis men; in her reflections on "Spirituality and Contemporary Culture," the Church's six contributions to Christian feminism (i.e., "What is Right with the Catholic Church?"); in her discussions of peacemaking and peace education ("Peacemaking and Prophetic Vision," "Haiti: Voices of Misery, Voices of Promise," "Peace is Worth Getting Riled About," and "Open Letter to the U.S. Bishops"); and finally, in her essays and interviews addressing ministry, Benedictine spirituality and its possibilities, and her clear love for the committed life she has chosen. (See "The Spirituality of St. Benedict" and "Ministering to the Wounded World."). This is a "WYSIWYG" (what you see is what you get) collection. There is no opening overview with the whys and wherefores of her writing, no attached bibliography, no synthesizing index. There is nothing here but sixteen gold pieces: all 24 karat, all the expression of her book's name, all the words of a feminist prophet, bridging women-church and womenstrength. **NOTE:** For additional work by Chittister see [**489**], and for an equally arresting collection directed almost entirely to her Christologically based activism (but not abstracted here), see her 1986 text, *Winds of Change: Women Challenge the Church* (Kansas City, MO: Sheed and Ward).

[**755**] Curran, Charles E., Margaret A. Farley, and Richard A. McCormick, eds. *Feminist Ethics and the Catholic Moral Tradition*. New York: The Paulist Press, 1996.
The 25 essays presented in this volume are grouped into the five categories of "Overview," "General Theory," "Interpersonal and Familial Relations," "Bioethics," and "Social Ethics," and all but a handful stem from works published in the early 1990s. Three are abstracted in the present bibliography (see [**268**], [**472**], [**483**]), and a number of others are excerpted from recent book length publications and include chapters from Hunt [**230**], Ruether [**235**], Isasi-Diaz [**256**], Townes [**638**], and Aquino [**926**]. Other contributions include, but are not limited to: "Encountering the Other: The Modern Papacy on Women" and "Western Religion and the Patriarchal Family," both by Christine Gudorf, Anne Patrick's "Toward Renewing 'The Life and Culture of Fallen Man': *Gaudium et Spes* as Catalyst for Catholic Feminist Theology," "Feminism, Liberalism and Catholicism" by Mary C. Segers, and "Healing the World: the Sacramental Tradition, by Rosemary R. Ruether. It is strong collection and especially keen on indicating the potential for dialogue between feminism, the church and social liberalism.

[**756**] Kolbenschlag, Madonna, ed. *Women in the Church I*. Washington, DC: The Pastoral Press, 1987.
Three frameworks provide the backdrop for the concerns of this text: the symbol and movement called 'women-church,' the Catholic feminism of American women religious, and an older, Catholic *aggiornamento*, seasoned by the post-conciliar experience of American Church life. The thirteen essays comprising this text are addresses given at the "Women in the Church Conference" sponsored by Time Consultants in Washington D.C. in October, 1986. Grouped into three categories ('The Tradition,' 'The Practice' and 'The Vision'), these essays each present arguments against a sexism sacralized as belief. Canonical, pastoral and theological issues are addressed and particularly strong are the entries by Mary Collins ("The Refusal of Women in Clerical Circles")

and Joan Chittister ("Agenda for the Next Decade"). These essays are prophetic, and they stand in stark contrast to keynoter Richard McBrien's address ("An Ecclesiology for Women and Men") which misses *widely* the mark of gender differentiation in Catholicism and the gender-aligned assumptions of its hierarchy of relations. NOTE: For an excellent theological discussion contemporary with this text, see Joann Wolski Conn, "A Discipleship of Equals: Past, Present, Future.'" *Horizons* 14 (1987): 231-261.

[757] Rader, Rosemary. "Catholic Feminism: Its Impact on United States Women." In *American Catholic Women*, edited by Karen Kennelly, 182-197. New York: Macmillan, 1989.
The title of Rader's essay will be misleading to those expecting an empirical discussion of the *impact* of Catholic feminism on American women. Rather, what Rader presents in this, the sixth volume of *The Bicentennial History of the Catholic Church in America Authorized by the National Conference of Catholic Bishops*, is a descriptive listing of several aspects of the women's movement within American Catholicism since the publication of Mary Daly's first volume, *The Church and the Second Sex* [157]. Rader defines Roman Catholic feminism in terms consonant with the motifs of the Second Vatican Council. It is "the movement among U.S. Catholics which regards sexism (the exploitation and domination of one sex by the other) as an injustice to be eliminated if the "good news" of true equality in Christ is to become a reality." Additionally, it is "the movement within the church that aims at the liberation of both women and men so as to allow their full and authentic response to the Spirit's call...[and it is]...an ongoing attempt to help bring about a radical renewal within the Catholic church, one that would celebrate the interdependence and collaborative efforts of men and women in building up the body of Christ the church" [p. 183]. Following her definition, Rader identifies the efforts of women's religious communities--and specifically the organizational networks of women's communities--as vanguards in the development of feminist consciousness in Catholicism. She then briefly summarizes Daly's critique of patriarchal Catholicism in *Beyond God the Father* [161] and selected aspects of three volumes by Ruether: her discussion of ideology and religious symbolisms in *New Woman/New Earth* [172], her understanding of experiences as foundational for theology in *Sexism and Godtalk* [190], and the invitational quality of her volume, *Women-church: Theology and Practice* [193]. Finally, she notes the contribution of Elisabeth Schüssler Fiorenza's *In Memory of Her* [195] (which she describes as a "neo-orthodox model") and the relevance of such works as Weaver's *New Catholic Women* [762]. This is an informative source for those seeking a preliminary and institutionally acceptable overview of the literature on Roman Catholic feminism. Because it is intended for a wide and general readership, it presumes no background in either feminism or theology, nor does Rader provide such a background. Finally, because its intent is informative and descriptive, Rader neither discusses the issues inherent in the literature she summarizes, nor does she take any position with regard to the literature. Hence, for more substantive historical and theological discussions of the materials reviewed by Rader, see Weaver [762], Carr [279] and Rader's cited works.

[758] Rosenblatt, Marie-Eloise, ed. *Where Can We Find Her: Searching for Women's Identity in the New Church.*New York: Paulist, 1991.
This highly readable anthology of ten essays prepared by (and largely for) Catholic sisters focuses the search for Catholic women's identity in terms of three theologically important and undeniable contexts: Scripture and its grounds for feminist Catholic identity, the experience of women responding to the second and third drafts of the American bishops' pastoral on sexism in the church [783], and, last, "the church" or what might be more specifically termed the hierarchy's moral capital as a source of teaching authority within the modern world. Overall, these essays do not break new ground in Catholic feminist theology. They do, however, serve to communicate its main lines and critical emphases to audiences wider than those of academe, and in ways that connect with lay and religious "yet to be radicalized" spiritualities. Each is grounded in feminist theology and exegesis, and each provides briefly annotated sources for further reading. Rosenblatt closes with general conclusions and study questions designed for group discussion(s).

[759] Ruether, Rosemary Radford. "Sexual Questions and the Challenge of Women." In *Contemporary Roman Catholicism: Crises and Challenges*, 24-46. Kansas City, MO: Sheed and Ward, 1987.
This chapter from entry [743] identifies six "sexual questions" currently facing Roman Catholic leadership and laity and about which Catholic leadership and laity are divided. These "questions" are: (1) mandatory celibacy as a requirement for priesthood; (2) the hierarchy's attempt to control women religious; (3) divorce; (4) women's reproductive rights; (5) homosexuality within the priesthood; and (6) the ordination of women. Tying them together are Catholicism's long standing,

historical amalgam of misogyny and the clericalization of asceticism (including celibacy) which Ruether deftly retraces at the beginning of the chapter. Further, as she unfolds the discussion, Ruether indicates several of the many cultural and ecclesiastical nuances of this amalgam--e.g., that while the reformation addressed the issue of mandatory celibacy, it yet retained a framework of male dominance for sexuality and ministry. This is easily readable by non-technical audiences, and although grounded in history and theology, it is in many ways confirmed by such studies as D'Antonio et al. [736] and Wallace [787]). NOTE: For Ruether's earlier analysis of clericalism and sexuality, see chapter 3 in *New Woman/New Earth* [172].

[760] Ruether, Rosemary Radford. "Catholic Women." In *In Our Own Voices,* edited by Rosemary Radford Ruether and Rosemary Skinner Keller, 1-60. HarperSanFrancisco, 1995.

Following the pattern of essays prevalent in all of the Ruether/Skinner documentary histories [132-135], this essay by Ruether provides not only a subject matter overview but with it, the numerous excerpts and sources that illustrate the discussion. And here, Ruether's topic could not be better. In four brief overviews she characterizes the history of women in American Catholicism, from "The Colonial Era," which witnesses the arrival of Ursuline nuns in New Orleans and Margaret Brent's demands for a seat in the Maryland Assembly, to multiple roles and structures of "Women Religious 1790-1950," to "Catholic Laywomen and Social Reform: 1890 to 1950" (*viz.,* Mother Jones, Katherine Conway, Frances Slattery and Dorothy Day) and, last, the "Birth of Catholic Feminism 1950-1993, " with its roots in the Grail, Christian Family, and Sister Formation Movements to its present women-church identity, both nationally and globally. The last portion of Ruether's essay (i.e., the birth of Catholic feminism) is in some ways the most instructive; for while several sources compile various Catholic women's histories, only a handful sketch the history of Catholic feminism *within* the institutional church per se--as contrasted, for example, with the wider history of feminist theology and the role played by Catholic feminists within it. It is a clear overview with well chosen supporting documents and its one primary limitation is the ambiguity of its title. In the book's Table of Contents it is as listed above. At the beginning of the essay, it is "Catholic Women in North America." Some of the latter are described, but the main discussion is in terms of the United States.

[761] Schneiders, Sandra M. *Beyond Patching: Faith and Feminism in the Catholic Church.* Mahwah, NJ: Paulist, 1991.

Possibly the most compact statement of Catholic feminism published in the 1990s, Schneider's three chapter text provides an introductory overview to the concepts and literature of feminism generally and the main theological questions facing Christian and Catholic feminists specifically. Last, this text highlights the connections between theology, justice, spirituality and American Catholic feminism (cf., e.g., [742]) by addressing the relative impacts of patriarchy, misogyny and sexism on "feminist Catholics" and "Catholic feminists." Schneiders begins with an overview of the many types and expressions of late 20th century Western feminism. She then turns to the main question facing contemporary Catholic women, i.e., whether the sexism of the Church is by divine or human design, and if the latter, a "corruption of the Gospel" to which Catholic women must respond. Her questions are posed theologically via Ricoer's understanding of symbol and hermeneutics, and they lead to an assessment of how Scripture itself can be life giving and empowering to women--in spite of its own sexism, misogyny and patriarchal teachings. Section III, a of issues, definitions and emphases in feminist spirituality, then surveys the responses Catholic women make to their own experience of sexism in the Church, and it is here that Schneiders unfolds her distinguishing criteria for the two main types of feminism within Catholicism, i.e., "feminist Catholics," women and men yet within the main stream of the church, and Catholic feminists--participants in women-church who do not necessarily maintain ties with Catholic culture and history. This is a packed, brilliant, and engaging text that some will chide for its lack of overt multicultural vocabulary and its seemingly insensitive use of such terms as "Judeo-Christian tradition." Its discussion cannot, however, be easily dismissed for these points, for its categories are directed to the foundational issues of revelation and theological anthropology, and thus, the ultimate range of women's experience, its Catholic focus notwithstanding. NOTE: Also by Schneiders are [391], [546], [547], and for her biblical work see *The Revelatory Text: Interpreting the New Testament as Sacred Scripture* [HarperSanFrancisco, 1991]. Although not abstracted here, it has received several positive and substantive reviews. See, for example, "Review Symposium: Sandra Schneiders' *The Revelatory Text: Interpreting the New Testament as Sacred Scripture." Horizons* 19 (1992): 288-303.

[762] Weaver, Mary Jo. *New Catholic Women: A Contemporary Challenge to Traditional Religious Authority.* New York: Harper & Row, 1985/1995.

According to its introduction, "this book is about women's attempts to create life for themselves in an environment that is often harmful to them." Weaver's volume is that--and more, for it provides: (1) an historical overview of women's experiences in American Catholic life; (2) a solid and reflective synthesis of the literature published in Catholic feminist theology and spirituality through 1983; and (3) an analysis of the structural bonds that both restrain and release Catholic lay and religious women as they grapple with Catholic patriarchal experience. Following her general introduction and historical overview of American Catholic women's history ("From Immigrants to Emigrants: Women in the Parish") Weaver addresses several religious issues deemed critical for Catholic women: the specifics of women's ordination, women in religious orders, the interplay of feminist theology and spirituality (including Catholic mysticism and goddess spirituality), and the tensions existing between lay and "religious" professional commitments. She provides an accurate and helpful history of the women's ordination movement through 1983, a substantive accounting of the similarities and differences existing within the theological writings of Anne Carr, Rosemary Radford Ruether, Elisabeth Schüssler Fiorenza and Mary Daly, and a critical discussion of the concept "sisterhood" and its significance for Roman Catholic feminist theologians. This is a highly readable and recommended text. Its extensive chapter notes include detailed bibliography, its index is thorough and well done, overall, it serves as a solid introduction to Catholic feminism through the mid-1980s. This noted, Catholic readers will, no doubt, understand Weaver's comments in the 1995 anniversary edition (published through the Indiana University Press), that when she wrote the book ten years earlier, she "...believed too much in the church and probably not enough in women..."(p. ix). **NOTE**: For additional surveys of early Roman Catholic feminist theological literature, see [184] and [185]. Also, for Weaver's work in feminist spirituality, see her *Springs of Water in A Dry Land: Spiritual Survival for Catholic Women Today.* [Boston: Beacon, 1993], which describes her developed understanding of Catholic women's "desert" experience, her revised understanding of goddess spirituality, and her own work in process spirituality.

NOTE: For related literature see Katzenstein [107] and Maguire [481].

B.   Topical Literatures

1.   The Ordination of Women

In 1977 the Vatican published a document listing its arguments prohibiting the admission of women into the ministerial priesthood within Catholicism . (See the "Declaration on the Question of the Admission of Women to the Ministerial Priesthood" in Swidler [781].) Because of its title the document is often referred to as the "Vatican Declaration" or, alternatively, "The 1977 Declaration." Further, because this document introduced a previously unmentioned criterion for entrance into the Catholic priesthood--namely, physical maleness [see paragraph 30 of the document], it generated extensive feminist theological, biblical, and ecumenical discussion. The literature below illustrates the range of this discussion, and while by no means exhaustive, it represents the main lines of Catholic "pre" and "post" declaration discussion on this topic. This literature was only a portion of the discussion, however, for on May 30, 1994, Pope John Paul II issued an apostolic letter entitled *Ordinatio Sacerdotalis*, which declared--in contrast to the bulk of published Catholic lay and professional theological opinion current to that time--that women may not be ordained within the Roman Catholic Church and that the discussion of the matter was to be closed. For the text of *Ordinatio Sacerdotalis,* and its initial discussion within the Catholic lay press, see *Ordinatio Sacerdotalis* and "Women's Ordination Discussion," *The National Catholic Reporter* 30 (June 17, 1994): 3-7, 9-12. For the discussion of this letter by by selected American Catholic bishops, see "Apostolic Letter on Ordination and Women," *Origins* 24, no. 1 (June 9, 1994): 49, 51-58. For an example of the clericalization attached to the discussion of women's ordination in Catholicism, see the essay by Avery Dulles, "Gender and Priesthood: Expanding the Teaching," in *Origins* 25, no. 45 (May 2, 1996): 778-784 and *Origins* 26 no. 11 (August 29, 1996): 177-180. While women are yet barred from the ministerial priesthood within Roman Catholicism (and no doubt will be through the papacy of John Paul II), the discussion of this topic has continued, with numerous studies indicating both the openness of American laity to women's ordination (cf. D'Antonio [734]) and the continued commitment to an alternative perspective on this topic. Again: the literature below provides a sampling of sources, and the reader is referred to material cited by Fox [738] and the *National Catholic Reporter*, a Roman Catholic news weekly, for current and thoughtful discussion on the matter. As a sidebar to this entire discussion, the Pope's 1994 announcement on women and ordination was followed by his stand against the New Revised Standard Version of the Bible as an inclusive translation suitable for liturgical use within parishes and other religious settings, and as a consequence of *this* decision (and its painful reception by the American hierarchy), public discussion soon emerged within the Catholic press about John Paul's capacity to "lead the church." See, for example, *The National Catholic Reporter*, November 11, 1994. The articles cited here from *The National Catholic Reporter* are readily available at almost any Catholic College or university, and the *NCR* website is *www.natcath.com*. Additionally, readers should see the *Catholic Periodical Index*, sources cited by Fox **[738]**, and other indices and internet sources.

a. Historical-theological Studies

An extended biblical-exegetical literature functions to ground several of the studies below and includes the following: Boucher **[392]**, Brown **[389]**, Schneiders **[391]**, and virtually all of Schüssler Fiorenza's early biblical work. Related pre-declaration sources include literature overviews by Patrick **[182]** and Carroll **[767]**, selected theological sources (e.g., Farley **[166, 167]**, and Ruether **[183]**), and the pre-declaration European literature as summarized by Weaver **[772]**. Important and related post-declaration literature includes virtually *all* of the feminist biblical literature on women's leadership (Catholic and Protestant), the full literature on feminist theological anthropology (see Chapter 8), and, of course, the literature in Chapter 16.

[763] Asen, Bernard A. "Women and the Ministerial Priesthood: An Annotated Bibliography." *Theology Digest* 29, no.4 (1981): 329-342.
This bibliography presents extended summaries of 64 articles written by Roman Catholic theologians in response to *Inter insigniores*, or what is else wise known as the Vatican's "Declaration on the Question of the Admission of Women to the Ministerial Priesthood." The declaration itself was completed in October of 1976, but it was not released officially until January of 1977. The material covered in the bibliography spans the period from February, 1977 to September, 1981, and it provides a clear sampling of the non-English journal literature written in response to the Declaration. The bibliographic summaries are in English, and the author's introductory comments provide a succinct overview of relevant ecclesiastical and ecumenical frameworks from within which the document was initially conceived.

[764] Brown, Raymond. "The Meaning of Modern New Testament Studies for the Possibility of Ordaining Women" In *Biblical Reflections on Crises Facing the Church*, 45-62. New York: Paulist , 1975.
In its time, this pre-declaration essay presented a Catholic "centrist" approach to the "ecumenical crisis" of women's ordination, with its patrimony and androcentrism less vivid to readers of even liberal Catholic persuasion. In the 1990s, it provides an almost voyeuristic look at the extent of Catholic clerical confusion about women. Brown's description of the many "non-theological factors" affecting Rome's possible decision(s) about ordaining women is presently outdated, but illustrates the not too recent historical evidence of androcentric theologizing among Roman Catholic biblical scholars as they step apart from the particular area of expertise, in Brown's case, New Testament Studies. The essay is a lecture delivered at Union Seminary in New York in 1975. In it, Brown cites (among other things) the "sexual problems" of having celibate male priests work closely with celibate female priests (e.g., they might fall in love); the "organizational problems" occasioned by the possibility of women as bishops (these are implied more than named); and the "ecumenical problems" afforded by women's ordination, about which Brown cites the now no longer relevant question of women's ordination (beyond the diaconate level) within the Anglican Communion in England. Brown's discussion here is more the genre of a cultural artifact than grounded debate, but it illustrates Catholic clericalism in its 'benign' form. For more skilled and insightful literature by Brown, see **[389]**.

[765] Byrne, Lavinia. *Women at the Altar: The Ordination of Women in the Roman Catholic Church.* Collegeville, MN: Liturgical Press, 1994.
This text argues for the priestly ordination of Roman Catholic women on the basis of the author's long-standing faith in the ultimate promises of Vatican II, her deep faith as a Catholic sister fully committed to well being of the church, and her professional role as the associate secretary for the Community of Women and Men in the Church for the Council of Churches of Britain and Ireland. It is a moving, pious and distinctive discussion, for its arguments are drawn more from a series of life long convictions than from formal training in either feminism or theology. Hence, it reflects

both the depth to which Roman authorities can misperceive women on this issue *and* the extent to which the issue itself can garner support within the context of a traditional parish and convent experience--giving lie to the charge of some critics [843] that the ordination movement represents the efforts of an educated American feminist elite. NOTE: See the closing comments of the Sectional Overview for more on this text and its destruction by the Vatican as reported in the *NCR*.

[766] Carr, Anne. "Women's 'Place,' Ordination, and Christian Thought: Old Answers to New Questions?" *Listening* 13 (1978): 158-175.
This essay begins with the recognition that the issue of women's ordination in Catholicism is symbolic of much of women's "place" in Christianity generally, and its synthesizing discussion provides an early benchmark for measuring Catholic progress on this issue. Carr begins by describing the two traditions that have conditioned women's historical experience in Christianity, i.e., the initial egalitarian impulse of Galatians 3:8 and the wider cultural forces of patriarchy and women's subordination. She then summarizes several theological issues that arise in conversation about women's ordination, including, issues of theological anthropology, Christology, God-language, ecclesiology, pastoral office, tradition and revelation. For closure, she then surveys ethical issues which arise as conversations about women's ordination take place (e.g., what to do with androcentric understandings of sin, human agency and responsibility). This is an archival discussion. It provides an overview of what was, so that one can gain a benchmark for what has happened theologically since its publication, i.e., quite a lot in feminist theology, and in terms of Catholic women's ordination, virtually nothing save further pronouncements against it. Its discussion of pastoral office and ecclesiology is particularly clear--and prophetic--for those churches that (more recently) have adopted sacramentalized and clericalized visions of ministry.

[767] Carroll, Elizabeth. "Women and Ministry." *Theological Studies* 36 (1975): 660-687.
Carroll's purpose here is three-fold. She wishes to explicate: (1) "Jesus' revelation about ministry [and] his assimilation of women into that ministry;" (2) the forces within the early church and subsequent history which seem "to have worked against" such an assimilation; and (3) "the dynamic of the contemporary women's movement as it may affect ministry" (p. 661). For the first part Carroll describes the scriptural understandings of ministry and the activities of women within such understandings. These include the involvement of women in discipleship, witnessing, apostleship, the reception and sharing of the Spirit, service to the community, the offering of intercessory prayer, ritual activities and community leadership. Carroll then addresses the impact of "venerable tradition," or more specifically, that tradition which developed to counter the involvement of women in ministerial roles, and which is cited in the contemporary period as the reason for "excluding women from official ministry" (p. 670). She finds such tradition invalid at four levels: (a) it does not develop from the teaching of Jesus; (b) contrary to much popular opinion, it is not a tradition that has been "constant" throughout the history of the church; (c) it does not rest on sound doctrine; and (d) it is (obviously) not unchangeable. Relationships of power and equality between women and men then become the focus of Carroll's closing remarks, and she closes with a discussion of baptism, renewed gender roles, and a call to "the Church" to embody a clearer revelation of Christ. Steeped in Catholic theology and teaching, Carroll's essay provides a clear introduction to the Catholic literature on women and ministry through 1975. It should be read with the related essays in the same *Theological Studies* issue [185], and with Carr [229], Schneiders [547], Weaver[772], LaCugna [780], Dyer [782] and Wallace [787].

[768] Gryson, Roger. *The Ministry of Women in the Early Church*. Translated by Jean LaPorte and Mary Louise Hall. Collegeville, MN: Liturgical Press, 1976.
This early, textual study examines the "ministry" of women--or more specifically, the "deaconess" and "widow" roles of women--during the first six centuries of Christianity. The author's sources range from the "Old Testament" to the Greek and Latin theological and "canonical" writings of the fourth to the sixth centuries, and Gryson's investigation concludes with traditional yet nudging interpretations concerning Catholic hierarchical and Vatican teaching on women's ordination. Thus, "The main obstacle is that, even though there were among Jesus's disciples women who, according to all evidence, possessed the qualities needed to accomplish this mission, he did not mandate women to preach the gospel with apostolic authority. It is not out of place, though, to ask whether the Jewish mentality at that period was ready to listen to the preaching of a women..." (p. 113). A subsequent appendix then addresses the possibility of ordaining women as deacons. Gryson's work reflects the assumptions, methodologies, and "ecclesiastical" biases necessary for discussion with Catholic hierarchs on this topic during the late 1960s and early 1970s (cf., e.g., pp. xvi, 11, 43, 59ff, 62 and 113). It thus fully reflects the harm of androcentrism to Christianity.

[769] Maguire, Daniel. "The Exclusion of Women from Orders." *Cross Currents* 34 (1984): 141-152.

This article presents a discussion of what Maguire sees as the "three-fold sinfulness" of the Roman church's institutional exclusion of women from the sacrament of orders. For Maguire, this exclusion is first, a "sin of injustice" because (among other things) "it confirms the church and extra-ecclesial society in its sexism." (pp. 141-142). Second it is "a sin against the church because it denies the church this distinctive service of women...thus impeding its mission as a witness to the possibilities of the Reign of God on this earth" (p. 142). Third, this exclusion is "a sin of sacrilege because the male monopoly on orders is presented as the will of God" (p. 142). Each of these judgments is documented from Catholic biblical, historical and theological literature on women and orders dating through 1984, and the "bad arguments, poor exegesis, uninformed scholarship and strident appeals to undefined authority" (p. 147) of the Roman Catholic hierarchical position are exposed. Parallels between this institutional exclusion the concordat between Nazi Germany and Pius XII which permitted the church liturgical freedom during Nazi rule are also drawn.

[770] Nilson, Jon. "'Let Bishops Give Proof of the Church's Motherly Concern': The Prospect of Women Bishops in Light of Vatican II." *Journal of Ecumenical Studies* 25 (1988): 511-523.

In contrast to discussions that debate the legitimacy of ordaining women to the Roman Catholic priesthood, this article examines whether women may be bishops in the Roman Catholic church, since elevation to the episcopacy is always an inherent possibility within the sacrament of holy orders. The discussion is a subtle and nuanced approach to the question of women's leadership within Roman Catholicism. To make his case Nilson examines the nature of the episcopal role as one of "service" with criteria for the latter developed from the documents of Vatican II (cf. pp. 514-ff). He finds, for example, that the bishop's role as servant entails teaching, shepherding and leadership (governing) tasks, and that the culmination of the bishop's service role is that of liturgical leader for the local community. Nilson finds also that *because these tasks are identified within conciliar documents, they do not require maleness as a grounding premise*, but rather service in the name of Christ and of the Church as a universal sign to all peoples. He thus concludes that no criteria exist that would bar women from episcopal positions within Roman Catholicism, and he challenges those who think otherwise to make their case. The discussion is thorough and while not unmindful of either the Vatican's 1977 Declaration [779] or the intricacies of ordination, delegation and representation, it is nonetheless premised on the authority of conciliar teaching, i.e., the authority of the episcopacy as described in *Lumen Gentium* and *Gaudium et Spes*.

[771] Schiessl, Johanna. "The Priesthood of Women." *Theology Digest* 41 (1994): 141-146.

This article was first published in 1993 in *Stimmen Der Zeit* (cf. vol 211, pp. 115-122) and is condensed in *Theology Digest* to demonstrate the cultural relativity attached to the Vatican's position in the 1977 Declaration. In brief, Schiessl makes five points. First, she reiterates both the theological research of Karl Rahner and the public position of the German Catholic hierarchy to note the "reformable" quality of the 1977 *Declaration*. Second, she summarizes the "tradition" and "symbolic" arguments used by the Vatican to bar women from the priesthood: i.e., that "Jesus did not call women to the twelve" and that maleness is required to represent him. Third, she identifies the three basic questions engendered by these positions: Is the teaching time-bound or borne of revelation? Is it based in scripture, and is there an unacceptable anthropology behind the "symbolic argument?" Fourth, she addresses these questions and finds fifth, that the teaching *is* time bound, *is not* supportable by scripture, and may well reflect a theological anthropology that devalues women, and particularly as it reflects a distinction between "the order of grace" and "the order of creation." She concludes with observations on the significance of this distinction and in particular that it is "not peripheral, but ultimately concerns the church's self-understanding as the people of God..." It is not merely an academic tiff, but a co-determinate of the church's future" (p. 145).

[772] Weaver, Mary Jo. "Ordination, Collective Power, and Sisterhood: Foundations for the Future." In Mary Jo Weaver, *New Catholic Women: A Contemporary Challenge to Traditional Religious Authority*, 109-144, San Francisco: Harper & Row, 1985.

This discussion by Weaver synthesizes several important "pre-declaration" sources supportive of women's ordination in Catholicism. In particular, Weaver summarizes American and European scriptural and canonical studies that challenge the traditional arguments *against* women's ordination, and she traces the history of the developing women's consciousness within Roman Catholicism, both before and after the 1977 Declaration. Of importance in her discussion is not only her excellent summary of pre- and early post-declaration literature (see her notes and bibliography), but as well, her analyses of: (1) the role played by women's religious congregations in the pressures for women's ordination during the late 1970s and early 1980s; (2) the establishment of the Women's Ordination Conference (WOC) in Detroit in 1978; and (3) the paralleling development of the "women-church" movement and its institutionalization with the development of the Women's Alliance for Theology Ritual and Ethics (WATER) in 1982 in Silver Spring, MD. WATER is an ecumenical group co-directed by Catholic feminist theologian Mary Hunt and Catholic liturgist Diann Neu. It serves as an organizing center and informational clearinghouse for the women-church movement in American Catholicism, and at a wider level, as a clearinghouse for feminist theology, ritual and ethics among feminists worldwide.

NOTE: For related literature see the entries in Chapter 8 on "Feminist Theology and Theological Anthropology," and Chapter 10 on "Women's Leadership in the Bible."

b. Canonical Studies

[773] Committee on Women in the Church. "The Canonist: Obstructionist or Enabler for Women in the Church?" *Proceedings from the Canon Law Society of America* 45 (1984): 126-153.
This is a panel discussion presented by the "Committee on Women" within the Canon Law Society of America (CLSA) at its 1984 annual meeting, and it identifies issues related to changes in Catholic canon law as they pertain to women. Additionally, it is the prelude to a "Learning Handout" (published with the essay) which focuses particular areas of change in canon law and relevant religious and theological discussions. The handout summarizes three things: a survey and analysis of the female membership within the CLSA; proposed models for the workshops on changes within the Revised Code and third, a survey of the "ecclesiastical offices, functions and ministries open to women in the Revised Code" (p. 134). The handout is the main portion of the article, and its workshop outlines identify numerous topics and issues (and these by canon number), several group and consciousness raising activities, additional bibliography, and last, the specific revised canons indicating wider roles and positions for women in church life.

[774] Coriden, James, ed. *Sexism and Church Law: Equal Rights and Affirmative Action.* New York: Paulist Press, 1977.
This volume presents a series of papers prepared for a "...symposium on Women and Canon Law, sponsored by the Canon Law Society of American and Rosemont College...October 9-11, 1976." As such it precedes the Vatican's 1977 "Declaration on the Question of the Admission of Women to the Ministerial Priesthood" [779], but it nonetheless addresses several of the assumptions present in the latter. Taken together, the symposium's eight papers discuss the juridical status of women in the church, the history and development of priesthood as an ecclesiastically grounded ministry in the early church, the status and perceptions of women within Vatican teaching from 1960-1975, and the range of feminist and "entrenched clericalist" approaches to the issues attached to the question of female priests in Roman Catholicism. A closing consensus statement presents recommendations for the Canon Law Society, the American hierarchy and the church at large. All papers are well documented and the volume includes both the 1975 "Biblical Commission Report: Can Women Be Priests?" and the Vatican's 1977 Declaration as appendices. An index and notes on contributors close the volume. Because of the ongoing shortage of priests within Roman Catholicism and the latter's continued resistance to the ordination of women, this volume remains an important source for those seeking historical and canonical literature on Catholicism and women's ordination. NOTE: For Catholic responses to the 1977 Declaration, see Swidler and Swidler [781]; for theological analyses of women's ordination in Roman Catholicism, see Weaver [772], Carr [229], LaCugna [780] and the historical theological entries listed above; for data on American lay attitudes towards the ordination of women to the Catholic priesthood, see D'Antonio et al. [736] and Wallace [787]. Additionally, see Vasquez' [778] discussion on canon law and the exclusion of women from the priesthood, and see the *National Catholic Reporter*, passim.

[775] Henning, Clara Maria. "Canon Law and the Battle of the Sexes." In *Religion and Sexism: Images of Woman in the Jewish and Christian Traditions*, edited by Rosemary Radford Ruether, 267-291. New York: Simon and Schuster, 1974.
Written prior to the revised code of canon law published in 1983, this essay argues for a virtual revolution in women's thinking vis a vis catholic church law, lest new discriminatory laws be written on the basis of old ones. It is a strong essay, written in frank and pointed language as it

rebukes Catholicism's "fossilized" law and the clericalism it sustains and is sustained by. Among other things, Henning cites numerous canons that evidence the misogyny of church teachings about women (relative to inadequate biology, male fears about women, and male disgust over women's menstrual cycles). Further, Henning documents the long history of discriminatory church attitudes towards women--both in terms of ecclesiastical control over women's bodies and reproductive capacities and the judgment that women are unfit for not only the sacrament of ordination, but even minor liturgical functions. Finally, Henning asserts clearly that the time for seeking recognition by Catholicism's "churchmen" is passed, and that the time for women's announcements, ordination and full participation in the church has come. She calls upon women to exercise their full strength in economic boycotts of the church and an all out educational effort "against empty theological excuses, discriminatory laws, and the collectively self-righteous ego trip of an all-male hierarchy" (p. 287).

[776] Huels, John M. "Women's Role in Church Law: Past and Present." *New Theology Review* 6, no. 2 (1993):19-31.
This article contrasts several perceptions of women evident in the 1917 and 1983 versions of Roman Catholic canon law to demonstrate the author's conviction that patterns of change in the ministerial activity in Roman Catholic women are real and evident. Its principal emphases address the progress of women as laity, who are, according to the author, no longer viewed negatively when contrasted with lay men. While the helpfulness of such comparisons may seem to many--in the 1990s--as at least moot, the discussion does endorse the ordination of women within Catholicism and the acknowledged support of at least two specific bishops on record for women's ordination. Its general tone, however, remains guarded and "obsequious" in the fullest Catholic loyalist use of the term (see Ladislas Orsy, *The Church...* [Wilmington, DE: Michael Glazier, Inc., 1987, p. 82]) despite its statements of support for feminist Catholic women. Moreover, it virtually ignores the entire feminist theological movement within Catholicism, save the fact that many women are alienated from the eucharistic celebrations and pastoral leadership of local parish life. In sum, the article reflects both the tensions and fears surrounding discussions of women, leadership and church law in Catholicism, as the conservatism of Catholic leadership increases.

[777] Ranges, Joan. "Legal Exclusion of Women from Church Orders." *The Jurist* 34 (1974): 112-127.
This article examines an important source of institutionalized sexism within Roman Catholic history and canon law, for it surveys the laws "which indicate that women are excluded from church office as these laws appear in the *Decretum* of Gratain" (p. 112). The Decretum is a compendium of laws dating from the twelfth century (c.1140) and Ranges examines both it and the sources from which it is derived to identify: (1) the tradition that Gratain inherited, and (2) his own uncritical adoption of the gender and sexuality norms within this tradition and then current and inimical to women. In her discussion, Ranges calls attention to the 11th and 12th century enforcement of clerical celibacy (and the misogyny upon which it was premised), the cultural separation of Eastern and Western churches borne of the schism with Constantinople in 1054, the interpretive assumptions Gratian used in identifying women as beings subordinate to men, and fourth, the relatively fluid understanding of sacraments prior to the twelfth century. All of these, she argues, contributed to the growth of clericalism and the norms governing the exclusion of women from church office. She argues that a reconsideration of these factors from within the modern assumption of women's equality with men may shed light on Gratian's own reading of women's ability for "orders" and subsequently, that of 20th century canonists. This is an interesting and fascinating article, both for its arguments and historical sensitivities and, too, the parallels it can evidence with late 20th century conversations on women's ordination within Catholicism.

[778] Vasquez, Lucy. "The Position of Women According to the Code." *The Jurist* 34 (1974): 128-142.
Along with Henning [775], this essay is one of the few sources providing detailed information on the status and perceptions of women within the 1917 Code of Canon law in Roman Catholicism. And, like Henning's discussion, this one also seeks to educate the reader on the nuances of canon laws dealing with women, and thus it focuses largely (but not exclusively) on the experience of women in religious and convent communities, rather than lay positions of either religious or secular work. Space does not permit a detailed overview of the material covered by Vasquez, but it is important to note that as she begins her discussion, she notes the absence of any prior research on this topic and second, that curiously enough, there is no single canon which is "openly against women or unequivocally classifies them as being inferior to men in the Church" (p. 129). This

said, she unfolds on a canon by canon basis the many "antifeminist" assumptions of the 1917 code.
NOTE: For additional work by Vasquez, see the "NOTE" in [783].

c. The 1977 Vatican Declaration

[779] Sacred Congregation for the Doctrine of the Faith. *Declaration on the Question of
the Admission of Women to the Ministerial Priesthood.* In *Women Priests: A
Catholic Commentary on the Vatican Declaration,* edited by Leonard Swidler and
Arlene Swidler, 37-52. New York: Paulist Press, 1977.
This document argues that women cannot be ordained to the ministry of the Catholic priesthood. It
lists several long standing theological and doctrinal assumptions generally offered as reasons for
this prohibition, and it adds an additional reason, new to this Declaration, i.e., that women cannot
physically represent Christ because they are not male. It has been heavily criticized (cf. Asen
[763] and Swidler and Swidler [781]), and it continues as a symbol of the sexist misogyny so
deeply ingrained in the Catholic doctrine of the priesthood.

d. Responses to the Declaration

[780] LaCugna, Catherine Mowry. "Catholic Women as Ministers and Theologians."
America 167 (1992): 238-248.
This extended essay reviews the main lines of both the rise of feminist theology within Roman
Catholicism and the history of women's ordination within mainline American Protestantism to
indicate the theological assumptions attached to the question of women's ordained ministry within
the Roman Catholic church. It is LaCugna's thesis that the Vatican's resistance to women's
ordination is based upon a faulty theology of not simply sex and gender, but as well, the
ecclesiological premises of sacramental ministry itself, given that sacramental ministers are to
"represent...the Christian community...*in persona Christi*..." (pp. 247, 248), and that women are
de facto precluded from this opportunity, *and with it,* the grace that this sacrament can provide.
Hence she argues for a theological consideration of the "anthropology" at the heart of the Vatican's
resistance to the ordination of women (as expressed in the 1977 Declaration [779]), and she closes
by affirming the necessity *and* possibility of rooting this discussion in current trinitarian theology.

[781] Swidler, Arlene and Leonard Swidler, eds. *Women Priests: A Catholic
Commentary on the Vatican Declaration.* New York: Paulist Press, 1977.
On October 15, 1976 the Sacred Congregation for the Doctrine of the Faith released its "Declaration
on the Question of the Admission of Women to the Ministerial Priesthood," a document that
expresses the Vatican's continued decision to forbid the ordination of women within Roman
Catholicism. Simultaneous with its release, the Vatican issued a "Commentary" on the Declaration
for the purpose of further clarifying the intent of the Declaration. Both the Declaration and
Commentary received immediate response from the Catholic theological community. The contours
of that response are presented here in this anthology edited by Swidler and Swidler. Specifically,
this anthology provides a series of forty-four commentaries by Roman Catholic theologians on
virtually every aspect of the Vatican Declaration and Commentary, including its central arguments,
its theological, methodological, canonical and hermeneutical assumptions, its use of scripture,
tradition and historical research, its assumptions concerning the nature of sexuality, sacramentality,
scholasticism, authority, leadership, priestly vocation, sex and gender roles, and the nature of
gender discrimination, to name but a few. Leonard Swidler's excellent "Introduction: 'Roma
Locuta, Causa Finita?'" locates the documents historically and surveys the international response to
the "Declaration" and its accompanying "Commentary." The entries then follow as brief
discussions directed to specific arguments within the Declaration. For example, one argument
within the Declaration lifts up the fact that women are not numbered among "The Twelve" within
the New Testament literature. An exegetical essay by Elisabeth Schüssler Fiorenza, entitled "The
Twelve," addresses this argument by surveying New Testament research on "the twelve" (current
through the mid-1970s) to identify the multiple meanings and uses of the term, and with these, the
conventional although exegetically inaccurate assumptions attached to "the twelve" as an argument
against the ordination of women. Similarly, the Vatican assumption that women were not among
the apostles is also examined in "The Apostleship of Women in Early Christianity" [401], and
again challenged with exegetical scholarship. The contributors here are too numerous to cite, but all
are well-recognized within the Catholic theological community, and in many cases well beyond it.
Thus, the volume is an excellent reference for those seeking scholarly literature on the "Declaration"
and its "Commentary," *and* its reception by a sizable--and knowledgeable--segment of the Catholic
theological world.

e. The Present Reality

[782] Dyer, George, ed. "Women--Theology and Ministry." *Chicago Studies* 35, no. 2 (1996): 115-184.
This thematic issue of *Chicago Studies* presents five articles on facets of "women, theology and ministry" within Catholicism, with each evidencing the widening, but still ecclesiastically restricted frames of of gender and theology from within which the question of women's *ordained* ministry (in Catholicism) is [elsewhere] discussed. Contributors include the following: (1) Kathleen Hughes, whose essay, "Inclusive Language Revisited," summarizes the tensions yet surrounding the use and discussion of "inclusive language" in Catholic liturgy and worship; (2) Anne Carr, who locates "Feminist Views of Chistology" within the context of religious symbolism and the scope of various Christological questions addressed across the feminist/womanist spectrum; (3) Agnes Cunningham, who presents "Feminist Spirituality: The State of the Question," a good summary of feminist spirituality and its varying implications; (4) Kathleen O'Brien and Margaret Early who in describing "Women: Leadership in Ministry," survey a wide range of secular and religious publications on the shape and diversity of leadership skills and behaviors; and (5) Ronald Lewinski, whose discussion, "Women in Parish Minisry," focuses traditional, renewed and expanded roles indicative of women's work in the context of parish organization(s).

[783] National Conference of Catholic Bishops [NCCB]. "Partners in the Mystery of Redemption: A Pastoral Response to Women's Concerns for Church and Society." *Origins, NC Documentary Service* 17, no. 45 (April 21, 1988): 757-788.
This issue of *Origins* presents the text of the American Catholic bishops' first draft of a (now defunct) statement attempting to respond to the voices of women in American Catholicism concerning sexism and other injustices in the church and society. By way of format and focus it is divided into four sections addressing various contexts of "partnership" in the mystery of redemption (i.e., "personhood," "relationships," "society" and "the Church"), with each further formatted to reflect various "voices," i.e., those of *women* (speaking both affirmation and alienation), *Catholic heritage*, and last, *the bishops* as respondents to these earlier sets. The document was based on "listening sessions" with over 75,000 American women, and it attempts to addresses a variety of topics (e.g., gender and family roles, equity in the work place, lesbianism, inclusive language and women's ordination) from within the context of both the listening sessions and past Catholic teaching. It is at points almost inspiring (e.g., the title alone reflects an important symbolism) but its final section on ordination belies its first three portions, for in section IV, the 1977 Declaration ultimately governs the discussion. This document took ten years to develop and was used as a vehicle for study and discussion groups in local parishes. It was, however, widely criticized by theologians and laity, and in the end not passed by the bishops at their annual meeting. Subsequent drafts have also failed, with the 1977 Declaration constituting at least one obviously clear stumbling block. For discussion of the document and its history see, e.g., Aggeler [753], and Rosenblatt [758], together with the other literature in this section. Additionally see the analysis (not abstracted here) by canonist Lucy Vazquez: "The Womens' Pastoral: Process, Myth and Present Reality." *Proceedings from the Canon Law Society of America* 50 (1990): 113-122.

[784] Slusser, Michael. "The Ordination of Male Infants." *Theological Studies* 57(1996): 313-321.
This brief theological note in such a prestigious journal as *Theological Studies* summarizes the historical arguments for ordaining male infants, as drawn from medieval manuals, Pope Benedict XIV, Thomas Aquinas, *and* the East/West ecumenical implications of the Catholic teaching on the validity of ordaining male infants. The author concludes that "There is, in short, much to recommend and nothing to prevent the Church from ceasing to claim, even in the most abstract and theoretical way, that it has the power to ordain male infants" (p. 321), and the article is included here as an example of the *incredible range of canonical insight* on this point.

[785] Sweetser, Thomas. "Authority and Ordination." *America* 171, no. 12 (October 22, 1994): 4-7.
As a social science based parish consultant, Sweetser has annually surveyed Catholic parishes and registered parishioners on a battery of more than 150 items for several years. In this essay he reports the data trends on three items: (1) whether priests may marry and still function as priests; (2) whether women should be permitted ordination to the priesthood; and (3) whether respondents agree with the statement, "Catholics should follow the teachings of the Pope and not take it on themselves to decide differently." Samples of parish staff and parish leaders, together with random

samples of registered parishioners indicate steadily increasing support (since 1980) for the first two items, with the 1993-1994 data indicating agreement levels of 67%, 55% and 44%, respectively, by the three types of groups on the item, "women should be allowed to be ordained to the priesthood." What is more, these same groups are the least likely to agree with item #3: Thus, only 18%, 27%, and 26%, respectively, agree with the item that "Catholics should follow the teachings of the Pope and not take it on themselves to decide differently," while the remaining proportions either disagree with or have mixed feelings about the item. While Sweetser's N-sizes here are small, his data are consistent with other data surveying Catholic attitudes (cf. [739]). In addition to these data, Sweetser also presents various breakouts by age, education and gender, and he expresses a positive hope for church leadership on these issues.

[786] Wallace, Ruth R. "Catholic Women and the Creation of a New Social Reality." In
     The Sociology of Gender: A Text-Reader, edited by Laura Kramer, 435-447. New
     York: St. Martin's Press, 1991.
Working from within the sociology of knowledge as developed by Peter Berger and Thomas Luckmann [*The Sociology of Knowledge.* Garden City, NY: Doubleday, 1966], Wallace locates the Post-Vatican II experience of Roman Catholic women within the framework of externalized new realities that are being internalized and objectivated as a series of resistances to the "retrenchment atmosphere of John Paul II's papacy" (p. 445). These new realities include (among other things) the positioning of women (albeit sparsely) in diocesan and chancellery offices, and their services as: parish administrators, eucharistic ministers, canon lawyers and members of seminary boards--and in non-canonical religious women's communities--whole organizations geared to social justice issues as new foci for ministry. Factors contributing to these new and changed realities for women include the increased educational levels of Catholic women, their experience of and exposure to insights from alternative service organizations (ranging from the Peace Corps during the sixties to current feminist organizations), and the emergence of broadly based theological and ecclesial religious organizations such as *Catholics For Free Choice,* the *Women-Church Convergence* and the *Women's Ordination Conference.* The first of these groups reflects the declining moral authority of church officials with respect to (non-rhythm) birth control as an enforceable church teaching. The second and third reflect specific movements for the incorporation of women into officially ordained positions within the structure of Catholic leadership. Such organizations (and the networks they represent) provide the presence of resistance factors to current papal retrenchment on women's roles, and they will not (in Wallace's judgment) recede in the near future.

[787] Wallace, Ruth R. *They Call Her Pastor. A New Role for Catholic Women.* Albany,
     NY: SUNY Press, 1992.
Roman Catholic canon law reserves the title, "pastor" for those ordained to the Roman Catholic priesthood, but as Wallace's volume indicates, Catholic practice among selected groups of laity has widened the horizons of this term. Directed to popular audiences (with more formal presentations restricted to professional papers, e.g., [786, 788]), Wallace's volume presents descriptive data from an availability sample of twenty female parish administrators who serve as "pastors" to priestless parishes in all capacities except those of the "sacramental minister" who administrates the sacraments in circuit rider fashion. Thus, canon law notwithstanding, parishioners in these priestless parishes have come to call their administrators "pastors" and with both respect and support for all roles available to these "pastors." Wallace's interview data with parishioners, their women "pastors" and visiting "sacramental ministers" detail the distinctive capacities of these church leaders and the supports and constraints that condition their work. The discussion is located within the context of Vatican II teaching on laity and clergy expectations, and while Wallace suggests that parallels do not exist with Protestant clergywomen (by virtue of their ordination status and the absence of ordination among these Catholic parish administrators), several parallels are nonetheless clear to those familiar with the experiences of Protestant women clergy. Where differences do exist, however, are with the understandings of sexuality attached to clerical roles, i.e., heterosexist marriage in the case of Protestant clergy and misogynous celibacy in the Catholic case. Professional and lay users will find this book useful, both academically and pastorally. Notes, bibliography and a well prepared index close the volume.

[788] Wallace, Ruth R. "The Social Construction of a New Leadership Role: Catholic
     Women Pastors." *Journal of Religion* 54 (1993): 31-42.
Elsewhere Wallace has described the marginalization of women in the church [696], the circumstances surrounding the recruitment and deployment of lay women as pastoral leaders [786, 787] and last, the constraints laywomen experience in such leadership roles [See "Women Administrators of Priestless Parishes: Constraints and Opportunities." *Review of Religious*

Research 32 (1991): 290-304.]. Here, she draws out the implications of such leadership for the church as a whole. Namely, that women pastoring in priestless parishes portend a declericalization of Catholic leadership with significant and long term ramifications for the church's life. Wallace begins her discussion with a review of the factors facilitating the advent of women in pastoring positions--these include external circumstances such as the American women's movement and internal circumstances such as Vatican II, changes in canon law and the growing priest shortage. She then develops her discussion around the social constructionist framework developed by Peter Berger and Thomas Luckmann in their sociology of knowledge. (See above, [786].) She points to the collaborative leadership style used by these women and describes the ways in which such leadership works to declericalize Catholic religious authority.

2. The "Women-church" Movement

a. Descriptive Studies

[789] Hunt, Mary E. "Defining 'Women-Church.'" *Waterwheel* 3 (Summer, 1990): 1-3. This brief essay by Hunt defines the women-church movement as a "global ecumenical movement made up of local feminist base communities of justice seeking friends who engage in sacrament and solidarity" (p. 1). Additionally, it describes what the women-church movement is *not*, and it expands briefly on each of the emphases presented by Hunt in her more formalized definition. Women-church is not, says Hunt, "an organization with members;" nor is it a "club," or a "women's auxiliary of the larger church, nor simply a respite from patriarchy, nor an association precluding local parish or congregational involvement. Rather, it is a "...religious expression of [the] historical stirrings of feminism and womanism..." and in this it is a synthesis of women's creativity--both locally and globally, as women's groups in local communities each articulate a "praxis of radical love" on behalf of women and their needs. **NOTE**: Also by Hunt are [217] (co-authored with Carter Heyward), [230], [479], and [918].

[790] Neu, Diann. "Women-Church on the Road to Change." In *Defecting in Place: Women Claiming Responsibility for Their Own Spiritual Lives*, by M.T. Winter, Adair Lummis and Allison Stokes, 241-247. New York: Crossroad, 1994. Included among the theological articles that comment on the Winter, Lummis, Stokes text, *Defecting in Place* [153], Neu's essay provides a practitioner's perspective on the women-church phenomenon. As a co-founder and co-director of the Women's Alliance for Theology, Ethics and Ritual (WATER), and as a woman trained professionally for both ordination and social work, Neu summarizes the theological, organizational and grassroots character of the women-church phenomenon. Organizationally, "women-church" is a gathering largely Catholic in origin, but it encompasses a far wider spiritual arena than Catholicism only, and it is affiliated with several other similar organizations. It provides liturgical and theological resources at local, national and international levels, it is a source of spiritual direction and counseling for women struggling to gain affirmation after years of patriarchal religious socialization, and it is a context within which women can think about (and/or re-think) the types of commitments (if any) they wish to have with their original ecclesial/denominational affiliations. In addition to her descriptive overview, Neu indicates various publications available from WATER, including sources that introduce women to feminist theology, liturgy and spirituality. Additionally, see Hunt [789] and Neu below [795], and see Neu's entry, "Women-Church Transforming Liturgy" in [526].

[791] Trebbi, Diana. "Women-Church: Catholic Women Produce an Alternative Spirituality." In *In Gods We Trust: New Patterns of Religious Pluralism in America*, edited by Thomas Robbins and Dick Anthony, 347-351. 2d ed., New Brunswick, NJ: Transaction, 1990. This article succinctly traces the development of women-church spirituality from its roots in the rise of the Catholic women's movement following Vatican II, through its dialogue with the Vatican's "suppress[ion] of public discussion of women's ordination" (p. 348) to its current and now organized commitment "to struggle for redress of social injustices on local, national and international levels" (p. 350). Trebbi notes several limitations to the women-church movement-- e.g., given the dearth of men in the women-church movement, "family structures among members is lacking," and she identifies the ambivalence within the movement concerning its possible future directions, since it roots in both biblically based traditions and the recognition of some members that Christianity is hopelessly patriarchal and should be rejected in factor of "goddess-worshipping traditions" (p. 351). **NOTE**: For a more substantive overview, see Ruether [193] and [449].

[792] Troch, Lieve. "The Feminist Movement in and on the Edge of the Churches in the Netherlands: From Consciousness-raising to Womenchurch." *Journal of Feminist Studies in Religion* 5, no. 2 (1989): 113-128.

This article describes selected aspects of the growth and development of feminist theology in the Netherlands. Its primary focus is on the extra-denominational efforts of Christian feminists (both Protestant and Catholic) to establish networks and centers for feminist reflection on feminist (theological) praxis. To this end, therefore, Troch describes: (1) the development of the "women and faith movement" in the Netherlands since its inception in the 1970s; (2) the varying occupational and ecclesiastical factors that constrain the "women and faith movement;" (3) key events that have solidified the "women and faith movement;" (4) contrasts between the Netherlands' "women and faith movement" and the American "Women-church" movement; and (5) the emerging points of consensus between the "women and faith movement" and the American "women-church" movement. An important emphasis throughout this discussion is the extra-ecclesial dimension of the women and faith movement, for while it receives some financial and organizational support from both Protestant and Catholic church sources, its growth has been characterized largely by the autonomous networks of women theologians interacting with grass roots women's groups, a process that has engendered the first meeting of a Dutch "women's synod." Further, this process has helped to describe both the differences and rising similarities between the women and faith movement and the women-church movement: e.g., the differential academic and cultural resources available to each, the differing political and liturgical emphases of each, and within the Netherlands, the political nature of the women-church symbol vis a vis women and the Roman Catholic hierarchy. Last, in the light of these and other points of contrast, the author summarizes the emphases and goals of the women and faith movement, and she indicates several "questions and challenges for the future" of feminist theology in the Netherlands. This is an important article both for its bibliographic references and the discussion itself since it highlights social as well as theological issues within the contexts of feminism's critique of androcentric and/or patriarchal Christianity in a secularized European society. NOTE: For a mainstream introduction to Catholic feminism in Europe see *The Voice of the Turtledove: New Catholic Women in Europe*, edited by Anne Brotherton [Mahwah, NJ: Paulist Press, 1992], a collection of ten essays which, together with overview discussions, detail "New Catholic Women..." in Belgium, England, France, Germany, Ireland, Italy, The Netherlands and Spain.

[793] Winter, Miriam Therese. "The Women-Church Movement." *The Christian Century* 106 (1988): 258-260.

This article identifies the American women-church movement as both "a national network of feminist base communities and a coalition of feminist organizations that seek to support one another in the living out of their own faith experience" (p. 258). Further, it unfolds that definition through a variety of additional women-church descriptions: (1) its character as "an initiative of the Holy Spirit among those who are religiously marginalized and oppressed" (p. 258); (2) its concern for justice in both church and society; (3) its ultimate goal of "genuinely inclusive communities of women and men in the *ecclesia* of Jesus Christ" (p. 258); and (4) its availability as a space of support for those in transition from patriarchy--whether through anger, attempts at church re-construction or alternatively, the need for an additional faith community that presents religious support and self-affirmation through feminist consciousness and worship. Author Winter is both an advocate of and liturgical writer within the women-church movement (cf. [153]), and as she reflects on these aspects of women-church identity and spirituality, she calls attention both to the prophetic implications of the movement for traditional church life and to its own internal limitations, *viz.*, its need for vehicles that provide both communal and gender specific means of religious nurture for women and men, and the need for the movement to articulate its relationship to other experiences of feminist worship and spirituality. NOTE: Also by Winter is [531].

[794] Zeigenhals, Gretchen E. "Meeting the Women of Women-Church." *The Christian Century* 106 (May 10, 1989): 492-494.

This article presents the author's observations and reflections on the women-church movement as drawn from her attendance at a "tri-state (Maine, New Hampshire and Vermont)" women-church conference held in Portsmith, New Hampshire in April, 1989. The author is a feminist raised in the Lutheran Church/Missouri Synod, and she describes the conference as an "intriguing glimpse into a community of worship which [she] had inaccurately envisioned" (p. 492). In particular, she notes that the women-church movement is "not an umbrella term for Christian feminists" (p. 294), but rather: (1) a highly liturgical effort of Catholic and Protestant women to *be* "church" in response to structures that marginalize and exclude them; (2) a movement directed to justice efforts on behalf of women and all marginalized persons; (3) a movement seeking to move constructively beyond the anger engendered by women's exclusion from Christian church structures; (4) a movement self-defined as inclusive of women and men but lacking male participation (at least at this conference); and (5) a movement currently in dialogue with womanism, as both womanism and the women-church movement struggle to overcome the historical and ecclesial tensions of race and gender in church and society.

b. Theological Studies

[795] Neu, Diann. "Our Name is Church: The Experience of Catholic Christian Feminist Liturgies." In *Can We Always Celebrate the Eucharist?* edited by Mary Collins and David Power, 75-84. New York: Seabury Press, 1982.
In a series of three motifs that parallel the development of feminist religious consciousness (i.e., an initial emphasis on identifying one's self with a positive religious tradition, a bonding with other women, and a re-claiming of the power to give birth to a new vision of faith in community) Neu describes and details three examples of feminist liturgy: a liturgy of "Naming," of "the laying on of hands," and last, "the eucharistic meal." The rubrics and theological rationales are presented for each liturgy, and at the close of her discussion Neu highlights the many questions posed by the "ecclesia of women:" *viz.*, "Can the institutional [presumably Catholic] Church change enough to welcome this energy of women? Can women move from the fringe into the mainstream of a church that is life for all...? Can women continue to be both Roman Catholic and feminist? Can the dualities of the hierarchical patristical church and the ecclesia of women co-exist?" (p. 83). The questions are pointed, and although presented in the early 1980s, they remain relevant for at least two reasons. First, they reflect the early moments of the now widened women-church movement. Second, they continue to reflect the voices of Catholic women who struggle against the Vatican's ongoing opposition to women's ordination. Similarly, the liturgies detailed by Neu remain, and they are sufficiently described to permit immediate use and adaptation. NOTE: Also by Neu (but not abstracted here) is "Celebration in a Different Key" [*Daughters of Sarah* 16, no. 6 (1990): 3-6] which details specifically how women may introduce and expand feminist liturgical celebrations.

[796] Ruether, Rosemary Radford. "Christian Quest for Redemptive Community." *Cross Currents* 38 (1988): 3-16.
At its widest reach this article unfolds the women-church phenomenon as one expressive vehicle for a Christian feminist liberation spirituality. To accomplish this task and to say more directly what "women-church" and a "Christian feminist liberation spirituality" are each about, Ruether develops a four-pronged discussion. She first describes several alternative images of Christianity, or several "models of the church" as she calls them, in order to delineate the assumptions about "redemption" that each has. That is, are these assumptions "inner-" or "other-worldly" in nature, and are they social and political in nature, rather than individual and privatized? By and large, those which are inner worldly (as well as social and political) are those which fall within a liberationist ecclesiology. Following this portion of her discussion, Ruether identifies key emphases in North American feminism (i.e., its organizational and normative emphasis on gender inclusivity and its parallels with biblical and prophetic quests for justice) and she aligns these with the emphases of liberationist theology to indicate the main contours of her Christian-feminist liberationist spirituality. That is, the latter is an orientation that is justice directed, liturgically grounded, defined by a praxis-based understanding of truth, and non-separatist in that it seeks the *reformation* of older, more established church structures. Ruether's last point of discussion then unfolds the women-church phenomenon as an expression of this spirituality, for the women-church movement provides the space in which women can do this "spiritual, cultural and political work" (p. 15) while experiencing themselves as safe from patriarchy. NOTE: This is a compactly presented discussion, and its primary emphases are helpfully examined in the light of Ruether's other women-church (e.g., [449]) and feminist-ecological, ethical writings (e.g., [235]).

NOTE: The bulk of the theological literature on the women-church movement has been presented earlier in the bibliography. Hence for additional theological sources see Schüssler Fiorenza's extended work on the "discipleship of equals" and the "ecclesia" of women ([236], [237], [369], and [370]), see Ruether's *Women-Church* [193] and her essay overview of the history of the women-church phenomenon [449], see the data cited by Winter, Lummis, and Stokes [153] and Lummis and Stokes [742], and see Katzenstein [285].

3. Feminism and Women in Religious Communities

a. American Sisters and Ecclesial Change

[797] Ebaugh, Helen Rose Fuchs. *Women in the Vanishing Cloister: Organizational Decline in Catholic Religious Orders in the United States.* New Brunswick, NJ: Rutger's Univ. Press, 1993.
This text is a richly written case study that examines the processes of organizational change experienced within an American [Catholic women's] "religious community," which in contrast to all research on secular organizations in decline, appears to be: (1) aware of its probable death and dismantlement and (2) at peace with the latter, with grace, equanimity, and a sense of contribution to the larger purpose of the church. The study is descriptive and more the advance of an hypothesis than its actual test, but its many observations and insights keep the reader engaged. Thus, where secular organizations face decline and probable death with informational closure and authoritarian rigidity, Ebaugh's selected community of study, the "Sisters of Service," become open and egalitarian. Or, where secular organizations engage in turf battles, fear risk taking, and experience low morale and cynicism, the Sisters of Service identify with a larger purpose, i.e., efforts at accommodation and planning for the inevitable. Or last, where secular organizations compete to survive, the Sisters of Service prepare to die with grace and peace. Ebaugh focuses her study around the loss of religious life's "organizational niche" within American society (*viz.,* the provision and maintenance of parochial schools and education), and she examines virtually all of the relevant historical literature on American Catholic women in "religious life," i.e., studies on recruitment and member retention, the role of Vatican II in the changes experienced by American convent communities, and so forth. Her insights bridge historical and statistical sources on convent communities, and they have rich implications for other struggling religious organizations (e.g., many mainline Protestant seminaries). **NOTE:** For Ebaugh on Vatican II, see [737].

[798] Neal, Marie Augusta. *From Nuns to Sisters: An Expanded Vocation.* Mystic, CT: Twenty-Third Pubs., 1990.
The substance of this text is condensed in [799] below, but its presentation here lifts up both the sociology of Catholicism's changing "female religious" occupational structure and the theological issues perceived by "female religious" as the driving forces behind the changes of that structure. The text is divided into five chapters. Chapter I details the social and historical forces defining Catholic women's religious congregations (i.e., "communities" or "orders") throughout the history of the Church, but with special attention to mid-20th century issues. These issues then transition one to Chapters 2 and 3 which identify: (1) a renewed sense of mission for women religious (as synthesized through 19th and 20th century church teaching on social justice issues); (2) the theological response of women religious to that teaching (*viz.,* the recognition of religious vocation as a call to support the global human rights movement); and (3) the organizational structures developed by Catholic women religious (during the 1960s and 1970s) to respond to that sense of mission. The remaining chapters then detail the implications of this renewed sense of mission for both the "vows" and "governance" (i.e., the communal structures) of Catholic women religious. This is an important text, for although it addresses topics seemingly important to only a limited audience, its sociological (and theological) significance should not be underestimated: it evidences the institutional witness of *non-clerical religious structures* to human rights as *the focus* of Christian mission in the late twentieth century, and it does so as an interpretation of Vatican II's imperative for the Church to "read the signs of the times." Further, it does so not through an organized process of preaching and evangelization designed to engage laity to take up the risks of political commitment on behalf of third world peoples and needs, but through the behavioral and "apostolic" commitment of women's communities' own members. And this, according to Neal, is both the driving force behind the changing perception of religious commitment held by the majority of Catholicism's female religious *and* its expression as a ministry of prophetic risk. **NOTE:** see also Neal [147] and Quinonez and Turner [800].

[799] Neal, Marie Augusta. "Democratic Process in the Experience of American Catholic Women Religious." In *A Democratic Catholic Church: The Reconstruction of Roman Catholicism,* edited by Eugene Bianchi and Rosemary Radford Ruether, 172-188. New York: Crossroad, 1993.
As one of the many fine entries in this reader (see [733]), Neal's essay begins with the observation that women in Catholic religious institutes no longer hold "'blind obedience'... in faith as holy..." and she asks: (1) "What is the historical origin of the radical change in the faith position of Catholic

women in institutes of religious life regarding authority and obedience in the late twentieth century..." and (2) "...what are the implications for the immediate future of the Catholic Church in the United States?" (p. 172). For answers, Neal discusses several historical points, but four are particularly relevant. The first is American society's heightened awareness (during the middle of the twentieth century) of the global human rights movement, as evidenced, for example, by the United Nations in the 1950s and mid-60s and by (at the same time) Catholicism's gradual recognition of such institutionalized evils as "...the Holocaust, the repression of native populations in Latin America, and racial segregation" within the United States just prior to the time of Vatican II. This heightened awareness was a factor that challenged the stability of previous generations. Factor #2 is the history of democratization within Christianity and specifically from the Reformation on, with its differing Protestant and Catholic ideas of work and community, and work and family relations--all realities which condition notions of commitment. Factors #3 and #4 are the coming together of these ideas during a period of increased education and literacy among women generally (Factor #3), and their carryover into the education and experience of Catholic women religious during the 1950s and early 1960s (Factor #4). In effect, Neal explains the abandonment of "blind obedience" through an analysis "secularization," but without the often tacit assumptions that (i) secularization is a linear process that (ii) necessarily means the death of Christianity. Moreover, to support her discussion, she draws upon data from her 1966 and 1982 "Sisters' Surveys" that indicate (a) the growing attention of sisters to the use of governing structures on behalf of community directed "mission" [goals and priorities] and (b) the widened attention of sisters to numerous sources of religious insight and not that of institutional authority only. This is an important and persuasive discussion, and while some might challenge Neal's interpretation of the data, it nonetheless illuminates not only the diminished appropriation of "holy obedience" among many contemporary Catholic sisters, but also, the changed climate of authority, overall, within Roman Catholicism. Hence it bears close and studied reading. **NOTE**: Also by Neal are **[145]**, **[146]**, **[147]**, and for the comparative details on her Sisters' Surveys (which form the basis of the article above), see her *Catholic Sisters in Transition: From the 1960s to the 1980s*. [Wilmington, DE: Michael Glazier, Inc., 1984]. While not abstracted here this text provides demographic, organizational, congregational, and communal data from the two population surveys of American Catholic sisters Neal conducted in 1966 and 1982, and it presents her provocative hypotheses and interpretations of the data, together with copies of survey instruments and her bibliography of publications from the data. Finally, for alternative interpretations of the changes evident in women's religious communities, see Ebaugh **[797]** and Wittberg **[803]**.

[800] Quinonez, Lora Ann and Mary Daniel Turner. *The Transformation of American Catholic Sisters*. Philadelphia: Temple Univ. Press, 1992.
Together with such sources as Neal **[798, 799]**, Ebaugh **[797]**, and Wittberg **[803]**, this text chronicles the changing shape of "religious life" for American Catholic sisters and nuns from the years just prior to the beginnings of the Second Vatican Council in 1962 to the publication of their text in 1992. What distinguishes this text from the others, however, are the premises driving its analysis: (1) a conscious effort to detail the organizational and normative development of the Leadership Conference of Women Religious (the "LCWR") as an ecclesial (albeit not clerical) reality, and (2) an equally conscious effort to highlight the character of women religious as "churchwomen:" that is, as vowed women redefining themselves in terms of both gender and justice directed commitments. And it succeeds on both counts. The discussion develops in six chapters and addresses (among other things): (1) the American religious and social climate into which Vatican II was received by [American] women religious; (2) the impact of American democratic values on the LCWR's leadership procedures; (3) its concomitantly developing commitment to human rights (as evidenced, for example, by its securing of NGO status at the UN); (4) the process of "feminization" within the LCWR (i.e., its recognition of sexism in both the Church and society and its increased attention to the effects of sexism in ecclesiastical procedures); and (4) a recognition of the struggles and conflicts yet to come as the LCWR comes to terms with its structural dependency on Rome as a religious organization within Catholicism. Finally, as a backdrop to each of these, the text regularly documents the character of the LCWR as an organization reflecting the thinking and concerns of large majorities of sisters in communities nationwide. As with other texts addressing change in women's religious communities, this one, too, is passionate about its subject matter. And well it should be, for it details clearly both the events that shaped the LCWR as a process of moral discourse seeking organizational shape and structure, and as a process grounded in the developing emotional and ecclesial adulthood of women who for decades built the church in the US, and who now speak with a public voice no longer identified as "child-like" and/or of the "good sisters."

[801] Ware, Ann P. *Midwives of the Future: American Sisters Tell Their Story*. Kansas City, MO: Leaven Press, 1985.
This volume is a collection of nineteen essays by Roman Catholic women religious who have lived in community since the period prior to Vatican II, and who with but few exceptions still do. The essays delve deeply into the reasons they entered community life and more importantly why they have continued to stay in community life. Among others, the contributors include such notables as Joan Chittister [754], Maureen Fiedler, Caridad Inda, Margaret Traxler, May Luke Tobin, and Elisabeth Carroll [767], and for virtually all of the contributors, the thematic emphases are the same. They are a generation and more of Catholic women who initially learned prayer, obedience, and more obedience, but who in the light of conciliar teaching learned to reconsider obedience as a "charism" to be used for justice, a gift for those who lack voice because of social and/or political oppression. Their stories are powerful and whether directed to the justice issues of Central and South America or those among secular, lay and "religious" women in the United States, they well reflect the hopes so prevalent in the post-conciliar Catholicism of the 1970s and early 1980s.

[802] Wittberg, Patricia. "Non-Ordained Workers in the Catholic Church: Power and Mobility Among American Nuns." *Journal for the Scientific Study of Religion* 28 (1989): 148-161.
Drawing upon interviews with 24 Catholic sisters employed in "in congregational schools and hospitals, as well as in diocesan middle management [positions] and parish work" (p. 152), Wittberg explores the patterns of organizational power and autonomy sisters have relative to discretion in decision making, professional recognition, job satisfaction and job stability. Her discussion is rooted in the organizational literature suggesting that personal power in organizational contexts is "structurally rooted and...related to opportunities for promotion and independent decision making" and that the circumstance of such power generates worker satisfaction and job commitment. While exploratory, her interviews generally confirm this pattern in that sisters working in organizations run by their own staffs tend to experience more structural power and autonomy (with its attendant possibilities) while those working in parish and diocesan office positions experience less structural power, and subsequently, less satisfaction with their work. Test hypotheses for further research are developed. In a subsequent discussion using both Catholic data collected by Gallup from the National Association of Church Personnel Administrators (NACPA), and data collected by Wittberg from a sample of non-NACPA, Catholic religious administrators [See Wittberg, *Review of Religious Research* 35 (1993): 19-33], Wittberg found that priests who experienced "both high commitment and greater autonomy and career opportunity scored highest...[over sisters and laity]...on all measures of job satisfaction and job stability" (with job stability understood as remaining in church employment), while sisters and laity (in varying degrees) experienced commitment and satisfaction, but less projected job stability--with laity experiencing lowest levels of satisfaction and projected job stability (p. 29). In turn, she noted the need for church leaders to examine the policy implications of her data given that priests and sisters are the largest employee pool for diocesan structures. Also by Wittberg is [803] below.

[803] Wittberg, Patricia. *The Rise and Fall of Catholic Religious Orders: A Social Movement Perspective*. Albany, NY: SUNY Press, 1994.
In an earlier publication *(Creating A Future for Religious Life: A Sociological Perspective*, Mahwah, NJ: Paulist Press, 1991) Wittberg contrasts the commitment mechanisms, recruitment and retention issues assumed by three models of religious life: i.e., its casting as "intentional community," as an object of bureaucratization, and as a developing form of "associational ties." Here, in an effort to synthesize insights from that text (as well as various histories of European and American religious life), Wittberg analyzes the decline of American women's religious orders and congregations from their membership high point of 181,421 in 1966 through the early 1990s when by the publication of her text in 1994, community membership had dropped by almost 50% to 94,022. The analysis is developed through two main theoretical frameworks, those of "resource mobilization" and "frame alignment," with each of these used to detail--first the history of religious life as mobilization on behalf of religious virtuosi (chapters 1-11), and second, the loss of its ideological and structural consistency (chapters 12-16). The heart of her analysis comes in these last chapters where she addresses the contemporary situation. Why the decline? Several factors are named, but in brief, three are critical: (1) the collapse of religious life's established ideological frames surrounding its definition as the task of religious virtuosity; (2) a variety of structural events that both evidence and contribute to that collapse, and (3) the loss of role model recruits and recruit mobilization efforts typically handled by hierarchical others to shore up declining membership numbers. This is a fascinating study and its discussion of the virtuosi ideology with its related structural pushes and pulls (such as, e.g., conciliar directed renewals and a climate of

democratization--but at the same time, role and function ambiguities within and across communities and organizational conflicts between Rome and the Leadership Conference of Women Religious over the goals of and for American women religious) is strong. Second, it is interestingly supported by Wittberg's content analysis of articles drawn from the *Review for Religious* from 1950-1992. Moreover, Wittberg's "Glossary" of technical religious terms is helpful for readers unfamiliar with the conceptual terrain, and the extended notes, bibliography and indices are especially thorough (although not helpfully formatted). Last, Wittberg's own passion for this life is clear, as she draws out several potential benefits for further sociological research. These points notwithstanding, Wittberg's text needs reading back to back with Neal [798] and Quinonez and Turner [800], for at bottom, it challenges the prophetic ministry arguments put forth by both, albeit here from within sociological rather than theological interpretation.

b. Supplemental Sources

[804] Ewens, Mary. "The Leadership of Nuns in Immigrant Catholicism." In *Women and Religion in America, Volume 1: The Nineteenth Century, A Documentary History,* edited by Rosemary Radford Ruether and Rosemary Skinner, 101-149. San Francisco: Harper & Row, 1981.
This article and the documentary sources accompanying it attest the impact of Roman Catholic sisters on the development of American Catholic schools, Catholic hospitals and nursing activities-- and as a consequence of the latter--the lowering of anti-Catholic prejudice during the middle and latter decades of the nineteenth century. To illustrate these points, Ewens identifies several factors of Catholic women's community experience prevalent during the nineteen century and evident to those involved with Catholic sisters. These factors include: (1) the statistical preponderance of sisters over priests; (2) their institutional autonomy from local episcopal governance; (3) the points of potential conflict between episcopal and community leadership; (4) the friendship, prejudice and pain suffered by American sisters; (5) their own structural bases of stratification and conflict; and (6) the opportunities provided to women by community life, i.e., "involvement in meaningful work, access to administrative positions, freedom from the responsibilities of marriage and motherhood, opportunities to live in sisterhood, and egalitarian friendships" (p. 107). Source documents include letters from nuns describing: (a) teaching experiences; (b) cross-country travel on behalf of mission activity; (c) experiences of anti-Catholic bigotry and violence; and (d) experiences of nursing efforts during the Civil War and the yellow fever epidemics in the 1850s in Charleston, South Carolina. Additional documents include a letter from John Carroll (the first American Archbishop) to Elizabeth Seton, correspondence between local superiors and church administrators, and publicized accounts of the "convent riots" at the Ursuline convent in Charleston, Massachusetts. **NOTE**: For a more recent discussion, see Ewens' essay, "Women in the Convent " in *American Catholic Women: Historical Exploration*, 17-42, edited by Karen Kennelly [749].

[805] Kolmer, Elizabeth. *Religious Women in the United States: A Survey of the Influential Literature from 1950 to 1983.* Wilmington, DE: Michael Glazier, 1984.
This brief volume synthesizes an array of sources generally unpublicized beyond the contexts of women's convent communities. By way of format it is structured into three bibliographic essays that divide the journal literature on Catholic sisters and nuns into three historically important, albeit general, categories: "Pre Vatican II" sources, sources dating from the "Vatican Council and After" and "Recent Trends." A fourth chapter offers the author's reflections on the literature and provides a list of 11 suggestions for researching Catholic women's religious orders. A bibliography of source listings then closes the volume. This is a specialized and focused bibliography which identifies papal and other documents for researching women's religious orders. Its use is limited, but it provides a goldmine for the researcher on this topic.

[806] Thomas, Evangeline, ed. with Joyce L. White and Lois Wachtel. *Women Religious History Sources: A Guide to Repositories in the United States.* New York: R. R. Bowker Co., 1983.
This reference volume is an excellent resource for those seeking both descriptive and historical information on the ministries, locations, foundresses, founding dates, membership levels and archival holdings of women's religious communities in the United States. It is well organized and its four main divisions include the following: (1) a set of descriptive community profiles arranged alphabetically within state and town locations; (2) a bibliography of community and/or order based literatures; (3) a "Table of U.S. Founding Dates" (which actually includes founding dates, 'country of origin,' and the community's first and current American locations); and (4) a "Biographical

Register of Foundresses and Major Superiors" which identifies foundresses and superiors by their community, 'personal dates' and years of community leadership. Moreover, each of these four sections are clearly cross-referenced to each other so that the reader can turn directly to related sources and information. Several prefatory chapters aid the reader's use of this reference with 'how to instructions,' a glossary of terms and a complete listing of order abbreviations. A comprehensive index referencing all materials by entry number closes the volume.

NOTE: For current statistical data on women in religious communities see the regularly updated article, "Statistical Summary of the Church in the U.S.," in the annually published *Catholic Almanac*, edited by Felician A. Foy and Rose M. Avato [Huntington, IN: Our Sunday Visitor Publishing Division/Our Sunday Visitor, Inc.]. Additionally, see the several web sites described in Fox **[738]**.

20

Feminist Theology, the Academy and Theological Education

The literature on "feminism, the academy and theological education" is, at once, focused, yet unsynthesized. On the one hand, there is a clear and consciously directed literature that seeks to shape the structures and processes of theological education by bringing feminist theological insights to the socialization of religious professionals. Thus some authors have set benchmark expectations for feminist theological education (e.g., The Mud Flower Collective [807] Ruether [808] and Sanders [809]), while others have sought to incorporate feminist and womanist values within the content and curricula of theological education (e.g., Cannon et al. [810], Chopp [811-812], Dewey [813], Leanard [815], Rader [816], Schüssler Fiorenza [817] and Gilpin [819]).

These sources noted, there is a wider literature of feminist theological education, i.e., what might be called a "literature of implications," or a literature that "hints at" the possibilities of theological education from a feminist perspective. This literature exists, however, in an unsynthesized and presently underdeveloped form, largely because its "hints" are couched in the discussion of other or differently directed topics.

For example, while much of the early feminist theological literature was critical of the fact that church structures and religious organizations in the 1960s and 1970s continued to embody exclusivist and patriarchal traditions (cf. Hageman [168] and Schüssler Fiorenza [175]), little systematic research was done then (cf., Neal [145]) on exactly *how* women's presence in theological education might shape the latter--or alternatively, be shaped by the latter. Moreover, while literature through the mid-1990s (e.g., [663:59-60]) recognizes the general impact of more gender sensitized faculties at seminaries, additional research is needed in this area.

In particular, while much clergywomen research has confirmed that numerically small and "organizationally struggling" churches have largely been the "first call" settings for women clergy, no research has, as of the mid 1990s, addressed the fact that it is now seminaries that are increasingly the "struggling" organizations, and that they are "calling" women as an "FTE" ("full time equivalency") resource. To what extent does this feed the dual tracking potentials of various denominations *and/or* open the "resource markets" as identified by Zikmund, Lummis and Chang [663]? And, further, to what extent does the increased presence of women affect the funding patterns of theological education? The sheer "demography" of women in theological education is a very underresearched topic--in spite of the statistics on the increased numbers of women students at seminaries (cf., Carpenter [644], King [661], Larson and Shopshire [699], O'Neil and Murphy [702], Carroll, Hargrove and Lummis [657], Lehman [712], Lincoln and Mamiya [141], and Nesbitt [662]).

Similarly, the literature on "mentoring" and "gatekeeping" in theological education is underdeveloped. Mentoring and gatekeeping are those aspects of professional socialization by which some occupational entrants (but not others) experience helpful movement and support into positions of power, security and/or prestige within the occupation, and they exist in the religious as well as other professions. Are female seminarians penalized by such processes? While Lehman [715] and Zikmund, Lummis and Chang [663] have opened the discussion, the experience of women in denominations requiring parish or internship experience as a degree or ordination requirement seems especially relevant for research.

A final example of topics "hinted at" but underresearched in the area of "feminism, the academy and feminist theological education" returns one to the women who are themselves, engaged in the process of theological education: *viz.*, the women faculty and administrators, staff and clerical support, board members, and financial contributors. Little is known about the identifying characteristics of such groups and how their varying *types and levels of presence* in seminary education affect female seminarians and the theological issues they address.

To be sure, Carroll, Hargrove and Lummis [657] collected some faculty data early on for their *Women of the Cloth* study, but as of the mid to late 1990s, data are absent for identifying the location, theological orientation(s), academic standing, career histories, religious (and other) role sets, professional visions, administrative and professional conflicts, general demographic, and other key variables distinguishing women who contribute to and/or give shape to theological education. What *is* known about these women, however, is that as regards *faculty* levels, their numbers are dwindling. Following a steady rise from 1991-1994, the ranks of women faculty in theological education (as indicated by ATS statistics) are dropping--and in dramatic ways.

As reported in the ATS *Factbook on Theological Education* for academic year 1995-1996, after a steady increase in women faculty from 1991-1994, the overall totals for women faculty dropped by 11% among full professors, and by 2.6 % and 7.7 % for associate and assistant professors. By comparison, however, males increased in full and associate categories and remained the same at the assistant level. These numbers are especially striking since women comprise only 13.2%, 26.7% and 36.7 % of these ranks, respectively. Moreover, the only category of female increase for the 1995-1996 academic year was that of "other," in which women rose by 28% (from n=32 to n=41) while males rose by 13% (from n=77 to n=87). (For the specific data here, see Table 3.1, "Number of Full-Time Faculty at All Member Schools by Race/Ethnicity, Rank and Gender," p. 69 in *Factbook on Theological Education*, edited by Daniel Aleshire and Jonathan Strom, The Association of Theological Schools in the United States and Canada, Pittsburgh: PA, 1996.)

Clearly some of this decline is demographic, given that churches are themselves aging institutions [686]. But demography alone cannot explain such faculty patterns, and one is pressed to ask how society's wider backlash against feminism and other social movements is now affecting seminaries and other schools of theological education. Indeed, perhaps what is needed overall, is a book about women theological educators that parallels Jessie Bernard's early text, *Academic Women* [University Park: Penn State University Press, 1964]. Written at the beginning of the feminist movement in an effort to document sexism in university settings, Bernard argued that (among other things) what distinguished women from men faculty was that women were "teachers," not "professors," "distributors," but not the creators of the knowledge to be delivered. Helpful now might be a similarly cast text, but with attention to the roles of theological mentors and gatekeepers, and the *scope* of society's backlash against feminist theology in seminary education, and its diffusion across church-wide structures.

In the current chapter on "feminism, the academy and theological education," attention is directed to the more consciously directed works addressing feminist expectations, standards, pedagogy and the hopes for an institutional grounding of feminist theological insight. But the "hinted at" literature of feminist theological education can not be ignored and is present throughout the various chapters of the bibliography.

A.   Feminist and Womanist Critiques of Theological Education

[807] The Mud Flower Collective [Katie Cannon, Beverly W. Harrison, Carter Heyward,
       Ada Maria Isasi-Diaz, Bess B. Johnson, Mary D. Pellauer, and Nancy D.
       Richardson.] *God's Fierce Whimsy: Christian Feminism and Theological
       Education.* New York: Pilgrim, 1985.
Initially published as a statement of feminist needs within theological education by a group of women faculty and students who readily acknowledge their limitations as a "representative sampling," this text argues that theological education should be "a process in learning and in doing the work of liberation" (p. 6). Moreover, it synthesizes the many tensions inherent in such perspective: (1) the need for justice directed institutional change within churches and theological education--and yet the lack of institutional resources and commitment toward such change; (2) the need to recognize the deep social organizational roots of the "problems" facing theological educators committed to justice and liberation education (e.g., the connections between racism, sexism and classism and their ties to women's poverty)--and yet the individual as well as social constraints in overcoming such problems; (3) the need for self-conscious feminist theological work--and yet the potential stigmatization of anything labeled "feminist," given that to be labeled "feminist" is virtually synonymous with being labeled "radical lesbian"; and (4) the need to connect with women in

theological education when networks of support and funding are absent, and where feminist connections are themselves caught within denominational and academic commitments that seem to presume priority over feminist need. This is a frankly presented series of essays, with the majority being open dialogues on several of feminist theology's grounding topics (e.g., inclusivity, praxis, feminist spirituality, sexuality, images of alienation and God sharing) and the remainder further theoretical reflections and expressions of correspondence between womanist ethicist Katie Cannon and feminist ethicist Carter Heyward. Although now an historical text perhaps surpassed by the more recent works of tradition reconstruction, *God's Fierce Whimsy* remains a benchmark. It is an initial and courageous measure for the expectations of the feminist theological movement *within theological education*, the acknowledged "limitations" of its contributors as all professional women from the Northeast and from only four denominations etc., notwithstanding.

[808] Ruether, Rosemary Radford. "The Future of Feminist Theology in the Academy." *Journal of the Academy of Religion* 53 (1985): 703-713.
Readers seeking a thematic overview of American feminist theology will want to contrast this essay with Trible's brief discussion [356], for like Trible, Ruether also identifies three historical moments in the development of American feminist theological thought. However, unlike Trible, Ruether prefaces her overview with a description of feminist theology as a critique of misogynist patriarchy, and specifically the capacity of patriarchy, historically, to close off the feminist impulse. She then notes the present potential and past successes of patriarchy at silencing women teachers and the concomitant necessity for feminist theologians to "be seen as a network of solidarity between many feminist communities engaged in the critique of patriarchalism in distinct cultural and religious milieux, rather than one dominant form of feminism that claims to speak for the whole of womenkind" (p. 704). These points made, Ruether identifies the three "moments" (i.e., phases) that have typified American feminist theological thought: first, a critique of the masculinist bias in theology, (i.e., a critique of androcentrism as a world view and base for understanding sin, redemption and revelation); second, the development of alternative traditions that support the "autonomous personhood of women;" and third, the attempt of feminist theology to re-state the norms and methods of theology itself as a result of these first two moments. Ruether finds this third moment especially significant, for the feminist theologian must function not "to repristinate a past revelation, but to make a new beginning...where woman is not defined as object, but defines herself as subject...[and in which the]...redefinition of the central tradition itself is taught to the next generation of theological students" (p. 711). This task requires strength, intellectual and cultic pluralism, a classical base within the academy, and the development of autonomous institutions so that once beyond patriarchy, a "truly human and humanizing" theology may emerge.

[809] Sanders, Cheryl. "Afrocentrism and Womanism in the Seminary." *Christianity and Crisis* 52 (1992): 123-126.
This brief discussion synthesizes the grounding emphases of Afrocentrism and womanism as interpretive frameworks for African American experience. Important to each are its celebrative and constructive emphases vis a vis African American experience, i.e., the critique of Eurocentric hegemenous thinking, and--following the black feminist epistemology developed by Collins (cf. [21] and [99]), the accountability of black scholars to the lived experience of African American communities. Sanders argues that these emphases find their theological expression in the "witness of the Spirit" tradition(s) of Black churches and in the "witness of history" tradition(s) basic to womanism. For the former, these emphases attain expression through the community's endorsing "Amen" which simultaneously engenders credibility for and accountability from local church leadership. For the latter, the themes of celebration, critique and (communal) construction come via black women's resistance to slavery and their mother-to-daughter, oral and family based traditions of support. Sanders concludes by noting the usefulness of these perspectives as criteria for meaning in African American theological education and as criteria for dialogue across African American and predominantly white, theological institutions. **NOTE**: Also by Sanders and supplemental to this is her essay, "Afrocentric and Womanist Approaches to Theological Education" in her edited reader, *Living the Intersection* [637].

B. Feminist and Womanist Pedagogies

[810] Cannon, Katie G., Kelly Brown Douglas, Toinette M. Eugene, and Cheryl Townsend Gilkes. "Metalogues and Dialogues: Teaching the Womanist Idea." *Journal of Feminist Studies in Religion* 8, no. 2 (1992): 125-154.
This entry is comprised by papers "originally presented at a session of the Womanist Approaches to Religion and Society Group of the 1991 Annual Meeting of the American Academy of Religion" (p.

125). Overall, the authors summarize their understandings of the term "womanism" and its pedagogical significance for their work. First, Katie Cannon organizes her assumptions and basic pedagogical strategies through the multiply grounded image of "metalogues." Not quite the level of a "metatheory," "metalogues" is an image that permits the interface of students' experience, its characterization by traditional academic discourse and the contemporary African American culture in which her students live, such that the "whats," "hows," and "whys" of race, sex and class oppression surface for critique and reconstruction. Contributor #2 to this discussion is Kelly Brown Douglas whose approach is expanded [814] below. Contributor #3 is Toinette Eugene who summarizes the epistemological and ethical paradigm shifts associated with womanism and their implications for courses on African American families and womanist ethics (cf. [626]). Finally, sociologist Cheryl T. Gilkes synthesizes the work of Black feminist sociologists such as Patricia Hill-Collins ([21] and [99]) to communicate the role of narrative, history, experience, class and oral tradition within the communal experience of African American women and to highlight their significance for "interdisciplinary dialogue and multidisciplinary investigations," and particularly in terms of how women "continue to account for and foster the integrity of the community in sacred and secular spaces."

[811] Chopp, Rebecca S. "Educational Process, Feminist Practice." *The Christian Century* 112, no. 4 (Feb. 1-8, 1995): 111-115.
Working with the assumption that specific theological movements provide a unique opportunity to examine the *process* of theological education (as contrasted with its products), Chopp considers feminism and its praxis epistemology as one avenue of entree into developing a more creative pattern for theological education. She argues that the feminist theological emphases of justice, dialogue and imagination each have bearing on the ways in which theological education can and should happen. In particular, she suggests that "new relationships of imagination, of justice,... [and]... dialogue should be formed in the midst of a pluralistic world... [and that]... new forms of relating, teaching, and community building will have to be developed" (p. 114). Further, of critical importance here is that students become engaged in the tasks understanding and addressing global "cultural problematics" (including both old and new symbol systems) so that they "can flourish amid various symbolic patterns" to imagine alternative possibilities for the future.

[812] Chopp, Rebecca S. *Saving Work: Feminist Practices of Theological Education.* Louisville, KY: Westminster/John Knox, 1995.
In her article length discussion [811], Chopp identified feminist theology as one avenue of entree into an understanding of the theological education process per se. Here she examines three feminist theological "practices" as examples of feminist pedagogy to spell out the "saving work" of feminist theological education. The discussion is rooted in a response to the crisis literature of theological education (those sources from the late 1970s that try to identify the meaning of theological education to undo its current crisis like status--cf. [821]), and the three feminist pedagogical practices Chopp examines are (1) "narrativity" (the re-writing of personal lives in the light of the major Christian story); "ekklesiality" (the justice and spirituality grounded spaces provided by women-church like experiences students may have while at seminary); and (3) "feminist theology" itself (the reconstruction of Christianity's major symbols along inclusive, justice directed and dialogical lines). Chopp fleshes her discussion out with several sources of information: the changing demographics of the seminary student population, the wider demography of women outside the seminary world, the points of compatibility between traditional theology and its feminist reconstructions, recollections from student interviews she conducted for this book etc., and in the end, she invites an important dialogue about the future of theological education. Her chapter notes and general index close the volume. This is an important text, and while it does not meet the benchmark issues identified in [807], it does illustrate the potential of Lilly funding for preliminary feminist work by the dean of a major theological school [Candler at Emory]. This said, sociologists seeking "interview data" and/or others wanting specific pedagogical strategies may be disappointed by the discursive quality of Chopp's text--her student illustrations notwithstanding. NOTE: For Chopp's related discussion of feminist theology, narrative structures, and local congregations, see her above article [811], and see her essay, "In the Real World: A Feminist Theology for the Church," *Quarterly Review* 16 (1996): 3-22 (not abstracted here).

[813] Dewey, Joanna. "Teaching the New Testament from a Feminist Perspective." *Theological Education* 26 (1989): 86-105.
This essay was prepared at the request of the Multicultural Workshop of the ATS Committee on Underrepresented Constituencies for "an inclusive, feminist, non-racist perspective" on the teaching of New Testament (p. 86). It describes the author's own initial biases borne of her personal and

professional socialization and the sources and strategies she uses to enable her students to begin the task of interpreting the New Testament from a non-androcentric, feminist-liberationist perspective. The author details: (1) feminist hermeneutical considerations; (2) the types of information and materials to which students need exposure in order to re-learn the tasks of exegesis and interpretation; and (3) the author's own selection of "methodological tools [needed] to overcome androcentrism." The author's grounding premises are clearly stated and she appends a copy of her semester-long introductory New Testament course syllabus to her essay. Her definition of a "feminist" follows Sakenfeld [410], and she roots the bulk of her discussion in the awareness that no teaching or interpretation about the New Testament is ever value free, but conditioned by the teacher (or interpreter's) constituencies in their social historical location (as summarized by Osiek [354]).

[814] Douglas, Kelly Brown. "Teaching Womanist Theology." In *Living the Intersections: Womanism and Afrocentrism in Theology*, edited by Cheryl Sanders, 147-155. Minneapolis, MN: Fortress, 1994.
With Alice Walker's definition of "womanist" as her focusing axis, Douglas describes her first experience teaching womanist theology and the lessons she learned from it: that its pedagogy must be dialogical not monological; that womanist theology is both academically and community oriented; and that as rooted in the history of black women's experience, womanist theology provides students the opportunities to dialogue with not only one another, but with, as well, community women rooted in a history that has nurtured the survival and freedom of African Americans throughout their history. In her discussion Douglas describes the theological dialogue with womanism as one that must "...help students to name the social, economic, political, religious and cultural barriers to black people's freedom...[and]...compel [them] to recognize their points of privilege and how they are themselves complicit in black oppression" (p. 153). She indicates that the theological discussion emerging through womanism is directed to both African American students (women and men) and students "not female and African American," and that it is a pedagogy fully mindful of the necessity for local community involvement and accountability to contemporary womanist experience.

[815] Leanard, Joan. "Teaching Introductory Feminist Spirituality: Tracing the Trajectory through Women Writers." *Journal of Feminist Studies in Religion* 6, no. 2 (1990): 121-135.
Following Anne Carr's description of feminist spirituality ([549]) Leanard describes both the literature she uses as sources for course development (e.g., *The Mists of Avalon*) and the journaling and discussion techniques she uses in her class. The framework is dialogical, and students develop at their own pace over the course of class meetings. Leanard's discussion reflects her initial experience of teaching feminist spirituality, and she projects the need to move to literature by Womanist and other communally grounded authors.

[816] Rader, Rosemary. "Recovering Women's History: Early Christianity." *Horizons* 11 (1984): 113-124.
Using the literature available through 1983, Radar traces the beginnings of her teaching activities at Arizona State University for her course on "Women and the Christian Tradition," which is offered to university undergraduates. Course planning suggestions, readings, paper topics and an annotated bibliography are included.

[817] Schüssler Fiorenza, Elisabeth. "To Set the Record Straight: Biblical Women's Studies." In *Mainstreaming*, edited by Arlene Swidler and Walter Conn, 21-32. Lanham, MD: University Press of America, 1985.
First published in *Horizons* [10 (1983): 111-121], this essay describes the core bibliography Schüssler Fiorenza used in her initial undergraduate course on women and men in the Bible. Divided into three parts, the course takes up (a) "issues in biblical interpretation" (for which Schüssler Fiorenza suggests an initial 9 references); (b) "wo/men [sic] in the Bible" (13 references); and (c) "current biblical theological issues" (15 references). Schüssler Fiorenza's own texts *In Memory of Her* [195] and *Bread Not Stone* [196] together with Letty Russell's *The Liberating Word* and *Feminist Interpretation of the Bible* [210] and the eight 1982 Society of Biblical Literature papers edited by Trible [351] are also indicated as standard references. In addition to the bibliographic material, Schüssler Fiorenza also describes the assumptions, strategies and conceptual frameworks that underlie her course, and the types of tasks, discussions and papers her students prepare. In all, Schüssler Fiorenza presents 49 books and/or articles as source

materials, together with a description of her own understanding of women's studies, feminist biblical theology and current and past "issues of interpretation." NOTE: Although this is an early publication, it is a helpful source for seeing the development of Schüssler Fiorenza's own work. Alternatively, for a different approach, see Dewey above [813]. Also, for an approach that draws upon *In Memory of Her* (but is directed to the wider concerns of feminist theology as a whole), see Chester Gillis, "Teaching Feminist Theology: A Male Perspective." *Horizons* 17 (1990): 244-255 (not abstracted in this volume). Finally, for Schüssler Fiorenza's own analysis and "update" of her work in feminist theological education, see Chapter 6, "Prisca--Teacher of Wisdom: Feminist Theological Education: Discourse of Possibility," in *But She Said* [236].

C. Related Sources

[818] Carroll, Jackson and Penny Long Marler. "Culture Wars? Insights from Ethnographies of Two Protestant Seminaries." *Sociology of Religion* 56 (1995): 1-20.

Using James Davison Hunter's *Culture Wars* [NY: Basic Books, 1991] as their starting point, Carroll and Marler contrast ethnographic data from two prototypical (and pseudonymously named) seminaries: "Evangelical Theological Seminary" (or "ES"), a conservative seminary with the mission of "sound interpretation of inerrant Scripture," and "Mainline Seminary," ("MS"), its more liberal counterpart. The contrast provides information on several aspects of seminary life, pedagogy, culture and teaching. And, it highlights as well, a possible misreading of the conflicts beneath Hunter's thesis. To be sure, the authors note the depths of conflict Hunter details. But following Coser's conflict theory, they find, too, that evangelical and mainline voices are typically in conflict with other evangelical and mainline voices internal to their own cultures. Hence, the authors conclude that these seminaries (and by implication, Hunter's cultures) may be less at "war" with each other, and more at cross purposes with each other. For example, at ES biblical truth is "out there" but the issue can be contentious, because some evangelicals are accommodating to a more flexible "self-directed" perspective. Likewise, MS is experiential in its pedagogy, worship and theological study, but its students are at times conflicted over commitments to diversity. The authors locate the culture and postures of the two seminaries in responses to modernity and post-modern thought, and they suggest that the historic Black Church might provide a mediating model of perspective for these cross purposes, given its commitment to the "out thereness" of Scriptural truth and its simultaneous focus on justice needs in society.

[819] Gilpin, W. Clark, ed. "Commitment and Critical Inquiry in Theological Education." *Theological Education* 25 (1989): 5-114.

This issue of *Theological Education* examines the ways in which "…commitment and critical inquiry are interrelated and interdependent components of theological education…" (p. 6). The contributors include Edward Farley, Vincent Wimbush, Harry Stout, John Coleman, Sallie McFague, David Kelsey, and editor Gilpin, with each examining nuances of "advocacy" and "the pursuit of knowledge." Farley's essay sets the opening tone by arguing that commitment and advocacy are not "oppositional terms." In turn, Wimbush discusses the role of "standpoint" and autobiography as factors in the theologizing process, and McFague argues the moral necessity of advocacy on the part of theologians, given the enormity of late twentieth century moral and social problems. Stout's essay examines commitment and inquiry as reflected in studies of American Puritanism and the Great Awakening, and Coleman attempts a specific framework for objectivity and commitment vis a vis religion and social science. The final piece (by Kelsey) provides a synthetic overview, and editor Gilpin lists relevant bibliography. Although by no means "radical," these essays provide an initial response to the kinds of questions raised by such discussions as those by The Mud Flower Collective [807] and Ruether [808].

[820] Schecter, Patricia, Beverly W. Harrison, Kwok Pui-lan, Margaret Miles, Renita J. Weems, and Majorie Suchocki. "Roundtable: A Vision of Feminist Religious Scholarship." *Journal of Feminist Studies in Religion* 3, no. 1 (1986): 91-111.

This "roundtable" presents a "vision of feminist religious scholarship" as developed by Schecter on the basis of her more than six years of graduate school experience at Graduate Theological Union (GTU), with Beverly Harrison, Kwok Pui-lan, Margaret Miles, Renita Weems and Majorie Suchocki serving as respondents to the presentation. Schecter begins by recounting her history at GTU: her traditional doctoral studies in systematics, her conversion to feminist consciousness upon reading *The Mists of Avalon*, and, last, her subsequent withdrawal from the Ph.D. program to write an MA level thesis based on her feminist experience. She indicates that at the time of her "withdrawing," GTU had no women faculty in systematics and by implication, no space in which to do feminist theology. It is in the light of this experience--with its insights and conflicts--that Schecter suggests a series of: (1) "alternate sources and content for women doing theology," namely, women's stories, experience and lived history; (2) an alternative form of thesis methodology and presentation, i.e., "poetry, dance, drama, art and music;" and (3) alternate processes of thesis research and composition, *viz.*, "collaborative dialogue" engendering joint theses and dissertations. By way of overview, most respondents readily acknowledged the conflicts recounted by Schecter, but raised several questions about her specific proposals, including questions of certification, peer review, and faculty competence to judge artistic methodologies. With her characteristic realism, however, Harrison suggested "dedicated networking" among feminist scholars, both for support and collaborative research and writing.

[**821**] Wheeler, Barbara G. "Critical Junctures: Theological Education Confronts Its
    Futures." *The Annals* 527 (May, 1993): 84-96.
This article identifies two streams of thinking prevalent within the theological educational literature, with each having implications and arguments for the restructuring of theological education. The first stream is an ethos directed to "clarity and coherence" in theological education. It is an emphasis that highlights the irrelevance of the established "practical theological" paradigm, and it favors, instead, the development of a wisdom-formation model, a vision of theological education as the giving of a "wisdom that shapes the whole person who seeks to understand and respond to God" (p. 91). Alternatively, a second approach to theological education stresses the many economic and social factors conditioning contemporary theological education, but notably those of a changed seminary population and clientele and the survival dynamics suggested by such changes. Hence this second approach favors "greater multiplicity and dispersion" within theological education, with attention directed to distance learning and creative entrepreneurial responses to the changing seminary student base. Wheeler sees both perspectives as responses to the "clericalism" inherent in the established theological educational milieux, and she cites literature from Jewish, Protestant and Roman Catholic sources to make her case. She reviews various other hypotheses about the perceived inadequacies of theological education (e.g., seminaries are suffering from the decline of mainline religion generally), and she summarizes key sources through 1992. Her final preference is toward the normative socialization model, but with only a limited discussion of its feminist possibilities.

NOTE: For related literature, see "Womanism, Ministry and Theological Education" in Chapter 17, *viz.*, entries [**643-646**]); see the entries on "Mainline Christianity: History and Sociology" in Chapter 21, *viz.*, entries [**683-688**], see Thistlethwaite and Engel [**276**], and see the literature on "standpoint" theology in Chapter 23.

VI

Responses and Recent Developments

Responses to social movements vary, and given the breadth of the women's movement in religion, it is not surprising that responses to feminist and womanist theologies have included both reaction and rejection, adaptation and specific applications, and in academia and the churches, a variety of dialogues which cut deeply across the traditional lines of Asian, Jewish, and Christian faith traditions. This final section of the bibliography presents literature evidencing this range of responses. It is divided into four chapters.

Chapter 21 presents the reactionary responses to feminist theology. It presents literature on "Antifeminism" in church and society, with sociological citations indicating examples of recent research on American antifeminism, and other citations evidencing examples of antifeminist "rhetoric" in both biblical and theological literature, and--one regrets to say--at least some sociological sources. The reactionary tone of these various sources is intense. It is frequently grounded in a fundamentalist reading of not only the Bible, but historical doctrines as well, and it typically has little regard for either the symbolic or the anthropomorphic character of religious language. Indeed, there is an intense hostility within the theological antifeminist literature--and particularly as it addresses feminist trinitarian theology, for in some sources (e.g., Oddie [842]), the distinction between issues and individuals is virtually irrelevant--a circumstance sociologists recognize as a precondition for bigoted and totalitarian perspectives. (Cf. the discussion in James M. Henslin, *Sociology: A Down to Earth Approach*, 3d ed., Boston: Allyn and Bacon, 1997, pp. 421-423.) The literature in Chapter 21 is serious and cannot be ignored, for at root, it is a literature deeply opposed to the flourishing of women in both church and society.

By way of contrast, the literatures in Chapters 22 and 23 are more positive. Chapter 22 presents literature condemning both violence to women and sexual harassment within Christian churches, and Chapter 23 provides literature on the global reach of the feminist theological movement, with particular attention to the international efforts of feminist, *Mujerista* and womanist theologians on behalf of justice issues for women. These literatures are newly developing and quite strong, although as the notes internal to the Chapter 22 indicate, this particular literature is not without its problems. In particular, the literature on domestic and ecclesial violence frequently lacks definitional clarity and is subsequently open to ideological distortion, and with this, co-optation by reactionary and New Right agendas. These points are detailed in notes internal to the chapter.

Chapter 24 closes the bibliography. It surveys the developing dialogue between Jewish and Christian feminist theological perspectives, and particularly that portion of the dialogue addressing anti-Judaism in Christian feminist theology. This dialogue is one of the most important theological literatures currently in process (for both feminist *and* androcentric perspectives), for it raises anew the questions of androcentric ecumenism in the study of First and Second Testament writings, and these, as theologians of good will struggle to respond to feminism within their own historical settings and milieux.

A final note: Sources relevant to this section occur variously throughout the bibliography, but of particular relevance to Chapter 21 are the materials in Chapter 12 on feminist ethics, while entries from Chapter 1 addressing global violence to women (*viz.*, Morgan [9], Neft and Levine [10], Schmittroth [11], The United Nations Report [12], French [24] and Heise [28]) are especially salient to much of Chapter 23. Additionally, the literatures on feminist ethics, spirituality and theological anthropology are especially relevant to the discussions in Chapters 22 and 24.

21

Antifeminism and Antifeminist Theology

The backlash against feminism and the women's movement in secular society finds its religious analogue in the theological literature of those who oppose feminist thinking and theology in virtually all areas of American religious life. The most virulent and hostile of antifeminist theology, however, lies with two things: reactions to the use of feminist language for God (e.g., God as Sophia and/or Mother) and with the general assumption that women--both as well as men and in contradistinction to men--might legitimately construct, interpret and reconstruct theological tradition(s). This chapter summarizes the meanings of "backlash" **[822]** and "antifeminist" thinking **[823]** and it details five characteristics of antifeminist theology. It provides critical background literature on the social sources of antifeminist belief and attitudes (e.g., Chafetz and Dworkin **[827]**, and Gibson and Tedin **[831]**, Himmelstein **[832]**, and Klatch **[833]**) and it is fruitfully read in conjunction with materials in Sections II, III and IV. Notes internal to the chapter detail the characteristics of antifeminist theological writing and the reader is referred back to the sectional overview for further discussion of the chapter materials.

A. Antifeminism in American Society

1. Reference Works

[822] Faludi, Susan. *Backlash: The Undeclared War Against Women.* New York: Crown, 1991.
This text documents the process of backlash that occurred during the 1980s against the accomplishments of the American feminist movement. It details the character, scope and content of this backlash, and it argues persuasively that "The important question to ask about the current backlash, is not *whether* women are resisting, but how effectively" (p. 455). Faludi begins by defining and locating the current backlash. It is "the attempt...[in the decade of the '80s]...to retract the handful of small and hard-won victories that the feminist movement did manage to win for women" (p. xviii), and like backlashes of previous eras (e.g., against Seneca Falls, The National Woman's Party, women in the labor movement, and working women after World War II) it, too, occurred as women were succeeding at self determination. What distinguishes this particular backlash, however, are two things: (a) the possibilities of feminist change felt by non-feminists during the movement's heyday of the late '70s and early '80s, and (b) its character as a cumulative and culturally subliminal process, unorchestrated but sympathetic to privatized fears. Put differently, this backlash is unlike any other precisely because it was not overtly organized, but was instead, culturally amorphous, co-opting of feminist hope, and cast as a mythology of misery-cum-equality. Its conduits were multiple and included the media, corporate America, various once-liberal thinkers from the academy, the preachers of the New Right, and the policies of Ronald Reagan and George Bush, and their message was clear: To the extent that women are experiencing psychological, economic or emotional pain (all potentials at time of change), it is because feminism has been a two-edged sword, bringing both possibilities and problems, with the latter widening as

women make gains. Hence, the real problem facing women in their quest for social equality is feminism itself, and smart women will recognize this. Few topics go unexplored as Faludi exposes the co-opting of feminist rhetoric and hope, and her documentation is substantial as she literally gets down to cases (e.g., the founding of Operation Rescue, job stratification at companies such as American Cyanimid and Sears and the discrimination suits brought against them, the writings of Alan Bloom etc.). In effect, what Faludi documents is an antifeminist mythology which worked as if anonymously as women internalized its message and became its main carriers. Hence, her final question is especially valid. Critics have challenged her work, but her discussion and documentation leave little room for doubting her thesis, and her commitment remains to feminism's demand for women's social, economic, sexual and political self determination.

[823] Kinnard, Cynthia D. *Antifeminism in American Religious Thought: An Annotated Bibliography*. Boston: G. K. Hall, 1986.
This bibliography contains 1,331 entries on American "antifeminism" culled from literature published or printed between 1776 (the year of American Independence) and 1921, the year American women won the right to vote. The dates are important, Kinnard notes, because her principal concern here is *antifeminism*, and not misogyny. The latter, she indicates, can stand alone, but "antifeminism" needs "feminism," or those who "perceive inequalities between men and women in their treatment, prospects, education, opportunities for employment, roles in the family etc....[and those who]...write and speak about the inequalities, seek to explain them, and work to remove them." Hence, anyone who "opposes these activities, is by definition, an antifeminist" and thus, if in print from 1776 to 1921, a candidate for this book. Kinnard locates her material under eight subject headings: (1) "Women's Rights and Feminism;" (2) "Women's Suffrage" (including "Antisuffrage Periodicals"); (3) "Domesticity, Femininity and Motherhood;" (4) "Education of Girls and Women;" (5) "Women's Intellect and Character;" (6) "Women's Work, Professional Employment and Creativity;" (7) "Women and Religion;" and (8) "Women's Bodies." Students of religion--and especially students of the New Testament literature on Paul and women--will find section 7 illuminating: thirty-seven entries evidence the 'ecumenical' character of antifeminism in established churches between 1822 and 1920 and (contemporary apologists aside) its roots in traditional Pauline teaching. Entries are indexed by name, but not subject. **NOTE:** For related literature, see Bendroth [825] and DeBerg [828].

NOTE: Although not abstracted in the present volume, the *Journal of Feminist Studies in Religion* "Roundtable" discusson of "Backlash" well illustrates the patterns and dynamics of social control indicated by the Faludi and Kinnard sources. [See Beverly W. Harrison and Carter Heyward et al., *Journal of Feminist Studies in Religion* 10, no. 1 (Spring, 1994): 91-112.] Participants in the discussion include the following: (1) Harrison and Heyward who identify the ways in which the contemporary backlash against feminism has changed feminists: *viz.*, many feminists are becoming more [read: too] comfortable with single rather than multiple issue politics, while at the same time, others have been awakened to the scope of male rage borne of women's gains; (2) Mary Hunt, who characteristically identifies the ways in which the symbols and tactics of solidarity hide their more ominous function(s); (3) Emilie M. Townes, who identifies the effects of backlash on African American women, *viz.*, "Black women are accused of complicity with the white male system of domination in their depiction of Black men" while they experience at the same time their "commodification" as the "ultimate (and dangerous) Other by Black men (as well as [by] large elements of white society and culture)" (p. 100); (4) Starhawk, who identifies the suppressing effect of patriarchal backlash on humanity's capacity for appreciating, enjoying and protecting the creation and its wonders; (5) Anne L. Barstow, who correctly names the rhetoric of the 1994 Republican national convention as violence against women; and (6) Paula Cooey [495], who also examines the rhetoric of the 1994 Republican convention and highlights the range of violence permitted by the power norms that continue to define the "public/private," or "society/family" values split.

2.   Critical and Historical Studies

[824] Arnott, Catherine. "Feminist and Anti-feminists As 'True Believers.'" *Sociology and Social Research* 57 (1973): 300-306.
Using data from a purposive sample of 61 married women ("20 active in feminist and 41 active in antifeminist groups" [p. 300]), Arnott addressed the question: "Are feminists and antifeminists drawn from the same sociological pool?" (p. 300). Background variables, measures of autonomy, role perceptions and future goals were used as bases of contrast and tested with 2-tailed tests of

differences in means and proportions. Arnott found two populations--feminists (or liberals) and antifeminists (or reactionaries)--that permit the conclusion that feminists and antifeminists do come from differing social worlds. Specifically, Arnott found that feminists (or liberals) were more likely to be educated, to be married to professionals and engaged in (their own) professional career development, and more likely to have fewer children, a strong sense of self-determination and career goals outside the home. Additionally, they were less likely to be involved in institutionalized religion. Anti-feminists had opposite characteristics. Areas of no significant difference included divorce rates and respondents' perception of their spouses' "tension over the wife's role."

[825] Bendroth, Margaret Lamberts. *Fundamentalism and Gender: 1875 to the Present.* New Haven, CT: Yale Univ. Press, 1993.
This text in many ways parallels DeBerg [828], in that its five chapters trace the religious debates over American gender roles as inherited from the 19th century, and its broad thesis is that fundamentalism attempted a re-masculinization of religion following its feminization in the 19th century. Where it differs from DeBerg, however, is in its nuance and level of abstraction. Bendroth's main question is that "If modern evangelicalism is not inherently antifeminist, then what is the source of energy behind the incessant debates over feminism and women's roles and what purpose do these arguments serve?" (p. 2). Generally speaking, her answer is three-fold. At one level, the debates are what they are: they are the tensions of the remasculinization process. At a deeper level, however, they are the long term conflicts of fundamentalism's sense of preached family and household "order" (as developed in the 1940's and 1950s) being caught off guard by the second wave of feminism, and responding with a reassertion of strict family roles as defined by biblical literalism (i.e., woman must be obedient to males, husband authority etc.). At the same time, the debates over gender are fueled by the rise of *evangelical* feminism among neo-evangelicals and a lack of religious leadership roles for women sufficiently powerful to stave off feminist arguments available from the wider society. Bendroth identifies Letha D. Scanzoni's work ([251]) as critical to the rising 1970s debate, and she concludes that there is a near fundamentalist/feminist impasse, with fundamentalism's "men's movement" serving to widen the divide. This widening, she suggests, is especially problematic given that evangelicalism's idea of masculinity lacks both a gender language (apart from antifeminist terms), and a critique of its own scope. Moreover, masculinity is the issue to be addressed, she says, if healing and a feminist/fundamentalist rapprochement are to occur.

[826] Burris, Val. "Who Opposed the ERA? An Analysis of the Social Basis of Antifeminism." *Social Science Quarterly* 64 (1983): 305-317.
Using data collected from voters in the 1980 national election, Burris found three factors that worked against support for the Equal Rights Amendment: (1) a low level of ERA support among politically influential groups; (2) an uneven geographic distribution of ERA support; and (3) a strong association between ERA opposition and a broadly based right-wing backlash. Burris' discussion presents percentages of ERA support by respondent's race, age, region, marital status, religion, type of household, church attendance, educational, and personal and family income levels.

[827] Chafetz, Janet Saltzman, and Anthony Gary Dworkin. "In the Face of Threat: Organized Antifeminism in Comparative Perspective." In *The Sociology of Gender: A Text-Reader*, edited by Laura Kramer, 471-486. NY: St. Martin's Press, 1991.
This article examines worldwide nineteenth and twentieth century antifeminist movements to test two predictive hypotheses: that (1) "orthodox religious institutions, through their clergy would play a visible and active role in anti-feminism" (p. 473) and (2) "economic-vested interest groups that perceived threats from women's movements would support antifeminist activities, but often covertly" (p. 475). The premise for these predictions is that *organized* backlash movements arise only after change-directed movements appear to be achieving their goals and thus constitute a threat to established interests or patterns. The data for the predictions were gathered from "a comprehensive literature search of English language sources that have anything to say about [anti-women's/antifeminist] movements, and the discussion is directed to *organized* opposition evidenced by "nongovernmental organizations and institutions which predate the women's movements" (p. 473) they seek to oppose. By way of findings, both predictions were sustained, albeit with some modification. Specifically, the authors found that: (1) oppositions to women's movements do mount as such movements achieve their goals; (2) the largest source of opposition comes from economic vested interests with religious vested interests entering the opposition openly only after the covert economic efforts seem to have failed; and (3) the contours of opposition after the apparent failure of economic efforts are often cast ideologically through patriotic and family related symbols that, in turn, mask class and economic interests. The support for finding #3 rests

with research attesting: (1) the predominantly elite male financial support of "voluntary" antifeminist groups (whose membership is largely generated by their wives), and (2) the perceived threat of working class males that women will "take" their jobs. Lastly, the exceptions to the prediction on religious leadership are based on American rather than international observations: i.e., the role of Catholicism in the anti-abortion movement and the mobilization of New Right religious leadership that provided the symbolic imagery of patriotic and familistic sentiment for antifeminist organizational efforts (cf. the entries by Marshall below [835-836]).

[828] DeBerg, Betty A. *Ungodly Women: Gender and the First Wave of American Feminism.* Minneapolis, MN: Fortress Press, 1990.
Working from both the current historical literature on fundamentalism and a variety of sermons, premilleniarist journals and other popular level sources drawn from the period 1880-1930, DeBerg summarizes the "rhetoric about gender used by the fundamentalists and their turn of the century predecessors" to argue that (1) contemporary historians of fundamentalism have missed an important dimension of its central turn of the century character and (2) they have thus inaccurately portrayed the more recent New Right's attack on gender as, in fact, new, rather than an "heir" of first wave fundamentalism. It is an important thesis, and while the text is not self-identified as feminist, it obviously dovetails with much in feminist and women studies literature. In brief, DeBerg first summarizes the main emphases of Victorian gender roles (as consequences of the industrial revolution) to indicate not only the realities of "separate spheres" and women's roles in religion, but the three main realities that defined masculinity for western [white] males prior to (and lost with) industrialization: *viz.*, the physical strength demands of work, a hunter/warrior capacity for ruthless competition, and the role of family patriarch--described here as the ability to produce sons and ensure patriarchal continuity via inheritance and deeded property. Second, DeBerg notes the liberating forces of Victorian mores for women (e.g., suffrage, temperance etc.) and the widened public role of women as guardians of society. In turn, she details the threat these mores provided to fundamentalist and conservative male church leaders and their subsequent need to remasculinize both Christianity and the ministry position. Subsequent chapters then provide specifics in terms of the lost masculinity needs listed above, and a closing chapter indicates the omission of this "Gender Agenda" in contemporary histories of evangelical work. Although sociologists accustomed to content analysis will perhaps wish for a more specific statement of study methodology, this is a persuasive and well documented text, and particularly so for readers seeking early antifeminist fundamentalist literature. Also by DeBerg is [678].

[829] Dworkin, Andrea. *Right-Wing Women.* New York: G. P. Putnam's Sons, 1983.
This volume is an intense, frank critique of Right-Wing social and political thinking as the latter is directed to American women's fears of exploitation and dependency. It identifies the ideological scope of antifeminist thinking, its grounds and roots in male violence against women, its subsequent "benefits" for women who choose traditional rather than feminist roles, and the ideological consistency of Right-Wing thinking on such issues as abortion, homosexuality, and female poverty. It is powerful reading and recommended for those seeking an exposition of how antifeminism can and does mobilize both women and men against the feminist movement.

[830] Eisenstein, Zillah. "The Sexual Politics of the New Right: Understanding the Crisis in Liberalism in the 1980s." In *Feminist Theory: A Critique of Ideology,* edited by O. Keohane, Michelle Z. Rosaldo, and Barbara C. Gelpi, 77-98. Chicago: University of Chicago Press, 1982.
This essay presents a detailed account of how the New Right emerged through the early 1980s to challenge feminism and reestablish the white-male patriarchal family unit as the norm for American social/domestic policy. The argument develops in terms of two main points and the discussion provides supportive statistics in terms of specific New Right leaders and constituencies, the role of neo-conservatives, the interaction of racial and gender ideologies, and Reagan administration policies. In brief, Eisenstein first advances her thesis that in its efforts to solve the problems of the American family, the New Right misread history and thus inaccurately assessed the crisis of American political liberalism. That is, it viewed the growth of the welfare state as the cause of problems within the traditional American family unit, and not a response to problems already present. And here, Eisenstein notes the presumed normativeness of the white, two parent, mother at home, father working family model and the various New Right groups that worked to support this perspective. Second, Eisenstein exposes the real crisis of liberalism in the early 1980s, i.e., that as married women entered the paid labor force but were *yet* required to perform full time at home duties, they perceived the "conflict between liberalism as an ideology about equality and the sexual inequality of patriarchy as a structural requisite of the capitalist market" (p. 90). Hence, the New

Right attack on wage earning women and the development of New Right anti-feminism cast as pro-familism. Third, Eisenstein details the role of feminist legislation in this process, and particularly the possibility of it engendering additional progressive change. While her data are dated, the argument rings true and particularly so in the light of such analyses as, e.g., Marshall [835-836] below.

[831] Gibson, James L., and Kent Tedin. "The Etiology of Intolerance of Homosexual Politics." *Social Science Quarterly* 69 (1988): 587-604.
Using telephone interview data from representative samples of voters (n=372) and non-voters (n= 247) registered at the time of a Houston, Texas referendum against gay rights, the authors examine factors influencing the sources and maintenance of intolerance for homosexual rights. They test a general model that "posits that tolerance of gay rights is a direct function of attitudes toward democratic norms as well as perception of threats from gays" (p. 593) and they find support for its many specific hypotheses. Namely, that (1) "greater support for the norms of democracy is associated with greater political tolerance of homosexuals"; (2) "greater political activism is associated with willingness to tolerate homosexual rights"; (3) "liberals are more tolerant [than conservatives] of the rights of homosexuals"; (4) "greater support for New Right issues is associated with greater intolerance of homosexual rights"; (5) "those who are especially threatened by homosexuals are more likely to favor political repression against them"; (6) "those who are more dogmatic are more intolerant of homosexuals"; and (7) "consistent with existing literature...high levels of education and income, youth and low levels of religiosity contribute to the tolerance of homosexual rights" (pp. 590-593). Gibson and Tedin find strong support for their model, with their path analysis indicating that support for democratic values is the strongest predictor of tolerance and perceived threats from gays the strongest predict of intolerance. Among their conclusions they note the role of education in exposure to diversity, the association between psychological inflexibility and intolerant attitudes and given the growing conservatism in America, the need to continue to monitor intolerance of homosexual rights. NOTE: For early related literature, see Nancy Henley and Fred Pincus, "Interrelationship of Sexist, Racist and Antihomosexual Attitudes." *Psychological Reports* 42 (1978): 83-90.

[832] Himmelstein, Jerome. "The Social Bases of Antifeminism: Religious Networks and Culture." *Journal for the Scientific Study of Religion* 25 (1986): 1-15.
Using data from studies published principally during the ten year period, 1975-1984, Himmelstein examines and rejects two currently held theories about opposition both to abortion and the ERA: i.e., theory #1, which argues that "Anti-abortion and anti-ERA movements have disproportionate appeal among lower SES, rural and older constituencies...[whether for]...status anxiety engendered by social change" or class conflicts over a range of issues (p. 1); and theory #2, "antifeminist sentiments are...paradoxically more prevalent among women who are the most vulnerable to and dependent upon men" (p. 2). Himmelstein argues that survey data from several sources do not support either of these theories. Rather, what explains antifeminist postures (including sentiments and activities directed against abortion and the ERA) is church attendance, regardless of denomination. This is because church attendance places one in a culture that supports traditional images of women and family life, and additionally, in a network of relationships readily available for antifeminist recruitment by those seeking such adherents. This is a tightly argued study based on secondary data with a solid theoretical discussion of religion, antifeminism and the intermediary linkages between public and private work-family spheres. For the discussion of religion and antifeminism world wide see Chafetz and Dworkin [827].

[833] Klatch, Rebecca E. *Women of the New Right.* Philadelphia: Temple Univ. Press, 1987.
This study identifies two types of political conservatism among women of the New Right. The first is "social conservatism." It views American history and experience through the lens of religious fundamentalism and finds that: (a) "traditional religion" is and should be the basis for society's values and social policies, and (b) the family unit is *the* moral cornerstone of society. The second type of conservatism identified by Klatch is "laissez-faire conservatism." This conservatism focuses American experience and history through the lens of individual achievement, or the assumption that all individuals are rational self-interested actors seeking to maximize their own abilities. Klatch's discussion is based on interviews with white middle class women from the Massachusetts area (N=30), participant observation in conference and organizational meetings, and an analysis of New Right documents and literature. After contrasting the two "world views" of New Right women, Klatch analyzes several uniting symbols ("Communism," "Big Government," and "Feminism") that are differentially understood by these two types of conservatives, and she discusses their

ideological implications for the future of New Right women. This is an insightful look at the social and political assumptions of New Right *women*, with strong, testable implications for understanding various responses to feminism by *ordained* women in both liberal and conservative churches.

[834] Küng, Hans and Jürgen Moltmann, eds. *Fundamentalism as an Ecumenical Challenge.* London: SCM Press, 1992.
Five divisions make up this *Concilium* reader. Definitions of fundamentalism come first, with Martin Marty providing the lead essay: "What Is Fundamentalism? Theological Perspectives." Social psychological, psychiatric and sociological perspectives then follow, by respectively, G. Müller-Fahrenholz, G. Hole, and John Coleman. Discussions of Jewish, Islamic and Christian fundamentalisms are handled separately, with the format comprised by descriptive and responsive essays: e.g., "What is the Challenge of Contemporary Jewish [or Islamic or Christian] Fundamentalism?" and "What Shall be the Answer to Contemporary Jewish [Islamic, Christian] Fundamentalism?" Essays by the volume editors then synthesize the discussions and offer responses to Catholic and Protestant fundamentalisms particularly. Contributors include Jacob Neusner and S.E. Karff for Jewish fundamentalism; E. Elshahed and M. Salim Abdullah for Islamic fundamentalism; and C. Yannaras, P. Hebblethwaite, and M. Volf for three pieces, "Orthodox Traditionalism," "A Fundamentalist Pope?" and "The Challenge of Protestant Fundamentalism," respectively. While by no means the scope of the "Fundamentalism Project," [see, e.g., "Book Review Symposia," *Review of Religious Research* 36 (1995): 389-402] the collection fulfills its purpose of providing informative overviews, although feminist frameworks are notably absent.

[835] Marshall, Susan E. "Keep Us on the Pedestal: Women Against Feminism in Twentieth Century America." In *Women: A Feminist Perspective* (4th ed.) edited by Jo Freeman, 567-580. Mountain View, CA: Mayfield, 1989.
This article is a helpful introduction to the issues of antifeminism as organized activity against the establishment of feminist values. Marshall provides a brief history of antifeminist attitudes among American women and in turn, identifies three elements of antifeminist ideology. These are: "...the reaffirmation of divinely ordained sex differences, support for the traditional family as a necessary basis for the continuation of society, and [the] alignment of antifeminism with unselfish patriotism" (p. 569). In her discussion Marshal analyzes Phyllis Schafly's political use of these three themes and she identifies antifeminism as a form of status politics engaging specific class interests and frustrations. The article is clear, well documented and particularly helpful if read as a preamble to Marshall's more recent discussion, **[836]** below.

[836] Marshall, Susan E. "Who Speaks for American Women? The Future of Antifeminism." *The Annals of the American Academy of Political and Social Science* 515 (May, 1991): 50-62.
This article examines the "antifeminist movement in the post-ERA decade" to review relevant research on antifeminist activities and to posit explanations about the relative successes of recent antifeminist activity. The two antifeminist groups Marshall examines are the Eagle Forum (led by Phyllis Schafly) and Conservative Women for America (led by Beverly LaHaye). This is an important article. Its discussion is clear and informative and its analyses are on the mark. It identifies abortion, comparable worth, child care and parental leave as significant antifeminist issues for the 1990s (p. 58), and it identifies the "major appeal" of the current antifeminist movement as its "linkage of class resentments, parental authority and moral righteousness" (p. 60). Moreover, Marshall underscores the alignment of antifeminist efforts and the work of the Christian Right. By way of closure, Marshall notes the potential for antifeminist decline, given the scandals attached to TV evangelists throughout the 1980s and the demise of communism as an American foe in the late 1980s. However, Marshall readily acknowledges the potential for mobilization among currently frustrated antifeminist adherents, and she suggests feminism's recognition of antifeminism as a "worthy opponent" to the feminist movement. **NOTE:** See Marshall's analysis, "Confrontation and Cooptation in Antifeminist Organizations," pp. 323-355, in Ferree and Martin **[119]**.

[837] Petchesky, Rosalind Pollack. "Anti-abortion, Antifeminism, and the Rise of the New Right." *Feminist Studies* 7 (1981): 206-246.
This is an extremely lucid account of the early years of the American New Right as a specifically "backlash," "pro-family" movement. The author argues persuasively that the "pro-family" motifs of the New Right constitute, in fact, an ideological gloss covering an antifeminist, anti-social welfare backlash, and that the conceptual linchpin of this ideological gloss is the concept of privacy

and the "reprivatization" of morality. Where the glossing *begins* is in the New Right's use of the anti-abortion movement to engender the idea that individuals must work against government intrusion into private matters; where it *actually occurs* is in the *corporate* (i.e., business and church but not individual) underwriting of efforts to bar government intrusion, and *where it is completed* is in the fact of individuals' buying the package, such that male patriarchal family structures are kept intact and all departures from its heterosexist assumptions are viewed as the cause of society's ills (of which there were many by 1980). To counter this ideological process, Petchetsky cites the feminist observation and argument that the bourgeoisie distinction between public and private spheres holds only for men and not for women, and that it is women's taking hold of their sexuality (by means of the ability and opportunity to make choices about reproduction) that is most threatening to New Right patriarchal, profamily advocates. Data from then current marriage, divorce, and working-women statistics bolster her discussion, and she concludes to the clear linkage between anti-abortion and reprivatization as elements of the backlash movements being played out at that time. A number of clear and related supportive discussions run through this article (e.g., an analysis of the Protestant Catholic ecumenism of the New Right and a review of the 1980 election and the New Right's involvement in it), and in spite of its now sporadically outdated statistics, it remains a theoretically strong analysis and relevant discussion of religion and its backlash possibilities.

B. Antifeminism in Biblical, Sociological and Theological Discourse

The following entries by no means exhaust the scope of antifeminist writings found in theological and popular religious journals. They do, however, illustrate the emphases and types of arguments--both subtle and strident--that opponents of feminist theology tend to employ. Generally speaking, the literature published in opposition to feminist theology is characterized by five features. *First*, it specifically *opposes* the feminist theological literature, rather than engage in dialogue with it on either its own behalf or that of a larger vision. *Second*, the oppositional literature frequently engages in polemics against specific feminist theologians, rather than discuss important issues about which there needs to be--at least initially, a search for some common ground. Moreover, it typically does not recognize feminist theologians as peers within a community of scholars and/or the ecclesial-theological community. *Third*, the antifeminist literature frequently employs ridicule and trivialization as vehicles of "discussion about" feminist insights, and in tones typically patronizing and theologically dismissive. *Fourth*, the antifeminist literature often attempts a *delegitimation* of feminist insight through the reassertion of misogynist and non-egalitarian gender roles vis a vis religious imagery, and typically without attending to the acknowledged pain that such imagery can generate. Last, *a fifth* characteristic of the oppositional literature is its reactionary attention to the feminist critique of patriarchy and misogyny (and particularly the feminist reading of biblical literature) and its lack of constructive attention to the feminist literature on the issues of inclusivity (i.e., pluralism and catholicity), peace making, and an ecumenical effort against violence toward women in both church and society. Indeed, in addition to the trivialization of women's voices and the personalized attacks on individual theologians, it is this selective and limited attention to the literature that is most obvious, as nuanced statements are pulled out of context and set against "traditions" without the benefit of collegial or peer measured discourse. Each of the entries below exhibits one or more of these characteristics and each is, for that reason, classified as "antifeminist" or oppositional to the feminist theological literature.

1. Biblical-theological Antifeminism

[838] Achtemeier, Elizabeth. "The Impossible Possibility: Evaluating the Feminist Approach to Bible and Theology." *Interpretation* 42 (1988): 45-57.
After indicating several disclaimers concerning the scope and sources for her task, Achtemeier "evaluates" what she describes as "the feminist approach to the Bible." Five sources inform her discussion: two essays by Schüssler Fiorenza [369, 483], selections from Ruether's hermeneutical work [366, 545], her texts *Sexism and God-Talk* [190] and *Women-Church* [193], and selected elements from Letty Russell's early work (*Growth in Partnership*). The task is "difficult," says Achtemeier, both because Protestant women do not always know how to "deal fairly" with the "rage" of "some Roman Catholics" (p. 47), and because "an appeal to the Bible...immediately calls into question, for many feminists, any critique of their positions" (p. 48). These difficulties notwithstanding, Achtemeier finds three problems with "the feminist approach to the Bible." First, feminists make "their own experience the authoritative judge of what is or is not the word of God" (p. 50). Second, "Many of them do not want to trust a Lord..." (p. 54). Third, "because some males have arrogated to themselves the rule of God...feminists...try to eliminate all

masculine language for God in liturgy, theology and the Bible..." (p. 55). According to Achtemeier, problems #1-2 may be solved by letting "scripture interpret itself." Problem #3 is insoluble, however, for by eliminating masculine language for God--and by substituting female, "mother" language for God--the "personal" and "holy other" quality of God's being is lost (pp. 55-56). As an "evaluation," Achtemeier's discussion is limited in at least three ways: (1) it lacks clearly developed criteria for assessing the adequacy of feminist approaches to the both the Bible and theology; (2) it ignores the plurality of feminist approaches to the Bible; and (3) it is exegetically uninformed and reflects, thereby, the very misogyny feminist theology seeks to dismantle. For a discussion that deals substantively with the full range of feminist biblical literature and issues through the late 1980s, see Tolbert, [284] "Protestant Feminists and the Bible: On the Horns of a Dilemma."

[839] Brighton, I. A. "The Ordination of Women: A Twentieth-Century Gnostic Heresy?" *Concordia Journal* 8 (1982): 12-18.
This essay examines Gnostic literature to survey its affirmations of women's social and religious equality with men and the use of masculine and feminine language for God. By way of development, Brighton presents a series of contrasts between Gnostic statements and "orthodox Christianity," that permit him the conclusion that [the] "orthodox Christianity of the early church with its theology of a Triune God could not but reject the practice of the ordination of women into the public ministry" (p. 16). Brighton's essay is clearly written, and given the copious quality of its notes, seemingly well-documented. It is, however, seriously flawed. First, although Brighton roots his discussion in a notion of the early church, he presents no criteria by which to distinguish this early church Christianity from "orthodox Christianity." Rather, absent criteria are simply presumed. Second, while some biblical literature is presented to illuminate the discussion of Sophia as a source of feminine language for God (e.g., citations from Proverbs and Wisdom literature), the biblical literature on women's leadership roles is noticeably absent. This is a serious omission, given the subject at hand. Finally, while Brighton's title suggests a specific question, Brighton ignores it. Instead, the question is rhetorical, as is the reader's (presumably positive) response to it. For more informed discussions of gnosticism and gendered God-language, see Ruether's *Sexism and God-Talk* [190], Clark's *Women in the Early Church* [296], Farley [167], Schüssler Fiorenza [401-402] and LaCugna [234, 458].

[840] Kimel, Alvin F., Jr. "The God Who Likes His Name: Holy Trinity, Feminism, and the Language of Faith." *Interpretation* 45 (1991): 147-158.
In a discussion heavily indebted to the work of Protestant theologian Robert Jenson [*The Triune Identity: God According to the Gospel.* Philadelphia: Fortress Press, 1982] this article argues for a literal reading of the trinitarian formula "Father-Son-Spirit" as an actual, proper, and personal name for the Christian God, as distinct, e.g., from other gods. The circumstance occasioning this discussion is Sally McFague's [244] attempt at an inclusive recasting of traditional trinitarian language (from the language of Father-Son-Spirit to that of "Creator-Redeemer-Sustainer" or alternatively, "Mother-Lover-Friend"), and in Kimel's judgment, this attempt is an apostasy from Christian tradition and an act that "must result in an alienation from the gospel." Thus he argues, "The triune God has named himself, and he likes his name" (p. 147). To support his thesis Kimel summarizes Basil's "grammar" of the triune name and its significance for Christian identity and belonging: As the source of an individual's incorporation into the Christian church, this triune name constitutes both God and the baptized Christian's fundamental identity, and thus departures from it--or attempts to replace it--are acts of apostasy that threaten the substance of the gospel and should be named as such. Kimel's position is similar to that of other trinitarian fundamentalists (cf., e.g., Wainwright [845], and the passion of his commitment to the appellation of "Father-Son-Spirit" as, literally, God's proper name, is unmistakable. His discussion lacks, however, an attention to the theoretical nuances underlying McFague's work, and it relies, instead, upon a literalist reading of religious language per se. For additional fundamentalist trinitarian literature, see Wainwright [845]. Alternatively, for a feminist discussion of God's "name," see Collins [517], and for feminist interpretations of trinitarian doctrine, see Farley [166], LaCugna [234], and Duck [457].

[841] Mannion, M. Francis. "The Church and the Voices of Feminism." *America* 165 (1991): 212-216.
Mannion's essay attempts a functional definition of feminism along a continuum of "narrow" to "wide" definitions. Narrow definitions present feminism as "a self-conscious movement aimed at the radical renewal of society and religion and the ending of patriarchy and the historical oppression of women." Wide definitions present feminism as "a complex and many sided movement dedicated

to advancing and securing the appropriate roles (however understood) of women in church and society" (p. 212). In this light, the author indicates five types of "church-related feminism." These are "affirmative," "corrective," "reformist," "reconstructive" and "separatist." Linchpin emphases for these categories of "church-feminism" include the extent to which potential category members affirm both (a) traditional sex role ideologies (including that of "complementarity") and (b) the legitimacy of hierarchical church authorities as the normative definers of "appropriate roles." Thus, to the extent that theologians depart from (a) or (b) they are slated accordingly, and Mannion locates selected contemporary feminist theologians within his constructed categories. Prima facie, Mannion's article seems helpful with its proposed typology, but in fact, it is seriously flawed. First, the variable better described by the Mannion's categories and discussion is *patriarchal authority*, not feminism; that is, it is male religious hierarchs and not women who here are identified as the legitimate interpreters of women's roles. Second, as used by Mannion, the concept "feminism" itself changes across typology categories and affirms as similar various concepts that are clearly opposed in both meaning and (empirical) referents, or indicators. This is an extremely reactionary piece, and for more helpful classificatory literature, the reader is referred to Osiek [354], to Chopp's definitional article on feminist theology [264], or Russell and Clarkson [272].

[842] Oddie, William. *What Will Happen to God? Feminism and the Reconstruction of Christian Belief.* San Francisco: St. Ignatius Press, 1988.
This work is ostensibly a critique of feminist theology and specifically, feminist theology as it appears in the Episcopal Church in the United States. More realistically, it is admittedly (pp. xvi-xvii) a frightened and angry condemnation of four things: feminist consciousness as expressed by Betty Friedan's *Feminine Mystique*; the use of inclusive language in prayer and liturgy as expressed in a particular service used by Episcopal priest Carter Heyward; feminist religious consciousness as expressed by Mary Daly and Naomi Goldenberg; and fourth, feminist Christian scholarship as expressed by Rosemary Radford Ruether and Elisabeth Schüssler Fiorenza. The body of literature addressed by Oddie is scant, and especially so in the cases of Ruether and Schüssler Fiorenza. Further, materials from each of these writers are quoted out of context (see, e.g., chapter 19), and works by male scholars and/or exegetes (e.g., Throckmorton [355]) who support feminist scholarship are ignored. Rather, according to Oddie, the task at hand is to save Christian tradition *as a context of male authority,* with Ephesians 5 and the theology of Karl Barth as the primary rationales (see especially chapters 8, "Hierarchy and Equality" and 19, "The Big Lie"). A final, almost epiphenomenal argument is also made: *viz.*, that given the technological state of modern life, *males* as well as females are alienated and suffering as much or more than females, and feminist theologians don't seem--in Oddie's judgment--to notice or care about this (cf. chapter 17). Oddie's discussion here borders on "victim blaming" of the worst kind, and his closing reassertions of "Christian authority and subordination" as the "...necessary and complimentary foundations of an authentically Christian ecclesial and social order" are appalling, and especially so, as he ignores such feminist theological concerns as efforts at peace-making, ecological ethics, and the eradication of women's poverty, illiteracy and sexual exploitation across the globe.

[843] Steichen, Donna. *Ungodly Rage: The Hidden Face of Catholic Feminism.* San Francisco: St. Ignatius Press, 1991.
This volume selectively examines Catholic feminist theological literature to argue that feminism is ultimately destructive of Catholicism, and particularly American Catholicism. It is particularly critical of Mary Daly, Rosemary Radford Ruether, Sandra Schneiders and Elisabeth Schüssler Fiorenza and its grounding implication is that Catholic feminism is, in effect, the work of a small group of women opposed to church authority and who are, thereby, unfaithful to Catholic tradition and (at best) "brainwashing" the church with its new [feminist] teachings. The text is passionately written and seemingly documented as it pits Catholicism's uncritical conservatism against the writings of these four women. At root, however, it ignores the scholarship of these theologians and rests on ideology, and it is more an experience of what Coleman and others describe as "Catholic Fundamentalism." See e.g., John Coleman, "Who Are the Catholic Fundamentalists?" *Commonweal* 115 (Jan. 27, 1989): 42-47 and Patrick M. Arnold "The Rise of Catholic Fundamentalism" and M. Timothy Iglesias "CUFF and Dissent: A Case Study in Religious Conservatism" in *America* 156 (April 11, 1987): 297-306.

[844] Stroup, George W. "Between Echo and Narcissus: The Role of the Bible in Feminist Theology." *Interpretation* 42 (1988): 19-32.
After an extended comparison between feminist and patriarchal theologies as, respectively, the condemned voice of Echo and the self-serving Narcissus of ancient myth, the author presents a series of questions he derives from his reading of Osiek [354], Ruether [190, 366], Russell

[249], Schüssler Fiorenza [196] and Tolbert [372]. He focuses primarily on the feminist use of women's experience as a framework for biblical interpretation (and especially as articulated by Ruether) and he argues, that feminism does not guarantee any less an ideological reading of the Bible than does patriarchy or androcentrism. Moreover, he affirms that it is "not the critical principle of full humanity, but the Bible itself, witnessing to God's judgment on human sin and God's promise of grace, [that] is the only adequate basis for Christian theology" (p. 32). Stroup's position is, prima facie, one response (albeit dogmatic) to feminist theology; but what classifies it as antifeminist here are two things. First, it bears an intensely ridiculing and mocking tone. This is evident in the opening Echo/Narcissus introduction, the author's selective characterization of Schüssler Fiorenza's work as a "paranoid style of feminist hermeneutics" (p. 25), and on page 26, his visibly clear misreading of Ruether's carefully nuanced characterization of women's experience as a "key" to feminist hermeneutics. None of Stroup's statements here suggest an endeavor on behalf of dialogue and mutually worked at truth. Second, Stroup's essay bears no "what if" statements about the legitimacy of the feminist theological critique of Christian tradition, but presents instead, a near knee-jerk reaction to what are (else wise) accepted principles of theological methodology. Put differently, although Stroup argues strenuously that the issue of women's experience in interpretation is not the issue of exegesis vs. eisegesis (objective vs. subjective readings of the Bible), he nonetheless concludes to an almost reified understanding of the process of scriptural interpretation, with little or no attention to the role of culture and historical consciousness (including issues of gender and experience) as factors in the interpretive process. This lack suggests an inattentiveness to the practices and experience of the *entire* believing community as members of the interpretive setting, and it suggests thereby, that women who are feminists may not accurately or adequately interpret Scripture by virtue of this fact. This eclipsed perspective, together with the ridiculing, demeaning and almost combative tone of his discussion, all suggest a misogynist and deeply antifeminist agenda in an article that purports to raise theological questions on behalf of the Scripture it seeks to uphold.

[845] Wainwright, Geoffrey. "The Doctrine of the Trinity: Where the Church Stands or Falls." *Interpretation* 45 (1991): 117-132.
Wainwright's chief contention in this article is that "Once more the understanding, and perhaps the attainment [*sic.*], of salvation is at stake, or certainly the message of the church, and the church's visible composition" (p. 117) [is at stake] because of the current attempt to re-conceptualize the traditional trinitarian language as an appropriate name for God. The challenge comes from three camps (feminists, deists and religionists), but the bulk of Wainwright's attention here is directed to a critique of feminist trinitarian theology. According to Wainwright, feminists cite two factors as the primary reasons for re-conceptualizing the traditional trinitarian language for God. First, such language implies "a paternalistic or worse, a patriarchal society and church" (p. 118). Second, such language should be re-cast in cultural motifs more appropriate to the contemporary period, since all language is ultimately metaphorical. Wainwright's targeted sources are, respectively, Mary Daly (who argues in *Beyond God the Father* [161] that Christianity is hopelessly and irretrievably patriarchal); and Sally McFague, who argues in *Metaphorical Theology* [200] that "mother" and "friend" language may also be used for God, as well as the language of "Creator, Revealer, and Sustainer." To these arguments Wainwright offers several of his own. First, the term Fatherhood does not mean the "masculinity" of God, but rather, it is the term Jesus used for God. Moreover, fourth century theology also recognizes the symbolic quality of God language and evidences this in the creedal language for the second person who is said to be "begotten, not made" (and with such begetting not limited to male imagery only). However, says Wainwright, the use of "Abba" by Jesus suggests a primary and "unsubstitutable" metaphor for God, for "how...[asks Wainwright]...could we ever know that another [metaphor] was 'equivalent?'" (p. 120). Therefore, concludes Wainwright, the traditional language should be maintained. Second, the "Creator, Sustainer, Redeemer" appellation is also unacceptable, because it permits the possibility of Sabellianism [the heresy that God is in three-fold relation to the world, but not three persons *in se*]. In contrast, says Wainwright, traditional trinitarian theology affirms a communion of persons in God, not functional relations to the world only. Third, (and related) the term Creator can imply Arianism, making God the creator of evil. Fourth, there is an inherent connection between trinitarian language and atonement, given both the Incarnation and its scope. Hence, the feminist attempt to re-conceptualize this traditional language is to be thwarted. Wainwright continues his critique in terms of deist and religionist attempts to alter trinitarian language and in a closing summary point addressing the charge that this language is culturally parochial, he responds that "it is reasonable to suppose that it [such language] was divinely meant to remain intelligible as long as human beings remain recognizably human beings..." (p. 131). Wainwright's discussion expresses a dogmatic fundamentalism that appears hostile to positions different from his own, and it is

unfamiliar with both the exegetical literature dismantling the Jesus/ABBA special relationship hypothesis, and the current state of trinitarian theology (feminist *or* androcentric). Hence, for a more scholarly treatment of contemporary trinitarian theology from within the mainstream Protestantism, see, e.g., Jurgen Moltmann, The *Crucified God: The Cross of Christ as the Foundation and Criticism of Christian Theology* (New York: Harper & Row, 1974). While not recognized as a feminist text, it lacks the doctrinaire and hostile tone of Wainwright's discussion. Likewise, for representative Catholic feminist literature on the Trinity, see LaCugna [234], and Carr [229]; while for representative Protestant feminist literature see McFague [200, 244], Suchocki [427], and in terms of worship, Duck [457] and Ramshaw [523].

[846] Witherington, Ben. *Women in the Ministry of Jesus: A Study of Jesus' Attitudes Toward Women and their Roles as Reflected in His Earthly Life.* Cambridge: Cambridge U. Press, 1984.

This volume incorporates article material published earlier by Witherington ["On the Road with Mary Magdalene, Joanna, Susanna, and Other Disciples--Luke 8:1-3." *Zeitschrift fur die Neutestamentliche Wissenschaft* 70(1979): 243-248 and "Rites and Rights for Women--Galatians 3:28" *New Testament Studies* 27(1981): 593-604] and is the published version of Witherington's doctoral dissertation. It thus represents an extended and heavily foot-noted summary of Witherington's research on women in the New Testament. Additionally, it is the first of Witherington's three books on this subject (see below). It is a scrupulously detailed work that presumes a passable reading knowledge of Koine Greek, and it argues consistently for the thesis that Christianity did not seek to reject patriarchy, but rather to reform it within the context of the Christian community. Witherington's argument is twofold: First, he argues that while Jesus was obviously different from his Jewish contemporaries in terms of his interactions with women and his teachings on divorce, celibacy and the norms governing sexual behaviors (of women and men), he cannot for these facts be considered a feminist (or alternatively) one who sought to reject patriarchal leadership. Second, because Jesus did choose "twelve men to be leaders of His new community" (p. 126) it is clear that he desired to reform, but not reject patriarchy as a form of religious-social organization. Witherington's arguments here seem strong, but his discussion is, in fact, moot. First, while virtually every sentence is footnoted, the discussion at no point seriously examines feminist exegetical work on "the twelve" (cf. e.g., Schüssler Fiorenza in [401]), or relatedly, the notion of apostleship implied by Witherington's own assumptions about leadership. Second, Witherington does not address the hermeneutical issues implicit throughout his argument, i.e., the role of both the Bible and other (more secular) sources of insight into the question of Christian leadership, and specifically the forms leadership might be expected take in late twentieth century culture and society. These limitations cast doubts on the "objectivity" that Witherington's "biblical theology" so stridently seeks to achieve. Further, they mask his central affirmation that patriarchy is a legitimate dimension of Christianity, both in terms of its beginnings *and* current practice. Hence the location of Witherington's work within antifeminist rather than feminist biblical scholarship.

[847] Witherington, Ben. *Women in the Earliest Churches.* Cambridge: Cambridge Univ. Press, 1988.

As with his earlier work [846], this second of Witherington's books is highly technical and it requires a familiarity with both New Testament exegesis and Koine Greek. By way of content, Witherington stresses four main points: First is the argument that neither Jesus nor Paul intended to reject patriarchy, but rather to reform it within the Christian community. Witherington's logic here is two-fold: (a) because Jesus chose twelve men to lead the Christian community but differed from Jewish teaching on marital and sex role expectations, he thereby evidenced a desire to reform but not repudiate patriarchy as a form of social and religious organization; (b) because Paul's writings are rooted in an awareness of Christ as the redemption of creation through its own reformation, Paul also sought a reformation but not a rejection of patriarchy. Witherington's second point addresses "women's roles" (in early Christianity) and it is two-tracked. On the one hand, women's roles within the early church are discussed under the rubric of the "physical family," and here Christianity adds nothing save the possibility of women learning such roles through the call to discipleship. On the other hand, the "family of faith" clearly opens out *new* roles for women, for in the "family of faith" women in fact *do* all the tasks that in later times will be associated with the behaviors of ordained clergy. Thus, Witherington's third point is that the New Testament provides no impediment to the ordination of women. Witherington's last point raises the question of the Bible's authority for understanding contemporary women's roles, and particularly their familial roles. However, his discussion here remains incomplete. He suggests on the one hand that some writers seem to import a "selective hermeneutic" as the final arbiter of faith and practice within the

Church--or that they use a standard of judgment external to the Bible to serve as the norm for the Church's faith and practice. Witherington rejects this strategy for he sees it as illegitimate within the context of biblical studies. At the same time, Witherington does not offer any extended solution to the question, but instead suggests a theological possibility. This theological possibility is that it is the *direction of the New Testament data towards reformation* that should serve as the normative principle for current issues (about women's roles) and that it is theoretically possible that the Church may ultimately reform itself to the point of abandoning patriarchy and no longer need such reformation. Witherington then concludes that howsoever this issue is resolved, it should rest on solid historical exegesis, and he offers his research as an aid in that process. As with Witherington's earlier work, this too ignores the available exegetical literature on both leadership and "the twelve" **[401]** and the role of power in community development. Thus, just as he suggests of the New Testament, Witherington too leaves patriarchy in tact and established as a normative value of the Christian community. Hence his work remains decidedly androcentric in spite of its seemingly "objective" analysis, and it should be read in conjunction with other and specifically feminist sources.

[848] Witherington, Ben. *Women and the Genesis of Christianity.* Cambridge: Cambridge Univ. Press, 1990.
This volume is Witherington's popularized synthesis of his two previously published technical works **[846-847]** on women in the New Testament. As such, it presents no new material, but provides readers with an accessible discussion of Witherington's various exegetical notes and his consistent argument that neither Jesus nor Paul sought to repudiate patriarchy, but rather to reform it. For the technical sources see entries **[846-847]** above.

2. Antifeminist Sociology

[849] DeSanto, Charles and Margaret Poloma, eds. *Social Problems: Christian Perspectives.* Winston-Salem, NC: Hunter Textbooks, 1985.
Readers expecting an informed discussion between social science and mainstream theological perspectives will be disappointed by this volume. This is because DeSanto and Poloma have presented a collection of ideologically based essays that read sociological data from within the assumptions of Pentecostal Christianity in its most judgmental of forms. A major emphasis is on sexuality and the condemnation of all sexual experience apart from monogamous heterosexual marriage relations. While this may serve to bolster American fundamentalism, it does not qualify as serious sociology, either theoretically or methodologically. Further, the tone and grounding assumptions are openly antifeminist. This is illustrated clearly in the entries by, for example, Frank Houser on "The Family" (pp. 166-178) and Sandra Miller and John S. Miller on "Changing Sex Roles," (pp. 179-194). For those seeking a perspective that balances both a skilled sociological honesty and a respect for evangelical Christianity, the reader is referred to the regularly updated text by Letha D. Scanzoni and John Scanzoni *Men, Women and Change: A Sociology of Marriage and Family.* 3d ed. New York: McGraw Hill, 1988, or any of Scanzoni's more recent works on families, friendship and sexuality.

[850] Hammersley, Martyn. "On Feminist Methodology." *Sociology* 26, no. 2 (1992): 187-206.
Working largely from British sources, Hammersley sets out to "assess the arguments in support of the claim that there is a distinctively feminist [sociological] methodology" and to this end he summarizes literature on "...the four themes...widely taken to mark its distinctiveness..." (p. 187.) *viz.*, (1) "the ubiquitous significance of gender and gender asymmetry," (2) "the validity of experience as against method," (3) "rejection of hierarchy in the research relationship," and (4) "emancipation as the goal of research and the criterion of validity." He then provides his critique of each theme through a discussion of several standard arguments that would seemingly oppose the emphases he has described. Thus he argues, in effect, 'of course gender is significant and several studies now demonstrate this fact...'; or to cite a different example 'of course experience is important, and Blumer's early work demonstrates this...'. What distinguishes this work as antifeminist, however, is not that Hammersley challenges the literature. Rather, it is that he minimizes and/or reduces various emphases to cast their points in an absurd fashion so that an alternative perspective (his) may be stated as the correct one. Thus, to cite but one (albeit) extreme example, Hammersley challenges the feminist attention to women's experience as "an appeal to a genetic criterion," and he likens it to the work of Nazi scientist Johannes Stark (cf. pp. 192-193) to discredit it. This borders on rhetoric of the most insensitive kind. Additional examples of Hammersley's flawed logic could be cited, but the two articles following his discussion (by

Caroline Ramazanoglu and Loraine Gelsthorpe) note the major limitations of his work: a selective reading of his authors' works, the assumption of a single, univocal feminist methodology, and the subsequent critique of a problem that does not really exist. NOTE: For sources on the plurality of feminist "sociological method," see Reinharz [112].

[851] Hunter, James Davison and Kimon Howland Sargeant. "Religion, Women and the Transformation of Public Culture." *Social Research* 60 (1993): 545-570.
Drawing from early feminist theological publications (e.g., [157, 161, 193, 196, 206, 558]) and variously rooted data discussions about the characteristics of women clergy (e.g., [657]), Hunter and Sargeant argue that while "...the cultural productivity of feminist theology seems obscure, the questions it raises are, anthropologically speaking, at the core of very civilization..." and thus "...the development of feminist theology clearly warrants further tracking" (p. 570). On the face of it, their point seems reasonable enough, yet the tone and development of this essay suggest an antifeminist rather than research directed agenda. Hunter and Sargeant develop their discussion in terms of five key steps. They begin by documenting what they see as key indicators of an almost evil like force: *viz.*, there is a growing feminization of the clergy profession across Christian and Jewish denominations, female clergy are often more liberal than male clergy in their theological, political and social attitudes and they are bringing an agenda for "significant ideological and vocational change" (p. 552), and, last, feminist theologians want only women's experience (e.g., the "church of women") as their source of understanding the Bible and religious symbols, including symbols of religious authority. Second, Hunter and Sargeant turn to the potential impacts of feminist theology (now descibed as "the project") to note that visibly radical feminist theologians such as Mary Daly, Judith Christ, and Naomi Goldenberg (and "the witch Starhawk") advocate separatism, witchcraft, goddess worship and the need only for the god or goddess within themselves, while other feminist theologians ("Ruether, Fiorenza and Letty Russell") seek to reconstruct Christianity from within. At stake in such a reconstruction, however, is the "foundation of the normative order of the traditions, that is, a normative order that makes patriarchy possible if not necessary" (pp. 562-563). Nor, the authors argue, can one count on sufficient opposition to this endeavor from evangelicals, for many female evangelicals are also buying into these perspectives and stressing "...egalitarianism both within the church and society as a whole" (p. 567). For step #3 of their discussion, Hunter and Sargeant back off from some of the more perilous implications of their discussion, to suggest that "feminist theological discourse does not have much currency in popular religious experience in America..." and that it "defines itself primarily in negative terms." They then (step #4) ask "For what does the movement stand?" and in step #5 of their argument, they conclude to the need for tracking feminst theology, specifically, because the beliefs of this movement challenge "...the cultural meaning of womanhood...[which]...is...related to the larger questions about the nature of moral authority, the meaning of tradition, the ontology of sacredness and the relation of the human experience to the sacred..." questions that are at "the very core of civilization." The argument, the innuendoes of unqualified and out of context citations (including comments about witchcraft and goddess worship) are at least inflammatory, and they imply either that feminist theology is bad for society, or alternatively, that laity shouldn't worry because sociologists of religion will track it to check its impact, and presumably do something about it.

22

Patriarchy, Violence and Sexual Harassment in the Churches

Several literatures provide the framework for focusing the material of this chapter. First, as noted in Chapter 18, the feminist reading of theological anthropology has identified numerous assumptions traditionally thought to reflect "gendered" patterns of reality. These assumptions include the idea that there are "higher" and "lower" levels of reality, and that among the higher levels are the characteristics typically attached to definitions of maleness, *viz.*, that maleness is to be identified with rationality, soul, spirit, goodness and a tendency toward the supernatural. Alternatively, femaleness has been associated with the "lower" levels of reality, i.e., such characteristics as emotions, carnality (body and matter), a tendency toward evil, or most simply, that which is "base."

Second, the literature in feminist ethics has also identified "gendered" assumptions about reality, and in particular, assumptions that reflect a devaluation of women, their experience and worth. More concretely, feminist ethics has identified a masculine devaluing of women, of women's work, intellectual capacities and sexuality, including the rights to reproductive freedom and affectional preference.

Finally, a third literature is relevant here, i.e., the literature on feminist spirituality. This literature is particularly important, for with its rejection of gender dualisms and its affirmation of "embodiment," this literature has in various ways exposed the normative links between patriarchal ownership and the presumption of violence as a tool of patriarchal self extension, in both religion and society. These three literatures and the themes they identify--that reality is *gendered and hierarchically so, that women may thereby be legitimately devalued, and that hierarchical ownership and violence are intimately linked*---have all contributed to the culturally encoded assumption that women may be owned and/or used for male pleasure, whether the latter includes physical and sexual violence, or at emotional and social levels, women's disempowerment through degradation and/or forced dependence on males. To each of these themes, the developing anti-harassment, anti-abuse, and anti-violence literature--the "survivors" literature--responds: NO.

This literature is developing at two levels. First, a formal theological literature is specifying how Christianity has sacralized violence against women through its anthropological and ethical dualisms concerning men, women, rationality and nature. And it is here that the anthropological, ethical and spirituality literatures have had a foundational impact. (See, e.g., Harrison and Heyward [867] and the entries found in the reader edited by Brown and Bohn [863].)

To some extent, these entries parallel the themes of feminist theology's early (1968-1973) critiques of patriarchy and misogyny. A key difference, however, is that now, three and more decades later, these critiques are directed specifically to the patriarchal dimensions of the family as an emotionally (if not legally) owned unit. In particular, these more recent critiques challenge the emotional privilege attached to roles of male headship whether in clergy or lay families, and whether biological or social, as is the case, at times, in Christian congregations. Some examples here are Redmond's critique of "christian virtues" and violence (as found in Brown and Bohn) and Tave's critique of violence in clergy marriages as found in the *Memoirs of Abigail Abbot Bailey* [875].

At the same time as this formally theological literature has developed, a programmatic and more popularized literature has also been developing. This second literature attempts to combat sexual and domestic violence through education, the establishment of social and religious centers seeking to curb such violence, the development of healing rituals, and last, a pastoral counseling literature which seeks to aid congregational members whose families are in crisis. Additionally, this programmatic literature has sought to address the issue of sexual harassment in the ministry, and particularly parishioner-directed sexual harassment by members of the clergy, i.e., the involvement of clergy in sexually exploitative pastor-parishioner relationships (although see [879] for data on clergy-peer sexual harrassment as well as the presence of consenting amorous relations across clergy role sets).

The literature below evidences both the theological and programmatic emphases. It is a complex literature, beset in various places with definitional problems concerning the concepts of abuse, violence and sexual harassment (each of which is further described in notes throughout the chapter), and beset, too, with the tensions of competing and near paradigm-like perspectives: the latter being the pressure for an *ethical* analysis and resolution of clergy-parishioner sexual interaction and the simultaneous *medicalization* of such interaction through the use of--and one wants almost to say the often *uncritical* use of--an addiction/recovery framework (given the absence of *any* definition of sexual addiction as a specific disorder within the *Diagnostic and Statistical Manual of Mental Disorders*, Third Edition, Revised [i.e., DSM-III-R]). These limitations notwithstanding--and they are by no means small given the "temperance" like polemic grounding much discussion--this is an enormously important literature. It connects feminist values and feminist praxis across often else wise divisive lines, and because it involves laity and legal cases within the secular courts, its "cost control" dimensions have generated both religious and secular visibility.

The sources on "Theology and Violence to Women" are presented first. They are prefaced with several social science entries; first to demonsrate the range of perspectives available for an interdisciplinary discussion of this topic, and second, to emphasizethe necessity for such interdisciplinary discussion. The literatures on "clergy sexual misconduct" and "clergy sexual harassment" then follow, and with the clear recognition that these terms constitute two of the concepts most obscured by polemics and analytically unclear discussion.

Again: Ths literature is important. From the perspective of feminist theology, it represents one of the last bastions of patriarchy in Christianity in that it challenges the patriarchal ownership of all sexuality and authority. Similarly, from a sociological perspective, it represents a secularization (but not a "depatriarchalization") of the historically defined male ministerial role, in that it evidences a competition between "traditional" (or sacralized) and professional (or rational legal and bureaucratized) understandings of ministry. It is, therefore, a discussion likely to continue and likely to have an enormous impact regardless of its ultimate shape.

A. Introductory and Background Sources

1. Partner Abuse, Domestic and Family Violence

[852] Fineman, Martha Albertson, and Roxanne Mykitiuk, eds. *The Public Nature of Private Violence: the Discovery of Domestic Abuse.* NY: Routledge, 1994.
Three general frameworks provide the setting for the 13 essays of this text that both revisit and unfold the "public" nature of private violence. The first framework provides "images" of private or "domestic" violence. These include the need to "reframe" domestic violence by noting its analogies to the terrorism and its impacts; the need to understand and challenge attitudinal and legal assumptions (such as "coverture") that continue to keep domestic violence "private;" the need for wider visions of women than those of victim or agent only, (with paralleling stay or leave choices only); and last, the need to recognize the "intersectionality" of violence to women, its hiddenness as defined by varying categories of ethnic and communal identity (e.g., race/ethnicity). Section II then addresses "feminist theory and legal norms" (within the U.S.) and the challenges to feminist theory posed by (1) the needs of children abused by their mothers, (2) intralesbian violence, (3) the role of alternative normative cultures (such as religion) in both the self-definition of children and the power balance between parents and the state, and (4) the continued vulnerability of women to "crimes of passion" yet sanctioned by marital rights normed by patriarchy. Last, Section III assesses the difficulties of naming--and stopping--domestic violence in cultures where wife-beating is still acceptable, and/or where domestic violence continues to be a private rather than social (or public) problem--or at its widest level, a human rights issue. A provocative overview then addresses the role of rationality in policy development.

[853] Hamberger, Kevin, and Claire Renzetti, eds., *Domestic Partner Abuse*. NY: Routledge, 1994.

This text presents seven essays that review or present current research on abuse in intimate relationships. Both its editors and contributors describe it as "controversial," for germane to its essays is the commitment of its contributors to conceptualize domestic abuse in frameworks which transcend gender and sociocultural frameworks only, since contributors view the latter as too limited. The editors provide a helpful introductory overview, and the essay titles and/or topics include: (1) "Gay and Bisexual Male Domestic Violence Victimization;" (2) mutual victimization in bi-directional violent couples; (3) heterosexual women arrested for domestic violence; (4) lesbian battering; (5) head injured males and relationship aggression (6) "Patriarchy and Wife Assault--the Ecological Fallacy"; and (7) "Psychopharmacological Treatment of Aggressive Behavior: Implications for Domestically Violent Men." Commentaries on the literature as a whole follow the specific discussions, with sociologists Susan Miller and editor Renzetti responding on behalf of feminist of the "women are as violent as men" argument grounding the text. In their reviews they challenge the privatized perspectives grounding much of the literature, and they note the need for theories that combine gender as well as sexual orientation, race, class and age "as interconnected...[and]...organizing variables in domestic violence, perpetration, victimization *and institutionalized* response" (p. 220). (Italics mine.) **NOTE**: For a framework which seeks to ameliorate both perspectives, see Hampton et al. below **[854]**.

[854] Hampton, Robert L., Thomas P. Gullotta, Gerald R. Adams, Earl H. Potter III, and Roger P. Weissberg, eds. *Family Violence: Prevention and Treatment*. Newbury Park, CA: Sage, 1993.

This twelve essay reader on the prevention and treatment of family violence surveys key aspects of family violence research available through the early 1990s. Richard Gelles' opening essay sets the tone by reviewing both his past work and the history of family violence research, as well as several of the controversies he and Loseke describe elsewhere **[856]**. It is a solid introductory overview and a preferred starting point for both the general literature and the longer Gelles and Loseke collection. Additional contributors (too numerous to list) address the following: "Physical Child Abuse," "Sexual Abuse of Children," "Psychological Aggression and Abuse in Marriage," "Physical and Sexual Violence in Marriage," "Elder Abuse," "Violence in Families of Color," "Legal Perspectives on Family Violence Against Children," "The Assessment and Treatment of Violent Families," "Male Batterers," "What Can Be Done to Prevent Child Maltreatment," and "Substance Abuse and Family Violence." As with all Sage publications, this is a substantive synthesis of published research, clearly presented and intentionally directed to various levels of readership. It comfortably introduces the issues and can be readily supplemented by the varioius sources in this chapter of the bibliography.

[855] Gelles, Richard and Murray Straus. "Violence in the American Family." *Journal of Social Issues* 35 (1979): 15-39.

Using data from a "nationally representative sample of 2,143 American couples, of whom 1,146 had one or more children aged 3 to 17 years old living at home at the time of the interview" the authors examine the incidence, demographic distribution and probable causes of violence within American families. Their data suggest a considerable expansion of mid-1970 estimates of family violence (i.e., estimates of violence to children, violence between spouses, and violence between siblings) and their discussion focuses on multivariate social and psychological explanations of such violence within families rather than traditional 'medical-psychiatric' explanations. Of importance in their explanations are the factors of (1) conflict within families as groups; (2) the presence of stressors; and (3) cultural norms which permit violence as a remedy to felt stress. Measures include the use of the "Conflict Tactics Scales," and the authors' discussion of abuse to children distinguishes between violent acts and reported injuries, together with other social and legal definitional factors. Readers unfamiliar with statistical formats of data presentation will appreciate the authors' narrative reporting style, together with their lack of polemical tone. For literature through 1993 see the following: Gelles's 1985 discussion, "Family Violence" [*Annual Review of Sociology* 11 (1985): 347-357, not reviewed here] and his introductory survey ["Family Violence"] to Hampton et al. **[854]**. Additionally, see Gelles and Loseke **[856]**.

[856] Gelles, Richard, and Donileen Loseke, eds. *Current Controversies on Family Violence*. Newbury Park, CA: Sage, 1993.

Four areas of current "controversy" provide the parameters for the 21 entries in this policy directed and research grounded reader on family violence. These issues include questions about the conceptualization and definition of family violence, its causes and measurement, the role(s) of researchers and practitioners relative to case specific interventions, and more widely, the formally "political" issues attached to family violence research and the potentials of structured social intervention. Detailed introductions precede each unit of discussion, and the essay entries readily highlight the multiplicity of issues--and perspectives--surrounding the study of family violence. For example, should family violence be conceptualized primarily through psychological, sociological, or feminist lenses? Or again, what are the meanings and measures of date rape, or of the *consequences* of violence against women? That is, does battering really generate a syndrome? Or to cite one last example, what is the role of abuse history among the elderly and their abusive offspring? These are just a few of the issues addressed by this text. As the editors draw their closing remarks, they find only two constants: (1) that all of the text's contributors agree that family violence is terrible and should be stopped; and (2) that while scientific and advocacy postures have numerous tensions and conflicts, these perspectives must be exploited productively. Thus the editors call for an engaged dialogue that addresses (1) issues (and not individuals), and (2) the mechanics of the *political process and its use* of formal research. This is an informative overview which well illustrates the controversies it describes, but see Fineman and Mykitiuk [852] and Hamburger and Renzetti [853] for more substantive feminist analysis.

[857] Shupe, Anson, William A. Stacey, and Lonnie R. Hazlewood. *Violent Men, Violent Couples: The Dynamics of Family Violence.* Lexington, MA: Lexington Books, 1987.
In three sections of discussion this brief volume: (1) traces the evolution of domestic violence as a specific social problem; (2) provides data on several aspects of violence as a cultural and structural norm; and (3) examines several strategies for dealing with violence at the local community level. While each of its subsections is engaging, informative and clearly written, its second section is particularly salient. It provides data from a study of "military family violence:" a contrast in the severity of family violence among civilians, "active" and "veteran" military families, and the "conservative" and (at other times) creative dimensions of religion as a factor in such family violence. The study's closing chapters provide additional (and comparative) data on intervention strategies. The study questionnaire, endnotes and a brief index close the volume.

[858] *Violence and Victimization: An Annotated Bibliography.* Bethesda, MD: NOVA Research Company, 1991.
This annotated bibliography provides extensive summaries of recently published literature on violence to women, as drawn from major social work and social psychological journals. The annotations are organized topically in terms 'incidence and prevalence,' specific populations, patterns of abuse history, 'effects and consequences' of violence to women, counseling and intervention issues and 'theoretical, legal and ethical issues.' It is directed to both researchers and professional practitioners, and a helpful closing note lists materials for clients to read. As prepared for the National Institute on Drug Abuse (NIDA, Contract # 271-88-8240), it is public domain material and may be reproduced without permission.

2. Definitions of Sexual Harassment

[859] Martin, Susan Ehrlich. "Sexual Harassment: The Link Joining Gender Stratification, Sexuality and Women's Economic Status." In *Women: A Feminist Perspective* (5th ed.) edited by Jo Freeman, 22-46. Mountain View, CA: Mayfield, 1995.
Drawing upon studies published through the early 1990s, this essay "reviews...the nature and extent of sexual harassment, analyzes the meaning of harassment from a feminist perspective, and examines the responses of individuals to harassment experience." Last, it "examines the government's responses [harassment] through the development of case law and public policy" (p. 22). The discussion develops at several levels. First, Martin presents a brief overview of sexual harassment as understood in the late 1970s, as, for example, "the unwanted imposition of sexual requirements in the context of a relationship of unequal power." She then works her way through sociological and other studies to identify both the characteristics of victims and offenders and the overlapping power dimensions which structurally sustain sexual harassment (i.e., social patterns that stress female subordination and the "genderizing" of professional and occupational roles, and with these, organizational patterns which stress informal responses to sexual harassment rather than legal reporting). Last, in a review of specific cases, Martin traces the development of legal and policy issues surrounding sexual harassment, including its widened but more specified EEOC

definitions as *quid pro quo* sexual favors and/or the presence of a hostile working environment. This discussion is clearly written and well documented with extended notes and bibliography; it has obvious implications for the study of sexual harassment in the ministry, and together with the other sources in this chapter, it should be read with Freeman [88] and subsequent legal decisions: e.g., the June 26, 1998 Supreme Court decisions establishing employer responsibility for supervisor behaviors in the workplace. (See, for example, *The Washington Post*, 6/27/98 as well as various feminist and women's studies web sites on the Internet.)

[860] Rutter, Paul. *Sex in the Forbidden Zone: When Men in Power--Therapists, Doctors, Clergy, Teachers and Others--Betray Women's Trust.* Los Angeles: Jeremy P. Tarcher, Inc., 1989.

This text is both an empathic 'call to honor' to all male professionals who deal with women in superordinate/subordinate trust relationships and an expose of the extent to which that honor is routinely violated by male professionals. It stems from several sources: first, the author's own awareness of how an acting out of sexual fantasies with a female client might affect the quality of the therapist-client relationship; second, the disappointing knowledge that one of his own mentors had regularly so acted for a period of many years, and last, his own frustration at the professional world's silent collusion on this subject. It is a clearly and movingly written book, based on the author's interviews with a number of women who agreed to tell their stories for the sake of exposing this 'shadow' dimension to male-female professional-client relations. The discussion develops in seven chapters with an addendum indicating supplemental bibliography and resources where women can seek help if caught by the dynamics of 'sex in the forbidden zone.' Rutter's seven chapters address the roots and patterning of professional-client sexual misconduct, the warning signals and warding off strategies which professionals (and women) may employ, and last, an epilogue vignette of what respectful trust can accomplish. Rutter's own background is in Jungian psychology, and while his descriptions of women and the 'feminine' will appear sexist to many, this frequently cited source has nonetheless broken important ground. Remaining unaddressed in the text, however, is the role of [male] "honor" as a normative contributor to both the problem and proposed solution to professional-client sexual (or other) exploitation, and the necessity for finding strategies which respectfully empower women while disabling the patriarchal protective "ownership" that male "honor" implies.

[861] Weeks, Elaine Lunsford, Jacqueline M. Boles, Albeno P. Garbin, and John Blount. "The Transformation of Sexual Harassment from a Private Trouble into a Public Issue." *Sociological Inquiry* 56 (1986): 432-455.

Following the perspective developed by Spector and Kitsuse [Malcolm Spector and John I. Kitsuse, *Constructing Social Problems*. Menlo Park, CA: Cummings, 1977], the authors trace the life history of sexual harassment from its status as a private, individually rooted behavioral act to that of a specifically redefined behavior, *viz.*, unwanted or unsolicited sexual behavior which is "detrimental to the workplace and elsewhere" (p. 432). The authors identify early literature, interest groups and their activities, collective activities, indicators of social recognition of sexual harassment as a problem, and the emergence of and reactions to public policy formation. Their discussion is foundational in terms of definitional material and the circumstances under which such redefined behavior(s) can continue to hold legitimacy as a social problem. **NOTE**: For additional literature see M. Dawn McCaghy, *Sexual Harassment: A Guide to Resources* [Boston: G. K. Hall, 1985] as reviewed by Dretha M. Phillips, *Sociological Inquiry* 56 (1986): 156-157, and see the literature cited by Martin [859]. Also, see Diana E. H. Russell's *Sexual Exploitation: Rape, Child Sexual Abuse, and Workplace Harassment* [Newbury Park, CA: Sage, 1984]. While not abstracted for this chapter, it remains a grounding sociological text detailing causal theories (together with detailed data from random rather than self-selecting samples), in the links between rape, childhood sexual abuse, and workplace sexual harassment.

3. Family Violence and Child Sexual Abuse

[862] Haugaard, Jeffrey J., and N. Dickon Reppucci. *The Sexual Abuse of Children: A Comprehensive Guide to Current Knowledge and Intervention Strategies.* San Francisco, CA: Jossey Bass, 1988.

This volume reviews the psychological literature on sexual abuse of children through the mid-1980s to identify both the extensive definitional problems existing within this literature and areas of yet needed research and analytical investigation. The authors argue that there is a "myth of shared definition" (i.e., that lay and professional discussions often assume there is a common understanding of "the sexual abuse of children"), and they demonstrate the fallacy of the myth.

Legal, moral, social, psychological and operational definitions vary, they argue, and research is better served by such redefinitions of abuse as "the sexual molestation of children by their parents" or "forced intercourse with an adult..." The authors review literally hundreds of studies and virtually every analytical perspective on this topic.

B. Feminist Critiques of Patriarchy and Sacralized Violence

1. The Emerging Literature

[863] Brown, Joanne Carlson, and Carole R. Bohn, eds. *Christianity, Patriarchy and Abuse*. New York: Pilgrim, 1989.
This collection of ten essays opens with Joanne C. Brown and Dorothy Parker's: "For God So Loved the World?" which surveys Christianity's major theological models of suffering and atonement and concludes that "Christianity is an abusive theology that glorifies suffering" (p. 26). Other contributors echo similar themes. Thus, Rosemary R. Ruether surveys the history of domestic violence as refracted through Christian tradition. Rita N. Brock re-examines abuse and vulnerability, Sheila Redmond discusses "Christian 'Virtues' and Child Sexual Abuse," and Karen Bloomquist addresses patriarchy and sexual violence. Additional contributors then widen the discussion: *viz.*, Catholic theologian/ethicist Mary Hunt traces themes of ownership and pornography within corporate structures and editor Bohn examines patriarchy and ownership as elements to be routed from ecclesiology and church leadership. Polly Young-Eisendrath and Demaris Wehr address individualism and suffering, Marie Fortune reexamines biblical assumptions about suffering, and Bev Harrison and Carter Heyward trace the history of eroticized domination as Christianity's leadership leitmotif [867]. This is a helpful introductory anthology with extensive notes following individual pieces, but it lacks indices and supplemental bibliographies. **NOTE**: For an essay discussion of how violence is sacralized in worship at Mother's Day sevices, see Sheila Redmond, "'Remember the Good: Forget the Bad': Denial and Family Violence in a Christian Worship Service," pp. 71-82 in Procter-Smith and Walton's *Women At Worship* [526].

[864] Brown, Joanne Carlson. "Divine Child Abuse." *Daughters of Sarah* 18, no. 3 (1992): 24-28.
This essay is a condensation of the Brown/Parker discussion in [863]. It briefly identifies and examines the "christus-victor," the "satisfaction," and the "moral influence" theories of atonement within Christian history, together with contemporary 'critical' theories, theories of God's suffering, and theories of the inevitability of [Christian] suffering. The authors suggest the abandonment of atonement as a grounding dimension of Christianity, and they present several Christological statements as imaged though justice-directed rather than sacrificially based constructs. A number of writers respond to Brown's essay and although this *Daughters of Sarah* issue is not exclusively directed to Brown's presentation, related articles and reviews also appear in this issue. Respondents to Brown include Presbyterian theologian Margaret Houts, child welfare clinician John Howell, Weaver Santaniello, a graduate theology student at Garret, and editor Reta Finger.

[865] Cooper-White, Pamela. *The Cry of Tamar: Violence Against Women and the Church's Response*. Philadelphia: Fortress, 1995.
This text is a significant and empowering resource for clergy and laity who work to combat social and religiously sanctioned violence against women. By way of overview, it opens with a strong reading of both the classical text of "The Rape of Tamar" [2 Samuel 13] and a feminist reconstruction of the text from within the perspective of a niece named for her aunt, but now anxiously mindful of this horror and its perduring, intergenerational character. Two theoretical chapters then identify the cultural and structural roots of violence to women, while subsequent chapters detail several specific "Forms of Violence Against Women," and "The Church's Response" to violence against women. By far, the middle section of the text (i.e., "Forms of Violence...") is the longest, with specific chapters addressing, respectively, sexual harassment, rape, battering, clergy sexual abuse, child sexual abuse, and ritual abuse. In turn, "The Church's Response" takes up "The Pastor as Wounded Healer," "Ministry with Violent Men," and "Empowering Women." A "Conclusion" then addresses issues of forgiveness and community restoration as it details "A Call to Reconciliation." By way of particulars, Cooper-White locates the roots of society's violence to women in both structural and cultural terms. The former are the interlocking structures of "power over" embedded in and protected by social structures which erase I-Thou relationality and provide opportunities for women's control and objectification. In turn, cultural sources are the normed permissions for violence as sustained by a pornographic culture

with its eroticized objectification of women and/or women's sexuality. This is a strong text and its various discussions of the forms of violence provide the reader with: (a) an opening vignette to illustrate the issues at hand; (b) a summary of both the facts and myths connected to the particular type of violence under analysis; (c) lists of signals or indicators to watch for to the extent that such are known; and (d) a summary of "pastoral response(s)" to the type of abuse under analysis. The closing chapters then describe the burnout and boundary problems faced by clergy, indicators and strategies for working with violent men, and last, the counseling/therapeutic needs of women in crisis and the role demands of functioning as an empowering force for women in such crisis. Are there limitations to the text? Given its scope, one is tempted to say no, but in its discussion of clergy sexual abuse, it continues the definitional problems attached to a framework rooted in the clericalized understanding of the ministry's "numinous power" as virtually "almighty." While the latter is often true, it is also empirically more varied than Cooper-White presents here, and it thereby deserves a more sophisticated ethic, e.g., **[878]**.

[866] Gudorf, Christine. "The Worst Sexual Sin: Sexual Violence and the Church." *The Christian Century* 110 (January 6-13, 1993): 19-21.
This refreshingly frank and theologically hard hitting article examines the problem of sexual violence in American society and argues that "a real concern about sexual violence [on the part of the churches] would produce a number of changes in the church's life and teachings" (p. 20). Among these would be that: (1) churches would explicitly condemn sexual violence from the pulpit; (2) clergy and laity would receive training in crisis intervention and long term recovery work; (3) churches would renounce the tradition of defining masculinity and femininity in terms of dominance and passivity--and "servant" models of church leadership would reflect this rejection of stereotypical role norms; (4) members would be taught appropriate ways to recognize and respond to victims of sexual violence--and thereby avoid well-intentioned but offensive and often harm giving comments to victims, including premature statements about the necessity of forgiveness. Fifth, churches would expose and help diffuse the elements of racism embedded in society's understanding of sexual violence, and last, churches (as a whole) would begin to think critically about the consequences of their interpretations of Jesus' passion, crucifixion and resurrection. In particular they might realize that "Christianity is about vanquishing sin and suffering not idolizing it" and that interpretations to the contrary support rather than combat victimization.

[867] Harrison, Beverly W., and Carter Heyward. "Pain and Pleasure: Avoiding the Confusions of Christian Tradition in Feminist Theory." In *Christianity, Patriarchy and Abuse*, edited by Joanne Carlson Brown and Carole R. Bohn, 148-173. Cleveland, OH: Pilgrim, 1989.
This essay traces the history of "eroticized domination" as an image of clerical leadership within Christianity. The authors ground their discussion in the gradual development of 'pain' as a religious reality borne of Christianity's early dualisms. They highlight the interactive aspects of suffering and liturgical development, the rise of a normative and disembodied Christian spirituality, the presence of sadomasochism in Christian tradition, and all of these as they correlate with Christianity's often misogynous understanding of women, sexuality and transcendence. The authors apply their discussion to current literature on violence within feminist philosophy, and they argue for a reading of eroticism which affirms the (rare) simultaneity of both personal independence and other-integrity within erotic experience. This is an important, difficult and prophetic essay-- helpfully read in the light of the authors' earlier and individual works: *viz.*, Heyward's **[198]**, **[199]**, **[242]** and **[570]**, and Harrison's **[207]**, **[497]**, **[502-503]**, and **[569]**.

[868] Pellauer, Mary. "Moral Callousness and Moral Sensitivity: Violence Against Women." In *Women's Consciousness, Women's Conscience: A Reader in Feminist Ethics*, edited by Barbara Hilkert Andolsen, Christine E. Gudorf and Mary D. Pellauer, 33-50. Minneapolis, MN: Winston Press, 1985.
Working from her own early life observations of domestic violence, Pellauer first describes her "forgetting" of this violence, and then her eventual, years later acknowledgment of it. She employs the metaphor of a "callous" to indicate the literal numbness and insensitivity one can develop about violence against women (including rape, incest and childhood sexual abuse), and after tracing some of the generally known effects of such violence upon women, she calls for the replacement of moral callousness with moral sensitivity. She recognizes the difficulty in developing this kind of sensitivity--too much of society's violence is invisible and unseen by many "good" people--and she readily acknowledges that "how we understand male power and dominance in the harsh light of violence against women...[and]...express its meaning and importance is a fundamental issue for feminist ethics" (p. 46). Pellauer's call for a sensitive awareness of society's violence against

women is not unusual, for much literature highlights this need. What makes this essay distinctive, however, is its recognition of the general invisibility of violence among *good* people and their obedience to cultural norms. Her discussion echoes Milgram's now classic studies on authority [cf. Stanley Milgram, *Obedience to Authority: An Experimental View*, NY: Harper & Row, 1973] and the early Lewis Coser and Kurt Wolff pieces on "The Visibility of Evil" and "For A Sociology of Evil," respectively, [*Journal of Social Issues* 25, no. 1 (1969): 101-125] and it is fruitfully read against this backdrop.

[869] Schüssler Fiorenza, Elisabeth, and M. Shawn Copeland, eds. *Violence Against Women.* London: SCM Press, 1994.

The eleven essays in this reader on violence against women--physical, emotional, domestic, interpersonal, institutionalized, ecclesiastical, economic, political, racial-ethnic and international-- are among some of the strongest of theological essays on this topic published through the mid-90s. Schüssler Fiorenza's introduction presents the devastating statistics and her analysis of institutional Christianity's collusion with violence and feminist theology's three options for combating it are equally clear. To the extent that churches do not publicly, unequivocally denounce any and all religious legitimations of violence against women--in effect, do not take up the cause--women have only two choices: to remain silent (and thus both victim and 'christian') or, alternatively, to resist and thus risk losing their church and its [potential] salvation. Currently, Schüssler Fiorenza sees only three feminist theological responses to this circumstance: (1) actually get women to leave their churches; (2) empower women to take a liberation perspective (i.e., Christ supports them not their abusers) within their tradition; or (3) empower women to address "the contradiction between the lived experience of survivors' agency and the discursive theological meanings that negate such agency" (p. xxi). Option #3 is Schüssler Fiorenza's here preferred strategy, and as the basis for a more systemically directed feminist theological effort, it grounds the essays that follow. Thus, biblical themes are addressed by JoAnn Carlson Brown (I Cor. 11:2-10) and Irmgard Fischer (Gen. 16, 21); E. Ann Matter and Eileen J. Stenzel depict ecclesial violence and violence in medieval religious images; Zilda F. Ribiero summarizes "Prostitution and Rape in the Colonial Period," and Beatrix Schiele addresses legal-philosophical ideas of justice and violence. In turn, African American domestic and white supremacist violence are addressed respectively by Delores Williams and Mark Taylor; and Mary John Mananzan and Felisa Elizondo detail patterns of women's complicity within and resistance to violence, respectively. Last, Marie Fortune discusses clergy malfeasance and co-editor Copeland provides closing reflections. **NOTE:** There are several provocative (and currently unresearched) implications to the essays in this text, not the least of which is the empirical scope of ecclesiastical (i.e., religious organizational) violence to women who do not meet or fit the religious organizational molds of various traditions and/or denominations.

[870] Thistlethwaite, Susan Brooks. "Every Two Minutes: Battered Women and Feminist Interpretation." In *Feminist Interpretation of the Bible*, edited by Letty Russell, 96-107. Philadelphia: Westminster, 1985.

Citing data collected in 1980-1981 by the United Methodist Church for a survey on the prevalence of male violence as experienced by Methodist women, Thistlethwaite directs the reader to four considerations which may be of help for those ministering to battered women. First, Thistlethwaite describes feminist "methodology" vis a vis the Bible: as a dialectic borne of women's experience interacting with the biblical text, it is a method which permits the re-grounding of texts from their depicting of women as victims to women as agents. Additionally, it is a necessary method given the role of the Bible in supporting women's victimization. Second, Thistlethwaite points to the necessity of aiding women in their need for establishing self esteem, taking control over their lives and finding their anger; third and fourth, she cites several biblical texts which can be used toward these ends. Although brief, Thistlethwaite's discussion is powerful, for it rests on the premise that the Bible need not--and indeed, ought not--to be used as vehicle of patriarchal violence. Further, she exposes the ideological base attached to the exegesis of Genesis 2:18-23 and Eph. 5:4-23: i.e., that when divorced from the observations of experience and their cultural patternings, these texts do divinize male superiority over females, the exegetical disclaimers of biblical scholars notwithstanding.

NOTE: For related literature see Gray [241] and Brock [432], and see Day [382], Setel [384], Trible [385] and Bird [360, 377] for examples of biblical-exegetical literature.

2. Related Interdisciplinary Sources

[871] Bartkowski, John P. "Spare the Rod..., Or Spare the Child? Divergent Perspectives on Conservative Protestant Child Discipline." *Review of Religious Research* 37 (1995): 97-116.
This essay reiterates several of the themes presented by Bartkowsi and Ellison below **[872]**. In particular, it contrasts the presuppositions of "mainstream" and conservative Protestant parenting ideologies, but here with an additional nuance. Namely, the restriction of "mainstream" sources to prominent sociologists of religion and anti child abuse social researchers--but notably Donald Capps and Murray Straus. In Bartkowski's judgment these and other writers require strong critique, for their works are theoretically biased against mild to moderate forms of child corporal punishment as advocated by conservative Protestant childrearing experts. In contrast, Bartkowski calls for more scholarship in this area. Specifically, an empirical test of the practice of conservative Protestant parenting techniques (i.e., Do they harm children? Do "ritualized" techniques escalate to abuse and result in physical injury; and last, do they physically or psychologically impair "the development and social adjustment of youngsters"?). As with **[872]** below, this discussion also ignores wide questions surrounding this topic, and because its empirical questions are descriptive and program evaluative in nature, they do not promise any significant scientific advance as envisioned by the author. A related and solo piece by Ellison ["Conservative Protestantism and the Corporal Punishment of Children: Clarifying the Issues" *JSSR* 35 (1996): 1-17] provides a more sociologically based "test" of the ideology: Namely, a longitudinal assessment (using e.g., NSFH panel data) to assess "(1) how parents decide to use corporal punishment; (2) how they administer corporal and other types of punishment; (3) whether effects are harmful and (4) how these affects vary by context, age, religious background and other dimensions of social location and culture." (*JSSR art. cit.*, p. 14).

[872] Bartkowski, John P. and Christopher G. Ellison. "Divergent Models of Childrearing in Popular Manuals: Conservative Protestants vs. the Mainline Experts." *Sociological Analysis* 56 (1995): 21-34.
This essay is one of at least three (see **[871]** above) which identifies the ideology of "mild-to moderate" corporal punishment for children as advocated by Conservative (i.e., Fundamentalist and Evangelical) Protestantism. The identification is based upon a content analysis of child rearing documents published (or broadcast) by "the most prominent, best selling childrearing experts" within Conservative Protestantism, and it is presented through a comparison of "mainline" and conservative Protestant parenting ideologies. The authors' purpose is threefold: First, they wish to identify the ideology of conservative Protestant parenting--that is, indicate its legitimating premises, its long term goals, its parent child roles and role set expectations. Second, they wish to counter the inaccurate bias they perceive around this topic, as expressed, for example, by "mainline" experts. Third, they wish to demonstrate the importance of this topic (i.e., scientifically legitimate it) and spell out its research implications. The authors' attention to ideology is important; for the emphasis here is on the authoritative inerrancy of the Bible, the sinfulness of human nature and its presumed need for control and internalized attitudes of obedience--and the ways in which parents are exhorted to embody these themes through loving but routinized corporal punishment of children for their willful disobedience. By way of research implications, the authors call for an empirical test of the ideology: *viz.*, does it do what it says it will with respect to long term goals etc. In turn, by virtue of this test, the importance of the topic will be demonstrated. **NOTE**: While the authors pose no critique of the ideology, nor necessarily should they, they *do not* address the wider social and sociological questions implicit in the latent functions of this ideology, *viz.*, its potentials as an infrastructure inimical to egalitarian and democratic processes.

[873] Capps, Donald. "Religion and Child Abuse: Perfect Together." *Journal for the Social Scientific Study of Religion* 31 (1992): 1-14.
This 1991 presidential SSSR address identifies three thematic emphases which suggest that religion and child abuse are 'perfect together.' The first of these emphases is that there is much religious literature which supports the use of the physical punishment for children, and not infrequently, the physical abuse of children. Second, Capps describes specific religious ideas which can function to torment children, and last, he suggests various ways in which religion can permit adults to detach from their own perceptions of religious childhood suffering and as well the traumas and suffering of other children. His thesis and the exposition of this last emphasis are--to say the least-- provocative. More pointedly, Capps argues that an effect of the religious teaching of the Virgin Birth of Jesus is that it shrouds the actual circumstances of Jesus' birth, and it thus causes adults to dissociate the facts of Jesus early life. This is important, he says, for if the development of the

biblical texts was, in fact, to hide the illegitimacy of Jesus' conception and the likelihood of his mother having been raped, it then shrouds violence to two children--the one Jesus, and the other Mary his very young girl-mother--and it teaches adults to dissociate from the pain of children around them in their own setting and present space. This is a poignant and powerful article with several implications for understanding the development and use of religious doctrine as religiously sanctioned mechanisms of secrecy and social control. **NOTE**: For an exegetical discussion which supports much of Capps' thesis, see Jane Schaberg's *The Illegitimacy of Jesus: A Feminist Theological Interpretation of the New Testament Infancy Narratives.* New York: Crossroad, 1990. Alternatively, for her article length discussions, see Schaberg's entry in the *Women's Bible Commentary* [343:275-292] on the Gospel of Luke, and see her discussion,"Feminist Interpretation of the Infancy Narrative of Matthew" [387].

[874] Fortune, Marie and Frances Wood. "The Center for Prevention of Sexual and Domestic Violence: A Study in Applied Feminist Theology and Ethics." *Journal of Feminist Studies in Religion* 4, no. 1 (1988): 115-122.
Marie Fortune is a UCC pastor whose ministerial portfolio has been almost consistently directed towards the eradication of sexual and domestic violence against women. Frances Wood is her professional associate and with Fortune is the Co-Founder of the Center for the Prevention of Sexual and Domestic Violence in Seattle, Washington. In this article they describe the conceptual, organization and logistical realities attached to the founding of their center, together with the feminist ethical and theological norms it presumes. The Center's quarterly newsletter is entitled *Working Together*, and it serves as a clearinghouse for religion related abuse reports, investigations, publications, teaching aids and the like.

[875] Taves, Ann, ed. *Religion and Domestic Violence in Early New England: The Memoirs of Abigail Abbot Bailey.* Bloomingdale and Indianapolis: Indiana Univ. Press, 1989.
First published in 1815, these memoirs depict the physical and psychological abuse inflicted on Abigail Abbot Bailey, by her husband Asa Bailey. Of striking note is the religiously grounded adulterous (rather than abusive) perception Abigail held of Asa's incestuous relationship with their daughter Phoebe (their second daughter and fourth of seventeen children), and his relationships outside of their marriage: an affair with one hired woman and the attempted rape of another. Taves' editorial introduction locates the religious and legal context of these memoirs (both for their own time and that of the present) and provides an illuminating historical case study of the social construction of child sexual abuse perceptions.

NOTE: For additional and related literature here, see Roy Herndon SteinhoffSmith [sic], "The Boundary Wars Mystery," *Religious Studies Review* 24, no. 2 (April, 1998): 131-141. SteinhoffSmith reviews twelve recent texts addressing the issues of caring and relationship boundaries in an attempt to mediate between the seemingly irreconcilable frameworks cutting across much of the literature. It is helpful review, with SteinhoffSmith's main contribution being his articulation of the two issues authors often fuse and confuse when discussing this topic. Namely, that for some (e.g., Cooper-White [865, 883] and Fortune [877]) the appropriate issue of discussion here is client "agency," or more accurately its absence in the circumstance of pastor-parishioner sexual relationship (given the pastor's authority of office). For others, however, (e.g., Lebacqz and Barton [878]), the key issue for discussion is "mutuality," or the ability of each member of the professional-client dyad to participate in postures of friendship that reach across diffucult and often patriarchally defined roles and/or role-set expectations. This is a helpful discussion, free of the many terminological and definitional problems within the literature and with substantive reviews of several recent sources not addressed in this bibliography. Additionally, its focus on "agency" and "mutuality" as the two perspectives counter-opposed in this literature presses one to reread McFague's discussion of "agency" and religious imagination in [244].

C. Malfeasance as Sexual Misconduct

A difficulty confounding the discussion of theology and sexual harassment is the absence of clear definitions surrounding what is called "clergy sexual harassment." The literature below evidences this difficulty, but nonetheless coalesces around the theme of power that is used for the sake of either unwanted, adult-to-adult sexual advances or quid pro quo sexual favors, and these, again, within the contexts of either: (a) *pastorally grounded* clergy-laity relationships (whether in congregational or paracongregational settings); or (b) *gender-defined* super- and subordinate relations (i.e, "peer" collegiality relations) within the clergy profession. Similarly, the literature is also often confused about the differences between *sexual harassment* (i.e., unsolicited sexual advances and/or "quid pro quo" requests for sexual favors), *sexual addiction* (a seemingly specific but not fully understood--or yet formally defind--sexual disorder), and *sexual abuse*, i.e., the singular or patterned forcing of physical intimacies. Finally, a further factor cutting across definitional issues is the developing "survivors movement" and the extensive media and legal attention it has generated toward Catholic pedophelia.

The survivors movement is an important if at times ambiguously applied framework for addressing clergy sexual misconduct, for where the Catholic literature addresses the sexual abuse of children (either pre-pubescent [ages 6-12] as in the case of pedophelia) or post-pubescent (ages 13-17, the circumstance of ephebophelia), the Protestant literature focuses almost exclusively on the "sexual abuse" of adult women congregants (by clergy) but through categories and motifs drawn from the child sex abuse problematic, and often with significant but inaccurate implications. In particular, to the extent that types of victimization are not differentiated (e.g., pedophilia vs. the sexual exploitation of an adult)--but are, rather, lumped together as "clergy sexual abuse," *types of victimizers remain undifferentiated*, as do appropriate treatment modalities, sanctions and/or prognoses for changed clergy behavior. This is a serious limitation in the literature, borne largely from the concern of victim advocates for victims' rights and compensations, but it nonetheless clouds the ethical, empirical, theoretical, and administrative discussions of the "clergy sex abuse/clergy malfeasance" problem. And, as a further consequence, it lends disproportionate and often inaccurate support both to the currently regnant addiction/recovery model grounding this literature, and its assumption that by definition, *all* clergy-parishioner sexual interaction is de facto an expression of the clergy person's "sexual addiction," or "his" permanent and (by definition) incurable disease. Clearly, that some forms of sexual abuse (e.g., pedophilia) are deemed incurable is in fact the case, but not all experiences of clergy parishioner sexual interaction are disease based, nor are all cases of abuse. Rather, the variation is real, and the empirical and theoretical need for distinguishing between harassment, abuse and mutually consenting amorous relations is evident. (See, e.g., Lebacqz and Barton [878] and Majka [879]).

A final complicating--and inadequately addressed--factor in this literature is that of same-sex relations between consenting adults, and here the issues turn on the uncritical equation of privacy with exploitative "secrecy," and the institutionalized discrimination which most denominations hold toward gay and lesbian clergy. More specifically, because "secrecy" is a major component in the dynamics of a sexually abusive relationship, and because many same-sex oriented couples or individuals in ministry must for reasons of professional survival remain "off record" about their relationships, the potential for discrimination against gay and lesbian church leaders is significantly enhanced in that "undesirables" can be purged through false but (given the fact of a "secret" relationship), seemingly air-tight charges of harassment. This circumstance--which, in effect, permits a structural blackmail of closeted gay and lesbian individuals serving in ordained or other professionally salient church leadership positions--is but one of the many ethical problems besetting the current literature on harassment and "sexual abuse" in the ministry.

A sampling of the literature follows, with Wolf's bibliography [881] serving to synthesize the rapidly growing professional, journal, and newspaper literature on this subject, and with Shupe's text [880] synthesizing much of the popular literature through 1994. A final note on this topic: Because of extensive popular literature on this topic, readers should consult the many general bibliographic library sources, as well as such computerized media news sources as *Lexus-Nexus*.

1. Sexual Harassment in Mainline Denominations

a. Bibliography and Background Literature

[876] Capps, Donald. "Sex in the Parish: Social Scientific Explanations for Why It Occurs." *The Journal of Pastoral Care* 47, no. 4 (1993): 350-361.
In contrast to the bulk of literature that attempts either an ethical or addiction based analysis of clergy sexual misconduct (that is, an analysis of the participation of ordained clergy in sexually exploitative relationships with parishioners against their will), this piece attempts a description of two theories that Capps feels may shed light on the advent of clergy affairs within congregations. These theories are those of Erving Goffman's "total institutions" and Rene Girard's concept of "scapegoating" within religious settings or organizations. Capps notes that the conventional literature adopts a power differential approach to clergy- parishioner sexual interaction, with the parishioner understood as the non-powered individual facing the powerful clergy figure and thus, unable to provide informed consent within sexual interaction. (Additionally, and to his credit, Capps also notes the nuanced discussion by Lebaczk and Barton [878] which permits some

variation within this more dogmatic perspective.) However, in contrast to the power differential which puts the parishioner at the disadvantage, Capps unfolds the notion of the congregation as an institution, and following Goffman's "asylum model," he identifies the pastor as caught by the same dynamics as the asylum inhabitant, and thus, he the pastor--and not the parishioner--is without power in the circumstance of parishioner initiated sexual interaction. Capps' second theoretical framework depicts the group need of the congregation to safely vent its anger and frustrations over various conflicts, and these on someone who is easily blamable "for escalating strife," a circumstance well met by the presence of a pastor engaged sexually with married woman within the congregation. Concretely, it is Capps' contention that pastors at times accommodate the scapegoating process precisely by having an affair with a married congregational member, and thus engaging in a behavior which by definition can require punishment, but which is not necessarily an abuse of pastoral power or privilege. rather, the congregation has a reason to get rid of the pastor and its angry feelings which may have little or nothing to do with the affair at hand. Capps' discussion here is subtle, provocative, sure to be controversial, and in need of empirical test.

[877] Fortune, Marie. *Is Nothing Sacred? When Sex Invades the Pastoral Relationship.* San Francisco: Harper & Row, 1989.
This text is in many ways the catalyst for the Protestant literature on ministry and clergy-parishioner "sex abuse." Because of her previous pastoral work with victims of sexual abuse and domestic violence, Fortune was asked to mediate a situation involving a pastor and the allegations of sexual abuse made against him by a number of parishioners (all women) within his congregation. This text recounts the process of that mediation. It provides an overview of the church and its leadership history; its call to the pastor accused and (ultimately found guilty) of sexual misconduct within the congregation; a discussion of the personality dynamics apparently associated with such behavior (on the part of clergy offender); Fortune's synthesis of her interviews with the victims of this pastor's misconduct; her assessment of the theological needs facing a congregation recovering from such disclosure; and in a separate appendix, a statement of formal guidelines to be used by church administrators facing similar situations. A premise to all of Fortune's discussion here is the factor of power associated with or presumed inherent in the pastoral role, and the related assumption that in the face of such power, parishioners are unable to say no when faced with sexual advances from the pastor. Further, on the basis of her experience with this congregation and earlier abuse victims, Fortune identifies sexual addiction as the cause of such clergy advances.

[878] Lebacqz, Karen and Ronald G. Barton. *Sex in the Parish.* Louisville, KY: Westminster/John Knox, 1991.
This volume addresses the theological, practical and ethical issue(s) attached to sexuality in ministry. Its focus is towards the development of a professional ethic for determining appropriate and inappropriate sexual behavior between clergy and parishioners and clergy and [clergy] colleagues. The authors draw heavily from the works of Marie Fortune [877] and Paul Rutter [860], and they illustrate their own discussions with interview and questionnaire data drawn from an availability sample of over 200 clergy. Principal emphases include the recognition that there are "forbidden zones" which de facto compromise the pastoral role, and further, that the responsibility for behavior in clergy parishioner sexual interaction lies primarily with the clergy professional and entails his or her capacity to demonstrate *clearly* and *publicly* that the parishioner involved is behaving in terms of full and free consent. The authors examine issues of co-dependence, sexual and relationship addictions, the differences between paternalism and abuse, the differing religious and cultural powers of male and female clergy, and the legitimacy for differential ethical considerations for married and single, and gay and lesbian clergy--whether closeted or covenanted. The authors close with particular suggestions for "bishops" and denominational leaders responsible for adjudicating claims of sexual abuse, harassment and/or other inappropriate behavior on the part of rostered clergy, and they include an "Appendix" of procedural guidelines developed by the United Church of Christ for dealing with "allegations of inappropriate sexual contact between clergy and parishioners." The authors' focus is singularly Protestant in that it does not deal with the issues of pederasty and/or parishioner-priest contact in Roman Catholicism. This book is not a "clergy taboos" discussion--at least it is not so, for heterosexual clergy. However, because it does not openly affirm the ethical and theological legitimacy of lesbian and gay ordained church leadership and the implications of partnered unions within *this light* in Christian ministry, it discriminates *de facto* against lesbian and gay clergy, in spite of its presumed fair treatment of issues vis a vis clergy questions of marital status and sexual orientation. Hence the effects of prejudice and discrimination functioning through lay attitudes and church structures remain unacknowledged, and the public criterion of pastor-parishioner relations is precluded--and with this, the development of just norms for gay and lesbian clergy, their relationships and their

parishioners. Thus, although ground breaking for its openness and attempted understanding of a 'theology of sexuality,' (and for these reasons likely to become a standard in the literature), this work leaves much to be desired in terms of ethical analysis. For a more comprehensive discussion of ethics applicable to the circumstances of both clergy and non-clergy, see Farley **[568]** and the developing literature on lesbian and gay spirituality, Nugent and Gramick **[587]**.

[879] Majka, Linda. "Sexual Harassment in the Church." *Society* 28 (1991): 14-21.
Using data from a 1990 national sample of United Methodist clergy, laity, students and church employees (N=1,578), Majka reports the frequency of sexual harassment experiences identified by members of these groups. The variable sexual harassment was defined as "an incident in which [respondents] received unwanted and unsolicited sexual attention" (p. 15) and specific study measures were patterned after "behaviors listed in surveys conducted by the United States Merit Systems Protection Board" (p. 15). Measures thus included behaviors ranging from unsolicited (and unwanted) looks (or leers) to unsolicited touching, kissing, use of influence in return for sexual favors, attempted and actual sexual assault and rape. Important findings included (but were not limited to) the following: (1) that clergy were the most likely of the four groups to report having experienced sexual harassment, with female clergy being more likely than male clergy to report having experienced sexual harassment and female clergy reporting a significantly higher frequency of harassing behaviors; (2) the predominant type of reported harassment behaviors were those of unsolicited looks, leers, jokes and unwanted touching (with female clergy more likely than male to report harassment experiences of all types); (3) clear variation in the settings of harassment behaviors with females reporting behaviors largely in church and worship settings and males those of parishioners' homes; (4) variations both in the means by which clergy handled such experiences and the effectiveness of those coping strategies--with most clergy preferring informal to formal coping means and with males more likely to have success at informal means than females. Additional frequencies are cited for other subsample members, for the sources (initiator and status) of harassing behavior(s), and for factors affecting perceptions of behaviors as sexually harassing. Majka discusses the study findings in terms of gender and power differentials and notes that study measures do not address findings about consensual amorous relationships or the differences between exploitation and harassment. As the first national denominational study on sexual harassment in church populations, Majka's work will no doubt be extended to other church bodies.

[880] Shupe, Anson. *In the Name of All That's Holy: A Theory of Clergy Malfeasance.* Westport, CT: Praeger, 1995.
This text develops a preliminary theoretical framework for interpreting "clergy malfeasance." It defines clergy malfeasance (hereafter CM) most fundamentally as "clerical dereliction of spiritual fiduciary responsibility" (p. 35), and although it identifies three types of CM (i.e., "sexual, financial and authoritarian"), its principal concern is with sexual CM, described frequently as "clergy sex abuse." Overall, Shupe argues 4 points. First, that a genuinely *theoretical* perspective for CM is needed, because CM is largely thought of in either individualized or moral terms (e.g., "there are always a few bad apples") that, by definition, do not account for either the structural factors facilitating CM, or the social movement quality that has surrounded its public salience in the early 1990s. Second, because CM represents the meeting of two sociological frameworks (i.e., the sociologies of religion and "deviance"), an accounting of it should be drawn from these fields and focus on the role of religious structure(s) in deviance. Thus, after critically reviewing the main sociological models for deviance, Shupe settles on "labeling/conflict theory," both because it focuses analysis in the social production of meaning imputed to or attached to actors and/or organizations and because its many concepts, but notably that of "opportunity structures," can be theoretically useful. Shupe's third point then addresses the nature and function of religious structures relative to deviance and religious authority, and after identifying both (a) the power imbalance typical to clergy/laity relations generally *and* (b) the characterization of church structures overall as either "hierarchical" or "congregational," he focuses a key premise of his argument. Namely, that religious structure is the mediating variable that affects (i.e., makes a difference in) "clergy perpetrations," "victims' responses" to clergy perpetrations, and, last, (church) organizational responses to both. Finally, for his fourth point, Shupe expands this main premise through a series of detailed propositions that spell out its structural implications. Overall, Shupe's text is a theoretical ground breaker, both because it attempts to provide a structural framework for understanding clergy sexual misconduct, and because--as a theory of *clergy malfeasance*--it transcends sexual misconduct only and permits an examination of other fiduciary failures, such as the more empirically varied (and in all likelihood more frequent) authoritarian exploitation of congregants or other clergy role set members by ministers. (Cf. Schüssler Fiorenza and Copeland for less recognized expressions of ecclesiastical violence **[869]**). While the content, tone, and style

of theorizing of this text may make it a difficult source for those unfamiliar with the literature, its general framework can be most useful to both sociologists and feminist theologians.

[881] Wolf, Ann. "Special Bibliography Issue: Sexual Abuse Issues: An Annotated Bibliography." *Theology Digest* 41, no. 3 (1994): 203-250.
This special issue of *Theology Digest* is the first of a two part series, with part two of the series presented in the Winter issue of TD's volume 41. [See Wolf, "Sexual Abuse issues: An Annotated Bibliography." *Theology Digest* 41, no. 4 (1994): 331-344]. Here, in Part I, however, Wolf briefly surveys 274 references on clergy sexual abuse, harassment and/or sexual misconduct. The entries--all books and articles drawn from professional and popular sources--are listed alphabetically by author, but in the case of several religious weeklies, sources are typically listed within a journal or newspaper's consecutive issues. This manner of listing is especially helpful for sources such as *The National Catholic Reporter*, *America* or *Christianity Today*, where the periodical or newspaper becomes the organizing title and articles about important cases or personalities are chronicled accordingly. Part II of Wolf's bibliography surveys resources for dealing with experiences of clergy sexual abuse and harassment. It briefly identifies a variety of booklets, books, audio tapes, videotapes, treatment and victim resource centers, and it lists the names of centers and resources outside the United States. Part II is particularly "user friendly" and practically directed in that it presents the names and telephone numbers for contact persons associated with all listed treatment or victim resource centers.

b. Pastoral and Congregational Perspectives

[882] Blanchard, Gerald T. "Sexually Abusive Clergyman: A Conceptual Framework for Intervention and Recovery." *Pastoral Psychology* 39, no. 4 (1991): 237-246.
In an attempt to describe the strategies and benefits of an effective intervention in the circumstance of clergy/parishioner "sexual exploitation" within a congregation, Blanchard highlights eight similarities between father-daughter incest and exploitative pastor-parishioner relationships. These similarities revolve around the differing (but in Blanchard's judgment similarly paired) levels of power and authority and adulation and trust which can be attributed to the father/pastor and daughter/parishioner roles. In brief, Blanchard argues that sexual relations with a parishioner and father/daughter incest are virtually the same (*viz.*, "Sexual relations with a parishioner is [sic] the exploitation of a power imbalance, a betrayal of trust and is equivalent to abusing a family member. It differs little from incest." p. 244), and he then describes the strategies and norms necessary for a successful intervention: e.g., one must plan and rehearse for anger, maintain a frank and resolute posture, etc. By way of closure, Blanchard notes that the success of an intervention is similar to that of any effective therapy: Two persons meet and are changed by their experience; only here, the persons are those of "confronter" and the confronted. This article is clearly written, and as with much of the literature on this topic, it presumes an addiction-recovery framework together with the ideology of victim (and thus victimizer) similarities, whether the victims are under-aged children or adult women. For an alternative perspective see Beal [894, 895] or Cimbolic [897].

[883] Cooper-White, Pamela. "Soul Stealing: Power Relations in Pastoral Sexual Abuse." *The Christian Century* 108 (Feb. 20, 1991): 196-199.
Following the framework developed by Fortune [877] that 'there can be no authentic consent in a relationship involving unequal power" (p. 197), Cooper-White argues for the absolute prohibition of all sexually intimate relations between pastors and parishioners. She develops her discussion in terms of three primary themes: the total power of the clergy role as a "man of God" [sic] enactment, a series of parishioner/battered women comparisons, and last, an overview of reasons why "women neither stop nor report pastoral abuse" (p. 199). Cooper-White's discussion is based on the experiences detailed by women who are members of a "survivors of clergy exploitation" support group. Cooper-White emphasizes that it is the misuse of the power inherent in the clergy role that is really what is at stake in this issue, and that clear denominational guidelines for clergy ethical behavior need to be established, as well as policies and procedures that ensure justice and restitution for victims. Additionally, she affirms the need for church personnel to closely monitor the education and counseling of offending clergy to prevent future parishioner harm.

[884] DeVogel, Susan Harrington. "Sexual Harassment in the Church." *Christian Ministry* 19 (July-August, 1988): 12-14.
This brief discussion identifies the many liabilities churches face when pastors engage in sexually harassing behaviors, with sexual harassment defined as "repeated, unwanted attention of a sexual

(but not necessarily physical) nature given to a person in a subordinate relationship" (p. 13). It provides several vignettes to concretize this definition, and following the Minnesota Annual Conference of the United Methodist Church's practice, it distinguishes and defines gender harassment in addition to sexual harassment. ("Gender harassment exists when the work environment is charged with sexist bias.") It is written by a Methodist minister cognizant of EEOC guidelines, and it avoids the definitional confusion evident in much clergy malfeasance literature, viz., the assumption that *all* clergy parishioner sexual interaction is *de facto*, abusive and/or the result of sexual addiction.

[885] Graham, Larry Kent, [guest] ed. *Pastoral Psychology* 41 (1993): 273-345.
This issue of *Pastoral Psychology* presents five papers addressing the topics of "abuse" and "sexual, and domestic violence." The papers were initially presented at a workshop on "sexual abuse and domestic violence" held at Illif School of Theology in October of 1991, and the conference participants attempt a synthesis of findings and insights from various helping professions. Legal and ethical issues, coping and educational strategies, and various offender characteristics are described, with contributors including editor Graham, Marie Fortune, Karen Steinhauser and numerous panel respondents. The discussions are directed to the problems of violence and abuse involving members of congregational families, and the presenters readily acknowledge pastors as frequent participants in sexually abusive relationships. Last, the participants' application of secular insights to the religious sphere generally presumes an addictive/recovery model for the treatment and response to specific cases.

[886] Graham, Larry Kent and Marie M. Fortune. "Empowering the Congregation to Respond to Sexual Abuse and Domestic Violence." *Pastoral Psychology* 41 (1993): 337-345.
Graham and Fortune are panel respondents here to questions posed at a day-long workshop on sexual abuse and domestic violence held in October, 1991 at Illif School of Theology in Denver, Colorado. The questions focus largely on how pastors might handle different types of abuse issues such as reporting and confidentiality, help for women in rural churches, and education of congregational members. Additionally, the fact of *clergy* sexual abuse (in congregations) is acknowledged and Graham and Fortune note that : (1) victims of clergy abuse are often persons who have experienced prior abuse or family violence, and (2) laity in congregations need to work with clergy leadership to make congregations safe spaces for all persons.

[887] Hopkins, Nancy M. "Congregational Intervention When the Pastor Has Committed Sexual Misconduct." *Pastoral Psychology* 39 (1991): 247-255.
This article describes the two principal psychological dynamics which may follow the disclosure of a male pastor's involvement in the sexual exploitation of a female parishioner. These dynamics are denial and congregational anger, and Hopkin's purpose here is to indicate the need for intervention with the *congregation* as a victim of the minister's misconduct. Hopkins then describes 12 points important to intervention strategies. Among others, these include: (1) intervention teams need at least two members so that both sexes are represented; (2) congregations need healing at both individual and small group levels; and (3) education and low threat group work may be necessary to help congregations through their period of denial as they deal with the shock of clergy misconduct. Hopkins closes with a request for response from readers and an affirmation that congregational healing can take place. A family systems, addiction/recovery model is presumed.

[888] Hopkins, Nancy M. *The Congregation Is Also a Victim: Sexual Abuse and the Violation of Pastoral Trust.* Washington, DC: Alban Institute, 1992.
This report focuses on the study of "after pastor" congregations, i.e., congregations which have new pastors who, in ignorance and innocence, succeed other pastors who have "sexually violated pastoral trusts." Hopkins begins by presenting a variety of Catholic and Protestant vignettes which illustrate the concept of "sexually violated pastoral trusts." She then summarizes (qualitative) data drawn from the participants of an all day workshop (attended by pastors and lay leaders seeking to address the needs of "after pastor" congregations), and in two subsequent conceptual discussions she details the distinctiveness of the pastoral role together with various models which can shed light on the experience of "after pastor" congregations. Hopkins' "after pastor" concept is provocative, as is her discussion of socially homogenous churches as "incestuous systems." Her study is limited, however, in three ways: (1) several measures for her data lack clear indicators; (2) the data lack controls beyond those of the author's own framework; and (3) the "incestuous congregation" model (while provocative) is itself limited because of the social homogeneity needed for its empirical definition. A subsequent collection of papers with several authors contributing to the

discussion of congregational interventions, and with a more explicit attention to the use of Friedman's "family systems theory" (Nancy Hopkins, ed., *Clergy Sexual Misconduct: A Systems Approach,* Washington, DC: Alban Institute, 1993) addresses some of these problems, but for more helpful literature, the reader is referred to Horton and Williamson **[900]** below.

[889] Laaser, Mark, [guest] ed. *Pastoral Psychology* 39 (1991): 211-273.
This issue of *Pastoral Psychology* presents four articles on "sexual addiction and clergy." Following Laaser's introduction, separate articles by Laaser **[890]** and Gerald Blanchard **[882]** provide descriptions of sexual addiction as discernible from clergy inpatients receiving treatment at a major medical facility. Nancy Hopkins then suggests elements of "Congregational Intervention When the Pastor has Committed Sexual Misconduct" **[887]** and last, Laaser introduces the subject of "Recovering Sexually Addicted Clergy." Anonymous recovery stories by a Lutheran pastor, a female Episcopal priest and a male Roman Catholic priest then follow.

[890] Laaser, Mark. "Sexual Addiction and Clergy." *Pastoral Psychology* 39 (1991): 213-235.
Readers familiar with the paradigm of addiction and recovery as a framework for personal growth and change will find their assumptions well validated by this discussion. In it Laaser details both the numerous ways in which clergy can be sexually addicted (i.e., caught by "repetitive, uncontrollable sexual activity of any kind...to escape or avoid feelings" p. 215) and the trauma of clergy in their beginning experiences of recovery. Last, Laaser details the several ways in which "pastoral identity and sexual addiction mesh together to form a fit of sexually addicted clergy" (p. 221). Laaser's discussion is based upon observations drawn from the many clergy who have sought (or been required to seek) medical treatment for their addiction at Laaser's facility. In the light of this self-selecting population, sociologists will find Laaser's discussion descriptively interesting but ungrounded in controls beyond those of Laaser's own discussion. By way of illustration, as Laaser cites the numerous sexual activities which can be indicators of sexual addiction, he notes the possibility of an individual having either 500+ partners a year or simply one relationship over many years--even a stable monogamous relationship. From a sociological perspective, the latter tends to approximate marriage (whether that of a 'first and always' or the beginning of a serial marriage career), and in the absence of indicators to demonstrate what is normal and non-addictive (as well as what is distinctively addictive), Laaser's discussion may seem (with the exception of culturally repugnant extreme cases) unclear to those used to more multi-variate, analytical models.

c. Related literature

[891] Clark, Donald C., Jr. "The Law Steps In: Sexual Abuse in the Church." *The Christian Century* 110 (April 14, 1993): 396-398.
This article summarizes the changing climate of the church/civil courts interface relative to the sexual conduct of [male Protestant] clergy vis a vis women parishioners. The author raises the question: "Why is the legal system getting so involved in monitoring and regulating ministers' conduct?" and he argues that the courts are filling a "void, a vacuum of leadership caused by the religious community's failure to act promptly and adequately" on this issue (p. 397). Clark identifies the court's role as one of regulating power rather than ministerial conduct per se, and he argues that "Equality of power does not exist in pastor-parishioner relationships" (p. 397). He says religious institutions must abandon strategies which are interpretable as "conspiratorial silence," and he argues that while the law may establish monetary compensations for victims of clergy exploitation, it is the religious community's responsibility to: (1) help rebuild victims' self esteem; (2) educate future clergy against exploitation (and work toward early intervention when it does occur); (3) recognize the gravity of the problem, and (4) "strive for justice and mercy" along the lines presented by Fortune **[877]** in her discussion of restitution and reconciliation.

[892] Cowen, Jennifer R. "Survey Finds 70% of Women Rabbis Sexually Harassed." *Moment: The Magazine of Jewish Culture and Opinion* 18, no. 5 (October, 1993): 34-37.
Written for a popularized audience, this brief article summarizes the main findings of a sexual harassment survey mailed to 325 women rabbis world wide by the American Jewish Congress Commission for Women's Equality. The response rate was 43% (N=140), and the majority of the respondents (65%) were congregational rabbis. The variable, sexual harassment, was defined by EEOC guidelines and 70% of the survey respondents reported having experienced sexual

harassment at least "once or twice during their careers...and one in four say they are harassed once a month or more" (p. 34). Other elements of the survey dealt with the rabbis' perceptions of gender discrimination, sex-typing within the rabbinate, role satisfaction, discriminatory salary levels, a "women-rabbis" glass ceiling, and the need for lay and rabbi education (across the board) concerning sexual harassment, inappropriate interview questions, and the ways by which women rabbis can safely report sexual harassment experiences. Many of these findings approximate those of Gentile women clergy, and like the early research on the latter, this study is also descriptive, without comparative male data, and indicative of an important research agenda. **NOTE**: For additional literature on women rabbis, see Simon, Scanlon and Nadel [719].

[893] Franklin, James L. "Sex Abuse by Clergy Called Crisis for Churches." *Working Together* 11 no. 3 (Spring/Summer, 1991): 1, 10.
First printed in *The Boston Globe* on 7/17/91, this article illustrates the general format of *Working Together*, the quarterly newsletter for the Center for the Prevention of Sexual and Domestic Violence, directed by Marie Fortune in Seattle, Washington. Second, it highlights the many tensions facing mainline churches as they grapple with issues of sexuality. Of immediate import are the data Franklin cites on "clergy sexual abuse" across the denominations. Quoting Fortune, he indicates that the clergy profession is twice as likely as others to have incidents of professional-to-client sexual abuse, and he describes the administrative difficulties church leaders have in dealing with this problem. Further, his discussion implies the ideological conflict hidden in this issue: i.e., that with churches focusing on the ordination of homosexuals, attention is deflected away from heterosexuals and their potential problems. This is significant for Franklin, since "over 90 % of those involved in clergy sex abuse are heterosexual men, and over 90% of those involved in same-sex sexual abuse are self-identified heterosexual men." Absent from the discussion are suggested solutions addressing the needs of both same-sex and heterosexual clergy. Rather, the article appears scapegoating and trivializing of same-sex clergy.

2. Priests and Pedophilia in Roman Catholicism

a. Canonical Literature

[894] Beal, John P. "Doing What One Can: Canon Law and Clerical Sexual Misconduct." *The Jurist* 52 (1992): 642-683.
This discussion comprehensively reviews the Roman Catholic canonical literature and discussion surrounding the legalities of priests accused of child sex abuse, whether in terms of pedophilia (the sexual violation of pre-pubescent children, ages 6-12) or ephebophilia, (the sexual violation of post-pubescent children, ages 13-17). The author reviews the canonical procedures, protections, rights and responsibilities for all involved, and as well, the norms governing these procedures, protections, rights and responsibilities. These norms include the presumption of innocence until the 'denounced' priest is proved guilty, a respect for the privacy of all involved individuals (and especially so in the early moments of investigation), and the need for *immediate* episcopal response to the reporting of a violation. In keeping with the traditional understanding of Roman Catholic priesthood as a sacramental reality which cannot be 'undone,' Beal considers the various options available to bishops when priests are found guilty (including that of retirement on disability if the priest is found to be suffering from an incurable sexual addiction), together with the legal implications of all options surveyed. Although written from the perspective of the institutional church rather than that of the abused victim, this discussion is informative, fair-minded, and free of institutional polemics. It is recommended for readers new to this topic, both for its discussion and extended synopsis of current literature. **NOTE**: At their November, 1993 annual meeting in Washington DC, the National Conference of Catholic Bishops voted to petition the Vatican for amended canonical procedures permitting the laicization of priests found guilty of the sexual abuse of children. See, *The Washington Post*, 11/18/93 and *The National Catholic Reporter*, 12/3/93.

[895] Beal, John P. "Administrative Leave: Canon 1722 Revisited." *Studia Canonica* 27, no. 2 (1993): 293-320.
This discussion reviews both the contemporary (lay) interest in the [secular] concept of "administrative leave" and the history of canon 1722 (in the 1983 Revised Code of Canon Law) which provides an ecclesiastical facsimile for this concept. Occasioning the discussion are the increasing numbers of pedophelia charges against U.S. Roman Catholic priests and the perceived need for some means of immediate redress and sanction for these charges. Citing canon 18 (which states that "laws which establish a penalty or restrict free exercise of rights, or which contain an exception to the law, are subject to a strict interpretation"), Beal argues the need for extreme

carefulness in case handling in order to protect the rights of an accused priest, pending the findings of a penal investigation and a shift in the priest's status from that of being accused to that of being an actual defendant having to respond formally to charges. As with his discussion above (see [894]) it must be noted that the status of some form of "administrative leave" as a sanction for handling pedophelia cases is now pending modification since the annual meeting of the American Catholic bishops in Washington, in November, 1993. NOTE: For related canonical literature, which (among other things) illustrates portions of Shupe's structural argument [880]) above, see John A. Alesandro, "Dismissal from the Clerical State in Cases of Sexual Misconduct: Recent Derogations," *Canon Law Society of America Proceedings* 56 (1994): 28-67.

[896] Carfardi, Nicholas. "Stones Instead of Bread: Sexually Abusive Priests in Ministry." *Studia Canonica* 27 (1993): 145-172.
The responsibility of the [Catholic] Church to its local communities together with the communal nature of priesthood are the foci of this article. After reviewing an extended litany of the many cases of priests who have sexually abused children in their parishes, Carfardi examines the question of whether priest pedophiles (or priest ephebophiles) should ever be allowed to return to parish ministry. The context of his analysis is that of community vs. priestly rights, with the latter borne of the indelibility of ordination and the former borne of the Church's "authority to regulate the rights of individual members of the community in the interest of the common good" (p. 157). Carfardi argues clearly for the right of the community to be free from violation. In particular, he argues that one cannot talk about priestly ministry apart from community, and that if a priest is a known pedophile, "determined to be incurable," then there is no community to which this priest can minister because his ministry "would violate the common good of the community" (p. 171). Throughout his discussion Carfardi addresses the many issues facing bishops as they struggle with this question, e.g., their stewardship of duties and the various therapies and treatment options etc. available for priests in need.

[897] Cimbolic, Peter. "The Identification and Treatment of Sexual Disorders and the Priesthood." *The Jurist* 52 (1992): 598-614.
This article summarizes the two principal sexual disorders which make up the bulk of child sex abuse charges currently facing American Roman Catholic priests. These are pedophelia and ephebophelia which are, respectively, recurring sexual urges or activity with children, with pedophilia involving pre-pubescent children (ages 6-12) and ephebophelia involving post-pubescent children, ages 13-17. Cimbolic's discussion is drawn from several sources including the *Diagnostic and Statistical Manual of Mental Disorders*, Third Edition (Revised) known more popularly as DSM-III-R, and it includes an overview of the various therapies available for treating each of these sexual disorders. NOTE: Curiously, and in contrast to the general tenor, tone and assumptions of most literature addressing the subject of clergy sexual misconduct, the DSM-III-R contains no listing for "sexual addition" as a specific sexual disorder.

b. Pastoral Perspectives

[898] Rigali, Norbert. "Church Responses to Pedophilia." *Theological Studies* 55 (1994): 124-139.
This entry within "Notes on Moral Theology: 1993" provides a succinct overview of the pedophilia problem in American Catholicism through December, 1993. Norbert begins with an overview of the pedophilia problem in Canada and the United States and then carefully reviews the various USCC, NCCB and specific diocesan policy and committee statements developed in Salt Lake City, Sioux City, Chicago, and Boston. He distinguishes between pedophilia and ephebophilia, and in the light of data extrapolated from Greeley's research on the Chicago archdiocesan priest population, he concludes that "...unless Chicago is completely atypical of the Church elsewhere in the country, pedophilia is a very small part and ephebophilia a much larger part of the problem" (p. 139). He thus discusses sexuality and adulthood relative to ephebophilia (for both gay and straight priests), he affirms the need for more specific and clear definitions of terms, he calls for an end "to apriori declarations about the nature of the problem," and he insists on a discussion rooted in a clear and up front statement of facts. Extensive footnotes detail both the publicized and lesser known ecclesiastical literatures.

NOTE: For ongoing and current coverage of the discussion of priest pedophilia, consult the general periodical indices and see the *National Catholic Reporter* and/or its web site at www.natcath.com.

D. Healing and the Hope of Recovery

[899] Berry, Jason. "Listening to the Survivors: Voices of People of God." *America* 169, no. 15 (Nov. 13, 1993): 4-9.
Jason Berry is the author of *Lead Us Not Into Temptation* [Doubleday, 1992], an in-depth study of the scope, pain and costs of pedophilia in American Catholicism, and his discussion here chronicles the rise of the "survivors" movement in American Catholicism. Among other things Berry details: (1) the mid-1991 beginnings of the "Victims of Clergy Abuse Link-up," a computer-based network of pedophilia survivors started in a Chicago suburb in an effort to prod Catholic officials toward a more pastoral and timely response to the needs of clergy abuse survivors; and (2) the Survivors Network for those Abused by Priests (SNAP), also Chicago based, and Survivor Connections, a group launched by Frank Fitzpatrick, "the insurance investigator who tracked down James Porter" (p. 5). According to Berry, these groups together number approximately 6100 members and their purpose is to call the American Catholic Church to accountability for the behavior of its priests. Although unaffiliated with other internally based Catholic reform groups (e.g., Women's Ordination Conference), they seek a "dialogue of truth" with Church officials and will not be dissuaded until this happens--whether in the church or the civil courts.

[900] Horton, Anne L., and Judith A. Williamson, eds. *Abuse and Religion: When Praying Isn't Enough.* Lexington, MA: Lexington Books, 1988.
This anthology of 30 essays addresses virtually every aspect of abuse and religion and is geared to practical use by persons in positions of parish leadership, whether lay or clerical. Its three sections include "Guidelines" from, respectively, abuse experts, religious leaders, and victims and perpetrators, and within each of these three sections, "special considerations" are addressed, such as: "Culture and Ethnicity in Family Violence," "Counseling the Adult Survivor of Child Sexual Abuse: Concepts and Cautions for Clergy," and "Wife Abuse and Scripture." Practical considerations include a victim's perception of a shelter and the discussion of a "model treatment program" together with guidelines for congregations seeking to help both victims and perpetrators.

[901] Jacobs, Janet. "The Effects of Ritualist Healing on Female Victims of Abuse: A Study of Empowerment and Transformation." *Sociological Analysis* 50 (1989): 265-279.
Using data from extended interviews, questionnaire responses, and participant observation with a group of 30 women engaged in goddess based ritual healing services, Jacobs identifies and describes the healing and empowerment dynamics which the women experience in these rituals. Elements of her analysis include the women's ability to: (1) name and reject their perpetrator; (2) experience bonding with other women experiencing the same reality; and (3) become sufficiently empowered to confront their abuser (at least symbolically) through either goddess-based self-images as 'avengers' or, in the majority of cases, goddess-based self-images as confronters able to overwhelm their abusers by their own strength of presence. Study implications include the necessity for research on the women's needs to maintain their empowerment through continued group participation, since their experiences of empowerment tended to recede over time.

[902] Jacobs, Janet. "Victimized Daughters: Sexual Violence and the Empathic Female Self." *Signs* 19 (1993): 126-145.
This uncommonly clear article describes the dynamics by which the "capacity for empathy" in young girls is deflected *away from* an identification with and activation by the girl's mother and is directed instead toward an identification with and activation by the girl-child's father, who in the cases of Jacobs' sample members is also an incest offender. Jacobs draws her discussion from a series of extended interviews with 50 women from the Denver area, all incest survivors and all referred to Jacobs by mental health professionals. She thus works with a "non-probabilistic" sample, but this fact notwithstanding, her sample members cut across race, class and sexual orientation variables, and her discussion highlights differences from within these categories. Jacobs' principal focus is on the social construction of the young girl's capacity for empathy and its subsequent attachment to the girl's father-violator rather than her (potential) mother-protector. Additionally, Jacobs describes the young girl's internalization of shame, her subsequent need to protect and rescue her father-perpetrator, and the implications of this experience for the girl's later, adult life. This is an exceptional discussion, and its clear theoretical and non-polemical tone make it one of the best available within the feminist sociological (and theological) literature.

[903] Keene, Jane A. *A Winter's Song: A Liturgy for Women Seeking Healing from Sexual Abuse in Childhood.* New York: Pilgrim, 1991.
The liturgy presented in this text is prefaced by the author's own acknowledgment of her early abuse history and her subsequent awareness of the many pains, ambiguities and feelings of guilt which can arise from such an experience: the sense of self-guilt which typically accompanies later life recollections of early childhood abuse, the inability of the abused person to "forgive herself" for such abuse, her inability to forgive a silent and seemingly complicit community which may have known nothing about it but was nonetheless presumed an advocate, the abused person's inability to forgive her abuser, and last, the complicating possibility of multiple personalities and the circumstances they may impose. The liturgy which follows this moving preface incorporates these sensitivities into a variety of prayers and expressions of the many levels of forgiveness and acceptance that can be healing to an abuse survivor. The liturgical "God-language" is gender inclusive, and the author's intention is that users of this liturgy may feel free to adapt its intents to their specific situations--including the possibility of a survivor's inability to forgive her abuser.

[904] Saussy, Carroll. *God Images and Self Esteem: Empowering Women in a Patriarchal Society.* Louisville, KY: Westminster/John Knox, 1991.
This discussion reports on the empowerment experiences of twenty-one women Saussy interviewed in an attempt to examine how women re-write their personal ideologies in post-patriarchal ways. The women were given a brief questionnaire on self-esteem, together with a series of open-ended questions asking them to identify both the types of "goal directed messages" they had received from parents and significant others during their childhoods and the conflicts these messages engendered. Additionally, Saussy asked respondents to recall images of God and important religious experiences. Saussy recounts her interview data in terms of each woman's search for "good enough self-esteem," and she describes the ways in which her sample members work to overcome internalized patriarchy and its negative effects on self esteem. She describes how her sample members sort out "true" from "false" selves, and she highlights the role of goddess imagery, women's bonding and feminist insights for these re-writings of self and self-ideologies. Saussy does not extend her findings beyond her initial 21 sample members, but she presents them as statements which may echo realities for others, and particularly, women who have experienced abuse. For related literature see Jacobs above **[901, 902]**.

23

Feminist Theology's Global Voices

As the women's movement has developed worldwide, the "hermeneutic of women's experience" has expanded considerably (in terms of cultural pluralism), and the doing of feminist theology has become formalized in terms of "social location" and its advocacy implications. Listed below are the sources that evidence this emphasis. These sources are now generally recognized as feminist theology's "global voices," and they include the voices of Native American women, Hispanic and Latina women, Asian and Asian-American women.

Social location is an important concept in contemporary theological methodology. It attempts a specification of the social forces conditioning theological thought, and because it often does so in categories drawn from the sociology of knowledge (cf., e.g., **[909]** and **[912]**), it emphasizes that history and culture play a larger epistemological role in the theologizing process than has generally been presumed. There are several implications to such a perspective, and not the least of these are the many problems of historical relativism, and for some, the dynamics of nihilism and atomistic philosophy (cf., e.g., **[327]** and **[330]**). But the methodology of social location also suggests that the women's movement in theology is grounded in the elements of social rather than formal organization, and that it is thereby sensitized to factors of injustice. Hence the women's movement in theology signals an ecumenical attention to the material, social and cultural problems of women, *and* the material, social and cultural solutions to such problems. Expressed differently, "social location" (or "standpoint theology" as it is also called) suggests that: (1) "women's experience" is de facto embedded in racial-ethnic and historically defined gendered networks; (2) it is thus inherently pluralistic; and (3) it is existentially and visibly justice-directed. This last point is particularly important, for uniting the racial-ethnic and historically evident gender-pluralism of women's experience are the facts of poverty, violence, and the devaluation of women's worth and women's experience by more powerful (and typically "hierarchically ordered") sectors of economies around the world. The entries below evidence these points, and their range of perspectives indicates the ecumenical reach of contemporary feminist theology.

A final note: In several entries reference is made to an organization identified as EATWOT, the *Ecumenical Association of Third World Theologians*, founded in 1976. (See George Gisper-Sauch, "Asian Theology" in *The Modern Theologians*, edited by David F. Ford, 455-476. Cambridge: Blackwell, 1997.)

A. Social Location and Theological Method

[905] Broderick y Guerra, Cecily P. "Annotated Bibliography." In *Inheriting Our Mothers' Gardens: Feminist Theology in Third World Perspective*, edited by Letty M. Russell, Kwok Pui-Lan, Ada Maria Isasi-Diaz and Katie Geneva Cannon, 165-181. Louisville, KY: Westminster, 1988.

The eighty-five entries in this annotated bibliography are dispersed across six sections, identified by the compiler as: "African and Afro-American women," "Asian and Asian-American Women,"

"Latin-American/Hispanic Women," "White American Women and The Third World," "Global Resources," and "Periodicals Related to Third World Feminist Theology." While many annotations are no more than paraphrased titles, this is an excellent beginning resource for one unfamiliar with the literature and seeking a list of sources by which to quickly "get on board."

[906] Eugene, Toinette, Ada Maria Isasi-Diaz, Kwok Pui Lan, Judith Plaskow, and Mary Hunt. "Appropriation and Reciprocity in Womanist/Mujerista Feminist Work." *Journal of Feminist Studies in Religion* 8, no. 2 (1992): 91-122.
This seminar-like discussion addresses the "problem" of "difference" between feminist, womanist, and *Mujerista* theological communities, with Eugene's lead essay acknowledging both the unfulfilled dream of genuine pluralism and at least three factors which (in the U.S.) work against it: the ideology of "professionalism" which splits praxis and scholarship; the "antifeminism of many women of color" (p. 94); and last, the homophobia evident in various women's communities. To combat the three social factors blocking the development of genuine pluralism, Eugene argues for the "cultivation" of "integrity, awareness, courage, and a redefining [of] one's own [idea of] 'success'" (p. 95). Moreover, she identifies an additional factor blocking the recognition of "genuine pluralism," i.e., the mechanism of "non-interactive acknowledgment," or the process of acknowledging difference and its location as beyond one's self, and thus removed from one's responsibility. This mechanism is similar to what Kanter **[728]** terms "trivialization," and in Eugene's discussion, it functions as a form of power which permits dominant persons to disclaim responsibility to respond to non-dominants, such that the latter thereby become more dependent on the former. Respondents to Eugene's discussion include Ada Maria Isasi-Diaz, who discusses the nature of respect for other people's work; Kwok Pui-lan, who examines the need for respecting intellectual boundaries; Judith Plaskow, who returns to the theme of power and violations of community symbols; and Mary Hunt, who with customary insight synthesizes much discussion through helpful imagery: here, "neighborly borrowing" and the range of its expectations.

[907] Haddad, Y. Y., and E. B. Findley, eds. *Women, Religion and Social Change.* Albany, NY: SUNY Press, 1985.
The 20 papers presented in this volume stem from the "Symposium on Women, Religion and Social Change" held at Hartford Seminary in Hartford, Connecticut, October 21-22, 1983. They are grouped into four categories which distinguish: (1) "Women and the Formation of Religious Tradition" (2) "Social Transformation [and] the Role of women in Traditional Institutions;" (3) "Women, Religion and Revolution;" and last, (4) "Women, Religion and the Transformation of Society in North America." A hallmark of the book is its attention to the pluralism and global scope of women's experience and involvement in religious traditions. Together, the papers reflect Asian, Latin American, Jewish, Muslim and Christian concerns, with particular attention directed to the liberationist efforts of women within these cultural frames.

[908] King, Ursula ed. *Feminist Theology from the Third World: A Reader.* Maryknoll, NY: Orbis, 1994.
Written as a parallel to Loades' reader on [first world] feminist theology **[274]**, this collection unfolds the global voices of feminist theology, both from within specifically geographic third world countries *and* the experiences of "minority" women living in first world countries such as the United States. It is a strong and informative text. Its opening introduction skillfully details the history of "third world" feminist theology (both in terms of key writers and formative institutions [e.g., the WCC, and the "Women's Commission of EATWOT"]), and it highlights the cross cutting themes which unite, but yet distinguish first and third world feminist theologians, *viz.*, an attention to: the economic oppression and suffering of third world women, to their possibilities for "dreaming" of new and better worlds, to the use of church and church based structures for liberation and empowerment and, grounding all, the tasks of justice-making activities. Virtually all noted third world feminists are represented among the contributors to the volume, and the entries well represent the biblical, empowerment, spirituality and prophetically directed methodologies of women doing theology in the "third world." Authors are helpfully identified in remarks prefatory to their works, and a supplemental bibliography and index close out the text.

[909] Pobee, John S., and Barbel von Wartenberg-Potter, eds. *New Eyes for Reading: Biblical and Theological Reflections by Women from the Third World.* Geneva: World Council of Churches, 1986.
This collection of 18 essays grouped into the two categories, "New Eyes for Reading" and "New Eyes for Seeing," presents work by several of the increasingly known feminist theologians of Africa, Asia and Latin America. The lead essays, by Ghanaian Elizabeth Amoah and Latin

American theologian Elsa Tamez, respectively, set the tone of this brief volume with reflections on Mark 5:25-29 and Gen. 16:1-4 and 21:8-20, all stories of poor women's needs and the authority such need engenders: a breaking of the rules in Mark, where a hemorrhaging woman touches Jesus, and a wilderness tradition in Genesis, as Hagar demands accountability first from Sara and then from God. The remaining essays fit the experience of materially poor and violently abused women—*third* worldwide—against this perception of needful authority and the new ears and eyes the authors demand privileged readers to develop. Among the noted contributors are Nigerian feminist theologian Mercy Oduyoye, Indian Aruna Gnanadason, Filipinos Elizabeth Dominguez and Virginia Fabella, and Kwok Pui Lan. Among less well known writers are Cameroun Grace Eneme, Korean Lee Oo Chung, and Egyptian Coptic Orthodox Marie Assaad. This was a "sleeper" text: written mid-80s, but salient by the mid-90s and especially so in the light of the widening theological critique of violence against women worldwide.

[910] Russell, Letty M., Kwok Pui-lan, Ada Maria Isasi-Diaz, and Katie Geneva Cannon, eds. *Inheriting Our Mothers' Gardens: Feminist Theology in Third World Perspective*. Louisville, KY: Westminster, 1988.
This work provides autobiographical essays by eight feminist theologians. The majority of these theologians were born and nurtured in "third" rather than first or second world cultures and milieux, and for each, the metaphors of "search" and "inheritance" allow a sketch of what personally and historically has shaped the development of her theology. The contributors include: two "white" [*sic*] feminist first world theologians--Presbyterian feminist Letty Russell and lay theologian Joann Nash Eakin; African-American ethicist and womanist scholar Katie Cannon; two voices bespeaking Asian women's theological experience--*viz.*, Chinese New Testament scholar Kwok Pui-Lan and Korean Chung Hyun Kyung, a graduate student in systematics at the time of the book's printing (but now author of *Struggle to Be the Sun Again* **[935]**); Ghanaian Methodist Mercy Amba Oduyoye; Salvadoran Marta Benavides; and *Mujerista* theologian, Ada Maria Isasi-Diaz. A ninth contributor is Cecily P. Broderick y Guerra, a "native New Yorker" whose entry is an annotated bibliography **[905]** rather than an autobiographical sketch. The essays are personal in nature, and they provide a bedrock of insight into the professional concerns of many current and rising stars within the globally based feminist theological community.

[911] Russell, Letty M.. "Affirming Cross-Cultural Diversity: A Missiological Issue in Feminist Perspective." *International Review of Mission* 81 (1992): 253-258.
This article summarizes Russell's reflections on her experience of a cross-cultural theological dialogue involving 35 Asian and Western women "seeking ways to understand and teach the gospel in their own context as well as a global one" (p. 353). Of primary import for Russell is the "contextual" method of feminist theology, a style of theologizing which is: (1) premised upon a unity in diversity; (2) fostering of an action-reflection strategy for theology; and (3) seeking to disclose the 'mission of God' as the activity of women building this unity through justice-directed activity on behalf of women everywhere. Russell emphasizes the use of "sources" in this contextual method. These include: "biblical and church tradition, reason, experience and action" and here, in contrast to feminist discussions which speak generally of women's experience as a source of revelation, Russell suggests that "the critical principle of discernment in feminist theologies is not just women's experience, but rather the experience of women of faith and struggle who are engaged in the work of new creation and willing to articulate what they are learning about struggle and new life seeking to be born" (p. 256). Russell's is an important suggestion for it identifies justice-seeking endeavors as the ecumenical ground of globally directed feminist theologies. **NOTE**: Additional articles in this thematic journal issue also echo Russell's themes and the reader is referred to Oduyoye **[920]**. Also, for an organizational discussion of this cross-cultural dialogue, see Teo Geok Lian, "Purpose of China 1990: Dialogue Among Theologically Trained Women of Asia and US." *Asia Journal of Theology* 5 (1991): 233-236.

[912] Segovia, Fernando F., and Mary Ann Tolbert, eds. *Reading from This Place: Social Location and Biblical Interpretation in the United States*. and *Reading from This Place: Social Location and Biblical Interpretation in Global Perspective*. Minneapolis, MN: Fortress, 1995.
This two volume set synthesizes the key theological, philosophical and hermeneutical essays grounding the epistemic dimensions of social location as critical to the genesis of religious symbols. Volume 1 presents papers given at Vanderbilt Divinity School in January of 1993. It focuses the American literature with 17 contributions organized around the three themes of "Social Location and Hermeneutics," "Contestations: Locations in Conflict," and "Social Location and Accountability," and with entries from such authors as Fernando Segovia, Herman Waetjen, Vincent Wimbush,

Tina Pippin, Antoinette Wire, and Mary Ann Tolbert. In April, 1993, Vanderbuilt again provided the forum, but here for the global literature, with contributors from Africa, Asia, Europe, Latin and North America (e.g., Amba Oduyoye, Naim Ateek, Luise Schotroff, and Teresa Calvalcanti). This is a solid source with *extended* notes and embedded bibliography.

[913] Webster, John C. B., and Ellen Low Webster, eds. *The Church and Women in the Third World.* Philadelphia: Westminster, 1985.
This text is an anthology of eight scholarly essays that highlight the ecclesiastical and missionary assumptions grounding Christian evangelization from the nineteenth century to the present time. The essays stem from critiques leveled at both the 1981 WCC Conference on "Women and Men in the Church" and the 1986 EATWOT conference on the theological challenges of the Third World. At each, the concerns of women were either marginalized or trivialized by a lack of sensitivity to the diversity of women's experiences within third world countries. Hence the editors here attempt a corrective with discussions of "Christian Images of Women" (in China and India); "The Role of Women in the Church" (six essays surveying the experiences of Latin American, Indian and African women); a discussion of women in Philippine base communities; and last, a brief, 46 item annotated bibliography on "The Church and Women in the Third World." The essays are well documented, and the bibliography stresses social rather than theological literature.

NOTE: For additional bibliography see Fenton and Heffron [45], Tierney [57] and Thistlethwaite and Engel [276].

B.   The Ecumenism of Women

1.   Women's Ecumenism and Feminist Spirituality

[914] Benavides, Marta. "Spirituality for the Twenty-First Century: Women, Mission and the 'New World Order.'" *International Review of Mission* 81 (1992): 213-226.
This article argues strongly for a spirituality grounded in the assumption of "justice" as the basis for Christian activity and ecumenism throughout the world. Its particular focus is for economic justice among "third world" and "developing" nations, and to make the point Benavides cites the disproportionate lack of resources available to "developing" nations and the impact of American and Gulf War ideology in maintaining the economically privileged positions of Europe and the United States. By way of closure, Benavides identifies sexism, racism and fascism as the pervasive 'causes' of injustice in the world, and she calls upon both religious and secular leaders to educate people for peace, for ecological sensitivity and "solidarious" societies across the world, which evidence the kind of community implied and exemplified in the life of Jesus. For background on Benavides, see her chapter in Russell et al. [910].

[915] Finger, Reta, ed. "Global Women's Communities." *Daughters of Sarah* 17, no. 2 (1991): 1-27.
This brief issue of *DOS* again evidences the strength of Reta Finger's editorial abilities, for it pulls together several discussions, resources and reviews of books on issues and concerns reflecting feminist theology in the "third world." Finger's own editorial is clear and powerful as it previews the journal issue: on all three continents (Latin America, Africa and Asia) women are oppressed; they take the biblical message of liberation seriously; they are vital to the church; they focus strongly on Christology, *and* they are beginning their theologies. The essays then follow. An introductory essay by Rosemary Radford Ruether ("Feminist Theology in Global Context") provides an historical overview of feminism and the initial resistance of third world male theologians to it--a resistance named and (successfully) challenged at EATWOT conferences by Mercy Oduyoye, now Deputy General Secretary of the WCC. Marion Jacobson, a medical technologist, and theologian Virginia Fabella introduce the reader to women in India, both in terms of religious and cultural values (Jacobson) and the possibilities for an Asian Christology (Fabella). Wanda Deifelt, a Brazilian Lutheran theologian, identifies several helpful (and harmful) religious-political connections among Brazilian women; Rev. Linda Gesling introduces Russian Orthodox women; and last, women-church liturgist Diane Neu provides a "Blessing of Many Breads." Several organizational resources and book reviews then follow.

[916] Gnanadason, Aruna. "A Spirituality That Sustains Our Struggles." *International Review of Mission* 80 (1991): 29-41.
The linkages between ecology, the rising consciousness of women, efforts to transcend and undo caste structures, and the struggle for validations of human dignity all coalesce in the "spirituality for

struggle" described here by Indian theologian, Aruna Gnanadason, who is also the Director for the World Council of Churches' "Women in Church and Society" subunit. Several specifics indicate the spirituality Gnanadason describes: the resurgence of *Shakti* (or "strength") spirituality among women in the lower Himalayas, the rise of the "Dalit movement for liberation" against India's caste system, India's ecology movement and numerous tribal movements against industrialization, and among Indian women and Asian feminist theologians specifically, an emerging theology which speaks loudly against the violence imposed by poverty, "caste gradation," prostitution tourism, and the use of women as both cheap labor and vehicles of violence for male prestige (pp. 39-40). Each of these elements, suggests Gnanadason, is evidence of a new and growing spirituality which is poised for struggle, but positively directed. In terms of specifics, this spirituality is characterized by five features: (1) an emphasis on "earthiness" and an attention to the "grim realities of life;" (2) the efforts of people--presently without a name--to find one deep in the recesses of their painful history; (3) a celebration of pluralism as the grounding of reality--and within this an acknowledged recognition of the oppression of specific and concrete groups; (4) a clear demand for "inclusion" and the eradication of racial, caste-based, gender and religious marginalizations; and (5) a recognition that "unity" is an "unfinished dream." This is an important article: it reflects the *very wide* reaches of the women's theological movement currently developing in Asia and it exhibits its connection to mainstream church structures. For related discussions see: Benavides **[914]**, Gnanadason **[917]**, Russell **[911]**, Oduyoye **[920]**, Kyung **[935]** and Park **[936-937]**.

[917] Gnanadason, Aruna. "Women in the Ecumenical Movement." *International Review of Mission* 81 (1992): 237-246.
This essay summarizes the historical involvement of women in 20th century ecumenism, with a particular emphasis on women and the identification of Christianity's mission priorities worldwide. Gnanadason begins with the observation that women's ecumenical work has typically been ignored, largely because such service is usually seen as "natural" to women. She then notes that women's ecumenical efforts are frequently viewed as elements of a "power play" rather than efforts at participation and mission development, and she sets about the task of identifying the history of activities of women in Christian mission from 1910 to the mid and late 1980s. Her discussion synthesizes a variety of recent sources on the history of women's ecumenical activity, and it identifies several important but previously unknown contributors to the discussion of organized Christianity and its world wide mission. By way of closure Gnanadason calls attention to several justice issues facing the church worldwide: (1) the global character of the women's movement and its implications for a "mission agenda for women in the churches"; (2) the need of churches to recognize both a theological pluralism and social diversity among their members; and (3) the need of churches to recognize that the struggle for justice by (and for) churchwomen is not a 'power play,' but a longing for a church "more responsive to the prophetic role it has to play in the midst of a bleeding humanity" (p. 246).

[918] Hunt, Mary E. "Feminist Ecumenism: Models for the Mainstream." *The Christian Century* 108 (1991): 996-999.
Hunt's purpose here is to describe three types of feminist ecumenism that contrast sharply with the "patriarchal ecumenism" of established church/denominational structures. These types include (1) feminist ecumenism *within* established ecumenical circles; (2) the women-church movement and (3) the "women's spirituality movement." The first type focuses on the inclusion of women into leadership positions and an attention to women's secular and religious needs, experiences, and contributions. The second type exhibits the mutual and inclusive nature of women's worship. As a regular and periodic gathering of women, the women-church movement pertains to "no single denomination" but provides a horizon of support and liturgical life for women seeking the inclusive reform of their traditional faith communities. The third type of feminist ecumenism is the women's spirituality movement. It is more eclectic in nature than the previous two types in that it includes women's religious groups from both established and non-traditional faith communities, e.g., "Native American and other indigenous traditions." This third type of feminist ecumenism stresses a justice seeking and creation based ethic, and its message to the broader ecumenical world "is the need to embrace without prejudice that which is different." **NOTE:** For related entries, see the women-church literature in Chapter 19.

[919] May, Melanie A. *Women and Church: The Challenge of Ecumenical Solidarity in an Age of Alienation.* Grand Rapids, MI: William B. Eerdmans [for the Commission on Faith and Order, NCCCCUSA], 1991.
In her forward to this anthology of twenty-three essays by women from virtually every mainline Christian denomination, Monika Hellwig describes the voices in this book as "voices to be heard."

She is correct. They are voices which seek women's solidarity both within and beyond the confines of organized religion, and they speak to issues which both permeate and transcend church life. The issues are three-fold and include *ministry*: its characterization as an official but yet ambivalent task for women in organized religion; *authority*: its recognized historical abuse by church*men* and the need for its redefinition; and last, the use of language in religion: i.e., its continuing androcentric character and the recognized need for greater inclusivity. Section I of this three-part text is "Women and Church," and with fourteen entries it is the longest section of the book. It is also the most frank, with discussions ranging from Edith Blumhofer's "Women in Evangelicalism and Pentecostalism" to Virginia Mollenkott's "Heterosexism as a Challenge to Ecclesial Solidarity." Part II looks at "Women in the Ecumenical Movement" and includes entries from Joan B. Campbell, Kathy Hurtz, Eileen Lindner, Mary Motte and Margaret O'Gara. Part III, "Toward a New Ecumenical Movement," addresses global and multi-cultural concerns with entries by Annie Machisale-Musopole, Letty Russell, Sun Ai Lee Park and Mary Tanner. All essays are brief, readable, feminist, and frank, but the volume lacks indices and supplemental bibliographies.

[920] Oduyoye, Mercy Amba. "Guest Editorial: The Pact of Love Across All Borders." *International Review of Mission* 81 (1992): 173-176.
This essay is Oduyoye's introduction to the special "women in mission" issue of the *International Review of Mission*. In it she examines "women's style of relating to systems and structures" to indicate five key emphases: the efforts of women "to work *with* rather than *for*" others; a related emphasis on "partnership, interdependence and solidarity;" a strong commitment to issues of justice for women as grounded in a "theology of self-inclusion," a recognition of the "diversity of gifts" which women bring to mission activity; and a subsequent recognition of mission as itself an *instrument* of unity. Seventeen articles then follow and address various historical and theological perspectives on women's mission activity. Abstracted for the present volume are essays by Benavides **[914]**, Gnanadason **[916, 917]**, Russell **[911]** and Sun Ai Lee Park **[937]**. Additionally, see Russell et al. **[910]**, Gnanadason **[934]**, and Kwok Pui-lan (**[219]** and **[281]**) for related literature.

[921] O'Connor, Francis Bernard. *Like Bread, Their Voices Rise!* Notre Dame, IN; Ave Maria Press, 1993.
Using interview and questionnaire data from selected samples of Catholic women in four countries [Brazil (n=408), the United States (n=485), Uganda (n=215), and Bangladesh (n=153)] O'Connor presents compelling arguments to refute "...Rome's assumption that women's desire for full participation in the church is only a North American 'problem...'" (p. 16). Her discussion focuses on the ways in which women feel excluded from full participation in the church and its leadership, including ordination and equal power in decision making. Because her study is directed to the tasks of education and consciousness raising on behalf of women in the church worldwide, O'Connor's discussion is pastorally toned and organized thematically around each sample's perceptions of 'full participation.' Hence a number of O'Connor's more technical considerations are reserved for an appendix presentation, with Rodney Ganey, the Director of the Social Science Training and Research Laboratory at Notre Dame, highlighting variable measures, data frequencies, and relevant significance tests. It is important to note that while the international samples are purposive rather than random, the American sample is comprised by three subsets: a random sample from the membership of the Women's Ordination Conference; a sample of parish women identified "by pastoral ministers, both lay and religious" and a sample of Catholic women identified by The Gallup Organization. An appendix of tables and bar graphs helpfully portray the data, and a copy of O'Connor's instrument as prepared for the American sample is included. Endnotes and a bibliography close the text.

[922] O'Neill, Maura. *Women Speaking, Women Listening: Women in Interreligious Dialogue*. Maryknoll, NY: Orbis, 1990.
This detailed and thought provoking study roots the tasks of interreligious dialogue in both feminist epistemology and the practical insight that differences and conflict are opportunities for growth, not problems to be solved. O'Neill begins with a critique of the androcentrism in philosophical anthropology and the implications of feminism for epistemology. Women, she argues, have been left out of inter-religious dialogues because traditional anthropologies take maleness as the norm. Feminist anthropologies, however, acknowledge the variability of gender and thus of the philosophical category of "persons," *and* the gendered character of all knowledge. With her framework thus set, O'Neill then reviews several emphases in feminist ethics and theology, and after identifying various conflicts that exist between first and third world feminists, she argues for dialogue that roots in personal narratives as a means of: (1) establishing trust; (2) clarifying diverse

perspectives; (3) keeping feminist theory from becoming too abstract and (4) providing "opportunities for common ground." Her discussion is frank about the painful differences which exist between variously grounded communities of women, and she advocates a serious listening by academic feminists to the religious experiences of women in traditions distinct from American and European academic theology--e.g., Islamic, Jewish, Asian, lay Christian, Goddess and Wiccan movements.

[923] Parvey, Constance F. "Re-membering: A Global Perspective on Women." In *Christian Feminism: Visions of a New Humanity,* edited by Judith Weidman, 158-179. San Francisco: Harper & Row, 1984.

"Re-membering" is the task of asking not only "when and where, but also why" (p. 159), and it is the task and invitation of this essay. It is the essay's task because Parvey calls to mind the accomplishments of women worldwide in late twentieth century, but with serious questions: "Does not technology enable one educated woman to use a computer and thereby displace the work of five or twenty or more? And if so, how does one come to terms with this?" (p. 162). These and other questions pulse through the essay as Parvey surveys women's accomplishments. But "re-membering" is also the invitation of this essay and readers are asked to reflect upon (among other things) the privatization of home life that removes individuals from responsibility in the public sphere (p. 168); and further, the fact that "the apex of the last women's movement was a decade before Hitler" (p. 170). Parvey's discussion synthesizes several elements of the women's movement worldwide, and it argues that women in the church, specifically, are called to global re-membering to network for peace, food-bearing, community and the liturgical empowerment of all people(s).

2. Global Voices

a. Native American Women's Theologies

[924] Parker, Kay. "American Indian Women and Religion on the Southern Plains." In *Women and Religion in America, Volume III: 1900-1968,* edited by Rosemary Radford Ruether and Rosemary Skinner Keller, 48-79. New York: Harper and Row, 1986.

This article briefly describes the history of American Indians in the Southern Plains and identifies three specific "religious contexts" within which women have had visible (although not always primary) religious roles. These contexts are (1) Native American traditions per se, in which women have frequently been Medicine Women; (2) Christian missions and denominations--in which women have participated socially and educationally; and (3) Pan-Indian Religion, and particularly the Peyote Cult which had (and yet has) varying expectations for women. Among others, the latter include the role of "water carrier" (for specific Peyote Services) and in the Native American Church (which the Peyote Cult officially became in 1955), the expectation that women are (or will be) keepers of the music traditionally associated with the cult. Fourteen documentary sources illustrating Parker's discussion then follow. **NOTE:** While Native Americans across the board have experienced tribal and cultural decimation throughout United States history, the Plains Indians received particularized brutality as settlers and states expanded westward and sought either genocide or "population transfer." In turn, much Native American culture was lost and/or destroyed, with a major effect being the lack of resources by which to reconstruct Native American women's history.

[925] Peterson, Jaqueline, and Mary Druke. "American Indian Women and Religion." In *Women and Religion in America, Volume II: The Colonial and Revolutionary Periods,* edited by Rosemary Radford Ruether and Rosemary Skinner Keller, 1-41. New York: Harper and Row, 1983.

Drawing upon examples from the many Native American tribes and confederations which originally peopled the American states prior to 1800, Peterson and Druke detail: (1) the difficulties in obtaining unbiased and indigenous sources for women's experiences in Native American religion; (2) the varying cosmologies, earth symbols, and gender assumptions particular to Native American religion generally; and (3) the interface between Christianity and Native Americans as Protestant and Catholic missionaries sought Native American conversions. The discussion here is closely informed by the 21 source documents following Peterson and Druke's introductory essay, and it is from these documents that Peterson and Druke identify the major roles women played in Native American traditions: e.g., those of visionary, shaman, healer, defender of the ancestral traditions, hunter and believer. The documents further expand upon these roles and in many cases highlight the ethnocentric perceptions of the traders, clergy and others describing specific incidents. **NOTE**: For additional historical information on Native American women, see Bass and Boyd [130]; see the article entries in Mankiller et al. [52], and see Evans [74], Loeb, Searing and Stineman [51], DuBois and Ruiz [73], Zinn and Dill [83], Freeman [88], and Inez Maria Talamantez's discussion in Ruether and Keller [135].

b. *Mujerista* Theology and Latin American Feminist Theologies

[926] Aquino, Maria Pilar. *Our Cry for Life: Feminist Theology from Latin America.*
    Maryknoll, NY: Orbis, 1993.
This text introduces new readers to the literature, issues and methodologies of "Latina" or Latin American feminist theology. It focuses Latina feminist theology as a grassroots movement borne of *Latin American women's* long history of race, gender and class oppression, and it argues consistently for the recognition of Latin American feminist theology as distinct from Latin American Liberation Theology, on the one hand, and First World (or North American) feminist theology on the other. This task of differentiation is important, because as Aquino persuasively argues, Latin American women have a history of "race, gender and class" oppression that was forged with the melding of colonialism, machista social structure and (eventually) capitalist investment, and it is against this backdrop that Latina women work to develop self-worth and self-determination through justice-directed social and religious structures. But there is a second reason for enhancing the visibility of Latina feminist theology (as contrasted with liberationist and other perspectives), and this reason focuses on the "daily" and "lived life" quality of Latina theology, for while liberation theology addresses issues of economic injustice, it does so only in the public sphere and not the private sphere where the racial and social dimensions of the machista world remain in place. Hence, while Latina feminist theology collaborates and dialogs with the well recognized horizons of Latin American "liberation theology," Latina feminist theology does not lump women as among "the [androcentrized] poor." Rather, Latina feminist theology speaks precisely on behalf of justice for *women* (who admittedly are among the poor), so that a justice critique may be made against the class gendered roles of *both the public and private spheres*. **NOTE**: Aquino is presently an associate professor at the University of San Diego. Her essay work appears in [322] and [323].

[927] Isasi-Diaz, Ada Maria. "Toward an Understanding of *Feminismo Hispano* in the
    U.S.A." In *Women's Consciousness, Women's Conscience: A Reader in Feminist
    Ethics*, edited by Barbara Hilkert Andolsen, Christine E. Gudorf and Mary D.
    Pellauer, 51-61. Minneapolis, MN: Winston Press, 1985.
The assimilation of culturally distinct groups into a majority pattern and/or experience has regularly generated its own tensions for both established groups and groups seeking an existence within the dominant pattern. This essay addresses this point by delineating the tensions that exist for *Feministas Hispanas* as they seek an affirmed space within the contexts of American culture and feminist theory. To identify these tensions Isasi-Diaz employs the concept "invisible invisibility." This concept refers to two things. The first is that Hispanic feminists are vulnerable to both racial-ethnic and gender prejudice--and these with all of the consequences they engender, including horizontal violence across culturally distinct groups of women. Second, "invisible invisibility" refers to the tension internal to women in Hispanic culture as they espouse feminist values vis a vis Hispanic males seeking equality in American society. To describe the latter, Isasi-Diaz contrasts the goals of equality and liberation as sought, respectively, by Hispanic men and women. To describe the former (i.e., the effects of racial-ethnic prejudice, and particularly horizontal violence), Isasi-Diaz contrasts the experiences and learnings of Hispanic and African-American women, with an attention to the values of "honor" and "time" as perceived within Hispanic culture. Last, Isasi-Diaz contrasts *Feministas Hispanas* and white/Anglo feminists to indicate the perceived needs, tensions and expectations Hispanic women have of white American feminists, and she identifies the need for a community of "familia" among Hispanic women as their efforts toward liberation and justice continue. **NOTE**: Also by Isasi-Diaz are [928-929], [255] (as co-author) and [256].

[928] Isasi-Diaz, Ada Maria. "*Mujeristas*: A Name of Our Own." In *The Future of
    Liberation Theology: Essays in Honor of Gustavo Gutierrez*, edited by Marc H.
    Ellis and Otto Maduro, 410-419. Maryknoll, NY: Orbis, 1989.
In her earlier work [927] Isasi-Diaz has identified Hispanic feminists as "Feministas Hispanas:" that is, as feminist Hispanic women seeking the dismantlement of racist, classist and sexist structures which oppress all peoples generally, and Hispanic women particularly. In this discussion Isasi-Diaz suggests that "*Mujeristas*" is a more appropriate naming of feminist Hispanic

women, because: (1) the name "Mujeristas" stems from the indigenous cultural experience of American feminist Hispanic women and (2) it avoids the potential divisiveness which the term "feminist" has for Hispanic males. Additionally, this name permits the exposition of a "mujerista theology" which is itself borne of the communal and action-reflective nature of Hispanic feminist women's experience. To make this point clear, Isasi-Diaz describes the two themes characteristic of this "mujerista theology." First is the affirmation that it is the mujerista community itself which acts as the agent of its theologizing process. That is, it is the community as a whole and not individual theologians who do "mujerista theology." Second, because the mujerista's epistemological standpoint is that of "the poor and the oppressed," (a theme consonant with emphases in Latin American liberation theology), this standpoint permits, and indeed requires, an action-reflection community model for the theologizing process. Three final points complete the discussion: (1) the recognition of a non-oppressive and "horizon" directed use of the Bible; (2) an exegesis of the Shiphrah and Puah story in Exodus 1:15-22 to evidence the efforts of community directed life-giving women; and (3) the need for an analysis of power for "Mujeristas" and "Mujerista theology," so that "self-determination" (including the leadership of women in priestly, liturgical roles) is clear as the goal of Mujerista theology.

[929] Isasi-Diaz, Ada Maria et al. "Roundtable: *Mujeristas*: Who We Are and What We Are About." *Journal of Feminist Studies in Religion* 8, no. 1 (1992): 105-127.
The "Roundtable" discussion is a regular feature in *JFSR* and here, the use of the term "mujerista" is explored as an identifying framework for the experience and theological efforts of Hispanic/Latina women. As elsewhere ([926, 927]) Isasi-Diaz describes the significance of the term *Mujerista*. It intends first, the theological task of empowering Hispanic women to understand and change oppressive structures, and to affirm, thereby, the reality of God in Hispanic women's daily life. Second, *Mujerista* intends the empowering of Hispanic women to define their own preferred social future and subsequently the necessary self and social structural changes that can work towards that future. Thus, *Mujerista* can function theologically as a term of conversion and eschatological hope, for it can aid Hispanic women in their task of divesting themselves of internalized oppressions. Last, *Mujerista* empowers Hispanic women to name themselves publicly and thus reject all definitions of suffering and self-effacement that may or have been assigned by others to Hispanic women. Among the points made by respondents to Isasi-Diaz's proposed liberationist/praxis identification process are: (1) the acknowledged value of Hispanic women having a distinct, self-chosen, Spanish and public name and (2) the affirmation of Hispanic women's solidarity with both "La Communidad" and its familial, religious heritage. At a more selective level, individual respondents suggested the need for: (a) locally grounded appropriations of the term *mujerista*, and particularly by women in the Puerto Rican community; (b) a religious framework which includes not only Catholic but also Protestant Hispanic women's experience; and (c) the need for *mujerista* theology to be open to lesbian and ecological theology and ethics, if the term is to be truly inclusive of the diversity of Latina women's experience and values. A brief and closing statement by Isasi-Diaz expresses her gratitude and enthusiasm for the discussion.

[930] Tamez, Elsa. *Against Machismo*. Oak Park, IL: Meyer Stone Books, 1987.
Phrasing her question in a variety of ways (e.g., "Juan Luis [Segundo], what do you think about women's liberation from the point of view of the theology of liberation?" or again, "Rubem [Alves], is the oppression of women in Latin America a reality or not?" or yet again, "Leonardo, [Boff] from your own experience, how do you see the oppression of women in Latin America?") Tamez interviews 15 Protestant and Catholic, Latin American, male liberation theologians to get their perceptions of women's experiences and oppression(s) in Latin America and the possibilities these theologians envision for Latin American women. The interviews are candid and clearly reported, and in their light Tamez highlights five broad conclusions: (1) the subject of women's oppression in Latin America is difficult to discuss because it raises the polemics of gender privilege and the need for strategies to change this; (2) the position of women in the church is (in Latin America) a matter of institutionalized, historical sin and tied to the various confessional expressions of the church; (3) there is a need for women to be theologizing, but neither the roles nor the contents of this effort are yet clear except that it must occur within the framework of liberation theology; (4) a number of biblical questions remain, and especially what to do with difficult texts and questions about inclusive language; and (5) it is clear that the journey must be undertaken.

[931] Tamez, Elsa, ed. *Through Her Eyes: Women's Theology from Latin America*. Maryknoll, NY: Orbis, 1989.
These essays by ten Latin American women theologians reflect the now established synthesis of Latin American liberationist themes and "women's experience" as a grounding "source" for the

theologizing process, with the latter clearly evident as these women reflect upon God, the Trinity, Christ, the Church and the social conditions which ground their lives. An important emphasis throughout these essays is the author(s)' experience of theologizing within an anchored or base communal setting. Thus, the authors' religious symbols speak to their *lived* experience and not its reification by those beyond the women's setting. By way of example, as Aracely de Rocchietti discusses "Women and the People of God," she does so specifically from within the context of "The Churches' Internal Debt to Latin America." Additional writers take up related themes and the text closes with the affirmations of women at the *Latin American Conference* (Buenos, Aries, Argentina, October 30-November 3, 1985) sponsored by the EATWOT. A "Forward" by Delores Williams sets the ecumenical tone of Catholic and Protestant contributors and notes both the gratitude and discomfort some Womanist readers may have with the collection because it does not directly address racial oppression among Latin American women. **NOTE:** For biblical work by Tamez see her commentary on "James" in Schüssler Fiorenza **[345]**.

c. Asian and Asian-American Women's Theology

[932] Fabella, Virginia, and Sun Ai Lee Park, eds. *We Dare to Dream: Doing Theology as Asian Women.* Maryknoll, NY: Orbis, 1990.
This collection of sixteen essays by prominent, emerging Asian feminist theologians is grounded in the need to think theologically about the context(s) and experiences of Asian women. It thus reflects a threefold "theological, inclusive and contextual emphasis." Six essays "rework theological themes," addressing christological and ecclesial questions from both Catholic and Protestant perspectives. An additional five essays address contextual issues from within specific theological motifs, e.g., the biblical concept of sexuality and its implications for tourism--*and prostitution.* Five final essays then address "Doing Theology as Asian Women," and here Korean, Indian, Filipino and Chinese women speak, both from within the context of (1) Asian women's theological conferences and organizational meetings (two entries) and (2) the symbolic motifs indigenous to local and national based cultures (three entries). Contributors include Fabella and Park, Chinese theologians Kwok Pui-Lan and Christine Tse; Yong Ting Jin of Malaysia; Aruna Gnanadason, Monica Melanchton and Crescy John from India, Lee Oo Chung, Ahn Sang Nim and Chung Hyun Kyung from Korea, and Elizabeth Dominguez and Mary John Mananzun from the Philippines.

[933] Fabella, Virginia, Peter K. H. Lee, and David Kwang-sun Suh, eds. *Asian Christian Spirituality: Reclaiming Traditions.* Maryknoll, NY: Orbis, 1992.
Together with Fabella's earlier co-edited collection **[932]**, this text is a grounding source for understanding Asian spirituality and the diverse cultural, religious, social and political streams which inform it. Fabella's introduction sets the tone with an overview of past EATWOT conferences that have eventuated in the present collection. Additionally, she highlights the material and "spiritual" needs of Asian peoples, as focused specifically by their respective Korean, Indonesian, Indian, Filipino, Chinese and Sri Lanken group and/or individual presenters. This is an informative and readable collection of sources that introduce one to the biblical and liberationist dimensions of Asian spirituality, as it is being crafted by the "miniscule" minority of Asian Christians committed to respecting both Christianity *and* the indigenous history and experiences of Asia's vast and pluralized but mostly poor peoples. Virtually all relevant topics are addressed: variations in religiosity, the impact of the caste hierarchy, patterns of military, economic and political violence, sex tourism, Asia's ecology movement and last, the efforts of tribal peoples to sustain cultural experiences in the face of industrialization.

[934] Gnanadason, Aruna. "Feminist Theology: An Indian Perspective." *Asia Journal of Theology* 2 (1988): 109-118.
This essay describes the need for a feminist theology for women in India. It critiques the religious legitimation of androcentrism and patriarchy, and on the basis of works published by Ruether, McFague and Schüssler Fiorenza, it argues for a re-reading of biblical texts in the light of the violence and subordination Indian women have historically experienced. This is a very important discussion. First, it highlights the rigidity of social and religious roles to which feminist theological analysis in India must speak. Second, it evidences the global application of several North American feminist theological sources. Gnanadason does not deny that much feminist thinking is "splintered...[by the]...contradictions of class and ideology within its ranks," but she insists that "the Church and its theologians need to stand by women in solidarity" (p. 88) because their humanity has been crushed into the dust by the history of India's caste system. As with her other writings (**[916]**, **[917]**), this is a clear and powerfully written piece, and it evidences Gnanadason's strong and well placed voice of justice within the World Council of Churches.

[935] Kyung, Chung Hyun. *Struggle to be the Sun Again: Introducing Asian Women's Theology.* Maryknoll, NY: Orbis, 1990.
In her comments for the back cover of this text, feminist ethicist Beverly Harrison describes it as a "truly artful presentation of many voices...." Her words are accurate and apt. This is an important--and difficult--text. Its importance lies with the material it delivers: (1) an overview of the development of Asian women's feminist theology as it has grown within EATWOT and other Christian/Asian organization settings; (2) an overview of the literature from "first" and "second generation" Asian feminist theologians, including Chung's discussion of several essays published in the Asian feminist journal *In God's Image*; (3) her brief but honed syntheses of the Asian feminist theological literature on the symbols God, Christ, and Mary; and (4) her reflections on the developing "spirituality" of Asian women. These contributions mark the text as "required reading," for they organize much literature currently dispersed in several sources. But the text is also difficult. First, it demands a sustained concentration for one unfamiliar with either liberation theology or other Asian feminist theological sources, for the writing is tight and tied clearly to the needs of a constituency which is itself pluralized and finding its wider voice. Second, Chung's text demands an honesty of response from readers, for it challenges easy assumptions about feminist theology vis a vis women in "third world" nations and the role of Western feminists in that encounter. Put differently, it is eminently clear that for Chung, Asian feminist theology is and must be about the advocacy needed on behalf of the poverty, suffering and violence done to women throughout Asia, and the accountability of Asian feminist theology to that experience. Hence, Chung speaks of the anger and "gut feeling" commitments she (and others) have on behalf of Asian women's liberation, the syncretism necessary to the integrity of Asian religious symbols, and the struggle of Asian women to be "authentic" and "self-defining" within their own context and over against those who now--and would in Kyung's perception--continue to define them.

[936] Park, Sun Ai Lee. "Asian Women's Theological Reflection." *East Asia Journal of Theology* 3 (1985): 172-182.
In this article Park identifies what she sees as the three main characteristics of Asian women's reflection on theology: "It is relevant theology. It is truthful to the tradition of Judeo-Christian religion and the event of Jesus Christ. It is liberation theology" (p. 172.) While few would dispute these characteristics for almost any designation of Christian theology, their articulation in the context of Asian women and their experience is particularly salient. This is because the element of relevance derives from Asia's extensive material poverty and its continued maintenance through "dictators and military regimes" and a "totalitarian culture" that both grounds and is grounded in the patriarchal constraint of women. Similarly, the truthful dimension of Asian women's theological reflection is also salient, in that it arises from a country by country social analysis of women's experience and the necessity for a liberationist perspective by which to address that experience. Park highlights these emphases with several examples: the experience of Korean women involved in anti-nuclear peace efforts and efforts against sex-tourism and western imperialism; the work of women in India as they struggle against the dowry death issue (cf. [939]); the efforts of Himalayan women as they work to protect the environment, their children and themselves; the labor struggles of women in textile and other factories, and the gathering organizational efforts of women across Asia as they meet to study and incorporate feminist theological motifs for the benefit of Asian women and Asian communities. All of these efforts reflect the relevant, truthful and liberationist emphases of Asian women's theology, and for Park particularly so, since only two percent of Asians are Christian and the church is not allied with the concerns of the poor in Asia.

[937] Park, Sun Ai Lee. "Asian Women in Mission." *International Review of Mission* 81 (1992): 265-280.
This informative article provides a basic introduction for readers unfamiliar with Korean women's theology, for it describes three factors crucial to the development of that theology: (1) the varying impacts of Western supported "development" on Korea's "Minjung" or "alienated and oppressed" population--and particularly Korea's Minjung women; (2) the differing traditional and radical women's groups which have worked for justice and peace concerns under the general umbrella of Christian ecumenism since the mid and late 1960s; and (3) the specific development of the Asian Women's Resource Center for Culture and Theology (i.e., the AWRC). As regards the latter, it emerged from the Women's Commission of EATWOT in 1983 and was formalized in 1988, with a focus on doing theology from within a "contextual" method. That is, with an approach that requires one to experience an "economic, political and religious-cultural analysis of one's own country from [within] women's perspective[s] before going...[on to]...biblical exegesis or theological reflection" about one's country (p. 278). Together with the AWRC, this method contributes to the development of indigenous feminist theologies and the generation of extra-

theological networks working on behalf of women. Further, because this method focuses on social analysis from within the perspective of women's experiences, it addresses directly the multiple contexts of violence Minjung women face: an economic violence created by the necessities to support families through low-paying factory work which provides exports to the U.S.; a social violence created by the disruption of rural women to urbanized centers to obtain this low-paying factory work; and third, a sexual violence arising from the high levels of prostitution made available to tourists from the U.S. and other countries. All of these elements make for Asian women's theological reflection, and for Park, all contribute to the sense of "mission" endemic to that reflection: an emphasis on "building a just and peaceful community of women and men" who work in an interfaith dialogue with numerous others also seeking justice-directed outcomes in [church and] society.

[938] Talbot, Rosemary. "What Do Korean Women Feminist Theologians Have to Offer Towards An Ecumenical Pakeha Women's Feminist Theology in Aotearoa?" *Asian Journal of Theology* 7 (1993): 103-113.

This article provides an introductory overview to the methodologies of Asian feminist theology as described by the author's reading of Chung Hyun Kyung [935], and it describes particularly the two "toanga" or treasures Korean women bring to this discussion. These are (1) a commitment to the liberationist strategies of Asian feminist theology generally (i.e., to the processes of women's story-telling, critical social analysis and empowering theological reflection) and (2) a capacity for re-imaging traditional Christian themes in categories that reflect "Han-pu-ri" or "life giving" theology. Among the latter and of empowering significance for Korean women in Aotearoa [New Zealand] is the task of reimagining a "Theology of Partnership" to address cultural and racial divisiveness.

[939] Teays, Wanda. "The Burning Bride: The Dowry Problem in India." *Journal of Feminist Studies in Religion* 7, no. 2 (1992): 29-52.

Readers unfamiliar with Indian culture and caste structure will find their first reading of this article a bit difficult, given both the sources and subject of its discussion. Additionally, sociologists will feel the need for greater numbers as Teays makes her case. These points notwithstanding, Teays's discussion undertakes the difficult task of identifying a social problem that has extensive cultural support--but little legal identity--in that the bride price, its bartering customs and violent outcomes for women have theoretically been illegal in India since 1961. The "Dowry Prohibition Act" was passed in 1961 (and amended, according to Teays, in 1987), but as Teays's discussion indicates, there are numerous factors precluding its legislative and political force: greed, economics, culture and religion--to name but four, which in India, still foster the denigration of women, and their value as commodities--and as necessary--their value as sacrifices on behalf of male pride. **NOTE**: See also Kwok Pui-lan [281] in Section III-3, and see Glenn Yocum, "Burning 'Widows,' Sacred 'Prostitutes,' and 'Perfect Wives': Recent Studies of Hindu Women." *Religious Studies Review* 20 (1994): 277-285.

24

The Jewish-Christian Feminist
Theological Dialogue

An important development within the feminist theological community is the growth of Jewish feminist theology. This theology has evolved from a discussion grounded self-consciously in a feminist dialogue with Jewish experience, Torah and tradition, and its principal emphases include: (1) an identification of the questions and issues which ground Jewish feminist theology (cf., e.g., Plaskow [953], Greenberg [952], Setel [956], Davidman [973] and Umansky [957]); (2) a related discussion identifying the religious experience(s) and spiritualities of Jewish women (Ackelsberg [958], Falk [960], Plaskow [954] and Umansky [962]); and (3) an emerging dialogue with Christian feminist theology, and within this, an effort to expose the assumptions of anti-Judaism embedded within Christian feminist theology (cf. Plaskow [970-971]). In all ways, this is a "cutting edge" literature. It is rich in implications for the "between" and "within" variations of bonded dialogue, its religious organizational significance is immeasurable, and its potential to model religious dialogue is unquestionable. Among its religious authors perhaps most well known to a Christian readership are Judith Plaskow and Ellen Umansky, but other contributors include Diane Ashton, Ann Braude, Susan Elwell, Marcia Falk, Judith Hauptman, and Susannah Heschel, all of whose works are listed below, and Esther Fuchs, Naomi Goldenberg and Lynn Gottlieb, whose works appear earlier in the bibliography ([383], [139] and [261]). In addition, sociologist Lynn Davidman's work provides a variety of essay-length observations: first (as the title to her co-edited work suggests) a series of "feminist perspectives on Jewish studies" [949]; and second, a sociological read of women newly returning to Orthodoxy ([973, 974]). While by no means exhaustive, these sources and those indicated above introduce readers to the key issues and authors in this important and developing literature.

A second dimension to the literature of Jewish feminism is the evolving "Witness Literature" (cf. Goldenberg [964-965]): the writings by and about women Holocaust survivors. This literature represents the intersection of several discussions: a variety of literatures in women's studies (including women's studies in religion and the critique of racist and religious misogyny); the sociologies of race, ethnicity and gender stratification; feminist history and historiography; the "interstructuring" of racial, sexual and heterosexual prejudice; and as point and counterpoint to all of these, the dialogue now developing between Jewish and Christian feminist theologians. Myrna Goldenberg, a professor of Women's Studies at Montgomery College in Rockville, Maryland and a Holocaust scholar of international standing, identifies the collection edited by Rittner and Roth [945] as the definitive starting point for readers seeking exposure to the Witness Literature. Additionally, her 1996 essay [965], together with the discussion by Ringelheim [966], provides extensive grounding bibliography.

Quite clearly, the "Witness Literature" could merit its own category of inclusion within the wider context of the present volume, as several recent sources would suggest. (Cf., the recently published *Women in the Holocaust*, edited by Dalia Ofer and Lenore J. Weitzman [New London: Yale University Press, 1998] and see the various bibliographic listings available via the internet. The distinctiveness of this literature noted, this literature is presented here both to maximize its exposure as a significant discussion within American Jewish feminism, and to indicate the enormous "moral demography" yet to be addressed within the Jewish-Christian dialogue--feminist, womanist, multicultural, *and* androcentric.

A final note: Several works by Judith Plaskow have been abstracted at earlier points in the bibliography. These include her early work in feminist theological method [170], her doctoral thesis on gender, theological anthropology and women's studies methodology [203], her principle work in Jewish feminist theology [262], her early [206] and later [544] co-edited works in feminist spirituality, her summary discussion of feminist theology and its dialogue with women's studies [340], and her participation in a variety of "roundtable" feminist theological discussions while co-editor of the *Journal of Feminist Studies in Religion* (e.g., [339]). Her related works are included in the present chapter and the specific literatures now follow.

A. Bibliography and Background Sources

1. Introductory Overviews

[940] Braude, Ann. "The Jewish Woman's Encounter with American Culture." In *Women and Religion in America, Volume 1: The Colonial and Revolutionary Periods*, edited by Rosemary Radford Ruether and Rosemary Skinner Keller, 150-192. San Francisco: Harper & Row, 1981.
This entry from Volume I Ruether-Keller series [132-135] on women and religion in America highlights the encounter between the gender norms of orthodox Judaism and the harsh and varying milieux awaiting immigrants from European and other cultures during the settlement of the United States from its beginnings through the late 19th century. Braude's discussion is compact and informative. It provides a brief overview of Jewish immigration patterns through the late 1880s, it contrasts the outcomes of Jewish and secular interactions for early Sephardic and Ashkenazik Jewish settlers and for German and Russian Jews arriving during the mid and late 19th century, and last, it details directly, the impact of immigration and religious-secular interaction for women in each of these Jewish worlds. Of central import is the effect of education on Jewish women and the increasing involvement of Jewish women in synagogue life as a means of strengthening Jewish survival in the United States. Braude's attentive reading of the various publications, personal letters and religious organizational histories produced by American Jewish women does much to dispel early and often uncritical Christian feminist readings of biblical and rabbinic Judaism as the source of all-encompassing patriarchal restrictions on women.

[941] Braude, Ann. "Jewish Women in the Twentieth Century: Building a Life in America." In *Women and Religion in America, Volume 3: 1960-1968*, edited by Rosemary Radford Ruether and Rosemary Skinner Keller, 131-174. San Francisco: Harper & Row, 1986.
In an earlier discussion [940] Braude has discussed the impact of "Americanization" on women's roles within Sephardic, Ashkenazik and Russian Judaism during the period of 19th century immigration. Here she describes the leadership and commitment of Jewish women within the American labor movement, the extended implications of American Judaism's separation of home and synagogue as spheres of religious activity for women (in contrast to the "orthodoxy" of familial activities for Jewish women prior to American immigration and including the press for women's entrance into the rabbinate), and last, the long range impact of Americanization, i.e., the education of Jewish women and the establishment of numerous organizations directed to international aspects of Jewish life and the establishment of peace and women's rights around the world. NOTE: For Braude's own update of her work in the Ruether Keller series, see her entry, "Jewish Feminism," in [135].

[942] Hauptman, Judith. "Images of Women in the Talmud." In *Religion and Sexism: Images of Women in Jewish and Christian Traditions*. edited by Rosemary Radford Ruether, 184-211. New York: Simon and Schuster, 1974.
This early essay serves as an historical marker for the feminist movement in American Judaism, and although it has since been surpassed by discussions such as Greenberg's below [975], it nonetheless remains a preliminary source. In brief, Hauptman details nine areas of Talmudic teaching which historically have focused the roles of women within Judaism, and she evidences the struggle of traditional rabbinical exegesis--and mid-70s feminist religious exegesis--with these areas. Selected topics include Betrothal, Ketubah, The Marriage Ceremony, Divorce Law, Women and Commandments, Civil and Criminal Law, Laws of Inheritance, prayer ('That Thou Didst Not Make Me a Woman') and Aggadah. The last is the most developed and Hauptman concludes to the plurality of images, the location of gender roles within the "goals" of Judaism (as understood

through rabbinical experience), the dynamic nature of rabbinic legislation and the need to discard "all traces of legal and social discrimination..." and find instead "...Ways...to involve women more in the life of the religious community" (pp. 209-210). NOTE: For additional bibliography on women in rabbinic Judaism see the essay by Hauptman in Davidman and Tenenbaum [949], and see "The Separation of Women in Rabbinic Judaism," by Baskin in Haddad and Findley [907].) The latter extends Hauptman's early work in two important ways. It demonstrates how both the distinction between public and private life and the metaphor of a nature/culture dualism dovetail to keep Jewish women separated from positions of social and religious authority; second, it links these patterns with the analysis of patriarchy as a social form congruent with--but distinct from-- historic rabbinic Judaism.

[943] Heschel, Susannah, ed. *On Being a Jewish Feminist*. New York: Schocken, 1983. This reader presents 24 essays addressing the social, historical, religious and theological circumstance of [American] feminist Jewish women. Several essays examine the reality of women's invisibility in Halakhah (Jewish law) and the effects of this invisibility in Jewish women's life and experience: the traditional and long standing prohibition against women's religious leadership (apart from familial roles), the regulation of women as 'sexual temptress,' and the related severity of Jewish law on divorce. Additional writings discuss alternatives to such traditional expectations: e.g., Jewish lesbianism, Jewish feminist poetry and the entrance of women into the rabbinate. A final section examines issues pertinent to the development of a Jewish feminist theology. In this final section Judith Plaskow [953] argues that a theological rather than a legal (or halakhic) analysis of Jewish women's (religious) identity is needed, for it is Judaism's male language for God--and not Jewish law--which has grounded the religious invisibility of women in Judaism. Thus, for Plaskow, it is a theological analysis which alone can evidence the historic presence of women in Torah and tradition. Subsequent essays then provide a range of feminist readings vis a vis Jewish history, experience and religious teaching.

[944] Pratt, Norma Fain. "Transitions in Judaism: The Jewish American Woman Through the 1930s." In *Women in American Religion,* edited by Janet Wilson James, 207-228. Philadelphia: University of Pennsylvania Press, 1980. Working from both archival and formalized historical sources, Pratt describes the widening social, religious, and religious-organizational roles available to American Jewish women during the period 1920-1940. She locates her discussion in the patterns established by Jewish immigration between 1840-1920: *viz.,* the already present but numerically small proportion of Sephardic Jews living in the US as approximately 250,000 German Ashkenazik Jews arrived and settled in the eastern and midwestern US; the class differences which quickly were evident between Sephardic, German and the newly arriving 2.5 million Eastern European Jews during the years 1880-1920; the turn of the century differentiation of these groups into Conservative, Reform and Orthodox Jews; the rise of secular Judaism with its intellectual and radical political emphases; and last, the tensions presented to Jewish women and men, as Jewish communities everywhere faced the conflicts of assimilation and anti-Semitism endemic in the early to mid-20th century period. Within these overlapping developments Pratt distinguishes the numerous American and international women's religious organizations which developed; the varying differentiations of Jewish women's family, social and religious roles; the tensions expressed by some Jewish leaders (e.g., Kaplan) over such developments; and as postscript, the 1970s rise of feminism among American Jewish women.

[945] Rittner, Carol, and John K. Roth, eds. *Different Voices: Women and the Holocaust.* New York Paragon House, 1993. This text presents the voices--the accounts of women in and women of the Holocaust, "Nazi Germany's planned total destruction of the Jewish people and the actual murder of nearly six million of them" (p. 1). It is set against the life and poetry of Gertrud Kolmar, a German Jewish woman who died (most likely) at Auschwitz (in 1942), and who wished her story to be told. But this is not a book of poetry. It is a book which presents and contrasts the voices of survivors, interpreters and historians with that which is indescribable. In all, 26 women present their experiences and/or Holocaust research, under the three-fold rubric of "Voices of... Experience, Interpretation, and Reflection." Additionally, the editors provide an informative overview locating the context and history of Hitler's Third Reich and the particular vulnerabilities of women during the Holocaust. And--to dispel any thoughts to the contrary--both the editors and several contributors provide maps, diagrams, and documentation--again and again--of workers, women, deaths, deportations, transports and more deaths. This is a text which defies simple description, but the contributors and editors each are to be commended for their courage, honesty, and tenacity-- and in the case of the editors specifically--their thoughtfulness for readers numbed by such reality.

For at points gently throughout the text, Kolmer's voice is again present: completed, but not silenced for this fact. **NOTE:** Although not abstracted here, the recently released *Women in the Holocaust*, edited by Dalia Ofer and Lenore J. Weitzman (New London: Yale Univ. Press, 1998) is a superlative companion to Rittner and Roth, with contributions from Holocaust scholars who variously examine four settings of women's experience in and of the Holocaust: "Before the War," "Life in the Ghettos," "Resistance and Rescue" and "Labor Camps and Concentration Camps."

[946] Umansky, Ellen M. "Women in Judaism: From the Reform Movement to Contemporary Jewish Religious Feminism." In *Women of Spirit: Female Leadership in Jewish and Christian Traditions*, edited by Rosemary Radford Ruether and Eleanor McLaughlin, 333-354. New York: Simon and Schuster, 1979.
This detailed essay by Umansky chronicles two types of leadership among Liberal, Reform and Reconstructionist Jewish women from the late 19th century to the last quarter of the 20th century. These are (1) the efforts and successes of American (and to some extent German) Jewish women seeking ordination to the rabbinate through the decade of the early 1970s, (when in 1972 Sally Priesand became the first woman rabbi in American Reform Judaism); and (2) the leadership of Jewish lay women such as British Magistrate Lily Montagu and American Paula Ackerman, who sought in various ways to deepen the piety of European and American Jews precluded from religious studies and/or formal theological education. This is a well documented discussion which introduces beginning students to numerous sources on American Jewish experience and the beginnings of American Jewish feminism. For Umansky's follow-up discussion addressing literature through 1984 see her "Feminism and the Reevaluation of Women's Roles within American Jewish Life" in *Women, Religion and Social Change*, edited by Yvonne Haddad and E. Findley **[907]**. There Umansky further details the discussion of women's ordination within Judaism--a summary with clearly stated empirical questions yet to be addressed by sociological research--and she highlights what she perceives as tensions existing between feminism and Judaism as exemplified within conservative and academic contexts.

[947] Umansky, Ellen M. "Females, Feminists, and Feminism: A Review of Recent Literature on Jewish Feminism and the Creation of a Feminist Judaism." *Feminist Studies* 14 (1988): 349-365.
This review essay critically assesses seven texts on Jewish feminism in the United States published during the early and mid 1980s. The texts under review include: Evelyn Torton Beck's edited anthology, *Nice Jewish Girls: A Lesbian Anthology*, [Crossing, 1982]; Elizabeth Koltun's 1983 reader *The Jewish Woman: New Perspectives* [Schocken]; Heschel's *On Being A Jewish Feminist*: **[943]**; Blue Greenberg's *On Women and Judaism: A View from Tradition* [Philadelphia: Jewish Publication Society, 1981]; Susan Weidman Schneider's *Jewish and Female: Choices and Changes in Our Lives Today* [Simon and Schuster, 1984]; *The Tribe of Dian: A Jewish Woman's Anthology*, edited by Melanie Kay/Kantrowist and Irena Klepfisz [Montpelier, VT: Sinister Wisdom Books, 1986] and last, Penina Adelman's *Miriam's Well: Rituals for Jewish Women Around the Year* [Biblio Press, 1986]. Umansky locates these texts within the history of American Jewish feminism and she details the potential conflicts between feminist commitment and Judaism as a specifically *religious* tradition.

2. Bibliographies and Recent Anthologies

[948] Baskin, Judith. *Jewish Women in Historical Perspective*. Detroit, MI: Wayne State Univ. Press, 1991.
Twelve essays, each addressing a specific aspect of Jewish women's historical experience, make up this well documented introduction to the study of women in Judaism. Although ungrouped, the papers fall generally into three types of discussion. These are: (1) descriptive overviews of Jewish women's experience in specific historical periods (e.g., Baskin's own essay, "Jewish Women in the Middle Ages" and Renee Melammed's "Sephardi Women in the Medieval and Early Modern Periods"); (2) demographic overviews such as Paula Hyman's "Gender and the Immigrant Jewish Experience in the United States" and Howard Adelman's "Italian Jewish Women;" and (3) synthesized overviews of Jewish women and Jewish religiosity (viz., "Portrayals of Women in the Hebrew Bible" [Susan Niditch], "Jewish Women in the Diaspora World of Late Antiquity" [Ross Kraemer], "The Image and Status of Women in Classical Rabbinic Judaism" [Judith Wegner], and "Prayers in Yiddish and the Religious World of Ashkenazic Women" [Chava Weissler]). Other entries such as Deborah Hertz's "Emancipation through Intermarriage in Old Berlin" and Marion Kaplan's "Traditions and Transition: Jewish Women in Imperial Germany" address highly specific experiences. Last, Joan Ringelheim's "Women and the Holocaust: A Reconsideration of Research"

(also printed in Rittner and Roth [945]) and Ellen Umansky's "Spiritual Expressions: Jewish Women's Religious Lives in the Twentieth-Century United States" close the volume. Baskin's introduction sets the wide frame for discussion, the essays provide extensive notes and bibliography, and a subject index closes the text.

[949] Davidman, Lynn, and Shelly Tenenbaum. *Feminist Perspectives on Jewish Studies.* New Haven: Yale Univ. Press, 1994.

Eleven entries examining the status of women, women's images, expectations and roles within Judaism make up this collection which synthesizes religious, philosophical, sociological, anthropological and historical feminist research on women in--for the most part--American Judaism. The editors' purpose is to synthesize feminist scholarship from several fields, with the term feminist used specifically to indicate gender as a formally analytical concept which opens out patterns existing among several variables, but notably those indicating power and its distributions. Three entries addressing the religious status of women in Judaism follow the editors' well written introduction. These are: (1) "The Bible and Women's Studies," a very readable overview of Jewish (and Christian) feminist exegesis by Reform scholar Tivka Frymer-Kensky; (2) Judith Hauptman's "Feminist Perspectives on Rabbinic Texts," a technical discussion comparing the feminist approaches to Mishnah used by Jacob Neusner and Judith Wegner; and last, as an exceptionally succinct statement of her work, Judith Plaskow's "Jewish Theology in Feminist Perspective" [955]. Remaining essays address philosophy, cinema, modern Jewish history, American and Hebrew literature and the sociology of gender in various Jewish communities. The editors' own essay, "Toward a Feminist Sociology of American Jews" and those by Paula Hyman ("Feminist Studies and Modern Jewish History") and Susan Starr Sered ("'She Perceives her Work to Be Rewarding': Jewish Women in a Cross-Cultural Perspective") provide overviews of recent research on several fronts--family life, education, religion etc., using American, Israeli and other data.

[950] "Judaism." In *Women and Religion: A Bibliographic Guide to Christian Feminist Liberation Theology,* compiled by Shelly Davis Finson, 51-56. Toronto: Univ. of Toronto Press, 1991.

As with other chapters of this bibliographic guide [269], this chapter also lists books, articles, reviews and doctoral theses published and/or completed between 1975 and 1988, and with the material here divided into two categories: "Women in Judaism" and the "Jewish-Christian Feminist Dialogue." The listings are drawn from standard computerized sources and are comprehensive, although one limitation is that because works from *Tikkun* and *Lilith* are not indexed in the standard source materials, they are not represented in Finson's guide. Thus, for these journal sources, readers must seek on-line university or consortium systems carrying these journals.

[951] Ruud, Inger Marie. *Women and Judaism: A Selected Bibliography.* New York: Garland, 1988.

This bibliography is Volume 136 Garland Reference Library of the Social Sciences. It presents 842 alphabetized and annotated entries on women and Judaism, with the majority of sources focusing on women and Judaism in Israel and the United States, but with a significant proportion addressing women and Judaism internationally. Ruud's annotations are brief and by her own decision, "without evaluation...of the quality" of their contents. Entries are numbered serially, and the volume's topographical, subject and author indices indicate appropriate cross-references.

B. Dimensions of Jewish Feminist Theology

1. Judaism and Feminist Theological Method

[952] Greenberg, Blu. "Confrontation and Change: Women and the Jewish Tradition." In *Women of Faith in Dialogue,* edited by Virginia Ramey Mollenkott, 17-28. New York: Crossroad, 1988.

This essay describes the tensions, assumptions and change based strategies the author has developed for confronting patriarchy within Orthodox Judaism. It is a practically directed discussion, and the author's primary objects of confrontation are Jewish scholarship and Jewish divorce law: the former because it should "...culminat[e] in the ordination of women" and the latter because in discriminating against one woman, "such law discriminates against all" (p. 25). Greenberg argues that her tradition-directed confrontation is itself religious, for "[I]n Judaism...study is equatable with prayer," and thus an informed confrontation with the Torah is religious and binding of membership in the community. Hence the legitimacy of both her challenge and her patience, as she argues for women's full equality within Orthodox experience and law. For an alternative perspective see Plaskow ([953-955]) below, and for research on the resurgence of Orthodoxy among American Jewish women see Davidman [973].

[953] Plaskow, Judith. "The Right Question is Theological." In *On Being A Jewish Feminist*, edited by Susannah Heschel, 223-232. New York: Schocken, 1983.
This essay is a grounding source for those seeking insight into the development of Plaskow's work, for it is here that Plaskow clearly contrasts the differences between asking *halakhic* and theological questions about the religious standing of women in both historical and contemporary Judaism. Thus, in contrast to those who argue that the religious role of women in Judaism has been defined historically *by the constraints of Jewish law* (with the net effect being that Jewish women have been religiously invisible apart from their religiously grounded familial roles) Plaskow argues two points. First, that the appropriate question is theological rather than halakhic; that is to say, it is the androcentric language of *Torah as Torah* (rather than Jewish law) which has defined women as a category of 'other' in Jewish tradition. Second, it is only with women's participation in the redefinition of Torah, God, and Israel that the 'otherness' of women in Judaism will be overcome. Plaskow illustrates her discussion with an emphasis on the function of halakhah as a tool which regulates the Torah-defined irregularity of women's existence apart from male authority, and she calls for a "new understanding of the community of Israel which includes the whole of Israel and which therefore allows women to "speak" and reclaim their own names and experiences" (p. 232). Her 1991 volume, *Standing Again At Sinai* [262], undertakes this task.

[954] Plaskow, Judith. "Jewish Memory from a Feminist Perspective." In *Weaving the Visions: New Patterns in Feminist Spirituality*, edited by Judith Plaskow and Carol Christ, 39-50. HarperSanFrancisco, 1987.
Published first in 1986 in the Jewish periodical *Tikkun*, this article lays the groundwork for Plaskow's more developed discussion, *Standing Again At Sinai* [262]. Plaskow begins with the presumed invisibility of women at Sinai, as indicated by the command of Moses in Ex. 19:15: that "men should not...go near a woman..." (as contrasted with the possible alternative command, 'that women and men should stay away from one another.'). She notes the setting and premise of Moses' command--it is just prior to the giving of the covenant and Moses addresses the community through an address to its men--and she moves to the significance of this point. First, while the assumption of women's invisibility has become the pattern for Judaism's religious history, it simply is not true. This is because women were present at Sinai, and have been actively present throughout the history of the community. Second, because the Torah is Judaism's living and still grounding and revelatory document, *and* because Jews are obligated to be defined through the memory of their history, the assumption of women's invisibility cannot be dismissed as merely a fact of the then current historical times--with women viewed as objects rather than subjects during the founding of the people. Rather, the "invisibility" of women must be addressed and then redressed in the light of women's experience throughout Judaism, for women have always been a part of the Jewish community and *as subjects* not objects. Hence, Jewish women must reclaim their history, and in doing so begin the redefinition of the people, the revelation, and the tradition. Plaskow then identifies the strategies for this redefinition. They are: (1) the *recovery* of women's presence in Torah and the tradition (a task requiring historical and historiographic skills); (2) the development of feminist midrash; and (3) the realities of women "speaking/acting," *viz.*, the development of feminist ritual. Plaskow provides illustrations for all three strategies and as with her longer text [262] her emphasis is clear: what needs discussion are the foundational assumptions of Torah as revelation, by and on behalf of women (as well as men) within the Jewish community overall.

[955] Plaskow, Judith. "Jewish Theology in Feminist Perspective." In *Feminist Perspective on Jewish Studies*, edited by Lynn Davidman and Shelly Tenenbaum, 62-84. New Haven: Yale Univ. Press, 1994.
Synthesizing many themes from her book length work, *Standing Again at Sinai* [262], Plaskow here explains the need for and the boundaries of Jewish theology in feminist perspective. First, although "theology" is typically heard as a Christian term indicating "beliefs" rather than "behaviors," and although Judaism is a tradition largely about behaviors (rather than beliefs), Judaism can and does engender theological thinking, and especially so if theology is understood as "sustained and coherent reflection on the experiences and categories of a particular religious tradition, and as reflection on the world in the light of that tradition" (p. 64). Second, it makes practical sense to think of Judaism in theological terms (and particularly so for feminists), because Judaism is already defined by theological criteria. On the one hand, there is Judaism's generally

agreed upon universal endpoint concerning the "messianic significance of Jesus" (i.e., to affirm the latter is to step beyond the Jewish pale); likewise, there is Judaism's debate over the significance of "Goddess" religion and Jewish feminist involvement within it. A third factor affecting the need to think theologically within Judaism, suggests Plaskow, is the issue of "meaning." This is because "law" and the tradition are often separated from one another within the perception of Judaism and its grounding moments. And it is here, with respect to this separation, that theology and especially feminist theology can help, for "Jewish feminist theology approaches the tradition with both a profound critique of its sexism and a vision of the religious meaning of women's full participation in Jewish life" (p. 65). Plaskow's discussion then unfolds some of the possibilities inherent in this approach to the tradition: (1) an articulation of Jewish feminist theology's basic starting point-- namely that "a woman is not simply a Jew, but always a female Jew," a person defined theologically as "other"(p. 69); (2) the possibility of an intratheological conversation within Jewish feminist theology--could one, e.g., "demonstrate Rosenzweig's androcentrism ...[and]...what would be the effects of that knowledge?"; (3) a discussion of how God and Holiness should be construed by Jewish feminists; (4) an exploration of whether there is a "Women's Torah;" and (5) a discussion of how the tradition can be empowered for change without "collusion with patriarchy in silencing women's voices." To respond to these issues and close her discussion, Plaskow details the main foci of Jewish feminist theology: (1) language, God and Torah; (2) feminist suspicion, Godwrestling, and midrash; and (3) feminist historiography as a bridge to each. This is vintage Plaskow: clear, challenging, and true to her earliest convictions (cf. [170]).

[956] Setel, T. Drorah et al. "Feminist Reflections on Separation and Unity in Jewish Theology." *Journal of Feminist Studies in Religion* 2, no. 1 (1986): 113-130.
This discussion is a *JFSR* "roundtable" essay, with an initial paper by Drorah Setel who attempts an integration of feminist and Jewish perspectives around the feminist value of relationship and the traditional Jewish concept of holiness as separation. Setel notes the clear establishment of holiness as a theme of separation within Judaism, but she notes too, the relational and justice directed emphases of 'tikkun olam' and their congruence with the feminist perception of the relationality and the simultaneous unity of God/dess and creation. She describes alternative translations of the image "Shechinah," and while acknowledging the difficulty of developing a Jewish practice based on relational values, she nonetheless argues that new and relational constructs must be developed. Respondents to her discussion include Catherine Keller, Marcia Falk, Anne M. Solomon and Rita M. Gross who lift up: (1) the methodological issues of Setel's discussion (Keller); (2) a paralleling psychological model of separation and differentiation (Falk); (3) a critique of Setel's use of *Kadosh* (Solomon); and (4) additional models of separation and relationality within the context of monotheistic constructs (Gross). For a related methodological discussion by Setel, see her earlier essay, "Feminist Insights and the Question of Method," in *Feminist Perspectives on Biblical Scholarship* [349], edited by Adela Yarbro Collins, 35-42. Additionally, see her brief--and brilliant--essay, "The Prophets and Pornography: Female Sexual Imagery in Hosea" [384], and see her commentary on "Exodus" in *The Women's Bible Commentary* [343:26-35]

[957] Umansky, Ellen M. "Creating a Jewish Feminist Theology." In *Weaving the Visions: New Patterns in Feminist Spirituality*, edited by Judith Plaskow and Carol Christ, 187-198. HarperSanFrancisco, 1989.
This essay locates the task of creating a Jewish feminist theology under the wider rubric of "responsive theology," with the latter understood as the "subjective response of the theologian to a set of experiences," and here specifically, "Jewish sources and Jewish beliefs" as apprehended by Jewish women (pp. 194-195). Umansky begins by identifying the fundamental criterion for a Jewish feminist theology: Namely, that it must be a "specifically Jewish" feminist theology or that the Jewish dimensions of its articulation must predominate in that articulation. Hence she rejects both the attempt to rename God as Goddess and/or the effort to incorporate Goddess religion into Judaism. Both betray the monotheistic emphasis of Judaism and both reflect the virtual endemic tension between 'personal experience and tradition,' or the fact that one may be forced to choose between a loyalty to one's self vs. a loyalty to one's Judaism. This tension notwithstanding, Umansky recognizes that Jewish women have received a male created and male directed heritage and tradition, and thus Jewish women legitimately can and must re-write that tradition, since the tradition received by Jewish women is incomplete. The parameters of that rewriting, however, are set by the need for a specifically Jewish women's "responsive theology," and Umansky suggests that the latter will, in all likelihood, draw upon the "aggadah" (or legends) of Judaism to incorporate and reflect the experience of contemporary women and their linkages to the past. By way of illustration, Umansky presents a "responsive" reading of the story of Sarah and the feelings Sarah

may have faced at the binding of her son. Umansky suggests that it is this kind of re-visioning which will generate the sources for a specifically Jewish feminist theology.

2. Community and Spirituality

[958] Ackelsberg, Martha. "Spirituality, Community, and Politics: B'not Esh and the Feminist Reconstruction of Judaism." *Journal of Feminist Studies in Religion* 2, no. 2 (1986): 109-120.

This article describes the formative years of B'not Esh, a group of Jewish feminist women seeking a Judaism compatible with women's experience. Among other things it details the significance of the traditional Sabboth 'davvening' ritual for these women and their emerging insights about spirituality, community and politics. With respect to the Sabboth 'davvening,' the ritual has served to focus--and often to redefine--the varying tensions between feminist and traditional theologies and feminist and traditional worship possibilities. Similarly, with respect to 'spirituality, politics and community,' it has become the group's perception that: (1) spirituality and politics are the "same impulse toward wholeness and fulfillment," with (2) the task of community building becoming that of taking on "the responsibility to make the world safe for each and all of us to be 'whole.'" Ackelsberg is a political scientist, who writes--as a Jewish feminist--from an awareness of the spiritual and political dimensions of group process issues. She thus exhibits several emphases which invite comparison and contrast with both the growing Catholic and Protestant literatures on spirituality (cf. Ruether [191], Schneiders [546] and Heyward [555]), and the justice building concerns of the Christian women-church and international feminist theological movements (e.g., Hunt [789, 918], Troch [792], Russell [911], and Gnanadason [916]).

[959] Elwell, Sue Levi. "Reclaiming Jewish Women's Oral Tradition? An Analysis of Rosh Hodesh." In *Women at Worship: Interpretations of North American Diversity*, edited by Majorie Procter-Smith and Janet R Walton, 111-126. Louisville, KY: Westminster/John Knox Press, 1993.

"Rosh Hodesh" is the "celebration of the new moon...the welcoming of the first day of every new Hebrew month" and here, for Elwell, it is a symbol of the extent to which Jewish feminist ritual has developed since the mid-1970s. Elwell begins by noting the feminist experience of Jewish women reclaiming their voices within the tradition: Jewish women have moved from early compensatory rituals to those which now seek to integrate women's experience and biology over the course of the life cycle. Still lacking however, are the many possibilities she identifies with two questions: First, how can the multiplicity of women's rites of passage actually be ritualized? Second, how can the tradition "expand sufficiently to accommodate this and...other celebrative needs of Jewish women's lives and life passages?" The weaving together of midrash, the values of women's bodies (and specifically women's uteruses) *and* the reality of women now expecting feminist events at synagogues are all elements Jewish feminism that can be expressed through Rosh Hodesh rituals, for the monthly nuances of this celebration lend themselves to such themes. By way of illustration, Elwell cites specific monthly emphases and ritualized celebrations, and she likens the developing history of women's Rosh Hodesh rituals to an oral tradition among Jewish women which will "enable Jewish women to share their truths with one another, and finally with the world" (p. 123).

[960] Falk, Marcia. "Notes on Composing New Blessings: Toward A Feminist Jewish Reconstruction of Prayer." *Journal of Feminist Studies in Religion* 3, no. 1 (1987): 39-49.

Working from the perspective that the composition of prayers (and specifically "blessings") is a distinct form of Jewish feminist theologizing (and her discussion leaves no doubt of this fact), Falk describes the premises and assumptions which guide her construction of new feminist "b'rakhot." To engage in the task of re-writing traditional blessings is to engage in the task of identifying metaphors which open out rather than restrict God-images, she argues, and in a feminist context it is to reclaim the authority of women's voices in the naming of reality. To demonstrate her discussion, Falk describes the syntax, theology and assumptions of traditional Jewish blessings and the elements of their reconstruction. All begin with the standard opening, "Blessed are you, Lord our God, king of the world,...who..." makes, does, brings forth etc., and it is this address to monotheism which Falk first reconstructs: i.e., "Let us bless the source of life...which..." makes, does, brings forth etc. Additionally, as she focuses each blessing (whether for bread, wine, meals or a particular event) Falk reexamines the assumptions of the traditional metaphor to identify both its central emphases and restrictive patterns so that more inclusive, more multi-leveled, more communal and creation based imageries can be used. For her major theological work, see [260].

[961] Umansky, Ellen M. "Piety, Persuasion and Friendship: Female Jewish Leadership in Modern Times." In *Embodied Love: Sensuality and Relationship as Feminist Values,* edited by Paul Cooey, Sharon A. Farmer and Mary Ellen Ross, 189-206. San Francisco: Harper & Row, 1987.

This essay contrasts the writings, speeches and religious perceptions of two well-known 20th century Jewish women leaders: The Honorable Lily H. Montagu, a British Magistrate whose "lay ministry" (p. 194) to varying groups of English Jewish women spanned the years 1893-1944 (and then continued intermittently through 1965), and Palestinian born, Tehilla Lichtenstein, whose leadership of the American based Society of Jewish Science continued for thirty-five years following the death of her husband, Morris, in 1938. By way of overview Umansky highlights the role of personalized piety in the faith development of each of these women, and she contrasts their personalized appropriations of faith with the more "rational" and/or "principled" styles of the men closest to them: *viz.,* Lichtenstein's husband Morris, and in the case of Montagu, Claude Montefiore, an early 20th century leader in Reform Judaism and Montagu's acknowledged personal mentor. For her conclusions, Umansky notes the creative adaptability of these women as religious leaders and the possibility that their personalized piety was, in fact, a centuries old and necessary 'tradition' among Jewish women. Last, she suggests that the 'visions' of these leaders "echoed the visions of earlier generations of women...[unable to]...articulate or record their own" (p. 203). For an expanded version of this essay, see the introduction to Umansky and Ashton [263].

[962] Umansky, Ellen M. "Finding God: Women in the Jewish Tradition." *Cross Currents* 41 (1991-1992): 521-537.

This essay provides an historical overview of the religious and prayer activities of Jewish women from the beginnings of the Common Era to the present time, and with a particular attention to their characterization as a tradition of personalized piety on the part of Jewish women. The discussion thus continues Umansky's earlier work [961], and widens it to include both the participation of women in synagogue activities in Reform and Reconstructionist Judaism in the 19th and 20th centuries and, additionally, the religious activities of modern Israeli women who worship at the Wall apart from--and in spite of--ultra-Orthodox authorities. Umansky concludes to: (a) the plurality of Jewish women's pieties throughout history; and (b) the significance of personalized piety (as contrasted with formal studies and theology) for apprehending both the faith of the Jewish community and the ability to "turn it over intact to all the generations that will come after" (p. 534).

[963] Wenig, Margaret Moers. "Reform Jewish Worship: How Shall We Speak of Torah, Israel and God?" In *Women at Worship: Interpretations of North American Diversity,* edited by Majorie Procter-Smith and Janet R Walton, 31-42. Louisville, KY: Westminster/John Knox Press, 1993.

This article briefly summarizes both the gains Reform Judaism has made on behalf of women since the early 1970s and the needs Reform Judaism has yet to address if the authority of Jewish feminism is to be fully incorporated into Reform teaching and practice. Identified as gains are: (1) the ordination of women to the rabbinate (since 1972); (2) the "ritual naming of daughters"; and (3) the "incorporation of women's words and songs in the official liturgies of the Reform movement" and specifically Reform Judaism's two prayerbooks, the *Gates of Prayer* and the *Gates of Repentance* (p. 31-32). Still needed, says Wenig, however, is the recognition of women's authority in worship and particularly with respect to the questions, "What is Torah (revelation)," "Who is Israel," and "How shall we speak of God?" (p. 34). The authority of women's voices at worship is needed vis a vis the Torah, says Wenig, because portions of the Torah destructive to women are still read aloud at worship, and thus, as if "revelation." Similarly, the authority of women's voices is needed in the self-description of Israel and the address of God, for much of Reform's liturgical language is still exclusionary and sexist in nature. Wenig cites several examples illustrating these points and she acknowledges the reality of the ongoing struggle.

C. Jewish Feminism and the Holocaust

[964] Goldenberg, Myrna. "Different Horrors, Same Hell: Women Remembering the Holocaust." In *Thinking the Unthinkable: Meanings of the Holocaust,* edited by Roger Gottlieb, 150-166. New York: Paulist Press, 1990.

A difficulty recognized by Goldenberg and others (cf., e.g., Ringleheim [966]) is the tension surrounding the depiction of women's experiences during the Holocaust. The risk is that of politicizing the Holocaust: of creating a circumstance in which sexism and anti-Semitism are pitted against each other such that either (a) the historicity of Jewish suffering is lost (or else wise de-moralized); or (b) sexism and anti-Semitism each become the foil by which the one may be reduced into the other. Hence, the intellectual trap: Does it matter that Jewish women were *women* in the Holocaust? Or is the latter simply an analytical detail which highlights the already known facts of Nazi brutality, cruelty and degradation? In this and its companion article below [965], Goldenberg both avoids the trap and movingly educates to the experience and values of telling about "different horrors" within the same hell. She unfolds the narratives of women survivors and depicts strengths and vulnerabilities alike to teach us, the readers: (1) *what* women endured--and at times resisted and at other times survived; (2) how patterns of gender socialization differently disadvantaged *and* empowered the women of her words; and (3) how the experiences of these women and the "ethic of care" exhibited by and among them (see below) pose the "value of [teaching nurture] to any society...growing more and more fragmented and violent." A gifted writer, Goldenberg is as sensitive to the needs of her readers, as she is her subjects.

[965] Goldenberg, Myrna. "Lessons Learned from Gentle Heroism: Women's Holocaust Narratives." *The Annals of the American Academy of Political and Social Science.* 548 (November, 1996): 78-93.

Together with [964] above, this essay takes the reader into the experiences of women Holocaust survivors. It opens with a review of the methodological issues grounding the task and moves quickly to the double experience Jewish women survivors describe: that the vulnerabilities of women in the camps were tied--as one might expect--to the realities of sexuality, socialization and reproduction, and that the capacities of these women for sustaining one another were tied, as well, to the same realities. By way of illustration, Goldenberg details specifics from various survivor narratives: that as much as women were sexually brutalized, they learned that sexuality at times afforded a measure of control over their future; that to protect their children from fear and the ultimate unknown, they often went to the gas chambers with them--or alternatively, went to work on their behalf thinking they would be safe in other portions of the camps; that to provide social and emotional support to one another they forged surrogate families, engaged in conversations transcending the confines of camp experience, helped one another get better camp work (i.e., jobs with more food, clothing or water); and when possible, participated in secreted acts of resistance. That to combat hunger they planned menus, exchanged recipes and thought openly of food, and in the worst of circumstances, smothered infants born in the camps to protect both themselves and the newborns from additional cruelties and eventual starvation. As with her earlier discussion [964], Goldenberg's essay here speaks of both cruelty and courage. And, while it does so in ways which lay bare vulnerabilities, it does so without a revictimization from within those vulnerabilities. Rather, the pain, the courage, the convictions, the anger, the care and the dignity of Goldenberg's sources are all clear, and all the more powerful as Goldenberg indicts both the racist misogynies of Nazi thought and the elements of their support--including Christian--beyond the Third Reich. This is an important contribution to the Witness Literature. It introduces readers to the range of Jewish women's survivor narratives, it lists extensive bibliography, and as with [964] above, it asks again the meaning of nurture in societies increasingly defined by violence and social fragmentation. NOTE: For additional work by Goldenberg, see her essay, "From a World Beyond: Women in the Holocaust," *Feminist Studies* 22, no. 3 (1996): 667-687.

[966] Ringelheim, Joan. "Thoughts About Women and the Holocaust." In *Thinking the Unthinkable: Meanings of the Holocaust,* edited by Roger Gottlieb, 141-149. New York: Paulist Press, 1990.

This article lays out some of the most difficult and radically painful questions twentieth century capacities can envision, and it does so precisely on behalf of those capacities. Most simply, it summarizes the deep tensions surrounding the discussion of "religion," "race" and "sex" as frameworks for identifying, analyzing, understanding *and* respecting the experiences of Holocaust survivors, and it exposes the pitfalls of attempts to pit one of the frameworks against any other to calculate the range of suffering--one wants to say victim authority--of any one particular group. It is a discussion for deep and close reading, if only for the enormity of its issues. But there is more. For in addition to the questions it raises, this discussion also sets a table for dialogue where the agenda items are the racism and misogyny of genocide and its ideologies, and the strengths of the human spirit for seeing not only that women and men--Jewish, gypsy and gay--suffered and at times survived, but *how* these women and men suffered and at times survived. And how, thereby, the world must be rebuilt and regrounded to respect the "Never Again" premise of this experience. In particular, Ringelheim identifies the interactive dimensions of misogyny, race, and gender, and the differential outcomes such interaction produces: death--for women specifically--where the racist goal is genocide and patriarchy and enslavement when the goal is labor unending. Neither has rights, and Ringelheim says so loudly.

D. Jewish and Christian Feminists in Dialogue

1. Introductory Discussions

[967] McCauley, Deborah, and Annette Daum. "Jewish-Christian Feminist Dialogue: A Wholistic Vision." *Union Seminary Quarterly Review* 38 (1983): 147-190.
This essay provides some of the earliest discussion for dismantling the anti-Judaism of feminism and feminist theological literature during the mid-1980s. The authors argue accurately that despite several specific efforts, formal Jewish-Christian dialogue receives only marginal attention from institutional religious personnel, and further, that "feminists of faith" are effectively barred from the discussion, given the male dominance and clericalism of official Jewish and Christian circles. Dividing feminists of faith, however, are anti-Jewish attitudes and motifs carried uncritically by Christian and Post-Christian writers who seek either to (1) critique Christian patriarchy through an analysis of its history, or (2) highlight what is non-patriarchal in Christian biblical and theological teaching. Almost inevitable to each strategy are (a) the projection of the Hebrew Scriptures and/or biblical and rabbinical Judaism as the ultimate source bed of religious and social sexism, and (b) the depiction of Jesus as somehow transcending his own (presumably sexist) Jewish milieux in favor of an ethic compatible with [Christian] feminist values, with the net effect being a devaluing and inaccurate reading of Jesus, Judaism and its teachings. Moreover, to the extent that feminists and feminist theologians retain and/or uncritically hold such assumptions in their own work, they provide de facto support for Christian triumphalist and other anti-Semitic perspectives (e.g., anti-Zionism) both within and beyond organized religion. McCauley and Daum detail several examples of these anti-Judaism beliefs and motifs, and while feminist theologians are increasingly sensitive to the need for more inclusive cross traditional conversation (cf. the decade of Jewish-Christian co-editorship of the *Journal of Feminist Studies in Religion*), clearly additional work is needed--both as detailed by Plaskow [971] and as implied by the ways women can "re-write patriarchy" (cf., e.g., Smith [114]) within gendered denominational commitments which yet require hierarchical images of transcendence.

[968] Plaskow, Judith. "Anti-Semitism: The Unacknowledged Racism." In *Women's Consciousness, Women's Conscience*, edited by Barbara Hilkert Andolsen, Christine Gudorf and Mary Pellauer, 75-84. Minneapolis, MN: Winston Press, 1985.
This essay is an expansion of Plaskow's similar discussion in *Woman's Spirit Bonding* [208], and as it expands the latter, it focuses Anti-Semitism as one axis of "the complexity of oppression" existing in American society for Jewish and other women. Plaskow's discussion focuses on the "psychic toll" of Anti-Semitism in the United States, and it recounts childhood and adult memories of passing and marginalization, the numerous insensitivities which Christians and American society generally have exhibited to Jews, and last, the bigotries attached to cultural stereotypes about Jews, both socially and economically. Additionally, Plaskow describes her own sense of powerlessness at being a "white middle class woman" who is caught both by the prejudices she experiences and her own abilities for prejudices to others. These all on the table, she at the same time affirms the need for bridge building across the conflicts and differences that maintain such complexities, and she urges feminists from all quarters to get beyond their own oppressions to learn those of others. It is a strong essay, written in her consistently powerful style, and it models the commitments and abilities so characteristic of her work as a whole.

[969] Umansky, Ellen M. "Racism, Classism and Sexism: A Jewish Woman's Perspective." In *Women of Faith in Dialogue*, edited by Virginia Ramey Mollenkott, 110-119. New York: Crossroad, 1988.
In this essay Umansky describes her feelings of "invisibility as an American Jewish woman" (p. 110) and her "sense of powerlessness" (p. 111) before the competing pressures of her three primary reference groups: her status as a woman in "our fathers' world;" her status as a feminist who continues to hold "to that 'hopelessly patriarchal and clannish' religion, Judaism;" and last, her status as an Americanized "other" by virtue of both her gender and her Judaism. Following the specifics of these competing expectations, Umansky describes the limited analysis of feminist Jewish organizations within American society and the felt pressures of the Christian based anti-Semitism Umansky regularly experiences. She synthesizes her discussion through the categories of racism, classism and sexism and describes experiences in ways comparable to those of women else wise marginalized from majority perspectives.

2. The Critique of Anti-Judaism in Christian Feminism

[970] Plaskow, Judith. "Feminist Anti-Judaism and the Christian God." *Journal of Feminist Studies in Religion* 7, no. 2 (1991): 99-108.
As background to this essay the reader should see Siegele-Wenschkewitz's brief overview [972] of anti-Judaism within feminism and feminist theology per se. Here, however, Plaskow identifies three areas within Christian feminist literature where feminist anti-Judaism is yet evident and yet unaddressed. These are: (1) the uncritical use by feminists of Christianity's dichotomous depictions of God as a God of wrath and love in, respectively, the "Old" and "New" testaments; (2) feminism's blaming of Judaism for the 'death of the goddess'; and (3) the highlighting of Jesus' theological uniqueness for women by his portrayal as either a 'feminist' or as a Jew distinct from others of his time. With respect to the wrath/love dichotomy, Plaskow notes that both features are evident in both testaments, and that to say differently is to "...project a tension that exists within both Judaism and Christianity...as a tension between them" (p. 102). Similarly, the "realization that the biblical writers helped to suppress female imagery comes with a sense of betrayal that easily attaches itself to traditional anti-Jewish themes" (p. 103). Finally, to portray Jesus as "unique" may be the Christian task, but if so, it should be done without negating either *his* Jewishness or that of his peers; this is because both strategies scapegoat Jews and continue the groundwork by which Jews have been dehumanized throughout history. This is a frank discussion by a theologian well versed in Jewish *and* Christian feminist theology, and it should be required reading for all who seek the universality Jewish and Christian traditions each proclaim.

[971] Plaskow, Judith. "Anti-Judaism in Feminist Christian Interpretation." In *Searching the Scriptures: A Feminist Introduction*, edited by Elisabeth Schüssler Fiorenza, 117-129. NY: Crossroad, 1993.
This essay is one of several critical pieces which seeks, within the context of Schüssler Fiorenza's collection [344], to generate "feminist frames of meaning" for "changing patriarchal blueprints." Overall, it repeats much of Plaskow's earlier anti-Judaism discussion [970], but it advances her earlier work in two important ways. First, in citing Katharina von Kellenbach's dissertation, "Anti-Judaism in Christian-Rooted Feminist Writing..." (Temple U., 1990 [288]), Plaskow focuses what is relevant and dispenses with what is not. Thus she cites the three "rules of formation" which for von Kellenback ground "the anti-Jewish myth and define the Christian representation of Judaism" (p. 118). In brief, these are the rules of *antithesis* or dualism, i.e., Old and New testaments; the rule of *scapegoat* or blaming Jews for the evil of the world; and third, the rule of *prologue* in which Judaism is "Christian pre-history" (pp. 118-119). Second, after reviewing several implications of these 'rules' and their identification, Plaskow describes five ways in which Christian feminists can "address rather than reproduce this sorry aspect of Christian self-understanding." Over all, these entail the recognition of anti-Judaism within Christianity (wherever it appears: scripture, prayer, theology etc.), the systematic incorporation of its critique by Christian feminist writers, and last, the abandonment of feminist Christianity's institutional isolation from Jewish feminists, and the incorporation of Jewish feminists within feminist theological interreligious dialogue.

[972] Siegele-Wenschkewitz, Leonore. "The Discussion of Anti-Judaism in Feminist Theology—A New Area of Jewish-Christian Dialogue." *Journal of Feminist Studies in Religion* 7, no. 2 (1991): 95-98.
This essay introduces American readers to the papers presented at the "third conference of the European Society of Women for Theological Research," held at the Protestant Academy in Arnoldshain, Germany, in September of 1989. The theme of the conference was "Images of God" and the ways in which such images are "simultaneously images of our own oppression and liberation..." (p. 95), and here particularly, images "which reflect anti-Jewish sentiment." A Christian theologian responding generally to Plaskow's critique of anti-Judaism within Christian feminist theology, Siegele-Wenschkewitz raises two important questions: (1) "How do Christian feminist theologians, as part of the new women's movement, look upon their church tradition, which is the history of denominational women's organizations?" (p. 97); and (2) how might feminist theology and the Jewish-Christian dialogue (hitherto distinct and separate) become combined? (p. 97-98). Siegele-Wenschkewitz does not address the first question, but for the second, she argues that current participants in the Jewish-Christian dialogue will need to take seriously feminism's critique of patriarchy and traditional theology. Similarly, feminist theologians will need to move beyond the critique of patriarchy (and androcentrism) and to the critiques of anti-Semitism, ethnocentrism and racism, in both past *and present* theologies and experience.

NOTE: For related literature on Jewish and Christian feminists in dialogue see Ruether [299], Briggs [306], Klein [312], and D'Angelo [433]. The Ruether text is a critical exposure of the anti-Semitism endemic to Christianity since its beginnings. The essay by Briggs contrasts assumptions held about "Women and Jews in 19-Century German Theology," while Klein's (infrequently cited) 1978 text analyzes the anti-Judaism prevalent in German Christian theology of the 1930s-1940s. In turn, D'Angelo's work identifies and dismantles 20th century New Testament scholarship that has supported anti-Semitic ideology. Other sources here include essays and bibliography embedded in both D'Angelo [433] and Schüssler Fiorenza [238]. Last, for empirical literature contrasting ordained Jewish and Christian women, see Simon, Scanlon and Nadell [719] and the literature cited there.

E. Orthodox Resurgence

[973] Davidman, Lynn. "Accommodation and Resistance to Modernity." *Sociological Analysis* 51 (1990): 35-52.
Focused within the framework of secularization theory and seeking to further document the pluriform response of religious traditions to the modernizing trends of pluralism, individualism and modern society's changing gender and family roles, Davidman skillfully contrasts the responses of two Orthodox Jewish groups to such trends. Group #1 is "Modern Orthodoxy." Although highly traditional, this group stresses an accommodation to society's wider cultural values and their incorporation into the values of Orthodoxy and its membership needs. Davidman illustrates this process and with it, the socialization mechanisms involved in a new recruit's community entrance. Over all, the grounding emphases are those of self care and self fulfillment via Orthodoxy's clear answers to the pain experienced by modern individuals, with the net effect being a developed, two-fold identity of modernism grounded in Orthodoxy. Group #2 is the Lubavitch Chassidism. This group seeks to resist modernizing trends and is separatist and sectarian in orientation. Moreover, as it socializes new recruits, it does so through the portrayal of one's self as the sum of one's roles, and an orientation that sees role enactment (and especially gender role enactment) as fundamentally natural. Hence community compliance here is gained through normative rather than coercive means, and without an incorporation of modern values such as "the self." Davidman supports her discussion with several examples drawn from the wider ethnographic research of her doctoral dissertation, *Tradition in a Rootless World: Women Turn to Orthodox Judaism*, Berkeley: University of California Press, 1991.

[974] Davidman, Lynn, and Arthur L. Griel. "Gender and the Experience of Conversion: The Case of 'Returnees' to Modern Orthodox Judaism." *Sociology of Religion* 54 (1993): 83-100.
As abstracted by the authors..."This essay develops a gendered analysis of the experience of conversion to one particular religious perspective, that of modern Orthodox Judaism. Based on interviews with newly Orthodox men and women, our analysis reveals important gender differences in the processes of recruitment and resocialization. Male recruits were more likely to have been active seekers and to have found Orthodoxy 'on their own,' while women were more likely to enter through personal contacts. Men emphasized ethical and workplace concerns in discussing the appeal of Orthodoxy; women stressed issues related to family and personal relationships. Men reported higher levels of belief in an anthropomorphic God. Questions of gender role were more salient for the women. These differences are consistent with gender role distinctions both in the wider society and within Orthodox Judaism. Future research should employ gender as a category in the analysis of all forms of religious experience."

[975] Greenberg, Blu. "Female Sexuality and Bodily Functions in the Jewish Tradition." In *Women Religion and Sexuality: Studies on the Impact of Religions Teachings on Women*, edited by Jeanne Becher, 1-44. Philadelphia: Trinity Press International, 1990.
This succinct discussion is an extremely readable overview of Jewish law and practice relative to women and sexuality within Conservative and Orthodox frameworks. It addresses virtually every aspect of women's experience as defined by Torah and tradition and from within the explicit awareness of a dialectic which sees women as "distinctive, special and equal on the one hand, and subordinate and inferior on the other" (p. 4). Greenberg begins with a summary of the literature "...intended to contain and transmit Judaism... [namely]...the Bible, the Talmud, halakha, [Jewish] philosophy, theology and exegesis" and she roots Conservatism's reading of the equal/subordinate dialectic in the creation stories of Genesis 1-2 and subsequent biblical narratives. She then expertly summarizes past and present Conservative and Orthodox thinking on four multiply directed topics

("Life Cycles and Ceremonies," "Generativity," "Sexuality," and "The Transmission of Values"), and she concludes to the necessity for maintaining a balance in interpreting traditional statements. She suggests that overall, such statements are neither fully misogynous nor fully egalitarian, and thus she argues for the "role distinctiveness" of women and men and a definition of sexual equality which means "...not sameness, nor identicality but human dignity, value and [an] appreciation of the godliness in male and female, body and soul alike" (p. 40).

[976] Levinson, Pnina Nave. "Women and Sexuality: Traditions and Progress." In *Women Religion and Sexuality: Studies on the Impact of Religious Teachings on Women,* edited by Jeanne Becher, 45-63. Philadelphia: Trinity Press International, 1990.

This essay summarizes Reform and liberal Jewish perspectives on women and sexuality and is intended as a complement to Greenburg [975]. Levinson begins by noting the differing assumptions made about halakha and theology in Orthodox and liberal perspectives (these are differences which largely parallel fundamentalist and non-fundamentalist orientations to revelation and tradition), and she continues with an overview of contrasts between Orthodoxy and liberal and Reform thinking on twelve different topics. As identified by Levinson these include "Plural Judaism," "Authority," "Statements" [on the integration of women into Reform religious practices]," "Abolishing Castes," "Releasing the 'Anchored' Wife,'" "No Bondage for the Childless Widow," "No Silent Brides," "Welcoming a Daughter," "Coming of Age: Bat-Mitzvah," "Menstruation Is a Private Thing," and "The Ordination of Women as Rabbis." Important to Levinson's overview is its international framework, with examples from Europe and the United States, but with clear attention to the emphases of Reform Judaism in Israel.

NOTE: For additional literature in Jewish feminism, see the journal *Lillith* [228].

Author Index

Listed below are the authors of all entries abstracted in the bibliography. Numbers in brackets refer to individual abstract entries.

Subject Index

Listed below are the main topics addressed by the abstracts presented in the bibliography. They are listed alphabetically and referenced by abstract numbers (presented in brackets as in the text), and because all abstracts are numbered sequentially throughout the bibliography, page numbers are omitted.

Title Index

Listed below are the titles of all entries abstracted in the bibliography. With the exception of initial definite and indefinite articles, these titles are arrayed in strict letter by letter alphabetical order. The numbers in brackets refer to individual abstract entry numbers within the bibliography, and because all abstracts are numbered sequentially throughout the bibliography, page numbers are neither needed nor listed.

About the Author

MARY-PAULA WALSH is a sociologist with specializations in feminist and religious studies. She was formerly on the faculty of the Lutheran Theological Seminary, where she served as Professor of Church and Society for eight years. Currently, she is the Senior Research Analyst and Training Evaluation Project Director for AFYA, a private consulting firm in Washington, D.C.

ISBN 0-313-26419-8